Almanac of
Business
and
Industrial
Financial
Ratios

2011 Edition

LEO TROY, Ph.D.

CCH
a Wolters Kluwer business

Editorial Staff

Production..Christopher Zwirek

Design ....Craig Arritola

This publication is designed to provide accurate and authoritative information in regard to the subject matter covered. It is sold with the understanding that the publisher is not engaged in rendering legal, accounting, or other professional service and that the author is not offering such advice in this publication. If legal advice or other professional assistance is required, the services of a competent professional person should be sought.

ISBN: 978-0-8080-2495-8

No claim is made to original government works; however, within this Product or Publication, the following are subject to CCH's copyright: (1) the gathering, compilation, and arrangement of such government materials; (2) the magnetic translation and digital conversion of data, if applicable; (3) the historical, statutory and other notes and references; and (4) the commentary and other materials.

Printed in the United States of America

Dedicated

**To Alexander, Suzannah, Dale, Ariel Sarah Troy, Abigayle Hannah Troy,
and Rachel Ilana Troy**

Preface

Now in its 42nd Edition, the *Almanac of Business and Industrial Financial Ratios* provides a precise benchmark for evaluating an individual company's financial performance. The performance data is derived from the latest available IRS figures on U.S. and international companies, and tracks 50 operating and financial factors in nearly 200 industries. The *Almanac* provides competitive norms in actual dollar amounts for revenue and capital factors, as well as important average operating costs in percent of net sales. It also provides other critical financial factors in percentage, including debt ratio, return on assets, return on equity, profit margin, and more. Beyond its reliable insights into corporate behavior, the *Almanac* can be used by other countries looking to model their economies on American performance.

Also included with the text, in a special pocket provided in the inside cover of the book, is a CD-ROM that contains all the materials found in the book including the explanatory discussion, the data tables, and the supporting index. Also included on the CD, but not in the book itself, is a special template that allows the reader to add individual company data of interest to compare and contrast with data from the book.

2011 Edition Highlights

The 2011 Edition of the *Almanac of Business and Industrial Financial Ratios* has been updated to include the following:

- **Broad scope:** *2011 Almanac* features the North American Industry Classification System (NAICS), so you can benchmark or analyze results consistently with corporations in the United States, Canada, and Mexico.

- **Most industry types:** *2011 Almanac* highlights most industry types, including industries with advanced technologies and newly emerging industries such as paging and wireless communications.

- **A truer picture** of corporate financial performance, since the data isn't based on a mixed bag of averages that might include partnerships or sole proprietors. *2011 Almanac* features a homogeneous universe of American corporate financial performance.

- **Many classifications:** *2011 Almanac* analyzes 195 industries with 50 financial performance items.

- **Benchmarks:** *2011 Almanac* provides 13 benchmarks, including such critical measures as Receipts to Cash Flow, Debt to Total Assets, and Return on Equity both before and after taxes.

- **Analytical tables:** *Table I, Corporations with and without Net Income (All Corporations), and Table II, Corporations with Net Income.*

- **Easier apples-to-apples comparisons:** Each table is divided into 13 asset sizes.

- **More comprehensive:** Total receipts of all corporations covered by *2011 Almanac* is $28.8 trillion, making the *Almanac* the Anatomy of American Corporate Capitalism.

Leo Troy, Ph. D.

October 2010

About the Author

Dr. Leo Troy is Professor of Economics at Rutgers University. He has been a faculty member of Rutgers for 50 years. In addition to authoring the widely praised *Almanac*, he has written many other books and articles published in leading journals. Professor Troy has been the recipient of numerous awards including two from the National Science Foundation, and two Fulbright grants. In addition, he has received numerous awards from private foundations. Dr. Troy received his Ph.D. from Columbia University and is a member of Phi Beta Kappa. He is a veteran of World War II with three battle stars and the combat infantry badge. He is the father of two children and is also a grandfather of three girls, including twins.

Acknowledgments

I wish to acknowledge the contributions of five people in particular for the development of the 42nd Edition of the *Almanac:* Phil Wilson, Alan Kovar of Brighton Best, Lawrence R. Chodor, CPA, CVA, Wiss & Company, Marvin Sunshine, and Karen Kane.

Philip is responsible for the programming, which dealt with a very large amount of data, covering both the current and trend information. Alan, drawing upon his knowledge and experience as a CPA and Partner of Wiss and Company of Livingston, N.J., contributed significantly to the new content of the book. To Marvin Sunshine, Esq, my appreciation for actions and support that helped make the *Almanac* a continuing publication. Karen Kane is acknowledged for her contributions to the graphics of this issue.

Special acknowledgement is due my late friends and colleagues, Stan Katz, CPA, and Professor Emeritus of Accounting, Rutgers University, John Gilmour. I thank, too, Professor of Accounting, Rutgers University, David Zaumeyer, Ph.D., CPA, for recommending several ratios that continue to be included in the *Almanac*. I thank Mr. Ka-Neng Au, Business Librarian, Rutgers University, for significant contributions to the *Almanac*.

I wish to recognize, too, the cooperation of members of the Statistics of Income Division of the Internal Revenue Service—in particular, Ken Szeflinksi, Martha A. Harris, and Phyllis J. Whiles of the Corporation Returns Analysis Section. Without their data and its reliability, the Almanac would not be possible. Responsibility for the use of their facts and figures is, of course, solely my own. In this regard, I recall the valuable assistance I received from Barry Rosenstein, MBA, CPA, in checking procedures, in earlier editions, and which have continued into the current one. Finally, I wish to recognize the help of Suzannah B. Troy in bringing about the 42nd annual edition of the *Almanac*. I anticipate continuation of her valuable assistance in subsequent editions.

INTRODUCTION

QUESTIONS, ANSWERS AND COMMENTS ON THE *ALMANAC*
Some users have requested further information on the use of the *Almanac's* ratios and statistics. This Q & A addition to the *Almanac* is in response to that demand.

1. What are the general purposes of the Almanac?

The goal of the *Almanac* is to provide users with a reliable and comprehensive source of standard financial ratios and financial statistics on all corporations, public and private, including those filing 1120S returns in the United States. Excluded are all individual proprietorships and partnerships. The *Almanac* makes available key business and financial statistics, which are consistent and neutral (unbiased by any commercial publisher or trade association).

2. What is the source and reliability of the Almanac's results?

The *Almanac's* results are computed from the Department of the Treasury, Internal Revenue Service's statistical sampling of the tax returns of all corporations. Dividends received from foreign corporations are included in total receipts of those corporations affected. The statistics apply to the company rather than the establishment.

3. Are international comparisons available?

Yes. Because of the adoption of a common system of industrial classification by the U.S., Canada and Mexico, known as the North American Industrial Classification System of industries (NAICS), under the North American Free Trade Agreement, users in Canada and Mexico can compare and contrast their results with those corporations in the United States.

4. What about comparisons within the U.S?

These are the most important applications of the *Almanac*. Results are available for each and every corporation within the U.S., whether public or private, and include small business corporations, those which file the 1120S tax return. Therefore, users can compare their corporate performance with that of their industry and asset size group of corporate enterprise in the United States.

5. How many corporations are covered in the Almanac?

The *Almanac's* results are derived from more than 5.8 million corporation tax returns. Furthermore, the user can easily determine the number of enterprises for the total of each industry and by each of the 12 asset size groups. This makes for a total of 13 asset size comparisons.

6. What about differences in the size of corporations?

In addition to the results for each industry, the *Almanac* displays 12 columns of performance by the size of assets. Again, this makes for a total of 13 asset size comparisons.

7. Does the Almanac distinguish between the profitability of corporations?

In a word, yes. Each industry is divided between two tables: Table I reports the results of all corporations in an industry, that is, those with and without net income. It is followed by a second table for the same industry, Table II, which reports only those corporations with net income.

8. How many items of information are there for each industry?

There are 50 indicators of corporate performance in each table and each industry and for all asset size groups, except where the IRS' data sample is too small, or it does not supply the necessary information.

9. Who are the users of the Almanac?

Accountants, corporate managers, business consultants, investors evaluating a corporate takeover, entrepreneurs considering new businesses, lawyers, and students of accounting, business, and management.

10. What accounting time period is covered?

The Internal Revenue Service provides the most recent statistics publicly available for the *Almanac.* For the 2011 *Almanac,* these statistics apply to the accounting period from July 2007 through June 2008.

WHAT'S NEW IN THIS EDITION

Beginning with the year 2002, the *Almanac of Business and Industrial Financial Ratios* began using the North American Industry Classification System (NAICS). NAICS replaces the Internal Revenue Service's own system, which it had used for many years, an adaptation of Standard Industrial Classification (SIC); all previous *Almanacs* had used that adaptation.

The new industrial classification system is the product of the North American Free Trade Agreement (NAFTA), and it replaces the existing classification systems not only of the United States but also of Canada and Mexico. Hence, the new system applies uniformly to the three countries, and users of the *Almanac 2011,* utilizing the new international industrial classification system, can now compare their results with corporations in all three nations.

In the United States, the new manual was created by the Office of Management and Budget (OMB). The NAICS system gives special attention to industries producing and furnishing advanced technologies, new and emerging industries, as well as service industries in general. NAICS divides the economy into 21 sectors, five in the predominantly goods-producing area, and 16 in the service producing area.

INDUSTRY SECTORS

In 2007, NAICS was revised and reorganized; several of those changes apply to the *Almanac 2011.* The Real Estate Investment Trust category (525930) was deleted. In its place, Mortgage REIT's were reclassified to Other Financial Vehicles (525995) while Equity REIT's were reclassified either to Lessors of Buildings (531115) or Lessors of Miniwarehouses, Self-Storage Units and other Real Estate (531135), depending on the content of the REIT portfolio.

The other major changes were in the information sector. The Internet Publishing and Broadcasting category (516100) was deleted and reclassified with Other Information Services (519100). Internet Service Providers (518115) were reclassified to Telecommunications (517000). Web Search Portals (also part of 518115) were reclassified to the expanded category, Other Information Services (519100). The remainder of the 518115 category was reorganized as Data processing, Hosting and Related Services (518210).

The source of the IRS's data are the tax returns of all *active* public and private corporations. Because the *Almanac's* data are derived only from corporate tax returns, there is a mixture of corporate with the financial performance of partnerships and individual proprietorships; the *Almanac's* information constitutes a **homogeneous universe**. The tax returns are classified by the IRS on the basis of the business activity which accounts for a corporation's largest percentage of total receipts. Large corporations with dissimilar business activities are included in only one industry, despite operations that are unrelated to the industry in which they are grouped.

The data developed by the IRS are derived from a stratified probability sample of corporation income tax returns. Where the sample data from the sample are small and should those numbers be used in a denominator, the result is reported as a dot (·) in the *Almanac*. Returns of the largest corporations are generally in the sample from year to year, but comparability can be affected by consolidations and mergers, changes in the law and the tax forms, and changes in the industrial classification system used over the years.

REPRESENTATIVE INDUSTRIES

The *Almanac* reports on nearly 200 industries. Minor industries are denoted by a six-digit code; major industries are designated by a three-digit industry code; industrial sectors by a two-digit code; and industrial divisions by a two-digit code. When the data are the same for minor, major, sector, and industrial division, the IRS reports only the industrial division, and similarly for other identities applicable to the major and sectoral industries; the *Almanac* follows this procedure.

Almanac 2011 continues the previous coverage of reporting information: for all industries, **Table I, Corporations with and without Net Income** (that is, the entire universe of active reporting corporations), and **Table II, Corporations with Net Income**, a subset of the universe. In the *Almanac 2011*, Table I covers over 5.8 million enterprises (corporations), and Table II covers 3.4 million corporations with net income. This implies that 2.4 million corporations reported deficits. The IRS defines net income (or deficit) as the companies' net profit or loss from taxable sources of income reduced by allowable deductions. Total receipts of the 5.8 million corporations reported in *Almanac 2011* was $28.8 trillion, up by $1.4 trillion.

The *Almanac* continues to report performance results not only by the total for each industry, but by 12 other asset size groups (a total of 13 asset size groups), providing 50 items of data and/or ratios on corporate performance:

Total

Zero
$1 to $500,000
$500,001 to $1,000,000
$1,000,001 to $5,000,000
$5,000,001 to $10,000,000
$10,000,001 to $25,000,000
$25,000,001 to $50,000,000
$50,000,001 to $100,000,000
$100,000,001 to $250,000,000
$250,000,001 to $500,000,000
$500,000,001 to $2,500,000,000
$2,500,000,001 or more

All data in Tables I and II cover an accounting period identified on all tables and are the most recent information available from the IRS. For the *Almanac 2011*, the accounting period is July 2007 through June 2008. The dating of the data is counterbalanced by the most extensive industrial coverage available in any report on financial performance, the number of items of corporate performance, and their availability in thirteen asset size groups. Moreover, the timing of the data are also counterbalanced by the stability of the *Almanac's* values as past trends have indicated. Therefore, the *Almanac's* financial results are reliable in assessing current corporate performance.

Beyond its reliable insights into corporate behavior on a micro basis, its comprehensive and detailed coverage make the *Almanac* the **Anatomy of American Corporate Capitalism**. In this macro sense, it constitutes **the** example to those countries desirous of modeling their economies on the American performance.

HOW TO USE THE ALMANAC

On the micro level, the *Almanac* multiplies manyfold the power of financial analysis to evaluate an individual company's financial performance: In contrast to many standard reports, the *Almanac* gives management, and analysts independent of any company, more of the fundamental analytical tools needed to compare their company with companies in the same industry and of the same asset size. The *Almanac* can enhance the value of any company's annual report because it affords the analyst and the stockholder detailed background of financial information for comparison.

All items and ratios are listed in Both Table I and Table II. No figures are reported in the *Almanac* when the IRS has either suppressed the underlying data, or the sample size, or other reasons affecting a calculated result, and where the ratio/item was not applicable to an industry. The 50 tax-based items that provide that financial analysis are as follows:

1. Number of Enterprises

These are the count of corporate tax returns filed by active corporations on one of the Form 1120-series returns.

> SPECIAL NOTE: Net Sales is used to compute the percentage of items 3 to 7 to Net Sales for all industries, except Finance, Insurance, and Real Estate (FIRE). For the FIRE industries, Total Receipts are used to compute the percentage of items 3 to 7.

REVENUES ($ IN THOUSANDS), ITEMS 2 TO 9

2. Operating Income (Net Sales)

This is the IRS item Business Receipts, the gross operating receipts reduced by the cost of returned goods and allowances.

3. Interest

Taxable interest includes interest on U.S. Government obligations, loans, notes, mortgages, arbitrage bonds, nonexempt private activity bonds, corporate bonds, bank deposits, and tax refunds; interest received from tax-exempt state or local municipal bonds and ESOP loans are not included in this item.

4. Rents

These are the gross amounts received from the use or occupancy of property by corporations whose principal activities did not involve operating rental properties.

5. Royalties

These are gross payments received for the use of property rights before taking deductions.

6. Other Portfolio Income

These consist of cash, notes, and accounts receivable, less allowance for bad debts and inventories.

7. Other Receipts

These receipts include such items as income from minor operations, cash discounts, claims, license rights, judgments, and joint ventures.

8. Total Receipts

Total receipts are the sum of ten items: 1. Business receipts; 2. Interest; 3. Interest on government obligations: state and local; 4. Rents; 5. Royalties; 6. Net capital gains (excluding long-term gains from regulated investment companies); 7. Net gain, noncapital assets; 8. Dividends received from domestic corporations; 9. Dividends received from foreign corporations; 10. Other receipts.

9. Average Total Receipts

Total receipts divided by the number of enterprises.

OPERATING COSTS/OPERATING INCOME, ITEMS 10 TO 22

10. Cost of Operations

This is the IRS's Costs of Goods Sold; it consists of the costs incurred in producing the goods or furnishing the services that generated the corporations' business receipts.

11. Salaries and Wages

These include the amount of salaries and wages paid as well as bonuses and director's fees, but no contributions to pension plans (see item 16) nor compensation of officers (see item 20).

12. Taxes Paid

Excludes Federal Income Taxes; they are the amounts paid for ordinary state and local taxes, social security, payroll taxes, unemployment insurance taxes, excise taxes, import and tariff duties, and business license and privilege taxes.

13. Interest Paid

These amounts consist of interest paid on all business indebtedness.

14. Depreciation

The charges allowed are governed principally by the IRS rules in effect in 1997, basically enacted in 1986, but also include other modifications. Hence, depreciation could represent amounts computed by different sets of rules.

15. Amortization and Depletion

Most amortization is calculated on a straight-line basis. Depletion is allowed for the exhaustion of natural deposits and timber.

16. Pensions, Profit-Sharing, Stock Bonus, and Annuity Plans

These are amounts deducted during the current year for qualified pension, profit-sharing, or other funded deferred compensation plans.

17. Employee Benefits

These are employer contributions to death benefit, insurance, health, accident, and sickness, and other welfare plans.

18. Advertising

Amounts include promotion and publicity expenses.

19. Other Expenses

These include expenses for repairs, bad debts, rent paid on business property, domestic production activities, contributions and gifts, and expenses not allocable to specific deductible items.

20. Officers' Compensation

Salaries, wages, stock bonuses, bonds, and other forms of compensation are included in this item.

21. Operating Margin

This is the net income after all operating costs have been deducted.

22. Operating Margin Before Officers' Compensation

This measure takes into account the effect of Officers' Compensation on the operating margin.

Selected Average Balance Sheet Items ($ in thousands) Items 23 to 29

23. *Average Net Receivables*

The total of Notes and Accounts Receivable, less Allowance for Bad Debts, divided by the number of enterprises. Notes and Accounts Receivable are the gross amounts arising from business sales or services to customers on credit in the course of ordinary trade or business. This includes commercial paper, charge accounts, current intercompany receivables, property investment loans, and trade acceptances.

24. *Average Inventories*

Total inventories are divided by the number of enterprises. Inventories include finished goods, partially finished goods, new materials and supplies acquired for sale, merchandise on hand or in transit, and growing crops reported as assets by agricultural enterprises.

25. *Average Net Property, Plant and Equipment*

This includes depreciable assets less accumulated depreciation, depletable assets less accumulated depletion, and land; the sum is divided by the number of enterprises. Depreciable assets consist of end-of-year balance sheet tangible property, such as buildings and equipment used in trade or business, or held for the production of income, and that has a useful life of one year or more. The amount of accumulated depreciation represents the portion written off in the current year, as well as in prior years. Depletable assets represent the end-of-year value of mineral property, oil and gas wells, and other natural resources; standing timber; intangible development and drilling costs capitalized; and leases and leaseholds, subject to depletion. Accumulated depletion represents the cumulative adjustment of these assets.

26. *Average Total Assets*

Total Assets (and Total Liabilities) are amounts reported in the end-of-year balance sheet. Total Assets are net amounts after reduction from accumulated depreciation, accumulated amortization, accumulated depletion, and the reserve for bad debts. Total Liabilities include the claims of creditors and stockholders' equity, and were net after reduction by the cost of treasury stock. The average of total assets was obtained by dividing it by the number of enterprises.

27. *Average of Notes and Loans Payable, and Mortgages*

These liabilities were separated on the balance sheet according to the time to maturity of the obligations. Time to maturity was based on the date of the balance sheet, rather than the date of issue of the obligations. The total was divided by the number of enterprises.

28. *Average of All Other Liabilities*

These included accounts payable, and other liabilities including other current liabilities. The total was divided by the number of enterprises.

29. *Average Net Worth*

Net Worth represents the stockholders' equity in the corporation (total assets minus the claims of creditors). It consists of Capital Stock, Paid-In Capital Surplus, Retained Earnings Appropriated, Retained Earnings Unappropriated, less cost of treasury stock.

SELECTED FINANCIAL RATIOS, NUMBER OF TIMES TO ONE, RATIOS 30 TO 44

30. Current Ratio

The items that used Current Assets for this ratio are Cash; Notes and Accounts Receivable, Less: Allowance for Bad Debts; Inventories; Government Obligations; Tax-Exempt Securities; and Other Current Assets. For Current Liabilities, the following items were included: Accounts Payable; Mortgages and Notes Maturing in Less than 1 Year; and Other Current Liabilities.

This ratio, rated highest by CPAs as a measure of liquidity, gauges the ability of a company to meet its short-term financial obligations should it be compelled to liquidate its assets. However, it is not an absolute measure of the company's ability to meet its obligations. It is obtained by dividing current assets by current liabilities. The standard guideline has been a ratio of 2 to 1; however, some companies have found that in their experience, a ratio less than 2 to 1 is adequate, while others consider a larger one to be necessary. The ratio is affected by the method of valuation of inventory (LIFO or FIFO) and by inflation. The *Almanac* provides measures that can be treated as standards by size of asset.

31. Quick Ratio

This ratio is also known as the "Acid Test Ratio" because it is often used to estimate a company's general liquidity. There is some disagreement about the inclusion of inventory in the numerator because it may be slow moving, obsolete, or pledged to specific creditors, and, therefore, not be readily convertible into cash. The *Almanac* adopts a conservative approach and does not include the item in calculating the ratio. Excluding inventories and other current assets, the numerator is the same as that used in determining current assets. The denominator, current liabilities, is unchanged. The ratio of 1 to 1 has been considered a reasonable standard, but it is jeopardized because accounts and notes receivable may not be convertible into cash at face value and at short notice. The *Almanac* provides measures that can be treated as standards by size of asset.

32. Net Sales to Working Capital

This is an efficiency, or turnover, ratio that measures the rate at which current assets less current liabilities (Working Capital) is used in making sales. (In industries in Finance, Insurance, and Real Estate, total receipts rather than net sales is used.) A low ratio indicates a less efficient (profitable) use of working capital in making sales. The *Almanac* provides measures that can be treated as standards by size of asset. Working Capital is the difference between current assets and current liabilities.

33. Coverage Ratio

This ratio measures the number of times all interest paid by the company is covered by earnings before interest charges and taxes (EBIT). For that reason, the ratio is also known as the "times interest earned ratio." The ratio indicates the company's ability to service its debt based on its income.

34. Total Asset Turnover

The ratio is an efficiency ratio because it indicates the effectiveness of the company's use of its total assets in generating sales. It is measured by dividing net sales by total assets.

35. Inventory Turnover

Inventory turnover measures the liquidity of the inventory. It is computed by dividing the cost of goods sold by the average inventory. The result shows the number of times that the average inventory can be converted into receivables or cash. The ratio reflects both on the quality of the inventory and the efficiency of management. Typically, the higher the turnover rate, the more likely profits will be higher.

SPECIAL NOTE: Inventory turnover is not computed for industries in Finance, Insurance, and Real Estate.

36. Receivables Turnover

This ratio measures the liquidity of accounts receivable. It indicates the average collection period throughout the year. It is obtained by dividing sales average by net receivables. It is not computed in the Finance, Insurance, and Real Estate industries (although it is calculated for all other industries even though conventional analysis typically omits it) for many of the industries in the *Almanac*.

37. Total Liabilities to Net Worth

This ratio indicates the extent to which the company's funds are supplied by short- and long-term creditors compared to its owners. It is an indicator of the company's long-term debt paying ability. The ratio is one of the most important bearing on the company's capital structure. Net worth is defined in ratio 29.

38. Current Assets to Working Capital

The dependence of Working Capital in part on current assets is important to understanding this part of the source of Working Capital. Current Assets are defined in ratio 30 and Working Capital is defined in ratio 32.

39. Current Liabilities to Working Capital

The dependence of Working Capital in part on current liabilities is important to understanding this part of the source of Working Capital. Current Liabilities are defined in ratio 30 and Working Capital is defined in ratio 32.

40. Working Capital to Net Sales or Total Receipts

The purpose of this ratio is to determine the working capital needed in relation to projected sales or receipts. Working Capital is defined in ratio 32.

41. Inventory to Working Capital

This ratio, by showing the proportion of Working Capital invested in Inventory, indicates the part of Current Assets that are least liquid. Inventories which exceed working capital indicate that current liabilities exceed liquid current assets. Working Capital is defined in ratio 32.

42. Total Receipts to Cash Flow

Cash Flow is the difference between cash receipts and cash disbursements. The ratio of total receipts to cash flow could suggest steps which management might take to improve the company's cash position.

43. Cost of Goods to Cash Flow

This ratio can be the basis for projections of cash requirements needed to fund projected costs of production. Cash flow is defined in ratio 42.

44. Cash Flow to Total Debt

This ratio indicates the extent to which a company could service its total debt from cash flow. It is analogous to the coverage ratio; refer to ratio 33. Cash flow is defined in ratio 42.

SELECTED FINANCIAL FACTORS (IN PERCENTAGES), ITEMS 45 TO 50

45. Debt Ratio (Total Liabilities to Total Assets)

This ratio indicates the company's ability to pay all its debts. It measures the creditors' and owners' of the company's ability to withstand losses. It is an indicator of the long-run solvency of the firm.

46. Return on Total Assets

The ratio combines the turnover and profit ratios (Sales/Total Assets x [times] Profit/Sales) and yields the return on investment (Total Assets). The result is the end product of the DuPont System of financial analysis. The system takes into account both operating income and operating assets. In Table I of each industry, the Return on Investment (ROI) is net income less deficit before income taxes divided by total assets. In Table II of each industry, the ROI is net income before income taxes divided by Total Assets. Total Assets are used because management has discretion in the investment of the resources provided by both the creditors and owners.

47. Return on Equity Before Income Taxes

This ratio measures the profitability of the company's operations to owners, before income taxes. For Table I this is net income, less deficit before income taxes and before credits. For Table II this is net income minus income tax before credits.

48. Return on Equity After Income Taxes

This ratio measures the profitability of the company's operations to owners, after income taxes. For Table I this is net income, less deficit and minus income tax before credits. For Table II this is net income minus income tax and before credits.

49. Profit Margin (Before Income Tax)

This is net income before income tax divided by net sales (or total receipts) and indicates the contribution of sales to the profitability of the company. Competition, capital structure, and operating characteristics cause the margin to vary within and among industries. For Table I, net income less deficit and before income taxes is the numerator; for Table II it is net income before tax.

50. Profit Margin (After Income Tax)

This ratio is the same as ratio 49 except that income taxes are taken into account.

Table of Contents

Page references to tables for industries with net income are in italic

PRINCIPAL BUSINESS ACTIVITY (BASED ON NAICS)

ALMANAC
of Business and Industrial
FINANCIAL RATIOS

42nd ANNUAL EDITION
2011

Table I

Corporations with and without Net Income

AGRICULTURAL PRODUCTION

MONEY AMOUNTS AND SIZE OF ASSETS IN THOUSANDS OF DOLLARS

Item Description for Accounting Period 7/07 Through 6/08	Total	Zero Assets	Under 500	500 to 1,000	1,000 to 5,000	5,000 to 10,000	10,000 to 25,000	25,000 to 50,000	50,000 to 100,000	100,000 to 250,000	250,000 to 500,000	500,000 to 2,500,000	2,500,000 and over
Number of Enterprises 1	102153	12728	57027	16229	14336	928	589	139	96	54	16	7	3
Revenues ($ in Thousands)													
Net Sales 2	98851427	1975708	12231453	8799271	20491600	6040152	9408574	3583037	7411146	8389473	6002457	3369886	11148670
Interest 3	437108	10863	90473	40606	99436	40027	22877	15647	22404	27003	18678	18214	30882
Rents 4	859290	19660	165986	158472	299467	42636	22369	14081	36509	35059	15618	40583	8852
Royalties 5	108829	1015	7136	12108	20659	5385	5721	20	5139	23949	848	13827	13023
Other Portfolio Income 6	1582832	193497	324288	194142	369613	109279	120782	71865	50387	84717	34227	20527	9507
Other Receipts 7	9904257	560444	2591802	1797805	2763212	762545	690481	96609	220733	180714	84271	131888	23747
Total Receipts 8	111743743	2761187	15411138	11002404	24043987	7000024	10270804	3781259	7746318	8740915	6156099	3594925	11234681
Average Total Receipts 9	1094	217	270	678	1677	7543	17438	27203	80691	161869	384756	513561	3744894
Operating Costs/Operating Income (%)													
Cost of Operations 10	49.9	58.6	17.7	28.3	28.8	38.5	70.0	64.8	73.3	59.4	78.5	64.0	81.7
Salaries and Wages 11	8.1	4.9	10.6	9.8	11.6	10.6	5.6	7.2	5.3	7.1	1.8	9.1	4.9
Taxes Paid 12	2.3	2.6	3.4	3.5	3.1	2.4	1.5	1.7	1.5	1.5	1.6	1.4	0.7
Interest Paid 13	3.0	3.6	3.4	3.8	3.7	4.4	2.3	3.5	1.7	2.1	1.7	2.0	2.9
Depreciation 14	5.3	6.9	8.0	9.2	7.2	6.5	3.3	4.3	3.0	3.5	2.2	3.1	1.9
Amortization and Depletion 15	0.3	0.0	0.0	0.2	0.1	0.3	0.2	0.3	0.4	0.7	0.7	1.2	0.2
Pensions and Other Deferred Comp. 16	0.3	0.2	0.2	0.1	0.2	0.2	0.1	0.2	0.2	0.2	0.8	0.2	0.5
Employee Benefits 17	1.1	0.4	1.3	1.4	0.9	1.0	0.7	0.6	0.7	1.0	0.8	3.0	1.4
Advertising 18	0.4	0.3	0.5	0.3	0.3	0.2	0.4	0.4	0.4	0.2	0.2	1.3	0.4
Other Expenses 19	37.5	52.3	70.2	61.0	56.1	47.6	22.1	21.0	13.7	25.8	8.4	11.1	7.6
Officers' Compensation 20	2.1	1.5	4.5	4.6	2.6	2.2	1.4	1.0	1.0	0.7	0.5	0.6	0.3
Operating Margin 21	•	•	•	•	•	•	•	•	•	•	2.9	3.0	•
Operating Margin Before Officers' Comp. 22	•	•	•	•	•	•	•	•	•	•	3.4	3.6	•

Selected Average Balance Sheet ($ in Thousands)

Net Receivables 23	77	0	3	27	62	417	1769	3061	11533	19923	45331	81087	328867
Inventories 24	104	0	10	49	138	974	2636	4467	10832	16910	41158	135127	435208
Net Property, Plant and Equipment 25	463	0	82	413	1068	3901	6075	15070	26011	54398	119517	197780	872009
Total Assets 26	1018	0	174	702	1894	6995	15212	32286	70315	145315	325755	701293	3629922
Notes and Loans Payable 27	545	0	157	361	1141	4707	7880	18123	27129	56694	80625	160265	1627756
All Other Liabilities 28	160	0	7	40	156	842	2373	3387	14479	25124	75793	183125	1712188
Net Worth 29	314	0	10	301	597	1447	4959	10776	28707	63497	169337	357904	289978

Selected Financial Ratios (Times to 1)

Current Ratio 30	1.4	•	1.7	1.4	1.4	1.2	1.5	1.3	1.6	1.4	2.1	1.2	1.0
Quick Ratio 31	0.7	•	1.1	0.8	0.7	0.6	0.7	0.6	0.8	0.7	0.9	0.7	0.4
Net Sales to Working Capital 32	10.6	•	10.6	11.2	11.2	16.6	7.4	10.6	6.3	9.5	4.9	11.5	399.3
Coverage Ratio 33	2.0	3.4	2.8	1.7	1.7	1.5	1.6	1.1	3.0	1.8	4.1	5.8	0.5
Total Asset Turnover 34	1.0	•	1.2	0.8	0.8	0.9	1.1	0.8	1.1	1.1	1.2	0.7	1.0
Inventory Turnover 35	4.6	•	3.7	3.1	3.0	2.6	4.2	3.7	5.2	5.5	7.2	2.3	7.0
Receivables Turnover 36	13.2	•	55.6	20.5	26.1	15.7	10.0	7.4	7.0	8.2	9.8	3.2	22.6
Total Liabilities to Net Worth 37	2.2	•	16.0	1.3	2.2	3.8	2.1	2.0	1.4	1.3	0.9	1.0	11.5
Current Assets to Working Capital 38	3.5	•	2.4	3.4	3.7	5.4	3.0	4.6	2.6	3.6	1.9	5.5	94.1
Current Liabilities to Working Capital 39	2.5	•	1.4	2.4	2.7	4.4	2.0	3.6	1.6	2.6	0.9	4.5	93.1
Working Capital to Net Sales 40	0.1	•	0.1	0.1	0.1	0.1	0.1	0.1	0.2	0.1	0.2	0.1	0.0
Inventory to Working Capital 41	1.2	•	0.5	1.1	1.0	2.3	1.2	1.8	0.9	1.2	0.6	1.3	46.8
Total Receipts to Cash Flow 42	3.3	2.1	2.0	2.1	2.3	2.4	5.3	5.9	7.0	4.1	9.1	5.9	26.9
Cost of Goods to Cash Flow 43	1.6	1.2	0.3	0.6	0.7	0.9	3.7	3.8	5.1	2.4	7.2	3.8	21.9
Cash Flow to Total Debt 44	0.4	•	0.7	0.6	0.5	0.5	0.3	0.2	0.3	0.5	0.3	0.2	0.0

Selected Financial Factors (in Percentages)

Debt Ratio 45	69.2	•	94.1	57.1	68.5	79.3	67.4	66.6	59.2	56.3	48.0	49.0	92.0
Return on Total Assets 46	5.6	•	11.7	5.1	4.8	6.0	4.0	3.2	5.6	4.1	8.0	8.1	1.5
Return on Equity Before Income Taxes 47	8.9	•	127.4	5.1	6.2	9.1	4.7	1.1	9.2	4.2	11.6	13.1	•
Return on Equity After Income Taxes 48	6.6	•	114.8	4.2	5.0	5.6	3.5	•	7.2	2.2	7.4	8.2	•
Profit Margin (Before Income Tax) 49	2.9	8.5	6.1	2.8	2.6	2.0	1.5	0.5	3.4	1.7	5.3	9.8	•
Profit Margin (After Income Tax) 50	2.1	7.2	5.5	2.3	2.1	1.2	1.1	•	2.7	0.9	3.4	6.1	•

1

AGRICULTURAL PRODUCTION

Table II

Corporations with Net Income

MONEY AMOUNTS AND SIZE OF ASSETS IN THOUSANDS OF DOLLARS

Item Description for Accounting Period 7/07 Through 6/08	Total	Zero Assets	Under 500	500 to 1000	251 to 500	501 to 1,000	1,001 to 5,000	5,001 to 10,000	10,001 to 25,000	25,001 to 50,000	50,001 to 100,000	100,001 to 250,000	250,001 and over
Number of Enterprises **1**	55619	5986	28911	10115	9552	533	331	83	60	•	•	•	0
Revenues ($ in Thousands)													
Net Sales **2**	61537598	1602966	7928345	6014122	13872502	4549586	5452222	2536941	5542722	•	•	•	0
Interest **3**	311871	10754	32870	39903	89697	32716	15496	4629	17772	•	•	•	0
Rents **4**	642867	7818	87207	123905	263611	36587	19575	12032	33869	•	•	•	0
Royalties **5**	89960	1004	5964	12108	14991	1517	4650	20	151	•	•	•	0
Other Portfolio Income **6**	1292190	169603	257164	154533	318885	92150	92797	58255	37250	•	•	•	0
Other Receipts **7**	7164048	411731	1769068	1062924	2418443	582829	408923	53776	134547	•	•	•	0
Total Receipts **8**	71038534	2203876	10080618	7407495	16978129	5295385	5993663	2665653	5766311	•	•	•	0
Average Total Receipts **9**	1277	368	349	732	1777	9935	18108	32116	96105	•	•	•	•
Operating Costs/Operating Income (%)													
Cost of Operations **10**	46.4	56.5	14.2	28.4	28.8	32.0	65.9	62.8	75.3	•	•	•	•
Salaries and Wages **11**	8.0	3.4	7.8	7.1	12.5	11.5	4.7	7.5	4.4	•	•	•	•
Taxes Paid **12**	2.3	1.9	2.7	3.4	3.3	2.2	1.4	1.6	1.4	•	•	•	•
Interest Paid **13**	2.5	3.3	2.7	2.8	3.6	3.1	2.0	2.3	1.4	•	•	•	•
Depreciation **14**	5.2	5.4	7.3	7.9	7.7	5.3	3.0	4.0	2.6	•	•	•	•
Amortization and Depletion **15**	0.3	0.0	0.0	0.2	0.1	0.3	0.2	0.2	0.4	•	•	•	•
Pensions and Other Deferred Comp. **16**	0.3	0.3	0.3	0.1	0.3	0.2	0.2	0.2	0.2	•	•	•	•
Employee Benefits **17**	1.1	0.2	1.2	1.3	1.0	1.0	0.6	0.7	0.5	•	•	•	•
Advertising **18**	0.3	0.2	0.3	0.3	0.3	0.2	0.5	0.2	0.2	•	•	•	•
Other Expenses **19**	34.7	36.2	64.2	54.1	50.3	48.8	20.3	17.0	9.5	•	•	•	•
Officers' Compensation **20**	2.4	1.4	4.6	5.2	2.9	2.6	1.3	0.7	0.8	•	•	•	•
Operating Margin **21**	•	•	•	•	•	•	•	2.8	3.2	•	•	•	•
Operating Margin Before Officers' Comp. **22**	•	•	•	•	•	1.1	1.1	3.6	4.0	•	•	•	•

Selected Average Balance Sheet ($ in Thousands)

Net Receivables **23**	84	0	5	27	52	414	2059	3414	13043
Inventories **24**	112	0	7	40	138	819	2651	3757	10669
Net Property, Plant and Equipment **25**	481	0	87	381	1017	3566	5821	16190	24989
Total Assets **26**	1094	0	197	717	1836	7057	15200	33073	69847
Notes and Loans Payable **27**	432	0	100	262	843	3822	5725	15277	24896
All Other Liabilities **28**	175	0	5	42	145	859	1988	3724	15247
Net Worth **29**	487	0	91	413	848	2375	7487	14073	29704

Selected Financial Ratios (Times to 1)

Current Ratio **30**	1.7	•	2.2	1.7	1.4	1.3	1.7	1.7	1.6
Quick Ratio **31**	1.0	•	1.7	1.0	0.8	0.7	1.0	1.1	0.9
Net Sales to Working Capital **32**	7.9	•	8.6	8.3	10.8	17.6	5.6	6.8	7.0
Coverage Ratio **33**	5.8	9.6	9.0	5.3	4.2	4.0	5.7	4.5	6.2
Total Asset Turnover **34**	1.0	•	1.4	0.8	0.8	1.2	1.1	0.9	1.3
Inventory Turnover **35**	4.6	•	5.3	4.2	3.0	3.3	4.1	5.1	6.5
Receivables Turnover **36**	13.8	•	46.9	22.0	32.6	•	8.4	7.4	•
Total Liabilities to Net Worth **37**	1.2	•	1.2	0.7	1.2	2.0	1.0	1.4	1.4
Current Assets to Working Capital **38**	2.5	•	1.9	2.5	3.4	4.5	2.4	2.4	2.6
Current Liabilities to Working Capital **39**	1.5	•	0.9	1.5	2.4	3.5	1.4	1.4	1.6
Working Capital to Net Sales **40**	0.1	•	0.1	0.1	0.1	0.1	0.2	0.1	0.1
Inventory to Working Capital **41**	0.8	•	0.2	0.6	1.1	1.7	0.8	0.7	0.8
Total Receipts to Cash Flow **42**	2.7	1.9	1.6	2.0	2.1	2.0	3.9	5.1	7.1
Cost of Goods to Cash Flow **43**	1.3	1.1	0.2	0.6	0.6	0.6	2.6	3.2	5.3
Cash Flow to Total Debt **44**	0.7	•	1.6	1.0	0.7	0.9	0.5	0.3	0.3

Selected Financial Factors (in Percentages)

Debt Ratio **45**	55.5	•	53.6	42.3	53.8	66.3	50.7	57.4	57.5
Return on Total Assets **46**	14.5	•	34.0	12.5	11.8	15.0	12.7	9.4	11.4
Return on Equity Before Income Taxes **47**	27.0	•	65.1	17.7	19.4	33.3	21.2	17.1	22.5
Return on Equity After Income Taxes **48**	24.3	•	62.3	16.6	18.3	29.5	19.7	15.2	19.5
Profit Margin (Before Income Tax) **49**	11.9	28.8	21.7	12.3	11.3	9.3	9.6	7.9	7.2
Profit Margin (After Income Tax) **50**	10.7	27.1	20.8	11.5	10.7	8.2	9.0	7.0	6.3

2

Table I

Corporations with and without Net Income

FORESTRY AND LOGGING

MONEY AMOUNTS AND SIZE OF ASSETS IN THOUSANDS OF DOLLARS

Item Description for Accounting Period 7/07 Through 6/08	Total	Zero Assets	Under 500	500 to 1,000	1,000 to 5,000	5,000 to 10,000	10,000 to 25,000	25,000 to 50,000	50,000 to 100,000	100,000 to 250,000	250,000 to 500,000	500,000 to 2,500,000	2,500,000 and over
Number of Enterprises 1	10097	1428	6012	1101	1382	24	110	21	8	0	4	7	0
Revenues ($ in Thousands)													
Net Sales 2	14178897	781642	3167331	2052106	4056536	564049	1629374	374076	366717	0	653399	533666	0
Interest 3	306657	36	2804	407	6073	46	4861	6362	968	0	11311	273787	0
Rents 4	43399	364	0	573	4268	250	4643	4598	206	0	3183	25314	0
Royalties 5	3265	0	0	2055	0	0	947	0	0	0	0	263	0
Other Portfolio Income 6	316716	749	13622	56331	124214	1359	34052	29666	4501	0	34234	17987	0
Other Receipts 7	265750	179	3834	28845	46326	8999	13428	-2136	1086	0	78963	86232	0
Total Receipts 8	15114684	782970	3187591	2140317	4237417	574703	1687305	412566	373478	0	781090	937249	0
Average Total Receipts 9	1497	548	530	1944	3066	23946	15339	19646	46685	•	195272	133893	•
Operating Costs/Operating Income (%)													
Cost of Operations 10	59.8	72.9	67.7	28.8	45.6	84.1	75.6	81.2	88.2	•	79.0	88.8	•
Salaries and Wages 11	9.2	8.6	5.0	14.6	13.8	2.6	7.9	2.2	3.4	•	4.4	3.6	•
Taxes Paid 12	2.2	0.5	1.8	2.1	3.2	0.7	1.5	2.9	1.5	•	1.3	3.5	•
Interest Paid 13	5.2	0.6	1.8	2.2	2.1	1.6	2.5	4.3	3.5	•	2.3	85.6	•
Depreciation 14	5.4	1.1	3.7	9.4	7.9	1.4	3.4	3.3	4.5	•	1.5	5.2	•
Amortization and Depletion 15	0.5	0.1	0.0	•	0.0	•	0.3	1.3	1.9	•	4.2	5.9	•
Pensions and Other Deferred Comp. 16	0.2	•	0.0	0.0	0.2	0.2	0.7	0.3	0.2	•	0.4	0.9	•
Employee Benefits 17	0.9	1.0	1.0	1.1	1.1	0.2	0.7	0.6	0.5	•	1.4	0.2	•
Advertising 18	0.2	0.2	0.1	0.1	0.1	0.1	0.4	0.1	0.2	•	0.1	0.3	•
Other Expenses 19	18.6	11.6	14.6	34.7	21.1	9.9	8.1	7.9	7.3	•	13.3	33.9	•
Officers' Compensation 20	3.3	0.5	5.7	3.4	3.7	1.9	2.3	0.8	1.3	•	1.1	0.8	•
Operating Margin 21	•	3.0	•	3.5	1.2	•	•	•	•	•	•	•	•
Operating Margin Before Officers' Comp. 22	•	3.4	4.2	6.9	4.9	•	•	•	•	•	•	•	•

Selected Average Balance Sheet ($ in Thousands)

Net Receivables 23	64	0	1	23	121	919	707	1294	4251	48917	12821
Inventories 24	87	0	7	10	145	1784	3603	4814	4044	3796	5791
Net Property, Plant and Equipment 25	916	0	61	483	1064	2367	7089	20850	37103	63562	721524
Total Assets 26	1909	0	104	676	1906	7577	16716	36658	68730	299900	1533264
Notes and Loans Payable 27	1055	0	112	529	1221	5333	5948	6654	20536	113554	881447
All Other Liabilities 28	162	0	6	13	124	574	1348	1824	6116	33378	146580
Net Worth 29	692	0	-15	134	561	1670	9420	28180	42078	152968	505238

Selected Financial Ratios (Times to 1)

Current Ratio 30	3.1	•	1.4	0.9	1.5	0.9	2.0	4.0	1.3	2.3	7.9
Quick Ratio 31	2.4	•	0.9	0.4	0.9	0.2	0.8	1.6	1.0	1.6	7.3
Net Sales to Working Capital 32	3.4	•	62.2	•	16.4	•	4.8	3.7	14.4	3.8	0.2
Coverage Ratio 33	1.2	6.6	0.6	4.5	3.7	0.5	1.0	2.2	•	5.6	0.4
Total Asset Turnover 34	0.7	•	5.1	2.8	1.5	3.1	0.9	0.5	0.7	0.5	0.0
Inventory Turnover 35	9.6	•	50.2	55.0	9.2	11.1	3.1	3.0	10.0	34.0	11.7
Receivables Turnover 36	20.8	•	473.3	42.9	25.6	36.4	18.5	8.7	10.2	4.2	6.1
Total Liabilities to Net Worth 37	1.8	•	•	4.1	2.4	3.5	0.8	0.3	0.6	1.0	2.0
Current Assets to Working Capital 38	1.5	•	3.7	•	3.0	•	2.0	1.3	4.3	1.8	1.1
Current Liabilities to Working Capital 39	0.5	•	2.7	•	2.0	•	1.0	0.3	3.3	0.8	0.1
Working Capital to Net Sales 40	0.3	•	0.0	•	0.1	•	0.2	0.3	0.1	0.3	6.1
Inventory to Working Capital 41	0.2	•	1.3	•	0.7	•	1.1	0.7	0.7	0.1	0.0
Total Receipts to Cash Flow 42	6.9	8.8	8.9	2.9	4.8	13.2	22.5	17.7	•	7.7	•
Cost of Goods to Cash Flow 43	4.1	6.5	6.0	0.8	2.2	11.1	17.0	14.4	6.1	•	•
Cash Flow to Total Debt 44	0.2	•	0.5	1.2	0.5	0.3	0.1	0.1	•	0.1	•

Selected Financial Factors (in Percentages)

Debt Ratio 45	63.7	•	114.1	80.2	70.6	78.0	43.6	23.1	38.8	49.0	67.0
Return on Total Assets 46	4.6	•	5.0	27.6	12.0	2.6	2.3	4.5	•	7.0	1.6
Return on Equity Before Income Taxes 47	2.2	•	28.3	108.7	29.7	•	0.2	3.1	•	11.2	•
Return on Equity After Income Taxes 48	1.1	•	29.3	108.7	28.3	•	•	0.6	•	11.0	•
Profit Margin (Before Income Tax) 49	1.1	3.1	•	7.8	5.7	0.1	0.1	5.0	•	10.5	•
Profit Margin (After Income Tax) 50	0.5	3.1	7.8	5.4	•	•	•	0.9	•	10.3	•

Table II
Corporations with Net Income

FORESTRY AND LOGGING

Money Amounts and Size of Assets in Thousands of Dollars

Item Description for Accounting Period 7/07 Through 6/08	Total	Zero Assets	Under 500	500 to 1,000	1,000 to 5,000	5,000 to 10,000	10,000 to 25,000	25,000 to 50,000	50,000 to 100,000	100,000 to 250,000	250,000 to 500,000	500,000 to 2,500,000	2,500,000 and over
Number of Enterprises **1**	4848	453	2901	672	756	7	46	•	0	0	0	0	0
Revenues ($ in Thousands)													
Net Sales **2**	8536880	681754	1124273	1516159	2818394	275651	1127702	•	0	0	0	0	0
Interest **3**	111523	15	2472	36	3816	46	4817	•	0	0	0	0	0
Rents **4**	18718	0	0	0	441	250	4629	•	0	0	0	0	0
Royalties **5**	499	0	0	0	0	0	239	•	0	0	0	0	0
Other Portfolio Income **6**	240915	624	5449	34545	105620	309	31845	•	0	0	0	0	0
Other Receipts **7**	236302	140	3371	13406	42210	972	4396	•	0	0	0	0	0
Total Receipts **8**	9144837	682533	1135565	1564146	2970481	277228	1173628	•	0	0	0	0	0
Average Total Receipts **9**	1886	1507	391	2328	3929	39604	25514	•	•	•	•	•	•
Operating Costs/Operating Income (%)													
Cost of Operations **10**	51.2	79.2	54.5	17.6	40.3	90.3	72.1	•	•	•	•	•	•
Salaries and Wages **11**	11.2	6.7	4.0	17.0	17.2	0.1	8.2	•	•	•	•	•	•
Taxes Paid **12**	2.0	0.0	1.1	2.1	3.4	0.6	1.4	•	•	•	•	•	•
Interest Paid **13**	2.8	0.0	2.2	1.8	2.0	0.7	1.0	•	•	•	•	•	•
Depreciation **14**	5.6	0.0	5.3	9.0	8.3	1.1	1.9	•	•	•	•	•	•
Amortization and Depletion **15**	0.4	0.0	•	•	0.0	•	0.3	•	•	•	•	•	•
Pensions and Other Deferred Comp. **16**	0.2	•	•	0.0	0.2	0.3	0.9	•	•	•	•	•	•
Employee Benefits **17**	0.8	•	0.1	1.2	1.1	0.2	0.6	•	•	•	•	•	•
Advertising **18**	0.1	0.0	0.2	0.0	0.0	0.1	0.5	•	•	•	•	•	•
Other Expenses **19**	19.1	9.0	17.2	39.2	18.8	2.5	8.6	•	•	•	•	•	•
Officers' Compensation **20**	3.2	•	5.8	2.5	4.5	3.7	2.3	•	•	•	•	•	•
Operating Margin **21**	3.3	5.0	9.7	9.5	4.2	0.4	2.3	•	•	•	•	•	•
Operating Margin Before Officers' Comp. **22**	6.5	5.0	15.4	12.0	8.7	4.1	4.6	•	•	•	•	•	•

Selected Average Balance Sheet ($ in Thousands)

Net Receivables 23	87	0	0	26	174	2306	1171
Inventories 24	88	0	4	3	137	4545	3911
Net Property, Plant and Equipment 25	437	0	38	531	945	2152	7894
Total Assets 26	1268	0	87	725	1773	9712	17204
Notes and Loans Payable 27	507	0	55	552	1151	3688	3714
All Other Liabilities 28	222	0	5	14	189	633	1941
Net Worth 29	539	0	27	159	434	5391	11549

Selected Financial Ratios (Times to 1)

Current Ratio 30	1.8	•	10.9	0.9	1.2	2.0	2.9
Quick Ratio 31	1.1	•	10.1	0.4	0.9	0.7	1.4
Net Sales to Working Capital 32	13.0	•	14.0	•	34.0	11.1	5.5
Coverage Ratio 33	4.7	189.7	5.9	8.1	5.7	2.5	7.4
Total Asset Turnover 34	1.4	•	4.5	3.1	2.1	4.1	1.4
Inventory Turnover 35	10.2	•	56.1	142.1	10.9	7.8	4.5
Receivables Turnover 36	19.0	•	905.9	51.7	22.3	•	17.7
Total Liabilities to Net Worth 37	1.4	•	2.2	3.6	3.1	0.8	0.5
Current Assets to Working Capital 38	2.2	•	1.1	•	5.2	2.0	1.5
Current Liabilities to Working Capital 39	1.2	•	0.1	•	4.2	1.0	0.5
Working Capital to Net Sales 40	0.1	•	0.1	•	0.0	0.1	0.2
Inventory to Working Capital 41	0.5	•	0.1	•	0.3	1.3	0.8
Total Receipts to Cash Flow 42	4.2	8.7	4.1	2.2	4.8	31.0	9.4
Cost of Goods to Cash Flow 43	2.2	6.9	2.2	0.4	1.9	28.0	6.8
Cash Flow to Total Debt 44	0.6	•	1.6	1.8	0.6	0.3	0.5

Selected Financial Factors (in Percentages)

Debt Ratio 45	57.5	•	68.8	78.1	75.5	44.5	32.9
Return on Total Assets 46	18.4	•	57.2	45.0	24.5	6.5	10.5
Return on Equity Before Income Taxes 47	34.1	•	152.4	180.0	82.4	7.0	13.6
Return on Equity After Income Taxes 48	31.2	•	151.3	179.9	79.0	6.8	9.8
Profit Margin (Before Income Tax) 49	10.4	5.1	10.7	12.7	9.6	1.0	6.4
Profit Margin (After Income Tax) 50	9.5	5.1	10.6	12.7	9.2	0.9	4.6

SUPPORT ACTIVITIES AND FISHING, HUNTING AND TRAPPING

Table I

Corporations with and without Net Income

MONEY AMOUNTS AND SIZE OF ASSETS IN THOUSANDS OF DOLLARS

Item Description for Accounting Period 7/07 Through 6/08	Total	Zero Assets	Under 500	500 to 1,000	1,000 to 5,000	5,000 to 10,000	10,000 to 25,000	25,000 to 50,000	50,000 to 100,000	100,000 to 250,000	250,000 to 500,000	500,000 to 2,500,000	2,500,000 and over
Number of Enterprises 1	29929	7002	17943	2717	1761	316	136	39	11	4	0	0	0
Revenues ($ in Thousands)													
Net Sales 2	27041006	307852	6875273	2305813	7806199	2912921	3434985	1000442	759679	1637841	0	0	0
Interest 3	33285	0	4271	1746	13480	3882	4905	413	1148	3440	0	0	0
Rents 4	30746	41	1018	6034	16786	4868	1972	4	0	24	0	0	0
Royalties 5	1279	0	0	0	0	535	0	22	0	722	0	0	0
Other Portfolio Income 6	171811	9636	28567	25604	41200	33225	27673	2266	1170	2467	0	0	0
Other Receipts 7	696913	105032	132017	270515	301163	-396677	181905	42497	41117	19348	0	0	0
Total Receipts 8	27975040	422561	7041146	2609712	8178828	2558754	3651440	1045644	803114	1663842	0	0	0
Average Total Receipts 9	935	60	392	961	4644	8097	26849	26811	73010	415960	•	•	•
Operating Costs/Operating Income (%)													
Cost of Operations 10	60.7	43.2	42.3	28.7	73.7	53.1	83.0	73.4	80.3	74.4	•	•	•
Salaries and Wages 11	8.8	3.4	11.6	10.4	6.8	13.7	4.4	5.5	5.4	9.3	•	•	•
Taxes Paid 12	1.9	3.5	2.1	2.2	1.8	2.0	1.5	1.4	1.2	2.6	•	•	•
Interest Paid 13	1.2	6.0	1.0	1.9	0.8	0.9	1.2	3.0	1.3	1.2	•	•	•
Depreciation 14	2.9	3.1	2.8	6.3	2.4	3.9	1.9	2.6	2.1	2.2	•	•	•
Amortization and Depletion 15	0.1	•	0.1	0.2	0.1	0.1	0.1	0.0	0.1	0.3	•	•	•
Pensions and Other Deferred Comp. 16	0.2	•	0.1	0.2	0.1	0.4	0.2	0.4	0.3	0.0	•	•	•
Employee Benefits 17	0.6	3.0	0.5	0.9	0.5	0.7	0.5	0.3	0.6	0.6	•	•	•
Advertising 18	0.2	0.9	0.5	0.2	0.1	0.2	0.1	0.3	0.1	0.4	•	•	•
Other Expenses 19	18.3	64.9	29.3	42.0	11.8	8.7	9.6	10.6	10.8	4.6	•	•	•
Officers' Compensation 20	3.3	6.1	4.9	5.8	3.3	1.3	1.7	1.6	0.6	1.5	•	•	•
Operating Margin 21	1.7	•	4.7	1.1	•	15.1	•	0.9	•	2.7	•	•	•
Operating Margin Before Officers' Comp. 22	5.0	•	9.7	6.9	2.0	16.3	•	2.5	•	4.2	•	•	•

Selected Average Balance Sheet ($ in Thousands)

Net Receivables 23	65	0	7	65	239	993	3161	6208	8936	33722	•	•	•	•
Inventories 24	57	0	6	17	144	758	2536	5609	11530	88988	•	•	•	•
Net Property, Plant and Equipment 25	180	0	38	316	866	3260	3997	7239	17619	68820	•	•	•	•
Total Assets 26	480	0	92	692	1875	7292	14941	33017	67727	292750	•	•	•	•
Notes and Loans Payable 27	219	0	82	307	863	1667	6557	16755	23357	101848	•	•	•	•
All Other Liabilities 28	106	0	20	60	288	2481	4302	6767	24809	63463	•	•	•	•
Net Worth 29	155	0	-9	325	725	3145	4083	9496	19562	127439	•	•	•	•

Selected Financial Ratios (Times to 1)

Current Ratio 30	1.6	•	1.8	3.2	2.1	1.2	1.2	1.5	1.3	2.1	•	•	•	•
Quick Ratio 31	1.0	•	1.4	2.9	1.4	0.8	0.6	0.9	0.6	0.9	•	•	•	•
Net Sales to Working Capital 32	10.5	•	23.4	4.7	11.7	15.1	17.1	4.1	7.2	4.4	•	•	•	•
Coverage Ratio 33	5.3	1.5	7.8	8.4	5.4	4.1	2.5	2.8	3.2	4.5	•	•	•	•
Total Asset Turnover 34	1.9	•	4.2	1.2	2.4	1.3	1.7	0.8	1.0	1.4	•	•	•	•
Inventory Turnover 35	9.7	•	26.2	14.2	22.7	6.5	8.3	3.4	4.8	3.4	•	•	•	•
Receivables Turnover 36	15.1	•	47.3	18.3	21.5	9.3	9.2	4.6	8.2	10.4	•	•	•	•
Total Liabilities to Net Worth 37	2.1	•	•	1.1	1.6	1.3	2.7	2.5	2.5	1.3	•	•	•	•
Current Assets to Working Capital 38	2.6	•	2.3	1.5	1.9	5.2	5.9	2.9	3.9	1.9	•	•	•	•
Current Liabilities to Working Capital 39	1.6	•	1.3	0.5	0.9	4.2	4.9	1.9	2.9	0.9	•	•	•	•
Working Capital to Net Sales 40	0.1	•	0.0	0.2	0.1	0.1	0.1	0.2	0.1	0.2	•	•	•	•
Inventory to Working Capital 41	0.7	•	0.3	0.1	0.5	1.6	1.9	0.7	1.8	1.0	•	•	•	•
Total Receipts to Cash Flow 42	5.3	1.6	3.5	2.1	8.0	12.1	12.7	6.7	8.2	13.2	•	•	•	•
Cost of Goods to Cash Flow 43	3.2	0.7	1.5	0.6	5.9	6.4	10.5	4.9	6.6	9.8	•	•	•	•
Cash Flow to Total Debt 44	0.5	•	1.1	1.1	0.5	0.2	0.2	0.2	0.2	0.2	•	•	•	•

Selected Financial Factors (in Percentages)

Debt Ratio 45	67.7	•	109.9	53.1	61.3	56.9	72.7	71.2	71.1	56.5	•	•	•	•
Return on Total Assets 46	11.9	•	34.2	19.8	9.8	4.8	5.3	6.5	4.3	7.7	•	•	•	•
Return on Equity Before Income Taxes 47	30.0	•	•	37.3	20.7	8.5	11.8	14.6	10.3	13.7	•	•	•	•
Return on Equity After Income Taxes 48	28.3	•	•	37.0	18.9	6.5	9.1	13.5	8.3	12.9	•	•	•	•
Profit Margin (Before Income Tax) 49	5.1	3.2	7.2	14.3	3.4	2.9	1.9	5.4	2.9	4.3	•	•	•	•
Profit Margin (After Income Tax) 50	4.9	3.1	7.1	14.1	3.1	2.2	1.5	5.0	2.4	4.0	•	•	•	•

SUPPORT ACTIVITIES AND FISHING, HUNTING AND TRAPPING

Table II

Corporations with Net Income

MONEY AMOUNTS AND SIZE OF ASSETS IN THOUSANDS OF DOLLARS

Item Description for Accounting Period 7/07 Through 6/08	Total	Zero Assets	Under 500	500 to 1,000	1,000 to 5,000	5,000 to 10,000	10,000 to 25,000	25,000 to 50,000	50,000 to 100,000	100,000 to 250,000	250,000 to 500,000	500,000 to 2,500,000	2,500,000 and over
Number of Enterprises **1**	15094	2470	9039	2073	1134	260	85	•	8	•	0	0	0
Revenues ($ in Thousands)													
Net Sales **2**	22791522	216647	5197912	1933047	6994271	2690655	2794330	•	659421	•	0	0	0
Interest **3**	22088	0	1512	619	11168	3609	2923	•	964	•	0	0	0
Rents **4**	20692	4	693	348	16772	1725	1146	•	0	•	0	0	0
Royalties **5**	530	0	0	0	0	508	0	•	0	•	0	0	0
Other Portfolio Income **6**	150546	9610	23235	19474	37419	33225	23687	•	1087	•	0	0	0
Other Receipts **7**	365672	23337	65444	223601	211882	-385999	141889	•	36979	•	0	0	0
Total Receipts **8**	23351050	249598	5288796	2177089	7271512	2343723	2963975	•	698451	•	0	0	0
Average Total Receipts **9**	1547	101	585	1050	6412	9014	34870	•	87306	•	•	•	•
Operating Costs/Operating Income (%)													
Cost of Operations **10**	60.2	28.1	39.1	28.0	74.4	49.4	84.3	•	80.3	•	•	•	•
Salaries and Wages **11**	8.5	3.6	11.6	9.4	6.3	14.3	3.8	•	4.2	•	•	•	•
Taxes Paid **12**	1.8	3.0	1.9	1.9	1.8	2.1	1.1	•	0.7	•	•	•	•
Interest Paid **13**	0.8	•	0.8	0.9	0.5	0.9	1.0	•	1.1	•	•	•	•
Depreciation **14**	2.5	1.1	2.5	5.5	1.9	3.7	1.8	•	1.4	•	•	•	•
Amortization and Depletion **15**	0.1	•	0.0	0.2	0.1	0.1	0.0	•	0.1	•	•	•	•
Pensions and Other Deferred Comp. **16**	0.2	•	0.1	0.2	0.2	0.4	0.2	•	0.3	•	•	•	•
Employee Benefits **17**	0.6	3.3	0.5	0.9	0.5	0.7	0.3	•	0.5	•	•	•	•
Advertising **18**	0.2	0.1	0.3	0.1	0.1	0.2	0.1	•	0.1	•	•	•	•
Other Expenses **19**	15.6	31.9	26.9	38.7	9.6	8.2	8.1	•	10.8	•	•	•	•
Officers' Compensation **20**	3.4	7.8	5.4	5.9	3.6	1.3	1.7	•	0.6	•	•	•	•
Operating Margin **21**	6.0	21.1	10.8	8.2	1.0	18.6	•	•	•	•	•	•	•
Operating Margin Before Officers' Comp. **22**	9.4	28.9	16.2	14.1	4.6	19.9	•	•	0.5	•	•	•	•

Selected Average Balance Sheet ($ in Thousands)

Net Receivables 23	105	0	10	83	250	1113	3798	•	10136
Inventories 24	90	0	8	13	143	1115	3030	•	18848
Net Property, Plant and Equipment 25	226	0	45	270	750	2852	3870	•	16609
Total Assets 26	680	0	120	685	2019	7368	15037	•	72458
Notes and Loans Payable 27	215	0	72	203	454	1597	5714	•	19846
All Other Liabilities 28	170	0	19	65	364	2850	5155	•	30766
Net Worth 29	295	0	29	418	1201	2921	4168	•	21845

Selected Financial Ratios (Times to 1)

Current Ratio 30	1.7	•	3.1	4.6	2.0	1.2	1.2	•	1.2
Quick Ratio 31	1.1	•	2.6	4.5	1.3	0.8	0.6	•	0.6
Net Sales to Working Capital 32	10.2	•	14.6	3.8	13.2	17.0	23.4	•	9.4
Coverage Ratio 33	11.3	•	17.5	23.2	10.7	7.3	4.7	•	6.2
Total Asset Turnover 34	2.2	•	4.8	1.4	3.1	1.4	2.2	•	1.1
Inventory Turnover 35	10.1	•	29.9	19.7	32.2	4.6	9.1	•	3.5
Receivables Turnover 36	15.3	•	46.1	18.0	26.1	•	9.3	•	•
Total Liabilities to Net Worth 37	1.3	•	3.2	0.6	0.7	1.5	2.6	•	2.3
Current Assets to Working Capital 38	2.5	•	1.5	1.3	2.0	5.9	7.1	•	5.0
Current Liabilities to Working Capital 39	1.5	•	0.5	0.3	1.0	4.9	6.1	•	4.0
Working Capital to Net Sales 40	0.1	•	0.1	0.3	0.1	0.1	0.0	•	0.1
Inventory to Working Capital 41	0.7	•	0.1	0.0	0.5	1.8	2.6	•	2.1
Total Receipts to Cash Flow 42	4.9	1.6	3.1	1.9	8.1	9.3	12.3	•	6.5
Cost of Goods to Cash Flow 43	3.0	0.4	1.2	0.5	6.0	4.6	10.3	•	5.2
Cash Flow to Total Debt 44	0.8	•	2.0	1.8	0.9	0.2	0.2	•	0.2

Selected Financial Factors (in Percentages)

Debt Ratio 45	56.7	•	76.1	39.0	40.5	60.4	72.3	•	69.9
Return on Total Assets 46	20.7	•	63.6	29.5	16.7	9.2	10.2	•	7.9
Return on Equity Before Income Taxes 47	43.4	•	250.6	46.3	25.5	20.1	29.0	•	21.8
Return on Equity After Income Taxes 48	41.7	•	249.4	46.0	23.8	17.5	24.6	•	19.4
Profit Margin (Before Income Tax) 49	8.5	36.3	12.5	20.8	5.0	5.7	3.7	•	5.8
Profit Margin (After Income Tax) 50	8.1	36.3	12.5	20.6	4.6	4.9	3.1	•	5.2

Table I

Corporations with and without Net Income

OIL AND GAS EXTRACTION

MONEY AMOUNTS AND SIZE OF ASSETS IN THOUSANDS OF DOLLARS

Item Description for Accounting Period 7/07 Through 6/08		Total	Zero Assets	Under 500	500 to 1,000	1,000 to 5,000	5,000 to 10,000	10,000 to 25,000	25,000 to 50,000	50,000 to 100,000	100,000 to 250,000	250,000 to 500,000	500,000 to 2,500,000	2,500,000 and over
Number of Enterprises	1	19441	3238	11672	1114	1746	679	421	201	129	109	46	55	30
Revenues ($ in Thousands)														
Net Sales	2	16698539	1734596	5393718	1013015	3084162	3243430	2816388	2626758	3896279	6107883	5620327	18893134	112559847
Interest	3	2473481	21944	7600	6098	21235	17351	32192	39079	38938	123431	77977	255169	1832466
Rents	4	179823	0	0	1017	17125	1200	52351	14158	5489	20816	913	11422	55333
Royalties	5	588501	51166	15806	0	31872	56282	90328	7868	39749	33795	12425	81158	168052
Other Portfolio Income	6	9571691	775101	65030	40065	261644	144728	207684	239764	415075	281084	338705	1506032	5296777
Other Receipts	7	13427206	320033	247349	4628	148195	295282	403990	232176	222170	581041	326617	1624248	9021481
Total Receipts	8	193230241	2902840	5729503	1064823	3564233	3758273	3602933	3159803	4617700	7148050	6376964	22371163	128933956
Average Total Receipts	9	9939	896	491	956	2041	5535	8558	15720	35796	65578	138630	406748	4297799
Operating Costs/Operating Income (%)														
Cost of Operations	10	49.1	4.9	38.5	12.8	25.5	47.7	23.3	32.8	46.9	34.9	39.2	30.5	56.8
Salaries and Wages	11	4.2	3.5	2.7	4.5	16.5	5.6	9.1	9.9	6.2	8.9	4.3	4.2	3.4
Taxes Paid	12	3.5	5.1	2.2	5.8	4.4	2.8	4.4	4.2	3.6	3.4	3.1	3.5	3.5
Interest Paid	13	5.1	13.7	0.7	0.1	1.5	1.3	2.8	5.0	3.8	5.5	3.4	8.2	5.1
Depreciation	14	5.1	7.5	2.2	2.2	5.1	3.8	7.9	7.2	6.6	9.0	6.5	8.0	4.3
Amortization and Depletion	15	6.0	11.1	1.3	1.2	3.8	2.8	4.7	7.6	7.3	6.8	9.4	14.7	4.6
Pensions and Other Deferred Comp.	16	0.3	0.0	0.8	0.4	0.3	0.3	0.6	0.4	0.2	0.6	0.4	0.2	0.3
Employee Benefits	17	0.4	1.6	0.4	0.1	0.9	0.4	1.1	1.2	0.6	0.7	0.7	0.4	0.4
Advertising	18	0.0	0.0	0.2	0.0	0.2	0.1	0.2	0.2	0.0	0.0	0.0	0.0	0.0
Other Expenses	19	29.2	66.6	45.5	36.8	29.0	22.1	39.0	38.4	27.7	32.7	25.1	39.3	25.9
Officers' Compensation	20	1.4	6.7	4.4	4.6	6.6	2.9	4.0	2.8	2.0	1.6	2.5	1.2	0.8
Operating Margin	21	•	•	1.1	31.5	6.2	10.1	3.1	•	•	•	5.3	•	•
Operating Margin Before Officers' Comp.	22	•	•	5.5	36.1	12.8	13.0	7.1	•	•	•	7.9	•	•

Selected Average Balance Sheet ($ in Thousands)

Item													
Net Receivables 23	2357	0	16	104	250	1233	1844	4158	7754	19127	29509	106769	1077121
Inventories 24	185	0	6	1	23	46	120	234	1004	2321	2896	9062	79440
Net Property, Plant and Equipment 25	12036	0	57	99	594	1733	4476	14284	30951	75402	173501	714772	5558375
Total Assets 26	22607	0	156	672	2262	7193	15582	35843	69561	163427	348316	1154712	10267032
Notes and Loans Payable 27	5923	0	76	10	649	1889	2862	10269	19863	46865	84405	379531	2537612
All Other Liabilities 28	6778	0	36	168	705	1565	3992	8300	12933	33290	65571	272329	3408026
Net Worth 29	9906	0	44	494	909	3739	8729	17274	36764	83272	198339	502853	4321395

Selected Financial Ratios (Times to 1)

Item													
Current Ratio 30	0.9	•	1.6	3.2	1.6	1.7	1.4	1.2	1.5	1.8	1.3	1.0	0.7
Quick Ratio 31	0.7	•	1.4	3.0	1.3	1.3	1.1	0.9	1.2	1.4	1.0	0.8	0.6
Net Sales to Working Capital 32	•	•	15.4	3.0	4.1	3.3	3.4	8.5	3.8	2.5	7.4	•	•
Coverage Ratio 33	3.5	4.5	11.7	313.8	15.0	20.0	12.0	3.1	4.6	3.3	6.7	2.0	3.3
Total Asset Turnover 34	0.4	•	3.0	1.4	0.8	0.7	0.4	0.4	0.4	0.3	0.4	0.3	0.4
Inventory Turnover 35	22.8	•	31.5	200.1	19.9	49.2	13.0	18.3	14.1	8.4	16.6	11.6	26.8
Receivables Turnover 36	4.2	•	23.5	8.1	7.4	4.4	3.4	3.4	4.5	2.9	3.8	3.3	4.2
Total Liabilities to Net Worth 37	1.3	•	2.5	0.4	1.5	0.9	0.8	1.1	0.9	1.0	0.8	1.3	1.4
Current Assets to Working Capital 38	•	•	2.6	1.5	2.7	2.5	3.5	6.9	3.0	2.2	4.0	•	•
Current Liabilities to Working Capital 39	•	•	1.6	0.5	1.7	1.5	2.5	5.9	2.0	1.2	3.0	•	•
Working Capital to Net Sales 40	•	•	0.1	0.3	0.2	0.3	0.3	0.1	0.3	0.4	0.1	•	•
Inventory to Working Capital 41	•	•	0.2	•	0.1	0.0	0.1	0.2	0.1	0.1	0.2	•	•
Total Receipts to Cash Flow 42	2.8	1.0	2.9	1.4	2.4	2.2	1.6	2.6	2.9	2.4	2.6	2.5	3.0
Cost of Goods to Cash Flow 43	1.4	0.1	1.1	0.2	0.6	1.0	0.4	0.9	1.4	0.8	1.0	0.7	1.7
Cash Flow to Total Debt 44	0.2	•	1.4	3.6	0.6	0.6	0.6	0.3	0.3	0.3	0.3	0.2	0.2

Selected Financial Factors (in Percentages)

Item													
Debt Ratio 45	56.2	•	71.8	26.4	59.8	48.0	44.0	51.8	47.1	49.0	43.1	56.5	57.9
Return on Total Assets 46	6.8	•	23.7	49.7	18.0	17.9	14.3	5.6	7.5	6.2	8.0	5.0	6.2
Return on Equity Before Income Taxes 47	11.1	•	76.9	67.3	41.7	32.8	23.5	7.8	11.0	8.5	11.9	5.9	10.2
Return on Equity After Income Taxes 48	7.4	•	73.5	66.6	38.7	31.6	20.5	5.4	8.9	5.2	8.0	3.8	6.0
Profit Margin (Before Income Tax) 49	12.9	48.3	7.3	36.6	21.5	25.7	30.6	10.3	13.4	12.6	19.4	8.6	11.8
Profit Margin (After Income Tax) 50	8.5	37.6	7.0	36.2	19.9	24.8	26.8	7.2	10.8	7.8	13.1	5.5	6.9

Table II

Corporations with Net Income

OIL AND GAS EXTRACTION

MONEY AMOUNTS AND SIZE OF ASSETS IN THOUSANDS OF DOLLARS

Item Description for Accounting Period 7/07 Through 6/08	Total	Zero Assets	Under 500	500 to 1,000	1,000 to 5,000	5,000 to 10,000	10,000 to 25,000	25,000 to 50,000	50,000 to 100,000	100,000 to 250,000	250,000 to 500,000	500,000 to 2,500,000	2,500,000 and over
Number of Enterprises **1**	11871	2093	6159	1066	1361	559	319	106	72	66	22	30	16
Revenues ($ in Thousands)													
Net Sales **2**	120706717	1269862	2927361	932150	2820623	2804449	2470067	1972086	2355331	5043920	4577397	11516770	82016701
Interest **3**	2120087	20021	4118	3842	16799	9224	27176	20133	18556	79045	54103	185255	1681816
Rents **4**	137212	0	0	1017	14367	1200	51017	9288	5038	18237	515	11141	25391
Royalties **5**	521900	49690	15083	0	30563	38814	90170	2614	38462	24180	9545	55780	167000
Other Portfolio Income **6**	8758728	772976	64393	39229	188585	143522	201215	199582	346799	245177	262722	1415217	4879311
Other Receipts **7**	10681314	313954	109698	4133	111973	295840	386175	164758	177146	492681	179501	1123783	7321670
Total Receipts **8**	142925958	2426503	3120653	980371	3182910	3293049	3225820	2368461	2941332	5903240	5083783	14307946	96091889
Average Total Receipts **9**	12040	1159	507	920	2339	5891	10112	22344	40852	89443	231081	476932	6005743
Operating Costs/Operating Income (%)													
Cost of Operations **10**	50.0	1.3	19.0	9.4	23.3	45.0	21.4	30.1	29.8	36.5	40.9	32.2	59.1
Salaries and Wages **11**	3.9	2.9	2.9	3.4	12.7	5.5	8.4	8.4	7.0	7.8	3.8	4.2	3.0
Taxes Paid **12**	3.8	4.7	2.3	5.9	4.1	2.9	4.6	4.2	4.9	3.4	2.9	3.3	3.9
Interest Paid **13**	4.1	17.3	0.2	0.1	1.1	1.0	2.3	1.9	2.2	2.4	1.3	5.6	4.5
Depreciation **14**	4.3	6.3	2.3	2.1	4.2	3.8	7.6	5.7	6.4	7.1	4.9	6.7	3.6
Amortization and Depletion **15**	4.5	13.3	2.3	1.3	3.4	1.3	4.0	4.3	6.2	4.3	5.8	10.6	3.7
Pensions and Other Deferred Comp. **16**	0.3	0.0	0.4	0.3	0.3	0.3	0.6	0.4	0.3	0.7	0.2	0.1	0.3
Employee Benefits **17**	0.4	2.0	0.2	0.1	0.7	0.4	1.1	0.8	0.7	0.6	0.5	0.3	0.4
Advertising **18**	0.0	0.0	0.1	0.0	0.2	0.0	0.2	0.1	0.0	0.0	0.0	0.0	0.0
Other Expenses **19**	24.0	63.2	46.9	35.8	25.6	17.7	30.2	21.9	22.5	22.5	15.1	35.4	21.5
Officers' Compensation **20**	1.5	8.3	5.0	4.5	6.6	2.7	3.9	2.4	2.3	1.1	2.5	1.2	0.9
Operating Margin **21**	3.2	•	18.3	37.0	17.8	19.4	15.7	19.8	17.7	13.6	22.2	0.3	•
Operating Margin Before Officers' Comp. **22**	4.7	•	23.4	41.5	24.4	22.1	19.6	22.2	20.0	14.7	24.7	1.5	0.0

Selected Average Balance Sheet ($ in Thousands)

Net Receivables 23	3121	0	18	109	254	1297	1917	4245	9666	21722	46894	151745	1685834
Inventories 24	221	0	3	1	20	50	140	325	642	3621	3835	9756	113854
Net Property, Plant and Equipment 25	10896	0	53	94	559	1549	4465	10798	24038	60018	161481	609926	6073695
Total Assets 26	22513	0	165	668	2337	7183	15683	34541	69074	161044	349330	1173743	11947668
Notes and Loans Payable 27	5237	0	64	10	391	950	2304	4827	11737	29556	49506	294302	2921486
All Other Liabilities 28	6057	0	17	175	782	1285	3526	6822	13252	38166	65579	254212	3465112
Net Worth 29	11218	0	83	483	1165	4948	9852	22892	44085	93322	234245	625229	5561070

Selected Financial Ratios (Times to 1)

Current Ratio 30	1.2	•	3.2	3.1	1.7	2.0	1.8	1.6	1.8	2.4	2.1	1.3	1.0
Quick Ratio 31	1.0	•	3.0	3.0	1.4	1.6	1.4	1.4	1.6	1.9	1.8	1.2	0.8
Net Sales to Working Capital 32	13.3	•	7.7	2.8	3.8	2.7	2.4	4.3	2.5	2.1	4.6	6.6	•
Coverage Ratio 33	6.8	5.3	166.5	494.6	28.8	37.6	20.8	21.5	20.6	13.4	26.3	5.5	5.3
Total Asset Turnover 34	0.5	•	2.9	1.3	0.9	0.7	0.5	0.5	0.5	0.5	0.6	0.3	0.4
Inventory Turnover 35	22.9	•	28.0	135.1	24.0	44.7	11.9	17.2	15.2	7.7	22.2	12.7	26.6
Receivables Turnover 36	3.6	•	18.8	7.9	8.3	4.3	3.7	4.5	3.9	3.5	4.8	2.7	3.5
Total Liabilities to Net Worth 37	1.0	•	1.0	0.4	1.0	0.5	0.6	0.5	0.6	0.7	0.5	0.9	1.1
Current Assets to Working Capital 38	6.3	•	1.4	1.5	2.5	2.0	2.3	2.6	2.3	1.7	1.9	4.0	•
Current Liabilities to Working Capital 39	5.3	•	0.4	0.5	1.5	1.0	1.3	1.6	1.3	0.7	0.9	3.0	•
Working Capital to Net Sales 40	0.1	•	0.1	0.4	0.3	0.4	0.4	0.2	0.4	0.5	0.2	0.2	•
Inventory to Working Capital 41	0.4	•	0.1	•	0.1	0.0	0.0	0.1	0.0	0.1	0.1	0.1	•
Total Receipts to Cash Flow 42	2.4	0.9	1.9	1.3	2.1	1.9	1.5	2.0	1.8	2.0	2.3	2.0	2.8
Cost of Goods to Cash Flow 43	1.2	0.0	0.4	0.1	0.5	0.9	0.3	0.6	0.5	0.7	0.9	0.6	1.7
Cash Flow to Total Debt 44	0.4	•	3.0	3.6	0.8	1.2	0.9	0.8	0.7	0.6	0.8	0.3	0.3

Selected Financial Factors (in Percentages)

Debt Ratio 45	50.2	•	49.5	27.7	50.2	31.1	37.2	33.7	36.2	42.1	32.9	46.7	53.5
Return on Total Assets 46	12.6	•	72.5	55.4	27.9	26.1	23.9	22.4	21.1	15.5	21.1	10.0	10.2
Return on Equity Before Income Taxes 47	21.5	•	142.6	76.5	54.0	36.9	36.2	32.2	31.4	24.8	30.2	15.4	17.8
Return on Equity After Income Taxes 48	16.1	•	139.3	75.7	51.0	35.9	32.7	28.8	28.2	20.1	23.3	12.3	11.7
Profit Margin (Before Income Tax) 49	23.7	74.1	24.9	42.2	30.3	36.4	46.0	39.6	42.3	30.3	34.0	25.1	19.3
Profit Margin (After Income Tax) 50	17.8	59.9	24.4	41.8	28.6	35.4	41.6	35.4	37.9	24.5	26.3	20.1	12.7

Table I

Corporations with and without Net Income

COAL MINING

MONEY AMOUNTS AND SIZE OF ASSETS IN THOUSANDS OF DOLLARS

Item Description for Accounting Period 7/07 Through 6/08	Total	Zero Assets	Under 500	500 to 1,000	1,000 to 5,000	5,000 to 10,000	10,000 to 25,000	25,000 to 50,000	50,000 to 100,000	100,000 to 250,000	250,000 to 500,000	500,000 to 2,500,000	2,500,000 and over
Number of Enterprises **1**	1232	•	610	•	210	127	52	•	12	11	0	11	5
Revenues ($ in Thousands)													
Net Sales **2**	27139791	•	271342	•	1223293	832616	2220917	•	1080549	1759970	0	6550201	11547248
Interest **3**	513082	•	517	•	2249	3342	630	•	429	8940	0	50286	445095
Rents **4**	30404	•	0	•	8700	98	1592	•	0	633	0	2590	16583
Royalties **5**	253161	•	0	•	3413	1446	17	•	447	9636	0	33346	177419
Other Portfolio Income **6**	547219	•	938	•	19491	24433	24356	•	6402	114259	0	111669	215806
Other Receipts **7**	1311779	•	3722	•	9053	30720	-6564	•	19388	24966	0	617651	562795
Total Receipts **8**	29795436	•	276519	•	1266199	892655	2240948	•	1107215	1918404	0	7365743	12964946
Average Total Receipts **9**	24185	•	453	•	6030	7029	43095	•	92268	174400	•	669613	2592989
Operating Costs/Operating Income (%)													
Cost of Operations **10**	68.0	•	50.5	•	38.1	58.9	88.8	•	68.7	75.8	•	82.7	59.9
Salaries and Wages **11**	3.7	•	•	•	10.1	9.0	1.2	•	3.8	2.8	•	1.5	4.2
Taxes Paid **12**	6.7	•	11.6	•	4.4	4.8	1.3	•	5.8	4.4	•	7.7	8.0
Interest Paid **13**	4.6	•	0.1	•	0.3	1.4	0.9	•	1.6	5.0	•	5.4	6.4
Depreciation **14**	5.4	•	5.6	•	3.6	9.1	2.0	•	5.9	7.5	•	6.0	5.3
Amortization and Depletion **15**	5.4	•	•	•	•	2.4	1.2	•	2.6	3.5	•	6.1	7.9
Pensions and Other Deferred Comp. **16**	0.8	•	4.7	•	1.8	0.1	0.1	•	0.2	0.5	•	0.7	1.1
Employee Benefits **17**	3.2	•	•	•	1.8	0.7	1.0	•	2.2	2.6	•	2.2	4.8
Advertising **18**	0.1	•	•	•	0.0	0.0	0.0	•	0.0	0.0	•	0.1	0.1
Other Expenses **19**	12.8	•	12.4	•	40.8	31.8	5.3	•	16.0	12.6	•	5.6	12.4
Officers' Compensation **20**	0.6	•	16.1	•	0.5	0.9	0.4	•	0.5	0.6	•	0.3	0.4
Operating Margin **21**	•	•	•	•	0.2	•	•	•	•	•	•	•	•
Operating Margin Before Officers' Comp. **22**	•	•	15.0	•	0.7	•	•	•	•	•	•	•	•

Selected Average Balance Sheet ($ in Thousands)

Net Receivables 23	9799	0	334	800	2076	11896	22478	117716	1979105
Inventories 24	865	0	20	80	1338	4108	4203	25749	113859
Net Property, Plant and Equipment 25	15070	33	650	1974	5456	33070	72972	498556	2169078
Total Assets 26	39357	141	2119	7381	15320	70627	200660	1060003	6117060
Notes and Loans Payable 27	11957	20	1154	1027	6261	20003	72656	352326	1712735
All Other Liabilities 28	18812	112	509	1032	3613	30181	59320	499930	3168957
Net Worth 29	8588	9	456	5322	5446	20443	68683	207746	1235368

Selected Financial Ratios (Times to 1)

Current Ratio 30	1.2	0.8	2.3	1.7	1.0	0.7	1.3	1.1	1.2
Quick Ratio 31	1.0	0.4	2.0	1.6	0.7	0.5	1.0	0.8	1.0
Net Sales to Working Capital 32	10.7	•	9.4	8.2	•	•	12.3	30.8	5.7
Coverage Ratio 33	0.7	10.0	12.0	•	•	•	•	•	1.3
Total Asset Turnover 34	0.6	3.1	2.7	0.9	2.8	1.3	0.8	0.6	0.4
Inventory Turnover 35	17.3	•	111.0	48.5	28.3	15.1	28.9	19.1	12.1
Receivables Turnover 36	3.3	•	15.6	9.9	17.7	6.2	11.0	4.8	1.9
Total Liabilities to Net Worth 37	3.6	14.4	3.6	0.4	1.8	2.5	1.9	4.1	4.0
Current Assets to Working Capital 38	6.6	•	1.8	2.4	•	•	4.3	10.7	6.1
Current Liabilities to Working Capital 39	5.6	•	0.8	1.4	•	•	3.3	9.7	5.1
Working Capital to Net Sales 40	0.1	•	0.1	0.1	•	•	0.1	0.0	0.2
Inventory to Working Capital 41	0.5	•	0.0	0.1	•	•	0.4	1.4	0.3
Total Receipts to Cash Flow 42	14.4	7.7	2.7	11.7	39.0	17.4	•	•	10.2
Cost of Goods to Cash Flow 43	9.8	3.9	1.0	6.9	34.6	11.9	•	•	6.1
Cash Flow to Total Debt 44	0.0	0.4	1.3	0.3	0.1	0.1	•	•	0.0

Selected Financial Factors (in Percentages)

Debt Ratio 45	78.2	93.5	78.5	27.9	64.5	71.1	65.8	80.4	79.8
Return on Total Assets 46	1.8	2.8	10.6	•	•	•	•	•	3.0
Return on Equity Before Income Taxes 47	•	39.1	45.3	•	•	•	•	•	3.0
Return on Equity After Income Taxes 48	•	37.5	45.1	•	•	•	•	•	1.8
Profit Margin (Before Income Tax) 49	•	0.8	3.6	•	•	•	•	•	1.6
Profit Margin (After Income Tax) 50	•	0.8	3.5	•	•	•	•	•	0.9

9

Table II

Corporations with Net Income

COAL MINING

MONEY AMOUNTS AND SIZE OF ASSETS IN THOUSANDS OF DOLLARS

Item Description for Accounting Period 7/07 Through 6/08	Total	Zero Assets	Under 500	500 to 1,000	1,000 to 5,000	5,000 to 10,000	10,000 to 25,000	25,000 to 50,000	50,000 to 100,000	100,000 to 250,000	250,000 to 500,000	500,000 to 2,500,000	2,500,000 and over
Number of Enterprises **1**	618	0	188	169	170	31	36	9	3	4	0	•	•
Revenues ($ in Thousands)													
Net Sales **2**	14757283	0	271342	304290	859260	423310	1792056	554119	325576	826038	0	•	•
Interest **3**	474583	0	444	132	1413	3334	620	1462	0	2839	0	•	•
Rents **4**	23638	0	0	193	8700	98	1592	15	0	614	0	•	•
Royalties **5**	217786	0	0	27436	3413	1340	17	0	0	1586	0	•	•
Other Portfolio Income **6**	347384	0	938	12715	1343	24259	21093	14421	4179	111182	0	•	•
Other Receipts **7**	839244	0	3722	32	498	22684	10996	41721	11092	22078	0	•	•
Total Receipts **8**	1665918	0	276446	344798	874627	475025	1826374	611738	340847	964337	0	•	•
Average Total Receipts **9**	26958	•	1470	2040	5145	15323	50733	67971	113616	241084	•	•	•
Operating Costs/Operating Income (%)													
Cost of Operations **10**	62.2	•	50.5	39.8	37.4	58.9	86.9	54.6	44.8	83.5	•	•	•
Salaries and Wages **11**	3.0	•	•	0.2	8.8	5.6	1.4	14.0	10.3	1.6	•	•	•
Taxes Paid **12**	6.1	•	11.1	5.7	4.7	3.4	1.1	6.9	2.3	3.9	•	•	•
Interest Paid **13**	5.2	•	0.1	0.1	0.0	1.1	0.7	0.8	1.3	3.8	•	•	•
Depreciation **14**	5.2	•	5.6	6.1	3.7	7.5	2.2	4.8	3.0	4.5	•	•	•
Amortization and Depletion **15**	5.5	•	•	0.6	•	1.5	1.3	1.5	2.9	3.9	•	•	•
Pensions and Other Deferred Comp. **16**	1.1	•	4.7	•	•	0.1	0.1	0.1	•	0.2	•	•	•
Employee Benefits **17**	4.2	•	•	4.2	2.5	0.9	0.4	0.5	2.5	0.8	•	•	•
Advertising **18**	0.1	•	•	•	•	0.0	0.0	0.0	•	0.0	•	•	•
Other Expenses **19**	14.9	•	7.1	29.4	35.8	22.2	6.1	21.7	33.1	6.4	•	•	•
Officers' Compensation **20**	0.8	•	16.1	1.0	0.8	0.9	0.5	0.2	0.3	0.3	•	•	•
Operating Margin **21**	•	•	4.8	12.9	6.4	•	•	•	•	•	•	•	•
Operating Margin Before Officers' Comp. **22**	•	•	20.9	13.8	7.1	•	•	•	•	•	•	•	•

Selected Average Balance Sheet ($ in Thousands)

Net Receivables 23	17517	•	0	110	333	1639	2069	6860	21874	13139
Inventories 24	992	•	0	0	30	187	1812	1026	9774	6599
Net Property, Plant and Equipment 25	15328	•	108	397	623	3549	5999	18043	23294	88758
Total Assets 26	49202	•	228	917	1864	8340	15403	33890	68392	187455
Notes and Loans Payable 27	13937	•	64	532	1204	2358	5819	32889	16937	34962
All Other Liabilities 28	26750	•	297	12	398	2403	3992	14646	16937	61891
Net Worth 29	8514	•	-133	373	262	3579	5593	-13645	34518	90602

Selected Financial Ratios (Times to 1)

Current Ratio 30	1.3	•	0.3	3.0	2.8	1.5	1.1	0.6	1.4	1.2
Quick Ratio 31	1.1	•	0.2	2.7	2.7	1.3	0.8	0.5	1.3	0.8
Net Sales to Working Capital 32	5.3	•	•	5.2	7.6	11.9	71.5	•	13.4	32.5
Coverage Ratio 33	1.9	•	75.6	195.8	579.9	10.4	2.7	7.9	4.2	3.0
Total Asset Turnover 34	0.5	•	6.3	2.0	2.7	1.6	3.2	1.8	1.6	1.1
Inventory Turnover 35	15.0	•	•	•	64.1	43.0	23.9	32.7	5.0	26.1
Receivables Turnover 36	2.2	•	32.8	•	11.4	18.5	12.1	•	2.3	31.4
Total Liabilities to Net Worth 37	4.8	•	1.5	6.1	1.3	1.8	•	•	1.0	1.1
Current Assets to Working Capital 38	4.9	•	1.5	1.6	3.2	9.7	•	•	3.4	7.3
Current Liabilities to Working Capital 39	3.9	•	0.5	0.6	2.2	8.7	•	•	2.4	6.3
Working Capital to Net Sales 40	0.2	•	0.2	0.1	0.1	0.0	0.0	•	0.1	0.0
Inventory to Working Capital 41	0.3	•	•	0.0	0.2	2.8	•	•	0.1	1.0
Total Receipts to Cash Flow 42	6.5	•	7.4	2.2	2.3	3.6	17.2	5.0	3.4	•
Cost of Goods to Cash Flow 43	4.1	•	3.7	0.9	0.9	2.1	15.0	2.7	1.5	•
Cash Flow to Total Debt 44	0.1	•	0.5	1.5	1.3	0.8	0.3	0.3	1.0	•

Selected Financial Factors (in Percentages)

Debt Ratio 45	82.7	•	158.1	59.4	86.0	57.1	63.7	140.3	49.5	51.7
Return on Total Assets 46	4.8	•	42.6	51.7	21.8	18.4	6.3	11.2	8.8	12.8
Return on Equity Before Income Taxes 47	13.0	•	•	126.5	154.9	38.8	10.9	•	13.3	17.8
Return on Equity After Income Taxes 48	10.8	•	•	117.9	154.5	33.8	10.5	•	13.3	17.5
Profit Margin (Before Income Tax) 49	4.6	•	6.7	26.2	8.0	10.2	1.2	5.4	4.2	7.8
Profit Margin (After Income Tax) 50	3.8	•	6.6	24.4	8.0	8.9	1.2	4.8	4.2	7.7

Table I

Corporations with and without Net Income

METAL ORE MINING

MONEY AMOUNTS AND SIZE OF ASSETS IN THOUSANDS OF DOLLARS

Item Description for Accounting Period 7/07 Through 6/08	Total	Zero Assets	Under 500	500 to 1,000	1,000 to 5,000	5,000 to 10,000	10,000 to 25,000	25,000 to 50,000	50,000 to 100,000	100,000 to 250,000	250,000 to 500,000	500,000 to 2,500,000	2,500,000 and over
Number of Enterprises **1**	2459	•	1911	•	130	27	42	•	16	15	6	10	9
Revenues ($ in Thousands)													
Net Sales **2**	44733094	•	37302	•	4832	4632	250459		219703	240112	2200669	2794662	38661120
Interest **3**	1159653	•	962	•	5054	1506	5103	•	6773	16569	32250	69182	1020174
Rents **4**	29742	•	6289	•	0	1109	0	•	45	816	31	68	21383
Royalties **5**	387988	•	13433	•	0	53	0	•	0	0	0	63747	310755
Other Portfolio Income **6**	4574668	•	5312	•	18603	5458	1667	•	23883	52875	1638	143055	4269209
Other Receipts **7**	196615	•	38825	•	7906	11816	28002	•	212658	4480	16892	140782	-288882
Total Receipts **8**	51081760	•	102123	•	36395	24574	285231	•	463062	314852	2251480	3211496	43993759
Average Total Receipts **9**	20773	•	53	•	280	910	6791	•	28941	20990	375247	321150	4888195
Operating Costs/Operating Income (%)													
Cost of Operations **10**	46.9	•	6.7	•	144.0	265.7	97.8	•	60.5	52.7	74.0	64.7	43.4
Salaries and Wages **11**	1.9	•	9.0	•	250.5	267.0	4.1	•	5.0	10.6	0.3	1.2	1.8
Taxes Paid **12**	1.9	•	13.6	•	55.4	36.4	0.1	•	2.9	2.2	0.1	2.3	2.0
Interest Paid **13**	3.2	•	4.9	•	254.4	58.7	0.2	•	1.8	7.6	2.4	1.4	3.3
Depreciation **14**	3.5	•	3.1	•	143.0	87.5	0.8	•	5.0	15.7	2.1	5.4	3.3
Amortization and Depletion **15**	11.3	•	33.0	•	40.6	61.2	5.8	•	13.8	13.8	6.7	12.3	11.5
Pensions and Other Deferred Comp. **16**	0.3	•	14.1	•	•	•	•	•	0.0	0.4	0.2	0.8	0.2
Employee Benefits **17**	0.7	•	3.1	•	3.9	32.3	1.0	•	0.2	0.9	1.4	0.1	0.7
Advertising **18**	0.0	•	•	•	24.0	4.4	0.0	•	0.2	0.0	•	0.0	0.0
Other Expenses **19**	11.5	•	243.5	•	1323.2	960.9	18.1	•	51.4	42.7	9.5	5.6	11.0
Officers' Compensation **20**	0.6	•	72.8	•	183.8	95.4	1.4	•	2.1	6.0	0.0	0.6	0.4
Operating Margin **21**	18.3	•	•	•	•	•	•	•	•	•	3.4	5.5	22.4
Operating Margin Before Officers' Comp. **22**	18.9	•	•	•	•	•	•	•	•	•	3.4	6.1	22.8

Selected Average Balance Sheet ($ in Thousands)

Net Receivables 23	10419	•	0	5	214	1812	•	5290	3171	21717	26764	2771139
Inventories 24	1999	•	0	4	34	123	•	1880	3863	20400	75352	436881
Net Property, Plant and Equipment 25	15515	•	8	968	2786	2582	•	15338	40933	202249	434746	3462707
Total Assets 26	56051	•	89	2796	7001	17011	•	63510	144742	336315	985206	13422613
Notes and Loans Payable 27	5583	•	206	684	84	8944	•	20495	35685	20787	91805	1189604
All Other Liabilities 28	19152	•	48	314	8201	6048	•	14708	46159	148793	161019	4771887
Net Worth 29	31316	•	-165	1798	-1283	2019	•	28308	62898	166735	732382	7461122

Selected Financial Ratios (Times to 1)

Current Ratio 30	1.4	•	0.3	2.4	0.6	0.7	•	3.6	1.8	1.0	2.8	1.4
Quick Ratio 31	1.1	•	0.3	2.3	0.5	0.5	•	2.0	1.3	0.7	1.8	1.1
Net Sales to Working Capital 32	3.7	•	•	0.1	•	•	•	1.0	0.9	•	1.7	3.9
Coverage Ratio 33	11.7	•	•	•	•	•	•	39.7	•	3.4	15.8	12.4
Total Asset Turnover 34	0.3	•	0.2	0.0	0.0	0.4	•	0.2	0.1	1.1	0.3	0.3
Inventory Turnover 35	4.3	•	•	13.1	13.5	47.5	•	4.4	2.2	13.3	2.4	4.3
Receivables Turnover 36	1.9	•	•	8.5	1.0	2.3	•	4.2	7.0	14.1	5.5	1.7
Total Liabilities to Net Worth 37	0.8	•	•	0.6	•	7.4	•	1.2	1.3	1.0	0.3	0.8
Current Assets to Working Capital 38	3.3	•	•	1.7	•	•	•	1.4	2.3	•	1.6	3.6
Current Liabilities to Working Capital 39	2.3	•	•	0.7	•	•	•	0.4	1.3	•	0.6	2.6
Working Capital to Net Sales 40	0.3	•	•	11.9	•	•	•	1.0	1.1	•	0.6	0.3
Inventory to Working Capital 41	0.5	•	•	0.0	•	•	•	0.2	0.3	•	0.4	0.5
Total Receipts to Cash Flow 42	2.5	•	1.2	•	•	44.8	•	0.9	•	8.2	4.0	2.3
Cost of Goods to Cash Flow 43	1.2	•	0.1	•	•	43.8	•	0.6	•	6.1	2.6	1.0
Cash Flow to Total Debt 44	0.3	•	0.1	•	•	0.0	•	0.4	•	0.3	0.3	0.3

Selected Financial Factors (in Percentages)

Debt Ratio 45	44.1	•	284.2	35.7	118.3	88.1	•	55.4	56.5	50.4	25.7	44.4
Return on Total Assets 46	12.1	•	•	•	•	•	•	15.0	•	8.8	6.5	13.1
Return on Equity Before Income Taxes 47	19.7	•	15.6	•	179.0	•	•	32.9	•	12.6	8.2	21.8
Return on Equity After Income Taxes 48	13.4	•	15.9	•	179.0	•	•	31.7	•	7.2	6.0	14.9
Profit Margin (Before Income Tax) 49	33.9	•	•	•	•	•	•	67.8	•	5.7	21.4	37.8
Profit Margin (After Income Tax) 50	23.0	•	•	•	•	•	•	65.3	•	3.3	15.6	25.8

11

Table II

Corporations with Net Income

METAL ORE MINING

MONEY AMOUNTS AND SIZE OF ASSETS IN THOUSANDS OF DOLLARS

Item Description for Accounting Period 7/07 Through 6/08	Total	Zero Assets	Under 500	500 to 1,000	1,000 to 5,000	5,000 to 10,000	10,000 to 25,000	25,000 to 50,000	50,000 to 100,000	100,000 to 250,000	250,000 to 500,000	500,000 to 2,500,000	2,500,000 and over
Number of Enterprises **1**	1270	•	1198	0	33	0	6	3	3	4	•	•	9
Revenues ($ in Thousands)													
Net Sales **2**	43697764	•	36577	0	0	0	248860	169983	106039	140310	•	•	38661120
Interest **3**	1129297	•	0	0	4143	0	2310	58	2615	9954	•	•	1020174
Rents **4**	21770	•	0	0	0	0	0	0	0	289	•	•	21383
Royalties **5**	385937	•	13433	0	0	0	0	0	0	0	•	•	310755
Other Portfolio Income **6**	4544276	•	103	0	18603	0	0	535	7082	52665	•	•	4269209
Other Receipts **7**	80460	•	34021	0	0	0	18266	0	210787	3061	•	•	-288882
Total Receipts **8**	49859504	•	84134	0	22746	0	269436	170576	326523	206279	•	•	43993759
Average Total Receipts **9**	39259	•	70	•	689	•	44906	56859	108841	51570	•	•	4888195
Operating Costs/Operating Income (%)													
Cost of Operations **10**	45.9	•	•	•	•	•	98.4	44.6	74.5	48.3	•	•	43.4
Salaries and Wages **11**	1.8	•	•	•	•	•	•	18.7	1.4	3.0	•	•	1.8
Taxes Paid **12**	1.9	•	8.6	•	•	•	•	2.1	1.3	1.2	•	•	2.0
Interest Paid **13**	3.1	•	4.5	•	•	•	0.0	0.2	0.0	7.0	•	•	3.3
Depreciation **14**	3.3	•	2.6	•	•	•	•	4.2	2.3	7.9	•	•	3.3
Amortization and Depletion **15**	11.3	•	8.1	•	•	•	0.0	•	7.2	9.8	•	•	11.5
Pensions and Other Deferred Comp. **16**	0.3	•	14.4	•	•	•	•	0.2	•	•	•	•	0.2
Employee Benefits **17**	0.7	•	•	•	•	•	•	1.3	•	0.1	•	•	0.7
Advertising **18**	0.0	•	•	•	•	•	•	0.0	0.0	0.0	•	•	0.0
Other Expenses **19**	10.6	•	50.0	•	•	•	0.8	15.1	9.0	22.6	•	•	11.0
Officers' Compensation **20**	0.5	•	57.6	•	•	•	•	0.1	•	2.8	•	•	0.4
Operating Margin **21**	20.6	•	•	•	•	•	0.8	13.6	4.2	•	•	•	22.4
Operating Margin Before Officers' Comp. **22**	21.1	•	11.8	•	•	•	0.8	13.7	4.2	0.1	•	•	22.8

Selected Average Balance Sheet ($ in Thousands)

Net Receivables 23	20070	0	2878	22046	18919	6974	2771139
Inventories 24	3619	0	0	2329	6380	9170	436881
Net Property, Plant and Equipment 25	27718	8	0	13141	10042	59576	3462707
Total Assets 26	103686	86	11120	43823	68139	155004	13422613
Notes and Loans Payable 27	9326	38	0	2065	1341	43216	1189604
All Other Liabilities 28	35789	46	3050	15935	12388	38810	4771887
Net Worth 29	58571	2	8070	25822	54410	72978	7461122

Selected Financial Ratios (Times to 1)

Current Ratio 30	1.4	1.4	33.7	3.7	2.0	4.5	1.2
Quick Ratio 31	1.1	1.4	33.6	2.6	2.0	3.5	0.8
Net Sales to Working Capital 32	3.7	6.2	•	5.0	3.5	1.4	2.7
Coverage Ratio 33	12.6	19.7	36.0	3239.9	67.4	18744.1	12.4
Total Asset Turnover 34	0.3	0.4	•	3.7	1.3	0.5	0.3
Inventory Turnover 35	4.4	•	•	10.8	4.1	1.8	4.3
Receivables Turnover 36	1.9	•	•	4.7	3.2	10.1	1.7
Total Liabilities to Net Worth 37	0.8	48.9	0.1	0.4	0.7	1.1	0.8
Current Assets to Working Capital 38	3.3	3.8	1.0	1.4	2.0	5.8	3.6
Current Liabilities to Working Capital 39	2.3	2.8	0.0	0.4	1.0	4.8	2.6
Working Capital to Net Sales 40	0.3	0.2	•	0.2	0.3	0.4	0.3
Inventory to Working Capital 41	0.5	•	•	•	0.2	0.7	0.5
Total Receipts to Cash Flow 42	2.4	0.8	0.8	10.1	6.0	3.7	2.3
Cost of Goods to Cash Flow 43	1.1	•	•	9.9	2.7	1.8	1.0
Cash Flow to Total Debt 44	0.3	0.4	0.6	1.3	0.5	0.1	0.3

Selected Financial Factors (in Percentages)

Debt Ratio 45	43.5	98.0	6.8	27.4	41.1	52.9	44.4
Return on Total Assets 46	13.1	31.5	26.7	34.0	18.3	11.6	13.1
Return on Equity Before Income Taxes 47	21.3	1491.5	27.8	46.8	30.5	21.3	21.8
Return on Equity After Income Taxes 48	14.7	1436.2	18.4	30.7	28.4	17.8	14.9
Profit Margin (Before Income Tax) 49	36.2	84.2	•	9.1	13.9	44.3	37.8
Profit Margin (After Income Tax) 50	25.0	81.1	•	6.0	12.9	37.0	25.8

Table I

Corporations with and without Net Income

NONMETALLIC MINERAL MINING AND QUARRYING

MONEY AMOUNTS AND SIZE OF ASSETS IN THOUSANDS OF DOLLARS

Item Description for Accounting Period 7/07 Through 6/08

	Total	Zero Assets	Under 500	500 to 1,000	1,000 to 5,000	5,000 to 10,000	10,000 to 25,000	25,000 to 50,000	50,000 to 100,000	100,000 to 250,000	250,000 to 500,000	500,000 to 2,500,000	2,500,000 and over
Number of Enterprises **1**	6004	•	3110	•	907	259	160	•	31	24	7	5	3
Revenues ($ in Thousands)													
Net Sales **2**	27424435	•	304349	•	3118128	2437055	2589381	•	1960056	2966578	2489406	2635890	6580354
Interest **3**	85957	•	250	•	1421	7681	4635	•	9827	10672	2323	17995	24857
Rents **4**	36325	•	0	•	2041	270	1339	•	685	4615	372	808	21841
Royalties **5**	27828	•	411	•	8	1214	0	•	0	1440	4167	5267	14523
Other Portfolio Income **6**	379851	•	22313	•	75626	13071	6222	•	47552	39144	9518	10426	131945
Other Receipts **7**	575102	•	16016	•	20251	29787	44312	•	20898	55436	16064	252109	89936
Total Receipts **8**	28529498	•	343339	•	3217475	2489078	2645889	•	2039018	3077885	2521850	2922495	6863456
Average Total Receipts **9**	4752	•	110	•	3547	9610	16537	•	65775	128245	360264	584499	2287819
Operating Costs/Operating Income (%)													
Cost of Operations **10**	63.7	•	43.8	•	61.8	67.0	63.0	•	66.9	68.9	66.4	69.7	57.2
Salaries and Wages **11**	5.2	•	5.8	•	5.0	3.5	4.1	•	6.1	3.9	3.7	4.1	7.7
Taxes Paid **12**	2.4	•	3.4	•	2.4	2.5	2.7	•	2.0	1.8	1.7	2.1	2.5
Interest Paid **13**	2.6	•	6.1	•	2.1	2.0	1.9	•	2.1	2.0	2.8	5.2	2.6
Depreciation **14**	5.9	•	18.8	•	5.2	4.3	6.1	•	5.5	6.9	4.3	4.9	7.1
Amortization and Depletion **15**	2.7	•	0.0	•	0.3	1.1	3.1	•	1.8	2.6	3.4	4.9	3.6
Pensions and Other Deferred Comp. **16**	0.7	•	•	•	0.1	0.8	0.5	•	0.6	0.9	0.8	0.8	0.8
Employee Benefits **17**	2.0	•	0.0	•	1.3	2.4	1.7	•	2.1	1.8	2.1	3.2	1.9
Advertising **18**	0.2	•	0.9	•	0.3	0.4	0.2	•	0.2	0.1	0.2	0.3	0.1
Other Expenses **19**	11.7	•	27.2	•	16.9	9.9	9.0	•	9.8	7.0	9.2	12.1	13.7
Officers' Compensation **20**	1.7	•	0.0	•	3.1	2.4	2.2	•	1.6	1.5	1.4	0.8	1.1
Operating Margin **21**	1.4	•	•	•	1.5	3.6	5.4	•	1.2	2.6	3.9	•	1.7
Operating Margin Before Officers' Comp. **22**	3.1	•	•	•	4.5	6.0	7.6	•	2.8	4.1	5.3	•	2.8

Selected Average Balance Sheet ($ in Thousands)

Net Receivables 23	562	0	366	1177	2151	7853	18186	44539	85791	241773
Inventories 24	430	6	159	506	1851	6771	17381	32380	110104	252540
Net Property, Plant and Equipment 25	2473	28	919	2660	7203	29086	65665	172649	330131	1859237
Total Assets 26	6215	57	2054	6262	16269	71777	159535	360496	948796	5027332
Notes and Loans Payable 27	2163	38	1052	2538	4498	18980	30638	157626	224194	2100062
All Other Liabilities 28	1414	2	245	1255	2518	14620	30103	49915	380852	1224546
Net Worth 29	2638	17	757	2468	9253	38178	98794	152955	343750	1702724

Selected Financial Ratios (Times to 1)

Current Ratio 30	1.2	5.2	1.9	2.0	2.8	2.3	2.3	1.2	1.5	0.5
Quick Ratio 31	0.7	2.4	1.4	1.4	1.8	1.4	1.3	0.6	0.7	0.2
Net Sales to Working Capital 32	17.1	6.4	6.4	6.9	3.6	4.0	3.6	21.8	7.9	•
Coverage Ratio 33	3.2	2.1	3.2	3.9	4.9	3.8	4.1	2.9	1.6	3.3
Total Asset Turnover 34	0.7	1.7	1.7	1.5	1.0	0.9	0.8	1.0	0.6	0.4
Inventory Turnover 35	6.8	7.0	13.3	12.5	5.5	6.2	4.9	7.3	3.3	5.0
Receivables Turnover 36	7.9	125.8	8.0	11.2	6.6	6.8	6.0	8.7	3.4	18.1
Total Liabilities to Net Worth 37	1.4	2.4	1.7	1.5	0.8	0.9	0.6	1.4	1.8	2.0
Current Assets to Working Capital 38	6.1	1.2	2.1	2.0	1.6	1.8	1.8	6.3	3.1	•
Current Liabilities to Working Capital 39	5.1	0.2	1.1	1.0	0.6	0.8	0.8	5.3	2.1	•
Working Capital to Net Sales 40	0.1	0.2	0.2	0.1	0.3	0.3	0.3	0.0	0.1	•
Inventory to Working Capital 41	1.7	0.3	0.3	0.4	0.4	0.5	0.4	2.1	0.8	•
Total Receipts to Cash Flow 42	8.2	4.5	6.8	8.4	7.7	8.4	10.2	9.8	9.3	7.7
Cost of Goods to Cash Flow 43	5.2	2.0	4.2	5.6	4.9	5.6	7.0	6.5	6.5	4.4
Cash Flow to Total Debt 44	0.2	0.5	0.4	0.3	0.3	0.2	0.2	0.2	0.1	0.1

Selected Financial Factors (in Percentages)

Debt Ratio 45	57.6	70.8	63.2	60.6	43.1	46.8	38.1	57.6	63.8	66.1
Return on Total Assets 46	5.9	21.9	11.4	11.6	9.4	7.0	6.4	8.0	4.5	3.8
Return on Equity Before Income Taxes 47	9.5	39.4	21.3	21.9	13.1	9.7	7.8	12.2	4.6	7.9
Return on Equity After Income Taxes 48	7.3	39.2	20.5	19.7	12.1	7.7	5.5	9.0	2.5	4.7
Profit Margin (Before Income Tax) 49	5.5	6.7	4.7	5.7	7.5	5.9	6.3	5.3	3.0	6.1
Profit Margin (After Income Tax) 50	4.2	6.7	4.5	5.2	6.9	4.6	4.4	3.9	1.6	3.6

Table II

Corporations with Net Income

NONMETALLIC MINERAL MINING AND QUARRYING

MONEY AMOUNTS AND SIZE OF ASSETS IN THOUSANDS OF DOLLARS

Item Description for Accounting Period 7/07 Through 6/08		Total	Zero Assets	Under 500	500 to 1,000	1,000 to 5,000	5,000 to 10,000	10,000 to 25,000	25,000 to 50,000	50,000 to 100,000	100,000 to 250,000	250,000 to 500,000	500,000 to 2,500,000	2,500,000 and over
Number of Enterprises	1	3334	•	1739	292	601	201	126	52	19	16	•	•	0
Revenues ($ in Thousands)														
Net Sales	2	21930578	•	271559	59005	2705145	2086672	2238452	1474006	1600160	2389249	•	•	0
Interest	3	43439	•	250	0	967	3512	3491	4495	9249	7046	•	•	0
Rents	4	32621	•	0	0	2041	80	1249	3229	541	4181	•	•	0
Royalties	5	20147	•	411	0	8	1	0	686	0	1440	•	•	0
Other Portfolio Income	6	229003	•	6940	0	38176	11073	6061	11132	4128	33526	•	•	0
Other Receipts	7	232132	•	15970	-2202	18820	8044	40146	24126	15676	48785	•	•	0
Total Receipts	8	22487920	•	295130	56803	2765157	2109382	2289399	1517674	1666754	2484227	•	•	•
Average Total Receipts	9	6745	•	170	195	4601	10494	18170	29186	87724	155264	•	•	•
Operating Costs/Operating Income (%)														
Cost of Operations	10	62.0	•	44.6	21.4	64.1	64.3	63.6	65.5	67.0	69.0	•	•	•
Salaries and Wages	11	5.1	•	4.8	17.0	5.5	3.1	4.0	3.5	6.6	3.8	•	•	•
Taxes Paid	12	2.2	•	2.8	4.2	2.2	2.4	2.7	2.4	1.9	1.6	•	•	•
Interest Paid	13	2.1	•	1.6	2.3	1.8	1.8	1.5	1.0	1.5	1.6	•	•	•
Depreciation	14	5.7	•	8.8	0.3	4.3	4.4	5.6	6.2	5.3	6.5	•	•	•
Amortization and Depletion	15	2.6	•	0.1	7.2	0.1	1.2	2.8	2.0	1.5	2.7	•	•	•
Pensions and Other Deferred Comp.	16	0.7	•	•	•	0.1	0.8	0.6	0.7	0.6	1.1	•	•	•
Employee Benefits	17	1.8	•	0.0	0.4	1.4	2.1	1.5	1.4	2.1	1.9	•	•	•
Advertising	18	0.2	•	1.0	•	0.3	0.4	0.2	0.4	0.2	0.1	•	•	•
Other Expenses	19	9.8	•	26.1	26.7	12.3	9.0	7.4	7.0	7.6	5.1	•	•	•
Officers' Compensation	20	1.6	•	•	•	3.2	2.5	2.0	1.5	1.4	1.3	•	•	•
Operating Margin	21	6.1	•	10.3	20.4	4.7	7.9	8.2	8.4	4.2	5.3	•	•	•
Operating Margin Before Officers' Comp.	22	7.8	•	10.3	20.4	7.9	10.4	10.2	9.9	5.6	6.6	•	•	•

Selected Average Balance Sheet ($ in Thousands)

Net Receivables 23	825	•	1	54	393	1301	2411	3421	10034	22898
Inventories 24	633	•	7	48	252	451	1746	3247	8107	19430
Net Property, Plant and Equipment 25	3397	•	30	387	899	2779	7346	13657	33245	70893
Total Assets 26	8149	•	79	890	1925	6123	16647	34380	74328	171767
Notes and Loans Payable 27	2750	•	40	59	1026	2470	3769	5443	15374	22136
All Other Liabilities 28	1770	•	1	189	270	1095	2493	5236	16411	34321
Net Worth 29	3629	•	38	641	629	2559	10386	23701	42543	115309

Selected Financial Ratios (Times to 1)

Current Ratio 30	1.3	•	9.4	2.6	2.6	1.9	3.1	2.8	2.2	2.6
Quick Ratio 31	0.8	•	4.3	1.9	1.9	1.5	2.1	1.8	1.5	1.4
Net Sales to Working Capital 32	14.7	•	5.3	•	7.4	9.1	3.5	3.6	4.7	3.4
Coverage Ratio 33	5.2	•	12.7	8.2	4.7	5.9	8.0	12.1	7.0	6.9
Total Asset Turnover 34	0.8	•	2.0	0.2	2.3	1.7	1.1	0.8	1.1	0.9
Inventory Turnover 35	6.4	•	9.9	0.9	11.5	14.8	6.5	5.7	7.0	5.3
Receivables Turnover 36	7.2	•	231.1	1.6	•	11.6	6.4	7.3	6.9	5.9
Total Liabilities to Net Worth 37	1.2	•	1.1	0.4	2.1	1.4	0.6	0.5	0.7	0.5
Current Assets to Working Capital 38	4.7	•	1.1	•	1.6	2.1	1.5	1.5	1.8	1.6
Current Liabilities to Working Capital 39	3.7	•	0.1	•	0.6	1.1	0.5	0.5	0.8	0.6
Working Capital to Net Sales 40	0.1	•	0.2	0.1	0.1	0.1	0.3	0.3	0.2	0.3
Inventory to Working Capital 41	1.4	•	0.3	0.4	0.4	0.4	0.3	0.5	0.5	0.4
Total Receipts to Cash Flow 42	7.2	•	3.1	3.5	7.7	7.1	6.5	6.2	7.8	9.1
Cost of Goods to Cash Flow 43	4.5	•	1.4	0.7	5.0	4.6	4.2	4.1	5.2	6.3
Cash Flow to Total Debt 44	0.2	•	1.2	0.2	0.4	0.4	0.4	0.4	0.3	0.3

Selected Financial Factors (in Percentages)

Debt Ratio 45	55.5	•	51.8	27.9	67.3	58.2	37.6	31.1	42.8	32.9
Return on Total Assets 46	8.8	•	40.6	4.3	20.5	18.3	12.7	10.2	12.2	9.3
Return on Equity Before Income Taxes 47	15.9	•	77.6	5.3	49.5	36.4	17.9	13.6	18.3	11.8
Return on Equity After Income Taxes 48	12.9	•	77.4	5.3	48.1	33.7	16.8	12.7	15.3	8.8
Profit Margin (Before Income Tax) 49	8.8	•	19.0	16.7	6.9	9.0	10.5	11.4	9.3	9.1
Profit Margin (After Income Tax) 50	7.1	•	18.9	16.7	6.7	8.3	9.8	10.6	7.7	6.8

Table I

Corporations with and without Net Income

SUPPORT ACTIVITIES FOR MINING

MONEY AMOUNTS AND SIZE OF ASSETS IN THOUSANDS OF DOLLARS

Item Description for Accounting Period 7/07 Through 6/08	Total	Zero Assets	Under 500	500 to 1,000	1,000 to 5,000	5,000 to 10,000	10,000 to 25,000	25,000 to 50,000	50,000 to 100,000	100,000 to 250,000	250,000 to 500,000	500,000 to 2,500,000	2,500,000 and over
Number of Enterprises **1**	9979	1218	6096	1440	816	153	119	34	30	19	14	24	16
Revenues ($ in Thousands)													
Net Sales **2**	84872306	1594411	3260697	2670345	3481296	2486026	2207246	1211565	1785393	2612309	2213855	19279752	42069408
Interest **3**	1180681	51431	1401	1940	8072	4742	8114	2685	6115	6715	39597	113144	936725
Rents **4**	620956	1	877	11	5	462	1140	0	296	104	69282	146785	401992
Royalties **5**	379370	171	0	398	0	34004	1545	0	408	0	1227	9030	332588
Other Portfolio Income **6**	2930696	28835	11870	2109	20268	15594	1943	16712	41648	38488	116107	241240	2395882
Other Receipts **7**	2482138	184570	523	35445	35978	218929	59594	34874	44221	36430	70067	308339	1453171
Total Receipts **8**	92466147	1859419	3275368	2710248	3545619	2759757	2279582	1265836	1878081	2694046	2510135	20098290	47589766
Average Total Receipts **9**	9266	1527	537	1882	4345	18038	19156	37230	62603	141792	179295	837429	2974360
Operating Costs/Operating Income (%)													
Cost of Operations **10**	42.6	52.5	24.3	36.1	35.5	34.0	37.0	33.7	42.2	64.2	43.7	43.3	44.0
Salaries and Wages **11**	10.9	11.9	20.8	14.6	11.8	15.3	15.3	17.4	15.6	9.7	12.3	8.8	9.9
Taxes Paid **12**	2.1	1.4	3.9	2.7	2.1	2.7	3.4	3.2	2.5	1.1	2.7	2.4	1.8
Interest Paid **13**	3.5	2.9	0.8	1.1	0.6	0.9	1.5	1.9	3.8	4.1	2.9	2.8	4.8
Depreciation **14**	8.4	4.1	3.4	4.1	4.9	6.3	8.2	6.0	11.4	6.1	11.0	12.4	7.7
Amortization and Depletion **15**	0.7	0.1	0.1	0.1	0.1	0.3	0.3	0.4	1.2	0.9	1.8	1.3	0.6
Pensions and Other Deferred Comp. **16**	0.5	0.8	1.2	0.3	0.3	0.2	0.3	0.3	0.6	0.2	0.5	0.3	0.7
Employee Benefits **17**	1.8	0.8	0.7	0.5	1.8	1.2	0.9	1.5	1.5	0.9	1.1	1.2	2.5
Advertising **18**	0.2	0.1	0.4	0.2	0.3	0.2	0.2	0.3	0.1	0.2	0.1	0.1	0.1
Other Expenses **19**	18.6	25.3	21.7	19.8	25.2	39.2	22.4	26.1	22.7	10.7	20.9	18.0	16.3
Officers' Compensation **20**	1.6	3.4	8.2	4.8	7.7	1.9	2.5	1.8	1.3	0.7	2.0	1.0	0.6
Operating Margin **21**	9.1	•	14.6	15.7	9.5	•	8.2	7.3	•	1.4	0.9	8.3	11.2
Operating Margin Before Officers' Comp. **22**	10.7	0.2	22.8	20.4	17.2	•	10.6	9.1	•	2.1	2.9	9.3	11.7

Selected Average Balance Sheet ($ in Thousands)

	1	2	3	4	5	6	7	8	9	10	11	12
Net Receivables 23	1676	5	117	531	1383	2794	8279	10620	28369	90197	169091	568192
Inventories 24	423	1	10	37	284	458	1230	1628	4718	5292	32821	189492
Net Property, Plant and Equipment 25	4979	53	217	694	2604	4991	9357	27687	53872	80239	644993	1794832
Total Assets 26	13229	117	666	1999	6611	14334	36577	70247	164713	335105	1257383	5290236
Notes and Loans Payable 27	3852	60	258	520	2347	4251	16196	27947	74884	51278	315486	1582301
All Other Liabilities 28	2846	18	194	263	1375	3097	11675	15919	36666	97411	257696	1131060
Net Worth 29	6531	39	214	1216	2889	6985	8705	26381	53163	186416	684201	2576875

Selected Financial Ratios (Times to 1)

	1	2	3	4	5	6	7	8	9	10	11	12
Current Ratio 30	1.9	•	2.3	1.5	3.3	1.7	1.7	1.5	1.4	1.6	2.2	1.9
Quick Ratio 31	1.3	•	2.1	1.2	3.0	1.4	1.4	1.2	1.0	1.1	1.6	1.1
Net Sales to Working Capital 32	5.0	•	18.5	18.6	5.4	13.6	6.8	9.6	7.8	3.2	4.8	4.1
Coverage Ratio 33	6.4	5.7	20.8	16.2	20.6	10.4	8.6	7.2	6.0	5.5	6.6	6.6
Total Asset Turnover 34	0.6	•	4.6	2.8	2.1	2.5	1.3	1.0	0.8	0.5	0.6	0.5
Inventory Turnover 35	8.6	•	112.5	67.7	41.0	19.5	15.0	9.8	15.4	18.7	13.0	6.1
Receivables Turnover 36	4.7	•	65.9	23.0	7.5	10.2	5.4	4.4	5.2	4.5	4.2	4.3
Total Liabilities to Net Worth 37	1.0	•	2.0	2.1	0.6	1.3	1.1	3.2	1.7	2.1	0.8	1.1
Current Assets to Working Capital 38	2.1	•	1.8	3.2	1.4	2.5	2.4	3.1	3.8	2.7	1.8	2.2
Current Liabilities to Working Capital 39	1.1	•	0.8	2.2	0.4	1.5	1.4	2.1	2.8	1.7	0.8	1.2
Working Capital to Net Sales 40	0.2	•	0.1	0.1	0.2	0.1	0.1	0.1	0.1	0.3	0.2	0.2
Inventory to Working Capital 41	0.3	•	0.0	0.1	0.0	0.3	0.1	0.1	0.3	0.2	0.2	0.4
Total Receipts to Cash Flow 42	3.4	4.7	3.1	3.0	3.7	2.5	3.7	3.5	5.3	7.6	4.3	3.0
Cost of Goods to Cash Flow 43	1.4	2.5	0.8	1.1	1.3	0.8	1.4	1.2	2.2	4.9	1.6	1.3
Cash Flow to Total Debt 44	0.4	•	2.2	1.4	1.5	1.8	0.7	0.4	0.3	0.2	0.3	0.3

Selected Financial Factors (in Percentages)

	1	2	3	4	5	6	7	8	9	10	11	12
Debt Ratio 45	50.6	66.7	67.9	39.2	56.3	51.3	76.2	62.4	67.7	44.4	45.6	51.3
Return on Total Assets 46	14.6	72.6	50.9	25.5	23.5	16.8	13.3	5.1	7.2	8.3	10.0	15.5
Return on Equity Before Income Taxes 47	25.0	207.6	148.8	39.9	48.5	30.4	48.1	5.1	11.7	12.5	15.0	27.1
Return on Equity After Income Taxes 48	17.6	204.8	144.1	35.5	41.2	26.2	42.4	2.6	7.2	8.3	9.8	18.4
Profit Margin (Before Income Tax) 49	19.2	15.1	17.2	11.4	8.6	11.5	11.8	2.3	4.5	14.7	12.7	26.5
Profit Margin (After Income Tax) 50	13.5	14.9	16.6	10.1	7.3	9.9	10.4	1.2	2.8	9.7	8.3	18.0

Table II

Corporations with Net Income

SUPPORT ACTIVITIES FOR MINING

MONEY AMOUNTS AND SIZE OF ASSETS IN THOUSANDS OF DOLLARS

Item Description for Accounting Period 7/07 Through 6/08	Total	Zero Assets	Under 500	500 to 1,000	1,000 to 5,000	5,000 to 10,000	10,000 to 25,000	25,000 to 50,000	50,000 to 100,000	100,000 to 250,000	250,000 to 500,000	500,000 to 2,500,000	2,500,000 and over
Number of Enterprises **1**	8294	•	5410	1050	737	126	82	25	17	12	•	21	•
Revenues ($ in Thousands)													
Net Sales **2**	77846870	•	2984439	2191704	3314126	2381122	1928380	970894	1345924	2032226	•	17992832	•
Interest **3**	1061143	•	1401	1509	6580	2349	6688	-461	2408	5607	•	106034	•
Rents **4**	619306	•	877	11	5	0	1140	0	154	104	•	146755	•
Royalties **5**	377343	•	0	398	0	33983	0	0	94	0	•	9012	•
Other Portfolio Income **6**	2849767	•	2801	2095	20268	15594	1917	16706	15493	35277	•	239856	•
Other Receipts **7**	2353112	•	522	35426	32433	218378	27873	33116	4695	33472	•	300692	•
Total Receipts **8**	85107541	•	2990040	2231143	3373412	2651426	1965998	1020255	1368768	2106686	•	18795181	•
Average Total Receipts **9**	10261	•	553	2125	4577	21043	23976	40810	80516	175557	•	895009	•
Operating Costs/Operating Income (%)													
Cost of Operations **10**	42.6	•	22.9	37.2	34.8	32.5	40.5	33.9	34.1	65.5	•	42.5	•
Salaries and Wages **11**	10.8	•	18.7	13.1	11.3	15.7	13.0	16.8	17.5	10.1	•	9.1	•
Taxes Paid **12**	2.2	•	3.8	2.6	2.1	2.7	3.2	3.6	2.6	1.0	•	2.5	•
Interest Paid **13**	3.2	•	0.7	0.8	0.5	0.8	1.2	1.9	1.7	1.8	•	2.7	•
Depreciation **14**	8.0	•	2.7	3.2	4.9	6.1	6.6	6.2	9.5	4.0	•	12.1	•
Amortization and Depletion **15**	0.7	•	0.0	0.1	0.1	0.3	0.2	0.2	0.3	0.7	•	1.3	•
Pensions and Other Deferred Comp. **16**	0.5	•	1.3	0.2	0.4	0.2	0.3	0.3	0.7	0.2	•	0.3	•
Employee Benefits **17**	1.8	•	0.7	0.3	1.7	1.2	0.9	1.5	1.3	0.6	•	1.3	•
Advertising **18**	0.2	•	0.4	0.2	0.3	0.2	0.2	0.3	0.1	0.2	•	0.1	•
Other Expenses **19**	17.6	•	21.7	19.6	25.5	39.9	17.1	19.9	20.7	10.0	•	17.9	•
Officers' Compensation **20**	1.5	•	8.7	2.6	7.7	2.0	2.2	1.6	1.3	0.6	•	1.0	•
Operating Margin **21**	11.0	•	18.5	20.1	10.8	•	14.5	13.9	10.2	5.3	•	9.3	•
Operating Margin Before Officers' Comp. **22**	12.6	•	27.2	22.7	18.5	0.5	16.7	15.5	11.5	5.9	•	10.2	•

Selected Average Balance Sheet ($ in Thousands)

Net Receivables 23	1850	•	3	100	576	1678	2942	8279	12881	35647	179656
Inventories 24	476	•	1	10	23	162	625	1295	1110	7144	36068
Net Property, Plant and Equipment 25	5044	•	41	198	722	2896	4490	10373	25030	33190	677075
Total Assets 26	13903	•	107	681	2004	6567	13947	36787	68994	151800	1305159
Notes and Loans Payable 27	3826	•	47	195	514	2111	4277	11892	19849	40197	327059
All Other Liabilities 28	2963	•	7	223	252	1506	1738	5194	17374	39942	261557
Net Worth 29	7115	•	52	263	1237	2950	7931	19701	31771	71661	716543

Selected Financial Ratios (Times to 1)

Current Ratio 30	1.9	•	3.1	1.6	3.7	1.6	2.2	2.8	1.8	1.6	2.3
Quick Ratio 31	1.4	•	3.0	1.2	3.4	1.4	1.8	2.6	1.6	1.1	1.7
Net Sales to Working Capital 32	4.9	•	15.4	16.8	5.2	15.8	7.1	3.9	6.1	6.8	4.6
Coverage Ratio 33	7.7	•	29.3	28.8	26.7	13.9	14.5	11.2	8.0	6.1	6.1
Total Asset Turnover 34	0.7	•	5.2	3.1	2.2	2.9	1.7	1.1	1.1	1.1	0.7
Inventory Turnover 35	8.4	•	159.3	81.1	69.1	37.9	15.2	10.2	24.3	15.5	10.1
Receivables Turnover 36	4.6	•	203.1	29.9	9.2	10.4	5.3	4.2	7.3	4.3	4.0
Total Liabilities to Net Worth 37	1.0	•	1.0	1.6	0.6	1.2	0.8	0.9	1.2	1.1	0.8
Current Assets to Working Capital 38	2.1	•	1.5	2.8	1.4	2.7	1.8	1.6	2.2	2.6	1.8
Current Liabilities to Working Capital 39	1.1	•	0.5	1.8	0.4	1.7	0.8	0.6	1.2	1.6	0.8
Working Capital to Net Sales 40	0.2	•	0.1	0.1	0.2	0.1	0.1	0.3	0.2	0.1	0.2
Inventory to Working Capital 41	0.3	•	0.0	0.1	0.0	0.2	0.1	0.0	0.1	0.2	0.2
Total Receipts to Cash Flow 42	3.2	•	2.8	2.6	3.5	2.3	3.6	3.4	3.6	5.8	4.2
Cost of Goods to Cash Flow 43	1.4	•	0.6	1.0	1.2	0.8	1.5	1.1	1.2	3.8	1.8
Cash Flow to Total Debt 44	0.4	•	3.7	1.9	1.7	2.2	1.1	0.7	0.6	0.4	0.3

Selected Financial Factors (in Percentages)

Debt Ratio 45	48.8	•	50.9	61.4	38.3	55.1	43.1	46.4	54.0	52.8	45.1
Return on Total Assets 46	16.8	•	100.0	69.6	29.3	30.8	29.8	21.9	15.6	12.0	10.9
Return on Equity Before Income Taxes 47	28.5	•	196.6	174.0	45.7	63.7	48.8	37.3	29.7	21.2	16.7
Return on Equity After Income Taxes 48	20.4	•	194.3	168.8	40.9	55.0	43.4	33.9	26.0	16.0	11.0
Profit Margin (Before Income Tax) 49	21.6	•	18.7	21.9	12.6	9.9	16.4	18.9	11.9	9.0	13.9
Profit Margin (After Income Tax) 50	15.5	•	18.5	21.2	11.3	8.6	14.6	17.2	10.5	6.8	9.2

16

Table I

Corporations with and without Net Income

ELECTRIC POWER GENERATION, TRANSMISSION AND DISTRIBUTION

MONEY AMOUNTS AND SIZE OF ASSETS IN THOUSANDS OF DOLLARS

Item Description for Accounting Period 7/07 Through 6/08	Total	Zero Assets	Under 500	500 to 1,000	1,000 to 5,000	5,000 to 10,000	10,000 to 25,000	25,000 to 50,000	50,000 to 100,000	100,000 to 250,000	250,000 to 500,000	500,000 to 2,500,000	2,500,000 and over
Number of Enterprises 1	1187	6	487	336	81	65	37	33	20	30	11	34	46
Revenues ($ in Thousands)													
Net Sales 2	328017143	246762	1347	1116031	19765	241938	601611	1655802	1440168	3400647	1109780	15577170	302606123
Interest 3	6189712	4617	235	261	21361	3676	3128	35171	24521	65070	38459	581992	5411222
Rents 4	1572125	2050	0	0	0	1486	0	389	674	517	252	16804	1549953
Royalties 5	34922	0	0	0	0	0	0	21	0	7	0	22577	12317
Other Portfolio Income 6	14832601	0	28630	0	160693	5524	43	1062	241	39580	6959	133327	14456540
Other Receipts 7	10531358	59691	1	13399	801	10966	1892	23615	45972	107488	89750	411762	9766021
Total Receipts 8	361177861	313120	30213	1129691	202620	263590	606674	1716060	1511576	3613309	1245200	16743632	333802176
Average Total Receipts 9	304278	52187	62	3362	2501	4055	16397	52002	75579	120444	113200	492460	7256569
Operating Costs/Operating Income (%)													
Cost of Operations 10	59.4	16.5	1442.3	81.4	•	14.2	73.8	80.5	68.0	71.4	51.3	59.8	59.1
Salaries and Wages 11	3.8	2.7	52.5	1.7	48.8	22.7	2.2	8.0	2.0	3.1	1.4	4.4	3.8
Taxes Paid 12	3.3	3.2	33.3	0.9	7.1	7.5	3.3	0.9	0.9	1.2	2.6	2.3	3.4
Interest Paid 13	6.4	40.9	0.9	0.3	923.8	8.0	2.5	1.8	2.5	3.6	14.0	7.3	6.4
Depreciation 14	5.8	24.4	12.8	0.2	13.5	6.7	4.6	0.9	1.1	2.5	8.3	7.5	5.8
Amortization and Depletion 15	0.8	8.5	•	0.0	1.4	2.6	0.5	0.1	1.2	0.5	0.3	1.1	0.8
Pensions and Other Deferred Comp. 16	0.9	0.1	•	0.0	•	1.8	1.1	0.5	0.2	0.1	0.4	0.7	0.9
Employee Benefits 17	1.0	0.2	•	0.0	10.3	3.1	0.5	1.9	0.2	0.4	0.8	0.8	1.0
Advertising 18	0.1	0.0	1.5	0.1	9.1	0.3	0.1	0.3	0.1	0.2	1.0	0.1	0.1
Other Expenses 19	20.2	29.0	1055.8	9.3	182.8	27.9	15.5	10.4	24.0	21.5	27.4	23.2	20.1
Officers' Compensation 20	0.4	•	•	4.3	25.8	3.5	0.3	1.0	0.8	0.4	1.4	0.5	0.3
Operating Margin 21	•	•	•	1.8	•	1.8	•	•	•	•	•	•	•
Operating Margin Before Officers' Comp. 22	•	•	•	6.1	•	5.3	•	•	•	•	•	•	•

Selected Average Balance Sheet ($ in Thousands)

Net Receivables 23	39948	0	0	123	136	670	2146	11391	11606	14950	15082	89777	934092
Inventories 24	10440	4	0	14	0	87	826	167	899	1836	18928	35036	236379
Net Property, Plant and Equipment 25	344101	1	0	97	54	3445	9818	9173	20436	54678	148548	672005	8282394
Total Assets 26	687848	17	0	729	2026	7140	19853	36525	73621	157764	363528	1231531	16556038
Notes and Loans Payable 27	253228	53	0	23	401	4516	10016	17639	22979	90447	192164	549277	5984949
All Other Liabilities 28	240186	0	0	475	381	1900	4527	24296	27167	43187	114935	375741	5824765
Net Worth 29	194433	-36	0	230	1244	724	5310	-5410	23475	24131	56430	306513	4746324

Selected Financial Ratios (Times to 1)

Current Ratio 30	1.0	•	57.1	1.3	2.8	1.8	1.1	0.9	1.0	1.3	1.7	1.0	1.0
Quick Ratio 31	0.6	•	35.2	1.3	0.9	1.7	0.8	0.6	0.9	1.0	1.2	0.6	0.5
Net Sales to Working Capital 32	239.2	•	0.2	20.5	0.2	3.1	25.4	•	355.7	12.5	6.0	197.4	482.7
Coverage Ratio 33	2.3	1.0	•	12.2	0.8	2.3	•	•	2.5	1.4	1.2	1.0	2.4
Total Asset Turnover 34	0.4	•	0.2	4.6	0.1	0.5	0.8	1.4	1.0	0.7	0.3	0.4	0.4
Inventory Turnover 35	15.7	•	11.4	192.5	•	6.1	14.5	242.2	54.4	44.1	2.7	7.8	16.4
Receivables Turnover 36	7.1	•	0.2	51.2	3.6	8.4	5.5	7.7	3.9	8.4	5.1	4.8	7.2
Total Liabilities to Net Worth 37	2.5	•	•	2.2	0.6	8.9	2.7	•	2.1	5.5	5.4	3.0	2.5
Current Assets to Working Capital 38	95.7	•	1.0	3.9	1.5	2.2	8.9	•	104.0	4.1	2.5	117.6	189.0
Current Liabilities to Working Capital 39	94.7	•	0.0	2.9	0.5	1.2	7.9	•	103.0	3.1	1.5	116.6	188.0
Working Capital to Net Sales 40	0.0	•	5.5	0.0	4.7	0.3	0.0	•	0.0	0.1	0.2	0.0	0.0
Inventory to Working Capital 41	10.0	•	0.1	0.1	•	0.1	1.5	•	5.6	0.3	0.3	19.3	19.2
Total Receipts to Cash Flow 42	4.4	3.9	11.0	3.1	•	•	12.3	14.8	4.2	5.4	3.7	5.7	4.4
Cost of Goods to Cash Flow 43	2.6	0.6	9.0	0.4	•	•	9.1	11.9	2.9	3.9	1.9	3.4	2.6
Cash Flow to Total Debt 44	0.1	•	0.6	0.2	•	•	0.1	0.1	0.3	0.2	0.1	0.1	0.1

Selected Financial Factors (in Percentages)

Debt Ratio 45	71.7	•	316.3	68.4	38.6	89.9	73.3	114.8	68.1	84.7	84.5	75.1	71.3
Return on Total Assets 46	5.8	•	•	15.1	87.5	9.8	•	•	6.1	3.5	4.7	2.6	6.0
Return on Equity Before Income Taxes 47	11.5	•	27.1	43.8	•	55.2	•	23.8	11.6	6.1	5.5	•	12.2
Return on Equity After Income Taxes 48	7.6	•	81.8	41.4	•	46.0	•	26.9	8.3	2.2	3.9	•	8.2
Profit Margin (Before Income Tax) 49	8.1	1.3	3.0	3.0	•	10.7	•	•	3.8	1.3	3.1	•	8.8
Profit Margin (After Income Tax) 50	5.4	•	2.9	2.9	•	8.9	•	•	2.7	0.5	2.2	•	5.9

Table II

Corporations with Net Income

ELECTRIC POWER GENERATION, TRANSMISSION AND DISTRIBUTION

MONEY AMOUNTS AND SIZE OF ASSETS IN THOUSANDS OF DOLLARS

Item Description for Accounting Period 7/07 Through 6/08		Total	Zero Assets	Under 500	500 to 1,000	1,000 to 5,000	5,000 to 10,000	10,000 to 25,000	25,000 to 50,000	50,000 to 100,000	100,000 to 250,000	250,000 to 500,000	500,000 to 2,500,000	2,500,000 and over
Number of Enterprises	1	956	•	•	315	19	28	18	•	10	20	6	19	38
Revenues ($ in Thousands)														
Net Sales	2	296757929	•	•	1114086	18991	179828	354900	•	978131	2894352	427223	10033006	279060927
Interest	3	5206762	•	•	188	456	460	1129	•	6884	47703	16163	343741	4781892
Rents	4	1542691	•	•	0	0	0	0	•	0	384	0	11397	1528831
Royalties	5	34783	•	•	0	0	0	0	•	0	0	0	22577	12207
Other Portfolio Income	6	14554420	•	•	0	11357	5524	0	•	241	36451	6918	76551	14387702
Other Receipts	7	11735246	•	•	10981	0	8528	1697	•	29909	95846	78805	262825	11174918
Total Receipts	8	329831831	•	•	1125255	30804	194340	357726	•	1015165	3074736	529109	10750097	310946477
Average Total Receipts	9	345012	•	•	3572	1621	6941	19874	•	101516	153737	88185	565795	8182802
Operating Costs/Operating Income (%)														
Cost of Operations	10	59.0	•	•	81.1	•	•	67.7	•	85.1	77.3	37.6	65.6	58.3
Salaries and Wages	11	3.9	•	•	1.1	•	26.8	1.2	•	1.7	3.1	1.0	4.9	3.9
Taxes Paid	12	3.5	•	•	0.9	1.1	2.4	4.0	•	1.1	0.9	2.3	2.7	3.6
Interest Paid	13	5.6	•	•	0.2	0.4	6.4	1.9	•	1.2	2.7	11.3	4.1	5.8
Depreciation	14	5.7	•	•	0.2	8.5	2.3	3.8	•	0.5	1.2	7.6	5.3	5.8
Amortization and Depletion	15	0.7	•	•	0.0	0.3	3.4	0.8	•	1.1	0.3	0.4	1.0	0.7
Pensions and Other Deferred Comp.	16	0.9	•	•	0.0	•	2.0	0.4	•	0.3	0.1	0.2	1.0	0.9
Employee Benefits	17	1.0	•	•	•	•	2.9	0.5	•	0.2	0.3	0.4	1.0	1.1
Advertising	18	0.1	•	•	0.0	•	0.4	•	•	0.0	0.1	2.6	0.1	0.1
Other Expenses	19	20.5	•	•	7.2	57.6	29.4	11.0	•	2.8	14.5	37.7	13.3	20.9
Officers' Compensation	20	0.4	•	•	4.3	•	4.2	•	•	0.8	0.4	2.9	0.6	0.4
Operating Margin	21	•	•	•	5.0	32.0	19.6	8.6	•	5.2	•	•	0.4	•
Operating Margin Before Officers' Comp.	22	•	•	•	9.3	32.0	23.8	8.6	•	6.0	•	•	1.0	•

Selected Average Balance Sheet ($ in Thousands)

Net Receivables 23	42358	•	•	130	500	2	3590	•	•	11291	17890	13270	121888	984746
Inventories 24	11248	•	•	9	0	0	310	•	•	924	2275	19918	28661	263872
Net Property, Plant and Equipment 25	378468	•	•	98	23	3878	10420	•	•	19615	38485	96291	598748	9170912
Total Assets 26	753051	•	•	724	3335	7561	20318	•	•	74159	155237	345818	1207744	18147767
Notes and Loans Payable 27	264037	•	•	25	22	4529	8242	•	•	14972	79035	119103	444858	6339454
All Other Liabilities 28	263514	•	•	344	719	1022	4573	•	•	22706	39895	160831	414596	6345469
Net Worth 29	225500	•	•	355	2593	2011	7504	•	•	36481	36307	65885	348290	5462845

Selected Financial Ratios (Times to 1)

Current Ratio 30	1.0	•	•	1.9	6.3	20.4	1.6	•	•	1.6	1.4	2.6	1.2	1.0
Quick Ratio 31	0.5	•	•	1.8	1.3	19.2	1.2	•	•	1.5	1.1	2.0	0.8	0.5
Net Sales to Working Capital 32	•	•	•	12.2	0.4	3.9	8.3	•	•	13.8	10.6	2.2	10.6	•
Coverage Ratio 33	2.8	•	•	33.8	222.0	5.3	5.9	•	•	8.2	2.8	2.7	2.8	2.8
Total Asset Turnover 34	0.4	•	•	4.9	0.3	0.8	1.0	•	•	1.3	0.9	0.2	0.4	0.4
Inventory Turnover 35	16.3	•	•	313.5	•	•	43.1	•	•	90.1	49.2	1.3	12.1	16.2
Receivables Turnover 36	7.7	•	•	54.3	4.0	7052.1	5.1	•	•	3.9	9.8	2.8	5.5	7.8
Total Liabilities to Net Worth 37	2.3	•	•	1.0	0.3	2.8	1.7	•	•	1.0	3.3	4.2	2.5	2.3
Current Assets to Working Capital 38	•	•	•	2.2	1.2	1.1	2.8	•	•	2.6	3.2	1.6	7.0	•
Current Liabilities to Working Capital 39	•	•	•	1.2	0.2	0.1	1.8	•	•	1.6	2.2	0.6	6.0	•
Working Capital to Net Sales 40	•	•	•	0.1	2.8	0.3	0.1	•	•	0.1	0.1	0.4	0.1	•
Inventory to Working Capital 41	•	•	•	0.0	•	•	0.2	•	•	0.1	0.2	0.1	0.6	•
Total Receipts to Cash Flow 42	4.1	•	•	10.0	1.1	2.0	5.0	•	•	9.2	6.2	1.9	5.8	4.0
Cost of Goods to Cash Flow 43	2.4	•	•	8.1	•	•	3.4	•	•	7.9	4.8	0.7	3.8	2.3
Cash Flow to Total Debt 44	0.1	•	•	1.0	1.2	0.6	0.3	•	•	0.3	0.1	0.1	0.1	0.1

Selected Financial Factors (in Percentages)

Debt Ratio 45	70.1	•	•	51.0	22.2	73.4	63.1	•	•	50.8	76.6	80.9	71.2	69.9
Return on Total Assets 46	6.4	•	•	30.4	28.4	28.9	10.9	•	•	13.5	7.2	6.3	5.1	6.4
Return on Equity Before Income Taxes 47	13.7	•	•	60.2	36.3	88.4	24.6	•	•	24.0	20.0	20.7	11.3	13.5
Return on Equity After Income Taxes 48	9.5	•	•	58.5	23.8	80.7	20.2	•	•	19.8	16.1	18.3	8.1	9.4
Profit Margin (Before Income Tax) 49	9.9	•	•	6.0	94.2	27.7	9.4	•	•	9.0	5.0	19.2	7.4	10.1
Profit Margin (After Income Tax) 50	6.9	•	•	5.9	61.7	25.3	7.7	•	•	7.4	4.0	16.9	5.3	7.0

Table I

Corporations with and without Net Income

NATURAL GAS DISTRIBUTION

MONEY AMOUNTS AND SIZE OF ASSETS IN THOUSANDS OF DOLLARS

Item Description for Accounting Period 7/07 Through 6/08	Total	Zero Assets	Under 500	500 to 1,000	1,000 to 5,000	5,000 to 10,000	10,000 to 25,000	25,000 to 50,000	50,000 to 100,000	100,000 to 250,000	250,000 to 500,000	500,000 to 2,500,000	2,500,000 and over
Number of Enterprises 1	618	•	262	122	86	39	25	13	10	•	•	8	21

Revenues ($ in Thousands)

Net Sales 2	112511451	•	19956	118908	231132	645359	608369	1272634	367293	•	•	9142635	89837813
Interest 3	2946662	•	2	1218	1729	2211	747	2394	4240	•	•	152533	2743818
Rents 4	102826	•	0	2047	0	54	0	0	2585	•	•	1668	96448
Royalties 5	50674	•	0	0	0	0	0	0	19	•	•	3211	43743
Other Portfolio Income 6	4869187	•	0	0	0	1943	1499	96	979	•	•	237875	4595723
Other Receipts 7	82804	•	0	1398	12911	1962	4634	1254	5923	•	•	109382	-149131
Total Receipts 8	120563604	•	19958	123571	245772	651529	615249	1276378	381039	•	•	9647304	97168414
Average Total Receipts 9	195087	•	76	1013	2858	16706	24610	98183	38104	•	•	1205913	4627067

Operating Costs/Operating Income (%)

Cost of Operations 10	69.9	•	98.2	•	71.0	82.7	89.9	90.3	73.5	•	•	82.6	65.7
Salaries and Wages 11	3.4	•	•	•	6.2	0.9	1.1	2.0	4.1	•	•	2.6	3.9
Taxes Paid 12	2.5	•	1.1	0.8	1.0	0.8	0.8	0.7	2.7	•	•	2.7	2.8
Interest Paid 13	5.3	•	•	0.0	1.1	0.4	1.9	0.4	4.5	•	•	3.0	6.2
Depreciation 14	4.4	•	•	•	4.3	1.9	1.6	0.4	5.1	•	•	3.1	5.0
Amortization and Depletion 15	0.4	•	•	•	0.0	0.3	0.0	•	0.1	•	•	0.4	0.4
Pensions and Other Deferred Comp. 16	0.4	•	•	•	1.4	0.2	0.1	0.1	0.9	•	•	0.3	0.4
Employee Benefits 17	1.3	•	•	•	0.4	0.3	0.3	0.1	1.6	•	•	0.8	1.5
Advertising 18	0.0	•	•	0.3	0.1	0.0	0.0	0.0	0.0	•	•	0.1	0.0
Other Expenses 19	14.2	•	115.2	91.5	12.1	3.2	4.1	1.2	6.2	•	•	5.2	16.6
Officers' Compensation 20	0.4	•	•	10.2	2.4	1.1	0.7	0.6	1.6	•	•	0.4	0.4
Operating Margin 21	•	•	•	•	•	8.2	•	4.1	•	•	•	•	•
Operating Margin Before Officers' Comp. 22	•	•	•	7.4	2.3	9.3	0.2	4.8	1.2	•	•	•	•

Selected Average Balance Sheet ($ in Thousands)

Net Receivables 23	72734	•	•	0	205	171	597	2314	16758	8240	•	•	85155	2035843
Inventories 24	9435	•	•	0	0	173	183	1049	2316	4792	•	•	123022	197417
Net Property, Plant and Equipment 25	184385	•	•	0	28	749	2774	7784	6541	29829	•	•	708823	5057819
Total Assets 26	425541	•	•	6	627	1821	7102	14574	31770	72965	•	•	1583264	11613630
Notes and Loans Payable 27	151995	•	•	1	170	604	460	7540	4965	18559	•	•	709938	4127910
All Other Liabilities 28	215820	•	•	4	383	311	1474	3463	14602	20430	•	•	483247	6052425
Net Worth 29	57727	•	•	1	74	906	5168	3571	12203	33976	•	•	390079	1433295

Selected Financial Ratios (Times to 1)

Current Ratio 30	1.2	•	•	1.1	1.6	2.0	1.2	1.5	1.0	•	•	•	1.1	1.2
Quick Ratio 31	0.7	•	•	1.1	1.2	1.8	0.8	1.3	0.7	•	•	•	0.5	0.7
Net Sales to Working Capital 32	8.7	•	•	127.9	4.5	9.0	17.7	33.3	12.8	•	•	•	39.5	7.6
Coverage Ratio 33	1.9	•	•	431.0	6.7	26.0	1.4	13.5	1.8	•	•	•	2.4	1.9
Total Asset Turnover 34	0.4	•	•	13.2	1.6	1.5	2.3	1.7	3.1	0.5	•	•	0.7	0.4
Inventory Turnover 35	13.5	•	•	•	11.1	74.6	20.8	38.2	5.6	•	•	•	7.7	14.2
Receivables Turnover 36	3.1	•	•	4.8	4.9	33.9	•	6.5	3.5	•	•	•	•	2.6
Total Liabilities to Net Worth 37	6.4	•	•	8.7	7.5	1.0	3.1	1.6	1.1	•	•	•	3.1	7.1
Current Assets to Working Capital 38	6.5	•	•	9.7	2.8	2.7	6.6	3.0	•	•	•	•	11.9	6.7
Current Liabilities to Working Capital 39	5.5	•	•	8.7	1.8	1.7	1.0	5.6	2.0	•	•	•	10.9	5.7
Working Capital to Net Sales 40	0.1	•	•	0.0	0.2	0.1	0.1	0.0	0.1	•	•	•	0.0	0.1
Inventory to Working Capital 41	0.5	•	•	•	0.6	0.0	1.4	0.3	•	•	•	•	4.2	0.4
Total Receipts to Cash Flow 42	6.8	•	•	127.9	1.2	6.9	8.5	23.9	18.8	•	•	•	16.4	5.9
Cost of Goods to Cash Flow 43	4.7	•	•	125.6	•	4.9	7.0	21.4	17.0	9.2	•	•	13.5	3.9
Cash Flow to Total Debt 44	0.1	•	•	0.1	1.5	0.4	1.0	0.1	0.3	•	•	•	0.1	0.1

Selected Financial Factors (in Percentages)

Debt Ratio 45	86.4	•	•	89.6	88.3	50.2	75.5	27.2	61.6	53.4	•	•	75.4	87.7
Return on Total Assets 46	4.4	•	•	1.7	10.8	21.7	4.3	14.8	4.0	•	•	•	5.2	4.3
Return on Equity Before Income Taxes 47	15.6	•	•	14.4	18.5	28.7	4.8	35.6	3.6	•	•	•	12.5	16.1
Return on Equity After Income Taxes 48	10.3	•	•	11.6	18.5	21.9	1.1	32.9	1.7	•	•	•	8.1	10.4
Profit Margin (Before Income Tax) 49	4.9	•	•	1.1	6.2	9.0	0.7	4.4	3.4	•	•	•	4.3	5.4
Profit Margin (After Income Tax) 50	3.3	•	•	0.9	6.2	6.8	0.2	4.1	1.5	•	•	•	2.8	3.5

Table II

Corporations with Net Income

NATURAL GAS DISTRIBUTION

MONEY AMOUNTS AND SIZE OF ASSETS IN THOUSANDS OF DOLLARS

Item Description for Accounting Period 7/07 Through 6/08	Total	Zero Assets	Under 500	500 to 1,000	1,000 to 5,000	5,000 to 10,000	10,000 to 25,000	25,000 to 50,000	50,000 to 100,000	100,000 to 250,000	250,000 to 500,000	500,000 to 2,500,000	2,500,000 and over
Number of Enterprises **1**	•	0	•	61	67	39	9	•	7	•	•	•	18
Revenues ($ in Thousands)													
Net Sales **2**	•	0	•	3452	217751	645359	529279	•	327168	•	•	•	78180556
Interest **3**	•	0	•	0	1601	2211	133	•	3156	•	•	•	2500873
Rents **4**	•	0	•	0	0	54	0	•	2585	•	•	•	58266
Royalties **5**	•	0	•	0	0	0	0	•	19	•	•	•	43743
Other Portfolio Income **6**	•	0	•	0	0	1943	14	•	915	•	•	•	4332993
Other Receipts **7**	•	0	•	0	11869	1962	2011	•	6673	•	•	•	-1360231
Total Receipts **8**	•	0	•	3452	231221	651529	531437	•	340516	•	•	•	83756200
Average Total Receipts **9**	•	•	•	57	3451	16706	59049	•	48645	•	•	•	4653122
Operating Costs/Operating Income (%)													
Cost of Operations **10**	•	•	•	•	69.5	82.7	92.4	•	74.6	•	•	•	66.1
Salaries and Wages **11**	•	•	•	•	6.6	0.9	0.9	•	3.0	•	•	•	3.6
Taxes Paid **12**	•	•	•	5.0	1.0	0.8	0.2	•	2.7	•	•	•	2.6
Interest Paid **13**	•	•	•	•	1.2	0.4	0.4	•	2.6	•	•	•	6.1
Depreciation **14**	•	•	•	•	2.5	1.9	0.0	•	5.0	•	•	•	5.0
Amortization and Depletion **15**	•	•	•	•	0.0	0.3	0.0	•	0.1	•	•	•	0.4
Pensions and Other Deferred Comp. **16**	•	•	•	•	1.5	0.2	0.0	•	0.9	•	•	•	0.4
Employee Benefits **17**	•	•	•	•	0.5	0.3	0.3	•	1.5	•	•	•	1.6
Advertising **18**	•	•	•	•	0.0	0.0	0.0	•	0.0	•	•	•	0.0
Other Expenses **19**	•	•	•	47.2	11.7	3.2	1.7	•	5.4	•	•	•	13.9
Officers' Compensation **20**	•	•	•	•	2.5	1.1	0.3	•	1.3	•	•	•	0.4
Operating Margin **21**	•	•	•	47.8	3.0	8.2	3.8	•	2.8	•	•	•	•
Operating Margin Before Officers' Comp. **22**	•	•	•	47.8	5.5	9.3	4.1	•	4.1	•	•	•	0.3

Selected Average Balance Sheet ($ in Thousands)

Line							
Net Receivables 23	409	215	597	4927	5149	•	1351691
Inventories 24	0	220	183	2202	4790	•	221298
Net Property, Plant and Equipment 25	57	678	2774	16	37411	•	5179809
Total Assets 26	526	1734	7102	11988	76302	•	10765379
Notes and Loans Payable 27	39	619	460	3868	20835	•	4116624
All Other Liabilities 28	336	398	1474	4749	17876	•	3733914
Net Worth 29	150	717	5168	3371	37591	•	2914840

Selected Financial Ratios (Times to 1)

Line							
Current Ratio 30	1.4	1.6	2.0	1.9	1.1	•	1.4
Quick Ratio 31	1.4	1.2	1.8	1.0	0.6	•	0.8
Net Sales to Working Capital 32	0.4	8.3	17.7	13.2	26.3	•	5.6
Coverage Ratio 33	•	9.0	26.0	11.8	3.6	•	2.2
Total Asset Turnover 34	0.1	1.9	2.3	4.9	0.6	•	0.4
Inventory Turnover 35	•	10.3	74.6	24.7	7.3	•	13.0
Receivables Turnover 36	0.1	5.9	34.1	8.4	•	•	•
Total Liabilities to Net Worth 37	2.5	1.4	0.4	2.6	1.0	•	2.7
Current Assets to Working Capital 38	3.5	2.6	2.0	2.1	9.9	•	3.7
Current Liabilities to Working Capital 39	2.5	1.6	1.0	1.1	8.9	•	2.7
Working Capital to Net Sales 40	2.3	0.1	0.1	0.1	0.0	•	0.2
Inventory to Working Capital 41	•	0.6	0.0	0.6	2.7	•	0.3
Total Receipts to Cash Flow 42	1.7	5.9	8.5	17.3	9.4	•	6.0
Cost of Goods to Cash Flow 43	4.1	7.0	16.0	7.0	•	•	4.0
Cash Flow to Total Debt 44	0.1	0.5	1.0	0.4	0.1	•	0.1

Selected Financial Factors (in Percentages)

Line							
Debt Ratio 45	71.4	58.6	27.2	71.9	50.7	•	72.9
Return on Total Assets 46	5.1	19.4	21.7	22.5	5.8	•	5.4
Return on Equity Before Income Taxes 47	18.0	41.8	28.7	73.2	8.5	•	10.7
Return on Equity After Income Taxes 48	15.3	41.8	21.9	62.2	5.9	•	7.4
Profit Margin (Before Income Tax) 49	47.8	9.2	9.0	4.2	6.8	•	7.1
Profit Margin (After Income Tax) 50	40.6	9.2	6.8	3.6	4.8	•	5.0

20

Table I

Corporations with and without Net Income

WATER, SEWAGE AND OTHER SYSTEMS

MONEY AMOUNTS AND SIZE OF ASSETS IN THOUSANDS OF DOLLARS

Item Description for Accounting Period 7/07 Through 6/08		Total	Zero Assets	Under 500	500 to 1,000	1,000 to 5,000	5,000 to 10,000	10,000 to 25,000	25,000 to 50,000	50,000 to 100,000	100,000 to 250,000	250,000 to 500,000	500,000 to 2,500,000	2,500,000 and over
Number of Enterprises	1	5824	•	4097	619	417	147	54	33	8	•	•	9	3
Revenues ($ in Thousands)														
Net Sales	2	8296070	•	835049	230722	306336	577296	207088	259299	89586	•	•	1731446	3525773
Interest	3	103633	•	1777	1080	3206	3903	607	13034	2278	•	•	15381	32824
Rents	4	23348	•	423	0	2122	0	437	2523	10	•	•	11365	3842
Royalties	5	59	•	0	0	0	0	0	58	0	•	•	0	0
Other Portfolio Income	6	102209	•	111	636	1631	2930	1961	5884	3	•	•	27886	5399
Other Receipts	7	-2284	•	52983	3187	24260	1515	6775	13163	2014	•	•	36941	-154941
Total Receipts	8	8523035	•	890343	235625	337555	585644	216868	293961	93891	•	•	1823019	3412897
Average Total Receipts	9	1463	•	217	381	809	3984	4016	8908	11736	•	•	202558	1137632
Operating Costs/Operating Income (%)														
Cost of Operations	10	32.5	•	12.5	24.2	16.5	50.5	46.6	21.2	37.0	•	•	49.6	28.7
Salaries and Wages	11	7.1	•	3.8	10.1	17.4	6.4	9.4	11.2	6.4	•	•	6.1	7.2
Taxes Paid	12	6.8	•	3.3	4.6	5.2	5.3	4.6	10.9	6.7	•	•	5.0	8.8
Interest Paid	13	9.4	•	0.5	4.5	8.0	2.5	7.3	6.4	9.3	•	•	11.0	12.4
Depreciation	14	11.9	•	2.8	6.2	17.9	7.1	9.1	10.0	9.2	•	•	11.7	14.3
Amortization and Depletion	15	0.7	•	0.0	0.6	0.1	0.1	0.3	0.3	0.6	•	•	0.3	1.2
Pensions and Other Deferred Comp.	16	1.8	•	1.0	0.9	0.4	0.6	0.6	0.7	1.3	•	•	1.3	2.6
Employee Benefits	17	2.6	•	1.5	2.1	2.0	2.6	2.2	2.4	2.0	•	•	2.7	3.0
Advertising	18	0.3	•	0.1	2.6	0.4	0.4	0.1	0.1	0.0	•	•	0.2	0.2
Other Expenses	19	19.6	•	37.8	54.1	44.7	20.1	17.3	35.5	27.3	•	•	10.3	12.6
Officers' Compensation	20	3.6	•	21.6	6.5	7.5	2.8	2.5	2.4	1.7	•	•	1.5	0.3
Operating Margin	21	3.7	•	15.2	•	•	1.5	0.1	•	0.0	•	•	0.3	8.7
Operating Margin Before Officers' Comp.	22	7.3	•	36.8	•	•	4.3	2.7	1.4	0.2	•	•	1.8	9.0

Selected Average Balance Sheet ($ in Thousands)

Net Receivables 23	224	•	11	36	85	343	1562	1302	1443	•	48702	164349
Inventories 24	43	•	1	48	17	7	68	62	259	•	12351	3258
Net Property, Plant and Equipment 25	4186	•	79	321	2111	3900	11054	19254	43058	•	565428	4598471
Total Assets 26	6268	•	126	753	2523	6725	16193	31526	70448	•	874823	6749235
Notes and Loans Payable 27	2279	•	52	404	1113	4060	4092	6966	23393	•	358752	2367904
All Other Liabilities 28	2002	•	26	74	817	1387	8542	12237	24273	•	273155	2187699
Net Worth 29	1987	•	48	274	593	1279	3558	12323	22782	•	242916	2193632

Selected Financial Ratios (Times to 1)

Current Ratio 30	1.3	•	1.6	0.6	1.8	2.2	1.0	1.9	3.8	•	0.9	1.1
Quick Ratio 31	0.7	•	1.5	0.4	1.6	2.0	0.8	1.4	1.6	•	0.5	0.5
Net Sales to Working Capital 32	10.1	•	12.8	•	5.0	3.5	3.8	3.8	0.9	•	•	41.5
Coverage Ratio 33	1.7	•	41.7	•	•	2.2	1.7	2.9	1.4	•	1.5	1.4
Total Asset Turnover 34	0.2	•	1.6	0.5	0.3	0.6	0.2	0.2	0.2	•	0.2	0.2
Inventory Turnover 35	10.8	•	34.4	1.9	7.1	299.7	26.4	27.0	16.0	•	7.7	103.4
Receivables Turnover 36	6.6	•	16.4	14.3	3.3	14.5	2.4	6.1	8.0	•	4.4	8.2
Total Liabilities to Net Worth 37	2.2	•	1.6	1.7	3.3	4.3	3.6	1.6	2.1	•	2.6	2.1
Current Assets to Working Capital 38	5.0	•	2.8	•	2.2	1.8	2.1	2.1	1.4	•	•	15.8
Current Liabilities to Working Capital 39	4.0	•	1.8	•	1.2	0.8	1.1	1.1	0.4	•	•	14.8
Working Capital to Net Sales 40	0.1	•	0.1	0.2	0.2	0.3	0.3	0.3	1.1	•	•	0.0
Inventory to Working Capital 41	0.3	•	0.0	•	0.2	0.0	0.0	0.0	0.0	•	•	0.1
Total Receipts to Cash Flow 42	4.6	•	1.9	3.1	3.8	7.1	5.4	2.4	3.7	•	9.7	6.2
Cost of Goods to Cash Flow 43	1.5	•	0.2	0.7	0.6	3.6	2.5	0.5	1.4	•	4.8	1.8
Cash Flow to Total Debt 44	0.1	•	1.4	0.3	0.1	0.1	0.1	0.2	0.1	•	0.0	0.0

Selected Financial Factors (in Percentages)

Debt Ratio 45	68.3	•	62.1	63.6	76.5	81.0	78.0	60.9	67.7	•	72.2	67.5
Return on Total Assets 46	3.6	•	36.2	•	•	3.2	2.9	4.7	2.0	•	3.6	3.1
Return on Equity Before Income Taxes 47	4.6	•	93.1	•	•	9.1	5.2	7.8	1.6	•	4.4	2.9
Return on Equity After Income Taxes 48	3.3	•	92.9	•	•	8.5	2.1	5.7	0.6	•	2.2	2.1
Profit Margin (Before Income Tax) 49	6.4	•	21.8	•	•	3.0	4.9	12.3	3.3	•	5.6	5.5
Profit Margin (After Income Tax) 50	4.6	•	21.8	•	•	2.8	2.0	8.9	1.2	•	2.7	3.9

WATER, SEWAGE AND OTHER SYSTEMS

Table II

Corporations with Net Income

MONEY AMOUNTS AND SIZE OF ASSETS IN THOUSANDS OF DOLLARS

Item Description for Accounting Period 7/07 Through 6/08	Total	Zero Assets	Under 500	500 to 1,000	1,000 to 5,000	5,000 to 10,000	10,000 to 25,000	25,000 to 50,000	50,000 to 100,000	100,000 to 250,000	250,000 to 500,000	500,000 to 2,500,000	2,500,000 and over
Number of Enterprises 1	3737	•	2879	124	184	67	25	•	4	•	•	•	•
Revenues ($ in Thousands)													
Net Sales 2	7197372	•	794376	10884	174462	456084	157556	•	61503	•	•	•	•
Interest 3	92480	•	1749	840	1986	3009	323	•	535	•	•	•	•
Rents 4	18440	•	423	0	0	0	437	•	10	•	•	•	•
Royalties 5	0	•	0	0	0	0	0	•	0	•	•	•	•
Other Portfolio Income 6	75216	•	111	636	633	1688	1961	•	0	•	•	•	•
Other Receipts 7	-37936	•	52982	1326	2345	690	6024	•	1996	•	•	•	•
Total Receipts 8	7345572	•	849641	13686	179426	461471	166301	•	64044	•	•	•	•
Average Total Receipts 9	1966	•	295	110	975	6888	6652	•	16011	•	•	•	•
Operating Costs/Operating Income (%)													
Cost of Operations 10	31.4	•	10.1	•	1.9	53.6	57.3	•	50.5	•	•	•	•
Salaries and Wages 11	6.7	•	3.5	11.0	14.7	4.8	8.3	•	3.4	•	•	•	•
Taxes Paid 12	7.0	•	3.0	2.6	4.0	5.2	3.1	•	6.4	•	•	•	•
Interest Paid 13	8.4	•	0.6	0.2	7.5	1.0	3.3	•	4.2	•	•	•	•
Depreciation 14	11.5	•	2.7	17.6	13.8	6.3	6.1	•	6.8	•	•	•	•
Amortization and Depletion 15	0.7	•	0.0	•	0.0	0.1	0.2	•	0.2	•	•	•	•
Pensions and Other Deferred Comp. 16	2.0	•	1.0	•	0.1	0.6	0.6	•	1.9	•	•	•	•
Employee Benefits 17	2.7	•	1.5	1.2	1.1	3.2	2.0	•	1.3	•	•	•	•
Advertising 18	0.2	•	0.0	•	0.2	0.5	0.1	•	0.0	•	•	•	•
Other Expenses 19	17.5	•	35.7	58.9	44.9	15.7	8.9	•	17.2	•	•	•	•
Officers' Compensation 20	3.5	•	22.1	5.8	4.8	3.4	3.0	•	1.5	•	•	•	•
Operating Margin 21	8.4	•	19.9	2.7	7.1	5.5	7.2	•	6.8	•	•	•	•
Operating Margin Before Officers' Comp. 22	11.9	•	42.0	8.5	11.9	9.0	10.2	•	8.3	•	•	•	•

Selected Average Balance Sheet ($ in Thousands)

Net Receivables 23	246	15	122	725	3017		1756
Inventories 24	38	0	11	15	135		506
Net Property, Plant and Equipment 25	5606	104	309	1766	4287	10063	53252
Total Assets 26	8029	152	696	2370	6663	17847	67431
Notes and Loans Payable 27	2614	59		952	3527	3506	13639
All Other Liabilities 28	2665	25		293	1216	8276	28012
Net Worth 29	2751	69		691	1919	6064	25780

Selected Financial Ratios (Times to 1)

Current Ratio 30	1.3	1.6	812.7	3.2	1.5	1.0	2.0
Quick Ratio 31	0.7	1.5	776.6	3.1	1.1	0.9	1.6
Net Sales to Working Capital 32	9.7	17.3	0.2	3.3	13.7	61.8	3.1
Coverage Ratio 33	2.2	49.6	120.0	2.3	7.6	4.9	3.6
Total Asset Turnover 34	0.2	1.8	0.1	0.4	1.0	0.4	0.2
Inventory Turnover 35	16.0	148.5		1.6	251.4	26.7	15.3
Receivables Turnover 36	9.4	18.9	3.2	2.4	12.0	2.4	
Total Liabilities to Net Worth 37	1.9	1.2	0.0	1.1	2.5	1.9	1.6
Current Assets to Working Capital 38	3.9	2.8	1.0	1.4	3.1	37.6	2.0
Current Liabilities to Working Capital 39	2.9	1.8	0.0	0.4	2.1	36.6	1.0
Working Capital to Net Sales 40	0.1	0.1	4.4	0.3	0.1	0.0	0.3
Inventory to Working Capital 41	0.1	0.0		0.0	0.0	0.8	0.1
Total Receipts to Cash Flow 42	4.2	1.8	1.3	2.1	8.0	5.2	4.2
Cost of Goods to Cash Flow 43	1.3	0.2		0.0	4.3	3.0	2.1
Cash Flow to Total Debt 44	0.1	1.9	15.6	0.4	0.2	0.1	0.1

Selected Financial Factors (in Percentages)

Debt Ratio 45	65.7	55.0	0.6	52.5	71.2	66.0	61.8
Return on Total Assets 46	4.5	49.6	3.6	6.9	7.9	5.7	3.4
Return on Equity Before Income Taxes 47	7.3	108.0	3.6	8.3	23.8	13.3	6.5
Return on Equity After Income Taxes 48	5.8	107.8	3.5	6.6	23.0	9.3	4.6
Profit Margin (Before Income Tax) 49	10.5	26.9	28.4	9.9	6.7	12.8	10.9
Profit Margin (After Income Tax) 50	8.3	26.8	27.4	7.8	6.5	8.9	7.8

Table I

Corporations with and without Net Income

COMBINATION GAS AND ELECTRIC

MONEY AMOUNTS AND SIZE OF ASSETS IN THOUSANDS OF DOLLARS

Item Description for Accounting Period 7/07 Through 6/08	Total	Zero Assets	Under 500	500 to 1,000	1,000 to 5,000	5,000 to 10,000	10,000 to 25,000	25,000 to 50,000	50,000 to 100,000	100,000 to 250,000	250,000 to 500,000	500,000 to 2,500,000	2,500,000 and over
Number of Enterprises **1**	32	•	0	0	0	0	0	0	0	•	•	3	26

Revenues ($ in Thousands)

Item Description for Accounting Period 7/07 Through 6/08	Total	Zero Assets	Under 500	500 to 1,000	1,000 to 5,000	5,000 to 10,000	10,000 to 25,000	25,000 to 50,000	50,000 to 100,000	100,000 to 250,000	250,000 to 500,000	500,000 to 2,500,000	2,500,000 and over
Net Sales **2**	216094226	•	0	0	0	0	0	0	0	•	•	770198	209989850
Interest **3**	1679119	•	0	0	0	0	0	0	0	•	•	6445	1643156
Rents **4**	865037	•	0	0	0	0	0	0	0	•	•	3292	849827
Royalties **5**	15676	•	0	0	0	0	0	0	0	•	•	0	15676
Other Portfolio Income **6**	2013739	•	0	0	0	0	0	0	0	•	•	2018	2011467
Other Receipts **7**	3068778	•	0	0	0	0	0	0	0	•	•	16098	2824760
Total Receipts **8**	223736575	•	0	0	0	0	0	0	0	•	•	798051	217234736
Average Total Receipts **9**	6991768	•	•	•	•	•	•	•	•	•	•	266017	8355182

Operating Costs/Operating Income (%)

Item Description for Accounting Period 7/07 Through 6/08	Total	Zero Assets	Under 500	500 to 1,000	1,000 to 5,000	5,000 to 10,000	10,000 to 25,000	25,000 to 50,000	50,000 to 100,000	100,000 to 250,000	250,000 to 500,000	500,000 to 2,500,000	2,500,000 and over
Cost of Operations **10**	62.6	•	•	•	•	•	•	•	•	•	•	61.7	63.3
Salaries and Wages **11**	4.1	•	•	•	•	•	•	•	•	•	•	1.3	4.1
Taxes Paid **12**	3.4	•	•	•	•	•	•	•	•	•	•	3.5	3.3
Interest Paid **13**	4.3	•	•	•	•	•	•	•	•	•	•	4.1	4.3
Depreciation **14**	5.3	•	•	•	•	•	•	•	•	•	•	6.1	5.3
Amortization and Depletion **15**	0.7	•	•	•	•	•	•	•	•	•	•	0.2	0.7
Pensions and Other Deferred Comp. **16**	0.6	•	•	•	•	•	•	•	•	•	•	2.4	0.6
Employee Benefits **17**	1.2	•	•	•	•	•	•	•	•	•	•	0.6	1.2
Advertising **18**	0.1	•	•	•	•	•	•	•	•	•	•	0.2	0.1
Other Expenses **19**	15.8	•	•	•	•	•	•	•	•	•	•	13.8	15.3
Officers' Compensation **20**	0.4	•	•	•	•	•	•	•	•	•	•	0.8	0.4
Operating Margin **21**	1.4	•	•	•	•	•	•	•	•	•	•	5.4	1.5
Operating Margin Before Officers' Comp. **22**	1.9	•	•	•	•	•	•	•	•	•	•	6.1	1.9

Selected Average Balance Sheet ($ in Thousands)

Net Receivables	23	720462	25283	881831
Inventories	24	354891	15002	428015
Net Property, Plant and Equipment	25	6895027	411539	8423764
Total Assets	26	12293945	811490	15011241
Notes and Loans Payable	27	4593474	222530	5618532
All Other Liabilities	28	4650618	321664	5675741
Net Worth	29	3049852	267295	3716968

Selected Financial Ratios (Times to 1)

Current Ratio	30	1.0	0.5	1.0
Quick Ratio	31	0.6	0.2	0.6
Net Sales to Working Capital	32	130.6	•	111.1
Coverage Ratio	33	2.2	3.2	2.2
Total Asset Turnover	34	0.5	0.3	0.5
Inventory Turnover	35	11.9	10.6	11.9
Receivables Turnover	36	9.0	•	8.9
Total Liabilities to Net Worth	37	3.0	2.0	3.0
Current Assets to Working Capital	38	36.0	•	31.4
Current Liabilities to Working Capital	39	35.0	•	30.4
Working Capital to Net Sales	40	0.0	•	0.0
Inventory to Working Capital	41	7.0	•	6.1
Total Receipts to Cash Flow	42	5.7	5.3	5.8
Cost of Goods to Cash Flow	43	3.6	3.3	3.7
Cash Flow to Total Debt	44	0.1	0.1	0.1

Selected Financial Factors (in Percentages)

Debt Ratio	45	75.2	67.1	75.2
Return on Total Assets	46	5.1	4.2	5.0
Return on Equity Before Income Taxes	47	11.0	8.6	10.9
Return on Equity After Income Taxes	48	7.2	5.7	7.1
Profit Margin (Before Income Tax)	49	5.0	9.0	5.0
Profit Margin (After Income Tax)	50	3.2	5.9	3.3

23

Table II

Corporations with Net Income

COMBINATION GAS AND ELECTRIC

MONEY AMOUNTS AND SIZE OF ASSETS IN THOUSANDS OF DOLLARS

Item Description for Accounting Period 7/07 Through 6/08	Total	Zero Assets	Under 500	500 to 1,000	1,000 to 5,000	5,000 to 10,000	10,000 to 25,000	25,000 to 50,000	50,000 to 100,000	100,000 to 250,000	250,000 to 500,000	500,000 to 2,500,000	2,500,000 and over
Number of Enterprises **1**	•	•	0	0	0	0	0	0	0	•	3	0	•

Revenues ($ in Thousands)

Item Description for Accounting Period 7/07 Through 6/08	Total	Zero Assets	Under 500	500 to 1,000	1,000 to 5,000	5,000 to 10,000	10,000 to 25,000	25,000 to 50,000	50,000 to 100,000	100,000 to 250,000	250,000 to 500,000	500,000 to 2,500,000	2,500,000 and over
Net Sales **2**	•	•	0	0	0	0	0	0	0	•	1013883	0	•
Interest **3**	•	•	0	0	0	0	0	0	0	•	9386	0	•
Rents **4**	•	•	0	0	0	0	0	0	0	•	5313	0	•
Royalties **5**	•	•	0	0	0	0	0	0	0	•	0	0	•
Other Portfolio Income **6**	•	•	0	0	0	0	0	0	0	•	2018	0	•
Other Receipts **7**	•	•	0	0	0	0	0	0	0	•	17697	0	•
Total Receipts **8**	•	•	0	0	0	0	0	0	0	•	1048297	0	•
Average Total Receipts **9**	•	•	•	•	•	•	•	•	•	•	349432	•	•

Operating Costs/Operating Income (%)

Item Description for Accounting Period 7/07 Through 6/08	Total	Zero Assets	Under 500	500 to 1,000	1,000 to 5,000	5,000 to 10,000	10,000 to 25,000	25,000 to 50,000	50,000 to 100,000	100,000 to 250,000	250,000 to 500,000	500,000 to 2,500,000	2,500,000 and over
Cost of Operations **10**	•	•	•	•	•	•	•	•	•	•	63.6	•	•
Salaries and Wages **11**	•	•	•	•	•	•	•	•	•	•	1.6	•	•
Taxes Paid **12**	•	•	•	•	•	•	•	•	•	•	3.2	•	•
Interest Paid **13**	•	•	•	•	•	•	•	•	•	•	4.4	•	•
Depreciation **14**	•	•	•	•	•	•	•	•	•	•	6.0	•	•
Amortization and Depletion **15**	•	•	•	•	•	•	•	•	•	•	0.2	•	•
Pensions and Other Deferred Comp. **16**	•	•	•	•	•	•	•	•	•	•	2.2	•	•
Employee Benefits **17**	•	•	•	•	•	•	•	•	•	•	0.9	•	•
Advertising **18**	•	•	•	•	•	•	•	•	•	•	0.1	•	•
Other Expenses **19**	•	•	•	•	•	•	•	•	•	•	11.2	•	•
Officers' Compensation **20**	•	•	•	•	•	•	•	•	•	•	0.9	•	•
Operating Margin **21**	•	•	•	•	•	•	•	•	•	•	5.7	•	•
Operating Margin Before Officers' Comp. **22**	•	•	•	•	•	•	•	•	•	•	6.6	•	•

Selected Average Balance Sheet ($ in Thousands)

Net Receivables 23	30815
Inventories 24	15002
Net Property, Plant and Equipment 25	471038
Total Assets 26	784166
Notes and Loans Payable 27	280637
All Other Liabilities 28	293048
Net Worth 29	210480

Selected Financial Ratios (Times to 1)

Current Ratio 30	1.0
Quick Ratio 31	0.4
Net Sales to Working Capital 32	
Coverage Ratio 33	3.1
Total Asset Turnover 34	0.4
Inventory Turnover 35	14.3
Receivables Turnover 36	21.9
Total Liabilities to Net Worth 37	2.7
Current Assets to Working Capital 38	
Current Liabilities to Working Capital 39	
Working Capital to Net Sales 40	
Inventory to Working Capital 41	
Total Receipts to Cash Flow 42	5.9
Cost of Goods to Cash Flow 43	3.8
Cash Flow to Total Debt 44	0.1

Selected Financial Factors (in Percentages)

Debt Ratio 45	73.2
Return on Total Assets 46	5.8
Return on Equity Before Income Taxes 47	14.6
Return on Equity After Income Taxes 48	10.2
Profit Margin (Before Income Tax) 49	9.1
Profit Margin (After Income Tax) 50	6.4

24

Table I

Corporations with and without Net Income

CONSTRUCTION OF BUILDINGS

MONEY AMOUNTS AND SIZE OF ASSETS IN THOUSANDS OF DOLLARS

Item Description for Accounting Period 7/07 Through 6/08	Total	Zero Assets	Under 500	500 to 1,000	1,000 to 5,000	5,000 to 10,000	10,000 to 25,000	25,000 to 50,000	50,000 to 100,000	100,000 to 250,000	250,000 to 500,000	500,000 to 2,500,000	2,500,000 and over
Number of Enterprises 1	230865	44746	131416	19961	25384	5061	2953	760	305	175	40	49	14
Revenues ($ in Thousands)													
Net Sales 2	664987858	8322961	81447857	32879860	103833370	64717976	83530492	43972165	38033583	44586291	18825517	68386703	76451083
Interest 3	2002546	24002	23949	30190	124556	61420	81439	38825	37609	59100	53605	598132	869718
Rents 4	498158	4806	36129	23716	67988	17128	29968	26142	20886	47473	70543	143015	10365
Royalties 5	12805	0	0	0	0	0	399	0	18	12064	0	304	20
Other Portfolio Income 6	2295336	9170	57659	70307	139193	34646	103746	48210	57979	49461	96314	680028	948624
Other Receipts 7	5529340	2190	716273	84582	483959	230881	534965	266870	286654	268309	615138	976951	1062569
Total Receipts 8	675326043	8363129	82281867	33088655	104649066	65062051	84281009	44352212	38436729	45022698	19661117	70785133	79342379
Average Total Receipts 9	2925	187	626	1658	4123	12856	28541	58358	126022	257273	491528	1444595	5667313
Operating Costs/Operating Income (%)													
Cost of Operations 10	84.4	69.3	71.5	76.6	84.1	87.3	88.3	90.0	89.8	91.0	91.5	88.1	82.2
Salaries and Wages 11	3.5	4.7	5.7	4.8	3.3	2.3	2.4	2.5	2.4	2.5	3.2	3.7	4.8
Taxes Paid 12	1.0	1.3	1.7	1.6	1.0	0.9	0.7	0.6	0.7	0.6	0.7	0.8	1.1
Interest Paid 13	0.9	1.5	0.7	1.4	0.8	0.5	0.6	0.8	0.7	0.8	0.8	1.5	1.5
Depreciation 14	0.5	0.9	0.9	0.8	0.5	0.5	0.4	0.3	0.3	0.4	0.4	0.5	0.4
Amortization and Depletion 15	0.1	0.1	0.0	0.0	0.0	0.0	0.0	0.0	0.0	0.0	0.0	0.3	0.2
Pensions and Other Deferred Comp. 16	0.2	0.5	0.3	0.2	0.2	0.2	0.2	0.2	0.2	0.2	0.2	0.3	0.1
Employee Benefits 17	0.5	0.5	0.7	0.6	0.5	0.5	0.5	0.4	0.4	0.4	0.3	0.4	0.5
Advertising 18	0.3	0.2	0.5	0.4	0.2	0.2	0.2	0.2	0.2	0.3	0.3	0.4	0.7
Other Expenses 19	7.1	18.0	12.2	9.4	5.3	3.5	3.1	2.6	2.8	2.4	3.2	4.5	19.8
Officers' Compensation 20	1.9	3.3	4.7	2.9	2.7	2.0	1.7	1.2	1.0	0.8	0.7	0.7	0.2
Operating Margin 21	•	•	1.2	1.3	1.2	2.0	1.8	1.1	1.5	0.7	•	•	•
Operating Margin Before Officers' Comp. 22	1.4	3.0	5.9	4.2	3.8	4.0	3.4	2.3	2.5	1.5	•	•	•

Selected Average Balance Sheet ($ in Thousands)

Net Receivables 23	321	0	12	89	368	1633	4089	9217	20720	42998	88136	211868	454785
Inventories 24	471	0	15	186	577	1759	3664	7779	16876	36129	94385	189497	2726598
Net Property, Plant and Equipment 25	189	0	26	133	311	650	1435	4283	6043	13785	36790	199711	245665
Total Assets 26	1659	0	101	708	2135	6880	15189	33925	69773	147427	339528	1088967	5857042
Notes and Loans Payable 27	647	0	65	437	1010	2702	5822	12534	22907	46056	104623	329181	2191959
All Other Liabilities 28	603	0	27	179	733	2937	6416	14865	31353	64919	130405	390129	1644461
Net Worth 29	409	0	8	92	391	1241	2951	6526	15512	36451	104500	369658	2020622

Selected Financial Ratios (Times to 1)

Current Ratio 30	1.6	•	1.6	1.6	1.4	1.5	1.4	1.3	1.4	1.5	1.9	1.5	2.2
Quick Ratio 31	0.7	•	0.6	0.6	0.5	0.6	0.7	0.7	0.7	0.8	1.0	0.8	0.6
Net Sales to Working Capital 32	6.8	•	25.4	9.1	8.4	7.0	7.9	9.2	8.1	6.8	3.8	6.8	2.8
Coverage Ratio 33	2.2	1.2	4.2	2.3	3.4	5.8	5.2	3.6	4.7	3.1	4.8	2.5	•
Total Asset Turnover 34	1.7	•	6.1	2.3	1.9	1.9	1.9	1.7	1.8	1.7	1.4	1.3	0.9
Inventory Turnover 35	5.2	•	30.2	6.8	6.0	6.3	6.8	6.7	6.6	6.4	4.6	6.5	1.6
Receivables Turnover 36	9.0	•	55.0	17.8	10.7	8.5	7.0	6.6	6.1	6.2	5.5	7.0	9.0
Total Liabilities to Net Worth 37	3.1	•	11.6	6.7	4.5	4.5	4.1	4.2	3.5	3.0	2.2	1.9	1.9
Current Assets to Working Capital 38	2.8	•	2.7	2.8	3.4	3.1	3.5	4.1	3.7	3.1	2.1	3.0	1.8
Current Liabilities to Working Capital 39	1.8	•	1.7	1.8	2.4	2.1	2.5	3.1	2.7	2.1	1.1	2.0	0.8
Working Capital to Net Sales 40	0.1	•	0.0	0.1	0.1	0.1	0.1	0.1	0.1	0.1	0.3	0.1	0.4
Inventory to Working Capital 41	1.0	•	0.6	1.0	1.0	1.0	1.0	1.2	1.1	0.9	0.7	0.9	1.1
Total Receipts to Cash Flow 42	14.6	6.4	7.9	10.0	16.2	19.8	20.6	25.9	22.4	29.4	18.6	20.5	10.0
Cost of Goods to Cash Flow 43	12.3	4.4	5.6	7.6	13.6	17.3	18.2	23.3	20.1	26.8	17.0	18.0	8.2
Cash Flow to Total Debt 44	0.2	•	0.8	0.3	0.1	0.1	0.1	0.1	0.1	0.1	0.1	0.1	0.1

Selected Financial Factors (in Percentages)

Debt Ratio 45	75.3	•	92.1	87.1	82.0	81.7	80.6	80.8	77.8	75.3	69.2	66.1	65.5
Return on Total Assets 46	3.5	•	17.6	7.9	5.6	5.3	6.1	4.6	5.8	4.1	5.3	4.9	•
Return on Equity Before Income Taxes 47	7.6	•	169.0	34.9	25.8	20.3	25.5	17.3	20.5	11.2	13.5	8.7	•
Return on Equity After Income Taxes 48	5.6	•	165.8	32.7	24.1	18.8	24.1	16.2	18.4	10.1	12.0	5.5	•
Profit Margin (Before Income Tax) 49	1.1	0.3	2.2	1.9	2.5	1.9	2.7	2.0	2.5	1.6	3.0	2.3	•
Profit Margin (After Income Tax) 50	0.8	0.1	2.1	1.8	2.3	1.8	2.5	1.8	2.3	1.5	2.7	1.5	•

Table II

Corporations with Net Income

CONSTRUCTION OF BUILDINGS

MONEY AMOUNTS AND SIZE OF ASSETS IN THOUSANDS OF DOLLARS

Item Description for Accounting Period 7/07 Through 6/08		Total	Zero Assets	Under 500	500 to 1,000	1,000 to 5,000	5,000 to 10,000	10,000 to 25,000	25,000 to 50,000	50,000 to 100,000	100,000 to 250,000	250,000 to 500,000	500,000 to 2,500,000	2,500,000 and over
Number of Enterprises	1	131875	18538	80764	11291	14725	3704	1990	468	208	121	31	31	5
Revenues ($ in Thousands)														
Net Sales	2	509217237	4290891	60389098	23246720	80478020	55672336	72467784	36723246	33015121	38294115	17215697	54756565	32667640
Interest	3	750146	17058	15948	18634	86013	53246	66726	34549	28029	48510	39443	228114	113875
Rents	4	328002	1704	21845	11331	23451	8528	17622	6280	18038	35340	68743	110415	4705
Royalties	5	12789	0	0	0	0	0	399	0	18	12064	0	304	3
Other Portfolio Income	6	2120806	2556	47560	63879	118717	29092	85635	36548	50669	35805	95947	660989	893407
Other Receipts	7	4504852	34301	626449	35086	386711	203088	475565	239446	237390	263788	529849	701993	771194
Total Receipts	8	516933832	4346510	61100900	23375650	81092912	55966290	73113731	37040069	33349265	38689622	17949679	56458380	34450824
Average Total Receipts	9	3920	234	757	2070	5507	15110	36741	79145	160333	319749	579022	1821238	6890165
Operating Costs/Operating Income (%)														
Cost of Operations	10	84.6	60.1	70.0	72.8	82.7	86.5	87.9	89.4	89.2	91.0	91.5	88.0	90.0
Salaries and Wages	11	3.1	4.1	5.5	4.4	3.0	2.1	2.2	2.2	2.2	2.2	2.6	3.2	4.5
Taxes Paid	12	0.9	1.5	1.6	1.6	1.0	0.9	0.7	0.5	0.6	0.5	0.7	0.8	1.0
Interest Paid	13	0.4	0.8	0.5	0.8	0.6	0.3	0.3	0.4	0.3	0.4	0.5	0.6	0.2
Depreciation	14	0.5	0.8	0.7	0.9	0.5	0.5	0.3	0.3	0.3	0.4	0.4	0.4	0.4
Amortization and Depletion	15	0.0	0.1	0.0	0.0	0.0	0.0	0.0	0.0	0.0	0.0	0.0	0.1	0.1
Pensions and Other Deferred Comp.	16	0.2	0.0	0.2	0.2	0.2	0.2	0.2	0.2	0.2	0.2	0.2	0.4	0.3
Employee Benefits	17	0.5	0.6	0.6	0.8	0.6	0.5	0.6	0.4	0.4	0.4	0.3	0.4	0.6
Advertising	18	0.2	0.2	0.4	0.4	0.2	0.1	0.1	0.2	0.2	0.2	0.2	0.2	0.5
Other Expenses	19	4.5	16.6	11.5	10.3	4.7	3.0	2.7	2.0	2.4	1.7	2.6	3.2	3.2
Officers' Compensation	20	1.9	3.6	4.3	3.2	2.6	2.0	1.6	1.2	1.0	0.8	0.7	0.7	0.2
Operating Margin	21	3.1	11.6	4.5	4.7	3.8	4.0	3.4	3.1	3.2	2.1	0.3	2.0	•
Operating Margin Before Officers' Comp.	22	5.0	15.2	8.9	7.9	6.4	5.9	5.0	4.3	4.2	2.9	0.9	2.7	•

Selected Average Balance Sheet ($ in Thousands)

Net Receivables 23	463	0	14	98	481	1997	5399	12660	27044	54018	91420	315823	585614
Inventories 24	543	0	14	174	587	1594	3203	7284	14363	33407	70780	100188	5787384
Net Property, Plant and Equipment 25	182	0	24	134	275	598	1072	2874	6243	14190	40234	189255	130932
Total Assets 26	1729		102	707	2239	6806	15345	34138	71054	148533	341150	1080499	6058985
Notes and Loans Payable 27	471	0	45	340	804	2013	3887	7262	13777	30596	83442	196477	1775526
All Other Liabilities 28	755	0	20	181	880	3289	7808	18744	39376	77896	141856	489444	1865014
Net Worth 29	503	0	37	186	555	1504	3650	8132	17901	40040	115852	394578	2418446

Selected Financial Ratios (Times to 1)

Current Ratio 30	1.5	•	2.1	1.6	1.5	1.5	1.4	1.3	1.3	1.4	1.7	1.2	2.0
Quick Ratio 31	0.8	•	1.4	0.7	0.7	0.8	0.8	0.9	0.9	0.9	1.0	0.9	0.7
Net Sales to Working Capital 32	9.2	•	22.4	11.3	9.3	7.7	10.2	11.8	10.8	9.0	5.8	14.0	3.2
Coverage Ratio 33	11.6	17.9	12.0	7.6	9.3	17.9	14.8	11.6	15.7	8.6	10.1	8.9	27.3
Total Asset Turnover 34	2.2	•	7.3	2.9	2.4	2.2	2.4	2.3	2.2	2.1	1.6	1.6	1.1
Inventory Turnover 35	6.0	•	38.8	8.6	7.7	8.2	10.0	9.6	9.9	8.6	7.2	15.5	1.0
Receivables Turnover 36	8.0	•	•	19.6	10.5	8.5	7.0	6.3	6.1	6.1	6.0	•	4.8
Total Liabilities to Net Worth 37	2.4	•	1.8	2.8	3.0	3.5	3.2	3.2	3.0	2.7	1.9	1.7	1.5
Current Assets to Working Capital 38	3.1	•	1.9	2.8	3.0	3.0	3.7	4.3	4.0	3.4	2.5	5.1	2.0
Current Liabilities to Working Capital 39	2.1	•	0.9	1.8	2.0	2.0	2.7	3.3	3.0	2.4	1.5	4.1	1.0
Working Capital to Net Sales 40	0.1	•	0.0	0.1	0.1	0.1	0.1	0.1	0.1	0.1	0.2	0.1	0.3
Inventory to Working Capital 41	0.8	•	0.4	0.9	0.8	0.7	0.8	0.8	0.8	0.7	0.5	0.8	1.3
Total Receipts to Cash Flow 42	12.7	3.7	6.4	7.0	12.1	15.2	16.7	18.4	17.6	23.4	16.0	16.1	22.7
Cost of Goods to Cash Flow 43	10.8	2.3	4.5	5.1	10.0	13.1	14.7	16.4	15.7	21.3	14.6	14.1	20.5
Cash Flow to Total Debt 44	0.2	•	1.8	0.6	0.3	0.2	0.2	0.2	0.2	0.1	0.2	0.2	0.1

Selected Financial Factors (in Percentages)

Debt Ratio 45	70.9	•	64.0	73.7	75.2	77.9	76.2	76.2	74.8	73.0	66.0	63.5	60.1
Return on Total Assets 46	11.3	•	45.6	17.5	12.5	10.5	10.8	10.0	9.9	7.5	8.0	9.3	5.3
Return on Equity Before Income Taxes 47	35.5	•	116.3	57.8	44.8	44.7	42.2	38.3	36.7	24.5	21.3	22.6	12.8
Return on Equity After Income Taxes 48	32.7	•	115.1	55.9	43.0	42.8	40.5	36.9	34.1	23.1	19.5	18.0	8.3
Profit Margin (Before Income Tax) 49	4.6	12.9	5.7	5.2	4.6	4.5	4.2	4.0	4.1	3.1	4.4	5.0	4.7
Profit Margin (After Income Tax) 50	4.3	12.5	5.7	5.1	4.4	4.3	4.1	3.8	3.8	2.9	4.1	4.0	3.1

Table I

Corporations with and without Net Income

HEAVY AND CIVIL ENGINEERING CONSTRUCTION

MONEY AMOUNTS AND SIZE OF ASSETS IN THOUSANDS OF DOLLARS

Item Description for Accounting Period 7/07 Through 6/08	Total	Zero Assets	Under 500	500 to 1,000	1,000 to 5,000	5,000 to 10,000	10,000 to 25,000	25,000 to 50,000	50,000 to 100,000	100,000 to 250,000	250,000 to 500,000	500,000 to 2,500,000	2,500,000 and over
Number of Enterprises 1	25883	2025	11324	3869	5430	1751	958	276	145	68	17	15	4
Revenues ($ in Thousands)													
Net Sales 2	226461519	7237091	12824628	7584325	27534954	27433869	31170657	20120821	18376664	17016988	10826055	21180259	25155207
Interest 3	555268	20467	8774	9102	47477	37842	38030	20853	28282	24382	25638	120050	174372
Rents 4	135950	4511	5479	16550	14465	5284	28078	8671	18803	14195	3634	12659	3622
Royalties 5	81642	0	0	0	0	0	2260	329	33363	52	9394	6931	29313
Other Portfolio Income 6	1676714	37557	80901	37473	218824	63333	154738	73545	67394	60106	30463	138928	713449
Other Receipts 7	2404095	148088	22642	15096	173680	150154	199172	94126	193640	204168	71250	165344	966738
Total Receipts 8	231315188	7447714	12942424	7662546	27989400	27690482	31592935	20318345	18718146	17319891	10966434	21624171	27042701
Average Total Receipts 9	8937	3678	1143	1980	5155	15814	32978	73617	129091	254704	645084	1441611	6760675
Operating Costs/Operating Income (%)													
Cost of Operations 10	75.7	74.7	62.6	56.3	64.9	74.8	78.9	78.2	79.8	76.7	81.1	80.8	85.4
Salaries and Wages 11	3.8	2.4	8.1	7.9	4.9	2.9	2.7	2.5	2.7	3.5	3.8	3.0	4.7
Taxes Paid 12	1.6	0.2	2.0	2.3	2.3	1.8	1.5	1.3	1.5	1.1	0.9	2.3	0.9
Interest Paid 13	0.7	0.2	0.6	0.8	0.9	0.6	0.6	0.6	0.5	0.7	0.8	0.9	0.8
Depreciation 14	2.8	1.2	2.4	3.8	4.8	3.3	2.8	2.7	2.7	2.8	2.4	2.1	1.4
Amortization and Depletion 15	0.2	0.8	0.0	0.0	0.0	0.0	0.1	0.1	0.1	0.1	0.4	0.4	0.3
Pensions and Other Deferred Comp. 16	0.3	0.2	0.2	0.3	0.5	0.6	0.4	0.4	0.3	0.4	0.2	0.2	0.1
Employee Benefits 17	0.9	0.4	0.8	1.6	1.0	1.0	1.0	0.9	1.0	1.1	1.0	0.7	0.4
Advertising 18	0.1	0.1	0.3	0.2	0.1	0.1	0.1	0.1	0.0	0.1	0.0	0.1	0.0
Other Expenses 19	7.2	7.8	13.3	16.7	11.9	7.0	4.8	6.8	5.1	5.7	4.7	7.2	2.8
Officers' Compensation 20	2.2	1.1	4.6	5.0	4.6	2.7	2.0	1.8	1.1	1.3	0.8	0.7	0.9
Operating Margin 21	4.6	10.9	5.1	5.1	4.0	5.1	5.1	4.8	5.3	6.5	3.8	1.6	2.4
Operating Margin Before Officers' Comp. 22	6.7	12.0	9.7	10.1	8.6	7.8	7.2	6.6	6.3	7.8	4.7	2.2	3.3

Selected Average Balance Sheet ($ in Thousands)

Net Receivables 23	1236	0	18	155	616	2344	5725	11715	22098	42459	94626	238836	931581
Inventories 24	110	0	3	8	51	235	434	902	1857	5706	12633	21584	62470
Net Property, Plant and Equipment 25	1147	0	77	282	853	1762	3957	8495	16016	36378	92624	203461	1113949
Total Assets 26	4605	0	171	714	2241	6957	15589	34207	67904	147538	360988	947453	6385581
Notes and Loans Payable 27	878	0	105	230	674	1692	3140	6486	12618	29048	65710	173900	421368
All Other Liabilities 28	1753	0	26	159	566	2246	5320	13802	25221	52734	129874	452818	3080322
Net Worth 29	1974	0	40	325	1001	3020	7129	13919	30065	65755	165404	320735	2883891

Selected Financial Ratios (Times to 1)

Current Ratio 30	1.5	•	1.7	1.7	1.9	1.8	1.7	1.6	1.6	1.7	1.6	1.2	1.0
Quick Ratio 31	1.2	•	1.4	1.5	1.5	1.5	1.4	1.3	1.3	1.4	1.2	0.9	0.8
Net Sales to Working Capital 32	10.5	•	36.0	14.4	8.8	7.8	7.4	7.9	7.9	7.2	9.3	13.8	•
Coverage Ratio 33	10.8	84.0	11.9	9.1	7.1	10.8	11.2	11.2	14.4	13.1	7.4	5.3	14.0
Total Asset Turnover 34	1.9	•	6.6	2.7	2.3	2.3	2.1	2.1	1.9	1.7	1.8	1.5	1.0
Inventory Turnover 35	60.0	•	271.7	140.8	64.3	49.9	59.2	63.2	54.5	33.6	40.9	52.9	85.9
Receivables Turnover 36	7.0	•	70.1	13.8	8.4	6.9	5.7	5.9	5.9	6.2	7.7	5.9	5.5
Total Liabilities to Net Worth 37	1.3	•	3.3	1.2	1.2	1.3	1.2	1.3	1.3	1.2	1.2	2.0	1.2
Current Assets to Working Capital 38	3.1	•	2.3	2.4	2.1	2.3	2.4	2.5	2.7	2.5	2.7	5.0	•
Current Liabilities to Working Capital 39	2.1	•	1.3	1.4	1.1	1.3	1.4	1.5	1.7	1.5	1.7	4.0	•
Working Capital to Net Sales 40	0.1	•	0.0	0.1	0.1	0.1	0.1	0.1	0.1	0.1	0.1	0.1	•
Inventory to Working Capital 41	0.1	•	0.0	0.1	0.1	0.1	0.1	0.1	0.1	0.2	0.2	0.2	•
Total Receipts to Cash Flow 42	9.3	5.0	6.9	6.1	7.6	10.8	11.5	9.9	10.8	8.9	12.2	11.4	9.7
Cost of Goods to Cash Flow 43	7.0	3.7	4.3	3.4	4.9	8.1	9.1	7.8	8.6	6.8	9.9	9.2	8.2
Cash Flow to Total Debt 44	0.4	•	1.3	0.8	0.5	0.4	0.3	0.4	0.3	0.3	0.3	0.2	0.2

Selected Financial Factors (in Percentages)

Debt Ratio 45	57.1	•	76.5	54.5	55.3	56.6	54.3	59.3	55.7	55.4	54.2	66.1	54.8
Return on Total Assets 46	14.2	•	43.8	18.9	14.9	15.0	14.9	13.4	14.2	15.1	10.4	6.7	11.3
Return on Equity Before Income Taxes 47	30.0	•	170.7	36.9	28.6	31.3	29.6	30.1	29.8	31.3	19.6	16.1	23.2
Return on Equity After Income Taxes 48	26.8	•	165.6	36.2	26.8	29.0	27.5	26.8	27.9	28.4	17.6	11.9	17.9
Profit Margin (Before Income Tax) 49	6.8	13.8	6.1	6.1	5.6	6.0	6.5	5.7	7.1	8.2	5.1	3.7	10.7
Profit Margin (After Income Tax) 50	6.1	13.7	5.9	5.3	5.3	5.6	6.0	5.1	6.6	7.5	4.6	2.7	8.2

Table II

Corporations with Net Income

HEAVY AND CIVIL ENGINEERING CONSTRUCTION

MONEY AMOUNTS AND SIZE OF ASSETS IN THOUSANDS OF DOLLARS

Item Description for Accounting Period 7/07 Through 6/08	Total	Zero Assets	Under 500	500 to 1,000	1,000 to 5,000	5,000 to 10,000	10,000 to 25,000	25,000 to 50,000	50,000 to 100,000	100,000 to 250,000	250,000 to 500,000	500,000 to 2,500,000	2,500,000 and over
Number of Enterprises **1**	18295	1333	6717	2785	4531	1577	880	247	131	61	•	•	4
Revenues ($ in Thousands)													
Net Sales **2**	201280531	2072083	10549956	5014229	23216315	25062800	29066996	18791215	17267485	15561605	•	•	25155207
Interest **3**	496851	1417	2355	6600	38278	36524	35617	20305	22748	21475	•	•	174372
Rents **4**	121679	4511	1279	16550	13742	4755	23838	7948	15155	13986	•	•	3622
Royalties **5**	79798	0	0	0	0	0	808	329	33363	52	•	•	29313
Other Portfolio Income **6**	1553784	23667	76615	32098	186539	57735	135699	58394	48211	54531	•	•	713449
Other Receipts **7**	2252532	52155	16430	13018	200529	147595	183804	84305	181970	178139	•	•	966738
Total Receipts **8**	205785175	2153833	10646635	5082495	23655403	25309409	29446762	18962496	17568932	15829788	•	•	27042701
Average Total Receipts **9**	11248	1616	1585	1825	5221	16049	33462	76771	134114	259505	•	•	6760675
Operating Costs/Operating Income (%)													
Cost of Operations **10**	75.8	33.2	65.7	53.3	64.6	74.5	78.4	77.5	79.5	76.0	•	•	85.4
Salaries and Wages **11**	3.5	1.5	6.1	8.1	4.5	3.0	2.7	2.4	2.6	3.5	•	•	4.7
Taxes Paid **12**	1.6	0.4	1.6	2.3	2.3	1.8	1.4	1.3	1.4	1.2	•	•	0.9
Interest Paid **13**	0.6	0.3	0.4	0.7	0.8	0.6	0.6	0.5	0.5	0.6	•	•	0.8
Depreciation **14**	2.7	2.1	2.0	3.8	4.5	3.1	2.8	2.5	2.7	2.6	•	•	1.4
Amortization and Depletion **15**	0.1	0.0	0.0	0.0	0.0	0.0	0.1	0.0	0.1	0.1	•	•	0.3
Pensions and Other Deferred Comp. **16**	0.3	0.6	0.2	0.0	0.5	0.4	0.4	0.3	0.3	0.4	•	•	0.1
Employee Benefits **17**	0.8	0.3	0.5	1.4	1.0	1.0	0.9	0.9	0.9	1.1	•	•	0.4
Advertising **18**	0.1	0.1	0.2	0.2	0.1	0.1	0.1	0.1	0.0	0.1	•	•	0.0
Other Expenses **19**	6.4	4.7	12.1	14.3	10.8	6.9	4.7	6.9	4.7	5.3	•	•	2.8
Officers' Compensation **20**	2.1	1.0	3.5	6.2	4.9	2.8	2.1	1.8	1.1	1.4	•	•	0.9
Operating Margin **21**	5.8	55.7	7.6	9.6	5.9	5.9	5.9	5.8	6.1	7.7	•	•	2.4
Operating Margin Before Officers' Comp. **22**	8.0	56.8	11.1	15.7	10.8	8.6	7.9	7.6	7.2	9.0	•	•	3.3

Selected Average Balance Sheet ($ in Thousands)

Item												
Net Receivables 23	1576	0	21	148	605	2354	5666	12099	22349	41591	•	931581
Inventories 24	126	0	2	4	55	142	432	881	1750	5063	•	60064
Net Property, Plant and Equipment 25	1426	0	87	270	819	1722	4035	8300	16090	35173	•	1113949
Total Assets 26	5877	0	206	724	2198	6917	15543	34080	67082	147450	•	6385581
Notes and Loans Payable 27	990	0	92	201	601	1565	3017	5967	11568	24361	•	421368
All Other Liabilities 28	2238	0	25	126	557	2279	5125	14065	23898	51461	•	3080322
Net Worth 29	2649	0	89	397	1040	3074	7402	14048	31616	71628	•	2883891

Selected Financial Ratios (Times to 1)

Item												
Current Ratio 30	1.5	•	2.5	2.2	1.9	1.8	1.6	1.8	1.7	1.7	•	1.0
Quick Ratio 31	1.2	•	2.2	2.0	1.6	1.5	1.4	1.5	1.4	1.4	•	0.8
Net Sales to Working Capital 32	10.3	•	26.6	10.0	8.7	8.0	8.1	7.3	7.7	6.9	•	•
Coverage Ratio 33	14.0	181.1	20.8	15.7	10.2	13.3	14.7	13.3	18.2	16.9	•	14.0
Total Asset Turnover 34	1.9	•	7.6	2.5	2.3	2.3	2.2	2.1	2.0	1.7	•	1.0
Inventory Turnover 35	66.2	•	447.4	232.2	60.6	83.6	67.0	59.9	59.9	38.3	•	89.4
Receivables Turnover 36	7.3	•	•	13.1	8.8	6.8	5.9	5.8	6.5	6.8	•	13.5
Total Liabilities to Net Worth 37	1.2	•	1.3	0.8	1.1	1.3	1.4	1.1	1.1	1.1	•	1.2
Current Assets to Working Capital 38	3.1	•	1.7	1.8	2.1	2.3	2.5	2.3	2.5	2.4	•	•
Current Liabilities to Working Capital 39	2.1	•	0.7	0.8	1.1	1.3	1.5	1.3	1.5	1.4	•	•
Working Capital to Net Sales 40	0.1	•	0.0	0.1	0.1	0.1	0.1	0.1	0.1	0.1	•	•
Inventory to Working Capital 41	0.1	•	0.0	0.0	0.1	0.1	0.1	0.1	0.1	0.2	•	•
Total Receipts to Cash Flow 42	8.6	1.6	6.3	4.7	7.0	9.9	9.0	10.8	10.3	8.2	•	9.7
Cost of Goods to Cash Flow 43	6.6	0.5	4.1	2.5	4.6	7.3	7.0	8.5	8.2	6.3	•	8.2
Cash Flow to Total Debt 44	0.4	•	2.1	1.2	0.6	0.4	0.4	0.4	0.4	0.4	•	0.2

Selected Financial Factors (in Percentages)

Item												
Debt Ratio 45	54.9	•	57.1	45.2	52.7	55.6	58.8	52.4	52.9	51.4	•	54.8
Return on Total Assets 46	16.4	•	68.3	29.0	20.2	17.1	15.9	16.5	16.1	17.2	•	11.3
Return on Equity Before Income Taxes 47	33.9	•	151.4	49.6	38.4	35.5	36.0	32.0	32.4	33.3	•	23.2
Return on Equity After Income Taxes 48	30.6	•	147.5	48.8	36.4	33.1	32.4	29.8	30.4	30.4	•	17.9
Profit Margin (Before Income Tax) 49	8.2	59.6	8.5	10.9	7.8	6.9	6.7	7.2	7.8	9.3	•	10.7
Profit Margin (After Income Tax) 50	7.4	59.3	8.3	10.8	7.4	6.4	6.0	6.7	7.3	8.5	•	8.2

28

Table I

Corporations with and without Net Income

LAND SUBDIVISION

MONEY AMOUNTS AND SIZE OF ASSETS IN THOUSANDS OF DOLLARS

Item Description for Accounting Period 7/07 Through 6/08	Total	Zero Assets	Under 500	500 to 1,000	1,000 to 5,000	5,000 to 10,000	10,000 to 25,000	25,000 to 50,000	50,000 to 100,000	100,000 to 250,000	250,000 to 500,000	500,000 to 2,500,000	2,500,000 and over
Number of Enterprises **1**	43883	6057	20271	5075	9335	1529	896	289	133	60	16	21	0
Revenues ($ in Thousands)													
Net Sales **2**	40840081	1548747	2773241	2188415	9410980	6252323	4691679	2918512	2328863	2677691	1429976	4619652	0
Interest **3**	361546	27034	7848	3498	59428	12271	12404	19465	19674	31352	38418	130154	0
Rents **4**	565096	69909	17720	29034	23471	40073	42208	24772	35872	147490	30624	103923	0
Royalties **5**	18136	0	0	0	7931	8106	256	893	83	826	0	42	0
Other Portfolio Income **6**	735767	149177	25416	19350	41629	39044	54125	39628	22521	55459	34564	254855	0
Other Receipts **7**	1300312	8012	131715	23121	365073	55193	93519	170367	193116	120500	12991	126704	0
Total Receipts **8**	43820938	1802879	2955940	2263418	9908512	6407010	4894191	3173637	2600129	3033318	1546573	5235330	0
Average Total Receipts **9**	1003	298	146	446	1061	4190	5462	10981	19550	50555	96661	249301	•
Operating Costs/Operating Income (%)													
Cost of Operations **10**	77.2	92.9	61.9	62.8	75.8	87.2	80.1	74.4	78.7	77.3	63.1	79.8	•
Salaries and Wages **11**	5.6	1.1	3.0	9.8	4.4	2.1	4.9	8.5	6.5	6.5	13.9	8.8	•
Taxes Paid **12**	2.1	1.7	2.3	2.9	1.7	0.8	1.5	2.4	2.0	2.1	2.3	4.4	•
Interest Paid **13**	5.4	7.2	2.9	3.3	4.4	3.4	4.8	6.9	7.2	8.2	5.8	9.1	•
Depreciation **14**	1.7	3.3	1.6	1.3	1.5	0.5	1.4	2.6	1.9	2.7	3.0	1.7	•
Amortization and Depletion **15**	0.0	0.1	0.0	0.3	0.0	0.0	0.1	0.2	0.2	0.2	0.3	•	•
Pensions and Other Deferred Comp. **16**	0.3	0.1	0.9	0.1	0.6	0.1	0.1	0.2	0.1	0.3	0.8	0.1	•
Employee Benefits **17**	0.6	0.0	0.4	1.0	0.4	0.1	0.3	0.6	0.6	0.8	0.6	1.6	•
Advertising **18**	0.8	0.2	0.7	0.1	0.4	1.0	1.0	1.1	1.4	0.9	2.1	1.0	•
Other Expenses **19**	12.4	9.0	18.3	12.8	11.6	7.0	10.5	14.3	12.2	14.3	14.9	17.7	•
Officers' Compensation **20**	2.3	0.8	9.5	2.4	2.3	0.9	1.7	1.4	2.6	3.2	0.5	1.6	•
Operating Margin **21**	•	•	•	3.2	•	•	•	•	•	•	•	•	•
Operating Margin Before Officers' Comp. **22**	•	8.0	5.6	•	•	•	•	•	•	•	•	•	•

Selected Average Balance Sheet ($ in Thousands)

	1	2	3	4	5	6	7	8	9	10	11	12	13
Net Receivables 23	160	0	6	30	216	219	704	3016	3728	12325	54940	35438	•
Inventories 24	666	0	33	204	528	2566	4738	7851	20783	32726	109369	264901	•
Net Property, Plant and Equipment 25	606	0	47	174	499	1816	3813	9200	14600	36399	68546	282273	•
Total Assets 26	2370	0	144	729	2179	6800	15412	34373	67487	153172	343103	894196	•
Notes and Loans Payable 27	1460	0	130	402	1350	4871	10002	22810	40596	86988	131864	512260	•
All Other Liabilities 28	355	0	69	102	256	900	2119	5843	7264	33261	45514	122184	•
Net Worth 29	555	0	-55	226	574	1028	3291	5720	19627	32923	165725	259752	•

Selected Financial Ratios (Times to 1)

	1	2	3	4	5	6	7	8	9	10	11	12	13
Current Ratio 30	2.3	•	3.2	2.8	2.6	3.1	2.3	1.9	2.5	1.6	4.8	1.6	•
Quick Ratio 31	0.5	•	1.0	0.5	0.8	0.3	0.4	0.6	0.5	0.4	1.7	0.3	•
Net Sales to Working Capital 32	1.3	•	2.9	1.6	1.4	1.4	1.0	1.2	0.8	1.8	0.5	1.5	•
Coverage Ratio 33	0.8	1.0	2.7	3.0	1.5	0.8	0.5	0.4	0.7	0.6	1.1	•	•
Total Asset Turnover 34	0.4	•	0.9	0.6	0.5	0.6	0.3	0.3	0.3	0.3	0.3	0.2	•
Inventory Turnover 35	1.1	•	2.6	1.3	1.4	1.4	0.9	1.0	0.7	1.1	0.5	0.7	•
Receivables Turnover 36	5.2	•	15.5	6.4	4.8	25.9	6.8	3.5	4.1	4.0	1.6	3.3	•
Total Liabilities to Net Worth 37	3.3	•	•	2.2	2.8	5.6	3.7	5.0	2.4	3.7	1.1	2.4	•
Current Assets to Working Capital 38	1.8	•	1.5	1.6	1.6	1.5	1.8	2.1	1.7	2.7	1.3	2.6	•
Current Liabilities to Working Capital 39	0.8	•	0.5	0.6	0.6	0.5	0.8	1.1	0.7	1.7	0.3	1.6	•
Working Capital to Net Sales 40	0.7	•	0.3	0.6	0.7	0.7	1.0	0.8	1.3	0.6	1.9	0.7	•
Inventory to Working Capital 41	0.9	•	0.6	1.0	0.7	1.0	1.0	1.0	0.9	1.3	0.7	1.6	•
Total Receipts to Cash Flow 42	12.7	64.5	5.1	6.1	8.6	23.1	18.0	13.7	12.1	16.6	9.2	•	•
Cost of Goods to Cash Flow 43	9.8	59.9	3.1	3.8	6.5	20.1	14.5	10.2	9.5	12.8	5.8	•	•
Cash Flow to Total Debt 44	0.0	0.1	0.1	0.1	0.1	0.0	0.0	0.0	0.0	0.0	0.1	•	•

Selected Financial Factors (in Percentages)

	1	2	3	4	5	6	7	8	9	10	11	12	13
Debt Ratio 45	76.6	•	138.2	69.0	73.7	84.9	78.6	83.4	70.9	78.5	51.7	71.0	•
Return on Total Assets 46	1.7	•	7.6	5.9	3.0	1.6	0.9	0.9	1.4	1.4	1.7	•	•
Return on Equity Before Income Taxes 47	•	•	•	12.6	3.7	•	•	•	•	•	0.5	•	•
Return on Equity After Income Taxes 48	•	•	•	12.5	3.1	•	•	•	•	•	•	•	•
Profit Margin (Before Income Tax) 49	•	•	5.1	6.6	2.1	•	•	•	•	•	0.9	•	•
Profit Margin (After Income Tax) 50	•	•	4.7	6.5	1.8	•	•	•	•	•	•	•	•

Table II

Corporations with Net Income

LAND SUBDIVISION

MONEY AMOUNTS AND SIZE OF ASSETS IN THOUSANDS OF DOLLARS

Item Description for Accounting Period 7/07 Through 6/08	Total	Zero Assets	Under 500	500 to 1,000	1,000 to 5,000	5,000 to 10,000	10,000 to 25,000	25,000 to 50,000	50,000 to 100,000	100,000 to 250,000	250,000 to 500,000	500,000 to 2,500,000	2,500,000 and over
Number of Enterprises 1	16214	2630	6060	2705	3639	617	352	106	55	29	•	•	0

Revenues ($ in Thousands)

	Total	Zero Assets	Under 500	500 to 1,000	1,000 to 5,000	5,000 to 10,000	10,000 to 25,000	25,000 to 50,000	50,000 to 100,000	100,000 to 250,000	250,000 to 500,000	500,000 to 2,500,000	2,500,000 and over
Net Sales 2	25408575	1332756	1570630	1854694	5885365	4913322	2686432	1546167	1137890	2096054	•	•	0
Interest 3	244061	15152	7184	2930	48012	11776	8136	8463	11345	22332	•	•	0
Rents 4	409895	18556	11902	23543	21637	31577	34517	10163	17218	110136	•	•	0
Royalties 5	17129	0	0	0	7816	8106	256	0	83	826	•	•	0
Other Portfolio Income 6	576513	116634	13556	16689	17268	35671	44506	10911	12754	47760	•	•	0
Other Receipts 7	1226892	11463	81003	19456	344720	42381	115723	133578	145319	61423	•	•	0
Total Receipts 8	27883065	1494561	1684275	1917312	6324818	5042833	2889570	1709282	1324609	2338531	•	•	0
Average Total Receipts 9	1720	568	278	709	1738	8173	8209	16125	24084	80639	•	•	•

Operating Costs/Operating Income (%)

	Total	Zero Assets	Under 500	500 to 1,000	1,000 to 5,000	5,000 to 10,000	10,000 to 25,000	25,000 to 50,000	50,000 to 100,000	100,000 to 250,000	250,000 to 500,000	500,000 to 2,500,000	2,500,000 and over
Cost of Operations 10	74.3	87.7	54.5	57.9	72.9	86.9	77.5	74.7	67.1	74.6	•	•	•
Salaries and Wages 11	4.1	0.8	2.2	11.4	2.5	1.1	3.1	6.3	5.2	5.1	•	•	•
Taxes Paid 12	1.4	1.0	1.9	2.8	1.3	0.4	1.1	1.5	1.7	1.8	•	•	•
Interest Paid 13	3.0	2.8	1.6	1.7	2.9	1.8	2.2	3.2	3.8	3.7	•	•	•
Depreciation 14	1.4	1.1	1.5	1.2	1.7	0.3	0.8	1.2	1.8	2.6	•	•	•
Amortization and Depletion 15	0.1	0.0	0.0	0.0	0.0	0.0	0.1	0.1	0.1	0.1	•	•	•
Pensions and Other Deferred Comp. 16	0.2	0.1	0.4	0.2	0.3	0.1	0.2	0.3	0.0	0.4	•	•	•
Employee Benefits 17	0.4	0.0	0.4	1.1	0.2	0.0	0.2	0.3	0.6	0.7	•	•	•
Advertising 18	0.5	0.1	0.2	0.1	0.4	0.3	0.3	0.7	0.8	0.8	•	•	•
Other Expenses 19	8.0	4.0	10.9	13.5	6.9	4.0	6.5	7.7	9.2	11.8	•	•	•
Officers' Compensation 20	1.9	0.6	4.4	2.5	1.9	0.4	2.3	1.0	3.2	3.3	•	•	•
Operating Margin 21	4.7	1.8	22.0	7.5	8.8	4.7	5.6	3.2	6.5	•	•	•	•
Operating Margin Before Officers' Comp. 22	6.7	2.4	26.4	10.0	10.7	5.1	8.0	4.2	9.7	•	•	•	•

Selected Average Balance Sheet ($ in Thousands)

Net Receivables 23	223	0	12	37	250	387	1041	3509	3714	13027
Inventories 24	922	0	53	145	612	2434	5119	9886	27188	43472
Net Property, Plant and Equipment 25	623	0	27	188	520	1031	2948	5823	10693	36843
Total Assets 26	2735.	0	182	764	2469	6578	15459	32225	66101	150968
Notes and Loans Payable 27	1402	0	93	389	1146	4223	9193	20296	31847	78295
All Other Liabilities 28	370	0	11	97	294	648	2172	4385	7737	31136
Net Worth 29	963	0	78	278	1029	1706	4093	7545	26516	41538

Selected Financial Ratios (Times to 1)

Current Ratio 30	2.7	•	4.4	2.6	3.2	3.1	2.4	2.3	3.1	2.0
Quick Ratio 31	0.8	•	2.0	0.8	1.2	0.5	0.5	0.7	0.8	0.4
Net Sales to Working Capital 32	1.7	•	3.3	3.2	1.7	2.9	1.3	1.3	0.8	1.6
Coverage Ratio 33	5.8	6.0	19.0	7.3	6.6	5.2	6.9	5.3	7.0	2.7
Total Asset Turnover 34	0.6	•	1.4	0.9	0.7	1.2	0.5	0.5	0.3	0.5
Inventory Turnover 35	1.3	•	2.7	2.7	1.9	2.8	1.2	1.1	0.5	1.2
Receivables Turnover 36	5.6	•	•	9.1	6.5	29.4	6.9	3.4	3.7	7.3
Total Liabilities to Net Worth 37	1.8	•	1.3	1.8	1.4	2.9	2.8	3.3	1.5	2.6
Current Assets to Working Capital 38	1.6	•	1.3	1.6	1.5	1.5	1.7	1.8	1.5	2.0
Current Liabilities to Working Capital 39	0.6	•	0.3	0.6	0.5	0.5	0.7	0.8	0.5	1.0
Working Capital to Net Sales 40	0.6	•	0.3	0.3	0.6	0.4	0.7	0.8	1.3	0.6
Inventory to Working Capital 41	0.8	•	0.7	0.8	0.5	0.9	0.8	0.9	0.8	0.9
Total Receipts to Cash Flow 42	5.2	8.6	2.7	4.7	4.7	10.0	5.8	5.0	3.3	7.7
Cost of Goods to Cash Flow 43	3.9	7.6	1.5	2.7	3.4	8.7	4.5	3.8	2.2	5.8
Cash Flow to Total Debt 44	0.2	0.9	0.3	0.3	0.2	0.2	0.1	0.1	0.2	0.1

Selected Financial Factors (in Percentages)

Debt Ratio 45	64.8	•	57.3	63.7	58.3	74.1	73.5	76.6	59.9	72.5
Return on Total Assets 46	10.0	•	44.1	11.3	12.5	11.1	7.6	7.6	8.3	4.9
Return on Equity Before Income Taxes 47	23.5	•	97.8	26.8	25.5	34.5	24.6	26.2	17.8	11.4
Return on Equity After Income Taxes 48	21.7	•	95.7	26.6	24.7	33.2	23.0	25.5	17.0	9.9
Profit Margin (Before Income Tax) 49	14.4	13.9	29.3	10.9	16.2	7.4	13.2	13.6	22.8	6.5
Profit Margin (After Income Tax) 50	13.4	11.6	28.6	10.8	15.7	7.1	12.3	13.2	21.7	5.7

Table I

Corporations with and without Net Income

ELECTRICAL CONTRACTORS

MONEY AMOUNTS AND SIZE OF ASSETS IN THOUSANDS OF DOLLARS

Item Description for Accounting Period 7/07 Through 6/08	Total	Zero Assets	Under 500	500 to 1,000	1,000 to 5,000	5,000 to 10,000	10,000 to 25,000	25,000 to 50,000	50,000 to 100,000	100,000 to 250,000	250,000 to 500,000	500,000 to 2,500,000	2,500,000 and over
Number of Enterprises 1	57940	8803	41205	3732	2998	740	336	72	39	12	3	0	0
Revenues ($ in Thousands)													
Net Sales 2	91270080	1114197	21439152	9113609	16379585	12347504	12883368	5985812	6356278	4086779	1563796	0	0
Interest 3	164574	270	9508	8136	22833	12396	6072	5773	3571	2822	93194	0	0
Rents 4	16002	0	7286	0	3334	437	1873	76	617	2380	0	0	0
Royalties 5	19074	0	0	0	1	0	4	0	0	0	19069	0	0
Other Portfolio Income 6	102491	3168	17619	11648	10667	17023	10719	4138	2769	7864	16875	0	0
Other Receipts 7	799500	20087	24594	36875	13594	54746	62834	20145	50063	11407	505154	0	0
Total Receipts 8	92371721	1137722	21498159	9170268	16430014	12432106	12964870	6015944	6413298	4111252	2198088	0	0
Average Total Receipts 9	1594	129	522	2457	5480	16800	38586	83555	164444	342604	732696	•	•
Operating Costs/Operating Income (%)													
Cost of Operations 10	67.9	51.8	49.9	65.2	70.1	78.4	74.3	77.6	78.2	77.4	78.2	•	•
Salaries and Wages 11	7.2	8.5	11.0	6.6	7.4	4.3	4.9	4.2	5.3	6.2	15.9	•	•
Taxes Paid 12	2.4	1.9	3.2	2.9	2.7	1.6	2.3	1.7	1.8	1.4	3.1	•	•
Interest Paid 13	0.7	1.4	0.7	0.6	0.5	0.6	0.5	0.3	0.2	0.6	7.1	•	•
Depreciation 14	1.1	2.8	1.6	0.9	1.2	0.8	0.8	0.9	0.6	0.8	4.4	•	•
Amortization and Depletion 15	0.1	0.0	0.0	0.1	0.0	0.0	0.0	0.1	0.0	0.3	3.0	•	•
Pensions and Other Deferred Comp. 16	0.6	0.0	0.7	0.7	0.4	0.6	0.5	0.4	0.4	0.7	2.0	•	•
Employee Benefits 17	2.3	1.0	1.3	2.2	2.3	2.2	4.4	3.9	1.4	2.2	2.2	•	•
Advertising 18	0.3	1.6	0.6	0.3	0.2	0.1	0.2	0.1	0.1	0.1	0.2	•	•
Other Expenses 19	9.3	25.1	17.7	9.7	7.5	5.7	5.0	3.3	3.9	4.9	19.0	•	•
Officers' Compensation 20	4.4	9.0	8.1	5.0	4.0	2.5	2.9	2.5	2.0	2.0	0.3	•	•
Operating Margin 21	3.8	•	5.2	5.8	3.7	3.2	4.4	4.9	6.0	3.5	•	•	•
Operating Margin Before Officers' Comp. 22	8.1	5.7	13.3	10.9	7.7	5.6	7.3	7.4	8.0	5.5	•	•	•

Selected Average Balance Sheet ($ in Thousands)

	•	•	•	•	•	•	•	•	•	•	•
Net Receivables 23	247	0	16	283	911	3329	8447	19169	35951	83391	247334	•
Inventories 24	25	0	8	43	147	267	292	1541	1129	4957	13618	•
Net Property, Plant and Equipment 25	73	0	26	105	246	578	1276	3260	4506	13368	203305	•
Total Assets 26	585	0	93	704	2018	6945	14880	35143	66720	172710	1338321	•
Notes and Loans Payable 27	107	0	45	166	295	1046	2353	3396	5529	29168	164105	•
All Other Liabilities 28	241	0	23	234	870	3149	7289	17798	34925	87581	355174	•
Net Worth 29	236	0	26	303	853	2749	5238	13949	26267	55962	819042	•

Selected Financial Ratios (Times to 1)

	•	•	•	•	•	•	•	•	•	•	•
Current Ratio 30	1.7	•	1.7	2.2	1.7	1.6	1.6	1.5	1.6	1.6	1.7	•
Quick Ratio 31	1.3	•	1.3	1.9	1.4	1.2	1.4	1.4	1.3	1.3	1.3	•
Net Sales to Working Capital 32	9.2	•	21.9	8.6	8.3	8.4	7.5	8.3	8.5	7.4	2.1	•
Coverage Ratio 33	8.6	0.1	9.2	11.8	8.7	8.0	11.8	18.5	34.5	7.5	1.7	•
Total Asset Turnover 34	2.7	•	5.6	3.5	2.7	2.4	2.6	2.4	2.4	2.0	0.4	•
Inventory Turnover 35	42.2	•	31.8	36.9	26.1	49.0	97.5	41.9	112.9	53.2	29.9	•
Receivables Turnover 36	6.5	•	32.2	8.0	5.6	4.4	4.7	4.9	5.9	3.4	4.2	•
Total Liabilities to Net Worth 37	1.5	•	2.6	1.3	1.4	1.5	1.8	1.5	1.5	2.1	0.6	•
Current Assets to Working Capital 38	2.5	•	2.5	1.8	2.4	2.8	2.5	2.9	2.8	2.8	2.4	•
Current Liabilities to Working Capital 39	1.5	•	1.5	0.8	1.4	1.8	1.5	1.9	1.8	1.8	1.4	•
Working Capital to Net Sales 40	0.1	•	0.0	0.1	0.1	0.1	0.1	0.1	0.1	0.1	0.5	•
Inventory to Working Capital 41	0.1	•	0.3	0.1	0.2	0.2	0.1	0.1	0.1	0.1	0.1	•
Total Receipts to Cash Flow 42	8.2	4.6	4.9	7.1	10.9	12.4	11.9	14.0	10.9	14.7	5.1	•
Cost of Goods to Cash Flow 43	5.6	2.4	2.4	4.6	9.7	8.9	8.9	10.9	8.5	11.4	4.0	•
Cash Flow to Total Debt 44	0.5	•	1.6	0.9	0.4	0.3	0.3	0.3	0.4	0.2	0.2	•

Selected Financial Factors (in Percentages)

	•	•	•	•	•	•	•	•	•	•	•
Debt Ratio 45	59.6	•	72.5	56.9	57.7	60.4	64.8	60.3	60.6	67.6	38.8	•
Return on Total Assets 46	15.2	•	34.4	24.5	12.2	10.7	14.0	13.5	17.4	9.2	4.7	•
Return on Equity Before Income Taxes 47	33.1	•	111.4	52.1	25.6	23.6	36.4	32.2	42.9	24.7	3.2	•
Return on Equity After Income Taxes 48	30.9	•	110.1	51.4	23.3	21.1	34.4	30.4	37.9	20.3	1.5	•
Profit Margin (Before Income Tax) 49	5.0	•	5.5	6.5	4.0	3.9	5.0	5.4	6.9	4.1	5.1	•
Profit Margin (After Income Tax) 50	4.6	•	5.4	6.4	3.6	3.5	4.7	5.1	6.1	3.3	2.3	•

Table II

Corporations with Net Income

ELECTRICAL CONTRACTORS

MONEY AMOUNTS AND SIZE OF ASSETS IN THOUSANDS OF DOLLARS

Item Description for Accounting Period 7/07 Through 6/08		Total	Zero Assets	Under 500	500 to 1,000	1,000 to 5,000	5,000 to 10,000	10,000 to 25,000	25,000 to 50,000	50,000 to 100,000	100,000 to 250,000	250,000 to 500,000	500,000 to 2,500,000	2,500,000 and over
Number of Enterprises	1	40437	4436	29897	2742	2326	619	303	63	•	•	0	0	0
Revenues ($ in Thousands)														
Net Sales	2	75619155	557968	15164046	7180262	13992682	10945079	11951127	5419635	•	•	0	0	0
Interest	3	75314	269	5297	4359	17696	12159	5458	4742	•	•	0	0	0
Rents	4	9464	0	1562	0	2522	437	1873	74	•	•	0	0	0
Royalties	5	4	0	0	0	0	0	4	0	•	•	0	0	0
Other Portfolio Income	6	84948	8	15763	7284	10212	12570	9265	3954	•	•	0	0	0
Other Receipts	7	738659	20087	23019	7200	3336	54008	54293	17763	•	•	0	0	0
Total Receipts	8	76527544	578332	15209687	7199105	14026448	11024253	12022020	5446168	•	•	0	0	0
Average Total Receipts	9	1893	130	509	2625	6030	17810	39677	86447	•	•	•	•	•
Operating Costs/Operating Income (%)														
Cost of Operations	10	67.4	42.7	46.8	63.5	67.8	76.6	74.1	77.1	•	•	•	•	•
Salaries and Wages	11	6.6	5.6	9.4	6.7	7.5	4.2	4.9	4.1	•	•	•	•	•
Taxes Paid	12	2.4	2.5	3.0	2.9	2.7	1.7	2.4	1.8	•	•	•	•	•
Interest Paid	13	0.4	1.5	0.5	0.4	0.4	0.4	0.4	0.3	•	•	•	•	•
Depreciation	14	1.0	1.6	1.5	0.8	1.2	0.8	0.5	0.7	•	•	•	•	•
Amortization and Depletion	15	0.1	0.0	0.0	0.1	0.0	0.0	0.0	0.0	•	•	•	•	•
Pensions and Other Deferred Comp.	16	0.6	0.0	0.6	0.7	0.5	0.6	0.5	0.4	•	•	•	•	•
Employee Benefits	17	2.5	0.1	1.3	2.3	2.3	2.4	4.5	3.9	•	•	•	•	•
Advertising	18	0.2	1.1	0.4	0.3	0.2	0.1	0.2	0.1	•	•	•	•	•
Other Expenses	19	8.3	21.7	17.9	7.5	7.3	5.4	4.6	3.2	•	•	•	•	•
Officers' Compensation	20	4.3	9.9	8.7	4.7	4.1	2.7	2.9	2.5	•	•	•	•	•
Operating Margin	21	6.3	13.2	9.9	10.0	6.0	5.0	5.0	5.8	•	•	•	•	•
Operating Margin Before Officers' Comp.	22	10.6	23.1	18.6	14.7	10.1	7.7	7.9	8.4	•	•	•	•	•

Selected Average Balance Sheet ($ in Thousands)

Net Receivables 23	305	0	17	255	956	3653	8621	19823
Inventories 24	29	0	7	52	160	294	310	1482
Net Property, Plant and Equipment 25	82	0	25	95	274	484	1110	2632
Total Assets 26	702	0	97	732	2082	6874	14730	34304
Notes and Loans Payable 27	102	0	32	117	292	770	2222	2917
All Other Liabilities 28	289	0	20	203	889	3218	7432	18326
Net Worth 29	311	0	45	412	901	2886	5075	13061

Selected Financial Ratios (Times to 1)

Current Ratio 30	1.8	•	2.4	2.4	1.8	1.7	1.6	1.6
Quick Ratio 31	1.4	•	2.0	2.0	1.5	1.4	1.4	1.4
Net Sales to Working Capital 32	8.2	•	13.5	8.4	8.2	7.0	7.9	8.0
Coverage Ratio 33	17.8	12.5	23.2	26.4	14.6	16.0	13.5	24.4
Total Asset Turnover 34	2.7	•	5.2	3.6	2.9	2.6	2.7	2.5
Inventory Turnover 35	43.0	•	34.3	32.0	25.5	46.1	94.4	44.8
Receivables Turnover 36	6.3	•	•	9.2	6.2	4.2	4.6	4.8
Total Liabilities to Net Worth 37	1.3	•	1.2	0.8	1.3	1.4	1.9	1.6
Current Assets to Working Capital 38	2.3	•	1.7	1.7	2.3	2.4	2.6	2.8
Current Liabilities to Working Capital 39	1.3	•	0.7	0.7	1.3	1.4	1.6	1.8
Working Capital to Net Sales 40	0.1	•	0.1	0.1	0.1	0.1	0.1	0.1
Inventory to Working Capital 41	0.1	•	0.2	0.2	0.2	0.1	0.1	0.1
Total Receipts to Cash Flow 42	7.3	2.7	3.9	6.1	9.0	10.3	11.5	12.4
Cost of Goods to Cash Flow 43	4.9	1.2	1.8	3.9	6.1	7.9	8.6	9.6
Cash Flow to Total Debt 44	0.7	•	2.5	1.3	0.6	0.4	0.4	0.3

Selected Financial Factors (in Percentages)

Debt Ratio 45	55.7	•	53.5	43.7	56.7	58.0	65.5	61.9
Return on Total Assets 46	21.1	•	55.9	38.3	19.3	15.7	16.1	16.5
Return on Equity Before Income Taxes 47	44.9	•	115.0	65.5	41.6	35.2	43.3	41.6
Return on Equity After Income Taxes 48	42.4	•	113.9	64.8	38.8	32.3	41.0	39.3
Profit Margin (Before Income Tax) 49	7.5	16.8	10.2	10.3	6.2	5.7	5.6	6.3
Profit Margin (After Income Tax) 50	7.0	16.0	10.2	10.2	5.8	5.3	5.3	6.0

Table I

Corporations with and without Net Income

PLUMBING, HEATING, AND AIR-CONDITIONING CONTRACTORS

MONEY AMOUNTS AND SIZE OF ASSETS IN THOUSANDS OF DOLLARS

Item Description for Accounting Period 7/07 Through 6/08	Total	Zero Assets	Under 500	500 to 1,000	1,000 to 5,000	5,000 to 10,000	10,000 to 25,000	25,000 to 50,000	50,000 to 100,000	100,000 to 250,000	250,000 to 500,000	500,000 to 2,500,000	2,500,000 and over
Number of Enterprises 1	76676	7030	60386	3970	4032	768	363	97	19	7	4	0	0
Revenues ($ in Thousands)													
Net Sales 2	12521838	877351	40394556	10403604	25501752	14799365	13461552	8207888	3337788	1695146	6539336	0	0
Interest 3	89400	1493	10740	7913	32084	8664	8741	2510	1337	3284	12634	0	0
Rents 4	10215	0	4268	107	1315	1234	1154	172	318	0	1647	0	0
Royalties 5	0	0	0	0	0	0	0	0	0	0	0	0	0
Other Portfolio Income 6	122684	15	64097	12302	31500	5378	5028	1291	674	155	2244	0	0
Other Receipts 7	475729	92951	61128	32050	129257	30107	64597	28492	14298	9472	13378	0	0
Total Receipts 8	125916366	971810	40534789	10455976	25695908	14844748	13541072	8240353	3354415	1708057	6569239	0	0
Average Total Receipts 9	1642	138	671	2634	6373	19329	37303	84952	176548	244008	1642310	•	•
Operating Costs/Operating Income (%)													
Cost of Operations 10	65.1	58.1	49.9	59.4	70.1	72.7	78.8	78.3	82.9	67.8	78.3	•	•
Salaries and Wages 11	8.3	4.3	13.5	7.8	6.3	6.4	4.2	4.3	4.1	9.0	4.4	•	•
Taxes Paid 12	2.6	2.5	3.4	3.1	2.3	2.2	1.9	1.6	1.7	3.7	2.5	•	•
Interest Paid 13	0.5	0.3	0.6	0.6	0.5	0.3	0.4	0.2	0.1	1.6	0.2	•	•
Depreciation 14	1.2	1.5	1.7	2.0	1.1	0.7	0.6	0.4	0.5	0.5	0.4	•	•
Amortization and Depletion 15	0.1	0.2	0.0	0.0	0.0	0.0	0.0	0.0	0.1	0.7	0.3	•	•
Pensions and Other Deferred Comp. 16	0.5	0.6	0.4	0.5	0.6	0.8	0.4	0.8	0.3	0.4	0.1	•	•
Employee Benefits 17	2.0	1.1	1.5	2.3	2.1	2.2	2.7	2.8	1.2	2.6	2.5	•	•
Advertising 18	0.7	0.7	1.0	1.5	0.8	0.5	0.1	0.1	0.1	0.1	0.1	•	•
Other Expenses 19	10.4	27.8	16.4	13.2	9.0	6.1	4.7	4.2	1.5	11.8	5.4	•	•
Officers' Compensation 20	5.1	16.9	8.2	6.1	4.5	3.7	2.3	1.8	1.2	1.7	1.8	•	•
Operating Margin 21	3.5	•	3.5	3.4	2.8	4.4	3.8	5.5	6.3	0.1	4.0	•	•
Operating Margin Before Officers' Comp. 22	8.7	2.8	11.7	9.6	7.2	8.0	6.1	7.2	7.5	1.8	5.8	•	•

Selected Average Balance Sheet ($ in Thousands)

Net Receivables 23	•	227	0	24	256	1018	3782	8374	18943	37612	62038	483486	•
Inventories 24	•	25	0	7	54	163	342	427	1450	1363	2417	17633	•
Net Property, Plant and Equipment 25	•	68	0	34	174	227	786	1150	2198	6877	6047	39015	•
Total Assets 26	•	504	0	113	712	2152	6852	14381	34192	70098	144487	1037271	•
Notes and Loans Payable 27	•	109	0	58	201	461	819	2048	2365	4257	34200	72946	•
All Other Liabilities 28	•	239	0	33	273	975	3556	8040	20480	39758	75956	604627	•
Net Worth 29	•	155	0	22	239	717	2478	4293	11347	26083	34330	359698	•

Selected Financial Ratios (Times to 1)

Current Ratio 30	•	1.5	•	1.6	1.6	1.7	1.6	1.5	1.4	1.5	1.1	1.4	•
Quick Ratio 31	•	1.3	•	1.4	1.2	1.4	1.4	1.2	1.1	1.3	1.0	1.2	•
Net Sales to Working Capital 32	•	12.4	•	25.9	13.6	9.1	8.9	9.3	11.1	9.7	21.1	8.7	•
Coverage Ratio 33	•	9.5	•	7.2	8.0	8.3	14.7	10.9	28.2	46.4	1.5	23.4	•
Total Asset Turnover 34	•	3.2	•	5.9	3.7	2.9	2.8	2.6	2.5	2.5	1.7	1.6	•
Inventory Turnover 35	•	42.1	•	46.7	28.9	27.2	41.0	68.4	45.7	106.8	67.9	72.6	•
Receivables Turnover 36	•	7.5	•	27.3	9.9	6.0	5.9	4.5	4.9	4.8	1.5	6.8	•
Total Liabilities to Net Worth 37	•	2.2	•	4.1	2.0	2.0	1.8	2.4	2.0	1.7	3.2	1.9	•
Current Assets to Working Capital 38	•	2.9	•	2.6	2.6	2.5	2.7	3.1	3.7	3.2	8.3	3.6	•
Current Liabilities to Working Capital 39	•	1.9	•	1.6	1.6	1.5	1.7	2.1	2.7	2.2	7.3	2.6	•
Working Capital to Net Sales 40	•	0.1	•	0.0	0.1	0.1	0.1	0.1	0.1	0.1	0.0	0.1	•
Inventory to Working Capital 41	•	0.2	•	0.3	0.3	0.2	0.2	0.1	0.2	0.1	0.1	0.1	•
Total Receipts to Cash Flow 42	•	8.2	5.0	5.7	7.0	9.8	11.2	13.3	12.5	12.9	9.1	12.7	•
Cost of Goods to Cash Flow 43	•	5.3	2.9	2.8	4.1	6.9	8.2	10.5	9.8	10.7	6.2	9.9	•
Cash Flow to Total Debt 44	•	0.6	•	1.3	0.8	0.4	0.4	0.3	0.3	0.3	0.2	0.2	•

Selected Financial Factors (in Percentages)

Debt Ratio 45	•	69.1	•	80.3	66.5	66.7	63.8	70.2	66.8	62.8	76.2	65.3	•
Return on Total Assets 46	•	14.8	•	26.3	16.6	11.8	14.1	12.4	15.1	17.4	4.2	7.3	•
Return on Equity Before Income Taxes 47	•	43.0	•	115.2	43.4	31.2	36.2	37.9	43.8	45.8	6.2	20.1	•
Return on Equity After Income Taxes 48	•	40.4	•	113.3	42.1	28.6	34.4	35.8	42.0	43.8	6.2	12.9	•
Profit Margin (Before Income Tax) 49	•	4.1	•	3.8	4.0	3.5	4.7	4.4	5.9	6.8	0.9	4.4	•
Profit Margin (After Income Tax) 50	•	3.8	•	3.8	3.8	3.2	4.4	4.1	5.6	6.5	0.9	2.8	•

Table II

Corporations with Net Income

PLUMBING, HEATING, AND AIR-CONDITIONING CONTRACTORS

MONEY AMOUNTS AND SIZE OF ASSETS IN THOUSANDS OF DOLLARS

Item Description for Accounting Period 7/07 Through 6/08	Total	Zero Assets	Under 500	500 to 1,000	1,000 to 5,000	5,000 to 10,000	10,000 to 25,000	25,000 to 50,000	50,000 to 100,000	100,000 to 250,000	250,000 to 500,000	500,000 to 2,500,000	2,500,000 and over
Number of Enterprises **1**	47209	2982	36716	3161	3195	716	319	94	•	•	•	0	0
Revenues ($ in Thousands)													
Net Sales **2**	106132443	326730	29854241	8732656	21732129	13805757	12363172	8150224	•	•	•	0	0
Interest **3**	77307	1480	7608	6987	28529	8659	7708	2507	•	•	•	0	0
Rents **4**	8369	0	2906	107	1260	810	1154	172	•	•	•	0	0
Royalties **5**	0	0	0	0	0	0	0	0	•	•	•	0	0
Other Portfolio Income **6**	115652	15	60315	11990	29803	4321	4865	1291	•	•	•	0	0
Other Receipts **7**	307379	775	41896	21429	96862	29388	60551	28440	•	•	•	0	0
Total Receipts **8**	106641150	329000	29966966	8773169	21888583	13848935	12437450	8182634	•	•	•	0	0
Average Total Receipts **9**	2259	110	816	2775	6851	19342	38989	87049	•	•	•	•	•
Operating Costs/Operating Income (%)													
Cost of Operations **10**	66.1	43.2	50.7	59.4	68.7	72.2	78.5	78.4	•	•	•	•	•
Salaries and Wages **11**	7.5	5.2	11.8	7.8	6.6	6.7	4.3	4.2	•	•	•	•	•
Taxes Paid **12**	2.5	2.5	3.2	3.0	2.2	2.2	1.9	1.6	•	•	•	•	•
Interest Paid **13**	0.4	0.2	0.5	0.5	0.4	0.3	0.4	0.2	•	•	•	•	•
Depreciation **14**	1.0	1.6	1.4	1.8	1.0	0.6	0.5	0.4	•	•	•	•	•
Amortization and Depletion **15**	0.0	•	0.0	0.0	0.0	0.0	0.0	0.0	•	•	•	•	•
Pensions and Other Deferred Comp. **16**	0.5	1.5	0.4	0.5	0.6	0.8	0.4	0.8	•	•	•	•	•
Employee Benefits **17**	2.1	1.6	1.5	2.2	2.2	1.7	2.7	2.8	•	•	•	•	•
Advertising **18**	0.6	0.6	0.8	1.4	0.7	0.5	0.1	0.1	•	•	•	•	•
Other Expenses **19**	9.3	17.7	15.1	12.5	9.1	6.2	4.2	4.0	•	•	•	•	•
Officers' Compensation **20**	4.7	9.4	8.0	5.9	4.3	3.8	2.5	1.8	•	•	•	•	•
Operating Margin **21**	5.2	16.6	6.5	5.0	4.1	5.0	4.5	5.6	•	•	•	•	•
Operating Margin Before Officers' Comp. **22**	10.0	26.1	14.5	10.9	8.4	8.8	7.0	7.3	•	•	•	•	•

Selected Average Balance Sheet ($ in Thousands)

Net Receivables 23	322	0	24	267	1021	3752	8696	19530
Inventories 24	34	0	8	51	178	324	446	1403
Net Property, Plant and Equipment 25	80	0	35	153	218	723	977	2256
Total Assets 26	680	0	128	708	2176	6765	14456	34267
Notes and Loans Payable 27	113	0	44	190	433	747	1776	2378
All Other Liabilities 28	322	0	35	283	889	3398	7926	20849
Net Worth 29	245	0	50	235	853	2620	4754	11040

Selected Financial Ratios (Times to 1)

Current Ratio 30	1.6	•	1.8	1.6	1.9	1.7	1.5	1.4
Quick Ratio 31	1.3	•	1.5	1.2	1.5	1.4	1.3	1.2
Net Sales to Working Capital 32	11.2	•	24.5	13.4	8.2	8.4	8.7	11.1
Coverage Ratio 33	16.1	109.8	15.9	11.2	12.3	19.3	14.5	28.6
Total Asset Turnover 34	3.3	•	6.4	3.9	3.1	2.9	2.7	2.5
Inventory Turnover 35	44.1	•	52.5	32.2	26.2	43.0	68.2	48.5
Receivables Turnover 36	7.3	•	32.2	11.0	6.3	6.0	4.4	5.0
Total Liabilities to Net Worth 37	1.8	•	1.6	2.0	1.5	1.6	2.0	2.1
Current Assets to Working Capital 38	2.7	•	2.3	2.6	2.2	2.5	2.8	3.7
Current Liabilities to Working Capital 39	1.7	•	1.3	1.6	1.2	1.5	1.8	2.7
Working Capital to Net Sales 40	0.1	•	0.0	0.1	0.1	0.1	0.1	0.1
Inventory to Working Capital 41	0.2	•	0.2	0.3	0.2	0.1	0.1	0.2
Total Receipts to Cash Flow 42	7.8	3.5	5.2	6.5	8.7	10.4	12.7	12.6
Cost of Goods to Cash Flow 43	5.2	1.5	2.6	3.9	6.0	7.5	10.0	9.8
Cash Flow to Total Debt 44	0.7	•	2.0	0.9	0.6	0.4	0.3	0.3

Selected Financial Factors (in Percentages)

Debt Ratio 45	64.0	•	61.2	66.8	60.8	61.3	67.1	67.8
Return on Total Assets 46	20.1	•	46.6	23.4	16.4	16.0	14.7	15.6
Return on Equity Before Income Taxes 47	52.3	•	112.6	64.1	38.4	39.1	41.5	46.9
Return on Equity After Income Taxes 48	49.6	•	111.2	62.5	35.7	37.3	39.4	45.0
Profit Margin (Before Income Tax) 49	5.7	17.3	6.9	5.5	4.8	5.3	5.1	6.0
Profit Margin (After Income Tax) 50	5.4	17.2	6.8	5.3	4.5	5.1	4.8	5.7

Table I

Corporations with and without Net Income

OTHER SPECIALTY TRADE CONTRACTORS

MONEY AMOUNTS AND SIZE OF ASSETS IN THOUSANDS OF DOLLARS

Item Description for Accounting Period 7/07 Through 6/08		Total	Zero Assets	Under 500	500 to 1,000	1,000 to 5,000	5,000 to 10,000	10,000 to 25,000	25,000 to 50,000	50,000 to 100,000	100,000 to 250,000	250,000 to 500,000	500,000 to 2,500,000	2,500,000 and over
Number of Enterprises	1	345559	65848	242805	15292	17696	2275	1214	271	89	42	16	12	0
Revenues ($ in Thousands)														
Net Sales	2	439142111	8024753	141751946	39833845	101793108	38444513	43016529	19773933	12491877	12245445	5218740	16547423	0
Interest	3	389978	4297	36773	29887	83615	36063	31256	17450	23741	16669	46140	64086	0
Rents	4	371683	0	35761	7648	38046	11712	8751	8769	2828	1007	4918	252243	0
Royalties	5	59567	0	222	0	17	0	4621	4413	16	5	44431	5843	0
Other Portfolio Income	6	1151708	158793	256316	71602	251419	71313	76987	57427	32610	37334	4176	133731	0
Other Receipts	7	1802980	97473	292497	211070	310437	201903	286776	95912	121730	40111	63717	81353	0
Total Receipts	8	442918027	8285316	142373515	40154052	102476642	38765504	43424920	19957904	12672802	12340571	5382122	17084679	0
Average Total Receipts	9	1282	126	586	2626	5791	17040	35770	73645	142391	293823	336383	1423723	•
Operating Costs/Operating Income (%)														
Cost of Operations	10	64.4	43.0	53.4	58.7	68.5	73.8	75.9	76.1	77.1	78.6	73.6	69.3	•
Salaries and Wages	11	7.3	7.6	10.3	9.0	6.2	4.9	4.3	3.9	4.6	3.7	6.7	5.5	•
Taxes Paid	12	2.2	2.2	2.6	2.8	2.3	1.8	1.7	1.7	1.5	1.3	1.3	1.8	•
Interest Paid	13	0.7	0.7	0.7	0.8	0.7	0.5	0.6	0.6	0.5	0.8	3.1	1.7	•
Depreciation	14	1.9	2.6	1.7	2.2	2.0	1.4	1.8	1.9	1.6	1.8	3.1	2.3	•
Amortization and Depletion	15	0.1	0.1	0.0	0.0	0.0	0.0	0.0	0.0	0.1	0.3	1.1	1.3	•
Pensions and Other Deferred Comp.	16	0.4	0.8	0.3	0.3	0.5	0.6	0.3	0.6	0.4	0.2	0.2	0.5	•
Employee Benefits	17	1.3	0.7	1.2	0.9	1.5	1.5	1.8	1.7	1.1	0.9	0.7	1.6	•
Advertising	18	0.5	1.1	0.7	0.5	0.3	0.2	0.1	0.2	0.1	0.1	0.3	1.9	•
Other Expenses	19	12.7	29.7	18.6	15.1	10.5	7.0	6.3	7.0	7.1	5.7	6.9	10.5	•
Officers' Compensation	20	4.3	7.6	6.6	4.9	4.0	3.4	2.3	1.5	1.7	1.4	0.8	0.4	•
Operating Margin	21	4.1	3.9	3.9	4.8	3.5	5.0	4.7	4.7	4.1	5.1	2.1	3.1	•
Operating Margin Before Officers' Comp.	22	8.4	11.5	10.5	9.7	7.5	8.3	7.0	6.2	5.8	6.5	2.9	3.5	•

Selected Average Balance Sheet ($ in Thousands)

Net Receivables 23	142	0	12	178	791	3350	6800	15326	29992	60555	77759	241181	•
Inventories 24	20	0	5	42	114	371	567	1379	2192	4641	3600	54177	•
Net Property, Plant and Equipment 25	96	0	32	217	472	968	2909	6153	10722	22542	58503	293585	•
Total Assets 26	433	0	88	711	2091	6879	15169	34597	70661	152254	324000	1569533	•
Notes and Loans Payable 27	146	0	57	271	666	1184	3145	6597	12383	31387	109290	706679	•
All Other Liabilities 28	144	0	20	135	671	2997	6445	16243	32152	68811	114997	373419	•
Net Worth 29	142	0	12	304	754	2699	5580	11757	26127	52055	99714	489434	•

Selected Financial Ratios (Times to 1)

Current Ratio 30	1.6	•	1.4	2.3	1.7	1.6	1.5	1.5	1.5	1.5	1.4	1.3
Quick Ratio 31	1.2	•	1.1	1.8	1.4	1.3	1.2	1.2	1.2	1.3	0.9	0.8
Net Sales to Working Capital 32	13.4	•	47.4	10.9	9.8	8.5	9.7	8.8	8.5	8.5	7.6	15.2
Coverage Ratio 33	8.0	10.7	7.6	8.4	7.5	13.5	11.1	10.5	11.1	8.4	2.7	5.0
Total Asset Turnover 34	2.9	•	6.6	3.7	2.8	2.5	2.3	2.1	2.0	1.9	1.0	0.9
Inventory Turnover 35	41.8	•	68.3	36.7	34.5	33.6	47.4	40.3	49.4	49.4	66.7	17.6
Receivables Turnover 36	9.2	•	46.1	13.3	7.3	5.2	5.4	4.8	4.7	4.7	5.2	9.0
Total Liabilities to Net Worth 37	2.1	•	6.4	1.3	1.8	1.5	1.7	1.9	1.7	1.9	2.2	2.2
Current Assets to Working Capital 38	2.8	•	3.5	1.8	2.5	2.7	3.0	3.1	3.1	2.9	3.7	4.8
Current Liabilities to Working Capital 39	1.8	•	2.5	0.8	1.5	1.7	2.0	2.1	2.1	1.9	2.7	3.8
Working Capital to Net Sales 40	0.1	•	0.0	0.1	0.1	0.1	0.1	0.1	0.1	0.1	0.1	0.1
Inventory to Working Capital 41	0.2	•	0.4	0.2	0.2	0.2	0.2	0.2	0.1	0.1	0.1	0.9
Total Receipts to Cash Flow 42	7.0	3.0	5.2	5.9	8.8	10.4	10.8	9.9	9.2	11.9	10.4	6.8
Cost of Goods to Cash Flow 43	4.5	1.3	2.8	3.5	6.0	7.7	8.2	7.5	7.1	9.4	7.6	4.7
Cash Flow to Total Debt 44	0.6	•	1.5	1.1	0.5	0.4	0.3	0.3	0.3	0.2	0.1	0.2

Selected Financial Factors (in Percentages)

Debt Ratio 45	67.2	•	86.5	57.2	63.9	60.8	63.2	66.0	63.0	65.8	69.2	68.8
Return on Total Assets 46	16.7	•	33.1	23.2	13.4	15.4	14.4	13.0	12.0	12.6	8.4	7.7
Return on Equity Before Income Taxes 47	44.6	•	213.5	47.7	32.2	36.3	35.6	34.7	29.5	32.5	17.1	19.8
Return on Equity After Income Taxes 48	41.9	•	211.3	46.3	30.3	33.4	33.2	32.6	26.3	30.2	14.4	13.7
Profit Margin (Before Income Tax) 49	5.0	7.1	4.4	5.6	4.2	5.8	5.6	5.6	5.5	5.8	5.2	7.0
Profit Margin (After Income Tax) 50	4.7	6.7	4.3	5.4	4.0	5.3	5.2	5.3	4.9	5.4	4.4	4.9

35

Table II

Corporations with Net Income

OTHER SPECIALTY TRADE CONTRACTORS

MONEY AMOUNTS AND SIZE OF ASSETS IN THOUSANDS OF DOLLARS

Item Description for Accounting Period 7/07 Through 6/08	Total	Zero Assets	Under 500	500 to 1,000	1,000 to 5,000	5,000 to 10,000	10,000 to 25,000	25,000 to 50,000	50,000 to 100,000	100,000 to 250,000	250,000 to 500,000	500,000 to 2,500,000	2,500,000 and over
Number of Enterprises 1	233091	38249	165650	12255	13560	1968	1034	236	79	•	•	7	0
Revenues ($ in Thousands)													
Net Sales 2	364804470	5438582	110657185	32649169	82343806	34046011	38952343	17437404	11760779	•	•	15291601	0
Interest 3	322162	2703	24979	22710	71349	33896	28419	14960	19017	•	•	42375	0
Rents 4	303190	0	33398	2955	30421	10701	8726	8628	2828	•	•	199608	0
Royalties 5	58380	0	222	0	17	0	4621	4413	16	•	•	4655	0
Other Portfolio Income 6	887367	152810	168253	58972	156856	47386	66931	52112	29595	•	•	115148	0
Other Receipts 7	1563278	86388	205048	169324	256849	218297	265707	86039	113591	•	•	76629	0
Total Receipts 8	367938847	5680483	111089085	32903130	82859298	34356291	39326747	17603556	11925826	•	•	15730016	0
Average Total Receipts 9	1579	149	671	2685	6111	17457	38034	74591	150960	•	•	2247145	•
Operating Costs/Operating Income (%)													
Cost of Operations 10	64.1	40.3	52.6	56.3	67.6	72.5	75.4	76.0	77.3	•	•	67.8	•
Salaries and Wages 11	7.0	6.3	10.0	9.1	6.1	4.9	4.3	3.6	4.4	•	•	5.4	•
Taxes Paid 12	2.1	1.8	2.5	2.8	2.2	1.9	1.7	1.6	1.3	•	•	1.9	•
Interest Paid 13	0.6	0.6	0.5	0.7	0.5	0.4	0.4	0.4	0.4	•	•	1.0	•
Depreciation 14	1.6	1.4	1.4	2.2	1.8	1.3	1.6	1.9	1.4	•	•	2.1	•
Amortization and Depletion 15	0.1	0.0	0.0	0.0	0.0	0.0	0.0	0.0	0.0	•	•	1.3	•
Pensions and Other Deferred Comp. 16	0.4	0.5	0.2	0.4	0.5	0.7	0.4	0.6	0.3	•	•	0.5	•
Employee Benefits 17	1.3	0.7	1.0	0.9	1.3	1.5	1.8	1.7	1.2	•	•	1.7	•
Advertising 18	0.4	0.8	0.5	0.4	0.3	0.2	0.1	0.1	0.1	•	•	2.0	•
Other Expenses 19	12.0	28.1	17.8	15.0	10.3	7.0	6.1	6.2	6.8	•	•	10.2	•
Officers' Compensation 20	4.1	6.0	6.2	5.2	3.7	3.5	2.5	1.5	1.7	•	•	0.4	•
Operating Margin 21	6.4	13.8	7.3	7.0	5.7	6.1	5.7	6.2	5.1	•	•	5.5	•
Operating Margin Before Officers' Comp. 22	10.5	19.7	13.4	12.2	9.4	9.7	8.2	7.7	6.8	•	•	5.9	•

Selected Average Balance Sheet ($ in Thousands)

Net Receivables 23	176	0	12	169	801	3429	7145	15564	32417	•	314376
Inventories 24	22	0	5	34	104	370	477	1328	1953	•	115022
Net Property, Plant and Equipment 25	104	0	30	215	426	970	2613	6245	10106	•	381442
Total Assets 26	513	0	91	701	2071	6844	15149	34952	71269	•	2083948
Notes and Loans Payable 27	144	0	46	225	528	1122	2580	6148	10275	•	917474
All Other Liabilities 28	168	0	18	117	611	2800	6576	15688	33683	•	480715
Net Worth 29	201	0	27	358	933	2922	5993	13115	27311	•	685759

Selected Financial Ratios (Times to 1)

Current Ratio 30	1.7	•	1.7	2.6	2.1	1.7	1.6	1.6	1.5	•	1.5
Quick Ratio 31	1.4	•	1.3	2.1	1.7	1.4	1.3	1.3	1.3	•	0.9
Net Sales to Working Capital 32	11.2	•	35.1	10.3	7.8	7.4	9.0	8.0	8.8	•	11.9
Coverage Ratio 33	14.0	33.6	15.3	12.7	13.6	17.2	16.4	19.0	17.7	•	9.6
Total Asset Turnover 34	3.1	•	7.3	3.8	2.9	2.5	2.5	2.1	2.1	•	1.0
Inventory Turnover 35	46.6	•	68.7	44.5	39.3	33.9	59.5	42.3	58.9	•	12.9
Receivables Turnover 36	9.1	•	53.4	14.5	7.3	5.3	5.5	4.7	4.7	•	•
Total Liabilities to Net Worth 37	1.6	•	2.4	1.0	1.2	1.3	1.5	1.7	1.6	•	2.0
Current Assets to Working Capital 38	2.3	•	2.5	1.6	1.9	2.4	2.8	2.8	3.1	•	3.2
Current Liabilities to Working Capital 39	1.3	•	1.5	0.6	0.9	1.4	1.8	1.8	2.1	•	2.2
Working Capital to Net Sales 40	0.1	•	0.0	0.1	0.1	0.1	0.1	0.1	0.1	•	0.1
Inventory to Working Capital 41	0.2	•	0.3	0.1	0.2	0.1	0.1	0.1	0.1	•	0.6
Total Receipts to Cash Flow 42	6.2	2.3	4.6	5.2	7.5	9.4	9.8	9.2	8.6	•	6.1
Cost of Goods to Cash Flow 43	4.0	0.9	2.4	2.9	5.1	6.8	7.4	7.0	6.7	•	4.1
Cash Flow to Total Debt 44	0.8	•	2.2	1.5	0.7	0.5	0.4	0.4	0.4	•	0.3

Selected Financial Factors (in Percentages)

Debt Ratio 45	60.8	•	70.8	48.9	55.0	57.3	60.4	62.5	61.7	•	67.1
Return on Total Assets 46	24.1	•	59.9	32.1	20.1	18.9	17.8	15.9	14.2	•	10.5
Return on Equity Before Income Taxes 47	57.0	•	191.7	57.9	41.3	41.7	42.1	40.2	34.9	•	28.7
Return on Equity After Income Taxes 48	54.2	•	190.3	56.4	39.3	38.7	39.6	38.0	31.5	•	21.2
Profit Margin (Before Income Tax) 49	7.3	18.2	7.6	7.8	6.3	7.0	6.7	7.1	6.4	•	9.0
Profit Margin (After Income Tax) 50	7.0	17.9	7.6	7.6	6.0	6.5	6.3	6.7	5.8	•	6.7

ANIMAL FOOD AND GRAIN AND OILSEED MILLING

Table I

Corporations with and without Net Income

MONEY AMOUNTS AND SIZE OF ASSETS IN THOUSANDS OF DOLLARS

Item Description for Accounting Period 7/07 Through 6/08	Total	Zero Assets	Under 500	500 to 1,000	1,000 to 5,000	5,000 to 10,000	10,000 to 25,000	25,000 to 50,000	50,000 to 100,000	100,000 to 250,000	250,000 to 500,000	500,000 to 2,500,000	2,500,000 and over
Number of Enterprises 1	1496	52	787	0	352	117	76	52	21	23	6	5	5
Revenues ($ in Thousands)													
Net Sales 2	104693420	526955	127442	0	2721994	2714662	3038612	5303262	3074935	6429211	2253059	3414389	75088900
Interest 3	622314	877	166	0	4872	1096	2742	2255	6386	11537	3059	27047	562277
Rents 4	192729	326	0	0	0	0	63	804	216	251	3109	1231	186729
Royalties 5	423108	0	0	0	0	42	0	0	36	1264	1126	55079	365561
Other Portfolio Income 6	974781	21977	0	0	8541	1075	737	21955	8037	14227	21556	62110	814567
Other Receipts 7	1468689	1015	0	0	26124	18765	7227	38710	31539	29704	7198	33697	1274708
Total Receipts 8	108375041	551150	127608	0	2761531	2735640	3049381	5366986	3121149	6486194	2289107	3593553	78292742
Average Total Receipts 9	72443	10599	162	•	7845	23382	40123	103211	148626	282008	381518	718711	15658548
Operating Costs/Operating Income (%)													
Cost of Operations 10	80.0	85.9	68.3	•	84.8	81.9	82.1	84.1	82.3	83.0	71.5	79.2	79.3
Salaries and Wages 11	2.9	3.3	4.7	•	5.0	5.0	3.4	3.1	3.3	2.7	6.3	3.1	2.5
Taxes Paid 12	0.7	0.8	8.0	•	1.0	0.7	0.8	0.7	0.8	0.9	1.2	0.8	0.7
Interest Paid 13	2.0	1.2	0.6	•	0.6	0.9	0.4	1.0	1.4	1.2	2.6	4.2	2.2
Depreciation 14	1.6	1.5	1.5	•	1.2	2.7	1.6	1.5	1.9	2.1	2.4	3.6	1.4
Amortization and Depletion 15	0.2	0.0	0.9	•	0.0	0.0	0.0	0.2	0.2	0.3	0.7	1.8	0.2
Pensions and Other Deferred Comp. 16	0.3	0.4	•	•	0.0	0.2	0.2	0.2	0.2	0.3	0.7	0.4	0.3
Employee Benefits 17	0.7	0.6	3.9	•	0.3	0.6	0.4	0.6	0.9	0.8	0.6	1.5	0.7
Advertising 18	4.8	0.1	0.2	•	0.4	0.5	0.3	0.3	0.6	0.3	1.0	0.7	6.5
Other Expenses 19	5.2	6.4	12.7	•	5.6	8.3	5.0	6.0	6.4	6.7	8.6	8.0	4.6
Officers' Compensation 20	0.4	0.2	9.6	•	1.6	0.2	1.1	0.9	0.7	0.7	1.4	1.5	0.2
Operating Margin 21	1.2	•	•	•	•	•	4.8	1.5	1.3	1.0	3.0	•	1.4
Operating Margin Before Officers' Comp. 22	1.6	•	•	•	1.1	•	5.8	2.3	2.0	1.7	4.3	•	1.6

Selected Average Balance Sheet ($ in Thousands)

Item													
Net Receivables 23	5147	0	3	•	514	1851	3980	9057	15249	31075	46722	70125	972071
Inventories 24	6073	0	17	•	801	788	2477	9833	14777	29365	44861	55469	1293089
Net Property, Plant and Equipment 25	10152	0	12	•	702	3183	6233	10248	22264	50289	95127	279505	1991800
Total Assets 26	52820	0	41	•	2362	7002	14408	38257	74099	160872	343851	874528	12512018
Notes and Loans Payable 27	23392	0	10	•	976	2250	2741	12102	27270	61539	139004	281816	5862136
All Other Liabilities 28	15400	0	30	•	751	3036	4037	13709	16236	39008	81685	188028	3741323
Net Worth 29	14029	0	1	•	635	1715	7630	12446	30593	60326	123161	404685	2908559

Selected Financial Ratios (Times to 1)

Item													
Current Ratio 30	1.0	•	•	0.6	1.4	1.1	1.9	1.3	1.7	1.8	1.8	1.3	0.9
Quick Ratio 31	0.4	•	•	0.2	0.6	0.7	1.4	0.7	0.9	0.8	0.9	0.7	0.3
Net Sales to Working Capital 32	145.6	•	•	•	18.7	96.8	10.7	18.1	9.6	8.6	5.6	14.7	•
Coverage Ratio 33	3.6	4.5	•	•	2.5	0.7	12.6	3.6	3.0	2.5	2.7	1.2	3.9
Total Asset Turnover 34	1.3	•	3.9	•	3.3	3.3	2.8	2.7	2.0	1.7	1.1	0.8	1.2
Inventory Turnover 35	9.2	•	6.6	•	8.2	24.1	13.3	8.7	8.2	7.9	6.0	9.8	9.2
Receivables Turnover 36	15.9	•	20.0	•	14.9	22.6	9.5	12.6	10.4	10.7	9.6	11.9	18.2
Total Liabilities to Net Worth 37	2.8	•	31.0	•	2.7	3.1	0.9	2.1	1.4	1.7	1.8	1.2	3.3
Current Assets to Working Capital 38	35.2	•	•	•	3.8	15.5	2.1	4.2	2.5	2.3	2.3	4.2	•
Current Liabilities to Working Capital 39	34.2	•	•	•	2.8	14.5	1.1	3.2	1.5	1.3	1.3	3.2	•
Working Capital to Net Sales 40	0.0	•	•	•	0.1	0.0	0.1	0.1	0.1	0.1	0.2	0.1	•
Inventory to Working Capital 41	14.5	•	•	•	1.9	4.5	0.5	1.9	1.0	1.0	0.8	1.5	•
Total Receipts to Cash Flow 42	13.0	12.7	•	•	18.9	19.6	11.1	13.0	13.4	13.4	9.2	16.1	12.7
Cost of Goods to Cash Flow 43	10.4	10.9	•	•	16.0	16.1	9.1	10.9	11.0	11.1	6.6	12.8	10.1
Cash Flow to Total Debt 44	0.1	•	•	•	0.2	0.2	0.5	0.3	0.3	0.2	0.2	0.1	0.1

Selected Financial Factors (in Percentages)

Item													
Debt Ratio 45	73.4	•	96.9	•	73.1	75.5	47.0	67.5	58.7	62.5	64.2	53.7	76.8
Return on Total Assets 46	9.7	•	•	•	5.0	1.9	15.5	9.8	8.3	5.3	7.6	4.0	10.5
Return on Equity Before Income Taxes 47	26.4	•	•	•	11.0	26.9	21.7	13.5	8.5	13.2	1.7	•	33.5
Return on Equity After Income Taxes 48	17.5	•	•	•	7.3	24.4	20.6	10.1	5.9	11.5	•	•	21.8
Profit Margin (Before Income Tax) 49	5.3	•	4.2	•	0.9	1.9	5.1	2.7	2.8	1.8	4.3	1.0	6.5
Profit Margin (After Income Tax) 50	3.5	•	3.5	•	0.6	1.3	4.7	2.5	1.8	1.3	3.8	•	4.2

Table II

Corporations with Net Income

ANIMAL FOOD AND GRAIN AND OILSEED MILLING

MONEY AMOUNTS AND SIZE OF ASSETS IN THOUSANDS OF DOLLARS

Item Description for Accounting Period 7/07 Through 6/08	Total	Zero Assets	Under 500	500 to 1,000	1,000 to 5,000	5,000 to 10,000	10,000 to 25,000	25,000 to 50,000	50,000 to 100,000	100,000 to 250,000	250,000 to 500,000	500,000 to 2,500,000	2,500,000 and over
Number of Enterprises **1**	708	10	241	0	200	98	70	41	17	18	•	•	5
Revenues ($ in Thousands)													
Net Sales **2**	99411900	464280	4399	0	2093672	2509836	2872780	3896282	2449834	5490709	•	•	75088900
Interest **3**	618446	837	0	0	4493	615	2645	2126	6276	11002	•	•	562277
Rents **4**	192530	326	0	0	0	0	63	730	216	251	•	•	186729
Royalties **5**	423108	0	0	0	0	42	0	0	36	1264	•	•	365561
Other Portfolio Income **6**	939497	21922	0	0	7637	1075	522	5445	6930	1233	•	•	814567
Other Receipts **7**	1427251	2629	0	0	22159	313	6828	29166	33198	24460	•	•	1274708
Total Receipts **8**	103012732	489994	4399	0	2127961	2511881	2882838	3933749	2496490	5528919	•	•	78292742
Average Total Receipts **9**	145498	48999	18	•	10640	25631	41183	95945	146852	307162	•	•	15658548
Operating Costs/Operating Income (%)													
Cost of Operations **10**	79.7	86.9	50.8	•	86.2	81.9	81.6	82.1	81.0	81.9	•	•	79.3
Salaries and Wages **11**	2.8	3.0	1.3	•	4.5	4.9	3.3	3.1	3.6	2.8	•	•	2.5
Taxes Paid **12**	0.7	0.7	3.5	•	0.8	0.6	0.8	0.9	0.6	0.9	•	•	0.7
Interest Paid **13**	2.0	1.1	•	•	0.7	0.6	0.4	0.9	1.3	1.2	•	•	2.2
Depreciation **14**	1.5	1.2	0.8	•	0.9	2.1	1.5	1.7	1.8	1.9	•	•	1.4
Amortization and Depletion **15**	0.2	•	0.6	•	0.0	0.1	0.0	0.1	0.3	0.2	•	•	0.2
Pensions and Other Deferred Comp. **16**	0.3	0.5	•	•	0.1	0.2	0.2	0.2	0.3	0.3	•	•	0.3
Employee Benefits **17**	0.7	0.5	•	•	0.3	0.6	0.4	0.7	0.9	0.9	•	•	0.7
Advertising **18**	5.1	0.1	3.4	•	0.5	0.3	0.3	0.3	0.7	0.3	•	•	6.5
Other Expenses **19**	4.9	5.1	12.8	•	4.1	7.2	4.9	5.6	5.9	5.7	•	•	4.6
Officers' Compensation **20**	0.4	•	•	•	1.8	0.1	1.1	0.8	0.8	0.8	•	•	0.2
Operating Margin **21**	1.7	0.9	26.8	•	0.2	1.3	5.7	3.4	2.7	3.0	•	•	1.4
Operating Margin Before Officers' Comp. **22**	2.1	0.9	26.8	•	2.0	1.5	6.7	4.3	3.5	3.7	•	•	1.6

Selected Average Balance Sheet ($ in Thousands)

Net Receivables 23	10139	0	0	•	485	2120	4069	9715	14399	33892	•	972071
Inventories 24	12022	0	0	•	1118	685	2459	10287	14743	33674	•	1293089
Net Property, Plant and Equipment 25	20180	0	0	•	735	2606	6253	10835	21119	48840	•	1991800
Total Assets 26	106903	0	3	•	2602	6746	14672	38584	75059	159449	•	12512018
Notes and Loans Payable 27	47161	0	0	•	914	2135	2507	11965	25275	60329	•	5862136
All Other Liabilities 28	31183	0	64	•	856	2559	3796	12176	16611	41584	•	3741323
Net Worth 29	28558	0	-60	•	832	2053	8368	14443	33173	57536	•	2908559

Selected Financial Ratios (Times to 1)

Current Ratio 30	1.0	0.0	•	•	1.6	1.4	2.0	1.6	1.7	1.8	•	0.9
Quick Ratio 31	0.4	0.0	•	•	0.7	1.0	1.4	0.8	0.9	0.8	•	0.3
Net Sales to Working Capital 32	189.4	•	•	•	15.3	21.9	10.2	11.3	9.1	8.8	•	•
Coverage Ratio 33	4.0	6.7	•	•	3.6	3.3	16.6	5.9	4.4	4.0	•	3.9
Total Asset Turnover 34	1.3	•	5.5	•	4.0	3.8	2.8	2.5	1.9	1.9	•	1.2
Inventory Turnover 35	9.3	•	559.0	•	8.1	30.6	13.6	7.6	7.9	7.4	•	9.2
Receivables Turnover 36	16.3	•	•	•	19.8	22.6	9.7	10.6	•	10.1	•	18.2
Total Liabilities to Net Worth 37	2.7	•	•	•	2.1	2.3	0.8	1.7	1.3	1.8	•	3.3
Current Assets to Working Capital 38	45.4	•	•	•	2.6	3.5	2.0	2.8	2.4	2.3	•	•
Current Liabilities to Working Capital 39	44.4	•	•	•	1.6	2.5	1.0	1.8	1.4	1.3	•	•
Working Capital to Net Sales 40	0.0	•	•	•	0.1	0.0	0.1	0.1	0.1	0.1	•	•
Inventory to Working Capital 41	18.6	•	•	•	1.4	0.9	0.5	1.2	0.9	1.1	•	•
Total Receipts to Cash Flow 42	12.4	11.3	2.7	•	20.3	18.0	10.2	11.1	11.2	12.0	•	12.7
Cost of Goods to Cash Flow 43	9.9	9.8	1.4	•	17.5	14.8	8.3	9.1	9.1	9.8	•	10.1
Cash Flow to Total Debt 44	0.1	•	0.1	•	0.3	0.3	0.6	0.4	0.3	0.2	•	0.1

Selected Financial Factors (in Percentages)

Debt Ratio 45	73.3	1929.2	•	•	68.0	69.6	43.0	62.6	55.8	63.9	•	76.8
Return on Total Assets 46	10.5	147.9	•	•	10.5	7.6	17.9	13.0	11.3	9.3	•	10.5
Return on Equity Before Income Taxes 47	29.4	•	•	•	23.7	17.5	29.5	28.9	19.8	19.4	•	33.5
Return on Equity After Income Taxes 48	20.2	•	•	•	18.7	16.3	27.0	27.7	15.9	15.9	•	21.8
Profit Margin (Before Income Tax) 49	6.0	6.4	26.8	•	1.9	1.4	6.0	4.4	4.6	3.7	•	6.5
Profit Margin (After Income Tax) 50	4.1	5.6	26.7	•	1.5	1.3	5.5	4.2	3.7	3.0	•	4.2

Table I

Corporations with and without Net Income

SUGAR AND CONFECTIONERY PRODUCT

MONEY AMOUNTS AND SIZE OF ASSETS IN THOUSANDS OF DOLLARS

Item Description for Accounting Period 7/07 Through 6/08	Total	Zero Assets	Under 500	500 to 1,000	1,000 to 5,000	5,000 to 10,000	10,000 to 25,000	25,000 to 50,000	50,000 to 100,000	100,000 to 250,000	250,000 to 500,000	500,000 to 2,500,000	2,500,000 and over
Number of Enterprises 1	1002	386	314	53	126	35	33	22	17	0	6	4	5
Revenues ($ in Thousands)													
Net Sales 2	46751478	17071	817524	106196	390302	546008	1624343	1217667	2138689	0	2064358	2320080	35509241
Interest 3	496187	346	0	0	136	381	703	1112	4329	0	12291	31113	445777
Rents 4	57642	0	0	0	0	61	137	3203	1396	0	48	21730	31068
Royalties 5	298068	0	0	0	0	0	10871	1405	0	0	8836	2015	274940
Other Portfolio Income 6	830309	0	0	0	0	0	6650	170	5738	0	5258	32940	779555
Other Receipts 7	507445	288	1763	0	1288	382	2726	8076	-10325	0	116265	24983	361994
Total Receipts 8	48941129	17705	819287	106196	391726	546832	1645430	1231633	2139827	0	2207056	2432861	37402575
Average Total Receipts 9	48843	46	2609	2004	3109	15624	49862	55983	125872	•	367843	608215	7480515
Operating Costs/Operating Income (%)													
Cost of Operations 10	54.7	54.9	65.2	42.9	59.4	64.3	79.5	78.7	69.6	•	71.1	74.3	49.1
Salaries and Wages 11	5.9	2.2	6.0	25.4	7.6	7.9	3.7	3.0	6.6	•	6.1	3.7	6.1
Taxes Paid 12	1.3	1.3	4.6	4.0	2.1	1.4	1.2	1.2	1.2	•	1.3	0.8	1.2
Interest Paid 13	4.2	0.1	0.2	2.8	1.0	1.3	1.0	1.4	3.4	•	4.7	3.0	4.7
Depreciation 14	2.4	1.3	1.3	1.0	0.8	3.0	1.1	3.1	2.2	•	3.1	4.8	2.2
Amortization and Depletion 15	1.1	1.1	•	0.0	0.8	0.3	0.0	0.3	0.6	•	1.2	0.4	1.3
Pensions and Other Deferred Comp. 16	0.7	0.0	•	•	1.9	0.2	0.4	0.1	0.7	•	1.0	1.1	0.7
Employee Benefits 17	1.2	0.1	•	•	4.0	1.0	0.7	0.5	1.7	•	2.2	0.8	1.2
Advertising 18	5.6	2.3	2.2	0.9	0.1	1.0	0.7	0.6	2.3	•	4.1	0.2	6.9
Other Expenses 19	21.0	20.2	16.0	21.9	10.1	14.3	7.7	8.9	11.9	•	10.5	13.2	24.0
Officers' Compensation 20	0.7	5.9	0.7	2.3	7.2	1.8	1.9	1.7	1.2	•	1.8	0.7	0.5
Operating Margin 21	1.3	10.6	3.9	•	4.9	3.5	2.0	0.4	•	•	•	•	2.1
Operating Margin Before Officers' Comp. 22	2.0	16.5	4.5	1.1	12.2	5.3	3.8	2.1	•	•	•	•	2.6

Selected Average Balance Sheet ($ in Thousands)

Net Receivables 23	6252	0	99	11	627	919	3032	5919	11063	•	53675	220236	900089
Inventories 24	4336	0	62	731	294	1534	5533	7271	19640	•	68222	92294	548112
Net Property, Plant and Equipment 25	10252	0	22	314	174	2489	4796	12209	18778	•	108928	372390	1450075
Total Assets 26	66882	0	449	866	1243	7250	17801	32100	80542	•	359511	1052573	11477642
Notes and Loans Payable 27	33721	0	323	982	514	1848	6062	8896	36251	•	230677	235805	6033371
All Other Liabilities 28	17414	0	212	47	436	997	5619	6955	24563	•	20891	360516	2993393
Net Worth 29	15746	0	-86	-162	293	4405	6119	16249	19729	•	107944	456252	2450878

Selected Financial Ratios (Times to 1)

Current Ratio 30	0.7	•	1.1	2.2	1.8	2.1	1.6	1.8	1.0	•	1.8	1.5	0.6
Quick Ratio 31	0.3	•	1.0	0.1	1.3	1.2	0.6	0.8	0.4	•	0.9	0.8	0.2
Net Sales to Working Capital 32	•	•	55.4	6.7	6.5	8.8	12.0	7.3	446.0	•	4.2	4.0	•
Coverage Ratio 33	2.7	164.1	24.7	0.6	6.2	3.9	4.3	2.1	0.6	•	1.3	1.6	2.9
Total Asset Turnover 34	0.7	•	5.8	2.3	2.5	2.2	2.8	1.7	1.6	•	1.0	0.6	0.6
Inventory Turnover 35	5.9	•	27.4	1.2	6.3	6.5	7.1	6.0	4.5	•	3.6	4.7	6.4
Receivables Turnover 36	6.4	•	23.7	2.9	7.3	12.7	13.5	10.8	10.6	•	6.8	2.7	6.4
Total Liabilities to Net Worth 37	3.2	•	•	1.8	3.2	0.6	1.9	1.0	3.1	•	2.3	1.3	3.7
Current Assets to Working Capital 38	•	•	9.1	1.8	2.2	1.9	2.7	2.2	140.3	•	2.2	3.0	•
Current Liabilities to Working Capital 39	•	•	8.1	0.8	1.2	0.9	1.7	1.2	139.3	•	1.2	2.0	•
Working Capital to Net Sales 40	•	•	0.0	0.2	0.2	0.1	0.1	0.1	0.0	•	0.2	0.2	•
Inventory to Working Capital 41	•	•	1.2	1.7	0.6	0.7	1.5	1.0	70.0	•	0.9	0.6	•
Total Receipts to Cash Flow 42	4.1	3.3	7.6	9.4	8.7	6.2	11.3	11.2	11.1	•	12.2	7.6	3.5
Cost of Goods to Cash Flow 43	2.2	1.8	4.9	4.0	5.2	4.0	9.0	8.8	7.8	•	8.7	5.7	1.7
Cash Flow to Total Debt 44	0.2	•	0.6	0.2	0.4	0.9	0.4	0.3	0.2	•	0.1	0.1	0.2

Selected Financial Factors (in Percentages)

Debt Ratio 45	76.5	•	119.1	118.7	76.4	39.2	65.6	49.4	75.5	•	70.0	56.7	78.6
Return on Total Assets 46	8.0	•	24.7	3.8	15.8	10.6	11.7	5.1	3.2	•	5.7	2.7	8.5
Return on Equity Before Income Taxes 47	21.4	•	•	14.1	56.2	13.0	26.1	5.4	•	•	3.9	2.5	26.0
Return on Equity After Income Taxes 48	14.3	•	•	14.1	49.8	9.2	23.5	4.4	•	•	2.1	1.1	17.4
Profit Margin (Before Income Tax) 49	7.2	14.3	4.1	5.3	3.7	3.2	1.6	•	•	•	1.2	1.9	9.0
Profit Margin (After Income Tax) 50	4.8	14.3	4.1	4.7	2.6	2.9	1.3	•	•	•	0.6	0.8	6.0

39

Table II

Corporations with Net Income

SUGAR AND CONFECTIONERY PRODUCT

MONEY AMOUNTS AND SIZE OF ASSETS IN THOUSANDS OF DOLLARS

Item Description for Accounting Period 7/07 Through 6/08	Total	Zero Assets	Under 500	500 to 1,000	1,000 to 5,000	5,000 to 10,000	10,000 to 25,000	25,000 to 50,000	50,000 to 100,000	100,000 to 250,000	250,000 to 500,000	500,000 to 2,500,000	2,500,000 and over
Number of Enterprises 1	874	377	304	0	98	•	28	14	10	0	•	•	5
Revenues ($ in Thousands)													
Net Sales 2	42769365	16781	816130	0	319951	•	1482027	952436	1254695	0	•	•	35509241
Interest 3	490903	0	0	0	136	•	542	1056	681	0	•	•	445777
Rents 4	57017	0	0	0	0	•	22	3137	1393	0	•	•	31068
Royalties 5	297969	0	0	0	0	•	10773	1405	0	0	•	•	274940
Other Portfolio Income 6	824612	0	0	0	0	•	6644	170	1966	0	•	•	779555
Other Receipts 7	487605	283	1760	0	1278	•	2269	7560	12498	0	•	•	361994
Total Receipts 8	44927471	17064	817890	0	321365	•	1502277	965764	1271233	0	•	•	37402575
Average Total Receipts 9	51404	45	2690	•	3279	•	53653	68983	127123	•	•	•	7480515
Operating Costs/Operating Income (%)													
Cost of Operations 10	52.3	54.3	65.2	•	54.0	•	80.0	77.9	65.8	•	•	•	49.1
Salaries and Wages 11	6.0	1.8	6.0	•	9.2	•	3.6	2.3	6.1	•	•	•	6.1
Taxes Paid 12	1.3	1.1	4.6	•	2.0	•	1.1	1.0	1.3	•	•	•	1.2
Interest Paid 13	4.1	•	0.2	•	0.7	•	1.0	1.0	1.3	•	•	•	4.7
Depreciation 14	2.2	1.3	1.3	•	0.8	•	1.1	2.7	2.2	•	•	•	2.2
Amortization and Depletion 15	1.1	1.1	•	•	0.9	•	0.0	0.2	0.3	•	•	•	1.3
Pensions and Other Deferred Comp. 16	0.7	0.0	•	•	2.3	•	0.3	0.1	0.9	•	•	•	0.7
Employee Benefits 17	1.2	0.0	•	•	4.7	•	0.7	0.5	2.2	•	•	•	1.2
Advertising 18	6.0	2.3	2.2	•	0.1	•	0.3	0.6	1.8	•	•	•	6.9
Other Expenses 19	22.2	18.7	14.1	•	10.5	•	7.8	8.6	13.7	•	•	•	24.0
Officers' Compensation 20	0.7	5.2	0.7	•	8.1	•	1.7	1.8	1.4	•	•	•	0.5
Operating Margin 21	2.1	14.1	5.8	•	6.7	•	2.2	3.2	2.9	•	•	•	2.1
Operating Margin Before Officers' Comp. 22	2.8	19.3	6.5	•	14.7	•	3.9	5.1	4.3	•	•	•	2.6

Selected Average Balance Sheet ($ in Thousands)

Net Receivables 23	6088	0	101	•	639	•	3147	7470	13166	•	900089
Inventories 24	4383	0	64	•	226	•	5949	7232	22235	•	548112
Net Property, Plant and Equipment 25	10181	0	23	•	150	•	4956	13178	23189	•	1450075
Total Assets 26	71827	0	462	•	1235	•	18382	33419	77919	•	11477642
Notes and Loans Payable 27	36046	0	0	•	482	•	6523	9621	20828	•	6033371
All Other Liabilities 28	17983	0	153	•	464	•	5607	6697	18492	•	2993393
Net Worth 29	17798	0	309	•	288	•	6252	17101	38600	•	2450878

Selected Financial Ratios (Times to 1)

Current Ratio 30	0.6	•	2.9	•	2.0	•	1.7	1.7	1.7	•	0.6
Quick Ratio 31	0.3	•	2.5	•	1.5	•	0.7	0.9	0.9	•	0.2
Net Sales to Working Capital 32	•	•	9.4	•	6.3	•	11.4	9.1	7.9	•	•
Coverage Ratio 33	3.0	•	36.1	•	11.1	•	4.6	5.8	4.3	•	2.9
Total Asset Turnover 34	0.7	•	5.8	•	2.6	•	2.9	2.0	1.6	•	0.6
Inventory Turnover 35	5.8	•	27.3	•	7.8	•	7.1	7.3	3.7	•	6.4
Receivables Turnover 36	6.7	•	23.7	•	8.7	•	14.5	11.3	8.1	•	6.4
Total Liabilities to Net Worth 37	3.0	•	0.5	•	3.3	•	1.9	1.0	1.0	•	3.7
Current Assets to Working Capital 38	•	•	1.5	•	2.0	•	2.5	2.5	2.4	•	•
Current Liabilities to Working Capital 39	•	•	0.5	•	1.0	•	1.5	1.5	1.4	•	•
Working Capital to Net Sales 40	•	•	0.1	•	0.2	•	0.1	0.1	0.1	•	•
Inventory to Working Capital 41	•	•	0.2	•	0.5	•	1.4	0.9	0.9	•	•
Total Receipts to Cash Flow 42	3.7	3.3	7.4	•	7.0	•	10.8	8.4	6.2	•	3.5
Cost of Goods to Cash Flow 43	2.0	1.8	4.8	•	3.8	•	8.6	6.5	4.1	•	1.7
Cash Flow to Total Debt 44	0.2	•	2.4	•	0.5	•	0.4	0.5	0.5	•	0.2

Selected Financial Factors (in Percentages)

Debt Ratio 45	75.2	•	33.1	•	76.6	•	66.0	48.8	50.5	•	78.6
Return on Total Assets 46	8.5	•	36.0	•	20.6	•	13.2	11.4	8.9	•	8.5
Return on Equity Before Income Taxes 47	23.1	•	52.3	•	80.4	•	30.5	18.4	13.8	•	26.0
Return on Equity After Income Taxes 48	15.9	•	52.3	•	72.0	•	27.5	16.9	12.5	•	17.4
Profit Margin (Before Income Tax) 49	8.4	15.7	6.0	•	7.1	•	3.6	4.6	4.2	•	9.0
Profit Margin (After Income Tax) 50	5.8	15.7	6.0	•	6.4	•	3.2	4.3	3.8	•	6.0

Table I

Corporations with and without Net Income

FRUIT AND VEGETABLE PRESERVING AND SPECIALTY FOOD

Money Amounts and Size of Assets in Thousands of Dollars

Item Description for Accounting Period 7/07 Through 6/08		Total	Zero Assets	Under 500	500 to 1,000	1,000 to 5,000	5,000 to 10,000	10,000 to 25,000	25,000 to 50,000	50,000 to 100,000	100,000 to 250,000	250,000 to 500,000	500,000 to 2,500,000	2,500,000 and over
Number of Enterprises	1	1221	391	387	0	213	59	77	30	25	18	6	8	5
Revenues ($ in Thousands)														
Net Sales	2	44327763	365282	1367	0	1482430	1165142	2430503	1470179	2843273	4947688	2889265	11943203	14789433
Interest	3	142481	751	19	0	453	6	1394	2719	1841	11224	5340	81100	37633
Rents	4	24938	1822	0	0	1399	0	1004	443	1406	157	5430	12428	849
Royalties	5	268781	0	0	0	0	0	134	0	101	0	0	43913	224633
Other Portfolio Income	6	658874	34	0	0	61	0	14102	32701	688	4442	47097	18956	540796
Other Receipts	7	753782	5532	9	0	689	2570	7122	67268	32902	10922	36509	191484	398771
Total Receipts	8	46176619	373421	1395	0	1485032	1167718	2454259	1573310	2880211	4974433	2983641	12291084	15592115
Average Total Receipts	9	37819	955	4	•	6972	19792	31873	52444	115208	276357	497274	1536386	3198423
Operating Costs/Operating Income (%)														
Cost of Operations	10	67.5	84.9	46.0	•	82.2	74.3	75.9	76.9	78.5	77.6	73.9	66.8	56.6
Salaries and Wages	11	4.7	1.2	19.2	•	1.9	3.4	5.2	4.2	3.0	3.2	3.8	6.6	4.8
Taxes Paid	12	1.2	4.0	5.9	•	2.2	1.2	1.1	1.2	1.0	1.2	2.1	1.6	0.5
Interest Paid	13	2.6	1.7	1.5	•	1.0	0.7	1.6	2.0	1.9	1.4	1.1	2.6	3.9
Depreciation	14	2.2	1.7	6.8	•	1.8	1.2	1.5	3.0	1.8	1.8	3.6	2.4	2.2
Amortization and Depletion	15	1.1	0.1	•	•	0.4	0.8	0.2	0.4	0.5	0.1	0.3	1.0	2.2
Pensions and Other Deferred Comp.	16	0.4	0.4	•	•	0.2	0.0	0.1	0.2	0.3	0.3	0.1	0.7	0.5
Employee Benefits	17	1.3	0.5	0.7	•	0.6	1.7	1.0	0.5	1.3	0.8	1.3	2.9	0.5
Advertising	18	3.3	1.1	•	•	0.2	0.4	1.8	1.4	0.5	0.4	2.1	5.7	4.1
Other Expenses	19	14.2	8.4	24.5	•	3.8	14.7	8.5	10.5	7.8	9.1	9.8	10.7	23.4
Officers' Compensation	20	0.8	0.4	6.0	•	3.7	0.4	1.0	1.0	0.8	0.7	0.6	0.3	0.9
Operating Margin	21	0.6	•	•	•	2.0	1.1	2.0	•	2.6	3.5	1.1	•	0.4
Operating Margin Before Officers' Comp.	22	1.3	•	•	•	5.7	1.6	3.1	•	3.4	4.2	1.7	•	1.3

Selected Average Balance Sheet ($ in Thousands)

Net Receivables 23	3053	0	0	•	520	2068	3161	6006	11369	24420	39747	114714	238160
Inventories 24	5221	0	0	•	427	1273	6722	9027	27765	62239	64380	196052	330241
Net Property, Plant and Equipment 25	6534	0	2	•	1038	1554	3291	9874	18551	43755	135897	290684	544608
Total Assets 26	38593	0	63	•	2621	7080	16096	34048	71841	156325	341284	1210695	5503486
Notes and Loans Payable 27	11990	0	42	•	1092	4642	6046	11774	27153	46026	82351	507723	1447086
All Other Liabilities 28	8956	0	1	•	530	2571	6280	8165	16499	41924	103651	254146	1224024
Net Worth 29	17646	0	19	•	999	-133	3770	14109	28188	68375	155282	448827	2832376

Selected Financial Ratios (Times to 1)

Current Ratio 30	1.4	•	8.5	•	1.5	0.8	1.3	1.7	1.5	1.8	1.6	2.3	0.9
Quick Ratio 31	0.5	•	7.9	•	0.9	0.4	0.5	0.8	0.5	0.5	0.5	0.9	0.4
Net Sales to Working Capital 32	11.9	•	0.2	•	19.0	•	12.7	6.4	8.1	6.0	9.4	6.0	•
Coverage Ratio 33	3.1	•	•	•	3.3	2.9	2.9	3.9	3.0	4.0	4.8	1.6	3.7
Total Asset Turnover 34	0.9	•	0.1	•	2.7	2.8	2.0	1.4	1.6	1.8	1.4	1.2	0.5
Inventory Turnover 35	4.7	•	19.4	•	13.4	11.5	3.6	4.2	3.2	3.4	5.5	5.1	5.1
Receivables Turnover 36	11.1	•	9.1	•	18.0	15.9	9.2	8.4	9.3	12.4	15.0	15.0	8.6
Total Liabilities to Net Worth 37	1.2	•	2.2	•	1.6	•	3.3	1.4	1.5	1.3	1.2	1.7	0.9
Current Assets to Working Capital 38	3.5	•	1.1	•	2.9	•	4.5	2.5	3.1	2.3	2.7	1.7	•
Current Liabilities to Working Capital 39	2.5	•	0.1	•	1.9	•	3.5	1.5	2.1	1.3	1.7	0.7	•
Working Capital to Net Sales 40	0.1	•	5.0	•	0.1	•	0.1	0.2	0.1	0.2	0.1	0.2	•
Inventory to Working Capital 41	1.8	•	0.0	•	1.2	•	2.7	1.2	2.0	1.5	1.5	0.8	•
Total Receipts to Cash Flow 42	6.0	24.0	9.5	•	20.6	7.3	10.3	8.4	10.0	8.9	8.7	10.2	3.4
Cost of Goods to Cash Flow 43	4.0	20.4	4.4	•	16.9	5.4	7.9	6.5	7.9	6.9	6.4	6.8	1.9
Cash Flow to Total Debt 44	0.3	•	0.0	•	0.2	0.4	0.2	0.3	0.3	0.4	0.3	0.2	0.3

Selected Financial Factors (in Percentages)

Debt Ratio 45	54.3	•	69.1	•	61.9	101.9	76.6	58.6	60.8	56.3	54.5	62.9	48.5
Return on Total Assets 46	7.5	•	•	•	8.5	5.7	9.0	11.0	9.1	9.5	7.7	5.2	7.8
Return on Equity Before Income Taxes 47	11.1	•	•	•	15.4	•	25.3	19.7	15.5	16.3	13.3	5.5	11.0
Return on Equity After Income Taxes 48	7.6	•	•	•	14.7	•	24.8	15.2	14.0	13.8	9.4	3.8	6.9
Profit Margin (Before Income Tax) 49	5.4	•	•	•	2.2	1.3	3.0	5.7	3.8	4.0	4.3	1.7	10.5
Profit Margin (After Income Tax) 50	3.7	•	•	•	2.1	1.3	3.0	4.4	3.5	3.4	3.0	1.2	6.6

Table II
Corporations with Net Income

FRUIT AND VEGETABLE PRESERVING AND SPECIALTY FOOD

MONEY AMOUNTS AND SIZE OF ASSETS IN THOUSANDS OF DOLLARS

Item Description for Accounting Period 7/07 Through 6/08	Total	Zero Assets	Under 500	500 to 1,000	1,000 to 5,000	5,000 to 10,000	10,000 to 25,000	25,000 to 50,000	50,000 to 100,000	100,000 to 250,000	250,000 to 500,000	500,000 to 2,500,000	2,500,000 and over
Number of Enterprises **1**	353	3	0	•	184	35	55	21	19	•	6	•	•
Revenues ($ in Thousands)													
Net Sales **2**	37980559	309613	0	•	1277650	839666	1798365	1061989	2095074	•	2889265	•	•
Interest **3**	130225	738	0	•	453	0	729	2649	1427	•	5340	•	•
Rents **4**	23196	1817	0	•	1399	0	4	443	670	•	5430	•	•
Royalties **5**	268261	0	0	•	0	0	0	0	0	•	0	•	•
Other Portfolio Income **6**	658488	34	0	•	0	0	14022	32573	676	•	47097	•	•
Other Receipts **7**	665240	5198	0	•	175	2467	2828	20043	20913	•	36509	•	•
Total Receipts **8**	39725969	317400	0	•	1279677	842133	1815948	1117697	2118760	•	2983641	•	•
Average Total Receipts **9**	112538	105800	•	•	6955	24061	33017	53224	111514	•	497274	•	•
Operating Costs/Operating Income (%)													
Cost of Operations **10**	66.5	84.7	•	•	80.5	74.1	71.5	75.8	78.1	•	73.9	•	•
Salaries and Wages **11**	4.9	1.2	•	•	2.0	2.7	6.1	4.0	3.0	•	3.8	•	•
Taxes Paid **12**	1.3	4.5	•	•	2.5	1.3	1.1	1.3	1.0	•	2.1	•	•
Interest Paid **13**	2.3	1.9	•	•	1.0	0.6	1.3	1.6	1.5	•	1.1	•	•
Depreciation **14**	2.3	1.9	•	•	1.7	1.2	1.5	2.3	1.9	•	3.6	•	•
Amortization and Depletion **15**	1.0	0.1	•	•	0.5	0.1	0.1	0.4	0.1	•	0.3	•	•
Pensions and Other Deferred Comp. **16**	0.5	0.0	•	•	0.2	•	0.1	0.3	0.4	•	0.1	•	•
Employee Benefits **17**	1.4	0.2	•	•	0.6	2.1	0.9	0.6	1.2	•	1.3	•	•
Advertising **18**	2.8	0.2	•	•	0.2	•	2.4	1.0	0.6	•	2.1	•	•
Other Expenses **19**	14.5	3.9	•	•	4.0	12.0	8.6	6.4	6.4	•	9.8	•	•
Officers' Compensation **20**	0.8	0.3	•	•	4.0	•	1.0	1.2	1.0	•	0.6	•	•
Operating Margin **21**	1.7	1.1	•	•	2.9	5.9	5.3	4.9	4.7	•	1.1	•	•
Operating Margin Before Officers' Comp. **22**	2.5	1.4	•	•	6.9	5.9	6.3	6.1	5.7	•	1.7	•	•

Selected Average Balance Sheet ($ in Thousands)

Net Receivables 23	9135	0	559	2659	2750	6546	10918	39747
Inventories 24	15518	0	363	1694	6629	8425	28566	64380
Net Property, Plant and Equipment 25	19527	0	1052	1747	3098	8394	18920	135897
Total Assets 26	118836		2699	7553	15669	31294	70630	341284
Notes and Loans Payable 27	33239	0	1110	3993	5076	9223	23949	82351
All Other Liabilities 28	27562	0	499	2330	6388	6791	17121	103651
Net Worth 29	58035	0	1090	1230	4205	15279	29559	155282

Selected Financial Ratios (Times to 1)

Current Ratio 30	1.4		1.7	1.3	1.4	2.4	1.6	1.6
Quick Ratio 31	0.5		1.1	0.7	0.5	1.2	0.5	0.5
Net Sales to Working Capital 32	10.6		16.1	19.0	9.5	4.1	6.7	9.4
Coverage Ratio 33	4.1	2.9	4.2	10.7	6.0	7.5	4.8	4.8
Total Asset Turnover 34	0.9		2.6	3.2	2.1	1.6	1.6	1.4
Inventory Turnover 35	4.6		15.4	10.5	3.5	4.6	3.0	5.5
Receivables Turnover 36	10.8		17.6	15.7	11.7	8.2	9.2	15.0
Total Liabilities to Net Worth 37	1.0		1.5	5.1	2.7	1.0	1.4	1.2
Current Assets to Working Capital 38	3.2		2.5	4.3	3.3	1.7	2.7	2.7
Current Liabilities to Working Capital 39	2.2		1.5	3.3	2.3	0.7	1.7	1.7
Working Capital to Net Sales 40	0.1		0.1	0.1	0.1	0.2	0.1	0.1
Inventory to Working Capital 41	1.7		0.8	1.8	2.0	0.8	1.7	1.5
Total Receipts to Cash Flow 42	5.4	17.6	17.1	6.4	7.7	8.3	9.4	8.7
Cost of Goods to Cash Flow 43	3.6	14.9	13.8	4.7	5.5	6.3	7.3	6.4
Cash Flow to Total Debt 44	0.3		0.3	0.6	0.4	0.4	0.3	0.3

Selected Financial Factors (in Percentages)

Debt Ratio 45	51.2		59.6	83.7	73.2	51.2	58.1	54.5
Return on Total Assets 46	8.5		10.3	21.8	15.7	18.9	11.4	7.7
Return on Equity Before Income Taxes 47	13.2		19.5	121.6	48.9	33.5	21.5	13.3
Return on Equity After Income Taxes 48	9.5		18.8	121.6	48.3	27.6	19.6	9.4
Profit Margin (Before Income Tax) 49	7.1	3.6	3.1	6.2	6.3	10.1	5.8	4.3
Profit Margin (After Income Tax) 50	5.2	2.8	3.0	6.2	6.2	8.3	5.2	3.0

Table I

Corporations with and without Net Income

DAIRY PRODUCT

MONEY AMOUNTS AND SIZE OF ASSETS IN THOUSANDS OF DOLLARS

Item Description for Accounting Period 7/07 Through 6/08	Total	Zero Assets	Under 500	500 to 1,000	1,000 to 5,000	5,000 to 10,000	10,000 to 25,000	25,000 to 50,000	50,000 to 100,000	100,000 to 250,000	250,000 to 500,000	500,000 to 2,500,000	2,500,000 and over
Number of Enterprises 1	929	0	620	0	165	36	45	21	18	11	7	6	0
Revenues ($ in Thousands)													
Net Sales 2	39707573	0	306108	0	2368585	747421	2355488	2049072	2632185	3808833	4655335	20784547	0
Interest 3	46928	0	15	0	890	1125	1825	989	5951	11518	15168	9448	0
Rents 4	16873	0	0	0	0	102	826	137	505	948	111	14243	0
Royalties 5	74374	0	0	0	0	0	0	0	3482	0	32288	38604	0
Other Portfolio Income 6	25016	0	1226	0	141	330	7163	3475	1969	1356	1105	8252	0
Other Receipts 7	162502	0	13	0	13606	539	9411	30488	7083	11190	42793	47376	0
Total Receipts 8	40033266	0	307362	0	2383222	749517	2374713	2084161	2651175	3833845	4746800	20902470	0
Average Total Receipts 9	43093	•	496	•	14444	20820	52771	99246	147288	348531	678114	3483745	•
Operating Costs/Operating Income (%)													
Cost of Operations 10	80.3	•	50.4	•	88.4	84.2	80.5	78.3	81.4	82.3	82.1	79.0	•
Salaries and Wages 11	4.1	•	6.6	•	2.2	3.2	4.6	6.1	5.2	3.2	3.4	4.3	•
Taxes Paid 12	1.0	•	4.5	•	1.0	1.3	1.2	1.3	1.0	0.8	0.8	1.0	•
Interest Paid 13	1.5	•	0.4	•	0.5	1.0	1.1	0.5	0.9	0.3	1.7	2.1	•
Depreciation 14	1.9	•	1.4	•	0.8	1.3	1.9	1.7	2.0	1.8	1.7	2.0	•
Amortization and Depletion 15	0.4	•	•	•	0.0	0.1	0.0	0.0	0.1	0.0	0.5	0.7	•
Pensions and Other Deferred Comp. 16	0.4	•	0.8	•	0.2	0.1	0.3	0.5	0.3	0.4	0.3	0.4	•
Employee Benefits 17	0.8	•	1.1	•	0.7	0.9	0.6	1.1	1.0	1.0	0.9	0.7	•
Advertising 18	1.2	•	8.4	•	0.1	1.1	0.6	0.5	0.7	0.9	1.5	1.4	•
Other Expenses 19	6.6	•	27.6	•	2.7	5.7	6.0	7.9	5.4	5.1	8.5	6.6	•
Officers' Compensation 20	0.4	•	2.4	•	0.7	1.2	1.2	0.9	0.6	0.5	0.2	0.2	•
Operating Margin 21	1.5	•	•	•	2.9	•	2.2	1.2	1.4	3.7	•	1.7	•
Operating Margin Before Officers' Comp. 22	1.9	•	•	•	3.5	1.2	3.4	2.1	2.0	4.2	•	1.9	•

Selected Average Balance Sheet ($ in Thousands)

Item										
Net Receivables 23	3324	•	928	1441	4096	8239	12876	24608	58252	269052
Inventories 24	2455	5	560	2335	4179	4776	12566	24680	42106	170019
Net Property, Plant and Equipment 25	6863	36	774	2467	6705	12991	23359	47171	107400	645146
Total Assets 26	21757	75	2838	6585	16723	35688	70474	154507	355019	2084221
Notes and Loans Payable 27	10477	53	818	2255	6863	8755	19186	43115	179310	1152802
All Other Liabilities 28	6283	24	1024	1605	4307	9551	18873	35214	102112	626518
Net Worth 29	4997	-2	997	2726	5553	17382	32415	76178	73597	304900

Selected Financial Ratios (Times to 1)

Item										
Current Ratio 30	1.6	0.6	1.3	2.0	2.0	1.5	1.7	1.8	1.2	1.6
Quick Ratio 31	0.8	0.3	0.8	1.2	1.0	0.8	0.8	0.9	0.7	0.7
Net Sales to Working Capital 32	14.5	•	30.2	10.3	10.6	16.1	9.9	10.9	37.8	13.7
Coverage Ratio 33	2.5	•	7.9	1.2	3.7	6.2	3.3	15.2	1.4	2.0
Total Asset Turnover 34	2.0	6.5	5.1	3.2	3.1	2.7	2.1	2.2	1.9	1.7
Inventory Turnover 35	14.0	45.3	22.7	7.5	10.1	16.0	9.5	11.5	13.0	16.1
Receivables Turnover 36	14.4	110.0	20.6	7.3	15.5	11.5	12.1	18.2	13.0	14.6
Total Liabilities to Net Worth 37	3.4	•	1.8	1.4	2.0	1.1	1.2	1.0	3.8	5.8
Current Assets to Working Capital 38	2.8	•	3.9	2.0	2.0	3.0	2.4	2.3	7.0	2.6
Current Liabilities to Working Capital 39	1.8	•	2.9	1.0	1.0	2.0	1.4	1.3	6.0	1.6
Working Capital to Net Sales 40	0.1	•	0.0	0.1	0.1	0.1	0.1	0.1	0.0	0.1
Inventory to Working Capital 41	0.9	•	1.5	0.7	0.8	0.9	0.9	1.0	2.7	0.7
Total Receipts to Cash Flow 42	13.8	24.8	19.9	20.4	13.2	10.9	15.9	11.4	13.1	14.0
Cost of Goods to Cash Flow 43	11.1	12.5	17.6	17.2	10.6	8.5	13.0	9.4	10.7	11.1
Cash Flow to Total Debt 44	0.2	0.3	0.4	0.3	0.4	0.5	0.2	0.4	0.2	0.1

Selected Financial Factors (in Percentages)

Item										
Debt Ratio 45	77.0	102.5	64.9	58.6	66.8	51.3	54.0	50.7	79.3	85.4
Return on Total Assets 46	7.6	•	20.2	3.9	13.0	9.2	6.1	10.5	4.3	7.2
Return on Equity Before Income Taxes 47	19.7	826.1	50.3	1.8	28.4	15.8	9.3	19.9	5.7	25.3
Return on Equity After Income Taxes 48	16.7	826.1	49.7	•	24.5	14.1	7.2	18.5	5.4	20.3
Profit Margin (Before Income Tax) 49	2.3	3.5	3.0	0.2	3.0	2.8	2.1	4.4	0.6	2.2
Profit Margin (After Income Tax) 50	2.0	3.4	•	0.2	2.6	2.5	1.6	4.1	0.6	1.8

43

Table II

Corporations with Net Income

DAIRY PRODUCT

MONEY AMOUNTS AND SIZE OF ASSETS IN THOUSANDS OF DOLLARS

Item Description for Accounting Period 7/07 Through 6/08	Total	Zero Assets	Under 500	500 to 1,000	1,000 to 5,000	5,000 to 10,000	10,000 to 25,000	25,000 to 50,000	50,000 to 100,000	100,000 to 250,000	250,000 to 500,000	500,000 to 2,500,000	2,500,000 and over
Number of Enterprises 1	614	0	375	0	120	•	40	15	15	•	0	6	0

Revenues ($ in Thousands)

Net Sales 2	34597372	0	190199	0	1738045	•	2037757	1334882	2060803	•	0	20784547	0
Interest 3	29958	0	0	0	643	•	903	459	4637	•	0	9448	0
Rents 4	16092	0	0	0	0	•	535	91	172	•	0	14243	0
Royalties 5	42086	0	0	0	0	•	0	0	3482	•	0	38604	0
Other Portfolio Income 6	21623	0	0	0	9	•	7119	2733	1824	•	0	8252	0
Other Receipts 7	131307	0	0	0	12478	•	9267	29648	6528	•	0	47376	0
Total Receipts 8	34838438	0	190199	0	1751175	•	2055581	1367813	2077446	•	0	20902470	0
Average Total Receipts 9	56740	•	507	•	14593	•	51390	91188	138496	•	•	3483745	•

Operating Costs/Operating Income (%)

Cost of Operations 10	80.7	•	51.7	•	87.5	•	81.8	80.9	81.2	•	•	79.0	•
Salaries and Wages 11	3.8	•	•	•	1.9	•	3.4	4.8	4.3	•	•	4.3	•
Taxes Paid 12	0.9	•	2.6	•	0.7	•	1.0	1.2	1.0	•	•	1.0	•
Interest Paid 13	1.5	•	•	•	0.3	•	1.3	0.4	0.9	•	•	2.1	•
Depreciation 14	1.8	•	1.1	•	0.6	•	1.9	1.3	2.0	•	•	2.0	•
Amortization and Depletion 15	0.4	•	•	•	•	•	0.0	0.1	0.1	•	•	0.7	•
Pensions and Other Deferred Comp. 16	0.4	•	•	•	0.3	•	0.1	0.4	0.2	•	•	0.4	•
Employee Benefits 17	0.7	•	0.9	•	0.8	•	0.4	0.8	0.8	•	•	0.7	•
Advertising 18	1.1	•	11.8	•	0.0	•	0.4	0.4	0.8	•	•	1.4	•
Other Expenses 19	6.0	•	31.7	•	2.0	•	5.2	6.1	6.0	•	•	6.6	•
Officers' Compensation 20	0.4	•	•	•	0.2	•	1.2	1.1	0.5	•	•	0.2	•
Operating Margin 21	2.3	•	0.2	•	5.7	•	3.3	2.5	2.1	•	•	1.7	•
Operating Margin Before Officers' Comp. 22	2.7	•	0.2	•	5.9	•	4.5	3.6	2.7	•	•	1.9	•

Selected Average Balance Sheet ($ in Thousands)

Net Receivables 23	4361	0	840	3955	7844	12399	269052
Inventories 24	2948	0	560	4308	5341	14511	179407
Net Property, Plant and Equipment 25	9006	32	531	6412	9001	22882	645146
Total Assets 26	28380	35	2449	16144	33794	71022	2084221
Notes and Loans Payable 27	13501	24	399	7555	8272	18425	1152802
All Other Liabilities 28	8339	11	989	4170	7108	17827	626518
Net Worth 29	6540	0	1061	4419	18414	34770	304900

Selected Financial Ratios (Times to 1)

Current Ratio 30	1.7	0.3	1.4	2.1	1.6	2.1	1.6
Quick Ratio 31	0.8	0.3	0.8	1.0	0.7	1.0	0.7
Net Sales to Working Capital 32	12.6	•	28.3	10.3	12.5	7.3	13.7
Coverage Ratio 33	2.9	•	22.1	4.2	13.8	4.3	2.0
Total Asset Turnover 34	2.0	14.4	5.9	3.2	2.6	1.9	1.7
Inventory Turnover 35	15.4	•	22.6	9.7	13.5	7.7	15.3
Receivables Turnover 36	15.3	•	22.1	15.7	10.9	•	•
Total Liabilities to Net Worth 37	3.3	346.5	1.3	2.7	0.8	1.0	5.8
Current Assets to Working Capital 38	2.4	•	3.3	1.9	2.7	1.9	2.6
Current Liabilities to Working Capital 39	1.4	•	2.3	0.9	1.7	0.9	1.6
Working Capital to Net Sales 40	0.1	•	0.0	0.1	0.1	0.1	0.1
Inventory to Working Capital 41	0.8	•	1.3	0.9	0.9	0.8	0.7
Total Receipts to Cash Flow 42	13.4	43.6	13.4	12.5	10.7	12.5	14.0
Cost of Goods to Cash Flow 43	10.8	22.5	11.7	10.2	8.7	10.1	11.1
Cash Flow to Total Debt 44	0.2	0.3	0.8	0.3	0.5	0.3	0.1

Selected Financial Factors (in Percentages)

Debt Ratio 45	77.0	99.7	56.7	72.6	45.5	51.0	85.4
Return on Total Assets 46	9.0	3.4	39.8	17.1	13.8	7.3	7.2
Return on Equity Before Income Taxes 47	25.9	1171.1	87.8	47.8	23.6	11.4	25.3
Return on Equity After Income Taxes 48	22.4	1171.1	87.0	42.4	21.4	9.0	20.3
Profit Margin (Before Income Tax) 49	3.0	0.2	6.4	4.1	4.9	2.9	2.2
Profit Margin (After Income Tax) 50	2.6	0.2	6.4	3.7	4.4	2.3	1.8

Table I

Corporations with and without Net Income

MEAT AND SEAFOOD PROCESSING

MONEY AMOUNTS AND SIZE OF ASSETS IN THOUSANDS OF DOLLARS

Item Description for Accounting Period 7/07 Through 6/08	Total	Zero Assets	Under 500	500 to 1,000	1,000 to 5,000	5,000 to 10,000	10,000 to 25,000	25,000 to 50,000	50,000 to 100,000	100,000 to 250,000	250,000 to 500,000	500,000 to 2,500,000	2,500,000 and over
Number of Enterprises 1	2731	393	1584	110	292	101	114	51	34	33	8	8	3
Revenues ($ in Thousands)													
Net Sales 2	104468858	768741	597087	193989	4146218	1623519	6532911	6212209	6302470	12993603	5066724	15390309	44641079
Interest 3	147571	2624	114	531	1065	1087	2290	3329	1022	36078	969	39738	58723
Rents 4	35721	1722	0	288	666	273	958	823	49	3190	871	2664	24216
Royalties 5	30921	0	0	0	0	0	0	0	0	228	0	26496	4197
Other Portfolio Income 6	214822	8586	61	2290	9284	1625	1324	3525	2352	46241	9166	35823	94547
Other Receipts 7	493929	9108	679	34	6248	5647	24793	20263	29975	78554	19142	165124	134361
Total Receipts 8	105391822	790781	597941	197132	4163481	1632151	6562276	6240149	6335868	13157894	5096872	15660154	44957123
Average Total Receipts 9	38591	2012	377	1792	14258	16160	57564	122356	186349	398724	637109	1957519	14985708
Operating Costs/Operating Income (%)													
Cost of Operations 10	85.2	78.8	58.6	69.5	77.0	81.4	84.7	85.6	83.4	83.7	85.5	84.4	87.6
Salaries and Wages 11	3.1	7.9	15.7	5.5	2.7	2.8	3.1	3.5	3.0	2.9	2.6	5.0	2.3
Taxes Paid 12	0.8	1.3	2.8	3.0	1.3	1.9	0.9	1.0	0.8	0.8	1.0	0.4	0.6
Interest Paid 13	0.9	1.0	0.8	0.1	0.6	0.9	0.7	0.7	0.7	0.9	1.5	0.9	1.0
Depreciation 14	1.7	0.9	2.4	1.3	1.4	3.1	1.1	1.4	1.8	1.9	1.7	1.4	1.7
Amortization and Depletion 15	*	*	0.5	*	0.0	0.2	0.1	0.1	0.0	0.2	0.4	0.1	*
Pensions and Other Deferred Comp. 16	0.3	0.0	0.1	0.1	0.1	0.2	0.1	0.2	0.1	0.2	0.2	0.3	0.5
Employee Benefits 17	0.8	0.5	0.8	0.6	0.6	0.6	0.8	0.4	0.9	0.8	1.2	1.7	0.5
Advertising 18	0.6	0.7	0.7	3.6	0.1	0.2	0.7	0.6	2.1	0.7	0.3	0.5	0.5
Other Expenses 19	5.3	10.7	20.1	12.1	9.5	7.2	4.7	4.8	4.9	5.3	4.1	7.1	4.2
Officers' Compensation 20	0.6	1.3	3.7	4.6	4.8	2.3	1.3	0.6	0.5	0.3	0.6	0.3	0.2
Operating Margin 21	0.8	*	*	*	1.9	*	1.8	1.0	1.7	2.2	0.9	*	1.1
Operating Margin Before Officers' Comp. 22	1.4	*	*	4.1	6.7	1.7	3.1	1.6	2.2	2.5	1.5	1.1	1.3

Selected Average Balance Sheet ($ in Thousands)

Net Receivables 23	2399	0	19	97	722	919	3704	7219	13696	26352	50802	143534	842634
Inventories 24	3475	0	0	94	168	813	2926	8197	17358	34999	79109	221532	1482118
Net Property, Plant and Equipment 25	5331	0	25	92	1112	2930	5015	12759	26855	62471	108446	271486	2216887
Total Assets 26	17329	0	132	751	3162	6540	15980	35938	73023	167726	342874	1202710	7137570
Notes and Loans Payable 27	5610	0	138	5	2473	3058	6124	13667	21390	50912	173346	347457	2033568
All Other Liabilities 28	4794	0	8	24	1060	1036	2990	9722	17078	48286	98056	273958	2224925
Net Worth 29	6926	0	-14	722	-371	2446	6866	12549	34555	68528	71471	581295	2879076

Selected Financial Ratios (Times to 1)

Current Ratio 30	1.6	•	2.3	9.1	1.2	1.5	2.0	1.4	1.5	1.4	1.2	1.7	
Quick Ratio 31	0.6	•	2.2	5.8	0.8	0.9	1.2	0.7	0.6	0.5	0.5	0.4	
Net Sales to Working Capital 32	13.2	•	18.6	8.9	65.3	16.5	12.6	21.6	15.5	17.2	26.8	6.6	13.8
Coverage Ratio 33	2.8	0.9	•	12.2	5.2	0.9	4.2	3.1	4.0	4.7	2.0	0.6	2.8
Total Asset Turnover 34	2.2	•	2.8	2.3	4.5	2.5	3.6	3.4	2.5	2.3	1.8	1.6	2.1
Inventory Turnover 35	9.4	•	513.3	13.0	65.2	16.1	16.6	12.7	8.9	9.4	6.8	7.3	8.8
Receivables Turnover 36	17.1	•	18.5	15.7	29.4	9.7	15.1	15.7	13.2	16.1	12.4	16.3	19.4
Total Liabilities to Net Worth 37	1.5	•	•	0.0	•	1.7	1.3	1.9	1.1	1.4	3.8	1.1	1.5
Current Assets to Working Capital 38	2.7	•	1.8	1.1	6.1	2.9	2.0	3.5	3.0	3.4	6.3	2.4	2.5
Current Liabilities to Working Capital 39	1.7	•	0.8	0.1	5.1	1.9	1.0	2.5	2.0	2.4	5.3	1.4	1.5
Working Capital to Net Sales 40	0.1	•	0.1	0.1	0.0	0.1	0.1	0.0	0.1	0.1	0.0	0.2	0.1
Inventory to Working Capital 41	1.3	•	0.0	0.4	1.1	0.6	0.6	1.4	1.5	1.7	3.4	0.8	1.5
Total Receipts to Cash Flow 42	17.0	11.2	15.3	12.1	11.1	19.3	17.4	19.4	15.6	13.1	19.9	19.6	18.4
Cost of Goods to Cash Flow 43	14.5	8.8	9.0	8.4	8.6	15.7	14.7	16.6	13.0	11.0	17.0	16.5	16.1
Cash Flow to Total Debt 44	0.2	•	0.2	5.0	0.4	0.2	0.4	0.3	0.3	0.3	0.1	0.2	0.2

Selected Financial Factors (in Percentages)

Debt Ratio 45	60.0	•	110.4	3.9	111.7	62.6	57.0	65.1	52.7	59.1	79.2	51.7	59.7
Return on Total Assets 46	5.8	•	•	2.4	12.9	1.9	10.6	7.9	7.5	10.3	5.4	0.8	6.1
Return on Equity Before Income Taxes 47	9.3	•	165.2	2.2	•	•	18.7	15.3	11.9	19.9	13.2	•	9.8
Return on Equity After Income Taxes 48	6.7	•	166.6	2.0	•	•	16.9	14.1	11.5	17.4	9.5	•	6.5
Profit Margin (Before Income Tax) 49	1.7	•	•	0.9	2.3	•	2.2	1.6	2.2	3.5	1.5	•	1.9
Profit Margin (After Income Tax) 50	1.2	•	•	0.8	2.2	•	2.0	1.5	2.1	3.0	1.1	•	1.3

45

Table II

Corporations with Net Income

MEAT AND SEAFOOD PROCESSING

MONEY AMOUNTS AND SIZE OF ASSETS IN THOUSANDS OF DOLLARS

Item Description for Accounting Period 7/07 Through 6/08		Total	Zero Assets	Under 500	500 to 1,000	1,000 to 5,000	5,000 to 10,000	10,000 to 25,000	25,000 to 50,000	50,000 to 100,000	100,000 to 250,000	250,000 to 500,000	500,000 to 2,500,000	2,500,000 and over
Number of Enterprises	1	1014	7	397	•	229	71	96	39	26	25	•	4	3
Revenues ($ in Thousands)														
Net Sales	2	80652352	399509	317615	•	2485672	956002	5342490	4904533	4008955	10865986	•	3672687	44641079
Interest	3	116381	2201	29	•	1064	513	2184	2866	658	29869	•	17291	58723
Rents	4	32723	0	0	•	666	66	875	594	32	3138	•	1977	24216
Royalties	5	4517	0	0	•	0	0	0	0	0	228	•	91	4197
Other Portfolio Income	6	193459	8565	0	•	9281	8	1307	2253	2235	45519	•	24485	94547
Other Receipts	7	439048	3183	658	•	6296	2527	24115	12336	27535	76101	•	123866	134361
Total Receipts	8	81438480	413458	318302	•	2502979	959116	5370971	4922582	4039415	11020841	•	3840397	44957123
Average Total Receipts	9	80314	59065	802	•	10930	13509	55948	126220	155362	440834	•	960099	14985708
Operating Costs/Operating Income (%)														
Cost of Operations	10	84.8	85.4	54.3	•	74.3	80.8	83.1	85.5	79.2	83.1	•	79.2	87.6
Salaries and Wages	11	2.6	3.9	22.4	•	3.0	2.4	3.4	2.6	3.0	3.0	•	2.2	2.3
Taxes Paid	12	0.8	1.0	2.5	•	1.5	1.3	0.9	1.0	0.7	0.8	•	1.2	0.6
Interest Paid	13	0.9	0.8	0.7	•	0.8	1.0	0.7	0.4	0.7	0.7	•	0.9	1.0
Depreciation	14	1.8	0.8	1.6	•	2.1	3.2	1.0	1.3	2.0	2.0	•	2.8	1.7
Amortization and Depletion	15	•	•	0.8	•	0.0	0.2	0.1	0.0	0.0	0.1	•	0.0	•
Pensions and Other Deferred Comp.	16	0.3	0.0	•	•	0.1	0.1	0.1	0.2	0.2	0.2	•	0.6	0.5
Employee Benefits	17	0.7	0.6	0.0	•	1.0	0.3	0.9	0.5	1.1	0.7	•	1.8	0.5
Advertising	18	0.7	0.7	1.1	•	0.1	0.1	0.9	0.7	3.0	0.8	•	0.1	0.5
Other Expenses	19	4.9	3.8	13.3	•	7.5	5.5	4.7	4.3	5.5	5.2	•	9.4	4.2
Officers' Compensation	20	0.6	2.4	0.0	•	4.2	2.1	1.5	0.6	0.7	0.3	•	0.8	0.2
Operating Margin	21	2.0	0.6	3.2	•	5.3	3.1	2.7	2.8	3.8	3.1	•	1.2	1.1
Operating Margin Before Officers' Comp.	22	2.6	3.0	3.2	•	9.6	5.1	4.2	3.4	4.5	3.4	•	2.0	1.3

Selected Average Balance Sheet ($ in Thousands)

Net Receivables 23	4855	0	6	596	659	3494	7716	12855	27753	58821	842634
Inventories 24	6137	0	0	122	870	2765	7624	16760	35805	363181	1601895
Net Property, Plant and Equipment 25	11982	0	35	1219	2736	5039	12591	25863	70243	257368	2216887
Total Assets 26	36618	0	352	3032	5936	15840	37430	72790	173796	813578	7137570
Notes and Loans Payable 27	10819	0	291	2691	2967	5318	11533	18008	47017	141543	2033568
All Other Liabilities 28	10567	0	24	841	938	2857	8608	14968	50765	221678	2224925
Net Worth 29	15232	0	36	-500	2031	7664	17289	39814	76015	450357	2879076

Selected Financial Ratios (Times to 1)

Current Ratio 30	1.6	•	1.7	1.3	1.4	2.2	1.5	1.7	1.5	1.5	1.7
Quick Ratio 31	0.6	•	1.7	0.9	1.0	1.2	0.8	0.7	0.7	0.5	0.5
Net Sales to Working Capital 32	14.0	•	46.9	40.3	19.6	11.4	17.3	10.3	17.2	10.6	13.8
Coverage Ratio 33	4.3	5.9	6.2	9.0	4.5	5.8	8.9	7.2	7.0	7.9	2.8
Total Asset Turnover 34	2.2	•	2.3	3.6	2.3	3.5	3.4	2.1	2.5	1.1	2.1
Inventory Turnover 35	11.0	•	948.5	65.8	12.5	16.7	14.1	7.3	10.1	2.0	8.1
Receivables Turnover 36	19.8	•	•	25.1	7.4	16.2	16.6	12.6	•	5.7	35.3
Total Liabilities to Net Worth 37	1.4	•	8.7	•	1.9	1.1	1.2	0.8	1.3	0.8	1.5
Current Assets to Working Capital 38	2.6	•	2.4	4.0	3.5	1.8	2.9	2.4	3.1	3.0	2.5
Current Liabilities to Working Capital 39	1.6	•	1.4	3.0	2.5	0.8	1.9	1.4	2.1	2.0	1.5
Working Capital to Net Sales 40	0.1	•	0.0	0.0	0.1	0.1	0.1	0.1	0.1	0.1	0.1
Inventory to Working Capital 41	1.3	•	0.0	0.6	0.9	0.6	1.2	1.2	1.4	1.1	1.5
Total Receipts to Cash Flow 42	14.4	13.7	6.9	9.4	13.6	15.0	15.2	10.8	11.7	7.2	18.4
Cost of Goods to Cash Flow 43	12.2	11.7	3.7	7.0	11.0	12.4	13.0	8.5	9.7	5.7	16.1
Cash Flow to Total Debt 44	0.3	•	0.4	0.3	0.3	0.5	0.4	0.4	0.4	0.3	0.2

Selected Financial Factors (in Percentages)

Debt Ratio 45	58.4	•	89.6	116.5	65.8	51.6	53.8	45.3	56.3	44.6	59.7
Return on Total Assets 46	8.5	•	9.3	24.2	9.8	13.6	12.5	11.3	13.1	7.7	6.1
Return on Equity Before Income Taxes 47	15.6	•	75.2	•	22.4	23.4	24.1	17.8	25.6	12.1	9.8
Return on Equity After Income Taxes 48	12.7	•	72.9	•	22.0	21.4	23.0	17.4	22.7	8.3	6.5
Profit Margin (Before Income Tax) 49	3.0	4.1	6.0	3.4	3.4	3.2	3.3	4.6	4.5	5.9	1.9
Profit Margin (After Income Tax) 50	2.4	3.7	5.8	3.3	3.3	2.9	3.2	4.5	4.0	4.0	1.3

Table I

Corporations with and without Net Income

BAKERIES AND TORTILLA

MONEY AMOUNTS AND SIZE OF ASSETS IN THOUSANDS OF DOLLARS

Item Description for Accounting Period 7/07 Through 6/08	Total	Zero Assets	Under 500	500 to 1,000	1,000 to 5,000	5,000 to 10,000	10,000 to 25,000	25,000 to 50,000	50,000 to 100,000	100,000 to 250,000	250,000 to 500,000	500,000 to 2,500,000	2,500,000 and over
Number of Enterprises **1**	4587	307	3805	30	180	83	107	25	23	9	8	10	0
Revenues ($ in Thousands)													
Net Sales **2**	39661995	305835	1065370	112904	753091	1152778	3377232	1717000	3160732	2056622	4636142	21324290	0
Interest **3**	79643	0	6	16	239	256	2069	806	1342	8422	7234	59254	0
Rents **4**	14045	0	1095	1697	67	0	0	201	4802	199	69	5916	0
Royalties **5**	40069	0	0	0	0	0	0	0	0	22778	5963	11328	0
Other Portfolio Income **6**	1488574	17783	40720	0	9689	250	5006	393	3104	763	16414	1394450	0
Other Receipts **7**	178821	11719	4781	193	10069	1176	16644	4350	22748	-13598	-19257	139996	0
Total Receipts **8**	41463147	335337	1111972	114810	773155	1154460	3400951	1722750	3192728	2075186	4646565	22935234	0
Average Total Receipts **9**	9039	1092	292	3827	4295	13909	31785	68910	138814	230576	580821	2293523	•
Operating Costs/Operating Income (%)													
Cost of Operations **10**	63.0	67.5	44.7	73.6	50.7	79.5	71.5	68.0	60.2	68.1	68.9	60.2	•
Salaries and Wages **11**	8.6	11.6	15.3	4.0	11.6	2.4	5.5	6.6	12.8	5.9	7.9	8.8	•
Taxes Paid **12**	2.0	1.0	3.7	2.9	3.5	1.3	1.9	1.7	2.1	2.2	1.5	2.1	•
Interest Paid **13**	2.2	0.9	1.9	1.4	0.5	1.2	0.8	2.0	0.8	2.6	2.0	2.9	•
Depreciation **14**	2.9	7.8	2.2	0.1	2.3	3.9	2.7	3.6	3.1	3.3	2.5	2.9	•
Amortization and Depletion **15**	0.7	•	0.4	•	0.1	0.0	0.1	0.7	0.1	0.8	1.1	0.8	•
Pensions and Other Deferred Comp. **16**	1.3	0.1	0.0	0.8	0.3	0.2	0.2	0.3	2.1	0.3	0.4	1.9	•
Employee Benefits **17**	3.2	0.1	0.6	0.3	0.9	1.5	1.1	0.9	3.7	2.6	1.5	4.4	•
Advertising **18**	1.8	0.9	2.3	0.9	1.3	0.1	0.6	0.6	1.0	1.6	1.6	2.3	•
Other Expenses **19**	14.4	22.0	27.0	14.8	15.6	11.4	9.6	13.7	9.5	15.5	9.5	16.2	•
Officers' Compensation **20**	1.0	0.8	8.2	2.8	6.1	1.2	2.0	2.1	1.2	1.1	0.5	0.3	•
Operating Margin **21**	•	•	•	•	7.3	•	3.9	•	3.3	•	2.7	•	•
Operating Margin Before Officers' Comp. **22**	•	•	1.8	1.1	13.3	•	6.0	1.9	4.5	•	3.1	•	•

Selected Average Balance Sheet ($ in Thousands)

Net Receivables 23	706	0	15	146	195	1000	2798	5899	11015	21807	79593	152521	•
Inventories 24	813	0	9	193	163	466	1550	3439	6051	15069	36117	280731	•
Net Property, Plant and Equipment 25	2004	0	36	683	792	3069	7168	18184	33905	65080	109942	517075	•
Total Assets 26	6224	0	96	941	2255	5654	14995	37810	71425	160647	398612	1845240	•
Notes and Loans Payable 27	1893	0	75	108	301	2960	5510	20828	18610	39956	90728	547275	•
All Other Liabilities 28	2054	0	21	200	338	2533	3131	9119	18809	58382	115392	662274	•
Net Worth 29	2277	0	1	632	1616	161	6354	7864	34006	62309	192493	635692	•

Selected Financial Ratios (Times to 1)

Current Ratio 30	0.9	•	1.6	1.1	3.4	0.9	1.4	1.0	1.4	1.1	1.5	0.6	•
Quick Ratio 31	0.5	•	1.3	0.7	1.5	0.6	0.9	0.6	0.9	0.6	1.0	0.3	•
Net Sales to Working Capital 32	•	•	14.5	270.1	4.5	•	19.0	3121.8	21.6	62.5	11.7	•	•
Coverage Ratio 33	3.0	•	1.0	19.7	•	•	6.6	1.1	6.3	•	2.5	3.3	•
Total Asset Turnover 34	1.4	•	2.9	4.0	1.9	2.5	2.1	1.8	1.9	1.4	1.5	1.2	•
Inventory Turnover 35	6.7	•	14.0	14.4	13.0	23.7	14.6	13.6	13.7	10.3	11.1	4.6	•
Receivables Turnover 36	7.8	•	22.5	19.1	20.4	20.0	11.3	12.2	11.9	8.8	8.8	6.1	•
Total Liabilities to Net Worth 37	1.7	•	103.2	0.5	0.4	34.1	1.4	3.8	1.1	1.6	1.1	1.9	•
Current Assets to Working Capital 38	•	•	2.5	17.9	1.4	•	3.7	570.9	3.8	13.0	3.1	•	•
Current Liabilities to Working Capital 39	•	•	1.5	16.9	0.4	•	2.7	569.9	2.8	12.0	2.1	•	•
Working Capital to Net Sales 40	•	•	0.1	0.0	0.2	•	0.1	0.0	0.0	0.0	0.1	•	•
Inventory to Working Capital 41	•	•	0.5	5.0	0.2	•	0.9	178.7	1.0	4.3	0.8	•	•
Total Receipts to Cash Flow 42	6.9	6.9	9.0	10.2	4.8	16.8	8.1	8.5	9.1	12.4	9.5	5.7	•
Cost of Goods to Cash Flow 43	4.3	4.7	4.0	7.5	2.4	13.4	5.8	5.8	5.5	8.5	6.6	3.4	•
Cash Flow to Total Debt 44	0.3	•	0.3	1.2	1.4	0.2	0.5	0.3	0.4	0.2	0.3	0.3	•

Selected Financial Factors (in Percentages)

Debt Ratio 45	63.4	•	99.0	32.8	28.3	97.1	57.6	79.2	52.4	61.2	51.7	65.5	•
Return on Total Assets 46	9.4	•	•	5.7	19.4	•	11.5	3.9	9.8	•	7.0	11.0	•
Return on Equity Before Income Taxes 47	17.2	•	•	•	25.7	•	22.9	1.3	17.3	•	8.7	22.3	•
Return on Equity After Income Taxes 48	11.2	•	•	•	24.7	•	22.0	0.8	15.5	•	6.7	13.6	•
Profit Margin (Before Income Tax) 49	4.5	•	•	9.9	9.9	•	4.6	0.1	4.3	•	2.9	6.6	•
Profit Margin (After Income Tax) 50	3.0	•	•	9.6	9.6	•	4.4	0.1	3.8	•	2.2	4.0	•

Table II

Corporations with Net Income

BAKERIES AND TORTILLA

MONEY AMOUNTS AND SIZE OF ASSETS IN THOUSANDS OF DOLLARS

Item Description for Accounting Period 7/07 Through 6/08		Total	Zero Assets	Under 500	500 to 1,000	1,000 to 5,000	5,000 to 10,000	10,000 to 25,000	25,000 to 50,000	50,000 to 100,000	100,000 to 250,000	250,000 to 500,000	500,000 to 2,500,000	2,500,000 and over
Number of Enterprises	1	1489	3	1198	•	95	40	74	12	•	4	5	7	0
Revenues ($ in Thousands)														
Net Sales	2	29220736	170408	421273	•	544962	662464	2377621	899001	•	1001223	3387373	16668026	0
Interest	3	58482	0	4	•	122	0	990	63	•	4698	4267	47427	0
Rents	4	13098	0	649	•	67	0	0	0	•	1	69	5904	0
Royalties	5	14267	0	0	•	0	0	0	0	•	0	5320	8947	0
Other Portfolio Income	6	1447343	0	40699	•	9689	0	3877	91	•	756	3491	1385633	0
Other Receipts	7	187982	11719	4591	•	3683	0	12852	4145	•	4030	-10102	134720	0
Total Receipts	8	30941908	182127	467216	•	558523	662464	2395340	903300	•	1010708	3390418	18266657	0
Average Total Receipts	9	20780	60709	390	•	5879	16562	32369	75275	•	252677	678084	2609522	•
Operating Costs/Operating Income (%)														
Cost of Operations	10	63.2	51.5	51.4	•	48.9	70.1	70.3	67.4	•	69.6	66.8	62.0	•
Salaries and Wages	11	7.5	10.5	11.4	•	9.5	2.5	5.3	7.0	•	5.0	9.3	6.8	•
Taxes Paid	12	1.8	1.7	2.6	•	2.3	0.5	1.5	1.7	•	2.1	1.8	1.8	•
Interest Paid	13	2.1	0.8	0.0	•	0.7	1.6	0.7	1.4	•	0.6	0.4	3.2	•
Depreciation	14	2.9	3.4	1.5	•	2.1	3.4	2.3	3.4	•	2.2	2.5	3.2	•
Amortization and Depletion	15	0.5	•	0.0	•	0.1	•	0.1	0.4	•	0.6	0.7	0.7	•
Pensions and Other Deferred Comp.	16	1.1	0.1	0.0	•	0.2	0.0	0.3	0.3	•	0.5	0.5	1.4	•
Employee Benefits	17	2.8	0.2	0.3	•	0.5	0.3	1.2	0.3	•	2.7	1.9	3.5	•
Advertising	18	1.8	1.7	2.2	•	1.6	0.1	0.5	0.5	•	2.0	0.6	2.5	•
Other Expenses	19	14.4	21.0	16.1	•	13.4	15.1	7.7	11.8	•	11.3	11.0	17.1	•
Officers' Compensation	20	0.9	1.4	12.8	•	3.4	1.7	2.0	1.8	•	1.0	0.4	0.4	•
Operating Margin	21	0.8	7.6	1.8	•	17.3	4.5	8.1	4.1	•	2.5	4.1	•	•
Operating Margin Before Officers' Comp.	22	1.8	9.0	14.6	•	20.7	6.3	10.2	5.9	•	3.5	4.6	•	•

Selected Average Balance Sheet ($ in Thousands)

Net Receivables 23	1656	0	11	•	273	•	887	2763	7360	•	26330	102158	177287	•
Inventories 24	2232	0	16	•	237	•	392	1538	3781	•	22790	39916	385406	•
Net Property, Plant and Equipment 25	4505	0	13	•	740	•	2660	6785	19769	•	68162	104188	605629	•
Total Assets 26	14842	0	104	•	1971	•	5700	14700	40351	•	162448	380239	2270465	•
Notes and Loans Payable 27	4336	0	13	•	455	•	3153	3785	19930	•	30616	48130	716527	•
All Other Liabilities 28	4490	0	10	•	398	•	1038	2636	8779	•	48726	138234	713419	•
Net Worth 29	6015	0	81	•	1118	•	1510	8279	11642	•	83107	193875	840519	•

Selected Financial Ratios (Times to 1)

Current Ratio 30	0.9	•	7.6	•	2.0	•	2.2	1.9	1.5	•	1.4	1.3	0.6	•
Quick Ratio 31	0.5	•	6.2	•	1.3	•	2.0	1.4	1.1	•	0.7	1.0	0.3	•
Net Sales to Working Capital 32	•	•	4.8	•	11.4	•	12.4	11.0	13.9	•	14.2	14.7	•	•
Coverage Ratio 33	4.8	18.9	442.6	•	29.7	•	3.9	13.2	4.2	•	7.0	11.2	4.0	•
Total Asset Turnover 34	1.3	•	3.4	•	2.9	•	2.9	2.2	1.9	•	1.5	1.8	1.0	•
Inventory Turnover 35	5.6	•	11.5	•	11.8	•	29.6	14.7	13.3	•	7.6	11.3	3.8	•
Receivables Turnover 36	6.8	•	•	•	21.5	•	21.7	11.0	10.6	•	7.8	8.1	5.3	•
Total Liabilities to Net Worth 37	1.5	•	0.3	•	0.8	•	2.8	0.8	2.5	•	1.0	1.0	1.7	•
Current Assets to Working Capital 38	•	•	1.2	•	2.0	•	1.8	2.1	2.9	•	3.3	3.9	•	•
Current Liabilities to Working Capital 39	•	•	0.2	•	1.0	•	0.8	1.1	1.9	•	2.3	2.9	•	•
Working Capital to Net Sales 40	•	•	0.2	•	0.1	•	0.1	0.1	0.1	•	0.1	0.1	•	•
Inventory to Working Capital 41	•	•	0.2	•	0.5	•	0.2	0.5	0.8	•	1.2	0.9	•	•
Total Receipts to Cash Flow 42	5.5	3.0	8.1	•	3.4	•	6.1	6.6	6.8	•	7.4	7.6	4.8	•
Cost of Goods to Cash Flow 43	3.5	1.6	4.2	•	1.7	•	4.3	4.7	4.6	•	5.1	5.1	3.0	•
Cash Flow to Total Debt 44	0.4	•	1.9	•	2.0	•	0.6	0.8	0.4	•	0.4	0.5	0.3	•

Selected Financial Factors (in Percentages)

Debt Ratio 45	59.5	•	21.8	•	43.3	•	73.5	43.7	71.1	•	48.8	49.0	63.0	•
Return on Total Assets 46	13.6	•	43.1	•	59.7	•	17.6	21.0	11.1	•	6.3	8.3	13.4	•
Return on Equity Before Income Taxes 47	26.6	•	55.0	•	101.7	•	49.5	34.4	29.4	•	10.5	14.7	27.1	•
Return on Equity After Income Taxes 48	19.7	•	45.3	•	99.1	•	49.5	33.3	28.8	•	10.4	11.6	17.7	•
Profit Margin (Before Income Tax) 49	8.1	14.5	12.7	•	19.8	•	4.5	8.9	4.6	•	3.5	4.2	9.5	•
Profit Margin (After Income Tax) 50	6.0	14.5	10.5	•	19.3	•	4.5	8.6	4.5	•	3.5	3.3	6.2	•

Table I

Corporations with and without Net Income

OTHER FOOD

MONEY AMOUNTS AND SIZE OF ASSETS IN THOUSANDS OF DOLLARS

Item Description for Accounting Period 7/07 Through 6/08	Total	Zero Assets	Under 500	500 to 1,000	1,000 to 5,000	5,000 to 10,000	10,000 to 25,000	25,000 to 50,000	50,000 to 100,000	100,000 to 250,000	250,000 to 500,000	500,000 to 2,500,000	2,500,000 and over
Number of Enterprises **1**	3718	656	1771	390	430	170	144	61	42	29	15	8	3
Revenues ($ in Thousands)													
Net Sales **2**	104171393	347711	140252	1170473	2551840	2777785	4966767	3488349	4894518	7305984	6373540	9504606	60649567
Interest **3**	2788249	1106	5	0	1952	2368	4435	3064	9423	15694	37579	39368	2673256
Rents **4**	108922	0	0	0	107	0	2029	1485	1701	979	16772	1337	84514
Royalties **5**	1005670	7	0	0	0	465	0	8919	32415	14429	9993	786	938656
Other Portfolio Income **6**	486135	1385	0	0	4650	8858	898	7467	16368	56550	93094	79682	217187
Other Receipts **7**	1113093	24442	1	2104	-8019	5159	30522	20319	23822	48579	64994	124346	776816
Total Receipts **8**	109673462	374651	140258	1172577	2550530	2794635	5004651	3529603	497247	7442215	6595972	9750125	65333996
Average Total Receipts **9**	29498	571	79	3007	5931	16439	34755	57862	118530	256628	439731	1218766	21779999
Operating Costs/Operating Income (%)													
Cost of Operations **10**	71.0	73.8	25.8	62.3	68.0	68.0	72.8	73.0	74.6	67.3	70.5	73.0	71.2
Salaries and Wages **11**	5.6	4.8	11.5	13.4	6.7	7.7	6.9	5.3	6.3	5.9	7.5	4.7	5.1
Taxes Paid **12**	1.3	0.6	3.5	2.3	1.8	2.1	1.3	1.3	1.3	1.5	1.1	1.3	1.3
Interest Paid **13**	4.1	3.3	3.4	1.3	0.8	1.2	1.1	1.6	1.6	2.4	2.0	3.1	5.6
Depreciation **14**	1.5	3.7	8.5	1.4	2.1	1.5	2.1	1.9	2.0	2.4	2.9	2.2	1.1
Amortization and Depletion **15**	0.3	0.9	0.4	0.0	0.1	0.1	0.1	0.4	0.8	0.5	0.5	1.3	0.2
Pensions and Other Deferred Comp. **16**	0.3	0.4	•	•	0.3	0.3	0.2	0.5	0.3	0.4	0.5	0.6	0.3
Employee Benefits **17**	1.2	2.3	•	0.1	1.0	0.9	1.2	1.5	1.0	1.5	1.3	1.5	1.1
Advertising **18**	3.5	2.8	7.3	0.8	0.6	0.5	1.0	2.0	1.8	3.6	2.5	0.8	4.7
Other Expenses **19**	10.5	22.7	52.0	9.1	12.3	10.1	8.8	9.9	8.0	10.6	10.3	12.2	10.4
Officers' Compensation **20**	0.6	0.8	6.0	3.9	4.7	3.1	1.3	1.1	1.1	1.0	0.8	0.4	0.1
Operating Margin **21**	•	•	•	5.5	1.6	4.3	3.3	1.6	1.3	2.7	0.2	•	•
Operating Margin Before Officers' Comp. **22**	0.5	•	•	9.4	6.3	7.4	4.6	2.7	2.3	3.8	0.9	•	•

Selected Average Balance Sheet ($ in Thousands)

Net Receivables 23	68587	0	7	72	457	1665	3524	5673	10378	23373	42248	109528	83669653
Inventories 24	2062	0	2	117	428	1469	3981	9819	13279	26590	44439	155363	924454
Net Property, Plant and Equipment 25	5173	0	28	241	894	2313	6113	8509	19441	39785	107852	250813	3772258
Total Assets 26	114009	0	53	855	2184	7125	16497	32925	69564	151712	338635	1106395	131890138
Notes and Loans Payable 27	11750	0	52	358	817	3446	5327	11768	24285	74306	104008	589390	10527680
All Other Liabilities 28	72531	0	16	223	350	2226	3780	9516	17025	44275	90455	286836	87416869
Net Worth 29	29727	0	-15	274	1017	1453	7391	11641	28253	33131	144172	230170	33945589

Selected Financial Ratios (Times to 1)

Current Ratio 30	0.9	•	1.1	1.5	2.3	1.3	1.9	1.4	1.7	1.6	1.8	1.4	0.9
Quick Ratio 31	0.9	•	0.8	0.8	1.3	0.7	1.1	0.6	0.9	0.8	0.8	0.6	0.9
Net Sales to Working Capital 32	•	•	50.5	27.9	8.4	15.9	7.6	11.1	8.4	9.3	6.8	13.8	•
Coverage Ratio 33	2.4	•	•	5.3	2.8	5.0	4.7	2.8	2.8	2.9	2.9	1.6	2.3
Total Asset Turnover 34	0.2	•	1.5	3.5	2.7	2.3	2.1	1.7	1.7	1.7	1.3	1.1	0.2
Inventory Turnover 35	9.7	•	8.4	16.0	9.4	7.6	6.3	4.3	6.5	6.4	6.7	5.6	15.6
Receivables Turnover 36	0.4	•	20.1	33.8	17.2	9.6	9.3	8.7	13.0	9.9	11.2	10.4	0.2
Total Liabilities to Net Worth 37	2.8	•	•	2.1	1.1	3.9	1.2	1.8	1.5	3.6	1.3	3.8	2.9
Current Assets to Working Capital 38	•	•	10.5	3.1	1.7	4.0	2.1	3.4	2.4	2.7	2.3	3.6	•
Current Liabilities to Working Capital 39	•	•	9.5	2.1	0.7	3.0	1.1	2.4	1.4	1.7	1.3	2.6	•
Working Capital to Net Sales 40	•	•	0.0	0.0	0.1	0.1	0.1	0.1	0.1	0.1	0.1	0.1	•
Inventory to Working Capital 41	•	•	2.8	0.9	0.7	1.4	0.8	1.7	1.0	1.0	0.8	1.7	•
Total Receipts to Cash Flow 42	7.4	11.1	5.4	8.6	9.5	7.8	9.2	9.1	11.1	7.5	9.7	8.4	6.6
Cost of Goods to Cash Flow 43	5.2	8.2	1.4	5.4	6.5	5.3	6.7	6.7	8.3	5.0	6.9	6.2	4.7
Cash Flow to Total Debt 44	0.0	•	0.2	0.6	0.5	0.4	0.4	0.3	0.3	0.3	0.2	0.2	0.0

Selected Financial Factors (in Percentages)

Debt Ratio 45	73.9	•	128.8	68.0	53.5	79.6	55.2	64.6	59.4	78.2	57.4	79.2	74.3
Return on Total Assets 46	2.4	•	•	24.4	6.6	14.2	10.8	7.5	11.9	7.0	5.4	•	2.0
Return on Equity Before Income Taxes 47	5.2	•	95.6	62.0	9.1	55.7	18.9	13.5	12.3	35.8	10.7	9.7	4.3
Return on Equity After Income Taxes 48	3.6	•	104.2	62.0	7.4	51.4	17.5	11.1	9.2	28.2	7.9	3.6	2.8
Profit Margin (Before Income Tax) 49	5.6	•	•	5.7	1.6	5.0	4.1	2.8	3.0	4.7	3.6	1.9	7.3
Profit Margin (After Income Tax) 50	3.8	•	•	5.7	1.3	4.6	3.8	2.3	2.2	3.7	2.7	0.7	4.8

49

Table II

Corporations with Net Income

OTHER FOOD

MONEY AMOUNTS AND SIZE OF ASSETS IN THOUSANDS OF DOLLARS

Item Description for Accounting Period 7/07 Through 6/08	Total	Zero Assets	Under 500	500 to 1,000	1,000 to 5,000	5,000 to 10,000	10,000 to 25,000	25,000 to 50,000	50,000 to 100,000	100,000 to 250,000	250,000 to 500,000	500,000 to 2,500,000	2,500,000 and over
Number of Enterprises **1**	2359	272	1076	266	378	144	106	44	32	22	11	5	3
Revenues ($ in Thousands)													
Net Sales **2**	93482430	217272	86915	1097882	2123605	2441167	3971750	2885932	3765603	5670682	4795558	5776497	60649567
Interest **3**	2772508	980	5	0	1393	2174	3196	2752	5635	12863	33952	36301	2673256
Rents **4**	106888	0	0	0	107	0	2029	1145	1451	951	16270	422	84514
Royalties **5**	1004199	0	0	0	0	465	0	8919	31304	14182	9886	786	938656
Other Portfolio Income **6**	460870	1254	0	0	0	8791	840	7366	15368	55921	88730	65414	217187
Other Receipts **7**	1025075	30838	1	2105	7801	3053	22801	20016	18481	10735	64214	68215	776816
Total Receipts **8**	98851970	250344	86921	1099987	2132906	2455650	4000616	2926130	3837842	5765334	5008610	5947635	65339996
Average Total Receipts **9**	41904	920	81	4135	5643	17053	37742	66503	119933	262061	455328	1189527	21779999
Operating Costs/Operating Income (%)													
Cost of Operations **10**	70.3	76.3	23.4	64.0	68.0	67.3	71.0	70.8	73.3	63.8	68.9	69.0	71.2
Salaries and Wages **11**	5.5	3.1	0.7	14.0	6.5	7.4	6.6	5.5	6.3	6.0	7.5	4.4	5.1
Taxes Paid **12**	1.3	0.2	2.6	2.1	2.0	2.0	1.4	1.3	1.2	1.4	1.0	1.3	1.3
Interest Paid **13**	4.3	1.5	0.0	0.6	0.9	1.0	0.8	1.4	1.5	2.2	1.9	3.7	5.6
Depreciation **14**	1.4	1.6	8.6	0.6	1.9	1.5	2.1	1.5	1.8	2.5	2.7	2.4	1.1
Amortization and Depletion **15**	0.3	0.1	0.1	•	0.1	0.1	0.0	0.4	0.6	0.3	0.5	1.4	0.2
Pensions and Other Deferred Comp. **16**	0.3	0.6	•	•	0.2	0.4	0.3	0.6	0.3	0.5	0.4	0.5	0.3
Employee Benefits **17**	1.2	2.9	•	0.0	1.0	0.9	1.1	1.6	0.6	1.3	1.1	2.1	1.1
Advertising **18**	3.8	•	1.2	0.8	0.3	0.6	0.8	2.2	1.9	4.4	3.3	0.8	4.7
Other Expenses **19**	10.3	17.5	50.1	6.8	10.2	10.0	8.4	9.9	7.7	10.5	10.6	11.7	10.4
Officers' Compensation **20**	0.6	0.3	•	3.6	4.5	3.0	1.4	1.2	1.2	1.1	0.9	0.5	0.1
Operating Margin **21**	0.7	•	13.2	7.6	4.3	6.0	6.3	3.5	3.5	5.8	1.1	2.0	•
Operating Margin Before Officers' Comp. **22**	1.2	•	13.2	11.2	8.8	9.0	7.6	4.7	4.7	6.9	2.0	2.5	•

Selected Average Balance Sheet ($ in Thousands)

Net Receivables 23	107680	0	12	76	471	1760	3824	6189	10429	25262	41326	104148	83669653
Inventories 24	2681	0	2	106	369	1390	3760	9748	14235	25976	33355	156996	924454
Net Property, Plant and Equipment 25	7195	0	8	118	851	2387	6087	8314	18779	40126	98603	274231	3772258
Total Assets 26	176391	0	33	801	2116	7164	16249	34165	68080	148833	339121	1189604	131890138
Notes and Loans Payable 27	16615	0	20	149	649	2517	4534	12194	21845	65199	106716	523479	10527680
All Other Liabilities 28	113297	0	5	275	355	2366	3059	8669	17481	43868	85018	259575	87416869
Net Worth 29	46480	0	7	378	1112	2281	8656	13302	28755	39766	147386	406550	33945589

Selected Financial Ratios (Times to 1)

Current Ratio 30	0.9	•	6.7	1.2	2.6	1.3	2.3	1.5	1.9	1.8	1.7	1.5	0.9
Quick Ratio 31	0.9	•	5.6	0.5	1.5	0.8	1.4	0.6	0.9	1.0	0.8	0.6	0.9
Net Sales to Working Capital 32	•	•	4.0	80.7	7.6	19.8	7.0	11.1	7.4	7.7	8.8	10.8	•
Coverage Ratio 33	2.6	8.6	1643.4	13.8	6.5	7.3	10.0	4.5	4.6	4.4	3.9	2.5	2.3
Total Asset Turnover 34	0.2	•	2.5	5.2	2.7	2.4	2.3	1.9	1.7	1.7	1.3	1.0	0.2
Inventory Turnover 35	10.4	•	8.0	24.9	10.3	8.2	7.1	4.8	6.1	6.3	9.0	5.1	15.6
Receivables Turnover 36	0.4	•	13.3	•	17.5	10.6	10.2	9.2	13.7	9.0	12.6	•	0.2
Total Liabilities to Net Worth 37	2.8	•	3.4	1.1	0.9	2.1	0.9	1.6	1.4	2.7	1.3	1.9	2.9
Current Assets to Working Capital 38	•	•	1.2	6.4	1.6	4.6	1.8	3.2	2.1	2.2	2.5	2.9	•
Current Liabilities to Working Capital 39	•	•	0.2	5.4	0.6	3.6	0.8	2.2	1.1	1.2	1.5	1.9	•
Working Capital to Net Sales 40	•	•	0.2	0.0	0.1	0.1	0.1	0.1	0.1	0.1	0.1	0.1	•
Inventory to Working Capital 41	•	•	0.2	2.1	0.6	1.7	0.6	1.5	1.0	0.8	0.8	1.5	•
Total Receipts to Cash Flow 42	6.8	3.7	1.9	8.6	8.4	6.9	7.5	7.6	9.0	6.3	8.4	6.9	6.6
Cost of Goods to Cash Flow 43	4.8	2.9	0.5	5.5	5.7	4.7	5.3	5.4	6.6	4.0	5.8	4.8	4.7
Cash Flow to Total Debt 44	0.0	•	1.7	1.1	0.7	0.5	0.7	0.4	0.3	0.4	0.3	0.2	0.0

Selected Financial Factors (in Percentages)

Debt Ratio 45	73.6	•	77.3	52.8	47.5	68.2	46.7	61.1	57.8	73.3	56.5	65.8	74.3
Return on Total Assets 46	2.5	•	32.8	43.1	14.9	18.0	17.9	12.1	12.0	17.1	9.6	8.9	2.0
Return on Equity Before Income Taxes 47	5.9	•	144.1	84.8	24.0	48.8	30.2	24.2	22.1	49.4	16.4	15.7	4.3
Return on Equity After Income Taxes 48	4.2	•	115.0	84.8	22.2	45.6	28.5	21.2	18.2	41.0	12.7	10.2	2.8
Profit Margin (Before Income Tax) 49	6.9	11.2	13.2	7.8	4.8	6.6	7.0	4.9	5.4	7.6	5.6	5.5	7.3
Profit Margin (After Income Tax) 50	4.9	11.2	10.6	7.8	4.4	6.1	6.6	4.3	4.5	6.3	4.3	3.6	4.8

Table I

Corporations with and without Net Income

SOFT DRINK AND ICE

MONEY AMOUNTS AND SIZE OF ASSETS IN THOUSANDS OF DOLLARS

Item Description for Accounting Period 7/07 Through 6/08	Total	Zero Assets	Under 500	500 to 1,000	1,000 to 5,000	5,000 to 10,000	10,000 to 25,000	25,000 to 50,000	50,000 to 100,000	100,000 to 250,000	250,000 to 500,000	500,000 to 2,500,000	2,500,000 and over
Number of Enterprises **1**	677	316	0	103	142	12	29	31	13	15	7	3	6
Revenues ($ in Thousands)													
Net Sales **2**	58337679	10927	0	223828	904562	132808	1463830	2336634	1468864	3371930	3271775	2898601	42253921
Interest **3**	1320446	342	0	17	1628	378	2584	1742	3622	3741	17264	1288	1287840
Rents **4**	85825	0	0	0	1662	6	314	128	593	1337	9146	4402	68238
Royalties **5**	1408002	0	0	0	0	0	0	0	0	89	8488	33	1399392
Other Portfolio Income **6**	1394015	21458	0	0	2613	3845	1581	3623	1507	8283	21950	6862	1322297
Other Receipts **7**	2143660	836	0	0	889	34961	15726	11908	-727	126744	58426	36411	1858479
Total Receipts **8**	64689627	33563	0	223845	911354	171998	1484035	2354035	1473859	3512124	3387049	2947597	48190167
Average Total Receipts **9**	95553	106	•	2173	6418	14333	51174	75937	113374	234142	483864	982532	8031694
Operating Costs/Operating Income (%)													
Cost of Operations **10**	54.3	55.1	•	49.0	69.1	66.7	79.9	66.7	70.3	70.7	51.1	58.9	50.4
Salaries and Wages **11**	12.7	28.5	•	8.2	13.7	17.7	4.8	8.6	9.1	9.8	18.3	11.8	13.2
Taxes Paid **12**	1.8	4.7	•	2.9	2.1	2.7	0.9	1.3	1.5	1.5	2.6	1.8	1.8
Interest Paid **13**	4.6	0.0	•	1.5	1.1	0.0	0.4	1.0	1.4	1.1	3.4	3.2	5.6
Depreciation **14**	3.2	6.4	•	4.0	1.9	2.4	1.7	2.2	3.6	2.9	5.0	2.6	3.2
Amortization and Depletion **15**	0.9	0.4	•	0.8	0.1	0.1	0.1	0.1	0.3	0.7	1.1	1.4	1.0
Pensions and Other Deferred Comp. **16**	0.6	•	•	1.5	0.5	1.0	0.1	0.3	0.2	0.4	0.5	0.2	0.6
Employee Benefits **17**	2.0	7.6	•	0.2	1.7	2.7	0.7	1.3	2.7	2.3	1.9	2.6	2.0
Advertising **18**	7.0	2.0	•	1.6	1.2	0.8	1.1	6.6	1.0	0.9	1.9	0.5	8.9
Other Expenses **19**	14.8	194.9	•	23.4	6.9	34.6	7.3	7.9	7.6	8.6	11.8	17.3	16.2
Officers' Compensation **20**	0.5	3.2	•	7.2	5.0	0.2	0.8	1.1	1.8	0.6	0.6	1.0	0.2
Operating Margin **21**	•	•	•	•	1.7	•	2.2	2.7	0.4	0.5	1.7	•	•
Operating Margin Before Officers' Comp. **22**	•	•	•	6.8	1.7	•	3.0	3.9	2.2	1.1	2.3	•	•

Selected Average Balance Sheet ($ in Thousands)

Net Receivables 23	16484	•	103	831	1198	4764	6152	15968	20482	47359	224683	1527924
Inventories 24	4050	0	156	125	912	2358	4703	6362	12047	35535	45460	305769
Net Property, Plant and Equipment 25	20031	0	126	571	1383	3944	8479	23089	46227	133540	242619	1736156
Total Assets 26	122053	0	608	1983	6675	17138	35537	69102	151712	406172	904844	11979150
Notes and Loans Payable 27	51648	0	391	591	12	2875	13579	19215	34238	227937	522321	5068484
All Other Liabilities 28	28469	0	73	428	968	3478	9820	17122	32056	156383	317404	2672955
Net Worth 29	41936	0	144	964	5696	10784	12138	32766	85419	21852	65119	4237711

Selected Financial Ratios (Times to 1)

Current Ratio 30	1.0	•	4.2	1.3	4.5	2.2	1.6	2.2	1.9	1.1	1.2	0.9
Quick Ratio 31	0.7	•	2.2	1.1	3.6	1.6	1.0	1.5	1.2	0.7	1.0	0.7
Net Sales to Working Capital 32	211.7	•	9.2	23.0	3.4	9.4	12.2	7.2	8.7	38.0	16.5	•
Coverage Ratio 33	3.2	164.3	0.8	•	23.7	9.4	4.3	1.6	5.3	2.5	1.2	3.3
Total Asset Turnover 34	0.7	•	3.6	3.2	1.7	2.9	2.1	1.6	1.5	1.2	1.1	0.6
Inventory Turnover 35	11.5	•	6.8	35.4	8.1	17.1	10.7	12.5	13.2	6.7	12.5	11.6
Receivables Turnover 36	5.3	•	21.4	6.6	7.9	12.0	10.6	7.5	13.5	8.7	4.4	4.7
Total Liabilities to Net Worth 37	1.9	•	3.2	1.1	0.2	0.6	1.9	1.1	0.8	17.6	12.9	1.8
Current Assets to Working Capital 38	67.5	•	1.3	4.4	1.3	1.8	2.6	1.9	2.1	8.5	5.2	•
Current Liabilities to Working Capital 39	66.5	•	0.3	3.4	0.3	0.8	1.6	0.9	1.1	7.5	4.2	•
Working Capital to Net Sales 40	0.0	•	0.1	0.0	0.3	0.1	0.1	0.1	0.1	0.0	0.1	•
Inventory to Working Capital 41	10.4	•	0.6	0.6	0.3	0.4	0.7	0.4	0.5	3.1	0.8	•
Total Receipts to Cash Flow 42	4.8	•	7.1	31.7	5.1	10.8	10.3	16.6	8.5	7.5	7.1	4.1
Cost of Goods to Cash Flow 43	2.6	•	3.5	21.9	3.4	8.6	6.8	11.7	6.0	3.8	4.2	2.0
Cash Flow to Total Debt 44	0.2	•	0.7	0.2	2.2	0.7	0.3	0.2	0.4	0.2	0.2	0.2

Selected Financial Factors (in Percentages)

Debt Ratio 45	65.6	•	76.3	51.4	14.7	37.1	65.8	52.6	43.7	94.6	92.8	64.6
Return on Total Assets 46	10.3	•	4.1	•	1.0	11.9	9.4	3.5	8.4	10.0	4.0	10.8
Return on Equity Before Income Taxes 47	20.6	•	•	•	1.1	16.9	21.1	2.6	12.1	111.6	7.5	21.2
Return on Equity After Income Taxes 48	13.8	•	•	•	•	14.9	19.3	1.7	10.3	76.3	•	14.1
Profit Margin (Before Income Tax) 49	10.0	4.5	•	0.6	0.6	3.6	3.4	0.8	4.6	5.2	0.5	12.8
Profit Margin (After Income Tax) 50	6.7	•	•	•	•	3.2	3.1	0.5	3.9	3.6	•	8.5

Table II
Corporations with Net Income

SOFT DRINK AND ICE

Money Amounts and Size of Assets in Thousands of Dollars

Item Description for Accounting Period 7/07 Through 6/08	Total	Zero Assets	Under 500	500 to 1000	251 to 500	501 to 1,000	1,001 to 5,000	5,001 to 10,000	10,001 to 25,000	25,001 to 50,000	50,001 to 100,000	100,001 to 250,000	250,001 and over
Number of Enterprises 1	332	82	0	51	111	9	•	20	9	•	•	0	6

Revenues ($ in Thousands)

	Total	Zero Assets	Under 500	500 to 1000	251 to 500	501 to 1,000	1,001 to 5,000	5,001 to 10,000	10,001 to 25,000	25,001 to 50,000	50,001 to 100,000	100,001 to 250,000	250,001 and over
Net Sales 2	55040516	6872	0	161627	702943	120545	•	1897225	893945	•	•	0	42253921
Interest 3	1317946	103	0	17	334	378	•	1742	3129	•	•	0	1287840
Rents 4	84163	0	0	0	0	6	•	128	593	•	•	0	68238
Royalties 5	1408002	0	0	0	0	0	•	0	0	•	•	0	1399392
Other Portfolio Income 6	1390576	21458	0	0	2613	3845	•	2394	405	•	•	0	1322297
Other Receipts 7	210194	378	0	0	73	34962	•	11651	-141	•	•	0	1858479
Total Receipts 8	61342397	28811	0	161644	705963	159736	•	1913140	897931	•	•	0	48190167
Average Total Receipts 9	184766	351	•	3169	6360	17748	•	95657	99770	•	•	•	8031694

Operating Costs/Operating Income (%)

	Total	Zero Assets	Under 500	500 to 1000	251 to 500	501 to 1,000	1,001 to 5,000	5,001 to 10,000	10,001 to 25,000	25,001 to 50,000	50,001 to 100,000	100,001 to 250,000	250,001 and over
Cost of Operations 10	53.0	26.3	•	65.1	67.2	66.9	•	63.1	64.4	•	•	•	50.4
Salaries and Wages 11	13.0	38.2	•	0.4	15.7	16.4	•	8.9	11.4	•	•	•	13.2
Taxes Paid 12	1.9	4.8	•	2.5	2.1	2.7	•	1.2	1.7	•	•	•	1.8
Interest Paid 13	4.7	0.0	•	0.3	0.7	0.0	•	0.7	1.1	•	•	•	5.6
Depreciation 14	3.1	8.4	•	3.5	0.6	2.5	•	1.7	2.8	•	•	•	3.2
Amortization and Depletion 15	0.9	0.6	•	0.4	•	0.1	•	0.1	0.4	•	•	•	1.0
Pensions and Other Deferred Comp. 16	0.6	•	•	2.1	0.5	1.1	•	0.3	0.2	•	•	•	0.6
Employee Benefits 17	2.0	12.1	•	0.3	1.5	3.0	•	1.3	3.1	•	•	•	2.0
Advertising 18	7.4	3.1	•	2.0	1.0	0.8	•	7.5	1.1	•	•	•	8.9
Other Expenses 19	14.9	31.7	•	17.3	3.4	29.3	•	7.9	8.7	•	•	•	16.2
Officers' Compensation 20	0.5	5.1	•	2.8	5.7	0.2	•	1.4	0.8	•	•	•	0.2
Operating Margin 21	•	•	•	3.2	1.7	•	•	5.9	4.1	•	•	•	•
Operating Margin Before Officers' Comp. 22	•	•	•	6.1	7.4	•	•	7.2	4.9	•	•	•	•

Selected Average Balance Sheet ($ in Thousands)

Net Receivables 23	32695	•	208	1002	1237	•	6954	16106	•	1527924
Inventories 24	7655	•	316	97	720	•	5912	6422	•	305769
Net Property, Plant and Equipment 25	38421	•	46	324	1734	•	7322	17357	•	1736156
Total Assets 26	241517	•	716	1791	6687	•	35805	68746	•	11979150
Notes and Loans Payable 27	101118	•	240	569	0	•	8343	16519	•	5068484
All Other Liabilities 28	56427	•	147	358	749	•	8151	11577	•	2672955
Net Worth 29	83973	•	330	864	5938	•	19311	40651	•	4237711

Selected Financial Ratios (Times to 1)

Current Ratio 30	1.0	•	4.2	1.3	5.1	•	2.3	3.1	•	0.9
Quick Ratio 31	0.7	•	2.2	1.1	4.1	•	1.4	2.1	•	0.7
Net Sales to Working Capital 32	495.4	•	6.6	19.9	4.9	•	9.4	5.2	•	•
Coverage Ratio 33	3.4	6621.3	10.8	3.8	879.9	•	10.4	4.9	•	3.3
Total Asset Turnover 34	0.7	•	4.4	3.5	2.0	•	2.6	1.4	•	0.6
Inventory Turnover 35	11.5	•	6.5	44.0	12.4	•	10.1	10.0	•	11.6
Receivables Turnover 36	5.1	•	15.4	11.2	8.7	•	10.9	•	•	4.7
Total Liabilities to Net Worth 37	1.9	•	1.2	1.1	0.1	•	0.9	0.7	•	1.8
Current Assets to Working Capital 38	160.2	•	1.3	3.9	1.2	•	1.7	1.5	•	•
Current Liabilities to Working Capital 39	159.2	•	0.3	2.9	0.2	•	0.7	0.5	•	•
Working Capital to Net Sales 40	0.0	•	0.2	0.1	0.2	•	0.1	0.2	•	•
Inventory to Working Capital 41	23.8	•	0.6	0.5	0.2	•	0.5	0.3	•	•
Total Receipts to Cash Flow 42	4.5	1.1	6.4	20.0	4.6	•	7.4	9.1	•	4.1
Cost of Goods to Cash Flow 43	2.4	0.3	4.2	13.4	3.0	•	4.7	5.9	•	2.0
Cash Flow to Total Debt 44	0.2	•	1.3	0.3	3.9	•	0.8	0.4	•	0.2

Selected Financial Factors (in Percentages)

Debt Ratio 45	65.2	•	54.0	51.7	11.2	•	46.1	40.9	•	64.6
Return on Total Assets 46	10.9	•	15.8	10.0	19.0	•	19.4	8.1	•	10.8
Return on Equity Before Income Taxes 47	22.0	•	31.3	15.4	21.4	•	32.6	11.0	•	21.2
Return on Equity After Income Taxes 48	15.0	•	24.2	14.6	15.8	•	30.9	9.9	•	14.1
Profit Margin (Before Income Tax) 49	11.1	289.0	3.3	2.1	9.5	•	6.6	4.5	•	12.8
Profit Margin (After Income Tax) 50	7.6	240.8	2.5	2.0	7.0	•	6.3	4.0	•	8.5

Table I

Corporations with and without Net Income

BREWERIES

MONEY AMOUNTS AND SIZE OF ASSETS IN THOUSANDS OF DOLLARS

Item Description for Accounting Period 7/07 Through 6/08	Total	Zero Assets	Under 500	500 to 1,000	1,000 to 5,000	5,000 to 10,000	10,000 to 25,000	25,000 to 50,000	50,000 to 100,000	100,000 to 250,000	250,000 to 500,000	500,000 to 2,500,000	2,500,000 and over
Number of Enterprises 1	141	8	81	0	27	0	12	3	4	3	0	0	3
Revenues ($ in Thousands)													
Net Sales 2	26560305	0	54955	0	104660	0	236929	113703	236721	688002	0	0	25125334
Interest 3	93746	6	473	0	0	0	313	0	438	2906	0	0	89609
Rents 4	32967	0	0	0	0	0	0	0	194	682	0	0	32091
Royalties 5	350989	0	0	0	0	0	0	0	0	0	0	0	350989
Other Portfolio Income 6	406179	0	0	0	0	0	352	0	271	1821	0	0	403735
Other Receipts 7	179845	0	1	0	0	0	1090	0	11947	5003	0	0	161805
Total Receipts 8	27624031	6	55429	0	104660	0	238684	113703	249571	698414	0	0	26163563
Average Total Receipts 9	195915	1	684	•	3876	•	19890	37901	62393	232805	•	•	8721188
Operating Costs/Operating Income (%)													
Cost of Operations 10	44.2	•	64.9	•	87.8	•	60.3	48.4	67.6	51.3	•	0	43.4
Salaries and Wages 11	9.2	•	•	•	4.4	•	4.7	10.0	5.6	6.5	•	•	9.4
Taxes Paid 12	12.6	•	6.0	•	0.1	•	5.4	3.3	3.4	3.4	•	•	13.1
Interest Paid 13	3.4	•	•	•	•	•	2.4	3.0	1.2	0.0	•	•	3.6
Depreciation 14	4.0	•	•	•	•	•	5.5	4.5	5.5	2.3	•	•	4.1
Amortization and Depletion 15	0.4	•	0.1	•	•	•	0.1	0.1	0.0	0.1	•	•	0.4
Pensions and Other Deferred Comp. 16	0.8	•	•	•	•	•	0.7	0.6	0.1	0.5	•	•	0.8
Employee Benefits 17	1.3	•	•	•	•	•	1.2	2.9	0.6	0.7	•	•	1.3
Advertising 18	7.2	•	•	•	2.2	•	1.8	6.9	1.3	3.8	•	•	7.4
Other Expenses 19	8.7	•	18.1	•	2.4	•	7.1	11.6	9.2	16.3	•	•	8.5
Officers' Compensation 20	0.4	•	•	•	•	•	3.5	0.9	1.6	0.9	•	•	0.3
Operating Margin 21	7.8	•	10.9	•	3.1	•	7.3	7.9	3.9	14.4	•	•	7.7
Operating Margin Before Officers' Comp. 22	8.2	•	10.9	•	3.1	•	10.9	8.8	5.6	15.3	•	•	8.0

Selected Average Balance Sheet ($ in Thousands)

Net Receivables 23	11898	0	86	•	95	1462	2637	14304	14291	•	514192
Inventories 24	6548	0	59	•	540	1341	4528	3166	8630	•	280669
Net Property, Plant and Equipment 25	76063	0	0	•	0	8850	34253	44157	39683	•	3406770
Total Assets 26	237984	0	348	•	1535	14538	40790	66383	185988	•	10788572
Notes and Loans Payable 27	164828	0	0	•	1324	5752	18924	22620	3358	•	7659557
All Other Liabilities 28	22470	0	48	•	92	2805	3966	8902	25656	•	1001236
Net Worth 29	50686	0	301	•	118	5980	17900	34860	156974	•	2127779

Selected Financial Ratios (Times to 1)

Current Ratio 30	0.8	•	3.6	•	16.6	•	1.4	1.4	2.6	4.4	•	0.7
Quick Ratio 31	0.5	•	2.1	•	11.0	•	0.8	0.7	2.1	4.0	•	0.4
Net Sales to Working Capital 32	•	•	5.4	•	2.7	•	17.6	21.2	4.8	2.6	•	•
Coverage Ratio 33	4.7	•	•	•	•	•	4.4	3.6	9.0	1183.9	•	4.5
Total Asset Turnover 34	0.8	•	1.9	•	2.5	•	1.4	0.9	0.9	1.2	•	0.8
Inventory Turnover 35	12.7	•	7.4	•	6.3	•	8.9	4.1	12.6	13.6	•	13.0
Receivables Turnover 36	17.0	•	11.8	•	2.6	•	16.4	9.7	8.3	15.8	•	17.7
Total Liabilities to Net Worth 37	3.7	•	0.2	•	12.0	•	1.4	1.3	0.9	0.2	•	4.1
Current Assets to Working Capital 38	•	•	1.4	•	1.1	•	3.8	3.5	1.6	1.3	•	•
Current Liabilities to Working Capital 39	•	•	0.4	•	0.1	•	2.8	2.5	0.6	0.3	•	•
Working Capital to Net Sales 40	•	•	0.2	•	0.4	•	0.1	0.0	0.2	0.4	•	•
Inventory to Working Capital 41	•	•	0.5	•	0.4	•	1.5	1.6	0.3	0.1	•	•
Total Receipts to Cash Flow 42	5.6	•	6.9	•	18.1	•	8.0	5.2	5.8	3.2	•	5.7
Cost of Goods to Cash Flow 43	2.5	•	4.5	•	15.9	•	4.8	3.9	3.9	1.6	•	2.5
Cash Flow to Total Debt 44	0.2	•	2.1	•	0.2	•	0.3	0.3	0.3	2.5	•	0.2

Selected Financial Factors (in Percentages)

Debt Ratio 45	78.7	•	13.7	•	92.3	•	58.9	56.1	47.5	15.6	•	80.3
Return on Total Assets 46	12.7	•	22.9	•	7.8	•	14.2	10.1	9.3	19.3	•	12.6
Return on Equity Before Income Taxes 47	46.9	•	26.5	•	101.9	•	26.7	16.7	15.7	22.9	•	49.9
Return on Equity After Income Taxes 48	31.1	•	21.4	•	101.9	•	17.4	16.7	15.4	20.0	•	32.6
Profit Margin (Before Income Tax) 49	12.6	•	11.7	•	3.1	•	8.1	7.9	9.3	15.6	•	12.7
Profit Margin (After Income Tax) 50	8.4	•	9.5	•	3.1	•	5.3	7.9	9.1	13.7	•	8.3

53

Table II

Corporations with Net Income

BREWERIES

MONEY AMOUNTS AND SIZE OF ASSETS IN THOUSANDS OF DOLLARS

Item Description for Accounting Period 7/07 Through 6/08	Total	Zero Assets	Under 500	500 to 1,000	1,000 to 5,000	5,000 to 10,000	10,000 to 25,000	25,000 to 50,000	50,000 to 100,000	100,000 to 250,000	250,000 to 500,000	500,000 to 2,500,000	2,500,000 and over
Number of Enterprises 1	138	8	81	0	27	0	9	3	4	3	0	0	3
Revenues ($ in Thousands)													
Net Sales 2	26513363	0	54955	0	104660	0	189987	113703	236721	688002	0	0	25125334
Interest 3	93745	6	473	0	0	0	312	0	438	2906	0	0	89609
Rents 4	32967	0	0	0	0	0	0	0	194	682	0	0	32091
Royalties 5	350989	0	0	0	0	0	0	0	0	0	0	0	350989
Other Portfolio Income 6	406178	0	0	0	0	0	351	0	271	1821	0	0	403735
Other Receipts 7	179318	0	1	0	0	0	564	0	11947	5003	0	0	161805
Total Receipts 8	27576560	6	55429	0	104660	0	191214	113703	249571	698414	0	0	26163563
Average Total Receipts 9	199830	1	684	•	3876	•	21246	37901	62393	232805	•	•	8721188
Operating Costs/Operating Income (%)													
Cost of Operations 10	44.2	•	64.9	•	87.8	•	58.7	48.4	67.6	51.3	•	•	43.4
Salaries and Wages 11	9.2	•	•	•	4.4	•	3.9	10.0	5.6	6.5	•	•	9.4
Taxes Paid 12	12.6	•	6.0	•	0.1	•	6.1	3.3	3.4	3.4	•	•	13.1
Interest Paid 13	3.4	•	•	•	•	•	1.6	3.0	1.2	0.0	•	•	3.6
Depreciation 14	4.0	•	•	•	•	•	5.0	4.5	5.5	2.3	•	•	4.1
Amortization and Depletion 15	0.4	•	0.1	•	•	•	0.1	0.1	0.0	0.1	•	•	0.4
Pensions and Other Deferred Comp. 16	0.8	•	•	•	•	•	0.9	0.6	0.1	0.5	•	•	0.8
Employee Benefits 17	1.3	•	•	•	•	•	0.7	2.9	0.6	0.7	•	•	1.3
Advertising 18	7.2	•	•	•	2.2	•	2.2	6.9	1.3	3.8	•	•	7.4
Other Expenses 19	8.7	•	18.1	•	2.4	•	7.1	11.6	9.2	16.3	•	•	8.5
Officers' Compensation 20	0.4	•	•	•	•	•	3.7	0.9	1.6	0.9	•	•	0.3
Operating Margin 21	7.8	•	10.9	•	3.1	•	10.0	7.9	3.9	14.4	•	•	7.7
Operating Margin Before Officers' Comp. 22	8.2	•	10.9	•	3.1	•	13.8	8.8	5.6	15.3	•	•	8.0

Selected Average Balance Sheet ($ in Thousands)

Net Receivables 23	12135	0	86	95	•	1617	2637	14304	14291	514192
Inventories 24	6621	0	59	371	•	1233	4528	3166	8630	280669
Net Property, Plant and Equipment 25	77444	0	0	0	•	7607	34253	44157	39683	3406770
Total Assets 26	242782	0	348	1535	•	13637	40790	66383	185988	10788572
Notes and Loans Payable 27	168205	0	0	1324	•	4509	18924	22620	3358	7659557
All Other Liabilities 28	22915	0	48	92	•	3075	3966	8902	25656	1001236
Net Worth 29	51662	0	301	118	•	6053	17900	34860	156974	2127779

Selected Financial Ratios (Times to 1)

Current Ratio 30	0.8	•	3.6	16.6	•	1.6	1.4	2.6	4.4	0.7
Quick Ratio 31	0.5	•	2.1	11.0	•	1.0	0.7	2.1	4.0	0.4
Net Sales to Working Capital 32	•	•	5.4	2.7	•	11.8	21.2	4.8	2.6	•
Coverage Ratio 33	4.7	•	•	•	•	7.7	3.6	9.0	1183.9	4.5
Total Asset Turnover 34	0.8	•	1.9	2.5	•	1.5	0.9	0.9	1.2	0.8
Inventory Turnover 35	12.8	•	7.4	9.2	•	10.0	4.1	12.6	13.6	13.0
Receivables Turnover 36	17.0	•	11.8	2.7	•	16.5	9.7	8.3	15.8	17.7
Total Liabilities to Net Worth 37	3.7	•	0.2	12.0	•	1.3	1.3	0.9	0.2	4.1
Current Assets to Working Capital 38	•	•	1.4	1.1	•	2.6	3.5	1.6	1.3	•
Current Liabilities to Working Capital 39	•	•	0.4	0.1	•	1.6	2.5	0.6	0.3	•
Working Capital to Net Sales 40	•	•	0.2	0.4	•	0.1	0.0	0.2	0.4	•
Inventory to Working Capital 41	•	•	0.5	0.4	•	0.9	1.6	0.3	0.1	•
Total Receipts to Cash Flow 42	5.6	•	6.9	18.1	•	6.8	5.2	5.8	3.2	5.7
Cost of Goods to Cash Flow 43	2.5	•	4.5	15.9	•	4.0	2.5	3.9	1.6	2.5
Cash Flow to Total Debt 44	0.2	•	2.1	0.2	•	0.4	0.3	0.3	2.5	0.2

Selected Financial Factors (in Percentages)

Debt Ratio 45	78.7	•	13.7	92.3	•	55.6	56.1	47.5	15.6	80.3
Return on Total Assets 46	12.7	•	22.9	7.8	•	19.0	10.1	9.3	19.3	12.6
Return on Equity Before Income Taxes 47	47.0	•	26.5	101.9	•	37.3	16.7	15.7	22.9	49.9
Return on Equity After Income Taxes 48	31.2	•	21.4	101.9	•	25.1	16.7	15.4	20.0	32.6
Profit Margin (Before Income Tax) 49	12.6	•	11.7	3.1	•	10.7	7.9	9.3	15.6	12.7
Profit Margin (After Income Tax) 50	8.4	•	9.5	3.1	•	7.2	7.9	9.1	13.7	8.3

54

Table I
Corporations with and without Net Income

WINERIES AND DISTILLERIES

MONEY AMOUNTS AND SIZE OF ASSETS IN THOUSANDS OF DOLLARS

Item Description for Accounting Period 7/07 Through 6/08	Total	Zero Assets	Under 500	500 to 1,000	1,000 to 5,000	5,000 to 10,000	10,000 to 25,000	25,000 to 50,000	50,000 to 100,000	100,000 to 250,000	250,000 to 500,000	500,000 to 2,500,000	2,500,000 and over
Number of Enterprises **1**	1522	602	0	211	464	140	26	36	26	6	3	3	4
Revenues ($ in Thousands)													
Net Sales **2**	22221221	51628	0	165283	730323	498933	231792	723844	1555525	509096	1310547	4242406	12199845
Interest **3**	225114	0	0	530	1595	989	1768	608	4935	299	7723	15539	191126
Rents **4**	13478	0	0	0	19	0	0	148	3160	0	615	7399	2136
Royalties **5**	508122	0	0	0	131	0	0	2507	1	0	0	164	505319
Other Portfolio Income **6**	269811	3675	0	0	12153	82170	27906	9879	26024	1269	15875	3561	87299
Other Receipts **7**	525000	3543	0	450	9021	15958	15702	17405	25792	41165	8608	56863	330495
Total Receipts **8**	23760746	58846	0	166263	753242	598050	277168	754391	1615437	551829	1343368	4325932	13316220
Average Total Receipts **9**	15612	98	•	788	1623	4272	10660	20955	62132	91972	447789	1441977	3329055
Operating Costs/Operating Income (%)													
Cost of Operations **10**	54.6	44.1	•	53.5	34.1	36.9	50.5	46.8	64.4	60.0	73.9	56.9	52.9
Salaries and Wages **11**	6.7	9.5	•	•	19.7	20.1	10.1	11.1	6.7	8.5	5.0	6.6	5.4
Taxes Paid **12**	10.9	7.5	•	5.5	5.0	3.9	5.7	3.1	5.7	8.8	3.3	17.0	11.6
Interest Paid **13**	6.2	3.5	•	3.8	1.7	7.1	3.3	2.2	2.7	3.8	1.6	1.5	9.5
Depreciation **14**	2.7	5.2	•	2.3	5.5	10.7	3.8	7.1	3.2	5.3	2.3	3.2	1.7
Amortization and Depletion **15**	1.7	2.6	•	0.3	0.5	0.3	0.0	0.1	0.7	3.0	0.1	0.5	2.7
Pensions and Other Deferred Comp. **16**	0.4	•	•	•	0.3	0.2	0.2	0.5	0.4	0.3	0.7	0.5	0.4
Employee Benefits **17**	1.2	•	•	0.5	2.2	1.0	1.3	1.2	0.6	1.4	0.9	1.0	1.3
Advertising **18**	5.0	1.8	•	3.0	3.8	0.6	1.1	1.0	2.6	3.0	1.5	2.7	7.1
Other Expenses **19**	8.7	38.8	•	13.5	26.7	17.3	17.9	14.1	9.7	6.4	3.3	8.3	7.2
Officers' Compensation **20**	1.2	•	•	17.7	7.0	0.9	2.5	1.8	2.9	1.6	0.6	0.1	0.9
Operating Margin **21**	0.5	•	•	•	•	0.9	3.5	11.1	0.3	•	6.9	1.6	•
Operating Margin Before Officers' Comp. **22**	1.8	•	•	17.6	0.5	1.9	6.0	12.9	3.2	•	7.5	1.8	0.3

Selected Average Balance Sheet ($ in Thousands)

Net Receivables 23	2409	0	•	10	61	447	945	2434	6854	12687	28788	116194	693110
Inventories 24	4948	0	•	377	1033	2540	5213	9293	19026	54440	369364	473079	876396
Net Property, Plant and Equipment 25	4124	0	•	376	452	4078	3929	14505	22832	54340	98938	328453	647618
Total Assets 26	24477	0	•	833	1762	7473	13474	35379	70178	140735	392802	1364619	6412179
Notes and Loans Payable 27	11725	0	•	789	409	5583	4409	8732	20872	43356	135639	359246	3497658
All Other Liabilities 28	4700	0	•	7	158	450	2618	7677	12166	27108	90307	303747	1252607
Net Worth 29	8052	0	•	37	1196	1440	6447	18971	37140	70272	166856	701626	1661914

Selected Financial Ratios (Times to 1)

Current Ratio 30	2.4	•	•	5.5	5.6	4.5	2.2	2.2	2.0	2.4	2.0	2.1	2.4
Quick Ratio 31	0.7	•	•	1.0	0.7	1.2	0.4	0.7	0.6	0.5	0.3	0.3	0.8
Net Sales to Working Capital 32	2.6	•	•	2.4	1.5	1.4	1.9	2.4	3.5	1.9	3.6	3.6	2.5
Coverage Ratio 33	2.3	1.3	•	1.1	•	3.9	7.9	7.9	2.5	2.6	6.8	3.5	2.0
Total Asset Turnover 34	0.6	•	•	0.9	0.9	0.5	0.7	0.6	0.9	0.6	1.1	1.0	0.5
Inventory Turnover 35	1.6	•	•	1.1	0.5	0.5	0.9	1.0	2.0	0.9	0.9	1.7	1.8
Receivables Turnover 36	5.2	•	•	43.2	13.5	8.0	10.7	8.3	8.8	6.5	3.2	24.3	3.8
Total Liabilities to Net Worth 37	2.0	•	•	21.8	0.5	4.2	1.1	0.9	0.9	1.0	1.4	0.9	2.9
Current Assets to Working Capital 38	1.7	•	•	1.2	1.2	1.3	1.8	1.8	2.0	1.7	2.0	1.9	1.7
Current Liabilities to Working Capital 39	0.7	•	•	0.2	0.2	0.3	0.8	0.8	1.0	0.7	1.0	0.9	0.7
Working Capital to Net Sales 40	0.4	•	•	0.4	0.7	0.7	0.5	0.4	0.3	0.5	0.3	0.3	0.4
Inventory to Working Capital 41	0.9	•	•	1.0	1.0	0.9	1.3	1.1	1.2	1.3	1.5	1.2	0.8
Total Receipts to Cash Flow 42	7.3	4.9	•	12.7	6.2	5.5	2.8	3.9	9.2	9.4	9.6	10.2	6.9
Cost of Goods to Cash Flow 43	4.0	2.1	•	6.8	2.1	2.0	1.4	1.8	5.9	5.6	7.1	5.8	3.7
Cash Flow to Total Debt 44	0.1	•	•	0.1	0.4	0.1	0.4	0.3	0.2	0.1	0.2	0.2	0.1

Selected Financial Factors (in Percentages)

Debt Ratio 45	67.1	•	•	95.6	32.1	80.7	52.2	46.4	47.1	50.1	57.5	48.6	74.1
Return on Total Assets 46	8.5	•	•	4.1	•	13.3	17.3	9.9	5.9	6.0	12.3	5.2	9.1
Return on Equity Before Income Taxes 47	14.7	•	•	11.0	•	51.5	31.7	16.1	6.7	7.4	24.7	7.3	17.9
Return on Equity After Income Taxes 48	10.1	•	•	6.1	•	36.3	27.2	15.0	5.0	7.3	19.7	4.7	11.5
Profit Margin (Before Income Tax) 49	8.1	•	•	0.5	•	20.8	22.9	15.2	4.2	6.1	9.4	3.6	9.7
Profit Margin (After Income Tax) 50	5.6	1.0	•	0.3	•	14.7	19.7	14.1	3.1	6.1	7.5	2.3	6.3

55

Table II

Corporations with Net Income

WINERIES AND DISTILLERIES

MONEY AMOUNTS AND SIZE OF ASSETS IN THOUSANDS OF DOLLARS

Item Description for Accounting Period 7/07 Through 6/08	Total	Zero Assets	Under 500	500 to 1,000	1,000 to 5,000	5,000 to 10,000	10,000 to 25,000	25,000 to 50,000	50,000 to 100,000	100,000 to 250,000	250,000 to 500,000	500,000 to 2,500,000	2,500,000 and over
Number of Enterprises **1**	300	5	0	51	76	88	23	29	16	•	•	0	•

Revenues ($ in Thousands)

Item Description for Accounting Period 7/07 Through 6/08	Total	Zero Assets	Under 500	500 to 1,000	1,000 to 5,000	5,000 to 10,000	10,000 to 25,000	25,000 to 50,000	50,000 to 100,000	100,000 to 250,000	250,000 to 500,000	500,000 to 2,500,000	2,500,000 and over
Net Sales **2**	19270518	19032	0	45960	292891	313777	223236	528388	1082027	•	•	0	•
Interest **3**	212648	0	0	530	1543	975	711	263	1370	•	•	0	•
Rents **4**	11214	0	0	0	19	0	0	30	2573	•	•	0	•
Royalties **5**	508121	0	0	0	131	0	0	2507	0	•	•	0	•
Other Portfolio Income **6**	246827	0	0	0	12153	82011	22769	1702	23938	•	•	0	•
Other Receipts **7**	514991	1	0	394	7932	12713	15662	16878	21472	•	•	0	•
Total Receipts **8**	20764319	19033	0	46884	314669	409476	262378	549768	1131380	•	•	0	•
Average Total Receipts **9**	69214	3807	•	919	4140	4653	11408	18958	70711	•	•	•	•

Operating Costs/Operating Income (%)

Item Description for Accounting Period 7/07 Through 6/08	Total	Zero Assets	Under 500	500 to 1,000	1,000 to 5,000	5,000 to 10,000	10,000 to 25,000	25,000 to 50,000	50,000 to 100,000	100,000 to 250,000	250,000 to 500,000	500,000 to 2,500,000	2,500,000 and over
Cost of Operations **10**	55.0	•	•	45.1	42.5	41.0	49.1	36.4	66.5	•	•	•	•
Salaries and Wages **11**	6.2	25.8	•	•	18.5	13.2	9.1	10.8	6.2	•	•	•	•
Taxes Paid **12**	11.6	0.0	•	5.9	2.9	4.4	5.7	3.2	2.0	•	•	•	•
Interest Paid **13**	6.1	•	•	3.0	2.5	4.6	2.7	1.5	2.4	•	•	•	•
Depreciation **14**	2.1	•	•	5.5	3.8	5.9	3.7	7.3	2.6	•	•	•	•
Amortization and Depletion **15**	1.9	•	•	•	0.1	0.3	0.0	0.0	0.7	•	•	•	•
Pensions and Other Deferred Comp. **16**	0.5	•	•	•	0.8	0.2	0.2	0.4	0.4	•	•	•	•
Employee Benefits **17**	1.2	•	•	1.6	2.4	1.2	1.3	1.0	0.6	•	•	•	•
Advertising **18**	5.1	•	•	1.9	1.9	0.6	1.1	1.4	3.0	•	•	•	•
Other Expenses **19**	7.5	0.3	•	16.3	20.4	16.9	17.6	14.6	8.6	•	•	•	•
Officers' Compensation **20**	0.9	•	•	17.2	3.9	1.1	2.6	2.1	1.5	•	•	•	•
Operating Margin **21**	1.8	74.0	•	3.6	0.3	10.7	6.8	21.3	5.5	•	•	•	•
Operating Margin Before Officers' Comp. **22**	2.8	74.0	•	20.8	4.2	11.8	9.5	23.5	7.0	•	•	•	•

Selected Average Balance Sheet ($ in Thousands)

Net Receivables 23	10602	0	•	•	253	358	1025	1934	7044
Inventories 24	20213	0	•	887	1421	3038	6194	8950	20927
Net Property, Plant and Equipment 25	14682	0	•	477	635	3599	4029	13331	20172
Total Assets 26	101937	0	•	705	2539	6969	13359	33050	69788
Notes and Loans Payable 27	50667	0	•	378	902	4507	3681	6800	21419
All Other Liabilities 28	20156	0	•	2	519	223	2842	5637	9593
Net Worth 29	31114	0	•	325	1118	2239	6835	20613	38776

Selected Financial Ratios (Times to 1)

Current Ratio 30	2.3	•	•	31.9	2.8	12.6	2.1	2.5	2.1
Quick Ratio 31	0.7	•	•	31.9	0.7	3.9	0.4	0.8	0.8
Net Sales to Working Capital 32	2.8	•	•	5.6	3.6	1.2	2.1	2.1	3.9
Coverage Ratio 33	2.7	•	•	2.9	4.1	10.0	10.0	17.7	5.2
Total Asset Turnover 34	0.6	•	•	1.3	1.5	0.5	0.7	0.6	1.0
Inventory Turnover 35	1.7	•	•	0.5	1.2	0.5	0.8	0.7	2.1
Receivables Turnover 36	5.1	•	•	16.6	17.2	6.9	•	9.0	8.3
Total Liabilities to Net Worth 37	2.3	•	•	1.2	1.3	2.1	1.0	0.6	0.8
Current Assets to Working Capital 38	1.7	•	•	1.0	1.6	1.1	1.9	1.6	1.9
Current Liabilities to Working Capital 39	0.7	•	•	0.0	0.6	0.1	0.9	0.6	0.9
Working Capital to Net Sales 40	0.4	•	•	0.2	0.3	0.9	0.5	0.5	0.3
Inventory to Working Capital 41	0.9	•	•	•	1.1	0.7	1.3	1.0	1.1
Total Receipts to Cash Flow 42	6.7	1.3	•	6.4	5.5	3.5	2.7	2.7	6.8
Cost of Goods to Cash Flow 43	3.7	•	•	2.9	2.3	1.4	1.3	1.0	4.5
Cash Flow to Total Debt 44	0.1	•	•	0.4	0.5	0.2	0.6	0.5	0.3

Selected Financial Factors (in Percentages)

Debt Ratio 45	69.5	•	•	53.9	56.0	67.9	48.8	37.6	44.4
Return on Total Assets 46	10.4	•	•	10.9	15.6	23.4	19.5	14.8	12.1
Return on Equity Before Income Taxes 47	21.3	•	•	15.5	26.8	65.6	34.4	22.3	17.5
Return on Equity After Income Taxes 48	15.2	•	•	13.2	23.9	50.0	29.6	21.0	14.9
Profit Margin (Before Income Tax) 49	10.3	74.0	•	5.6	7.8	41.2	24.2	25.3	10.0
Profit Margin (After Income Tax) 50	7.4	74.0	•	4.8	6.9	31.4	20.8	23.8	8.6

Table I

Corporations with and without Net Income

TOBACCO MANUFACTURING

MONEY AMOUNTS AND SIZE OF ASSETS IN THOUSANDS OF DOLLARS

Item Description for Accounting Period 7/07 Through 6/08	Total	Zero Assets	Under 500	500 to 1,000	1,000 to 5,000	5,000 to 10,000	10,000 to 25,000	25,000 to 50,000	50,000 to 100,000	100,000 to 250,000	250,000 to 500,000	500,000 to 2,500,000	2,500,000 and over
Number of Enterprises 1	34	0	0	0	0	9	6	10	0	0	0	5	4
Revenues ($ in Thousands)													
Net Sales 2	45405179	0	0	0	0	292318	153583	883198	0	0	0	4495412	39580667
Interest 3	440197	0	0	0	0	9802	776	19051	0	0	0	43563	367005
Rents 4	1629174	0	0	0	0	0	0	73	0	0	0	0	1629101
Royalties 5	235660	0	0	0	0	0	0	5040	0	0	0	6	230614
Other Portfolio Income 6	5219977	0	0	0	0	0	19975	24085	0	0	0	126221	5049698
Other Receipts 7	2380649	0	0	0	0	33	255	25488	0	0	0	56025	2298847
Total Receipts 8	55310836	0	0	0	0	302153	174589	956935	0	0	0	4721227	49155932
Average Total Receipts 9	1626789	•	•	•	•	33573	29098	95694	•	•	•	944245	12288983
Operating Costs/Operating Income (%)													
Cost of Operations 10	45.3	•	•	•	•	50.2	57.1	82.1	•	•	•	30.1	46.2
Salaries and Wages 11	3.7	•	•	•	•	0.5	13.2	3.9	•	•	•	4.7	3.6
Taxes Paid 12	15.5	•	•	•	•	36.6	1.8	0.5	•	•	•	10.2	16.3
Interest Paid 13	3.9	•	•	•	•	0.2	0.9	3.0	•	•	•	3.9	4.0
Depreciation 14	2.1	•	•	•	•	0.7	0.9	0.5	•	•	•	0.9	2.2
Amortization and Depletion 15	0.5	•	•	•	•	0.0	0.1	0.4	•	•	•	2.0	0.3
Pensions and Other Deferred Comp. 16	1.2	•	•	•	•	0.2	1.6	0.1	•	•	•	1.0	1.2
Employee Benefits 17	3.1	•	•	•	•	0.5	1.5	0.3	•	•	•	0.8	3.4
Advertising 18	2.4	•	•	•	•	0.2	6.2	1.6	•	•	•	0.4	2.6
Other Expenses 19	12.5	•	•	•	•	1.0	22.3	9.3	•	•	•	23.7	11.4
Officers' Compensation 20	0.7	•	•	•	•	11.6	6.2	1.0	•	•	•	2.0	0.5
Operating Margin 21	9.1	•	•	•	•	•	•	•	•	•	•	20.3	8.3
Operating Margin Before Officers' Comp. 22	9.8	•	•	•	•	10.0	•	•	•	•	•	22.3	8.7

Selected Average Balance Sheet ($ in Thousands)

Net Receivables	23	44578	•	335	2630	4249	•	31009	324830
Inventories	24	90158	•	2724	6193	7370	•	317851	645118
Net Property, Plant and Equipment	25	129662	•	2827	900	2517	•	152690	897262
Total Assets	26	2029388	•	6211	12776	70093	•	1346552	15358233
Notes and Loans Payable	27	476110	•	1600	2134	26203	•	502306	3346746
All Other Liabilities	28	851905	•	1592	3142	15606	•	470159	6606188
Net Worth	29	701372	•	3019	7501	28284	•	374087	5405299

Selected Financial Ratios (Times to 1)

Current Ratio	30	1.2	•	2.0	4.9	3.2	•	1.5	1.1
Quick Ratio	31	0.7	•	0.5	2.3	2.0	•	0.4	0.7
Net Sales to Working Capital	32	16.0	•	19.1	3.1	2.4	•	8.0	21.5
Coverage Ratio	33	11.0	•	11.0	3.1	2.9	•	7.6	11.5
Total Asset Turnover	34	0.7	•	5.2	2.0	1.3	•	0.7	0.6
Inventory Turnover	35	6.7	•	6.0	2.4	9.8	•	0.9	7.1
Receivables Turnover	36	47.2	•	85.2	5.7	31.9	•	20.2	60.9
Total Liabilities to Net Worth	37	1.9	•	1.1	0.7	1.5	•	2.6	1.8
Current Assets to Working Capital	38	6.6	•	2.0	1.3	1.5	•	3.0	8.9
Current Liabilities to Working Capital	39	5.6	•	1.0	0.3	0.5	•	2.0	7.9
Working Capital to Net Sales	40	0.1	•	0.1	0.3	0.4	•	0.1	0.0
Inventory to Working Capital	41	1.3	•	1.5	0.6	0.3	•	1.9	1.4
Total Receipts to Cash Flow	42	2.5	•	37.3	7.5	8.5	•	2.3	2.4
Cost of Goods to Cash Flow	43	1.1	•	18.7	4.3	6.9	•	0.7	1.1
Cash Flow to Total Debt	44	0.4	•	0.3	0.6	0.2	•	0.4	0.4

Selected Financial Factors (in Percentages)

Debt Ratio	45	65.4	•	51.4	41.3	59.6	•	72.2	64.8
Return on Total Assets	46	28.1	•	10.1	5.5	11.0	•	19.6	29.3
Return on Equity Before Income Taxes	47	73.9	•	18.9	6.3	18.0	•	61.4	75.9
Return on Equity After Income Taxes	48	48.4	•	12.5	6.3	13.2	•	43.5	49.5
Profit Margin (Before Income Tax)	49	38.8	•	1.8	1.8	5.8	•	25.5	41.5
Profit Margin (After Income Tax)	50	25.4	•	1.2	1.8	4.2	•	18.1	27.0

Table II
Corporations with Net Income

TOBACCO MANUFACTURING

MONEY AMOUNTS AND SIZE OF ASSETS IN THOUSANDS OF DOLLARS

Item Description for Accounting Period 7/07 Through 6/08	Total	Zero Assets	Under 500	500 to 1,000	1,000 to 5,000	5,000 to 10,000	10,000 to 25,000	25,000 to 50,000	50,000 to 100,000	100,000 to 250,000	250,000 to 500,000	500,000 to 2,500,000	2,500,000 and over
Number of Enterprises **1**	28	0	0	0	0	9	•	5	0	0	0	5	•
Revenues ($ in Thousands)													
Net Sales **2**	44930093	0	0	0	0	292318	•	419029	0	0	0	4495412	•
Interest **3**	439421	0	0	0	0	9802	•	19051	0	0	0	43563	•
Rents **4**	1629174	0	0	0	0	0	•	73	0	0	0	0	•
Royalties **5**	235660	0	0	0	0	0	•	5040	0	0	0	6	•
Other Portfolio Income **6**	5199958	0	0	0	0	0	•	24040	0	0	0	126221	•
Other Receipts **7**	2378147	0	0	0	0	33	•	23168	0	0	0	56025	•
Total Receipts **8**	54812453	0	0	0	0	302153	•	490401	0	0	0	4721227	•
Average Total Receipts **9**	1957588	•	•	•	•	33573	•	98080	•	•	•	944245	•
Operating Costs/Operating Income (%)													
Cost of Operations **10**	44.9	•	•	•	•	50.2	•	76.4	•	•	•	30.1	•
Salaries and Wages **11**	3.7	•	•	•	•	0.5	•	3.2	•	•	•	4.7	•
Taxes Paid **12**	15.6	•	•	•	•	36.6	•	0.3	•	•	•	10.2	•
Interest Paid **13**	3.9	•	•	•	•	0.2	•	5.5	•	•	•	3.9	•
Depreciation **14**	2.1	•	•	•	•	0.7	•	0.2	•	•	•	0.9	•
Amortization and Depletion **15**	0.5	•	•	•	•	0.0	•	0.7	•	•	•	2.0	•
Pensions and Other Deferred Comp. **16**	1.2	•	•	•	•	0.2	•	•	•	•	•	1.0	•
Employee Benefits **17**	3.1	•	•	•	•	0.5	•	0.2	•	•	•	0.8	•
Advertising **18**	2.4	•	•	•	•	0.2	•	2.0	•	•	•	0.4	•
Other Expenses **19**	12.6	•	•	•	•	1.0	•	12.9	•	•	•	23.7	•
Officers' Compensation **20**	0.7	•	•	•	•	11.6	•	0.8	•	•	•	2.0	•
Operating Margin **21**	9.3	•	•	•	•	•	•	•	•	•	•	20.3	•
Operating Margin Before Officers' Comp. **22**	10.0	•	•	•	•	10.0	•	•	•	•	•	22.3	•

Selected Average Balance Sheet ($ in Thousands)

Net Receivables 23	31009	6918	335	53782
Inventories 24	317851	10560	2724	108015
Net Property, Plant and Equipment 25	152690	860	2827	156622
Total Assets 26	1346552	98890	6211	2456351
Notes and Loans Payable 27	502306	45032	1600	576360
All Other Liabilities 28	470159	23661	1592	1032963
Net Worth 29	374087	30198	3019	847028

Selected Financial Ratios (Times to 1)

Current Ratio 30	1.5	4.0	2.0	1.2
Quick Ratio 31	0.4	3.0	0.5	0.7
Net Sales to Working Capital 32	8.0	1.3	19.1	16.2
Coverage Ratio 33	7.6	3.7	11.0	11.0
Total Asset Turnover 34	0.7	0.8	5.2	0.7
Inventory Turnover 35	0.9	6.1	6.0	6.7
Receivables Turnover 36	20.2	24.2	85.2	47.7
Total Liabilities to Net Worth 37	2.6	2.3	1.1	1.9
Current Assets to Working Capital 38	3.0	1.3	2.0	6.7
Current Liabilities to Working Capital 39	2.0	0.3	1.0	5.7
Working Capital to Net Sales 40	0.1	0.8	0.1	0.1
Inventory to Working Capital 41	1.9	0.2	1.5	1.4
Total Receipts to Cash Flow 42	2.3	4.6	37.3	2.4
Cost of Goods to Cash Flow 43	0.7	3.5	18.7	1.1
Cash Flow to Total Debt 44	0.4	0.3	0.3	0.4

Selected Financial Factors (in Percentages)

Debt Ratio 45	72.2	69.5	51.4	65.5
Return on Total Assets 46	19.6	17.1	10.1	28.2
Return on Equity Before Income Taxes 47	61.4	40.9	18.9	74.3
Return on Equity After Income Taxes 48	43.5	31.9	12.5	48.8
Profit Margin (Before Income Tax) 49	25.5	14.7	1.8	39.2
Profit Margin (After Income Tax) 50	18.1	11.5	1.2	25.7

Table I

Corporations with and without Net Income

TEXTILE MILLS

MONEY AMOUNTS AND SIZE OF ASSETS IN THOUSANDS OF DOLLARS

Item Description for Accounting Period 7/07 Through 6/08	Total	Zero Assets	Under 500	500 to 1,000	1,000 to 5,000	5,000 to 10,000	10,000 to 25,000	25,000 to 50,000	50,000 to 100,000	100,000 to 250,000	250,000 to 500,000	500,000 to 2,500,000	2,500,000 and over
Number of Enterprises 1	1953	3	1311	290	165	63	69	10	16	15	5	5	0
Revenues ($ in Thousands)													
Net Sales 2	13976873	30930	981827	505813	548934	722125	2096204	398591	1616460	2721374	1963347	2391267	0
Interest 3	93303	81	519	1672	4122	3546	2744	1937	4402	8569	5359	60351	0
Rents 4	6604	0	0	0	0	884	1064	244	766	673	2772	202	0
Royalties 5	46777	0	0	0	0	0	0	0	7	5127	0	41644	0
Other Portfolio Income 6	160027	0	6872	20422	0	11144	3484	2108	50715	24816	8521	31943	0
Other Receipts 7	105545	86	1031	2055	2061	10218	20384	1156	11108	43722	12343	1383	0
Total Receipts 8	14389129	31097	990249	529962	555117	747917	2123880	404036	1683458	2804281	1992342	2526790	0
Average Total Receipts 9	7368	10366	755	1827	3364	11872	30781	40404	105216	186952	398468	505358	•
Operating Costs/Operating Income (%)													
Cost of Operations 10	74.9	102.9	52.2	77.8	71.8	79.0	81.7	80.9	80.0	74.8	74.0	72.9	•
Salaries and Wages 11	5.8	5.1	4.8	4.2	4.4	4.2	6.1	4.5	5.6	6.1	6.0	6.9	•
Taxes Paid 12	1.8	2.0	3.1	2.1	2.2	2.0	1.1	1.6	1.7	1.3	2.2	2.2	•
Interest Paid 13	2.6	2.4	2.1	0.6	0.4	0.9	1.6	3.8	0.7	3.2	1.8	5.9	•
Depreciation 14	2.4	•	0.3	0.9	1.3	2.1	1.9	4.8	1.9	3.2	3.2	2.7	•
Amortization and Depletion 15	0.4	•	0.0	•	0.0	0.2	0.1	0.9	0.0	0.3	0.3	1.5	•
Pensions and Other Deferred Comp. 16	0.7	•	1.4	0.0	0.8	0.4	0.0	0.4	0.8	0.9	0.7	0.8	•
Employee Benefits 17	1.4	2.9	•	0.2	1.8	1.0	1.2	0.7	0.8	1.8	0.9	2.7	•
Advertising 18	0.4	0.0	2.0	0.1	0.3	0.0	0.2	0.1	0.8	0.2	0.5	0.1	•
Other Expenses 19	10.3	56.3	20.6	11.6	10.7	9.9	4.9	6.0	10.5	9.3	7.4	14.0	•
Officers' Compensation 20	2.3	0.4	13.7	6.5	2.7	1.5	1.1	1.4	1.3	0.9	1.4	1.0	•
Operating Margin 21	•	•	•	•	3.5	•	0.0	•	0.0	0.3	1.6	•	•
Operating Margin Before Officers' Comp. 22	•	13.4	•	2.6	6.2	0.2	1.1	•	•	3.0	•	•	•

Selected Average Balance Sheet ($ in Thousands)

Net Receivables 23	1133	0	87	198	534	1493	3851	4975	9933	20915	70587	143483	•
Inventories 24	1042	0	16	64	659	1810	4663	8381	15980	25829	72928	73647	•
Net Property, Plant and Equipment 25	1346	0	10	222	222	1880	4458	12634	20581	40837	100677	103310	•
Total Assets 26	6251	0	230	676	1923	7457	18117	37085	67885	151838	390243	797659	•
Notes and Loans Payable 27	2288	0	66	163	838	3866	6644	16895	15615	56693	89003	355949	•
All Other Liabilities 28	1261	0	93	95	521	2113	3008	4858	12465	37589	75664	139407	•
Net Worth 29	2702	0	71	418	564	1478	8464	15332	39805	57556	225576	302304	•

Selected Financial Ratios (Times to 1)

Current Ratio 30	2.0	•	2.1	2.1	2.8	2.3	1.9	3.1	2.3	1.7	1.8	2.0	•
Quick Ratio 31	1.1	•	1.4	1.5	1.8	1.1	0.9	1.9	0.9	0.9	0.8	1.2	•
Net Sales to Working Capital 32	5.0	•	6.8	7.7	3.5	4.2	5.1	3.8	5.1	6.4	5.4	3.7	•
Coverage Ratio 33	1.0	•	1.0	2.6	12.6	3.4	1.8	0.1	0.9	1.3	2.8	0.2	•
Total Asset Turnover 34	1.1	•	3.3	2.6	1.7	1.5	1.7	1.1	1.5	1.2	1.0	0.6	•
Inventory Turnover 35	5.1	•	24.5	21.1	3.6	5.0	5.3	3.8	5.1	5.3	4.0	4.7	•
Receivables Turnover 36	6.5	•	•	•	4.3	8.5	8.5	5.7	10.3	7.7	6.2	3.7	•
Total Liabilities to Net Worth 37	1.3	•	2.2	0.6	2.4	4.0	1.1	1.4	0.7	1.6	0.7	1.6	•
Current Assets to Working Capital 38	2.0	•	1.9	1.9	1.6	1.8	2.1	1.5	1.7	2.4	2.2	2.0	•
Current Liabilities to Working Capital 39	1.0	•	0.9	0.9	0.6	0.8	1.1	0.5	0.7	1.4	1.2	1.0	•
Working Capital to Net Sales 40	0.2	•	0.1	0.1	0.3	0.2	0.2	0.3	0.2	0.2	0.2	0.3	•
Inventory to Working Capital 41	0.7	•	0.1	0.3	0.5	0.7	0.8	0.5	0.9	0.9	1.1	0.6	•
Total Receipts to Cash Flow 42	14.4	•	7.8	15.6	8.0	12.2	20.1	•	15.4	13.3	10.9	23.2	•
Cost of Goods to Cash Flow 43	10.8	•	4.1	12.1	5.8	9.6	16.4	•	12.3	10.0	8.0	16.9	•
Cash Flow to Total Debt 44	0.1	•	0.6	0.4	0.3	0.2	0.2	•	0.2	0.1	0.2	0.0	•

Selected Financial Factors (in Percentages)

Debt Ratio 45	56.8	•	69.2	38.2	70.7	80.2	53.3	58.7	41.4	62.1	42.2	62.1	•
Return on Total Assets 46	3.1	•	6.7	3.7	8.7	4.9	4.9	0.3	1.0	5.0	5.0	0.8	•
Return on Equity Before Income Taxes 47	0.3	•	•	3.7	27.3	17.4	4.8	•	•	3.2	5.5	•	•
Return on Equity After Income Taxes 48	•	•	•	3.6	26.8	11.0	4.7	•	•	1.5	4.0	•	•
Profit Margin (Before Income Tax) 49	0.1	•	0.9	0.9	4.6	2.2	1.3	•	•	1.0	3.2	•	•
Profit Margin (After Income Tax) 50	•	•	0.9	4.5	1.3	1.4	1.3	•	0.5	2.3	•	•	•

Table II

Corporations with Net Income

TEXTILE MILLS

MONEY AMOUNTS AND SIZE OF ASSETS IN THOUSANDS OF DOLLARS

Item Description for Accounting Period 7/07 Through 6/08	Total	Zero Assets	Under 500	500 to 1,000	1,000 to 5,000	5,000 to 10,000	10,000 to 25,000	25,000 to 50,000	50,000 to 100,000	100,000 to 250,000	250,000 to 500,000	500,000 to 2,500,000	2,500,000 and over
Number of Enterprises **1**	1284	0	942	161	64	48	41	4	11	•	0	0	0
Revenues ($ in Thousands)													
Net Sales **2**	8898806	0	614256	334955	402743	610676	1343571	148121	1120602	•	0	0	0
Interest **3**	27412	0	0	911	761	3480	0	1651	2885	•	0	0	0
Rents **4**	4555	0	0	0	0	24	848	244	14	•	0	0	0
Royalties **5**	12	0	0	0	0	0	0	0	0	•	0	0	0
Other Portfolio Income **6**	124022	0	6872	20422	0	1541	580	2108	50625	•	0	0	0
Other Receipts **7**	87977	0	0	2054	701	8939	11078	360	12320	•	0	0	0
Total Receipts **8**	9142784	0	621128	358342	404205	624660	1356077	152484	1186446	•	0	0	0
Average Total Receipts **9**	7121	•	659	2226	6316	13014	33075	38121	107859	•	•	•	•
Operating Costs/Operating Income (%)													
Cost of Operations **10**	72.0	•	52.9	70.7	69.8	78.4	80.3	79.2	79.7	•	•	•	•
Salaries and Wages **11**	5.9	•	2.5	4.4	2.9	4.4	6.9	3.9	6.3	•	•	•	•
Taxes Paid **12**	1.6	•	2.3	2.8	2.0	1.6	0.9	1.5	1.8	•	•	•	•
Interest Paid **13**	1.8	•	3.3	0.3	0.3	0.5	1.4	1.1	0.4	•	•	•	•
Depreciation **14**	1.9	•	0.3	0.7	1.1	1.3	0.9	3.8	1.1	•	•	•	•
Amortization and Depletion **15**	0.2	•	0.0	•	0.0	0.2	0.0	•	0.0	•	•	•	•
Pensions and Other Deferred Comp. **16**	0.6	•	0.7	0.0	0.0	0.5	0.0	0.7	0.8	•	•	•	•
Employee Benefits **17**	1.2	•	•	0.3	2.1	0.6	0.7	0.0	0.7	•	•	•	•
Advertising **18**	0.3	•	0.0	0.1	0.0	0.1	0.3	0.1	1.1	•	•	•	•
Other Expenses **19**	9.4	•	18.7	13.3	9.5	9.6	4.2	4.8	7.2	•	•	•	•
Officers' Compensation **20**	2.1	•	10.8	8.1	1.5	1.2	1.2	2.3	1.3	•	•	•	•
Operating Margin **21**	2.9	•	8.3	•	10.8	1.5	3.4	2.6	•	•	•	•	•
Operating Margin Before Officers' Comp. **22**	5.0	•	19.2	7.4	12.3	2.8	4.6	4.9	0.9	•	•	•	•

Selected Average Balance Sheet ($ in Thousands)

Net Receivables 23	857	•	95	117	956	1660	2016	4196	9349
Inventories 24	945	•	10	98	976	2604	5658	4891	17756
Net Property, Plant and Equipment 25	1192	•	13	203	402	1279	3393	10059	14660
Total Assets 26	4875	•	162	619	2556	7508	17890	29392	63862
Notes and Loans Payable 27	1458	•	62	88	178	4790	4707	2944	8642
All Other Liabilities 28	997	•	90	103	790	2294	3083	5432	10292
Net Worth 29	2420	•	10	428	1588	425	10101	21016	44929

Selected Financial Ratios (Times to 1)

Current Ratio 30	1.9	•	1.4	3.0	3.3	2.3	2.1	3.5	2.4
Quick Ratio 31	0.9	•	1.3	1.3	1.9	1.2	0.8	2.6	0.9
Net Sales to Working Capital 32	5.6	•	17.7	8.3	4.2	4.1	4.7	2.7	5.0
Coverage Ratio 33	4.1	•	3.5	19.6	44.6	7.9	4.2	6.0	14.7
Total Asset Turnover 34	1.4	•	4.0	3.4	2.5	1.7	1.8	1.3	1.6
Inventory Turnover 35	5.3	•	34.6	15.0	4.5	3.8	4.6	6.0	4.6
Receivables Turnover 36	8.0	•	9.9	16.9	7.3	•	10.9	11.1	•
Total Liabilities to Net Worth 37	1.0	•	14.5	0.4	0.6	16.7	0.8	0.4	0.4
Current Assets to Working Capital 38	2.1	•	3.5	1.5	1.4	1.7	1.9	1.4	1.7
Current Liabilities to Working Capital 39	1.1	•	2.5	0.5	0.4	0.7	0.9	0.4	0.7
Working Capital to Net Sales 40	0.2	•	0.1	0.1	0.2	0.2	0.2	0.4	0.2
Inventory to Working Capital 41	0.8	•	0.3	0.5	0.6	0.8	0.7	0.3	0.9
Total Receipts to Cash Flow 42	8.6	•	4.9	9.1	5.5	9.4	13.4	12.0	13.4
Cost of Goods to Cash Flow 43	6.2	•	2.6	6.4	3.9	7.4	10.7	9.5	10.7
Cash Flow to Total Debt 44	0.3	•	0.9	1.2	1.2	0.2	0.3	0.4	0.4

Selected Financial Factors (in Percentages)

Debt Ratio 45	50.4	•	93.6	30.8	37.9	94.3	43.5	28.5	29.6
Return on Total Assets 46	10.5	•	46.8	22.6	28.1	7.4	10.4	8.2	9.3
Return on Equity Before Income Taxes 47	16.0	•	519.4	31.0	44.2	114.0	14.0	9.6	12.4
Return on Equity After Income Taxes 48	13.8	•	511.6	30.7	43.8	85.1	14.0	9.4	9.4
Profit Margin (Before Income Tax) 49	5.6	•	8.3	6.4	11.2	3.8	4.3	5.4	5.5
Profit Margin (After Income Tax) 50	4.8	•	8.2	6.3	11.0	2.8	4.3	5.3	4.1

Table I

Corporations with and without Net Income

TEXTILE PRODUCT MILLS

MONEY AMOUNTS AND SIZE OF ASSETS IN THOUSANDS OF DOLLARS

Item Description for Accounting Period 7/07 Through 6/08		Total	Zero Assets	Under 500	500 to 1,000	1,000 to 5,000	5,000 to 10,000	10,000 to 25,000	25,000 to 50,000	50,000 to 100,000	100,000 to 250,000	250,000 to 500,000	500,000 to 2,500,000	2,500,000 and over
Number of Enterprises	1	1744	9	783	446	310	58	65	42	7	11	5	7	0
Revenues ($ in Thousands)														
Net Sales	2	26813836	259157	416483	774123	2168705	808171	2709352	2731039	980235	2571613	1641105	11753852	0
Interest	3	84065	0	25	1553	1540	784	2360	970	514	3413	14182	58723	0
Rents	4	3574	0	22	0	0	0	0	323	161	2465	0	602	0
Royalties	5	41435	0	0	0	0	0	0	0	0	0	906	40529	0
Other Portfolio Income	6	146855	2094	0	0	243	0	20576	25861	6997	53808	222	37054	0
Other Receipts	7	324944	243	4826	2361	8118	10920	17624	29969	1343	19679	102787	127078	0
Total Receipts	8	27414709	261494	421356	778037	2178606	819875	2749912	2788162	989250	2650978	1759202	12017838	0
Average Total Receipts	9	15719	29055	538	1744	7028	14136	42306	66385	141321	240998	351840	1716834	•
Operating Costs/Operating Income (%)														
Cost of Operations	10	70.4	74.1	54.7	68.7	52.1	75.6	81.3	76.2	77.7	76.6	71.4	68.0	•
Salaries and Wages	11	10.2	6.2	11.8	5.4	15.0	5.4	5.1	6.6	4.8	4.9	4.7	14.4	•
Taxes Paid	12	1.7	1.2	4.4	2.5	2.4	1.7	0.9	1.6	1.5	1.5	1.4	1.7	•
Interest Paid	13	1.9	3.5	0.8	1.9	0.7	1.8	1.7	1.2	1.4	1.7	4.6	1.9	•
Depreciation	14	2.1	1.3	0.7	3.1	2.3	0.8	1.1	1.5	1.3	1.9	1.7	2.8	•
Amortization and Depletion	15	0.3	0.1	•	0.4	0.0	0.2	0.0	0.1	0.5	0.6	0.1	0.5	•
Pensions and Other Deferred Comp.	16	0.5	0.0	0.0	0.3	0.4	0.4	0.2	0.7	0.1	0.3	1.2	0.6	•
Employee Benefits	17	1.8	0.2	0.0	1.3	1.2	0.2	1.0	1.5	1.8	1.2	1.7	2.6	•
Advertising	18	0.8	0.1	0.9	0.4	0.8	0.6	0.4	0.4	0.5	1.1	1.1	0.9	•
Other Expenses	19	9.2	7.8	11.1	11.7	18.2	10.4	6.7	7.8	6.4	7.7	16.6	7.6	•
Officers' Compensation	20	1.9	3.9	15.4	10.0	3.3	8.4	1.2	1.5	0.5	1.7	0.9	0.7	•
Operating Margin	21	•	1.6	0.2	•	3.6	•	0.3	0.8	3.5	0.9	•	•	•
Operating Margin Before Officers' Comp.	22	1.2	5.6	15.6	4.3	6.9	2.8	1.5	2.3	4.0	2.6	•	•	•

Selected Average Balance Sheet ($ in Thousands)

Net Receivables 23	1328	0	139	632	2273	4752	8862	19105	27614	46145	81077	•
Inventories 24	2408	0	136	685	1953	6903	12900	24236	45821	59584	260195	•
Net Property, Plant and Equipment 25	1967	0	275	428	1893	2794	7093	13859	31455	63288	259257	•
Total Assets 26	12210	0	771	2689	8208	16373	39229	70617	155091	298644	1884407	•
Notes and Loans Payable 27	3654	0	575	682	4192	5337	8647	19367	56363	164594	479883	•
All Other Liabilities 28	2810	0	227	776	3561	4280	11915	17764	25919	76131	393428	•
Net Worth 29	5746	0	-31	1232	455	6755	18667	33486	72809	57919	1011096	•

Selected Financial Ratios (Times to 1)

Current Ratio 30	1.6	•	1.2	0.7	1.9	1.3	2.1	1.8	2.1	1.6	1.9	1.5
Quick Ratio 31	0.8	•	1.1	0.5	1.1	0.7	0.9	0.9	1.2	0.7	0.8	0.7
Net Sales to Working Capital 32	7.6	•	80.0	•	7.0	8.9	6.1	5.1	6.1	7.4	5.4	8.3
Coverage Ratio 33	1.8	1.7	2.7	•	6.5	•	2.1	3.3	2.5	3.3	1.4	1.3
Total Asset Turnover 34	1.3	•	9.3	2.3	2.6	1.7	2.5	1.7	2.0	1.5	1.1	0.9
Inventory Turnover 35	4.5	•	79.3	8.7	5.3	5.4	4.9	3.8	4.5	3.9	3.9	4.4
Receivables Turnover 36	11.5	•	•	•	12.3	7.9	9.9	7.8	6.3	7.4	7.9	18.8
Total Liabilities to Net Worth 37	1.1	•	50.0	•	1.2	17.1	1.4	1.1	1.1	1.1	4.2	0.9
Current Assets to Working Capital 38	2.6	•	5.8	•	2.1	3.9	1.9	2.2	1.9	2.6	2.1	2.9
Current Liabilities to Working Capital 39	1.6	•	4.8	•	1.1	2.9	0.9	1.2	0.9	1.6	1.1	1.9
Working Capital to Net Sales 40	0.1	•	0.0	•	0.1	0.1	0.2	0.2	0.2	0.1	0.2	0.1
Inventory to Working Capital 41	1.1	•	0.6	•	0.8	1.6	1.0	0.9	0.8	1.3	1.0	1.2
Total Receipts to Cash Flow 42	12.1	15.3	8.7	26.6	5.2	42.2	15.1	10.9	11.3	12.2	5.8	17.4
Cost of Goods to Cash Flow 43	8.5	11.3	4.8	18.3	2.7	31.9	12.2	8.3	8.8	9.3	4.2	11.9
Cash Flow to Total Debt 44	0.2	•	1.1	0.1	0.9	0.0	0.3	0.3	0.2	0.2	0.2	0.1

Selected Financial Factors (in Percentages)

Debt Ratio 45	52.9	•	98.0	104.0	54.2	94.5	58.7	52.4	52.6	53.1	80.6	46.3
Return on Total Assets 46	4.2	•	20.3	12.5	•	•	9.0	6.8	11.3	8.6	7.0	2.3
Return on Equity Before Income Taxes 47	4.0	•	648.5	296.9	23.1	•	11.2	10.1	18.1	12.7	10.3	1.0
Return on Equity After Income Taxes 48	2.1	•	614.2	306.3	20.9	•	9.6	9.7	17.3	10.7	3.8	•
Profit Margin (Before Income Tax) 49	1.5	2.6	1.4	4.1	•	1.8	2.9	4.3	4.0	1.8	0.6	•
Profit Margin (After Income Tax) 50	0.8	2.6	1.3	3.7	•	1.6	2.8	4.1	4.0	3.3	0.7	•

Table II
Corporations with Net Income

TEXTILE PRODUCT MILLS

MONEY AMOUNTS AND SIZE OF ASSETS IN THOUSANDS OF DOLLARS

Item Description for Accounting Period 7/07 Through 6/08	Total	Zero Assets	Under 500	500 to 1,000	1,000 to 5,000	5,000 to 10,000	10,000 to 25,000	25,000 to 50,000	50,000 to 100,000	100,000 to 250,000	250,000 to 500,000	500,000 to 2,500,000	2,500,000 and over
Number of Enterprises 1	1135	4	510	191	301	36	43	30	•	•	5	0	0
Revenues ($ in Thousands)													
Net Sales 2	20055825	56665	415400	461904	2092065	570957	1791031	1980183	•	•	9543104	0	0
Interest 3	53010	0	25	541	1463	447	1323	531	•	•	45394	0	0
Rents 4	3448	0	22	0	0	0	0	323	•	•	476	0	0
Royalties 5	7456	0	0	0	0	0	0	0	•	•	7456	0	0
Other Portfolio Income 6	109084	2094	0	0	142	0	6754	23713	•	•	15658	0	0
Other Receipts 7	255830	63	4826	-1	7999	1871	417	29498	•	•	191380	0	0
Total Receipts 8	20484653	58822	420273	462444	2101669	573275	1799525	2034248	•	•	9803468	0	0
Average Total Receipts 9	18048	14706	824	2421	6982	15924	41849	67808	•	•	1960694	•	•
Operating Costs/Operating Income (%)													
Cost of Operations 10	66.0	48.4	54.7	61.5	50.6	72.8	81.9	75.2	•	•	61.5	•	•
Salaries and Wages 11	10.9	3.2	11.8	7.4	15.2	4.7	3.8	6.3	•	•	14.8	•	•
Taxes Paid 12	1.7	1.1	4.4	2.4	2.4	1.9	0.6	1.6	•	•	1.7	•	•
Interest Paid 13	1.5	•	0.8	0.6	0.6	1.8	0.8	0.8	•	•	2.0	•	•
Depreciation 14	2.0	0.2	0.7	0.6	2.3	0.6	1.0	1.4	•	•	2.5	•	•
Amortization and Depletion 15	0.2	•	•	0.0	0.0	•	0.0	0.1	•	•	0.3	•	•
Pensions and Other Deferred Comp. 16	0.5	•	•	0.4	0.4	0.5	0.1	0.4	•	•	0.7	•	•
Employee Benefits 17	1.8	0.2	0.0	0.7	1.2	0.3	1.4	1.4	•	•	2.6	•	•
Advertising 18	0.7	0.3	0.9	0.4	0.8	0.8	0.2	0.2	•	•	0.9	•	•
Other Expenses 19	10.1	4.3	11.1	11.4	18.1	5.1	5.2	6.9	•	•	10.9	•	•
Officers' Compensation 20	1.9	13.9	15.4	9.1	3.3	10.8	1.2	1.7	•	•	0.4	•	•
Operating Margin 21	2.7	28.4	0.2	5.8	5.1	0.9	3.9	3.9	•	•	1.9	•	•
Operating Margin Before Officers' Comp. 22	4.7	42.3	15.6	15.0	8.4	11.7	5.1	5.6	•	•	2.3	•	•

Selected Average Balance Sheet ($ in Thousands)

Net Receivables 23	1252	0	20	180	644	2615	4407	8267	•	56415
Inventories 24	2539	0	3	362	544	3193	7067	10581	•	269968
Net Property, Plant and Equipment 25	2115	0	24	157	423	1144	2738	6365	•	299165
Total Assets 26	13097	0	87	753	2730	7720	16113	37743	•	1964490
Notes and Loans Payable 27	3644	0	28	236	622	3172	3299	6440	•	555957
All Other Liabilities 28	2871	0	56	274	777	1391	3920	10189	•	409447
Net Worth 29	6582	0	3	243	1331	3156	8893	21114	•	999086

Selected Financial Ratios (Times to 1)

Current Ratio 30	1.7	•	1.2	1.5	2.0	2.7	2.3	2.4	•	1.5
Quick Ratio 31	0.8	•	1.1	1.0	1.2	1.4	1.0	1.2	•	0.7
Net Sales to Working Capital 32	6.9	•	71.1	13.0	6.4	3.9	5.9	3.9	•	8.3
Coverage Ratio 33	4.3	•	2.7	11.0	10.1	1.7	6.7	9.1	•	3.3
Total Asset Turnover 34	1.3	•	9.4	3.2	2.5	2.1	2.6	1.7	•	1.0
Inventory Turnover 35	4.6	•	173.8	4.1	6.5	3.6	4.8	4.7	•	4.3
Receivables Turnover 36	14.8	•	80.4	8.7	14.5	•	9.5	10.4	•	1.0
Total Liabilities to Net Worth 37	1.0	•	29.2	2.1	1.1	1.4	0.8	0.8	•	1.0
Current Assets to Working Capital 38	2.3	•	5.0	2.8	2.0	1.6	1.8	1.7	•	2.9
Current Liabilities to Working Capital 39	1.3	•	4.0	1.8	1.0	0.6	0.8	0.7	•	1.9
Working Capital to Net Sales 40	0.1	•	0.0	0.1	0.2	0.3	0.2	0.3	•	0.1
Inventory to Working Capital 41	1.0	•	0.4	1.0	0.7	0.8	1.0	0.7	•	1.2
Total Receipts to Cash Flow 42	7.9	2.8	8.7	7.0	4.8	17.6	12.2	8.1	•	7.5
Cost of Goods to Cash Flow 43	5.2	1.4	4.8	4.3	2.4	12.8	10.0	6.1	•	4.6
Cash Flow to Total Debt 44	0.3	•	1.1	0.7	1.0	0.2	0.5	0.5	•	0.3

Selected Financial Factors (in Percentages)

Debt Ratio 45	49.7	•	96.7	67.8	51.2	59.1	44.8	44.1	•	49.1
Return on Total Assets 46	8.5	•	20.8	21.0	15.6	6.3	13.2	13.1	•	6.3
Return on Equity Before Income Taxes 47	13.0	•	396.0	59.1	28.8	6.6	20.3	20.8	•	8.7
Return on Equity After Income Taxes 48	10.4	•	375.3	56.4	26.7	4.7	18.5	20.4	•	5.7
Profit Margin (Before Income Tax) 49	4.8	32.2	1.4	5.9	5.5	1.3	4.3	6.7	•	4.5
Profit Margin (After Income Tax) 50	3.9	32.2	1.3	5.7	5.1	0.9	3.9	6.5	•	3.0

Table I

Corporations with and without Net Income

APPAREL KNITTING MILLS

MONEY AMOUNTS AND SIZE OF ASSETS IN THOUSANDS OF DOLLARS

Item Description for Accounting Period 7/07 Through 6/08	Total	Zero Assets	Under 500	500 to 1,000	1,000 to 5,000	5,000 to 10,000	10,000 to 25,000	25,000 to 50,000	50,000 to 100,000	100,000 to 250,000	250,000 to 500,000	500,000 to 2,500,000	2,500,000 and over
Number of Enterprises **1**	109	0	0	0	65	3	27	6	0	4	4	0	0
Revenues ($ in Thousands)													
Net Sales **2**	7327461	0	0	0	224591	84002	704034	542091	0	672513	5100229	0	0
Interest **3**	9055	0	0	0	2601	0	1507	87	0	1168	3692	0	0
Rents **4**	61	0	0	0	0	0	17	37	0	7	0	0	0
Royalties **5**	47536	0	0	0	0	0	0	212	0	13015	34308	0	0
Other Portfolio Income **6**	86422	0	0	0	0	4170	1284	1845	0	7481	71642	0	0
Other Receipts **7**	29109	0	0	0	505	926	8950	1400	0	1304	16026	0	0
Total Receipts **8**	7499644	0	0	0	227697	89098	715792	545672	0	695488	5225897	0	0
Average Total Receipts **9**	68804	•	•	•	3503	29699	26511	90945	•	173872	1306474	•	•
Operating Costs/Operating Income (%)													
Cost of Operations **10**	73.7	•	•	•	74.4	92.7	80.0	82.4	•	74.1	71.6	•	•
Salaries and Wages **11**	7.0	•	•	•	3.5	7.8	5.4	4.3	•	5.3	7.9	•	•
Taxes Paid **12**	1.5	•	•	•	4.5	0.8	2.0	2.1	•	1.7	1.3	•	•
Interest Paid **13**	4.0	•	•	•	1.5	2.3	1.2	1.8	•	1.0	5.1	•	•
Depreciation **14**	1.3	•	•	•	1.5	1.4	1.3	1.6	•	2.2	1.1	•	•
Amortization and Depletion **15**	0.3	•	•	•	0.0	•	0.1	0.5	•	0.6	0.3	•	•
Pensions and Other Deferred Comp. **16**	0.3	•	•	•	0.0	0.0	0.0	0.2	•	0.4	0.3	•	•
Employee Benefits **17**	1.8	•	•	•	1.4	0.1	0.6	0.2	•	1.3	2.2	•	•
Advertising **18**	3.5	•	•	•	1.4	0.1	0.1	0.1	•	4.2	4.4	•	•
Other Expenses **19**	6.5	•	•	•	10.0	14.3	7.3	5.0	•	7.6	6.1	•	•
Officers' Compensation **20**	0.7	•	•	•	5.4	2.2	1.3	1.2	•	0.4	0.4	•	•
Operating Margin **21**	•	•	•	•	•	•	0.9	0.6	•	1.2	•	•	•
Operating Margin Before Officers' Comp. **22**	0.1	•	•	•	1.8	•	2.2	1.8	•	1.6	•	•	•

Selected Average Balance Sheet ($ in Thousands)

	1	2	3	4	5	6	7
Net Receivables 23	8811	218	954	3137	11254	27135	170644
Inventories 24	15488	753	10126	1774	28654	51038	283158
Net Property, Plant and Equipment 25	5825	174	2949	2130	9569	30314	94637
Total Assets 26	48853	2168	7041	14359	52187	132204	983332
Notes and Loans Payable 27	30492	299	1193	3055	20121	23817	750522
All Other Liabilities 28	13180	259	3612	2717	9508	34461	285169
Net Worth 29	5182	1610	2236	8586	22558	73926	-52359

Selected Financial Ratios (Times to 1)

	1	2	3	4	5	6	7
Current Ratio 30	2.5	3.3	1.2	1.9	3.9	2.4	2.6
Quick Ratio 31	1.0	0.9	0.5	1.2	1.6	1.0	0.9
Net Sales to Working Capital 32	4.1	4.3	52.0	7.0	3.4	3.7	3.9
Coverage Ratio 33	1.6	•	•	3.1	1.7	5.6	1.5
Total Asset Turnover 34	1.4	1.6	4.0	1.8	1.7	1.3	1.3
Inventory Turnover 35	3.2	3.4	2.6	11.8	2.6	2.4	3.2
Receivables Turnover 36	8.0	10.2	2.5	15.0	7.2	5.6	8.6
Total Liabilities to Net Worth 37	8.4	0.3	2.1	0.7	1.3	0.8	•
Current Assets to Working Capital 38	1.6	1.4	7.6	2.1	1.3	1.7	1.6
Current Liabilities to Working Capital 39	0.6	0.4	6.6	1.1	0.3	0.7	0.6
Working Capital to Net Sales 40	0.2	0.2	0.0	0.1	0.3	0.3	0.3
Inventory to Working Capital 41	0.9	1.0	2.1	0.7	0.7	1.0	0.9
Total Receipts to Cash Flow 42	15.7	32.8	•	13.6	20.7	9.4	16.1
Cost of Goods to Cash Flow 43	11.6	24.4	•	10.9	17.0	7.0	11.5
Cash Flow to Total Debt 44	0.1	0.2	•	0.3	0.1	0.3	0.1

Selected Financial Factors (in Percentages)

	1	2	3	4	5	6	7
Debt Ratio 45	89.4	25.7	68.2	40.2	56.8	44.1	105.3
Return on Total Assets 46	8.5	•	•	6.5	5.3	7.0	9.8
Return on Equity Before Income Taxes 47	28.3	•	•	7.3	5.2	10.3	•
Return on Equity After Income Taxes 48	24.1	•	•	6.0	3.5	9.0	•
Profit Margin (Before Income Tax) 49	2.2	•	•	2.4	1.3	4.5	2.4
Profit Margin (After Income Tax) 50	1.9	•	2.0	2.0	0.9	4.0	2.2

Table II

Corporations with Net Income

APPAREL KNITTING MILLS

MONEY AMOUNTS AND SIZE OF ASSETS IN THOUSANDS OF DOLLARS

Item Description for Accounting Period 7/07 Through 6/08	Total	Zero Assets	Under 500	500 to 1,000	1,000 to 5,000	5,000 to 10,000	10,000 to 25,000	25,000 to 50,000	50,000 to 100,000	100,000 to 250,000	250,000 to 500,000	500,000 to 2,500,000	2,500,000 and over
Number of Enterprises **1**	46	0	0	0	20	0	14	•	0	•	•	0	0
Revenues ($ in Thousands)													
Net Sales **2**	6231649	0	0	0	41692	0	452565	•	0	•	•	0	0
Interest **3**	7535	0	0	0	2601	0	102	•	0	•	•	0	0
Rents **4**	44	0	0	0	0	0	0	•	0	•	•	0	0
Royalties **5**	47245	0	0	0	0	0	0	•	0	•	•	0	0
Other Portfolio Income **6**	78736	0	0	0	0	0	1045	•	0	•	•	0	0
Other Receipts **7**	22643	0	0	0	0	0	8787	•	0	•	•	0	0
Total Receipts **8**	6387852	0	0	0	44293	0	462499	•	0	•	•	0	0
Average Total Receipts **9**	138866	•	•	•	2215	•	33036	•	•	•	•	•	•
Operating Costs/Operating Income (%)													
Cost of Operations **10**	72.1	•	•	•	68.4	•	77.4	•	•	•	•	•	•
Salaries and Wages **11**	7.3	•	•	•	2.3	•	5.4	•	•	•	•	•	•
Taxes Paid **12**	1.5	•	•	•	5.6	•	2.5	•	•	•	•	•	•
Interest Paid **13**	4.3	•	•	•	0.5	•	0.7	•	•	•	•	•	•
Depreciation **14**	1.2	•	•	•	0.4	•	1.1	•	•	•	•	•	•
Amortization and Depletion **15**	0.3	•	•	•	•	•	0.0	•	•	•	•	•	•
Pensions and Other Deferred Comp. **16**	0.3	•	•	•	0.1	•	0.0	•	•	•	•	•	•
Employee Benefits **17**	1.8	•	•	•	0.6	•	0.2	•	•	•	•	•	•
Advertising **18**	4.1	•	•	•	5.8	•	0.0	•	•	•	•	•	•
Other Expenses **19**	6.1	•	•	•	11.0	•	7.1	•	•	•	•	•	•
Officers' Compensation **20**	0.5	•	•	•	4.6	•	1.1	•	•	•	•	•	•
Operating Margin **21**	0.5	•	•	•	0.8	•	4.4	•	•	•	•	•	•
Operating Margin Before Officers' Comp. **22**	1.0	•	•	•	5.4	•	5.5	•	•	•	•	•	•

Selected Average Balance Sheet ($ in Thousands)

Net Receivables 23	17457	229	4969
Inventories 24	19701	135	1147
Net Property, Plant and Equipment 25	11739	121	1509
Total Assets 26	100308	2510	15967
Notes and Loans Payable 27	66384	0	3216
All Other Liabilities 28	27038	252	2983
Net Worth 29	6886	2258	9768

Selected Financial Ratios (Times to 1)

Current Ratio 30	2.5	2.0	1.3
Quick Ratio 31	0.9	1.5	1.1
Net Sales to Working Capital 32	4.3	8.2	16.5
Coverage Ratio 33	1.8	14.6	9.9
Total Asset Turnover 34	1.4	0.8	2.0
Inventory Turnover 35	5.0	10.6	21.8
Receivables Turnover 36	11.2	8.6	•
Total Liabilities to Net Worth 37	13.6	0.1	0.6
Current Assets to Working Capital 38	1.7	2.0	4.0
Current Liabilities to Working Capital 39	0.7	1.0	3.0
Working Capital to Net Sales 40	0.2	0.1	0.1
Inventory to Working Capital 41	0.9	0.5	0.6
Total Receipts to Cash Flow 42	13.6	9.2	8.7
Cost of Goods to Cash Flow 43	9.8	6.3	6.7
Cash Flow to Total Debt 44	0.1	0.9	0.6

Selected Financial Factors (in Percentages)

Debt Ratio 45	93.1	10.1	38.8
Return on Total Assets 46	10.6	6.2	14.4
Return on Equity Before Income Taxes 47	69.3	6.5	21.2
Return on Equity After Income Taxes 48	61.8	5.1	18.9
Profit Margin (Before Income Tax) 49	3.5	7.0	6.4
Profit Margin (After Income Tax) 50	3.1	5.5	5.7

Table I

Corporations with and without Net Income

CUT AND SEW APPAREL CONTRACTORS AND MFRS.

MONEY AMOUNTS AND SIZE OF ASSETS IN THOUSANDS OF DOLLARS

Item Description for Accounting Period 7/07 Through 6/08	Total	Zero Assets	Under 500	500 to 1,000	1,000 to 5,000	5,000 to 10,000	10,000 to 25,000	25,000 to 50,000	50,000 to 100,000	100,000 to 250,000	250,000 to 500,000	500,000 to 2,500,000	2,500,000 and over
Number of Enterprises **1**	7090	2036	3780	442	478	119	137	53	19	13	9	•	4
Revenues ($ in Thousands)													
Net Sales **2**	41718735	122280	1949620	759342	3077173	2246942	5101414	3486343	2174078	2947027	4608850	•	15245666
Interest **3**	82920	43	188	106	4348	6	4360	2018	2469	13000	5222	•	51163
Rents **4**	25142	0	0	0	664	0	0	0	1891	521	1373	•	20692
Royalties **5**	897217	0	0	0	423	0	1925	18568	303	96	68759	•	807141
Other Portfolio Income **6**	359574	74	1296	0	14027	72	748	73083	2146	2215	16302	•	249611
Other Receipts **7**	915077	1334	1538	69	23160	33194	55962	-3968	38973	11508	155085	•	598222
Total Receipts **8**	43998665	123731	1952642	759517	3119795	2280214	5164409	3576044	2219860	2974367	4855591	•	16972495
Average Total Receipts **9**	6206	61	517	1718	6527	19161	37696	67473	116835	228797	539510		4243124
Operating Costs/Operating Income (%)													
Cost of Operations **10**	63.3	27.7	24.8	59.9	69.2	66.6	75.6	70.5	66.2	65.0	59.0	•	61.7
Salaries and Wages **11**	10.7	24.0	15.0	19.6	8.9	11.3	5.9	8.2	12.3	10.0	11.8	•	11.7
Taxes Paid **12**	1.9	4.1	3.7	3.0	1.5	2.6	2.4	2.1	2.6	1.6	1.7	•	1.5
Interest Paid **13**	1.9	4.4	0.4	0.9	1.8	1.5	1.4	1.5	1.3	2.4	1.1	•	2.7
Depreciation **14**	1.0	1.7	1.2	1.0	0.5	0.3	0.3	0.7	1.1	1.1	1.3	•	1.4
Amortization and Depletion **15**	0.7	1.5	0.0	0.0	0.2	0.1	0.0	0.5	0.1	0.4	0.3	•	1.4
Pensions and Other Deferred Comp. **16**	0.4	0.1	0.0	0.0	0.1	0.1	0.4	0.2	0.7	0.4	0.3	•	0.5
Employee Benefits **17**	1.3	0.7	1.1	0.6	0.6	0.4	0.4	0.9	1.2	1.4	1.6	•	1.9
Advertising **18**	2.5	1.2	0.4	0.8	0.4	3.4	0.6	1.2	1.8	2.4	3.6	•	4.0
Other Expenses **19**	15.1	70.7	46.7	24.9	12.3	10.1	7.9	11.0	10.3	7.2	14.5	•	17.2
Officers' Compensation **20**	2.4	7.0	5.2	3.1	3.2	2.8	3.3	2.3	1.4	1.8	1.3	•	2.1
Operating Margin **21**	•	•	1.4	•	1.4	0.9	1.8	1.1	1.0	6.2	3.5	•	•
Operating Margin Before Officers' Comp. **22**	1.2	•	6.6	•	4.6	3.7	5.2	3.3	2.4	8.0	4.8	•	•

Selected Average Balance Sheet ($ in Thousands)

Net Receivables 23	848	0	11	116	450	2165	3363	7550	15411	23244	123272	• 719849
Inventories 24	898	0	20	130	1466	3479	5094	12081	26592	34421	88517	• 507338
Net Property, Plant and Equipment 25	420	0	12	143	104	433	1585	3740	8613	18697	53233	• 365945
Total Assets 26	4113	0	72	734	2302	7558	15423	32973	70976	149444	471407	• 3791988
Notes and Loans Payable 27	1198	0	27	438	895	3063	3878	8781	15898	51536	72306	• 1196522
All Other Liabilities 28	1225	0	29	167	864	1304	5750	8964	16948	27948	156796	• 1143313
Net Worth 29	1690	0	16	129	543	3192	5795	15229	38130	69961	242305	• 1452152

Selected Financial Ratios (Times to 1)

Current Ratio 30	1.8	•	2.0	1.4	2.3	1.9	1.4	1.7	2.3	2.4	2.3	• 1.6
Quick Ratio 31	0.9	•	1.3	0.7	0.9	0.7	0.5	0.6	1.0	1.0	1.3	• 0.9
Net Sales to Working Capital 32	5.9	•	18.3	19.1	5.3	5.9	10.6	6.5	3.9	4.7	3.1	• 6.9
Coverage Ratio 33	3.4	•	5.4	•	2.6	2.6	3.2	3.4	3.3	3.9	8.8	• 3.3
Total Asset Turnover 34	1.4	•	7.1	2.3	2.8	2.5	2.4	2.0	1.6	1.5	1.1	• 1.0
Inventory Turnover 35	4.1	•	6.4	7.9	3.0	3.6	5.5	3.8	2.8	4.3	3.4	• 4.6
Receivables Turnover 36	7.0	•	48.7	18.6	8.7	8.8	9.0	10.6	7.1	8.9	4.4	• 5.7
Total Liabilities to Net Worth 37	1.4	•	3.4	4.7	3.2	1.4	1.7	1.2	0.9	1.1	0.9	• 1.6
Current Assets to Working Capital 38	2.2	•	2.0	3.4	1.7	2.1	3.3	2.4	1.7	1.7	1.8	• 2.7
Current Liabilities to Working Capital 39	1.2	•	1.0	2.4	0.7	1.1	2.3	1.4	0.7	0.7	0.8	• 1.7
Working Capital to Net Sales 40	0.2	•	0.1	0.1	0.2	0.2	0.1	0.2	0.3	0.2	0.3	• 0.1
Inventory to Working Capital 41	0.9	•	0.6	1.7	1.0	1.3	1.6	1.2	0.8	0.8	0.6	• 0.9
Total Receipts to Cash Flow 42	6.5	•	2.7	38.5	8.7	9.0	10.9	7.9	9.5	8.3	5.1	• 5.6
Cost of Goods to Cash Flow 43	4.1	•	0.7	23.1	6.0	6.0	8.2	5.6	6.3	5.4	3.0	• 3.5
Cash Flow to Total Debt 44	0.4	•	3.4	0.1	0.4	0.5	0.4	0.5	0.4	0.3	0.4	• 0.3

Selected Financial Factors (in Percentages)

Debt Ratio 45	58.9	•	77.5	82.4	76.4	57.8	62.4	53.8	46.3	53.2	48.6	• 61.7
Return on Total Assets 46	9.4	•	13.8	•	12.6	9.5	10.7	10.1	7.1	14.5	10.8	• 9.2
Return on Equity Before Income Taxes 47	16.2	•	50.2	•	32.5	13.9	19.7	15.5	9.3	23.1	18.6	• 16.7
Return on Equity After Income Taxes 48	12.6	•	49.4	•	31.6	13.2	18.7	15.2	7.4	20.4	14.5	• 11.8
Profit Margin (Before Income Tax) 49	4.7	•	1.6	•	2.7	2.3	3.1	3.6	3.1	7.1	8.8	• 6.4
Profit Margin (After Income Tax) 50	3.6	•	1.6	•	2.7	2.2	2.9	3.5	2.5	6.3	6.9	• 4.5

65

Table II

Corporations with Net Income

CUT AND SEW APPAREL CONTRACTORS AND MFRS.

MONEY AMOUNTS AND SIZE OF ASSETS IN THOUSANDS OF DOLLARS

Item Description for Accounting Period 7/07 Through 6/08	Total	Zero Assets	Under 500	500 to 1,000	1,000 to 5,000	5,000 to 10,000	10,000 to 25,000	25,000 to 50,000	50,000 to 100,000	100,000 to 250,000	250,000 to 500,000	500,000 to 2,500,000	2,500,000 and over
Number of Enterprises **1**	3743	295	2515	264	388	•	94	34	15	10	•	•	•
Revenues ($ in Thousands)													
Net Sales **2**	34140000	17509	1604491	421509	2610504	•	3806700	2357179	1959549	2713498	•	•	•
Interest **3**	52658	0	20	0	3691	•	4209	564	2357	12361	•	•	•
Rents **4**	14690	0	0	0	388	•	0	0	1787	104	•	•	•
Royalties **5**	752620	0	0	0	423	•	1925	1574	303	96			•
Other Portfolio Income **6**	323481	0	0	0	78	•	220	72770	1727	2215	•	•	•
Other Receipts **7**	761288	826	176	0	17534	•	43429	19754	33470	10625	•	•	•
Total Receipts **8**	36044737	18335	1604687	421509	2632618	•	3856483	2451841	1999193	2738899	•	•	•
Average Total Receipts **9**	9630	62	638	1597	6785	•	41026	72113	133280	273890			
Operating Costs/Operating Income (%)													
Cost of Operations **10**	62.9	69.3	23.8	65.6	68.5	•	73.9	70.2	66.9	63.4	•	•	•
Salaries and Wages **11**	10.0	7.0	10.5	12.2	9.0	•	5.2	7.6	11.8	10.4	•	•	•
Taxes Paid **12**	1.8	0.6	3.5	1.2	1.4	•	2.2	2.2	2.6	1.7	•	•	•
Interest Paid **13**	1.9	0.9	0.0	1.6	1.2	•	1.2	1.3	1.2	2.5	•	•	•
Depreciation **14**	1.0	0.6	1.2	0.6	0.6	•	0.3	0.6	0.9	1.0	•	•	•
Amortization and Depletion **15**	0.6	0.1	•	0.0	0.0		0.0	0.2	0.1	0.5	•	•	•
Pensions and Other Deferred Comp. **16**	0.3	0.2	•	•	0.1		0.1	0.3	0.7	0.4	•	•	•
Employee Benefits **17**	1.4	1.0	0.9	0.8	0.6	•	0.4	1.1	1.2	1.3	•	•	•
Advertising **18**	2.4	1.6	0.4	0.3	0.4	•	0.7	0.8	1.9	2.4	•	•	•
Other Expenses **19**	14.5	18.2	51.0	10.5	11.7	•	7.5	8.6	9.3	7.3	•	•	•
Officers' Compensation **20**	2.3	0.6	4.4	3.4	3.2	•	4.0	2.3	1.4	1.7	•	•	•
Operating Margin **21**	1.1	•	4.2	3.9	3.4		4.5	4.9	2.0	7.4			•
Operating Margin Before Officers' Comp. **22**	3.3	0.5	8.6	7.3	6.5	•	8.5	7.2	3.4	9.1			•

Selected Average Balance Sheet ($ in Thousands)

Net Receivables 23	1117	0	•	81	371	•	3797	8643	14417	27237
Inventories 24	1453	0	•	124	1445	•	5753	11475	26621	44155
Net Property, Plant and Equipment 25	615	0	•	162	114	•	1027	4506	7831	22404
Total Assets 26	6250	0	•	677	2386	•	15723	32806	70693	155649
Notes and Loans Payable 27	1800	0	•	319	776	•	2856	8752	13082	60816
All Other Liabilities 28	1850	0	•	135	773	•	5762	7453	17040	29500
Net Worth 29	2600	0	•	223	837	•	7105	16601	40571	65333

Selected Financial Ratios (Times to 1)

Current Ratio 30	1.9	•	1.9	2.7	•	1.5	2.0	2.8	2.5
Quick Ratio 31	0.9	•	1.3	1.0	•	0.6	0.8	1.1	1.1
Net Sales to Working Capital 32	6.1	•	19.6	129.7	4.7	9.9	5.3	3.8	4.6
Coverage Ratio 33	4.6	6.0	433.3	3.4	4.4	5.7	8.0	4.4	4.3
Total Asset Turnover 34	1.5	•	8.2	2.4	2.8	2.6	2.1	1.8	1.7
Inventory Turnover 35	3.9	•	6.1	8.5	3.2	5.2	4.2	3.3	3.9
Receivables Turnover 36	7.0	•	54.9	16.2	9.7	8.1	9.4	•	•
Total Liabilities to Net Worth 37	1.4	•	1.3	2.0	1.8	1.2	1.0	0.7	1.4
Current Assets to Working Capital 38	2.2	•	2.1	14.7	1.6	3.0	2.0	1.6	1.7
Current Liabilities to Working Capital 39	1.2	•	1.1	13.7	0.6	2.0	1.0	0.6	0.7
Working Capital to Net Sales 40	0.2	•	0.1	0.0	0.2	0.1	0.2	0.3	0.2
Inventory to Working Capital 41	0.9	•	0.7	5.7	0.9	1.4	0.8	0.8	0.7
Total Receipts to Cash Flow 42	5.7	4.5	2.3	10.3	7.8	8.7	6.3	9.7	7.4
Cost of Goods to Cash Flow 43	3.6	3.1	0.5	6.8	5.4	6.4	4.4	6.5	4.7
Cash Flow to Total Debt 44	0.4	•	6.3	0.3	0.6	0.5	0.7	0.4	0.4

Selected Financial Factors (in Percentages)

Debt Ratio 45	58.4	•	56.9	67.1	•	54.8	49.4	42.6	58.0
Return on Total Assets 46	13.1	•	34.8	12.9	•	18.1	21.3	9.6	18.9
Return on Equity Before Income Taxes 47	24.7	•	80.4	27.8	•	33.0	36.8	12.9	34.6
Return on Equity After Income Taxes 48	20.3	•	79.9	23.4	•	31.8	36.4	10.7	30.9
Profit Margin (Before Income Tax) 49	7.0	4.6	4.2	3.9	4.2	5.8	8.8	4.0	8.3
Profit Margin (After Income Tax) 50	5.8	4.6	4.2	3.3	4.1	5.6	8.7	3.3	7.4

Table I

Corporations with and without Net Income

APPAREL ACCESSORIES AND OTHER APPAREL

MONEY AMOUNTS AND SIZE OF ASSETS IN THOUSANDS OF DOLLARS

Item Description for Accounting Period 7/07 Through 6/08	Total	Zero Assets	Under 500	500 to 1,000	1,000 to 5,000	5,000 to 10,000	10,000 to 25,000	25,000 to 50,000	50,000 to 100,000	100,000 to 250,000	250,000 to 500,000	500,000 to 2,500,000	2,500,000 and over
Number of Enterprises **1**	3891	1723	1181	339	518	18	78	20	7	5	0	0	0
Revenues ($ in Thousands)													
Net Sales **2**	9894060	475483	1026374	472053	2325915	313986	1690093	1071756	691905	1826495	0	0	0
Interest **3**	8137	0	12	0	3324	330	1393	1269	155	1654	0	0	0
Rents **4**	137	0	0	0	0	0	8	129	0	0	0	0	0
Royalties **5**	1023	0	0	0	0	32	0	0	94	897	0	0	0
Other Portfolio Income **6**	23335	9	5	0	18349	184	2503	538	807	940	0	0	0
Other Receipts **7**	109676	28858	6175	21649	22502	2795	9381	2995	10270	5051	0	0	0
Total Receipts **8**	10036368	504350	1032566	493702	2370090	317327	1703378	1076687	703231	1835037	0	0	0
Average Total Receipts **9**	2579	293	874	1456	4575	17629	21838	53834	100462	367007	•	•	•
Operating Costs/Operating Income (%)													
Cost of Operations **10**	63.4	73.1	64.8	73.4	66.1	68.5	65.6	66.0	73.8	45.6	•	•	•
Salaries and Wages **11**	11.7	29.6	8.8	7.3	9.4	10.2	11.5	7.0	8.7	16.9	•	•	•
Taxes Paid **12**	3.1	5.7	1.6	2.4	2.2	2.3	2.2	2.5	1.5	6.5	•	•	•
Interest Paid **13**	2.2	3.0	0.1	1.7	1.3	0.9	2.4	3.2	1.9	4.0	•	•	•
Depreciation **14**	1.1	0.9	0.1	0.9	0.6	0.6	1.6	1.5	1.3	1.5	•	•	•
Amortization and Depletion **15**	0.3	0.5	0.0	0.3	0.0	0.1	0.2	0.5	0.1	0.9	•	•	•
Pensions and Other Deferred Comp. **16**	0.4	0.0	0.6	0.0	0.5	0.3	0.3	0.2	1.3	0.0	•	•	•
Employee Benefits **17**	1.1	0.9	0.2	0.2	1.2	4.0	1.3	1.2	1.0	1.2	•	•	•
Advertising **18**	1.6	1.2	1.2	0.3	1.3	1.6	0.8	2.7	0.8	2.7	•	•	•
Other Expenses **19**	12.5	22.0	11.6	13.3	10.6	6.4	10.8	10.3	10.0	17.8	•	•	•
Officers' Compensation **20**	2.8	3.1	4.8	3.7	5.4	2.3	1.5	1.2	2.0	0.7	•	•	•
Operating Margin **21**	•	•	6.2	•	1.3	2.9	2.0	3.7	•	2.0	•	•	•
Operating Margin Before Officers' Comp. **22**	2.7	•	11.0	0.1	6.7	5.1	3.5	4.9	•	2.7	•	•	•

Selected Average Balance Sheet ($ in Thousands)

Net Receivables 23	304	0	70	91	524	1598	3346	10076	19072	34654
Inventories 24	448	0	63	405	631	2733	4987	12103	27247	71904
Net Property, Plant and Equipment 25	156	0	2	29	205	796	1692	4991	6089	39992
Total Assets 26	1490	0	219	627	2033	8490	14479	37320	72352	347380
Notes and Loans Payable 27	736	0	28	444	451	1033	12905	18008	40376	156009
All Other Liabilities 28	498	0	97	290	765	6230	2421	10241	16303	141584
Net Worth 29	256	0	94	-107	818	1228	-848	9070	15673	49788

Selected Financial Ratios (Times to 1)

Current Ratio 30	1.8	•	2.0	2.3	1.8	3.4	1.9	2.0	2.0	1.3
Quick Ratio 31	0.7	•	1.4	0.5	0.9	1.7	0.7	0.8	0.7	0.4
Net Sales to Working Capital 32	5.8	•	8.0	4.6	7.0	4.0	4.1	3.6	3.6	10.9
Coverage Ratio 33	1.6	•	69.6	1.6	3.5	5.5	2.2	2.3	0.6	1.6
Total Asset Turnover 34	1.7	•	4.0	2.2	2.2	2.1	1.5	1.4	1.4	1.1
Inventory Turnover 35	3.6	•	9.0	2.5	4.7	4.4	2.8	2.9	2.7	2.3
Receivables Turnover 36	8.6	•	11.8	11.2	9.7	21.8	7.1	5.2	4.4	10.8
Total Liabilities to Net Worth 37	4.8	•	1.3	•	1.5	5.9	•	3.1	3.6	6.0
Current Assets to Working Capital 38	2.3	•	2.0	1.8	2.2	1.4	2.1	2.0	2.0	4.9
Current Liabilities to Working Capital 39	1.3	•	1.0	0.8	1.2	0.4	1.1	1.0	1.0	3.9
Working Capital to Net Sales 40	0.2	•	0.1	0.2	0.1	0.3	0.2	0.3	0.3	0.1
Inventory to Working Capital 41	1.1	•	0.5	1.3	1.1	0.6	1.1	0.9	1.0	2.5
Total Receipts to Cash Flow 42	9.6	•	6.8	9.5	8.5	11.1	9.3	7.9	13.0	7.4
Cost of Goods to Cash Flow 43	6.1	•	4.4	7.0	5.6	7.6	6.1	5.2	9.6	3.4
Cash Flow to Total Debt 44	0.2	•	1.0	0.2	0.4	0.2	0.2	0.2	0.1	0.2

Selected Financial Factors (in Percentages)

Debt Ratio 45	82.8	•	56.9	117.0	59.8	85.5	105.9	75.7	78.3	85.7
Return on Total Assets 46	6.0	•	27.6	5.8	10.0	9.9	7.9	10.5	1.7	6.8
Return on Equity Before Income Taxes 47	13.3	•	63.1	•	17.8	56.0	•	24.4	•	17.8
Return on Equity After Income Taxes 48	7.3	•	63.1	•	15.2	53.5	•	20.0	•	6.5
Profit Margin (Before Income Tax) 49	1.3	•	6.8	1.0	3.2	3.9	2.8	4.1	•	2.4
Profit Margin (After Income Tax) 50	0.7	•	6.8	1.0	2.8	3.8	2.2	3.4	•	0.9

67

Table II

Corporations with Net Income

APPAREL ACCESSORIES AND OTHER APPAREL

MONEY AMOUNTS AND SIZE OF ASSETS IN THOUSANDS OF DOLLARS

Item Description for Accounting Period 7/07 Through 6/08		Total	Zero Assets	Under 500	500 to 1,000	1,000 to 5,000	5,000 to 10,000	10,000 to 25,000	25,000 to 50,000	50,000 to 100,000	100,000 to 250,000	250,000 to 500,000	500,000 to 2,500,000	2,500,000 and over
Number of Enterprises	1	1623	457	431	132	518	•	48	•	4	•	0	0	0
Revenues ($ in Thousands)														
Net Sales	2	7033121	99214	766201	213978	2325915	•	1291644	•	383164	•	0	0	0
Interest	3	7419	0	12	0	3324	•	1064	•	149	•	0	0	0
Rents	4	112	0	0	0	0	•	0	•	0	•	0	0	0
Royalties	5	1023	0	0	0	0	•	0	•	94	•	0	0	0
Other Portfolio Income	6	19533	0	0	0	18349	•	59	•	0	•	0	0	0
Other Receipts	7	53724	-1	9	21290	22502	•	4492	•	2288	•	0	0	•
Total Receipts	8	7114932	99213	766222	235268	2370090	•	1297259	•	385695	•	0	0	•
Average Total Receipts	9	4384	217	1778	1782	4575	•	27026	•	96424	•	•	•	•
Operating Costs/Operating Income (%)														
Cost of Operations	10	65.1	89.4	65.7	76.8	66.1	•	65.2	•	69.8	•	•	•	•
Salaries and Wages	11	8.6	9.5	7.8	5.1	9.4	•	10.0	•	6.1	•	•	•	•
Taxes Paid	12	2.6	•	1.5	1.5	2.2	•	2.0	•	1.4	•	•	•	•
Interest Paid	13	1.7	0.0	0.0	1.4	1.3	•	2.5	•	1.3	•	•	•	•
Depreciation	14	0.8	0.0	0.1	1.5	0.6	•	1.1	•	0.8	•	•	•	•
Amortization and Depletion	15	0.2	•	0.0	•	0.0	•	0.1	•	0.1	•	•	•	•
Pensions and Other Deferred Comp.	16	0.4	•	0.8	0.0	0.5	•	0.3	•	0.0	•	•	•	•
Employee Benefits	17	1.1	•	•	0.5	1.2	•	1.0	•	0.7	•	•	•	•
Advertising	18	1.5	0.3	0.0	0.3	1.3	•	0.8	•	1.4	•	•	•	•
Other Expenses	19	9.5	0.7	8.3	11.3	10.6	•	9.4	•	12.5	•	•	•	•
Officers' Compensation	20	3.2	•	5.1	0.6	5.4	•	1.6	•	3.0	•	•	•	•
Operating Margin	21	5.4	0.2	10.6	0.9	1.3	•	6.1	•	2.8	•	•	•	•
Operating Margin Before Officers' Comp.	22	8.6	0.2	15.7	1.6	6.7	•	7.7	•	5.9	•	•	•	•

Selected Average Balance Sheet ($ in Thousands)

	•	•	•	•	•	•	•	•	•
Net Receivables 23	523	0	191	75	524	•	2949	•	10479
Inventories 24	674	0	95	305	613	•	7205	•	24840
Net Property, Plant and Equipment 25	220	0	4	61	205	•	1575	•	3756
Total Assets 26	2260	0	375	577	2033	•	15191	•	68045
Notes and Loans Payable 27	817	0	33	355	451	•	8102	•	20549
All Other Liabilities 28	553	0	174	416	765	•	2067	•	6415
Net Worth 29	890	0	168	-194	818	•	5022	•	41081

Selected Financial Ratios (Times to 1)

	•	•	•	•	•	•	•	•	•
Current Ratio 30	2.1	•	1.8	2.2	1.8	•	1.9	•	2.0
Quick Ratio 31	0.9	•	1.8	0.5	0.9	•	0.5	•	0.4
Net Sales to Working Capital 32	5.1	•	10.9	5.9	7.0	•	4.9	•	3.6
Coverage Ratio 33	4.9	6.4	4786.2	8.7	3.5	•	3.6	•	3.6
Total Asset Turnover 34	1.9	•	4.7	2.8	2.2	•	1.8	•	1.4
Inventory Turnover 35	4.2	•	12.3	4.1	4.8	•	2.4	•	2.7
Receivables Turnover 36	9.0	•	8.8	16.4	10.1	•	•	•	7.8
Total Liabilities to Net Worth 37	1.5	•	1.2	•	1.5	•	2.0	•	0.7
Current Assets to Working Capital 38	1.9	•	2.3	1.8	2.2	•	2.1	•	2.0
Current Liabilities to Working Capital 39	0.9	•	1.3	0.8	1.2	•	1.1	•	1.0
Working Capital to Net Sales 40	0.2	•	0.1	0.2	0.1	•	0.2	•	0.3
Inventory to Working Capital 41	0.9	•	0.0	1.3	1.1	•	1.3	•	1.0
Total Receipts to Cash Flow 42	7.1	587.1	5.9	5.5	8.5	•	7.1	•	6.6
Cost of Goods to Cash Flow 43	4.6	524.9	3.9	4.3	5.6	•	4.7	•	4.6
Cash Flow to Total Debt 44	0.4	•	1.5	0.4	0.4	•	0.4	•	0.5

Selected Financial Factors (in Percentages)

	•	•	•	•	•	•	•	•	•
Debt Ratio 45	60.6	•	55.2	133.5	59.8	•	66.9	•	39.6
Return on Total Assets 46	15.7	•	50.3	34.6	10.0	•	16.0	•	6.8
Return on Equity Before Income Taxes 47	31.7	•	112.4	•	17.8	•	35.1	•	8.2
Return on Equity After Income Taxes 48	27.6	•	112.4	•	15.2	•	30.7	•	7.2
Profit Margin (Before Income Tax) 49	6.5	0.2	10.6	10.9	3.2	•	6.5	•	3.5
Profit Margin (After Income Tax) 50	5.7	0.2	10.6	10.9	2.8	•	5.7	•	3.1

Table I

Corporations with and without Net Income

LEATHER AND ALLIED PRODUCT MANUFACTURING

MONEY AMOUNTS AND SIZE OF ASSETS IN THOUSANDS OF DOLLARS

Item Description for Accounting Period 7/07 Through 6/08		Total	Zero Assets	Under 500	500 to 1,000	1,000 to 5,000	5,000 to 10,000	10,000 to 25,000	25,000 to 50,000	50,000 to 100,000	100,000 to 250,000	250,000 to 500,000	500,000 to 2,500,000	2,500,000 and over
Number of Enterprises	1	1775	458	1043	66	151	0	26	11	6	5	3	6	0
Revenues ($ in Thousands)														
Net Sales	2	8788622	91037	215050	19023	519122	0	800632	628583	752638	1180591	1373631	3208314	0
Interest	3	56389	33	0	14	1023	0	432	1293	1826	3611	8361	39794	0
Rents	4	1360	0	0	386	5	0	104	114	0	0	382	370	0
Royalties	5	179599	0	0	0	0	0	0	0	2941	0	44462	132196	0
Other Portfolio Income	6	75815	0	0	19576	1868	0	1286	0	231	43	36412	16399	0
Other Receipts	7	42426	1	33	13	357	0	-2766	4115	428	-43	1031	39259	0
Total Receipts	8	9144211	91071	215083	39012	522375	0	799688	634105	758064	1184202	1464279	3436332	0
Average Total Receipts	9	5152	199	206	591	3459	•	30757	57646	126344	236840	488093	572722	•
Operating Costs/Operating Income (%)														
Cost of Operations	10	63.5	91.7	35.1	85.3	64.8	•	57.6	80.7	60.8	54.1	73.4	62.3	•
Salaries and Wages	11	10.0	2.6	11.4	•	9.5	•	11.9	4.1	11.4	7.6	6.6	13.0	•
Taxes Paid	12	2.0	1.2	1.7	8.4	2.8	•	0.9	2.2	2.2	1.4	1.7	2.4	•
Interest Paid	13	2.2	0.5	0.0	0.4	0.1	•	0.6	1.0	1.4	2.0	2.6	3.4	•
Depreciation	14	1.3	0.3	0.5	3.0	0.4	•	1.0	2.6	0.8	1.0	1.5	1.5	•
Amortization and Depletion	15	0.6	0.0	0.3	0.0	0.0	•	0.1	0.0	0.4	0.6	0.2	1.2	•
Pensions and Other Deferred Comp.	16	0.5	0.3	0.2	0.1	0.3	•	0.4	0.1	0.3	0.2	1.6	0.4	•
Employee Benefits	17	1.0	•	•	•	0.3	•	2.0	1.5	0.9	0.2	1.4	0.9	•
Advertising	18	2.8	0.0	1.0	0.9	2.0	•	3.7	0.1	2.8	3.2	2.2	3.6	•
Other Expenses	19	13.3	5.0	32.1	13.0	17.2	•	12.4	4.9	13.1	16.6	13.4	12.4	•
Officers' Compensation	20	2.1	0.6	8.0	20.7	3.0	•	2.3	1.3	1.0	3.9	1.3	1.6	•
Operating Margin	21	0.6	•	9.5	•	•	•	7.2	1.4	4.9	9.2	•	•	•
Operating Margin Before Officers' Comp.	22	2.7	•	17.6	•	2.6	•	9.5	2.7	5.9	13.1	•	•	•

Selected Average Balance Sheet ($ in Thousands)

Net Receivables 23	1037	0	21	106	37	•	3881	9518	21817	35269	94595	168131	•
Inventories 24	852	0	47	14	491	•	4617	10098	27137	60514	65127	96926	•
Net Property, Plant and Equipment 25	426	0	1	2	191	•	1138	9175	7693	14195	44631	57589	•
Total Assets 26	5421	0	96	646	1629	•	17695	36241	79907	150377	388531	996377	•
Notes and Loans Payable 27	2145	0	35	30	44	•	2035	12611	15748	46491	238720	421254	•
All Other Liabilities 28	1501	0	1	77	896	•	3623	4277	18181	31206	124923	290460	•
Net Worth 29	1775	0	61	539	689	•	12037	19354	45978	72679	24887	284663	•

Selected Financial Ratios (Times to 1)

Current Ratio 30	1.8	•	31.4	8.4	1.4	•	3.2	1.9	3.2	3.2	1.5	1.5	•
Quick Ratio 31	1.0	•	17.4	8.2	0.3	•	1.8	1.1	1.4	1.6	0.8	0.8	•
Net Sales to Working Capital 32	4.0	•	2.4	0.5	10.1	•	3.2	5.4	3.0	3.0	6.8	4.1	•
Coverage Ratio 33	3.4	•	855.2	203.2	0.4	•	12.7	3.3	5.0	5.7	2.1	2.5	•
Total Asset Turnover 34	0.9	•	2.1	0.4	2.1	•	1.7	1.6	1.6	1.6	1.2	0.5	•
Inventory Turnover 35	3.7	•	1.5	18.2	4.5	•	3.8	4.6	2.8	2.1	5.2	3.4	•
Receivables Turnover 36	5.6	•	10.4	5.4	60.6	•	8.8	5.1	6.2	5.9	9.7	3.7	•
Total Liabilities to Net Worth 37	2.1	•	0.6	0.2	1.4	•	0.5	0.9	0.7	1.1	14.6	2.5	•
Current Assets to Working Capital 38	2.3	•	1.0	1.1	3.8	•	1.5	2.1	1.5	1.5	3.1	3.1	•
Current Liabilities to Working Capital 39	1.3	•	0.0	0.1	2.8	•	0.5	1.1	0.5	0.5	2.1	2.1	•
Working Capital to Net Sales 40	0.2	•	0.4	2.0	0.1	•	0.3	0.2	0.3	0.3	0.1	0.2	•
Inventory to Working Capital 41	0.7	•	0.5	0.0	1.5	•	0.6	0.8	0.7	0.7	1.0	0.7	•
Total Receipts to Cash Flow 42	6.5	67.7	2.7	•	8.6	•	5.4	16.2	6.1	4.2	8.8	7.0	•
Cost of Goods to Cash Flow 43	4.2	62.0	1.0	•	5.5	•	3.1	13.1	3.7	2.3	6.5	4.4	•
Cash Flow to Total Debt 44	0.2	•	2.2	•	0.4	•	1.0	0.2	0.6	0.7	0.1	0.1	•

Selected Financial Factors (in Percentages)

Debt Ratio 45	67.3	•	36.6	16.5	57.7	•	32.0	46.6	42.5	51.7	93.6	71.4	•
Return on Total Assets 46	6.8	•	20.5	32.9	0.1	•	13.3	5.1	11.1	18.1	6.4	4.5	•
Return on Equity Before Income Taxes 47	14.6	•	32.3	39.2	•	•	18.0	6.7	15.5	30.9	53.2	9.5	•
Return on Equity After Income Taxes 48	11.5	•	30.9	32.2	•	•	16.9	6.7	13.0	27.0	29.9	6.6	•
Profit Margin (Before Income Tax) 49	5.2	•	9.5	73.3	•	•	7.0	2.3	5.7	9.5	2.9	5.1	•
Profit Margin (After Income Tax) 50	4.1	•	9.1	60.2	•	•	6.6	2.3	4.8	8.3	1.6	3.5	•

Table II

Corporations with Net Income

LEATHER AND ALLIED PRODUCT MANUFACTURING

MONEY AMOUNTS AND SIZE OF ASSETS IN THOUSANDS OF DOLLARS

Item Description for Accounting Period 7/07 Through 6/08	Total	Zero Assets	Under 500	500 to 1,000	1,000 to 5,000	5,000 to 10,000	10,000 to 25,000	25,000 to 50,000	50,000 to 100,000	100,000 to 250,000	250,000 to 500,000	500,000 to 2,500,000	2,500,000 and over
Number of Enterprises **1**	977	0	750	•	117	0	22	•	•	5	0	3	0
Revenues ($ in Thousands)													
Net Sales **2**	7111669	0	201966	•	227107	0	800632	•	•	1916435	0	2707948	0
Interest **3**	21740	0	0	•	105	0	432	•	•	9988	0	8155	0
Rents **4**	1001	0	0	•	5	0	104	•	•	382	0	10	0
Royalties **5**	120513	0	0	•	0	0	0	•	•	2042	0	115530	0
Other Portfolio Income **6**	28482	0	0	•	1282	0	1286	•	•	6332	0	6	0
Other Receipts **7**	37585	0	0	•	101	0	2667	•	•	470	0	29848	0
Total Receipts **8**	7320990	0	201966	•	228600	0	805121	•	•	1935649	0	2861497	0
Average Total Receipts **9**	7493	•	269	•	1954	•	36596	•	•	387130	•	953832	•
Operating Costs/Operating Income (%)													
Cost of Operations **10**	63.2	•	32.0	•	46.6	•	57.6	•	•	66.6	•	62.9	•
Salaries and Wages **11**	9.5	•	12.2	•	8.9	•	11.8	•	•	6.5	•	11.7	•
Taxes Paid **12**	2.0	•	1.8	•	4.6	•	0.8	•	•	1.4	•	2.3	•
Interest Paid **13**	0.5	•	0.0	•	0.1	•	0.6	•	•	0.5	•	0.4	•
Depreciation **14**	1.2	•	0.2	•	0.5	•	0.7	•	•	1.2	•	1.4	•
Amortization and Depletion **15**	0.4	•	0.3	•	0.0	•	0.1	•	•	0.1	•	0.8	•
Pensions and Other Deferred Comp. **16**	0.3	•	0.2	•	0.1	•	0.3	•	•	0.4	•	0.3	•
Employee Benefits **17**	0.9	•	•	•	0.3	•	2.0	•	•	0.7	•	0.6	•
Advertising **18**	2.9	•	1.0	•	3.8	•	3.7	•	•	2.2	•	3.9	•
Other Expenses **19**	10.8	•	25.0	•	29.9	•	10.9	•	•	9.5	•	10.3	•
Officers' Compensation **20**	2.5	•	8.6	•	4.9	•	2.3	•	•	3.2	•	1.9	•
Operating Margin **21**	5.9	•	18.8	•	0.4	•	9.0	•	•	7.6	•	3.5	•
Operating Margin Before Officers' Comp. **22**	8.4	•	27.4	•	5.3	•	11.3	•	•	10.7	•	5.4	•

Selected Average Balance Sheet ($ in Thousands)

Net Receivables 23	1560	29	37	4585	59972	294346
Inventories 24	1220	15	317	5324	63160	149714
Net Property, Plant and Equipment 25	557	1	142	1332	27502	86167
Total Assets 26	5057	92	1326	18388	229305	789334
Notes and Loans Payable 27	561	3	20	2405	41256	28242
All Other Liabilities 28	1514	1	885	4273	61454	278929
Net Worth 29	2982	88	420	11711	126595	482163

Selected Financial Ratios (Times to 1)

Current Ratio 30	2.1	21.0	1.2	2.9	1.9	2.0
Quick Ratio 31	1.3	17.3	0.2	1.5	1.1	1.4
Net Sales to Working Capital 32	3.8	3.5	12.4	3.8	5.0	3.3
Coverage Ratio 33	17.6	1651.8	4.9	16.8	17.1	27.8
Total Asset Turnover 34	1.4	2.9	1.5	2.0	1.7	1.1
Inventory Turnover 35	3.8	5.9	2.9	3.9	4.0	3.8
Receivables Turnover 36	5.2	9.8	23.2	9.0	•	0.6
Total Liabilities to Net Worth 37	0.7	0.0	2.2	0.6	0.8	0.6
Current Assets to Working Capital 38	1.9	1.0	6.8	1.5	2.1	2.0
Current Liabilities to Working Capital 39	0.9	0.0	5.8	0.5	1.1	1.0
Working Capital to Net Sales 40	0.3	0.3	0.1	0.3	0.2	0.3
Inventory to Working Capital 41	0.6	0.2	2.0	0.7	0.8	0.5
Total Receipts to Cash Flow 42	5.8	2.3	4.6	5.1	6.3	5.7
Cost of Goods to Cash Flow 43	3.7	0.7	2.1	3.0	4.2	3.6
Cash Flow to Total Debt 44	0.6	29.7	0.5	1.1	0.6	0.5

Selected Financial Factors (in Percentages)

Debt Ratio 45	41.0	4.2	68.3	36.3	44.8	38.9
Return on Total Assets 46	13.7	55.0	0.8	20.0	15.5	11.3
Return on Equity Before Income Taxes 47	22.0	57.4	2.1	29.6	26.4	17.9
Return on Equity After Income Taxes 48	18.7	56.1	1.7	28.2	21.4	14.4
Profit Margin (Before Income Tax) 49	9.0	18.8	0.5	9.5	8.7	9.5
Profit Margin (After Income Tax) 50	7.7	18.4	0.4	9.1	7.1	7.7

Table I

Corporations with and without Net Income

WOOD PRODUCT MANUFACTURING

MONEY AMOUNTS AND SIZE OF ASSETS IN THOUSANDS OF DOLLARS

Item Description for Accounting Period 7/07 Through 6/08	Total	Zero Assets	Under 500	500 to 1,000	1,000 to 5,000	5,000 to 10,000	10,000 to 25,000	25,000 to 50,000	50,000 to 100,000	100,000 to 250,000	250,000 to 500,000	500,000 to 2,500,000	2,500,000 and over
Number of Enterprises 1	11265	510	6623	1085	2178	360	297	91	56	39	10	14	0
Revenues ($ in Thousands)													
Net Sales 2	73997131	924710	4614179	1824384	10739599	7362071	8508036	5238513	5236808	7763498	5498083	16287250	0
Interest 3	251562	246	994	434	9303	5516	4639	7590	6713	19121	32844	164262	0
Rents 4	30715	0	0	0	6319	720	8924	2800	3100	1277	2225	5350	0
Royalties 5	16723	0	0	286	0	0	97	1208	14	4027	691	10400	0
Other Portfolio Income 6	245584	29849	15767	3919	8292	10088	39829	37057	11817	32336	7708	48925	0
Other Receipts 7	645601	20527	20616	655	37316	32710	39640	41427	39249	93299	87749	232408	0
Total Receipts 8	75187316	975332	4651556	1829678	10800829	7411105	8601065	5328595	5297701	7913558	5629300	16748595	0
Average Total Receipts 9	6674	1912	702	1686	4959	20586	28960	58556	94602	202912	562930	1196328	•
Operating Costs/Operating Income (%)													
Cost of Operations 10	75.7	83.8	54.6	66.9	71.7	81.8	76.7	81.9	79.0	81.4	82.4	73.6	•
Salaries and Wages 11	6.4	4.6	12.0	9.3	7.3	4.2	4.8	4.1	4.5	5.2	4.7	8.2	•
Taxes Paid 12	1.8	0.9	3.3	2.3	2.1	1.4	1.9	1.6	1.6	1.6	1.1	1.9	•
Interest Paid 13	1.8	4.5	1.1	1.3	1.1	0.7	1.4	1.1	1.8	2.1	2.2	3.0	•
Depreciation 14	3.2	8.0	2.2	2.7	1.7	1.9	3.2	2.4	3.0	3.6	3.6	4.8	•
Amortization and Depletion 15	0.5	1.6	0.1	0.1	0.0	0.0	0.1	0.1	0.8	0.3	0.5	1.4	•
Pensions and Other Deferred Comp. 16	0.4	0.2	0.2	0.1	0.2	0.2	0.5	0.3	0.3	0.1	0.3	0.7	•
Employee Benefits 17	1.4	0.5	1.8	0.8	1.0	1.1	1.2	1.1	1.2	1.2	1.2	2.1	•
Advertising 18	0.6	0.5	0.4	0.2	0.2	0.7	0.3	0.3	0.6	0.4	1.3	1.2	•
Other Expenses 19	8.5	14.6	18.0	12.9	10.0	4.7	8.9	5.3	7.0	6.9	8.4	7.6	•
Officers' Compensation 20	1.8	2.5	8.1	4.8	3.2	1.9	1.3	1.2	0.7	0.8	0.5	0.5	•
Operating Margin 21	•	•	•	•	1.5	1.3	•	0.7	•	•	•	•	•
Operating Margin Before Officers' Comp. 22	•	•	6.3	3.5	4.7	3.2	1.1	1.9	0.1	•	•	•	•

Selected Average Balance Sheet ($ in Thousands)

Item													
Net Receivables 23	514	0	23	170	461	1457	2336	6164	8228	17491	44525	77399	•
Inventories 24	790	0	17	191	665	2254	4162	9977	15686	24721	53165	128820	•
Net Property, Plant and Equipment 25	1618	0	56	133	519	2288	5847	11981	25514	69224	142215	526932	•
Total Assets 26	4451	0	152	660	2082	7522	14957	35050	70572	154105	384873	1409445	•
Notes and Loans Payable 27	1598	0	114	371	838	1992	6053	10662	24470	55803	86405	508782	•
All Other Liabilities 28	964	0	37	139	419	1305	2393	6143	11531	34326	141436	315350	•
Net Worth 29	1889	0	1	150	825	4225	6511	18245	34570	63977	157032	585313	•

Selected Financial Ratios (Times to 1)

Item													
Current Ratio 30	1.8	•	1.4	2.8	1.9	2.2	1.8	2.0	1.7	1.8	1.8	1.6	
Quick Ratio 31	0.8	•	0.9	1.4	1.0	0.9	0.8	0.8	0.8	0.8	0.8	0.6	
Net Sales to Working Capital 32	8.3	•	36.8	5.5	8.0	7.9	8.0	6.1	7.0	7.1	8.8	9.2	
Coverage Ratio 33	0.8	•	0.2	0.2	2.9	3.8	1.6	3.2	1.3	0.1	•	0.3	
Total Asset Turnover 34	1.5	•	4.6	2.5	2.4	2.7	1.9	1.6	1.3	1.3	1.4	0.8	
Inventory Turnover 35	6.3	•	21.8	5.9	5.3	7.4	5.3	4.7	4.7	6.6	8.5	6.6	
Receivables Turnover 36	12.1	•	23.6	11.6	8.9	16.6	11.5	8.2	10.9	10.9	12.4	14.6	
Total Liabilities to Net Worth 37	1.4	•	110.5	3.4	1.5	0.8	1.3	0.9	1.0	1.4	1.5	1.4	
Current Assets to Working Capital 38	2.3	•	3.8	1.6	2.2	1.9	2.2	2.0	2.3	2.2	2.3	2.8	
Current Liabilities to Working Capital 39	1.3	•	2.8	0.6	1.2	0.9	1.2	1.0	1.3	1.2	1.3	1.8	
Working Capital to Net Sales 40	0.1	•	0.0	0.2	0.1	0.1	0.1	0.2	0.1	0.1	0.1	0.1	
Inventory to Working Capital 41	1.0	•	0.6	0.6	0.9	1.0	1.1	0.9	1.2	0.9	0.9	1.0	
Total Receipts to Cash Flow 42	17.0	•	8.3	14.6	10.5	19.3	13.0	17.3	16.2	26.8	36.5	28.0	
Cost of Goods to Cash Flow 43	12.9	•	4.5	9.8	7.5	15.7	10.0	14.1	12.8	21.8	30.1	20.6	
Cash Flow to Total Debt 44	0.2	•	0.6	0.2	0.4	0.3	0.3	0.2	0.2	0.1	0.1	0.1	

Selected Financial Factors (in Percentages)

Item													
Debt Ratio 45	57.6	•	99.1	77.3	60.4	43.8	56.5	47.9	51.0	58.5	59.2	58.5	
Return on Total Assets 46	2.0	•	1.0	0.7	7.4	7.5	4.3	5.7	3.1	0.3	•	0.7	
Return on Equity Before Income Taxes 47	•	•	•	•	12.2	9.8	3.8	7.5	1.5	•	•	•	
Return on Equity After Income Taxes 48	•	•	•	•	11.1	9.0	3.0	5.4	0.4	•	•	•	
Profit Margin (Before Income Tax) 49	•	•	•	•	2.0	2.0	0.9	2.4	0.5	•	•	•	
Profit Margin (After Income Tax) 50	•	•	•	•	1.9	1.9	0.7	1.7	0.2	•	•	•	

Table II

Corporations with Net Income

WOOD PRODUCT MANUFACTURING

MONEY AMOUNTS AND SIZE OF ASSETS IN THOUSANDS OF DOLLARS

Item Description for Accounting Period 7/07 Through 6/08	Total	Zero Assets	Under 500	500 to 1,000	1,000 to 5,000	5,000 to 10,000	10,000 to 25,000	25,000 to 50,000	50,000 to 100,000	100,000 to 250,000	250,000 to 500,000	500,000 to 2,500,000	2,500,000 and over
Number of Enterprises **1**	5406	19	2575	725	1524	287	164	65	27	13	3	5	0
Revenues ($ in Thousands)													
Net Sales **2**	45145152	491548	2349382	1385072	8457701	6559559	4944432	3763368	2923501	2095851	2001514	10173223	0
Interest **3**	47432	129	78	426	8522	3495	1807	4942	3113	4311	1	20609	0
Rents **4**	17894	0	0	0	6211	389	6806	1719	1643	173	183	768	0
Royalties **5**	11550	0	0	286	0	0	0	1208	0	0	0	10056	0
Other Portfolio Income **6**	130238	21081	14885	3530	8009	6988	20420	19978	3103	3567	1452	27225	0
Other Receipts **7**	365802	19737	2012	617	25476	22237	14873	29010	20900	36761	40655	153526	0
Total Receipts **8**	45718068	532495	2366357	1389931	8505919	6592668	4988338	3820225	2952260	2140663	2043805	10385407	0
Average Total Receipts **9**	8457	28026	919	1917	5581	22971	30417	58773	109343	164666	681268	2077081	•
Operating Costs/Operating Income (%)													
Cost of Operations **10**	71.7	77.7	51.8	71.5	69.7	82.1	73.5	79.0	76.9	67.1	79.1	65.5	•
Salaries and Wages **11**	6.9	6.6	12.4	5.3	7.4	4.1	4.4	3.9	4.0	6.2	4.7	10.8	•
Taxes Paid **12**	1.8	0.7	3.0	1.8	2.1	1.3	1.8	1.6	1.2	2.3	1.6	2.0	•
Interest Paid **13**	1.0	0.9	0.8	0.8	0.7	0.5	1.2	0.9	1.2	1.6	0.5	1.6	•
Depreciation **14**	2.3	3.5	1.9	1.7	1.5	1.8	2.8	2.4	2.1	2.7	2.2	2.9	•
Amortization and Depletion **15**	0.2	0.1	0.2	0.1	0.0	0.0	0.0	0.1	0.1	0.2	0.0	0.8	•
Pensions and Other Deferred Comp. **16**	0.5	0.0	0.2	0.1	0.2	0.2	0.5	0.4	0.5	0.2	0.3	1.0	•
Employee Benefits **17**	1.4	0.1	1.7	0.9	1.0	1.0	0.9	1.2	1.1	1.7	0.8	2.5	•
Advertising **18**	0.7	0.7	0.4	0.2	0.2	0.6	0.3	0.2	0.7	1.0	1.2	1.6	•
Other Expenses **19**	7.6	6.2	14.2	7.5	9.0	4.1	8.5	4.9	6.3	9.6	7.6	8.0	•
Officers' Compensation **20**	2.0	4.6	7.2	5.8	3.6	1.6	1.4	1.2	0.7	1.4	0.7	0.5	•
Operating Margin **21**	3.9	•	6.2	4.2	4.7	2.6	4.7	4.2	5.3	5.9	1.3	2.8	•
Operating Margin Before Officers' Comp. **22**	5.9	3.3	13.4	10.0	8.3	4.2	6.1	5.4	5.9	7.4	2.0	3.3	•

Selected Average Balance Sheet ($ in Thousands)

	•	•	•	•	•	•	•	•	•	•	•	•
Net Receivables 23	0	640	45	187	440	1412	2503	6365	9385	17674	47958	135708
Inventories 24	0	1008	23	206	672	2461	4339	11447	16871	24469	59118	187334
Net Property, Plant and Equipment 25	0	1268	54	108	463	2360	5612	11588	19025	60748	134477	374634
Total Assets 26	0	4529	211	574	2104	7583	14516	35001	69810	133719	328008	1775748
Notes and Loans Payable 27	0	1229	68	174	647	1324	5623	9753	18330	56394	46431	411030
All Other Liabilities 28	0	1075	42	143	320	1386	2149	5003	11241	29277	97451	611581
Net Worth 29	0	2225	100	257	1137	4874	6744	20245	40239	48047	184125	753137

Selected Financial Ratios (Times to 1)

	•	•	•	•	•	•	•	•	•	•	•	•
Current Ratio 30	•	1.8	1.9	2.7	2.4	2.5	2.1	2.3	2.2	1.5	1.7	1.0
Quick Ratio 31	•	0.8	1.5	1.9	1.3	1.1	1.0	1.0	0.9	0.9	0.8	0.3
Net Sales to Working Capital 32	•	9.3	18.2	6.5	7.8	7.5	5.1	7.2	5.7	10.3	10.1	99.6
Coverage Ratio 33	8.5	6.1	9.8	6.9	8.9	7.2	5.8	7.2	6.2	6.1	7.8	4.0
Total Asset Turnover 34	•	1.8	4.3	3.3	2.6	3.0	2.1	1.7	1.6	1.2	2.0	1.1
Inventory Turnover 35	•	5.9	20.3	6.6	5.7	7.6	5.1	4.0	4.9	4.4	8.9	7.1
Receivables Turnover 36	•	10.7	14.7	10.4	9.2	18.0	9.8	7.1	•	6.4	•	14.1
Total Liabilities to Net Worth 37	•	1.0	1.1	1.2	0.9	0.6	1.2	0.7	0.7	1.8	0.8	1.4
Current Assets to Working Capital 38	•	2.3	2.1	1.6	1.7	1.7	1.9	1.7	1.8	3.1	2.4	23.6
Current Liabilities to Working Capital 39	•	1.3	1.1	0.6	0.7	0.7	0.9	0.7	0.8	2.1	1.4	22.6
Working Capital to Net Sales 40	•	0.1	0.1	0.1	0.2	0.1	0.1	0.2	0.2	0.1	0.1	0.0
Inventory to Working Capital 41	•	1.0	0.2	0.4	0.7	0.9	0.9	0.8	0.9	0.9	0.9	8.9
Total Receipts to Cash Flow 42	8.5	9.3	6.0	10.4	8.5	16.9	8.7	11.1	8.8	6.5	10.1	8.9
Cost of Goods to Cash Flow 43	6.6	6.7	3.1	7.5	5.9	13.9	6.4	8.8	6.7	4.4	8.0	6.0
Cash Flow to Total Debt 44	•	0.4	0.6	0.6	0.7	0.5	0.4	0.4	0.4	0.3	0.5	0.2

Selected Financial Factors (in Percentages)

	•	•	•	•	•	•	•	•	•	•	•	•
Debt Ratio 45	•	50.9	52.3	55.3	46.0	35.7	53.5	42.2	42.4	64.1	43.9	57.6
Return on Total Assets 46	•	11.4	33.3	17.6	15.7	10.9	14.1	11.0	11.5	11.6	7.8	7.6
Return on Equity Before Income Taxes 47	•	19.3	62.8	33.6	25.7	14.6	25.1	16.4	16.7	26.9	12.1	13.4
Return on Equity After Income Taxes 48	•	17.3	62.7	33.2	24.6	13.8	23.7	13.8	14.9	20.9	11.9	10.8
Profit Margin (Before Income Tax) 49	7.0	5.1	6.9	4.5	5.3	3.1	5.6	5.7	6.2	8.0	3.3	5.0
Profit Margin (After Income Tax) 50	6.2	4.6	6.9	4.5	5.0	2.9	5.3	4.8	5.5	6.2	3.3	4.0

Table I

Corporations with and without Net Income

PULP, PAPER, AND PAPERBOARD MILLS

Money Amounts and Size of Assets in Thousands of Dollars

Item Description for Accounting Period 7/07 Through 6/08	Total	Zero Assets	Under 500	500 to 1,000	1,000 to 5,000	5,000 to 10,000	10,000 to 25,000	25,000 to 50,000	50,000 to 100,000	100,000 to 250,000	250,000 to 500,000	500,000 to 2,500,000	2,500,000 and over
Number of Enterprises **1**	368	•	0	0	233	•	•	25	15	13	8	20	10

Revenues ($ in Thousands)

	Total	Zero Assets	Under 500	500 to 1,000	1,000 to 5,000	5,000 to 10,000	10,000 to 25,000	25,000 to 50,000	50,000 to 100,000	100,000 to 250,000	250,000 to 500,000	500,000 to 2,500,000	2,500,000 and over
Net Sales **2**	98309855	•	•	0	854800	•	•	1441890	1675359	2168589	2774992	24939197	62711912
Interest **3**	1896956	•	•	0	1	•	•	3723	8556	17421	12434	238882	1608606
Rents **4**	25344	•	•	0	0	•	•	118	702	1	2127	3502	18462
Royalties **5**	145491	•	•	0	0	•	•	0	0	0	0	55885	89605
Other Portfolio Income **6**	2321709	•	•	0	8330	•	•	21106	78462	19318	3051	532434	1656310
Other Receipts **7**	1062862	•	•	0	1401	•	•	12568	23146	-2786	11111	195947	841264
Total Receipts **8**	103762217	•	•	0	864532	•	•	1479405	1786225	2202543	2803715	25965847	66926159
Average Total Receipts **9**	281963	•	•	•	3710	•	•	59176	119082	169426	350464	1298292	6692616

Operating Costs/Operating Income (%)

	Total	Zero Assets	Under 500	500 to 1,000	1,000 to 5,000	5,000 to 10,000	10,000 to 25,000	25,000 to 50,000	50,000 to 100,000	100,000 to 250,000	250,000 to 500,000	500,000 to 2,500,000	2,500,000 and over
Cost of Operations **10**	77.6	•	•	•	79.5	•	•	86.9	77.3	79.4	77.0	78.0	77.1
Salaries and Wages **11**	4.8	•	•	•	2.5	•	•	3.6	3.3	4.1	6.0	4.4	5.1
Taxes Paid **12**	1.3	•	•	•	0.5	•	•	1.1	1.1	1.1	1.0	1.3	1.4
Interest Paid **13**	4.6	•	•	•	1.0	•	•	1.1	1.9	2.9	2.5	2.7	5.7
Depreciation **14**	2.9	•	•	•	0.5	•	•	2.4	4.0	3.7	3.8	3.5	2.5
Amortization and Depletion **15**	0.5	•	•	•	0.2	•	•	0.0	0.3	0.2	0.6	0.3	0.5
Pensions and Other Deferred Comp. **16**	0.8	•	•	•	0.0	•	•	0.8	1.8	0.7	1.4	0.7	0.8
Employee Benefits **17**	1.6	•	•	•	0.3	•	•	3.0	1.1	1.8	2.4	1.6	1.6
Advertising **18**	0.3	•	•	•	0.2	•	•	0.1	0.4	0.4	0.1	0.5	0.2
Other Expenses **19**	7.7	•	•	•	11.5	•	•	6.1	10.9	6.0	6.6	7.3	7.9
Officers' Compensation **20**	0.3	•	•	•	2.4	•	•	1.0	1.0	0.8	0.4	0.4	0.2
Operating Margin **21**	•	•	•	•	1.3	•	•	•	•	•	•	•	•
Operating Margin Before Officers' Comp. **22**	•	•	•	•	3.7	•	•	•	•	•	•	•	•

Selected Average Balance Sheet ($ in Thousands)

Net Receivables 23	38595	287	•	7623	12696	17545	34419	239377	831913
Inventories 24	24314	128	•	4278	8757	22225	39655	134840	527076
Net Property, Plant and Equipment 25	123855	148	•	7698	24757	53509	150416	468800	3351081
Total Assets 26	421500	1353	•	33573	68141	162541	331669	1186506	12392356
Notes and Loans Payable 27	173318	768	•	9882	36186	48333	129417	333485	5406303
All Other Liabilities 28	103496	66	•	18959	20165	43791	92122	418864	2739857
Net Worth 29	144686	519	•	4733	11790	70417	110130	434157	4246196

Selected Financial Ratios (Times to 1)

Current Ratio 30	1.3	•	1.2	1.6	1.3	2.1	1.6	1.1
Quick Ratio 31	0.7	•	0.7	0.9	0.8	0.7	1.0	0.5
Net Sales to Working Capital 32	15.1	•	22.9	8.8	14.5	4.2	7.5	33.7
Coverage Ratio 33	1.7	•	•	3.0	1.1	0.7	2.3	1.7
Total Asset Turnover 34	0.6	•	1.7	1.6	1.0	1.0	1.1	0.5
Inventory Turnover 35	8.5	•	11.7	9.9	6.0	6.7	7.2	9.2
Receivables Turnover 36	7.2	•	12.7	10.9	7.1	9.5	6.0	7.5
Total Liabilities to Net Worth 37	1.9	•	1.6	4.8	1.3	2.0	1.7	1.9
Current Assets to Working Capital 38	4.8	•	1.1	2.7	4.1	1.9	2.7	10.2
Current Liabilities to Working Capital 39	3.8	•	6.6	1.7	3.1	0.9	1.7	9.2
Working Capital to Net Sales 40	0.1	•	0.0	0.1	0.1	0.2	0.1	0.0
Inventory to Working Capital 41	1.4	•	1.3	0.9	1.5	0.5	0.8	2.9
Total Receipts to Cash Flow 42	12.6	•	371.9	11.3	22.6	22.3	14.4	11.3
Cost of Goods to Cash Flow 43	9.8	•	323.2	8.8	17.9	17.2	11.2	8.7
Cash Flow to Total Debt 44	0.1	•	0.0	0.2	0.1	0.1	0.1	0.1

Selected Financial Factors (in Percentages)

Debt Ratio 45	65.7	•	85.9	82.7	56.7	66.8	63.4	65.7
Return on Total Assets 46	5.0	•	•	9.0	3.3	1.8	6.5	4.8
Return on Equity Before Income Taxes 47	6.1	•	•	34.7	0.7	•	10.1	5.6
Return on Equity After Income Taxes 48	4.8	•	•	22.5	•	•	8.1	4.6
Profit Margin (Before Income Tax) 49	3.3	•	•	3.7	0.3	•	3.5	3.8
Profit Margin (After Income Tax) 50	2.6	•	•	2.4	•	•	2.8	3.1

Table II

Corporations with Net Income

PULP, PAPER, AND PAPERBOARD MILLS

MONEY AMOUNTS AND SIZE OF ASSETS IN THOUSANDS OF DOLLARS

Item Description for Accounting Period 7/07 Through 6/08	Total	Zero Assets	Under 500	500 to 1,000	1,000 to 5,000	5,000 to 10,000	10,000 to 25,000	25,000 to 50,000	50,000 to 100,000	100,000 to 250,000	250,000 to 500,000	500,000 to 2,500,000	2,500,000 and over
Number of Enterprises **1**	224	•	0	0	136	•	•	16	9	8	5	15	7

Revenues ($ in Thousands)

Net Sales **2**	81810475	•	0	0	803953	•	•	954391	928140	1646187	1571885	19034730	56036426
Interest **3**	1797245	•	0	0	1	•	•	2889	6386	6002	8910	227027	1546029
Rents **4**	24348	•	0	0	0	•	•	0	702	1	2127	3153	18365
Royalties **5**	137856	•	0	0	0	•	•	0	0	0	0	53611	84246
Other Portfolio Income **6**	2136131	•	0	0	8329	•	•	995	78462	17934	3051	490272	1536635
Other Receipts **7**	984929	•	0	0	198	•	•	2083	11072	-2983	-12515	132731	849148
Total Receipts **8**	86890984	•	0	0	812481	•	•	960358	1024762	1667141	1573458	19941524	60070849
Average Total Receipts **9**	387906	•	•	•	5974	•	•	60022	113862	208393	314692	1329435	8581550

Operating Costs/Operating Income (%)

Cost of Operations **10**	76.5	•	•	•	80.8	•	•	82.6	82.2	76.8	67.9	75.6	76.7
Salaries and Wages **11**	5.2	•	•	•	2.6	•	•	3.5	2.8	3.6	6.7	5.0	5.4
Taxes Paid **12**	1.4	•	•	•	0.5	•	•	1.1	1.0	1.1	1.3	1.4	1.5
Interest Paid **13**	4.5	•	•	•	0.6	•	•	1.1	1.3	2.0	2.6	2.6	5.5
Depreciation **14**	2.7	•	•	•	0.2	•	•	1.7	3.1	3.0	4.6	3.4	2.4
Amortization and Depletion **15**	0.4	•	•	•	•	•	•	0.0	0.3	0.2	0.4	0.4	0.5
Pensions and Other Deferred Comp. **16**	0.7	•	•	•	•	•	•	0.3	2.1	0.6	1.6	0.7	0.7
Employee Benefits **17**	1.5	•	•	•	0.2	•	•	1.2	1.5	1.5	1.7	1.6	1.5
Advertising **18**	0.3	•	•	•	0.2	•	•	0.0	0.1	0.6	0.1	0.6	0.3
Other Expenses **19**	7.8	•	•	•	9.4	•	•	4.4	4.1	5.8	8.0	7.5	8.1
Officers' Compensation **20**	0.3	•	•	•	2.6	•	•	1.2	1.5	1.0	0.6	0.4	0.2
Operating Margin **21**	•	•	•	•	2.9	•	•	2.8	0.2	3.8	4.6	0.9	•
Operating Margin Before Officers' Comp. **22**	•	•	•	•	5.5	•	•	4.0	1.7	4.8	5.2	1.3	•

Selected Average Balance Sheet ($ in Thousands)

Net Receivables 23	47008	427	7208	7686	22396	34620	176148	1033500
Inventories 24	30543	210	4064	9331	25341	30787	104814	640375
Net Property, Plant and Equipment 25	163287	123	9437	19970	58543	163375	462440	3987067
Total Assets 26	587155	1425	34283	67332	155750	365611	1148011	15657535
Notes and Loans Payable 27	234078	426	9309	38680	41436	135409	280520	6656031
All Other Liabilities 28	134221	28	8332	23775	34549	93068	361982	3355398
Net Worth 29	218857	971	16643	4878	79765	137134	505509	5646106

Selected Financial Ratios (Times to 1)

Current Ratio 30	1.3	45.6	2.0	1.6	2.1	2.6	2.0	1.1
Quick Ratio 31	0.6	32.5	1.2	0.9	1.3	0.8	1.1	0.5
Net Sales to Working Capital 32	15.8	4.7	6.1	8.0	6.4	2.7	6.8	56.5
Coverage Ratio 33	2.1	7.2	4.1	9.3	3.6	2.8	3.2	1.8
Total Asset Turnover 34	0.6	4.1	1.7	1.5	1.3	0.9	1.1	0.5
Inventory Turnover 35	9.1	22.8	12.1	9.1	6.2	6.9	9.2	9.6
Receivables Turnover 36	7.5	12.7	9.8	12.4	7.4	7.8	7.8	•
Total Liabilities to Net Worth 37	1.7	0.5	1.1	12.8	1.0	1.7	1.3	1.8
Current Assets to Working Capital 38	4.8	1.0	2.1	2.7	1.9	1.6	2.0	16.9
Current Liabilities to Working Capital 39	3.8	0.0	1.1	1.7	0.9	0.6	1.0	15.9
Working Capital to Net Sales 40	0.1	0.2	0.2	0.1	0.2	0.4	0.1	0.0
Inventory to Working Capital 41	1.3	0.3	0.4	1.0	0.7	0.3	0.7	4.5
Total Receipts to Cash Flow 42	10.5	11.9	14.5	19.0	11.6	9.0	11.1	10.2
Cost of Goods to Cash Flow 43	8.0	9.6	12.0	15.6	8.9	6.1	8.4	7.8
Cash Flow to Total Debt 44	0.1	1.1	0.2	0.1	0.2	0.2	0.2	0.1

Selected Financial Factors (in Percentages)

Debt Ratio 45	62.7	31.9	51.5	92.8	48.8	62.5	56.0	63.9
Return on Total Assets 46	5.9	19.2	7.9	18.2	9.4	6.3	9.2	5.2
Return on Equity Before Income Taxes 47	8.2	24.3	12.3	224.7	13.2	10.7	14.3	6.5
Return on Equity After Income Taxes 48	6.8	24.2	11.9	175.3	10.4	7.5	12.0	5.4
Profit Margin (Before Income Tax) 49	4.9	4.0	3.4	10.6	5.1	4.7	5.7	4.6
Profit Margin (After Income Tax) 50	4.1	4.0	3.3	8.3	4.0	3.3	4.8	3.8

Table I

Corporations with and without Net Income

CONVERTED PAPER PRODUCT

MONEY AMOUNTS AND SIZE OF ASSETS IN THOUSANDS OF DOLLARS

Item Description for Accounting Period 7/07 Through 6/08	Total	Zero Assets	Under 500	500 to 1,000	1,000 to 5,000	5,000 to 10,000	10,000 to 25,000	25,000 to 50,000	50,000 to 100,000	100,000 to 250,000	250,000 to 500,000	500,000 to 2,500,000	2,500,000 and over
Number of Enterprises **1**	2762	•	659	202	1171	•	•	104	38	25	10	13	6
Revenues ($ in Thousands)													
Net Sales **2**	93642402	•	932416	512826	7698573	•	•	6816564	3924257	5443649	3680459	12692101	40460938
Interest **3**	2127375	•	2083	101	42	•	•	4426	6055	3378	15522	31104	2050986
Rents **4**	69067	•	0	437	0	•	•	2771	3151	196	1628	10463	46569
Royalties **5**	1071173	•	0	0	0	•	•	611	0	3076	3783	1843	1061859
Other Portfolio Income **6**	2082823	•	0	987	56757	•	•	16934	21525	9332	56267	43475	1593259
Other Receipts **7**	1454762	•	17	131	7348	•	•	34527	21531	3740	95297	66788	111266
Total Receipts **8**	100447602	•	934516	514482	7762720	•	•	6875833	3976519	5463371	3852956	12845774	46324877
Average Total Receipts **9**	36368	•	1418	2547	6629	•	•	66114	104645	218535	385296	988136	7720813
Operating Costs/Operating Income (%)													
Cost of Operations **10**	70.2	•	83.3	70.0	66.7	•	•	77.4	77.8	72.6	73.7	74.3	65.7
Salaries and Wages **11**	8.5	•	3.8	7.4	9.9	•	•	5.5	5.2	5.9	7.2	4.8	11.6
Taxes Paid **12**	2.0	•	1.6	2.0	2.1	•	•	1.6	1.4	1.3	1.8	1.5	2.4
Interest Paid **13**	3.7	•	2.3	0.9	1.4	•	•	1.3	1.9	1.8	1.6	3.7	5.8
Depreciation **14**	2.9	•	1.1	2.4	1.9	•	•	3.1	2.9	2.3	2.6	3.4	3.3
Amortization and Depletion **15**	0.7	•	0.0	0.2	0.2	•	•	0.1	0.2	0.4	0.6	1.8	0.8
Pensions and Other Deferred Comp. **16**	0.9	•	0.4	0.1	0.4	•	•	0.4	0.2	0.4	0.6	0.9	1.3
Employee Benefits **17**	1.9	•	0.0	0.6	2.3	•	•	1.5	1.6	1.6	1.5	2.3	2.0
Advertising **18**	0.6	•	0.0	0.2	0.2	•	•	0.2	0.2	0.6	0.8	0.2	1.1
Other Expenses **19**	8.0	•	10.6	11.9	9.1	•	•	5.7	6.6	10.3	7.0	6.7	8.2
Officers' Compensation **20**	1.0	•	0.2	6.7	2.7	•	•	1.4	1.0	0.7	0.9	0.3	0.5
Operating Margin **21**	•	•	•	•	3.0	•	•	1.7	1.0	2.1	1.5	0.1	•
Operating Margin Before Officers' Comp. **22**	0.6	•	4.4	•	5.8	•	•	3.1	2.0	2.8	2.4	0.4	•

Selected Average Balance Sheet ($ in Thousands)

Net Receivables 23	4900	135	340	758	•	7124	13764	26127	57303	138415	1158859
Inventories 24	2901	46	81	391	•	6023	13970	21976	47174	108524	518983
Net Property, Plant and Equipment 25	8108	17	175	720	•	12958	22586	37773	87085	335757	1896928
Total Assets 26	45428	351	681	2390	•	34472	67697	126793	330916	977897	15335531
Notes and Loans Payable 27	16123	1098	427	1006	•	11031	24972	46339	66937	501404	5004762
All Other Liabilities 28	9825	110	296	707	•	8524	15666	40682	87726	256237	3031112
Net Worth 29	19480	-857	-42	676	•	14917	27059	39772	176253	220257	7299657

Selected Financial Ratios (Times to 1)

Current Ratio 30	1.1	2.2	1.6	1.5	•	1.6	1.5	1.6	1.5	1.2	1.0
Quick Ratio 31	0.5	1.7	1.3	1.0	•	0.9	0.7	0.8	0.8	0.7	0.4
Net Sales to Working Capital 32	26.0	7.8	13.9	12.7	•	10.3	9.3	9.8	8.0	19.9	•
Coverage Ratio 33	3.2	•	•	3.7	•	3.0	2.2	2.3	4.9	1.4	3.5
Total Asset Turnover 34	0.7	4.0	3.7	2.8	•	1.9	1.5	1.7	1.1	1.0	0.4
Inventory Turnover 35	8.2	25.7	21.8	11.2	•	8.4	5.8	7.2	5.7	6.7	8.5
Receivables Turnover 36	6.7	9.9	•	9.2	•	8.6	7.9	9.1	6.8	6.3	5.5
Total Liabilities to Net Worth 37	1.3	•	•	2.5	•	1.3	1.5	2.2	0.9	3.4	1.1
Current Assets to Working Capital 38	9.6	1.8	2.6	2.8	•	2.6	3.0	2.7	3.1	5.6	•
Current Liabilities to Working Capital 39	8.6	0.8	1.6	1.8	•	1.6	2.0	1.7	2.1	4.6	•
Working Capital to Net Sales 40	0.0	0.1	0.1	0.1	•	0.1	0.1	0.1	0.1	0.1	•
Inventory to Working Capital 41	2.4	0.2	0.4	0.9	•	1.0	1.3	1.1	1.1	1.9	•
Total Receipts to Cash Flow 42	8.4	102.8	21.1	11.2	•	15.7	14.9	9.7	9.3	15.6	6.1
Cost of Goods to Cash Flow 43	5.9	85.6	14.7	7.5	•	12.2	11.6	7.0	6.9	11.6	4.0
Cash Flow to Total Debt 44	0.2	0.0	0.2	0.3	•	0.2	0.2	0.3	0.3	0.1	0.1

Selected Financial Factors (in Percentages)

Debt Ratio 45	57.1	344.4	106.2	71.7	•	56.7	60.0	68.6	46.7	77.5	52.4
Return on Total Assets 46	8.8	•	•	14.6	•	7.5	6.6	7.2	9.0	5.0	9.1
Return on Equity Before Income Taxes 47	14.2	5.0	123.6	37.6	•	11.4	9.1	13.0	13.4	5.9	13.6
Return on Equity After Income Taxes 48	9.4	5.1	124.3	37.4	•	9.8	7.6	10.9	11.6	4.6	8.2
Profit Margin (Before Income Tax) 49	8.2	•	•	3.9	•	2.6	2.4	2.4	6.4	1.3	14.8
Profit Margin (After Income Tax) 50	5.4	•	•	3.8	•	2.2	2.0	2.0	5.5	1.0	8.9

Table II
Corporations with Net Income

CONVERTED PAPER PRODUCT

MONEY AMOUNTS AND SIZE OF ASSETS IN THOUSANDS OF DOLLARS

Item Description for Accounting Period 7/07 Through 6/08	Total	Zero Assets	Under 500	500 to 1,000	1,000 to 5,000	5,000 to 10,000	10,000 to 25,000	25,000 to 50,000	50,000 to 100,000	100,000 to 250,000	250,000 to 500,000	500,000 to 2,500,000	2,500,000 and over
Number of Enterprises **1**	1910	•	451	99	760	•	•	79	26	20	7	8	6
Revenues ($ in Thousands)													
Net Sales **2**	82981016	•	918820	287957	6316712	•	•	5659281	2830070	4041420	2802219	9773777	40460938
Interest **3**	2092771	•	2083	12	5	•	•	4227	5739	1759	12678	6023	2050986
Rents **4**	58333	•	0	0	0	•	•	1659	3142	31	128	2953	46569
Royalties **5**	1068986	•	0	0	0	•	•	611	0	2021	3173	1320	1061859
Other Portfolio Income **6**	2052853	•	0	0	56756	•	•	10556	17617	6756	50729	34313	1593259
Other Receipts **7**	1446832	•	16	0	4332	•	•	37397	18598	14934	90818	63400	111266
Total Receipts **8**	89700791	•	920919	287969	6377805	•	•	5713731	2875166	4066921	2959745	9881786	46324877
Average Total Receipts **9**	46964	•	2042	2909	8392	•	•	72326	110583	203346	422821	1235223	7720813
Operating Costs/Operating Income (%)													
Cost of Operations **10**	69.5	•	82.8	62.2	66.1	•	•	76.2	76.9	74.0	71.6	73.9	65.7
Salaries and Wages **11**	8.7	•	0.7	10.7	10.1	•	•	5.7	5.2	5.8	8.4	4.4	11.6
Taxes Paid **12**	2.1	•	1.1	1.5	2.0	•	•	1.7	1.4	1.3	2.0	1.5	2.4
Interest Paid **13**	3.8	•	0.2	0.0	1.3	•	•	1.2	1.4	1.7	1.6	3.7	5.8
Depreciation **14**	2.9	•	0.5	3.2	1.8	•	•	2.8	2.6	2.3	2.3	3.3	3.3
Amortization and Depletion **15**	0.7	•	•	0.0	0.1	•	•	0.1	0.2	0.2	0.7	2.1	0.8
Pensions and Other Deferred Comp. **16**	0.9	•	0.4	0.0	0.4	•	•	0.5	0.2	0.4	0.7	0.8	1.3
Employee Benefits **17**	1.9	•	0.0	0.5	2.0	•	•	1.5	1.7	1.4	1.5	2.1	2.0
Advertising **18**	0.6	•	0.0	0.3	0.1	•	•	0.1	0.3	0.4	0.8	0.2	1.1
Other Expenses **19**	7.6	•	7.9	10.4	8.6	•	•	5.6	6.1	7.7	6.4	6.4	8.2
Officers' Compensation **20**	0.9	•	0.2	5.0	2.7	•	•	1.3	1.0	0.8	0.9	0.3	0.5
Operating Margin **21**	0.4	•	6.3	6.4	4.7	•	•	3.2	3.0	3.8	3.1	1.3	•
Operating Margin Before Officers' Comp. **22**	1.3	•	6.5	11.4	7.4	•	•	4.5	3.9	4.6	4.0	1.6	•

Selected Average Balance Sheet ($ in Thousands)

Net Receivables 23	6155	171	322	770	•	7619	14738	25104	56889	146387	1158859
Inventories 24	3592	62	64	498	•	6426	13962	19468	42819	137625	518983
Net Property, Plant and Equipment 25	10223	14	247	892	•	12981	20856	33145	75098	403817	1896928
Total Assets 26	61102	474	724	2587	•	35424	67843	123877	318826	1134223	15335531
Notes and Loans Payable 27	20770	46	3	1011	•	10874	21619	41696	68093	562862	5004762
All Other Liabilities 28	12898	140	303	843	•	8525	15226	35357	61218	307939	3031112
Net Worth 29	27435	288	417	733	•	16025	30998	46825	189515	263421	7299657

Selected Financial Ratios (Times to 1)

Current Ratio 30	1.1	2.5	1.6	1.5	•	1.6	1.8	1.9	1.7	1.4	1.0
Quick Ratio 31	0.5	1.8	1.3	0.9	•	0.9	0.9	1.1	0.9	0.7	0.4
Net Sales to Working Capital 32	26.1	7.4	17.1	15.6	•	10.1	7.0	7.2	6.3	14.0	•
Coverage Ratio 33	3.6	43.9	1313.7	5.4	•	4.5	4.2	3.5	6.5	1.7	3.5
Total Asset Turnover 34	0.7	4.3	4.0	3.2	•	2.0	1.6	1.6	1.3	1.1	0.4
Inventory Turnover 35	8.4	27.2	28.1	11.0	•	8.5	6.0	7.7	6.7	6.6	8.5
Receivables Turnover 36	6.8	11.0	•	11.4	•	8.3	8.0	9.5	7.8	7.0	5.5
Total Liabilities to Net Worth 37	1.2	0.6	0.7	2.5	•	1.2	1.2	1.6	0.7	3.3	1.1
Current Assets to Working Capital 38	9.8	1.7	2.8	3.1	•	2.5	2.3	2.1	2.4	3.6	•
Current Liabilities to Working Capital 39	8.8	0.7	1.8	2.1	•	1.5	1.3	1.1	1.4	2.6	•
Working Capital to Net Sales 40	0.0	0.1	0.1	0.1	•	0.1	0.1	0.1	0.2	0.1	•
Inventory to Working Capital 41	2.3	0.2	0.4	1.2	•	1.0	0.9	0.8	0.8	1.4	•
Total Receipts to Cash Flow 42	7.7	13.0	8.0	9.3	•	12.9	12.4	10.3	8.1	14.1	6.1
Cost of Goods to Cash Flow 43	5.4	10.8	5.0	6.1	•	9.8	9.6	7.6	5.8	10.4	4.0
Cash Flow to Total Debt 44	0.2	0.8	1.2	0.5	•	0.3	0.2	0.3	0.4	0.1	0.1

Selected Financial Factors (in Percentages)

Debt Ratio 45	55.1	39.3	42.3	71.7	•	54.8	54.3	62.2	40.6	76.8	52.4
Return on Total Assets 46	9.8	28.7	25.7	22.3	•	10.8	9.6	9.9	13.3	6.6	9.1
Return on Equity Before Income Taxes 47	15.7	46.2	44.5	64.4	•	18.5	16.0	18.8	19.0	11.2	13.6
Return on Equity After Income Taxes 48	10.8	46.0	44.3	64.1	•	16.6	14.1	16.5	16.5	9.4	8.2
Profit Margin (Before Income Tax) 49	9.9	6.5	6.4	5.7	•	4.1	4.6	4.3	9.0	2.4	14.8
Profit Margin (After Income Tax) 50	6.8	6.5	6.4	5.6	•	3.7	4.0	3.8	7.8	2.0	8.9

Table I

Corporations with and without Net Income

PRINTING AND RELATED SUPPORT ACTIVITIES

MONEY AMOUNTS AND SIZE OF ASSETS IN THOUSANDS OF DOLLARS

Item Description for Accounting Period 7/07 Through 6/08	Total	Zero Assets	Under 500	500 to 1,000	1,000 to 5,000	5,000 to 10,000	10,000 to 25,000	25,000 to 50,000	50,000 to 100,000	100,000 to 250,000	250,000 to 500,000	500,000 to 2,500,000	2,500,000 and over
Number of Enterprises **1**	31937	2726	22278	2821	3176	415	321	118	36	15	15	11	4
Revenues ($ in Thousands)													
Net Sales **2**	90336370	777795	10828219	5482339	16710945	5712070	8175374	5892897	3316808	2550870	5599691	13061729	12227632
Interest **3**	306414	33	7325	2759	14948	7454	7200	6903	6861	6469	27671	44050	174740
Rents **4**	29670	0	81	5318	6454	2449	1955	2053	146	2172	3625	3276	2140
Royalties **5**	102591	0	1677	0	0	0	8354	21	0	18827	44037	0	29675
Other Portfolio Income **6**	416601	64489	39252	3800	61068	16527	22368	55691	24717	7598	35163	17642	68286
Other Receipts **7**	812786	14940	70963	41647	78205	62051	60066	142881	28450	3623	60174	157241	92548
Total Receipts **8**	92004432	857257	10947517	5535863	16871620	5800551	8275317	6100446	3376982	2589559	5770361	13283938	12595021
Average Total Receipts **9**	2881	314	491	1962	5312	13977	25780	51699	93805	172637	384691	1207631	3148755
Operating Costs/Operating Income (%)													
Cost of Operations **10**	60.7	62.8	43.2	49.7	62.1	67.4	64.7	69.3	65.3	66.7	64.2	64.1	61.0
Salaries and Wages **11**	10.5	5.4	12.0	14.2	11.2	10.1	9.4	9.0	8.0	7.6	10.1	9.4	11.6
Taxes Paid **12**	2.4	2.1	3.1	3.0	2.7	2.1	2.3	2.0	2.1	2.4	2.0	1.7	2.5
Interest Paid **13**	2.4	2.2	0.8	1.8	1.4	1.6	1.8	1.9	2.6	4.1	2.5	3.2	5.2
Depreciation **14**	3.3	3.5	2.2	3.5	2.8	3.5	3.9	3.3	3.3	4.2	3.6	4.0	3.1
Amortization and Depletion **15**	0.5	0.7	0.1	0.2	0.2	0.2	0.2	0.3	0.8	1.0	1.4	0.9	0.8
Pensions and Other Deferred Comp. **16**	0.5	0.5	0.5	0.8	0.2	0.3	0.4	0.5	0.3	0.4	1.3	0.4	0.3
Employee Benefits **17**	1.6	1.7	1.2	1.1	1.4	1.0	1.6	1.8	1.9	1.3	3.2	2.0	1.3
Advertising **18**	0.8	0.3	0.6	0.7	0.5	0.2	0.6	0.5	0.4	2.0	0.4	2.3	0.4
Other Expenses **19**	12.0	17.8	22.4	16.7	11.4	10.5	10.1	7.7	10.9	10.1	11.7	8.5	9.7
Officers' Compensation **20**	3.5	5.2	11.3	5.6	4.7	3.6	2.9	2.4	1.8	1.1	1.0	0.2	0.6
Operating Margin **21**	1.9	•	2.5	2.9	1.5	•	2.1	1.2	2.5	•	•	3.1	3.6
Operating Margin Before Officers' Comp. **22**	5.4	3.0	13.8	8.5	6.2	3.2	4.9	3.6	4.3	0.3	•	•	4.2

Selected Average Balance Sheet ($ in Thousands)

Net Receivables 23	365	0	25	175	613	1905	3694	8170	13215	21227	60645	168772	538060
Inventories 24	145	0	7	45	208	934	1856	4153	8429	17835	19548	62361	167024
Net Property, Plant and Equipment 25	531	0	39	285	790	2188	5535	8674	19321	45548	85242	357123	623083
Total Assets 26	2100	0	110	740	2138	6803	14511	34423	69907	163562	395298	1070938	5383951
Notes and Loans Payable 27	918	0	86	539	994	2643	5524	12848	26540	85236	134297	510428	2118632
All Other Liabilities 28	648	0	35	206	561	1746	3946	8158	19123	34768	103860	368817	1949300
Net Worth 29	534	0	-11	-5	582	2415	5041	13418	24244	43558	157141	191693	1316020

Selected Financial Ratios (Times to 1)

Current Ratio 30	1.2	•	1.3	1.9	1.4	1.6	1.6	1.5	1.5	0.7	1.6	1.0	0.9
Quick Ratio 31	0.8	•	1.1	1.6	1.0	1.1	1.1	1.2	0.9	0.5	1.0	0.7	0.5
Net Sales to Working Capital 32	20.8	•	35.3	11.1	15.6	9.4	9.8	7.7	8.1	•	7.7	•	•
Coverage Ratio 33	2.6	4.6	5.4	3.1	2.8	1.7	2.8	3.5	2.6	1.2	1.8	2.5	2.4
Total Asset Turnover 34	1.3	•	4.4	2.6	2.5	2.0	1.8	1.5	1.3	1.0	0.9	1.1	0.6
Inventory Turnover 35	11.8	•	30.0	21.4	15.7	9.9	8.9	8.3	7.1	6.4	12.2	12.2	11.2
Receivables Turnover 36	7.6	•	19.3	9.6	8.9	6.9	6.1	6.4	7.2	5.4	8.6	5.8	6.2
Total Liabilities to Net Worth 37	2.9	•	•	•	2.7	1.8	1.9	1.6	1.9	2.8	1.5	4.6	3.1
Current Assets to Working Capital 38	5.5	•	4.2	2.1	3.4	2.6	2.8	2.6	3.0	•	2.6	•	•
Current Liabilities to Working Capital 39	4.5	•	3.2	1.1	2.4	1.6	1.8	1.6	2.0	•	1.6	•	•
Working Capital to Net Sales 40	0.0	•	0.0	0.1	0.1	0.1	0.1	0.1	0.1	•	0.1	•	•
Inventory to Working Capital 41	1.0	•	0.4	0.2	0.6	0.6	0.7	0.6	0.8	•	0.5	•	•
Total Receipts to Cash Flow 42	8.5	4.5	5.4	6.6	10.9	13.7	9.9	10.7	8.0	12.2	9.7	9.5	7.0
Cost of Goods to Cash Flow 43	5.1	2.8	2.3	3.3	6.7	9.2	6.4	7.4	5.2	8.2	6.2	6.1	4.3
Cash Flow to Total Debt 44	0.2	•	0.8	0.4	0.3	0.2	0.3	0.2	0.3	0.1	0.2	0.1	0.1

Selected Financial Factors (in Percentages)

Debt Ratio 45	74.6	•	109.6	100.6	72.8	64.5	65.3	61.0	65.3	73.4	60.2	82.1	75.6
Return on Total Assets 46	8.4	•	19.5	15.0	9.4	5.6	8.9	9.8	9.0	5.1	4.3	8.8	7.1
Return on Equity Before Income Taxes 47	20.3	•	•	•	22.1	6.6	16.5	17.8	16.0	3.1	4.8	29.8	16.7
Return on Equity After Income Taxes 48	16.5	•	•	•	21.0	6.1	14.5	15.4	13.5	1.8	2.9	22.5	10.6
Profit Margin (Before Income Tax) 49	3.8	8.0	3.6	3.9	2.4	1.2	3.3	4.8	4.2	0.8	2.0	4.8	7.2
Profit Margin (After Income Tax) 50	3.1	8.0	3.6	3.8	2.3	1.1	2.9	4.1	3.6	0.4	1.2	3.6	4.6

Table II

Corporations with Net Income

PRINTING AND RELATED SUPPORT ACTIVITIES

Money Amounts and Size of Assets in Thousands of Dollars

Item Description for Accounting Period 7/07 Through 6/08	Total	Zero Assets	Under 500	500 to 1,000	1,000 to 5,000	5,000 to 10,000	10,000 to 25,000	25,000 to 50,000	50,000 to 100,000	100,000 to 250,000	250,000 to 500,000	500,000 to 2,500,000	2,500,000 and over
Number of Enterprises **1**	19686	2022	13218	•	2170	263	•	86	23	10	11	8	•
Revenues ($ in Thousands)													
Net Sales **2**	70689054	238797	8424273	•	12451717	3995815	•	4521087	2453408	1640779	4522489	11787097	•
Interest **3**	237434	0	1283	•	13650	3072	•	5379	5321	6217	23944	9116	•
Rents **4**	20031	0	0	•	5459	1142	•	1094	80	2172	3625	3276	•
Royalties **5**	101849	0	1677	•	0	0	•	0	0	18670	44037	0	•
Other Portfolio Income **6**	390216	62873	29668	•	56124	16143	•	50303	23350	7598	35158	17482	•
Other Receipts **7**	709326	12889	63884	•	65295	55726	•	134492	24324	17300	57142	119695	•
Total Receipts **8**	72147910	314559	8520785	•	12592245	4071898	•	4712355	2506483	1692736	4686395	11936666	•
Average Total Receipts **9**	3665	156	645	•	5803	15483	•	54795	108978	169274	426036	1492083	•
Operating Costs/Operating Income (%)													
Cost of Operations **10**	60.5	57.9	42.8	•	64.6	66.1	•	69.1	62.4	61.5	62.5	63.4	•
Salaries and Wages **11**	9.9	3.7	11.0	•	9.6	9.8	•	8.2	8.8	9.7	11.0	8.9	•
Taxes Paid **12**	2.3	0.8	2.6	•	2.4	2.0	•	2.0	2.1	2.4	2.1	1.8	•
Interest Paid **13**	1.8	0.6	0.6	•	1.0	1.0	•	1.4	2.4	1.8	1.4	2.6	•
Depreciation **14**	3.0	1.3	2.0	•	2.1	3.1	•	3.4	2.9	3.7	3.5	4.2	•
Amortization and Depletion **15**	0.4	0.0	0.1	•	0.2	0.1	•	0.2	0.6	1.3	0.8	0.9	•
Pensions and Other Deferred Comp. **16**	0.5	0.2	0.5	•	0.2	0.3	•	0.5	0.3	0.3	1.6	0.5	•
Employee Benefits **17**	1.4	0.1	1.2	•	1.1	0.9	•	1.6	1.9	1.3	3.3	1.8	•
Advertising **18**	0.8	0.3	0.5	•	0.5	0.2	•	0.5	0.4	2.0	0.5	2.6	•
Other Expenses **19**	11.5	23.8	21.4	•	9.8	10.9	•	7.2	11.3	12.8	12.5	8.5	•
Officers' Compensation **20**	3.4	3.0	11.5	•	4.5	4.0	•	2.4	2.1	1.3	1.2	0.2	•
Operating Margin **21**	4.4	8.2	5.9	•	4.1	1.6	•	3.4	4.8	2.0	•	4.7	•
Operating Margin Before Officers' Comp. **22**	7.8	11.2	17.4	•	8.6	5.6	•	5.9	6.9	3.3	0.9	4.9	•

Selected Average Balance Sheet ($ in Thousands)

Net Receivables 23	473	0	634	32	2131	•	8041	14964	21706	67643	207848
Inventories 24	183	0	190	6	1008	•	3921	9387	21879	21213	76292
Net Property, Plant and Equipment 25	654	0	651	38	1843	•	9210	19815	40006	98012	470912
Total Assets 26	2587	0	2090	130	6745	•	34498	70696	164978	399132	1211308
Notes and Loans Payable 27	925	0	752	74	2025	•	10217	28144	54974	89936	556173
All Other Liabilities 28	841	0	563	40	1656	•	7726	17664	28911	120408	450571
Net Worth 29	821	0	775	16	3064	•	16555	24888	81092	188788	204564

Selected Financial Ratios (Times to 1)

Current Ratio 30	1.3	1.4	1.5	1.8	•	1.9	1.6	1.3	1.6	0.9
Quick Ratio 31	0.8	1.3	1.2	1.2	•	1.3	1.1	0.8	1.0	0.6
Net Sales to Working Capital 32	18.9	29.1	13.9	8.4	•	7.1	7.8	14.3	7.4	•
Coverage Ratio 33	4.7	12.8	6.3	4.4	•	6.3	3.9	4.0	3.8	3.3
Total Asset Turnover 34	1.4	4.9	2.7	2.3	•	1.5	1.5	1.0	1.0	1.2
Inventory Turnover 35	11.9	48.6	19.5	10.0	•	9.3	7.1	4.6	12.1	12.2
Receivables Turnover 36	7.3	23.9	9.3	6.2	•	7.1	7.0	5.4	10.8	•
Total Liabilities to Net Worth 37	2.2	7.1	1.7	1.2	•	1.1	1.8	1.0	1.1	4.9
Current Assets to Working Capital 38	5.0	3.4	2.9	2.2	•	2.2	2.6	4.1	2.6	•
Current Liabilities to Working Capital 39	4.0	2.4	1.9	1.2	•	1.2	1.6	3.1	1.6	•
Working Capital to Net Sales 40	0.1	0.0	0.1	0.1	•	0.1	0.1	0.1	0.1	•
Inventory to Working Capital 41	0.9	0.3	0.4	0.4	•	0.5	0.7	1.1	0.6	•
Total Receipts to Cash Flow 42	7.0	4.6	9.5	10.5	1.6	8.6	6.5	6.7	7.9	8.5
Cost of Goods to Cash Flow 43	4.3	2.0	6.1	6.9	0.9	5.9	4.1	4.1	5.0	5.4
Cash Flow to Total Debt 44	0.3	1.2	0.5	0.4	•	0.3	0.4	0.3	0.2	0.2

Selected Financial Factors (in Percentages)

Debt Ratio 45	68.3	87.6	62.9	54.6	•	52.0	64.8	50.8	52.7	83.1
Return on Total Assets 46	11.6	37.4	17.1	10.3	•	13.9	13.9	7.1	5.3	10.4
Return on Equity Before Income Taxes 47	28.8	278.5	38.7	17.5	•	24.4	29.4	10.8	8.2	42.9
Return on Equity After Income Taxes 48	24.8	277.1	37.4	16.9	•	21.7	25.6	9.7	6.0	33.5
Profit Margin (Before Income Tax) 49	6.6	39.9	7.0	5.2	3.5	7.7	6.9	5.4	3.8	5.9
Profit Margin (After Income Tax) 50	5.7	39.8	7.0	5.1	3.4	6.8	6.0	4.8	2.8	4.7

Table I

Corporations with and without Net Income

PETROLEUM REFINERIES (INCLUDING INTEGRATED)

MONEY AMOUNTS AND SIZE OF ASSETS IN THOUSANDS OF DOLLARS

Item Description for Accounting Period 7/07 Through 6/08	Total	Zero Assets	Under 500	500 to 1,000	1,000 to 5,000	5,000 to 10,000	10,000 to 25,000	25,000 to 50,000	50,000 to 100,000	100,000 to 250,000	250,000 to 500,000	500,000 to 2,500,000	2,500,000 and over
Number of Enterprises **1**	661	55	425	0	109	9	15	3	4	10	0	12	18
Revenues ($ in Thousands)													
Net Sales **2**	1793586160	5501436	0	0	3492	48783	343435	794	705541	4501488	0	39808715	1742672475
Interest **3**	22811671	0	0	0	705	770	2925	789	4312	9235	0	120513	22672422
Rents **4**	1513602	0	0	0	0	0	273	0	0	165	0	17266	1495898
Royalties **5**	1057331	0	0	0	0	0	0	0	0	0	0	48	1057283
Other Portfolio Income **6**	24424549	0	0	0	0	0	1725	0	5147	9531	0	93537	24314611
Other Receipts **7**	42383661	431429	0	0	109110	10081	351	16	1204	32390	0	596659	41202420
Total Receipts **8**	1885776974	5932865	0	0	113307	59634	348709	1599	716204	4552809	0	40636738	1833415109
Average Total Receipts **9**	2852915	107870	0	•	1040	6626	23247	533	179051	455281	•	3386395	101856395
Operating Costs/Operating Income (%)													
Cost of Operations **10**	88.6	98.3	•	•	134.0	56.9	65.9	5.2	95.9	92.0	•	86.4	88.6
Salaries and Wages **11**	1.4	•	•	•	72.4	28.1	7.0	299.1	0.8	1.5	•	1.9	1.4
Taxes Paid **12**	1.7	0.0	•	•	121.1	1.1	1.4	77.3	0.1	0.3	•	1.9	1.7
Interest Paid **13**	1.6	0.0	•	•	57.5	1.8	0.7	544.5	0.3	0.4	•	0.6	1.7
Depreciation **14**	0.9	•	•	•	15.8	2.2	1.7	43.8	0.6	1.3	•	1.0	0.9
Amortization and Depletion **15**	0.3	•	•	•	8.5	0.3	•	941.2	0.0	0.0	•	0.4	0.3
Pensions and Other Deferred Comp. **16**	0.2	•	•	•	•	0.4	0.4	•	0.1	0.1	•	0.1	0.2
Employee Benefits **17**	0.2	•	•	•	•	0.6	0.2	46.1	0.3	0.2	•	0.2	0.2
Advertising **18**	0.1	•	•	•	7.1	•	0.0	•	0.0	0.1	•	0.0	0.1
Other Expenses **19**	3.6	0.4	•	•	878.8	24.6	17.8	2036.1	1.1	2.0	•	3.4	3.7
Officers' Compensation **20**	0.1	•	•	•	1.7	5.7	3.7	125.6	0.1	0.2	•	0.3	0.1
Operating Margin **21**	1.3	1.2	•	•	•	•	1.1	•	0.6	1.9	•	3.7	1.3
Operating Margin Before Officers' Comp. **22**	1.4	1.2	•	•	•	•	4.7	•	0.8	2.1	•	4.0	1.4

Selected Average Balance Sheet ($ in Thousands)

Net Receivables 23	1058532	0	0	•	6	2176	2328	117	8778	60052	•	181616	38712179
Inventories 24	49814	0	0	•	1	78	1751	1568	19790	20337	•	213941	1669225
Net Property, Plant and Equipment 25	329269	0	0	•	60	1577	2242	13101	16285	33553	•	513945	11721382
Total Assets 26	2825439	0	0	•	1939	8492	15522	48137	68877	171180	•	1321759	102727863
Notes and Loans Payable 27	321367	0	49	•	104	1131	1990	4281	13842	33758	•	326830	11556861
All Other Liabilities 28	1350530	0	0	•	62	3892	1811	15797	18327	62052	•	461987	49241477
Net Worth 29	1153541	0	-49	•	1773	3468	11722	28059	36708	75370	•	532942	41929524

Selected Financial Ratios (Times to 1)

Current Ratio 30	1.0	•	•	•	1.1	1.6	4.1	0.1	0.9	1.6	•	1.6	1.0
Quick Ratio 31	0.9	•	•	•	1.0	1.2	3.2	0.1	0.9	1.1	•	0.8	0.9
Net Sales to Working Capital 32	2831.5	•	•	•	3.2	2.3	3.5	•	•	10.5	•	15.2	•
Coverage Ratio 33	5.8	319.8	•	•	34.9	1.3	4.8	•	8.5	8.3	•	10.6	5.7
Total Asset Turnover 34	1.0	•	•	•	0.0	0.6	1.5	0.0	2.6	2.6	•	2.5	0.9
Inventory Turnover 35	48.2	•	•	•	32.5	39.4	8.6	0.0	8.5	20.4	•	13.4	51.4
Receivables Turnover 36	2.3	•	•	•	6.6	5.0	7.9	0.0	6.1	11.4	•	20.0	2.3
Total Liabilities to Net Worth 37	1.4	•	•	•	0.1	1.4	0.3	0.7	0.9	1.3	•	1.5	1.5
Current Assets to Working Capital 38	1265.1	•	1.0	•	12.8	2.7	1.3	•	•	2.7	•	2.7	•
Current Liabilities to Working Capital 39	1264.1	•	•	•	11.8	1.7	0.3	•	•	1.7	•	1.7	•
Working Capital to Net Sales 40	0.0	•	•	•	0.3	0.4	0.3	•	•	0.1	•	0.1	•
Inventory to Working Capital 41	55.0	•	•	•	0.1	0.0	0.3	•	•	0.7	•	1.1	•
Total Receipts to Cash Flow 42	10.9	10.5	•	•	0.0	5.6	5.2	•	45.1	21.4	•	12.7	10.9
Cost of Goods to Cash Flow 43	9.7	10.3	•	•	0.0	3.2	3.5	•	43.3	19.6	•	11.0	9.6
Cash Flow to Total Debt 44	0.1	•	•	•	5.4	0.2	1.1	•	0.1	0.2	•	0.3	0.1

Selected Financial Factors (in Percentages)

Debt Ratio 45	59.2	•	12661.4	•	8.6	59.2	24.5	41.7	46.7	56.0	•	59.7	59.2
Return on Total Assets 46	9.0	•	•	•	33.1	1.5	4.9	•	6.2	9.2	•	15.9	8.9
Return on Equity Before Income Taxes 47	18.2	•	3.3	•	35.2	0.8	5.2	•	10.2	18.4	•	35.7	18.0
Return on Equity After Income Taxes 48	11.8	•	3.3	•	32.2	0.8	4.2	•	6.8	16.4	•	23.8	11.7
Profit Margin (Before Income Tax) 49	7.7	9.1	•	•	1947.9	0.5	2.6	•	2.1	3.1	•	5.7	7.8
Profit Margin (After Income Tax) 50	5.0	5.8	•	•	1783.6	0.5	2.2	•	1.4	2.7	•	3.8	5.1

Table II

Corporations with Net Income

PETROLEUM REFINERIES (INCLUDING INTEGRATED)

MONEY AMOUNTS AND SIZE OF ASSETS IN THOUSANDS OF DOLLARS

Item Description for Accounting Period 7/07 Through 6/08	Total	Zero Assets	Under 500	500 to 1,000	1,000 to 5,000	5,000 to 10,000	10,000 to 25,000	25,000 to 50,000	50,000 to 100,000	100,000 to 250,000	250,000 to 500,000	500,000 to 2,500,000	2,500,000 and over
Number of Enterprises **1**	160	•	0	0	105	6	11	0	•	7	0	•	•
Revenues ($ in Thousands)													
Net Sales **2**	1766097167	•	0	0	0	48783	335807	0	•	2172093	0	•	•
Interest **3**	22600650	0	0	0	620	0	1186	0	•	4488	0	•	•
Rents **4**	1504046	•	0	0	0	0	273	0	•	165	0	•	•
Royalties **5**	1057331	•	0	0	0	0	0	0	•	0	0	•	•
Other Portfolio Income **6**	24304706	•	0	0	0	0	1725	0	•	9337	0	•	•
Other Receipts **7**	43387429	•	0	0	108984	10081	408	0	•	30034	0	•	•
Total Receipts **8**	1858951329	•	0	0	109604	58864	339399	0	•	2216117	0	•	•
Average Total Receipts **9**	11618446	•	•	•	1044	9811	30854	•	•	316588	•	•	•
Operating Costs/Operating Income (%)													
Cost of Operations **10**	88.5	•	•	•	•	56.9	61.4	•	•	87.0	•	•	•
Salaries and Wages **11**	1.4	•	•	•	•	20.4	6.7	•	•	2.1	•	•	•
Taxes Paid **12**	1.7	•	•	•	•	0.6	1.4	•	•	0.4	•	•	•
Interest Paid **13**	1.6	•	•	•	•	1.4	0.6	•	•	0.6	•	•	•
Depreciation **14**	0.9	•	•	•	•	0.4	1.6	•	•	1.3	•	•	•
Amortization and Depletion **15**	0.3	•	•	•	•	•	0.4	•	•	0.1	•	•	•
Pensions and Other Deferred Comp. **16**	0.2	•	•	•	•	0.4	0.4	•	•	0.1	•	•	•
Employee Benefits **17**	0.2	•	•	•	•	•	0.2	•	•	0.3	•	•	•
Advertising **18**	0.1	•	•	•	•	•	0.0	•	•	0.2	•	•	•
Other Expenses **19**	3.6	•	•	•	•	10.2	16.8	•	•	0.9	•	•	•
Officers' Compensation **20**	0.1	•	•	•	•	5.7	3.6	•	•	0.3	•	•	•
Operating Margin **21**	1.4	•	•	•	•	4.0	7.3	•	•	6.9	•	•	•
Operating Margin Before Officers' Comp. **22**	1.5	•	•	•	•	9.7	10.9	•	•	7.1	•	•	•

Selected Average Balance Sheet ($ in Thousands)

Net Receivables 23	4353333	4	3263	2905	43317
Inventories 24	202178	0	117	1978	32816
Net Property, Plant and Equipment 25	1334508	28	1444	2601	23567
Total Assets 26	11555179	1927	8008	15299	148128
Notes and Loans Payable 27	1301578	0	825	2289	26062
All Other Liabilities 28	5546612	-13	5748	2048	52613
Net Worth 29	4706989	1940	1435	10962	69453

Selected Financial Ratios (Times to 1)

Current Ratio 30	1.0		1.0	4.0	1.4
Quick Ratio 31	0.9		0.7	2.8	0.9
Net Sales to Working Capital 32	1642.1		32.7	4.8	10.5
Coverage Ratio 33	5.9		18.0	15.0	15.7
Total Asset Turnover 34	1.0		1.0	2.0	2.1
Inventory Turnover 35	48.3		39.4	9.5	8.2
Receivables Turnover 36	2.3		5.0	8.3	
Total Liabilities to Net Worth 37	1.5		4.6	0.4	1.1
Current Assets to Working Capital 38	740.9	1.0	24.8	1.3	3.3
Current Liabilities to Working Capital 39	739.9		23.8	0.3	2.3
Working Capital to Net Sales 40	0.0		0.0	0.2	0.1
Inventory to Working Capital 41	31.8		0.5	0.4	1.1
Total Receipts to Cash Flow 42	10.7		3.5	4.2	11.2
Cost of Goods to Cash Flow 43	9.5		2.0	2.6	9.7
Cash Flow to Total Debt 44	0.2		0.4	1.7	0.4

Selected Financial Factors (in Percentages)

Debt Ratio 45	59.3		82.1	28.3	53.1
Return on Total Assets 46	9.1	52.2	26.5	17.9	19.9
Return on Equity Before Income Taxes 47	18.6	51.8	139.5	23.3	39.8
Return on Equity After Income Taxes 48	12.2	49.0	139.5	21.9	36.7
Profit Margin (Before Income Tax) 49	7.9		24.6	8.4	8.9
Profit Margin (After Income Tax) 50	5.2		24.6	7.9	8.2

Table I

Corporations with and without Net Income

ASPHALT PAVING, ROOFING, OTHER PETROLEUM AND COAL PRODUCTS

MONEY AMOUNTS AND SIZE OF ASSETS IN THOUSANDS OF DOLLARS

Item Description for Accounting Period 7/07 Through 6/08		Total	Zero Assets	Under 500	500 to 1,000	1,000 to 5,000	5,000 to 10,000	10,000 to 25,000	25,000 to 50,000	50,000 to 100,000	100,000 to 250,000	250,000 to 500,000	500,000 to 2,500,000	2,500,000 and over
Number of Enterprises	1	628	6	101	58	244	98	72	16	13	14	0	5	0
Revenues ($ in Thousands)														
Net Sales	2	16335276	101642	315999	140845	1760743	1629765	1769654	1349539	1647976	2858004	0	4761109	0
Interest	3	58184	97	0	25	720	934	3949	1619	2931	10695	0	37213	0
Rents	4	6712	0	0	0	20	846	62	3330	3	717	0	1734	0
Royalties	5	10777	470	0	0	0	3	0	1576	0	6446	0	2283	0
Other Portfolio Income	6	97176	10192	0	0	1124	1942	6668	1767	1617	20419	0	53448	0
Other Receipts	7	205914	3874	0	195	26289	2163	19928	4641	23940	56292	0	68590	0
Total Receipts	8	16714039	116275	315999	141065	1788896	1635653	1800261	1362472	1676467	2952573	0	4924377	0
Average Total Receipts	9	26615	19379	3129	2432	7332	16690	25004	85154	128959	210898	•	984875	•
Operating Costs/Operating Income (%)														
Cost of Operations	10	72.5	71.7	72.6	63.3	55.7	74.5	71.8	77.5	80.2	77.0	•	71.9	•
Salaries and Wages	11	5.3	13.7	•	7.1	13.4	3.8	5.5	3.1	2.3	5.9	•	4.2	•
Taxes Paid	12	1.2	1.4	1.3	2.0	1.8	1.3	1.9	1.0	0.7	1.1	•	1.0	•
Interest Paid	13	3.1	1.7	1.3	0.4	1.3	1.4	0.8	0.7	1.2	2.7	•	7.0	•
Depreciation	14	2.4	4.7	2.3	4.9	1.7	2.3	2.5	2.6	1.9	2.2	•	2.7	•
Amortization and Depletion	15	0.3	2.2	•	•	0.1	0.1	0.3	0.2	0.1	0.5	•	0.3	•
Pensions and Other Deferred Comp.	16	0.3	0.0	•	0.0	0.5	0.3	0.1	0.4	0.2	0.3	•	0.3	•
Employee Benefits	17	1.2	1.4	•	•	1.1	0.8	1.3	1.1	0.7	0.7	•	1.9	•
Advertising	18	0.9	0.0	4.8	0.1	0.3	2.7	0.9	0.3	1.5	0.2	•	0.7	•
Other Expenses	19	10.3	14.0	19.4	11.5	13.7	8.4	8.5	7.0	5.1	6.7	•	14.5	•
Officers' Compensation	20	2.2	2.0	20.7	9.4	3.3	4.9	2.8	3.3	0.8	0.7	•	0.3	•
Operating Margin	21	0.4	•	•	1.3	7.2	•	3.6	2.7	5.2	2.1	•	•	•
Operating Margin Before Officers' Comp.	22	2.6	•	•	10.7	10.5	4.4	6.4	6.0	6.1	2.8	•	•	•

Selected Average Balance Sheet ($ in Thousands)

Net Receivables 23	2933	0	151	404	712	1951	2831	7175	18777	29843	91534	•
Inventories 24	2498	0	0	0	206	628	2635	7274	15340	15831	126980	•
Net Property, Plant and Equipment 25	4935	0	215	298	639	2698	4586	12019	13894	36588	284965	•
Total Assets 26	19175	0	392	722	2478	7432	14568	36974	66399	189293	1094803	•
Notes and Loans Payable 27	6513	0	657	151	2286	3235	4000	7143	15839	72893	302374	•
All Other Liabilities 28	8122	0	440	324	1779	1663	2923	9830	18203	46568	636809	•
Net Worth 29	4540	0	-705	247	-1587	2534	7645	20000	32357	69833	155620	•

Selected Financial Ratios (Times to 1)

Current Ratio 30	1.9	•	0.4	1.3	1.0	1.5	1.9	1.8	2.9	1.9	2.3	•
Quick Ratio 31	0.9	•	0.3	1.3	0.7	1.1	1.3	0.9	1.7	0.8	0.6	•
Net Sales to Working Capital 32	6.9	•	•	24.0	•	14.2	7.4	9.1	4.4	5.5	4.7	•
Coverage Ratio 33	1.9	1.8	•	4.6	7.9	0.8	7.4	6.1	6.8	3.1	0.8	•
Total Asset Turnover 34	1.4	•	8.0	3.4	2.9	2.2	1.7	2.3	1.9	1.1	0.9	•
Inventory Turnover 35	7.6	•	•	19.5	19.7	6.7	9.0	6.6	9.9	5.4	•	•
Receivables Turnover 36	8.5	•	•	12.5	9.5	7.3	9.0	6.4	8.5	12.3	•	•
Total Liabilities to Net Worth 37	3.2	•	•	1.9	•	1.9	0.9	2.2	1.1	1.7	6.0	•
Current Assets to Working Capital 38	2.2	•	•	4.2	•	2.9	2.2	2.2	1.5	2.2	1.8	•
Current Liabilities to Working Capital 39	1.2	•	•	3.2	•	1.9	1.2	1.2	0.5	1.2	0.8	•
Working Capital to Net Sales 40	0.1	•	•	0.0	•	0.1	0.1	0.1	0.2	0.2	0.2	•
Inventory to Working Capital 41	0.7	•	•	•	•	0.7	0.6	0.8	0.5	0.6	0.7	•
Total Receipts to Cash Flow 42	9.9	7.1	8.7	5.1	•	14.6	8.0	11.0	9.0	9.1	13.7	•
Cost of Goods to Cash Flow 43	7.2	5.1	5.5	2.8	•	10.9	5.7	8.6	7.3	7.0	9.8	•
Cash Flow to Total Debt 44	0.2	•	0.6	0.3	•	0.2	0.4	0.5	0.4	0.2	0.1	•

Selected Financial Factors (in Percentages)

Debt Ratio 45	76.3	•	279.8	65.8	164.0	65.9	47.5	45.9	51.3	63.1	85.8	•
Return on Total Assets 46	7.8	•	•	6.4	29.4	2.6	10.3	9.9	15.5	8.7	5.0	•
Return on Equity Before Income Taxes 47	15.4	•	98.8	14.5	•	17.0	15.3	27.2	15.9	•	•	•
Return on Equity After Income Taxes 48	11.6	•	98.8	12.3	•	15.2	12.4	24.1	11.9	•	•	•
Profit Margin (Before Income Tax) 49	2.7	1.4	•	1.5	8.8	5.3	3.6	6.9	5.4	•	•	•
Profit Margin (After Income Tax) 50	2.0	1.4	•	1.3	8.7	4.7	2.9	6.1	4.1	•	•	•

81

Table II

Corporations with Net Income

ASPHALT PAVING, ROOFING, OTHER PETROLEUM AND COAL PRODUCTS

MONEY AMOUNTS AND SIZE OF ASSETS IN THOUSANDS OF DOLLARS

Item Description for Accounting Period 7/07 Through 6/08	Total	Zero Assets	Under 500	500 to 1,000	1,000 to 5,000	5,000 to 10,000	10,000 to 25,000	25,000 to 50,000	50,000 to 100,000	100,000 to 250,000	250,000 to 500,000	500,000 to 2,500,000	2,500,000 and over
Number of Enterprises 1	418	•	0	58	207	53	60	•	•	11	0	•	0
Revenues ($ in Thousands)													
Net Sales 2	10844443	•	0	140845	1696478	1084472	1635665	•	•	1737181	0	•	0
Interest 3	43657	•	0	25	71	108	2244	•	•	10030	0	•	0
Rents 4	6470	•	0	0	20	846	62	•	•	475	0	•	0
Royalties 5	2668	•	0	0	0	3	0	•	•	383	0	•	0
Other Portfolio Income 6	82878	•	0	0	724	1942	6185	•	•	7094	0	•	0
Other Receipts 7	183266	•	0	195	26166	2163	18265	•	•	54153	0	•	0
Total Receipts 8	11163382	•	0	141065	1723459	1089534	1662421	•	•	1809316	0	•	0
Average Total Receipts 9	26707	•	•	2432	8326	20557	27707	•	•	164483	•	•	•
Operating Costs/Operating Income (%)													
Cost of Operations 10	69.6	•	•	63.3	55.2	67.0	70.4	•	•	68.6	•	•	•
Salaries and Wages 11	6.1	•	•	7.1	13.6	4.9	5.5	•	•	7.5	•	•	•
Taxes Paid 12	1.4	•	•	2.0	1.8	1.5	1.8	•	•	1.3	•	•	•
Interest Paid 13	1.7	•	•	0.4	1.3	0.7	0.7	•	•	2.1	•	•	•
Depreciation 14	2.3	•	•	4.9	1.4	1.3	2.5	•	•	2.1	•	•	•
Amortization and Depletion 15	0.3	•	•	•	0.1	0.0	0.3	•	•	0.7	•	•	•
Pensions and Other Deferred Comp. 16	0.4	•	•	0.0	0.5	0.4	0.2	•	•	0.4	•	•	•
Employee Benefits 17	1.1	•	•	•	1.1	0.6	1.2	•	•	0.9	•	•	•
Advertising 18	1.0	•	•	0.1	0.3	4.0	0.9	•	•	0.3	•	•	•
Other Expenses 19	8.9	•	•	11.5	13.0	7.0	7.5	•	•	7.6	•	•	•
Officers' Compensation 20	2.5	•	•	9.4	3.2	7.3	2.9	•	•	0.8	•	•	•
Operating Margin 21	4.7	•	•	1.3	8.5	5.2	5.9	•	•	7.8	•	•	•
Operating Margin Before Officers' Comp. 22	7.3	•	•	10.7	11.7	12.5	8.8	•	•	8.6	•	•	•

Selected Average Balance Sheet ($ in Thousands)

Net Receivables 23	3108	404	720	2307	3169	29274
Inventories 24	2603	0	336	1073	2307	21414
Net Property, Plant and Equipment 25	3871	298	695	1935	5017	26584
Total Assets 26	16577	722	2544	6731	15308	169848
Notes and Loans Payable 27	5358	151	2326	1706	4227	51672
All Other Liabilities 28	5230	324	1990	1621	3110	34331
Net Worth 29	5989	247	-1772	3404	7972	83846

Selected Financial Ratios (Times to 1)

Current Ratio 30	2.0	1.3	0.9	2.0	1.9	2.3
Quick Ratio 31	1.0	1.3	0.7	1.3	1.2	1.2
Net Sales to Working Capital 32	6.1	24.0		9.9	7.9	4.2
Coverage Ratio 33	5.6	4.6	9.1	9.2	11.0	6.7
Total Asset Turnover 34	1.6	3.4	3.2	3.0	1.8	0.9
Inventory Turnover 35	6.9		13.5	12.8	8.3	5.1
Receivables Turnover 36	7.6	7.4		7.9	9.5	5.1
Total Liabilities to Net Worth 37	1.8	1.9		1.0	0.9	1.0
Current Assets to Working Capital 38	2.0	4.2		2.0	2.1	1.8
Current Liabilities to Working Capital 39	1.0	3.2		1.0	1.1	0.8
Working Capital to Net Sales 40	0.2	0.0		0.1	0.1	0.2
Inventory to Working Capital 41	0.6			0.6	0.7	0.4
Total Receipts to Cash Flow 42	7.2	8.7	4.9	9.0	7.1	5.4
Cost of Goods to Cash Flow 43	5.0	5.5	2.7	6.0	5.0	3.7
Cash Flow to Total Debt 44	0.3	0.6	0.4	0.7	0.5	0.3

Selected Financial Factors (in Percentages)

Debt Ratio 45	63.9	65.8	169.7	49.4	47.9	50.6
Return on Total Assets 46	14.6	6.4	36.7	19.2	14.7	13.2
Return on Equity Before Income Taxes 47	33.2	14.5		33.8	25.8	22.8
Return on Equity After Income Taxes 48	28.9	12.3		30.2	23.6	18.5
Profit Margin (Before Income Tax) 49	7.7	1.5	10.1	5.6	7.5	12.1
Profit Margin (After Income Tax) 50	6.7	1.3	10.0	5.0	6.9	9.8

Table I

Corporations with and without Net Income

BASIC CHEMICAL

Money Amounts and Size of Assets in Thousands of Dollars

Item Description for Accounting Period 7/07 Through 6/08	Total	Zero Assets	Under 500	500 to 1,000	1,000 to 5,000	5,000 to 10,000	10,000 to 25,000	25,000 to 50,000	50,000 to 100,000	100,000 to 250,000	250,000 to 500,000	500,000 to 2,500,000	2,500,000 and over
Number of Enterprises 1	1244	25	517	57	288	57	121	52	26	27	14	36	25
Revenues ($ in Thousands)													
Net Sales 2	178019490	4402760	379945	184414	1362857	772696	3413584	2572978	2781849	5214146	4269397	33581730	119083131
Interest 3	3975426	26025	0	7	2204	2418	8068	3343	4093	34974	44114	493111	3357068
Rents 4	279711	116	0	0	0	0	5972	1564	471	5797	1300	29214	235277
Royalties 5	3308772	6231	0	0	1351	0	22	571	0	18941	35343	216268	3030044
Other Portfolio Income 6	4740119	58360	0	0	8111	155	2050	1014	9192	12890	51284	1272028	3325033
Other Receipts 7	4699182	15637	0	11902	12465	561	27388	6797	23476	99210	39809	775931	3686014
Total Receipts 8	195022700	4509129	379945	196323	1386988	775830	3457084	2586267	2819081	5385958	4441247	36368282	132716567
Average Total Receipts 9	156771	180365	735	3444	4816	13611	28571	49736	108426	199480	317232	1010230	5308663
Operating Costs/Operating Income (%)													
Cost of Operations 10	78.6	79.9	72.0	59.0	70.5	74.9	72.7	67.0	75.1	75.9	69.5	77.5	80.0
Salaries and Wages 11	4.8	5.6	1.7	10.9	8.2	1.3	6.0	6.5	4.9	5.3	4.8	4.8	4.6
Taxes Paid 12	1.1	0.7	0.7	2.1	1.7	2.5	1.7	1.4	1.2	1.2	0.6	1.1	1.1
Interest Paid 13	4.6	2.2	0.0	1.1	0.5	•	1.3	1.1	2.2	2.3	2.1	3.5	5.5
Depreciation 14	3.2	4.8	0.7	1.1	2.2	3.7	2.3	2.6	3.7	3.0	3.7	3.8	3.0
Amortization and Depletion 15	0.9	1.0	•	•	0.0	•	0.2	0.3	0.6	0.6	0.8	1.0	1.0
Pensions and Other Deferred Comp. 16	0.9	0.2	0.0	•	0.3	0.3	0.3	0.5	0.3	0.5	0.7	1.1	0.9
Employee Benefits 17	1.4	1.7	0.7	2.4	1.7	0.4	1.3	1.7	0.8	1.2	1.5	1.9	1.3
Advertising 18	0.7	0.1	0.3	0.0	0.2	0.0	0.2	0.2	0.1	0.1	0.1	0.2	1.0
Other Expenses 19	8.8	6.7	12.5	12.8	10.9	5.0	7.8	9.2	9.9	9.7	16.2	10.1	8.1
Officers' Compensation 20	0.8	0.2	3.6	15.7	4.0	0.7	2.1	3.0	1.4	0.8	0.8	0.8	0.6
Operating Margin 21	•	•	7.8	•	•	11.3	4.1	6.5	•	•	•	•	•
Operating Margin Before Officers' Comp. 22	•	•	11.4	10.5	3.7	12.0	6.2	9.5	1.1	0.2	0.0	•	•

Selected Average Balance Sheet ($ in Thousands)

Net Receivables 23	54626	0	78	282	596	2641	3578	7882	15807	31926	84935	141374	2367280
Inventories 24	14067	0	27	539	244	1863	3007	6896	12966	18305	43920	116895	436033
Net Property, Plant and Equipment 25	42526	0	15	59	212	3208	4914	8514	21414	55472	126116	348306	1410058
Total Assets 26	261144	0	274	826	2097	7163	15417	33180	72368	174590	410607	1237279	10527422
Notes and Loans Payable 27	100498	0	0	428	336	9038	4432	8704	25176	57797	111416	391092	4221574
All Other Liabilities 28	78069	0	48	150	464	1337	3382	6862	21023	47664	103873	401824	3134229
Net Worth 29	82577	0	226	248	1296	-3212	7603	17615	26169	69130	195318	444363	3171618

Selected Financial Ratios (Times to 1)

Current Ratio 30	1.1	•	5.2	1.8	3.0	1.3	2.1	2.1	1.5	1.7	2.1	1.2	1.0
Quick Ratio 31	0.8	•	3.5	0.7	2.3	0.9	1.3	1.3	0.9	1.0	1.4	0.6	0.8
Net Sales to Working Capital 32	32.4	•	3.7	10.0	4.7	15.8	6.3	5.0	9.1	6.6	3.5	14.1	•
Coverage Ratio 33	2.1	0.7	1476.8	2.1	3.8	•	5.2	7.4	1.5	2.2	2.6	1.9	2.1
Total Asset Turnover 34	0.5	•	2.7	3.9	2.3	1.9	1.8	1.5	1.5	1.1	0.7	0.8	0.5
Inventory Turnover 35	8.0	•	19.5	3.5	13.7	5.5	6.8	4.8	6.2	8.0	4.8	6.2	8.7
Receivables Turnover 36	2.8	•	15.5	3.9	8.6	4.1	8.0	6.4	7.0	6.8	3.7	6.4	2.2
Total Liabilities to Net Worth 37	2.2	•	0.2	2.3	0.6	•	1.0	0.9	1.8	1.5	1.1	1.8	2.3
Current Assets to Working Capital 38	18.7	•	1.2	2.3	1.5	4.5	1.9	1.9	3.0	2.5	1.9	5.4	•
Current Liabilities to Working Capital 39	17.7	•	0.2	1.3	0.5	3.5	0.9	0.9	2.0	1.5	0.9	4.4	•
Working Capital to Net Sales 40	0.0	•	0.3	0.1	0.2	0.1	0.2	0.2	0.1	0.2	0.3	0.1	•
Inventory to Working Capital 41	3.2	•	0.1	1.4	0.3	0.4	0.7	0.7	1.1	0.7	0.5	1.6	•
Total Receipts to Cash Flow 42	9.7	27.9	6.1	8.1	10.2	6.5	8.9	6.8	11.1	9.2	5.6	10.3	9.7
Cost of Goods to Cash Flow 43	7.6	22.3	4.4	4.8	7.2	4.9	6.5	4.6	8.4	7.0	3.9	8.0	7.8
Cash Flow to Total Debt 44	0.1	•	2.5	0.7	0.6	0.2	0.4	0.5	0.2	0.2	0.3	0.1	0.1

Selected Financial Factors (in Percentages)

Debt Ratio 45	68.4	•	17.6	70.0	38.2	144.8	50.7	46.9	63.8	60.4	52.4	64.1	69.9
Return on Total Assets 46	5.3	•	20.9	9.4	4.6	22.1	12.1	12.1	4.9	5.7	4.0	5.0	5.2
Return on Equity Before Income Taxes 47	8.8	•	25.3	16.5	5.5	•	19.9	19.6	4.6	7.8	5.2	6.7	9.0
Return on Equity After Income Taxes 48	5.7	•	25.3	14.0	3.8	•	13.5	15.9	1.8	4.9	2.9	2.6	6.2
Profit Margin (Before Income Tax) 49	5.1	•	7.8	1.3	1.5	11.7	5.4	7.0	1.1	2.8	3.3	3.2	6.0
Profit Margin (After Income Tax) 50	3.3	•	7.8	1.1	1.1	11.5	3.6	5.7	0.4	1.7	1.9	1.2	4.1

Table II

Corporations with Net Income

BASIC CHEMICAL

MONEY AMOUNTS AND SIZE OF ASSETS IN THOUSANDS OF DOLLARS

Item Description for Accounting Period 7/07 Through 6/08	Total	Zero Assets	Under 500	500 to 1,000	1,000 to 5,000	5,000 to 10,000	10,000 to 25,000	25,000 to 50,000	50,000 to 100,000	100,000 to 250,000	250,000 to 500,000	500,000 to 2,500,000	2,500,000 and over
Number of Enterprises **1**	757	13	269	57	157	47	95	35	18	16	9	19	22
Revenues ($ in Thousands)													
Net Sales **2**	146242672	3327740	372410	184414	1087498	742594	3058981	1665681	2071614	3216856	2764605	16914986	110835293
Interest **3**	3528897	24234	0	7	2174	495	6209	1747	2568	23708	21938	333170	3112647
Rents **4**	268321	39	0	0	0	0	5972	1564	471	327	1267	24950	233731
Royalties **5**	2710406	6231	0	0	1204	0	22	571	0	14867	35343	175672	2476496
Other Portfolio Income **6**	4290637	58338	0	0	4088	155	2050	819	7309	11062	42884	1189474	2974459
Other Receipts **7**	3485196	10373	0	11902	12386	359	25358	3182	18777	90631	23367	571921	2716939
Total Receipts **8**	160526129	3426955	372410	196323	1107350	743603	3098592	1673564	2100739	3357451	2889404	19210173	122349565
Average Total Receipts **9**	212056	263612	1384	3444	7053	15821	32617	47816	116708	209841	321045	1011062	5561344
Operating Costs/Operating Income (%)													
Cost of Operations **10**	77.3	77.3	73.4	59.0	68.8	75.4	71.9	60.6	74.6	73.9	63.8	69.5	79.5
Salaries and Wages **11**	4.8	6.2	1.7	10.9	7.1	0.8	6.0	6.1	4.9	4.5	5.3	6.3	4.5
Taxes Paid **12**	1.1	0.8	0.7	2.1	1.7	2.5	1.8	1.3	1.3	1.3	0.4	1.5	1.0
Interest Paid **13**	4.3	2.3	0.0	1.1	0.7	•	0.9	0.8	1.1	1.1	1.5	3.2	5.0
Depreciation **14**	3.1	3.2	0.7	1.1	2.3	3.8	1.8	2.7	3.7	2.8	4.1	3.7	3.1
Amortization and Depletion **15**	0.9	0.7	•	•	•	•	0.2	0.0	0.5	0.2	0.9	1.4	0.9
Pensions and Other Deferred Comp. **16**	0.8	0.1	0.0	•	0.3	0.3	0.3	0.7	0.4	0.7	1.0	1.1	0.9
Employee Benefits **17**	1.4	2.0	0.7	2.4	1.6	0.1	1.2	1.9	0.9	1.1	1.1	2.3	1.3
Advertising **18**	0.8	0.1	0.3	0.0	0.1	0.0	0.2	0.1	0.2	0.1	0.1	0.2	1.0
Other Expenses **19**	8.5	5.5	7.9	12.8	10.4	4.3	7.0	10.1	8.0	9.6	18.1	12.8	7.7
Officers' Compensation **20**	0.6	0.2	3.7	15.7	4.8	0.5	2.1	2.6	1.1	1.0	1.1	0.9	0.3
Operating Margin **21**	•	1.6	10.8	•	2.2	12.4	6.8	13.1	3.4	3.6	2.7	•	•
Operating Margin Before Officers' Comp. **22**	•	1.8	14.5	10.5	7.0	12.9	8.8	15.7	4.5	4.6	3.7	•	•

Selected Average Balance Sheet ($ in Thousands)

Net Receivables 23	82593	0	149	282	950	3143	4082	7094	16979	37986	77679	160588	2585019
Inventories 24	18996	0	27	539	288	1995	3341	6975	12826	19473	44732	146330	450739
Net Property, Plant and Equipment 25	53185	0	21	59	292	3874	4683	8400	22468	47084	148804	312119	1402628
Total Assets 26	343046	0	404	826	2790	7472	15768	32595	68431	162278	399760	1315459	10167370
Notes and Loans Payable 27	124968	0	1	428	616	10961	3951	7146	20106	38132	75328	246788	3954554
All Other Liabilities 28	94213	0	92	150	574	1522	3451	6516	17658	43883	117102	393029	2773954
Net Worth 29	123864	0	312	248	1600	-5011	8367	18933	30667	80263	207330	675642	3438862

Selected Financial Ratios (Times to 1)

Current Ratio 30	1.0	•	4.1	1.8	2.4	1.0	2.4	2.8	1.8	1.9	1.9	1.6	1.0
Quick Ratio 31	0.8	•	2.4	0.7	1.7	0.9	1.4	1.8	1.1	1.3	1.3	0.8	0.8
Net Sales to Working Capital 32	40.1	•	4.9	10.0	6.4	•	6.0	4.0	7.0	5.0	4.0	5.6	•
Coverage Ratio 33	2.7	3.0	2019.3	2.1	7.0	•	10.4	18.1	5.4	8.3	6.1	4.7	2.3
Total Asset Turnover 34	0.6	•	3.4	3.9	2.5	2.1	2.0	1.5	1.7	1.2	0.8	0.7	0.5
Inventory Turnover 35	7.9	•	37.3	3.5	16.6	6.0	6.9	4.1	6.7	7.6	4.4	4.2	8.9
Receivables Turnover 36	2.4	•	18.5	3.9	8.3	4.0	8.0	5.8	7.4	5.9	3.3	4.7	2.1
Total Liabilities to Net Worth 37	1.8	•	0.3	2.3	0.7	•	0.9	0.7	1.2	1.0	0.9	0.9	2.0
Current Assets to Working Capital 38	24.7	•	1.3	2.3	1.7	•	1.7	1.6	2.3	2.1	2.2	2.6	•
Current Liabilities to Working Capital 39	23.7	•	0.3	1.3	0.7	•	0.7	0.6	1.3	1.1	1.2	1.6	•
Working Capital to Net Sales 40	0.0	•	0.2	0.1	0.2	•	0.2	0.3	0.1	0.2	0.3	0.2	•
Inventory to Working Capital 41	3.6	•	0.2	1.4	0.4	•	0.7	0.5	0.8	0.5	0.4	0.6	•
Total Receipts to Cash Flow 42	8.2	13.5	5.6	8.1	8.5	6.4	7.6	4.6	9.0	6.4	4.2	5.1	9.4
Cost of Goods to Cash Flow 43	6.3	10.4	4.1	4.8	5.9	4.8	5.5	2.8	6.7	4.8	2.7	3.5	7.5
Cash Flow to Total Debt 44	0.1	•	2.7	0.7	0.7	0.2	0.6	0.8	0.3	0.4	0.4	0.3	0.1

Selected Financial Factors (in Percentages)

Debt Ratio 45	63.9	•	22.9	70.0	42.7	167.1	46.9	41.9	55.2	50.5	48.1	48.6	66.2
Return on Total Assets 46	6.6	•	37.2	9.4	11.6	26.5	18.3	21.0	10.0	11.4	6.8	10.2	5.8
Return on Equity Before Income Taxes 47	11.5	•	48.2	16.5	17.4	•	31.1	34.1	18.1	20.2	10.9	15.6	9.8
Return on Equity After Income Taxes 48	8.3	•	48.2	14.0	14.9	•	23.7	28.9	14.7	16.0	7.6	10.6	7.0
Profit Margin (Before Income Tax) 49	7.4	4.6	10.8	1.3	4.0	12.6	8.1	13.6	4.8	8.1	7.4	11.8	6.7
Profit Margin (After Income Tax) 50	5.3	3.5	10.8	1.1	3.4	12.4	6.2	11.5	3.9	6.4	5.1	8.0	4.8

Table I

Corporations with and without Net Income

RESIN, SYNTHETIC RUBBER AND FIBERS AND FILAMENTS

MONEY AMOUNTS AND SIZE OF ASSETS IN THOUSANDS OF DOLLARS

Item Description for Accounting Period 7/07 Through 6/08	Total	Zero Assets	Under 500	500 to 1,000	1,000 to 5,000	5,000 to 10,000	10,000 to 25,000	25,000 to 50,000	50,000 to 100,000	100,000 to 250,000	250,000 to 500,000	500,000 to 2,500,000	2,500,000 and over
Number of Enterprises 1	1067	4	585	162	175	43	38	17	15	11	8	5	3
Revenues ($ in Thousands)													
Net Sales 2	40078009	156305	153070	322133	1070900	797540	985908	809047	1471197	2410563	3750345	5325744	22825258
Interest 3	1884090	141	0	0	0	237	1448	3173	3160	13210	8917	35576	1818228
Rents 4	66237	8	0	0	0	0	0	62	0	1408	544	1596	62619
Royalties 5	724449	0	0	0	0	0	0	76	0	7771	4166	7302	705133
Other Portfolio Income 6	491979	53	0	0	48	412	25	913	3565	4021	33410	228579	220953
Other Receipts 7	1447602	191	0	0	9281	34	1023	9904	3830	649	19816	82199	1320676
Total Receipts 8	44692366	156698	153070	322133	1080229	798223	988404	823175	1481752	2437622	3817198	5680996	26952867
Average Total Receipts 9	41886	39174	262	1988	6173	18563	26011	48422	98783	221602	477150	1136199	8984289
Operating Costs/Operating Income (%)													
Cost of Operations 10	72.3	77.2	60.0	44.5	59.5	67.6	74.4	73.3	73.7	83.7	83.5	78.1	68.9
Salaries and Wages 11	2.3	4.5	3.7	7.4	4.9	11.1	3.5	4.0	4.3	3.5	3.7	2.8	1.0
Taxes Paid 12	0.8	1.3	3.7	1.9	2.6	1.6	1.7	1.3	1.7	0.9	1.0	0.6	0.6
Interest Paid 13	6.4	0.7	0.9	0.0	2.1	0.9	1.8	4.0	1.0	2.3	3.4	2.6	9.4
Depreciation 14	3.5	2.6	2.3	0.6	2.1	0.8	3.3	2.9	2.5	2.2	3.4	3.5	3.9
Amortization and Depletion 15	0.2	0.2	•	0.0	•	0.0	0.0	0.1	0.4	0.2	0.4	0.1	0.3
Pensions and Other Deferred Comp. 16	0.4	0.3	•	0.0	1.8	0.0	0.2	0.2	0.7	0.3	0.4	0.4	0.4
Employee Benefits 17	2.1	1.3	2.4	0.7	3.8	0.4	1.7	1.0	1.0	1.4	1.0	0.7	2.8
Advertising 18	0.3	0.7	0.3	0.0	0.2	0.3	0.5	0.5	0.4	0.1	0.2	0.1	0.4
Other Expenses 19	15.6	9.5	46.3	18.1	10.4	10.6	8.4	9.8	4.3	4.5	5.2	6.3	22.1
Officers' Compensation 20	0.5	0.4	•	4.9	4.1	3.2	1.6	1.4	1.3	0.6	0.5	0.6	0.0
Operating Margin 21	•	1.3	•	21.9	8.5	3.5	3.0	1.5	8.6	0.4	•	4.0	•
Operating Margin Before Officers' Comp. 22	•	1.8	•	26.8	12.5	6.7	4.6	3.0	9.9	1.0	•	4.6	•

Selected Average Balance Sheet ($ in Thousands)

Net Receivables 23	9075	0	6	294	688	1372	3500	7456	15095	31758	60500	117907	2514504
Inventories 24	4759	0	4	93	577	2369	3655	4186	10632	24540	43995	152341	1034688
Net Property, Plant and Equipment 25	14278	0	31	77	703	1492	6877	12372	20400	45149	146758	392255	3535915
Total Assets 26	97192	0	222	544	3089	5722	16832	39653	70836	153372	362730	947682	30331660
Notes and Loans Payable 27	12943	0	370	84	285	2116	4981	16229	13917	43718	167248	341215	3080146
All Other Liabilities 28	36773	0	97	121	148	1706	5458	12078	15586	48288	85042	323012	11862733
Net Worth 29	47476	0	-244	340	2656	1900	6393	11346	41333	61365	110440	283456	15388781

Selected Financial Ratios (Times to 1)

Current Ratio 30	1.8	•	3.0	3.4	8.3	1.3	1.5	1.3	2.5	1.8	0.8	1.9	1.9
Quick Ratio 31	1.1	•	1.1	2.5	5.1	0.4	0.9	0.9	1.4	0.9	0.4	1.0	1.3
Net Sales to Working Capital 32	5.0	•	2.0	6.2	4.0	21.7	8.4	11.4	4.2	5.9	•	5.8	3.8
Coverage Ratio 33	2.3	3.2	•	552.3	5.5	4.8	2.8	1.8	10.6	1.7	1.2	5.1	2.0
Total Asset Turnover 34	0.4	•	1.2	3.7	2.0	3.2	1.5	1.2	1.4	1.4	1.3	1.1	0.3
Inventory Turnover 35	5.7	•	40.9	9.5	6.3	5.3	5.3	8.3	6.8	7.5	8.9	5.5	5.1
Receivables Turnover 36	4.2	•	35.0	7.8	9.6	10.8	5.4	7.6	7.8	7.7	7.1	6.7	3.2
Total Liabilities to Net Worth 37	1.0	•	•	0.6	0.2	2.0	1.6	2.5	0.7	1.5	2.3	2.3	1.0
Current Assets to Working Capital 38	2.3	•	1.5	1.4	1.1	4.9	2.9	3.9	1.7	2.2	•	2.1	2.1
Current Liabilities to Working Capital 39	1.3	•	0.5	0.4	0.1	3.9	1.9	2.9	0.7	1.2	•	1.1	1.1
Working Capital to Net Sales 40	0.2	•	0.5	0.2	0.2	0.0	0.1	0.1	0.2	0.2	•	0.2	0.3
Inventory to Working Capital 41	0.7	•	0.0	0.3	0.4	2.7	1.1	1.0	0.5	0.8	•	0.8	0.5
Total Receipts to Cash Flow 42	5.0	9.4	4.1	2.7	6.5	8.1	10.5	9.1	7.8	19.5	26.6	6.6	3.7
Cost of Goods to Cash Flow 43	3.6	7.3	2.4	1.2	3.9	5.4	7.8	6.6	5.7	16.3	22.2	5.1	2.6
Cash Flow to Total Debt 44	0.2	•	0.1	3.6	2.2	0.6	0.2	0.2	0.4	0.1	0.1	0.2	0.1

Selected Financial Factors (in Percentages)

Debt Ratio 45	51.2	•	209.9	37.6	14.0	66.8	62.0	71.4	41.6	60.0	69.6	70.1	49.3
Return on Total Assets 46	5.6	•	•	80.2	22.7	14.6	7.9	8.7	14.2	5.5	5.4	14.9	4.8
Return on Equity Before Income Taxes 47	6.4	•	20.9	128.3	21.5	34.9	13.4	13.8	22.0	5.5	3.3	40.1	4.8
Return on Equity After Income Taxes 48	4.4	•	20.9	128.3	21.5	34.7	11.5	10.4	18.9	1.6	0.3	30.6	3.1
Profit Margin (Before Income Tax) 49	8.1	1.5	•	21.9	9.4	3.6	3.3	3.3	9.3	1.5	0.8	10.7	9.8
Profit Margin (After Income Tax) 50	5.6	0.5	•	21.9	9.3	3.5	2.8	2.5	8.0	0.5	0.1	8.1	6.3

Table II
Corporations with Net Income

RESIN, SYNTHETIC RUBBER AND FIBERS AND FILAMENTS

MONEY AMOUNTS AND SIZE OF ASSETS IN THOUSANDS OF DOLLARS

Item Description for Accounting Period 7/07 Through 6/08		Total	Zero Assets	Under 500	500 to 1,000	1,000 to 5,000	5,000 to 10,000	10,000 to 25,000	25,000 to 50,000	50,000 to 100,000	100,000 to 250,000	250,000 to 500,000	500,000 to 2,500,000	2,500,000 and over
Number of Enterprises	1	648	•	263	101	175	40	21	11	•	7	•	•	3
Revenues ($ in Thousands)														
Net Sales	2	36063870	•	71542	267236	1070900	776682	679495	583105	•	1784551	•	•	22825258
Interest	3	1877522	•	0	0	0	48	1066	1303	•	10926	•	•	1818228
Rents	4	66175	•	0	0	0	0	0	0	•	1408	•	•	62619
Royalties	5	717449	•	0	0	0	0	0	76	•	773	•	•	705133
Other Portfolio Income	6	476028	•	0	0	48	412	25	911	•	4008	•	•	220953
Other Receipts	7	1448193	•	0	0	9281	35	818	6662	•	10098	•	•	1320676
Total Receipts	8	40649237	•	71542	267236	1080229	777177	681404	592057	•	1811764	•	•	26952867
Average Total Receipts	9	62730	•	272	2646	6173	19429	32448	53823	•	258823	•	•	8984289
Operating Costs/Operating Income (%)														
Cost of Operations	10	70.5	•	15.3	40.3	59.5	66.4	72.9	68.8	•	80.1	•	•	68.9
Salaries and Wages	11	2.2	•	•	8.9	4.9	11.3	4.0	3.4	•	4.7	•	•	1.0
Taxes Paid	12	0.8	•	2.4	1.6	2.6	1.6	1.5	1.3	•	0.8	•	•	0.6
Interest Paid	13	6.6	•	1.9	0.0	2.1	0.9	1.3	1.3	•	2.1	•	•	9.4
Depreciation	14	3.5	•	1.0	0.0	2.1	0.5	2.3	3.3	•	1.5	•	•	3.9
Amortization and Depletion	15	0.2	•	•	•	•	0.0	0.0	•	•	0.3	•	•	0.3
Pensions and Other Deferred Comp.	16	0.4	•	•	•	1.8	0.0	0.2	0.3	•	0.3	•	•	0.4
Employee Benefits	17	2.2	•	•	•	3.8	0.4	2.1	0.7	•	1.3	•	•	2.8
Advertising	18	0.3	•	•	0.0	0.2	0.3	0.7	0.4	•	0.1	•	•	0.4
Other Expenses	19	16.6	•	75.9	18.2	10.4	10.4	6.8	8.7	•	4.4	•	•	22.1
Officers' Compensation	20	0.5	•	3.6	3.6	4.1	3.3	2.0	1.4	•	0.7	•	•	0.0
Operating Margin	21	•	•	3.5	27.3	8.5	4.9	6.1	10.9	•	3.6	•	•	•
Operating Margin Before Officers' Comp.	22	•	•	3.5	30.9	12.5	8.2	8.1	12.2	•	4.3	•	•	•

Selected Average Balance Sheet ($ in Thousands)

Net Receivables 23	14279	•	0	•	351	688	1301	5724	9875	• 33811	• 2514504
Inventories 24	7059	•	0	•	126	577	2489	4746	5113	• 25305	• 1034688
Net Property, Plant and Equipment 25	21774	•	8		2	703	1131	4788	16920	• 40470	• 3535915
Total Assets 26	155575	•	84		555	3089	5373	17617	37994	• 164413	• 30031660
Notes and Loans Payable 27	18347	•	12		14	285	1788	5216	7363	• 32289	• 3080146
All Other Liabilities 28	59134	•	85		142	148	1782	6457	13720	• 55070	• 11862733
Net Worth 29	78095	•	-13		399	2656	1802	5943	16911	• 77054	• 15388781

Selected Financial Ratios (Times to 1)

Current Ratio 30	2.0	•	7.7	3.7	8.3	1.2	1.9	1.3	• 2.2	• 1.9
Quick Ratio 31	1.3	•	7.7	2.8	5.1	0.4	1.1	0.9	• 1.0	• 1.3
Net Sales to Working Capital 32	4.3	•	4.1	6.5	4.0	28.8	5.4	12.9	• 4.9	• 3.8
Coverage Ratio 33	2.5	•	2.8	570.5	5.5	6.5	5.9	10.5	• 3.4	• 2.0
Total Asset Turnover 34	0.4	•	3.2	4.8	2.0	3.6	1.8	1.4	• 1.6	• 0.3
Inventory Turnover 35	5.6	•	•	8.5	6.3	5.2	5.0	7.1	• 8.1	• 5.1
Receivables Turnover 36	4.0	•	•	7.6	9.6	11.0	4.4	6.2	• 8.0	• 3.2
Total Liabilities to Net Worth 37	1.0	•	•	0.4	0.2	2.0	2.0	1.2	• 1.1	• 1.0
Current Assets to Working Capital 38	2.0	•	1.1	1.4	1.1	6.3	2.1	4.4	• 1.8	• 2.1
Current Liabilities to Working Capital 39	1.0	•	0.1	0.4	0.1	5.3	1.1	3.4	• 0.8	• 1.1
Working Capital to Net Sales 40	0.2	•	0.2	0.2	0.2	0.0	0.2	0.1	• 0.2	• 0.3
Inventory to Working Capital 41	0.5	•	•	0.3	0.4	3.5	0.7	1.1	• 0.6	• 0.5
Total Receipts to Cash Flow 42	4.4	•	1.3	2.3	6.5	7.4	9.2	5.2	• 11.5	• 3.7
Cost of Goods to Cash Flow 43	3.1	•	0.2	0.9	3.9	4.9	6.7	3.6	• 9.2	• 2.6
Cash Flow to Total Debt 44	0.2	•	2.2	7.4	2.2	0.7	0.3	0.5	• 0.3	• 0.1

Selected Financial Factors (in Percentages)

Debt Ratio 45	49.8	•	115.1	28.1	14.0	66.5	66.3	55.5	• 53.1	• 49.3
Return on Total Assets 46	5.8	•	17.8	130.2	22.7	21.0	14.1	19.1	• 11.3	• 4.8
Return on Equity Before Income Taxes 47	6.9	•	•	180.7	21.5	53.0	34.7	38.8	• 17.0	• 4.8
Return on Equity After Income Taxes 48	4.9	•	•	180.7	21.5	52.7	31.1	35.3	• 12.2	• 3.1
Profit Margin (Before Income Tax) 49	9.7	•	3.5	27.3	9.4	4.9	6.4	12.4	• 5.1	• 9.8
Profit Margin (After Income Tax) 50	6.9	•	3.5	27.3	9.3	4.9	5.7	11.3	• 3.7	• 6.3

86

Table I

Corporations with and without Net Income

PHARMACEUTICAL AND MEDICINE

MONEY AMOUNTS AND SIZE OF ASSETS IN THOUSANDS OF DOLLARS

Item Description for Accounting Period 7/07 Through 6/08	Total	Zero Assets	Under 500	500 to 1,000	1,000 to 5,000	5,000 to 10,000	10,000 to 25,000	25,000 to 50,000	50,000 to 100,000	100,000 to 250,000	250,000 to 500,000	500,000 to 2,500,000	2,500,000 and over
Number of Enterprises **1**	1034	23	112	149	227	175	108	68	47	45	17	29	34
Revenues ($ in Thousands)													
Net Sales **2**	317414432	309502	90852	267204	418116	1767914	2143305	2072208	1932591	4894446	3799754	21249626	278468912
Interest **3**	10721209	204041	54	2668	3949	6767	25197	33748	51990	81721	66056	333652	9911366
Rents **4**	225010	60	1102	0	241	67	562	1081	78	1626	312	9338	210543
Royalties **5**	23521552	214162	0	0	58	647	1174	12173	17161	81756	161746	396572	22636104
Other Portfolio Income **6**	6723066	1476	0	18924	19293	45375	34596	10806	27519	304055	41175	217401	6002444
Other Receipts **7**	22733989	1112197	10844	184	1690	11480	27812	40734	186075	252555	208963	1426490	19454969
Total Receipts **8**	381339258	1841438	102852	288980	443347	1832250	2232646	2170750	2215414	5616159	4278006	23633079	336684338
Average Total Receipts **9**	368800	80063	918	1939	1953	10470	20673	31923	47136	124804	251647	814934	9902481
Operating Costs/Operating Income (%)													
Cost of Operations **10**	49.2	65.8	45.5	65.9	66.9	68.2	65.4	62.4	50.2	41.6	41.9	43.2	49.5
Salaries and Wages **11**	14.4	13.1	22.0	10.8	20.0	6.0	10.0	12.6	19.1	14.6	15.7	14.0	14.4
Taxes Paid **12**	1.5	8.0	0.9	3.6	3.1	3.1	2.1	2.2	3.2	2.7	2.1	1.5	1.4
Interest Paid **13**	5.0	2.8	7.9	0.3	8.5	1.6	1.9	2.3	2.4	2.7	3.1	3.4	5.3
Depreciation **14**	2.5	1.0	7.3	3.6	3.4	2.7	3.2	2.7	5.0	3.2	1.8	1.8	2.5
Amortization and Depletion **15**	1.5	2.5	4.7	0.2	2.5	0.1	2.6	2.0	2.5	2.7	2.6	2.3	1.4
Pensions and Other Deferred Comp. **16**	0.9	0.2	•	0.3	0.0	0.4	0.3	0.4	0.7	0.6	0.4	0.4	1.0
Employee Benefits **17**	2.9	1.1	0.7	1.2	2.6	2.2	1.7	1.8	2.4	2.7	2.9	2.0	3.0
Advertising **18**	5.0	1.4	•	0.1	0.9	0.6	0.9	2.0	1.7	3.1	2.9	4.0	5.3
Other Expenses **19**	22.7	320.9	50.1	19.8	59.3	12.7	23.3	27.4	36.0	32.9	22.5	27.0	21.7
Officers' Compensation **20**	0.6	2.7	0.4	5.5	5.9	4.8	3.1	3.7	3.7	3.0	2.2	1.4	0.4
Operating Margin **21**	•	•	•	•	•	•	•	•	•	•	2.0	•	•
Operating Margin Before Officers' Comp. **22**	•	•	•	•	•	2.3	•	•	•	•	•	•	0.5

Selected Average Balance Sheet ($ in Thousands)

Net Receivables 23	137035	0	60	160	241	1388	3037	4872	6883	14629	36647	85066	4018663
Inventories 24	38138	0	49	253	237	1500	3216	4293	6815	16350	34342	131295	970249
Net Property, Plant and Equipment 25	71319	0	202	138	454	3023	4344	6243	12021	23349	32870	99091	1974326
Total Assets 26	854188	0	327	727	1794	8254	18247	34650	72484	157900	338576	1015703	24446572
Notes and Loans Payable 27	277630	0	648	139	1358	2633	5657	9639	11512	35472	96013	289927	8022443
All Other Liabilities 28	244862	0	193	87	798	3353	6349	10837	15277	40911	94803	277567	7021822
Net Worth 29	331696	0	-514	501	-363	2268	6241	14174	45695	81517	147760	448208	9402306

Selected Financial Ratios (Times to 1)

Current Ratio 30	1.1	•	0.5	3.9	0.9	2.8	1.3	2.1	3.0	2.3	2.5	2.1	1.1
Quick Ratio 31	0.7	•	0.4	2.7	0.6	1.5	0.9	1.6	1.7	1.1	1.4	1.1	0.7
Net Sales to Working Capital 32	10.0	•	•	6.4	•	3.5	7.1	2.4	1.5	2.5	2.0	3.1	15.3
Coverage Ratio 33	4.1	64.6	•	•	1.7	•	•	•	•	2.9	6.8	4.2	4.2
Total Asset Turnover 34	0.4	•	2.5	2.5	1.0	1.2	1.1	0.9	0.6	0.7	0.7	0.7	0.3
Inventory Turnover 35	4.0	•	7.6	4.7	5.2	4.6	4.0	4.4	3.0	2.8	2.7	2.4	4.2
Receivables Turnover 36	2.4	•	11.1	10.5	5.0	7.4	5.7	7.2	4.9	6.0	5.6	3.7	2.2
Total Liabilities to Net Worth 37	1.6	•	•	0.5	•	2.6	1.9	1.4	0.6	0.9	1.3	1.3	1.6
Current Assets to Working Capital 38	8.3	•	•	1.3	•	1.5	3.9	1.9	1.5	1.8	1.7	1.9	13.1
Current Liabilities to Working Capital 39	7.3	•	•	0.3	•	0.5	2.9	0.9	0.5	0.8	0.7	0.9	12.1
Working Capital to Net Sales 40	0.1	•	•	0.2	•	0.3	0.1	0.4	0.7	0.4	0.5	0.3	0.1
Inventory to Working Capital 41	1.3	•	•	0.3	•	0.6	1.1	0.3	0.3	0.4	0.3	0.5	1.9
Total Receipts to Cash Flow 42	3.1	0.2	•	9.2	•	11.7	11.2	12.6	4.9	3.5	3.0	2.9	3.1
Cost of Goods to Cash Flow 43	1.5	0.1	•	6.1	•	7.9	7.3	7.8	2.5	1.4	1.2	1.2	1.5
Cash Flow to Total Debt 44	0.2	•	•	0.9	•	0.1	0.1	0.1	0.3	0.4	0.4	0.4	0.2

Selected Financial Factors (in Percentages)

Debt Ratio 45	61.2	•	257.2	31.1	120.2	72.5	65.8	59.1	37.0	48.4	56.4	55.9	61.5
Return on Total Assets 46	7.4	•	•	•	•	3.3	•	•	•	5.4	13.8	10.3	7.4
Return on Equity Before Income Taxes 47	14.5	•	41.7	•	340.5	4.8	•	•	•	6.8	26.9	17.7	14.7
Return on Equity After Income Taxes 48	9.4	41.7	•	•	343.3	•	•	•	•	1.1	18.9	13.0	9.7
Profit Margin (Before Income Tax) 49	15.6	175.5	•	•	•	1.1	•	•	•	5.1	17.8	10.9	16.8
Profit Margin (After Income Tax) 50	10.2	97.4	•	•	•	•	•	•	•	0.8	12.5	7.9	11.1

Table II

Corporations with Net Income

PHARMACEUTICAL AND MEDICINE

MONEY AMOUNTS AND SIZE OF ASSETS IN THOUSANDS OF DOLLARS

Item Description for Accounting Period 7/07 Through 6/08	Total	Zero Assets	Under 500	500 to 1,000	1,000 to 5,000	5,000 to 10,000	10,000 to 25,000	25,000 to 50,000	50,000 to 100,000	100,000 to 250,000	250,000 to 500,000	500,000 to 2,500,000	2,500,000 and over
Number of Enterprises **1**	611	•	94	117	63	132	59	24	•	27	•	24	31
Revenues ($ in Thousands)													
Net Sales **2**	305030640	•	90055	250426	125730	1476423	1362787	1484759	•	4124522	•	20086848	271745097
Interest **3**	10096220	•	38	2516	71	3252	11372	4754	•	36336	•	292056	9478050
Rents **4**	218362	•	1102	0	0	0	515	390	•	1487	•	3895	210522
Royalties **5**	22461159	•	0	0	0	0	234	7831	•	28481	•	315652	21750200
Other Portfolio Income **6**	6608079	•	0	18864	17949	45375	14451	524	•	302797	•	203528	5962584
Other Receipts **7**	21198010	•	9782	184	239	1223	17454	23290	•	230341	•	1373064	18108878
Total Receipts **8**	365612470	•	100977	271990	143989	1526273	1406813	1521548	•	4723964	•	22275043	327255331
Average Total Receipts **9**	598384	•	1074	2325	2286	11563	23844	63398	•	174962	•	928127	10556624
Operating Costs/Operating Income (%)													
Cost of Operations **10**	49.4	•	45.6	59.9	64.0	65.4	52.2	63.0	•	41.3	•	43.9	49.9
Salaries and Wages **11**	13.8	•	17.1	9.9	11.8	4.5	9.1	6.1	•	11.1	•	13.3	14.0
Taxes Paid **12**	1.5	•	0.3	3.3	1.8	3.0	2.2	1.6	•	2.5	•	1.5	1.4
Interest Paid **13**	4.8	•	1.8	0.3	1.0	1.6	0.8	1.1	•	1.9	•	3.0	5.1
Depreciation **14**	2.5	•	6.7	2.3	4.4	2.0	2.7	1.5	•	2.9	•	1.8	2.5
Amortization and Depletion **15**	1.5	•	•	0.0	0.2	0.4	0.1	0.2	•	2.0	•	2.1	1.4
Pensions and Other Deferred Comp. **16**	0.9	•	•	0.3	0.1	0.5	0.4	0.4	•	0.7	•	0.4	0.9
Employee Benefits **17**	2.9	•	•	•	0.3	2.4	1.7	1.0	•	2.3	•	2.0	3.0
Advertising **18**	4.9	•	•	0.1	0.1	0.3	1.1	1.3	•	3.0	•	3.7	5.1
Other Expenses **19**	21.7	•	17.1	16.1	15.6	7.8	18.9	12.8	•	23.8	•	26.5	21.2
Officers' Compensation **20**	0.4	•	5.8	5.8	1.1	4.7	2.6	2.5	•	2.6	•	1.2	0.3
Operating Margin **21**	•	•	5.7	2.0	0.6	7.4	8.3	8.4	•	5.8	•	0.7	•
Operating Margin Before Officers' Comp. **22**	•	•	11.5	7.9	1.7	12.1	10.9	10.8	•	8.5	•	1.9	•

Selected Average Balance Sheet ($ in Thousands)

Net Receivables 23	208732	•	71	193	363	1356	3854	8460	20258	91966	3981142
Inventories 24	60931	•	7	175	286	1664	4574	6765	22094	152093	1021529
Net Property, Plant and Equipment 25	112338	•	231	99	275	3120	4931	7355	28407	111034	2047772
Total Assets 26	1353129	•	325	762	1369	8192	18517	34926	160354	1034278	25443895
Notes and Loans Payable 27	428254	•	170	126	361	2456	2720	12686	34893	268533	8127228
All Other Liabilities 28	394346	•	83	80	314	1084	5772	8455	40784	288397	7446157
Net Worth 29	530529	•	72	556	694	4652	10025	13785	84677	477348	9870510

Selected Financial Ratios (Times to 1)

Current Ratio 30	1.1	•	1.1	4.2	3.5	3.5	2.2	1.9	2.1	2.1	1.0
Quick Ratio 31	0.7	•	0.9	3.3	2.5	1.8	1.4	1.3	0.8	1.1	0.6
Net Sales to Working Capital 32	17.7	•	87.4	7.1	2.6	3.7	3.7	5.0	3.7	3.3	40.8
Coverage Ratio 33	4.7	•	14.2	41.0	14.6	7.6	14.8	10.4	11.8	5.0	4.5
Total Asset Turnover 34	0.4	•	2.9	2.8	1.5	1.4	1.2	1.8	1.0	0.8	0.3
Inventory Turnover 35	4.0	•	60.8	7.3	4.5	4.4	2.6	5.8	2.9	2.4	4.3
Receivables Turnover 36	2.7	•	27.0	14.2	4.8	7.4	4.7	8.3	6.3	3.8	2.5
Total Liabilities to Net Worth 37	1.6	•	3.5	0.4	1.0	0.8	0.8	1.5	0.9	1.2	1.6
Current Assets to Working Capital 38	14.0	•	8.6	1.3	1.4	1.4	1.9	2.1	2.0	1.9	33.5
Current Liabilities to Working Capital 39	13.0	•	7.6	0.3	0.4	0.4	0.9	1.1	1.0	0.9	32.5
Working Capital to Net Sales 40	0.1	•	0.0	0.1	0.4	0.3	0.3	0.2	0.3	0.3	0.0
Inventory to Working Capital 41	2.2	•	1.2	0.2	0.3	0.6	0.6	0.5	0.5	0.5	5.0
Total Receipts to Cash Flow 42	3.0	•	3.0	4.9	6.9	7.6	3.6	4.9	2.9	2.8	3.0
Cost of Goods to Cash Flow 43	1.5	•	1.4	2.9	4.4	5.0	1.9	3.1	1.2	1.2	1.5
Cash Flow to Total Debt 44	0.2	•	1.3	2.1	0.4	0.4	0.8	0.6	0.7	0.5	0.2

Selected Financial Factors (in Percentages)

Debt Ratio 45	60.8	•	77.8	27.0	49.3	43.2	45.9	60.5	47.2	53.8	61.2
Return on Total Assets 46	8.3	•	74.8	30.7	22.0	16.8	15.4	21.2	21.4	12.2	7.8
Return on Equity Before Income Taxes 47	16.5	•	313.0	41.0	40.5	25.7	26.5	48.6	37.1	21.2	15.7
Return on Equity After Income Taxes 48	11.2	•	313.0	28.1	35.5	21.8	23.0	40.9	28.0	15.8	10.5
Profit Margin (Before Income Tax) 49	17.6	•	23.6	10.6	14.1	10.7	11.5	10.8	20.6	12.1	17.7
Profit Margin (After Income Tax) 50	11.9	•	23.6	7.3	12.4	9.1	10.0	9.1	15.5	9.0	11.8

Table I

Corporations with and without Net Income

PAINT, COATING, AND ADHESIVE

MONEY AMOUNTS AND SIZE OF ASSETS IN THOUSANDS OF DOLLARS

Item Description for Accounting Period 7/07 Through 6/08		Total	Zero Assets	Under 500	500 to 1,000	1,000 to 5,000	5,000 to 10,000	10,000 to 25,000	25,000 to 50,000	50,000 to 100,000	100,000 to 250,000	250,000 to 500,000	500,000 to 2,500,000	2,500,000 and over
Number of Enterprises	1	1411	•	•	•	775	120	57	33	19	7	4	11	5

Revenues ($ in Thousands)

		Total	Zero Assets	Under 500	500 to 1,000	1,000 to 5,000	5,000 to 10,000	10,000 to 25,000	25,000 to 50,000	50,000 to 100,000	100,000 to 250,000	250,000 to 500,000	500,000 to 2,500,000	2,500,000 and over
Net Sales	2	49486744	•	•	•	3389260	2039263	1716480	1877068	1781067	1411281	1449892	12287064	22132112
Interest	3	480902	•	•	•	289	1765	847	2755	4323	8928	3086	192805	264693
Rents	4	15631	•	•	•	0	401	1463	1321	227	0	1283	7880	2937
Royalties	5	461353	•	•	•	0	0	0	166	5196	2184	753	80029	369056
Other Portfolio Income	6	980919	•	•	•	8721	8618	2629	8754	1464	5688	6854	613205	322685
Other Receipts	7	353319	•	•	•	7515	9960	8465	5174	6924	3224	31828	182944	82516
Total Receipts	8	51778868	•	•	•	3405785	2060007	1729884	1895238	1799201	1431305	1493696	13363927	23173999
Average Total Receipts	9	36697	•	•	•	4395	17167	30349	57431	94695	204472	373424	1214902	4634800

Operating Costs/Operating Income (%)

		Total	Zero Assets	Under 500	500 to 1,000	1,000 to 5,000	5,000 to 10,000	10,000 to 25,000	25,000 to 50,000	50,000 to 100,000	100,000 to 250,000	250,000 to 500,000	500,000 to 2,500,000	2,500,000 and over
Cost of Operations	10	64.3	•	•	•	61.7	68.2	66.4	69.0	66.5	63.7	80.3	63.2	63.4
Salaries and Wages	11	9.6	•	•	•	8.3	6.1	9.7	8.2	8.5	9.9	5.0	10.9	9.8
Taxes Paid	12	1.9	•	•	•	3.1	3.5	1.5	1.6	2.0	1.9	1.7	1.8	1.5
Interest Paid	13	2.8	•	•	•	0.9	1.1	1.2	0.5	1.6	1.0	3.5	3.4	3.6
Depreciation	14	1.9	•	•	•	0.4	1.8	1.5	1.2	2.0	2.4	2.1	2.4	2.0
Amortization and Depletion	15	0.8	•	•	•	0.3	0.1	0.1	0.2	1.0	0.6	0.4	1.3	0.7
Pensions and Other Deferred Comp.	16	1.6	•	•	•	0.7	0.3	0.6	0.6	1.5	2.1	0.5	2.8	1.4
Employee Benefits	17	1.9	•	•	•	0.7	1.4	1.0	1.0	1.9	1.8	1.1	2.6	1.8
Advertising	18	1.2	•	•	•	0.9	0.7	1.0	0.2	0.5	0.9	0.3	0.8	1.8
Other Expenses	19	12.3	•	•	•	12.3	11.5	10.3	9.9	11.1	11.7	4.2	14.7	11.7
Officers' Compensation	20	1.3	•	•	•	5.7	4.4	2.3	1.6	1.7	1.1	0.6	0.7	0.4
Operating Margin	21	0.4	•	•	•	5.1	0.9	4.3	5.9	1.6	2.9	0.3	•	1.9
Operating Margin Before Officers' Comp.	22	1.7	•	•	•	10.7	5.2	6.6	7.5	3.3	4.0	0.9	•	2.4

Selected Average Balance Sheet ($ in Thousands)

Net Receivables 23	4783	439	1780	4035	8416	13636	26763	49932	149149	656559
Inventories 24	3415	406	1564	3696	7420	12014	30421	30918	98697	440420
Net Property, Plant and Equipment 25	5447	253	1337	3325	5389	16307	42604	45548	243729	687314
Total Assets 26	31968	1738	6302	14135	32467	72757	145519	375784	1231014	4685550
Notes and Loans Payable 27	11033	619	2250	4794	5971	16278	25400	162307	302275	1943653
All Other Liabilities 28	13025	415	1782	4180	6664	15297	36195	101802	687572	1754309
Net Worth 29	7911	704	2270	5161	19832	41182	83924	111675	241167	987587

Selected Financial Ratios (Times to 1)

Current Ratio 30	1.1	2.1	1.1	1.6	3.1	2.2	2.0	2.1	1.1	0.9
Quick Ratio 31	0.7	1.3	0.7	0.9	2.0	1.2	1.1	1.3	0.6	0.6
Net Sales to Working Capital 32	25.6	7.6	41.4	9.5	3.8	5.4	5.8	5.7	30.9	•
Coverage Ratio 33	2.9	6.9	2.7	5.1	14.3	2.7	5.3	2.0	2.4	3.0
Total Asset Turnover 34	1.1	2.5	2.7	2.1	1.8	1.3	1.4	1.0	0.9	0.9
Inventory Turnover 35	6.6	6.6	7.4	5.4	5.3	5.2	4.2	9.4	7.1	6.4
Receivables Turnover 36	7.2	9.0	8.7	8.2	7.1	6.9	5.8	14.5	7.6	6.4
Total Liabilities to Net Worth 37	3.0	1.5	1.8	1.7	0.6	0.8	0.7	2.4	4.1	3.7
Current Assets to Working Capital 38	9.0	1.9	8.7	2.8	1.5	1.8	2.0	1.9	11.9	•
Current Liabilities to Working Capital 39	8.0	0.9	7.7	1.8	0.5	0.8	1.0	0.9	10.9	•
Working Capital to Net Sales 40	0.0	0.1	0.0	0.1	0.3	0.2	0.2	0.2	0.0	•
Inventory to Working Capital 41	2.6	0.7	3.2	1.1	0.5	0.7	0.7	0.5	3.4	•
Total Receipts to Cash Flow 42	7.3	6.3	14.2	7.4	6.5	7.9	7.5	17.8	8.3	6.4
Cost of Goods to Cash Flow 43	4.7	3.9	9.7	4.9	4.5	5.3	4.8	14.3	5.3	4.1
Cash Flow to Total Debt 44	0.2	0.7	0.3	0.5	0.7	0.4	0.4	0.1	0.1	0.2

Selected Financial Factors (in Percentages)

Debt Ratio 45	75.3	59.5	64.0	63.5	38.9	43.4	42.3	70.3	80.4	78.9
Return on Total Assets 46	9.0	16.2	8.0	13.3	13.2	5.6	7.3	6.8	7.3	10.1
Return on Equity Before Income Taxes 47	23.9	34.3	14.1	29.3	20.2	6.2	10.3	11.4	21.4	32.0
Return on Equity After Income Taxes 48	16.0	33.8	12.8	27.1	17.7	3.7	7.9	7.2	12.9	20.4
Profit Margin (Before Income Tax) 49	5.4	5.5	1.9	5.0	7.0	2.7	4.3	3.5	4.6	7.1
Profit Margin (After Income Tax) 50	3.6	5.4	1.7	4.6	6.2	1.6	3.3	2.2	2.8	4.6

Table II

Corporations with Net Income

PAINT, COATING, AND ADHESIVE

MONEY AMOUNTS AND SIZE OF ASSETS IN THOUSANDS OF DOLLARS

Item Description for Accounting Period 7/07 Through 6/08	Total	Zero Assets	Under 500	500 to 1,000	1,000 to 5,000	5,000 to 10,000	10,000 to 25,000	25,000 to 50,000	50,000 to 100,000	100,000 to 250,000	250,000 to 500,000	500,000 to 2,500,000	2,500,000 and over
Number of Enterprises **1**	1260	0	91	235	721	104	45	27	14	7	•	•	•
Revenues ($ in Thousands)													
Net Sales **2**	40815412	0	78366	533111	3245459	1832480	1452546	1616371	1320805	1411281	•	•	•
Interest **3**	463600	0	0	387	197	1569	805	2687	3065	8928	•	•	•
Rents **4**	13323	0	0	0	0	401	0	1321	217	0	•	•	•
Royalties **5**	435190	0	0	0	0	0	0	166	5196	2184	•	•	•
Other Portfolio Income **6**	903302	0	0	1015	8665	8618	1347	8753	1031	5688	•	•	•
Other Receipts **7**	186234	0	3	748	7386	9706	6684	3505	3689	3224	•	•	•
Total Receipts **8**	42817061	0	78369	535261	3261707	1852774	1461382	1632803	1334003	1431305	•	•	•
Average Total Receipts **9**	33982	•	861	2278	4524	17815	32475	60474	95286	204472	•	•	•
Operating Costs/Operating Income (%)													
Cost of Operations **10**	63.5	•	63.6	63.8	60.9	66.8	65.0	67.8	65.7	63.7	•	•	•
Salaries and Wages **11**	9.3	•	6.0	6.5	8.2	5.8	9.9	7.9	7.3	9.9	•	•	•
Taxes Paid **12**	1.9	•	1.7	5.2	3.1	3.4	1.5	1.7	2.0	1.9	•	•	•
Interest Paid **13**	2.5	•	0.0	2.4	0.8	1.0	1.0	0.3	1.7	1.0	•	•	•
Depreciation **14**	1.9	•	0.2	3.0	0.3	1.6	1.4	1.2	1.9	2.4	•	•	•
Amortization and Depletion **15**	0.8	•	•	0.0	0.3	0.1	0.1	0.1	0.8	0.6	•	•	•
Pensions and Other Deferred Comp. **16**	1.3	•	•	•	0.7	0.3	0.6	0.7	0.4	2.1	•	•	•
Employee Benefits **17**	1.7	•	2.5	1.7	0.7	1.4	1.0	0.5	1.5	1.8	•	•	•
Advertising **18**	1.3	•	•	0.1	0.9	0.6	1.0	0.2	0.6	0.9	•	•	•
Other Expenses **19**	11.9	•	23.8	12.7	11.8	11.0	10.5	10.0	11.7	11.7	•	•	•
Officers' Compensation **20**	1.3	•	0.9	3.8	5.6	4.5	2.2	1.7	1.8	1.1	•	•	•
Operating Margin **21**	2.5	•	1.1	0.8	6.7	3.6	5.8	7.8	4.6	2.9	•	•	•
Operating Margin Before Officers' Comp. **22**	3.8	•	2.0	4.6	12.3	8.1	7.9	9.6	6.4	4.0	•	•	•

Selected Average Balance Sheet ($ in Thousands)

Net Receivables 23	4438	•	80	413	454	1733	4205	9010	13945	26763
Inventories 24	3084	•	91	167	389	1173	3513	7806	12268	30421
Net Property, Plant and Equipment 25	4661	•	24	219	200	1176	3684	5267	15228	42604
Total Assets 26	28854	•	202	844	1726	6201	14478	33356	71981	145519
Notes and Loans Payable 27	8300	•	0	514	533	2107	3804	2091	17844	25400
All Other Liabilities 28	10600	•	226	313	417	1809	4495	6413	15386	36195
Net Worth 29	9953	•	-24	17	776	2285	6179	24852	38750	83924

Selected Financial Ratios (Times to 1)

Current Ratio 30	1.1	•	0.8	1.1	2.1	1.1	1.6	4.4	2.1	2.0
Quick Ratio 31	0.7	•	0.4	0.7	1.3	0.6	0.9	3.0	1.1	1.1
Net Sales to Working Capital 32	24.4	•	•	51.7	7.4	73.2	9.3	3.3	5.8	5.8
Coverage Ratio 33	4.1	•	124.0	1.5	10.5	5.8	7.1	31.3	4.3	5.3
Total Asset Turnover 34	1.1	•	4.3	2.7	2.6	2.8	2.2	1.8	1.3	1.4
Inventory Turnover 35	6.7	•	6.0	8.7	7.0	10.0	6.0	5.2	5.1	4.2
Receivables Turnover 36	7.4	•	21.6	5.5	9.3	9.4	•	6.7	6.7	5.8
Total Liabilities to Net Worth 37	1.9	•	•	49.6	1.2	1.7	1.3	0.3	0.9	0.7
Current Assets to Working Capital 38	8.9	•	•	14.2	1.9	14.5	2.7	1.3	1.9	2.0
Current Liabilities to Working Capital 39	7.9	•	•	13.2	0.9	13.5	1.7	0.3	0.9	1.0
Working Capital to Net Sales 40	0.0	•	•	0.0	0.1	0.0	0.1	0.3	0.2	0.2
Inventory to Working Capital 41	2.4	•	•	4.0	0.7	5.4	1.0	0.4	0.7	0.7
Total Receipts to Cash Flow 42	6.6	•	6.7	13.6	5.9	11.0	6.6	5.8	6.2	7.5
Cost of Goods to Cash Flow 43	4.2	•	4.3	8.7	3.6	7.3	4.3	3.9	4.1	4.8
Cash Flow to Total Debt 44	0.3	•	0.6	0.2	0.8	0.4	0.6	1.2	0.5	0.4

Selected Financial Factors (in Percentages)

Debt Ratio 45	65.5	•	111.9	98.0	55.0	63.1	57.3	25.5	46.2	42.3
Return on Total Assets 46	11.5	•	4.7	9.6	20.7	16.3	16.4	16.7	9.6	7.3
Return on Equity Before Income Taxes 47	25.2	•	•	160.3	41.6	36.5	32.9	21.7	13.7	10.3
Return on Equity After Income Taxes 48	18.2	•	•	160.3	41.2	35.1	30.6	19.3	10.1	7.9
Profit Margin (Before Income Tax) 49	7.8	•	1.1	1.2	7.2	4.7	6.3	9.0	5.6	4.3
Profit Margin (After Income Tax) 50	5.6	•	1.1	1.2	7.1	4.5	5.9	8.0	4.2	3.3

Table I

Corporations with and without Net Income

SOAP, CLEANING COMPOUND, AND TOILET PREPARATION

MONEY AMOUNTS AND SIZE OF ASSETS IN THOUSANDS OF DOLLARS

Item Description for Accounting Period 7/07 Through 6/08		Total	Zero Assets	Under 500	500 to 1,000	1,000 to 5,000	5,000 to 10,000	10,000 to 25,000	25,000 to 50,000	50,000 to 100,000	100,000 to 250,000	250,000 to 500,000	500,000 to 2,500,000	2,500,000 and over
Number of Enterprises	1	1862	•	•	•	181	104	65	22	14	10	5	11	10
Revenues ($ in Thousands)														
Net Sales	2	139836602	•	•	•	1343172	998256	2281138	1033999	1337455	1802792	2936182	11449268	115732151
Interest	3	1057654	•	•	•	140	1321	991	7252	1095	9559	5074	72882	958408
Rents	4	64591	•	•	•	1822	803	865	84	110	0	240	45176	15491
Royalties	5	4192766	•	•	•	7573	0	992	1108	156	0	6506	423432	3753000
Other Portfolio Income	6	2820214	•	•	•	3339	186	1664	6776	9163	13731	31275	546312	2207771
Other Receipts	7	2534658	•	•	•	7115	29984	26163	9262	47816	51890	20492	184873	2157004
Total Receipts	8	150506485	•	•	•	1363161	1030550	2311813	1058481	1395795	1877972	2999769	12721943	124823825
Average Total Receipts	9	80831	•	•	•	7531	9909	35566	48113	99700	187797	599954	1156540	12482382
Operating Costs/Operating Income (%)														
Cost of Operations	10	61.2	•	•	•	61.0	53.7	66.9	57.5	63.5	54.4	60.8	50.3	62.4
Salaries and Wages	11	7.0	•	•	•	8.0	13.4	10.2	10.8	9.3	10.0	9.4	11.9	6.2
Taxes Paid	12	1.2	•	•	•	2.3	1.5	1.6	1.5	1.6	1.4	1.5	1.3	1.1
Interest Paid	13	3.2	•	•	•	0.6	0.6	1.2	1.2	1.3	3.3	1.1	5.0	3.2
Depreciation	14	1.4	•	•	•	0.3	1.2	1.7	1.0	1.9	1.3	2.2	1.4	1.4
Amortization and Depletion	15	1.0	•	•	•	0.0	0.0	0.2	0.5	0.5	1.7	0.5	0.8	1.1
Pensions and Other Deferred Comp.	16	0.9	•	•	•	0.7	0.2	0.4	0.3	0.2	0.6	0.9	0.7	0.9
Employee Benefits	17	1.2	•	•	•	0.5	0.7	2.3	1.3	1.4	1.1	1.3	2.6	1.1
Advertising	18	5.1	•	•	•	1.6	2.0	1.4	4.6	1.5	10.4	5.1	4.6	5.3
Other Expenses	19	17.2	•	•	•	15.4	14.6	10.3	17.2	11.8	14.6	13.5	24.3	16.9
Officers' Compensation	20	0.9	•	•	•	7.3	4.7	1.6	2.2	4.3	0.9	1.6	1.8	0.6
Operating Margin	21	•	•	•	•	2.3	7.4	2.3	1.8	2.6	0.3	2.1	•	•
Operating Margin Before Officers' Comp.	22	0.5	•	•	•	9.6	12.0	3.9	4.0	7.0	1.2	3.7	•	0.3

Selected Average Balance Sheet ($ in Thousands)

Net Receivables 23	16969	•	778	1362	4156	8383	16469	28178	85527	166059	2801265
Inventories 24	4823	•	519	958	3635	6944	12038	30647	70243	140871	594112
Net Property, Plant and Equipment 25	9033	•	209	1174	3962	4901	12774	22099	96256	162556	1359324
Total Assets 26	129203	•	2677	6021	14840	31958	64291	166631	397361	1345872	21808883
Notes and Loans Payable 27	36542	•	554	625	4425	9331	19092	63264	86942	769801	5743307
All Other Liabilities 28	28707	•	478	1518	4434	9711	16985	39088	132474	406131	4690580
Net Worth 29	63954	•	1645	3878	5981	12916	28214	64279	177944	169940	11374995

Selected Financial Ratios (Times to 1)

Current Ratio 30	1.0	•	2.4	2.5	1.6	1.9	1.5	1.4	1.6	1.2	0.9
Quick Ratio 31	0.7	•	1.2	1.5	0.9	1.0	0.8	0.8	1.0	0.6	0.7
Net Sales to Working Capital 32	•	•	5.8	3.9	9.1	5.7	7.5	8.7	9.3	17.6	•
Coverage Ratio 33	3.8	•	7.2	17.7	4.1	4.5	6.9	2.3	5.1	2.9	3.9
Total Asset Turnover 34	0.6	•	2.8	1.6	2.4	1.5	1.5	1.1	1.5	0.8	0.5
Inventory Turnover 35	9.5	•	8.7	5.4	6.5	3.9	5.0	3.2	5.1	3.7	12.2
Receivables Turnover 36	4.1	•	8.8	6.8	9.3	5.5	6.7	5.6	7.1	6.8	3.8
Total Liabilities to Net Worth 37	1.0	•	0.6	0.6	1.5	1.5	1.3	1.6	1.2	6.9	0.9
Current Assets to Working Capital 38	•	•	1.7	1.7	2.6	2.1	2.9	3.3	2.7	7.2	•
Current Liabilities to Working Capital 39	•	•	0.7	0.7	1.6	1.1	1.9	2.3	1.7	6.2	•
Working Capital to Net Sales 40	•	•	0.2	0.3	0.1	0.2	0.1	0.1	0.1	0.1	•
Inventory to Working Capital 41	•	•	0.4	0.5	1.1	0.7	1.1	1.3	1.0	2.3	•
Total Receipts to Cash Flow 42	4.5	•	6.1	4.4	8.0	5.2	6.0	5.7	6.5	3.8	4.4
Cost of Goods to Cash Flow 43	2.7	•	3.7	2.3	5.4	3.0	3.8	3.1	3.9	1.9	2.7
Cash Flow to Total Debt 44	0.3	•	1.2	1.0	0.5	0.5	0.4	0.3	0.4	0.2	0.3

Selected Financial Factors (in Percentages)

Debt Ratio 45	50.5	•	38.6	35.6	59.7	59.6	56.1	61.4	55.2	87.4	47.8
Return on Total Assets 46	7.1	•	11.8	17.9	11.3	7.9	13.2	8.1	7.9	11.2	6.8
Return on Equity Before Income Taxes 47	10.6	•	16.5	26.2	21.2	15.3	25.7	11.6	14.2	58.5	9.7
Return on Equity After Income Taxes 48	6.9	•	14.7	25.6	19.2	12.7	21.7	10.1	11.4	33.8	6.3
Profit Margin (Before Income Tax) 49	9.1	•	3.7	10.6	3.6	4.2	7.6	4.1	4.3	9.5	9.5
Profit Margin (After Income Tax) 50	5.9	•	3.3	10.3	3.3	3.5	6.4	3.6	3.5	5.5	6.2

Table II

Corporations with Net Income

SOAP, CLEANING COMPOUND, AND TOILET PREPARATION

MONEY AMOUNTS AND SIZE OF ASSETS IN THOUSANDS OF DOLLARS

Item Description for Accounting Period 7/07 Through 6/08	Total	Zero Assets	Under 500	500 to 1,000	1,000 to 5,000	5,000 to 10,000	10,000 to 25,000	25,000 to 50,000	50,000 to 100,000	100,000 to 250,000	250,000 to 500,000	500,000 to 2,500,000	2,500,000 and over
Number of Enterprises **1**	463	0	0	113	163	77	54	17	•	7	5	7	•
Revenues ($ in Thousands)													
Net Sales **2**	132901315	0	0	156598	1168742	806063	2032399	958182	•	1125511	2936182	9249640	•
Interest **3**	921015	0	0	24	135	451	990	5025	•	1635	5074	46184	•
Rents **4**	59396	0	0	0	0	803	865	84	•	0	240	45146	•
Royalties **5**	3970646	0	0	0	7573	0	992	100	•	0	6506	413745	•
Other Portfolio Income **6**	2776783	0	0	0	3339	168	1664	6776	•	4113	31275	542423	•
Other Receipts **7**	2443185	0	0	28	6509	29899	25272	6644	•	43792	20492	172713	•
Total Receipts **8**	143072340	0	0	156650	1186298	837384	2062182	976811	•	1175051	2999769	10469851	•
Average Total Receipts **9**	309012	•	•	1386	7278	10875	38189	57459	•	167864	599954	1495693	•
Operating Costs/Operating Income (%)													
Cost of Operations **10**	61.4	•	•	65.8	58.1	49.3	66.2	57.2	•	61.9	60.8	46.6	•
Salaries and Wages **11**	6.9	•	•	4.9	8.1	14.2	9.8	10.5	•	11.1	9.4	13.3	•
Taxes Paid **12**	1.1	•	•	2.2	2.3	1.3	1.6	1.5	•	1.5	1.5	1.4	•
Interest Paid **13**	3.0	•	•	1.2	0.4	0.3	0.8	1.1	•	2.9	1.1	3.6	•
Depreciation **14**	1.4	•	•	1.0	0.3	1.0	1.7	1.0	•	1.5	2.2	1.4	•
Amortization and Depletion **15**	1.0	•	•	•	0.0	0.0	0.2	0.4	•	1.5	0.5	0.7	•
Pensions and Other Deferred Comp. **16**	0.9	•	•	•	0.8	0.3	0.4	0.3	•	0.7	0.9	0.8	•
Employee Benefits **17**	1.2	•	•	2.5	0.5	0.8	2.2	1.3	•	1.6	1.3	2.9	•
Advertising **18**	4.9	•	•	0.0	1.7	2.3	1.4	4.7	•	2.0	5.1	3.8	•
Other Expenses **19**	17.2	•	•	12.3	16.8	12.2	10.2	17.0	•	10.9	13.5	26.2	•
Officers' Compensation **20**	0.8	•	•	6.9	8.0	4.9	1.7	2.2	•	0.9	1.6	1.7	•
Operating Margin **21**	0.3	•	•	3.2	3.1	13.4	3.7	2.8	•	3.4	2.1	•	•
Operating Margin Before Officers' Comp. **22**	1.1	•	•	10.1	11.0	18.3	5.4	5.0	•	4.2	3.7	•	•

Selected Average Balance Sheet ($ in Thousands)

Net Receivables 23	64458	148	763	1477	4431	9617	30337	85527	191207
Inventories 24	17550	81	438	788	3886	7674	32028	61451	162261
Net Property, Plant and Equipment 25	34032	89	192	1179	4218	4976	23165	96256	178323
Total Assets 26	489101	736	2537	6021	15455	31878	159290	397361	1322880
Notes and Loans Payable 27	132763	184	442	309	3893	5544	55777	86942	870459
All Other Liabilities 28	108961	65	424	1172	4335	11612	39186	132474	504224
Net Worth 29	247377	487	1670	4540	7227	14722	64327	177944	-51803

Selected Financial Ratios (Times to 1)

Current Ratio 30	1.0	7.5	3.0	3.3	1.7	1.9	2.2	1.6	1.1
Quick Ratio 31	0.7	4.0	1.5	2.0	1.0	1.0	1.2	1.0	0.5
Net Sales to Working Capital 32	•	2.6	5.0	3.6	8.7	5.9	4.2	9.3	50.9
Coverage Ratio 33	4.4	3.8	10.8	52.8	7.2	5.2	3.6	5.1	5.0
Total Asset Turnover 34	0.6	1.9	2.8	1.7	2.4	1.8	1.0	1.5	1.0
Inventory Turnover 35	10.0	11.2	9.5	6.6	6.4	4.2	3.1	5.8	3.8
Receivables Turnover 36	4.0	12.2	8.8	6.4	•	5.7	4.4	•	•
Total Liabilities to Net Worth 37	1.0	0.5	0.5	0.3	1.1	1.2	1.5	1.2	•
Current Assets to Working Capital 38	•	1.2	1.5	1.4	2.4	2.1	1.8	2.7	19.5
Current Liabilities to Working Capital 39	•	0.2	0.5	0.4	1.4	1.1	0.8	1.7	18.5
Working Capital to Net Sales 40	0.4	0.4	0.2	0.3	0.1	0.2	0.2	0.1	0.0
Inventory to Working Capital 41	•	0.2	0.3	0.3	0.9	0.8	0.7	1.0	6.3
Total Receipts to Cash Flow 42	4.3	9.2	5.5	3.6	7.1	5.2	5.7	6.5	3.1
Cost of Goods to Cash Flow 43	2.6	6.1	3.2	1.8	4.7	3.0	3.6	3.9	1.5
Cash Flow to Total Debt 44	0.3	0.6	1.5	2.0	0.6	0.6	0.3	0.4	0.3

Selected Financial Factors (in Percentages)

Debt Ratio 45	49.4	33.8	34.1	24.6	53.2	53.8	59.6	55.2	103.9
Return on Total Assets 46	7.6	8.3	13.6	30.7	14.6	10.4	10.8	7.9	17.9
Return on Equity Before Income Taxes 47	11.5	9.2	18.7	39.9	27.0	18.2	19.3	14.2	•
Return on Equity After Income Taxes 48	7.6	7.7	16.8	39.2	25.0	15.2	17.1	11.4	•
Profit Margin (Before Income Tax) 49	9.9	3.2	4.4	17.3	5.2	4.7	7.7	4.3	14.4
Profit Margin (After Income Tax) 50	6.6	2.7	3.9	17.0	4.8	4.0	6.9	3.5	9.4

Table I

Corporations with and without Net Income

CHEMICAL PRODUCT AND PREPARATION

MONEY AMOUNTS AND SIZE OF ASSETS IN THOUSANDS OF DOLLARS

Item Description for Accounting Period 7/07 Through 6/08		Total	Zero Assets	Under 500	500 to 1,000	1,000 to 5,000	5,000 to 10,000	10,000 to 25,000	25,000 to 50,000	50,000 to 100,000	100,000 to 250,000	250,000 to 500,000	500,000 to 2,500,000	2,500,000 and over
Number of Enterprises	1	2946	•	•	•	695	80	121	68	36	26	16	20	7
Revenues ($ in Thousands)														
Net Sales	2	84062534	•	•	•	2063823	1188153	3625642	3466185	3480542	5079410	6669873	20762882	35685940
Interest	3	662614	•	•	•	1467	1727	9018	14267	18118	11182	45348	180666	377056
Rents	4	21255	•	•	•	0	2691	907	1282	180	143	920	9291	3136
Royalties	5	517393	•	•	•	287	0	2262	34	1682	25849	17525	97913	371840
Other Portfolio Income	6	1283389	•	•	•	41670	873	15754	30297	29537	39746	103897	893691	121196
Other Receipts	7	2466847	•	•	•	1512	1506	24240	55156	10742	165355	165456	769103	1313459
Total Receipts	8	89014032	•	•	•	2108759	1194950	3677823	3567221	3540801	5321685	7003019	22713546	37872627
Average Total Receipts	9	30215	•	•	•	3034	14937	30395	52459	98356	204680	437689	1135677	5410375
Operating Costs/Operating Income (%)														
Cost of Operations	10	71.9	•	•	•	53.8	53.5	73.0	65.6	73.4	66.4	77.8	70.0	75.2
Salaries and Wages	11	6.4	•	•	•	9.5	11.5	6.0	8.7	6.0	9.1	6.0	6.4	5.6
Taxes Paid	12	1.2	•	•	•	2.9	2.6	1.5	1.5	1.3	1.5	1.2	1.4	0.8
Interest Paid	13	2.6	•	•	•	1.0	1.2	1.0	1.7	1.3	2.0	2.4	3.0	3.1
Depreciation	14	2.6	•	•	•	8.3	2.0	1.5	2.1	1.7	2.3	2.1	2.6	2.9
Amortization and Depletion	15	1.0	•	•	•	0.0	0.1	0.3	0.3	0.3	0.7	0.9	0.9	1.4
Pensions and Other Deferred Comp.	16	0.5	•	•	•	0.3	0.6	0.3	0.5	0.4	0.9	0.6	0.9	0.3
Employee Benefits	17	1.0	•	•	•	1.5	1.5	1.0	0.6	1.0	1.4	1.1	1.7	0.5
Advertising	18	0.6	•	•	•	0.2	0.4	0.7	0.6	0.5	0.6	0.4	1.4	0.2
Other Expenses	19	11.0	•	•	•	20.7	16.3	11.3	17.4	9.3	12.5	8.3	10.8	9.9
Officers' Compensation	20	1.0	•	•	•	6.3	4.7	1.9	2.5	1.3	1.2	0.6	0.9	0.1
Operating Margin	21	0.1	•	•	•	•	5.5	1.4	•	3.3	1.4	•	0.0	0.0
Operating Margin Before Officers' Comp.	22	1.1	•	•	•	1.8	10.2	3.3	1.1	4.6	2.6	•	0.9	0.1

Selected Average Balance Sheet ($ in Thousands)

Net Receivables 23	5068	•	•	•	•	275	1956	4296	7471	14773	30444	89643	157289	1074203
Inventories 24	2905	•	•	•	•	210	1954	3558	6562	15513	25165	47139	124825	407235
Net Property, Plant and Equipment 25	6121	•	•	•	•	719	2376	3503	9069	14283	31801	82881	239405	1256751
Total Assets 26	35867	•	•	•	•	1691	7717	15783	35626	75040	165239	364208	1324317	8553115
Notes and Loans Payable 27	9207	•	•	•	•	493	2237	4442	9744	17565	51032	127898	431284	1799686
All Other Liabilities 28	11198	•	•	•	•	213	2274	5028	10500	18999	50008	107405	387289	2827611
Net Worth 29	15462	•	•	•	•	985	3206	6313	15382	38476	64199	128905	505745	3925818

Selected Financial Ratios (Times to 1)

Current Ratio 30	1.4	•	•	•	•	2.7	2.0	2.0	1.8	1.8	1.6	1.4	1.5	1.2
Quick Ratio 31	0.8	•	•	•	•	1.9	1.1	1.1	1.1	1.0	0.8	0.9	0.9	0.7
Net Sales to Working Capital 32	8.3	•	•	•	•	6.7	6.4	5.5	5.3	5.2	6.7	8.2	6.2	13.6
Coverage Ratio 33	3.5	•	•	•	•	•	5.9	3.7	1.9	4.9	4.1	2.6	4.3	3.5
Total Asset Turnover 34	0.8	•	•	•	•	1.8	1.9	1.9	1.4	1.3	1.2	1.1	0.8	0.6
Inventory Turnover 35	7.1	•	•	•	•	7.6	4.1	6.1	5.1	4.6	5.2	6.9	5.8	9.4
Receivables Turnover 36	7.0	•	•	•	•	10.7	6.5	7.0	6.7	6.1	7.1	5.1	6.6	7.5
Total Liabilities to Net Worth 37	1.3	•	•	•	•	0.7	1.4	1.5	1.3	1.0	1.6	1.8	1.6	1.2
Current Assets to Working Capital 38	3.7	•	•	•	•	1.6	2.0	2.0	2.2	2.2	2.8	3.3	3.0	6.5
Current Liabilities to Working Capital 39	2.7	•	•	•	•	0.6	1.0	1.0	1.2	1.2	1.8	2.3	2.0	5.5
Working Capital to Net Sales 40	0.1	•	•	•	•	0.1	0.2	0.2	0.2	0.2	0.2	0.1	0.2	0.1
Inventory to Working Capital 41	0.9	•	•	•	•	0.4	0.7	0.6	0.6	0.8	1.0	0.9	0.8	1.3
Total Receipts to Cash Flow 42	6.7	•	•	•	•	8.4	4.9	8.1	6.2	8.3	5.8	10.2	5.7	6.8
Cost of Goods to Cash Flow 43	4.8	•	•	•	•	4.5	2.6	5.9	4.1	6.1	3.9	7.9	4.0	5.1
Cash Flow to Total Debt 44	0.2	•	•	•	•	0.5	0.7	0.4	0.4	0.3	0.3	0.2	0.2	0.2

Selected Financial Factors (in Percentages)

Debt Ratio 45	56.9	•	•	•	•	41.7	58.5	60.0	56.8	48.7	61.1	64.6	61.8	54.1
Return on Total Assets 46	7.4	•	•	•	•	•	14.0	7.3	4.6	8.4	9.8	7.0	9.9	6.5
Return on Equity Before Income Taxes 47	12.4	•	•	•	•	•	•	28.0	13.4	13.0	19.1	12.2	19.9	10.1
Return on Equity After Income Taxes 48	8.8	•	•	•	•	•	•	24.1	9.2	9.2	14.0	7.7	14.9	7.4
Profit Margin (Before Income Tax) 49	6.7	•	•	•	•	•	6.0	2.8	1.5	6.3	5.2	3.8	9.7	7.8
Profit Margin (After Income Tax) 50	4.8	•	•	•	•	•	5.2	1.9	0.6	3.7	4.6	2.4	7.3	5.7

Table II

Corporations with Net Income

CHEMICAL PRODUCT AND PREPARATION

MONEY AMOUNTS AND SIZE OF ASSETS IN THOUSANDS OF DOLLARS

Item Description for Accounting Period 7/07 Through 6/08	Total	Zero Assets	Under 500	500 to 1,000	1,000 to 5,000	5,000 to 10,000	10,000 to 25,000	25,000 to 50,000	50,000 to 100,000	100,000 to 250,000	250,000 to 500,000	500,000 to 2,500,000	2,500,000 and over
Number of Enterprises 1	1773	•	668	178	233	67	92	44	•	17	12	15	•
Revenues ($ in Thousands)													
Net Sales 2	74270735	•	629425	137763	1683660	1009271	3208389	3000843	•	3807796	5355119	18979831	•
Interest 3	581909	•	0	29	1448	1716	5293	3967	•	7264	39808	152197	•
Rents 4	18963	•	0	1405	0	2691	659	1267	•	20	916	8935	•
Royalties 5	490729	•	0	0	287	0	255	34	•	19358	14511	88255	•
Other Portfolio Income 6	1266086	•	0	466	41670	845	15733	29854	•	27105	103739	891073	•
Other Receipts 7	2339346	•	4919	93	1461	1492	17323	25115	•	48586	164031	742908	•
Total Receipts 8	78967768	•	634344	139756	1728526	1016015	3247652	3061080	•	3910129	5678124	20863199	•
Average Total Receipts 9	44539	•	950	785	7419	15164	35301	69570	•	230008	473177	1390880	•
Operating Costs/Operating Income (%)													
Cost of Operations 10	72.2	•	45.0	42.3	55.4	47.6	72.3	64.0	•	63.3	77.0	70.6	•
Salaries and Wages 11	6.0	•	0.1	8.8	9.7	12.9	5.5	7.8	•	8.1	5.5	6.1	•
Taxes Paid 12	1.2	•	2.7	2.6	2.4	2.6	1.5	1.5	•	1.5	1.2	1.5	•
Interest Paid 13	2.1	•	0.1	2.3	0.5	1.1	0.6	1.0	•	1.1	2.1	2.6	•
Depreciation 14	2.1	•	0.5	1.9	0.9	1.9	1.4	1.7	•	2.1	1.7	2.4	•
Amortization and Depletion 15	0.8	•	•	•	•	0.1	0.1	0.1	•	0.7	0.8	0.9	•
Pensions and Other Deferred Comp. 16	0.5	•	1.7	2.4	0.3	0.7	0.3	0.5	•	0.8	0.7	0.9	•
Employee Benefits 17	1.0	•	0.4	•	1.6	1.5	1.1	0.5	•	1.5	1.1	1.7	•
Advertising 18	0.5	•	0.1	0.9	0.3	0.5	0.7	0.5	•	0.7	0.4	1.1	•
Other Expenses 19	10.7	•	21.3	24.7	17.0	18.8	9.8	15.5	•	10.9	8.5	10.7	•
Officers' Compensation 20	0.8	•	14.3	8.2	4.8	5.2	1.5	2.4	•	0.7	0.6	0.6	•
Operating Margin 21	2.2	•	13.8	6.0	7.0	7.1	5.3	4.7	•	8.5	0.5	1.0	•
Operating Margin Before Officers' Comp. 22	3.0	•	28.1	14.2	11.9	12.3	6.8	7.1	•	9.2	1.1	1.7	•

Selected Average Balance Sheet ($ in Thousands)

Net Receivables 23	7306	•	122	147	744	2006	4649	9438	•	33607	104350	184147	•
Inventories 24	3724	•	17	271	453	1818	3948	7165	•	26749	49704	163932	•
Net Property, Plant and Equipment 25	7309	•	27	57	418	2208	3327	9122	•	36788	58119	269758	•
Total Assets 26	46371	•	207	766	2222	7825	15682	36585	•	165701	376821	1438156	•
Notes and Loans Payable 27	11172	•	30	209	174	2048	3051	8136	•	44409	124052	478022	•
All Other Liabilities 28	14131	•	67	100	531	1879	4704	10176	•	41090	116271	470139	•
Net Worth 29	21068	•	110	456	1517	3898	7926	18273	•	80202	136498	489995	•

Selected Financial Ratios (Times to 1)

Current Ratio 30	1.3	•	2.6	1.5	2.7	2.5	2.1	1.9	•	1.6	1.6	1.5	•
Quick Ratio 31	0.8	•	2.3	0.7	2.0	1.3	1.2	1.1	•	0.8	1.0	0.8	•
Net Sales to Working Capital 32	9.8	•	8.5	6.1	6.5	5.1	5.7	6.3	•	6.9	6.4	6.8	•
Coverage Ratio 33	5.5	•	194.5	4.2	19.5	8.0	11.7	7.6	•	10.9	4.1	5.3	•
Total Asset Turnover 34	0.9	•	4.6	1.0	3.3	1.9	2.2	1.9	•	1.4	1.2	0.9	•
Inventory Turnover 35	8.1	•	25.0	1.2	8.8	3.9	6.4	6.1	•	5.3	6.9	5.4	•
Receivables Turnover 36	7.6	•	7.5	2.8	10.3	6.7	7.5	7.6	•	7.1	5.0	•	•
Total Liabilities to Net Worth 37	1.2	•	0.9	0.7	0.5	1.0	1.0	1.0	•	1.1	1.8	1.9	•
Current Assets to Working Capital 38	4.0	•	1.6	2.9	1.6	1.7	1.9	2.1	•	2.7	2.7	3.2	•
Current Liabilities to Working Capital 39	3.0	•	0.6	1.9	0.6	0.7	0.9	1.1	•	1.7	1.7	2.2	•
Working Capital to Net Sales 40	0.1	•	0.1	0.2	0.2	0.2	0.2	0.2	•	0.1	0.2	0.1	•
Inventory to Working Capital 41	1.0	•	0.2	1.5	0.4	0.6	0.6	0.7	•	0.9	0.7	0.9	•
Total Receipts to Cash Flow 42	5.8	•	3.2	3.3	4.5	4.1	6.9	5.2	•	4.9	7.9	5.3	•
Cost of Goods to Cash Flow 43	4.2	•	1.4	1.4	2.5	2.0	5.0	3.3	•	3.1	6.0	3.8	•
Cash Flow to Total Debt 44	0.3	•	3.1	0.8	2.3	0.9	0.7	0.7	•	0.5	0.2	0.2	•

Selected Financial Factors (in Percentages)

Debt Ratio 45	54.6	•	46.7	40.5	31.7	50.2	49.5	50.1	•	51.6	63.8	65.9	•
Return on Total Assets 46	10.3	•	66.7	9.8	33.3	17.2	15.7	14.4	•	16.6	10.4	12.2	•
Return on Equity Before Income Taxes 47	18.6	•	124.4	12.6	46.2	30.1	28.4	25.1	•	31.1	21.7	29.0	•
Return on Equity After Income Taxes 48	14.3	•	124.4	10.6	43.9	26.3	24.0	21.1	•	24.9	16.0	22.1	•
Profit Margin (Before Income Tax) 49	9.3	•	14.5	7.4	9.7	7.8	6.5	6.7	•	11.1	6.6	11.2	•
Profit Margin (After Income Tax) 50	7.2	•	14.5	6.3	9.2	6.8	5.5	5.7	•	8.9	4.9	8.6	•

Table I

Corporations with and without Net Income

PLASTICS PRODUCT

MONEY AMOUNTS AND SIZE OF ASSETS IN THOUSANDS OF DOLLARS

Item Description for Accounting Period 7/07 Through 6/08	Total	Zero Assets	Under 500	500 to 1,000	1,000 to 5,000	5,000 to 10,000	10,000 to 25,000	25,000 to 50,000	50,000 to 100,000	100,000 to 250,000	250,000 to 500,000	500,000 to 2,500,000	2,500,000 and over
Number of Enterprises 1	10910	1410	3743	1693	2650	592	384	184	107	90	30	24	4
Revenues ($ in Thousands)													
Net Sales 2	116472690	1039371	1827195	2969423	13886492	8446567	11524448	10425349	11187131	18127686	10816098	17561353	8661577
Interest 3	447643	5622	987	2681	10956	7646	8150	8230	44514	50400	61293	115252	131913
Rents 4	25737	61	0	471	1333	2843	663	2796	1675	5662	8760	611	862
Royalties 5	156481	0	0	0	791	85	132	2860	8268	9923	39262	48546	46616
Other Portfolio Income 6	584022	8742	14617	866	25074	23191	27067	43133	56392	78834	69451	138503	98153
Other Receipts 7	806422	14199	2653	1253	49931	43580	85041	111333	67514	153554	74156	118947	84257
Total Receipts 8	118492995	1067995	1845452	2974694	13974577	8523912	11645501	10593701	11365494	18426059	11069020	17983212	9023378
Average Total Receipts 9	10861	757	493	1757	5273	14398	30327	57574	106220	204734	368967	749300	2255844
Operating Costs/Operating Income (%)													
Cost of Operations 10	72.4	70.4	57.1	56.1	67.5	69.8	71.9	72.0	72.1	75.9	78.2	76.4	71.1
Salaries and Wages 11	5.3	5.3	7.5	7.9	5.7	6.0	5.9	6.5	6.0	4.5	3.8	4.5	4.7
Taxes Paid 12	1.6	2.3	2.4	2.7	2.3	1.8	1.9	1.7	1.6	1.5	1.1	1.1	1.3
Interest Paid 13	3.0	3.9	0.7	0.8	1.1	1.3	1.2	1.7	2.1	2.5	4.5	4.9	9.5
Depreciation 14	3.0	2.8	1.4	2.0	2.4	2.9	2.6	3.3	3.0	2.9	3.0	3.6	3.5
Amortization and Depletion 15	0.5	1.5	0.0	0.3	0.1	0.1	0.2	0.3	0.7	0.6	0.8	0.8	0.8
Pensions and Other Deferred Comp. 16	0.4	0.3	0.0	0.5	0.3	0.3	0.4	0.4	0.5	0.5	0.4	0.4	0.4
Employee Benefits 17	1.4	1.1	0.6	0.7	1.4	1.2	1.4	1.6	1.8	1.7	1.4	1.1	1.8
Advertising 18	0.4	0.2	1.5	0.9	0.4	0.7	0.4	0.4	0.5	0.6	0.4	0.2	0.2
Other Expenses 19	9.2	14.4	21.5	15.5	11.2	9.1	8.9	7.6	8.8	8.0	8.4	7.0	11.2
Officers' Compensation 20	1.8	2.3	5.1	9.0	4.6	2.7	2.0	1.7	0.9	0.8	0.6	0.4	0.6
Operating Margin 21	1.0	•	2.0	3.7	3.1	4.2	3.2	2.9	2.0	0.7	•	•	•
Operating Margin Before Officers' Comp. 22	2.7	•	7.1	12.6	7.7	6.9	5.2	4.6	2.9	1.5	0.0	•	•

Selected Average Balance Sheet ($ in Thousands)

Net Receivables 23	1367	0	30	168	556	1715	3763	7243	14071	25423	60849	116317	208970
Inventories 24	1141	0	20	113	424	1241	3446	6308	13246	25368	37948	92987	180743
Net Property, Plant and Equipment 25	2070	0	25	119	535	2425	4926	11925	19974	45854	72979	206441	484776
Total Assets 26	8515	0	128	704	2095	7106	15547	36336	70183	158195	333449	846845	4183122
Notes and Loans Payable 27	3462	0	77	251	866	2522	5553	12274	23453	52247	180828	408464	1608858
All Other Liabilities 28	2069	0	64	143	604	1813	4073	9409	18151	48140	102826	180725	607604
Net Worth 29	2984	0	-12	310	625	2771	5922	14653	28579	57808	49795	257656	1966660

Selected Financial Ratios (Times to 1)

Current Ratio 30	1.5	•	1.2	2.5	1.8	1.6	1.7	1.6	1.7	1.6	1.2	1.6	1.0
Quick Ratio 31	0.8	•	0.7	1.7	1.1	1.0	0.9	0.9	0.9	0.9	0.7	0.9	0.4
Net Sales to Working Capital 32	9.3	•	38.9	6.1	8.9	10.3	7.9	8.4	7.4	8.2	15.6	7.8	65.9
Coverage Ratio 33	1.9	0.6	5.2	5.6	4.3	4.9	4.6	3.7	2.8	2.0	1.0	1.5	0.9
Total Asset Turnover 34	1.3	•	3.8	2.5	2.5	2.0	1.9	1.6	1.5	1.3	1.1	0.9	0.5
Inventory Turnover 35	6.8	•	13.8	8.7	8.3	8.0	6.3	6.5	5.7	6.0	7.4	6.0	8.5
Receivables Turnover 36	7.6	•	•	•	9.6	8.8	7.9	7.9	7.3	8.0	6.5	5.3	9.9
Total Liabilities to Net Worth 37	1.9	•	•	1.3	2.4	1.6	1.6	1.5	1.5	1.7	5.7	2.3	1.1
Current Assets to Working Capital 38	2.9	•	7.4	1.7	2.3	2.8	2.4	2.7	2.5	2.6	5.4	2.6	21.5
Current Liabilities to Working Capital 39	1.9	•	6.4	0.7	1.3	1.8	1.4	1.7	1.5	1.6	4.4	1.6	20.5
Working Capital to Net Sales 40	0.1	•	0.0	0.2	0.1	0.1	0.1	0.1	0.1	0.1	0.1	0.1	0.0
Inventory to Working Capital 41	1.0	•	1.6	0.4	0.8	0.9	0.9	1.0	0.9	1.0	1.8	0.9	6.3
Total Receipts to Cash Flow 42	10.7	12.3	6.0	7.3	9.0	8.3	9.3	10.0	9.4	11.9	17.6	14.3	13.2
Cost of Goods to Cash Flow 43	7.8	8.7	3.4	4.1	6.1	5.8	6.7	7.2	6.8	9.0	13.8	10.9	9.4
Cash Flow to Total Debt 44	0.2	•	0.6	0.6	0.4	0.4	0.3	0.3	0.3	0.2	0.1	0.1	0.1

Selected Financial Factors (in Percentages)

Debt Ratio 45	65.0	•	109.6	56.0	70.2	61.0	61.9	59.7	59.3	63.5	85.1	69.6	53.0
Return on Total Assets 46	7.3	•	14.2	11.7	12.0	12.9	10.4	9.7	8.6	6.1	4.6	6.4	4.4
Return on Equity Before Income Taxes 47	10.0	•	•	21.9	31.0	26.3	21.4	17.6	13.5	8.2	•	7.2	•
Return on Equity After Income Taxes 48	8.1	•	•	20.5	29.3	24.9	19.1	15.5	11.0	6.4	•	5.4	•
Profit Margin (Before Income Tax) 49	2.8	•	3.0	3.9	3.7	5.1	4.2	4.5	3.7	2.4	0.9	2.5	•
Profit Margin (After Income Tax) 50	2.3	•	3.0	3.6	3.5	4.8	3.8	4.0	3.0	1.8	•	1.9	•

95

Table II

Corporations with Net Income

PLASTICS PRODUCT

MONEY AMOUNTS AND SIZE OF ASSETS IN THOUSANDS OF DOLLARS

Item Description for Accounting Period 7/07 Through 6/08		Total	Zero Assets	Under 500	500 to 1,000	1,000 to 5,000	5,000 to 10,000	10,000 to 25,000	25,000 to 50,000	50,000 to 100,000	100,000 to 250,000	250,000 to 500,000	500,000 to 2,500,000	2,500,000 and over
Number of Enterprises	1	6359	397	1747	1272	1863	480	299	129	79	58	•	•	0
Revenues ($ in Thousands)														
Net Sales	2	84384544	687696	854167	2371476	10704780	7392817	9596462	7928181	8740907	12935167	•	•	0
Interest	3	188840	5052	77	2191	7499	4499	7104	7003	19255	30271	•	•	0
Rents	4	19558	0	0	471	1333	2843	627	1455	1632	2531	•	•	0
Royalties	5	112245	0	0	0	791	0	0	2855	8168	5352	•	•	0
Other Portfolio Income	6	462241	8686	14617	866	24144	3038	25425	33864	44328	51838	•	•	0
Other Receipts	7	513654	11317	1935	1098	40114	38730	74226	52638	35188	100817	•	•	0
Total Receipts	8	85681082	712751	870796	2376102	10778661	7441927	9703844	8025996	8849478	13125976	•	•	0
Average Total Receipts	9	13474	1795	498	1868	5786	15504	32454	62217	112019	226310	•	•	•
Operating Costs/Operating Income (%)														
Cost of Operations	10	70.8	71.7	48.7	54.3	65.2	67.6	71.5	70.2	69.8	75.7	•	•	•
Salaries and Wages	11	5.3	3.8	7.8	6.4	5.8	6.0	5.8	6.2	6.1	4.2	•	•	•
Taxes Paid	12	1.6	1.5	2.3	2.6	2.2	1.8	2.0	1.6	1.6	1.5	•	•	•
Interest Paid	13	1.7	3.5	0.8	0.8	0.7	0.9	1.0	1.4	1.4	1.9	•	•	•
Depreciation	14	2.7	2.2	0.6	1.7	1.9	2.7	2.5	3.0	2.7	2.5	•	•	•
Amortization and Depletion	15	0.3	1.8	0.1	0.4	0.0	0.0	0.1	0.2	0.3	0.4	•	•	•
Pensions and Other Deferred Comp.	16	0.4	0.2	0.1	0.7	0.4	0.4	0.5	0.4	0.5	0.4	•	•	•
Employee Benefits	17	1.4	0.7	0.9	0.8	1.5	1.2	1.4	1.7	1.8	1.4	•	•	•
Advertising	18	0.4	0.2	1.4	0.8	0.4	0.8	0.4	0.3	0.6	0.5	•	•	•
Other Expenses	19	8.4	12.2	21.6	14.2	10.3	9.0	7.8	6.8	8.5	7.2	•	•	•
Officers' Compensation	20	1.9	0.7	3.3	9.9	4.9	2.7	1.7	1.6	1.0	0.8	•	•	•
Operating Margin	21	4.9	1.6	12.4	7.5	6.7	6.9	5.2	6.6	5.7	3.5	•	•	•
Operating Margin Before Officers' Comp.	22	6.8	2.2	15.7	17.4	11.6	9.6	6.9	8.3	6.7	4.3	•	•	•

Selected Average Balance Sheet ($ in Thousands)

Net Receivables **23**	1573	0	41	159	600	1801	4033	8074	14283	25543
Inventories **24**	1432	0	58	111	504	1307	3393	7013	14004	29974
Net Property, Plant and Equipment **25**	2421	0	21	112	467	2413	4798	11773	19911	48931
Total Assets **26**	9136	0	172	722	2147	6992	15708	36922	70578	156123
Notes and Loans Payable **27**	3170	0	94	198	582	1940	4504	11202	18500	46736
All Other Liabilities **28**	2323	0	28	139	572	1360	3930	8371	18499	44544
Net Worth **29**	3643	0	49	386	992	3692	7274	17348	33579	64843

Selected Financial Ratios (Times to 1)

Current Ratio **30**	1.6	•	2.2	2.5	2.1	2.0	2.0	1.8	1.9	1.8
Quick Ratio **31**	0.9	•	1.3	1.9	1.3	1.3	1.1	1.0	1.0	1.0
Net Sales to Working Capital **32**	8.4	•	6.7	6.4	7.4	7.7	6.8	6.9	6.2	7.1
Coverage Ratio **33**	4.7	2.5	19.1	10.7	12.1	9.0	7.1	6.8	6.0	3.6
Total Asset Turnover **34**	1.5	•	2.8	2.6	2.7	2.2	2.0	1.7	1.6	1.4
Inventory Turnover **35**	6.6	•	4.1	9.1	7.4	8.0	6.8	6.1	5.5	5.6
Receivables Turnover **36**	7.9	•	10.0	•	9.2	8.8	8.4	7.6	7.6	7.7
Total Liabilities to Net Worth **37**	1.5	•	2.5	0.9	1.2	0.9	1.2	1.1	1.1	1.4
Current Assets to Working Capital **38**	2.5	•	1.8	1.6	1.9	2.0	2.0	2.2	2.1	2.2
Current Liabilities to Working Capital **39**	1.5	•	0.8	0.6	0.9	1.0	1.0	1.2	1.1	1.2
Working Capital to Net Sales **40**	0.1	•	0.1	0.2	0.1	0.1	0.1	0.1	0.2	0.1
Inventory to Working Capital **41**	0.9	•	0.3	0.4	0.7	0.7	0.8	0.8	0.8	0.8
Total Receipts to Cash Flow **42**	8.0	6.4	3.5	5.9	6.9	6.9	8.5	7.9	7.1	9.4
Cost of Goods to Cash Flow **43**	5.7	4.6	1.7	3.2	4.5	4.6	6.1	5.6	5.0	7.2
Cash Flow to Total Debt **44**	0.3	•	1.1	0.9	0.7	0.7	0.4	0.4	0.4	0.3

Selected Financial Factors (in Percentages)

Debt Ratio **45**	60.1	•	71.3	46.6	53.8	47.2	53.7	53.0	52.4	58.5
Return on Total Assets **46**	12.0	•	43.0	22.0	21.6	18.7	14.9	15.4	13.2	9.9
Return on Equity Before Income Taxes **47**	23.8	•	141.9	37.3	42.8	31.5	27.8	28.0	23.2	17.3
Return on Equity After Income Taxes **48**	21.2	•	141.3	35.8	41.3	30.1	25.3	25.5	20.3	14.7
Profit Margin (Before Income Tax) **49**	6.5	5.2	14.3	7.7	7.4	7.5	6.3	7.9	7.0	5.0
Profit Margin (After Income Tax) **50**	5.8	4.5	14.3	7.4	7.1	7.2	5.7	7.2	6.2	4.3

Table I

Corporations with and without Net Income

RUBBER PRODUCT

MONEY AMOUNTS AND SIZE OF ASSETS IN THOUSANDS OF DOLLARS

Item Description for Accounting Period 7/07 Through 6/08	Total	Zero Assets	Under 500	500 to 1,000	1,000 to 5,000	5,000 to 10,000	10,000 to 25,000	25,000 to 50,000	50,000 to 100,000	100,000 to 250,000	250,000 to 500,000	500,000 to 2,500,000	2,500,000 and over
Number of Enterprises 1	718	11	87	0	431	59	59	24	19	12	4	9	4
Revenues ($ in Thousands)													
Net Sales 2	55052485	130783	74100	0	2105236	738624	2016270	1467800	1682889	1723256	1217350	10375912	33520265
Interest 3	455984	1119	1	0	4606	1991	1258	1414	4435	3315	11065	87290	339488
Rents 4	14558	0	0	0	0	0	0	2	3372	300	849	1778	8256
Royalties 5	854721	3662	0	0	0	0	0	1208	42	1982	945	49247	797637
Other Portfolio Income 6	1124835	0	2	0	712	437	776	1684	62793	11849	811	77680	968092
Other Receipts 7	462469	26158	1981	0	4893	4511	9840	11024	4213	3160	40487	54654	301548
Total Receipts 8	57965052	161722	76084	0	2115447	745563	2028144	1483132	1757744	1743862	1271507	10646561	35935286
Average Total Receipts 9	80731	14702	875	•	4908	12637	34375	61797	92513	145322	317877	1182951	8983822
Operating Costs/Operating Income (%)													
Cost of Operations 10	71.9	65.4	27.4	•	66.7	73.0	70.1	77.1	74.9	75.8	68.0	76.1	70.7
Salaries and Wages 11	6.1	7.5	11.8	•	10.2	5.7	4.8	5.7	5.3	5.0	4.1	4.1	6.7
Taxes Paid 12	1.3	2.3	3.8	•	2.2	1.3	1.7	2.1	2.3	1.8	0.6	0.8	1.3
Interest Paid 13	2.1	13.4	5.7	•	1.2	1.3	0.7	2.1	2.7	2.4	1.2	2.5	2.1
Depreciation 14	2.3	2.3	7.8	•	1.2	1.4	2.1	2.6	3.6	2.6	1.2	2.7	2.2
Amortization and Depletion 15	0.8	4.3	0.0	•	0.0	0.0	0.1	0.6	0.4	1.4	1.2	0.6	1.0
Pensions and Other Deferred Comp. 16	1.8	0.3	0.0	•	0.5	0.5	0.7	0.9	0.2	0.6	1.4	1.2	2.4
Employee Benefits 17	3.4	0.7	1.0	•	2.0	0.4	2.0	2.5	3.1	2.2	1.4	3.9	3.7
Advertising 18	1.2	0.8	0.0	•	0.2	0.3	2.9	0.4	0.7	0.1	1.5	0.6	1.5
Other Expenses 19	10.0	33.1	30.7	•	10.9	6.7	7.8	5.7	7.4	6.1	13.7	5.5	11.8
Officers' Compensation 20	0.6	4.3	5.8	•	5.1	5.1	1.3	1.1	0.9	0.8	0.5	0.6	0.1
Operating Margin 21	•	•	6.0	•	•	4.2	5.7	•	•	1.3	5.3	1.4	•
Operating Margin Before Officers' Comp. 22	•	•	11.8	•	4.9	9.3	7.0	0.3	•	2.0	5.8	1.9	•

Selected Average Balance Sheet ($ in Thousands)

Line Item													
Net Receivables 23	12196	0	76	•	676	1614	3820	8297	12883	24509	87465	139938	1447692
Inventories 24	9793	0	29	•	491	1849	2764	8115	13061	13968	62970	130709	1124153
Net Property, Plant and Equipment 25	14310	0	158	•	401	1184	4291	11597	20767	29372	43419	258412	1560000
Total Assets 26	67700	0	330	•	2295	6231	13815	35324	70972	135284	355728	1277779	7416331
Notes and Loans Payable 27	19185	0	253	•	685	1960	2973	12846	30487	49117	64006	379152	2005266
All Other Liabilities 28	29731	0	579	•	713	1375	3402	16705	18897	32816	116976	473122	3706434
Net Worth 29	18784	0	-502	•	897	2896	7439	5773	21488	53350	174746	425505	1704630

Selected Financial Ratios (Times to 1)

Line Item													
Current Ratio 30	1.6	•	0.8	•	1.8	2.7	2.2	1.6	1.3	1.9	2.2	1.2	1.8
Quick Ratio 31	1.0	•	0.6	•	1.1	1.8	1.3	0.8	0.7	1.1	1.4	0.6	1.1
Net Sales to Working Capital 32	6.8	•	•	•	6.7	4.5	7.3	7.7	13.1	5.3	3.7	20.0	5.8
Coverage Ratio 33	3.2	•	2.5	0.2	1.2	4.8	10.0	1.1	2.2	2.2	9.4	2.8	3.4
Total Asset Turnover 34	1.1	•	2.6	•	2.1	2.0	2.5	1.7	1.2	1.1	0.9	0.9	1.1
Inventory Turnover 35	5.6	•	7.9	•	6.6	4.9	8.7	5.8	5.1	7.8	3.3	6.7	5.3
Receivables Turnover 36	7.0	•	•	•	8.1	3.4	11.0	7.8	6.2	8.1	3.6	8.7	6.7
Total Liabilities to Net Worth 37	2.6	•	•	•	1.6	1.2	0.9	5.1	2.3	1.5	1.0	2.0	3.4
Current Assets to Working Capital 38	2.6	•	•	•	2.3	1.6	1.9	2.6	4.0	2.1	1.9	6.8	2.3
Current Liabilities to Working Capital 39	1.6	•	•	•	1.3	0.6	0.9	1.6	3.0	1.1	0.9	5.8	1.3
Working Capital to Net Sales 40	0.1	•	•	•	0.1	0.2	0.1	0.1	0.1	0.2	0.3	0.0	0.2
Inventory to Working Capital 41	0.9	•	•	•	0.7	0.5	0.6	1.1	1.6	0.7	0.5	2.5	0.8
Total Receipts to Cash Flow 42	9.3	•	4.8	•	11.5	10.2	8.0	20.4	17.2	13.8	4.4	11.9	8.5
Cost of Goods to Cash Flow 43	6.7	•	3.1	•	7.7	7.4	5.6	15.7	12.9	10.4	3.0	9.1	6.0
Cash Flow to Total Debt 44	0.2	•	•	0.3	0.3	0.4	0.7	0.1	0.1	0.1	0.4	0.1	0.2

Selected Financial Factors (in Percentages)

Line Item													
Debt Ratio 45	72.3	•	252.2	•	60.9	53.5	46.1	83.7	69.7	60.6	50.9	66.7	77.0
Return on Total Assets 46	7.7	•	37.0	•	3.1	13.0	17.2	4.0	7.4	5.8	9.3	6.4	8.1
Return on Equity Before Income Taxes 47	19.0	•	•	•	1.6	22.1	28.8	2.2	13.2	8.1	17.0	12.3	24.9
Return on Equity After Income Taxes 48	13.5	•	•	•	0.7	16.4	26.1	•	6.7	6.9	15.3	8.6	17.2
Profit Margin (Before Income Tax) 49	4.6	•	8.7	•	0.3	5.1	6.3	0.2	3.2	3.0	9.7	4.5	5.1
Profit Margin (After Income Tax) 50	3.3	•	8.7	•	0.1	3.8	5.7	•	1.6	2.6	8.8	3.2	3.5

Table II

Corporations with Net Income

RUBBER PRODUCT

MONEY AMOUNTS AND SIZE OF ASSETS IN THOUSANDS OF DOLLARS

Item Description for Accounting Period 7/07 Through 6/08		Total	Zero Assets	Under 500	500 to 1,000	1,000 to 5,000	5,000 to 10,000	10,000 to 25,000	25,000 to 50,000	50,000 to 100,000	100,000 to 250,000	250,000 to 500,000	500,000 to 2,500,000	2,500,000 and over
Number of Enterprises	1	455	8	87	0	231	36	51	9	12	8	•	•	•
Revenues ($ in Thousands)														
Net Sales	2	46012584	0	74100	0	1811254	647898	1843478	487094	1016707	1261737	•	•	•
Interest	3	360689	895	1	0	562	1991	1005	201	4076	2219	•	•	•
Rents	4	13994	0	0	0	0	0	0	0	3115	185	•	•	•
Royalties	5	843652	2610	0	0	0	0	0	0	42	1952	•	•	•
Other Portfolio Income	6	1116820	0	2	0	712	437	193	557	62081	10130	•	•	•
Other Receipts	7	458522	6021	1981	0	2163	610	8982	10022	5212	2162	•	•	•
Total Receipts	8	48806261	9526	76084	0	1814691	650936	1853658	497874	1091233	1278385	•	•	•
Average Total Receipts	9	107267	1191	875	•	7856	18082	36346	55319	90936	159798	•	•	•
Operating Costs/Operating Income (%)														
Cost of Operations	10	70.3	•	27.4	•	67.0	70.5	69.2	68.1	72.7	75.6	•	•	•
Salaries and Wages	11	6.4	•	11.8	•	9.6	5.9	4.9	7.9	6.3	4.9	•	•	•
Taxes Paid	12	1.4	•	3.8	•	2.2	1.5	1.7	2.5	2.4	1.7	•	•	•
Interest Paid	13	1.9	•	5.7	•	1.2	0.5	0.6	0.5	1.2	1.8	•	•	•
Depreciation	14	2.2	•	7.8	•	1.0	0.6	2.0	2.1	2.7	2.9	•	•	•
Amortization and Depletion	15	0.8	•	0.0	•	0.0	0.0	0.0	0.9	0.2	1.2	•	•	•
Pensions and Other Deferred Comp.	16	2.1	•	0.0	•	0.4	0.5	0.2	0.4	0.3	0.7	•	•	•
Employee Benefits	17	3.5	•	1.0	•	1.9	0.5	1.9	2.8	3.7	2.1	•	•	•
Advertising	18	1.4	•	0.0	•	0.2	0.4	3.1	0.7	1.0	0.1	•	•	•
Other Expenses	19	10.1	•	30.7	•	9.4	5.8	7.7	4.4	7.7	4.3	•	•	•
Officers' Compensation	20	0.6	•	5.8	•	5.5	5.6	1.2	1.7	1.2	0.7	•	•	•
Operating Margin	21	•	•	6.0	•	1.7	8.2	7.5	8.0	0.6	4.0	•	•	•
Operating Margin Before Officers' Comp.	22	•	•	11.8	•	7.1	13.8	8.7	9.7	1.8	4.6	•	•	•

Selected Average Balance Sheet ($ in Thousands)

Net Receivables	23	15795	0	76	•	1023	2039	3867	7962	12229	27606
Inventories	24	11902	0	29	•	771	2529	2607	9554	14681	12151
Net Property, Plant and Equipment	25	18971	0	158	•	438	702	4302	10153	18679	36362
Total Assets	26	86093	0	330	•	2752	6644	13406	35608	70697	140704
Notes and Loans Payable	27	23661	0	253	•	1004	606	2784	7621	18398	50531
All Other Liabilities	28	40785	0	579	•	1007	1818	3059	7946	13415	36020
Net Worth	29	21647	0	-502	•	741	4220	7562	20041	38884	54153

Selected Financial Ratios (Times to 1)

Current Ratio	30	1.6	•	0.8	•	1.7	2.3	2.6	2.9	1.8	1.8
Quick Ratio	31	1.0	•	0.6	•	0.9	1.5	1.5	1.7	1.0	1.1
Net Sales to Working Capital	32	6.6	3165.0	•	•	8.2	6.1	6.5	4.2	6.8	5.6
Coverage Ratio	33	4.3	•	2.5	•	2.6	17.4	13.6	19.8	8.4	4.0
Total Asset Turnover	34	1.2	•	2.6	•	2.8	2.7	2.7	1.5	1.2	1.1
Inventory Turnover	35	6.0	•	7.9	•	6.8	5.0	9.6	3.9	4.2	9.8
Receivables Turnover	36	7.3	•	22.3	•	8.5	3.2	11.8	5.7	6.0	9.6
Total Liabilities to Net Worth	37	3.0	•	•	•	2.7	0.6	0.8	0.8	0.8	1.6
Current Assets to Working Capital	38	2.5	•	•	•	2.4	1.8	1.6	1.5	2.2	2.2
Current Liabilities to Working Capital	39	1.5	•	•	•	1.4	0.8	0.6	0.5	1.2	1.2
Working Capital to Net Sales	40	0.2	•	•	•	0.1	0.2	0.2	0.2	0.1	0.2
Inventory to Working Capital	41	0.9	•	•	•	0.8	0.6	0.5	0.6	0.8	0.6
Total Receipts to Cash Flow	42	8.2	•	3.3	•	10.9	7.8	7.1	7.2	10.7	11.9
Cost of Goods to Cash Flow	43	5.7	•	0.9	•	7.3	5.5	4.9	4.9	7.8	9.0
Cash Flow to Total Debt	44	0.2	•	0.3	•	0.4	0.9	0.9	0.5	0.2	0.2

Selected Financial Factors (in Percentages)

Debt Ratio	45	74.9	252.2	•	•	73.1	36.5	43.6	43.7	45.0	61.5
Return on Total Assets	46	9.8	37.0	•	•	8.6	24.8	23.4	16.3	11.6	8.2
Return on Equity Before Income Taxes	47	29.9	•	•	•	19.6	36.8	38.4	27.4	18.6	15.9
Return on Equity After Income Taxes	48	22.4	•	•	•	17.7	30.4	35.3	24.9	12.8	14.0
Profit Margin (Before Income Tax)	49	6.4	8.7	•	•	1.8	8.6	8.0	10.2	8.5	5.4
Profit Margin (After Income Tax)	50	4.8	8.7	•	•	1.7	7.1	7.4	9.2	5.9	4.8

Table I

Corporations with and without Net Income

CLAY, REFRACTORY AND OTHER NONMETALLIC MINERAL PRODUCT

MONEY AMOUNTS AND SIZE OF ASSETS IN THOUSANDS OF DOLLARS

Item Description for Accounting Period 7/07 Through 6/08		Total	Zero Assets	Under 500	500 to 1,000	1,000 to 5,000	5,000 to 10,000	10,000 to 25,000	25,000 to 50,000	50,000 to 100,000	100,000 to 250,000	250,000 to 500,000	500,000 to 2,500,000	2,500,000 and over
Number of Enterprises	1	2891	318	1431	526	460	10	63	31	20	17	8	8	0
Revenues ($ in Thousands)														
Net Sales	2	20658994	412797	940890	948457	1990070	108346	1416110	1489269	1465213	1994971	2143551	7749320	0
Interest	3	239082	5430	885	990	1086	37	823	2312	2973	4482	12441	207623	0
Rents	4	93036	0	0	0	0	0	533	2	57	1599	1559	89286	0
Royalties	5	188163	0	0	0	0	5501	3041	0	223	1281	2738	175378	0
Other Portfolio Income	6	428285	613	2047	0	1570	2	914	2870	94387	3009	1625	321245	0
Other Receipts	7	274472	2054	142	5682	13600	3800	30979	23009	10595	96639	22646	65331	0
Total Receipts	8	21182032	420894	943964	955129	2006326	117686	1452400	1517462	1573448	2101981	2184560	8608183	0
Average Total Receipts	9	7569	1324	660	1816	4362	11769	23054	48950	78672	123646	273070	1076023	•
Operating Costs/Operating Income (%)														
Cost of Operations	10	66.2	64.5	40.8	65.8	67.0	84.7	69.4	68.7	68.3	73.2	55.0	68.8	•
Salaries and Wages	11	7.2	3.6	14.2	4.7	6.2	7.2	4.8	6.3	6.8	7.2	11.4	6.6	•
Taxes Paid	12	2.0	1.6	5.2	2.3	3.1	2.5	2.1	2.1	1.8	1.7	1.8	1.3	•
Interest Paid	13	2.8	0.8	0.6	0.5	0.6	2.6	1.2	1.2	2.2	2.0	1.5	5.3	•
Depreciation	14	3.6	8.5	3.9	0.8	1.9	3.0	2.5	2.6	4.8	5.1	3.9	3.7	•
Amortization and Depletion	15	0.6	•	0.0	0.6	0.3	0.2	0.6	0.2	0.7	0.4	0.8	0.8	•
Pensions and Other Deferred Comp.	16	1.1	1.4	•	3.6	0.3	0.2	0.4	0.5	0.5	0.5	1.3	1.6	•
Employee Benefits	17	1.6	0.8	0.2	2.2	1.1	1.5	1.1	1.9	1.0	2.1	1.7	1.9	•
Advertising	18	1.1	0.7	1.4	0.3	1.0	0.1	0.8	0.2	0.9	1.0	2.2	1.3	•
Other Expenses	19	23.1	19.6	26.4	9.9	9.8	11.2	6.7	8.5	8.0	10.1	14.2	42.6	•
Officers' Compensation	20	2.4	0.7	3.7	8.2	6.1	2.4	4.8	1.2	2.3	2.3	0.6	0.9	•
Operating Margin	21	•	•	3.6	1.0	2.5	•	5.8	6.5	2.7	•	5.7	•	•
Operating Margin Before Officers' Comp.	22	•	•	7.3	9.2	8.5	•	10.6	7.7	5.0	•	6.2	•	•

Selected Average Balance Sheet ($ in Thousands)

Net Receivables 23	3462	0	21	79	342	1207	2576	5890	11270	14706	65118	1053396	•
Inventories 24	1031	0	33	105	324	2076	3411	7897	12374	29389	41584	146140	•
Net Property, Plant and Equipment 25	2284	0	74	69	548	1100	5882	12797	26776	51504	100028	402426	•
Total Assets 26	11308	0	173	684	1734	8288	14102	34140	72071	131560	317552	2879772	•
Notes and Loans Payable 27	2673	0	120	177	599	1677	5186	10397	23308	39116	52638	620958	•
All Other Liabilities 28	4133	0	15	137	490	3968	2866	6821	12236	31174	80657	1222316	•
Net Worth 29	4502	0	38	369	645	2643	6050	16923	36527	61270	184257	1036498	•

Selected Financial Ratios (Times to 1)

Current Ratio 30	1.4	•	6.0	2.9	1.7	0.8	1.9	2.5	2.5	1.8	2.5	1.2	•
Quick Ratio 31	1.1	•	3.6	2.4	1.0	0.3	0.9	1.3	1.3	0.7	1.4	1.1	•
Net Sales to Working Capital 32	4.5	•	8.7	5.9	9.6	•	6.8	4.6	3.9	4.6	3.1	3.8	•
Coverage Ratio 33	•	0.5	7.6	4.4	6.4	•	8.2	8.0	5.7	0.9	6.1	•	•
Total Asset Turnover 34	0.6	•	3.8	2.6	2.5	1.3	1.6	1.4	1.0	0.9	0.8	0.3	•
Inventory Turnover 35	4.6	•	8.2	11.3	9.0	4.4	4.6	4.2	4.0	2.9	3.5	4.6	•
Receivables Turnover 36	2.4	•	20.3	15.6	12.9	5.4	8.1	8.0	6.4	5.5	5.9	1.1	•
Total Liabilities to Net Worth 37	1.5	•	3.6	0.9	1.7	2.1	1.3	1.0	1.0	1.1	0.7	1.8	•
Current Assets to Working Capital 38	3.3	•	1.2	1.5	2.4	•	2.1	1.7	1.7	2.3	1.7	5.1	•
Current Liabilities to Working Capital 39	2.3	•	0.2	0.5	1.4	•	1.1	0.7	0.7	1.3	0.7	4.1	•
Working Capital to Net Sales 40	0.2	•	0.1	0.2	0.1	•	0.1	0.2	0.3	0.2	0.3	0.3	•
Inventory to Working Capital 41	0.6	•	0.5	0.2	0.9	•	1.0	0.7	0.6	1.2	0.6	0.5	•
Total Receipts to Cash Flow 42	7.7	6.1	5.1	11.9	10.5	1305.4	7.5	6.5	9.8	12.1	5.3	7.6	•
Cost of Goods to Cash Flow 43	5.1	3.9	2.1	7.8	7.1	1105.6	5.2	4.4	6.7	8.9	2.9	5.2	•
Cash Flow to Total Debt 44	0.1	0	1.0	0.5	0.4	0.0	0.4	0.4	0.2	0.1	0.4	0.1	•

Selected Financial Factors (in Percentages)

Debt Ratio 45	60.2	•	78.1	46.0	62.8	68.1	57.1	50.4	49.3	53.4	42.0	64.0	•
Return on Total Assets 46	•	•	17.3	5.9	9.7	•	15.2	13.4	12.5	1.7	7.7	•	•
Return on Equity Before Income Taxes 47	•	•	68.6	8.4	22.0	•	31.1	23.7	20.3	•	11.1	•	•
Return on Equity After Income Taxes 48	•	•	67.5	7.8	21.9	•	29.7	19.2	14.3	•	6.5	•	•
Profit Margin (Before Income Tax) 49	•	•	4.0	1.7	3.3	•	8.4	8.4	10.1	•	7.6	•	•
Profit Margin (After Income Tax) 50	•	•	3.9	1.6	3.3	•	8.0	6.8	7.2	•	4.4	•	•

Table II

Corporations with Net Income

CLAY, REFRACTORY AND OTHER NONMETALLIC MINERAL PRODUCT

MONEY AMOUNTS AND SIZE OF ASSETS IN THOUSANDS OF DOLLARS

Item Description for Accounting Period 7/07 Through 6/08	Total	Zero Assets	Under 500	500 to 1,000	1,000 to 5,000	5,000 to 10,000	10,000 to 25,000	25,000 to 50,000	50,000 to 100,000	100,000 to 250,000	250,000 to 500,000	500,000 to 2,500,000	2,500,000 and over
Number of Enterprises 1	1673	9	897	269	394	0	38	•	•	9	•	4	0

Revenues ($ in Thousands)

	Total	Zero Assets	Under 500	500 to 1,000	1,000 to 5,000	5,000 to 10,000	10,000 to 25,000	25,000 to 50,000	50,000 to 100,000	100,000 to 250,000	250,000 to 500,000	500,000 to 2,500,000	2,500,000 and over
Net Sales 2	12484625	412797	849397	531866	1792688	0	1177438	•	•	1304978	•	2094749	0
Interest 3	121705	5430	751	990	710	0	474	•	•	3547	•	92395	0
Rents 4	3668	0	0	0	0	0	521	•	•	1496	•	32	0
Royalties 5	47756	0	0	0	0	0	3041	•	•	11	•	41742	0
Other Portfolio Income 6	284577	613	2047	0	1037	0	690	•	•	613	•	181598	0
Other Receipts 7	178741	2054	137	138	13281	0	29806	•	•	86964	•	-5666	0
Total Receipts 8	13121072	420894	852332	532994	1807716	0	1211970	•	•	1397609	•	2404850	0
Average Total Receipts 9	7843	46766	950	1981	4588	•	31894	•	•	155290	•	601212	•

Operating Costs/Operating Income (%)

	Total	Zero Assets	Under 500	500 to 1,000	1,000 to 5,000	5,000 to 10,000	10,000 to 25,000	25,000 to 50,000	50,000 to 100,000	100,000 to 250,000	250,000 to 500,000	500,000 to 2,500,000	2,500,000 and over
Cost of Operations 10	62.9	64.5	37.3	59.5	68.2	•	69.2	•	•	73.5	•	57.0	•
Salaries and Wages 11	7.0	3.6	15.6	4.4	5.5	•	4.1	•	•	6.8	•	7.2	•
Taxes Paid 12	2.3	1.6	5.3	3.0	3.3	•	2.0	•	•	1.6	•	1.6	•
Interest Paid 13	1.8	0.8	0.6	0.1	0.5	•	0.7	•	•	0.9	•	6.3	•
Depreciation 14	3.2	8.5	4.3	0.7	1.9	•	1.6	•	•	4.0	•	3.0	•
Amortization and Depletion 15	0.5	•	•	0.0	0.3	•	0.6	•	•	0.5	•	0.7	•
Pensions and Other Deferred Comp. 16	0.6	1.4	•	0.1	0.3	•	0.3	•	•	0.5	•	1.2	•
Employee Benefits 17	1.8	0.8	0.0	4.0	1.2	•	1.1	•	•	2.0	•	3.0	•
Advertising 18	0.5	0.7	1.6	0.2	0.4	•	0.7	•	•	1.2	•	0.1	•
Other Expenses 19	11.0	7.2	26.4	10.7	8.6	•	5.6	•	•	7.8	•	16.1	•
Officers' Compensation 20	2.6	0.7	2.7	8.8	5.8	•	5.1	•	•	1.1	•	1.0	•
Operating Margin 21	5.8	10.2	6.3	8.5	4.0	•	8.9	•	•	0.2	•	2.7	•
Operating Margin Before Officers' Comp. 22	8.5	10.9	8.9	17.3	9.9	•	14.0	•	•	1.3	•	3.7	•

Selected Average Balance Sheet ($ in Thousands)

Net Receivables **23**	1246	0	12	116	342	•	3261	•	16157	•	199252
Inventories **24**	973	0	39	102	257	•	4113	•	27881	•	76037
Net Property, Plant and Equipment **25**	1819	0	117	114	592	•	4885	•	51084	•	136524
Total Assets **26**	6697	0	226	637	1745	•	14655	•	140585	•	1010867
Notes and Loans Payable **27**	1838	0	145	146	608	•	3234	•	22418	•	372566
All Other Liabilities **28**	2242	0	4	119	483	•	2933	•	32520	•	554404
Net Worth **29**	2617	0	78	372	654	•	8488	•	85646	•	83898

Selected Financial Ratios (Times to 1)

Current Ratio **30**	2.1	•	25.9	3.6	1.8	•	2.1	•	2.4	•	1.6
Quick Ratio **31**	1.2	•	16.5	2.6	1.1	•	1.1	•	1.2	•	0.9
Net Sales to Working Capital **32**	4.4	16.5	10.1	5.7	9.7	•	7.4	•	3.7	•	3.0
Coverage Ratio **33**	7.2	•	11.6	119.9	11.2	•	18.3	•	8.7	•	4.0
Total Asset Turnover **34**	1.1	•	4.2	3.1	2.6	•	2.1	•	1.0	•	0.5
Inventory Turnover **35**	4.8	•	9.1	11.6	12.1	•	5.2	•	3.8	•	3.9
Receivables Turnover **36**	6.1	•	24.7	9.9	14.8	•	8.3	•	•	•	•
Total Liabilities to Net Worth **37**	1.6	•	1.9	0.7	1.7	•	0.7	•	0.6	•	11.0
Current Assets to Working Capital **38**	1.9	•	1.0	1.4	2.3	•	1.9	•	1.7	•	2.8
Current Liabilities to Working Capital **39**	0.9	•	0.0	0.4	1.3	•	0.9	•	0.7	•	1.8
Working Capital to Net Sales **40**	0.2	•	0.1	0.2	0.1	•	0.1	•	0.3	•	0.3
Inventory to Working Capital **41**	0.6	•	0.4	0.4	0.9	•	0.9	•	0.7	•	0.4
Total Receipts to Cash Flow **42**	5.4	6.1	4.5	6.2	10.3	•	6.4	•	7.1	•	3.2
Cost of Goods to Cash Flow **43**	3.4	3.9	1.7	3.7	7.0	•	4.4	•	5.2	•	1.8
Cash Flow to Total Debt **44**	0.3	•	1.4	1.2	0.4	•	0.8	•	0.4	•	0.2

Selected Financial Factors (in Percentages)

Debt Ratio **45**	60.9	•	65.6	41.6	62.6	•	42.1	•	39.1	•	91.7
Return on Total Assets **46**	14.5	•	30.2	27.3	13.9	•	26.6	•	8.5	•	13.0
Return on Equity Before Income Taxes **47**	31.8	•	80.4	46.4	33.8	•	43.3	•	12.4	•	117.4
Return on Equity After Income Taxes **48**	25.2	•	79.6	45.3	33.6	•	41.7	•	10.8	•	82.7
Profit Margin (Before Income Tax) **49**	11.2	12.0	6.6	8.7	4.9	•	11.9	•	7.3	•	18.8
Profit Margin (After Income Tax) **50**	8.8	7.8	6.5	8.5	4.8	•	11.4	•	6.4	•	13.2

Table I

Corporations with and without Net Income

GLASS AND GLASS PRODUCT

MONEY AMOUNTS AND SIZE OF ASSETS IN THOUSANDS OF DOLLARS

Item Description for Accounting Period 7/07 Through 6/08	Total	Zero Assets	Under 500	500 to 1,000	1,000 to 5,000	5,000 to 10,000	10,000 to 25,000	25,000 to 50,000	50,000 to 100,000	100,000 to 250,000	250,000 to 500,000	500,000 to 2,500,000	2,500,000 and over
Number of Enterprises **1**	2388	0	1365	641	273	40	29	13	8	6	4	8	0
Revenues ($ in Thousands)													
Net Sales **2**	23132499	0	683558	904894	1529842	540767	956277	750561	645596	1352557	1171758	14596688	0
Interest **3**	179697	0	0	391	1573	682	-2932	1059	2617	5374	18407	152526	0
Rents **4**	8489	0	0	0	0	970	930	253	738	183	1280	4136	0
Royalties **5**	102637	0	0	0	0	54	0	0	0	14930	9	87643	0
Other Portfolio Income **6**	1996241	0	0	0	216	935	968	151	33188	205	1226	1959350	0
Other Receipts **7**	81030	0	179	1394	1707	-1024	1978	330	3069	2030	24761	46609	0
Total Receipts **8**	25500593	0	683737	906679	1533338	542384	957221	752354	685208	1375279	1217441	16846952	0
Average Total Receipts **9**	10679	•	501	1414	5617	13560	33008	57873	85651	229213	304360	2105869	•
Operating Costs/Operating Income (%)													
Cost of Operations **10**	68.4	•	32.2	52.3	63.6	75.2	78.7	65.2	68.3	69.2	73.8	70.4	•
Salaries and Wages **11**	6.8	•	19.4	14.0	8.2	4.7	4.1	6.1	4.5	8.9	5.8	5.9	•
Taxes Paid **12**	2.3	•	2.9	2.5	2.3	2.0	1.8	2.9	2.6	2.8	1.8	2.2	•
Interest Paid **13**	3.5	•	0.1	1.2	1.5	0.9	1.4	1.6	2.1	2.1	4.8	4.4	•
Depreciation **14**	4.0	•	0.5	3.0	2.5	2.9	3.1	2.0	2.3	2.7	3.8	4.8	•
Amortization and Depletion **15**	0.5	•	0.0	0.0	0.0	0.3	0.1	0.9	0.3	0.6	0.4	0.7	•
Pensions and Other Deferred Comp. **16**	0.8	•	•	•	0.1	0.3	0.2	0.1	0.5	0.6	0.6	1.1	•
Employee Benefits **17**	2.7	•	0.3	0.5	0.9	2.1	1.8	1.6	2.4	2.1	1.1	3.5	•
Advertising **18**	0.6	•	2.7	0.8	0.6	0.3	0.2	0.7	0.1	0.5	2.3	0.3	•
Other Expenses **19**	11.5	•	19.7	20.4	9.8	7.5	6.9	13.3	8.6	10.6	8.2	11.5	•
Officers' Compensation **20**	1.8	•	12.1	6.2	9.3	3.9	1.7	0.3	1.5	0.8	0.8	0.4	•
Operating Margin **21**	•	•	10.1	•	1.1	•	0.1	5.3	6.9	•	•	•	•
Operating Margin Before Officers' Comp. **22**	•	•	22.2	5.3	10.4	3.8	1.7	5.7	8.4	•	•	•	•

Selected Average Balance Sheet ($ in Thousands)

Net Receivables 23	1209	•	32	145	633	2128	3012	5438	13231	22973	72601	225060	•
Inventories 24	1268	•	75	171	519	1102	3511	6455	9713	25976	48369	162607	•
Net Property, Plant and Equipment 25	2651	•	11	90	1132	2116	6341	7458	22187	41361	103528	593048	•
Total Assets 26	10595	•	169	620	2556	6517	14959	34835	77538	158814	361041	2476394	•
Notes and Loans Payable 27	3391	•	293	480	1373	1608	7254	16267	20346	52800	160536	675944	•
All Other Liabilities 28	3124	•	25	101	328	2205	4526	5312	23454	53867	109036	754567	•
Net Worth 29	4080	•	-149	38	855	2704	3179	13256	33738	52146	91469	1045884	•

Selected Financial Ratios (Times to 1)

Current Ratio 30	1.2	•	6.4	2.6	3.0	1.6	1.1	1.4	2.1	1.7	1.0	1.0	•
Quick Ratio 31	0.6	•	2.7	1.3	1.8	0.9	0.6	0.8	1.3	0.9	0.6	0.4	•
Net Sales to Working Capital 32	24.3	•	3.8	5.6	6.3	8.6	60.5	10.0	4.5	6.9	173.5	•	•
Coverage Ratio 33	3.8	•	90.1	0.4	1.9	1.2	1.1	4.4	7.2	1.4	1.1	4.1	•
Total Asset Turnover 34	0.9	•	3.0	2.3	2.2	2.1	2.2	1.7	1.0	1.4	0.8	0.7	•
Inventory Turnover 35	5.2	•	2.2	4.3	6.9	9.2	7.4	5.8	5.7	6.0	4.5	7.9	•
Receivables Turnover 36	7.9	•	15.0	14.0	7.8	6.5	9.2	10.0	7.7	9.2	3.1	10.5	•
Total Liabilities to Net Worth 37	1.6	•	•	15.3	2.0	1.4	3.7	1.6	1.3	2.0	2.9	1.4	•
Current Assets to Working Capital 38	7.5	•	1.2	1.6	1.5	2.7	14.5	3.2	1.9	2.4	87.2	•	•
Current Liabilities to Working Capital 39	6.5	•	0.2	0.6	0.5	1.7	13.5	2.2	0.9	1.4	86.2	•	•
Working Capital to Net Sales 40	0.0	•	0.3	0.2	0.2	0.1	0.0	0.1	0.2	0.1	0.0	•	•
Inventory to Working Capital 41	3.2	•	0.7	0.7	0.5	0.8	6.1	1.3	0.6	0.8	28.9	•	•
Total Receipts to Cash Flow 42	7.5	•	4.2	7.6	11.9	20.0	19.7	6.1	6.6	12.2	20.9	6.6	•
Cost of Goods to Cash Flow 43	5.1	•	1.4	4.0	7.5	15.1	15.5	4.0	4.5	8.4	15.4	4.6	•
Cash Flow to Total Debt 44	0.2	•	0.4	0.3	0.2	0.2	0.1	0.4	0.3	0.2	0.1	0.2	•

Selected Financial Factors (in Percentages)

Debt Ratio 45	61.5	•	188.2	93.9	66.6	58.5	78.7	61.9	56.5	67.2	74.7	57.8	•
Return on Total Assets 46	12.2	•	30.5	1.1	6.3	2.3	3.4	11.9	15.7	4.2	4.3	13.5	•
Return on Equity Before Income Taxes 47	23.2	•	•	•	8.9	1.0	1.4	24.3	31.2	3.9	1.5	24.3	•
Return on Equity After Income Taxes 48	20.4	•	•	•	7.8	•	•	19.4	23.3	1.8	0.1	21.7	•
Profit Margin (Before Income Tax) 49	9.8	•	10.2	•	1.4	0.2	0.1	5.6	13.0	0.9	0.5	13.9	•
Profit Margin (After Income Tax) 50	8.6	•	10.2	•	1.2	•	•	4.4	9.7	0.4	0.0	12.4	•

Table II

Corporations with Net Income

GLASS AND GLASS PRODUCT

MONEY AMOUNTS AND SIZE OF ASSETS IN THOUSANDS OF DOLLARS

Item Description for Accounting Period 7/07 Through 6/08	Total	Zero Assets	Under 500	500 to 1000	251 to 500	501 to 1,000	1,001 to 5,000	5,001 to 10,000	10,001 to 25,000	25,001 to 50,000	50,001 to 100,000	100,001 to 250,000	250,001 and over
Number of Enterprises **1**	1835	0	1063	457	249	27	13	•	•	6	0	5	0
Revenues ($ in Thousands)													
Net Sales **2**	17802388	0	683558	724057	1259700	374158	710243	•	•	1137096	0	11662885	0
Interest **3**	149503	0	0	391	1565	437	475	•	•	11028	0	132091	0
Rents **4**	6311	0	0	0	0	956	846	•	•	8	0	3510	0
Royalties **5**	82853	0	0	0	0	0	0	•	•	9	0	82843	0
Other Portfolio Income **6**	1994123	0	0	0	216	923	948	•	•	940	0	1957766	0
Other Receipts **7**	19732	0	179	1394	1290	576	594	•	•	10946	0	4046	0
Total Receipts **8**	20054910	0	683737	725842	1262771	377050	713106	•	•	1160027	0	13843141	0
Average Total Receipts **9**	10929	•	643	1588	5071	13965	54854	•	•	193338	•	2768628	•
Operating Costs/Operating Income (%)													
Cost of Operations **10**	65.6	•	32.2	41.1	59.9	70.0	79.5	•	•	67.5	•	68.5	•
Salaries and Wages **11**	7.0	•	19.4	14.9	9.0	5.1	3.0	•	•	6.7	•	6.1	•
Taxes Paid **12**	2.4	•	2.9	3.1	2.4	2.7	1.7	•	•	2.5	•	2.3	•
Interest Paid **13**	3.6	•	0.1	1.6	1.6	0.8	0.6	•	•	4.6	•	4.6	•
Depreciation **14**	4.1	•	0.5	3.8	2.8	3.1	2.0	•	•	3.9	•	5.0	•
Amortization and Depletion **15**	0.5	•	•	0.0	0.0	0.0	0.0	•	•	0.7	•	0.7	•
Pensions and Other Deferred Comp. **16**	0.8	•	•	•	0.1	0.3	0.1	•	•	0.8	•	1.1	•
Employee Benefits **17**	2.8	•	0.3	0.6	0.9	2.6	1.8	•	•	1.7	•	3.6	•
Advertising **18**	0.5	•	2.7	1.0	0.7	0.3	0.1	•	•	0.5	•	0.4	•
Other Expenses **19**	12.1	•	19.0	24.5	9.8	6.3	4.7	•	•	8.4	•	12.3	•
Officers' Compensation **20**	2.0	•	12.1	7.8	10.7	4.7	1.4	•	•	0.8	•	0.4	•
Operating Margin **21**	•	•	10.9	1.7	2.1	3.9	5.3	•	•	1.9	•	•	•
Operating Margin Before Officers' Comp. **22**	0.5	•	22.9	9.5	12.8	8.6	6.7	•	•	2.7	•	•	•

Selected Average Balance Sheet ($ in Thousands)

Net Receivables 23	1172	41	118	572	1541	4049	•	48618	274002
Inventories 24	1069	19	177	506	853	3489	•	25896	288878
Net Property, Plant and Equipment 25	2615	7	126	1197	2062	6855	•	62221	753584
Total Assets 26	10428	113	648	2486	5649	16726	•	219855	3127342
Notes and Loans Payable 27	3173	23	391	1356	1670	6207	•	94386	897283
All Other Liabilities 28	2948	32	123	302	1090	5538	•	53568	918014
Net Worth 29	4307	59	133	827	2888	4980	•	71902	1312045

Selected Financial Ratios (Times to 1)

Current Ratio 30	1.2	3.4	1.8	3.7	2.2	1.0	•	2.7	1.0
Quick Ratio 31	0.6	2.6	0.7	2.3	1.2	0.6	•	1.8	0.4
Net Sales to Working Capital 32	21.3	8.6	10.4	5.8	7.6	134.9	•	3.2	•
Coverage Ratio 33	4.9	96.5	2.3	2.5	7.0	11.1	•	1.8	5.0
Total Asset Turnover 34	0.9	5.7	2.4	2.0	2.5	3.3	•	0.9	0.7
Inventory Turnover 35	6.0	10.8	3.7	6.0	11.4	12.5	•	4.9	5.5
Receivables Turnover 36	8.8	15.0	21.4	7.2	7.6	9.5	•	•	•
Total Liabilities to Net Worth 37	1.4	0.9	3.9	2.0	1.0	2.4	•	2.1	1.4
Current Assets to Working Capital 38	6.2	1.4	2.3	1.4	1.9	22.4	•	1.6	•
Current Liabilities to Working Capital 39	5.2	0.4	1.3	0.4	0.9	21.4	•	0.6	•
Working Capital to Net Sales 40	0.0	0.1	0.1	0.2	0.1	0.0	•	0.3	•
Inventory to Working Capital 41	2.4	0.3	1.2	0.5	0.5	7.4	•	0.4	•
Total Receipts to Cash Flow 42	5.9	4.2	5.4	10.3	12.6	11.7	•	10.5	5.4
Cost of Goods to Cash Flow 43	3.9	1.4	2.2	6.2	8.8	9.3	•	7.1	3.7
Cash Flow to Total Debt 44	0.3	2.8	0.6	0.3	0.4	0.4	•	0.1	0.2

Selected Financial Factors (in Percentages)

Debt Ratio 45	58.7	48.0	79.4	66.7	48.9	70.2	•	67.3	58.0
Return on Total Assets 46	16.6	62.4	8.7	8.1	13.4	20.4	•	7.4	17.2
Return on Equity Before Income Taxes 47	32.0	118.7	23.6	14.5	22.5	62.2	•	10.3	32.9
Return on Equity After Income Taxes 48	28.4	118.7	22.4	13.1	14.9	50.5	•	7.7	29.5
Profit Margin (Before Income Tax) 49	14.2	10.9	2.0	2.4	4.7	5.7	•	3.9	18.5
Profit Margin (After Income Tax) 50	12.6	10.9	1.9	2.1	3.1	4.6	•	2.9	16.6

Table I

Corporations with and without Net Income

CEMENT, CONCRETE, LIME AND GYPSUM PRODUCT

MONEY AMOUNTS AND SIZE OF ASSETS IN THOUSANDS OF DOLLARS

Item Description for Accounting Period 7/07 Through 6/08	Total	Zero Assets	Under 500	500 to 1,000	1,000 to 5,000	5,000 to 10,000	10,000 to 25,000	25,000 to 50,000	50,000 to 100,000	100,000 to 250,000	250,000 to 500,000	500,000 to 2,500,000	2,500,000 and over
Number of Enterprises 1	5051	10	2466	727	1244	290	161	59	35	21	10	16	11
Revenues ($ in Thousands)													
Net Sales 2	82088473	3015948	1877528	1510247	6047061	3979104	3886403	3200711	3152293	4369473	4036139	10857809	36155757
Interest 3	968903	108067	1633	1951	9517	6829	8100	3144	2504	9473	17126	84093	716464
Rents 4	55578	1234	0	123	1459	1187	5627	1260	2395	419	8521	13170	20183
Royalties 5	61060	311	0	0	0	0	25	54	1603	754	16944	12111	29258
Other Portfolio Income 6	887846	60759	1111	20135	75165	4898	20236	7595	13826	12786	17983	93271	560079
Other Receipts 7	819553	7475	31107	9258	54447	38237	24518	12222	43525	12255	107391	116637	362485
Total Receipts 8	84481413	3193794	1911379	1541714	6187649	4030255	3944909	3224986	3216146	4405160	4204104	11177091	37844226
Average Total Receipts 9	16805	319379	775	2121	4974	13897	24503	54661	91890	209770	420410	698568	3440384
Operating Costs/Operating Income (%)													
Cost of Operations 10	67.5	57.3	65.3	61.5	65.5	69.5	67.5	72.6	70.3	69.6	69.3	67.0	67.8
Salaries and Wages 11	5.4	8.7	9.0	6.3	6.1	5.1	7.0	5.5	5.6	4.3	3.7	3.4	5.5
Taxes Paid 12	2.1	1.9	4.2	2.8	2.4	1.8	2.3	1.9	2.2	2.2	2.2	2.2	1.9
Interest Paid 13	3.9	6.6	1.1	0.8	1.7	1.5	1.0	1.1	1.6	2.0	1.1	2.6	6.2
Depreciation 14	4.7	6.0	4.1	2.5	3.3	3.7	4.5	4.2	4.8	4.7	4.2	6.1	4.8
Amortization and Depletion 15	1.2	1.9	0.0	•	0.0	0.0	0.2	0.2	0.3	0.9	0.8	2.1	1.6
Pensions and Other Deferred Comp. 16	0.7	0.4	•	1.3	0.3	0.4	0.6	0.5	0.6	0.6	0.4	0.6	0.9
Employee Benefits 17	1.8	1.7	1.3	3.0	1.2	1.8	1.4	1.1	1.9	2.0	1.4	1.6	2.0
Advertising 18	0.3	0.1	0.1	0.8	0.8	0.3	0.4	0.7	0.5	0.3	0.3	0.1	0.2
Other Expenses 19	10.0	14.7	19.3	14.6	12.9	9.4	10.8	8.0	7.8	5.5	7.0	7.3	10.6
Officers' Compensation 20	1.1	0.3	5.1	5.1	3.9	2.9	2.0	1.4	1.3	0.8	0.8	0.3	0.2
Operating Margin 21	1.4	0.4	•	1.2	1.9	3.6	2.3	2.9	3.0	7.1	8.7	6.6	•
Operating Margin Before Officers' Comp. 22	2.5	0.8	•	6.4	5.8	6.5	4.3	4.3	4.3	7.9	9.5	6.9	•

Selected Average Balance Sheet ($ in Thousands)

Net Receivables 23	3756	0	34	209	607	1934	3316	8909	13130	33027	52066	76596	1223884
Inventories 24	1463	0	15	71	254	968	1655	4729	6709	16456	22042	76532	375857
Net Property, Plant and Equipment 25	9806	0	84	187	869	2897	6415	14644	32167	62694	143490	490885	3057994
Total Assets 26	25314	0	159	771	2476	7233	15146	33984	67489	154237	355890	1018493	8347962
Notes and Loans Payable 27	8046	0	163	147	1157	3569	4265	11564	20616	47738	67894	203552	2784501
All Other Liabilities 28	10210	0	34	348	505	1445	3263	5559	12520	31273	67238	306146	3878809
Net Worth 29	7058	0	-38	276	815	2220	7618	16861	34354	75226	220758	508794	1684652

Selected Financial Ratios (Times to 1)

Current Ratio 30	1.5	•	0.9	2.2	1.8	1.9	1.9	2.1	1.8	1.9	2.7	1.8	1.4
Quick Ratio 31	1.1	•	0.6	1.9	1.3	1.2	1.4	1.4	1.2	1.2	2.0	0.8	1.0
Net Sales to Working Capital 32	6.8	•	•	7.6	8.2	7.3	6.6	6.1	7.3	7.3	4.4	6.6	6.2
Coverage Ratio 33	2.3	2.0	•	5.0	3.5	4.2	4.8	4.3	4.2	5.1	12.6	4.7	1.5
Total Asset Turnover 34	0.6	•	4.8	2.7	2.0	1.9	1.6	1.6	1.3	1.3	1.1	0.7	0.4
Inventory Turnover 35	7.5	•	34.0	18.1	12.6	9.9	9.9	8.3	9.4	8.8	12.7	5.9	5.9
Receivables Turnover 36	4.7	•	35.4	9.6	7.7	7.1	7.3	6.3	6.6	5.9	8.7	5.7	3.2
Total Liabilities to Net Worth 37	2.6	•	•	1.8	2.0	2.3	1.0	1.0	1.0	1.1	0.6	1.0	4.0
Current Assets to Working Capital 38	2.8	•	•	1.8	2.2	2.1	2.1	1.9	2.3	2.2	1.6	2.2	3.6
Current Liabilities to Working Capital 39	1.8	•	•	0.8	1.2	1.1	1.1	0.9	1.3	1.2	0.6	1.2	2.6
Working Capital to Net Sales 40	0.1	•	•	0.1	0.1	0.1	0.2	0.2	0.1	0.1	0.2	0.2	0.2
Inventory to Working Capital 41	0.7	•	•	0.2	0.5	0.6	0.5	0.5	0.6	0.5	0.3	0.8	0.8
Total Receipts to Cash Flow 42	8.3	5.3	6.8	17.2	7.7	8.8	8.9	10.6	9.5	9.0	5.8	6.7	9.3
Cost of Goods to Cash Flow 43	5.6	3.0	11.3	4.2	5.0	6.1	6.0	7.7	6.6	6.3	4.0	4.5	6.3
Cash Flow to Total Debt 44	0.1	•	0.2	0.6	0.4	0.3	0.3	0.3	0.3	0.3	0.5	0.2	0.1

Selected Financial Factors (in Percentages)

Debt Ratio 45	72.1	•	123.6	64.2	67.1	69.3	49.7	50.4	49.1	51.2	38.0	50.0	79.8
Return on Total Assets 46	5.6	•	•	11.2	11.6	12.2	7.6	7.7	8.8	13.3	15.8	8.2	3.6
Return on Equity Before Income Taxes 47	11.2	•	158.2	25.0	25.0	30.3	12.0	11.9	13.2	22.0	23.4	13.0	6.0
Return on Equity After Income Taxes 48	8.0	•	159.2	23.4	24.1	28.6	9.5	10.7	11.7	18.0	17.2	8.8	3.5
Profit Margin (Before Income Tax) 49	4.9	6.3	•	3.3	4.2	4.9	3.8	3.7	5.0	7.9	12.8	9.7	3.1
Profit Margin (After Income Tax) 50	3.5	4.2	•	3.1	4.0	4.6	3.0	3.3	4.5	6.5	9.4	6.6	1.8

Table II

Corporations with Net Income

CEMENT, CONCRETE, LIME AND GYPSUM PRODUCT

MONEY AMOUNTS AND SIZE OF ASSETS IN THOUSANDS OF DOLLARS

Item Description for Accounting Period 7/07 Through 6/08	Total	Zero Assets	Under 500	500 to 1,000	1,000 to 5,000	5,000 to 10,000	10,000 to 25,000	25,000 to 50,000	50,000 to 100,000	100,000 to 250,000	250,000 to 500,000	500,000 to 2,500,000	2,500,000 and over
Number of Enterprises **1**	2618	6	965	564	634	223	105	•	30	16	•	16	8

Revenues ($ in Thousands)

	Total	Zero Assets	Under 500	500 to 1,000	1,000 to 5,000	5,000 to 10,000	10,000 to 25,000	25,000 to 50,000	50,000 to 100,000	100,000 to 250,000	250,000 to 500,000	500,000 to 2,500,000	2,500,000 and over
Net Sales **2**	61919705	2039751	739642	1294798	3548274	3026282	2839611	•	2690704	3609664	•	10857809	24922672
Interest **3**	753398	106788	419	767	4548	3882	5105	•	465	7789	•	84093	519293
Rents **4**	48862	780	0	123	364	1187	2703	•	1947	196	•	13170	19724
Royalties **5**	59456	0	0	0	0	0	3	•	1603	682	•	12111	28114
Other Portfolio Income **6**	606983	60718	705	19633	54643	4148	12128	•	12820	8415	•	93271	319184
Other Receipts **7**	598401	-5823	3075	7789	18674	31873	19177	•	26147	12507	•	116637	249659
Total Receipts **8**	63986805	2202214	743841	1323110	3626503	3067372	2878727	•	2733686	3639253	•	11177091	26058646
Average Total Receipts **9**	24441	367036	771	2346	5720	13755	27416	•	91123	227453	•	698568	3257331

Operating Costs/Operating Income (%)

	Total	Zero Assets	Under 500	500 to 1,000	1,000 to 5,000	5,000 to 10,000	10,000 to 25,000	25,000 to 50,000	50,000 to 100,000	100,000 to 250,000	250,000 to 500,000	500,000 to 2,500,000	2,500,000 and over
Cost of Operations **10**	65.4	49.8	41.9	57.2	63.0	66.7	68.5	•	69.8	68.7	•	67.0	64.8
Salaries and Wages **11**	5.6	11.9	15.6	7.3	5.6	5.9	5.5	•	5.2	4.4	•	3.4	6.2
Taxes Paid **12**	2.3	2.0	6.2	2.8	2.3	1.8	2.1	•	2.3	2.3	•	2.2	2.4
Interest Paid **13**	3.8	7.3	0.7	0.9	1.0	1.4	0.8	•	1.2	1.3	•	2.6	6.7
Depreciation **14**	4.6	4.7	3.1	2.7	2.2	2.4	4.2	•	5.0	4.5	•	6.1	4.9
Amortization and Depletion **15**	1.3	2.4	0.0	•	0.1	0.0	0.2	•	0.2	0.6	•	2.1	1.8
Pensions and Other Deferred Comp. **16**	0.7	0.5	•	1.5	0.3	0.4	0.5	•	0.6	0.6	•	0.6	1.1
Employee Benefits **17**	1.8	1.0	0.8	3.4	1.6	1.9	1.2	•	1.6	1.7	•	1.6	2.2
Advertising **18**	0.3	0.1	0.2	0.7	1.1	0.3	0.4	•	0.6	0.4	•	0.1	0.2
Other Expenses **19**	8.8	17.4	23.7	15.0	10.4	9.7	8.3	•	7.4	5.4	•	7.3	8.8
Officers' Compensation **20**	1.1	0.3	5.6	5.7	5.0	3.3	2.0	•	1.4	0.7	•	0.3	0.1
Operating Margin **21**	4.2	2.6	2.1	2.7	7.5	6.1	6.4	•	4.8	9.5	•	6.6	0.9
Operating Margin Before Officers' Comp. **22**	5.3	3.0	7.7	8.4	12.5	9.5	8.4	•	6.2	10.2	•	6.9	1.0

Selected Average Balance Sheet ($ in Thousands)

Item													
Net Receivables 23	6289	0	6	197	800	2033	3431	•	13016	35731	•	76596	1493172
Inventories 24	2368	0	15	84	336	1005	2099	•	6941	16406	•	76532	432345
Net Property, Plant and Equipment 25	13217	0	75	176	574	2281	6128	•	32186	66457	•	490885	2637070
Total Assets 26	34158	0	132	796	2442	7202	15475	•	67223	153378	•	1018493	7297848
Notes and Loans Payable 27	12392	0	115	172	692	2925	3230	•	18898	33625	•	203552	3175306
All Other Liabilities 28	9327	0	13	342	458	1382	2882	•	12602	34324	•	306146	2074224
Net Worth 29	12439	0	3	281	1292	2895	9364	•	35723	85430	•	508794	2048318

Selected Financial Ratios (Times to 1)

Item													
Current Ratio 30	1.9	•	1.0	2.0	3.0	2.2	2.4	•	2.0	1.9	•	1.8	1.8
Quick Ratio 31	1.4	•	0.7	1.7	2.3	1.5	1.7	•	1.3	1.3	•	0.8	1.4
Net Sales to Working Capital 32	4.5	•	828.3	8.9	5.0	5.8	5.6	•	6.3	7.0	•	6.6	3.2
Coverage Ratio 33	3.0	2.4	4.6	6.3	10.4	6.2	10.9	•	6.3	8.6	•	4.7	1.8
Total Asset Turnover 34	0.7	•	5.8	2.9	2.3	1.9	1.7	•	1.3	1.5	•	0.7	0.4
Inventory Turnover 35	6.5	•	21.3	15.7	10.5	9.0	8.8	•	9.0	9.4	•	5.9	4.7
Receivables Turnover 36	3.9	•	165.1	10.9	5.6	6.6	6.7	•	•	5.9	•	5.7	•
Total Liabilities to Net Worth 37	1.7	•	38.9	1.8	0.9	1.5	0.7	•	0.9	0.8	•	1.0	2.6
Current Assets to Working Capital 38	2.1	•	43.9	2.0	1.5	1.8	1.7	•	2.0	2.1	•	2.2	2.2
Current Liabilities to Working Capital 39	1.1	•	42.9	1.0	0.5	0.8	0.7	•	1.0	1.1	•	1.2	1.2
Working Capital to Net Sales 40	0.2	•	0.0	0.1	0.2	0.2	0.2	•	0.2	0.1	•	0.2	0.3
Inventory to Working Capital 41	0.5	•	11.3	0.3	0.3	0.5	0.4	•	0.5	0.4	•	0.8	0.4
Total Receipts to Cash Flow 42	7.2	3.9	5.2	5.9	6.2	7.1	7.6	•	8.6	7.5	•	6.7	8.5
Cost of Goods to Cash Flow 43	4.7	1.9	2.2	3.4	3.9	4.7	5.2	•	6.0	5.2	•	4.5	5.5
Cash Flow to Total Debt 44	0.2	•	1.1	0.8	0.8	0.4	0.6	•	0.3	0.4	•	0.2	0.1

Selected Financial Factors (in Percentages)

Item													
Debt Ratio 45	63.6	•	97.5	64.6	47.1	59.8	39.5	•	46.9	44.3	•	50.0	71.9
Return on Total Assets 46	7.9	•	19.9	16.9	24.5	16.9	14.9	•	10.1	17.1	•	8.2	5.2
Return on Equity Before Income Taxes 47	14.4	•	623.6	40.1	41.9	35.2	22.3	•	16.0	27.1	•	13.0	8.3
Return on Equity After Income Taxes 48	10.9	•	593.8	38.1	40.8	33.5	19.3	•	14.4	22.4	•	8.8	5.4
Profit Margin (Before Income Tax) 49	7.6	10.6	2.7	4.9	9.7	7.5	7.7	•	6.4	10.2	•	9.7	5.4
Profit Margin (After Income Tax) 50	5.7	7.4	2.6	4.7	9.4	7.2	6.7	•	5.7	8.5	•	6.6	3.6

Table I

Corporations with and without Net Income

IRON, STEEL MILLS AND STEEL PRODUCT

MONEY AMOUNTS AND SIZE OF ASSETS IN THOUSANDS OF DOLLARS

Item Description for Accounting Period 7/07 Through 6/08	Total	Zero Assets	Under 500	500 to 1,000	1,000 to 5,000	5,000 to 10,000	10,000 to 25,000	25,000 to 50,000	50,000 to 100,000	100,000 to 250,000	250,000 to 500,000	500,000 to 2,500,000	2,500,000 and over
Number of Enterprises 1	3983	761	1694	346	562	241	170	78	41	40	18	19	12
Revenues ($ in Thousands)													
Net Sales 2	143590271	4110533	918035	972949	3977616	3495658	5427353	5595280	4449965	10061231	6722857	25573401	72285394
Interest 3	736339	27253	0	732	802	1174	6015	-1128	7717	56277	82392	78833	476273
Rents 4	62414	139	0	0	66	443	1625	2079	327	1831	12820	10720	32363
Royalties 5	403939	13	0	0	0	0	7177	0	4049	21716	1930	17347	351705
Other Portfolio Income 6	976367	147789	0	2758	336	706	7853	7948	2380	49324	142976	314437	299858
Other Receipts 7	1429072	57223	1861	23473	2346	27889	9237	20621	17871	64894	33411	305826	864422
Total Receipts 8	147198402	4342950	919896	999912	3981166	3525870	5459260	5624800	4482309	10255273	6996386	26300564	74310015
Average Total Receipts 9	36957	5707	543	2890	7084	14630	32113	72113	109325	256382	388688	1384240	6192501
Operating Costs/Operating Income (%)													
Cost of Operations 10	78.3	80.4	44.6	76.5	74.7	76.8	75.0	79.4	81.7	78.7	83.7	84.2	76.2
Salaries and Wages 11	2.9	5.0	20.9	6.6	5.1	4.7	4.5	3.3	2.8	3.3	2.9	2.4	2.3
Taxes Paid 12	1.2	0.7	2.4	1.8	1.3	1.7	1.5	1.2	1.2	1.6	0.9	0.9	1.3
Interest Paid 13	1.5	2.2	1.2	0.0	0.7	0.7	0.8	1.3	1.8	1.7	2.7	1.2	1.5
Depreciation 14	2.2	2.1	1.9	0.9	1.2	1.4	1.7	2.0	2.0	1.9	1.5	1.9	2.6
Amortization and Depletion 15	0.4	0.4	0.2	0.0	0.0	0.1	0.2	0.1	0.3	0.1	0.3	1.1	0.2
Pensions and Other Deferred Comp. 16	0.9	0.1	1.4	0.1	0.3	0.3	0.5	0.5	0.5	0.5	0.8	0.3	1.3
Employee Benefits 17	1.7	0.8	0.4	1.5	0.5	1.2	1.6	1.3	1.0	1.1	1.1	1.3	2.2
Advertising 18	0.1	0.2	0.4	0.1	0.2	0.2	0.2	0.2	0.1	0.3	0.1	0.1	0.0
Other Expenses 19	6.0	3.4	19.6	7.1	4.6	4.2	5.6	4.8	3.3	4.9	6.7	3.6	7.4
Officers' Compensation 20	0.8	1.2	4.2	2.7	5.4	2.7	2.3	1.4	1.0	0.6	0.7	0.7	0.3
Operating Margin 21	4.1	3.5	3.0	2.6	6.0	5.9	6.2	4.5	4.3	5.3	•	2.3	4.6
Operating Margin Before Officers' Comp. 22	4.9	4.7	7.1	5.3	11.4	8.6	8.5	5.9	5.3	5.9	•	3.0	5.0

Selected Average Balance Sheet ($ in Thousands)

	1	2	3	4	5	6	7	8	9	10	11	12	13
Net Receivables 23	5223	0	32	231	678	1619	4054	10739	13663	31109	51209	156551	1055947
Inventories 24	5025	0	21	59	725	2075	3957	7368	20954	44962	72226	269443	727346
Net Property, Plant and Equipment 25	8194	0	31	106	459	1831	3278	10119	15375	43389	58427	294878	1790256
Total Assets 26	32227		121	700	2371	7045	15291	35369	68234	158155	326790	1216830	6783313
Notes and Loans Payable 27	9792	0	81	145	1016	1334	4225	12766	22309	41014	94130	290865	2202468
All Other Liabilities 28	9446	0	40	245	666	1930	3928	10810	25312	47032	104631	407341	1881527
Net Worth 29	12990	0	0	311	689	3781	7137	11792	20613	70109	128030	518624	2699317

Selected Financial Ratios (Times to 1)

	1	2	3	4	5	6	7	8	9	10	11	12	13
Current Ratio 30	2.0	0.9	2.0	2.6	2.3	2.0	1.5	1.5	2.1	1.6	2.0	1.6	2.2
Quick Ratio 31	1.0	0.6	1.7	1.4	1.3	1.0	0.8	0.7	1.0	0.7	0.8	0.8	1.2
Net Sales to Working Capital 32	5.3	•	11.2	6.4	5.1	6.7	9.5	7.8	5.1	3.8	7.2	7.2	4.3
Coverage Ratio 33	5.5	5.1	316.0	9.7	10.6	9.6	4.9	3.7	5.4	2.0	5.5	5.5	5.8
Total Asset Turnover 34	1.1	•	4.0	3.0	2.1	2.1	2.0	1.6	1.6	1.1	1.1	1.1	0.9
Inventory Turnover 35	5.6	•	36.5	7.3	5.4	6.0	7.7	4.2	4.4	4.3	4.2	4.2	6.3
Receivables Turnover 36	7.9	•	19.2	10.6	8.1	7.5	8.2	7.7	7.8	7.5	7.0	7.0	7.6
Total Liabilities to Net Worth 37	1.5	5976	1.3	2.4	0.9	1.1	2.0	2.3	1.3	1.6	1.9	1.3	1.5
Current Assets to Working Capital 38	2.0	•	2.0	1.6	1.7	2.0	3.1	3.1	1.9	2.0	2.8	2.8	1.8
Current Liabilities to Working Capital 39	1.0	•	1.0	0.6	0.7	1.0	2.1	2.1	0.9	1.0	1.8	1.8	0.8
Working Capital to Net Sales 40	0.2	•	0.1	0.2	0.2	0.1	0.1	0.1	0.2	0.3	0.1	0.1	0.2
Inventory to Working Capital 41	0.7	•	0.3	0.6	0.7	0.8	1.2	1.5	0.9	0.8	1.2	1.2	0.6
Total Receipts to Cash Flow 42	9.9	9.9	9.6	11.0	10.2	10.0	11.9	13.3	9.7	15.0	13.5	13.5	8.6
Cost of Goods to Cash Flow 43	7.7	8.0	7.4	8.2	7.8	7.5	9.4	10.9	7.6	12.6	11.4	11.4	6.5
Cash Flow to Total Debt 44	0.2	•	0.8	0.4	0.4	0.4	0.3	0.2	0.3	0.1	0.1	0.1	0.2

Selected Financial Factors (in Percentages)

	1	2	3	4	5	6	7	8	9	10	11	12	13
Debt Ratio 45	59.7	99.8	55.6	70.9	46.3	53.3	66.7	69.8	55.7	60.8	57.4	57.4	60.2
Return on Total Assets 46	9.0	•	19.8	21.5	20.2	15.3	15.8	12.7	10.8	14.1	6.3	6.3	8.0
Return on Equity Before Income Taxes 47	18.3	8562.3	48.4	62.4	25.9	30.2	30.5	26.2	26.0	8.2	13.9	13.9	16.6
Return on Equity After Income Taxes 48	12.8	7519.3	48.0	60.8	23.6	27.4	27.8	22.5	19.0	2.0	8.7	8.7	11.3
Profit Margin (Before Income Tax) 49	6.6	3.2	5.3	6.1	6.7	6.8	5.0	5.0	7.2	2.8	5.4	5.4	7.4
Profit Margin (After Income Tax) 50	4.6	5.4	5.3	5.9	6.2	6.1	4.6	4.3	5.3	0.7	3.4	3.4	5.1

Table II

Corporations with Net Income

IRON, STEEL MILLS AND STEEL PRODUCT

MONEY AMOUNTS AND SIZE OF ASSETS IN THOUSANDS OF DOLLARS

Item Description for Accounting Period 7/07 Through 6/08	Total	Zero Assets	Under 500	500 to 1,000	1,000 to 5,000	5,000 to 10,000	10,000 to 25,000	25,000 to 50,000	50,000 to 100,000	100,000 to 250,000	250,000 to 500,000	500,000 to 2,500,000	2,500,000 and over
Number of Enterprises 1	3067	•	1365	•	466	237	152	69	30	36	14	13	•

Revenues ($ in Thousands)

	Total	Zero Assets	Under 500	500 to 1,000	1,000 to 5,000	5,000 to 10,000	10,000 to 25,000	25,000 to 50,000	50,000 to 100,000	100,000 to 250,000	250,000 to 500,000	500,000 to 2,500,000	2,500,000 and over
Net Sales 2	120747349	•	721762	•	3665319	3474440	5211712	5045271	3472593	8996887	5574125	20478665	•
Interest 3	508988	•	0	•	789	1118	5478	-1547	7048	53091	37421	48549	•
Rents 4	38836	•	0	•	66	443	1611	1171	202	1831	12641	8847	•
Royalties 5	401713	•	0	•	0	0	7177	0	4049	21372	1930	17347	•
Other Portfolio Income 6	941009	•	0	•	336	706	7851	6217	1064	48194	141488	302267	•
Other Receipts 7	1339449	•	1856	•	2337	27889	19440	19444	16635	63360	29681	285958	•
Total Receipts 8	123977344	•	723618	•	3668847	3504596	5253269	5070556	3501591	9184735	5779286	21141633	•
Average Total Receipts 9	40423	•	530	•	7873	14787	34561	73486	116720	255132	414092	1626279	•

Operating Costs/Operating Income (%)

	Total	Zero Assets	Under 500	500 to 1,000	1,000 to 5,000	5,000 to 10,000	10,000 to 25,000	25,000 to 50,000	50,000 to 100,000	100,000 to 250,000	250,000 to 500,000	500,000 to 2,500,000	2,500,000 and over
Cost of Operations 10	78.6	•	41.5	•	74.9	76.9	74.7	79.0	82.1	77.9	84.4	81.8	•
Salaries and Wages 11	2.7	•	21.8	•	4.8	4.7	4.4	3.0	2.1	3.4	2.6	2.4	•
Taxes Paid 12	1.1	•	2.0	•	1.3	1.7	1.5	1.1	1.2	1.7	0.8	0.9	•
Interest Paid 13	1.2	•	0.4	•	0.6	0.6	0.8	1.3	1.4	1.4	1.8	1.0	•
Depreciation 14	2.1	•	1.4	•	1.0	1.4	1.6	1.9	1.6	1.7	1.5	1.7	•
Amortization and Depletion 15	0.3	•	0.3	•	0.0	0.0	0.1	0.1	0.2	0.2	0.2	1.3	•
Pensions and Other Deferred Comp. 16	0.8	•	1.7	•	0.3	0.3	0.6	0.5	0.4	0.5	0.4	0.3	•
Employee Benefits 17	1.1	•	0.3	•	0.5	1.2	1.6	1.3	0.8	1.0	1.0	1.6	•
Advertising 18	0.1	•	0.3	•	0.2	0.2	0.2	0.2	0.1	0.3	0.1	0.1	•
Other Expenses 19	5.2	•	18.9	•	3.4	4.2	5.3	4.4	3.1	4.9	2.4	4.1	•
Officers' Compensation 20	0.8	•	4.1	•	5.7	2.7	2.3	1.5	1.1	0.6	0.5	0.2	•
Operating Margin 21	5.9	•	7.5	•	7.2	6.0	7.0	5.6	5.9	6.4	4.4	4.8	•
Operating Margin Before Officers' Comp. 22	6.7	•	11.6	•	13.0	8.7	9.3	7.0	7.0	6.9	4.9	5.0	•

Selected Average Balance Sheet ($ in Thousands)

Net Receivables 23	5749	30	689	1623	4288	11198	14573	31291	47658	180581
Inventories 24	5772	8	761	1914	4071	7563	22844	43082	90408	351867
Net Property, Plant and Equipment 25	8598	28	304	1841	3242	10083	14937	38966	63767	285742
Total Assets 26	34405	105	2335	7051	15297	35295	68252	154211	318344	1351791
Notes and Loans Payable 27	9945	64	894	1182	3934	13222	18603	29861	88642	298675
All Other Liabilities 28	9918	30	632	1935	4082	9939	27452	46944	102745	464959
Net Worth 29	14541	10	810	3934	7282	12133	22196	77405	126957	588157

Selected Financial Ratios (Times to 1)

Current Ratio 30	2.0	1.2	2.8	2.3	2.0	1.4	1.5	2.1	2.1	1.5
Quick Ratio 31	1.0	1.1	1.5	1.3	1.0	0.8	0.7	1.0	0.7	0.7
Net Sales to Working Capital 32	5.1	51.8	6.4	5.1	6.8	10.1	8.2	4.9	3.9	8.5
Coverage Ratio 33	7.9	21.3	13.7	13.2	11.3	5.7	5.8	7.1	5.6	9.3
Total Asset Turnover 34	1.1	5.1	3.4	2.1	2.2	2.1	1.7	1.6	1.3	1.2
Inventory Turnover 35	5.4	27.3	7.7	5.9	6.3	7.6	4.2	4.5	3.7	3.7
Receivables Turnover 36	7.4	9.3	12.2	8.3	7.8	8.4	7.6	7.9	•	6.2
Total Liabilities to Net Worth 37	1.4	9.1	1.9	0.8	1.1	1.9	2.1	1.0	1.5	1.3
Current Assets to Working Capital 38	2.0	5.1	1.6	1.7	2.0	3.3	3.2	1.9	1.9	3.0
Current Liabilities to Working Capital 39	1.0	4.1	0.6	0.7	1.0	2.3	2.2	0.9	0.9	2.0
Working Capital to Net Sales 40	0.2	0.0	0.2	0.2	0.1	0.1	0.1	0.2	0.3	0.1
Inventory to Working Capital 41	0.7	0.6	0.6	0.7	0.8	1.2	1.6	0.8	0.9	1.2
Total Receipts to Cash Flow 42	8.3	5.0	10.7	10.1	9.3	11.0	10.8	8.7	13.3	9.5
Cost of Goods to Cash Flow 43	6.5	2.1	8.0	7.8	6.9	8.7	8.9	6.8	11.2	7.8
Cash Flow to Total Debt 44	0.2	1.1	0.5	0.5	0.5	0.3	0.2	0.4	0.2	0.2

Selected Financial Factors (in Percentages)

Debt Ratio 45	57.7	90.1	65.3	44.2	52.4	65.6	67.5	49.8	60.1	56.5
Return on Total Assets 46	11.3	40.9	26.6	15.5	19.1	15.2	13.9	16.0	12.7	10.8
Return on Equity Before Income Taxes 47	23.3	393.8	71.2	25.6	36.6	36.5	35.4	27.3	26.3	22.2
Return on Equity After Income Taxes 48	16.9	368.6	69.7	23.4	33.5	33.5	30.7	20.2	18.1	15.5
Profit Margin (Before Income Tax) 49	8.6	7.7	7.3	6.9	7.8	6.1	6.8	8.5	8.4	8.3
Profit Margin (After Income Tax) 50	6.2	7.2	7.2	6.3	7.1	5.6	5.9	6.3	5.8	5.8

Table I

Corporations with and without Net Income

NONFERROUS METAL PRODUCTION AND PROCESSING

MONEY AMOUNTS AND SIZE OF ASSETS IN THOUSANDS OF DOLLARS

Item Description for Accounting Period 7/07 Through 6/08	Total	Zero Assets	Under 500	500 to 1,000	1,000 to 5,000	5,000 to 10,000	10,000 to 25,000	25,000 to 50,000	50,000 to 100,000	100,000 to 250,000	250,000 to 500,000	500,000 to 2,500,000	2,500,000 and over
Number of Enterprises 1	870	14	171	65	316	66	88	58	31	15	18	22	5
Revenues ($ in Thousands)													
Net Sales 2	112549558	5111804	165072	364621	1481223	2626584	3627965	5181378	4307489	2581895	11530278	35923149	39648099
Interest 3	2021186	16343	1	0	1127	387	2322	1412	20389	11723	38583	217070	1711829
Rents 4	45593	43	0	0	5400	2496	25	476	93	21	30280	2855	3905
Royalties 5	139429	0	0	0	0	0	541	0	4811	534	0	33670	99873
Other Portfolio Income 6	4424560	7527	0	40929	3548	3	1817	7681	15927	570	14314	89176	4243067
Other Receipts 7	1983699	56275	9	8	145	4198	13737	72235	55077	388508	283323	401188	708997
Total Receipts 8	121164025	5191992	165082	405558	1491443	2633668	3646407	5263182	4403786	2983251	11896778	36667108	46415770
Average Total Receipts 9	139269	370857	965	6239	4720	39904	41436	90745	142058	198883	660932	1666687	9283154
Operating Costs/Operating Income (%)													
Cost of Operations 10	84.4	88.0	56.0	79.7	71.8	92.4	84.2	87.6	85.7	81.6	88.3	85.7	81.5
Salaries and Wages 11	2.7	1.2	17.8	3.1	2.0	1.7	2.6	2.8	2.8	5.3	1.8	2.5	3.2
Taxes Paid 12	0.7	0.5	2.4	0.6	1.1	0.5	1.2	0.9	0.9	1.2	0.6	0.8	0.5
Interest Paid 13	3.2	1.6	0.1	0.1	1.4	0.6	0.7	1.2	1.3	1.9	1.9	1.7	6.3
Depreciation 14	1.6	1.0	1.3	1.2	2.3	0.7	1.0	1.4	1.6	1.7	1.2	1.3	2.2
Amortization and Depletion 15	0.7	0.2	•	0.0	0.0	0.1	0.0	0.4	0.2	0.1	0.2	0.2	1.7
Pensions and Other Deferred Comp. 16	0.3	0.3	•	3.3	0.4	0.1	0.3	0.3	0.3	0.3	0.4	0.2	0.3
Employee Benefits 17	1.0	0.3	1.2	0.3	0.4	0.5	0.8	1.0	0.8	2.7	1.1	0.8	1.1
Advertising 18	0.1	0.0	1.6	0.0	0.2	0.0	0.1	0.0	0.1	0.1	0.0	0.1	0.2
Other Expenses 19	5.3	2.7	23.1	3.8	10.9	1.6	3.3	3.5	4.3	15.0	3.7	5.1	6.1
Officers' Compensation 20	0.4	0.2	2.2	0.1	1.1	0.4	1.2	1.1	0.9	0.9	0.4	0.4	0.1
Operating Margin 21	•	4.0	•	7.8	8.4	1.3	4.7	•	1.1	•	0.2	1.2	•
Operating Margin Before Officers' Comp. 22	•	4.2	•	7.9	9.5	1.7	5.9	0.7	2.0	•	0.7	1.7	•

Selected Average Balance Sheet ($ in Thousands)

Net Receivables 23	58279	0	95	458	456	1798	5129	9100	17368	50388	78284	167046	8607340
Inventories 24	11130	0	5	2	378	2324	4020	12172	17670	28138	66079	161065	529364
Net Property, Plant and Equipment 25	23834	0	43	9	375	1440	3553	9148	16061	29243	81603	225624	2460258
Total Assets 26	187483	202	548	1330	6373	15639	35152	66783	151501	349947	1100875		24784613
Notes and Loans Payable 27	56151	0	152	33	1315	2907	4308	14509	19957	48816	130333	358506	7082170
All Other Liabilities 28	53902	0	50	205	278	2178	4944	10586	20108	72358	99206	422128	6562209
Net Worth 29	77430	0	-0	309	-264	1289	6386	10057	26718	30327	120408	320241	11140234

Selected Financial Ratios (Times to 1)

Current Ratio 30	1.2	•	1.5	2.4	3.0	1.2	1.9	1.4	1.8	1.3	1.8	1.8	1.1
Quick Ratio 31	0.9	•	1.1	2.4	2.0	0.6	1.2	0.7	1.0	0.8	0.9	0.8	1.0
Net Sales to Working Capital 32	10.3	•	21.5	18.0	7.9	43.4	7.8	13.6	7.3	8.3	8.1	7.8	13.6
Coverage Ratio 33	3.6	4.4	•	297.4	7.7	3.7	8.8	2.0	3.6	3.5	2.8	3.0	3.7
Total Asset Turnover 34	0.7	•	4.8	10.2	3.5	6.2	2.6	2.5	2.1	1.1	1.8	1.5	0.3
Inventory Turnover 35	9.8	•	104.3	2383.0	8.9	15.8	8.6	6.4	6.7	5.0	8.6	8.7	12.2
Receivables Turnover 36	2.3	•	10.0	24.5	9.1	20.1	7.4	8.3	6.9	4.1	9.9	9.2	1.0
Total Liabilities to Net Worth 37	1.4	•	•	0.8	•	3.9	1.4	2.5	1.5	4.0	1.9	2.4	1.2
Current Assets to Working Capital 38	6.2	•	3.2	1.7	1.5	5.2	2.1	3.4	2.3	4.7	2.3	2.3	16.6
Current Liabilities to Working Capital 39	5.2	•	2.2	0.7	0.5	4.2	1.1	2.4	1.3	3.7	1.3	1.3	15.6
Working Capital to Net Sales 40	0.1	•	0.0	0.1	0.1	0.0	0.1	0.1	0.1	0.1	0.1	0.1	0.1
Inventory to Working Capital 41	0.9	•	0.1	0.0	0.4	2.4	0.7	1.7	0.9	1.5	0.9	0.8	0.9
Total Receipts to Cash Flow 42	10.9	12.9	8.7	4.7	5.6	37.5	13.2	25.0	15.3	6.0	16.0	13.9	7.9
Cost of Goods to Cash Flow 43	9.2	11.4	4.9	3.8	4.0	34.6	11.1	21.9	13.2	4.9	14.2	11.9	6.5
Cash Flow to Total Debt 44	0.1	•	0.5	5.0	0.5	0.2	0.3	0.2	0.2	0.2	0.2	0.2	0.1

Selected Financial Factors (in Percentages)

Debt Ratio 45	58.7	•	100.0	43.5	119.8	79.8	59.2	71.4	60.0	80.0	65.6	70.9	55.1
Return on Total Assets 46	8.0	•	•	195.5	36.7	13.7	15.4	6.2	9.6	7.5	9.9		7.5
Return on Equity Before Income Taxes 47	13.9	•	55235.3	344.8	49.3	33.5	11.0	17.3	26.6	18.6	17.1		12.1
Return on Equity After Income Taxes 48	9.3	•	56958.8	344.8	43.0	31.6	9.2	11.5	16.2	11.4	11.9		7.9
Profit Margin (Before Income Tax) 49	8.3	5.6	•	19.0	9.1	1.6	5.2	1.2	3.3	4.7	3.5	3.4	17.0
Profit Margin (After Income Tax) 50	5.6	3.4	•	19.0	9.0	1.4	4.9	1.0	2.2	2.9	2.1	2.3	11.1

Table II

Corporations with Net Income

NONFERROUS METAL PRODUCTION AND PROCESSING

MONEY AMOUNTS AND SIZE OF ASSETS IN THOUSANDS OF DOLLARS

Item Description for Accounting Period 7/07 Through 6/08	Total	Zero Assets	Under 500	500 to 1,000	1,000 to 5,000	5,000 to 10,000	10,000 to 25,000	25,000 to 50,000	50,000 to 100,000	100,000 to 250,000	250,000 to 500,000	500,000 to 2,500,000	2,500,000 and over
Number of Enterprises **1**	658	•	85	•	260	63	82	•	21	10	•	17	5
Revenues ($ in Thousands)													
Net Sales **2**	92424769	•	65575	•	1384758	2455045	3370397	•	2953364	1912607	•	27623337	39648099
Interest **3**	1932567	•	1	•	144	387	2308	•	16159	6402	•	162731	1711829
Rents **4**	9320	•	0	•	2034	0	0	•	82	21	•	2731	3905
Royalties **5**	139196	•	0	•	0	0	541	•	4578	534	•	33670	99873
Other Portfolio Income **6**	4368393	•	0	•	3548	3	1558	•	15693	505	•	43419	4243067
Other Receipts **7**	1803174	•	-1	•	140	4152	10100	•	50881	329946	•	313743	708997
Total Receipts **8**	100677419	•	65575	•	1390624	2459587	3384904	•	3040757	2250015	•	28179631	46415770
Average Total Receipts **9**	153005	•	771	•	5349	39041	41279	•	144798	225002	•	1657625	9283154
Operating Costs/Operating Income (%)													
Cost of Operations **10**	83.2	•	69.1	•	72.4	92.1	83.4	•	83.5	81.0	•	84.3	81.5
Salaries and Wages **11**	2.8	•	3.9	•	2.1	1.6	2.6	•	3.4	5.6	•	2.7	3.2
Taxes Paid **12**	0.7	•	5.7	•	0.9	0.5	1.2	•	0.9	0.9	•	0.8	0.5
Interest Paid **13**	3.4	•	•	•	1.3	0.5	0.6	•	1.0	1.1	•	1.4	6.3
Depreciation **14**	1.6	•	0.8	•	2.4	0.7	0.9	•	1.2	0.7	•	1.3	2.2
Amortization and Depletion **15**	0.8	•	•	•	0.0	0.1	0.0	•	0.1	0.1	•	0.2	1.7
Pensions and Other Deferred Comp. **16**	0.3	•	•	•	0.5	0.1	0.2	•	0.2	0.2	•	0.3	0.3
Employee Benefits **17**	0.9	•	2.9	•	0.3	0.5	0.7	•	0.6	2.8	•	0.8	1.1
Advertising **18**	0.1	•	•	•	0.2	0.0	0.1	•	0.1	0.0	•	0.1	0.2
Other Expenses **19**	5.2	•	9.2	•	9.5	1.8	3.2	•	5.3	17.1	•	4.6	6.1
Officers' Compensation **20**	0.4	•	5.5	•	1.0	0.4	1.2	•	0.8	1.0	•	0.5	0.1
Operating Margin **21**	0.6	•	3.0	•	9.4	1.6	5.9	•	2.9	•	•	3.1	•
Operating Margin Before Officers' Comp. **22**	1.0	•	8.4	•	10.4	2.1	7.1	•	3.6	•	•	3.6	•

Selected Average Balance Sheet ($ in Thousands)

Net Receivables 23	74216	102	527	1761	5245	17842	52760	176410	8607340
Inventories 24	12338	9	215	2143	3608	20122	31964	170232	529364
Net Property, Plant and Equipment 25	27565	46	360	1314	3648	13613	17692	230655	2460258
Total Assets 26	231204	264	1322	6283	15742	68554	141576	1090205	24784613
Notes and Loans Payable 27	66823	0	1342	2681	3242	14489	38410	331574	7082170
All Other Liabilities 28	64932	12	295	2075	4663	20626	76250	403292	6562209
Net Worth 29	99448	252	-316	1528	7837	33439	26917	355340	11140234

Selected Financial Ratios (Times to 1)

Current Ratio 30	1.2	11.9	2.9	1.3	2.2	2.0	1.3	2.1	1.1
Quick Ratio 31	1.0	10.8	2.2	0.6	1.4	1.1	0.8	1.0	1.0
Net Sales to Working Capital 32	8.9	5.7	9.1	33.5	6.8	6.2	8.4	6.1	13.6
Coverage Ratio 33	4.2	•	8.3	4.5	12.0	6.8	7.5	4.6	3.7
Total Asset Turnover 34	0.6	2.9	4.0	6.2	2.6	2.1	1.4	1.5	0.3
Inventory Turnover 35	9.5	58.8	18.0	16.7	9.5	5.8	4.8	8.0	12.2
Receivables Turnover 36	1.9	7.3	•	19.6	7.5	6.0	4.0	8.7	1.0
Total Liabilities to Net Worth 37	1.3	0.0	•	3.1	1.0	1.1	4.3	2.1	1.2
Current Assets to Working Capital 38	6.1	1.1	1.5	4.1	1.8	2.0	4.4	1.9	16.6
Current Liabilities to Working Capital 39	5.1	0.1	0.5	3.1	0.8	1.0	3.4	0.9	15.6
Working Capital to Net Sales 40	0.1	0.2	0.1	0.0	0.1	0.2	0.1	0.2	0.1
Inventory to Working Capital 41	0.8	0.1	0.4	2.0	0.6	0.7	1.4	0.7	0.9
Total Receipts to Cash Flow 42	9.2	14.0	5.9	33.2	11.5	10.0	4.7	11.9	7.9
Cost of Goods to Cash Flow 43	7.7	9.7	4.3	30.5	9.6	8.3	3.8	10.1	6.5
Cash Flow to Total Debt 44	0.1	4.4	0.6	0.2	0.5	0.4	0.4	0.2	0.1

Selected Financial Factors (in Percentages)

Debt Ratio 45	57.0	4.7	123.9	75.7	50.2	51.2	81.0	67.4	55.1
Return on Total Assets 46	8.6	8.7	44.8	14.5	17.9	14.0	11.2	9.7	7.5
Return on Equity Before Income Taxes 47	15.3	9.1	•	46.5	32.9	24.5	50.9	23.3	12.1
Return on Equity After Income Taxes 48	10.6	7.8	•	40.9	31.3	17.6	33.3	17.2	7.9
Profit Margin (Before Income Tax) 49	10.9	3.0	9.8	1.8	6.3	5.8	7.2	5.1	17.0
Profit Margin (After Income Tax) 50	7.5	2.5	9.8	1.6	6.0	4.2	4.7	3.8	11.1

Table I

Corporations with and without Net Income

FOUNDRIES

MONEY AMOUNTS AND SIZE OF ASSETS IN THOUSANDS OF DOLLARS

Item Description for Accounting Period 7/07 Through 6/08		Total	Zero Assets	Under 500	500 to 1,000	1,000 to 5,000	5,000 to 10,000	10,000 to 25,000	25,000 to 50,000	50,000 to 100,000	100,000 to 250,000	250,000 to 500,000	500,000 to 2,500,000	2,500,000 and over
Number of Enterprises	1	1573	3	1075	0	294	99	53	17	13	7	6	6	0
Revenues ($ in Thousands)														
Net Sales	2	25592957	90447	1093504	0	2388368	1309299	1532239	997617	1370120	1756541	2674675	12380147	0
Interest	3	35043	14	0	0	3120	1235	1608	980	884	3559	2814	20828	0
Rents	4	5020	0	0	0	680	113	1207	22	224	95	1192	1488	0
Royalties	5	32302	0	0	0	0	7812	17	4	253	0	3511	20705	0
Other Portfolio Income	6	121487	6	0	0	25258	957	4114	316	6247	4305	3139	77145	0
Other Receipts	7	317920	168	0	0	54115	11428	4423	4874	11986	19531	18331	193063	0
Total Receipts	8	26104729	90635	1093504	0	2471541	1330844	1543608	1003813	1389714	1784031	2703662	12693376	0
Average Total Receipts	9	16596	30212	1017	•	8407	13443	29125	59048	106901	254862	450610	2115563	•
Operating Costs/Operating Income (%)														
Cost of Operations	10	73.2	60.3	63.2	•	65.7	79.7	73.9	76.8	78.5	78.8	80.6	71.6	•
Salaries and Wages	11	5.1	5.8	6.5	•	5.8	4.7	3.9	3.9	4.6	3.5	2.9	5.8	•
Taxes Paid	12	1.8	4.9	2.3	•	2.5	2.3	2.3	2.0	1.9	0.5	1.6	1.6	•
Interest Paid	13	1.5	6.2	0.2	•	0.5	1.4	1.0	1.8	1.3	3.0	2.2	1.5	•
Depreciation	14	2.5	2.7	1.8	•	1.3	2.7	2.7	2.6	3.1	3.8	3.5	2.2	•
Amortization and Depletion	15	0.4	0.5	0.2	•	0.0	0.1	0.0	0.1	0.1	0.5	0.4	0.6	•
Pensions and Other Deferred Comp.	16	0.6	0.0	0.7	•	0.4	0.3	0.9	0.5	0.5	0.2	0.5	0.7	•
Employee Benefits	17	2.3	2.4	0.3	•	2.5	2.0	1.8	1.2	0.7	4.0	2.7	2.6	•
Advertising	18	0.1	0.0	0.1	•	0.1	0.2	0.1	0.2	0.3	0.0	0.2	0.1	•
Other Expenses	19	5.1	41.7	8.7	•	9.9	5.8	5.3	3.7	4.1	5.9	6.1	3.4	•
Officers' Compensation	20	2.4	0.3	4.8	•	7.0	1.9	2.6	1.8	1.1	0.4	0.4	2.2	•
Operating Margin	21	5.1	•	11.2	•	4.4	0.8	5.6	5.4	3.7	•	7.8	•	•
Operating Margin Before Officers' Comp.	22	7.5	•	16.0	•	11.3	0.8	8.2	7.2	4.8	•	10.0	•	•

Selected Average Balance Sheet ($ in Thousands)

	•	•	•	•	•	•	•	•	•	•	•	•
Net Receivables 23	2100	0	129	•	990	2334	3903	8693	12549	29506	65495	254140
Inventories 24	1927	0	36	•	735	1455	2196	7856	14063	17884	57741	288037
Net Property, Plant and Equipment 25	2861	0	33	•	604	2201	5317	10543	28410	63583	108046	357692
Total Assets 26	12742	0	238	•	3261	7254	14839	34824	69696	185220	363969	2057496
Notes and Loans Payable 27	2622	0	143	•	363	3129	3971	13571	14516	92207	122424	257364
All Other Liabilities 28	2966	0	77	•	896	2183	3459	7869	15997	70215	77568	436711
Net Worth 29	7154	0	17	•	2002	1942	7408	13384	39183	22798	163977	1363421

Selected Financial Ratios (Times to 1)

	•	•	•	•	•	•	•	•	•	•	•	•
Current Ratio 30	1.9	•	2.3	•	2.4	2.1	1.9	1.8	2.1	1.0	2.1	1.9
Quick Ratio 31	1.1	•	1.8	•	1.6	1.3	1.2	1.1	1.2	0.6	1.2	1.0
Net Sales to Working Capital 32	7.0	•	9.8	•	6.0	5.4	7.5	6.5	5.6	•	6.6	6.5
Coverage Ratio 33	5.8	•	63.8	•	16.5	1.4	7.4	4.4	4.6	1.3	1.0	8.1
Total Asset Turnover 34	1.3	•	4.3	•	2.5	1.8	1.9	1.7	1.5	1.4	1.2	1.0
Inventory Turnover 35	6.2	•	18.0	•	7.3	7.2	9.7	5.7	5.9	11.1	6.2	5.1
Receivables Turnover 36	7.6	•	8.6	•	7.9	5.8	8.5	6.6	7.6	10.9	5.3	8.0
Total Liabilities to Net Worth 37	0.8	•	12.8	•	0.6	2.7	1.0	1.6	0.8	7.1	1.2	0.5
Current Assets to Working Capital 38	2.1	•	1.7	•	1.7	1.9	2.1	2.2	1.9	•	1.9	2.1
Current Liabilities to Working Capital 39	1.1	•	0.7	•	0.7	0.9	1.1	1.2	0.9	•	0.9	1.1
Working Capital to Net Sales 40	0.1	•	0.1	•	0.2	0.2	0.1	0.2	0.2	•	0.2	0.2
Inventory to Working Capital 41	0.8	•	0.3	•	0.5	0.7	0.6	0.8	0.6	•	0.7	0.9
Total Receipts to Cash Flow 42	9.7	6.5	6.0	•	6.8	17.7	10.1	11.1	12.7	32.7	20.7	8.3
Cost of Goods to Cash Flow 43	7.1	3.9	3.8	•	4.4	14.1	7.5	8.5	10.0	25.8	16.7	5.9
Cash Flow to Total Debt 44	0.3	•	0.8	•	1.0	0.1	0.4	0.2	0.3	0.0	0.1	0.4

Selected Financial Factors (in Percentages)

	•	•	•	•	•	•	•	•	•	•	•	•
Debt Ratio 45	43.9	•	92.8	•	38.6	73.2	50.1	61.6	43.8	87.7	54.9	33.7
Return on Total Assets 46	11.2	•	48.5	•	20.8	3.6	14.3	13.2	9.5	5.3	2.8	12.2
Return on Equity Before Income Taxes 47	16.5	•	659.9	•	31.8	3.6	24.8	26.5	13.2	10.4	0.1	16.1
Return on Equity After Income Taxes 48	11.8	•	659.9	•	31.1	1.7	18.8	23.8	10.8	10.4	•	10.7
Profit Margin (Before Income Tax) 49	7.3	•	11.2	•	7.8	0.5	6.4	6.0	4.9	0.9	0.0	10.7
Profit Margin (After Income Tax) 50	5.2	•	11.2	•	7.7	0.2	4.8	5.4	4.0	•	•	7.1

Table II

Corporations with Net Income

FOUNDRIES

MONEY AMOUNTS AND SIZE OF ASSETS IN THOUSANDS OF DOLLARS

Item Description for Accounting Period 7/07 Through 6/08	Total	Zero Assets	Under 500	500 to 1,000	1,000 to 5,000	5,000 to 10,000	10,000 to 25,000	25,000 to 50,000	50,000 to 100,000	100,000 to 250,000	250,000 to 500,000	500,000 to 2,500,000	2,500,000 and over
Number of Enterprises **1**	1434	•	989	0	279	81	45	•	10	3	•	6	0
Revenues ($ in Thousands)													
Net Sales **2**	22306717	•	991098	0	2111612	1021521	1358771	•	1155560	673840	•	12380147	0
Interest **3**	29350	•	0	0	1994	866	1436	•	714	388	•	20828	0
Rents **4**	4018	•	0	0	0	0	1207	•	224	0	•	1488	0
Royalties **5**	24489	•	0	0	0	0	17	•	253	0	•	20705	0
Other Portfolio Income **6**	114126	•	0	0	25254	957	1048	•	6247	43	•	77145	0
Other Receipts **7**	288573	•	0	0	52540	5743	4070	•	8227	5409	•	193063	0
Total Receipts **8**	22767273	•	991098	0	2191400	1029087	1366549	•	1171225	679680	•	12693376	0
Average Total Receipts **9**	15877	•	1002	•	7854	12705	30368	•	117122	226560	•	2115563	•
Operating Costs/Operating Income (%)													
Cost of Operations **10**	71.8	•	61.2	•	62.1	77.4	73.1	•	77.7	71.0	•	71.6	•
Salaries and Wages **11**	5.4	•	6.9	•	6.2	5.1	3.7	•	4.5	4.6	•	5.8	•
Taxes Paid **12**	1.8	•	2.0	•	2.5	2.4	2.3	•	1.9	1.3	•	1.6	•
Interest Paid **13**	1.3	•	0.2	•	0.5	1.7	0.9	•	1.2	2.1	•	1.5	•
Depreciation **14**	2.2	•	1.9	•	1.3	2.1	2.5	•	2.6	2.2	•	2.2	•
Amortization and Depletion **15**	0.4	•	0.3	•	0.0	0.2	0.0	•	0.0	0.6	•	0.6	•
Pensions and Other Deferred Comp. **16**	0.6	•	0.7	•	0.4	0.3	0.9	•	0.5	0.6	•	0.7	•
Employee Benefits **17**	2.2	•	0.2	•	2.6	1.8	2.0	•	0.7	2.6	•	2.6	•
Advertising **18**	0.1	•	0.1	•	0.1	0.2	0.1	•	0.4	0.0	•	0.1	•
Other Expenses **19**	4.6	•	9.6	•	11.4	5.0	5.1	•	3.9	4.5	•	3.4	•
Officers' Compensation **20**	2.6	•	4.2	•	7.6	1.9	2.6	•	1.1	0.4	•	2.2	•
Operating Margin **21**	6.9	•	12.7	•	5.2	1.9	6.8	•	5.4	10.1	•	7.8	•
Operating Margin Before Officers' Comp. **22**	9.5	•	16.9	•	12.8	3.9	9.4	•	6.6	10.6	•	10.0	•

Selected Average Balance Sheet ($ in Thousands)

Net Receivables 23	2000	134	924	2317	4231	12357	20383	254140
Inventories 24	1941	30	747	1437	2357	12914	32014	288037
Net Property, Plant and Equipment 25	2574	29	585	1953	5153	23765	48576	357692
Total Assets 26	12461	240	3227	6871	15184	67208	152798	2057496
Notes and Loans Payable 27	2141	154	299	3484	3710	10916	47916	257364
All Other Liabilities 28	2812	62	865	1869	3465	15310	72052	436711
Net Worth 29	7508	24	2064	1517	8009	40983	32830	1363421

Selected Financial Ratios (Times to 1)

Current Ratio 30	2.0	3.0	2.4	2.4	2.1	2.4	1.3	1.9
Quick Ratio 31	1.2	2.4	1.6	1.5	1.4	1.4	0.5	1.0
Net Sales to Working Capital 32	6.3	8.0	5.6	4.5	6.6	5.2	15.6	6.5
Coverage Ratio 33	7.9	71.2	20.5	2.6	9.5	6.6	6.2	8.1
Total Asset Turnover 34	1.2	4.2	2.3	1.8	2.0	1.7	1.5	1.0
Inventory Turnover 35	5.8	20.8	6.3	6.8	9.4	7.0	5.0	5.1
Receivables Turnover 36	7.4	8.8		5.5	8.2	9.1	7.6	8.0
Total Liabilities to Net Worth 37	0.7	8.9	0.6	3.5	0.9	0.6	3.7	0.5
Current Assets to Working Capital 38	2.0	1.5	1.7	1.7	1.9	1.7	3.9	2.1
Current Liabilities to Working Capital 39	1.0	0.5	0.7	0.7	0.9	0.7	2.9	1.1
Working Capital to Net Sales 40	0.2	0.1	0.2	0.2	0.2	0.2	0.1	0.2
Inventory to Working Capital 41	0.8	0.3	0.6	0.6	0.6	0.6	2.3	0.9
Total Receipts to Cash Flow 42	8.4	5.3	5.8	14.6	9.3	10.5	7.1	8.3
Cost of Goods to Cash Flow 43	6.0	3.3	3.6	11.3	6.8	8.2	5.0	5.9
Cash Flow to Total Debt 44	0.4	0.9	1.1	0.2	0.5	0.4	0.3	0.4

Selected Financial Factors (in Percentages)

Debt Ratio 45	39.7	89.9	36.0	77.9	47.3	39.0	78.5	33.7
Return on Total Assets 46	13.1	53.6	22.2	8.0	16.5	13.3	19.3	12.2
Return on Equity Before Income Taxes 47	19.0	522.1	33.1	22.3	27.9	18.5	75.3	16.1
Return on Equity After Income Taxes 48	14.1	522.1	32.4	19.2	21.5	15.6	58.2	10.7
Profit Margin (Before Income Tax) 49	9.2	12.7	9.0	2.7	7.4	6.6	11.0	10.7
Profit Margin (After Income Tax) 50	6.8	12.7	8.8	2.3	5.7	5.5	8.5	7.1

Table I

Corporations with and without Net Income

FORGING AND STAMPING

MONEY AMOUNTS AND SIZE OF ASSETS IN THOUSANDS OF DOLLARS

Item Description for Accounting Period 7/07 Through 6/08		Total	Zero Assets	Under 500	500 to 1,000	1,000 to 5,000	5,000 to 10,000	10,000 to 25,000	25,000 to 50,000	50,000 to 100,000	100,000 to 250,000	250,000 to 500,000	500,000 to 2,500,000	2,500,000 and over
Number of Enterprises	**1**	2927	•	•	•	575	151	162	35	18	17	7	3	0

Revenues ($ in Thousands)

Net Sales	**2**	21374618	•	•	•	2908701	1668731	5021248	1974554	1707922	3120127	2319627	1741956	0
Interest	**3**	28991	•	•	•	2097	975	2367	1667	2510	2672	6775	7171	0
Rents	**4**	3573	•	•	•	164	0	38	78	1249	1192	468	384	0
Royalties	**5**	323	•	•	•	0	0	0	2	0	0	322	0	0
Other Portfolio Income	**6**	52633	•	•	•	7679	16205	2266	5785	1525	9427	1634	243	0
Other Receipts	**7**	217157	•	•	•	7838	16196	57631	1326	15387	40461	57474	19962	0
Total Receipts	**8**	21677295	•	•	•	2926479	1702107	5083550	1983412	1728593	3173879	2386300	1769716	0
Average Total Receipts	**9**	7406	•	•	•	5090	11272	31380	56669	96033	186699	340900	589905	•

Operating Costs/Operating Income (%)

Cost of Operations	**10**	74.3	•	•	•	68.6	70.6	76.8	77.0	77.8	75.9	78.1	74.5	•
Salaries and Wages	**11**	4.2	•	•	•	4.4	6.9	4.5	3.4	4.5	4.0	2.6	3.6	•
Taxes Paid	**12**	1.7	•	•	•	2.4	1.9	1.6	1.8	1.6	1.9	1.1	0.9	•
Interest Paid	**13**	1.6	•	•	•	1.2	1.0	0.9	1.2	1.4	2.4	3.1	2.4	•
Depreciation	**14**	2.6	•	•	•	3.0	2.1	2.1	2.4	3.4	3.2	3.7	1.4	•
Amortization and Depletion	**15**	0.2	•	•	•	0.0	0.1	0.2	0.3	0.4	0.3	0.2	0.4	•
Pensions and Other Deferred Comp.	**16**	0.6	•	•	•	1.2	0.4	0.4	0.6	0.5	0.5	0.5	1.4	•
Employee Benefits	**17**	2.1	•	•	•	2.9	1.8	1.9	2.1	1.9	2.5	2.1	0.7	•
Advertising	**18**	0.1	•	•	•	0.2	0.4	0.1	0.1	0.1	0.1	0.0	0.1	•
Other Expenses	**19**	6.5	•	•	•	9.4	8.9	5.5	5.6	4.7	4.6	5.3	3.5	•
Officers' Compensation	**20**	2.5	•	•	•	4.7	2.6	1.9	1.1	1.4	1.3	1.5	0.4	•
Operating Margin	**21**	3.5	•	•	•	2.0	3.3	3.9	4.4	2.4	3.4	1.9	10.6	•
Operating Margin Before Officers' Comp.	**22**	5.9	•	•	•	6.7	6.0	5.8	5.5	3.8	4.7	3.4	11.0	•

Selected Average Balance Sheet ($ in Thousands)

Net Receivables 23	1048	621	1465	3935	8478	13881	27343	57592	111348
Inventories 24	964	428	2009	3048	7305	12129	27478	65714	185886
Net Property, Plant and Equipment 25	1473	732	1673	3828	11725	25220	40276	80249	271661
Total Assets 26	5289	2395	6753	14356	36497	64790	133679	321331	1096428
Notes and Loans Payable 27	1564	678	1990	3891	10399	20350	47919	107591	281323
All Other Liabilities 28	1504	1479	1107	3718	7821	15592	33754	77733	345994
Net Worth 29	2221	238	3657	6747	18276	28848	52006	136007	469111

Selected Financial Ratios (Times to 1)

Current Ratio 30	1.7	1.7	2.4	1.9	1.7	1.7	1.5	2.1	1.2
Quick Ratio 31	1.0	1.2	1.3	1.1	1.0	1.0	0.8	1.0	0.5
Net Sales to Working Capital 32	6.3	7.5	5.2	7.1	7.0	7.7	8.2	3.8	11.0
Coverage Ratio 33	4.0	3.1	6.2	6.6	4.8	3.5	3.1	2.5	6.1
Total Asset Turnover 34	1.4	2.1	1.6	2.2	1.5	1.5	1.4	1.0	0.5
Inventory Turnover 35	5.6	8.1	3.9	7.8	6.0	6.1	5.1	3.9	2.3
Receivables Turnover 36	6.8	8.2	4.8	8.3	5.9	5.9	6.2	5.3	10.4
Total Liabilities to Net Worth 37	1.4	9.1	0.8	1.1	1.0	1.2	1.6	1.4	1.3
Current Assets to Working Capital 38	2.3	2.4	1.7	2.1	2.4	2.5	2.9	1.9	6.8
Current Liabilities to Working Capital 39	1.3	1.4	0.7	1.1	1.4	1.5	1.9	0.9	5.8
Working Capital to Net Sales 40	0.2	0.1	0.2	0.1	0.1	0.1	0.1	0.3	0.1
Inventory to Working Capital 41	0.9	0.6	0.7	0.8	0.9	0.8	1.2	0.8	3.5
Total Receipts to Cash Flow 42	11.1	13.7	8.9	12.2	11.7	14.4	12.3	11.0	6.6
Cost of Goods to Cash Flow 43	8.2	9.4	6.3	9.4	9.0	11.2	9.3	8.6	4.9
Cash Flow to Total Debt 44	0.2	0.2	0.4	0.3	0.3	0.2	0.2	0.2	0.1

Selected Financial Factors (in Percentages)

Debt Ratio 45	58.0	90.1	45.9	53.0	49.9	55.5	61.1	57.7	57.2
Return on Total Assets 46	8.9	8.1	10.4	13.0	9.3	7.2	10.3	8.1	7.7
Return on Equity Before Income Taxes 47	16.0	55.2	16.1	23.5	14.7	11.6	17.9	11.5	15.1
Return on Equity After Income Taxes 48	13.6	51.2	14.1	21.3	12.4	10.1	14.2	9.1	13.2
Profit Margin (Before Income Tax) 49	4.9	2.6	5.3	5.1	4.8	3.5	5.1	4.7	12.2
Profit Margin (After Income Tax) 50	4.2	2.4	4.7	4.6	4.0	3.1	4.0	3.8	10.6

Table II

Corporations with Net Income

FORGING AND STAMPING

MONEY AMOUNTS AND SIZE OF ASSETS IN THOUSANDS OF DOLLARS

Item Description for Accounting Period 7/07 Through 6/08	Total	Zero Assets	Under 500	500 to 1,000	1,000 to 5,000	5,000 to 10,000	10,000 to 25,000	25,000 to 50,000	50,000 to 100,000	100,000 to 250,000	250,000 to 500,000	500,000 to 2,500,000	2,500,000 and over
Number of Enterprises **1**	2182	0	1217	283	389	107	127	23	•	14	•	0	0
Revenues ($ in Thousands)													
Net Sales **2**	15840814	0	105715	449776	2336810	1196247	3858177	1252327	•	2710599	•	0	0
Interest **3**	21638	0	40	191	1428	918	1646	1665	•	1669	•	0	0
Rents **4**	3528	0	0	0	164	0	0	78	•	1192	•	0	0
Royalties **5**	2	0	0	0	0	0	0	2	•	0	•	0	0
Other Portfolio Income **6**	46188	0	4958	5	7624	16099	448	5771	•	9057	•	0	0
Other Receipts **7**	159958	0	45	0	3587	16050	48148	594	•	10088	•	0	0
Total Receipts **8**	16072128	0	110758	449972	2349613	1229314	3908419	1260437	•	2732605	•	0	0
Average Total Receipts **9**	7366	•	91	1590	6040	11489	30775	54802	•	195186	•	•	•
Operating Costs/Operating Income (%)													
Cost of Operations **10**	71.9	•	33.1	61.3	67.1	65.3	75.8	74.0	•	73.8	•	•	•
Salaries and Wages **11**	4.2	•	1.1	1.9	4.3	7.4	4.1	3.4	•	3.9	•	•	•
Taxes Paid **12**	1.7	•	1.7	2.3	2.4	1.8	1.6	1.7	•	1.8	•	•	•
Interest Paid **13**	1.2	•	1.5	0.7	1.0	0.7	0.7	0.8	•	1.5	•	•	•
Depreciation **14**	2.5	•	6.6	0.3	2.8	2.3	2.0	2.8	•	2.8	•	•	•
Amortization and Depletion **15**	0.2	•	0.0	0.1	0.0	0.1	0.1	0.4	•	0.1	•	•	•
Pensions and Other Deferred Comp. **16**	0.8	•	•	0.5	1.4	0.5	0.5	0.5	•	0.5	•	•	•
Employee Benefits **17**	2.0	•	0.2	1.1	3.1	2.5	1.9	1.8	•	2.5	•	•	•
Advertising **18**	0.2	•	3.8	0.4	0.2	0.6	0.1	0.1	•	0.1	•	•	•
Other Expenses **19**	5.5	•	29.5	14.3	6.9	8.7	4.4	5.9	•	4.2	•	•	•
Officers' Compensation **20**	2.6	•	6.4	12.5	5.5	2.9	2.1	1.1	•	1.4	•	•	•
Operating Margin **21**	7.2	•	16.0	4.5	5.3	7.1	6.7	7.5	•	7.4	•	•	•
Operating Margin Before Officers' Comp. **22**	9.9	•	22.4	17.0	10.7	10.0	8.8	8.6	•	8.8	•	•	•

Selected Average Balance Sheet ($ in Thousands)

Line Item										
Net Receivables 23	1035	•	13	191	706	1520	3858	8828	•	29099
Inventories 24	975	•	4	248	472	2005	3478	8231	•	29300
Net Property, Plant and Equipment 25	1175	•	18	36	673	1602	3771	9720	•	39734
Total Assets 26	4791	•	51	894	2256	7230	13908	37530	•	133508
Notes and Loans Payable 27	1222	•	14	129	674	1449	3381	6368	•	37952
All Other Liabilities 28	1155	•	6	191	640	1012	3419	7473	•	34174
Net Worth 29	2413	•	32	574	941	4769	7108	23689	•	61382

Selected Financial Ratios (Times to 1)

Line Item										
Current Ratio 30	2.2	•	6.3	3.7	1.8	2.4	2.1	2.4	•	2.2
Quick Ratio 31	1.2	•	6.2	2.6	1.1	1.4	1.2	1.5	•	1.2
Net Sales to Working Capital 32	5.0	•	3.0	2.7	8.7	5.3	6.5	4.3	•	5.0
Coverage Ratio 33	8.0	•	14.5	7.4	7.0	14.9	11.9	11.4	•	6.4
Total Asset Turnover 34	1.5	•	1.7	1.8	2.7	1.5	2.2	1.5	•	1.5
Inventory Turnover 35	5.4	•	8.0	3.9	8.5	3.6	6.6	4.9	•	4.9
Receivables Turnover 36	6.7	•	4.9	6.0	8.2	5.8	•	5.4	•	•
Total Liabilities to Net Worth 37	1.0	•	0.6	0.6	1.4	0.5	1.0	0.6	•	1.2
Current Assets to Working Capital 38	1.8	•	1.2	1.4	2.2	1.7	1.9	1.7	•	1.8
Current Liabilities to Working Capital 39	0.8	•	0.2	0.4	1.2	0.7	0.9	0.7	•	0.8
Working Capital to Net Sales 40	0.2	•	0.3	0.4	0.1	0.2	0.2	0.2	•	0.2
Inventory to Working Capital 41	0.7	•	0.0	0.4	0.6	0.6	0.7	0.6	•	0.8
Total Receipts to Cash Flow 42	8.3	•	2.3	6.9	11.9	6.0	9.5	8.4	•	9.3
Cost of Goods to Cash Flow 43	5.9	•	0.7	4.3	8.0	3.9	7.2	6.2	•	6.8
Cash Flow to Total Debt 44	0.4	•	2.0	0.7	0.4	0.8	0.5	0.5	•	0.3

Selected Financial Factors (in Percentages)

Line Item										
Debt Ratio 45	49.6	•	37.5	35.8	58.3	34.0	48.9	36.9	•	54.0
Return on Total Assets 46	15.0	•	37.9	9.3	18.2	16.4	19.0	12.9	•	14.1
Return on Equity Before Income Taxes 47	26.1	•	56.4	12.5	37.3	23.2	34.0	18.6	•	25.8
Return on Equity After Income Taxes 48	23.3	•	56.3	11.9	35.8	21.0	31.4	15.8	•	21.9
Profit Margin (Before Income Tax) 49	8.7	•	20.8	4.5	5.8	9.9	8.0	8.1	•	8.2
Profit Margin (After Income Tax) 50	7.7	•	20.7	4.3	5.6	9.0	7.3	6.9	•	7.0

Table I

Corporations with and without Net Income

CUTLERY, HARDWARE, SPRING AND WIRE MACHINE SHOPS, NUT, BOLT

MONEY AMOUNTS AND SIZE OF ASSETS IN THOUSANDS OF DOLLARS

Item Description for Accounting Period 7/07 Through 6/08		Total	Zero Assets	Under 500	500 to 1,000	1,000 to 5,000	5,000 to 10,000	10,000 to 25,000	25,000 to 50,000	50,000 to 100,000	100,000 to 250,000	250,000 to 500,000	500,000 to 2,500,000	2,500,000 and over
Number of Enterprises	1	22397	4273	13105	1487	2569	475	336	78	28	22	11	13	0
Revenues ($ in Thousands)														
Net Sales	2	69173555	1646816	6115796	3084928	10507783	5800601	8983997	4088442	2656229	3692505	4094687	18501773	0
Interest	3	385679	641	5364	4358	14597	11267	6863	16472	4194	13593	6224	302105	0
Rents	4	36121	0	0	6264	7324	857	1654	5447	601	6776	807	6393	0
Royalties	5	128059	0	29	0	0	0	10	201	1784	3548	3370	119119	0
Other Portfolio Income	6	528843	31071	54386	9692	49731	2815	40056	4684	17288	18095	64343	236680	0
Other Receipts	7	810002	8850	10066	5856	72563	34401	51131	24280	13753	208327	8716	372057	0
Total Receipts	8	71062259	1687378	6185641	3111098	10651998	5849941	9083711	4139526	2693849	3942844	4178147	19538127	0
Average Total Receipts	9	3173	395	472	2092	4146	12316	27035	53071	96209	179220	379832	1502933	•
Operating Costs/Operating Income (%)														
Cost of Operations	10	64.1	66.9	50.6	60.7	63.1	65.1	68.8	71.8	68.7	72.4	64.8	62.7	•
Salaries and Wages	11	7.4	7.7	10.9	4.3	6.7	4.8	6.1	4.7	6.2	8.3	10.3	8.6	•
Taxes Paid	12	2.2	1.9	3.1	4.0	3.1	2.5	2.1	1.9	2.0	1.8	1.9	1.3	•
Interest Paid	13	2.8	1.0	1.0	1.8	1.7	0.9	1.3	1.1	1.6	1.9	3.8	6.1	•
Depreciation	14	2.7	3.3	3.5	4.8	4.0	2.8	2.4	2.5	2.9	2.7	2.0	1.4	•
Amortization and Depletion	15	0.8	0.1	0.0	0.1	0.1	0.0	0.2	0.3	0.5	0.6	1.2	2.2	•
Pensions and Other Deferred Comp.	16	0.5	1.3	0.8	0.8	0.4	0.5	0.5	0.5	0.5	0.8	0.6	0.3	•
Employee Benefits	17	1.9	1.1	1.1	2.8	1.9	1.5	2.0	1.5	1.6	2.0	2.5	2.2	•
Advertising	18	0.7	0.4	0.3	0.2	0.3	0.4	0.8	0.3	0.9	0.6	1.6	1.2	•
Other Expenses	19	11.3	13.9	16.4	10.6	9.7	9.3	8.1	7.2	6.8	8.4	10.0	15.1	•
Officers' Compensation	20	3.3	1.9	8.3	7.8	6.7	4.9	2.6	1.4	1.9	0.8	0.6	0.5	•
Operating Margin	21	2.3	0.4	4.0	2.2	2.4	7.1	5.2	6.8	6.5	•	0.8	•	•
Operating Margin Before Officers' Comp.	22	5.6	2.3	12.2	9.9	9.0	12.0	7.8	8.2	8.3	0.5	1.4	•	•

Selected Average Balance Sheet ($ in Thousands)

Net Receivables 23	534	0	34	186	434	1308	3392	7090	14259	30459	63839	463641
Inventories 24	362	0	19	100	373	1914	3927	8124	17057	27570	76424	151164
Net Property, Plant and Equipment 25	419	0	43	286	738	1783	4024	7551	18231	35039	44871	148960
Total Assets 26	3320	0	161	752	2192	6885	15386	31856	70170	168678	368848	3448861
Notes and Loans Payable 27	1393	0	93	441	1044	1384	5052	7319	18712	51800	182090	1541554
All Other Liabilities 28	682	0	85	184	493	1409	3006	6914	17090	35374	96919	621272
Net Worth 29	1245	0	-17	127	655	4092	7328	17622	34368	81504	89839	1286035

Selected Financial Ratios (Times to 1)

Current Ratio 30	1.9	•	1.0	1.4	1.7	2.4	2.0	2.6	2.3	1.9	1.7	2.1
Quick Ratio 31	1.2	•	0.8	1.0	1.1	1.3	1.1	1.3	1.2	0.9	0.8	1.6
Net Sales to Working Capital 32	5.7	•	113.1	17.5	9.1	4.7	5.5	4.4	4.5	4.7	5.4	3.8
Coverage Ratio 33	3.0	3.8	6.1	2.7	3.2	9.7	5.8	8.0	6.3	4.4	1.8	1.9
Total Asset Turnover 34	0.9	•	2.9	2.8	1.9	1.8	1.7	1.6	1.4	1.0	1.0	0.4
Inventory Turnover 35	5.5	•	12.5	12.6	6.9	4.2	4.7	4.6	3.8	4.4	3.2	5.9
Receivables Turnover 36	6.5	•	13.8	9.8	9.3	8.0	7.9	7.7	6.2	5.6	5.2	4.1
Total Liabilities to Net Worth 37	1.7	•	•	4.9	2.3	0.7	1.1	0.8	1.0	1.1	3.1	1.7
Current Assets to Working Capital 38	2.1	•	23.7	3.5	2.5	1.7	2.0	1.6	1.8	2.1	2.4	1.9
Current Liabilities to Working Capital 39	1.1	•	22.7	2.5	1.5	0.7	1.0	0.6	0.8	1.1	1.4	0.9
Working Capital to Net Sales 40	0.2	•	0.0	0.1	0.1	0.2	0.2	0.2	0.2	0.2	0.2	0.3
Inventory to Working Capital 41	0.7	•	4.3	0.8	0.7	0.8	0.7	0.7	0.7	0.8	1.0	0.4
Total Receipts to Cash Flow 42	7.4	7.9	6.0	9.6	10.3	7.9	8.2	7.3	7.6	7.5	10.4	5.8
Cost of Goods to Cash Flow 43	4.7	5.3	3.0	5.8	6.5	5.1	5.6	5.2	5.2	5.4	6.8	3.7
Cash Flow to Total Debt 44	0.2	•	0.4	0.3	0.3	0.6	0.4	0.5	0.3	0.3	0.1	0.1

Selected Financial Factors (in Percentages)

Debt Ratio 45	62.5	•	110.8	83.1	70.1	40.6	52.4	44.7	51.0	51.7	75.6	62.7
Return on Total Assets 46	7.6	•	17.7	13.3	10.2	15.7	13.2	15.1	13.3	8.3	6.9	4.7
Return on Equity Before Income Taxes 47	13.4	•	•	49.5	23.3	23.8	22.9	23.8	22.8	13.3	12.5	5.8
Return on Equity After Income Taxes 48	11.1	•	•	47.6	19.1	21.0	20.5	21.8	19.3	11.2	8.7	3.8
Profit Margin (Before Income Tax) 49	5.4	2.9	5.1	3.0	3.7	8.0	6.3	8.0	8.2	6.5	3.0	5.2
Profit Margin (After Income Tax) 50	4.5	2.8	5.0	2.9	3.1	7.0	5.6	7.3	7.0	5.4	2.1	3.4

Table II

Corporations with Net Income

CUTLERY, HARDWARE, SPRING AND WIRE MACHINE SHOPS, NUT, BOLT

MONEY AMOUNTS AND SIZE OF ASSETS IN THOUSANDS OF DOLLARS

Item Description for Accounting Period 7/07 Through 6/08	Total	Zero Assets	Under 500	500 to 1,000	1,000 to 5,000	5,000 to 10,000	10,000 to 25,000	25,000 to 50,000	50,000 to 100,000	100,000 to 250,000	250,000 to 500,000	500,000 to 2,500,000	2,500,000 and over
Number of Enterprises 1	12778	851	8415	1020	1721	383	266	66	23	16	7	9	0
Revenues ($ in Thousands)													
Net Sales 2	56770823	1119953	4679747	2502368	8038558	4941259	7518085	3379296	2300993	3044845	2944200	16301519	0
Interest 3	359733	144	3883	3465	11459	11121	4488	15785	3947	10718	4193	290530	0
Rents 4	23018	0	0	0	3808	857	981	5447	601	6637	807	3880	0
Royalties 5	125908	0	0	0	0	0	10	201	1784	3536	2340	118037	0
Other Portfolio Income 6	440256	26734	9977	745	33901	2800	39269	3081	16734	16797	60303	229913	0
Other Receipts 7	742531	10255	2723	5095	67152	30330	35617	26295	12518	201943	6376	344228	0
Total Receipts 8	58462269	1157086	4696330	2511673	8154878	4986367	7598450	3430105	2336577	3284476	3018219	17288107	0
Average Total Receipts 9	4575	1360	558	2462	4738	13019	28566	51971	101590	205280	431174	1920901	•
Operating Costs/Operating Income (%)													
Cost of Operations 10	62.7	72.4	51.4	60.5	61.1	62.4	67.6	68.5	67.3	69.9	63.8	60.8	•
Salaries and Wages 11	7.3	3.9	7.5	2.7	6.8	5.1	6.2	5.1	6.5	9.2	11.1	9.1	•
Taxes Paid 12	2.1	1.6	2.5	3.9	2.9	2.5	2.1	2.0	1.9	2.0	1.8	1.3	•
Interest Paid 13	2.8	0.5	0.7	1.1	1.3	0.7	1.1	1.1	1.4	1.3	3.0	6.7	•
Depreciation 14	2.4	2.0	3.6	4.4	3.5	2.6	2.3	2.8	2.4	2.6	1.4	1.3	•
Amortization and Depletion 15	0.8	0.0	0.0	0.0	0.1	0.0	0.1	0.2	0.3	0.3	0.6	2.3	•
Pensions and Other Deferred Comp. 16	0.5	1.8	0.6	0.9	0.5	0.6	0.5	0.5	0.4	0.9	0.5	0.2	•
Employee Benefits 17	2.0	1.3	0.8	2.9	1.8	1.6	2.0	1.8	1.7	2.1	2.5	2.3	•
Advertising 18	0.6	0.2	0.4	0.3	0.2	0.4	0.7	0.3	1.1	0.7	1.3	0.9	•
Other Expenses 19	11.4	6.7	15.4	10.2	9.6	10.0	7.6	7.6	7.1	9.0	9.9	15.8	•
Officers' Compensation 20	3.1	1.5	7.7	7.3	7.3	4.7	2.6	1.6	1.9	0.9	0.5	0.5	•
Operating Margin 21	4.4	8.1	9.5	6.0	5.0	9.5	7.2	8.4	8.1	1.0	3.5	•	•
Operating Margin Before Officers' Comp. 22	7.6	9.6	17.2	13.3	12.3	14.1	9.7	10.0	10.1	1.9	4.0	•	•

Selected Average Balance Sheet ($ in Thousands)

	•	•	•	•	•	•	•	•	•	•	•	•
Net Receivables 23	814	0	34	216	528	1362	3523	7202	15496	35008	77819	620723
Inventories 24	518	0	16	108	474	2145	4296	8723	17719	31737	78735	180752
Net Property, Plant and Equipment 25	538	0	47	227	650	1589	3972	8062	17145	36157	46718	180322
Total Assets 26	5019	0	154	766	2287	6975	15297	32048	70359	166398	359714	4718728
Notes and Loans Payable 27	2033	0	76	381	829	1103	4635	6839	18588	39292	153982	2142621
All Other Liabilities 28	955	0	32	175	458	1567	3024	7032	17653	35695	97975	826027
Net Worth 29	2031	0	45	210	1000	4305	7638	18177	34419	91410	107756	1750080

Selected Financial Ratios (Times to 1)

	•	•	•	•	•	•	•	•	•	•	•	•
Current Ratio 30	2.2	•	2.1	2.2	2.3	2.5	2.2	2.8	2.3	2.0	1.8	2.3
Quick Ratio 31	1.5	•	1.6	1.5	1.5	1.3	1.2	1.4	1.2	1.1	0.9	1.8
Net Sales to Working Capital 32	4.8	•	10.8	9.3	6.2	4.6	5.4	3.9	4.4	4.6	5.6	3.4
Coverage Ratio 33	3.8	24.5	15.0	6.9	6.0	16.1	8.3	9.7	8.3	7.8	3.1	1.9
Total Asset Turnover 34	0.9	•	3.6	3.2	2.0	1.8	1.8	1.6	1.4	1.1	1.2	0.4
Inventory Turnover 35	5.4	•	17.8	13.7	6.0	3.8	4.5	4.0	3.8	4.2	3.4	6.1
Receivables Turnover 36	6.2	•	16.9	11.1	8.6	7.6	7.7	•	6.2	5.4	4.5	•
Total Liabilities to Net Worth 37	1.5	•	2.4	2.6	1.3	0.6	1.0	0.8	1.1	0.8	2.3	1.7
Current Assets to Working Capital 38	1.8	•	1.9	1.9	1.8	1.7	1.8	1.5	1.8	2.0	2.3	1.8
Current Liabilities to Working Capital 39	0.8	•	0.9	0.9	0.8	0.7	0.8	0.5	0.8	1.0	1.3	0.8
Working Capital to Net Sales 40	0.2	•	0.1	0.1	0.2	0.2	0.2	0.3	0.2	0.2	0.2	0.3
Inventory to Working Capital 41	0.5	•	0.3	0.4	0.6	0.7	0.8	0.7	0.7	0.7	0.9	0.3
Total Receipts to Cash Flow 42	6.3	6.2	4.9	7.4	8.1	6.4	7.3	6.2	6.6	6.2	8.1	5.4
Cost of Goods to Cash Flow 43	3.9	4.5	2.5	4.4	5.0	4.0	5.0	4.2	4.4	4.3	5.2	3.3
Cash Flow to Total Debt 44	0.2	•	1.0	0.6	0.4	0.8	0.5	0.6	0.4	0.4	0.2	0.1

Selected Financial Factors (in Percentages)

	•	•	•	•	•	•	•	•	•	•	•	•
Debt Ratio 45	59.5	•	70.7	72.5	56.3	38.3	50.1	43.3	51.5	45.1	70.0	62.9
Return on Total Assets 46	9.4	•	38.3	24.0	15.7	20.4	17.3	17.7	16.3	11.7	10.7	5.0
Return on Equity Before Income Taxes 47	17.1	•	121.8	74.6	30.0	31.0	30.5	28.0	29.6	18.6	24.0	6.4
Return on Equity After Income Taxes 48	14.5	•	120.2	73.0	26.0	27.8	27.6	25.6	25.3	16.1	19.0	4.4
Profit Margin (Before Income Tax) 49	7.8	11.4	9.9	6.4	6.4	10.4	8.2	9.9	10.1	9.0	6.2	6.2
Profit Margin (After Income Tax) 50	6.6	11.3	9.8	6.3	5.6	9.3	7.5	9.1	8.6	7.7	4.9	4.2

Table I

Corporations with and without Net Income

ARCHITECTURAL AND STRUCTURAL METALS

MONEY AMOUNTS AND SIZE OF ASSETS IN THOUSANDS OF DOLLARS

Item Description for Accounting Period 7/07 Through 6/08	Total	Zero Assets	Under 500	500 to 1,000	1,000 to 5,000	5,000 to 10,000	10,000 to 25,000	25,000 to 50,000	50,000 to 100,000	100,000 to 250,000	250,000 to 500,000	500,000 to 2,500,000	2,500,000 and over
Number of Enterprises 1	6917	290	3350	671	1753	472	242	82	24	14	7	10	0
Revenues ($ in Thousands)													
Net Sales 2	56046682	554131	2532305	1954668	9375270	7137568	7966554	5342833	2825743	3529960	3048653	11778997	0
Interest 3	351611	424	856	3637	6263	5171	6749	6828	2100	10474	3787	305324	0
Rents 4	10367	0	0	0	756	1006	1965	424	325	567	0	5325	0
Royalties 5	34464	0	0	0	0	0	0	16	0	165	4	34279	0
Other Portfolio Income 6	541097	309	1298	222	22412	30621	3444	39594	8377	4638	1415	428766	0
Other Receipts 7	515692	10763	4892	8011	24182	24331	44943	25132	60093	15887	52069	245386	0
Total Receipts 8	57499913	565627	2539351	1966538	9428883	7198697	8023655	5414827	2896638	3561691	3105928	12798077	0
Average Total Receipts 9	8313	1950	758	2931	5379	15251	33156	66034	120693	254406	443704	1279808	•
Operating Costs/Operating Income (%)													
Cost of Operations 10	70.7	77.1	64.4	65.7	67.7	72.1	74.6	76.7	72.9	73.1	78.4	65.5	•
Salaries and Wages 11	6.1	5.1	6.3	6.7	5.8	5.0	5.5	5.8	4.7	7.4	5.0	7.9	•
Taxes Paid 12	2.0	2.8	2.5	2.9	2.4	2.0	1.5	1.6	1.7	1.8	1.2	2.1	•
Interest Paid 13	2.2	0.5	0.7	0.3	0.8	0.9	0.8	1.1	1.2	1.7	2.8	6.3	•
Depreciation 14	2.3	2.1	1.6	1.3	1.5	2.0	1.4	1.8	4.2	1.5	3.1	3.7	•
Amortization and Depletion 15	0.3	0.6	0.0	0.2	0.0	0.1	0.1	0.1	0.3	0.2	0.6	0.8	•
Pensions and Other Deferred Comp. 16	0.6	1.0	0.2	0.7	0.5	0.6	0.5	0.4	0.3	0.4	0.2	0.9	•
Employee Benefits 17	1.8	0.9	1.4	1.8	2.4	1.0	1.4	1.4	1.2	1.4	0.8	2.7	•
Advertising 18	0.6	0.6	0.2	0.6	0.3	0.3	0.2	0.5	0.5	0.9	0.3	1.3	•
Other Expenses 19	8.7	8.1	13.9	12.6	9.5	8.5	6.6	6.1	7.1	7.7	4.4	10.7	•
Officers' Compensation 20	2.1	0.2	5.8	4.3	3.6	3.1	1.8	1.2	1.0	1.1	0.8	0.6	•
Operating Margin 21	2.8	1.1	3.0	2.8	5.4	4.4	5.6	3.4	4.8	2.7	2.5	•	•
Operating Margin Before Officers' Comp. 22	4.9	1.3	8.8	7.1	9.0	7.5	7.4	4.6	5.7	3.8	3.3	•	•

Selected Average Balance Sheet ($ in Thousands)

Net Receivables 23	1339	0	68	198	760	2514	5390	9200	20437	32930	81198	280603
Inventories 24	699	0	22	198	390	1275	3168	6204	13968	28011	33560	110183
Net Property, Plant and Equipment 25	1136	0	31	127	464	1673	3166	7982	15988	40854	95297	302147
Total Assets 26	5063	0	163	695	2165	6697	15475	34560	72611	166266	307475	1425319
Notes and Loans Payable 27	1798	0	128	73	681	1813	4002	10498	17954	58502	121548	598262
All Other Liabilities 28	1471	0	53	96	698	1947	5294	8880	19623	57807	81903	392491
Net Worth 29	1795	0	-17	526	786	2938	6179	15183	35034	49957	104024	434566

Selected Financial Ratios (Times to 1)

Current Ratio 30	1.9	•	1.6	4.7	2.0	1.8	1.7	1.8	1.9	1.7	1.7	2.0
Quick Ratio 31	1.2	•	1.2	3.7	1.4	1.2	1.1	1.1	1.2	0.9	1.1	1.3
Net Sales to Working Capital 32	6.5	•	17.1	7.0	6.9	7.2	7.3	6.3	6.1	7.0	6.9	4.7
Coverage Ratio 33	3.6	7.2	5.8	13.0	8.9	6.7	8.6	5.4	6.9	3.1	2.6	2.0
Total Asset Turnover 34	1.6	•	4.6	4.2	2.5	2.3	2.1	1.9	1.6	1.5	1.4	0.8
Inventory Turnover 35	8.2	•	21.8	9.6	9.3	8.6	7.8	8.1	6.1	6.6	10.2	7.0
Receivables Turnover 36	6.1	•	12.0	9.8	6.7	7.2	6.3	7.8	6.5	6.0	6.6	4.0
Total Liabilities to Net Worth 37	1.8	•	•	0.3	1.8	1.3	1.5	1.3	1.1	2.3	2.0	2.3
Current Assets to Working Capital 38	2.1	•	2.8	1.3	2.0	2.2	2.4	2.3	2.1	2.5	2.5	2.0
Current Liabilities to Working Capital 39	1.1	•	1.8	0.3	1.0	1.2	1.4	1.3	1.1	1.5	1.5	1.0
Working Capital to Net Sales 40	0.2	•	0.1	0.1	0.1	0.1	0.1	0.2	0.2	0.1	0.1	0.2
Inventory to Working Capital 41	0.5	•	0.5	0.2	0.5	0.6	0.7	0.7	0.7	0.7	0.4	0.5
Total Receipts to Cash Flow 42	9.1	9.9	8.7	9.6	8.5	8.1	8.9	11.9	7.8	10.3	13.6	8.5
Cost of Goods to Cash Flow 43	6.4	7.7	5.6	6.3	5.7	5.9	6.6	9.1	5.7	7.5	10.7	5.6
Cash Flow to Total Debt 44	0.3	•	0.5	1.8	0.5	0.5	0.4	0.3	0.4	0.2	0.2	0.1

Selected Financial Factors (in Percentages)

Debt Ratio 45	64.6	•	110.6	24.3	63.7	56.1	60.1	56.1	51.8	70.0	66.2	69.5
Return on Total Assets 46	12.2	•	18.2	15.3	16.5	14.0	15.3	11.0	13.7	8.2	10.1	10.5
Return on Equity Before Income Taxes 47	24.8	•	•	18.7	40.4	27.2	33.8	20.4	24.4	18.4	18.2	17.5
Return on Equity After Income Taxes 48	20.3	•	•	18.3	36.8	24.5	30.7	16.6	22.4	14.7	12.2	10.6
Profit Margin (Before Income Tax) 49	5.5	3.2	3.2	3.4	5.9	5.3	6.3	4.7	7.3	3.6	4.4	6.4
Profit Margin (After Income Tax) 50	4.5	2.7	3.1	3.3	5.4	4.8	5.8	3.9	6.7	2.9	2.9	3.9

Table II

Corporations with Net Income

ARCHITECTURAL AND STRUCTURAL METALS

MONEY AMOUNTS AND SIZE OF ASSETS IN THOUSANDS OF DOLLARS

Item Description for Accounting Period 7/07 Through 6/08	Total	Zero Assets	Under 500	500 to 1,000	1,000 to 5,000	5,000 to 10,000	10,000 to 25,000	25,000 to 50,000	50,000 to 100,000	100,000 to 250,000	250,000 to 500,000	500,000 to 2,500,000	2,500,000 and over
Number of Enterprises **1**	4422	•	1961	422	1278	420	204	59	19	•	•	7	0
Revenues ($ in Thousands)													
Net Sales **2**	46745687	•	2159706	1477941	7008364	6155566	7227348	4215124	2325636	•	•	10646556	0
Interest **3**	333085	•	519	2902	5426	4930	6043	6333	615	•	•	294021	0
Rents **4**	9771	•	0	0	419	992	1965	424	325	•	•	5324	0
Royalties **5**	34308	•	0	0	0	0	0	16	0	•	•	34127	0
Other Portfolio Income **6**	525345	•	1298	213	20270	30511	2516	36938	8377	•	•	419196	0
Other Receipts **7**	387571	•	1844	4599	22327	17226	36161	13376	59384	•	•	176251	0
Total Receipts **8**	48035767	•	2163367	1485655	7056806	6209225	7274033	4272211	2394337	•	•	11575475	0
Average Total Receipts **9**	10863	•	1103	3521	5522	14784	35657	72410	126018	•	•	1653639	•
Operating Costs/Operating Income (%)													
Cost of Operations **10**	70.0	•	62.7	64.2	65.3	70.3	74.0	75.7	72.1	•	•	66.7	•
Salaries and Wages **11**	6.0	•	6.4	6.5	6.0	5.0	5.5	5.5	4.3	•	•	7.4	•
Taxes Paid **12**	1.9	•	2.5	2.6	2.4	2.0	1.5	1.6	1.7	•	•	2.1	•
Interest Paid **13**	1.9	•	0.7	0.3	0.6	0.8	0.7	0.8	0.9	•	•	5.7	•
Depreciation **14**	2.1	•	1.5	1.4	1.6	2.1	1.2	1.6	4.6	•	•	3.0	•
Amortization and Depletion **15**	0.2	•	0.0	0.2	0.0	0.1	0.0	0.0	0.2	•	•	0.7	•
Pensions and Other Deferred Comp. **16**	0.5	•	0.3	0.8	0.7	0.7	0.5	0.4	0.2	•	•	0.6	•
Employee Benefits **17**	1.5	•	0.9	1.3	1.6	0.9	1.4	1.3	0.7	•	•	2.8	•
Advertising **18**	0.5	•	0.2	0.7	0.3	0.3	0.2	0.3	0.3	•	•	1.3	•
Other Expenses **19**	8.3	•	13.4	12.8	9.0	8.6	6.4	5.3	7.2	•	•	10.2	•
Officers' Compensation **20**	2.1	•	5.7	2.9	4.0	3.3	1.8	1.2	1.0	•	•	0.5	•
Operating Margin **21**	4.8	•	5.7	6.2	8.6	6.0	6.9	6.3	6.9	•	•	6.9	•
Operating Margin Before Officers' Comp. **22**	6.8	•	11.5	9.1	12.5	9.3	8.7	7.4	7.8	•	•	7.8	•

Selected Average Balance Sheet ($ in Thousands)

Line Item									
Net Receivables 23	1737	107	202	824	2533	5682	9992	21508	322254
Inventories 24	886	24	209	325	1128	3279	7038	12952	156741
Net Property, Plant and Equipment 25	1300	35	150	440	1731	2991	6867	16326	299868
Total Assets 26	6257	230	689	2152	6674	15494	34284	72905	1675919
Notes and Loans Payable 27	2089	86	73	608	1514	3671	8476	14380	710463
All Other Liabilities 28	1789	76	82	650	1791	5443	8634	20127	448821
Net Worth 29	2379	68	534	893	3368	6380	17174	38398	516635

Selected Financial Ratios (Times to 1)

Line Item								
Current Ratio 30	1.9	1.5	4.2	2.2	1.8	2.0	1.8	1.9
Quick Ratio 31	1.3	1.2	3.5	1.7	1.2	1.2	1.1	1.1
Net Sales to Working Capital 32	6.4	18.9	8.6	5.9	6.8	5.9	6.8	5.4
Coverage Ratio 33	5.0	8.9	23.7	16.7	12.5	10.5	11.9	2.4
Total Asset Turnover 34	1.7	4.8	5.1	2.5	2.3	2.1	1.7	0.9
Inventory Turnover 35	8.4	28.9	10.8	11.0	8.0	7.7	6.8	6.5
Receivables Turnover 36	6.1	12.5	13.6	6.2	6.4	7.2	•	6.5
Total Liabilities to Net Worth 37	1.6	2.4	0.3	1.4	1.4	1.0	0.9	2.2
Current Assets to Working Capital 38	2.1	3.0	1.3	1.8	2.2	2.0	2.2	2.2
Current Liabilities to Working Capital 39	1.1	2.0	0.3	0.8	1.2	1.0	1.2	1.2
Working Capital to Net Sales 40	0.2	0.1	0.1	0.2	0.1	0.2	0.1	0.2
Inventory to Working Capital 41	0.5	0.4	0.2	0.3	0.6	0.6	0.7	0.6
Total Receipts to Cash Flow 42	7.8	7.4	7.5	7.0	8.1	9.5	6.5	7.8
Cost of Goods to Cash Flow 43	5.5	4.7	4.8	4.6	6.0	7.2	4.7	5.2
Cash Flow to Total Debt 44	0.3	0.9	3.0	0.6	0.5	0.4	0.5	0.2

Selected Financial Factors (in Percentages)

Line Item									
Debt Ratio 45	62.0	70.5	22.5	58.5	49.5	58.8	49.9	47.3	69.2
Return on Total Assets 46	16.1	31.9	35.8	25.0	16.7	18.7	17.5	18.0	12.4
Return on Equity Before Income Taxes 47	33.8	95.8	44.3	56.7	29.7	41.8	31.6	31.3	23.6
Return on Equity After Income Taxes 48	28.4	94.0	43.8	52.4	27.1	38.2	27.0	29.0	15.4
Profit Margin (Before Income Tax) 49	7.6	5.9	6.8	9.2	6.8	7.5	7.6	9.8	8.0
Profit Margin (After Income Tax) 50	6.4	5.8	6.7	8.5	6.2	6.9	6.5	9.1	5.2

Table I

Corporations with and without Net Income

BOILER, TANK, AND SHIPPING CONTAINER

MONEY AMOUNTS AND SIZE OF ASSETS IN THOUSANDS OF DOLLARS

Item Description for Accounting Period 7/07 Through 6/08	Total	Zero Assets	Under 500	500 to 1,000	1,000 to 5,000	5,000 to 10,000	10,000 to 25,000	25,000 to 50,000	50,000 to 100,000	100,000 to 250,000	250,000 to 500,000	500,000 to 2,500,000	2,500,000 and over
Number of Enterprises **1**	546	•	•	•	167	42	61	20	11	7	3	4	3
Revenues ($ in Thousands)													
Net Sales **2**	23362121	•	•	•	802466	728935	1803023	1133212	846637	1357786	1677486	3523868	10939150
Interest **3**	47378	•	•	•	585	527	3461	1008	1215	3019	19838	1233	16492
Rents **4**	14254	•	•	•	1815	1064	2	225	2	702	777	54	9613
Royalties **5**	124209	•	•	•	0	0	0	0	0	569	107	19529	104004
Other Portfolio Income **6**	98982	•	•	•	9540	22430	3736	14858	274	94	4465	2482	35376
Other Receipts **7**	135909	•	•	•	33	6419	11593	3687	-3812	7337	20818	36566	52790
Total Receipts **8**	23782853	•	•	•	814439	759375	1821815	1152990	844316	1369507	1723491	3583732	11157425
Average Total Receipts **9**	43558	•	•	•	4877	18080	29866	57650	76756	195644	574497	895933	3719142
Operating Costs/Operating Income (%)													
Cost of Operations **10**	79.7	•	•	•	69.2	75.3	71.9	72.7	69.8	76.8	79.6	79.7	84.3
Salaries and Wages **11**	3.9	•	•	•	8.0	5.3	6.6	4.4	5.5	3.9	5.0	3.1	3.0
Taxes Paid **12**	1.2	•	•	•	2.7	1.5	1.5	2.2	1.3	0.9	1.6	1.2	0.9
Interest Paid **13**	2.7	•	•	•	0.1	0.8	0.7	1.2	2.6	2.4	2.1	4.0	3.1
Depreciation **14**	2.5	•	•	•	0.6	1.2	1.3	1.5	1.8	2.9	1.6	3.5	3.0
Amortization and Depletion **15**	0.5	•	•	•	•	0.2	0.1	0.3	1.7	0.2	0.6	0.6	0.6
Pensions and Other Deferred Comp. **16**	0.6	•	•	•	0.7	0.6	0.3	0.2	0.3	0.4	0.3	0.4	0.9
Employee Benefits **17**	1.9	•	•	•	2.8	1.1	1.2	2.5	2.4	0.8	0.8	0.8	2.7
Advertising **18**	0.2	•	•	•	0.8	0.2	1.1	0.2	0.3	0.2	0.3	0.0	0.0
Other Expenses **19**	3.2	•	•	•	6.1	5.2	6.6	6.8	8.3	6.3	1.2	3.6	1.0
Officers' Compensation **20**	1.0	•	•	•	4.6	2.3	2.6	1.6	1.1	2.3	0.1	0.2	0.4
Operating Margin **21**	2.6	•	•	•	4.5	6.3	6.0	6.4	4.9	2.9	6.9	2.9	0.1
Operating Margin Before Officers' Comp. **22**	3.6	•	•	•	9.1	8.5	8.6	8.0	6.0	5.2	7.0	3.1	0.5

Selected Average Balance Sheet ($ in Thousands)

Net Receivables 23	4809	565	2316	4149	8810	13283	28308	82160	84292	348562
Inventories 24	4776	536	1025	4157	5481	11542	24468	65731	109967	384488
Net Property, Plant and Equipment 25	7343	109	1465	2500	5414	11247	39129	29432	198433	784378
Total Assets 26	42893	1637	6867	16678	30164	72608	172166	314947	881978	4877441
Notes and Loans Payable 27	17722	66	1528	2348	8485	33945	65057	93252	398216	2146617
All Other Liabilities 28	11408	361	3935	5191	9645	11830	60381	122594	233370	1200921
Net Worth 29	13763	1211	1404	9139	12034	26833	46728	99100	250392	1529903

Selected Financial Ratios (Times to 1)

Current Ratio 30	1.3	3.7	1.1	2.4	2.1	1.7	1.0	1.8	1.4	0.9
Quick Ratio 31	0.6	2.2	0.8	1.4	1.3	1.0	0.5	1.1	0.7	0.4
Net Sales to Working Capital 32	16.1	4.4	28.3	4.4	5.0	5.9	58.5	6.1	12.5	•
Coverage Ratio 33	2.7	117.5	13.9	11.1	7.6	2.9	2.6	5.5	2.2	1.8
Total Asset Turnover 34	1.0	2.9	2.5	1.8	1.9	1.1	1.1	1.8	1.0	0.7
Inventory Turnover 35	7.1	6.2	12.7	5.1	7.5	4.7	6.1	6.8	6.4	8.0
Receivables Turnover 36	6.1	8.4	7.3	6.5	5.0	5.1	8.9	7.1	10.5	5.0
Total Liabilities to Net Worth 37	2.1	0.4	3.9	0.8	1.5	1.7	2.7	2.2	2.5	2.2
Current Assets to Working Capital 38	4.7	1.4	8.2	1.7	1.9	2.4	22.5	2.2	3.4	•
Current Liabilities to Working Capital 39	3.7	0.4	7.2	0.7	0.9	1.4	21.5	1.2	2.4	•
Working Capital to Net Sales 40	0.1	0.2	0.0	0.2	0.2	0.2	0.0	0.2	0.1	•
Inventory to Working Capital 41	1.9	0.5	1.8	0.6	0.5	0.7	10.1	0.5	1.5	•
Total Receipts to Cash Flow 42	16.5	11.6	6.9	8.1	7.7	8.8	11.8	11.3	14.4	52.7
Cost of Goods to Cash Flow 43	13.1	8.0	5.2	5.8	5.6	6.1	9.0	9.0	11.4	44.4
Cash Flow to Total Debt 44	0.1	1.0	0.5	0.5	0.4	0.2	0.1	0.2	0.1	0.0

Selected Financial Factors (in Percentages)

Debt Ratio 45	67.9	26.0	79.6	45.2	60.1	63.0	72.9	68.5	71.6	68.6
Return on Total Assets 46	7.2	17.7	27.9	13.6	17.6	8.2	7.0	20.8	8.6	4.0
Return on Equity Before Income Taxes 47	14.0	23.8	126.7	22.6	38.3	14.6	15.7	54.1	16.3	5.5
Return on Equity After Income Taxes 48	10.9	20.5	111.3	20.5	36.0	12.6	12.3	35.3	10.7	4.4
Profit Margin (Before Income Tax) 49	4.5	6.0	10.3	7.0	8.1	5.1	3.8	9.6	4.6	2.3
Profit Margin (After Income Tax) 50	3.5	5.2	9.0	6.4	7.6	4.4	3.0	6.2	3.1	1.9

Table II

Corporations with Net Income

BOILER, TANK, AND SHIPPING CONTAINER

Money Amounts and Size of Assets in Thousands of Dollars

Revenues ($ in Thousands)

Item Description for Accounting Period 7/07 Through 6/08	Total	Zero Assets	Under 500	500 to 1,000	1,000 to 5,000	5,000 to 10,000	10,000 to 25,000	25,000 to 50,000	50,000 to 100,000	100,000 to 250,000	250,000 to 500,000	500,000 to 2,500,000	2,500,000 and over
Number of Enterprises 1	483	•	0	168	167	37	55	•	7	•	3	4	3
Net Sales 2	22779197	•	0	184597	802466	684324	1709866	•	670764	•	1677486	3523868	10939150
Interest 3	45064	•	0	0	585	527	1669	•	1136	•	19838	1233	16492
Rents 4	13551	•	0	0	1815	1064	2	•	2	•	777	54	9613
Royalties 5	124174	•	0	0	0	0	0	•	0	•	107	19529	104004
Other Portfolio Income 6	98542	•	0	0	9540	22430	3653	•	68	•	4465	2482	35376
Other Receipts 7	131765	•	0	439	33	6488	10197	•	-4287	•	20818	36566	52790
Total Receipts 8	23210293	•	0	185036	814439	714833	1725387	•	667683	•	1723491	3583732	11157425
Average Total Receipts 9	48054	•	•	1101	4877	19320	31371	•	95383	•	574497	895933	3719142

Operating Costs/Operating Income (%)

Item	Total	Zero Assets	Under 500	500 to 1,000	1,000 to 5,000	5,000 to 10,000	10,000 to 25,000	25,000 to 50,000	50,000 to 100,000	100,000 to 250,000	250,000 to 500,000	500,000 to 2,500,000	2,500,000 and over
Cost of Operations 10	79.8	•	•	59.7	69.2	73.7	72.0	•	68.5	•	79.6	79.7	84.3
Salaries and Wages 11	3.8	•	•	9.9	8.0	4.1	6.5	•	4.7	•	5.0	3.1	3.0
Taxes Paid 12	1.2	•	•	2.8	2.7	1.3	1.5	•	1.3	•	1.6	1.2	0.9
Interest Paid 13	2.5	•	•	0.3	0.1	0.8	0.5	•	1.1	•	2.1	4.0	3.1
Depreciation 14	2.5	•	•	0.5	0.6	1.2	1.2	•	1.2	•	1.6	3.5	3.0
Amortization and Depletion 15	0.5	•	•	•	•	0.2	0.0	•	0.5	•	0.6	0.6	0.6
Pensions and Other Deferred Comp. 16	0.6	•	•	0.8	0.7	0.7	0.3	•	0.2	•	0.3	0.4	0.9
Employee Benefits 17	1.9	•	•	0.2	2.8	0.9	1.2	•	1.9	•	0.8	0.8	2.7
Advertising 18	0.2	•	•	1.1	0.8	0.3	1.1	•	0.3	•	0.3	0.0	0.0
Other Expenses 19	3.0	•	•	8.6	6.1	4.8	6.6	•	8.0	•	1.2	3.6	1.0
Officers' Compensation 20	0.9	•	•	6.7	4.6	1.9	2.1	•	0.7	•	0.1	0.2	0.4
Operating Margin 21	3.1	•	•	9.4	4.5	10.1	6.8	•	11.5	•	6.9	2.9	0.1
Operating Margin Before Officers' Comp. 22	4.0	•	•	16.1	9.1	12.1	9.0	•	12.3	•	7.0	3.1	0.5

Selected Average Balance Sheet ($ in Thousands)

	1	2	3	4	5	6	7	8	9	10	11	12	13
Net Receivables 23	5222	•	•	170	565	2135	4414	•	16537	•	82160	84292	348562
Inventories 24	5180	•	•	110	507	1038	4078	•	8221	•	65731	109967	420257
Net Property, Plant and Equipment 25	8087	•	•	205	109	1566	2581	•	9925	•	29432	198433	784378
Total Assets 26	46618	•	•	580	1637	6776	16919	•	71063	•	314947	881978	4877441
Notes and Loans Payable 27	18627	•	•	73	66	1590	2138	•	19075	•	93252	398216	2146617
All Other Liabilities 28	12527	•	•	56	361	1778	5506	•	16052	•	122594	233370	1200921
Net Worth 29	15464	•	•	451	1211	3408	9275	•	35936	•	99100	250392	1529903

Selected Financial Ratios (Times to 1)

	1	2	3	4	5	6	7	8	9	10	11	12	13
Current Ratio 30	1.3	•	•	4.2	3.7	2.1	2.4	•	2.1	•	1.8	1.4	0.9
Quick Ratio 31	0.6	•	•	2.4	2.2	1.4	1.4	•	1.3	•	1.1	0.7	0.4
Net Sales to Working Capital 32	15.9	•	•	3.9	4.4	7.3	4.4	•	4.9	•	6.1	12.5	•
Coverage Ratio 33	3.0	•	•	38.7	117.5	18.4	15.4	•	10.9	•	5.5	2.2	1.8
Total Asset Turnover 34	1.0	•	•	1.9	2.9	2.7	1.8	•	1.3	•	1.8	1.0	0.7
Inventory Turnover 35	7.3	•	•	6.0	6.6	13.1	5.5	•	8.0	•	6.8	6.4	7.3
Receivables Turnover 36	9.1	•	•	4.3	9.3	•	•	•	•	•	7.1	10.5	•
Total Liabilities to Net Worth 37	2.0	•	•	0.3	0.4	1.0	0.8	•	1.0	•	2.2	2.5	2.2
Current Assets to Working Capital 38	4.5	•	•	1.3	1.4	1.9	1.7	•	1.9	•	2.2	3.4	•
Current Liabilities to Working Capital 39	3.5	•	•	0.3	0.4	0.9	0.7	•	0.9	•	1.2	2.4	•
Working Capital to Net Sales 40	0.1	•	•	0.3	0.2	0.1	0.2	•	0.2	•	0.2	0.1	•
Inventory to Working Capital 41	1.8	•	•	0.4	0.5	0.4	0.6	•	0.4	•	0.5	1.5	•
Total Receipts to Cash Flow 42	15.5	•	•	9.6	11.6	5.5	7.7	•	5.7	•	11.3	14.4	52.7
Cost of Goods to Cash Flow 43	12.4	•	•	5.7	8.0	4.0	5.6	•	3.9	•	9.0	11.4	44.4
Cash Flow to Total Debt 44	0.1	•	•	0.9	1.0	1.0	0.5	•	0.5	•	0.2	0.1	0.0

Selected Financial Factors (in Percentages)

	1	2	3	4	5	6	7	8	9	10	11	12	13
Debt Ratio 45	66.8	•	•	22.2	26.0	49.7	45.2	•	49.4	•	68.5	71.6	68.6
Return on Total Assets 46	7.7	•	•	18.7	17.7	41.5	15.1	•	16.4	•	20.8	8.6	4.0
Return on Equity Before Income Taxes 47	15.3	•	•	23.3	23.8	78.1	25.8	•	29.5	•	54.1	16.3	5.5
Return on Equity After Income Taxes 48	12.3	•	•	23.3	20.5	70.9	23.5	•	27.1	•	35.3	10.7	4.4
Profit Margin (Before Income Tax) 49	5.0	•	•	9.6	6.0	14.4	7.7	•	11.1	•	9.6	4.6	2.3
Profit Margin (After Income Tax) 50	4.0	•	•	9.6	5.2	13.1	7.0	•	10.2	•	6.2	3.1	1.9

Table I

Corporations with and without Net Income

COATING, ENGRAVING, HEAT TREATING, AND ALLIED ACTIVITIES

MONEY AMOUNTS AND SIZE OF ASSETS IN THOUSANDS OF DOLLARS

Item Description for Accounting Period 7/07 Through 6/08		Total	Zero Assets	Under 500	500 to 1,000	1,000 to 5,000	5,000 to 10,000	10,000 to 25,000	25,000 to 50,000	50,000 to 100,000	100,000 to 250,000	250,000 to 500,000	500,000 to 2,500,000	2,500,000 and over
Number of Enterprises	1	4076	•	•	•	700	101	57	17	11	9	0	5	0

Revenues ($ in Thousands)

Net Sales	2	16819059	•	•	•	3173061	958218	1066267	1142440	988278	1427386	0	5731383	0
Interest	3	123986	•	•	•	6649	3280	2424	1546	2121	10619	0	92007	0
Rents	4	10082	•	•	•	241	1924	0	917	1	817	0	686	0
Royalties	5	62984	•	•	•	0	0	0	0	21	16518	0	46393	0
Other Portfolio Income	6	53624	•	•	•	1981	55	219	1508	73	5440	0	10244	0
Other Receipts	7	112757	•	•	•	18177	9482	6121	3935	15049	7461	0	36190	0
Total Receipts	8	17182492	•	•	•	3200109	972959	1075031	1150346	1005543	1468241	0	5916903	0
Average Total Receipts	9	4216	•	•	•	4572	9633	18860	67667	91413	163138	•	1183381	•

Operating Costs/Operating Income (%)

Cost of Operations	10	64.0	•	•	•	53.2	63.0	57.4	75.0	71.8	66.5	•	75.1	•
Salaries and Wages	11	7.2	•	•	•	7.6	8.1	7.9	5.1	5.5	5.9	•	7.1	•
Taxes Paid	12	2.5	•	•	•	3.6	4.6	2.9	2.3	1.5	2.4	•	1.6	•
Interest Paid	13	3.1	•	•	•	1.3	1.6	1.6	1.3	1.8	5.0	•	5.6	•
Depreciation	14	2.7	•	•	•	2.9	3.0	4.0	3.2	4.0	4.9	•	1.8	•
Amortization and Depletion	15	0.6	•	•	•	0.0	0.1	0.3	0.2	0.4	1.9	•	1.2	•
Pensions and Other Deferred Comp.	16	0.8	•	•	•	1.2	1.7	1.1	0.3	0.6	0.4	•	0.7	•
Employee Benefits	17	1.8	•	•	•	3.0	2.1	2.1	1.9	1.5	1.8	•	1.3	•
Advertising	18	0.5	•	•	•	0.2	0.1	0.2	0.1	0.2	0.1	•	1.2	•
Other Expenses	19	11.3	•	•	•	12.8	9.1	9.9	4.7	7.1	6.4	•	9.2	•
Officers' Compensation	20	4.4	•	•	•	9.3	3.9	2.7	1.2	1.7	1.4	•	1.2	•
Operating Margin	21	1.0	•	•	•	4.8	2.8	9.8	4.6	4.0	3.4	•	•	•
Operating Margin Before Officers' Comp.	22	5.4	•	•	•	14.1	6.8	12.6	5.8	5.7	4.8	•	•	•

Selected Average Balance Sheet ($ in Thousands)

Net Receivables 23	702	508	1798	3073	7424	13230	26300	292616
Inventories 24	433	146	437	1038	6096	7295	31189	208963
Net Property, Plant and Equipment 25	866	696	2382	6093	14161	25239	59045	251946
Total Assets 26	4248	2043	7034	14883	35464	63710	182356	2161546
Notes and Loans Payable 27	1909	619	4781	5869	11106	14475	72530	1053002
All Other Liabilities 28	735	312	1300	2368	8265	19262	49786	320108
Net Worth 29	1604	1112	952	6646	16092	29973	60039	788436

Selected Financial Ratios (Times to 1)

Current Ratio 30	1.9	2.3	2.2	1.6	1.8	2.0	1.7	2.0
Quick Ratio 31	1.1	1.8	1.6	1.2	1.1	1.2	0.9	1.0
Net Sales to Working Capital 32	5.5	8.0	5.0	7.2	9.7	5.8	5.4	3.5
Coverage Ratio 33	2.0	5.4	3.7	7.6	4.9	4.2	2.3	0.5
Total Asset Turnover 34	1.0	2.2	1.3	1.3	1.9	1.4	0.9	0.5
Inventory Turnover 35	6.1	16.6	13.7	10.3	8.3	8.8	3.4	4.1
Receivables Turnover 36	6.5	8.8	6.2	6.9	6.8	8.5	4.2	5.0
Total Liabilities to Net Worth 37	1.6	0.8	6.4	1.2	1.2	1.1	2.0	1.7
Current Assets to Working Capital 38	2.1	1.7	1.8	2.7	2.3	2.0	2.3	2.0
Current Liabilities to Working Capital 39	1.1	0.7	0.8	1.7	1.3	1.0	1.3	1.0
Working Capital to Net Sales 40	0.2	0.1	0.2	0.1	0.1	0.2	0.2	0.3
Inventory to Working Capital 41	0.7	0.2	0.3	0.4	0.7	0.6	1.0	0.9
Total Receipts to Cash Flow 42	8.7	7.1	8.9	5.7	11.9	9.0	10.4	19.9
Cost of Goods to Cash Flow 43	5.6	3.8	5.6	3.3	8.9	6.5	6.9	14.9
Cash Flow to Total Debt 44	0.2	0.7	0.2	0.4	0.3	0.3	0.1	0.0

Selected Financial Factors (in Percentages)

Debt Ratio 45	62.2	45.6	86.5	55.3	54.6	53.0	67.1	63.5
Return on Total Assets 46	6.1	15.4	8.0	15.4	12.6	10.5	9.8	1.6
Return on Equity Before Income Taxes 47	8.3	23.1	43.3	29.9	22.1	17.1	16.6	
Return on Equity After Income Taxes 48	6.7	22.2	36.7	27.7	16.9	15.7	16.6	
Profit Margin (Before Income Tax) 49	3.2	5.7	4.3	10.6	5.3	5.7	7.3	
Profit Margin (After Income Tax) 50	2.6	5.5	3.7	9.8	4.0	5.2	6.3	2.8

Table II

Corporations with Net Income

COATING, ENGRAVING, HEAT TREATING, AND ALLIED ACTIVITIES

MONEY AMOUNTS AND SIZE OF ASSETS IN THOUSANDS OF DOLLARS

Item Description for Accounting Period 7/07 Through 6/08	Total	Zero Assets	Under 500	500 to 1,000	1,000 to 5,000	5,000 to 10,000	10,000 to 25,000	25,000 to 50,000	50,000 to 100,000	100,000 to 250,000	250,000 to 500,000	500,000 to 2,500,000	2,500,000 and over
Number of Enterprises 1	2445	•	1652	109	524	79	50	•	•	6	0	0	0
Revenues ($ in Thousands)													
Net Sales 2	9970531	•	1236959	264977	2453114	690759	991539	•	•	2304825	0	0	0
Interest 3	22810	•	1619	256	5081	3199	2424	•	•	7973	0	0	0
Rents 4	2744	•	0	0	241	1208	0	•	•	376	0	0	0
Royalties 5	17245	•	0	0	0	0	0	•	•	17245	0	0	0
Other Portfolio Income 6	43595	•	0	105	1981	55	219	•	•	6654	0	0	0
Other Receipts 7	72039	•	13864	99	6706	7205	4996	•	•	20430	0	0	0
Total Receipts 8	10128964	•	1252442	265437	2467123	702426	999178	•	•	2357503	0	0	0
Average Total Receipts 9	4143	•	758	2435	4708	8891	19984	•	•	392917	•	•	•
Operating Costs/Operating Income (%)													
Cost of Operations 10	59.3	•	35.7	35.8	51.3	59.1	56.9	•	•	70.1	•	•	•
Salaries and Wages 11	7.2	•	10.8	0.0	8.0	8.7	8.2	•	•	6.2	•	•	•
Taxes Paid 12	2.6	•	2.1	1.6	3.6	2.7	2.9	•	•	2.3	•	•	•
Interest Paid 13	1.6	•	0.4	1.0	1.4	1.9	1.3	•	•	2.7	•	•	•
Depreciation 14	2.8	•	1.8	1.4	2.6	2.7	3.6	•	•	2.9	•	•	•
Amortization and Depletion 15	0.3	•	0.0	•	0.0	0.0	0.0	•	•	0.9	•	•	•
Pensions and Other Deferred Comp. 16	0.9	•	0.4	1.9	1.3	2.3	1.2	•	•	0.5	•	•	•
Employee Benefits 17	1.9	•	0.8	1.1	2.8	2.9	2.3	•	•	1.3	•	•	•
Advertising 18	0.2	•	0.2	0.0	0.2	0.1	0.3	•	•	0.1	•	•	•
Other Expenses 19	10.6	•	15.9	51.7	13.1	7.8	9.0	•	•	6.8	•	•	•
Officers' Compensation 20	5.2	•	16.5	3.1	8.1	4.4	2.8	•	•	0.9	•	•	•
Operating Margin 21	7.6	•	15.4	2.4	7.6	7.5	11.4	•	•	5.2	•	•	•
Operating Margin Before Officers' Comp. 22	12.8	•	31.9	5.5	15.6	11.9	14.3	•	•	6.1	•	•	•

Selected Average Balance Sheet ($ in Thousands)

Net Receivables 23	527	42	299	537	2013	3166	57180
Inventories 24	369	9	194	155	386	1065	37104
Net Property, Plant and Equipment 25	806	56	49	746	2151	5766	97158
Total Assets 26	2719	186	681	2136	7104	14417	461029
Notes and Loans Payable 27	799	47	316	675	4219	4144	103497
All Other Liabilities 28	605	13	303	329	1240	2493	130789
Net Worth 29	1316	126	61	1133	1645	7781	226743

Selected Financial Ratios (Times to 1)

Current Ratio 30	2.2	9.1	1.6	1.9	2.4	1.6	2.6
Quick Ratio 31	1.5	7.9	1.2	1.5	1.8	1.2	1.6
Net Sales to Working Capital 32	6.6	6.9	11.9	10.1	4.2	7.0	4.7
Coverage Ratio 33	6.6	43.9	3.6	6.8	5.8	10.4	3.8
Total Asset Turnover 34	1.5	4.0	3.6	2.2	1.2	1.4	0.8
Inventory Turnover 35	6.5	30.4	4.5	15.5	13.4	10.6	7.3
Receivables Turnover 36	6.2	17.5	10.2	8.4		7.6	8.4
Total Liabilities to Net Worth 37	1.1	0.5	10.2	0.9	3.3	0.9	1.0
Current Assets to Working Capital 38	1.8	1.1	2.7	2.1	1.7	2.6	1.6
Current Liabilities to Working Capital 39	0.8	0.1	1.7	1.1	0.7	1.6	0.6
Working Capital to Net Sales 40	0.2	0.1	0.1	0.1	0.2	0.1	0.2
Inventory to Working Capital 41	0.4	0.1	0.6	0.4	0.2	0.4	0.5
Total Receipts to Cash Flow 42	6.1	3.8	2.2	5.9	6.7	5.5	8.3
Cost of Goods to Cash Flow 43	3.6	1.3	0.8	3.0	3.9	3.1	5.8
Cash Flow to Total Debt 44	0.5	3.3	1.8	0.8	0.2	0.5	0.2

Selected Financial Factors (in Percentages)

Debt Ratio 45	51.6	32.2	91.1	47.0	76.8	46.0	50.8
Return on Total Assets 46	16.2	68.7	12.3	20.9	13.6	18.6	8.5
Return on Equity Before Income Taxes 47	28.4	99.0	99.7	33.6	48.7	31.1	12.8
Return on Equity After Income Taxes 48	25.3	98.1	95.3	32.5	43.8	28.9	8.4
Profit Margin (Before Income Tax) 49	9.2	16.7	2.5	8.1	9.2	12.2	7.5
Profit Margin (After Income Tax) 50	8.2	16.5	2.4	7.9	8.2	11.4	5.0

Table I

Corporations with and without Net Income

OTHER FABRICATED METAL PRODUCT

MONEY AMOUNTS AND SIZE OF ASSETS IN THOUSANDS OF DOLLARS

Item Description for Accounting Period 7/07 Through 6/08	Total	Zero Assets	Under 500	500 to 1,000	1,000 to 5,000	5,000 to 10,000	10,000 to 25,000	25,000 to 50,000	50,000 to 100,000	100,000 to 250,000	250,000 to 500,000	500,000 to 2,500,000	2,500,000 and over
Number of Enterprises 1	16035	820	8758	2138	2976	682	343	150	68	47	23	22	9
Revenues ($ in Thousands)													
Net Sales 2	136598538	452092	5210337	3798729	17350480	9207218	10366782	9577833	7064105	7960436	6789308	18855792	39965427
Interest 3	1291111	2698	1885	3494	12711	6261	10911	11052	13468	28471	25206	154084	1020869
Rents 4	53530	156	11	49	6421	481	6	785	3111	1554	5738	3014	32204
Royalties 5	631886	0	0	0	46	324	2523	919	4580	19380	4998	73446	525670
Other Portfolio Income 6	1406583	52092	13149	135930	13259	3480	15692	14979	34319	62458	19206	145524	896493
Other Receipts 7	1658651	15597	22553	41997	167786	56414	86293	31516	82802	93312	80154	272666	707563
Total Receipts 8	141640299	522635	5247935	3980199	17550703	9274178	10482207	9637084	7202385	8165611	6924610	19504526	43148226
Average Total Receipts 9	8833	637	599	1862	5897	13599	30560	64247	105917	173736	301070	886569	4794247
Operating Costs/Operating Income (%)													
Cost of Operations 10	67.9	62.1	51.8	63.9	69.2	68.9	70.4	70.1	70.1	71.9	65.5	70.6	66.6
Salaries and Wages 11	6.6	8.9	13.0	11.5	5.3	6.1	6.3	7.0	6.8	6.6	8.7	5.9	6.0
Taxes Paid 12	2.0	3.5	3.2	3.2	2.8	2.1	1.8	1.6	1.7	1.6	1.9	1.7	1.9
Interest Paid 13	2.5	1.9	1.2	1.1	1.0	1.1	0.9	1.3	1.4	1.9	1.5	3.2	4.5
Depreciation 14	2.0	1.6	2.2	1.7	1.9	1.9	2.0	1.8	2.1	2.1	2.5	1.9	2.0
Amortization and Depletion 15	0.9	1.1	0.1	0.3	0.1	0.2	0.1	0.1	0.3	0.3	0.4	0.6	2.5
Pensions and Other Deferred Comp. 16	0.6	0.2	0.1	0.6	0.5	0.5	0.5	0.6	0.6	1.2	0.8	1.0	0.5
Employee Benefits 17	2.0	0.8	1.6	1.4	1.6	1.8	1.6	1.3	1.9	1.8	1.9	2.5	2.5
Advertising 18	0.8	0.0	0.3	0.4	0.4	0.4	0.4	0.7	0.5	0.5	1.1	0.3	1.6
Other Expenses 19	8.6	17.6	14.3	13.9	8.5	7.6	6.7	7.9	6.6	6.6	8.8	8.0	9.4
Officers' Compensation 20	2.2	5.8	8.4	5.4	4.5	4.4	2.4	2.0	1.4	1.3	1.2	0.8	0.6
Operating Margin 21	3.7	•	3.7	•	4.0	5.0	7.0	5.4	6.6	4.2	5.8	3.6	1.9
Operating Margin Before Officers' Comp. 22	5.9	2.3	12.1	2.0	8.5	9.5	9.4	7.4	8.0	5.5	7.0	4.4	2.5

Selected Average Balance Sheet ($ in Thousands)

Net Receivables 23	1503	0	33	171	760	1684	4012	9270	15361	24073	55747	144249	1182817
Inventories 24	1138	0	28	156	624	1972	4474	9300	17953	30976	56359	142663	492538
Net Property, Plant and Equipment 25	1174	0	49	133	558	1539	3802	8272	17146	28158	56883	128605	692695
Total Assets 26	16280	0	171	705	2468	6972	16177	34732	69740	140316	304319	969233	21725349
Notes and Loans Payable 27	6509	0	124	348	757	1849	3819	11112	15964	38097	75015	359319	9282198
All Other Liabilities 28	2167	0	30	185	701	1859	3737	9093	16562	35832	85017	269156	1934468
Net Worth 29	7604	0	17	171	1011	3265	8622	14527	37213	66386	144287	340759	10508683

Selected Financial Ratios (Times to 1)

Current Ratio 30	1.8	•	2.0	1.6	2.0	2.2	2.4	2.0	2.1	2.2	2.0	1.8	1.5
Quick Ratio 31	1.0	•	1.3	0.9	1.3	1.1	1.3	1.0	1.1	1.1	1.0	0.9	0.9
Net Sales to Working Capital 32	5.4	•	12.3	10.0	6.7	5.0	4.7	5.5	4.8	4.1	4.2	4.9	5.8
Coverage Ratio 33	4.1	7.2	4.6	2.2	6.0	6.4	10.1	5.5	7.3	4.7	6.5	3.2	3.4
Total Asset Turnover 34	0.5	•	3.5	2.5	2.4	1.9	1.9	1.8	1.5	1.2	1.0	0.9	0.2
Inventory Turnover 35	5.1	•	11.1	7.3	6.5	4.7	4.8	4.8	4.1	3.9	3.4	4.2	6.0
Receivables Turnover 36	5.3	•	13.4	9.8	7.7	8.4	7.2	7.4	6.5	6.8	5.4	6.0	3.2
Total Liabilities to Net Worth 37	1.1	•	8.9	3.1	1.4	1.1	0.9	1.4	0.9	1.1	1.1	1.8	1.1
Current Assets to Working Capital 38	2.3	•	2.0	2.6	2.0	1.9	1.7	2.0	1.9	1.8	2.0	2.3	2.9
Current Liabilities to Working Capital 39	1.3	•	1.0	1.6	1.0	0.9	0.7	1.0	0.9	0.8	1.0	1.3	1.9
Working Capital to Net Sales 40	0.2	•	0.1	0.1	0.1	0.2	0.2	0.2	0.2	0.2	0.2	0.2	0.2
Inventory to Working Capital 41	0.7	•	0.5	1.0	0.7	0.9	0.7	0.9	0.8	0.7	0.8	0.8	0.7
Total Receipts to Cash Flow 42	7.2	6.4	6.8	9.8	9.5	8.9	7.7	8.1	7.4	9.0	6.8	7.5	5.8
Cost of Goods to Cash Flow 43	4.9	4.0	3.5	6.2	6.6	6.1	5.4	5.7	5.2	6.5	4.4	5.3	3.8
Cash Flow to Total Debt 44	0.1	•	0.6	0.3	0.4	0.4	0.5	0.4	0.4	0.3	0.3	0.2	0.1

Selected Financial Factors (in Percentages)

Debt Ratio 45	53.3	•	89.9	75.7	59.1	53.2	46.7	58.2	46.6	52.7	52.6	64.8	51.6
Return on Total Assets 46	5.3	•	19.8	6.3	14.5	13.2	16.8	13.5	14.8	10.6	9.2	9.2	3.1
Return on Equity Before Income Taxes 47	8.6	•	152.3	14.1	29.6	23.8	28.4	26.4	23.9	17.6	16.4	18.0	4.5
Return on Equity After Income Taxes 48	6.5	•	148.8	12.3	27.9	22.0	26.2	23.9	20.1	12.9	13.2	12.2	2.9
Profit Margin (Before Income Tax) 49	7.7	12.0	4.4	1.4	5.1	5.8	8.1	6.0	8.5	6.9	8.0	7.2	10.6
Profit Margin (After Income Tax) 50	5.8	10.1	4.3	1.2	4.8	5.3	7.5	5.4	7.2	5.1	6.5	4.8	7.0

Table II

Corporations with Net Income

OTHER FABRICATED METAL PRODUCT

MONEY AMOUNTS AND SIZE OF ASSETS IN THOUSANDS OF DOLLARS

Item Description for Accounting Period 7/07 Through 6/08	Total	Zero Assets	Under 500	500 to 1,000	1,000 to 5,000	5,000 to 10,000	10,000 to 25,000	25,000 to 50,000	50,000 to 100,000	100,000 to 250,000	250,000 to 500,000	500,000 to 2,500,000	2,500,000 and over
Number of Enterprises **1**	11821	408	6960	1086	2212	598	292	123	58	40	18	18	9
Revenues ($ in Thousands)													
Net Sales **2**	121526316	296975	4574537	2196283	13229591	8199236	8855843	7977380	6241702	7125640	5982309	16881393	39965427
Interest **3**	1265096	932	1454	2248	8716	6090	10222	6057	10514	24930	24962	148102	1020869
Rents **4**	52443	156	11	0	6060	481	6	406	2900	1523	5738	2959	32204
Royalties **5**	630774	0	0	0	46	324	2523	493	4580	19380	4826	72933	525670
Other Portfolio Income **6**	1365485	43089	12894	135194	6273	2047	6811	12087	31185	59418	19195	140799	896493
Other Receipts **7**	1532552	14918	21135	11392	154465	43195	71225	24568	76566	89669	53047	264805	707563
Total Receipts **8**	126372666	356070	4610031	2345117	13405151	8251373	8946630	8020991	6367447	7320560	6090077	17510991	43148226
Average Total Receipts **9**	10691	873	662	2159	6060	13798	30639	65211	109784	183014	338338	972833	4794247
Operating Costs/Operating Income (%)													
Cost of Operations **10**	67.1	56.6	49.8	65.6	66.7	68.3	68.8	68.7	68.8	71.5	63.8	70.0	66.6
Salaries and Wages **11**	6.6	8.1	14.0	9.0	5.3	5.8	6.2	7.3	6.8	6.5	9.0	5.7	6.0
Taxes Paid **12**	2.0	4.9	3.3	2.8	2.8	2.1	1.8	1.5	1.6	1.6	2.0	1.7	1.9
Interest Paid **13**	2.4	1.0	1.1	1.0	0.8	1.0	0.7	1.1	1.1	1.5	1.0	2.9	4.5
Depreciation **14**	1.9	1.2	2.2	1.8	1.8	1.8	1.9	1.7	1.9	1.9	2.5	1.8	2.0
Amortization and Depletion **15**	1.0	0.0	0.1	0.3	0.1	0.0	0.1	0.1	0.2	0.2	0.2	0.5	2.5
Pensions and Other Deferred Comp. **16**	0.7	0.3	0.0	0.8	0.6	0.5	0.5	0.6	0.6	1.3	0.8	1.1	0.5
Employee Benefits **17**	2.0	0.9	1.6	1.3	1.4	1.9	1.6	1.3	1.9	1.7	1.9	2.6	2.5
Advertising **18**	0.9	0.1	0.3	0.6	0.5	0.3	0.4	0.8	0.5	0.5	1.0	0.3	1.6
Other Expenses **19**	8.4	4.3	14.1	12.1	8.3	7.0	6.1	7.5	6.8	6.3	8.4	8.0	9.4
Officers' Compensation **20**	2.1	8.7	8.1	6.4	4.8	4.6	2.5	2.1	1.5	1.4	1.2	0.8	0.6
Operating Margin **21**	5.0	14.1	5.4	•	6.9	6.6	9.4	7.4	8.2	5.5	8.1	4.4	1.9
Operating Margin Before Officers' Comp. **22**	7.1	22.8	13.5	4.7	11.7	11.3	11.9	9.5	9.7	6.9	9.3	5.3	2.5

Selected Average Balance Sheet ($ in Thousands)

Net Receivables 23	1839	29	155	736	1771	4087	9475	15882	25430	54045	153401	1182817
Inventories 24	1374	20	195	624	1983	4686	9806	18673	31712	55609	163464	492538
Net Property, Plant and Equipment 25	1401	55	130	515	1493	3588	7811	16600	27714	65344	139817	692695
Total Assets 26	21151	164	704	2486	6991	15890	34883	70515	137768	309041	1045100	21725349
Notes and Loans Payable 27	8326	113	253	575	1789	3211	9482	14030	29540	66886	343435	9282198
All Other Liabilities 28	2639	28	148	642	1811	3401	8746	16341	36450	79157	279544	1934468
Net Worth 29	10185	24	303	1270	3390	9277	16655	40145	71777	162998	422122	10508683

Selected Financial Ratios (Times to 1)

Current Ratio 30	1.9	•	2.2	1.8	2.4	2.3	2.6	2.2	2.3	2.3	1.8	1.5
Quick Ratio 31	1.0	•	1.5	1.0	1.5	1.1	1.5	1.1	1.2	1.1	0.9	0.9
Net Sales to Working Capital 32	5.2	•	13.2	10.1	5.6	4.8	4.4	5.0	4.4	4.2	4.7	5.8
Coverage Ratio 33	4.8	35.3	6.6	6.1	10.7	8.5	16.0	8.5	10.3	6.7	3.9	3.4
Total Asset Turnover 34	0.5	•	4.0	2.9	2.4	2.0	1.9	1.9	1.5	1.3	0.9	0.2
Inventory Turnover 35	5.0	•	16.0	6.8	6.4	4.7	4.5	4.5	4.0	4.0	3.8	6.0
Receivables Turnover 36	5.1	•	17.7	8.7	7.8	8.4	6.8	7.2	6.6	7.1	•	3.2
Total Liabilities to Net Worth 37	1.1	•	5.9	1.3	1.0	1.1	0.7	1.1	0.8	0.9	1.5	1.1
Current Assets to Working Capital 38	2.2	•	1.9	2.3	1.7	1.8	1.6	1.8	1.8	1.8	2.2	2.9
Current Liabilities to Working Capital 39	1.2	•	0.9	1.3	0.7	1.3	0.6	0.8	0.8	0.8	1.2	1.9
Working Capital to Net Sales 40	0.2	•	0.1	0.1	0.2	0.2	0.2	0.2	0.2	0.2	0.2	0.2
Inventory to Working Capital 41	0.7	•	0.4	0.9	0.6	0.9	0.6	0.8	0.8	0.8	0.7	0.7
Total Receipts to Cash Flow 42	6.6	3.0	6.1	8.6	7.3	8.2	6.7	7.2	6.5	8.1	6.1	5.8
Cost of Goods to Cash Flow 43	4.4	1.7	3.1	5.7	4.9	5.6	4.6	5.0	4.5	5.8	3.9	3.8
Cash Flow to Total Debt 44	0.1	0.8	0.6	0.7	0.5	0.7	0.5	0.8	0.5	0.3	0.2	0.1

Selected Financial Factors (in Percentages)

Debt Ratio 45	51.8	•	85.6	57.0	48.9	51.5	41.6	52.3	43.1	47.9	47.3	51.6
Return on Total Assets 46	5.7	•	29.1	17.6	21.8	16.2	21.2	16.7	17.2	12.8	12.0	10.1
Return on Equity Before Income Taxes 47	9.3	•	171.6	34.3	38.7	29.4	34.1	30.9	27.3	20.8	20.6	18.6
Return on Equity After Income Taxes 48	7.3	•	168.4	32.3	36.8	27.4	31.7	28.2	23.2	15.7	17.3	12.8
Profit Margin (Before Income Tax) 49	9.2	34.0	6.2	5.1	8.2	7.3	10.4	7.9	10.2	8.4	10.1	10.6
Profit Margin (After Income Tax) 50	7.2	31.1	6.1	4.8	7.8	6.8	9.7	7.2	8.6	6.3	5.8	7.0

Table I

Corporations with and without Net Income

AGRICULTURE, CONSTRUCTION, AND MINING MACHINERY

MONEY AMOUNTS AND SIZE OF ASSETS IN THOUSANDS OF DOLLARS

Item Description for Accounting Period 7/07 Through 6/08	Total	Zero Assets	Under 500	500 to 1,000	1,000 to 5,000	5,000 to 10,000	10,000 to 25,000	25,000 to 50,000	50,000 to 100,000	100,000 to 250,000	250,000 to 500,000	500,000 to 2,500,000	2,500,000 and over
Number of Enterprises **1**	3873	5	2228	143	1102	156	107	40	33	20	16	12	10
Revenues ($ in Thousands)													
Net Sales **2**	126751403	144315	790982	220668	5117889	1723013	2857572	2458541	3108449	4008608	5879406	18723660	81718299
Interest **3**	4662836	363	135	963	2977	665	7299	2687	6783	7083	47506	145612	4440762
Rents **4**	1368542	0	325	0	830	0	4691	531	656	2217	1835	88734	1268723
Royalties **5**	1184435	243	0	0	0	0	0	0	593	561	17284	256776	908977
Other Portfolio Income **6**	851423	1	0	3225	3841	1364	26630	10111	2509	11354	16175	204735	571478
Other Receipts **7**	2555687	7115	2206	0	33588	16025	14191	10815	11378	15929	180899	327275	1936269
Total Receipts **8**	137374326	152037	793648	224856	5159125	1741067	2910383	2482685	3130368	4045752	6143105	19746792	90844508
Average Total Receipts **9**	35470	30407	356	1572	4682	11161	27200	62067	94860	202288	383944	1645566	9084451
Operating Costs/Operating Income (%)													
Cost of Operations **10**	71.6	67.1	54.7	59.5	70.6	62.6	68.6	71.4	72.4	70.9	73.4	76.0	71.0
Salaries and Wages **11**	6.1	17.2	7.0	8.5	5.5	12.2	6.8	6.4	5.9	6.7	7.5	5.1	6.0
Taxes Paid **12**	1.0	2.6	2.6	2.7	1.2	2.6	2.1	1.7	1.5	1.4	1.4	1.0	0.8
Interest Paid **13**	3.7	6.4	1.4	1.0	0.9	1.1	1.9	1.0	1.5	1.7	2.4	2.4	4.6
Depreciation **14**	2.3	2.5	1.1	0.4	1.8	1.9	2.1	1.2	2.0	1.6	1.8	1.7	2.7
Amortization and Depletion **15**	0.4	3.0	0.0	*	0.1	0.1	0.2	0.2	0.4	0.5	0.8	0.4	0.4
Pensions and Other Deferred Comp. **16**	1.0	1.1	0.7	0.3	0.5	0.3	0.6	0.8	0.7	0.9	0.5	0.8	1.1
Employee Benefits **17**	1.6	2.0	0.8	0.2	0.9	2.0	2.1	1.4	1.4	1.5	1.1	1.1	1.8
Advertising **18**	0.4	0.3	0.4	0.9	0.7	1.7	1.5	0.5	0.6	0.8	0.8	0.6	0.2
Other Expenses **19**	11.6	33.8	11.0	9.2	7.7	10.2	8.6	7.2	7.0	8.8	7.5	7.9	13.5
Officers' Compensation **20**	0.8	0.7	7.1	8.2	3.8	2.4	2.2	1.8	1.0	0.9	0.7	1.0	0.3
Operating Margin **21**	*	*	13.2	9.2	6.3	2.9	3.5	6.5	5.7	4.5	2.1	2.2	*
Operating Margin Before Officers' Comp. **22**	0.4	*	20.3	17.3	10.2	5.3	5.6	8.3	6.7	5.3	2.8	3.1	*

Selected Average Balance Sheet ($ in Thousands)

Net Receivables 23	13271	0	18	40	435	1017	3409	8951	14045	28446	71011	237395	4497314
Inventories 24	4577	0	18	350	614	3124	5468	12630	17912	41134	71206	229639	1007401
Net Property, Plant and Equipment 25	4559	0	41	114	465	970	2964	5324	12507	21687	51626	173858	1259850
Total Assets 26	43247	0	110	663	2341	6073	15839	36001	68138	140364	342105	1356769	13368433
Notes and Loans Payable 27	18541	0	91	135	789	1171	5257	10677	19903	34874	86573	310369	6308236
All Other Liabilities 28	12376	0	37	165	596	1671	4963	13704	17908	53973	101060	462825	3698528
Net Worth 29	12331	0	-18	363	956	3231	5619	11620	30327	51517	154472	583576	3361669

Selected Financial Ratios (Times to 1)

Current Ratio 30	1.6	•	1.2	2.3	2.6	2.3	1.7	1.8	2.1	1.7	2.1	1.4	1.6
Quick Ratio 31	1.1	•	0.6	1.2	1.6	0.7	0.8	0.8	1.0	0.7	1.1	0.7	1.2
Net Sales to Working Capital 32	4.1	•	38.0	6.3	4.6	4.4	5.6	5.0	4.5	5.7	3.7	9.9	3.5
Coverage Ratio 33	3.7	•	10.7	12.3	8.6	4.6	3.8	8.3	5.4	4.2	3.9	4.6	3.4
Total Asset Turnover 34	0.8	•	3.2	2.3	2.0	1.8	1.7	1.7	1.4	1.4	1.1	1.2	0.6
Inventory Turnover 35	5.1	•	10.7	2.6	5.3	2.2	3.4	3.5	3.8	3.5	3.8	5.2	5.8
Receivables Turnover 36	2.5	•	18.2	20.9	11.1	7.8	8.0	6.9	6.8	7.7	6.6	6.6	1.8
Total Liabilities to Net Worth 37	2.5	•	•	0.8	1.4	0.9	1.8	2.1	1.2	1.7	1.2	1.3	3.0
Current Assets to Working Capital 38	2.6	•	6.9	1.8	1.6	1.8	2.4	2.2	1.9	2.5	1.9	3.6	2.7
Current Liabilities to Working Capital 39	1.6	•	5.9	0.8	0.6	0.8	1.4	1.2	0.9	1.5	0.9	2.6	1.7
Working Capital to Net Sales 40	0.2	•	0.0	0.2	0.2	0.2	0.2	0.2	0.2	0.2	0.3	0.1	0.3
Inventory to Working Capital 41	0.6	•	2.0	0.8	0.6	1.2	1.1	1.1	0.8	1.2	0.7	1.5	0.5
Total Receipts to Cash Flow 42	5.6	119.9	4.8	5.4	7.8	8.1	8.3	7.7	8.3	7.7	8.2	7.2	4.8
Cost of Goods to Cash Flow 43	4.0	80.4	2.6	3.2	5.5	5.1	5.7	5.5	6.0	5.5	6.0	5.5	3.4
Cash Flow to Total Debt 44	0.2	•	0.6	0.9	0.4	0.5	0.3	0.3	0.3	0.3	0.2	0.3	0.2

Selected Financial Factors (in Percentages)

Debt Ratio 45	71.5	•	116.7	45.2	59.1	46.8	64.5	67.7	55.5	63.3	54.8	57.0	74.9
Return on Total Assets 46	10.2	•	48.3	28.0	16.0	9.2	12.1	14.7	11.0	10.0	10.0	12.9	9.7
Return on Equity Before Income Taxes 47	26.2	•	•	47.0	34.6	13.5	25.1	40.0	20.1	20.8	16.4	23.5	27.3
Return on Equity After Income Taxes 48	17.9	•	•	32.4	32.7	11.9	17.9	31.7	14.8	15.6	10.6	15.7	18.3
Profit Margin (Before Income Tax) 49	9.9	•	13.6	11.1	7.1	3.9	5.3	7.6	6.5	5.3	6.9	8.8	11.2
Profit Margin (After Income Tax) 50	6.7	•	13.3	7.6	6.7	3.5	3.8	6.0	4.8	4.0	4.5	5.9	7.5

Table II
Corporations with Net Income

AGRICULTURE, CONSTRUCTION, AND MINING MACHINERY

MONEY AMOUNTS AND SIZE OF ASSETS IN THOUSANDS OF DOLLARS

Item Description for Accounting Period 7/07 Through 6/08		Total	Zero Assets	Under 500	500 to 1,000	1,000 to 5,000	5,000 to 10,000	10,000 to 25,000	25,000 to 50,000	50,000 to 100,000	100,000 to 250,000	250,000 to 500,000	500,000 to 2,500,000	2,500,000 and over
Number of Enterprises	1	3416	•	2049	83	999	83	92	33	27	14	•	•	•
Revenues ($ in Thousands)														
Net Sales	2	120947035	•	737296	151973	4881453	1117136	2471953	2094633	2628015	3246548	•	•	•
Interest	3	4620803	•	135	11	2450	665	7037	2622	6716	6268	•	•	•
Rents	4	1368342	•	325	0	684	0	4691	531	656	2163	•	•	•
Royalties	5	1135326	•	0	0	0	0	0	0	593	561			•
Other Portfolio Income	6	828016	•	0	3225	3841	265	16808	10021	2369	7214	•	•	•
Other Receipts	7	2424671	•	2206	0	30237	15622	14501	9176	10780	13682	•	•	•
Total Receipts	8	131324193	•	739962	155209	4918665	1133688	2514990	2116983	2649129	3276436	•	•	•
Average Total Receipts	9	38444	•	361	1870	4924	13659	27337	64151	98116	234031	•	•	•
Operating Costs/Operating Income (%)														
Cost of Operations	10	71.5	•	53.2	55.2	70.3	67.7	68.7	69.7	72.4	71.2	•	•	•
Salaries and Wages	11	5.8	•	6.8	5.2	5.4	7.4	6.7	6.4	5.1	6.2	•	•	•
Taxes Paid	12	1.0	•	2.4	2.4	1.2	2.1	2.2	1.7	1.4	1.3	•	•	•
Interest Paid	13	3.6	•	0.9	1.4	0.9	0.4	1.8	0.9	1.1	1.4	•	•	•
Depreciation	14	2.3	•	1.1	0.5	1.8	0.8	1.9	1.1	2.0	1.4	•	•	•
Amortization and Depletion	15	0.3	•	0.0	•	0.1	0.1	0.2	0.1	0.3	0.3	•	•	•
Pensions and Other Deferred Comp.	16	1.0	•	0.7	0.2	0.5	0.5	0.7	0.9	0.6	0.6	•	•	•
Employee Benefits	17	1.6	•	0.8	0.0	0.8	0.7	2.1	1.4	1.1	1.1	•	•	•
Advertising	18	0.3	•	0.4	0.9	0.7	2.4	0.9	0.4	0.5	0.8	•	•	•
Other Expenses	19	11.7	•	10.4	9.3	7.6	7.9	6.8	7.4	6.2	8.5	•	•	•
Officers' Compensation	20	0.7	•	7.6	8.6	3.9	3.0	2.1	1.5	0.9	0.9	•	•	•
Operating Margin	21	0.1	•	15.8	16.3	6.8	6.9	6.1	8.6	8.3	6.4	•	•	•
Operating Margin Before Officers' Comp.	22	0.9	•	23.4	24.9	10.7	9.9	8.2	10.1	9.3	7.3	•	•	•

Selected Average Balance Sheet ($ in Thousands)

Net Receivables 23	14518	16	41	456	1114	3558	8672	14170	29832
Inventories 24	4770	11	140	593	3245	4929	13754	16886	46596
Net Property, Plant and Equipment 25	4963	34	168	492	728	2941	5120	12714	19796
Total Assets 26	46590	91	652	2388	6272	15580	36558	67483	138235
Notes and Loans Payable 27	20315	63	233	797	523	4747	8714	17188	32507
All Other Liabilities 28	13059	22	128	615	1398	4602	13972	17969	49285
Net Worth 29	13216	6	290	976	4351	6231	13872	32326	56443

Selected Financial Ratios (Times to 1)

Current Ratio 30	1.7	1.3	1.6	2.6	3.6	1.9	1.9	2.3	1.8
Quick Ratio 31	1.2	0.7	0.8	1.6	1.2	0.9	0.8	1.2	0.8
Net Sales to Working Capital 32	3.9	34.2	16.1	4.8	3.9	5.0	4.8	4.1	5.9
Coverage Ratio 33	4.0	18.2	14.0	9.2	24.8	5.4	12.4	9.5	6.2
Total Asset Turnover 34	0.8	3.9	2.8	2.0	2.1	1.7	1.7	1.4	1.7
Inventory Turnover 35	5.3	17.3	7.2	5.8	2.8	3.7	3.2	4.2	3.5
Receivables Turnover 36	2.5	34.2	29.5	11.3	9.1	7.8	•	7.5	
Total Liabilities to Net Worth 37	2.5	14.0	1.2	1.4	0.4	1.5	1.6	1.1	1.4
Current Assets to Working Capital 38	2.5	5.0	2.6	1.6	1.4	2.1	2.1	1.8	2.3
Current Liabilities to Working Capital 39	1.5	4.0	1.6	0.6	0.4	1.1	1.1	0.8	1.3
Working Capital to Net Sales 40	0.3	0.0	0.1	0.2	0.3	0.2	0.2	0.2	0.2
Inventory to Working Capital 41	0.6	1.8	1.3	0.6	0.9	0.9	1.0	0.7	1.2
Total Receipts to Cash Flow 42	5.3	4.4	4.0	7.5	6.7	7.7	6.5	7.1	6.9
Cost of Goods to Cash Flow 43	3.8	2.3	2.2	5.3	4.5	5.3	4.5	5.2	4.9
Cash Flow to Total Debt 44	0.2	1.0	1.3	0.5	1.1	0.4	0.4	0.4	0.4

Selected Financial Factors (in Percentages)

Debt Ratio 45	71.6	93.3	55.5	59.1	30.6	60.0	62.1	52.1	59.2
Return on Total Assets 46	10.8	67.3	55.8	17.4	18.8	16.5	18.6	14.7	14.5
Return on Equity Before Income Taxes 47	28.4	954.7	116.4	38.0	26.0	33.6	45.0	27.6	29.8
Return on Equity After Income Taxes 48	19.6	938.8	84.8	36.0	23.7	26.1	36.6	21.4	23.0
Profit Margin (Before Income Tax) 49	10.6	16.2	18.4	7.6	8.4	7.8	9.8	9.2	7.3
Profit Margin (After Income Tax) 50	7.3	15.9	13.4	7.2	7.7	6.1	8.0	7.1	5.6

Table I

Corporations with and without Net Income

INDUSTRIAL MACHINERY

MONEY AMOUNTS AND SIZE OF ASSETS IN THOUSANDS OF DOLLARS

Item Description for Accounting Period 7/07 Through 6/08		Total	Zero Assets	Under 500	500 to 1,000	1,000 to 5,000	5,000 to 10,000	10,000 to 25,000	25,000 to 50,000	50,000 to 100,000	100,000 to 250,000	250,000 to 500,000	500,000 to 2,500,000	2,500,000 and over
Number of Enterprises	1	3068	28	1378	352	653	330	137	76	48	33	15	14	4
Revenues ($ in Thousands)														
Net Sales	2	55989056	578577	746884	197754	3855306	3260151	2969404	3415499	3970515	5659931	5487702	8690160	17157173
Interest	3	347746	30491	160	22	5094	3421	10042	15555	20461	50236	39599	56382	116284
Rents	4	39615	58	0	2539	531	123	1497	5081	2278	11946	2185	12053	1323
Royalties	5	281947	1010	0	0	31	0	5442	5503	2740	9065	29188	137783	91185
Other Portfolio Income	6	414993	770	4662	0	2196	1841	12449	7957	30759	36000	75563	170088	72712
Other Receipts	7	493425	11148	12625	1618	77085	17613	16986	33780	56392	43966	58485	210014	-46291
Total Receipts	8	57566782	622054	764331	201933	3940243	3283149	3015820	3483375	4083145	5811144	5692722	9276480	17392386
Average Total Receipts	9	18764	22216	555	574	6034	9949	22013	45834	85066	176095	379515	662606	4348096
Operating Costs/Operating Income (%)														
Cost of Operations	10	65.2	72.0	64.0	64.7	71.5	64.5	71.0	67.2	72.2	67.2	66.8	64.7	59.8
Salaries and Wages	11	10.0	6.8	6.5	3.3	5.9	10.8	9.0	9.4	7.0	10.3	7.9	12.3	11.4
Taxes Paid	12	1.6	1.8	3.2	4.2	2.5	2.5	2.3	2.0	1.7	1.3	1.9	1.5	1.0
Interest Paid	13	2.0	8.5	1.0	1.4	1.2	1.3	1.0	1.0	1.3	2.0	2.8	3.2	1.7
Depreciation	14	1.9	1.8	2.6	1.0	2.0	1.3	1.6	2.9	1.4	2.2	1.7	2.4	1.7
Amortization and Depletion	15	0.7	0.3	•	0.0	0.1	0.3	0.3	0.4	0.7	0.9	1.3	0.8	0.8
Pensions and Other Deferred Comp.	16	0.7	0.4	0.0	0.1	0.4	1.2	0.8	0.7	0.7	0.5	1.4	0.8	0.4
Employee Benefits	17	1.9	2.4	2.2	3.3	2.4	1.9	1.9	1.8	2.2	1.9	2.7	1.9	1.4
Advertising	18	0.5	0.4	0.4	0.5	0.3	0.4	0.7	0.8	0.4	0.3	0.6	0.4	0.5
Other Expenses	19	7.9	10.2	13.1	14.0	8.4	8.0	8.6	10.2	6.5	9.4	7.3	7.0	7.4
Officers' Compensation	20	1.6	0.8	6.8	10.3	3.5	4.6	2.8	2.4	1.5	1.2	1.2	1.1	0.5
Operating Margin	21	6.1	•	0.3	•	1.8	3.3	0.0	1.2	4.2	2.7	4.5	3.8	13.5
Operating Margin Before Officers' Comp.	22	7.7	•	7.0	7.4	5.3	7.9	2.8	3.6	5.7	4.0	5.7	4.8	13.9

Selected Average Balance Sheet ($ in Thousands)

Net Receivables 23	3882	0	45	113	881	1645	3613	8444	16418	36023	57543	210650	941684
Inventories 24	2441	0	49	50	730	2083	3817	9148	9935	25394	51143	74554	474234
Net Property, Plant and Equipment 25	2179	0	26	91	597	1374	1834	6520	10615	19232	49328	77065	516479
Total Assets 26	21001	0	139	795	2782	7308	15489	34824	73402	157590	360708	1049958	6532773
Notes and Loans Payable 27	4772	0	45	155	841	2700	2840	7236	14120	39120	122528	262884	1164716
All Other Liabilities 28	5739	0	52	341	1093	1348	5694	11401	24086	51093	129642	341616	1259953
Net Worth 29	10491	0	42	299	848	3259	6955	16187	35195	67377	108538	445458	4108104

Selected Financial Ratios (Times to 1)

Current Ratio 30	1.7	•	1.8	3.2	2.2	2.4	1.8	2.0	1.7	1.9	1.5	1.4	1.7
Quick Ratio 31	1.1	•	1.0	2.8	1.3	1.2	1.1	1.1	1.1	1.1	0.8	1.0	1.2
Net Sales to Working Capital 32	4.8	•	11.3	1.5	5.7	3.6	4.0	3.9	4.5	3.9	6.2	5.3	4.9
Coverage Ratio 33	5.8	1.2	3.6	0.5	4.4	4.2	2.5	4.3	6.2	3.7	4.3	4.7	10.2
Total Asset Turnover 34	0.9	•	3.9	0.7	2.1	1.4	1.4	1.3	1.1	1.1	1.0	0.6	0.7
Inventory Turnover 35	4.9	•	7.2	7.3	5.8	3.1	4.0	3.3	6.0	4.5	4.8	5.4	5.4
Receivables Turnover 36	4.6	•	12.7	3.4	6.7	6.1	6.3	5.1	5.4	5.4	5.4	3.8	3.7
Total Liabilities to Net Worth 37	1.0	•	2.3	1.7	2.3	1.2	1.2	1.2	1.1	1.3	2.3	1.4	0.6
Current Assets to Working Capital 38	2.4	•	2.3	1.4	1.9	1.7	2.2	2.0	2.4	2.1	2.9	3.6	2.5
Current Liabilities to Working Capital 39	1.4	•	1.3	0.4	0.9	0.7	1.2	1.0	1.4	1.1	1.9	2.6	1.5
Working Capital to Net Sales 40	0.2	•	0.1	0.7	0.2	0.3	0.2	0.3	0.2	0.3	0.2	0.2	0.2
Inventory to Working Capital 41	0.6	•	0.8	0.2	0.7	0.8	0.7	0.8	0.6	0.6	0.9	0.7	0.5
Total Receipts to Cash Flow 42	6.9	8.8	8.3	11.5	10.4	9.9	13.5	8.6	8.5	7.8	7.2	6.3	5.2
Cost of Goods to Cash Flow 43	4.5	6.3	5.3	7.4	7.4	6.4	9.6	5.8	6.1	5.2	4.8	4.1	3.1
Cash Flow to Total Debt 44	0.3	•	0.7	0.1	0.3	0.2	0.2	0.3	0.3	0.2	0.2	0.2	0.3

Selected Financial Factors (in Percentages)

Debt Ratio 45	50.0	•	69.6	62.4	69.5	55.4	55.1	53.5	52.1	57.2	69.9	57.6	37.1
Return on Total Assets 46	9.9	•	14.0	0.5	11.1	7.2	3.5	5.8	9.4	8.2	12.2	9.0	11.2
Return on Equity Before Income Taxes 47	16.3	•	33.4	•	28.0	12.2	4.7	9.6	16.5	13.9	31.1	16.6	16.1
Return on Equity After Income Taxes 48	11.3	•	31.4	•	24.9	11.0	2.4	7.4	12.4	10.3	20.2	12.0	10.6
Profit Margin (Before Income Tax) 49	9.4	2.0	2.6	•	4.0	4.0	1.5	3.4	7.0	5.5	9.2	11.9	15.4
Profit Margin (After Income Tax) 50	6.5	0.1	2.4	•	3.6	3.6	0.8	2.7	5.3	4.1	6.0	8.6	10.1

Table II

Corporations with Net Income

INDUSTRIAL MACHINERY

MONEY AMOUNTS AND SIZE OF ASSETS IN THOUSANDS OF DOLLARS

Item Description for Accounting Period 7/07 Through 6/08	Total	Zero Assets	Under 500	500 to 1,000	1,000 to 5,000	5,000 to 10,000	10,000 to 25,000	25,000 to 50,000	50,000 to 100,000	100,000 to 250,000	250,000 to 500,000	500,000 to 2,500,000	2,500,000 and over
Number of Enterprises 1	2051	•	•	94	434	283	94	54	40	23	•	14	4
Revenues ($ in Thousands)													
Net Sales 2	49131293	•	•	61378	2237740	3062479	2045224	2584336	3312948	4198610	•	8690160	17157173
Interest 3	323276	•	•	22	3027	3055	4935	12033	19413	38395	•	56382	116284
Rents 4	34883	•	•	670	531	123	267	3524	2256	11928	•	12053	1323
Royalties 5	271905	•	•	0	31	0	33	5503	1339	5832	•	137783	91185
Other Portfolio Income 6	386031	•	•	0	2016	1585	11419	6846	25183	28030	•	170088	72712
Other Receipts 7	434397	•	•	14	76725	17519	8532	28560	48085	31028	•	210014	-46291
Total Receipts 8	50581785	•	•	62084	2320070	3084761	2070410	2640802	3409224	4313823	•	9276480	17392386
Average Total Receipts 9	24662	•	•	660	5346	10900	22026	48904	85231	187558	•	662606	4348096
Operating Costs/Operating Income (%)													
Cost of Operations 10	63.7	•	•	54.0	61.9	64.6	68.9	64.4	71.7	66.9	•	64.7	59.8
Salaries and Wages 11	10.1	•	•	3.8	6.8	10.3	8.9	9.2	6.3	9.0	•	12.3	11.4
Taxes Paid 12	1.6	•	•	1.3	2.6	2.3	2.4	2.1	1.8	1.3	•	1.5	1.0
Interest Paid 13	1.9	•	•	3.3	0.8	1.1	0.6	1.1	1.1	1.7	•	3.2	1.7
Depreciation 14	1.8	•	•	2.4	1.8	1.1	1.2	2.9	1.5	1.8	•	2.4	1.7
Amortization and Depletion 15	0.6	•	•	0.0	0.1	0.2	0.3	0.3	0.5	0.6	•	0.8	0.8
Pensions and Other Deferred Comp. 16	0.7	•	•	0.1	0.5	1.3	0.7	0.8	0.8	0.5	•	0.8	0.4
Employee Benefits 17	1.9	•	•	0.1	2.7	1.8	2.0	1.8	2.1	1.9	•	1.9	1.4
Advertising 18	0.5	•	•	1.6	0.5	0.4	0.5	0.8	0.4	0.3	•	0.4	0.5
Other Expenses 19	7.6	•	•	17.9	10.1	7.6	5.8	10.0	6.2	8.9	•	7.0	7.4
Officers' Compensation 20	1.6	•	•	6.8	5.3	4.5	2.9	2.6	1.5	1.3	•	1.1	0.5
Operating Margin 21	8.0	•	•	8.6	7.0	5.0	5.9	4.0	5.9	5.8	•	3.8	13.5
Operating Margin Before Officers' Comp. 22	9.6	•	•	15.5	12.3	9.5	8.7	6.6	7.5	7.1	•	4.8	13.9

Selected Average Balance Sheet ($ in Thousands)

Net Receivables 23	5178	•	161	901	1710	3512	8507	15897	35232	•	210650	941684
Inventories 24	3150	•	156	724	2126	4182	9726	10160	27269	•	85627	474234
Net Property, Plant and Equipment 25	2812	•	248	509	1410	1704	6204	10675	18016	•	77065	516479
Total Assets 26	28645		827	2487	7536	14701	34194	74044	158114		1049958	6532773
Notes and Loans Payable 27	6041	•	443	508	2036	2315	7541	11803	33074	•	262884	1164716
All Other Liabilities 28	7535	•	84	602	1486	4917	10911	23812	57509	•	341616	1259953
Net Worth 29	15070	•	300	1378	4014	7468	15741	38428	67531	•	445458	4108104

Selected Financial Ratios (Times to 1)

Current Ratio 30	1.7	•	6.9	2.6	2.3	2.1	2.2	1.9	1.8	•	1.4	1.7
Quick Ratio 31	1.1	•	4.4	1.6	1.3	1.2	1.2	1.2	1.0	•	1.0	1.2
Net Sales to Working Capital 32	4.8	•	1.3	4.6	4.0	3.7	3.8	3.9	4.4	•	5.3	4.9
Coverage Ratio 33	7.2	•	3.9	14.6	6.4	11.8	6.8	9.2	6.0	•	4.7	10.2
Total Asset Turnover 34	0.8	•	0.8	2.1	1.4	1.5	1.4	1.1	1.2	•	0.6	0.7
Inventory Turnover 35	4.8	•	2.3	4.4	3.3	3.6	3.2	5.8	4.5	•	4.7	5.4
Receivables Turnover 36	4.5	•	1.9	5.2	6.3	6.2	5.0	5.5	5.6	•	•	3.7
Total Liabilities to Net Worth 37	0.9	•	1.8	0.8	0.9	1.0	1.2	0.9	1.3	•	1.4	0.6
Current Assets to Working Capital 38	2.5	•	1.2	1.6	1.8	2.0	1.9	2.2	2.3	•	3.6	2.5
Current Liabilities to Working Capital 39	1.5	•	0.2	0.6	0.8	1.0	0.9	1.2	1.3	•	2.6	1.5
Working Capital to Net Sales 40	0.2	•	0.8	0.2	0.2	0.3	0.3	0.3	0.2	•	0.2	0.2
Inventory to Working Capital 41	0.6	•	0.4	0.6	0.7	0.7	0.7	0.5	0.7	•	0.7	0.5
Total Receipts to Cash Flow 42	6.1	•	4.2	5.6	8.7	8.6	7.0	7.5	6.4	•	6.3	5.2
Cost of Goods to Cash Flow 43	3.9	•	2.3	3.5	5.6	5.9	4.5	5.4	4.3	•	4.1	3.1
Cash Flow to Total Debt 44	0.3	•	0.3	0.8	0.4	0.4	0.4	0.3	0.3	•	0.2	0.3

Selected Financial Factors (in Percentages)

Debt Ratio 45	47.4	•	63.8	44.6	46.7	49.2	54.0	48.1	57.3	•	57.6	37.1
Return on Total Assets 46	11.2	•	10.4	23.7	9.7	11.3	10.2	11.0	11.9	•	9.0	11.2
Return on Equity Before Income Taxes 47	18.3	•	21.3	39.8	15.3	20.5	18.8	18.9	23.2	•	16.6	16.1
Return on Equity After Income Taxes 48	13.1	•	17.1	37.0	14.2	17.4	15.7	14.4	18.1	•	12.0	10.6
Profit Margin (Before Income Tax) 49	11.5	•	9.8	10.6	5.7	7.0	6.2	8.8	8.6	•	11.9	15.4
Profit Margin (After Income Tax) 50	8.2	•	7.9	9.9	5.3	6.0	5.2	6.7	6.7	•	8.6	10.1

Table I

Corporations with and without Net Income

COMMERCIAL AND SERVICE INDUSTRY MACHINERY

MONEY AMOUNTS AND SIZE OF ASSETS IN THOUSANDS OF DOLLARS

Item Description for Accounting Period 7/07 Through 6/08	Total	Zero Assets	Under 500	500 to 1,000	1,000 to 5,000	5,000 to 10,000	10,000 to 25,000	25,000 to 50,000	50,000 to 100,000	100,000 to 250,000	250,000 to 500,000	500,000 to 2,500,000	2,500,000 and over
Number of Enterprises **1**	2433	875	900	222	199	106	66	22	12	12	7	8	4
Revenues ($ in Thousands)													
Net Sales **2**	38540405	682918	945543	340416	1342486	1016062	1482587	1010725	1003137	2347636	1831332	5251680	21285882
Interest **3**	729861	12	48	482	1528	2779	3042	4408	2722	18452	16838	25080	654468
Rents **4**	189366	0	1924	0	0	8	19	1256	653	8410	671	107552	68874
Royalties **5**	1186147	0	0	0	0	0	19	77	884	150	2067	22051	1160899
Other Portfolio Income **6**	1326568	0	941	5	348	447	22889	2092	7736	3830	54512	31312	1202456
Other Receipts **7**	1342934	5255	2091	1212	12556	7093	5435	7883	6007	46279	8021	48646	1192459
Total Receipts **8**	43315281	688185	950547	342115	1356918	1026389	1513991	1026441	1021139	2424757	1913441	5486321	25565038
Average Total Receipts **9**	17803	786	1056	1541	6819	9683	22939	46656	85095	202063	273349	685790	6391260
Operating Costs/Operating Income (%)													
Cost of Operations **10**	59.0	39.3	71.7	66.3	66.8	59.7	67.3	73.0	60.2	67.6	54.9	67.4	54.4
Salaries and Wages **11**	16.1	40.0	9.2	3.5	10.5	13.1	10.5	7.6	12.3	11.5	12.4	8.1	20.1
Taxes Paid **12**	2.4	6.4	3.1	2.7	2.0	2.6	2.2	1.9	2.3	1.7	1.5	2.0	2.6
Interest Paid **13**	3.8	0.0	0.8	1.4	0.6	1.4	1.2	0.9	1.5	1.6	3.7	4.4	4.8
Depreciation **14**	4.5	0.6	0.5	0.5	0.5	2.9	1.8	1.8	2.0	1.6	4.2	4.1	6.1
Amortization and Depletion **15**	0.8	•	•	0.1	0.0	0.2	0.3	0.3	0.7	0.5	1.9	0.8	0.9
Pensions and Other Deferred Comp. **16**	1.5	0.0	0.5	0.1	0.9	0.5	0.5	0.5	0.7	0.5	0.3	0.7	2.3
Employee Benefits **17**	4.2	6.3	1.3	1.3	2.4	3.2	1.6	1.4	3.0	2.3	1.8	2.6	5.6
Advertising **18**	1.6	1.8	0.2	0.4	0.9	3.1	1.0	0.8	1.5	1.0	0.9	0.6	2.0
Other Expenses **19**	12.8	0.6	11.5	25.7	8.2	12.7	8.3	8.8	13.8	10.2	15.3	9.0	14.7
Officers' Compensation **20**	1.3	4.2	3.5	7.6	5.1	3.0	2.2	2.1	2.9	0.8	1.4	0.8	0.7
Operating Margin **21**	•	0.7	•	•	2.1	•	3.2	0.9	•	0.7	1.8	•	•
Operating Margin Before Officers' Comp. **22**	•	4.9	1.3	•	7.1	0.5	5.3	3.0	1.8	1.5	3.2	0.3	•

Selected Average Balance Sheet ($ in Thousands)

Net Receivables 23	5002	0	110	117	607	1229	2807	8293	18024	40331	44061	188404	2227689
Inventories 24	1712	0	89	187	1650	1544	4339	11460	14113	41340	31308	82946	366095
Net Property, Plant and Equipment 25	2480	0	33	79	256	1432	2613	5581	9463	22461	40885	118701	967406
Total Assets 26	26572	0	321	785	2811	6176	14096	35517	70303	158064	335150	820847	12401752
Notes and Loans Payable 27	10431	0	82	682	647	1352	3341	4859	17903	35202	121348	335446	5096149
All Other Liabilities 28	8708	0	201	650	420	2881	3946	17022	20261	46726	57329	339821	3978452
Net Worth 29	7433	0	38	-547	1744	1944	6809	13636	32139	76135	156473	145580	3327150

Selected Financial Ratios (Times to 1)

Current Ratio 30	1.1	•	1.0	0.9	3.7	1.4	1.9	1.5	1.6	1.9	1.3	1.6	1.0
Quick Ratio 31	0.7	•	0.6	0.4	2.0	0.7	0.9	0.7	0.9	1.1	0.6	1.1	0.6
Net Sales to Working Capital 32	17.8	•	132.4	•	4.2	9.8	5.0	4.8	5.6	4.2	9.9	4.9	•
Coverage Ratio 33	2.7	47.2	•	•	5.9	•	5.5	3.7	1.5	3.5	2.7	2.0	2.9
Total Asset Turnover 34	0.6	•	3.3	2.0	2.4	1.6	1.6	1.3	1.2	1.2	0.8	0.8	0.4
Inventory Turnover 35	5.5	•	8.4	5.4	2.7	3.7	3.5	2.9	3.6	3.2	4.6	5.3	7.9
Receivables Turnover 36	3.0	•	10.5	18.9	4.7	7.9	8.2	5.8	4.6	3.9	8.4	3.6	2.2
Total Liabilities to Net Worth 37	2.6	•	7.4	•	0.6	2.2	1.1	1.6	1.2	1.1	1.1	4.6	2.7
Current Assets to Working Capital 38	10.9	•	32.7	•	1.4	3.6	2.2	3.0	2.8	2.1	4.1	2.6	•
Current Liabilities to Working Capital 39	9.9	•	31.7	•	0.4	2.6	1.2	2.0	1.8	1.1	3.1	1.6	•
Working Capital to Net Sales 40	0.1	•	0.0	•	0.2	0.1	0.2	0.2	0.2	0.2	0.1	0.2	•
Inventory to Working Capital 41	1.9	•	12.5	•	0.6	1.6	1.0	1.4	0.8	0.8	1.6	0.7	•
Total Receipts to Cash Flow 42	8.7	•	13.7	9.3	11.4	11.1	9.1	10.2	8.6	8.0	5.6	10.3	8.2
Cost of Goods to Cash Flow 43	5.1	•	9.8	6.1	7.6	6.6	6.1	7.4	5.2	5.4	3.1	6.9	4.4
Cash Flow to Total Debt 44	0.1	•	0.3	0.1	0.6	0.2	0.3	0.2	0.3	0.3	0.3	0.1	0.1

Selected Financial Factors (in Percentages)

Debt Ratio 45	72.0	•	88.1	169.8	38.0	68.5	51.7	61.6	54.3	51.8	53.3	82.3	73.2
Return on Total Assets 46	6.0	•	•	•	9.1	•	10.2	4.2	2.7	7.0	7.8	6.9	6.0
Return on Equity Before Income Taxes 47	13.6	•	•	25.4	12.2	•	17.4	8.0	1.9	10.4	10.5	19.0	14.5
Return on Equity After Income Taxes 48	9.0	•	•	26.1	11.9	•	15.2	4.6	•	7.3	6.8	12.9	9.6
Profit Margin (Before Income Tax) 49	6.4	1.4	•	3.1	•	•	5.3	2.4	0.7	4.0	6.3	4.2	9.1
Profit Margin (After Income Tax) 50	4.2	1.2	•	3.1	•	•	4.6	1.4	•	2.8	4.1	2.9	6.0

127

Table II

Corporations with Net Income

COMMERCIAL AND SERVICE INDUSTRY MACHINERY

MONEY AMOUNTS AND SIZE OF ASSETS IN THOUSANDS OF DOLLARS

Item Description for Accounting Period 7/07 Through 6/08		Total	Zero Assets	Under 500	500 to 1,000	1,000 to 5,000	5,000 to 10,000	10,000 to 25,000	25,000 to 50,000	50,000 to 100,000	100,000 to 250,000	250,000 to 500,000	500,000 to 2,500,000	2,500,000 and over
Number of Enterprises	1	1501	478	619	59	161	88	47	•	8	•	•	•	4
Revenues ($ in Thousands)														
Net Sales	2	35546494	644831	678048	41626	1317402	945019	1230042	•	700541	•	•	•	21285882
Interest	3	721901	12	0	181	965	1959	2421	•	1507	•	•	•	654468
Rents	4	184262	0	0	0	0	8	0	•	219	•	•	•	68874
Royalties	5	1185254	0	0	0	0	0	0	•	22	•	•	•	1160899
Other Portfolio Income	6	1322126	0	0	5	348	396	22668	•	4622	•	•	•	1202456
Other Receipts	7	1306713	5254	0	0	12550	6375	3569	•	4313	•	•	•	1192459
Total Receipts	8	40266750	650097	678048	41812	1331265	953757	1258700	•	711224	•	•	•	25565038
Average Total Receipts	9	26827	1360	1095	709	8269	10838	26781	•	88903	•	•	•	6391260
Operating Costs/Operating Income (%)														
Cost of Operations	10	58.3	37.4	70.0	75.7	66.6	60.1	67.1	•	59.6	•	•	•	54.4
Salaries and Wages	11	16.4	42.4	2.0	0.2	10.6	12.4	9.5	•	10.8	•	•	•	20.1
Taxes Paid	12	2.4	6.8	2.9	1.4	1.9	2.6	2.2	•	2.6	•	•	•	2.6
Interest Paid	13	3.7	0.0	0.2	0.0	0.4	1.0	0.6	•	1.4	•	•	•	4.8
Depreciation	14	4.7	0.6	0.4	0.2	0.4	1.3	1.3	•	1.4	•	•	•	6.1
Amortization and Depletion	15	0.7	•	•	•	0.0	0.1	0.1	•	0.5	•	•	•	0.9
Pensions and Other Deferred Comp.	16	1.6	0.0	0.2	0.1	0.9	0.6	0.5	•	0.8	•	•	•	2.3
Employee Benefits	17	4.3	6.6	•	0.0	2.4	3.2	1.8	•	3.5	•	•	•	5.6
Advertising	18	1.6	2.0	0.2	0.0	0.9	2.4	1.0	•	0.9	•	•	•	2.0
Other Expenses	19	12.5	•	8.7	10.7	7.1	11.0	7.3	•	11.8	•	•	•	14.7
Officers' Compensation	20	1.2	4.5	3.7	1.3	4.8	2.9	2.1	•	1.5	•	•	•	0.7
Operating Margin	21	•	1.2	11.6	10.4	3.8	2.3	6.4	•	5.3	•	•	•	•
Operating Margin Before Officers' Comp.	22	•	5.7	15.3	11.7	8.7	5.2	8.6	•	6.8	•	•	•	•

Selected Average Balance Sheet ($ in Thousands)

Net Receivables 23	7823	0	102	98	689	1358	3333	18153	•	2227689
Inventories 24	2221	0	97	213	1679	1202	4366	15417	•	370120
Net Property, Plant and Equipment 25	3739	0	10	1	280	970	2118	7899	•	967406
Total Assets 26	40919	0	275	627	3116	6034	14041	69103	•	12401752
Notes and Loans Payable 27	15690	0	39	2	392	852	1749	14810	•	5096149
All Other Liabilities 28	13508	0	79	165	499	3094	4454	17211	•	3978452
Net Worth 29	11721	0	157	460	2225	2088	7837	37081	•	3327150

Selected Financial Ratios (Times to 1)

Current Ratio 30	1.1	•	2.5	3.8	3.8	1.5	2.0	1.8	•	1.0
Quick Ratio 31	0.7	•	1.5	2.6	2.2	0.7	0.9	1.1	•	0.6
Net Sales to Working Capital 32	18.6	•	6.9	1.5	4.5	8.7	4.9	4.6	•	2.9
Coverage Ratio 33	3.1	62.7	57.3	411.8	12.4	4.1	16.2	5.7	•	2.9
Total Asset Turnover 34	0.6	•	4.0	1.1	2.6	1.8	1.9	1.3	•	0.4
Inventory Turnover 35	6.2	•	7.9	2.5	3.2	5.4	4.0	3.4	•	7.8
Receivables Turnover 36	3.1	•	9.5	5.6	6.0	9.9	8.6	4.5	•	2.7
Total Liabilities to Net Worth 37	2.5	•	0.8	0.4	0.4	1.9	0.8	0.9	•	•
Current Assets to Working Capital 38	11.7	•	1.7	1.4	1.4	3.0	2.0	2.2	•	•
Current Liabilities to Working Capital 39	10.7	•	0.7	0.4	0.4	2.0	1.0	1.2	•	•
Working Capital to Net Sales 40	0.1	•	0.1	0.7	0.2	0.1	0.2	0.2	•	•
Inventory to Working Capital 41	1.9	•	0.6	0.4	0.6	1.3	0.9	0.6	•	•
Total Receipts to Cash Flow 42	8.1	•	5.5	4.7	10.4	8.2	7.4	6.4	•	8.2
Cost of Goods to Cash Flow 43	4.7	•	3.9	3.6	6.9	4.9	5.0	3.8	•	4.4
Cash Flow to Total Debt 44	0.1	•	1.7	0.9	0.9	0.3	0.6	0.4	•	0.1

Selected Financial Factors (in Percentages)

Debt Ratio 45	71.4	•	43.0	26.7	28.6	65.4	44.2	46.3	•	73.2
Return on Total Assets 46	6.7	•	46.8	12.3	14.0	7.5	17.4	10.4	•	6.0
Return on Equity Before Income Taxes 47	15.9	•	80.7	16.7	18.0	16.4	29.2	16.1	•	14.5
Return on Equity After Income Taxes 48	11.2	•	80.7	13.5	17.8	11.4	26.5	13.2	•	9.6
Profit Margin (Before Income Tax) 49	7.9	2.0	11.6	10.9	4.9	3.2	8.8	6.8	•	9.1
Profit Margin (After Income Tax) 50	5.5	1.8	11.6	8.8	4.8	2.2	7.9	5.6	•	6.0

Table I

Corporations with and without Net Income

VENTILATION, HEATING, A.C. & COMMERCIAL REFRIGERATION EQUIP.

MONEY AMOUNTS AND SIZE OF ASSETS IN THOUSANDS OF DOLLARS

Item Description for Accounting Period 7/07 Through 6/08	Total	Zero Assets	Under 500	500 to 1,000	1,000 to 5,000	5,000 to 10,000	10,000 to 25,000	25,000 to 50,000	50,000 to 100,000	100,000 to 250,000	250,000 to 500,000	500,000 to 2,500,000	2,500,000 and over
Number of Enterprises 1	873	3	195	238	189	89	63	36	30	16	5	4	4

Revenues ($ in Thousands)

Item Description for Accounting Period 7/07 Through 6/08	Total	Zero Assets	Under 500	500 to 1,000	1,000 to 5,000	5,000 to 10,000	10,000 to 25,000	25,000 to 50,000	50,000 to 100,000	100,000 to 250,000	250,000 to 500,000	500,000 to 2,500,000	2,500,000 and over
Net Sales 2	36108833	366891	183422	466106	956147	1432203	1723798	2050788	3383300	2838114	1674586	7378132	13650346
Interest 3	117061	196	772	0	2321	451	2082	7864	6473	7668	6229	38721	44283
Rents 4	16896	0	3912	0	937	21	407	381	53	1183	335	5358	4309
Royalties 5	171225	1548	0	0	0	0	1132	1377	4583	3232	910	66993	91449
Other Portfolio Income 6	811162	73	2450	0	755	381	3572	28835	9279	8510	85984	45128	626191
Other Receipts 7	1186575	3470	322	-154	11402	14900	24886	4797	6417	23817	11017	909912	175796
Total Receipts 8	38411752	372178	190878	465952	971562	1447956	1755877	2094042	3415105	2882524	1779061	8444244	14592374
Average Total Receipts 9	44000	124059	979	1958	5141	16269	27871	58168	113837	180158	355812	2111061	3648094

Operating Costs/Operating Income (%)

Item Description for Accounting Period 7/07 Through 6/08	Total	Zero Assets	Under 500	500 to 1,000	1,000 to 5,000	5,000 to 10,000	10,000 to 25,000	25,000 to 50,000	50,000 to 100,000	100,000 to 250,000	250,000 to 500,000	500,000 to 2,500,000	2,500,000 and over
Cost of Operations 10	75.5	83.8	55.4	52.9	61.5	77.2	70.5	67.9	71.2	69.2	70.5	85.8	76.4
Salaries and Wages 11	7.3	30.2	16.0	3.4	10.6	5.9	9.0	8.8	6.1	8.1	5.8	5.0	7.8
Taxes Paid 12	1.0	0.6	3.2	1.0	2.8	1.4	1.5	1.6	1.7	1.7	1.0	1.0	0.3
Interest Paid 13	2.5	1.8	0.5	0.2	0.9	1.0	1.1	1.3	1.1	4.3	4.2	1.5	3.5
Depreciation 14	1.2	1.0	1.8	0.3	1.6	0.9	1.8	1.3	1.7	2.1	1.5	0.9	1.1
Amortization and Depletion 15	0.8	7.6	•	•	0.2	0.0	0.2	0.2	0.3	0.5	0.9	0.3	1.4
Pensions and Other Deferred Comp. 16	0.6	0.1	4.7	0.1	1.4	0.3	0.4	0.7	0.7	1.8	0.1	0.6	0.2
Employee Benefits 17	1.5	0.5	1.3	0.8	2.3	0.7	1.6	1.9	1.9	2.5	1.3	1.4	1.4
Advertising 18	0.9	0.3	0.3	0.3	3.4	0.3	0.4	0.9	0.6	0.7	0.7	1.3	0.9
Other Expenses 19	9.5	28.0	13.0	19.6	14.8	7.5	9.2	9.6	7.2	7.9	8.8	9.9	9.2
Officers' Compensation 20	1.3	0.4	12.0	2.9	6.0	2.5	2.4	1.1	1.9	1.7	0.6	1.3	0.4
Operating Margin 21	•	•	•	18.4	•	2.2	2.0	4.8	5.7	•	4.5	•	•
Operating Margin Before Officers' Comp. 22	•	•	3.7	21.3	0.4	4.7	4.4	5.9	7.6	1.2	5.1	•	•

Selected Average Balance Sheet ($ in Thousands)

Net Receivables 23	5920	0	56	162	568	2472	4077	8970	19261	25788	75509	153917	557104
Inventories 24	4084	0	4	70	602	1949	3989	6831	11827	24980	35040	181289	275810
Net Property, Plant and Equipment 25	3787	0	148	88	377	1601	3089	5064	14377	24577	34756	110385	306388
Total Assets 26	39474	0	373	702	2321	7358	14537	33238	70141	173546	395404	1507701	4531498
Notes and Loans Payable 27	12751	0	22	29	747	2423	3287	9921	17794	67127	109174	419696	1591776
All Other Liabilities 28	13520	0	57	103	790	1935	3752	10896	20649	56906	156760	389322	1736609
Net Worth 29	13202	0	294	570	784	2999	7498	12421	31698	49514	129470	698682	1203114

Selected Financial Ratios (Times to 1)

Current Ratio 30	1.4	•	2.4	4.8	1.9	3.1	2.0	1.9	1.7	1.1	1.6	2.0	1.1
Quick Ratio 31	0.8	•	2.3	4.2	1.1	1.8	1.1	1.2	1.1	0.6	1.0	1.2	0.5
Net Sales to Working Capital 32	9.6	•	10.6	4.1	6.2	4.5	5.6	4.8	6.2	22.2	5.5	7.3	31.3
Coverage Ratio 33	2.9	•	•	99.9	•	4.4	4.4	6.3	6.7	1.3	3.6	4.7	2.5
Total Asset Turnover 34	1.0	•	2.5	2.8	2.2	2.2	1.9	1.7	1.6	1.0	0.8	1.2	0.8
Inventory Turnover 35	7.7	•	130.0	14.7	5.2	6.4	4.8	5.7	6.8	4.9	6.7	8.7	9.5
Receivables Turnover 36	6.8	•	10.7	•	8.3	•	6.9	5.0	6.2	7.7	5.4	8.9	6.2
Total Liabilities to Net Worth 37	2.0	•	0.3	0.2	2.0	1.5	0.9	1.7	1.2	2.5	2.1	1.2	2.8
Current Assets to Working Capital 38	3.6	•	1.7	1.3	2.1	1.5	2.0	2.1	2.3	8.9	2.6	2.0	13.7
Current Liabilities to Working Capital 39	2.6	•	0.7	0.3	1.1	0.5	1.0	1.1	1.3	7.9	1.6	1.0	12.7
Working Capital to Net Sales 40	0.1	•	0.1	0.2	0.2	0.2	0.2	0.2	0.2	0.0	0.2	0.1	0.0
Inventory to Working Capital 41	0.9	•	0.0	0.1	0.7	0.6	0.8	0.5	0.7	3.4	0.6	0.5	2.7
Total Receipts to Cash Flow 42	9.8	•	15.4	2.8	12.1	10.1	8.8	6.7	8.1	13.9	7.3	7.7	12.7
Cost of Goods to Cash Flow 43	7.4	•	8.5	1.5	7.5	7.8	6.2	4.5	5.8	9.6	5.1	6.6	9.7
Cash Flow to Total Debt 44	0.2	•	0.8	5.4	0.3	0.4	0.4	0.4	0.4	0.1	0.2	0.3	0.1

Selected Financial Factors (in Percentages)

Debt Ratio 45	66.6	•	21.3	18.8	66.2	59.2	48.4	62.6	54.8	71.5	67.3	53.7	73.4
Return on Total Assets 46	7.4	•	•	51.8	•	9.3	9.2	13.8	12.3	5.6	12.7	8.6	6.6
Return on Equity Before Income Taxes 47	14.4	•	•	63.2	•	17.7	13.8	31.0	23.1	4.3	27.9	14.6	15.0
Return on Equity After Income Taxes 48	9.0	•	•	62.7	•	16.6	9.3	24.1	18.0	•	21.2	9.5	9.0
Profit Margin (Before Income Tax) 49	4.6	•	•	18.4	•	3.3	3.8	6.8	6.5	1.2	10.8	5.5	5.3
Profit Margin (After Income Tax) 50	2.9	•	•	18.3	•	3.1	2.5	5.3	5.0	•	8.2	3.6	3.2

Table II

Corporations with Net Income

VENTILATION, HEATING, A.C. & COMMERCIAL REFRIGERATION EQUIP.

MONEY AMOUNTS AND SIZE OF ASSETS IN THOUSANDS OF DOLLARS

Item Description for Accounting Period 7/07 Through 6/08		Total	Zero Assets	Under 500	500 to 1,000	1,000 to 5,000	5,000 to 10,000	10,000 to 25,000	25,000 to 50,000	50,000 to 100,000	100,000 to 250,000	250,000 to 500,000	500,000 to 2,500,000	2,500,000 and over
Number of Enterprises	1	653	•	•	•	144	61	46	29	23	12	5	4	•
Revenues ($ in Thousands)														
Net Sales	2	31664698	•	•	•	852760	1082571	1241879	1770448	2863270	2569142	1674586	7378132	•
Interest	3	104745	•	•	•	2193	419	1340	6783	5440	5817	6229	38721	•
Rents	4	16792	•	•	•	854	0	407	381	53	1183	335	5358	•
Royalties	5	169562	•	•	•	0	0	1132	1340	4583	3232	910	66993	•
Other Portfolio Income	6	807315	•	•	•	159	72	3184	28794	9253	8476	85984	45128	•
Other Receipts	7	1169424	•	•	•	4048	8311	15886	3763	6237	22761	11017	909912	•
Total Receipts	8	33932536	•	•	•	860014	1091373	1263828	1811509	2888836	2610611	1779061	8444244	•
Average Total Receipts	9	51964	•	•	•	5972	17891	27475	62466	125602	217551	355812	2111061	•
Operating Costs/Operating Income (%)														
Cost of Operations	10	75.1	•	•	•	58.8	77.5	68.9	65.9	69.2	68.2	70.5	85.8	•
Salaries and Wages	11	7.0	•	•	•	8.8	4.2	7.2	9.3	6.4	7.1	5.8	5.0	•
Taxes Paid	12	1.0	•	•	•	2.6	0.9	1.7	1.4	1.7	1.8	1.0	1.0	•
Interest Paid	13	1.9	•	•	•	0.3	0.8	0.7	0.4	1.2	2.0	4.2	1.5	•
Depreciation	14	1.2	•	•	•	1.6	0.6	1.5	1.2	1.4	2.1	1.5	0.9	•
Amortization and Depletion	15	0.4	•	•	•	0.2	0.0	0.3	0.1	0.2	0.5	0.9	0.3	•
Pensions and Other Deferred Comp.	16	0.6	•	•	•	1.5	0.4	0.6	0.7	0.8	2.0	0.1	0.6	•
Employee Benefits	17	1.6	•	•	•	1.9	0.3	1.2	2.0	1.9	2.6	1.3	1.4	•
Advertising	18	1.0	•	•	•	3.0	0.1	0.2	0.7	0.6	0.7	0.7	1.3	•
Other Expenses	19	9.3	•	•	•	12.3	6.2	7.0	9.4	6.9	7.3	8.8	9.9	•
Officers' Compensation	20	1.3	•	•	•	6.0	2.0	2.4	1.0	2.2	1.7	0.6	1.3	•
Operating Margin	21	•	•	•	•	3.0	7.1	8.4	7.8	7.7	4.1	4.5	•	•
Operating Margin Before Officers' Comp.	22	1.1	•	•	•	9.1	9.0	10.8	8.8	9.8	5.8	5.1	•	•

Selected Average Balance Sheet ($ in Thousands)

Net Receivables 23	7059	706	2956	4663	9430	21543	28007	75509	153917
Inventories 24	4751	728	2468	4178	7183	12229	29697	35040	123536
Net Property, Plant and Equipment 25	4392	444	1650	3006	5259	13874	29011	34756	110385
Total Assets 26	38746	2464	7478	15334	33729	73527	165040	395404	1507701
Notes and Loans Payable 27	13571	534	1974	3227	7558	15377	59367	109174	419696
All Other Liabilities 28	14641	808	2158	3444	1118	22219	64917	156760	389322
Net Worth 29	10533	1123	3346	8663	15053	35932	40755	129470	698682

Selected Financial Ratios (Times to 1)

Current Ratio 30	1.4	2.1	3.1	2.0	2.4	2.0	1.0	1.6	2.0
Quick Ratio 31	0.8	1.2	1.9	1.1	1.5	1.3	0.5	1.0	1.2
Net Sales to Working Capital 32	9.9	6.2	4.5	5.4	4.1	5.2	•	5.5	7.3
Coverage Ratio 33	4.8	15.6	11.4	16.3	25.6	8.5	4.0	3.6	4.7
Total Asset Turnover 34	1.3	2.4	2.4	1.8	1.8	1.7	1.3	0.8	1.2
Inventory Turnover 35	7.7	4.8	5.6	4.4	5.6	7.0	4.9	6.7	12.8
Receivables Turnover 36	6.6	7.6	6.0	6.2	4.9	6.0	•	5.4	•
Total Liabilities to Net Worth 37	2.7	1.2	1.2	0.8	1.2	1.0	3.0	2.1	1.2
Current Assets to Working Capital 38	3.7	1.9	1.5	2.0	1.7	2.0	•	2.6	2.0
Current Liabilities to Working Capital 39	2.7	0.9	0.5	1.0	0.7	1.0	•	1.6	1.0
Working Capital to Net Sales 40	0.1	0.2	0.2	0.2	0.2	0.2	•	0.2	0.1
Inventory to Working Capital 41	0.9	0.7	0.5	0.8	0.4	0.5	•	0.6	0.5
Total Receipts to Cash Flow 42	8.1	7.2	7.3	6.3	5.6	7.1	8.8	7.3	7.7
Cost of Goods to Cash Flow 43	6.0	4.2	5.7	4.3	3.7	4.9	6.0	5.1	6.6
Cash Flow to Total Debt 44	0.2	0.6	0.6	0.6	0.6	0.5	0.2	0.2	0.3

Selected Financial Factors (in Percentages)

Debt Ratio 45	72.8	54.4	55.3	43.5	55.4	51.1	75.3	67.3	53.7
Return on Total Assets 46	11.6	9.9	20.5	18.9	18.7	16.5	10.3	12.7	8.6
Return on Equity Before Income Taxes 47	33.9	20.4	41.8	31.4	40.3	29.8	31.4	27.9	14.6
Return on Equity After Income Taxes 48	24.7	17.9	40.4	26.1	33.2	23.9	23.1	21.2	9.5
Profit Margin (Before Income Tax) 49	7.4	3.9	7.9	10.1	9.9	8.6	6.0	10.8	5.5
Profit Margin (After Income Tax) 50	5.4	3.4	7.6	8.4	8.2	6.9	4.4	8.2	3.6

Table I

Corporations with and without Net Income

METALWORKING MACHINERY

MONEY AMOUNTS AND SIZE OF ASSETS IN THOUSANDS OF DOLLARS

Item Description for Accounting Period 7/07 Through 6/08	Total	Zero Assets	Under 500	500 to 1,000	1,000 to 5,000	5,000 to 10,000	10,000 to 25,000	25,000 to 50,000	50,000 to 100,000	100,000 to 250,000	250,000 to 500,000	500,000 to 2,500,000	2,500,000 and over
Number of Enterprises 1	6317	640	3565	516	1257	153	104	45	18	11	4	4	0
Revenues ($ in Thousands)													
Net Sales 2	24412072	158387	1817834	709368	5170199	1557682	1912672	2084796	1405035	1871125	1432573	6292400	0
Interest 3	73220	80	1772	331	10013	3426	1818	1712	9809	9933	3071	31256	0
Rents 4	9476	176	0	789	1112	2927	1048	918	0	894	968	644	0
Royalties 5	4188	0	0	0	0	0	214	249	2	1630	0	2093	0
Other Portfolio Income 6	172658	3572	57456	479	5554	891	2312	7074	3506	33177	0	58637	0
Other Receipts 7	249115	200	27967	9905	39631	6069	19928	30247	13162	28430	-2084	75661	0
Total Receipts 8	24920729	162415	1905029	720872	5226509	1570995	1937992	2124996	1431514	1945189	1434528	6460691	0
Average Total Receipts 9	3945	254	534	1397	4158	10268	18635	47222	79529	176835	358632	1615173	•
Operating Costs/Operating Income (%)													
Cost of Operations 10	64.9	59.8	33.5	62.2	67.6	66.7	65.7	70.0	67.4	64.9	71.5	67.7	•
Salaries and Wages 11	7.9	12.6	12.1	5.8	5.9	5.4	7.6	6.6	6.7	7.9	8.8	9.7	•
Taxes Paid 12	2.3	1.4	4.4	4.0	3.2	2.7	2.7	2.4	2.2	1.7	1.7	1.0	•
Interest Paid 13	1.9	1.6	2.2	1.6	1.1	1.5	1.5	1.2	1.3	2.5	1.6	3.1	•
Depreciation 14	2.5	0.8	3.3	3.1	2.6	3.6	2.9	3.3	2.5	1.4	1.3	2.1	•
Amortization and Depletion 15	0.4	0.1	0.0	0.0	0.0	0.3	0.2	0.1	0.5	0.5	0.1	1.1	•
Pensions and Other Deferred Comp. 16	0.5	0.5	0.3	0.8	0.4	0.5	0.4	0.9	0.8	0.6	0.4	0.5	•
Employee Benefits 17	2.6	2.1	1.3	4.6	1.9	1.7	3.1	2.1	1.9	2.5	1.7	3.9	•
Advertising 18	0.3	0.1	0.0	0.1	0.2	0.2	0.5	0.3	0.5	0.4	0.5	0.5	•
Other Expenses 19	10.7	9.0	34.3	8.1	8.7	9.8	9.6	8.9	8.1	7.2	6.8	9.4	•
Officers' Compensation 20	3.0	2.3	9.0	10.9	4.7	3.5	2.8	2.3	1.6	1.6	0.3	0.4	•
Operating Margin 21	2.9	9.9	•	•	3.6	3.9	3.0	1.9	6.6	8.8	5.0	0.5	•
Operating Margin Before Officers' Comp. 22	5.9	12.2	8.5	9.7	8.3	7.4	5.9	4.3	8.2	10.4	5.3	1.0	•

Selected Average Balance Sheet ($ in Thousands)

Item													
Net Receivables 23	558	0	32	210	635	1765	3236	8709	12573	39734	60555	149953	•
Inventories 24	547	0	14	140	581	1324	3228	8144	12943	25694	86523	209665	•
Net Property, Plant and Equipment 25	600	0	52	144	668	2120	3685	10279	13000	19172	44244	225284	•
Total Assets 26	3607	0	153	723	2481	7262	14781	35363	69452	157519	330962	2550473	•
Notes and Loans Payable 27	1215	0	163	345	869	1918	4114	7015	13658	53712	330962	973995	•
All Other Liabilities 28	912	0	44	139	598	1903	5413	9435	16404	37052	154124	546184	•
Net Worth 29	1479	0	-55	239	1015	3441	5254	18913	39390	66755	162420	1030294	•

Selected Financial Ratios (Times to 1)

Item													
Current Ratio 30	1.4	•	1.0	2.8	1.7	1.6	1.2	2.0	2.4	2.3	1.6	0.8	•
Quick Ratio 31	0.7	•	0.8	1.7	1.0	1.0	0.6	1.1	1.2	1.4	0.7	0.3	•
Net Sales to Working Capital 32	9.2	9.1	164.0	4.1	6.3	6.8	10.9	4.5	3.4	3.5	5.4	•	•
Coverage Ratio 33	3.7	•	2.9	1.3	5.2	4.1	3.9	4.2	7.3	7.2	4.2	2.2	•
Total Asset Turnover 34	1.1	•	3.3	1.9	1.7	1.4	1.2	1.3	1.1	1.1	1.1	0.6	•
Inventory Turnover 35	4.6	•	12.4	6.1	4.8	5.1	3.7	4.0	4.1	4.3	3.0	5.1	•
Receivables Turnover 36	6.4	•	14.2	5.9	5.8	5.9	5.9	5.1	6.6	4.1	7.3	7.7	•
Total Liabilities to Net Worth 37	1.4	•	•	2.0	1.4	1.1	1.8	0.9	0.8	1.4	1.0	1.5	•
Current Assets to Working Capital 38	3.6	•	28.5	1.6	2.3	2.7	5.2	2.0	1.7	1.8	2.8	•	•
Current Liabilities to Working Capital 39	2.6	•	27.5	0.6	1.3	1.7	4.2	1.0	0.7	0.8	1.8	•	•
Working Capital to Net Sales 40	0.1	•	0.0	0.2	0.2	0.1	0.1	0.2	0.3	0.3	0.2	•	•
Inventory to Working Capital 41	1.3	•	3.5	0.4	0.8	0.8	2.0	0.8	0.6	0.5	1.5	•	•
Total Receipts to Cash Flow 42	7.5	5.5	3.1	16.2	9.8	8.2	8.9	8.8	6.6	5.5	8.9	8.8	•
Cost of Goods to Cash Flow 43	4.9	3.3	1.0	10.1	6.6	5.5	5.9	6.2	4.5	3.6	6.4	5.9	•
Cash Flow to Total Debt 44	0.2	•	0.8	0.2	0.3	0.3	0.2	0.3	0.4	0.3	0.2	0.1	•

Selected Financial Factors (in Percentages)

Item													
Debt Ratio 45	59.0	•	135.9	67.0	59.1	52.6	64.5	46.5	43.3	57.6	50.9	59.6	•
Return on Total Assets 46	7.8	•	21.9	3.8	9.6	8.8	7.2	6.5	11.0	19.2	7.4	4.3	•
Return on Equity Before Income Taxes 47	13.9	•	•	2.6	18.9	14.0	15.1	9.3	16.8	39.0	11.5	5.8	•
Return on Equity After Income Taxes 48	11.4	•	•	1.9	17.8	12.0	13.3	7.8	13.6	33.0	7.2	3.9	•
Profit Margin (Before Income Tax) 49	5.3	13.3	4.3	0.4	4.7	4.7	4.3	3.8	8.5	15.3	5.2	3.8	•
Profit Margin (After Income Tax) 50	4.4	13.1	3.8	0.3	4.4	4.1	3.2	3.2	6.9	13.0	3.3	2.5	•

131

Table II

Corporations with Net Income

METALWORKING MACHINERY

Money Amounts and Size of Assets in Thousands of Dollars

Item Description for Accounting Period 7/07 Through 6/08	Total	Zero Assets	Under 500	500 to 1,000	1,000 to 5,000	5,000 to 10,000	10,000 to 25,000	25,000 to 50,000	50,000 to 100,000	100,000 to 250,000	250,000 to 500,000	500,000 to 2,500,000	2,500,000 and over
Number of Enterprises 1	4368	400	2552	297	847	122	84	33	•	•	0	4	0

Revenues ($ in Thousands)

	Total	Zero Assets	Under 500	500 to 1,000	1,000 to 5,000	5,000 to 10,000	10,000 to 25,000	25,000 to 50,000	50,000 to 100,000	100,000 to 250,000	250,000 to 500,000	500,000 to 2,500,000	2,500,000 and over
Net Sales 2	20988380	137252	1558814	444429	4060061	1274438	1575821	1621773	•	•	0	6292400	0
Interest 3	65379	80	1102	288	5809	2954	1623	1210	•	•	0	31256	0
Rents 4	7995	176	0	789	1112	2437	1026	918	•	•	0	644	0
Royalties 5	4188	0	0	0	0	0	214	249	•	•	0	2093	0
Other Portfolio Income 6	161726	3572	57456	479	2439	845	2280	5305	•	•	0	58637	0
Other Receipts 7	228254	200	27163	9905	36600	2752	18330	16605	•	•	0	75661	0
Total Receipts 8	21456922	141280	1644535	455890	4106021	1283426	1599294	1646060	•	•	0	6460691	0
Average Total Receipts 9	4912	353	644	1535	4848	10520	19039	49881	•	•	•	1615173	•

Operating Costs/Operating Income (%)

	Total	Zero Assets	Under 500	500 to 1,000	1,000 to 5,000	5,000 to 10,000	10,000 to 25,000	25,000 to 50,000	50,000 to 100,000	100,000 to 250,000	250,000 to 500,000	500,000 to 2,500,000	2,500,000 and over
Cost of Operations 10	64.1	64.1	28.6	61.9	66.9	65.4	65.0	66.5	•	•	•	67.7	•
Salaries and Wages 11	7.9	8.7	12.3	5.5	6.0	4.8	7.1	7.1	•	•	•	9.7	•
Taxes Paid 12	2.1	1.1	4.3	3.6	2.8	3.0	2.7	2.1	•	•	•	1.0	•
Interest Paid 13	1.9	1.9	1.8	1.1	0.9	1.1	1.2	1.1	•	•	•	3.1	•
Depreciation 14	2.4	0.9	3.2	3.1	2.4	3.9	3.1	3.5	•	•	•	2.1	•
Amortization and Depletion 15	0.4	0.1	0.0	•	0.0	0.0	0.0	0.1	•	•	•	1.1	•
Pensions and Other Deferred Comp. 16	0.5	0.5	0.4	1.0	0.4	0.6	0.4	1.0	•	•	•	0.5	•
Employee Benefits 17	2.5	2.4	1.1	3.0	1.7	1.9	2.7	2.0	•	•	•	3.9	•
Advertising 18	0.3	0.1	0.0	0.1	0.2	0.1	0.4	0.4	•	•	•	0.5	•
Other Expenses 19	10.4	5.7	36.4	9.9	7.9	9.4	9.2	8.7	•	•	•	9.4	•
Officers' Compensation 20	3.0	2.7	10.1	11.3	4.8	3.8	3.0	2.5	•	•	•	0.4	•
Operating Margin 21	4.3	11.9	1.6	•	5.9	6.1	5.2	5.1	•	•	•	0.5	•
Operating Margin Before Officers' Comp. 22	7.3	14.5	11.7	10.8	10.8	9.9	8.1	7.6	•	•	•	1.0	•

Selected Average Balance Sheet ($ in Thousands)

Net Receivables	23	670	0	29	232	723	1900	3454	8435	•	149953
Inventories	24	650	0	8	132	701	1337	3087	7872	•	218761
Net Property, Plant and Equipment	25	717	0	56	144	737	2145	3914	11080	•	225284
Total Assets	26	4537	0	165	730	2638	7338	14146	37189	•	2550473
Notes and Loans Payable	27	1503	0	144	344	834	1550	3050	7234	•	973995
All Other Liabilities	28	1115	0	50	111	669	1932	3491	9471	•	546184
Net Worth	29	1918	0	-29	275	1135	3855	7605	20483	•	1030294

Selected Financial Ratios (Times to 1)

Current Ratio	30	1.4	•	1.1	4.0	2.1	1.8	1.9	2.1	•	0.8
Quick Ratio	31	0.7	•	0.8	2.6	1.3	1.2	1.1	1.1	•	0.3
Net Sales to Working Capital	32	8.6	9.4	127.4	3.5	5.2	5.5	4.5	4.4	•	•
Coverage Ratio	33	4.6	9.4	4.9	3.0	8.5	7.3	6.4	6.8	•	2.2
Total Asset Turnover	34	1.1	•	3.7	2.0	1.8	1.4	1.3	1.3	•	0.6
Inventory Turnover	35	4.7	•	21.5	7.0	4.6	5.1	3.9	4.2	•	4.9
Receivables Turnover	36	6.7	•	34.8	5.6	5.9	5.4	5.9	5.7	•	•
Total Liabilities to Net Worth	37	1.4	•	•	1.7	1.3	0.9	0.9	0.8	•	1.5
Current Assets to Working Capital	38	3.3	•	19.2	1.3	1.9	2.2	2.1	1.9	•	•
Current Liabilities to Working Capital	39	2.3	•	18.2	0.3	0.9	1.2	1.1	0.9	•	•
Working Capital to Net Sales	40	0.1	•	0.0	0.3	0.2	0.2	0.2	0.2	•	•
Inventory to Working Capital	41	1.2	•	1.6	0.3	0.7	0.6	0.8	0.8	•	•
Total Receipts to Cash Flow	42	6.8	5.8	2.7	11.3	8.3	7.4	7.9	7.3	•	8.8
Cost of Goods to Cash Flow	43	4.4	3.7	0.8	7.0	5.5	4.8	5.1	4.8	•	5.9
Cash Flow to Total Debt	44	0.3	•	1.1	0.3	0.4	0.4	0.4	0.4	•	0.1

Selected Financial Factors (in Percentages)

Debt Ratio	45	57.7	•	117.8	62.3	57.0	47.5	46.2	44.9	•	59.6
Return on Total Assets	46	9.4	•	33.1	6.4	14.5	11.3	10.4	10.1	•	4.3
Return on Equity Before Income Taxes	47	17.4	•	•	11.3	29.8	18.5	16.3	15.6	•	5.8
Return on Equity After Income Taxes	48	14.6	•	•	10.3	28.4	16.2	14.8	13.8	•	3.9
Profit Margin (Before Income Tax)	49	6.9	15.8	7.1	2.1	7.1	6.8	6.6	6.5	•	3.8
Profit Margin (After Income Tax)	50	5.8	15.6	6.5	1.9	6.7	6.0	6.0	5.7	•	2.5

Table I

Corporations with and without Net Income

ENGINE, TURBINE AND POWER TRANSMISSION EQUIPMENT

MONEY AMOUNTS AND SIZE OF ASSETS IN THOUSANDS OF DOLLARS

Item Description for Accounting Period 7/07 Through 6/08	Total	Zero Assets	Under 500	500 to 1,000	1,000 to 5,000	5,000 to 10,000	10,000 to 25,000	25,000 to 50,000	50,000 to 100,000	100,000 to 250,000	250,000 to 500,000	500,000 to 2,500,000	2,500,000 and over
Number of Enterprises 1	332	10	97	0	122	26	30	12	9	9	5	7	5
Revenues ($ in Thousands)													
Net Sales 2	32410459	125456	1522	0	837962	230672	535266	358646	733157	1438796	2302714	6682564	19163706
Interest 3	258569	941	1	0	398	1004	757	5460	3213	19137	9378	26682	191598
Rents 4	8830	0	0	0	0	0	0	0	77	1044	141	1950	5619
Royalties 5	354407	0	0	0	0	0	0	0	442	508	9283	29696	314478
Other Portfolio Income 6	387886	13917	0	0	2103	0	3796	206	1006	2339	46620	63554	254346
Other Receipts 7	457465	-1	31577	0	114	70	1326	-219	23743	17463	55167	74402	253817
Total Receipts 8	33877616	140313	33100	0	840577	231746	541145	364093	761638	1479287	2423303	6878848	20183564
Average Total Receipts 9	102041	14031	341	•	6890	8913	18038	30341	84626	164365	484661	982693	4036713
Operating Costs/Operating Income (%)													
Cost of Operations 10	71.1	57.5	190.9	•	63.0	56.0	64.6	67.9	72.4	70.1	74.4	78.5	69.0
Salaries and Wages 11	6.8	7.9	1239.8	•	13.0	15.8	6.1	7.5	8.0	8.6	7.0	5.7	6.4
Taxes Paid 12	1.5	3.2	156.4	•	1.7	3.5	2.4	2.7	2.4	1.2	1.9	1.1	1.4
Interest Paid 13	2.8	3.9	29.5	•	3.0	0.4	1.6	1.9	1.7	2.1	1.4	1.8	3.4
Depreciation 14	1.8	2.6	23.3	•	2.1	3.0	2.6	3.5	1.3	2.0	1.3	1.9	1.8
Amortization and Depletion 15	1.1	•	•	•	0.0	0.3	0.4	0.0	0.3	0.5	1.0	0.8	1.4
Pensions and Other Deferred Comp. 16	1.4	0.3	47.5	•	1.9	0.2	0.5	0.6	1.4	0.7	0.9	1.6	1.5
Employee Benefits 17	2.9	0.1	155.9	•	0.5	0.7	1.7	2.8	2.2	2.6	2.1	0.4	4.2
Advertising 18	0.4	0.1	1.0	•	0.8	0.3	0.2	0.2	0.3	0.6	0.1	0.7	0.4
Other Expenses 19	10.2	13.4	2038.0	•	9.8	11.8	8.5	11.3	11.2	8.9	9.8	6.7	11.3
Officers' Compensation 20	0.8	1.0	569.3	•	0.8	1.5	4.1	1.1	1.8	1.2	0.7	0.4	0.7
Operating Margin 21	•	10.2	•	•	3.4	6.4	7.4	0.7	•	1.6	•	0.5	•
Operating Margin Before Officers' Comp. 22	•	11.2	•	•	4.1	8.0	11.5	1.8	•	2.7	•	0.9	•

Selected Average Balance Sheet ($ in Thousands)

Item													
Net Receivables **23**	14888	0	1	•	910	1191	1949	5314	21104	20187	93961	207001	477604
Inventories **24**	16406	0	9	•	861	1257	3804	9580	14135	25020	65325	130348	695206
Net Property, Plant and Equipment **25**	14458	0	27	•	1177	1296	3717	6658	8504	40048	38606	118273	594146
Total Assets **26**	104745	0	86	•	4063	7194	14300	34424	72456	177508	342220	988093	4472952
Notes and Loans Payable **27**	31721	0	235	•	1621	427	4801	9756	21193	43011	85654	197938	1529383
All Other Liabilities **28**	37670	0	131	•	671	713	3482	9595	29163	44698	146673	530173	1412860
Net Worth **29**	35354	0	-280	•	1771	6054	6016	15073	22099	89799	109894	259983	1530709

Selected Financial Ratios (Times to 1)

Item												
Current Ratio **30**	1.4	•	0.4	•	3.2	5.9	1.8	1.8	2.0	1.7	1.3	1.2
Quick Ratio **31**	0.7	•	0.3	•	1.7	3.8	1.1	1.1	1.0	1.0	0.5	0.7
Net Sales to Working Capital **32**	9.4	•	•	•	3.8	2.8	4.7	2.5	4.2	6.0	8.4	16.3
Coverage Ratio **33**	2.5	6.7	•	•	2.2	19.2	6.2	2.2	1.5	4.8	3.1	2.2
Total Asset Turnover **34**	0.9	•	0.2	1.7	1.2	1.2	0.9	1.1	0.9	1.3	1.0	0.9
Inventory Turnover **35**	4.2	•	3.4	5.0	4.0	3.0	2.1	4.2	4.5	5.8	5.2	3.8
Receivables Turnover **36**	4.5	•	23.1	10.1	•	7.8	6.2	4.8	7.0	4.2	5.1	4.1
Total Liabilities to Net Worth **37**	2.0	•	•	1.3	0.2	1.4	1.3	2.3	1.0	2.1	2.8	1.9
Current Assets to Working Capital **38**	3.8	•	•	1.4	1.2	2.2	2.2	2.3	2.0	2.5	4.8	5.3
Current Liabilities to Working Capital **39**	2.8	•	•	0.4	0.2	1.2	1.2	1.3	1.0	1.5	3.8	4.3
Working Capital to Net Sales **40**	0.1	•	•	0.3	0.4	0.4	0.4	0.2	0.2	0.2	0.1	0.1
Inventory to Working Capital **41**	1.3	•	•	0.7	0.4	1.0	0.8	0.7	0.8	0.6	1.4	1.9
Total Receipts to Cash Flow **42**	8.5	2.9	•	8.8	6.3	6.7	8.7	9.6	8.3	8.3	11.8	7.8
Cost of Goods to Cash Flow **43**	6.0	1.7	•	5.6	3.5	4.3	5.9	7.0	5.8	6.2	9.2	5.4
Cash Flow to Total Debt **44**	0.2	•	•	0.3	1.2	0.3	0.2	0.2	0.2	0.2	0.1	0.2

Selected Financial Factors (in Percentages)

Item											
Debt Ratio **45**	66.2	•	424.6	56.4	57.9	56.2	69.5	49.4	67.9	73.7	65.8
Return on Total Assets **46**	6.4	•	•	11.3	12.7	3.5	2.9	5.9	8.9	5.3	6.4
Return on Equity Before Income Taxes **47**	11.2	•	127.6	14.2	25.3	4.4	3.2	7.8	21.9	13.7	10.2
Return on Equity After Income Taxes **48**	7.7	•	127.6	12.0	22.0	0.2	•	5.1	13.7	8.8	7.2
Profit Margin (Before Income Tax) **49**	4.0	22.0	•	3.7	8.5	2.2	0.9	4.4	5.2	3.7	4.1
Profit Margin (After Income Tax) **50**	2.8	22.0	•	3.1	7.4	0.1	•	2.9	3.3	2.4	2.9

Table II

Corporations with Net Income

ENGINE, TURBINE AND POWER TRANSMISSION EQUIPMENT

MONEY AMOUNTS AND SIZE OF ASSETS IN THOUSANDS OF DOLLARS

Item Description for Accounting Period 7/07 Through 6/08	Total	Zero Assets	Under 500	500 to 1,000	1,000 to 5,000	5,000 to 10,000	10,000 to 25,000	25,000 to 50,000	50,000 to 100,000	100,000 to 250,000	250,000 to 500,000	500,000 to 2,500,000	2,500,000 and over
Number of Enterprises **1**	177	10	0	•	88	14	26	•	•	6	•	•	•
Revenues ($ in Thousands)													
Net Sales **2**	27915409	125456	0	•	704239	172153	460989	•	•	1112370	•	•	•
Interest **3**	234404	941	0	•	298	156	757	•	•	11752	•	•	•
Rents **4**	8579	0	0	•	0	0	0	•	•	818	•	•	•
Royalties **5**	344282	0	0	•	0	0	0	•	•	508	•	•	•
Other Portfolio Income **6**	328288	13917	0	•	2103	0	3796	•	•	2336	•	•	•
Other Receipts **7**	353771	-1	0	•	114	70	1326	•	•	7716	•	•	•
Total Receipts **8**	29184733	140313	0	•	706754	172379	466868	•	•	1135500	•	•	•
Average Total Receipts **9**	164885	14031	•	•	8031	12313	17956	•	•	189250	•	•	•
Operating Costs/Operating Income (%)													
Cost of Operations **10**	70.1	57.5	•	•	64.8	56.2	61.8	•	•	68.5	•	•	•
Salaries and Wages **11**	6.9	7.9	•	•	11.7	8.2	6.4	•	•	8.3	•	•	•
Taxes Paid **12**	1.5	3.2	•	•	1.5	3.0	2.7	•	•	0.8	•	•	•
Interest Paid **13**	2.4	3.9	•	•	2.9	0.6	1.9	•	•	1.5	•	•	•
Depreciation **14**	1.8	2.6	•	•	2.1	3.4	3.0	•	•	2.4	•	•	•
Amortization and Depletion **15**	0.7	•	•	•	0.0	0.1	0.4	•	•	0.2	•	•	•
Pensions and Other Deferred Comp. **16**	1.6	0.3	•	•	2.2	0.3	0.6	•	•	0.6	•	•	•
Employee Benefits **17**	3.2	0.1	•	•	0.4	0.9	1.8	•	•	1.7	•	•	•
Advertising **18**	0.3	0.1	•	•	0.3	0.4	0.1	•	•	0.8	•	•	•
Other Expenses **19**	10.2	13.4	•	•	8.2	7.9	7.6	•	•	7.2	•	•	•
Officers' Compensation **20**	0.8	1.0	•	•	0.8	2.1	4.8	•	•	1.2	•	•	•
Operating Margin **21**	0.6	10.2	•	•	5.1	16.9	8.8	•	•	6.8	•	•	•
Operating Margin Before Officers' Comp. **22**	1.4	11.2	•	•	5.9	19.0	13.5	•	•	8.0	•	•	•

Selected Average Balance Sheet ($ in Thousands)

Net Receivables 23	22470	0	•	1145	•	1795	2004	•	•	•	25022
Inventories 24	26862	0	•	1023	•	2606	3438	•	•	•	33079
Net Property, Plant and Equipment 25	19980	0	•	1224	•	1929	4280	•	•	•	32578
Total Assets 26	138064	0	•	4395	•	6862	14991	•	•	•	175686
Notes and Loans Payable 27	31718	0	•	1748	•	790	4628	•	•	•	42402
All Other Liabilities 28	55157	0	•	489	•	647	3260	•	•	•	50318
Net Worth 29	51190	0	•	2158	•	5426	7103	•	•	•	82966

Selected Financial Ratios (Times to 1)

Current Ratio 30	1.3	•	•	6.1	•	8.7	1.8	•	•	•	2.1
Quick Ratio 31	0.7	•	•	3.3	•	5.7	0.8	•	•	•	1.1
Net Sales to Working Capital 32	11.0	•	•	3.2	•	2.8	4.7	•	•	•	4.2
Coverage Ratio 33	3.3	6.7	•	2.9	•	31.3	6.3	•	•	•	6.8
Total Asset Turnover 34	1.1	•	•	1.8	•	1.8	1.2	•	•	•	1.1
Inventory Turnover 35	4.1	•	•	5.1	•	2.7	3.2	•	•	•	3.8
Receivables Turnover 36	4.6	•	•	9.4	•	6.1	7.8	•	•	•	5.9
Total Liabilities to Net Worth 37	1.7	•	•	1.0	•	0.3	1.1	•	•	•	1.1
Current Assets to Working Capital 38	4.0	•	•	1.2	•	1.1	2.2	•	•	•	1.9
Current Liabilities to Working Capital 39	3.0	•	•	0.2	•	0.1	1.2	•	•	•	0.9
Working Capital to Net Sales 40	0.1	•	•	0.3	•	0.4	0.2	•	•	•	0.2
Inventory to Working Capital 41	1.4	•	•	0.5	•	0.4	0.9	•	•	•	0.8
Total Receipts to Cash Flow 42	7.5	2.9	•	8.2	•	4.3	6.5	•	•	•	6.6
Cost of Goods to Cash Flow 43	5.3	1.7	•	5.3	•	2.4	4.0	•	•	•	4.5
Cash Flow to Total Debt 44	0.2	•	•	0.4	•	2.0	0.3	•	•	•	0.3

Selected Financial Factors (in Percentages)

Debt Ratio 45	62.9	•	•	50.9	•	20.9	52.6	•	•	•	52.8
Return on Total Assets 46	9.0	•	•	15.3	•	31.5	14.1	•	•	•	11.0
Return on Equity Before Income Taxes 47	17.0	•	•	20.3	•	38.6	25.1	•	•	•	19.8
Return on Equity After Income Taxes 48	12.4	•	•	17.7	•	31.1	21.9	•	•	•	15.4
Profit Margin (Before Income Tax) 49	5.5	22.0	•	5.5	•	17.0	10.0	•	•	•	8.9
Profit Margin (After Income Tax) 50	4.0	22.0	•	4.8	•	13.7	8.8	•	•	•	6.9

Table I

Corporations with and without Net Income

OTHER GENERAL PURPOSE MACHINERY

MONEY AMOUNTS AND SIZE OF ASSETS IN THOUSANDS OF DOLLARS

Item Description for Accounting Period 7/07 Through 6/08	Total	Zero Assets	Under 500	500 to 1,000	1,000 to 5,000	5,000 to 10,000	10,000 to 25,000	25,000 to 50,000	50,000 to 100,000	100,000 to 250,000	250,000 to 500,000	500,000 to 2,500,000	2,500,000 and over
Number of Enterprises **1**	6093	324	3962	188	1006	249	219	53	28	30	9	15	8
Revenues ($ in Thousands)													
Net Sales **2**	68407121	244245	1767754	247152	4026611	3215080	5786778	2499111	2446910	5088064	3595374	11954960	27536081
Interest **3**	743636	266	1850	219	4319	2412	4114	3664	5706	28514	17454	45211	629907
Rents **4**	14555	0	207	308	929	1981	2576	0	431	1289	1750	1640	3445
Royalties **5**	688415	0	0	0	3801	0	461	1423	2408	17096	4196	76342	582687
Other Portfolio Income **6**	2739511	3262	54976	0	5551	17252	6029	5650	42684	14298	7943	69019	2512842
Other Receipts **7**	511173	520	3064	800	13021	13460	45456	31519	27377	26120	33564	116076	200203
Total Receipts **8**	73104411	248293	1827851	248479	4054232	3250185	5845414	2540367	2525516	5175381	3660281	12263248	31465165
Average Total Receipts **9**	11998	766	461	1322	4030	13053	26691	47931	90197	172513	406698	817550	3933146
Operating Costs/Operating Income (%)													
Cost of Operations **10**	67.1	68.0	47.0	74.2	62.2	61.2	69.3	68.8	71.5	70.6	62.0	67.1	68.7
Salaries and Wages **11**	8.5	9.5	14.8	6.3	9.1	10.6	8.0	9.2	7.9	7.5	8.7	7.3	8.5
Taxes Paid **12**	1.7	1.3	2.5	2.5	2.5	2.2	1.9	1.4	1.6	1.7	1.5	2.0	1.2
Interest Paid **13**	3.4	1.9	1.1	1.8	1.0	1.2	1.2	1.9	1.5	2.0	2.0	1.8	6.2
Depreciation **14**	1.6	4.7	2.4	2.0	2.0	1.9	1.5	1.8	1.3	1.6	1.6	1.8	1.4
Amortization and Depletion **15**	0.8	0.3	0.1	0.3	0.0	0.1	0.3	0.5	0.5	0.9	0.9	0.6	1.3
Pensions and Other Deferred Comp. **16**	0.8	•	0.3	0.1	0.5	0.4	0.4	0.3	0.7	1.0	0.7	0.9	1.0
Employee Benefits **17**	2.6	1.7	1.2	1.7	1.8	1.9	2.3	1.9	1.8	2.0	2.8	3.4	2.9
Advertising **18**	0.6	0.5	0.6	0.7	0.7	0.8	0.4	0.4	0.5	0.5	0.4	0.5	0.7
Other Expenses **19**	10.1	6.0	17.1	14.0	10.9	9.7	7.0	9.6	8.5	7.9	11.7	8.2	11.4
Officers' Compensation **20**	1.6	0.7	5.9	2.0	4.6	3.2	2.5	1.2	1.8	1.0	1.0	2.2	0.6
Operating Margin **21**	1.1	5.3	6.8	•	4.7	6.7	5.2	3.0	2.3	3.3	6.6	4.3	•
Operating Margin Before Officers' Comp. **22**	2.8	6.0	12.8	•	9.3	9.9	7.7	4.2	4.1	4.2	7.7	6.4	•

Selected Average Balance Sheet ($ in Thousands)

Net Receivables 23	1862	0	24	120	512	1758	4768	8660	14312	31842	64934	123759	621872
Inventories 24	1405	0	25	298	433	1906	3731	7915	15455	22972	40334	110771	389220
Net Property, Plant and Equipment 25	1156	0	52	144	503	1126	2553	6039	9811	19680	44650	91114	314130
Total Assets 26	15544	0	142	634	1925	7107	14993	35365	68760	153424	352110	857745	7824910
Notes and Loans Payable 27	3832	0	94	715	651	1470	4546	8242	16418	40440	91341	125452	2001066
All Other Liabilities 28	5031	0	31	78	622	2170	4743	10628	27453	41782	62800	359326	2471423
Net Worth 29	6681	0	17	-158	651	3466	5704	16495	24889	71202	197969	372967	3352420

Selected Financial Ratios (Times to 1)

Current Ratio 30	1.4	•	2.0	4.4	1.9	1.9	2.0	1.5	1.9	1.4	1.2	1.2	
Quick Ratio 31	0.7	•	1.3	2.4	1.2	1.0	1.1	0.8	0.8	1.2	0.6	0.5	
Net Sales to Working Capital 32	8.1	•	12.3	5.1	6.4	5.2	4.2	6.8	4.6	8.4	13.2	10.9	
Coverage Ratio 33	3.5	4.6	10.0	•	6.3	7.7	3.5	5.0	3.5	5.1	2.8		
Total Asset Turnover 34	0.7	•	3.1	2.1	2.1	1.8	1.3	1.3	1.1	1.1	0.9	0.4	
Inventory Turnover 35	5.4	•	8.3	3.3	5.8	4.1	4.0	5.2	6.1	4.8	6.1		
Receivables Turnover 36	5.8	•	13.2	5.7	7.9	7.6	5.7	5.8	5.3	5.7	4.8	5.8	
Total Liabilities to Net Worth 37	1.3	•	7.6	•	2.0	1.1	1.1	1.8	1.2	0.8	1.3	1.3	
Current Assets to Working Capital 38	3.7	•	2.0	1.3	2.2	2.1	2.0	3.2	2.1	3.3	5.6	5.7	
Current Liabilities to Working Capital 39	2.7	•	1.0	0.3	1.2	1.1	1.0	2.2	1.1	2.3	4.6	4.7	
Working Capital to Net Sales 40	0.1	•	0.1	0.2	0.2	0.2	0.2	0.1	0.2	0.1	0.1	0.1	
Inventory to Working Capital 41	1.0	•	0.6	0.6	0.7	0.8	0.7	1.2	0.6	0.9	1.8	1.3	
Total Receipts to Cash Flow 42	8.1	9.7	5.3	18.0	7.1	7.0	8.6	8.1	8.3	9.1	5.5	7.2	9.6
Cost of Goods to Cash Flow 43	5.5	6.6	2.5	13.4	4.4	4.3	6.0	6.0	6.4	3.4	4.8	6.6	
Cash Flow to Total Debt 44	0.2	•	0.7	0.1	0.4	0.5	0.3	0.2	0.2	0.5	0.2	0.1	

Selected Financial Factors (in Percentages)

Debt Ratio 45	57.0	•	88.3	125.0	66.2	51.2	62.0	53.4	63.8	53.6	43.8	56.5	57.2
Return on Total Assets 46	8.7	•	35.7	•	13.3	16.4	13.0	8.8	9.3	7.8	11.9	8.4	7.8
Return on Equity Before Income Taxes 47	14.4	•	274.8	41.3	33.2	29.2	28.9	13.5	20.6	12.0	17.0	15.5	11.8
Return on Equity After Income Taxes 48	10.5	•	264.5	44.0	28.9	26.9	25.3	11.4	14.7	8.1	10.9	11.9	7.9
Profit Margin (Before Income Tax) 49	8.6	7.0	10.2	•	5.4	7.8	6.2	4.7	5.9	5.1	10.9	8.4	7.3	11.5
Profit Margin (After Income Tax) 50	6.2	6.5	9.8	•	4.7	7.2	5.5	4.0	4.2	3.4	5.4	5.5	7.7

Table II
Corporations with Net Income

OTHER GENERAL PURPOSE MACHINERY

MONEY AMOUNTS AND SIZE OF ASSETS IN THOUSANDS OF DOLLARS

Item Description for Accounting Period 7/07 Through 6/08	Total	Zero Assets	Under 500	500 to 1,000	1,000 to 5,000	5,000 to 10,000	10,000 to 25,000	25,000 to 50,000	50,000 to 100,000	100,000 to 250,000	250,000 to 500,000	500,000 to 2,500,000	2,500,000 and over
Number of Enterprises 1	3404	5	1944	158	786	218	182	38	22	24	•	•	•
Revenues ($ in Thousands)													
Net Sales 2	51711130	148017	1408972	245548	3197753	2775647	4930394	1993207	1995748	4060729	•	•	•
Interest 3	343244	209	1239	107	3571	1785	3036	3391	4604	26176	•	•	•
Rents 4	8843	0	207	308	541	208	2573	0	431	1289	•	•	•
Royalties 5	655123	0	0	0	3801	0	461	933	1856	4506	•	•	•
Other Portfolio Income 6	2716516	3001	54966	0	5254	17238	6003	4367	42516	13007	•	•	•
Other Receipts 7	391944	403	3012	799	11793	5378	42633	15472	14668	23430	•	•	•
Total Receipts 8	55826800	151630	1468396	246762	3222713	2800256	4985100	2017370	2059823	4129137	•	•	•
Average Total Receipts 9	16400	30326	755	1562	4100	12845	27391	53089	93628	172047	•	•	•
Operating Costs/Operating Income (%)													
Cost of Operations 10	64.5	61.5	46.0	74.5	58.1	58.9	67.3	66.1	69.3	67.9	•	•	•
Salaries and Wages 11	9.0	12.1	16.0	4.7	9.6	10.7	8.0	10.1	7.5	8.4	•	•	•
Taxes Paid 12	1.7	1.5	2.4	2.4	2.3	2.3	1.8	1.5	1.8	1.6	•	•	•
Interest Paid 13	3.3	0.9	1.1	1.8	1.0	0.9	0.8	1.1	1.6	1.8	•	•	•
Depreciation 14	1.5	5.5	1.0	2.0	1.7	2.0	1.3	1.8	1.3	1.6	•	•	•
Amortization and Depletion 15	0.8	0.2	0.0	0.2	0.0	0.0	0.1	0.3	0.7	0.8	•	•	•
Pensions and Other Deferred Comp. 16	0.7	•	0.4	0.1	0.6	0.5	0.5	0.3	0.8	0.9	•	•	•
Employee Benefits 17	2.4	1.3	1.1	1.6	1.5	2.0	2.3	2.1	2.0	1.4	•	•	•
Advertising 18	0.7	0.2	0.5	0.7	0.7	0.9	0.4	0.4	0.5	0.5	•	•	•
Other Expenses 19	10.0	0.3	14.9	8.7	11.0	9.6	6.6	8.2	7.7	8.6	•	•	•
Officers' Compensation 20	1.9	0.4	6.1	1.5	4.6	3.2	2.6	1.3	2.0	1.1	•	•	•
Operating Margin 21	3.6	16.0	10.5	1.9	8.9	8.9	8.3	6.9	4.8	5.6	•	•	•
Operating Margin Before Officers' Comp. 22	5.5	16.4	16.6	3.4	13.5	12.1	10.9	8.2	6.8	6.6	•	•	•

Selected Average Balance Sheet ($ in Thousands)

Net Receivables 23	2204	0	45	137	552	1623	4929	9286	12464	33755
Inventories 24	1957	0	28	157	449	1862	3301	7575	14808	23391
Net Property, Plant and Equipment 25	1499	0	80	170	411	1179	2553	6660	9725	21128
Total Assets 26	20687	0	207	572	1935	7076	15149	35986	68755	158632
Notes and Loans Payable 27	4585	0	72	227	534	1372	4127	6776	17520	35028
All Other Liabilities 28	6733	0	53	80	556	2121	4356	10274	24070	38470
Net Worth 29	9370	0	81	265	845	3584	6666	18935	27165	85135

Selected Financial Ratios (Times to 1)

Current Ratio 30	1.5	•	2.0	4.7	2.4	2.2	2.0	2.1	1.6	2.1
Quick Ratio 31	0.8	•	1.3	2.6	1.6	1.1	1.3	1.1	0.8	1.2
Net Sales to Working Capital 32	7.8	•	12.3	5.4	4.7	4.5	4.7	4.2	6.8	3.9
Coverage Ratio 33	4.7	21.3	14.3	2.3	11.1	11.4	12.6	8.7	6.2	5.2
Total Asset Turnover 34	0.7	•	3.5	2.7	2.1	1.8	1.8	1.5	1.3	1.1
Inventory Turnover 35	5.0	•	12.1	7.4	5.3	4.0	5.5	4.6	4.2	4.9
Receivables Turnover 36	6.1	•	13.2	•	7.2	8.2	6.8	•	6.2	5.4
Total Liabilities to Net Worth 37	1.2	•	1.6	1.2	1.3	1.0	1.3	0.9	1.5	0.9
Current Assets to Working Capital 38	3.2	•	2.0	1.3	1.7	1.9	2.0	1.9	2.8	1.9
Current Liabilities to Working Capital 39	2.2	•	1.0	0.3	0.7	0.9	1.0	0.9	1.8	0.9
Working Capital to Net Sales 40	0.1	•	0.1	0.2	0.2	0.2	0.2	0.2	0.1	0.3
Inventory to Working Capital 41	1.0	•	0.6	0.5	0.6	0.8	0.6	0.6	1.0	0.6
Total Receipts to Cash Flow 42	6.7	5.8	4.6	11.9	5.4	6.2	6.9	7.0	7.3	7.1
Cost of Goods to Cash Flow 43	4.3	3.6	2.1	8.8	3.1	3.6	4.6	4.6	5.1	4.8
Cash Flow to Total Debt 44	0.2	•	1.2	0.4	0.7	0.6	0.5	0.4	0.3	0.3

Selected Financial Factors (in Percentages)

Debt Ratio 45	54.7	•	60.8	53.6	56.3	49.4	56.0	47.4	60.5	46.3
Return on Total Assets 46	11.4	•	55.5	11.2	22.4	19.3	18.3	13.4	13.2	9.7
Return on Equity Before Income Taxes 47	19.9	•	131.6	13.8	46.6	34.8	38.2	22.6	27.9	14.6
Return on Equity After Income Taxes 48	14.9	•	127.3	11.9	42.3	32.3	34.5	20.1	21.1	10.5
Profit Margin (Before Income Tax) 49	12.3	18.4	14.7	2.4	9.7	9.8	9.4	8.2	8.4	7.3
Profit Margin (After Income Tax) 50	9.2	17.6	14.2	2.0	8.8	9.1	8.5	7.2	6.3	5.3

COMPUTER AND PERIPHERAL EQUIPMENT

Table I

Corporations with and without Net Income

MONEY AMOUNTS AND SIZE OF ASSETS IN THOUSANDS OF DOLLARS

Item Description for Accounting Period 7/07 Through 6/08	Total	Zero Assets	Under 500	500 to 1,000	1,000 to 5,000	5,000 to 10,000	10,000 to 25,000	25,000 to 50,000	50,000 to 100,000	100,000 to 250,000	250,000 to 500,000	500,000 to 2,500,000	2,500,000 and over
Number of Enterprises **1**	2987	364	1317	371	585	102	102	53	28	22	13	19	11
Revenues ($ in Thousands)													
Net Sales **2**	191110824	646460	134544	537193	2496115	1312435	2222410	2807555	2715353	3631724	3517180	16657907	154431951
Interest **3**	3043917	1264	485	520	10216	3569	19523	22312	18612	71736	56112	202890	2636678
Rents **4**	1051472	0	0	0	1192	0	1711	463	168	0	289	17100	1030550
Royalties **5**	26101283	0	0	0	97	0	496	12027	5890	4432	9748	428160	25640435
Other Portfolio Income **6**	2317635	33248	44634	3	5458	8737	5548	2349	26015	19202	11005	71747	2089685
Other Receipts **7**	3028977	19567	0	5862	6385	5376	6869	-17805	26553	195861	26072	426407	2327830
Total Receipts **8**	226654108	700539	179663	543578	2519463	1330117	2256557	2826901	2792591	3922955	3620406	17804211	188157129
Average Total Receipts **9**	75880	1925	136	1465	4307	13040	22123	53338	99735	178316	278493	937064	17105194
Operating Costs/Operating Income (%)													
Cost of Operations **10**	64.3	61.0	61.0	52.0	53.7	63.9	66.8	60.0	66.4	67.3	57.7	69.0	64.1
Salaries and Wages **11**	16.4	54.0	10.9	18.0	16.3	20.5	19.4	20.8	13.6	14.7	17.8	14.2	16.3
Taxes Paid **12**	1.8	4.1	3.2	2.2	2.6	2.7	2.0	1.9	2.0	1.2	1.7	1.6	1.8
Interest Paid **13**	1.5	5.3	0.1	2.9	0.8	1.2	1.0	1.0	1.7	1.7	0.7	1.2	1.6
Depreciation **14**	2.9	2.5	0.7	1.2	1.1	1.6	1.9	1.6	1.8	1.7	1.3	2.2	3.1
Amortization and Depletion **15**	0.8	1.5	•	0.7	1.6	1.2	0.8	0.7	1.1	1.4	2.0	1.4	0.7
Pensions and Other Deferred Comp. **16**	0.9	0.6	1.2	0.2	1.5	0.1	0.2	0.1	0.2	0.2	0.2	0.2	1.1
Employee Benefits **17**	1.7	1.4	•	2.2	2.3	2.0	2.0	1.5	1.7	2.0	1.2	1.9	1.6
Advertising **18**	1.7	1.6	0.9	1.0	0.7	0.6	1.1	2.0	0.7	1.6	1.4	3.7	1.5
Other Expenses **19**	21.1	16.9	37.7	28.6	16.8	8.8	10.1	15.2	15.3	12.0	19.1	8.7	23.2
Officers' Compensation **20**	0.7	4.2	14.6	4.8	6.5	2.9	3.1	2.1	1.5	2.0	1.8	0.7	0.4
Operating Margin **21**	•	•	•	•	•	•	•	•	•	•	•	•	•
Operating Margin Before Officers' Comp. **22**	•	•	•	•	2.7	•	•	•	•	•	•	•	•

Selected Average Balance Sheet ($ in Thousands)

Net Receivables 23	20854	0	3	229	424	2364	4192	10086	17340	28259	71732	188850	5011088
Inventories 24	3582	0	4	244	315	1857	2640	5355	12307	18731	28926	78681	645030
Net Property, Plant and Equipment 25	7307	0	0	45	129	611	1093	3053	6973	9890	16910	86757	1737864
Total Assets 26	104541	0	33	831	1846	7443	15860	36947	76686	165573	339538	1172968	24909597
Notes and Loans Payable 27	18813	0	38	607	1479	1552	2604	8201	15581	18062	29905	171471	4519456
All Other Liabilities 28	35918	0	11	292	1017	2624	4388	10570	34684	57641	146010	331955	8622687
Net Worth 29	49810	0	-16	-68	-650	3267	8867	18176	26421	89870	163624	669542	11767455

Selected Financial Ratios (Times to 1)

Current Ratio 30	1.3	•	0.5	2.5	2.2	1.9	2.5	2.3	1.5	1.9	1.7	1.8	1.2
Quick Ratio 31	0.8	•	0.5	1.1	1.6	1.1	1.7	1.5	0.8	1.3	1.1	1.1	0.8
Net Sales to Working Capital 32	6.2	•	•	3.1	5.5	5.0	3.0	3.4	5.5	3.5	3.0	3.9	7.3
Coverage Ratio 33	5.5	33.1	•	•	•	•	•	•	•	2.3	•	3.1	6.6
Total Asset Turnover 34	0.6	•	3.1	1.7	2.3	1.7	1.4	1.4	1.3	1.0	0.8	0.7	0.6
Inventory Turnover 35	11.5	•	14.0	3.1	7.3	4.4	5.5	5.9	5.2	5.9	5.4	7.7	14.0
Receivables Turnover 36	3.7	•	5.1	12.6	10.7	5.5	5.0	5.6	5.9	4.7	4.2	3.8	3.5
Total Liabilities to Net Worth 37	1.1	•	•	•	1.3	0.8	1.7	1.0	1.9	0.8	1.1	0.8	1.1
Current Assets to Working Capital 38	4.1	•	•	1.7	1.8	2.1	1.7	1.8	2.9	2.1	2.4	2.2	5.0
Current Liabilities to Working Capital 39	3.1	•	•	0.7	0.8	1.1	0.7	0.8	1.9	1.1	1.4	1.2	4.0
Working Capital to Net Sales 40	0.2	•	•	0.3	0.2	0.2	0.3	0.3	0.2	0.3	0.3	0.3	0.1
Inventory to Working Capital 41	0.4	•	•	0.5	0.4	0.8	0.3	0.4	0.7	0.4	0.3	0.3	0.3
Total Receipts to Cash Flow 42	4.2	111.7	•	8.0	9.1	70.0	142.9	14.1	10.6	8.1	6.4	12.3	3.7
Cost of Goods to Cash Flow 43	2.7	68.2	•	4.2	4.9	44.8	95.5	8.4	7.0	5.4	3.7	8.5	2.4
Cash Flow to Total Debt 44	0.3	•	0.0	0.2	0.2	0.0	0.2	0.2	0.2	0.3	0.2	0.1	0.3

Selected Financial Factors (in Percentages)

Debt Ratio 45	52.4	•	146.9	108.1	135.2	56.1	44.1	50.8	65.5	45.7	51.8	42.9	52.8
Return on Total Assets 46	5.1	•	10.4	•	•	•	•	•	•	3.9	•	2.7	5.8
Return on Equity Before Income Taxes 47	8.8	•	•	268.7	18.7	•	•	•	•	4.1	•	3.2	10.5
Return on Equity After Income Taxes 48	5.7	•	•	270.2	25.9	•	•	•	•	2.4	•	0.8	7.3
Profit Margin (Before Income Tax) 49	6.9	3.3	•	•	•	•	•	•	•	2.2	•	2.5	8.8
Profit Margin (After Income Tax) 50	4.4	2.6	•	•	•	•	•	•	•	1.3	•	0.6	6.1

Table II

Corporations with Net Income

COMPUTER AND PERIPHERAL EQUIPMENT

MONEY AMOUNTS AND SIZE OF ASSETS IN THOUSANDS OF DOLLARS

Item Description for Accounting Period 7/07 Through 6/08	Total	Zero Assets	Under 500	500 to 1,000	1,000 to 5,000	5,000 to 10,000	10,000 to 25,000	25,000 to 50,000	50,000 to 100,000	100,000 to 250,000	250,000 to 500,000	500,000 to 2,500,000	2,500,000 and over
Number of Enterprises **1**	1852	303	567	337	448	73	41	27	14	11	9	10	11
Revenues ($ in Thousands)													
Net Sales **2**	179420492	86235	134544	527567	2233668	955821	1263816	1717739	1937977	1762095	2335340	12033738	154431951
Interest **3**	2833809	387	485	61	6282	1494	3941	7537	5253	42295	46008	83387	2636678
Rents **4**	1046582	0	0	0	0	0	0	275	168	0	289	15300	1030550
Royalties **5**	25933469	0	0	0	97	0	496	9262	4293	11	7032	271845	25640435
Other Portfolio Income **6**	2268122	32399	44634	0	225	8737	2165	2132	20953	14350	6312	46531	2089685
Other Receipts **7**	2788667	19028	0	2754	4444	1124	3326	7773	6307	185576	51890	178615	2327830
Total Receipts **8**	214291141	138049	179663	530382	2244716	967176	1273744	1744718	1974951	2004327	2446871	12629416	188157129
Average Total Receipts **9**	115708	456	317	1574	5011	13249	31067	64619	141068	182212	271875	1262942	17105194
Operating Costs/Operating Income (%)													
Cost of Operations **10**	64.2	80.7	61.0	51.9	53.3	65.0	68.9	60.7	71.4	65.0	50.0	69.9	64.1
Salaries and Wages **11**	15.8	7.1	10.9	14.2	12.8	15.6	9.0	14.9	9.2	14.4	19.4	11.8	16.3
Taxes Paid **12**	1.8	1.6	2.6	1.8	2.1	2.4	1.1	1.6	1.9	1.1	1.6	1.6	1.8
Interest Paid **13**	1.4	1.3	0.1	2.7	0.5	1.2	0.4	0.4	1.3	1.0	0.2	0.6	1.6
Depreciation **14**	2.9	2.5	0.7	0.7	0.7	1.2	0.8	1.3	1.3	1.2	1.3	1.9	3.1
Amortization and Depletion **15**	0.7	1.4	•	0.6	0.0	0.5	0.0	0.3	0.3	0.4	1.0	1.0	0.7
Pensions and Other Deferred Comp. **16**	1.0	•	1.2	0.2	1.6	0.1	0.1	0.1	0.2	0.1	0.1	0.2	1.1
Employee Benefits **17**	1.6	1.0	•	1.9	2.1	1.2	0.6	1.0	1.4	1.5	1.1	2.0	1.6
Advertising **18**	1.6	0.7	0.9	0.8	0.4	0.3	0.5	1.6	0.5	2.0	1.9	3.9	1.5
Other Expenses **19**	21.1	17.2	33.0	16.9	11.0	5.2	6.4	12.2	9.8	12.4	19.7	3.9	23.2
Officers' Compensation **20**	0.5	3.2	14.6	4.3	5.8	1.7	2.0	1.6	1.2	0.9	1.9	0.5	0.4
Operating Margin **21**	•	•	•	3.8	9.6	5.7	10.0	4.3	1.7	0.0	1.8	2.8	•
Operating Margin Before Officers' Comp. **22**	•	•	•	8.0	15.4	7.3	12.0	5.9	2.8	0.9	3.7	3.3	•

Selected Average Balance Sheet ($ in Thousands)

Net Receivables 23	32242	0	6	246	435	2578	5060	10931	22060	22737	70835	242142	5011088
Inventories 24	5150	0	0	252	322	2002	4072	6416	19170	19983	25778	104266	667254
Net Property, Plant and Equipment 25	11232	0	0	21	103	573	993	3630	10370	6922	16825	107889	1737864
Total Assets 26	159023	0	76	836	1700	7116	15353	39105	80813	169904	340509	1114833	24909597
Notes and Loans Payable 27	27988	0	2	629	375	1728	1709	3192	15454	18552	13918	91138	4519456
All Other Liabilities 28	54414	0	22	224	473	2212	4193	12247	49935	43286	110210	279462	8622687
Net Worth 29	76620	0	52	-16	852	3176	9451	23666	15424	108067	216381	744233	11767455

Selected Financial Ratios (Times to 1)

Current Ratio 30	1.3	•	0.5	3.0	2.9	2.0	2.3	2.5	1.2	2.1	2.0	2.0	1.2
Quick Ratio 31	0.8	•	0.5	1.3	2.1	1.2	1.4	1.6	0.6	1.5	1.6	1.2	0.8
Net Sales to Working Capital 32	6.6	•	•	2.9	5.2	4.7	4.6	3.5	12.1	3.4	2.5	4.5	7.3
Coverage Ratio 33	7.0	36.6	84.6	2.6	21.4	7.0	27.9	15.1	4.1	15.3	37.5	15.5	6.6
Total Asset Turnover 34	0.6	•	3.1	1.9	2.9	1.8	2.0	1.6	1.7	0.9	0.8	1.1	0.6
Inventory Turnover 35	12.1	•	•	3.2	8.2	4.3	5.2	6.0	5.2	5.2	5.0	8.1	13.5
Receivables Turnover 36	3.6	•	•	12.7	13.0	5.4	5.5	5.6	7.0	5.3	4.1	3.4	•
Total Liabilities to Net Worth 37	1.1	•	0.4	•	1.0	1.2	0.6	0.7	4.2	0.6	0.6	0.5	1.1
Current Assets to Working Capital 38	4.4	•	•	1.5	1.5	2.0	1.7	1.7	5.1	1.9	2.0	2.0	5.0
Current Liabilities to Working Capital 39	3.4	•	•	0.5	0.5	1.0	0.7	0.7	4.1	0.9	1.0	1.0	4.0
Working Capital to Net Sales 40	0.2	•	•	0.3	0.2	0.2	0.2	0.3	0.1	0.3	0.4	0.2	0.1
Inventory to Working Capital 41	0.4	•	•	0.5	0.4	0.8	0.6	0.4	1.6	0.4	0.2	0.3	0.3
Total Receipts to Cash Flow 42	3.9	1.9	23.6	5.4	5.4	10.8	6.4	6.1	8.8	4.2	4.0	9.9	3.7
Cost of Goods to Cash Flow 43	2.5	1.6	14.4	2.8	2.9	7.1	4.4	3.7	6.3	2.7	2.0	6.9	2.4
Cash Flow to Total Debt 44	0.3	•	0.4	0.3	1.1	0.3	0.8	0.7	0.2	0.6	0.5	0.3	0.3

Selected Financial Factors (in Percentages)

Debt Ratio 45	51.8	•	30.9	101.9	49.8	55.4	38.4	39.5	80.9	36.4	36.5	33.2	52.8
Return on Total Assets 46	6.2	•	27.1	13.2	31.2	14.7	22.4	10.0	9.1	13.9	5.2	9.5	5.8
Return on Equity Before Income Taxes 47	11.0	•	38.7	•	59.3	28.3	35.1	15.5	36.1	20.4	7.9	13.3	10.5
Return on Equity After Income Taxes 48	7.8	•	35.8	•	52.0	24.4	31.4	13.2	27.6	17.6	6.5	9.1	7.3
Profit Margin (Before Income Tax) 49	8.7	47.0	8.5	4.3	10.1	6.9	10.7	5.8	4.0	13.8	6.6	8.2	8.8
Profit Margin (After Income Tax) 50	6.1	34.7	7.9	4.3	8.9	5.9	9.6	4.9	3.1	11.8	5.4	5.7	6.1

Table I

Corporations with and without Net Income

COMMUNICATIONS EQUIPMENT

MONEY AMOUNTS AND SIZE OF ASSETS IN THOUSANDS OF DOLLARS

Item Description for Accounting Period 7/07 Through 6/08	Total	Zero Assets	Under 500	500 to 1,000	1,000 to 5,000	5,000 to 10,000	10,000 to 25,000	25,000 to 50,000	50,000 to 100,000	100,000 to 250,000	250,000 to 500,000	500,000 to 2,500,000	2,500,000 and over
Number of Enterprises 1	1251	78	458	157	256	66	87	57	25	23	12	18	13
Revenues ($ in Thousands)													
Net Sales 2	138957567	1034176	172416	157442	1049038	422445	1933140	2500286	1798056	2834214	3939326	18225552	104891475
Interest 3	1764848	4832	12	3535	5178	2802	12281	10699	28516	45936	50666	168840	1431551
Rents 4	156361	0	0	0	493	268	1504	2206	124	0	36	1116	150613
Royalties 5	2024662	7779	0	0	0	0	415	0	900	14682	16119	63439	1921328
Other Portfolio Income 6	2034165	3598	0	719	19998	1	25671	26835	33355	17859	27086	371043	1508003
Other Receipts 7	912468	12425	1	72	1567	12775	10035	23639	20977	7980	12222	159889	650884
Total Receipts 8	145850071	1062810	172429	161768	1076274	438291	1983046	2563665	1881928	2920671	4045455	18989879	110553854
Average Total Receipts 9	116587	13626	376	1030	4204	6641	22794	44977	75277	126986	337121	1054993	8504143
Operating Costs/Operating Income (%)													
Cost of Operations 10	67.3	57.3	46.5	67.7	43.3	61.6	59.7	61.6	57.1	55.2	66.8	78.9	66.5
Salaries and Wages 11	15.5	24.0	17.2	15.1	28.1	21.7	16.2	15.6	15.4	18.4	11.9	6.8	16.8
Taxes Paid 12	1.4	2.9	4.2	2.5	3.1	2.9	3.3	1.7	1.8	2.1	1.2	0.9	1.4
Interest Paid 13	1.9	2.1	0.9	0.3	2.6	2.3	7.3	1.6	3.4	0.6	2.7	0.9	1.9
Depreciation 14	1.9	3.2	0.5	0.3	1.5	2.0	1.8	2.4	1.4	2.2	2.7	1.2	2.0
Amortization and Depletion 15	1.4	1.3	•	•	3.7	1.3	1.1	2.3	1.3	1.7	0.9	0.9	1.5
Pensions and Other Deferred Comp. 16	0.7	0.0	•	1.4	0.5	0.1	0.7	0.1	0.3	0.1	0.3	0.1	0.9
Employee Benefits 17	1.5	2.0	•	2.4	2.7	3.0	1.5	1.7	2.2	3.2	1.4	1.8	1.4
Advertising 18	1.0	0.4	0.5	1.1	1.9	1.3	1.1	0.6	0.7	0.8	0.5	0.4	1.1
Other Expenses 19	9.2	13.7	42.2	10.5	23.2	17.3	15.5	17.6	15.0	15.0	11.1	8.9	8.3
Officers' Compensation 20	0.8	2.7	12.0	2.9	8.6	6.6	4.3	2.1	2.1	1.4	0.6	0.6	0.5
Operating Margin 21	•	•	•	•	•	•	•	•	•	•	•	•	•
Operating Margin Before Officers' Comp. 22	•	•	•	•	•	•	•	1.4	•	•	•	0.7	0.5

Selected Average Balance Sheet ($ in Thousands)

Net Receivables 23	21218	0	18	69	431	1072	3008	7619	17441	28724	56202	140698	1641868
Inventories 24	8117	0	43	195	869	907	2698	6245	11498	12779	39840	87282	507793
Net Property, Plant and Equipment 25	10796	0	7	11	130	999	1415	4678	4131	8726	27564	48610	884845
Total Assets 26	161593	0	167	658	2386	6496	15576	35188	75905	153885	387656	1205117	12753169
Notes and Loans Payable 27	33211	0	148	19	1439	1392	17093	9276	25767	9184	140924	223763	2494331
All Other Liabilities 28	53065	0	103	222	1001	1724	7520	14949	24425	37991	107685	310591	4312235
Net Worth 29	75316	0	-84	417	-54	3380	-9037	10962	25713	106709	139048	670763	5946603

Selected Financial Ratios (Times to 1)

Current Ratio 30	1.4	•	1.0	2.9	1.1	1.5	1.4	2.5	2.4	2.1	1.7	1.3	
Quick Ratio 31	0.8	•	0.7	1.9	0.6	0.7	0.8	1.8	1.6	1.2	1.0	0.8	
Net Sales to Working Capital 32	6.3	•	176.5	2.4	37.7	5.8	7.5	2.5	2.5	3.5	4.8	7.4	
Coverage Ratio 33	3.0	•	•	•	•	1.4	2.2	5.3	1.9	4.2	3.5		
Total Asset Turnover 34	0.7	•	2.2	1.5	1.7	1.0	1.4	0.9	0.8	0.8	0.8	0.6	
Inventory Turnover 35	9.2	•	4.1	3.5	2.0	4.3	4.9	4.3	3.6	5.3	5.5	9.2	10.6
Receivables Turnover 36	5.4	•	22.5	25.8	6.9	8.3	6.8	3.9	5.1	5.0	8.0	5.0	
Total Liabilities to Net Worth 37	1.1	•	0.6	•	0.9	•	2.2	2.0	0.4	1.8	0.8	1.1	
Current Assets to Working Capital 38	3.3	•	73.7	1.5	18.1	3.2	3.7	1.7	1.7	1.9	2.5	3.9	
Current Liabilities to Working Capital 39	2.3	•	72.7	0.5	17.1	2.2	2.7	0.7	0.7	0.9	1.5	2.9	
Working Capital to Net Sales 40	0.2	•	0.0	0.4	0.0	0.2	0.1	0.4	0.4	0.3	0.2	0.1	
Inventory to Working Capital 41	0.5	•	24.1	0.5	6.6	0.8	1.1	0.3	0.3	0.4	0.4	0.5	
Total Receipts to Cash Flow 42	10.3	29.1	7.9	15.1	119.2	54.1	11.6	6.0	6.6	8.1	10.7	10.2	
Cost of Goods to Cash Flow 43	6.9	16.7	3.7	10.2	51.6	32.3	7.1	3.4	3.6	5.4	8.5	6.8	
Cash Flow to Total Debt 44	0.1	•	0.2	0.3	0.0	0.0	0.2	0.2	0.4	0.2	0.2	0.1	

Selected Financial Factors (in Percentages)

Debt Ratio 45	53.4	•	150.2	36.6	102.3	48.0	158.0	68.8	66.1	30.7	64.1	44.3	53.4
Return on Total Assets 46	3.9	•	•	•	•	•	•	7.3	2.4	4.4	3.3	4.3	
Return on Equity Before Income Taxes 47	5.5	•	107.8	•	1263.1	24.3	•	11.9	2.8	5.9	4.5	6.6	
Return on Equity After Income Taxes 48	3.3	•	107.9	•	1327.8	26.5	•	5.4	1.2	2.3	3.8	4.2	
Profit Margin (Before Income Tax) 49	3.7	•	•	•	•	•	•	4.3	2.5	2.5	2.9	4.8	
Profit Margin (After Income Tax) 50	2.3	•	•	•	•	•	•	1.9	1.0	1.0	2.5	3.1	

Table II

Corporations with Net Income

COMMUNICATIONS EQUIPMENT

MONEY AMOUNTS AND SIZE OF ASSETS IN THOUSANDS OF DOLLARS

Item Description for Accounting Period 7/07 Through 6/08	Total	Zero Assets	Under 500	500 to 1,000	1,000 to 5,000	5,000 to 10,000	10,000 to 25,000	25,000 to 50,000	50,000 to 100,000	100,000 to 250,000	250,000 to 500,000	500,000 to 2,500,000	2,500,000 and over
Number of Enterprises 1	777	54	293	131	142	51	34	23	11	12	8	9	9

Revenues ($ in Thousands)

	Total	Zero Assets	Under 500	500 to 1,000	1,000 to 5,000	5,000 to 10,000	10,000 to 25,000	25,000 to 50,000	50,000 to 100,000	100,000 to 250,000	250,000 to 500,000	500,000 to 2,500,000	2,500,000 and over
Net Sales 2	78566322	325157	17850	67518	619351	246079	1268493	1246594	1072085	1918583	1981752	12925935	56876925
Interest 3	862481	0	0	3511	2533	205	4318	632	13864	25618	31981	87700	692119
Rents 4	143163	0	0	0	493	0	0	2061	124	0	36	76	140372
Royalties 5	925035	0	0	0	0	0	0	0	49	14652	14748	21184	874401
Other Portfolio Income 6	1041234	0	0	0	19413	0	25162	19819	12473	12153	25363	316827	610029
Other Receipts 7	380135	0	0	73	234	2070	2332	11307	18241	4462	6812	100112	234490
Total Receipts 8	81918370	325157	17850	71102	642024	248354	1300305	1280413	1116836	1975468	2060692	13451834	59428336
Average Total Receipts 9	105429	6021	61	543	4521	4870	38244	55670	101531	164622	257586	1494648	6603148

Operating Costs/Operating Income (%)

	Total	Zero Assets	Under 500	500 to 1,000	1,000 to 5,000	5,000 to 10,000	10,000 to 25,000	25,000 to 50,000	50,000 to 100,000	100,000 to 250,000	250,000 to 500,000	500,000 to 2,500,000	2,500,000 and over
Cost of Operations 10	60.8	54.7	86.0	36.4	51.6	40.7	61.7	60.5	58.0	55.3	48.4	82.5	56.8
Salaries and Wages 11	18.1	28.9	•	28.2	15.6	19.1	7.2	10.8	11.3	14.4	18.0	3.8	22.0
Taxes Paid 12	1.6	2.4	1.4	5.2	2.0	2.1	2.3	1.7	1.4	1.9	1.5	0.8	1.8
Interest Paid 13	1.8	•	2.6	0.7	0.5	1.6	7.7	0.9	4.2	0.1	4.6	0.3	2.0
Depreciation 14	1.9	•	•	0.7	0.7	1.6	0.9	2.3	1.1	2.1	3.6	0.8	2.2
Amortization and Depletion 15	0.7	•	•	•	0.1	0.2	0.2	0.2	0.2	0.3	0.9	0.1	0.9
Pensions and Other Deferred Comp. 16	0.7	•	•	3.3	0.3	•	1.0	0.1	0.4	0.2	0.4	0.0	0.9
Employee Benefits 17	1.1	1.2	•	5.7	1.8	1.9	0.7	1.2	2.1	3.2	2.0	1.6	0.9
Advertising 18	1.0	•	•	2.6	2.0	1.2	0.8	0.5	0.5	0.9	0.9	0.3	1.2
Other Expenses 19	7.0	9.7	3.4	13.3	9.7	11.1	6.3	9.4	10.6	11.9	13.8	6.8	6.4
Officers' Compensation 20	0.9	1.9	•	6.9	6.8	8.7	3.1	1.8	1.5	1.5	0.8	0.6	0.7
Operating Margin 21	4.3	1.1	6.6	•	8.8	11.8	8.0	10.4	8.8	8.2	5.1	2.4	4.2
Operating Margin Before Officers' Comp. 22	5.2	3.1	6.6	4.1	15.6	20.5	11.1	12.2	10.4	9.7	5.9	3.0	5.0

Selected Average Balance Sheet ($ in Thousands)

Net Receivables 23	18607	0	0	15	347	799	4455	9971	22305	39527	59995	164504	1256050
Inventories 24	8910	0	3	167	1209	984	2280	7705	15735	15725	35050	131829	513375
Net Property, Plant and Equipment 25	12818	0	0	12	114	1058	1611	6684	4706	11993	27121	55540	974098
Total Assets 26	148316	0	107	587	2409	6008	15333	36203	75838	156564	388812	898866	11024166
Notes and Loans Payable 27	31830	0	81	23	1195	1108	30481	8958	37936	3726	146625	57702	2342442
All Other Liabilities 28	37761	0	7	22	776	555	7965	14765	25940	47629	105119	343709	2643897
Net Worth 29	78725	0	18	542	438	4345	-23114	12481	11962	105209	137067	497455	6037828

Selected Financial Ratios (Times to 1)

Current Ratio 30	1.4	•	1.2	26.5	1.2	8.8	2.5	1.4	2.6	2.7	2.4	1.7	1.2
Quick Ratio 31	0.9	•	1.2	16.9	0.6	5.5	1.1	0.9	1.8	2.1	1.7	1.0	0.8
Net Sales to Working Capital 32	7.8	•	3.4	0.9	11.1	1.1	3.7	7.8	2.6	2.7	2.7	6.5	10.7
Coverage Ratio 33	6.7	•	3.5	4.9	25.3	9.0	2.4	15.1	4.2	81.3	2.9	26.0	6.6
Total Asset Turnover 34	0.7	•	0.6	0.9	1.8	0.8	2.4	1.5	1.3	1.0	0.6	1.6	0.6
Inventory Turnover 35	6.9	•	20.7	1.1	1.9	2.0	10.1	4.3	3.6	5.6	3.4	9.0	7.0
Receivables Turnover 36	4.4	•	13.3	40.2	6.8	12.1	10.4	6.3	4.2	4.6	3.6	7.9	3.9
Total Liabilities to Net Worth 37	0.9	•	4.9	0.1	4.5	0.4	•	1.9	5.3	0.5	1.8	0.8	0.8
Current Assets to Working Capital 38	3.8	•	5.9	1.0	5.6	1.1	1.7	3.4	1.6	1.6	1.7	2.4	5.3
Current Liabilities to Working Capital 39	2.8	•	4.9	0.0	4.6	0.1	0.7	2.4	0.6	0.6	0.7	1.4	4.3
Working Capital to Net Sales 40	0.1	•	0.3	1.1	0.1	0.9	0.3	0.1	0.4	0.4	0.4	0.2	0.1
Inventory to Working Capital 41	0.6	•	0.1	0.4	2.5	0.2	0.3	0.9	0.4	0.2	0.3	0.5	0.7
Total Receipts to Cash Flow 42	7.5	17.2	10.0	8.5	6.0	4.7	7.4	5.2	4.6	4.7	4.8	8.8	7.7
Cost of Goods to Cash Flow 43	4.5	9.4	8.6	3.1	3.1	1.9	4.6	3.2	2.7	2.6	2.3	7.3	4.4
Cash Flow to Total Debt 44	0.2	•	0.1	1.4	0.4	0.6	0.1	0.4	0.3	0.7	0.2	0.4	0.2

Selected Financial Factors (in Percentages)

Debt Ratio 45	46.9	•	83.0	7.6	81.8	27.7	250.7	65.5	84.2	32.8	64.7	44.7	45.2
Return on Total Assets 46	8.2	•	5.2	2.8	23.5	11.5	44.3	20.9	22.4	11.5	8.5	10.8	7.5
Return on Equity Before Income Taxes 47	13.2	•	22.1	2.4	124.2	14.1	•	56.7	107.8	170	16.0	18.8	11.6
Return on Equity After Income Taxes 48	9.9	•	21.4	2.4	109.9	12.7	•	53.0	76.0	13.7	10.6	17.1	8.3
Profit Margin (Before Income Tax) 49	10.3	1.1	6.6	2.6	12.5	12.7	10.5	13.1	13.2	11.2	8.8	6.5	11.1
Profit Margin (After Income Tax) 50	7.7	1.1	6.4	2.5	11.0	11.4	9.1	12.2	9.3	9.0	5.9	6.5	7.9

Table I

Corporations with and without Net Income

AUDIO AND VIDEO EQUIP., REPRODUCING MAGNETIC & OPTICAL MEDIA

MONEY AMOUNTS AND SIZE OF ASSETS IN THOUSANDS OF DOLLARS

Item Description for Accounting Period 7/07 Through 6/08	Total	Zero Assets	Under 500	500 to 1,000	1,000 to 5,000	5,000 to 10,000	10,000 to 25,000	25,000 to 50,000	50,000 to 100,000	100,000 to 250,000	250,000 to 500,000	500,000 to 2,500,000	2,500,000 and over
Number of Enterprises 1	1351	28	765	68	337	57	43	12	13	11	7	10	0
Revenues ($ in Thousands)													
Net Sales 2	34168138	129747	235432	127755	1314543	380993	1082672	760614	912773	1615226	3422917	24185465	0
Interest 3	224254	12281	0	176	1050	10914	6761	2412	5049	10649	14424	160538	0
Rents 4	9396	0	0	0	0	32	0	2	214	722	3072	5354	0
Royalties 5	587900	0	0	0	5544	0	3050	73	0	661	99	578475	0
Other Portfolio Income 6	486622	17415	0	0	1848	104	281	55735	3119	12151	11274	384696	0
Other Receipts 7	464583	83194	0	3	26880	32936	7295	1323	34170	9870	16944	251965	0
Total Receipts 8	35940893	242637	235432	127934	1349865	424979	1100059	820159	955325	1649279	3468730	25566493	0
Average Total Receipts 9	26603	8666	308	1881	4006	7456	25583	68347	73487	149934	495533	2556649	•
Operating Costs/Operating Income (%)													
Cost of Operations 10	67.5	87.9	45.9	47.8	61.4	59.3	59.9	58.0	48.0	59.4	77.8	68.6	•
Salaries and Wages 11	11.1	20.3	7.5	17.9	8.3	17.7	14.7	15.2	17.8	13.2	9.3	10.6	•
Taxes Paid 12	1.2	7.1	2.2	2.1	2.1	1.7	1.2	1.5	2.2	2.0	0.8	1.0	•
Interest Paid 13	2.0	10.1	0.7	5.5	1.0	1.9	0.8	2.4	2.5	2.6	0.7	2.2	•
Depreciation 14	2.3	6.7	0.1	4.2	0.8	1.2	1.7	1.6	2.9	1.9	2.0	2.4	•
Amortization and Depletion 15	0.9	2.9	0.1	0.1	0.6	0.8	0.5	0.8	1.2	0.5	0.4	1.1	•
Pensions and Other Deferred Comp. 16	0.6	0.9	•	0.1	0.2	0.1	0.6	0.2	0.4	0.4	0.4	0.7	•
Employee Benefits 17	1.5	2.2	1.0	•	1.4	1.4	2.3	1.0	4.6	1.7	1.0	1.4	•
Advertising 18	2.1	3.6	10.9	0.3	2.3	1.0	0.9	2.7	1.2	2.3	1.1	2.2	•
Other Expenses 19	14.5	73.0	19.2	31.6	16.9	37.6	17.3	18.6	13.7	13.3	7.0	14.4	•
Officers' Compensation 20	0.8	5.0	7.3	0.8	3.3	8.9	2.6	2.0	2.2	0.9	0.5	0.3	•
Operating Margin 21	•	•	5.0	•	1.7	•	•	•	3.5	1.8	•	•	•
Operating Margin Before Officers' Comp. 22	•	•	12.2	•	5.1	•	•	•	5.7	2.7	•	•	•

Selected Average Balance Sheet ($ in Thousands)

Net Receivables 23	4205	0	72	321	410	1614	5009	8492	11638	37209	55331	410916	•
Inventories 24	2949	0	18	328	498	877	3984	10790	11560	32176	77792	156373	•
Net Property, Plant and Equipment 25	2387	0	1	125	124	247	1340	4272	9793	10301	46003	248880	•
Total Assets 26	28531	0	115	530	2187	6848	17480	37925	68706	158481	337751	3108704	•
Notes and Loans Payable 27	7869	0	6	1237	763	912	2438	24672	18226	50772	34948	879211	•
All Other Liabilities 28	7951	0	112	234	766	5391	6127	13957	19935	38991	137542	799246	•
Net Worth 29	12712	0	-3	-941	658	545	8916	-703	30544	68717	165261	1430247	•

Selected Financial Ratios (Times to 1)

Current Ratio 30	1.5	•	1.2	1.3	2.2	1.9	2.1	1.6	2.8	2.7	1.8	1.3	•
Quick Ratio 31	0.8	•	0.8	1.2	1.4	1.5	1.4	0.8	1.5	1.5	0.7	0.7	•
Net Sales to Working Capital 32	7.6	•	16.6	21.6	3.6	2.5	3.6	6.6	2.3	2.4	5.4	13.0	•
Coverage Ratio 33	1.5	•	8.1	•	5.1	•	•	2.7	4.5	2.4	1.7	1.4	•
Total Asset Turnover 34	0.9	•	2.7	3.5	1.8	1.0	1.4	1.7	1.0	0.9	1.4	0.8	•
Inventory Turnover 35	5.8	•	7.8	2.7	4.8	4.5	3.8	3.4	2.9	2.7	4.9	10.6	•
Receivables Turnover 36	5.6	•	8.6	2.9	9.0	3.1	5.0	3.7	5.1	4.0	9.2	8.4	•
Total Liabilities to Net Worth 37	1.2	•	•	•	2.3	11.6	1.0	•	1.2	1.3	1.0	1.2	•
Current Assets to Working Capital 38	3.2	•	5.9	4.6	1.8	2.1	1.9	2.5	1.6	1.6	2.3	4.9	•
Current Liabilities to Working Capital 39	2.2	•	4.9	3.6	0.8	1.1	0.9	1.5	0.6	0.6	1.3	3.9	•
Working Capital to Net Sales 40	0.1	•	0.1	0.0	0.3	0.4	0.3	0.2	0.4	0.4	0.2	0.1	•
Inventory to Working Capital 41	0.9	•	1.9	0.3	0.5	0.2	0.6	1.1	0.3	0.4	1.0	1.3	•
Total Receipts to Cash Flow 42	7.7	•	4.5	11.5	5.5	6.6	6.8	7.9	5.3	6.4	17.0	7.5	•
Cost of Goods to Cash Flow 43	5.2	•	2.1	5.5	3.4	3.9	4.1	4.6	2.5	3.8	13.2	5.2	•
Cash Flow to Total Debt 44	0.2	•	0.6	0.1	0.5	0.2	0.4	0.2	0.3	0.3	0.2	0.2	•

Selected Financial Factors (in Percentages)

Debt Ratio 45	55.4	•	102.8	277.7	69.9	92.0	49.0	101.9	55.5	56.6	51.1	54.0	•
Return on Total Assets 46	2.6	•	15.2	•	9.5	•	•	10.8	11.2	5.8	1.7	2.4	•
Return on Equity Before Income Taxes 47	2.0	•	•	20.3	25.3	•	•	•	19.5	7.9	1.4	1.6	•
Return on Equity After Income Taxes 48	0.4	•	•	20.3	21.7	•	•	•	15.7	3.4	0.1	0.5	•
Profit Margin (Before Income Tax) 49	1.0	•	5.0	•	4.3	•	•	4.0	8.5	3.7	0.5	0.9	•
Profit Margin (After Income Tax) 50	0.2	•	5.0	•	3.7	•	•	1.5	6.8	1.6	0.0	0.3	•

AUDIO AND VIDEO EQUIP., REPRODUCING MAGNETIC & OPTICAL MEDIA

Table II

Corporations with Net Income

MONEY AMOUNTS AND SIZE OF ASSETS IN THOUSANDS OF DOLLARS

Item Description for Accounting Period 7/07 Through 6/08	Total	Zero Assets	Under 500	500 to 1,000	1,000 to 5,000	5,000 to 10,000	10,000 to 25,000	25,000 to 50,000	50,000 to 100,000	100,000 to 250,000	250,000 to 500,000	500,000 to 2,500,000	2,500,000 and over
Number of Enterprises **1**	593	9	•	0	317	27	28	8	7	7	3	•	0

Revenues ($ in Thousands)

	Total	Zero Assets	Under 500	500 to 1,000	1,000 to 5,000	5,000 to 10,000	10,000 to 25,000	25,000 to 50,000	50,000 to 100,000	100,000 to 250,000	250,000 to 500,000	500,000 to 2,500,000	2,500,000 and over
Net Sales **2**	24716704	32656	•	0	1259853	192099	895980	546390	573075	1278020	1217765	•	0
Interest **3**	175270	11613	•	0	542	1883	2547	2233	45	8038	5603	•	0
Rents **4**	6025	0	•	0	0	0	0	2	214	0	455	•	0
Royalties **5**	500500	0	•	0	0	0	3050	0	0	661	0	•	0
Other Portfolio Income **6**	421674	17415	•	0	1848	0	133	55649	394	2504	7339	•	0
Other Receipts **7**	433931	77799	•	0	26679	31877	5121	2342	33941	9116	11826	•	0
Total Receipts **8**	26254104	139483	•	0	1288922	225859	906831	606616	607669	1298339	1242988	•	0
Average Total Receipts **9**	44273	15498	•	•	4066	8365	32387	75827	86810	185477	414329	•	•

Operating Costs/Operating Income (%)

	Total	Zero Assets	Under 500	500 to 1,000	1,000 to 5,000	5,000 to 10,000	10,000 to 25,000	25,000 to 50,000	50,000 to 100,000	100,000 to 250,000	250,000 to 500,000	500,000 to 2,500,000	2,500,000 and over
Cost of Operations **10**	64.4	161.4	•	•	61.3	43.5	61.3	51.6	52.4	59.0	71.0	•	•
Salaries and Wages **11**	11.3	42.8	•	•	6.4	14.5	8.7	15.5	10.8	10.6	15.9	•	•
Taxes Paid **12**	1.1	22.2	•	•	2.0	1.7	1.0	1.6	2.2	1.9	1.6	•	•
Interest Paid **13**	1.4	10.0	•	•	0.3	0.2	0.6	2.4	3.4	2.4	0.8	•	•
Depreciation **14**	2.0	18.5	•	•	0.8	1.4	1.3	1.6	1.6	1.4	2.5	•	•
Amortization and Depletion **15**	0.8	5.2	•	•	0.0	0.0	0.5	1.1	0.4	0.4	0.5	•	•
Pensions and Other Deferred Comp. **16**	0.6	3.0	•	•	0.2	0.2	0.2	0.3	0.5	0.5	0.9	•	•
Employee Benefits **17**	1.6	5.8	•	•	1.3	2.0	2.6	0.6	5.9	1.3	2.2	•	•
Advertising **18**	2.7	•	•	•	2.3	1.8	0.8	2.2	1.1	2.4	1.8	•	•
Other Expenses **19**	14.2	93.5	•	•	15.1	19.8	11.6	13.8	8.6	12.4	0.6	•	•
Officers' Compensation **20**	0.8	12.0	•	•	3.2	10.9	2.3	2.3	1.4	0.7	0.6	•	•
Operating Margin **21**	•	•	•	•	7.2	3.9	9.2	6.9	11.8	7.0	1.5	•	•
Operating Margin Before Officers' Comp. **22**	•	•	•	•	10.4	14.8	11.5	9.2	13.2	7.8	2.1	•	•

Selected Average Balance Sheet ($ in Thousands)

Net Receivables 23	49702	31982	12138	7786	6467	2340	404	•	0	6396
Inventories 24	85383	37991	13833	9092	4763	1169	476	•	0	5345
Net Property, Plant and Equipment 25	64926	9947	10300	4791	1548	340	92	•	0	3893
Total Assets 26	337135	165546	68920	38191	18690	7149	2142	•	0	51647
Notes and Loans Payable 27	67308	64238	31219	14586	2468	883	453	•	0	11374
All Other Liabilities 28	81727	48217	21722	11971	5143	7802	441	•	0	12222
Net Worth 29	188101	53091	15979	11634	11079	-1536	1247	•	0	28051

Selected Financial Ratios (Times to 1)

Current Ratio 30	2.8	2.3	2.9	1.7	2.6	2.8	2.8	•	•	1.7
Quick Ratio 31	1.3	1.2	1.3	0.9	1.6	2.2	1.8	•	•	0.9
Net Sales to Working Capital 32	3.3	3.4	2.7	7.4	3.6	1.8	3.2	•	•	5.7
Coverage Ratio 33	5.8	4.5	6.2	8.4	19.1	105.5	31.9	•	6.3	4.9
Total Asset Turnover 34	1.2	1.1	1.2	1.8	1.7	1.0	1.9	•	•	0.8
Inventory Turnover 35	3.4	2.8	3.1	3.9	4.1	2.6	5.1	•	•	5.0
Receivables Turnover 36	6.4	5.4	6.1	7.1	5.8	1.9	10.8	•	•	5.8
Total Liabilities to Net Worth 37	0.8	2.1	3.3	2.3	0.7	•	0.7	•	•	0.8
Current Assets to Working Capital 38	1.6	1.8	1.5	2.4	1.6	1.6	1.6	•	•	2.4
Current Liabilities to Working Capital 39	0.6	0.8	0.5	1.4	0.6	0.6	0.6	•	•	1.4
Working Capital to Net Sales 40	0.3	0.3	0.4	0.1	0.3	0.6	0.3	•	•	0.2
Inventory to Working Capital 41	0.6	0.6	0.4	1.0	0.6	0.2	0.5	•	•	0.7
Total Receipts to Cash Flow 42	37.5	5.1	4.2	5.2	4.8	2.5	4.6	•	1.1	5.8
Cost of Goods to Cash Flow 43	26.6	3.0	2.2	2.7	2.9	1.1	2.8	•	1.8	3.7
Cash Flow to Total Debt 44	0.1	0.3	0.4	0.5	0.9	0.3	1.0	•	•	0.3

Selected Financial Factors (in Percentages)

Debt Ratio 45	44.2	67.9	76.8	69.5	40.7	121.5	41.7	•	•	45.7
Return on Total Assets 46	5.8	12.1	25.1	36.3	18.7	21.5	18.0	•	•	5.5
Return on Equity Before Income Taxes 47	8.6	29.2	90.8	105.1	30.0	•	29.9	•	•	8.1
Return on Equity After Income Taxes 48	5.9	20.0	77.6	84.1	26.6	•	27.9	•	•	6.5
Profit Margin (Before Income Tax) 49	4.0	8.5	17.7	17.9	10.4	21.4	9.4	•	52.8	5.4
Profit Margin (After Income Tax) 50	2.8	5.8	15.1	14.3	9.2	21.3	8.8	•	39.4	4.4

Table I

Corporations with and without Net Income

SEMICONDUCTOR AND OTHER ELECTRONIC COMPONENT

MONEY AMOUNTS AND SIZE OF ASSETS IN THOUSANDS OF DOLLARS

Item Description for Accounting Period 7/07 Through 6/08	Total	Zero Assets	Under 500	500 to 1,000	1,000 to 5,000	5,000 to 10,000	10,000 to 25,000	25,000 to 50,000	50,000 to 100,000	100,000 to 250,000	250,000 to 500,000	500,000 to 2,500,000	2,500,000 and over
Number of Enterprises **1**	5730	388	2488	502	1379	417	243	80	56	49	49	53	26
Revenues ($ in Thousands)													
Net Sales **2**	208037646	1061246	1356096	954830	5467143	4919743	4632862	3111731	3382588	7704533	13770206	41350420	120322248
Interest **3**	3361624	9905	3864	1342	14109	13070	45929	25852	37876	98174	211671	728628	2171204
Rents **4**	73856	957	10204	0	0	1979	5252	4081	5113	2732	10107	17278	16154
Royalties **5**	5621485	70997	0	0	0	0	1387	2325	1868	57803	126962	1139145	4220998
Other Portfolio Income **6**	3478550	148858	123	51	4734	71676	12647	10100	35966	44127	91367	772896	2286002
Other Receipts **7**	3357064	13142	28482	221	19606	33952	69226	58135	59811	95090	403831	653257	1922314
Total Receipts **8**	223930225	1305105	1398769	956444	5505592	5040420	4767303	3212224	3523222	8002459	14614144	44661624	130942920
Average Total Receipts **9**	39080	3364	562	1905	3992	12087	19619	40153	62915	163315	298248	842672	5036266
Operating Costs/Operating Income (%)													
Cost of Operations **10**	65.8	55.4	63.9	54.0	56.2	65.8	66.9	64.1	65.7	70.9	62.9	66.6	66.1
Salaries and Wages **11**	11.8	24.0	6.2	12.1	16.4	11.3	13.8	9.9	14.1	10.5	15.0	13.6	10.6
Taxes Paid **12**	1.3	2.7	3.4	3.4	3.5	2.0	2.1	2.1	1.6	1.4	1.9	1.3	1.0
Interest Paid **13**	2.2	1.6	0.6	1.8	1.6	0.6	1.7	1.2	2.0	1.2	1.9	2.2	2.4
Depreciation **14**	4.6	2.8	0.4	1.3	2.3	1.4	2.6	2.7	3.3	2.2	3.4	4.0	5.6
Amortization and Depletion **15**	1.2	3.2	0.0	0.5	0.7	0.3	0.6	0.5	1.2	0.6	1.4	1.3	1.3
Pensions and Other Deferred Comp. **16**	0.5	1.6	•	0.5	0.9	0.5	0.4	0.9	2.4	0.3	0.5	0.5	0.4
Employee Benefits **17**	1.8	2.6	1.4	1.4	1.6	2.0	1.7	2.2	2.0	1.7	2.0	1.7	1.9
Advertising **18**	1.4	0.3	0.6	0.6	0.6	0.8	0.4	0.6	0.5	0.8	0.7	0.4	2.0
Other Expenses **19**	10.4	29.8	21.0	20.6	14.0	9.5	11.2	14.6	14.8	11.6	11.9	7.9	10.2
Officers' Compensation **20**	1.1	4.7	6.2	7.9	6.7	4.0	3.6	2.6	2.0	1.3	1.1	1.2	0.4
Operating Margin **21**	•	•	•	•	•	1.8	•	•	•	•	•	•	•
Operating Margin Before Officers' Comp. **22**	•	•	2.3	3.9	2.0	5.8	•	1.3	•	•	•	•	0.5

Selected Average Balance Sheet ($ in Thousands)

Net Receivables 23	9870	0	9	263	492	1700	3149	6981	12656	33658	63820	149088	1550096
Inventories 24	3529	0	15	206	510	1706	2690	5760	8942	25496	28267	67593	416734
Net Property, Plant and Equipment 25	7613	0	15	125	600	1086	2586	6898	10632	17814	51084	161971	1096437
Total Assets 26	59604	0	105	707	2404	6915	15992	34761	71045	167598	357992	112008	9206831
Notes and Loans Payable 27	11260	0	130	371	853	1340	4786	5733	15446	31927	68621	292937	1512821
All Other Liabilities 28	15485	0	19	198	623	1559	3881	8637	22852	47596	77616	282613	2424784
Net Worth 29	32859	0	-44	139	928	4015	7325	20391	32747	88075	211755	536458	5269226

Selected Financial Ratios (Times to 1)

Current Ratio 30	1.8	•	1.0	1.8	1.7	3.0	2.2	2.1	1.9	2.3	2.5	2.0	1.7
Quick Ratio 31	1.3	•	0.8	1.1	1.0	1.7	1.3	1.4	1.2	1.4	1.6	1.3	1.2
Net Sales to Working Capital 32	3.4	•	3635.6	8.1	6.8	3.4	3.2	3.4	3.3	2.8	2.6	3.4	3.5
Coverage Ratio 33	4.1	•	•	•	•	7.6	•	2.7	•	2.2	2.8	4.9	4.5
Total Asset Turnover 34	0.6	•	5.2	2.7	1.6	1.7	1.2	1.1	0.9	0.9	0.8	0.7	0.5
Inventory Turnover 35	6.8	•	23.2	5.0	4.4	4.5	4.7	4.3	4.4	4.4	6.2	7.7	7.3
Receivables Turnover 36	3.9	•	48.0	7.7	7.2	6.8	6.4	5.8	4.9	4.4	5.8	4.9	3.3
Total Liabilities to Net Worth 37	0.8	•	•	4.1	1.6	0.7	1.2	0.7	1.2	0.9	0.7	1.1	0.7
Current Assets to Working Capital 38	2.2	•	431.1	2.2	2.5	1.5	1.9	1.9	2.1	1.8	1.7	2.0	2.5
Current Liabilities to Working Capital 39	1.2	•	430.1	1.2	1.5	0.5	0.9	0.9	1.1	0.8	0.7	1.0	1.5
Working Capital to Net Sales 40	0.3	•	0.0	0.1	0.1	0.3	0.3	0.3	0.3	0.4	0.4	0.3	0.3
Inventory to Working Capital 41	0.3	•	92.0	0.8	0.8	0.5	0.5	0.5	0.5	0.4	0.3	0.3	0.3
Total Receipts to Cash Flow 42	7.4	5.2	8.0	10.4	19.9	10.2	16.1	6.9	16.2	9.2	8.1	7.8	6.7
Cost of Goods to Cash Flow 43	4.9	2.9	5.1	5.6	11.2	6.7	10.8	4.4	10.6	6.5	5.1	5.2	4.4
Cash Flow to Total Debt 44	0.2	0.5	0.3	0.1	0.4	0.1	0.1	0.4	0.1	0.2	0.2	0.2	0.2

Selected Financial Factors (in Percentages)

Debt Ratio 45	44.9	•	142.1	80.4	61.4	41.9	54.2	41.3	53.9	47.4	40.8	51.8	42.8
Return on Total Assets 46	5.4	•	•	•	•	8.4	•	3.5	•	2.6	4.2	7.6	5.4
Return on Equity Before Income Taxes 47	7.4	•	8.7	•	•	12.6	•	3.7	•	2.7	4.7	12.5	7.3
Return on Equity After Income Taxes 48	3.9	•	10.7	•	•	11.6	•	2.1	•	0.4	3.3	8.0	3.8
Profit Margin (Before Income Tax) 49	6.7	•	•	•	•	4.3	•	2.0	•	1.5	3.5	8.6	8.3
Profit Margin (After Income Tax) 50	3.5	•	•	•	•	3.9	•	1.1	•	0.2	2.5	5.5	4.3

Table II

Corporations with Net Income

SEMICONDUCTOR AND OTHER ELECTRONIC COMPONENT

MONEY AMOUNTS AND SIZE OF ASSETS IN THOUSANDS OF DOLLARS

Item Description for Accounting Period 7/07 Through 6/08	Total	Zero Assets	Under 500	500 to 1,000	1,000 to 5,000	5,000 to 10,000	10,000 to 25,000	25,000 to 50,000	50,000 to 100,000	100,000 to 250,000	250,000 to 500,000	500,000 to 2,500,000	2,500,000 and over
Number of Enterprises **1**	3335	354	•	294	816	330	123	47	23	28	29	36	•
Revenues ($ in Thousands)													
Net Sales **2**	133678158	325604	•	600996	4163476	3799042	3146840	2061928	2030318	4601220	8437187	30377340	•
Interest **3**	2316299	2212	•	1323	6051	5464	14370	14994	13709	43551	125724	514066	•
Rents **4**	52379	0	•	0	0	1979	4195	369	4656	784	4525	15743	•
Royalties **5**	4983115	0	•	0	0	0	1386	39	0	44891	107845	926049	•
Other Portfolio Income **6**	2504662	34964	•	51	2873	69558	8691	6606	22152	29863	65059	729777	•
Other Receipts **7**	1299294	208	•	221	9428	19966	62793	55750	13556	37111	300341	614152	•
Total Receipts **8**	144833907	362988	•	602591	4181828	3896009	3238275	2139686	2084391	4757420	9040681	33177127	•
Average Total Receipts **9**	43428	1025	•	2050	5125	11806	26327	45525	90626	169908	311748	921587	•
Operating Costs/Operating Income (%)													
Cost of Operations **10**	60.0	63.9	•	51.5	54.3	61.5	63.8	60.1	65.3	67.9	56.7	64.2	•
Salaries and Wages **11**	11.7	8.0	•	9.2	13.6	8.5	8.9	8.1	9.1	7.9	15.4	14.9	•
Taxes Paid **12**	1.3	1.5	•	2.6	3.2	1.5	1.8	2.0	1.3	1.5	2.0	1.3	•
Interest Paid **13**	1.5	0.4	•	0.3	1.2	0.5	0.6	0.5	1.1	1.3	1.4	2.0	•
Depreciation **14**	4.8	1.6	•	1.1	2.4	1.3	1.7	1.8	2.3	2.1	3.6	4.0	•
Amortization and Depletion **15**	0.9	0.1	•	0.1	0.2	0.3	0.3	0.5	0.2	0.5	1.1	0.9	•
Pensions and Other Deferred Comp. **16**	0.6	0.0	•	0.7	0.7	0.6	0.5	1.1	0.6	0.4	0.6	0.5	•
Employee Benefits **17**	2.1	1.4	•	1.2	1.6	1.4	1.4	1.5	1.7	1.3	2.3	1.8	•
Advertising **18**	1.6	0.2	•	0.0	0.5	0.9	0.4	0.6	0.4	1.0	0.5	0.4	•
Other Expenses **19**	8.2	5.5	•	22.0	10.6	9.6	7.6	10.6	8.4	9.8	11.1	5.4	•
Officers' Compensation **20**	1.2	8.3	•	10.2	6.4	3.8	3.3	2.5	1.6	1.2	1.0	1.5	•
Operating Margin **21**	6.2	9.0	•	1.0	5.2	10.1	9.6	10.8	8.1	5.0	4.3	3.0	•
Operating Margin Before Officers' Comp. **22**	7.4	17.3	•	11.2	11.6	13.9	12.9	13.3	9.7	6.3	5.2	4.5	•

Selected Average Balance Sheet ($ in Thousands)

Net Receivables 23	6877	0	•	316	521	1544	3875	8256	17576	32198	60098	173074
Inventories 24	3810	0	•	197	662	1623	3519	5994	11067	26769	33250	67357
Net Property, Plant and Equipment 25	8583	0	•	59	635	1189	2584	4831	10468	20734	51732	193732
Total Assets 26	52771	0	•	657	2405	6608	15664	34871	74072	167465	358177	1149480
Notes and Loans Payable 27	7390	0	•	67	795	1179	2825	3963	12251	25123	48834	296328
All Other Liabilities 28	12222	0	•	220	468	1267	3561	6530	22943	44273	78046	332392
Net Worth 29	33159	0	•	370	1143	4163	9278	24378	38878	98070	231297	520760

Selected Financial Ratios (Times to 1)

Current Ratio 30	2.4		•	2.0	2.2	3.2	2.3	3.2	2.0	2.4	2.7	2.1
Quick Ratio 31	1.5		•	1.4	1.3	1.9	1.4	2.2	1.3	1.5	1.7	1.4
Net Sales to Working Capital 32	3.1		•	7.9	6.3	3.5	4.0	2.7	3.8	3.1	2.6	3.3
Coverage Ratio 33	11.6	48.8	•	5.1	5.7	21.2	29.6	10.9	7.7	9.1	8.1
Total Asset Turnover 34	0.8		•	3.1	2.1	1.6	1.7	1.3	1.2	1.0	0.8	0.7
Inventory Turnover 35	6.3		•	5.3	4.2	4.4	4.6	4.4	5.2	4.2	5.0	8.0
Receivables Turnover 36	5.3		•	5.9	7.2	6.7	6.5	5.4	5.5	4.4	5.9	4.8
Total Liabilities to Net Worth 37	0.6		•	0.8	1.1	0.6	0.7	0.4	0.9	0.7	0.5	1.2
Current Assets to Working Capital 38	1.7		•	2.0	1.8	1.5	1.8	1.4	2.0	1.7	1.6	1.9
Current Liabilities to Working Capital 39	0.7		•	1.0	0.8	0.5	0.8	0.4	1.0	0.7	0.6	0.9
Working Capital to Net Sales 40	0.3		•	0.1	0.2	0.3	0.3	0.4	0.3	0.3	0.4	0.3
Inventory to Working Capital 41	0.3		•	0.5	0.7	0.5	0.6	0.4	0.5	0.4	0.3	0.2
Total Receipts to Cash Flow 42	4.9	7.2	•	5.6	8.2	5.3	5.6	4.3	6.0	5.0	6.6
Cost of Goods to Cash Flow 43	3.0	4.6	•	2.9	4.4	3.3	3.6	2.6	3.9	4.1	2.8	4.2
Cash Flow to Total Debt 44	0.4		•	1.3	0.5	0.9	0.7	1.0	0.4	0.4	0.5	0.2

Selected Financial Factors (in Percentages)

Debt Ratio 45	37.2		•	43.6	52.5	37.0	40.8	30.1	47.5	41.4	35.4	54.7
Return on Total Assets 46	13.3		•	4.9	14.6	22.9	21.4	18.9	14.0	9.9	10.6	11.7
Return on Equity Before Income Taxes 47	19.4		•	7.0	25.3	35.0	34.5	26.1	24.3	14.6	14.7	22.7
Return on Equity After Income Taxes 48	13.5		•	6.0	21.6	33.8	28.5	23.8	20.9	11.1	12.6	15.9
Profit Margin (Before Income Tax) 49	16.0	20.5	•	1.3	5.7	12.6	12.5	14.5	10.7	8.7	11.7	14.0
Profit Margin (After Income Tax) 50	11.2	17.9	•	1.1	4.8	10.3	12.2	13.2	9.2	6.6	10.0	9.8

Table I

Corporations with and without Net Income

NAVIGATIONAL, MEASURING, ELECTROMEDICAL, AND CONTROL

MONEY AMOUNTS AND SIZE OF ASSETS IN THOUSANDS OF DOLLARS

Item Description for Accounting Period 7/07 Through 6/08	Total	Zero Assets	Under 500	500 to 1,000	1,000 to 5,000	5,000 to 10,000	10,000 to 25,000	25,000 to 50,000	50,000 to 100,000	100,000 to 250,000	250,000 to 500,000	500,000 to 2,500,000	2,500,000 and over
Number of Enterprises 1	3438	48	1477	661	713	170	179	60	30	46	15	26	12
Revenues ($ in Thousands)													
Net Sales 2	87359366	1464010	515082	912573	4343255	1587219	4080965	2786410	2382411	6932867	3073113	20142440	39139020
Interest 3	1464029	3974	109	371	3884	2858	9286	7964	16351	64331	57847	212593	1084462
Rents 4	52436	0	0	1910	176	3454	2230	1500	6095	1452	2126	8475	25018
Royalties 5	864194	6945	0	0	0	0	73	290	2253	15646	2993	647079	188915
Other Portfolio Income 6	1061549	4467	48	0	1991	2447	14821	5526	22612	47110	44475	742127	175923
Other Receipts 7	2054471	7596	3546	2359	6302	17988	7168	44337	29654	115644	58194	950951	810734
Total Receipts 8	92856045	1486992	518785	917213	4355608	1613966	4114543	2846027	2459376	7177050	3238748	22703665	41424072
Average Total Receipts 9	27009	30979	351	1388	6109	9494	22986	47434	81979	156023	215917	873218	3452006
Operating Costs/Operating Income (%)													
Cost of Operations 10	59.8	53.8	26.4	56.5	61.0	67.2	60.5	50.0	60.0	61.2	47.6	57.9	62.5
Salaries and Wages 11	13.8	27.1	4.4	8.8	13.8	12.5	11.8	16.3	13.7	13.4	18.6	15.2	12.7
Taxes Paid 12	2.0	0.8	2.0	3.0	2.7	2.0	2.3	1.8	2.3	1.9	2.3	1.4	2.3
Interest Paid 13	3.5	2.1	0.7	0.7	0.9	0.5	1.1	1.5	1.8	1.7	1.7	2.6	5.6
Depreciation 14	1.7	0.7	1.2	0.6	1.0	1.1	1.6	1.6	1.4	1.8	2.3	2.0	1.6
Amortization and Depletion 15	1.4	0.1	•	0.1	0.1	0.2	0.2	1.1	0.8	0.7	1.3	2.7	1.4
Pensions and Other Deferred Comp. 16	1.0	0.3	•	0.4	0.4	0.4	0.6	1.2	0.5	0.4	0.7	0.7	1.4
Employee Benefits 17	2.2	2.1	1.6	1.7	2.4	2.2	1.9	2.7	2.0	2.0	2.4	2.1	2.2
Advertising 18	0.7	0.3	0.5	1.0	1.0	0.4	1.1	1.2	1.4	1.2	1.8	0.6	0.5
Other Expenses 19	12.9	16.0	53.3	19.0	13.4	13.1	9.6	16.5	11.9	15.2	16.7	15.4	10.3
Officers' Compensation 20	1.6	12.3	14.1	9.9	4.3	2.0	3.5	2.8	1.9	1.5	1.4	1.0	0.6
Operating Margin 21	•	•	•	•	•	•	5.8	3.4	2.3	•	3.1	•	•
Operating Margin Before Officers' Comp. 22	0.9	•	•	8.2	3.3	0.4	9.3	6.1	4.2	0.5	4.5	1.0	•

Selected Average Balance Sheet ($ in Thousands)

Net Receivables 23	5791	0	25	153	982	2116	3596	8124	16239	31427	81443	169344	835301
Inventories 24	2614	0	6	166	685	894	2992	4489	12161	20068	23555	83737	300372
Net Property, Plant and Equipment 25	2855	0	14	41	241	923	2577	4772	7700	17786	25122	105327	377290
Total Assets 26	45142	0	116	688	2926	6511	15118	35125	71478	170453	362089	1199409	8330303
Notes and Loans Payable 27	12412	0	90	153	802	659	3121	9046	16020	42392	43752	355765	2359670
All Other Liabilities 28	12535	0	26	149	1162	2445	3339	10756	14525	39518	98490	219894	2585312
Net Worth 29	20195	0	-1	387	962	3408	8658	15323	40933	88543	219847	623750	3385321

Selected Financial Ratios (Times to 1)

Current Ratio 30	1.2	•	1.9	3.9	1.6	2.2	2.4	1.5	2.2	1.8	2.4	1.4	0.8
Quick Ratio 31	0.7	•	1.7	2.6	0.9	1.6	1.4	0.9	1.3	1.1	1.7	0.9	0.5
Net Sales to Working Capital 32	13.6	•	13.4	3.0	7.4	3.7	3.8	7.0	3.4	4.1	1.9	6.4	•
Coverage Ratio 33	2.8	•	•	•	0.3	1.2	7.2	4.8	4.2	2.8	6.1	6.0	2.0
Total Asset Turnover 34	0.6	•	3.0	2.0	2.1	1.4	1.5	1.3	1.1	0.9	0.6	0.6	0.4
Inventory Turnover 35	5.8	•	14.2	4.7	5.4	7.0	4.6	5.2	3.9	4.6	4.1	5.4	6.8
Receivables Turnover 36	5.2	•	21.6	8.4	7.1	6.5	6.9	6.6	5.2	5.3	2.9	4.7	5.2
Total Liabilities to Net Worth 37	1.2	•	•	0.8	2.0	0.9	0.7	1.3	0.7	0.9	0.6	0.9	1.5
Current Assets to Working Capital 38	6.6	•	2.1	1.3	2.7	1.8	1.7	3.0	1.8	2.3	1.7	3.3	•
Current Liabilities to Working Capital 39	5.6	•	1.1	0.3	1.7	0.8	0.7	2.0	0.8	1.3	0.7	2.3	•
Working Capital to Net Sales 40	0.1	•	0.1	0.3	0.1	0.3	0.3	0.1	0.3	0.2	0.5	0.2	•
Inventory to Working Capital 41	1.6	•	0.2	0.4	0.9	0.5	0.6	0.8	0.6	0.6	0.2	0.7	•
Total Receipts to Cash Flow 42	6.4	200.7	2.2	7.8	10.6	8.8	6.9	4.9	6.7	6.3	4.5	4.6	7.6
Cost of Goods to Cash Flow 43	3.8	108.0	0.6	4.4	6.5	5.9	4.2	2.5	4.0	3.9	2.1	2.7	4.7
Cash Flow to Total Debt 44	0.2	•	1.3	0.6	0.3	0.3	0.5	0.5	0.4	0.3	0.3	0.3	0.1

Selected Financial Factors (in Percentages)

Debt Ratio 45	55.3	•	100.5	43.8	67.1	47.7	42.7	56.4	42.7	48.1	39.3	48.0	59.4
Return on Total Assets 46	5.6	•	•	•	0.5	0.8	11.5	9.4	8.4	4.2	5.8	10.0	4.4
Return on Equity Before Income Taxes 47	8.1	2051.0	•	•	•	0.2	17.3	16.9	11.2	5.2	8.1	15.9	5.5
Return on Equity After Income Taxes 48	5.5	2051.0	•	•	•	•	14.8	13.9	8.3	2.4	5.7	11.3	3.8
Profit Margin (Before Income Tax) 49	6.4	•	•	•	•	0.1	6.6	5.6	5.8	3.1	8.7	12.8	5.7
Profit Margin (After Income Tax) 50	4.4	•	•	•	•	•	5.6	4.6	4.3	1.4	6.1	9.1	4.0

Table II

Corporations with Net Income

NAVIGATIONAL, MEASURING, ELECTROMEDICAL, AND CONTROL

MONEY AMOUNTS AND SIZE OF ASSETS IN THOUSANDS OF DOLLARS

Item Description for Accounting Period 7/07 Through 6/08		Total	Zero Assets	Under 500	500 to 1,000	1,000 to 5,000	5,000 to 10,000	10,000 to 25,000	25,000 to 50,000	50,000 to 100,000	100,000 to 250,000	250,000 to 500,000	500,000 to 2,500,000	2,500,000 and over
Number of Enterprises	1	1532	19	•	373	459	118	150	42	21	31	11	•	•
Revenues ($ in Thousands)														
Net Sales	2	76880568	337875	•	661273	3216469	1452108	3668247	2269280	1697953	5452452	2757261	•	•
Interest	3	1374764	36	•	360	2223	295	6251	4713	11979	31125	45646	•	•
Rents	4	50289	0	•	1093	176	3454	2230	478	6086	1153	2126	•	•
Royalties	5	799606	24	•	0	0	0	73	77	2253	9041	2993	•	•
Other Portfolio Income	6	999545	4467	•	0	860	2257	7017	4804	15992	42437	44406	•	•
Other Receipts	7	1861577	154	•	14	4897	18886	5364	37091	25394	74749	40776	•	•
Total Receipts	8	81966349	342556	•	662740	3224625	1477000	3689182	2316443	1759657	5610957	2893208	•	•
Average Total Receipts	9	53503	18029	•	1777	7025	12517	24595	55153	83793	180999	263019	•	•
Operating Costs/Operating Income (%)														
Cost of Operations	10	60.0	65.2	•	52.9	57.0	68.1	60.1	47.8	61.0	61.8	49.2	•	•
Salaries and Wages	11	13.1	9.9	•	11.5	14.2	9.9	11.2	15.1	11.7	11.6	17.2	•	•
Taxes Paid	12	2.0	1.3	•	2.7	2.7	1.7	2.3	1.6	2.0	1.8	2.4	•	•
Interest Paid	13	3.3	1.3	•	0.1	0.5	0.5	0.9	0.6	0.9	1.6	1.7	•	•
Depreciation	14	1.6	1.0	•	0.5	1.0	1.0	1.4	1.3	1.4	1.6	2.0	•	•
Amortization and Depletion	15	1.3	0.1	•	0.1	0.0	0.1	0.1	0.5	0.5	0.5	1.0	•	•
Pensions and Other Deferred Comp.	16	1.0	0.9	•	0.6	0.3	0.4	0.6	1.3	0.6	0.4	0.8	•	•
Employee Benefits	17	2.1	1.5	•	1.3	2.1	2.1	1.9	2.4	2.0	1.9	2.5	•	•
Advertising	18	0.6	0.1	•	0.1	1.1	0.4	0.8	0.8	1.1	1.1	1.9	•	•
Other Expenses	19	12.2	6.4	•	17.9	12.6	7.4	7.7	15.2	10.4	13.0	14.6	•	•
Officers' Compensation	20	1.2	2.6	•	8.2	4.0	1.3	3.6	2.9	1.7	1.4	1.4	•	•
Operating Margin	21	1.5	9.9	•	4.2	4.6	7.0	9.3	10.5	6.8	3.4	5.3	•	•
Operating Margin Before Officers' Comp.	22	2.7	12.4	•	12.4	8.6	8.3	12.9	13.4	8.5	4.8	6.8	•	•

Selected Average Balance Sheet ($ in Thousands)

Net Receivables 23	11380	0	•	206	844	2788	3746	8891	15426	36773	69864
Inventories 24	5127	0	•	162	648	1021	3127	5377	13861	20706	26256
Net Property, Plant and Equipment 25	5524	0	•	28	282	1151	2352	5421	7912	19149	30272
Total Assets 26	88656	0	•	755	2775	6291	15025	34865	70066	167638	358478
Notes and Loans Payable 27	22226	0	•	72	562	763	2709	4911	8808	44608	39721
All Other Liabilities 28	25701	0	•	224	850	2482	3270	11018	14828	40620	101861
Net Worth 29	40729	0	•	459	1363	3046	9046	18936	46430	82410	216897

Selected Financial Ratios (Times to 1)

Current Ratio 30	1.2		•	3.3	2.3	1.8	2.5	1.7	2.8	1.6	2.7
Quick Ratio 31	0.7		•	2.6	1.2	1.2	1.4	1.0	1.6	1.0	1.8
Net Sales to Working Capital 32	14.7		•	3.6	6.2	5.6	3.9	5.7	2.9	5.6	2.1
Coverage Ratio 33	3.7	9.9	•	51.4	10.6	19.4	12.4	23.8	13.2	5.4	7.2
Total Asset Turnover 34	0.6		•	2.3	2.5	2.0	1.6	1.5	1.2	1.0	0.7
Inventory Turnover 35	5.9		•	5.8	6.2	8.2	4.7	4.8	3.6	5.2	4.7
Receivables Turnover 36	5.3		•	7.6	8.1	7.1	7.5	6.4	5.0	5.5	3.9
Total Liabilities to Net Worth 37	1.2		•	0.6	1.0	1.1	0.7	0.8	0.5	1.0	0.7
Current Assets to Working Capital 38	7.0		•	1.4	1.8	2.2	1.7	2.4	1.5	2.7	1.6
Current Liabilities to Working Capital 39	6.0		•	0.4	0.8	1.2	0.7	1.4	0.5	1.7	0.6
Working Capital to Net Sales 40	0.1		•	0.3	0.2	0.2	0.3	0.2	0.4	0.2	0.5
Inventory to Working Capital 41	1.7		•	0.2	0.6	0.7	0.6	0.6	0.4	0.8	0.2
Total Receipts to Cash Flow 42	5.7	6.1	•	5.6	7.2	6.8	6.2	3.8	5.4	5.7	4.6
Cost of Goods to Cash Flow 43	3.4	4.0	•	3.0	4.1	4.6	3.7	1.8	3.3	3.5	2.2
Cash Flow to Total Debt 44	0.2		•	1.1	0.7	0.6	0.7	0.9	0.6	0.4	0.4

Selected Financial Factors (in Percentages)

Debt Ratio 45	54.1		•	39.2	50.9	51.6	39.8	45.7	33.7	50.8	39.5
Return on Total Assets 46	7.0		•	10.7	13.5	18.0	17.5	20.5	13.4	9.0	8.5
Return on Equity Before Income Taxes 47	11.0		•	17.2	24.8	35.3	26.7	36.1	18.7	14.9	12.0
Return on Equity After Income Taxes 48	8.2		•	16.1	22.5	32.2	23.8	32.6	15.1	10.4	8.7
Profit Margin (Before Income Tax) 49	9.0	11.2	•	4.5	4.8	8.7	9.9	12.7	10.8	7.0	10.4
Profit Margin (After Income Tax) 50	6.7	10.8	•	4.2	4.4	8.0	8.8	11.4	8.7	4.9	7.5

Table I

Corporations with and without Net Income

ELECTRICAL LIGHTING EQUIPMENT AND HOUSEHOLD APPLIANCE

MONEY AMOUNTS AND SIZE OF ASSETS IN THOUSANDS OF DOLLARS

Item Description for Accounting Period 7/07 Through 6/08		Total	Zero Assets	Under 500	500 to 1,000	1,000 to 5,000	5,000 to 10,000	10,000 to 25,000	25,000 to 50,000	50,000 to 100,000	100,000 to 250,000	250,000 to 500,000	500,000 to 2,500,000	2,500,000 and over
Number of Enterprises	1	1281	314	470	0	170	136	121	23	7	20	9	9	3
Revenues ($ in Thousands)														
Net Sales	2	138529384	746409	39487	0	900162	1186099	4227817	1358230	603777	3613999	4580765	12310618	108962022
Interest	3	86972645	1731	3	0	3	3136	4404	1681	1200	16613	540	62825	86880510
Rents	4	12307019	0	0	0	0	0	6177	0	1435	1436	243	18016	12279712
Royalties	5	2262252	91	0	0	0	36	0	1391	0	2489	288	37730	2220226
Other Portfolio Income	6	15679126	458	55	0	1	590	5855	3	1178	7882	8726	57978	15596398
Other Receipts	7	31846612	701	119	0	4	10274	13332	21581	1951	68029	24666	136786	31569171
Total Receipts	8	287597038	749390	39664	0	900170	1200135	4257585	1382886	609541	3710448	4615228	12623953	257508039
Average Total Receipts	9	224510	2387	84	•	5295	8825	35187	60125	87077	185522	512803	1402661	85836013
Operating Costs/Operating Income (%)														
Cost of Operations	10	71.3	81.1	36.8	•	55.9	65.3	69.5	76.0	68.7	66.0	69.4	70.2	71.9
Salaries and Wages	11	12.3	18.9	17.6	•	16.6	13.5	8.6	4.7	6.5	8.2	6.2	6.6	13.6
Taxes Paid	12	1.0	0.6	1.8	•	1.2	2.9	1.6	1.0	1.4	1.6	1.3	1.3	0.8
Interest Paid	13	70.2	0.3	1.7	•	0.4	3.3	1.0	1.4	2.5	2.6	1.4	2.0	88.7
Depreciation	14	8.8	3.1	0.2	•	0.4	1.1	1.2	1.8	1.6	1.8	2.1	1.5	10.7
Amortization and Depletion	15	1.5	3.0	1.5	•	0.1	0.7	0.0	0.4	1.2	0.7	0.3	0.6	1.8
Pensions and Other Deferred Comp.	16	0.6	0.4	•	•	0.0	0.1	0.4	0.3	0.2	0.7	0.5	0.3	0.7
Employee Benefits	17	1.7	0.8	1.8	•	0.1	2.2	1.4	1.6	1.8	1.6	1.6	2.1	1.7
Advertising	18	1.1	0.4	2.0	•	0.4	0.7	0.7	0.9	2.6	1.0	5.0	2.1	0.8
Other Expenses	19	35.7	17.3	65.5	•	15.1	19.1	10.4	11.0	12.1	10.2	7.3	11.9	42.3
Officers' Compensation	20	0.4	1.3	4.2	•	1.8	1.5	1.3	1.5	1.1	1.2	2.5	0.3	0.3
Operating Margin	21	•	•	•	•	7.9	•	3.9	•	0.2	4.4	2.5	1.3	•
Operating Margin Before Officers' Comp.	22	•	•	•	•	9.7	•	5.2	1.0	1.4	5.6	4.9	1.5	•

Selected Average Balance Sheet ($ in Thousands)

Net Receivables 23	143305	0	3	•	687	1450	4166	8235	17295	31397	69642	214703	59752245
Inventories 24	9047	0	25	•	648	2030	4968	10280	13961	34579	68704	120325	2621110
Net Property, Plant and Equipment 25	39077	0	1	•	56	717	2603	6713	7892	21946	69816	140658	15697593
Total Assets 26	631815	0	38	•	1563	6608	16554	35228	70738	160836	338376	1358540	262125314
Notes and Loans Payable 27	443144	0	13	•	258	3164	3698	10140	27089	45606	98170	223380	187503339
All Other Liabilities 28	112217	0	56	•	718	2199	4866	12412	25100	40748	111618	481195	45367558
Net Worth 29	76455	0	-31	•	586	1244	7990	12676	18549	74482	128588	653964	29254416

Selected Financial Ratios (Times to 1)

Current Ratio 30	0.8	•	0.2	•	2.0	1.6	2.1	1.4	1.5	2.0	1.8	1.2	0.8
Quick Ratio 31	0.6	•	0.1	•	1.1	0.8	1.1	0.7	0.8	1.2	0.8	0.6	0.6
Net Sales to Working Capital 32	•	•	•	•	7.2	4.7	5.5	8.9	7.2	4.2	5.8	13.7	•
Coverage Ratio 33	1.1	•	•	•	22.0	•	5.7	1.9	1.5	3.8	3.3	3.1	1.1
Total Asset Turnover 34	0.2	•	2.2	•	3.4	1.3	2.1	1.7	1.2	1.1	1.5	1.0	0.1
Inventory Turnover 35	8.5	•	1.2	•	4.6	2.8	4.9	4.4	4.2	3.4	5.1	8.0	10.0
Receivables Turnover 36	0.8	•	37.0	•	9.9	4.9	8.9	6.9	6.0	5.1	8.7	7.5	0.6
Total Liabilities to Net Worth 37	7.3	•	•	•	1.7	4.3	1.1	1.8	2.8	1.2	1.6	1.1	8.0
Current Assets to Working Capital 38	•	•	•	•	2.0	2.6	1.9	3.5	3.1	2.0	2.2	5.1	•
Current Liabilities to Working Capital 39	•	•	•	•	1.0	1.6	0.9	2.5	2.1	1.0	1.2	4.1	•
Working Capital to Net Sales 40	•	•	•	•	0.1	0.2	0.2	0.1	0.1	0.2	0.2	0.1	•
Inventory to Working Capital 41	•	•	•	•	0.9	1.1	0.8	1.5	1.2	0.7	1.0	1.3	•
Total Receipts to Cash Flow 42	3.0	•	4.8	•	4.9	12.7	7.8	9.0	9.1	6.5	10.6	7.0	2.6
Cost of Goods to Cash Flow 43	2.1	•	1.8	•	2.7	8.3	5.4	6.8	6.3	4.3	7.4	4.9	1.8
Cash Flow to Total Debt 44	0.1	•	0.3	•	1.1	0.1	0.5	0.3	0.2	0.3	0.2	0.3	0.1

Selected Financial Factors (in Percentages)

Debt Ratio 45	87.9	•	181.4	•	62.5	81.2	51.7	64.0	73.8	53.7	62.0	51.9	88.8
Return on Total Assets 46	13.0	•	•	•	28.0	•	11.8	4.6	4.5	10.9	6.7	6.1	13.2
Return on Equity Before Income Taxes 47	8.2	•	88.8	•	71.2	•	20.1	6.1	5.5	17.3	12.2	8.6	8.1
Return on Equity After Income Taxes 48	5.3	•	88.8	•	70.8	•	17.7	1.4	•	13.9	10.9	5.4	5.3
Profit Margin (Before Income Tax) 49	5.8	•	•	•	7.9	•	4.6	1.3	1.2	7.1	3.1	4.1	6.6
Profit Margin (After Income Tax) 50	3.8	•	•	•	7.8	•	4.0	0.3	•	5.7	2.7	2.6	4.3

Table II

Corporations with Net Income

ELECTRICAL LIGHTING EQUIPMENT AND HOUSEHOLD APPLIANCE

MONEY AMOUNTS AND SIZE OF ASSETS IN THOUSANDS OF DOLLARS

Item Description for Accounting Period 7/07 Through 6/08	Total	Zero Assets	Under 500	500 to 1,000	1,000 to 5,000	5,000 to 10,000	10,000 to 25,000	25,000 to 50,000	50,000 to 100,000	100,000 to 250,000	250,000 to 500,000	500,000 to 2,500,000	2,500,000 and over
Number of Enterprises 1	976	293	384	0	139	16	96	15	•	16	5	•	0
Revenues ($ in Thousands)													
Net Sales 2	116436237	2726	8736	0	849413	314124	3825367	792061	•	2896261	2804178	•	0
Interest 3	86922099	0	3	0	3	107	1807	1449	•	10818	92	•	0
Rents 4	12304444	0	0	0	0	0	5187	0	•	1380	152	•	0
Royalties 5	1601517	0	0	0	0	0	0	1391	•	2307	288	•	0
Other Portfolio Income 6	15643418	0	55	0	1	32	4064	3	•	7740	5701	•	0
Other Receipts 7	31705135	0	111	0	0	2590	11738	22290	•	55353	14991	•	0
Total Receipts 8	264612850	2726	8905	0	849417	316853	3848163	817194	•	2973859	2825402	•	0
Average Total Receipts 9	271120	9	23	•	6111	19803	40085	54480	•	185866	565080	•	•
Operating Costs/Operating Income (%)													
Cost of Operations 10	71.0	43.2	25.1	•	55.8	58.9	69.2	67.7	•	64.7	70.7	•	•
Salaries and Wages 11	13.2	•	0.7	•	17.6	8.9	8.3	6.0	•	8.1	4.6	•	•
Taxes Paid 12	0.9	0.5	1.0	•	1.2	1.9	1.6	1.1	•	1.7	1.2	•	•
Interest Paid 13	83.1	29.4	0.2	•	0.4	0.7	0.8	2.1	•	2.2	0.9	•	•
Depreciation 14	10.2	•	0.1	•	0.3	0.5	1.1	2.1	•	1.9	2.1	•	•
Amortization and Depletion 15	1.7	•	•	•	0.1	0.0	0.0	0.6	•	0.4	0.3	•	•
Pensions and Other Deferred Comp. 16	0.5	•	•	•	0.0	0.1	0.2	0.3	•	0.8	0.4	•	•
Employee Benefits 17	1.7	•	0.0	•	0.1	0.8	1.3	1.7	•	1.8	1.0	•	•
Advertising 18	0.9	•	3.4	•	0.4	1.1	0.7	0.4	•	0.9	3.9	•	•
Other Expenses 19	39.4	21.6	66.5	•	13.4	14.3	9.7	10.8	•	9.5	8.2	•	•
Officers' Compensation 20	0.4	•	2.4	•	1.9	1.3	1.2	2.3	•	1.4	0.6	•	•
Operating Margin 21	•	5.3	0.5	•	8.7	11.6	6.0	4.8	•	6.7	6.0	•	•
Operating Margin Before Officers' Comp. 22	•	5.3	3.0	•	10.6	12.9	7.2	7.1	•	8.1	6.6	•	•

Selected Average Balance Sheet ($ in Thousands)

Net Receivables 23	170149	0	0	787	4738	1829	8120	32482	76059
Inventories 24	9714	0	18	414	5145	6348	10647	30939	98276
Net Property, Plant and Equipment 25	49495	0	0	58	2733	481	5942	23117	81460
Total Assets 26	780129	0	3	1597	16360	7641	35773	162567	369632
Notes and Loans Payable 27	572766	0	11	136	3020	1582	12764	37007	85488
All Other Liabilities 28	127057	0	-30	740	4863	2453	11068	42870	112513
Net Worth 29	80306	0	21	721	8477	3605	11941	82690	171631

Selected Financial Ratios (Times to 1)

Current Ratio 30	0.8	•	3.0	2.0	2.1	2.0	1.4	2.1	2.0
Quick Ratio 31	0.6	•	1.1	1.2	1.0	0.6	0.8	1.2	0.8
Net Sales to Working Capital 32	•	•	13.3	8.3	6.1	5.6	8.4	4.0	5.4
Coverage Ratio 33	1.1	1.2	13.6	23.7	9.6	19.0	4.8	5.4	8.3
Total Asset Turnover 34	0.2	•	8.9	3.8	2.4	2.6	1.5	1.1	1.5
Inventory Turnover 35	8.7	•	0.3	8.2	5.4	1.8	3.4	3.8	4.0
Receivables Turnover 36	0.7	•	25.4	12.8	9.4	5.7	6.2	•	•
Total Liabilities to Net Worth 37	8.7	•	•	1.2	0.9	1.1	2.0	1.0	1.2
Current Assets to Working Capital 38	•	•	1.5	2.0	1.9	2.0	3.4	1.9	2.0
Current Liabilities to Working Capital 39	•	•	0.5	1.0	0.9	1.0	2.4	0.9	1.0
Working Capital to Net Sales 40	•	•	0.1	0.1	0.2	0.2	0.1	0.2	0.2
Inventory to Working Capital 41	•	•	0.9	0.8	0.9	1.3	1.4	0.7	0.9
Total Receipts to Cash Flow 42	2.7	3.7	2.9	5.0	7.2	4.0	5.7	5.9	7.1
Cost of Goods to Cash Flow 43	1.9	1.6	0.7	2.8	5.0	2.4	3.9	3.8	5.0
Cash Flow to Total Debt 44	0.1	•	•	1.4	0.7	1.2	0.4	0.4	0.4

Selected Financial Factors (in Percentages)

Debt Ratio 45	89.7	•	•	54.8	48.2	52.8	66.6	49.1	53.6
Return on Total Assets 46	13.9	•	23.6	34.9	18.0	33.9	14.8	12.9	11.3
Return on Equity Before Income Taxes 47	11.2	•	2.6	73.9	31.1	68.1	35.1	20.7	21.4
Return on Equity After Income Taxes 48	7.6	•	2.6	73.6	28.2	63.2	27.4	16.8	19.6
Profit Margin (Before Income Tax) 49	7.5	5.3	2.5	8.7	6.6	12.5	7.9	9.4	6.5
Profit Margin (After Income Tax) 50	5.1	4.5	2.4	8.7	6.0	11.6	6.2	7.7	6.0

Table I
Corporations with and without Net Income

ELECTRICAL EQUIPMENT

MONEY AMOUNTS AND SIZE OF ASSETS IN THOUSANDS OF DOLLARS

Item Description for Accounting Period 7/07 Through 6/08	Total	Zero Assets	Under 500	500 to 1,000	1,000 to 5,000	5,000 to 10,000	10,000 to 25,000	25,000 to 50,000	50,000 to 100,000	100,000 to 250,000	250,000 to 500,000	500,000 to 2,500,000	2,500,000 and over
Number of Enterprises **1**	1382	44	586	173	316	142	53	23	11	15	6	8	5
Revenues ($ in Thousands)													
Net Sales **2**	49265330	382197	237626	420573	1697988	2711642	1307332	1053099	1132694	2563432	2760071	5744579	29254097
Interest **3**	982051	4672	0	23	667	1077	3785	3688	3720	17913	34287	91178	821042
Rents **4**	80967	0	0	549	423	68	1601	121	331	8	163	656	77046
Royalties **5**	370889	219	0	0	0	0	13	0	2527	658	12247	15120	340106
Other Portfolio Income **6**	1095223	54187	0	0	17153	154	26237	2966	8803	7806	20838	99585	857492
Other Receipts **7**	561893	25343	0	-1	1222	11192	13317	3757	3040	10200	27556	40704	425564
Total Receipts **8**	52356353	466618	237626	421144	1717453	2724133	1352285	1063631	1151115	2600017	2855162	5991822	31775347
Average Total Receipts **9**	37884	10605	406	2434	5435	19184	25515	46245	104647	173334	475860	748978	6355069
Operating Costs/Operating Income (%)													
Cost of Operations **10**	69.4	74.7	69.1	56.8	68.0	70.3	64.4	70.6	67.7	60.9	66.8	67.1	71.2
Salaries and Wages **11**	7.8	33.8	1.0	5.3	9.2	6.5	10.4	7.3	8.1	12.0	7.7	8.8	7.0
Taxes Paid **12**	1.7	2.6	2.3	2.5	2.2	1.8	2.1	1.5	1.3	1.8	2.0	1.3	1.8
Interest Paid **13**	3.9	3.6	0.5	0.4	1.0	0.7	0.7	2.2	1.2	1.9	2.1	5.8	4.7
Depreciation **14**	1.6	0.8	1.2	1.4	1.3	0.6	1.4	1.1	1.5	2.3	1.7	2.7	1.5
Amortization and Depletion **15**	1.0	1.1	0.2	0.0	0.0	0.0	0.2	0.9	0.3	1.6	1.2	4.0	0.6
Pensions and Other Deferred Comp. **16**	1.2	0.6	•	0.1	0.4	0.5	0.9	0.9	0.3	1.0	0.8	0.5	1.6
Employee Benefits **17**	1.8	1.0	1.6	1.2	1.0	1.1	2.1	1.7	1.1	2.7	1.4	2.3	1.9
Advertising **18**	0.4	0.6	0.0	0.4	0.3	0.1	0.6	0.3	0.5	0.9	0.1	0.8	0.4
Other Expenses **19**	10.9	38.5	13.3	13.4	9.3	6.5	12.6	8.2	10.2	13.2	12.3	20.3	8.8
Officers' Compensation **20**	1.1	1.1	8.8	13.7	4.1	2.4	2.4	2.3	2.1	2.1	0.4	0.6	0.5
Operating Margin **21**	•	•	2.0	4.7	3.2	9.3	2.2	3.1	5.8	•	3.3	•	0.1
Operating Margin Before Officers' Comp. **22**	0.2	•	10.8	18.4	7.3	11.7	4.6	5.4	7.9	1.9	3.7	•	0.6

Selected Average Balance Sheet ($ in Thousands)

Net Receivables 23	8674	51	0	275	562	2087	3286	7730	15960	32635	71465	169239	1727174
Inventories 24	3777	58	0	222	1072	2179	3849	7575	15991	25896	46315	144961	423739
Net Property, Plant and Equipment 25	4042	4	0	121	310	899	2590	3729	8801	25754	72228	108031	666663
Total Assets 26	53838	147	0	853	2203	7723	15064	35688	69325	175379	380628	1386260	10798303
Notes and Loans Payable 27	9699	46	0	99	701	1509	2538	10821	9868	35783	90960	465278	1525440
All Other Liabilities 28	10820	53	0	180	800	2450	4607	10665	22743	53988	100728	288303	1966101
Net Worth 29	33319	48	0	574	701	3764	7919	14202	36715	85608	188939	632678	7306762

Selected Financial Ratios (Times to 1)

Current Ratio 30	1.3	2.1	•	3.7	2.1	1.7	2.8	1.9	1.9	1.8	1.7	1.6	1.1
Quick Ratio 31	0.8	1.1	•	2.5	0.8	1.1	1.8	1.0	1.0	1.1	1.0	0.9	0.7
Net Sales to Working Capital 32	10.2	5.4	•	4.8	5.6	7.9	3.3	4.7	5.3	4.3	6.7	5.6	24.7
Coverage Ratio 33	2.6	5.4	•	12.6	5.4	14.5	8.5	2.9	7.2	1.6	4.7	•	3.0
Total Asset Turnover 34	0.7	2.8	•	2.8	2.4	2.5	1.6	1.3	1.5	1.0	1.2	0.5	0.5
Inventory Turnover 35	6.6	4.8	•	6.2	3.4	6.2	4.1	4.3	4.4	4.0	6.6	3.3	9.8
Receivables Turnover 36	4.2	7.1	•	9.5	10.7	8.5	7.1	5.8	5.8	5.0	7.7	2.7	3.9
Total Liabilities to Net Worth 37	0.6	2.1	•	0.5	2.1	1.1	0.9	1.5	0.9	1.0	1.0	1.2	0.5
Current Assets to Working Capital 38	4.7	1.9	•	1.4	1.9	2.3	1.5	2.1	2.1	2.2	2.4	2.7	12.2
Current Liabilities to Working Capital 39	3.7	0.9	•	0.4	0.9	1.3	0.5	1.1	1.1	1.2	1.4	1.7	11.2
Working Capital to Net Sales 40	0.1	0.2	•	0.2	0.2	0.1	0.3	0.2	0.2	0.2	0.2	0.2	0.0
Inventory to Working Capital 41	1.0	0.9	•	0.4	1.1	0.8	0.5	0.8	0.8	0.6	0.7	0.9	1.9
Total Receipts to Cash Flow 42	7.7	9.9	•	6.1	9.2	6.9	6.9	9.6	6.2	8.6	6.0	11.6	7.2
Cost of Goods to Cash Flow 43	5.4	6.9	•	3.4	6.3	4.9	4.5	6.8	4.2	5.2	4.0	7.8	5.2
Cash Flow to Total Debt 44	0.2	0.4	•	1.4	0.4	0.7	0.5	0.2	0.5	0.2	0.4	0.1	0.2

Selected Financial Factors (in Percentages)

Debt Ratio 45	38.1	67.3	•	32.7	68.2	51.3	47.4	60.2	47.0	51.2	50.4	54.4	32.3
Return on Total Assets 46	6.6	6.8	•	14.9	13.1	26.0	10.2	8.2	13.2	3.0	12.2	•	7.8
Return on Equity Before Income Taxes 47	6.5	16.9	•	20.4	33.4	49.7	17.1	13.6	21.5	2.4	19.4	•	7.7
Return on Equity After Income Taxes 48	4.2	13.4	•	19.0	30.0	48.6	12.4	6.2	17.1	•	12.8	•	5.5
Profit Margin (Before Income Tax) 49	6.1	2.0	•	4.8	4.4	9.8	5.5	4.2	7.7	1.2	8.0	•	9.6
Profit Margin (After Income Tax) 50	4.0	1.6	•	4.5	3.9	9.6	4.0	1.9	6.1	•	5.3	•	6.9

Table II

Corporations with Net Income

ELECTRICAL EQUIPMENT

MONEY AMOUNTS AND SIZE OF ASSETS IN THOUSANDS OF DOLLARS

Item Description for Accounting Period 7/07 Through 6/08	Total	Zero Assets	Under 500	500 to 1,000	1,000 to 5,000	5,000 to 10,000	10,000 to 25,000	25,000 to 50,000	50,000 to 100,000	100,000 to 250,000	250,000 to 500,000	500,000 to 2,500,000	2,500,000 and over
Number of Enterprises 1	771	11	102	173	276	125	41	12	•	8	•	4	•
Revenues ($ in Thousands)													
Net Sales 2	36219709	22866	124934	420573	1642103	2555569	1064178	675393	•	1633438	•	3902005	•
Interest 3	925213	3	0	23	411	798	2378	815	•	3138	•	83429	•
Rents 4	75240	0	0	549	423	68	77	0	•	0	•	150	•
Royalties 5	180745	0	0	0	0	0	0	0	•	0	•	9622	•
Other Portfolio Income 6	968959	35717	0	0	17153	138	26186	78	•	3205	•	18935	•
Other Receipts 7	371734	-1	0	-1	1339	11154	10072	2579	•	6265	•	14678	•
Total Receipts 8	38741600	58585	124934	421144	1661429	2567727	1102891	678865	•	1646046	•	4028819	•
Average Total Receipts 9	50249	5326	1225	2434	6020	20542	26900	56572	•	205756	•	1007205	•
Operating Costs/Operating Income (%)													
Cost of Operations 10	66.7	67.8	65.8	56.8	66.2	69.0	60.8	66.5	•	58.0	•	70.0	•
Salaries and Wages 11	7.4	25.1	1.0	5.3	9.1	6.5	9.1	6.0	•	11.9	•	8.4	•
Taxes Paid 12	1.7	0.5	2.6	2.5	2.1	1.8	2.1	1.3	•	1.6	•	1.0	•
Interest Paid 13	3.9	8.2	0.7	0.4	0.9	0.6	0.7	1.8	•	1.4	•	2.9	•
Depreciation 14	1.4	1.8	1.7	1.4	1.3	0.6	1.3	1.1	•	2.1	•	1.8	•
Amortization and Depletion 15	0.9	•	•	0.0	0.0	0.0	0.1	0.9	•	1.0	•	1.6	•
Pensions and Other Deferred Comp. 16	0.9	5.9	•	0.1	0.4	0.6	0.9	0.5	•	1.4	•	0.6	•
Employee Benefits 17	1.5	7.5	3.1	1.2	1.1	1.0	1.8	1.5	•	2.1	•	1.9	•
Advertising 18	0.5	•	0.0	0.4	0.3	0.1	0.6	0.4	•	1.0	•	0.8	•
Other Expenses 19	10.1	27.5	12.6	13.4	8.7	6.2	11.4	7.2	•	9.1	•	10.0	•
Officers' Compensation 20	1.2	8.6	7.8	13.7	4.1	2.5	2.5	1.4	•	1.2	•	0.7	•
Operating Margin 21	3.9	•	4.8	4.7	6.0	11.1	8.7	11.5	•	9.2	•	0.3	•
Operating Margin Before Officers' Comp. 22	5.1	•	12.6	18.4	10.0	13.6	11.2	12.8	•	10.4	•	0.9	•

Selected Average Balance Sheet ($ in Thousands)

Net Receivables	23	12612	0	165	275	509	2188	3267	7851	37905	•	222284
Inventories	24	4962	0	306	219	924	1902	3616	7905	24511	•	163417
Net Property, Plant and Equipment	25	5306	0	0	121	326	881	2382	3128	28647	•	149090
Total Assets	26	68896	0	474	853	2156	7872	14846	34985	159984	•	1682205
Notes and Loans Payable	27	9653	0	225	99	687	1385	2427	5237	31761	•	413747
All Other Liabilities	28	11882	0	192	180	554	1963	3035	12728	56391	•	357067
Net Worth	29	47361	0	57	574	914	4524	9384	17020	71833	•	911391

Selected Financial Ratios (Times to 1)

Current Ratio	30	1.4	•	1.8	3.7	2.9	2.0	3.3	2.3	2.1	•	1.4
Quick Ratio	31	0.8	•	0.6	2.5	1.0	1.2	2.2	1.3	1.4	•	0.7
Net Sales to Working Capital	32	7.1	•	5.9	4.8	5.0	7.1	3.3	5.4	4.8	•	7.0
Coverage Ratio	33	4.0	13.6	8.2	12.6	8.6	19.2	18.3	7.9	8.3	•	2.6
Total Asset Turnover	34	0.7	•	2.6	2.8	2.8	2.6	1.7	1.6	1.3	•	0.6
Inventory Turnover	35	6.3	•	2.6	6.3	4.3	7.4	4.4	4.7	4.8	•	4.2
Receivables Turnover	36	4.0	•	•	9.9	15.8	10.9	7.9	6.2	•	•	•
Total Liabilities to Net Worth	37	0.5	•	7.4	0.5	1.4	0.7	0.6	1.1	1.2	•	0.8
Current Assets to Working Capital	38	3.5	•	2.3	1.4	1.5	2.0	1.4	1.8	1.9	•	3.3
Current Liabilities to Working Capital	39	2.5	•	1.3	0.4	0.5	1.0	0.4	0.8	0.9	•	2.3
Working Capital to Net Sales	40	0.1	•	0.2	0.2	0.2	0.1	0.3	0.2	0.2	•	0.1
Inventory to Working Capital	41	0.7	•	1.5	0.4	0.9	0.7	0.4	0.7	0.6	•	1.2
Total Receipts to Cash Flow	42	5.8	•	9.5	6.1	7.6	6.3	5.0	5.7	5.7	•	8.7
Cost of Goods to Cash Flow	43	3.9	•	6.3	3.4	5.0	4.3	3.0	3.8	3.3	•	6.1
Cash Flow to Total Debt	44	0.4	•	0.3	1.4	0.6	1.0	1.0	0.5	0.4	•	0.1

Selected Financial Factors (in Percentages)

Debt Ratio	45	31.3	•	88.0	32.7	57.6	42.5	36.8	51.4	55.1	•	45.8
Return on Total Assets	46	10.6	•	14.0	14.9	22.3	31.7	22.5	22.4	14.4	•	4.3
Return on Equity Before Income Taxes	47	11.6	•	103.0	20.4	46.5	52.3	33.7	40.2	28.3	•	5.0
Return on Equity After Income Taxes	48	8.7	•	85.9	19.0	43.6	51.2	28.5	28.4	22.5	•	3.2
Profit Margin (Before Income Tax)	49	11.7	103.3	4.8	4.8	7.1	11.6	12.2	12.2	10.0	•	4.6
Profit Margin (After Income Tax)	50	8.8	103.3	4.0	4.5	6.7	11.3	10.3	8.6	7.9	•	3.0

Table I
Corporations with and without Net Income

OTHER ELECTRICAL EQUIPMENT AND COMPONENT

MONEY AMOUNTS AND SIZE OF ASSETS IN THOUSANDS OF DOLLARS

Item Description for Accounting Period 7/07 Through 6/08	Total	Zero Assets	Under 500	500 to 1,000	1,000 to 5,000	5,000 to 10,000	10,000 to 25,000	25,000 to 50,000	50,000 to 100,000	100,000 to 250,000	250,000 to 500,000	500,000 to 2,500,000	2,500,000 and over
Number of Enterprises **1**	3949	495	1011	703	897	370	238	103	62	31	18	15	5
Revenues ($ in Thousands)													
Net Sales **2**	66300010	707787	1001953	1670996	3982858	4268867	6922573	5130269	5256714	5853872	5703396	10561399	15239326
Interest **3**	622861	2319	241	184	4331	7611	10611	9263	29726	27028	66390	171004	294152
Rents **4**	28251	0	0	168	137	2063	415	31	1645	532	1033	5341	16885
Royalties **5**	213397	0	0	0	0	16	1916	12522	6369	13358	40859	19392	118964
Other Portfolio Income **6**	211284	0	19	1664	8373	1819	15400	15476	10248	27359	12314	47156	71456
Other Receipts **7**	575015	16391	23608	1808	126355	15236	22862	54109	59724	84959	36906	19151	113910
Total Receipts **8**	67950818	726497	1025821	1674820	4122054	4295612	6973777	5221670	5364426	6007108	5860898	10823443	15854693
Average Total Receipts **9**	17207	1468	1015	2382	4595	11610	29302	50696	86523	193778	325605	721563	3170939
Operating Costs/Operating Income (%)													
Cost of Operations **10**	68.4	76.8	51.0	60.5	58.4	68.1	73.8	67.4	70.7	69.0	65.1	70.1	69.5
Salaries and Wages **11**	9.1	3.5	21.8	8.4	13.8	10.4	6.7	10.1	8.5	9.4	10.4	8.7	7.4
Taxes Paid **12**	1.7	2.3	2.6	2.1	2.4	2.7	1.9	1.8	1.9	1.6	1.6	1.2	1.5
Interest Paid **13**	2.7	1.7	2.9	0.8	1.4	1.5	0.8	1.6	1.1	1.8	2.7	3.3	5.1
Depreciation **14**	1.7	1.5	1.2	0.7	1.7	1.0	1.5	2.1	2.1	1.6	2.4	2.0	1.3
Amortization and Depletion **15**	0.9	0.3	0.1	0.0	0.5	0.3	0.2	0.3	0.5	0.5	1.1	2.1	1.4
Pensions and Other Deferred Comp. **16**	0.6	1.8	0.0	0.1	0.6	0.2	0.4	0.8	0.4	0.5	0.9	1.0	0.6
Employee Benefits **17**	1.5	2.5	0.1	0.5	1.3	1.4	1.1	1.6	1.7	1.5	2.6	1.7	1.2
Advertising **18**	1.0	0.3	1.0	0.1	0.4	0.7	0.3	0.5	0.6	0.7	1.0	0.8	2.1
Other Expenses **19**	9.6	9.4	32.6	18.5	9.6	8.4	7.0	10.3	7.7	6.3	12.4	8.2	10.5
Officers' Compensation **20**	1.7	0.1	1.2	3.2	5.4	3.8	2.6	2.0	1.6	2.2	0.8	0.8	0.4
Operating Margin **21**	1.1	•	•	5.1	4.6	1.3	3.7	1.5	3.2	5.1	•	0.0	•
Operating Margin Before Officers' Comp. **22**	2.9	•	•	8.3	10.0	5.1	6.3	3.5	4.8	7.3	0.8	0.8	•

Selected Average Balance Sheet ($ in Thousands)

Net Receivables 23	2485	0	86	302	653	1478	4436	8958	15554	33734	43617	106607	401994
Inventories 24	2118	0	61	245	406	2210	3981	7677	12403	29283	42760	96102	264597
Net Property, Plant and Equipment 25	1873	0	28	61	420	1058	2726	6597	11129	22703	51336	97099	291108
Total Assets 26	24967	0	304	693	2142	6827	15896	36068	69282	164464	322772	1102196	10823403
Notes and Loans Payable 27	5175	0	972	167	615	2475	3521	11886	13790	42324	104019	330322	1362437
All Other Liabilities 28	12256	0	243	178	773	1591	4717	8909	19795	39209	95299	299615	7210720
Net Worth 29	7536	0	-911	348	754	2761	7658	15273	35696	82931	123454	472260	2250245

Selected Financial Ratios (Times to 1)

Current Ratio 30	1.3	•	0.9	2.3	1.6	1.7	1.9	2.2	2.2	2.3	2.1	1.6	1.1
Quick Ratio 31	0.4	•	0.5	1.6	1.1	0.8	1.1	1.3	1.2	1.2	1.0	0.8	0.1
Net Sales to Working Capital 32	5.4	•	•	6.7	7.9	5.8	5.7	3.8	3.7	3.9	3.9	5.5	7.9
Coverage Ratio 33	2.5	2.4	•	7.4	6.9	2.2	6.6	3.1	5.6	5.5	1.7	1.8	1.8
Total Asset Turnover 34	0.7	•	3.3	3.4	2.1	1.7	1.8	1.4	1.2	1.1	1.0	0.6	0.3
Inventory Turnover 35	5.4	•	8.3	5.9	6.4	3.6	5.4	4.4	4.8	4.4	4.8	5.1	8.0
Receivables Turnover 36	7.0	•	10.9	8.4	7.6	8.6	7.2	5.9	5.9	5.5	5.9	6.1	9.4
Total Liabilities to Net Worth 37	2.3	•	•	1.0	1.8	1.5	1.1	1.4	0.9	1.0	1.6	1.3	3.8
Current Assets to Working Capital 38	4.1	•	•	1.8	2.7	2.4	2.2	1.8	1.8	1.8	1.9	2.7	14.7
Current Liabilities to Working Capital 39	3.1	•	•	0.8	1.7	1.4	1.2	0.8	0.8	0.8	0.9	1.7	13.7
Working Capital to Net Sales 40	0.2	•	•	0.1	0.1	0.2	0.2	0.3	0.3	0.3	0.3	0.2	0.1
Inventory to Working Capital 41	0.7	•	•	0.5	0.7	1.2	0.8	0.6	0.6	0.6	0.6	0.8	0.9
Total Receipts to Cash Flow 42	8.8	•	7.5	4.7	6.7	11.4	10.0	8.4	8.7	8.2	8.2	11.0	8.8
Cost of Goods to Cash Flow 43	6.0	9.7	3.8	2.9	3.9	7.8	7.4	5.7	6.1	5.6	5.3	7.7	6.1
Cash Flow to Total Debt 44	0.1	7.4	0.1	1.5	0.5	0.2	0.4	0.3	0.3	0.3	0.2	0.1	0.0

Selected Financial Factors (in Percentages)

Debt Ratio 45	69.8	•	400.1	49.8	64.8	59.6	51.8	57.7	48.5	49.6	61.8	57.2	79.2
Return on Total Assets 46	4.5	•	•	20.9	19.6	5.9	9.6	6.7	7.8	11.2	4.5	3.8	2.6
Return on Equity Before Income Taxes 47	8.8	•	13.1	36.1	47.5	8.1	16.8	10.7	12.5	18.2	4.8	4.0	5.6
Return on Equity After Income Taxes 48	6.2	•	13.2	35.7	45.2	4.5	13.6	8.3	10.4	13.6	2.0	2.8	3.0
Profit Margin (Before Income Tax) 49	4.0	2.4	•	5.3	8.1	1.9	4.4	3.3	5.3	8.0	1.9	2.7	4.1
Profit Margin (After Income Tax) 50	2.8	•	•	5.2	7.7	1.1	3.6	2.6	4.4	6.0	0.8	1.9	2.2

Table II

Corporations with Net Income

OTHER ELECTRICAL EQUIPMENT AND COMPONENT

MONEY AMOUNTS AND SIZE OF ASSETS IN THOUSANDS OF DOLLARS

Item Description for Accounting Period 7/07 Through 6/08	Total	Zero Assets	Under 500	500 to 1000	251 to 500	501 to 1,000	1,001 to 5,000	5,001 to 10,000	10,001 to 25,000	25,001 to 50,000	50,001 to 100,000	100,001 to 250,000	250,001 and over
1 Number of Enterprises	2927	476	491	641	725	247	183	70	44	27	•	•	•
Revenues ($ in Thousands)													
2 Net Sales	53956329	622494	364589	1587403	3342051	3387015	5438871	4200744	4162167	5191920	•	•	•
3 Interest	462251	880	205	130	4114	5581	5394	4371	11864	23189	•	•	•
4 Rents	21601	0	0	168	137	1070	227	0	1457	532	•	•	•
5 Royalties	151074	0	0	0	0	0	1916	0	4414	13358	•	•	•
6 Other Portfolio Income	185265	0	0	0	8264	236	12109	7257	7473	27083	•	•	•
7 Other Receipts	418610	15856	79	753	118848	2850	19952	37910	32637	82752	•	•	•
8 Total Receipts	55195130	639230	364873	1588454	3473414	3396752	5478469	4250282	4220012	5338834	•	•	•
9 Average Total Receipts	18857	1343	743	2478	4791	13752	29937	60718	95909	197735	•	•	•
Operating Costs/Operating Income (%)													
10 Cost of Operations	67.9	76.3	51.8	61.7	56.2	67.0	71.4	68.3	69.3	69.9	•	•	•
11 Salaries and Wages	8.4	3.3	8.7	8.0	13.9	10.0	5.7	8.8	7.7	8.8	•	•	•
12 Taxes Paid	1.7	2.4	2.1	2.1	2.5	2.6	1.9	1.6	1.8	1.6	•	•	•
13 Interest Paid	2.2	1.6	0.3	0.5	1.3	1.4	0.8	1.1	1.1	1.7	•	•	•
14 Depreciation	1.5	1.2	1.7	0.7	1.2	0.9	1.2	1.6	1.8	1.5	•	•	•
15 Amortization and Depletion	0.6	•	0.1	0.0	0.2	0.3	0.1	0.2	0.4	0.4	•	•	•
16 Pensions and Other Deferred Comp.	0.5	2.0	0.1	0.1	0.6	0.2	0.4	0.3	0.4	0.3	•	•	•
17 Employee Benefits	1.4	2.5	0.0	0.5	1.3	1.4	0.9	1.4	1.4	1.5	•	•	•
18 Advertising	1.0	0.3	0.8	0.1	0.3	0.7	0.3	0.5	0.6	0.7	•	•	•
19 Other Expenses	8.3	2.6	28.7	16.9	8.7	6.4	6.2	9.3	6.5	5.3	•	•	•
20 Officers' Compensation	1.6	•	3.2	2.5	5.8	3.3	2.7	1.7	1.7	1.5	•	•	•
21 Operating Margin	4.9	7.8	2.6	7.0	8.0	5.9	8.3	5.2	7.2	7.0	•	•	•
22 Operating Margin Before Officers' Comp.	6.6	7.8	5.7	9.5	13.8	9.2	11.1	6.8	8.9	8.5	•	•	•

Selected Average Balance Sheet ($ in Thousands)

Net Receivables 23	2618	0	38	321	610	1800	4446	10274	16391	33631
Inventories 24	2219	0	32	150	343	2518	4240	7981	13399	30261
Net Property, Plant and Equipment 25	1915	0	9	62	320	896	2688	5943	11110	23792
Total Assets 26	27611	0	178	696	2013	7260	15768	34973	69806	165630
Notes and Loans Payable 27	4487	0	5	160	594	2554	3001	8907	14441	42237
All Other Liabilities 28	15072	0	67	189	585	1783	4340	9188	18815	38366
Net Worth 29	8052	0	106	347	834	2923	8428	16878	36551	85027

Selected Financial Ratios (Times to 1)

Current Ratio 30	1.3	•	2.3	2.2	1.8	1.8	2.0	2.1	2.0	2.4
Quick Ratio 31	0.3	•	1.5	1.6	1.3	0.9	1.2	1.2	1.1	1.2
Net Sales to Working Capital 32	5.0	•	8.2	7.1	6.6	5.7	5.4	4.6	4.5	3.8
Coverage Ratio 33	4.5	7.5	8.7	16.3	10.5	5.3	12.9	7.0	9.0	6.9
Total Asset Turnover 34	0.7	•	4.2	3.6	2.3	1.9	1.9	1.7	1.4	1.2
Inventory Turnover 35	5.6	•	12.2	10.2	7.5	3.6	5.0	5.1	4.9	4.4
Receivables Turnover 36	7.4	•	•	10.1	9.7	8.8	7.2	6.8	6.3	5.5
Total Liabilities to Net Worth 37	2.4	•	0.7	1.0	1.4	1.5	0.9	1.1	0.9	0.9
Current Assets to Working Capital 38	4.1	•	1.8	1.8	2.2	2.2	2.0	1.9	2.0	1.7
Current Liabilities to Working Capital 39	3.1	•	0.8	0.8	1.2	1.2	1.0	0.9	1.0	0.7
Working Capital to Net Sales 40	0.2	•	0.1	0.1	0.2	0.2	0.2	0.2	0.2	0.3
Inventory to Working Capital 41	0.7	•	0.3	0.5	0.6	1.1	0.8	0.7	0.7	0.6
Total Receipts to Cash Flow 42	7.3	8.4	4.0	4.6	5.6	9.2	7.2	7.0	7.2	7.6
Cost of Goods to Cash Flow 43	4.9	6.4	2.1	2.8	3.2	6.2	5.2	4.8	5.0	5.3
Cash Flow to Total Debt 44	0.1	•	2.6	1.5	0.7	0.3	0.6	0.5	0.4	0.3

Selected Financial Factors (in Percentages)

Debt Ratio 45	70.8	•	40.6	50.2	58.6	59.7	46.6	51.7	47.6	48.7
Return on Total Assets 46	6.5	•	12.4	26.6	30.1	14.4	18.6	12.8	13.1	13.7
Return on Equity Before Income Taxes 47	17.5	•	18.5	50.1	65.8	29.0	32.1	22.7	22.2	22.8
Return on Equity After Income Taxes 48	14.2	•	15.5	49.7	63.2	24.1	28.2	19.7	19.4	17.7
Profit Margin (Before Income Tax) 49	7.6	10.5	2.6	7.0	11.9	6.2	9.1	6.4	8.6	10.1
Profit Margin (After Income Tax) 50	6.2	7.7	2.2	7.0	11.4	5.1	8.0	5.5	7.5	7.8

Table I

Corporations with and without Net Income

MOTOR VEHICLES AND PARTS

MONEY AMOUNTS AND SIZE OF ASSETS IN THOUSANDS OF DOLLARS

Item Description for Accounting Period 7/07 Through 6/08	Total	Zero Assets	Under 500	500 to 1,000	1,000 to 5,000	5,000 to 10,000	10,000 to 25,000	25,000 to 50,000	50,000 to 100,000	100,000 to 250,000	250,000 to 500,000	500,000 to 2,500,000	2,500,000 and over
Number of Enterprises 1	4993	863	2057	506	619	255	217	134	119	94	51	56	22
Revenues ($ in Thousands)													
Net Sales 2	602727111	3262296	1903687	884125	3367863	3511216	7481806	8694222	14409641	24376982	30256665	69574185	435004423
Interest 3	28205916	33320	350	213	3774	2071	9928	17791	35300	56365	181620	772919	27092265
Rents 4	15023556	164	0	0	283	0	1267	2132	5959	10010	12759	105003	14885980
Royalties 5	8388646	3950	0	308	0	0	0	8220	4508	4742	8516	317335	8041067
Other Portfolio Income 6	17200161	66378	13167	1769	876	115	16512	40263	21910	35833	52667	818759	16131913
Other Receipts 7	18241154	82286	31789	5641	15377	43048	50844	71343	109587	186435	229097	661552	16754153
Total Receipts 8	689786544	3448394	1948993	892056	3388173	3556450	7560357	8833971	14586905	24670367	30741324	72249753	517909801
Average Total Receipts 9	138151	3996	947	1763	5474	13947	34840	65925	122579	262451	602771	1290174	23541355
Operating Costs/Operating Income (%)													
Cost of Operations 10	82.6	85.6	70.5	67.7	72.8	78.0	77.7	79.9	81.2	83.3	84.2	80.5	83.2
Salaries and Wages 11	3.5	3.7	12.8	10.2	7.0	5.6	5.0	5.3	3.9	3.5	2.8	4.7	3.2
Taxes Paid 12	1.0	2.2	2.2	1.8	1.9	1.6	1.7	1.5	1.6	1.4	1.2	1.3	0.9
Interest Paid 13	6.4	3.7	0.4	1.1	1.5	1.2	1.2	1.1	1.7	1.3	2.0	2.9	8.1
Depreciation 14	6.1	2.7	1.1	1.6	1.4	1.8	2.1	2.6	3.4	2.7	2.8	2.9	7.3
Amortization and Depletion 15	1.0	0.5	0.0	0.1	0.3	0.2	0.2	0.1	0.3	0.4	0.4	0.7	1.2
Pensions and Other Deferred Comp. 16	1.6	1.3	0.0	0.2	0.7	0.1	0.3	0.2	0.3	0.3	0.5	0.7	2.1
Employee Benefits 17	1.3	2.0	0.6	0.4	0.7	1.4	1.4	1.8	1.7	1.8	1.5	1.8	1.1
Advertising 18	1.6	0.1	0.7	0.9	0.4	0.2	0.8	0.3	0.5	0.2	0.2	0.6	2.1
Other Expenses 19	9.4	21.4	11.0	16.2	9.5	8.3	6.8	7.4	6.2	4.8	4.1	7.7	10.3
Officers' Compensation 20	0.2	0.1	3.4	4.0	3.3	1.1	1.9	0.8	0.6	0.4	0.4	0.3	0.1
Operating Margin 21	•	•	•	•	0.5	0.5	0.9	•	•	0.0	0.1	•	•
Operating Margin Before Officers' Comp. 22	•	0.7	0.7	•	3.8	1.6	2.8	•	•	0.4	0.5	•	•

Selected Average Balance Sheet ($ in Thousands)

Line Item													
Net Receivables 23	64749	0	20	308	386	1470	3573	8106	15343	32782	71973	205996	13659326
Inventories 24	9098	0	86	209	967	1725	4948	7098	12995	28545	55059	115292	1299371
Net Property, Plant and Equipment 25	42500	0	28	102	405	1547	4503	10818	25579	46553	97786	234682	8339569
Total Assets 26	219211	0	163	791	2227	6476	16086	34576	73430	152936	357115	1043082	44676901
Notes and Loans Payable 27	70254	0	89	311	1460	2824	6426	11063	28171	42156	116720	344245	14245142
All Other Liabilities 28	113399	0	62	127	1549	2091	5267	11397	24495	48631	110641	430377	23846102
Net Worth 29	35558	0	11	353	-782	1561	4393	12116	20765	62149	129754	268459	6585657

Selected Financial Ratios (Times to 1)

Line Item													
Current Ratio 30	1.3	•	1.4	2.6	1.4	1.6	1.3	1.3	1.2	1.3	1.4	1.1	1.3
Quick Ratio 31	0.9	•	0.4	1.6	0.6	0.7	0.7	0.7	0.6	0.7	0.8	0.7	0.9
Net Sales to Working Capital 32	5.4	•	25.4	4.4	12.7	8.2	13.8	12.9	23.3	13.8	12.0	25.9	4.3
Coverage Ratio 33	1.1	•	0.3	•	1.7	2.5	2.7	1.4	1.0	1.9	1.9	1.0	1.1
Total Asset Turnover 34	0.6	•	5.7	2.2	2.4	2.1	2.1	1.9	1.6	1.7	1.7	1.2	0.4
Inventory Turnover 35	11.0	•	7.5	5.7	4.1	6.2	5.4	7.3	7.6	7.6	9.1	8.7	12.7
Receivables Turnover 36	1.8	•	59.5	8.1	8.4	12.4	9.0	7.5	7.8	7.6	8.6	6.7	1.4
Total Liabilities to Net Worth 37	5.2	•	13.3	1.2	•	3.1	2.7	1.9	2.5	1.5	1.8	2.9	5.8
Current Assets to Working Capital 38	4.7	•	3.7	1.6	3.3	2.7	4.2	4.0	7.2	4.0	3.4	9.1	4.6
Current Liabilities to Working Capital 39	3.7	•	2.7	0.6	2.3	1.7	3.2	3.0	6.2	3.0	2.4	8.1	3.6
Working Capital to Net Sales 40	0.2	•	0.0	0.2	0.1	0.1	0.1	0.1	0.0	0.1	0.1	0.0	0.2
Inventory to Working Capital 41	0.4	•	2.5	0.6	1.6	1.4	1.8	1.5	2.7	1.4	1.2	2.4	0.3
Total Receipts to Cash Flow 42	13.6	•	12.3	17.0	13.0	13.5	14.5	17.9	22.1	20.7	20.9	16.9	12.3
Cost of Goods to Cash Flow 43	11.3	•	8.6	11.5	9.5	10.5	11.3	14.3	18.0	17.3	17.6	13.6	10.3
Cash Flow to Total Debt 44	0.0	•	0.5	0.2	0.1	0.2	0.2	0.2	0.1	0.1	0.1	0.1	0.0

Selected Financial Factors (in Percentages)

Line Item													
Debt Ratio 45	83.8	•	93.0	55.4	135.1	75.9	72.7	65.0	71.7	59.4	63.7	74.3	85.3
Return on Total Assets 46	3.8	•	0.6	•	6.4	6.4	6.7	3.0	2.8	4.3	6.2	3.5	3.8
Return on Equity Before Income Taxes 47	1.4	•	•	•	•	15.8	15.5	2.4	•	5.2	8.1	0.1	1.3
Return on Equity After Income Taxes 48	•	•	•	•	•	14.5	11.0	•	•	2.9	4.1	•	•
Profit Margin (Before Income Tax) 49	0.4	•	1.1	•	1.1	1.8	2.0	0.4	1.2	1.8	0.0	•	0.4
Profit Margin (After Income Tax) 50	•	•	0.9	•	•	1.6	1.4	•	0.7	0.9	•	•	0.4

Table II

Corporations with Net Income

MOTOR VEHICLES AND PARTS

MONEY AMOUNTS AND SIZE OF ASSETS IN THOUSANDS OF DOLLARS

Item Description for Accounting Period 7/07 Through 6/08	Total	Zero Assets	Under 500	500 to 1,000	1,000 to 5,000	5,000 to 10,000	10,000 to 25,000	25,000 to 50,000	50,000 to 100,000	100,000 to 250,000	250,000 to 500,000	500,000 to 2,500,000	2,500,000 and over
Number of Enterprises 1	1990	4	678	177	515	187	145	78	70	59	34	•	•
Revenues ($ in Thousands)													
Net Sales 2	414179334	1449813	234362	398753	2532795	3147611	5497289	5211035	9984807	15281370	20137686	•	•
Interest 3	20486884	6075	45	103	1891	1137	5460	10597	20564	39580	70509	•	•
Rents 4	8766818	160	0	0	283	0	964	1945	5348	1314	2548	•	•
Royalties 5	6972625	244	0	308	0	0	0	5558	3177	4460	4270	•	•
Other Portfolio Income 6	14771137	13897	7761	0	876	114	16031	8917	11008	14994	38613	•	•
Other Receipts 7	13119734	40287	0	908	13270	42601	43337	50054	58677	136019	138610	•	•
Total Receipts 8	478298532	1510476	242168	400072	2549115	3191463	5563081	5288106	10083581	15477737	20392236	•	•
Average Total Receipts 9	240351	377619	357	2260	4950	17067	38366	67796	144051	262335	599772	•	•
Operating Costs/Operating Income (%)													
Cost of Operations 10	80.5	83.8	53.8	55.6	69.1	77.3	75.9	76.4	80.5	82.3	82.5	•	•
Salaries and Wages 11	3.2	3.3	4.0	15.9	8.4	5.5	4.7	4.7	3.4	2.9	3.0	•	•
Taxes Paid 12	1.1	0.7	2.2	2.1	2.1	1.5	1.5	1.5	1.4	1.3	1.3	•	•
Interest Paid 13	6.4	0.6	0.5	1.1	1.5	0.8	1.1	0.8	1.0	0.9	1.2	•	•
Depreciation 14	6.1	0.9	2.6	1.9	1.2	1.5	1.8	2.2	2.9	2.5	2.6	•	•
Amortization and Depletion 15	1.0	0.1	•	0.2	0.1	0.1	0.1	0.0	0.1	0.4	0.3	•	•
Pensions and Other Deferred Comp. 16	2.1	0.1	•	0.2	0.9	0.1	0.3	0.2	0.3	0.2	0.4	•	•
Employee Benefits 17	0.9	1.0	1.4	0.6	0.8	1.4	1.3	1.5	1.4	1.5	1.6	•	•
Advertising 18	2.0	0.1	3.2	0.1	0.3	0.1	0.8	0.3	0.4	0.2	0.2	•	•
Other Expenses 19	9.4	4.0	19.9	13.6	9.3	7.8	6.0	6.7	4.9	4.4	3.4	•	•
Officers' Compensation 20	0.2	0.1	6.7	6.1	3.8	1.2	2.1	0.9	0.6	0.5	0.4	•	•
Operating Margin 21	•	5.4	5.6	2.7	2.3	2.7	4.2	4.9	3.1	2.9	3.1	•	•
Operating Margin Before Officers' Comp. 22	•	5.4	12.3	8.8	6.1	3.9	6.3	5.8	3.7	3.4	3.6	•	•

Selected Average Balance Sheet ($ in Thousands)

Net Receivables 23	110894	0	17	258	367	1839	3723	8338	17029	30561	75697
Inventories 24	11449	0	74	314	960	1441	5053	7809	14895	27659	58168
Net Property, Plant and Equipment 25	65233	0	35	110	338	1716	3999	9797	25594	42728	89291
Total Assets 26	321148	0	138	834	2026	6202	16285	34457	74857	147239	347219
Notes and Loans Payable 27	130871	0	42	300	1317	2039	5626	7666	21375	28064	90443
All Other Liabilities 28	146420	0	63	129	1758	1968	4399	9738	23853	45135	116451
Net Worth 29	43857	0	33	406	-1050	2196	6260	17053	29629	74039	140325

Selected Financial Ratios (Times to 1)

Current Ratio 30	1.3	•	1.3	4.0	1.5	1.4	1.7	1.7	1.5	1.5	1.6
Quick Ratio 31	1.0	•	0.3	2.1	0.6	0.8	0.8	1.0	0.8	0.8	0.9
Net Sales to Working Capital 32	6.1	•	16.0	4.4	11.1	13.9	8.3	7.9	10.4	10.8	8.6
Coverage Ratio 33	1.5	16.8	17.9	3.8	3.0	6.1	5.8	9.1	5.0	5.9	4.8
Total Asset Turnover 34	0.6	•	2.5	2.7	2.4	2.7	2.3	1.9	1.9	1.8	1.7
Inventory Turnover 35	14.6	•	2.5	4.0	3.5	9.0	5.7	6.5	7.7	7.7	8.4
Receivables Turnover 36	2.8	•	36.5	•	8.3	12.2	10.4	7.1	•	7.6	7.9
Total Liabilities to Net Worth 37	6.3	•	3.2	1.1	•	1.8	1.6	1.0	1.5	1.0	1.5
Current Assets to Working Capital 38	4.9	•	4.7	1.3	3.0	3.4	2.4	2.4	3.0	3.0	2.5
Current Liabilities to Working Capital 39	3.9	•	3.7	0.3	2.0	2.4	1.4	1.4	2.0	2.0	1.5
Working Capital to Net Sales 40	0.2	•	0.1	0.2	0.1	0.1	0.1	0.1	0.1	0.1	0.1
Inventory to Working Capital 41	0.4	•	3.6	0.6	1.7	1.3	1.2	0.9	1.1	1.1	0.8
Total Receipts to Cash Flow 42	9.8	7.7	4.4	19.3	11.1	10.8	10.1	8.9	12.9	12.9	14.3
Cost of Goods to Cash Flow 43	7.9	6.4	2.4	10.7	7.7	8.3	7.7	6.8	10.4	10.6	11.8
Cash Flow to Total Debt 44	0.1	•	0.7	0.3	0.1	0.4	0.4	0.4	0.2	0.3	0.2

Selected Financial Factors (in Percentages)

Debt Ratio 45	86.3	•	76.4	51.4	151.8	64.6	61.6	50.5	60.4	49.7	59.6
Return on Total Assets 46	6.3	•	23.7	11.0	10.8	13.3	15.2	14.0	9.8	9.0	9.5
Return on Equity Before Income Taxes 47	15.6	•	95.2	16.7	•	31.4	32.8	25.1	19.8	15.0	18.6
Return on Equity After Income Taxes 48	11.5	•	95.0	11.3	•	30.1	28.1	21.6	16.0	11.9	13.0
Profit Margin (Before Income Tax) 49	3.3	9.5	9.0	3.0	3.0	4.1	5.4.	6.4	4.1	4.3	4.4
Profit Margin (After Income Tax) 50	2.4	8.9	8.9	2.0	2.8	3.9	4.6	5.5	3.3	3.4	3.1

Table I

Corporations with and without Net Income

AEROSPACE PRODUCT AND PARTS

MONEY AMOUNTS AND SIZE OF ASSETS IN THOUSANDS OF DOLLARS

Item Description for Accounting Period 7/07 Through 6/08	Total	Zero Assets	Under 500	500 to 1,000	1,000 to 5,000	5,000 to 10,000	10,000 to 25,000	25,000 to 50,000	50,000 to 100,000	100,000 to 250,000	250,000 to 500,000	500,000 to 2,500,000	2,500,000 and over
Number of Enterprises 1	1867	21	1262	158	190	38	83	31	25	18	8	19	15
Revenues ($ in Thousands)													
Net Sales 2	272648670	1693594	1157473	146356	963304	416223	1982606	1368672	1538773	2406768	2372323	16672755	24192823
Interest 3	4439548	1364	1324	255	459	8289	6241	5283	8186	6191	27360	149205	4225389
Rents 4	1329335	305	0	0	0	0	3203	484	485	990	272	30658	1292936
Royalties 5	2014829	7544	0	0	0	0	341	0	0	3093	0	16308	1987543
Other Portfolio Income 6	2929618	11132	36184	241	6064	3629	23618	43047	2838	7179	798	23730	2771158
Other Receipts 7	4489037	51145	350	0	1137	786	16992	8191	48938	55956	65306	45001	4195239
Total Receipts 8	287851037	1765084	1195331	146852	970964	428927	2033001	1425677	1599220	2480177	2466059	16937657	255402088
Average Total Receipts 9	154178	84052	947	929	5110	11288	24494	45990	63969	137788	308257	891456	17093473
Operating Costs/Operating Income (%)													
Cost of Operations 10	73.6	74.6	49.7	50.0	71.7	63.9	62.9	65.9	64.5	69.0	82.5	69.4	74.2
Salaries and Wages 11	4.1	6.6	21.4	2.3	5.6	12.1	6.0	10.6	11.6	6.6	6.3	8.6	3.5
Taxes Paid 12	1.3	1.9	2.4	3.5	1.8	1.7	2.0	2.7	2.3	1.3	2.3	2.4	1.2
Interest Paid 13	2.6	3.9	1.3	0.8	0.6	4.0	1.5	2.4	2.0	3.0	9.3	3.5	2.5
Depreciation 14	2.1	3.0	0.8	3.1	1.0	2.2	2.6	3.0	2.6	2.5	3.2	2.1	2.1
Amortization and Depletion 15	0.8	0.5	0.0	0.1	0.0	0.2	0.2	0.3	1.2	0.5	3.6	1.3	0.7
Pensions and Other Deferred Comp. 16	1.6	1.1	0.0	2.5	0.3	0.4	0.5	1.1	1.2	0.2	0.6	0.9	1.8
Employee Benefits 17	2.4	2.5	0.3	0.5	0.6	1.5	2.1	2.6	2.4	0.9	2.4	2.6	2.4
Advertising 18	0.2	0.1	0.6	0.5	0.2	0.6	0.4	0.3	0.3	0.3	0.4	0.2	0.2
Other Expenses 19	9.7	9.1	18.1	17.7	6.3	14.4	12.8	6.2	12.7	8.0	4.6	4.4	10.0
Officers' Compensation 20	0.4	2.7	3.0	18.4	3.1	1.9	3.2	2.9	2.1	1.3	0.9	1.1	0.2
Operating Margin 21	1.2	•	2.4	0.5	8.8	•	5.9	1.9	•	6.4	•	3.4	1.2
Operating Margin Before Officers' Comp. 22	1.6	•	5.3	18.9	11.9	•	9.1	4.8	•	7.7	•	4.5	1.4

Selected Average Balance Sheet ($ in Thousands)

Net Receivables 23	20457	0	5	37	727	1217	3781	6006	10997	17462	56443	149990	2240418
Inventories 24	19350	0	8	302	687	5588	5209	11202	16262	41971	85149	193207	1962144
Net Property, Plant and Equipment 25	21682	0	31	49	157	955	3455	7045	13464	33152	58886	154212	2368540
Total Assets 26	170800	0	82	770	1971	7468	16460	34920	72886	155622	363287	1286645	18904963
Notes and Loans Payable 27	38687	0	90	356	450	3919	6007	10594	20206	51464	145425	426435	4020028
All Other Liabilities 28	77895	0	-9	8	476	1659	4810	7504	21649	38658	204917	427075	8910949
Net Worth 29	54217	0	1	407	1045	1890	5643	16822	31032	65500	12946	433135	5973987

Selected Financial Ratios (Times to 1)

Current Ratio 30	1.2	•	2.5	12.9	3.4	2.0	1.8	2.2	1.6	2.1	1.2	1.7	1.1
Quick Ratio 31	0.6	•	2.0	5.9	2.2	0.7	0.9	1.1	0.8	0.7	0.6	0.9	0.6
Net Sales to Working Capital 32	15.1	•	34.4	1.7	4.1	3.5	5.0	3.4	4.4	3.6	8.8	4.2	21.0
Coverage Ratio 33	3.7	0.5	5.3	2.0	16.2	1.0	6.4	3.4	1.5	4.2	•	2.5	4.0
Total Asset Turnover 34	0.9	•	11.2	1.2	2.6	1.5	1.5	1.3	0.8	0.9	0.8	0.7	0.9
Inventory Turnover 35	5.6	•	57.7	1.5	5.3	1.3	2.9	2.6	2.4	2.2	2.9	3.2	6.1
Receivables Turnover 36	7.2	•	49.7	19.3	7.4	5.3	6.7	5.4	5.1	7.3	4.7	5.8	7.3
Total Liabilities to Net Worth 37	2.2	•	101.1	0.9	0.9	3.0	1.9	1.1	1.3	1.4	27.1	2.0	2.2
Current Assets to Working Capital 38	6.1	•	1.7	1.1	1.4	2.0	2.3	1.8	2.8	1.9	6.0	2.3	8.2
Current Liabilities to Working Capital 39	5.1	•	0.7	0.1	0.4	1.0	1.3	0.8	1.8	0.9	5.0	1.3	7.2
Working Capital to Net Sales 40	0.1	•	0.0	0.6	0.2	0.3	0.2	0.3	0.2	0.3	0.1	0.2	0.0
Inventory to Working Capital 41	2.1	•	0.2	0.6	0.4	1.3	1.0	0.7	1.3	1.1	2.7	0.9	2.7
Total Receipts to Cash Flow 42	6.9	18.2	5.7	7.5	7.0	7.7	5.6	11.6	8.9	6.3	•	13.0	6.6
Cost of Goods to Cash Flow 43	5.1	13.6	2.8	3.7	5.0	4.9	3.5	7.6	5.8	4.3	•	9.0	4.9
Cash Flow to Total Debt 44	0.2	•	2.0	0.3	0.8	0.3	0.4	0.2	0.2	0.2	•	0.1	0.2

Selected Financial Factors (in Percentages)

Debt Ratio 45	68.3	•	99.0	47.2	47.0	74.7	65.7	51.8	57.4	57.9	96.4	66.3	68.4
Return on Total Assets 46	8.2	•	77.8	1.9	26.4	5.9	14.5	10.6	2.6	10.8	•	5.8	8.4
Return on Equity Before Income Taxes 47	18.9	•	6431.8	1.8	46.7	0.5	35.6	15.7	2.0	19.5	•	10.2	20.0
Return on Equity After Income Taxes 48	12.6	•	6178.1	•	44.2	0.5	31.1	11.9	•	17.5	•	7.5	13.3
Profit Margin (Before Income Tax) 49	7.0	•	5.6	0.8	9.6	0.1	8.4	6.0	1.0	9.6	•	5.0	7.4
Profit Margin (After Income Tax) 50	4.7	•	5.4	•	9.1	0.1	7.3	4.5	•	8.6	•	3.7	4.9

Table II

Corporations with Net Income

AEROSPACE PRODUCT AND PARTS

Money Amounts and Size of Assets in Thousands of Dollars

Item Description for Accounting Period 7/07 Through 6/08	Total	Zero Assets	Under 500	500 to 1,000	1,000 to 5,000	5,000 to 10,000	10,000 to 25,000	25,000 to 50,000	50,000 to 100,000	100,000 to 250,000	250,000 to 500,000	500,000 to 2,500,000	2,500,000 and over
Number of Enterprises 1	1481	•	1032	108	168	22	65	22	14	13	4	•	•
Revenues ($ in Thousands)													
Net Sales 2	262332502	•	1117766	146133	958625	284737	1680074	1080347	977577	2162614	1507902	•	•
Interest 3	4290015	•	1027	99	322	0	5478	2908	3218	4082	7706	•	•
Rents 4	1322536	•	0	0	0	0	3196	484	425	241	250	•	•
Royalties 5	2003975	•	0	0	0	0	341	0	0	2836	0	•	•
Other Portfolio Income 6	2893061	•	19549	213	6064	47	22528	43042	2598	1561	795	•	•
Other Receipts 7	4357394	•	348	0	262	490	7761	4691	16456	56608	40648	•	•
Total Receipts 8	277199483	•	1138690	146445	965273	285274	1719378	1131472	1000274	2227942	1557301	•	•
Average Total Receipts 9	187170	•	1103	1356	5746	12967	26452	51431	71448	171380	389325	•	•
Operating Costs/Operating Income (%)													
Cost of Operations 10	73.4	•	47.4	50.0	71.6	61.4	59.4	64.3	65.6	69.0	75.4	•	•
Salaries and Wages 11	4.0	•	21.6	1.1	5.2	8.5	5.7	10.2	6.7	5.3	5.7	•	•
Taxes Paid 12	1.3	•	2.4	3.3	1.7	1.2	1.8	2.5	2.0	1.3	2.1	•	•
Interest Paid 13	2.4	•	1.1	0.8	0.5	1.1	1.2	1.4	2.0	1.5	1.3	•	•
Depreciation 14	2.1	•	0.7	2.6	1.0	1.8	2.4	1.9	2.0	2.5	3.3	•	•
Amortization and Depletion 15	0.7	•	0.0	•	0.0	0.0	0.2	0.3	0.3	0.3	0.1	•	•
Pensions and Other Deferred Comp. 16	1.7	•	0.0	2.5	0.3	0.7	0.5	1.1	0.6	0.2	1.0	•	•
Employee Benefits 17	2.4	•	0.3	0.4	0.5	0.8	2.0	2.6	1.8	0.8	2.2	•	•
Advertising 18	0.2	•	0.7	0.4	0.2	0.1	0.4	0.2	0.3	0.2	0.3	•	•
Other Expenses 19	9.7	•	18.7	11.6	5.3	6.1	11.8	1.1	7.9	7.1	4.0	•	•
Officers' Compensation 20	0.4	•	3.1	17.8	2.8	1.2	3.5	2.0	2.4	1.4	1.2	•	•
Operating Margin 21	1.7	•	4.2	9.5	10.9	17.1	11.1	12.3	8.5	10.3	3.5	•	•
Operating Margin Before Officers' Comp. 22	2.1	•	7.3	27.3	13.7	18.4	14.6	14.4	10.9	11.8	4.6	•	•

Selected Average Balance Sheet ($ in Thousands)

	•	•	•	•	•	•	•	•	•	•
Net Receivables 23	24720	•	6	53	818	1770	3981	6881	14278	21892	82215
Inventories 24	22501	•	6	355	509	5711	7568	11081	18811	42113	113353
Net Property, Plant and Equipment 25	25623	•	38	44	164	912	3433	6420	9000	34314	67444
Total Assets 26	205706	•	92	773	1815	7298	16246	37582	74294	152767	379066
Notes and Loans Payable 27	44103	•	111	268	408	1764	4327	6454	14269	40037	65790
All Other Liabilities 28	94522	•	-11	0	532	820	3998	6887	20193	45021	153752
Net Worth 29	67081	•	-8	505	875	4714	7920	24241	39831	67709	159523

Selected Financial Ratios (Times to 1)

	•	•	•	•	•	•	•	•	•	•
Current Ratio 30	1.2	•	2.1	13.6	2.8	6.2	2.3	3.8	1.6	2.1	1.6
Quick Ratio 31	0.6	•	1.6	6.6	1.7	2.3	1.2	2.0	0.8	0.7	0.8
Net Sales to Working Capital 32	16.1	•	44.5	2.0	5.5	2.5	3.9	2.7	4.4	3.8	3.9
Coverage Ratio 33	4.2	•	6.5	13.2	25.3	16.3	12.2	13.3	6.3	10.0	6.2
Total Asset Turnover 34	0.9	•	11.8	1.8	3.1	1.8	1.6	1.3	0.9	1.1	1.0
Inventory Turnover 35	5.8	•	93.1	1.9	8.0	1.0	2.7	2.9	2.4	2.7	2.5
Receivables Turnover 36	7.3	•	•	•	9.6	4.2	6.6	5.5	3.8	8.7	•
Total Liabilities to Net Worth 37	2.1	•	•	0.5	1.1	0.5	1.1	0.6	0.9	1.3	1.4
Current Assets to Working Capital 38	6.4	•	1.9	1.1	1.6	1.2	1.7	1.4	2.6	1.9	2.6
Current Liabilities to Working Capital 39	5.4	•	0.9	0.1	0.6	0.2	0.7	0.4	1.6	0.9	1.6
Working Capital to Net Sales 40	0.1	•	0.0	0.5	0.2	0.4	0.3	0.4	0.2	0.3	0.3
Inventory to Working Capital 41	2.2	•	0.2	0.5	0.5	0.7	0.7	0.4	1.2	1.1	1.2
Total Receipts to Cash Flow 42	6.6	•	5.4	5.8	6.6	4.5	4.6	6.9	6.0	5.2	10.7
Cost of Goods to Cash Flow 43	4.9	•	2.6	2.9	4.7	2.8	2.7	4.4	3.9	3.6	8.1
Cash Flow to Total Debt 44	0.2	•	2.0	0.9	0.9	1.1	0.7	0.5	0.3	0.4	0.2

Selected Financial Factors (in Percentages)

	•	•	•	•	•	•	•	•	•	•
Debt Ratio 45	67.4	•	108.4	34.6	51.8	35.4	51.2	35.5	46.4	55.7	57.9
Return on Total Assets 46	8.7	•	84.6	18.3	37.9	32.7	23.3	24.1	12.1	16.4	8.0
Return on Equity Before Income Taxes 47	20.2	•	•	•	75.5	47.5	43.9	34.5	19.0	33.3	15.9
Return on Equity After Income Taxes 48	13.8	•	•	18.8	72.2	47.5	39.7	30.8	15.9	30.6	12.5
Profit Margin (Before Income Tax) 49	7.7	•	6.1	9.7	11.6	17.3	13.4	17.0	10.8	13.5	6.7
Profit Margin (After Income Tax) 50	5.2	•	5.8	7.0	11.1	17.3	12.2	15.2	9.1	12.5	5.3

Table I

Corporations with and without Net Income

SHIP AND BOAT BUILDING

MONEY AMOUNTS AND SIZE OF ASSETS IN THOUSANDS OF DOLLARS

Item Description for Accounting Period 7/07 Through 6/08	Total	Zero Assets	Under 500	500 to 1,000	1,000 to 5,000	5,000 to 10,000	10,000 to 25,000	25,000 to 50,000	50,000 to 100,000	100,000 to 250,000	250,000 to 500,000	500,000 to 2,500,000	2,500,000 and over
Number of Enterprises **1**	1873	773	505	190	211	69	61	34	17	8	5	0	0
Revenues ($ in Thousands)													
Net Sales **2**	36861031	132057	378139	335761	1521026	1298867	1823429	2090498	2166149	1711192	25403914	0	0
Interest **3**	58622	0	334	0	1580	779	1318	1449	1594	3813	47755	0	0
Rents **4**	65249	0	0	0	2790	0	30	15259	92	3635	43445	0	0
Royalties **5**	6070	0	0	0	0	0	0	2970	0	0	3100	0	0
Other Portfolio Income **6**	166658	2454	7223	12	4229	234	464	17040	13556	1633	119814	0	0
Other Receipts **7**	173053	301	2374	3429	11072	2055	22729	29435	40054	33920	27681	0	0
Total Receipts **8**	37330683	134812	388070	339202	1540697	1301935	1847970	2156651	2221445	1754193	25645709	0	0
Average Total Receipts **9**	19931	174	768	1785	7302	18869	30295	63431	130673	219274	5129142	•	•
Operating Costs/Operating Income (%)													
Cost of Operations **10**	76.8	67.4	55.6	46.3	76.3	73.0	78.3	74.0	77.7	81.1	77.6	•	•
Salaries and Wages **11**	3.2	4.7	0.7	19.8	3.1	8.3	5.2	4.1	2.5	3.1	2.6	•	•
Taxes Paid **12**	2.1	5.2	2.5	2.3	2.4	1.5	0.9	1.3	1.6	1.8	2.3	•	•
Interest Paid **13**	0.7	0.8	0.6	0.1	1.1	0.4	1.1	1.1	1.2	2.0	0.5	•	•
Depreciation **14**	1.1	1.9	2.0	0.5	1.1	1.1	2.4	1.8	2.7	2.4	0.8	•	•
Amortization and Depletion **15**	0.7	•	0.2	•	•	0.0	0.1	0.2	0.3	0.1	0.9	•	•
Pensions and Other Deferred Comp. **16**	0.5	0.2	0.0	0.1	0.3	0.2	0.3	0.5	0.6	0.3	0.6	•	•
Employee Benefits **17**	1.6	1.3	1.2	5.7	0.9	1.9	0.7	1.6	1.3	1.3	1.7	•	•
Advertising **18**	0.4	0.6	1.0	0.2	1.2	0.7	1.0	0.9	0.8	0.8	0.2	•	•
Other Expenses **19**	5.4	18.0	15.3	12.2	8.9	1.9	6.1	10.8	6.7	4.0	4.5	•	•
Officers' Compensation **20**	1.3	3.7	4.6	3.3	4.2	1.8	2.3	1.4	1.3	0.9	0.9	•	•
Operating Margin **21**	6.1	•	16.3	9.6	0.6	9.2	1.6	2.2	3.2	2.2	7.3	•	•
Operating Margin Before Officers' Comp. **22**	7.4	•	20.8	12.8	4.7	11.0	4.0	3.6	4.5	3.1	8.2	•	•

Selected Average Balance Sheet ($ in Thousands)

Net Receivables 23	1502	0	5	196	383	1190	2467	8182	12922	17809	363892
Inventories 24	2476	0	27	5	1803	3416	3416	5480	14432	19829	641603
Net Property, Plant and Equipment 25	2348	0	8	93	816	1389	4867	9776	29267	40582	531272
Total Assets 26	16219	0	166	672	2820	7789	16910	36984	74730	175821	4813671
Notes and Loans Payable 27	2693	0	20	96	1158	1236	10285	9411	16605	51804	608254
All Other Liabilities 28	5806	0	34	315	736	3436	5290	13247	26650	50872	1754584
Net Worth 29	7720	0	113	261	926	3117	1336	14326	31475	73146	2450832

Selected Financial Ratios (Times to 1)

Current Ratio 30	1.5	•	10.8	1.4	2.0	1.8	1.3	1.7	1.4	1.7	1.4
Quick Ratio 31	0.7		8.4	1.2	0.5	0.6	0.5	0.9	0.7	0.7	0.6
Net Sales to Working Capital 32	8.9		7.2	10.7	7.5	7.0	15.0	6.8	12.0	6.3	9.1
Coverage Ratio 33	11.9		30.3	72.9	2.6	24.7	3.8	6.1	6.0	3.3	17.6
Total Asset Turnover 34	1.2		4.5	2.6	2.6	2.4	1.8	1.7	1.7	1.2	1.1
Inventory Turnover 35	6.1		15.4	166.7	3.1	4.0	6.8	8.3	6.9	8.8	6.1
Receivables Turnover 36	13.2		9.7	11.1	18.5	15.5	13.0	9.9	11.2	10.2	13.8
Total Liabilities to Net Worth 37	1.1		0.5	1.6	2.0	1.5	11.7	1.6	1.4	1.4	1.0
Current Assets to Working Capital 38	3.1		1.1	3.4	2.0	2.3	4.5	2.5	3.7	2.4	3.4
Current Liabilities to Working Capital 39	2.1		0.1	2.4	1.0	1.3	3.5	1.5	2.7	1.4	2.4
Working Capital to Net Sales 40	0.1		0.1	0.1	0.1	0.1	0.1	0.1	0.1	0.2	0.1
Inventory to Working Capital 41	1.1		0.2	0.0	1.0	1.3	1.6	0.6	1.4	0.6	1.2
Total Receipts to Cash Flow 42	9.2	19.5	3.6	6.4	12.0	9.9	12.9	8.2	9.1	14.3	8.9
Cost of Goods to Cash Flow 43	7.0	13.1	2.0	3.0	9.2	7.2	10.1	6.0	7.1	11.6	6.9
Cash Flow to Total Debt 44	0.3	•	3.8	0.7	0.3	0.4	0.1	0.3	0.3	0.1	0.2

Selected Financial Factors (in Percentages)

Debt Ratio 45	52.4	•	32.3	61.1	67.2	60.0	92.1	61.3	57.9	58.4	49.1
Return on Total Assets 46	10.2	•	87.7	28.2	7.7	23.9	7.1	10.7	11.8	8.0	9.7
Return on Equity Before Income Taxes 47	19.6	•	125.3	71.6	14.4	57.3	66.5	23.0	23.3	13.4	18.0
Return on Equity After Income Taxes 48	13.7	•	125.0	71.6	11.1	57.1	60.5	18.9	19.5	11.4	11.6
Profit Margin (Before Income Tax) 49	7.7	•	18.8	10.6	1.9	9.5	3.0	5.4	5.8	4.6	8.7
Profit Margin (After Income Tax) 50	5.4	•	18.8	10.6	1.4	9.5	2.7	4.4	4.8	3.9	5.6

157

Table II

Corporations with Net Income

SHIP AND BOAT BUILDING

MONEY AMOUNTS AND SIZE OF ASSETS IN THOUSANDS OF DOLLARS

Item Description for Accounting Period 7/07 Through 6/08	Total	Zero Assets	Under 500	500 to 1,000	1,000 to 5,000	5,000 to 10,000	10,000 to 25,000	25,000 to 50,000	50,000 to 100,000	100,000 to 250,000	250,000 to 500,000	500,000 to 2,500,000	2,500,000 and over
Number of Enterprises 1	671	•	176	157	179	57	52	28	•	•	•	0	0
Revenues ($ in Thousands)													
Net Sales 2	33811438	•	357978	270687	1463537	1236544	1687263	1653561	•	•	•	0	0
Interest 3	52213	•	286	0	1580	372	1318	1449	•	•	•	0	0
Rents 4	49822	•	0	0	2790	0	30	15259	•	•	•	0	0
Royalties 5	6057	•	0	0	0	0	0	2970	•	•	•	0	0
Other Portfolio Income 6	156110	•	6882	0	4229	234	452	16059	•	•	•	0	0
Other Receipts 7	142071	•	86	0	7128	2045	28552	22837	•	•	•	0	0
Total Receipts 8	34217711	•	365232	270687	1479264	1239195	1717615	1712135	•	•	•	0	0
Average Total Receipts 9	50995	•	2075	1724	8264	21740	33031	61148	•	•	•	•	•
Operating Costs/Operating Income (%)													
Cost of Operations 10	76.6	•	53.5	28.7	76.0	72.4	77.3	71.0	•	•	•	•	•
Salaries and Wages 11	3.1	•	0.2	23.7	2.7	8.4	4.5	4.7	•	•	•	•	•
Taxes Paid 12	2.1	•	2.3	2.7	2.3	1.4	0.9	1.5	•	•	•	•	•
Interest Paid 13	0.6	•	0.5	0.2	0.8	0.4	1.2	1.1	•	•	•	•	•
Depreciation 14	0.9	•	1.0	0.6	1.0	1.1	2.5	1.9	•	•	•	•	•
Amortization and Depletion 15	0.7	•	0.0	•	•	0.0	0.1	0.3	•	•	•	•	•
Pensions and Other Deferred Comp. 16	0.6	•	0.0	0.1	0.2	0.2	0.3	0.5	•	•	•	•	•
Employee Benefits 17	1.6	•	1.3	7.0	1.0	1.9	0.7	1.5	•	•	•	•	•
Advertising 18	0.3	•	0.9	0.2	1.2	0.7	0.9	1.1	•	•	•	•	•
Other Expenses 19	4.8	•	13.4	9.2	8.1	1.4	6.2	10.8	•	•	•	•	•
Officers' Compensation 20	1.3	•	4.8	4.0	4.2	1.7	2.5	1.3	•	•	•	•	•
Operating Margin 21	7.3	•	22.0	23.6	2.4	10.4	2.9	4.3	•	•	•	•	•
Operating Margin Before Officers' Comp. 22	8.7	•	26.8	27.6	6.6	12.1	5.4	5.5	•	•	•	•	•

Selected Average Balance Sheet ($ in Thousands)

Net Receivables 23	3907	11	223	446	1438	2285	8296
Inventories 24	6243	62	5	1425	3473	3114	5494
Net Property, Plant and Equipment 25	5333	11	109	610	1635	5505	8634
Total Assets 26	41805	328	666	2903	8154	16537	35971
Notes and Loans Payable 27	5878	2	33	917	1384	5532	10377
All Other Liabilities 28	14675	20	49	648	3122	5456	10700
Net Worth 29	21253	307	584	1338	3649	5549	14893

Selected Financial Ratios (Times to 1)

Current Ratio 30	1.5	15.3	9.2	2.4	1.9	1.4	2.1
Quick Ratio 31	0.7	12.0	9.1	0.6	0.7	0.6	1.1
Net Sales to Working Capital 32	8.2	7.2	3.5	6.4	7.1	11.0	5.0
Coverage Ratio 33	15.8	47.0	153.9	5.2	28.7	5.1	7.8
Total Asset Turnover 34	1.2	6.2	2.6	2.8	2.7	2.0	1.6
Inventory Turnover 35	6.2	17.6	97.3	4.4	4.5	8.1	7.6
Receivables Turnover 36	13.0		15.0	20.6	14.8	14.6	9.5
Total Liabilities to Net Worth 37	1.0	0.1	0.1	1.2	1.2	2.0	1.4
Current Assets to Working Capital 38	2.9	1.1	1.1	1.7	2.1	3.2	1.9
Current Liabilities to Working Capital 39	1.9	0.1	0.1	0.7	1.1	2.2	0.9
Working Capital to Net Sales 40	0.1	0.1	0.3	0.2	0.1	0.1	0.2
Inventory to Working Capital 41	1.0	0.2	0.0	0.9	1.3	1.2	0.5
Total Receipts to Cash Flow 42	8.6	3.2	3.5	10.9	9.3	10.5	6.2
Cost of Goods to Cash Flow 43	6.6	1.7	1.0	8.3	6.8	8.1	4.4
Cash Flow to Total Debt 44	0.3	29.4	6.0	0.5	0.5	0.3	0.5

Selected Financial Factors (in Percentages)

Debt Ratio 45	49.2	6.5	12.3	53.9	55.3	66.4	58.6
Return on Total Assets 46	11.4	152.1	61.4	12.1	29.2	11.5	14.7
Return on Equity Before Income Taxes 47	21.1	159.2	69.6	21.2	63.0	27.6	30.9
Return on Equity After Income Taxes 48	15.1	158.9	69.6	18.5	62.8	25.9	26.2
Profit Margin (Before Income Tax) 49	8.9	24.0	23.6	3.5	10.6	4.7	7.8
Profit Margin (After Income Tax) 50	6.4	24.0	23.6	3.0	10.6	4.4	6.6

OTHER TRANSPORTATION EQUIPMENT AND RAILROAD ROLLING STOCK

Table I

Corporations with and without Net Income

MONEY AMOUNTS AND SIZE OF ASSETS IN THOUSANDS OF DOLLARS

Item Description for Accounting Period 7/07 Through 6/08	Total	Zero Assets	Under 500	500 to 1,000	1,000 to 5,000	5,000 to 10,000	10,000 to 25,000	25,000 to 50,000	50,000 to 100,000	100,000 to 250,000	250,000 to 500,000	500,000 to 2,500,000	2,500,000 and over
Number of Enterprises 1	2031	7	1470	101	300	53	51	13	13	7	5	11	0
Revenues ($ in Thousands)													
Net Sales 2	29036235	60361	244273	386083	1262529	1036272	1545271	1154840	1023632	1009169	3259966	18053840	0
Interest 3	809908	320	0	0	2997	162	2615	1195	3323	4536	14416	780344	0
Rents 4	70546	0	0	0	0	20	35	17	440	0	34	70001	0
Royalties 5	70783	0	0	0	28	102	0	0	98	0	0	70555	0
Other Portfolio Income 6	108598	107	0	0	11621	0	3605	140	741	2604	163	89616	0
Other Receipts 7	256507	573	2803	811	18404	1104	13630	4255	10323	3384	30890	170329	0
Total Receipts 8	30352577	61361	247076	386894	1295579	1037660	1565156	1160447	1038557	1019693	3305469	19234685	0
Average Total Receipts 9	14945	8766	168	3831	4319	19578	30689	89265	79889	145670	661094	1748608	•
Operating Costs/Operating Income (%)													
Cost of Operations 10	70.4	82.7	77.5	77.0	74.5	74.7	77.2	78.1	72.3	79.0	82.8	65.7	•
Salaries and Wages 11	6.0	24.7	4.9	1.1	7.0	8.3	7.6	5.3	5.6	5.5	3.1	6.4	•
Taxes Paid 12	1.5	2.0	5.7	0.9	1.7	1.3	1.7	1.7	1.5	1.9	0.6	1.5	•
Interest Paid 13	2.5	0.0	5.7	0.9	1.4	0.6	1.2	0.5	2.5	0.6	0.4	3.4	•
Depreciation 14	3.1	2.1	5.2	1.3	2.0	1.0	1.9	1.2	1.7	3.0	1.0	4.0	•
Amortization and Depletion 15	0.7	0.1	0.6	0.0	0.0	0.1	0.2	0.0	0.9	0.2	0.2	0.9	•
Pensions and Other Deferred Comp. 16	0.4	0.0	•	0.1	0.1	0.0	0.2	0.2	0.7	0.2	0.2	0.5	•
Employee Benefits 17	1.7	0.5	0.6	2.1	0.7	1.6	1.2	1.1	1.2	1.3	1.2	2.0	•
Advertising 18	0.7	1.4	2.5	0.7	0.4	0.2	0.7	0.8	0.2	0.5	1.2	0.6	•
Other Expenses 19	9.9	44.3	29.9	7.5	11.2	4.2	10.4	5.2	5.5	4.5	6.8	11.2	•
Officers' Compensation 20	0.9	1.5	3.2	7.3	6.0	1.2	2.0	1.8	1.7	0.5	0.4	0.3	•
Operating Margin 21	2.2	•	•	1.4	•	7.0	•	3.9	6.3	2.8	2.1	3.3	•
Operating Margin Before Officers' Comp. 22	3.1	•	•	8.6	1.1	8.2	•	5.7	7.9	3.2	2.5	3.7	•

Selected Average Balance Sheet ($ in Thousands)

Net Receivables 23	2807	0	6	178	608	2301	3357	6667	8147	20442	66113	411927	•
Inventories 24	2210	0	35	160	514	5348	3836	13783	14070	42556	112892	232961	•
Net Property, Plant and Equipment 25	2739	0	31	159	276	1269	4272	7876	7707	28415	40464	411716	•
Total Assets 26	11154	0	96	772	1980	8919	16729	34645	67682	148079	343136	1493690	•
Notes and Loans Payable 27	3775	0	114	248	902	1882	5129	7714	23383	37867	3710	559482	•
All Other Liabilities 28	3952	0	12	319	3714	3402	7155	10010	13024	26616	191198	443196	•
Net Worth 29	3427	0	-30	205	-2636	3635	4445	16921	31276	83596	148228	491012	•

Selected Financial Ratios (Times to 1)

Current Ratio 30	1.6	•	1.1	2.1	3.8	2.3	1.3	1.8	1.7	1.9	1.6	1.5	•
Quick Ratio 31	0.9	•	0.2	1.0	2.5	0.8	0.6	0.8	0.7	0.7	0.8	0.9	•
Net Sales to Working Capital 32	6.0	•	44.3	13.4	3.3	4.5	15.1	9.5	7.2	3.5	5.8	6.0	•
Coverage Ratio 33	3.7	•	•	2.8	•	12.2	•	9.6	4.2	7.7	10.7	3.9	•
Total Asset Turnover 34	1.3	•	1.7	5.0	2.1	2.2	1.8	2.6	1.2	1.0	1.9	1.1	•
Inventory Turnover 35	4.6	•	3.7	18.4	6.1	2.7	6.1	5.0	4.0	2.7	4.8	4.6	•
Receivables Turnover 36	5.2	•	18.9	20.7	5.9	10.0	7.7	9.4	8.4	4.2	9.3	4.3	•
Total Liabilities to Net Worth 37	2.3	•	•	2.8	•	1.5	2.8	1.0	1.2	0.8	1.3	2.0	•
Current Assets to Working Capital 38	2.7	•	17.1	1.9	1.4	1.8	4.7	2.3	2.4	2.1	2.6	3.0	•
Current Liabilities to Working Capital 39	1.7	•	16.1	0.9	0.4	0.8	3.7	1.3	1.4	1.1	1.6	2.0	•
Working Capital to Net Sales 40	0.2	•	0.0	0.1	0.3	0.2	0.1	0.1	0.1	0.3	0.2	0.2	•
Inventory to Working Capital 41	0.9	•	13.5	0.6	0.3	1.1	2.0	1.1	1.0	0.7	0.8	0.9	•
Total Receipts to Cash Flow 42	7.0	•	•	15.1	15.7	10.1	19.1	12.0	8.8	13.7	10.3	5.5	•
Cost of Goods to Cash Flow 43	4.9	•	•	11.6	11.7	7.5	14.7	9.4	6.4	10.8	8.5	3.6	•
Cash Flow to Total Debt 44	0.3	•	•	0.4	0.1	0.4	0.1	0.4	0.2	0.2	0.3	0.3	•

Selected Financial Factors (in Percentages)

Debt Ratio 45	69.3	•	130.7	73.5	233.1	59.2	73.4	51.2	53.8	43.5	56.8	67.1	•
Return on Total Assets 46	11.8	•	•	12.1	•	17.0	•	12.5	12.2	4.2	7.4	14.6	•
Return on Equity Before Income Taxes 47	28.1	•	193.4	29.7	3.7	38.3	•	22.9	20.1	6.5	15.4	33.1	•
Return on Equity After Income Taxes 48	17.1	•	193.4	19.7	4.4	36.5	•	19.7	15.7	4.6	11.8	20.4	•
Profit Margin (Before Income Tax) 49	6.7	•	1.6	•	•	7.1	•	4.4	8.0	3.7	3.5	9.9	•
Profit Margin (After Income Tax) 50	4.1	•	1.1	•	•	6.8	•	3.7	6.2	2.7	2.7	6.1	•

Table II

Corporations with Net Income

OTHER TRANSPORTATION EQUIPMENT AND RAILROAD ROLLING STOCK

MONEY AMOUNTS AND SIZE OF ASSETS IN THOUSANDS OF DOLLARS

Item Description for Accounting Period 7/07 Through 6/08	Total	Zero Assets	Under 500	500 to 1,000	1,000 to 5,000	5,000 to 10,000	10,000 to 25,000	25,000 to 50,000	50,000 to 100,000	100,000 to 250,000	250,000 to 500,000	500,000 to 2,500,000	2,500,000 and over
Number of Enterprises 1	602	•	274	50	160	53	25	9	•	•	•	7	0
Revenues ($ in Thousands)													
Net Sales 2	23429802	•	8389	281011	860189	1036272	750048	929453	•	•	•	15149716	0
Interest 3	799114	•	0	0	1125	162	1044	696	•	•	•	778364	0
Rents 4	69877	•	0	0	0	20	0	17	•	•	•	69366	0
Royalties 5	68024	•	0	0	0	102	0	0	•	•	•	67824	0
Other Portfolio Income 6	91430	•	0	0	0	0	2692	140	•	•	•	85225	0
Other Receipts 7	239688	•	0	808	18405	1104	20231	250	•	•	•	148859	0
Total Receipts 8	24697935	•	8389	281819	879719	1037660	774015	930556	•	•	•	16299354	0
Average Total Receipts 9	41026	•	31	5636	5498	19578	30961	103395	•	•	•	2328479	•
Operating Costs/Operating Income (%)													
Cost of Operations 10	67.4	•	62.9	75.8	74.7	74.7	65.2	79.0	•	•	•	62.4	•
Salaries and Wages 11	5.9	•	•	1.5	3.1	8.3	9.1	3.9	•	•	•	6.4	•
Taxes Paid 12	1.5	•	3.6	0.3	1.3	1.3	1.7	1.3	•	•	•	1.7	•
Interest Paid 13	2.4	•	2.7	0.3	0.5	0.6	0.8	0.2	•	•	•	3.4	•
Depreciation 14	3.3	•	4.5	1.6	1.4	1.0	1.9	0.6	•	•	•	4.5	•
Amortization and Depletion 15	0.6	•	•	•	0.0	0.1	0.0	0.0	•	•	•	0.9	•
Pensions and Other Deferred Comp. 16	0.5	•	•	•	0.1	0.0	0.2	0.2	•	•	•	0.6	•
Employee Benefits 17	1.8	•	•	2.8	0.2	1.6	1.2	1.1	•	•	•	2.2	•
Advertising 18	0.6	•	0.2	0.6	0.0	0.2	0.9	0.8	•	•	•	0.7	•
Other Expenses 19	9.7	•	17.0	6.3	3.4	4.2	11.2	5.1	•	•	•	11.7	•
Officers' Compensation 20	0.8	•	•	8.3	6.0	1.2	2.8	0.7	•	•	•	0.3	•
Operating Margin 21	5.3	•	9.0	2.4	9.1	7.0	5.1	7.1	•	•	•	5.3	•
Operating Margin Before Officers' Comp. 22	6.1	•	9.0	10.6	15.1	8.2	7.9	7.8	•	•	•	5.6	•

Selected Average Balance Sheet ($ in Thousands)

Net Receivables 23	8345	•	0	275	1112	2301	3742	6824	•	587148
Inventories 24	5547	•	7	158	552	5084	4337	15589	•	267046
Net Property, Plant and Equipment 25	8220	•	5	222	209	1269	5457	5587	•	604019
Total Assets 26	30252	•	10	917	2412	8919	17006	32760	•	1960937
Notes and Loans Payable 27	9533	•	6	108	842	1882	4467	5779	•	693101
All Other Liabilities 28	10058	•	-0	435	6632	3402	4621	8739	•	529034
Net Worth 29	10661	•	4	374	-5063	3635	7918	18242	•	738801

Selected Financial Ratios (Times to 1)

Current Ratio 30	1.7	•	0.9	2.3	3.5	1.5	2.3	2.5	•	1.6
Quick Ratio 31	1.1	•	0.1	1.6	2.6	0.8	0.8	1.2	•	1.1
Net Sales to Working Capital 32	5.1	•	•	14.1	3.3	4.5	8.8	7.2	•	5.0
Coverage Ratio 33	5.4	•	4.3	9.8	23.5	12.2	11.3	37.7	•	4.8
Total Asset Turnover 34	1.3	•	3.0	6.1	2.2	2.2	1.8	3.2	•	1.1
Inventory Turnover 35	4.7	•	2.7	27.0	7.3	2.9	4.5	5.2	•	5.1
Receivables Turnover 36	4.8	•	1.0	17.0	4.6	11.4	4.8	11.1	•	4.0
Total Liabilities to Net Worth 37	1.8	•	1.6	1.5	•	1.5	1.1	0.8	•	1.7
Current Assets to Working Capital 38	2.3	•	•	1.7	1.4	1.8	2.9	1.7	•	2.5
Current Liabilities to Working Capital 39	1.3	•	•	0.7	0.4	0.8	1.9	0.7	•	1.5
Working Capital to Net Sales 40	0.2	•	•	0.1	0.3	0.2	0.1	0.1	•	0.2
Inventory to Working Capital 41	0.7	•	•	•	0.3	1.1	1.0	0.8	•	0.7
Total Receipts to Cash Flow 42	5.6	•	4.5	15.8	7.4	10.1	6.0	9.0	•	4.6
Cost of Goods to Cash Flow 43	3.8	•	2.8	12.0	5.5	7.5	3.9	7.1	•	2.9
Cash Flow to Total Debt 44	0.4	•	1.1	0.7	0.1	0.4	0.5	0.8	•	0.4

Selected Financial Factors (in Percentages)

Debt Ratio 45	64.8	•	62.0	59.2	309.9	59.2	53.4	44.3	•	62.3
Return on Total Assets 46	17.0	•	35.1	18.0	26.5	17.0	16.1	23.2	•	18.0
Return on Equity Before Income Taxes 47	39.2	•	71.1	39.7	•	38.3	31.5	40.6	•	37.8
Return on Equity After Income Taxes 48	27.2	•	71.1	28.7	•	36.5	28.1	36.3	•	24.5
Profit Margin (Before Income Tax) 49	10.7	•	9.0	2.6	11.4	7.1	8.3	7.2	•	12.9
Profit Margin (After Income Tax) 50	7.5	•	9.0	1.9	10.8	6.8	7.4	6.4	•	8.4

Table I

Corporations with and without Net Income

FURNITURE AND RELATED PRODUCT MANUFACTURING

MONEY AMOUNTS AND SIZE OF ASSETS IN THOUSANDS OF DOLLARS

Item Description for Accounting Period 7/07 Through 6/08		Total	Zero Assets	Under 500	500 to 1,000	1,000 to 5,000	5,000 to 10,000	10,000 to 25,000	25,000 to 50,000	50,000 to 100,000	100,000 to 250,000	250,000 to 500,000	500,000 to 2,500,000	2,500,000 and over
Number of Enterprises	1	12025	2014	7658	625	1210	197	183	62	28	27	8	14	0
Revenues ($ in Thousands)														
Net Sales	2	67861589	973653	5418114	1549315	7444343	3559903	5385513	4360899	3229514	6320466	4043251	25576618	0
Interest	3	126369	513	838	258	6976	4702	5326	3520	4016	8757	18492	72971	0
Rents	4	41884	0	442	0	1127	0	719	4670	891	1231	11418	21385	0
Royalties	5	70855	0	0	0	0	0	0	1183	505	0	909	68257	0
Other Portfolio Income	6	340057	61602	7614	1400	11194	22430	6114	8334	6027	21233	38231	155875	0
Other Receipts	7	580931	59319	18278	693	14674	12840	42346	23616	9111	58878	-93312	434494	0
Total Receipts	8	69021685	1095087	5445286	1551666	7478314	3599875	5440018	4402222	3250064	6410565	4018989	26329600	0
Average Total Receipts	9	5740	544	711	2483	6180	18273	29727	71004	116074	237428	502374	1880686	•
Operating Costs/Operating Income (%)														
Cost of Operations	10	66.7	75.0	55.7	71.1	65.0	70.2	68.9	71.1	73.4	73.6	63.0	65.4	•
Salaries and Wages	11	8.3	16.0	12.1	4.6	8.6	8.4	8.1	7.5	6.2	5.6	8.4	8.4	•
Taxes Paid	12	2.0	1.6	3.0	1.7	2.4	1.8	2.0	2.1	1.6	1.8	1.8	1.9	•
Interest Paid	13	1.5	3.5	1.1	0.5	0.9	0.6	1.4	0.9	2.4	1.3	1.2	1.9	•
Depreciation	14	1.5	3.4	1.1	0.9	1.8	1.1	1.5	1.5	1.1	1.8	1.7	1.6	•
Amortization and Depletion	15	0.4	0.5	0.2	0.1	0.0	0.0	0.1	0.1	0.5	0.4	0.4	0.7	•
Pensions and Other Deferred Comp.	16	0.6	0.3	0.1	0.3	1.1	0.2	0.3	0.4	0.3	0.5	0.6	0.7	•
Employee Benefits	17	1.9	1.0	0.9	1.6	1.3	1.6	2.4	1.5	1.6	2.4	1.8	2.2	•
Advertising	18	2.0	1.6	0.5	0.4	0.8	1.3	1.3	1.1	1.2	1.1	4.3	3.0	•
Other Expenses	19	11.3	16.8	14.4	10.4	12.6	10.7	8.8	9.3	9.9	9.0	12.9	11.4	•
Officers' Compensation	20	1.8	3.9	6.5	4.0	3.1	2.7	2.5	1.4	1.1	0.7	0.5	0.5	•
Operating Margin	21	2.1	•	4.3	4.4	2.3	1.5	2.6	3.0	0.6	1.8	3.4	2.3	•
Operating Margin Before Officers' Comp.	22	3.9	•	10.8	8.4	5.5	4.2	5.1	4.4	1.7	2.5	3.9	2.9	•

Selected Average Balance Sheet ($ in Thousands)

Net Receivables 23	584	0	28	359	648	1754	3628	8563	16404	27315	48922	191054	•
Inventories 24	610	0	23	211	693	2826	3510	9739	17402	29284	46518	195506	•
Net Property, Plant and Equipment 25	619	0	36	66	511	1294	3387	9404	11058	35766	77683	225177	•
Total Assets 26	3118	0	149	730	2097	6247	14458	34615	69359	133961	337315	1362524	•
Notes and Loans Payable 27	1039	0	83	322	1065	1745	5011	9127	29309	38897	64065	440173	•
All Other Liabilities 28	919	0	45	234	1024	1817	3140	8324	19025	28518	117820	402210	•
Net Worth 29	1159	0	21	174	8	2685	6307	17164	21025	66545	155430	520140	•

Selected Financial Ratios (Times to 1)

Current Ratio 30	1.7	•	1.4	2.4	1.6	1.9	1.9	2.0	1.6	2.0	1.3	1.6
Quick Ratio 31	0.9	•	0.8	1.8	0.9	1.0	1.0	1.0	0.8	1.0	0.6	0.8
Net Sales to Working Capital 32	9.1	•	28.9	6.6	11.0	8.7	7.2	6.3	8.1	6.3	19.0	8.8
Coverage Ratio 33	3.6	•	5.4	9.9	3.9	5.3	3.6	5.3	1.5	3.5	3.2	3.8
Total Asset Turnover 34	1.8	•	4.8	3.4	2.9	2.9	2.0	2.0	1.7	1.7	1.5	1.3
Inventory Turnover 35	6.2	•	17.4	8.4	5.8	4.5	5.8	5.1	4.9	5.9	6.8	6.1
Receivables Turnover 36	8.3	•	25.0	5.8	8.5	8.3	8.2	7.7	7.4	8.3	9.0	7.3
Total Liabilities to Net Worth 37	1.7	•	6.1	3.2	268.9	1.3	1.3	1.0	2.3	1.0	1.2	1.6
Current Assets to Working Capital 38	2.5	•	3.7	1.7	2.7	2.1	2.1	2.0	2.8	2.0	4.6	2.6
Current Liabilities to Working Capital 39	1.5	•	2.7	0.7	1.7	1.1	1.1	1.0	1.8	1.0	3.6	1.6
Working Capital to Net Sales 40	0.1	•	0.0	0.2	0.1	0.1	0.1	0.2	0.1	0.2	0.1	0.1
Inventory to Working Capital 41	0.9	•	1.0	0.3	1.0	0.9	0.8	0.9	1.2	0.8	1.7	0.8
Total Receipts to Cash Flow 42	8.2	•	7.0	8.5	10.5	10.1	9.8	8.6	10.2	9.7	8.5	6.9
Cost of Goods to Cash Flow 43	5.5	63.8	3.9	6.1	6.8	7.1	6.8	6.1	7.5	7.1	5.3	4.5
Cash Flow to Total Debt 44	0.3	47.9	0.8	0.5	0.3	0.5	0.4	0.5	0.2	0.4	0.3	0.3

Selected Financial Factors (in Percentages)

Debt Ratio 45	62.8	•	85.9	76.1	99.6	57.0	56.4	50.4	69.7	50.3	53.9	61.8
Return on Total Assets 46	9.6	•	28.2	17.3	10.9	9.3	10.2	9.9	6.1	7.9	5.9	9.7
Return on Equity Before Income Taxes 47	18.7	•	163.0	65.1	2195.2	17.5	16.9	16.2	6.9	11.3	8.9	18.8
Return on Equity After Income Taxes 48	15.1	•	161.3	62.8	2041.0	16.0	14.6	14.6	5.4	9.7	6.0	13.9
Profit Margin (Before Income Tax) 49	3.8	•	4.8	4.6	2.8	2.6	3.6	4.0	1.3	3.2	2.7	5.3
Profit Margin (After Income Tax) 50	3.1	•	4.8	4.4	2.6	2.4	3.1	3.6	1.0	2.8	1.8	4.0

Table II

Corporations with Net Income

FURNITURE AND RELATED PRODUCT MANUFACTURING

MONEY AMOUNTS AND SIZE OF ASSETS IN THOUSANDS OF DOLLARS

Item Description for Accounting Period 7/07 Through 6/08	Total	Zero Assets	Under 500	500 to 1,000	1,000 to 5,000	5,000 to 10,000	10,000 to 25,000	25,000 to 50,000	50,000 to 100,000	100,000 to 250,000	250,000 to 500,000	500,000 to 2,500,000	2,500,000 and over
Number of Enterprises **1**	8039	•	5082	•	800	153	138	47	14	19	•	11	0
Revenues ($ in Thousands)													
Net Sales **2**	52369774	•	4153663	•	4844488	3031939	4185179	3511657	1928272	4268356	•	21611431	0
Interest **3**	100579	•	128	•	4573	4245	4866	2737	2707	4982	•	57518	0
Rents **4**	30142	•	0	•	1033	0	415	2072	876	1231	•	14702	0
Royalties **5**	53482	•	0	•	0	0	0	1183	505	0	•	50885	0
Other Portfolio Income **6**	241695	•	155	•	10905	18351	4377	4774	5041	5597	•	154127	0
Other Receipts **7**	459489	•	7798	•	10601	5021	40650	18212	4940	50153	•	416338	0
Total Receipts **8**	53255161	•	4161744	•	4871600	3059556	4235487	3540635	1942341	4330319	•	22305001	0
Average Total Receipts **9**	6625	•	819	•	6090	19997	30692	75333	138739	227912	•	2027727	•
Operating Costs/Operating Income (%)													
Cost of Operations **10**	65.2	•	50.8	•	64.8	68.4	67.6	69.5	71.8	71.6	•	65.7	•
Salaries and Wages **11**	8.6	•	13.5	•	8.7	8.6	7.8	7.7	6.7	5.6	•	8.7	•
Taxes Paid **12**	2.0	•	2.9	•	2.6	1.6	1.9	2.3	1.6	1.8	•	1.9	•
Interest Paid **13**	1.1	•	0.9	•	1.0	0.4	1.1	0.7	1.6	1.2	•	1.3	•
Depreciation **14**	1.5	•	1.0	•	1.4	1.2	1.4	1.5	1.1	1.8	•	1.7	•
Amortization and Depletion **15**	0.3	•	0.3	•	0.0	0.0	0.1	0.1	0.4	0.2	•	0.5	•
Pensions and Other Deferred Comp. **16**	0.6	•	0.1	•	1.7	0.2	0.3	0.4	0.3	0.5	•	0.7	•
Employee Benefits **17**	2.0	•	0.9	•	1.5	1.5	2.2	1.4	1.7	3.0	•	2.3	•
Advertising **18**	1.9	•	0.4	•	0.9	1.3	1.5	1.3	1.2	0.9	•	2.4	•
Other Expenses **19**	10.6	•	14.7	•	9.2	9.4	8.8	9.0	8.0	8.2	•	11.0	•
Officers' Compensation **20**	1.8	•	6.2	•	3.7	2.6	2.2	1.4	1.2	0.9	•	0.6	•
Operating Margin **21**	4.5	•	8.4	•	4.6	4.8	5.2	4.8	4.4	4.4	•	3.2	•
Operating Margin Before Officers' Comp. **22**	6.2	•	14.6	•	8.3	7.4	7.4	6.1	5.6	5.2	•	3.7	•

Selected Average Balance Sheet ($ in Thousands)

Net Receivables 23	661	33	551	1981	3917	9249	18359	26035	201792
Inventories 24	686	12	695	1742	3614	9676	19359	32806	161507
Net Property, Plant and Equipment 25	727	43	463	1114	3200	9329	11139	37005	254230
Total Assets 26	3521	157	2106	6328	14831	34269	68289	136678	1368460
Notes and Loans Payable 27	948	73	787	1384	3668	8278	24554	37815	358671
All Other Liabilities 28	1058	57	728	1783	3139	8653	14789	25626	440935
Net Worth 29	1516	26	591	3161	8024	17337	28945	73237	568853

Selected Financial Ratios (Times to 1)

Current Ratio 30	1.7	1.1	1.8	2.3	2.5	2.0	2.2	2.7	1.5
Quick Ratio 31	0.9	0.7	1.0	1.3	1.4	1.0	1.2	1.3	0.7
Net Sales to Working Capital 32	8.9	89.5	9.1	7.5	5.6	6.6	5.9	4.7	10.1
Coverage Ratio 33	6.6	10.1	6.3	16.3	6.8	8.7	4.3	5.9	5.9
Total Asset Turnover 34	1.8	5.2	2.9	3.1	2.0	2.2	2.0	1.6	1.4
Inventory Turnover 35	6.2	34.2	5.6	7.8	5.7	5.4	5.1	4.9	8.0
Receivables Turnover 36	7.8	27.3	8.4	•	7.9	7.2	7.2	7.5	•
Total Liabilities to Net Worth 37	1.3	5.1	2.6	1.0	0.8	1.0	1.4	0.9	1.4
Current Assets to Working Capital 38	2.4	9.8	2.3	1.8	1.7	2.0	1.8	1.6	2.9
Current Liabilities to Working Capital 39	1.4	8.8	1.3	0.8	0.7	1.0	0.8	0.6	1.9
Working Capital to Net Sales 40	0.1	0.0	0.1	0.1	0.2	0.2	0.2	0.2	0.1
Inventory to Working Capital 41	0.8	1.6	0.9	0.7	0.6	0.8	0.7	0.7	0.8
Total Receipts to Cash Flow 42	7.1	5.5	8.9	8.4	7.6	7.7	8.5	8.0	6.6
Cost of Goods to Cash Flow 43	4.6	2.8	5.8	5.8	5.2	5.3	6.1	5.7	4.3
Cash Flow to Total Debt 44	0.5	1.1	0.5	0.7	0.6	0.6	0.4	0.4	0.4

Selected Financial Factors (in Percentages)

Debt Ratio 45	57.0	83.6	71.9	50.0	45.9	49.4	57.6	46.4	58.4
Return on Total Assets 46	13.5	49.7	17.6	19.0	15.3	13.7	13.5	11.5	11.1
Return on Equity Before Income Taxes 47	26.5	272.3	52.8	35.8	24.2	24.0	24.5	17.8	22.3
Return on Equity After Income Taxes 48	22.4	270.1	49.8	34.2	21.7	21.9	22.2	15.8	16.6
Profit Margin (Before Income Tax) 49	6.2	8.6	5.2	5.7	6.4	5.6	5.1	5.8	6.4
Profit Margin (After Income Tax) 50	5.2	8.5	4.9	5.5	5.7	5.1	4.7	5.1	4.8

Table I

Corporations with and without Net Income

MEDICAL EQUIPMENT AND SUPPLIES

MONEY AMOUNTS AND SIZE OF ASSETS IN THOUSANDS OF DOLLARS

Item Description for Accounting Period 7/07 Through 6/08	Total	Zero Assets	Under 500	500 to 1,000	1,000 to 5,000	5,000 to 10,000	10,000 to 25,000	25,000 to 50,000	50,000 to 100,000	100,000 to 250,000	250,000 to 500,000	500,000 to 2,500,000	2,500,000 and over
Number of Enterprises **1**	8538	471	5731	540	1203	95	199	91	62	51	30	42	23

Revenues ($ in Thousands)

	Total	Zero Assets	Under 500	500 to 1,000	1,000 to 5,000	5,000 to 10,000	10,000 to 25,000	25,000 to 50,000	50,000 to 100,000	100,000 to 250,000	250,000 to 500,000	500,000 to 2,500,000	2,500,000 and over
Net Sales **2**	142253216	3810603	2418276	1004625	5766650	954503	3707025	4188358	4037247	6399248	6212584	24906355	78847743
Interest **3**	3732763	38816	1736	1800	7921	8222	45171	33291	33921	69237	59783	326564	3106302
Rents **4**	670166	9361	0	1	1190	6	285	2941	712	4051	903	31523	619192
Royalties **5**	3008224	46417	0	0	2028	732	1371	20425	8784	68919	19187	178724	2661637
Other Portfolio Income **6**	3486090	50523	12106	26328	2118	0	12175	61828	54373	116688	189081	213219	2747653
Other Receipts **7**	3556012	15173	4117	1215	24103	4041	32415	48128	70855	101677	80144	347844	2826296
Total Receipts **8**	156706471	3970893	2436235	1033969	5804010	967504	3798442	4354971	4205892	6759820	6561682	26004229	90080823
Average Total Receipts **9**	18354	8431	425	1915	4825	10184	19088	47857	67837	132545	218723	619148	3948210

Operating Costs/Operating Income (%)

	Total	Zero Assets	Under 500	500 to 1,000	1,000 to 5,000	5,000 to 10,000	10,000 to 25,000	25,000 to 50,000	50,000 to 100,000	100,000 to 250,000	250,000 to 500,000	500,000 to 2,500,000	2,500,000 and over
Cost of Operations **10**	58.0	48.0	36.2	50.8	61.5	53.0	56.5	56.9	49.7	50.7	43.1	52.8	63.1
Salaries and Wages **11**	16.5	12.4	13.1	9.8	12.1	14.5	17.4	16.5	16.6	16.2	19.6	14.2	17.8
Taxes Paid **12**	1.8	2.1	3.5	3.6	2.7	3.2	2.5	2.2	2.4	1.8	2.1	1.5	1.6
Interest Paid **13**	4.5	14.2	0.7	0.7	0.9	1.1	2.1	1.4	1.6	2.0	2.1	3.9	5.5
Depreciation **14**	2.6	2.7	1.9	0.5	1.0	2.2	2.1	2.2	2.7	2.7	2.7	2.3	2.8
Amortization and Depletion **15**	0.9	0.3	0.1	0.1	0.3	0.6	0.8	0.5	0.9	1.0	1.9	1.3	0.9
Pensions and Other Deferred Comp. **16**	1.2	6.4	0.2	0.4	0.6	0.2	0.5	0.6	0.5	0.5	0.8	0.6	1.5
Employee Benefits **17**	2.3	0.7	1.4	3.3	1.2	2.1	2.0	1.3	2.8	2.5	2.3	2.3	2.4
Advertising **18**	1.1	0.7	0.6	0.6	1.6	1.7	1.4	2.4	2.2	1.9	1.1	1.0	0.9
Other Expenses **19**	12.6	24.9	23.5	24.7	15.4	21.9	21.3	20.3	19.8	18.7	19.8	15.6	8.0
Officers' Compensation **20**	1.6	1.1	14.0	7.2	4.7	4.7	3.7	2.7	2.1	2.3	1.3	1.5	0.7
Operating Margin **21**	•	•	4.8	•	•	•	•	•	•	•	3.2	3.0	•
Operating Margin Before Officers' Comp. **22**	•	•	18.8	5.6	2.7	•	•	•	0.8	2.1	4.5	4.5	•

Selected Average Balance Sheet ($ in Thousands)

Net Receivables **23**	3765	0	16	159	691	1511	2985	7256	12537	26169	50214	129158	899901
Inventories **24**	1971	0	12	89	512	2204	3126	6138	8294	16987	25652	94426	373334
Net Property, Plant and Equipment **25**	2592	0	21	68	212	1019	2285	5151	10161	19000	31268	105258	597368
Total Assets **26**	29990	0	87	677	1983	7364	16668	34876	68823	153669	333267	970719	7945245
Notes and Loans Payable **27**	6432	0	42	498	466	2197	3476	6739	11610	29298	49324	282489	1598979
All Other Liabilities **28**	8561	0	24	354	692	2688	4334	10651	13234	34431	97260	230414	2377072
Net Worth **29**	14997	0	22	-174	825	2478	8858	17487	43979	89940	186684	457816	3969194

Selected Financial Ratios (Times to 1)

Current Ratio **30**	1.5	•	1.3	2.1	1.8	1.8	2.4	2.0	2.8	2.5	2.4	2.0	1.2
Quick Ratio **31**	0.9	•	0.9	1.3	1.1	1.0	1.5	1.3	1.7	1.6	1.3	1.2	0.7
Net Sales to Working Capital **32**	5.8	•	43.2	6.5	7.1	3.9	2.9	4.2	2.8	2.7	2.2	3.7	10.4
Coverage Ratio **33**	2.8	0.4	9.4	3.0	•	•	•	•	2.9	3.7	5.6	3.0	3.2
Total Asset Turnover **34**	0.6	•	4.8	2.7	2.4	1.4	1.1	1.3	0.9	0.8	0.6	0.6	0.4
Inventory Turnover **35**	4.9	•	12.3	10.6	5.8	2.4	3.4	4.3	3.9	3.7	3.5	3.3	5.8
Receivables Turnover **36**	5.0	•	26.3	10.8	6.8	5.5	5.5	5.7	5.5	4.5	4.2	4.1	4.9
Total Liabilities to Net Worth **37**	1.0	•	3.0	•	1.4	2.0	0.9	1.0	0.6	0.7	0.8	1.1	1.0
Current Assets to Working Capital **38**	3.1	•	4.8	1.9	2.3	2.3	1.7	2.0	1.6	1.7	1.7	2.0	5.9
Current Liabilities to Working Capital **39**	2.1	•	3.8	0.9	1.3	1.3	0.7	1.0	0.6	0.7	0.7	1.0	4.9
Working Capital to Net Sales **40**	0.2	•	0.0	0.2	0.1	0.3	0.3	0.2	0.4	0.4	0.5	0.3	0.1
Inventory to Working Capital **41**	0.8	•	1.2	0.3	0.7	0.9	0.5	0.5	0.4	0.3	0.3	0.5	1.4
Total Receipts to Cash Flow **42**	6.4	6.7	4.3	5.5	10.1	6.8	10.2	7.7	5.2	4.8	4.1	4.8	7.4
Cost of Goods to Cash Flow **43**	3.7	3.2	1.5	2.8	6.2	3.6	5.8	4.4	2.6	2.4	1.8	2.5	4.7
Cash Flow to Total Debt **44**	0.2	•	1.5	0.4	0.3	0.3	0.2	0.3	0.5	0.4	0.3	0.2	0.1

Selected Financial Factors (in Percentages)

Debt Ratio **45**	50.0	•	75.1	125.7	58.4	66.3	46.9	49.9	36.1	41.5	44.0	52.8	50.0
Return on Total Assets **46**	7.1	•	29.8	5.4	•	•	•	•	4.4	6.0	7.3	7.1	7.6
Return on Equity Before Income Taxes **47**	9.2	•	107.1	•	•	•	•	•	4.5	7.4	10.7	10.1	10.4
Return on Equity After Income Taxes **48**	5.9	•	104.3	•	•	•	•	•	2.1	4.5	7.3	7.6	6.8
Profit Margin (Before Income Tax) **49**	8.3	•	5.5	1.3	•	•	•	•	3.1	5.3	9.6	7.8	12.1
Profit Margin (After Income Tax) **50**	5.3	•	5.4	1.0	•	•	•	•	1.4	3.2	6.6	5.9	7.9

Table II

Corporations with Net Income

MEDICAL EQUIPMENT AND SUPPLIES

MONEY AMOUNTS AND SIZE OF ASSETS IN THOUSANDS OF DOLLARS

Item Description for Accounting Period 7/07 Through 6/08	Total	Zero Assets	Under 500	500 to 1,000	1,000 to 5,000	5,000 to 10,000	10,000 to 25,000	25,000 to 50,000	50,000 to 100,000	100,000 to 250,000	250,000 to 500,000	500,000 to 2,500,000	2,500,000 and over
Number of Enterprises **1**	5608	80	4038	349	810	44	104	45	38	36	20	30	14
Revenues ($ in Thousands)													
Net Sales **2**	114483726	507459	1958842	927802	4389834	563400	2906641	2858184	3140924	5343083	4846001	19950373	67091183
Interest **3**	3133488	3232	1621	611	1268	1118	10061	5914	13183	39149	33156	287267	2736907
Rents **4**	636880	609	0	1	0	6	28	2124	561	4010	848	9574	619119
Royalties **5**	2735546	0	0	0	0	475	1	8322	3350	57272	16334	161996	2487796
Other Portfolio Income **6**	3283879	4714	0	0	15	0	8332	57546	46854	106202	177847	167599	2699367
Other Receipts **7**	3152438	12831	4078	1211	12756	841	29218	20747	60149	99203	53007	262672	2595728
Total Receipts **8**	127425957	528845	1964541	945027	4403873	565840	2954281	2952837	3265021	5648919	5127193	20839481	78230100
Average Total Receipts **9**	22722	6611	487	2708	5437	12860	28407	65619	85922	156914	256360	694649	5587864
Operating Costs/Operating Income (%)													
Cost of Operations **10**	57.9	47.7	30.3	49.0	58.7	42.9	58.1	57.0	50.2	53.6	41.7	51.3	62.8
Salaries and Wages **11**	16.6	20.1	13.8	9.0	10.1	7.9	9.7	13.3	13.3	13.2	17.7	14.1	18.8
Taxes Paid **12**	1.8	1.2	3.9	3.5	2.7	3.1	1.9	1.8	2.1	1.6	2.1	1.5	1.7
Interest Paid **13**	3.9	1.1	0.6	0.5	0.4	1.0	0.7	0.8	1.6	1.7	2.1	3.1	5.2
Depreciation **14**	2.6	1.3	1.9	0.5	0.9	1.5	1.2	2.1	2.4	2.1	2.6	2.1	3.1
Amortization and Depletion **15**	0.7	0.5	0.0	0.1	0.0	0.2	0.2	0.0	0.8	0.8	1.5	1.1	0.6
Pensions and Other Deferred Comp. **16**	1.3	•	0.4	0.4	0.0	0.1	0.6	0.8	0.6	0.5	1.0	0.6	1.7
Employee Benefits **17**	1.9	1.1	1.6	3.1	0.9	0.7	1.4	0.8	2.6	2.3	2.3	2.3	1.8
Advertising **18**	1.0	0.6	0.4	0.6	1.8	1.6	1.1	1.4	2.2	1.8	0.9	1.0	0.8
Other Expenses **19**	10.0	8.4	20.1	21.2	11.8	15.2	13.3	12.0	15.9	15.1	19.4	14.8	6.5
Officers' Compensation **20**	1.5	2.4	16.3	6.1	4.4	4.4	2.6	2.6	1.7	1.8	1.2	1.6	0.6
Operating Margin **21**	0.9	15.7	10.9	6.0	7.8	21.4	9.1	7.3	6.6	5.5	7.4	6.4	•
Operating Margin Before Officers' Comp. **22**	2.4	18.1	27.2	12.1	12.2	25.8	11.7	9.9	8.4	7.3	8.6	8.0	•

Selected Average Balance Sheet ($ in Thousands)

Net Receivables 23	4281	0	7	239	750	1899	4710	8930	13441	29105	54291	131857	1122445
Inventories 24	2418	0	15	107	491	2177	4220	6487	9113	19945	28211	106201	530222
Net Property, Plant and Equipment 25	3016	0	21	94	220	722	2395	7194	12103	19074	36413	112039	769786
Total Assets 26	33667	0	84	700	1933	6730	16588	34042	70365	151212	333896	984440	9912565
Notes and Loans Payable 27	6060	0	28	724	318	1372	2541	6525	14584	29125	65090	219405	1661328
All Other Liabilities 28	9753	0	20	324	542	1529	3016	10398	11723	31882	86303	248732	3030776
Net Worth 29	17854	0	35	-347	1074	3828	11031	17120	44058	90205	182503	516303	5220461

Selected Financial Ratios (Times to 1)

Current Ratio 30	1.4	•	1.3	1.6	2.1	2.4	2.7	1.9	2.5	2.4	2.1	2.1	1.1
Quick Ratio 31	0.8	•	0.8	1.0	1.4	1.4	1.7	1.2	1.4	1.6	1.2	1.2	0.6
Net Sales to Working Capital 32	7.4	•	45.1	14.7	6.8	4.2	3.8	6.7	3.8	3.3	3.2	3.5	17.6
Coverage Ratio 33	4.5	19.1	20.2	16.5	19.0	23.8	15.8	13.7	7.8	7.5	7.7	4.6	3.9
Total Asset Turnover 34	0.6	•	5.8	3.8	2.8	1.9	1.7	1.9	1.2	1.0	0.7	0.7	0.5
Inventory Turnover 35	4.9	•	10.1	12.1	6.5	2.5	3.8	5.6	4.5	4.0	3.6	3.2	5.7
Receivables Turnover 36	5.1	•	32.6	10.1	6.9	6.6	5.4	6.0	6.3	4.7	4.4	4.2	5.1
Total Liabilities to Net Worth 37	0.9	•	1.4	•	0.8	0.8	0.5	1.0	0.6	0.7	0.8	0.9	0.9
Current Assets to Working Capital 38	3.6	•	3.9	2.8	1.9	1.7	1.6	2.2	1.7	1.7	2.0	1.9	8.9
Current Liabilities to Working Capital 39	2.6	•	2.9	1.8	0.9	0.7	0.6	1.2	0.7	0.7	1.0	0.9	7.9
Working Capital to Net Sales 40	0.1	•	0.0	0.1	0.1	0.2	0.3	0.1	0.3	0.3	0.3	0.3	0.1
Inventory to Working Capital 41	0.9	•	1.2	0.4	0.5	0.7	0.5	0.6	0.5	0.4	0.4	0.5	2.3
Total Receipts to Cash Flow 42	5.6	3.7	3.8	4.4	6.1	2.9	4.6	5.5	4.3	4.4	3.6	4.2	7.0
Cost of Goods to Cash Flow 43	3.2	1.8	1.2	2.2	3.6	1.2	2.7	3.1	2.1	2.3	1.5	2.2	4.4
Cash Flow to Total Debt 44	0.2	•	2.6	0.6	1.0	1.5	1.1	0.7	0.7	0.6	0.4	0.3	0.1

Selected Financial Factors (in Percentages)

Debt Ratio 45	47.0	•	57.9	149.6	44.5	43.1	33.5	49.7	37.4	40.3	45.3	47.6	47.3
Return on Total Assets 46	10.6	•	68.3	31.8	24.0	43.3	19.3	21.4	14.6	12.5	11.9	9.7	9.8
Return on Equity Before Income Taxes 47	15.5	•	154.1	•	40.9	73.0	27.2	39.4	20.3	18.1	18.9	14.6	13.9
Return on Equity After Income Taxes 48	11.2	•	151.7	•	39.1	66.0	23.4	35.7	16.3	14.0	13.8	11.5	9.4
Profit Margin (Before Income Tax) 49	13.6	19.9	11.2	7.9	8.1	21.8	10.7	10.6	10.8	11.0	14.3	11.3	15.2
Profit Margin (After Income Tax) 50	9.8	19.5	11.0	7.5	7.7	19.7	9.2	9.6	8.7	8.5	10.4	8.9	10.2

Table I

Corporations with and without Net Income

OTHER MISCELLANEOUS MANUFACTURING

MONEY AMOUNTS AND SIZE OF ASSETS IN THOUSANDS OF DOLLARS

Item Description for Accounting Period 7/07 Through 6/08	Total	Zero Assets	Under 500	500 to 1,000	1,000 to 5,000	5,000 to 10,000	10,000 to 25,000	25,000 to 50,000	50,000 to 100,000	100,000 to 250,000	250,000 to 500,000	500,000 to 2,500,000	2,500,000 and over
Number of Enterprises 1	25002	3444	16445	1949	1961	461	389	165	79	60	22	27	0
Revenues ($ in Thousands)													
Net Sales 2	104784547	575346	6595391	2960519	12833809	5525547	10069676	8365820	7680804	10434792	7057919	32684924	0
Interest 3	782659	442	2276	1732	16306	4584	9878	18467	17880	34783	44661	631651	0
Rents 4	90767	57	18	3650	3865	864	5280	873	342	5970	4996	64853	0
Royalties 5	742752	10251	77	0	2391	0	2542	9233	14727	17582	21446	664503	0
Other Portfolio Income 6	635477	21571	9375	4555	1412	30131	18916	6548	36852	157663	121864	226592	0
Other Receipts 7	1827831	54242	78900	510	29969	50595	102907	82915	44325	131008	226343	1026113	0
Total Receipts 8	108864033	661909	6686037	2970966	12887752	5611721	10209199	8483856	7794930	10781798	7477229	35298636	0
Average Total Receipts 9	4354	192	407	1524	6572	12173	26245	51417	98670	179697	339874	1307357	•
Operating Costs/Operating Income (%)													
Cost of Operations 10	64.2	71.9	50.5	54.8	67.4	60.4	68.1	66.8	66.9	66.0	61.6	64.5	•
Salaries and Wages 11	9.6	6.4	13.0	8.7	8.3	11.6	8.4	7.6	8.9	8.9	13.4	9.6	•
Taxes Paid 12	1.8	2.2	2.9	2.5	2.2	2.4	1.8	2.0	1.7	1.5	1.6	1.4	•
Interest Paid 13	2.7	1.9	1.4	1.6	1.0	1.8	1.4	1.6	1.9	2.8	4.5	4.5	•
Depreciation 14	1.9	1.0	1.2	1.7	1.4	2.3	1.7	1.8	1.8	2.2	2.4	2.0	•
Amortization and Depletion 15	0.7	0.0	0.3	0.3	0.1	0.3	0.4	0.4	0.5	0.8	1.1	1.4	•
Pensions and Other Deferred Comp. 16	0.5	0.1	0.5	0.1	0.4	0.3	0.4	0.5	0.5	0.6	0.5	0.6	•
Employee Benefits 17	1.5	1.1	1.1	1.6	1.3	2.2	1.5	1.4	1.7	1.6	1.6	1.4	•
Advertising 18	1.7	3.8	1.1	2.3	0.9	1.0	1.1	2.1	1.9	1.8	2.6	1.8	•
Other Expenses 19	12.9	23.7	19.0	16.2	11.8	14.2	10.3	11.3	10.6	12.3	11.6	13.6	•
Officers' Compensation 20	2.3	2.2	9.4	5.2	4.8	2.4	2.3	1.9	1.9	1.0	1.1	0.5	•
Operating Margin 21	0.2	•	•	5.1	0.3	0.9	2.6	2.7	1.7	0.4	•	•	•
Operating Margin Before Officers' Comp. 22	2.5	•	9.1	10.4	5.1	3.4	4.9	4.5	3.6	1.4	•	•	•

Selected Average Balance Sheet ($ in Thousands)

Net Receivables 23	567	0	23	171	782	1501	3770	7297	14913	27664	65753	159313	•
Inventories 24	591	0	31	198	915	2351	4624	8374	15944	29623	53458	118292	•
Net Property, Plant and Equipment 25	499	0	24	141	522	1320	2428	7348	11279	25401	65981	154350	•
Total Assets 26	3367	0	119	707	2861	6907	15251	34335	71576	162103	357657	1377550	•
Notes and Loans Payable 27	1249	0	91	350	995	3271	4721	10045	25200	52464	172647	487392	•
All Other Liabilities 28	1022	0	57	146	975	1525	3974	10106	24794	40819	105004	436435	•
Net Worth 29	1096	0	-29	211	892	2111	6556	14185	21582	68820	80006	453723	•

Selected Financial Ratios (Times to 1)

Current Ratio 30	1.4	•	1.1	1.8	2.1	1.8	1.7	1.7	1.5	1.7	1.7	1.0	•
Quick Ratio 31	0.7	•	0.6	1.0	1.1	0.7	0.8	0.8	0.8	0.9	0.9	0.5	•
Net Sales to Working Capital 32	9.8	•	48.9	7.5	5.7	5.5	6.0	5.5	7.2	5.4	5.4	•	•
Coverage Ratio 33	2.6	1.6	1.8	4.4	1.7	2.4	3.6	2.4	2.7	2.5	2.0	2.7	•
Total Asset Turnover 34	1.2	•	3.4	2.1	2.3	1.7	1.5	1.7	1.4	1.1	0.9	0.9	•
Inventory Turnover 35	4.5	•	6.6	4.2	4.8	3.1	4.0	3.8	4.1	3.9	3.7	6.6	•
Receivables Turnover 36	6.9	•	13.7	7.6	8.4	7.8	6.4	6.3	6.2	6.1	3.9	8.3	•
Total Liabilities to Net Worth 37	2.1	•	•	2.3	2.2	2.3	1.4	1.3	2.3	1.4	3.5	2.0	•
Current Assets to Working Capital 38	3.5	•	9.8	2.3	1.9	2.3	2.5	2.3	3.0	2.5	2.4	•	•
Current Liabilities to Working Capital 39	2.5	•	8.8	1.3	0.9	1.3	1.5	1.3	2.0	1.5	1.4	•	•
Working Capital to Net Sales 40	0.1	•	0.0	0.1	0.2	0.2	0.2	0.2	0.1	0.2	0.2	•	•
Inventory to Working Capital 41	1.4	•	3.9	0.8	0.8	1.2	1.0	1.0	1.1	1.0	0.8	•	•
Total Receipts to Cash Flow 42	7.0	4.6	6.9	6.0	10.9	7.6	8.5	7.4	8.6	7.5	7.4	5.4	•
Cost of Goods to Cash Flow 43	4.5	3.3	3.5	3.3	7.3	4.6	5.8	5.0	5.7	4.9	4.5	3.5	•
Cash Flow to Total Debt 44	0.3	•	0.4	0.5	0.3	0.3	0.3	0.3	0.2	0.2	0.2	0.2	•

Selected Financial Factors (in Percentages)

Debt Ratio 45	67.5	•	124.3	70.1	68.8	69.4	57.0	58.7	69.8	57.5	77.6	67.1	•
Return on Total Assets 46	8.9	•	8.2	15.1	4.1	7.4	9.2	8.3	7.1	7.4	8.2	10.4	•
Return on Equity Before Income Taxes 47	16.9	•	•	39.3	5.4	14.1	15.7	14.5	14.9	10.3	18.8	19.7	•
Return on Equity After Income Taxes 48	12.3	•	•	38.4	3.2	11.9	13.9	12.2	10.6	8.2	12.6	12.9	•
Profit Margin (Before Income Tax) 49	4.4	1.2	1.1	5.5	0.7	2.5	4.0	4.1	3.3	4.1	4.7	7.4	•
Profit Margin (After Income Tax) 50	3.2	1.0	0.9	5.3	0.4	2.1	3.5	3.4	2.4	3.3	3.2	4.8	•

Table II

Corporations with Net Income

OTHER MISCELLANEOUS MANUFACTURING

MONEY AMOUNTS AND SIZE OF ASSETS IN THOUSANDS OF DOLLARS

Item Description for Accounting Period 7/07 Through 6/08	Total	Zero Assets	Under 500	500 to 1,000	1,000 to 5,000	5,000 to 10,000	10,000 to 25,000	25,000 to 50,000	50,000 to 100,000	100,000 to 250,000	250,000 to 500,000	500,000 to 2,500,000	2,500,000 and over
Number of Enterprises 1	14216	1656	9001	1353	1376	300	290	113	52	41	15	19	0
Revenues ($ in Thousands)													
Net Sales 2	82499257	322840	4326119	2377260	10347337	4393732	7979598	6016255	5450322	8449225	5279492	27557076	0
Interest 3	657209	308	413	702	10323	2504	6057	11082	15082	23899	37008	549831	0
Rents 4	83551	43	18	3650	3797	864	1787	643	254	3201	4798	64496	0
Royalties 5	688204	10251	77	0	0	0	997	6664	2398	15760	7178	644879	0
Other Portfolio Income 6	488845	8594	6611	3720	563	5939	9845	5512	22364	134149	101831	189716	0
Other Receipts 7	1634398	56268	46286	4089	14948	32701	89398	58088	36944	128398	181907	985373	0
Total Receipts 8	86051464	398304	4379524	2389421	10376968	4435740	8087682	6098244	5527364	8754632	5612214	29991371	0
Average Total Receipts 9	6053	241	487	1766	7541	14786	27889	53967	106295	213528	374148	1578493	•
Operating Costs/Operating Income (%)													
Cost of Operations 10	62.5	63.1	43.9	55.3	67.0	57.8	66.6	65.4	63.6	64.1	59.5	63.2	•
Salaries and Wages 11	9.7	6.7	15.1	6.4	7.8	11.3	8.6	7.4	9.6	9.1	14.4	9.9	•
Taxes Paid 12	1.8	2.8	3.0	2.4	2.2	2.4	1.8	2.1	1.8	1.5	1.8	1.5	•
Interest Paid 13	2.4	1.9	0.7	1.4	0.8	1.1	1.2	1.2	1.3	2.4	4.1	4.2	•
Depreciation 14	1.8	0.9	1.0	1.6	1.2	2.2	1.3	1.6	1.6	2.3	2.5	2.1	•
Amortization and Depletion 15	0.7	0.1	0.3	0.2	0.1	0.2	0.2	0.3	0.4	0.6	0.9	1.4	•
Pensions and Other Deferred Comp. 16	0.5	0.1	0.7	0.1	0.5	0.4	0.4	0.6	0.6	0.7	0.6	0.5	•
Employee Benefits 17	1.5	1.5	1.3	1.5	1.2	2.3	1.5	1.2	1.6	1.6	1.8	1.4	•
Advertising 18	1.6	4.7	1.2	2.3	0.8	0.7	1.1	1.3	1.9	2.1	1.1	2.0	•
Other Expenses 19	11.5	11.8	16.4	14.7	10.1	13.0	8.9	10.0	9.4	9.9	10.7	12.9	•
Officers' Compensation 20	2.3	2.0	10.0	5.1	4.5	2.6	2.5	2.2	2.0	1.0	1.2	0.5	•
Operating Margin 21	3.6	4.4	6.5	8.9	3.9	6.1	5.9	6.7	6.2	4.7	1.5	0.5	•
Operating Margin Before Officers' Comp. 22	5.9	6.4	16.5	14.1	8.4	8.7	8.4	8.9	8.3	5.8	2.7	0.9	•

Selected Average Balance Sheet ($ in Thousands)

Net Receivables 23	•	158736	60506	30728	14275	7750	4081	1733	896	203	25	0	720
Inventories 24	•	139681	48468	33959	16840	8651	4413	2098	975	181	24	0	727
Net Property, Plant and Equipment 25	•	177390	72201	28797	10907	7127	2248	1518	567	159	16	0	651
Total Assets 26	•	1509223	360302	170221	69500	34768	15097	6903	2991	714	112	0	4301
Notes and Loans Payable 27	•	470913	169748	49289	18375	9359	3887	2276	844	361	39	0	1360
All Other Liabilities 28	•	531457	103658	44444	19475	9103	3887	1597	906	126	43	0	1331
Net Worth 29	•	506853	86895	76488	31651	16306	7324	3030	1241	227	30	0	1609

Selected Financial Ratios (Times to 1)

Current Ratio 30	•	0.9	1.9	1.7	1.8	1.8	2.0	1.9	2.5	1.6	1.5	•	1.4
Quick Ratio 31	•	0.4	1.0	0.8	1.0	0.9	1.0	0.8	1.4	1.2	1.0	•	0.7
Net Sales to Working Capital 32	•	•	5.3	5.6	6.1	5.3	5.5	6.6	5.5	9.9	18.3	•	9.9
Coverage Ratio 33	•	3.4	3.2	4.7	7.1	7.6	7.0	7.3	6.3	7.6	12.1	16.0	4.4
Total Asset Turnover 34	•	1.0	1.0	1.2	1.5	1.5	1.8	2.1	2.5	2.5	4.3	•	1.3
Inventory Turnover 35	•	6.6	4.3	3.9	4.0	4.0	4.2	4.0	5.2	5.4	8.8	•	5.0
Receivables Turnover 36	•	8.6	4.7	6.4	6.1	6.1	6.4	8.0	8.2	7.9	16.2	•	7.4
Total Liabilities to Net Worth 37	•	2.0	3.1	1.2	1.2	1.1	1.1	1.3	1.4	2.1	2.7	•	1.7
Current Assets to Working Capital 38	•	•	2.1	2.4	2.3	2.2	2.0	2.2	1.7	2.6	3.0	•	3.2
Current Liabilities to Working Capital 39	•	1.1	1.4	1.3	1.2	1.2	1.0	1.2	0.7	1.6	2.0	•	2.2
Working Capital to Net Sales 40	•	0.2	0.2	0.2	0.2	0.2	0.2	0.2	0.2	0.1	0.1	•	0.1
Inventory to Working Capital 41	•	0.7	0.9	0.9	0.8	0.8	0.8	1.0	0.7	0.6	0.8	•	1.2
Total Receipts to Cash Flow 42	•	4.9	6.0	6.4	6.7	6.1	7.2	6.1	8.7	5.2	5.3	2.7	5.9
Cost of Goods to Cash Flow 43	•	3.1	3.6	4.1	4.3	4.0	4.8	3.5	5.8	2.9	2.3	1.7	3.7
Cash Flow to Total Debt 44	•	0.3	0.2	0.3	0.4	0.5	0.5	0.6	0.5	0.7	1.1	•	0.4

Selected Financial Factors (in Percentages)

Debt Ratio 45	•	66.4	75.9	55.1	54.5	53.1	51.5	56.1	58.5	68.2	72.9	•	62.6
Return on Total Assets 46	•	13.8	12.6	13.6	13.6	14.2	15.3	17.3	12.4	26.8	36.2	•	14.6
Return on Equity Before Income Taxes 47	•	29.1	35.8	23.7	25.7	26.3	27.0	34.1	25.1	73.1	122.7	•	30.1
Return on Equity After Income Taxes 48	•	20.4	27.5	21.0	21.4	23.4	24.8	31.7	22.8	72.0	119.9	•	24.5
Profit Margin (Before Income Tax) 49	•	10.2	8.8	8.8	7.8	8.1	7.2	7.1	4.1	9.5	7.7	28.6	8.3
Profit Margin (After Income Tax) 50	•	7.1	6.8	7.8	6.5	7.2	6.6	6.6	3.8	9.3	7.6	28.2	6.8

Table I

Corporations with and without Net Income

MOTOR VEHICLE AND MOTOR VEHICLE PARTS AND SUPPLIES

MONEY AMOUNTS AND SIZE OF ASSETS IN THOUSANDS OF DOLLARS

Item Description for Accounting Period 7/07 Through 6/08	Total	Zero Assets	Under 500	500 to 1,000	1,000 to 5,000	5,000 to 10,000	10,000 to 25,000	25,000 to 50,000	50,000 to 100,000	100,000 to 250,000	250,000 to 500,000	500,000 to 2,500,000	2,500,000 and over
Number of Enterprises **1**	19167	1493	11304	2665	2616	466	381	115	52	33	17	18	7
Revenues ($ in Thousands)													
Net Sales **2**	294237482	5316436	10766087	5942162	16041018	8959875	16354524	9080701	7750409	8370403	16599292	43365661	145690914
Interest **3**	2870025	4924	535	7609	18101	9510	14445	8819	9360	26242	46457	243716	2480306
Rents **4**	699972	0	0	2667	5150	4044	9668	6563	7069	6242	9753	42221	606595
Royalties **5**	41707	0	0	0	0	86	210	196	11	1384	8625	9841	21355
Other Portfolio Income **6**	530109	466	25363	9130	32667	5539	16077	15293	10190	41157	21757	64178	288292
Other Receipts **7**	3143057	68462	28967	11614	234638	53898	94809	50512	73800	65707	32633	493931	1934086
Total Receipts **8**	301522352	5390288	10820952	5973182	16331574	9032952	16489733	9162084	7850839	8511135	16718517	44219548	151021548
Average Total Receipts **9**	15731	3610	957	2241	6243	19384	43280	79670	150978	257913	983442	2456642	21574507
Operating Costs/Operating Income (%)													
Cost of Operations **10**	82.1	91.5	85.5	79.9	76.6	82.0	81.8	78.0	82.8	78.0	86.9	83.9	81.7
Salaries and Wages **11**	3.6	1.4	3.5	6.2	6.0	5.7	6.1	6.5	6.0	6.1	2.6	3.9	2.4
Taxes Paid **12**	0.7	0.2	0.9	1.2	1.6	1.0	1.0	1.3	0.9	1.2	0.5	0.8	0.5
Interest Paid **13**	1.3	0.8	0.4	0.3	0.7	1.0	1.0	1.0	1.0	1.3	0.8	1.1	1.7
Depreciation **14**	3.2	0.1	0.4	0.4	0.5	0.4	0.8	1.2	0.9	1.1	0.7	1.0	5.7
Amortization and Depletion **15**	0.1	0.0	0.1	0.0	0.0	0.0	0.1	0.1	0.2	0.3	0.1	0.3	0.1
Pensions and Other Deferred Comp. **16**	0.2	0.1	0.1	0.1	0.2	0.2	0.2	0.2	0.1	0.2	0.1	0.2	0.2
Employee Benefits **17**	0.4	0.2	0.4	0.6	0.6	0.4	0.6	0.8	0.6	0.8	0.5	0.5	0.3
Advertising **18**	2.6	0.8	0.3	0.3	0.8	0.5	0.5	0.6	0.4	1.0	1.6	2.2	4.1
Other Expenses **19**	5.3	6.9	7.4	8.1	9.0	5.2	5.7	6.7	5.3	8.0	3.9	5.8	4.2
Officers' Compensation **20**	0.6	0.6	1.9	2.3	2.9	1.3	1.2	2.3	0.9	0.6	0.4	0.2	0.1
Operating Margin **21**	•	•	•	0.7	1.2	2.2	1.0	1.3	0.9	1.4	1.8	0.3	•
Operating Margin Before Officers' Comp. **22**	0.4	1.2	1.2	3.0	4.1	3.4	2.2	3.5	1.8	2.0	2.2	0.5	•

Selected Average Balance Sheet ($ in Thousands)

Item													
Net Receivables 23	2584	0	19	201	512	1799	4207	8771	16317	26356	72942	260398	5191996
Inventories 24	1693	0	50	248	808	3284	6984	14118	24251	52238	96288	388692	1669897
Net Property, Plant and Equipment 25	2293	0	17	49	279	605	1943	5379	9230	20939	47699	142130	5244770
Total Assets 26	9305	0	121	702	2195	6981	16064	35623	71467	145739	354400	1147979	17240564
Notes and Loans Payable 27	3057	0	81	190	566	2326	5917	11294	23179	42787	104396	394077	5652771
All Other Liabilities 28	3958	0	41	211	690	2097	5949	11854	25640	48209	128891	412714	7982024
Net Worth 29	2290	0	-1	300	939	2558	4198	12475	22649	54743	121113	341188	3605768

Selected Financial Ratios (Times to 1)

Item													
Current Ratio 30	1.4	•	1.8	2.2	2.0	1.9	1.4	1.6	1.5	1.6	1.6	1.3	1.3
Quick Ratio 31	0.8	•	0.7	1.2	0.9	0.8	0.6	0.7	0.6	0.7	0.7	0.6	0.8
Net Sales to Working Capital 32	10.3	•	24.0	7.1	7.3	6.9	11.0	7.6	9.4	7.2	12.7	13.4	10.0
Coverage Ratio 33	2.8	•	0.6	4.9	5.5	3.9	2.8	3.2	3.2	3.4	4.2	3.0	2.5
Total Asset Turnover 34	1.6	•	7.8	3.2	2.8	2.8	2.7	2.2	2.1	1.7	2.8	2.1	1.2
Inventory Turnover 35	7.4	•	16.4	7.2	5.8	4.8	5.0	4.4	5.1	3.8	8.8	5.2	10.2
Receivables Turnover 36	6.3	•	50.8	11.2	12.9	10.2	10.5	8.6	10.0	8.7	16.2	9.7	4.3
Total Liabilities to Net Worth 37	3.1	•	•	1.3	1.3	1.7	2.8	1.9	2.2	1.7	1.9	2.4	3.8
Current Assets to Working Capital 38	3.8	•	2.3	1.8	2.0	2.1	3.4	2.6	3.2	2.7	2.8	4.1	4.7
Current Liabilities to Working Capital 39	2.8	•	1.3	0.8	1.0	1.1	2.4	1.6	2.2	1.7	1.8	3.1	3.7
Working Capital to Net Sales 40	0.1	•	0.0	0.1	0.1	0.1	0.1	0.1	0.1	0.1	0.1	0.1	0.1
Inventory to Working Capital 41	1.2	•	1.4	0.7	1.0	1.2	1.9	1.3	1.6	1.4	1.4	2.0	0.9
Total Receipts to Cash Flow 42	15.1	19.0	19.9	14.2	10.4	15.1	16.6	13.7	16.5	10.5	17.5	14.3	15.7
Cost of Goods to Cash Flow 43	12.4	17.4	17.0	11.3	8.0	12.4	13.6	10.7	13.7	8.2	15.2	12.0	12.8
Cash Flow to Total Debt 44	0.1	•	0.4	0.4	0.5	0.3	0.2	0.2	0.2	0.2	0.2	0.2	0.1

Selected Financial Factors (in Percentages)

Item													
Debt Ratio 45	75.4	•	100.7	57.2	63.4	73.9	65.0	68.3	62.4	65.8	70.3	79.1	
Return on Total Assets 46	6.0	•	1.6	4.7	11.0	10.3	7.6	7.1	7.6	9.1	6.9	5.2	
Return on Equity Before Income Taxes 47	15.6	•	151.8	8.8	19.7	22.3	18.6	13.8	14.6	20.4	15.5	15.0	
Return on Equity After Income Taxes 48	10.9	•	217.4	7.0	18.8	20.2	16.1	12.3	11.8	16.6	9.8	9.4	
Profit Margin (Before Income Tax) 49	2.3	•	•	1.2	3.0	1.8	2.2	2.2	2.5	2.2	2.6		
Profit Margin (After Income Tax) 50	1.6	•	•	0.9	2.7	1.6	1.9	2.1	1.6	1.4	1.6		

Table II

Corporations with Net Income

MOTOR VEHICLE AND MOTOR VEHICLE PARTS AND SUPPLIES

MONEY AMOUNTS AND SIZE OF ASSETS IN THOUSANDS OF DOLLARS

Item Description for Accounting Period 7/07 Through 6/08	Total	Zero Assets	Under 500	500 to 1,000	1,000 to 5,000	5,000 to 10,000	10,000 to 25,000	25,000 to 50,000	50,000 to 100,000	100,000 to 250,000	250,000 to 500,000	500,000 to 2,500,000	2,500,000 and over
Number of Enterprises 1	11645	739	•	2063	2085	379	320	91	43	23	14	14	•
Revenues ($ in Thousands)													
Net Sales 2	236597360	2024544	•	5160035	13574900	6009063	14495384	7597996	6978198	6134071	15772028	38543273	•
Interest 3	2111663	496	•	6586	14883	8733	12039	6497	8951	23953	41161	242349	•
Rents 4	563716	0	•	2667	3621	1016	9557	6297	7069	6136	9402	41779	•
Royalties 5	37454	0	•	0	0	0	210	196	0	227	8625	8230	•
Other Portfolio Income 6	383700	466	•	9050	27984	5463	11071	9151	10190	40543	21451	43973	•
Other Receipts 7	2821215	17603	•	9611	237239	42094	75935	30944	60394	55734	46540	444796	•
Total Receipts 8	242515108	2043109	•	5187949	13858627	6066369	14604196	7651081	7064802	6260664	15899207	39324400	•
Average Total Receipts 9	20826	2765	•	2515	6647	16006	45638	84078	164298	272203	1135658	2808886	•
Operating Costs/Operating Income (%)													
Cost of Operations 10	82.6	89.4	•	81.4	77.7	76.3	81.7	77.7	82.1	76.5	86.8	83.9	•
Salaries and Wages 11	3.6	3.2	•	4.9	5.4	7.2	6.1	6.3	6.0	5.9	2.6	3.6	•
Taxes Paid 12	0.7	0.5	•	1.2	1.6	1.3	1.0	1.3	0.9	1.3	0.5	0.8	•
Interest Paid 13	1.0	0.2	•	0.2	0.6	1.0	1.0	0.8	1.0	1.1	0.6	1.0	•
Depreciation 14	2.0	0.1	•	0.3	0.4	0.6	0.7	1.1	0.9	1.2	0.8	0.8	•
Amortization and Depletion 15	0.1	0.0	•	0.0	0.0	0.0	0.1	0.1	0.1	0.2	0.1	0.1	•
Pensions and Other Deferred Comp. 16	0.2	0.1	•	0.1	0.2	0.3	0.2	0.2	0.1	0.2	0.1	0.1	•
Employee Benefits 17	0.4	0.4	•	0.5	0.3	0.6	0.6	0.6	0.6	0.7	0.5	0.4	•
Advertising 18	2.9	0.3	•	0.2	0.7	0.6	0.3	0.6	0.4	1.1	1.6	2.4	•
Other Expenses 19	5.1	4.0	•	6.7	8.0	6.4	5.1	6.5	5.1	8.1	3.8	5.8	•
Officers' Compensation 20	0.6	0.8	•	1.8	2.8	1.7	1.2	2.2	0.9	0.6	0.4	0.2	•
Operating Margin 21	0.9	0.9	•	2.6	2.3	4.0	2.1	2.7	1.7	3.0	2.2	0.7	•
Operating Margin Before Officers' Comp. 22	1.5	1.8	•	4.5	5.1	5.7	3.3	4.9	2.6	3.6	2.6	1.0	•

Selected Average Balance Sheet ($ in Thousands)

Net Receivables 23	2807	0	•	231	548	1829	4108	8817	16242	27982	76848	269146
Inventories 24	2314	0	•	228	802	3298	7146	15807	24609	58659	97742	424381
Net Property, Plant and Equipment 25	1998	0	•	35	174	570	1736	5237	9600	21166	55131	145634
Total Assets 26	10634	0	•	690	2099	7003	15825	36368	71305	146449	347039	1248495
Notes and Loans Payable 27	3052	0	•	174	446	1888	5737	9285	22825	43501	81753	383603
All Other Liabilities 28	4420	0	•	227	635	2161	5426	11727	23404	39679	133616	483129
Net Worth 29	3162	0	•	288	1017	2954	4662	15356	25075	63270	131670	381763

Selected Financial Ratios (Times to 1)

Current Ratio 30	1.4	•	•	2.3	2.1	2.0	1.5	1.8	1.5	1.8	1.7	1.3
Quick Ratio 31	0.7	•	•	1.3	1.0	0.8	0.6	0.8	0.7	0.8	0.7	0.6
Net Sales to Working Capital 32	11.3	•	•	7.3	7.6	5.2	10.2	6.9	9.0	6.1	12.6	13.6
Coverage Ratio 33	4.3	8.9	•	13.8	8.7	5.8	3.9	5.3	4.0	5.5	5.9	3.8
Total Asset Turnover 34	1.9	•	•	3.6	3.1	2.3	2.9	2.3	2.3	1.8	3.2	2.2
Inventory Turnover 35	7.3	•	•	8.9	6.3	3.7	5.2	4.1	5.4	3.5	10.0	5.4
Receivables Turnover 36	6.3	•	•	10.8	12.9	7.8	11.7	8.5	11.0	7.9	18.2	10.8
Total Liabilities to Net Worth 37	2.4	•	•	1.4	1.1	1.4	2.4	1.4	1.8	1.3	1.6	2.3
Current Assets to Working Capital 38	3.8	•	•	1.8	1.9	2.0	3.0	2.3	2.8	2.2	2.5	4.1
Current Liabilities to Working Capital 39	2.8	•	•	0.8	0.9	1.0	2.0	1.3	1.8	1.2	1.5	3.1
Working Capital to Net Sales 40	0.1	•	•	0.1	0.1	0.2	0.1	0.1	0.1	0.2	0.1	0.1
Inventory to Working Capital 41	1.2	•	•	0.7	1.0	1.1	1.7	1.2	1.4	1.2	1.2	2.0
Total Receipts to Cash Flow 42	13.3	21.4	•	12.6	9.6	10.8	15.2	12.0	15.4	8.7	16.6	13.3
Cost of Goods to Cash Flow 43	11.0	19.2	•	10.2	7.4	8.2	12.4	9.3	12.7	6.7	14.4	11.1
Cash Flow to Total Debt 44	0.2	•	•	0.5	0.6	0.4	0.3	0.3	0.2	0.4	0.3	0.2

Selected Financial Factors (in Percentages)

Debt Ratio 45	70.3	•	•	58.2	51.5	57.8	70.5	57.8	64.8	56.8	62.1	69.4
Return on Total Assets 46	8.3	•	•	12.4	15.4	13.4	10.8	9.5	8.8	11.1	11.6	8.2
Return on Equity Before Income Taxes 47	21.5	•	•	27.6	28.0	26.3	27.3	18.3	18.8	21.1	25.3	19.7
Return on Equity After Income Taxes 48	16.2	•	•	25.2	27.0	24.1	24.6	16.7	15.7	17.9	21.1	13.2
Profit Margin (Before Income Tax) 49	3.3	1.9	•	3.2	4.4	4.9	2.8	3.4	2.9	5.0	3.0	2.7
Profit Margin (After Income Tax) 50	2.5	1.6	•	2.9	4.2	4.5	2.5	3.1	2.4	4.2	2.5	1.8

Table I

Corporations with and without Net Income

LUMBER AND OTHER CONSTRUCTION MATERIALS

MONEY AMOUNTS AND SIZE OF ASSETS IN THOUSANDS OF DOLLARS

Item Description for Accounting Period 7/07 Through 6/08	Total	Zero Assets	Under 500	500 to 1,000	1,000 to 5,000	5,000 to 10,000	10,000 to 25,000	25,000 to 50,000	50,000 to 100,000	100,000 to 250,000	250,000 to 500,000	500,000 to 2,500,000	2,500,000 and over
Number of Enterprises **1**	15837	1665	7343	1478	3725	956	472	114	43	26	6	8	0
Revenues ($ in Thousands)													
Net Sales **2**	120853478	1345288	5185589	3577817	29375653	20514617	20533682	10922839	8392599	9465998	2952308	8587087	0
Interest **3**	219434	170	3589	6095	28040	8987	17367	12782	8018	5695	25869	102824	0
Rents **4**	32127	0	9	1799	9146	2123	3275	7947	3523	1066	1859	1378	0
Royalties **5**	15545	0	0	0	0	49	0	82	808	0	0	14606	0
Other Portfolio Income **6**	228694	22160	129	4907	54067	12711	18275	7011	6166	4584	7748	90935	0
Other Receipts **7**	616674	-8198	24474	2321	157457	111714	109387	60022	28466	60795	11683	58554	0
Total Receipts **8**	121965952	1359420	5213790	3592939	29624363	20650201	20681986	11010683	8439580	9538138	2999467	8855384	0
Average Total Receipts **9**	7701	816	710	2431	7953	21601	43818	96585	196269	366851	499911	1106923	•
Operating Costs/Operating Income (%)													
Cost of Operations **10**	79.0	86.1	62.4	76.2	77.3	82.1	79.4	82.0	82.4	80.7	69.9	80.5	•
Salaries and Wages **11**	6.6	2.6	6.3	5.4	6.8	5.5	7.3	6.7	6.3	6.7	10.7	7.4	•
Taxes Paid **12**	1.2	0.6	1.5	1.4	1.3	1.1	1.2	1.0	0.9	0.9	1.7	1.3	•
Interest Paid **13**	1.0	4.1	0.5	0.5	0.7	0.9	0.8	1.0	0.8	1.0	2.0	2.8	•
Depreciation **14**	1.0	1.4	0.6	0.9	0.7	0.7	0.9	0.8	0.8	1.4	1.9	3.4	•
Amortization and Depletion **15**	0.1	0.2	0.1	0.0	0.0	0.0	0.0	0.0	0.1	0.2	0.3	0.8	•
Pensions and Other Deferred Comp. **16**	0.3	0.0	0.7	0.5	0.4	0.2	0.3	0.2	0.2	0.3	0.5	0.5	•
Employee Benefits **17**	0.6	0.4	0.6	0.6	0.5	0.5	0.8	0.5	0.6	0.8	0.8	1.3	•
Advertising **18**	0.3	0.3	1.2	0.6	0.3	0.3	0.3	0.4	0.3	0.2	0.4	0.1	•
Other Expenses **19**	6.9	5.1	17.7	7.6	7.4	5.7	5.8	6.4	5.7	6.4	9.3	5.6	•
Officers' Compensation **20**	1.8	1.2	4.9	3.6	2.5	1.5	1.7	0.9	0.9	0.5	3.0	0.7	•
Operating Margin **21**	1.1	•	3.7	2.6	2.2	1.4	1.6	0.1	1.0	0.9	•	•	•
Operating Margin Before Officers' Comp. **22**	2.9	•	8.6	6.1	4.7	3.0	3.2	1.0	2.0	1.4	2.5	•	•

Selected Average Balance Sheet ($ in Thousands)

Net Receivables 23	843	0	35	192	958	2156	4590	10481	20957	42575	72671	172862
Inventories 24	811	0	23	204	710	2729	4846	12417	26935	44247	35069	111728
Net Property, Plant and Equipment 25	558	0	13	64	353	1229	2668	4922	10245	24778	97522	334328
Total Assets 26	2921	0	117	753	2550	7047	15508	35344	65282	143183	331439	1022872
Notes and Loans Payable 27	950	0	45	302	725	2298	4710	13718	18995	51089	105169	350764
All Other Liabilities 28	776	0	40	199	721	1585	3660	8398	20549	39257	79382	304504
Net Worth 29	1196	0	33	252	1104	3164	7138	13229	25739	52836	146887	367603

Selected Financial Ratios (Times to 1)

Current Ratio 30	1.8	•	1.5	2.6	2.0	2.0	1.9	1.8	1.6	1.8	1.5	1.1
Quick Ratio 31	1.0	•	1.1	1.3	1.2	0.9	1.0	0.8	0.8	0.9	0.9	0.7
Net Sales to Working Capital 32	8.8	•	25.8	6.0	7.7	7.8	7.9	8.3	10.7	8.5	12.4	25.3
Coverage Ratio 33	3.1	0.8	10.2	6.5	5.6	3.4	3.8	1.8	2.9	2.7	1.5	1.0
Total Asset Turnover 34	2.6	•	6.0	3.2	3.1	3.0	2.8	2.7	3.0	2.5	1.5	1.0
Inventory Turnover 35	7.4	•	18.8	9.0	8.6	6.5	7.1	6.3	6.0	6.6	9.8	7.7
Receivables Turnover 36	8.6	•	33.9	11.7	8.8	8.7	9.5	8.0	8.0	7.6	6.9	5.5
Total Liabilities to Net Worth 37	1.4	•	2.5	2.0	1.3	1.2	1.2	1.7	1.5	1.7	1.3	1.8
Current Assets to Working Capital 38	2.3	•	2.9	1.6	2.0	2.0	2.1	2.3	2.7	2.3	3.1	8.0
Current Liabilities to Working Capital 39	1.3	0.8	1.9	0.6	1.0	1.0	1.1	1.3	1.7	1.3	2.1	7.0
Working Capital to Net Sales 40	0.1	•	0.0	0.2	0.1	0.1	0.1	0.1	0.1	0.1	0.1	0.0
Inventory to Working Capital 41	0.9	•	0.8	0.7	0.7	0.9	0.9	1.0	1.3	1.0	0.9	1.9
Total Receipts to Cash Flow 42	14.2	42.8	5.8	12.1	11.5	15.8	16.0	18.3	18.5	15.4	12.3	35.2
Cost of Goods to Cash Flow 43	11.2	36.8	3.6	9.2	8.9	13.0	12.7	15.0	15.2	12.5	8.6	28.3
Cash Flow to Total Debt 44	0.3	•	1.4	0.4	0.5	0.3	0.3	0.2	0.3	0.3	0.2	0.0

Selected Financial Factors (in Percentages)

Debt Ratio 45	59.1	•	71.8	66.5	56.7	55.1	54.0	62.6	60.6	63.1	55.7	64.1
Return on Total Assets 46	8.1	•	28.1	11.4	11.4	9.0	8.7	5.2	7.2	6.8	4.6	2.8
Return on Equity Before Income Taxes 47	13.2	•	89.9	28.7	21.7	14.1	13.9	6.4	12.1	11.6	3.7	•
Return on Equity After Income Taxes 48	11.7	•	89.1	27.6	20.3	13.4	12.6	4.6	11.2	9.9	0.8	•
Profit Margin (Before Income Tax) 49	2.1	•	4.2	3.0	3.0	2.1	2.3	0.9	1.6	1.7	1.1	•
Profit Margin (After Income Tax) 50	1.8	•	4.2	2.9	2.8	2.0	2.1	0.6	1.5	1.4	0.2	•

Table II

Corporations with Net Income

LUMBER AND OTHER CONSTRUCTION MATERIALS

MONEY AMOUNTS AND SIZE OF ASSETS IN THOUSANDS OF DOLLARS

Item Description for Accounting Period 7/07 Through 6/08	Total	Zero Assets	Under 500	500 to 1,000	1,000 to 5,000	5,000 to 10,000	10,000 to 25,000	25,000 to 50,000	50,000 to 100,000	100,000 to 250,000	250,000 to 500,000	500,000 to 2,500,000	2,500,000 and over
Number of Enterprises 1	10247	665	4529	930	2864	751	371	75	31	23	3	4	0
Revenues ($ in Thousands)													
Net Sales 2	95821293	889071	2765954	2446525	24819345	17396310	16533632	7642849	6017473	7446868	2432966	7430301	0
Interest 3	109620	4	734	5085	22886	6223	13197	10236	6313	5653	22434	16855	0
Rents 4	24252	0	9	1438	7952	1889	2737	7928	30	551	1440	278	0
Royalties 5	14737	0	0	0	0	49	0	82	0	0	0	14606	0
Other Portfolio Income 6	180918	12776	126	568	47506	7969	16492	4828	5315	2869	6706	75761	0
Other Receipts 7	484093	1209	18229	1063	130109	91770	82153	43646	20181	55021	7843	32869	0
Total Receipts 8	96634913	903060	2785052	2454679	25027798	17504210	16648211	7709569	6049312	7510962	2471389	7570670	0
Average Total Receipts 9	9431	1358	615	2639	8739	23308	44874	102794	195139	326564	823796	1892668	•
Operating Costs/Operating Income (%)													
Cost of Operations 10	79.0	90.7	57.8	75.1	78.3	82.0	79.0	82.2	79.2	80.5	71.0	80.2	•
Salaries and Wages 11	6.4	0.6	4.3	3.9	6.4	5.7	6.9	6.3	7.2	6.5	8.7	7.7	•
Taxes Paid 12	1.1	0.5	1.7	1.3	1.2	1.1	1.1	0.9	1.1	0.9	1.6	1.3	•
Interest Paid 13	0.7	0.4	0.4	0.4	0.5	0.7	0.6	0.7	0.8	1.0	1.7	0.9	•
Depreciation 14	0.9	0.1	0.8	0.9	0.5	0.5	0.9	0.6	0.8	1.2	2.0	2.3	•
Amortization and Depletion 15	0.1	0.0	0.0	0.0	0.0	0.0	0.0	0.0	0.1	0.2	0.1	0.4	•
Pensions and Other Deferred Comp. 16	0.3	0.0	1.1	0.7	0.4	0.2	0.3	0.2	0.2	0.4	0.5	0.5	•
Employee Benefits 17	0.6	0.1	0.7	0.5	0.4	0.5	0.8	0.5	0.7	0.7	0.8	1.3	•
Advertising 18	0.3	0.1	1.5	0.4	0.2	0.2	0.3	0.2	0.3	0.2	0.5	0.0	•
Other Expenses 19	6.0	2.5	15.7	7.0	6.0	4.9	5.6	5.5	6.1	6.3	8.3	5.1	•
Officers' Compensation 20	1.8	0.3	5.6	3.6	2.5	1.6	1.7	1.0	1.2	0.6	3.1	0.7	•
Operating Margin 21	2.8	4.7	10.4	6.2	3.5	2.6	2.8	1.9	2.3	1.5	1.8	•	•
Operating Margin Before Officers' Comp. 22	4.6	4.9	16.0	9.8	6.0	4.2	4.4	2.8	3.5	2.1	4.9	0.2	•

Selected Average Balance Sheet ($ in Thousands)

Net Receivables 23	996	0	23	196	1036	2217	4516	10674	22712	40621	99930	218366
Inventories 24	1010	0	25	207	760	2921	5004	13072	23822	36360	55266	211685
Net Property, Plant and Equipment 25	566	0	14	65	304	1030	2684	4160	10364	24840	163298	336183
Total Assets 26	3259	0	89	793	2649	6945	15491	35667	66853	137483	373652	1167172
Notes and Loans Payable 27	855	0	29	159	645	1903	4123	11538	18475	47716	115877	197047
All Other Liabilities 28	832	0	32	242	697	1372	3377	7559	18900	36882	110294	387058
Net Worth 29	1572	0	28	391	1307	3670	7991	16570	29477	52884	147480	583066

Selected Financial Ratios (Times to 1)

Current Ratio 30	2.1	•	2.4	2.4	2.1	2.4	2.2	2.2	1.7	1.8	1.7	1.6
Quick Ratio 31	1.1	•	1.7	1.4	1.3	1.1	1.2	1.0	0.9	0.9	1.0	0.9
Net Sales to Working Capital 32	7.8	•	15.1	6.5	7.4	7.1	7.0	6.9	8.7	8.0	11.6	10.8
Coverage Ratio 33	6.4	18.6	27.0	16.2	9.2	5.8	6.5	4.7	4.5	3.4	3.0	3.9
Total Asset Turnover 34	2.9	•	6.8	3.3	3.3	3.3	2.9	2.9	2.9	2.4	2.2	1.6
Inventory Turnover 35	7.3	•	14.0	9.6	8.9	6.5	7.0	6.4	6.5	7.2	10.4	7.0
Receivables Turnover 36	8.4	•	42.4	10.2	8.7	8.7	9.3	7.4	•	7.1	•	6.7
Total Liabilities to Net Worth 37	1.1	•	2.1	1.0	1.0	0.9	0.9	1.2	1.3	1.6	1.5	1.0
Current Assets to Working Capital 38	1.9	•	1.7	1.7	1.9	1.7	1.8	1.8	2.3	2.2	2.5	2.7
Current Liabilities to Working Capital 39	0.9	•	0.7	0.7	0.9	0.7	0.8	0.8	1.3	1.2	1.5	1.7
Working Capital to Net Sales 40	0.1	•	0.1	0.2	0.1	0.1	0.1	0.1	0.1	0.1	0.1	0.1
Inventory to Working Capital 41	0.8	•	0.5	0.6	0.6	0.8	0.8	0.7	1.1	0.9	0.8	0.8
Total Receipts to Cash Flow 42	12.6	12.8	4.4	9.0	11.4	14.9	13.6	15.1	14.3	14.1	10.7	20.5
Cost of Goods to Cash Flow 43	10.0	11.6	2.5	6.7	8.9	12.2	10.8	12.5	11.3	11.3	7.6	16.4
Cash Flow to Total Debt 44	0.4	•	2.3	0.7	0.6	0.5	0.4	0.4	0.4	0.3	0.3	0.2

Selected Financial Factors (in Percentages)

Debt Ratio 45	51.8	•	68.2	50.6	50.7	47.2	48.4	53.5	55.9	61.5	60.5	50.0
Return on Total Assets 46	12.6	•	78.8	23.0	15.7	12.9	11.8	10.0	10.7	7.8	11.0	5.6
Return on Equity Before Income Taxes 47	22.0	•	238.8	43.7	28.4	20.3	19.3	16.9	18.8	14.4	18.5	8.4
Return on Equity After Income Taxes 48	20.3	•	237.2	42.6	26.9	19.5	17.8	14.7	17.8	12.5	12.8	5.4
Profit Margin (Before Income Tax) 49	3.7	6.3	11.1	6.5	4.3	3.2	3.5	2.8	2.9	2.3	3.4	2.6
Profit Margin (After Income Tax) 50	3.4	6.2	11.0	6.3	4.1	3.1	3.2	2.4	2.7	2.0	2.3	1.7

Table I

Corporations with and without Net Income

PROFESSIONAL AND COMMERCIAL EQUIPMENT AND SUPPLIES

MONEY AMOUNTS AND SIZE OF ASSETS IN THOUSANDS OF DOLLARS

Item Description for Accounting Period 7/07 Through 6/08	Total	Zero Assets	Under 500	500 to 1,000	1,000 to 5,000	5,000 to 10,000	10,000 to 25,000	25,000 to 50,000	50,000 to 100,000	100,000 to 250,000	250,000 to 500,000	500,000 to 2,500,000	2,500,000 and over
Number of Enterprises **1**	32105	4383	19279	3023	4126	583	412	130	60	60	15	24	10
Revenues ($ in Thousands)													
Net Sales **2**	219781897	9568743	13299492	6515191	23557483	19288557	18494120	11844796	7744367	19864672	6456127	35724252	47424097
Interest **3**	903049	9523	5352	4769	15323	13253	22055	12373	21874	49645	32409	260593	455883
Rents **4**	324964	11	307	847	5514	2871	1526	29	17897	2558	69958	68580	154866
Royalties **5**	101216	0	0	0	267	2	16643	489	1272	20523	12597	17352	32072
Other Portfolio Income **6**	396921	40	2039	12139	28566	11601	41925	3723	54349	29354	46554	29451	137181
Other Receipts **7**	1688490	38652	38844	130240	157126	127373	91227	92871	75094	114635	58925	359947	403551
Total Receipts **8**	223196537	9616969	13346034	6663186	23764279	19443657	18667496	11954281	7914853	20081387	6676570	36460175	48607650
Average Total Receipts **9**	6952	2194	692	2204	5760	33351	45309	91956	131914	334690	445105	1519174	4860765
Operating Costs/Operating Income (%)													
Cost of Operations **10**	76.8	91.5	61.7	64.5	64.5	83.9	77.6	75.0	75.8	78.9	74.6	79.1	80.8
Salaries and Wages **11**	8.0	3.8	9.1	11.6	11.2	7.0	7.7	9.9	9.0	7.0	8.5	7.9	6.8
Taxes Paid **12**	1.0	0.4	1.8	1.6	1.7	0.7	1.0	1.0	1.2	0.8	1.1	0.8	0.9
Interest Paid **13**	0.9	1.2	0.5	0.9	0.7	0.3	0.6	0.8	1.2	0.9	1.2	1.2	1.1
Depreciation **14**	1.0	0.1	0.6	0.4	1.0	0.4	0.7	1.1	1.4	0.8	1.3	1.2	1.5
Amortization and Depletion **15**	0.3	0.2	0.1	0.1	0.1	0.0	0.2	0.2	0.4	0.3	0.8	0.4	0.3
Pensions and Other Deferred Comp. **16**	0.2	0.1	0.3	0.3	0.3	0.2	0.2	0.2	0.2	0.3	0.2	0.2	0.2
Employee Benefits **17**	0.7	0.2	0.4	0.6	1.0	0.5	0.6	0.9	0.9	0.6	0.8	0.9	0.8
Advertising **18**	0.8	0.0	0.7	1.0	0.9	0.4	0.8	0.4	0.9	0.6	2.3	0.9	0.8
Other Expenses **19**	7.9	5.1	13.4	13.8	12.4	4.9	8.1	7.3	8.5	7.3	9.5	5.8	6.7
Officers' Compensation **20**	1.5	0.9	6.3	4.9	4.0	1.1	1.6	1.3	0.9	0.5	0.6	0.4	0.2
Operating Margin **21**	0.9	•	5.2	0.3	2.1	0.6	1.0	1.9	•	2.1	•	1.2	•
Operating Margin Before Officers' Comp. **22**	2.4	•	11.5	5.2	6.1	1.7	2.7	3.1	0.6	2.6	•	1.7	•

Selected Average Balance Sheet ($ in Thousands)

876	0	31	206	699	2819	5542	14049	22443	51502	98222	209138	732651
541	0	26	185	440	1984	3771	8374	15985	31711	53816	128651	394748
240	0	13	58	257	605	1452	3558	7607	10214	16111	76866	164422
3374	0	120	741	2077	7040	15122	37549	71233	159298	323012	928189	3904229
895	0	60	255	681	1531	3638	8533	16072	40717	90389	256101	957738
1210	0	44	331	942	2858	6892	16220	29371	64859	129767	366575	1010506
1270	0	16	155	453	2651	4593	12796	25790	53722	102856	305514	1935985

Row labels (top to bottom): Net Receivables 23; Inventories 24; Net Property, Plant and Equipment 25; Total Assets 26; Notes and Loans Payable 27; All Other Liabilities 28; Net Worth 29

Selected Financial Ratios (Times to 1)

Row													
Current Ratio 30	1.5	•	1.9	1.7	1.5	1.7	1.5	1.5	1.4	1.4	1.4	1.6	1.4
Quick Ratio 31	0.9	•	1.2	0.9	1.0	1.1	1.0	0.9	0.8	0.8	0.8	0.9	0.7
Net Sales to Working Capital 32	10.7	•	14.6	8.7	10.3	14.3	10.8	9.7	9.5	10.8	8.4	8.1	10.8
Coverage Ratio 33	3.9	•	11.1	3.8	5.1	6.0	4.5	4.5	2.7	4.9	3.4	4.0	2.9
Total Asset Turnover 34	2.0	•	5.7	2.9	2.7	4.7	3.0	2.4	1.8	2.1	1.3	1.6	1.2
Inventory Turnover 35	9.7	•	16.4	7.5	8.4	14.0	9.2	8.2	6.1	8.2	6.0	9.2	9.7
Receivables Turnover 36	7.8	•	23.3	9.5	8.2	13.1	8.1	7.1	6.4	6.9	4.3	6.6	6.2
Total Liabilities to Net Worth 37	1.7	•	6.4	3.8	3.6	1.7	2.3	1.9	1.8	2.0	2.1	2.0	1.0
Current Assets to Working Capital 38	3.0	•	2.1	2.4	2.9	2.5	2.9	2.9	3.5	3.5	3.7	2.6	3.7
Current Liabilities to Working Capital 39	2.0	•	1.1	1.4	1.9	1.5	1.9	1.9	2.5	2.5	2.7	1.6	2.7
Working Capital to Net Sales 40	0.1	•	0.1	0.1	0.1	0.1	0.1	0.1	0.1	0.1	0.1	0.1	0.1
Inventory to Working Capital 41	0.9	•	0.6	0.8	0.9	0.8	0.9	0.9	1.2	1.1	0.9	0.7	0.9
Total Receipts to Cash Flow 42	11.3	64.0	6.3	7.5	7.7	18.8	11.7	11.2	11.4	10.9	9.8	12.7	13.0
Cost of Goods to Cash Flow 43	8.7	58.6	3.9	4.9	5.0	15.8	9.1	8.4	8.6	8.6	7.3	10.0	10.5
Cash Flow to Total Debt 44	0.3	•	1.1	0.5	0.5	0.4	0.3	0.3	0.2	0.3	0.2	0.2	0.2

Selected Financial Factors (in Percentages)

Row													
Debt Ratio 45	62.4	•	86.5	79.1	78.2	62.3	69.6	65.9	63.8	66.3	68.2	67.1	50.4
Return on Total Assets 46	7.0	•	35.0	9.9	10.2	7.7	7.5	8.7	6.1	8.8	5.4	7.5	4.1
Return on Equity Before Income Taxes 47	13.7	•	235.8	35.1	37.5	17.1	19.1	19.9	10.6	20.8	11.9	17.2	5.4
Return on Equity After Income Taxes 48	10.5	•	234.7	33.0	33.5	14.8	15.4	17.3	6.8	16.4	6.3	11.3	3.5
Profit Margin (Before Income Tax) 49	2.5	•	5.5	2.5	3.0	1.4	2.0	2.8	2.1	3.4	2.9	3.5	2.2
Profit Margin (After Income Tax) 50	1.9	•	5.5	2.4	2.7	1.2	1.6	2.4	1.4	2.7	1.5	2.3	1.4

Table II

Corporations with Net Income

PROFESSIONAL AND COMMERCIAL EQUIPMENT AND SUPPLIES

MONEY AMOUNTS AND SIZE OF ASSETS IN THOUSANDS OF DOLLARS

Item Description for Accounting Period 7/07 Through 6/08	Total	Zero Assets	Under 500	500 to 1,000	1,000 to 5,000	5,000 to 10,000	10,000 to 25,000	25,000 to 50,000	50,000 to 100,000	100,000 to 250,000	250,000 to 500,000	500,000 to 2,500,000	2,500,000 and over
Number of Enterprises **1**	20816	1310	•	2451	2973	486	301	116	42	50	10	18	•
Revenues ($ in Thousands)													
Net Sales **2**	185383669	8266418	•	5494440	18613126	12807206	14494767	11091123	6439015	16774755	5009465	31616481	•
Interest **3**	734610	1036	•	3589	14220	9532	16400	10910	9616	44518	28595	224910	•
Rents **4**	314406	0	•	847	3643	2871	748	29	16632	2447	69798	65984	•
Royalties **5**	94324	0	•	0	267	0	16643	161	1267	20523	8425	14966	•
Other Portfolio Income **6**	373379	40	•	11421	27056	11423	38729	1003	48709	27821	39238	29176	•
Other Receipts **7**	1259969	55359	•	122451	140335	98145	73924	87321	40720	110786	35962	224665	•
Total Receipts **8**	188160357	8322853	•	5632748	18798647	12929177	14641211	11190547	6555959	16980850	5191483	32176182	•
Average Total Receipts **9**	9039	6353	•	2298	6323	26603	48642	96470	156094	339617	519148	1787566	•
Operating Costs/Operating Income (%)													
Cost of Operations **10**	76.3	94.0	•	63.7	61.5	78.3	75.6	75.5	75.8	78.6	71.7	79.4	•
Salaries and Wages **11**	7.7	2.2	•	10.7	11.5	8.9	7.7	9.7	8.0	6.8	9.0	7.4	•
Taxes Paid **12**	1.0	0.3	•	1.5	1.8	0.9	1.1	1.0	1.2	0.8	1.1	0.7	•
Interest Paid **13**	0.7	0.1	•	0.9	0.6	0.3	0.4	0.6	0.8	0.8	1.1	0.8	•
Depreciation **14**	0.9	0.0	•	0.3	1.0	0.5	0.7	0.9	1.3	0.8	1.5	1.2	•
Amortization and Depletion **15**	0.2	0.0	•	0.1	0.0	0.0	0.1	0.2	0.2	0.2	0.8	0.3	•
Pensions and Other Deferred Comp. **16**	0.2	0.0	•	0.2	0.4	0.2	0.2	0.3	0.2	0.3	0.2	0.2	•
Employee Benefits **17**	0.7	0.1	•	0.5	1.1	0.7	0.6	0.8	0.8	0.6	0.9	0.9	•
Advertising **18**	0.8	0.0	•	1.2	0.9	0.4	0.7	0.3	0.9	0.6	2.7	0.9	•
Other Expenses **19**	7.6	2.3	•	13.1	12.2	6.1	7.9	6.8	7.4	7.1	9.5	5.5	•
Officers' Compensation **20**	1.3	0.3	•	4.6	3.7	1.6	1.9	1.2	0.8	0.6	0.5	0.4	•
Operating Margin **21**	2.5	0.5	•	3.1	5.3	2.1	3.1	2.6	2.5	2.9	1.1	2.3	•
Operating Margin Before Officers' Comp. **22**	3.8	0.9	•	7.8	9.0	3.7	4.9	3.9	3.3	3.5	1.5	2.6	•

Selected Average Balance Sheet ($ in Thousands)

Net Receivables 23	1116	0	192	756	2746	5848	14782	22605	53489	84219	226012	•
Inventories 24	679	0	189	421	2057	4108	8001	19364	32896	55112	153454	•
Net Property, Plant and Equipment 25	311	0	60	285	594	1554	3173	9104	10968	21840	91847	•
Total Assets 26	4342	0	747	2162	7042	15204	37249	71620	157662	316931	999855	•
Notes and Loans Payable 27	1008	0	253	479	1117	2923	7510	13672	38812	80978	249941	•
All Other Liabilities 28	1494	0	227	887	2789	6322	16395	31132	62858	117905	404311	•
Net Worth 29	1840	0	267	796	3136	5959	13344	26816	55991	118048	345603	•

Selected Financial Ratios (Times to 1)

Current Ratio 30	1.6	•	2.4	1.8	1.8	1.7	1.6	1.4	1.5	1.3	1.6	•
Quick Ratio 31	0.9	•	1.2	1.2	1.1	1.1	0.9	0.8	0.9	0.7	0.9	•
Net Sales to Working Capital 32	10.2	•	6.3	8.7	10.5	9.3	9.6	10.3	9.4	13.0	8.7	•
Coverage Ratio 33	6.5	10.1	7.4	11.9	11.5	11.5	6.5	6.6	6.8	5.7	6.1	•
Total Asset Turnover 34	2.1	•	3.0	2.9	3.7	3.2	2.6	2.1	2.1	1.6	1.8	•
Inventory Turnover 35	10.0	•	7.5	9.1	10.0	8.9	9.0	6.0	8.0	6.5	9.1	•
Receivables Turnover 36	8.1	•	9.3	8.2	10.4	7.8	7.4	•	6.8	•	7.2	•
Total Liabilities to Net Worth 37	1.4	•	1.8	1.7	1.2	1.6	1.8	1.7	1.8	1.7	1.9	•
Current Assets to Working Capital 38	2.8	•	1.7	2.3	2.3	2.4	2.8	3.3	3.1	4.7	2.7	•
Current Liabilities to Working Capital 39	1.8	•	0.7	1.3	1.3	1.4	1.8	2.3	2.1	3.7	1.7	•
Working Capital to Net Sales 40	0.1	•	0.2	0.1	0.1	0.1	0.1	0.1	0.1	0.1	0.1	•
Inventory to Working Capital 41	0.8	•	0.6	0.6	0.8	0.8	0.8	1.3	0.9	1.4	0.8	•
Total Receipts to Cash Flow 42	9.8	30.2	6.4	6.3	12.5	9.5	10.8	9.7	9.8	8.2	12.0	•
Cost of Goods to Cash Flow 43	7.5	28.4	4.1	3.9	9.8	7.2	8.2	7.4	7.7	5.9	9.5	•
Cash Flow to Total Debt 44	0.4	•	0.7	0.7	0.5	0.5	0.4	0.4	0.3	0.3	0.2	•

Selected Financial Factors (in Percentages)

Debt Ratio 45	57.6	•	64.2	63.2	55.5	60.8	64.2	62.6	64.5	62.8	65.4	•
Return on Total Assets 46	9.9	•	19.6	19.9	12.7	14.2	10.7	10.9	10.9	9.8	9.1	•
Return on Equity Before Income Taxes 47	19.9	•	47.5	49.6	26.0	33.2	25.4	24.8	26.2	21.7	21.9	•
Return on Equity After Income Taxes 48	16.4	•	45.9	46.5	23.7	29.3	22.6	19.5	21.1	14.3	15.0	•
Profit Margin (Before Income Tax) 49	4.1	1.2	5.7	6.3	3.1	4.1	3.5	4.3	4.4	5.1	4.3	•
Profit Margin (After Income Tax) 50	3.4	1.1	5.5	5.9	2.8	3.6	3.2	3.4	3.5	3.4	3.0	•

Table I

Corporations with and without Net Income

METAL AND MINERAL (EXCEPT PETROLEUM)

MONEY AMOUNTS AND SIZE OF ASSETS IN THOUSANDS OF DOLLARS

Item Description for Accounting Period 7/07 Through 6/08		Total	Zero Assets	Under 500	500 to 1,000	1,000 to 5,000	5,000 to 10,000	10,000 to 25,000	25,000 to 50,000	50,000 to 100,000	100,000 to 250,000	250,000 to 500,000	500,000 to 2,500,000	2,500,000 and over
Number of Enterprises	1	5866	16	3456	480	1091	352	249	73	70	35	21	18	4
Revenues ($ in Thousands)														
Net Sales	2	149930396	1084115	1618448	1326899	10843261	9147817	11665396	7021902	12942011	14403751	15484652	33325975	30526168
Interest	3	490354	1813	632	1680	7987	5647	9109	7221	15291	26746	55900	71123	287206
Rents	4	182152	268	0	0	338	100	1362	872	1414	688	2604	32160	142345
Royalties	5	2843	0	0	0	2097	0	0	0	84	247	11	4	400
Other Portfolio Income	6	419882	3	0	2176	17839	707	10672	4671	81013	15872	15448	164244	107235
Other Receipts	7	936957	3121	1711	3291	37991	18042	110959	8689	52754	94890	112110	197580	295822
Total Receipts	8	151422584	1089320	1620791	1334046	10909513	9172313	11797498	7043355	13092567	14542194	15670725	33791086	31359176
Average Total Receipts	9	25814	68082	469	2779	10000	26058	47380	96484	187037	415491	746225	1877283	7839794
Operating Costs/Operating Income (%)														
Cost of Operations	10	88.0	92.9	63.6	76.4	84.9	87.5	86.7	88.9	87.3	89.8	89.4	88.6	89.2
Salaries and Wages	11	3.0	1.7	13.2	3.3	3.5	2.5	2.9	2.7	3.0	1.9	2.1	3.4	2.9
Taxes Paid	12	0.6	0.3	1.8	1.2	0.8	0.5	0.7	0.6	0.6	0.6	0.6	0.5	0.5
Interest Paid	13	1.3	0.3	0.6	0.3	0.4	0.6	0.5	0.8	0.7	0.9	0.8	1.4	2.8
Depreciation	14	0.5	0.2	0.4	0.4	0.3	0.2	0.5	0.6	0.5	0.3	0.5	0.5	0.8
Amortization and Depletion	15	0.2	0.0	0.1	0.0	0.0	0.0	0.0	0.1	0.0	0.1	0.2	0.2	0.4
Pensions and Other Deferred Comp.	16	0.2	0.1	0.7	0.9	0.3	0.1	0.2	0.1	0.1	0.2	0.2	0.3	0.1
Employee Benefits	17	0.4	0.2	0.6	0.9	0.4	0.3	0.3	0.3	0.3	0.3	0.4	0.7	0.4
Advertising	18	0.1	0.0	0.6	0.2	0.1	0.1	0.0	0.1	0.1	0.0	0.0	0.0	0.0
Other Expenses	19	3.2	1.9	9.1	5.3	4.7	2.5	3.2	2.5	3.0	2.2	3.7	3.0	2.9
Officers' Compensation	20	0.9	0.3	6.5	7.4	2.7	1.7	1.4	0.9	0.9	0.4	0.3	0.5	0.3
Operating Margin	21	1.8	2.0	2.9	3.6	2.0	4.0	3.4	2.5	3.2	3.3	1.8	1.0	•
Operating Margin Before Officers' Comp.	22	2.7	2.3	9.3	11.1	4.7	5.7	4.9	3.4	4.2	3.7	2.1	1.5	0.0

Selected Average Balance Sheet ($ in Thousands)

Net Receivables 23	3167	0	45	242	931	2125	5074	10501	20536	47096	89735	227805	1360157
Inventories 24	3097	0	25	90	752	2749	5603	16186	28550	73231	84892	260806	658796
Net Property, Plant and Equipment 25	2090	0	7	37	169	410	1579	3562	6678	11673	44427	166195	1609434
Total Assets 26	11378	0	142	739	2848	6661	15308	34960	70444	156021	363621	941066	4779028
Notes and Loans Payable 27	3898	0	55	104	333	2014	3861	10044	19543	52616	141020	316149	1998850
All Other Liabilities 28	4115	0	20	171	1004	2239	4452	12110	20739	47563	84316	374149	2122620
Net Worth 29	3365	0	67	465	1511	2409	6994	12807	30162	55842	138285	250767	657559

Selected Financial Ratios (Times to 1)

Current Ratio 30	1.7	•	2.7	2.4	2.1	1.7	1.9	1.6	1.9	2.0	1.7	2.0	1.4
Quick Ratio 31	0.9	•	2.0	1.8	1.3	0.9	1.0	0.8	0.8	0.8	0.9	0.9	0.8
Net Sales to Working Capital 32	7.9	•	6.2	8.2	7.9	10.4	7.7	8.6	6.6	6.6	8.0	6.4	11.4
Coverage Ratio 33	3.5	8.6	6.3	13.5	8.1	8.3	9.4	4.3	7.3	5.9	4.8	2.8	1.9
Total Asset Turnover 34	2.2	•	3.3	3.7	3.5	3.9	3.1	2.8	2.6	2.6	2.0	2.0	1.6
Inventory Turnover 35	7.2	•	11.9	23.4	11.2	8.3	7.3	5.3	5.7	5.0	7.8	6.3	10.3
Receivables Turnover 36	8.3	•	13.4	18.1	13.0	10.5	9.1	7.5	9.5	7.4	9.0	8.8	6.1
Total Liabilities to Net Worth 37	2.4	•	1.1	0.6	0.9	1.8	1.2	1.7	1.3	1.8	1.6	2.8	6.3
Current Assets to Working Capital 38	2.3	•	1.6	1.7	1.9	2.3	2.1	2.6	2.1	2.0	2.4	2.0	3.7
Current Liabilities to Working Capital 39	1.3	•	0.6	0.7	0.9	1.3	1.1	1.6	1.1	1.0	1.4	1.0	2.7
Working Capital to Net Sales 40	0.1	•	0.2	0.1	0.1	0.1	0.1	0.1	0.2	0.2	0.1	0.2	0.1
Inventory to Working Capital 41	1.0	•	0.3	0.4	0.7	1.1	1.0	1.1	1.1	1.0	0.9	0.9	1.0
Total Receipts to Cash Flow 42	19.6	24.9	9.6	12.8	16.1	16.3	14.5	22.3	16.1	16.7	16.7	22.9	33.7
Cost of Goods to Cash Flow 43	17.3	23.1	6.1	9.8	13.7	14.3	12.6	19.8	14.0	15.0	14.9	20.3	30.1
Cash Flow to Total Debt 44	0.2	•	0.6	0.8	0.5	0.4	0.4	0.2	0.3	0.2	0.2	0.1	0.1

Selected Financial Factors (in Percentages)

Debt Ratio 45	70.4	•	52.9	37.1	47.0	63.8	54.3	63.4	57.2	64.2	62.0	73.4	86.2
Return on Total Assets 46	9.9	•	11.8	16.4	10.4	18.8	15.6	9.9	13.4	13.5	7.7	7.5	8.3
Return on Equity Before Income Taxes 47	24.0	•	21.1	24.1	17.2	45.6	30.5	20.9	27.0	31.4	16.0	18.1	28.5
Return on Equity After Income Taxes 48	18.6	•	19.8	23.0	16.4	41.2	26.9	17.1	22.3	22.3	11.3	13.3	17.8
Profit Margin (Before Income Tax) 49	3.2	2.5	3.0	4.1	2.6	4.2	4.6	2.8	4.4	4.3	3.0	2.5	2.5
Profit Margin (After Income Tax) 50	2.5	1.9	2.8	3.9	2.5	3.8	4.0	2.3	3.6	3.0	2.1	1.8	1.5

Table II
Corporations with Net Income

METAL AND MINERAL (EXCEPT PETROLEUM)

MONEY AMOUNTS AND SIZE OF ASSETS IN THOUSANDS OF DOLLARS

Item Description for Accounting Period 7/07 Through 6/08	Total	Zero Assets	Under 500	500 to 1,000	1,000 to 5,000	5,000 to 10,000	10,000 to 25,000	25,000 to 50,000	50,000 to 100,000	100,000 to 250,000	250,000 to 500,000	500,000 to 2,500,000	2,500,000 and over
Number of Enterprises 1	3965	8	•	480	997	314	232	62	62	30	17	15	•
Revenues ($ in Thousands)													
Net Sales 2	128548710	1084115	•	1326899	10205654	8888036	10929616	6185863	11658671	13420037	12694379	24571202	•
Interest 3	429952	1813	•	1680	5685	3089	8660	7110	14625	21601	54091	56889	•
Rents 4	168252	268	•	0	155	100	1256	857	1325	618	907	20430	•
Royalties 5	1155	0	•	0	1015	0	0	0	84	41	11	4	•
Other Portfolio Income 6	403804	3	•	2176	14193	707	10672	4596	80718	15204	15099	153678	•
Other Receipts 7	833161	3121	•	3291	33527	19232	105845	6408	51656	90506	102935	172075	•
Total Receipts 8	130385034	1089320	•	1334046	10260229	8911164	11056049	6204834	11807079	13548007	12867422	24974278	•
Average Total Receipts 9	32884	136165	•	2779	10291	28380	47655	100078	190437	451600	756907	1664952	•
Operating Costs/Operating Income (%)													
Cost of Operations 10	87.7	92.9	•	76.4	85.4	87.5	86.1	88.5	86.6	89.7	89.3	85.6	•
Salaries and Wages 11	2.8	1.7	•	3.3	3.0	2.5	3.1	2.6	3.2	2.0	2.1	4.0	•
Taxes Paid 12	0.6	0.3	•	1.2	0.7	0.5	0.7	0.6	0.6	0.6	0.6	0.6	•
Interest Paid 13	1.0	0.3	•	0.3	0.3	0.5	0.5	0.8	0.7	0.8	0.3	1.6	•
Depreciation 14	0.5	0.2	•	0.4	0.2	0.2	0.5	0.6	0.6	0.2	0.5	0.6	•
Amortization and Depletion 15	0.1	0.0	•	0.0	0.0	0.0	0.0	0.0	0.0	0.0	0.2	0.2	•
Pensions and Other Deferred Comp. 16	0.2	0.1	•	0.9	0.3	0.1	0.2	0.1	0.2	0.2	0.2	0.2	•
Employee Benefits 17	0.4	0.2	•	0.9	0.3	0.3	0.4	0.3	0.3	0.3	0.4	0.8	•
Advertising 18	0.1	0.0	•	0.2	0.1	0.1	0.1	0.0	0.1	0.0	0.0	0.0	•
Other Expenses 19	3.1	1.9	•	5.3	4.1	2.3	3.3	2.4	3.0	2.0	3.3	3.6	•
Officers' Compensation 20	0.9	0.3	•	7.4	2.6	1.7	1.5	1.0	1.0	0.4	0.3	0.4	•
Operating Margin 21	2.6	2.0	•	3.6	2.8	4.4	3.7	3.0	3.8	3.8	2.7	2.3	•
Operating Margin Before Officers' Comp. 22	3.6	2.3	•	11.1	5.4	6.1	5.2	4.0	4.8	4.2	3.0	2.7	•

Selected Average Balance Sheet ($ in Thousands)

Net Receivables 23	4085	0	242	965	2158	5078	11008	20778	48334	87674	221031
Inventories 24	4061	0	144	773	2907	5748	16728	27817	80676	91474	240580
Net Property, Plant and Equipment 25	1569	0	37	133	428	1578	3557	7210	10051	46772	156653
Total Assets 26	14179	0	739	2870	6711	15396	35732	70236	159255	362485	876485
Notes and Loans Payable 27	4717	0	104	280	1802	3839	9267	18817	52287	84419	279029
All Other Liabilities 28	4400	0	171	1017	2370	4293	12811	20157	48322	113206	314367
Net Worth 29	5061	0	465	1574	2539	7264	13654	31262	58646	164859	283090

Selected Financial Ratios (Times to 1)

Current Ratio 30	1.9	•	2.4	2.2	1.7	2.0	1.7	1.9	2.0	1.8	2.2
Quick Ratio 31	1.0	•	1.8	1.3	0.8	1.0	0.8	0.8	0.8	0.9	1.1
Net Sales to Working Capital 32	7.3	•	8.2	7.8	11.5	7.4	8.2	6.9	6.7	7.5	5.7
Coverage Ratio 33	5.1	8.6	13.5	11.4	9.9	10.4	5.1	8.3	6.9	12.5	3.5
Total Asset Turnover 34	2.3	•	3.7	3.6	4.2	3.1	2.8	2.7	2.8	2.1	1.9
Inventory Turnover 35	7.0	•	14.6	11.3	8.5	7.1	5.3	5.9	5.0	7.3	5.8
Receivables Turnover 36	8.1	•	•	13.2	10.9	8.9	7.6	9.5	8.1	8.4	•
Total Liabilities to Net Worth 37	1.8	•	0.6	0.8	1.6	1.1	1.6	1.2	1.7	1.2	2.1
Current Assets to Working Capital 38	2.1	•	1.7	1.8	2.4	2.0	2.4	2.1	2.0	2.3	1.8
Current Liabilities to Working Capital 39	1.1	•	0.7	0.8	1.4	1.0	1.4	1.1	1.0	1.3	0.8
Working Capital to Net Sales 40	0.1	•	0.1	0.1	0.1	0.1	0.1	0.1	0.1	0.1	0.2
Inventory to Working Capital 41	0.9	•	0.4	0.7	1.1	0.9	1.1	1.1	1.0	0.8	0.8
Total Receipts to Cash Flow 42	16.3	24.9	12.8	15.4	15.8	13.8	20.6	14.8	16.1	15.3	16.0
Cost of Goods to Cash Flow 43	14.3	23.1	9.8	13.1	13.8	11.9	18.2	12.8	14.4	13.6	13.7
Cash Flow to Total Debt 44	0.2	•	0.8	0.5	0.4	0.4	0.2	0.3	0.3	0.2	0.2

Selected Financial Factors (in Percentages)

Debt Ratio 45	64.3	•	37.1	45.2	52.8	62.2	61.8	55.5	63.2	54.5	67.7
Return on Total Assets 46	11.6	•	16.4	13.2	16.6	21.8	11.5	15.4	15.6	9.0	10.4
Return on Equity Before Income Taxes 47	26.1	•	24.1	21.9	31.7	51.9	24.2	30.5	36.3	18.2	23.2
Return on Equity After Income Taxes 48	20.7	•	23.0	21.0	28.0	47.1	19.9	25.3	26.2	13.4	18.0
Profit Margin (Before Income Tax) 49	4.1	2.5	4.1	3.4	4.9	4.7	3.3	5.1	4.8	4.0	4.0
Profit Margin (After Income Tax) 50	3.2	1.9	3.9	3.2	2.7	4.2	2.7	4.2	3.4	2.9	3.1

Table I

Corporations with and without Net Income

ELECTRICAL GOODS

Money Amounts and Size of Assets in Thousands of Dollars

Item Description for Accounting Period 7/07 Through 6/08		Total	Zero Assets	Under 500	500 to 1,000	1,000 to 5,000	5,000 to 10,000	10,000 to 25,000	25,000 to 50,000	50,000 to 100,000	100,000 to 250,000	250,000 to 500,000	500,000 to 2,500,000	2,500,000 and over
Number of Enterprises	1	27133	3698	14317	3896	3709	668	422	168	125	62	24	33	11
Revenues ($ in Thousands)														
Net Sales	2	326093468	2730392	8888212	7806908	26987347	12941388	20658426	13263626	21091485	23022459	17414316	68823415	102465493
Interest	3	1173067	2196	8775	5469	18009	9686	19011	24635	73288	47535	43428	395991	525043
Rents	4	152538	632	1581	0	2161	3360	2210	312	3659	15222	1767	25064	96570
Royalties	5	1014977	2912	20	0	0	0	0	395	4891	3921	42288	23664	936886
Other Portfolio Income	6	624819	3128	7940	796	18842	5797	62818	3318	36881	30831	16370	86548	351548
Other Receipts	7	3090376	247105	46795	58204	186823	58119	135107	154788	163508	116341	136680	939633	847279
Total Receipts	8	332149245	2986365	8953323	7871377	27213182	13018350	20877572	13447074	21373712	23236309	17654849	70294315	105222819
Average Total Receipts	9	12242	808	625	2020	7337	19489	49473	80042	170990	374779	735619	2130131	9565711
Operating Costs/Operating Income (%)														
Cost of Operations	10	81.6	77.2	59.9	71.7	75.2	77.5	84.0	77.9	81.7	84.9	85.7	87.3	81.4
Salaries and Wages	11	6.1	15.7	11.4	8.8	7.7	8.0	6.2	8.1	6.6	5.3	5.5	4.8	5.3
Taxes Paid	12	0.8	1.1	2.0	1.4	1.2	1.1	0.8	1.0	0.9	0.8	0.5	0.8	0.5
Interest Paid	13	0.7	2.0	1.1	0.8	0.5	0.8	0.5	0.6	0.8	0.5	0.6	0.7	0.9
Depreciation	14	0.6	0.7	0.8	0.3	0.4	0.5	0.4	0.5	0.6	0.5	0.6	0.5	0.9
Amortization and Depletion	15	1.4	0.4	0.0	0.0	0.0	0.1	0.1	0.2	0.2	0.1	0.2	0.2	4.1
Pensions and Other Deferred Comp.	16	0.3	0.0	0.8	0.3	0.5	0.2	0.2	0.3	0.4	0.2	0.2	0.3	0.2
Employee Benefits	17	0.6	0.7	1.0	0.4	0.6	0.7	0.5	0.6	0.6	0.5	0.8	0.5	0.5
Advertising	18	1.2	0.6	0.5	0.7	1.0	0.4	0.3	0.7	0.6	0.8	0.8	0.8	2.2
Other Expenses	19	5.7	15.7	13.2	10.4	7.4	7.8	5.4	7.3	5.4	5.3	4.3	4.3	4.7
Officers' Compensation	20	1.0	2.2	7.9	4.5	3.2	1.9	1.2	1.1	0.9	0.4	0.5	0.2	0.2
Operating Margin	21	0.1	•	1.3	0.8	2.1	1.1	0.5	1.7	1.4	0.7	0.5	•	•
Operating Margin Before Officers' Comp.	22	1.1	•	9.2	5.2	5.3	3.0	1.7	2.8	2.4	1.1	0.9	•	•

Selected Average Balance Sheet ($ in Thousands)

Net Receivables 23	1830	0	31	179	842	2696	6364	13074	25478	60471	110227	329891	1658637
Inventories 24	1104	0	19	219	724	2610	4966	10101	18862	37943	85557	166829	758478
Net Property, Plant and Equipment 25	417	0	16	107	203	513	1056	1984	5589	9372	18097	54179	482001
Total Assets 26	5810	0	115	737	2407	7604	15753	34587	68760	152189	353096	999387	6107108
Notes and Loans Payable 27	1247	0	132	230	556	2143	4432	6276	17222	32301	43792	119901	1404783
All Other Liabilities 28	2422	0	61	266	991	3070	8068	14171	29107	68760	168599	432583	2370730
Net Worth 29	2141	0	-79	241	860	2391	3252	14140	22430	51128	140705	446903	2331595

Selected Financial Ratios (Times to 1)

Current Ratio 30	1.5	•	1.2	2.0	1.8	1.6	1.4	1.8	1.5	1.6	1.5	1.5	1.3
Quick Ratio 31	0.9	•	0.9	1.0	1.0	1.0	0.8	1.1	0.9	1.0	0.9	0.9	0.7
Net Sales to Working Capital 32	9.5	•	52.6	6.6	8.0	8.2	12.5	6.3	9.0	7.7	8.9	9.7	10.5
Coverage Ratio 33	3.8	•	2.9	3.1	7.3	3.2	4.3	6.1	4.7	4.4	4.5	4.0	3.2
Total Asset Turnover 34	2.1	•	5.4	2.7	3.0	2.5	3.1	2.3	2.5	2.4	2.1	2.1	1.5
Inventory Turnover 35	8.9	•	19.9	6.6	7.6	5.7	8.3	6.1	7.3	8.3	7.3	10.9	10.0
Receivables Turnover 36	6.9	•	19.9	12.0	9.1	6.8	7.7	5.8	7.0	5.6	6.2	7.3	6.0
Total Liabilities to Net Worth 37	1.7	•	•	2.1	1.8	2.2	3.8	1.4	2.1	2.0	1.5	1.2	1.6
Current Assets to Working Capital 38	3.1	•	6.9	2.0	2.3	2.7	3.5	2.2	3.0	2.6	3.0	3.0	4.1
Current Liabilities to Working Capital 39	2.1	•	5.9	1.0	1.3	1.7	2.5	1.2	2.0	1.6	2.0	2.0	3.1
Working Capital to Net Sales 40	0.1	•	0.0	0.2	0.1	0.1	0.1	0.2	0.1	0.1	0.1	0.1	0.1
Inventory to Working Capital 41	0.9	•	1.4	0.8	0.9	0.9	1.3	0.8	1.0	0.8	1.0	0.8	0.8
Total Receipts to Cash Flow 42	15.7	18.1	8.4	10.4	11.5	12.0	17.6	11.1	13.9	16.8	18.4	18.5	18.9
Cost of Goods to Cash Flow 43	12.8	13.9	5.0	7.5	8.6	9.3	14.8	8.6	11.3	14.3	15.7	16.2	15.4
Cash Flow to Total Debt 44	0.2	•	0.4	0.4	0.4	0.3	0.2	0.3	0.3	0.2	0.2	0.2	0.1

Selected Financial Factors (in Percentages)

Debt Ratio 45	63.1	•	168.5	67.2	64.3	68.6	79.4	59.1	67.4	66.4	60.2	55.3	61.8
Return on Total Assets 46	5.6	•	17.1	6.4	10.1	6.2	6.5	8.7	8.6	5.2	5.2	5.5	4.2
Return on Equity Before Income Taxes 47	11.1	•	•	13.2	24.5	13.6	24.1	17.7	20.8	11.9	10.1	9.1	7.5
Return on Equity After Income Taxes 48	8.5	•	•	11.7	22.0	11.1	18.3	15.3	17.0	8.8	8.0	6.0	5.8
Profit Margin (Before Income Tax) 49	2.0	•	2.1	1.6	2.9	1.7	1.6	3.2	2.8	1.6	2.0	2.0	1.9
Profit Margin (After Income Tax) 50	1.5	•	1.9	1.4	2.6	1.4	1.2	2.7	2.3	1.2	1.6	1.3	1.4

Table II

Corporations with Net Income

ELECTRICAL GOODS

MONEY AMOUNTS AND SIZE OF ASSETS IN THOUSANDS OF DOLLARS

Item Description for Accounting Period 7/07 Through 6/08		Total	Zero Assets	Under 500	500 to 1,000	1,000 to 5,000	5,000 to 10,000	10,000 to 25,000	25,000 to 50,000	50,000 to 100,000	100,000 to 250,000	250,000 to 500,000	500,000 to 2,500,000	2,500,000 and over
Number of Enterprises	1	16557	1640	8069	2607	3035	523	339	139	103	47	19	25	11
Revenues ($ in Thousands)														
Net Sales	2	291639241	1464885	6498469	6274402	24119365	11283037	17431877	12076998	17736993	18280386	15153417	58853918	102465493
Interest	3	1032133	653	6041	3821	16118	6941	13828	21236	59984	36923	33063	308483	525043
Rents	4	143111	160	1581	0	738	1128	1083	221	1100	14750	1533	24245	96570
Royalties	5	1002532	0	20	0	0	0	0	395	1825	3921	40736	18749	936886
Other Portfolio Income	6	566546	3047	6725	766	17515	5574	62657	3318	36815	24079	16338	38162	351548
Other Receipts	7	2540260	22398	46049	53073	177541	43649	123533	124229	131942	101599	126947	742025	847279
Total Receipts	8	296923823	1491143	6558885	6332062	24331277	11340329	17763978	12226397	17968659	18461658	15372034	59985582	105222819
Average Total Receipts	9	17933	909	813	2429	8017	21683	52015	87960	174453	392801	809054	2399423	9565711
Operating Costs/Operating Income (%)														
Cost of Operations	10	81.5	77.6	56.1	72.9	76.0	77.0	84.0	78.4	82.1	83.8	85.5	86.8	81.4
Salaries and Wages	11	6.0	4.3	12.6	8.3	7.3	7.7	5.9	7.5	6.2	5.7	6.0	4.9	5.3
Taxes Paid	12	0.8	0.6	2.0	1.3	1.1	1.1	0.7	0.9	0.9	0.9	0.5	0.9	0.5
Interest Paid	13	0.6	0.5	0.4	0.5	0.4	0.7	0.4	0.3	0.6	0.3	0.4	0.6	0.9
Depreciation	14	0.6	0.3	0.8	0.3	0.4	0.4	0.3	0.4	0.6	0.4	0.6	0.4	0.9
Amortization and Depletion	15	1.5	0.0	0.1	0.0	0.0	0.1	0.1	0.1	0.1	0.1	0.2	0.1	4.1
Pensions and Other Deferred Comp.	16	0.3	0.0	0.8	0.3	0.5	0.2	0.2	0.3	0.3	0.2	0.2	0.3	0.2
Employee Benefits	17	0.5	0.2	0.7	0.3	0.6	0.7	0.5	0.6	0.6	0.5	0.8	0.5	0.5
Advertising	18	1.2	0.2	0.5	0.4	1.1	0.4	0.2	0.5	0.4	0.7	0.4	0.7	2.2
Other Expenses	19	5.0	9.5	11.6	8.3	6.5	7.3	4.2	6.8	4.5	4.6	3.9	3.8	4.7
Officers' Compensation	20	0.9	0.7	8.4	3.9	3.0	1.5	1.3	1.1	1.0	0.4	0.5	0.2	0.2
Operating Margin	21	1.1	6.0	6.1	3.5	3.0	2.8	2.1	3.3	2.7	2.3	1.2	0.8	•
Operating Margin Before Officers' Comp.	22	2.0	6.7	14.5	7.4	6.0	4.3	3.4	4.3	3.7	2.7	1.7	1.0	•

Selected Average Balance Sheet ($ in Thousands)

Net Receivables 23	2658	0	37	199	930	2992	6571	14041	24940	60400	116638	350641	1658637
Inventories 24	1499	0	21	246	765	2680	5194	10592	19535	39145	91992	188819	688333
Net Property, Plant and Equipment 25	605	0	17	57	183	505	1067	1879	5783	8635	21881	62775	482001
Total Assets 26	8307	0	134	726	2461	7740	15925	34717	67410	146553	349794	1006619	6107108
Notes and Loans Payable 27	1568	0	56	123	469	2180	3017	4806	14907	20247	35086	92929	1404783
All Other Liabilities 28	3432	0	64	270	1018	3473	7087	14445	26354	64119	158225	458927	2370730
Net Worth 29	3307	0	14	333	973	2087	5821	15466	26149	62187	156483	454763	2331595

Selected Financial Ratios (Times to 1)

Current Ratio 30	1.5	•	1.3	2.2	1.8	1.5	1.6	2.0	1.6	1.7	1.6	1.5	1.3
Quick Ratio 31	0.9	•	1.1	1.2	1.1	0.9	0.9	1.2	1.0	1.1	1.0	1.0	0.7
Net Sales to Working Capital 32	9.4	•	35.8	6.5	8.4	9.9	9.8	5.9	8.1	7.5	8.7	10.1	10.5
Coverage Ratio 33	5.8	17.2	19.2	10.4	10.7	5.3	8.8	14.4	7.8	10.9	8.4	6.0	3.2
Total Asset Turnover 34	2.1	•	6.0	3.3	3.2	2.8	3.2	2.5	2.6	2.7	2.3	2.3	1.5
Inventory Turnover 35	9.6	•	21.4	7.1	7.9	6.2	8.3	6.4	7.2	8.3	7.4	10.8	11.0
Receivables Turnover 36	7.1	•	21.7	12.6	9.1	6.6	7.8	6.0	•	6.0	6.5	7.4	•
Total Liabilities to Net Worth 37	1.5	•	8.4	1.2	1.5	2.7	1.7	1.2	1.6	1.4	1.2	1.2	1.6
Current Assets to Working Capital 38	3.1	•	4.2	1.8	2.3	3.0	2.6	2.0	2.6	2.4	2.8	3.0	4.1
Current Liabilities to Working Capital 39	2.1	•	3.2	0.8	1.3	2.0	1.6	1.0	1.6	1.4	1.8	2.0	3.1
Working Capital to Net Sales 40	0.1	•	0.0	0.2	0.1	0.1	0.1	0.2	0.1	0.1	0.1	0.1	0.1
Inventory to Working Capital 41	0.8	•	0.7	0.8	0.8	1.0	1.0	0.7	0.9	0.7	0.9	0.8	0.8
Total Receipts to Cash Flow 42	14.7	6.4	6.3	9.6	11.1	10.5	15.9	10.0	13.2	14.2	17.3	17.3	18.9
Cost of Goods to Cash Flow 43	12.0	5.0	3.5	7.0	8.4	8.1	13.4	7.9	10.8	11.9	14.7	15.0	15.4
Cash Flow to Total Debt 44	0.2	•	1.1	0.6	0.5	0.4	0.3	0.5	0.3	0.3	0.2	0.2	0.1

Selected Financial Factors (in Percentages)

Debt Ratio 45	60.2	•	89.4	54.1	60.4	73.0	63.4	55.5	61.2	57.6	55.3	54.8	61.8
Return on Total Assets 46	7.5	•	44.4	16.0	13.8	11.2	11.7	12.3	11.9	9.6	7.2	7.8	4.2
Return on Equity Before Income Taxes 47	15.6	•	395.8	31.6	31.6	33.6	28.3	25.8	26.7	20.5	14.1	14.5	7.5
Return on Equity After Income Taxes 48	12.9	•	380.5	30.0	28.9	30.0	24.3	23.1	22.8	17.2	11.8	10.4	5.8
Profit Margin (Before Income Tax) 49	2.9	7.8	7.0	4.4	3.9	3.3	3.2	4.6	4.0	3.3	2.8	2.8	1.9
Profit Margin (After Income Tax) 50	2.4	7.3	6.7	4.1	3.5	2.9	2.7	4.1	3.5	2.7	2.3	2.0	1.4

Table I

Corporations with and without Net Income

HARDWARE, PLUMBING, HEATING EQUIPMENT, AND SUPPLIES

MONEY AMOUNTS AND SIZE OF ASSETS IN THOUSANDS OF DOLLARS

Item Description for Accounting Period 7/07 Through 6/08	Total	Zero Assets	Under 500	500 to 1,000	1,000 to 5,000	5,000 to 10,000	10,000 to 25,000	25,000 to 50,000	50,000 to 100,000	100,000 to 250,000	250,000 to 500,000	500,000 to 2,500,000	2,500,000 and over
Number of Enterprises **1**	15368	1380	8189	1843	2997	384	392	97	56	15	4	10	0
Revenues ($ in Thousands)													
Net Sales **2**	99292161	198042	3566531	5396364	17239271	6608389	16283905	8338103	8845781	5219651	2295539	25300583	0
Interest **3**	250617	251	1438	3281	22259	6167	10822	9654	10183	3370	2816	180377	0
Rents **4**	10769	0	350	0	3842	416	1962	586	1929	987	0	696	0
Royalties **5**	18480	0	0	0	0	4	6902	0	433	0	10990	151	0
Other Portfolio Income **6**	149165	104	48077	1138	31430	1279	13532	7800	11136	536	1373	32756	0
Other Receipts **7**	1043632	45867	19124	16910	206583	266440	98343	54400	110249	49169	36406	140147	0
Total Receipts **8**	100764824	244264	3635520	5417693	17503385	6882695	16415466	8410543	8979711	5273713	2347124	25654710	0
Average Total Receipts **9**	6557	177	444	2940	5840	17924	41876	86707	160352	351581	586781	2565471	•
Operating Costs/Operating Income (%)													
Cost of Operations **10**	71.6	79.5	58.0	67.0	71.7	71.2	74.7	75.9	75.4	77.4	65.5	69.1	•
Salaries and Wages **11**	10.1	6.1	9.1	10.4	9.1	11.0	10.3	8.8	9.3	7.5	10.6	11.6	•
Taxes Paid **12**	1.4	1.0	2.1	1.5	1.4	1.5	1.2	1.2	1.1	1.1	1.7	1.5	•
Interest Paid **13**	1.0	1.1	0.8	0.4	0.6	0.6	0.7	0.9	0.7	1.0	0.9	2.0	•
Depreciation **14**	0.7	0.0	1.0	0.3	0.5	1.1	0.4	0.6	0.7	0.8	1.3	1.0	•
Amortization and Depletion **15**	0.2	•	0.2	0.0	0.2	0.0	0.0	0.1	0.1	0.2	0.3	0.5	•
Pensions and Other Deferred Comp. **16**	0.5	0.1	2.6	0.7	0.6	0.5	0.3	0.5	0.4	0.2	0.7	0.4	•
Employee Benefits **17**	1.1	9.8	0.7	1.0	0.7	1.1	0.6	0.8	0.9	0.8	1.7	1.7	•
Advertising **18**	0.5	0.9	1.4	0.3	0.4	1.1	0.4	0.7	0.6	0.7	1.4	0.2	•
Other Expenses **19**	7.9	16.9	14.8	8.3	8.8	8.2	5.5	6.9	6.8	6.2	13.5	8.1	•
Officers' Compensation **20**	2.2	5.8	8.2	6.0	4.0	3.6	2.1	1.2	0.9	0.8	1.1	0.2	•
Operating Margin **21**	2.8	•	1.2	4.2	2.0	0.1	3.7	2.6	3.2	3.3	1.3	3.8	•
Operating Margin Before Officers' Comp. **22**	5.1	•	9.4	10.2	6.0	3.7	5.9	3.7	4.1	4.1	2.4	4.0	•

Selected Average Balance Sheet ($ in Thousands)

Net Receivables 23	863	0	24	275	668	1960	4817	9914	21432	45695	67099	480290	•
Inventories 24	886	0	19	206	724	3419	5715	14030	23579	68500	96566	326364	•
Net Property, Plant and Equipment 25	294	0	14	40	148	766	1173	2898	8670	23454	59384	178138	•
Total Assets 26	2947		93	693	2264	6524	15442	33236	68340	167170	281241	1721662	•
Notes and Loans Payable 27	868	0	56	178	464	1661	3860	9422	16478	43278	95954	614888	•
All Other Liabilities 28	775	0	42	258	734	1837	4347	7451	19183	60235	57670	355153	•
Net Worth 29	1303	0	-5	256	1066	3026	7235	16362	32679	63656	127616	751622	•

Selected Financial Ratios (Times to 1)

Current Ratio 30	2.2	•	1.3	1.8	2.3	2.1	2.0	2.1	2.1	1.7	1.8	2.6	•
Quick Ratio 31	1.1	•	0.9	1.1	1.2	0.9	1.0	0.9	1.0	0.8	0.6	1.5	•
Net Sales to Working Capital 32	5.8	•	36.2	10.7	5.6	5.9	6.5	6.1	5.6	6.8	6.8	4.5	•
Coverage Ratio 33	5.2	3.0	5.0	13.0	6.4	7.6	7.9	4.9	7.5	5.3	4.8	3.6	•
Total Asset Turnover 34	2.2	•	4.7	4.2	2.5	2.6	2.7	2.6	2.3	2.1	2.0	1.5	•
Inventory Turnover 35	5.2	•	13.6	9.5	5.7	3.6	5.4	4.6	5.0	3.9	3.9	5.4	•
Receivables Turnover 36	7.4	•	14.9	10.4	9.0	6.6	9.5	8.0	7.9	7.5	8.6	5.3	•
Total Liabilities to Net Worth 37	1.3	•	•	1.7	1.1	1.2	1.1	1.0	1.1	1.6	1.2	1.3	•
Current Assets to Working Capital 38	1.9	•	4.9	2.2	1.8	1.9	2.0	1.9	1.9	2.3	2.3	1.6	•
Current Liabilities to Working Capital 39	0.9	•	3.9	1.2	0.8	0.9	1.0	0.9	0.9	1.3	1.3	0.6	•
Working Capital to Net Sales 40	0.2	•	0.0	0.1	0.2	0.2	0.2	0.2	0.2	0.1	0.1	0.2	•
Inventory to Working Capital 41	0.8	•	1.5	0.8	0.7	1.0	0.9	1.0	0.9	1.3	1.1	0.6	•
Total Receipts to Cash Flow 42	10.0	6.5	7.3	9.2	10.0	9.7	12.4	12.1	10.4	11.6	6.8	9.2	•
Cost of Goods to Cash Flow 43	7.2	5.2	4.2	6.2	7.2	6.9	9.3	9.2	7.8	9.0	4.4	6.4	•
Cash Flow to Total Debt 44	0.4	•	0.6	0.7	0.5	0.5	0.4	0.4	0.4	0.3	0.6	0.3	•

Selected Financial Factors (in Percentages)

Debt Ratio 45	55.8	•	105.1	63.0	52.9	53.6	53.1	50.8	52.2	61.9	54.6	56.3	•
Return on Total Assets 46	11.8	•	17.8	21.2	10.5	12.8	14.1	11.2	12.5	11.1	9.2	10.5	•
Return on Equity Before Income Taxes 47	21.5	•	•	52.8	18.9	24.0	26.3	18.1	22.7	23.6	16.0	17.3	•
Return on Equity After Income Taxes 48	17.7	•	•	48.4	16.2	22.2	23.5	15.3	19.9	20.5	11.2	12.2	•
Profit Margin (Before Income Tax) 49	4.3	2.2	3.1	4.6	3.5	4.2	4.6	3.4	4.7	4.3	3.6	5.1	•
Profit Margin (After Income Tax) 50	3.6	2.1	2.8	4.2	3.0	3.9	4.1	2.9	4.1	3.8	2.5	3.6	•

Table II

Corporations with Net Income

HARDWARE, PLUMBING, HEATING EQUIPMENT, AND SUPPLIES

MONEY AMOUNTS AND SIZE OF ASSETS IN THOUSANDS OF DOLLARS

Item Description for Accounting Period 7/07 Through 6/08	Total	Zero Assets	Under 500	500 to 1,000	1,000 to 5,000	5,000 to 10,000	10,000 to 25,000	25,000 to 50,000	50,000 to 100,000	100,000 to 250,000	250,000 to 500,000	500,000 to 2,500,000	2,500,000 and over
Number of Enterprises 1	11066	665	5452	1688	2404	356	345	78	52	12	4	10	0
Revenues ($ in Thousands)													
Net Sales 2	91125759	41663	2856126	5284559	14067026	6407263	14938625	6990176	8347412	4596787	2295539	25300583	0
Interest 3	244743	250	1262	2580	21730	5835	9638	7399	9687	3171	2816	180377	0
Rents 4	9032	0	0	0	3842	416	1723	395	1929	30	0	696	0
Royalties 5	18480	0	0	0	0	4	6902	0	433	0	10990	151	0
Other Portfolio Income 6	136130	0	46522	339	21241	1194	13353	7679	11136	536	1373	32756	0
Other Receipts 7	995227	44163	9869	16906	194918	265113	86051	48445	104390	48819	36406	140147	0
Total Receipts 8	92529371	86076	2913779	5304384	14308757	6679825	15056292	7054094	8474987	4649343	2347124	25654710	0
Average Total Receipts 9	8362	129	534	3142	5952	18764	43641	90437	162981	387445	586781	2565471	•
Operating Costs/Operating Income (%)													
Cost of Operations 10	71.3	72.1	58.2	66.9	71.4	71.2	74.3	76.0	74.9	76.4	65.5	69.1	•
Salaries and Wages 11	10.1	2.2	8.6	10.5	8.4	11.1	10.3	8.8	9.2	7.7	10.6	11.6	•
Taxes Paid 12	1.4	1.3	2.0	1.4	1.3	1.5	1.2	1.2	1.2	1.1	1.7	1.5	•
Interest Paid 13	1.0	1.1	0.8	0.4	0.5	0.6	0.6	0.8	0.7	0.8	0.9	2.0	•
Depreciation 14	0.7	•	0.8	0.2	0.4	1.1	0.4	0.5	0.7	0.7	1.3	1.0	•
Amortization and Depletion 15	0.2	•	0.1	0.0	0.1	0.0	0.0	0.0	0.1	0.2	0.3	0.5	•
Pensions and Other Deferred Comp. 16	0.5	•	1.4	0.7	0.6	0.5	0.3	0.4	0.4	0.3	0.7	0.4	•
Employee Benefits 17	1.1	1.0	0.4	1.0	0.7	1.1	0.6	0.7	0.9	0.8	1.7	1.7	•
Advertising 18	0.5	1.9	1.5	0.3	0.2	1.1	0.4	0.7	0.6	0.5	1.4	0.2	•
Other Expenses 19	7.6	41.0	12.9	8.2	8.6	7.7	5.3	5.9	6.9	6.2	13.5	8.1	•
Officers' Compensation 20	2.2	2.7	8.2	5.9	4.4	3.7	2.2	1.1	0.9	0.8	1.1	0.2	•
Operating Margin 21	3.6	•	5.1	4.4	3.3	0.4	4.3	3.9	3.6	4.4	1.3	3.8	•
Operating Margin Before Officers' Comp. 22	5.8	•	13.3	10.3	7.7	4.1	6.5	5.0	4.4	5.2	2.4	4.0	•

Selected Average Balance Sheet ($ in Thousands)

	•	•	•	•	•	•	•	•	•	•	•	•
Net Receivables 23	1103	0	27	284	687	1998	4967	10183	21639	42476	67099	480290
Inventories 24	1089	0	12	213	729	3553	5987	14870	24536	65958	96566	319587
Net Property, Plant and Equipment 25	372	0	16	35	144	755	1060	2661	9049	24137	59384	178138
Total Assets 26	3713	0	73	703	2237	6490	15619	32574	68816	163817	281241	1721662
Notes and Loans Payable 27	1053	0	45	178	381	1377	3459	8818	15152	41996	95954	614888
All Other Liabilities 28	948	0	45	273	680	1794	4419	7514	19443	50542	57670	355153
Net Worth 29	1712	0	-16	253	1176	3319	7741	16241	34221	71278	127616	751622

Selected Financial Ratios (Times to 1)

	•	•	•	•	•	•	•	•	•	•	•	•
Current Ratio 30	2.3	•	1.4	1.8	2.5	2.2	2.1	2.2	2.1	1.8	1.8	2.6
Quick Ratio 31	1.2	•	1.1	1.0	1.4	1.0	1.0	1.0	1.0	0.8	0.6	1.5
Net Sales to Working Capital 32	5.7	•	36.4	11.8	5.1	5.9	6.3	6.1	5.6	7.4	6.8	4.5
Coverage Ratio 33	6.1	79.7	10.4	13.9	11.2	8.8	9.4	6.9	8.5	8.3	4.8	3.6
Total Asset Turnover 34	2.2	•	7.2	4.5	2.6	2.8	2.8	2.8	2.3	2.3	2.0	1.5
Inventory Turnover 35	5.4	•	26.2	9.8	5.7	3.6	5.4	4.6	4.9	4.4	3.9	5.5
Receivables Turnover 36	7.5	•	18.2	10.6	9.0	6.6	9.3	7.6	•	8.7	8.6	•
Total Liabilities to Net Worth 37	1.2	•	•	1.8	0.9	1.0	1.0	1.0	1.0	1.3	1.2	1.3
Current Assets to Working Capital 38	1.8	•	3.8	2.3	1.7	1.8	1.9	1.8	1.9	2.2	2.3	1.6
Current Liabilities to Working Capital 39	0.8	•	2.8	1.3	0.7	0.8	0.9	0.8	0.9	1.2	1.3	0.6
Working Capital to Net Sales 40	0.2	•	0.0	0.1	0.2	0.2	0.2	0.2	0.2	0.1	0.1	0.2
Inventory to Working Capital 41	0.8	•	0.6	0.9	0.7	1.0	0.9	0.9	0.9	1.2	1.1	0.6
Total Receipts to Cash Flow 42	9.5	0.9	6.1	9.2	8.9	9.7	12.0	11.4	9.9	10.2	6.8	9.2
Cost of Goods to Cash Flow 43	6.8	0.6	3.5	6.2	6.3	6.9	8.9	8.6	7.4	7.8	4.4	6.4
Cash Flow to Total Debt 44	0.4	•	1.0	0.8	0.6	0.6	0.5	0.5	0.5	0.4	0.6	0.3

Selected Financial Factors (in Percentages)

	•	•	•	•	•	•	•	•	•	•	•	•
Debt Ratio 45	53.9	•	121.8	64.1	47.4	48.9	50.4	50.1	50.3	56.5	54.6	56.3
Return on Total Assets 46	13.5	•	56.0	22.8	14.3	14.5	15.9	15.3	13.4	14.8	9.2	10.5
Return on Equity Before Income Taxes 47	24.5	•	58.8	•	24.9	25.2	28.6	26.3	23.8	29.9	16.0	17.3
Return on Equity After Income Taxes 48	20.6	•	53.9	•	21.8	23.5	25.7	22.8	21.0	26.4	11.2	12.2
Profit Margin (Before Income Tax) 49	5.1	83.3	7.1	4.7	5.0	4.6	5.1	4.8	5.1	5.6	3.6	5.1
Profit Margin (After Income Tax) 50	4.3	83.2	6.7	4.4	4.3	4.4	4.6	4.1	4.5	4.9	2.5	3.6

Table I

Corporations with and without Net Income

MACHINERY, EQUIPMENT, AND SUPPLIES

MONEY AMOUNTS AND SIZE OF ASSETS IN THOUSANDS OF DOLLARS

Item Description for Accounting Period 7/07 Through 6/08		Total	Zero Assets	Under 500	500 to 1,000	1,000 to 5,000	5,000 to 10,000	10,000 to 25,000	25,000 to 50,000	50,000 to 100,000	100,000 to 250,000	250,000 to 500,000	500,000 to 2,500,000	2,500,000 and over
Number of Enterprises	1	48396	4050	27946	4680	8498	1529	1072	334	141	82	36	22	6
Revenues ($ in Thousands)														
Net Sales	2	259461520	5584265	15547281	8535382	49555251	25602046	36366387	21391197	16671934	18943644	14114975	31017872	16131286
Interest	3	637157	8077	8274	8152	44822	17243	31883	33586	75973	70645	54034	55282	229185
Rents	4	234015	223	46797	8683	17187	12859	25077	25740	25629	43238	21450	1064	6068
Royalties	5	13728	0	0	0	0	20	18	72	2500	623	2100	3139	5257
Other Portfolio Income	6	1459001	2788	31584	70453	156305	91505	170528	192046	116102	211751	160555	233965	21417
Other Receipts	7	2741186	50899	325443	47822	310091	245108	354248	300966	243971	244084	231617	342075	44864
Total Receipts	8	264546607	5646252	15959379	8670492	50083656	25968781	36948141	21943607	17136109	19513985	14584731	31653397	16438077
Average Total Receipts	9	5466	1394	571	1853	5894	16984	34467	65699	121533	237975	405131	1438791	2739680
Operating Costs/Operating Income (%)														
Cost of Operations	10	75.2	93.5	65.5	70.1	73.6	75.0	77.0	77.3	77.2	75.6	74.0	77.7	73.0
Salaries and Wages	11	7.3	1.6	6.1	7.4	8.1	8.4	8.0	7.4	7.0	7.4	7.3	5.6	8.7
Taxes Paid	12	1.2	0.3	1.8	1.7	1.4	1.4	1.1	1.1	1.0	1.2	0.8	0.9	1.4
Interest Paid	13	1.1	0.2	0.4	0.7	0.8	0.8	1.0	1.1	1.3	1.7	1.8	1.4	1.6
Depreciation	14	1.7	0.2	0.6	1.2	0.9	0.9	1.5	2.1	2.3	2.9	4.4	2.6	1.0
Amortization and Depletion	15	0.2	0.0	0.0	0.0	0.1	0.1	0.1	0.1	0.2	0.4	0.1	0.4	0.4
Pensions and Other Deferred Comp.	16	0.4	0.1	1.3	0.2	0.4	0.4	0.3	0.3	0.3	0.4	0.2	0.5	1.0
Employee Benefits	17	0.9	0.3	1.2	0.8	0.7	0.9	0.8	0.8	0.8	1.4	1.5	1.1	1.1
Advertising	18	0.5	0.1	0.5	0.5	0.4	0.4	0.4	0.5	0.4	0.4	0.6	0.5	0.9
Other Expenses	19	7.3	3.5	14.7	10.6	8.3	6.8	6.2	6.7	7.0	6.5	8.0	5.1	5.7
Officers' Compensation	20	2.1	0.9	6.4	5.0	3.7	2.3	1.7	1.3	1.0	0.7	0.6	0.5	0.8
Operating Margin	21	2.0	•	1.4	1.9	1.6	2.6	1.9	1.2	1.7	1.5	0.6	3.8	4.5
Operating Margin Before Officers' Comp.	22	4.1	0.1	7.8	6.9	5.2	4.9	3.6	2.5	2.7	2.2	1.2	4.3	5.3

Selected Average Balance Sheet ($ in Thousands)

Net Receivables 23	641	0	27	193	565	1916	3687	8978	15187	34615	56256	162879	679838
Inventories 24	912	0	30	244	892	3299	5993	12834	21596	55547	106066	238928	357832
Net Property, Plant and Equipment 25	409	0	18	104	237	962	2033	5564	11061	29166	53795	178729	245316
Total Assets 26	2818	0	114	703	2235	7279	14894	34734	67753	164274	317784	889092	3031095
Notes and Loans Payable 27	860	0	58	220	701	2032	4652	11056	22144	55560	103315	282654	599229
All Other Liabilities 28	939	0	29	192	762	2329	5262	12516	21270	53689	99304	319608	973116
Net Worth 29	1020	0	26	291	772	2917	4979	11162	24339	55025	115166	286829	1458750

Selected Financial Ratios (Times to 1)

Current Ratio 30	1.7	•	2.6	2.4	1.7	1.7	1.5	1.5	1.6	1.6	1.5	1.7	1.9
Quick Ratio 31	0.7	•	1.5	1.3	0.8	0.7	0.6	0.7	0.7	0.7	0.5	0.7	1.0
Net Sales to Working Capital 32	7.0	•	10.7	5.6	8.1	6.8	8.0	7.4	6.6	5.7	5.7	6.8	4.1
Coverage Ratio 33	4.6	2.0	10.9	6.3	4.1	5.8	4.5	4.4	4.5	3.6	3.1	5.3	5.1
Total Asset Turnover 34	1.9	•	4.9	2.6	2.6	2.3	2.3	1.8	1.7	1.4	1.2	1.6	0.9
Inventory Turnover 35	4.4	•	12.0	5.2	4.8	3.8	4.4	3.9	4.2	3.1	2.7	4.6	5.5
Receivables Turnover 36	8.2	•	17.8	8.1	9.9	8.6	9.6	7.1	8.1	6.3	7.0	7.3	4.6
Total Liabilities to Net Worth 37	1.8	•	3.3	1.4	1.9	1.5	2.0	2.1	1.8	2.0	1.8	2.1	1.1
Current Assets to Working Capital 38	2.5	•	1.6	1.7	2.5	2.4	2.8	3.0	2.7	2.7	2.9	2.4	2.1
Current Liabilities to Working Capital 39	1.5	•	0.6	0.7	1.5	1.4	1.8	2.0	1.7	1.7	1.9	1.4	1.1
Working Capital to Net Sales 40	0.1	•	0.1	0.2	0.1	0.1	0.1	0.1	0.2	0.2	0.2	0.1	0.2
Inventory to Working Capital 41	1.2	•	0.5	0.6	1.2	1.3	1.5	1.5	1.3	1.3	1.6	1.0	0.7
Total Receipts to Cash Flow 42	10.4	29.8	6.9	8.7	11.1	10.8	11.9	10.9	10.0	11.1	9.7	10.4	9.2
Cost of Goods to Cash Flow 43	7.9	27.8	4.5	6.1	8.2	8.1	9.2	8.4	7.8	8.4	7.2	8.1	6.7
Cash Flow to Total Debt 44	0.3	•	0.9	0.5	0.4	0.4	0.3	0.2	0.3	0.2	0.2	0.2	0.2

Selected Financial Factors (in Percentages)

Debt Ratio 45	63.8	•	76.8	58.5	65.5	59.9	66.6	67.9	64.1	66.5	63.8	67.7	51.9
Return on Total Assets 46	9.7	•	21.6	10.7	9.1	11.1	10.4	9.0	10.1	8.7	7.2	11.5	7.2
Return on Equity Before Income Taxes 47	21.1	•	84.5	21.7	19.9	22.9	24.2	21.6	21.8	18.8	13.5	29.0	12.0
Return on Equity After Income Taxes 48	17.1	•	82.4	20.5	17.6	20.4	20.8	17.9	17.1	15.6	10.4	20.7	7.8
Profit Margin (Before Income Tax) 49	4.0	0.2	4.0	3.5	2.6	4.0	3.6	3.8	4.5	4.5	4.0	5.9	6.5
Profit Margin (After Income Tax) 50	3.3	0.0	3.9	3.3	2.3	3.6	3.1	3.1	3.5	3.7	3.1	4.2	4.2

Machinery, Equipment, and Supplies

Table II
Corporations with Net Income

MONEY AMOUNTS AND SIZE OF ASSETS IN THOUSANDS OF DOLLARS

Item Description for Accounting Period 7/07 Through 6/08	Total	Zero Assets	Under 500	500 to 1,000	1,000 to 5,000	5,000 to 10,000	10,000 to 25,000	25,000 to 50,000	50,000 to 100,000	100,000 to 250,000	250,000 to 500,000	500,000 to 2,500,000	2,500,000 and over
Number of Enterprises 1	30220	1141	•	3163	6360	1345	905	267	117	69	31	18	•
Revenues ($ in Thousands)													
Net Sales 2	217878441	4974033	•	6926693	40805734	24359471	32311101	18326280	14493510	16819298	12519206	18348425	•
Interest 3	586026	8015	•	5319	39596	13910	29272	25256	73114	65392	47058	46900	•
Rents 4	200866	19	•	6862	15665	12673	23644	22312	25334	33989	6703	803	•
Royalties 5	10898	0	•	0	0	20	18	12	2500	623	2100	369	•
Other Portfolio Income 6	1189981	895	•	49934	115181	72247	95208	149643	102360	175868	151727	224006	•
Other Receipts 7	2392158	47392	•	39143	262062	225351	306757	266268	228982	227550	221118	219660	•
Total Receipts 8	222258370	5030354	•	7027951	41238238	24683672	32766000	18789771	14925800	17322720	12947912	18840163	•
Average Total Receipts 9	7355	4409	•	2222	6484	18352	36206	70374	127571	251054	417675	1046676	•
Operating Costs/Operating Income (%)													
Cost of Operations 10	74.0	95.0	•	69.6	73.0	75.2	77.0	77.6	77.1	75.1	72.9	65.7	•
Salaries and Wages 11	7.5	1.2	•	6.9	7.9	8.3	7.9	7.1	6.8	7.4	7.2	8.3	•
Taxes Paid 12	1.2	0.2	•	1.6	1.3	1.4	1.1	1.1	1.0	1.2	0.9	1.4	•
Interest Paid 13	1.0	0.1	•	0.5	0.7	0.7	0.8	1.0	1.1	1.6	1.8	1.8	•
Depreciation 14	1.6	0.1	•	1.2	0.8	0.7	1.2	1.7	2.0	2.6	4.8	3.9	•
Amortization and Depletion 15	0.2	0.0	•	0.0	0.1	0.1	0.1	0.1	0.1	0.3	0.1	0.6	•
Pensions and Other Deferred Comp. 16	0.5	0.2	•	0.1	0.4	0.4	0.3	0.3	0.3	0.5	0.2	0.8	•
Employee Benefits 17	0.9	0.1	•	0.7	0.7	0.9	0.7	0.7	0.8	1.3	1.6	1.6	•
Advertising 18	0.4	0.0	•	0.5	0.4	0.4	0.4	0.5	0.3	0.3	0.7	0.5	•
Other Expenses 19	7.1	2.3	•	9.4	8.1	6.5	5.8	6.1	6.3	6.5	7.8	7.1	•
Officers' Compensation 20	2.1	0.3	•	4.7	3.8	2.3	1.6	1.3	1.0	0.7	0.6	0.8	•
Operating Margin 21	3.5	0.5	•	4.8	2.9	3.2	3.1	2.6	3.3	2.5	1.4	7.6	•
Operating Margin Before Officers' Comp. 22	5.5	0.7	•	9.5	6.7	5.5	4.7	3.8	4.2	3.2	2.0	8.4	•

Selected Average Balance Sheet ($ in Thousands)

Net Receivables 23	876	0	•	•	225	573	2024	3846	9520	15621	37039	55402	155480
Inventories 24	1251	0	•	•	251	912	3423	6126	13780	21939	58601	120315	226669
Net Property, Plant and Equipment 25	504	0	•	•	113	202	766	1645	5063	10198	25171	58243	190509
Total Assets 26	3648	0	•	•	696	2237	7305	14828	34927	68095	166525	317213	824390
Notes and Loans Payable 27	1070	0	•	•	204	656	1836	4151	9974	20302	51127	105719	291332
All Other Liabilities 28	1101	0	•	•	165	718	2272	5327	12387	21267	55947	94615	207420
Net Worth 29	1476	0	•	•	327	864	3196	5350	12566	26526	59452	116879	325638

Selected Financial Ratios (Times to 1)

Current Ratio 30	1.8	•	•	•	2.5	1.9	1.8	1.6	1.6	1.6	1.6	1.7	1.9
Quick Ratio 31	0.8	•	•	•	1.5	0.9	0.8	0.7	0.7	0.7	0.7	0.5	0.8
Net Sales to Working Capital 32	6.5	•	•	•	6.9	7.3	6.7	7.6	7.1	6.5	5.4	5.1	5.0
Coverage Ratio 33	6.4	13.9	•	•	12.6	6.8	7.5	6.3	6.3	6.7	4.5	3.7	6.7
Total Asset Turnover 34	2.0	•	•	•	3.1	2.9	2.5	2.4	2.0	1.8	1.5	1.3	1.2
Inventory Turnover 35	4.3	•	•	•	6.1	5.1	4.0	4.5	3.9	4.4	3.1	2.4	3.0
Receivables Turnover 36	7.9	•	•	•	7.9	10.7	8.7	9.9	7.0	8.6	6.3	•	1.5
Total Liabilities to Net Worth 37	1.5	•	•	•	1.1	1.6	1.3	1.8	1.8	1.6	1.8	1.7	1.5
Current Assets to Working Capital 38	2.3	•	•	•	1.7	2.2	2.2	2.6	2.8	2.6	2.6	2.5	2.2
Current Liabilities to Working Capital 39	1.3	•	•	•	0.7	1.2	1.2	1.6	1.8	1.6	1.6	1.5	1.2
Working Capital to Net Sales 40	0.2	•	•	•	0.1	0.1	0.1	0.1	0.1	0.2	0.2	0.2	0.2
Inventory to Working Capital 41	1.1	•	•	•	0.6	1.0	1.2	1.4	1.3	1.2	1.3	1.5	1.1
Total Receipts to Cash Flow 42	9.2	27.1	•	•	7.4	9.9	10.5	11.1	10.0	9.0	10.0	9.1	6.5
Cost of Goods to Cash Flow 43	6.8	25.7	•	•	5.2	7.2	7.9	8.6	7.8	7.0	7.5	6.6	4.3
Cash Flow to Total Debt 44	0.4	•	•	•	0.8	0.5	0.4	0.3	0.3	0.3	0.2	0.2	0.3

Selected Financial Factors (in Percentages)

Debt Ratio 45	59.5	•	•	•	53.1	61.4	56.2	63.9	64.0	61.0	64.3	63.2	60.5
Return on Total Assets 46	12.9	•	•	•	21.4	13.5	13.1	12.9	11.9	13.3	10.3	8.6	14.9
Return on Equity Before Income Taxes 47	26.8	•	•	•	41.9	29.7	25.9	30.0	27.9	29.2	22.5	17.1	32.2
Return on Equity After Income Taxes 48	22.5	•	•	•	40.3	27.0	23.4	26.3	23.7	23.9	19.0	13.5	23.3
Profit Margin (Before Income Tax) 49	5.5	1.6	•	•	6.2	4.0	4.6	4.5	5.1	6.2	5.5	4.9	10.3
Profit Margin (After Income Tax) 50	4.6	1.3	•	•	6.0	3.6	4.1	3.9	4.3	3.9	4.6	3.9	7.4

180

Table I
Corporations with and without Net Income

FURNITURE, SPORTS, TOYS, JEWELRY, OTHER DURABLE GOODS

MONEY AMOUNTS AND SIZE OF ASSETS IN THOUSANDS OF DOLLARS

Item Description for Accounting Period 7/07 Through 6/08	Total	Zero Assets	Under 500	500 to 1,000	1,000 to 5,000	5,000 to 10,000	10,000 to 25,000	25,000 to 50,000	50,000 to 100,000	100,000 to 250,000	250,000 to 500,000	500,000 to 2,500,000	2,500,000 and over
Number of Enterprises **1**	68582	10404	42123	6051	7054	1432	972	288	147	75	15	16	5
Revenues ($ in Thousands)													
Net Sales **2**	261809455	7958557	17080624	10723801	44407250	22553443	34019542	22116209	19962624	21678680	7537966	27010212	26760547
Interest **3**	645901	12574	5675	19332	27419	18119	45584	15153	40631	95706	52685	49120	263902
Rents **4**	78263	794	1706	242	7704	2549	3640	4570	7686	6237	3317	24803	15014
Royalties **5**	325931	3982	0	3560	27962	2461	5984	4622	57727	26226	62957	14039	116411
Other Portfolio Income **6**	598995	45176	18795	53661	48664	58239	87894	7384	35438	35616	17887	21034	169212
Other Receipts **7**	1757613	94170	148419	29603	259972	57764	268268	128392	164863	155594	50361	269086	131117
Total Receipts **8**	265216158	8115253	17255219	10830199	44778971	22692575	34430912	22276330	20268969	21998059	7725173	27388294	27456203
Average Total Receipts **9**	3867	780	410	1790	6348	15847	35423	77348	137884	293307	515012	1711768	5491241
Operating Costs/Operating Income (%)													
Cost of Operations **10**	78.1	83.8	62.5	72.4	73.0	74.7	78.8	81.2	79.5	78.9	78.1	84.3	88.3
Salaries and Wages **11**	5.9	6.0	7.3	6.7	6.8	7.5	6.5	5.2	5.5	5.5	6.3	4.1	4.0
Taxes Paid **12**	1.0	0.9	1.3	1.4	1.2	1.3	1.0	0.8	1.1	0.9	0.9	0.7	0.7
Interest Paid **13**	0.9	1.0	0.6	0.5	0.6	0.7	1.0	1.2	1.0	1.5	0.7	1.2	1.1
Depreciation **14**	0.6	0.6	0.5	0.7	0.5	0.6	0.5	0.6	0.7	0.9	1.0	0.8	0.4
Amortization and Depletion **15**	0.3	0.4	0.1	0.1	0.0	0.1	0.1	0.2	0.2	0.4	0.5	0.4	0.8
Pensions and Other Deferred Comp. **16**	0.2	0.2	0.7	0.1	0.3	0.2	0.2	0.2	0.2	0.2	0.1	0.2	0.1
Employee Benefits **17**	0.5	0.3	0.8	0.3	0.3	0.6	0.5	0.4	0.5	0.8	1.0	0.6	0.2
Advertising **18**	1.3	0.8	0.7	1.0	1.5	0.8	0.9	1.0	1.6	1.6	3.7	1.5	1.9
Other Expenses **19**	7.9	7.3	16.0	13.9	10.1	7.6	7.6	6.8	7.1	8.0	8.3	4.1	2.3
Officers' Compensation **20**	2.0	1.1	6.6	3.4	3.4	2.9	1.7	0.9	1.0	0.8	1.3	0.3	0.3
Operating Margin **21**	1.3	•	2.8	•	2.2	3.0	1.3	1.6	1.8	0.6	•	1.8	•
Operating Margin Before Officers' Comp. **22**	3.3	•	9.4	2.8	5.6	5.9	2.9	2.5	2.8	1.4	2.1	•	0.2

Selected Average Balance Sheet ($ in Thousands)

Net Receivables 23	441	0	14	143	582	1974	4762	11495	19954	38198	129988	165216	696922
Inventories 24	487	0	39	284	773	2860	5354	12317	21413	40293	71945	173010	351553
Net Property, Plant and Equipment 25	142	0	10	71	221	465	1263	3087	6200	14962	25499	80278	164131
Total Assets 26	1720	0	100	661	2245	6994	15059	34678	66943	149923	328608	898076	3776924
Notes and Loans Payable 27	512	0	64	264	542	1789	4679	10860	18997	51600	42365	294480	949602
All Other Liabilities 28	635	0	26	280	827	2570	5584	15032	24291	51159	137470	307984	1422115
Net Worth 29	573	0	11	117	876	2635	4797	8785	23655	47163	148774	295611	1405206

Selected Financial Ratios (Times to 1)

Current Ratio 30	1.5	•	2.3	1.6	1.8	1.7	1.5	1.4	1.7	1.6	1.7	1.5	1.1
Quick Ratio 31	0.7	•	1.1	0.7	0.8	0.8	0.7	0.7	0.8	0.8	1.2	0.7	0.4
Net Sales to Working Capital 32	9.0	•	9.1	8.9	8.0	6.3	8.7	9.0	6.6	7.8	5.3	11.9	28.6
Coverage Ratio 33	3.9	0.6	7.3	1.7	6.0	6.2	3.6	3.0	4.3	2.3	3.0	3.7	3.4
Total Asset Turnover 34	2.2	•	4.0	2.7	2.8	2.3	2.3	2.2	2.0	1.9	1.5	1.9	1.4
Inventory Turnover 35	6.1	•	6.6	4.5	5.9	4.1	5.1	5.1	5.0	5.7	5.5	8.2	13.4
Receivables Turnover 36	8.6	•	24.9	10.8	11.2	7.5	7.2	6.8	7.1	7.0	3.3	8.9	10.1
Total Liabilities to Net Worth 37	2.0	•	8.0	4.7	1.6	1.7	2.1	2.9	1.8	2.2	1.2	2.0	1.7
Current Assets to Working Capital 38	2.9	•	1.8	2.6	2.3	2.4	3.0	3.3	2.5	2.6	2.5	3.1	10.6
Current Liabilities to Working Capital 39	1.9	•	0.8	1.6	1.3	1.4	2.0	2.3	1.5	1.6	1.5	2.1	9.6
Working Capital to Net Sales 40	0.1	•	0.1	0.1	0.1	0.2	0.1	0.1	0.2	0.1	0.2	0.1	0.0
Inventory to Working Capital 41	1.2	•	0.8	1.3	1.0	1.1	1.3	1.5	1.1	1.1	0.5	1.1	2.5
Total Receipts to Cash Flow 42	12.0	19.0	6.5	11.1	9.8	11.1	12.3	12.9	11.0	12.6	14.0	16.5	26.1
Cost of Goods to Cash Flow 43	9.4	15.9	4.1	8.0	7.2	8.3	9.7	10.5	8.7	9.9	10.9	13.9	23.0
Cash Flow to Total Debt 44	0.3	•	0.7	0.3	0.5	0.3	0.3	0.2	0.3	0.2	0.2	0.2	0.1

Selected Financial Factors (in Percentages)

Debt Ratio 45	66.7	•	88.9	82.3	61.0	62.3	68.1	74.7	64.7	68.5	54.7	67.1	62.8
Return on Total Assets 46	8.0	•	17.9	2.3	10.3	9.7	8.0	7.7	8.8	7.0	3.0	8.4	5.2
Return on Equity Before Income Taxes 47	17.8	•	138.9	5.5	21.9	21.6	18.0	20.5	19.1	12.7	4.5	18.6	10.0
Return on Equity After Income Taxes 48	14.1	•	135.7	2.2	20.1	19.3	15.7	17.3	15.6	7.6	1.9	11.5	5.8
Profit Margin (Before Income Tax) 49	2.7	•	3.8	0.4	3.1	3.6	2.5	2.3	3.3	2.1	1.3	3.3	2.6
Profit Margin (After Income Tax) 50	2.1	•	3.7	0.1	2.8	3.2	2.2	2.0	2.7	1.2	0.6	2.0	1.5

Table II
Corporations with Net Income

FURNITURE, SPORTS, TOYS, JEWELRY, OTHER DURABLE GOODS

MONEY AMOUNTS AND SIZE OF ASSETS IN THOUSANDS OF DOLLARS

Item Description for Accounting Period 7/07 Through 6/08		Total	Zero Assets	Under 500	500 to 1,000	1,000 to 5,000	5,000 to 10,000	10,000 to 25,000	25,000 to 50,000	50,000 to 100,000	100,000 to 250,000	250,000 to 500,000	500,000 to 2,500,000	2,500,000 and over
Number of Enterprises	1	40193	3633	•	3951	5745	1183	727	211	115	54	12	12	•
Revenues ($ in Thousands)														
Net Sales	2	216903351	4771140	•	8074953	38897172	19632204	28388210	16363135	16605442	18198491	5995972	25417938	•
Interest	3	532762	8249	•	15390	23633	15769	30718	12190	24762	66946	37710	47171	•
Rents	4	68424	668	•	125	5715	2471	2881	4220	3023	4482	3317	24803	•
Royalties	5	206134	6	•	3560	26311	0	4608	3430	55098	26214	60518	13006	•
Other Portfolio Income	6	522817	42268	•	27398	42798	55803	73649	5340	30768	34019	16029	9840	•
Other Receipts	7	1400693	88744	•	26627	207311	46696	245096	89667	154771	110818	27868	187931	•
Total Receipts	8	219634181	4911075	•	8148053	39202940	19752943	28745162	16477982	16873864	18440970	6141414	25700689	•
Average Total Receipts	9	5464	1352	•	2062	6824	16697	39539	78095	146729	341499	511784	2141724	•
Operating Costs/Operating Income (%)														
Cost of Operations	10	78.8	83.1	•	72.1	73.1	75.5	79.4	81.0	79.9	80.1	78.3	84.9	•
Salaries and Wages	11	5.1	6.1	•	6.4	6.2	6.4	5.8	4.8	4.8	4.8	5.6	3.9	•
Taxes Paid	12	0.9	0.8	•	1.2	1.1	1.2	1.0	0.7	1.0	0.9	0.9	0.7	•
Interest Paid	13	0.7	0.8	•	0.4	0.5	0.6	0.7	1.0	0.7	1.0	0.8	0.9	•
Depreciation	14	0.5	0.8	•	0.6	0.5	0.6	0.5	0.5	0.5	0.7	1.1	0.8	•
Amortization and Depletion	15	0.1	0.3	•	0.1	0.0	0.0	0.0	0.1	0.1	0.3	0.4	0.3	•
Pensions and Other Deferred Comp.	16	0.2	0.2	•	0.2	0.2	0.2	0.2	0.1	0.1	0.2	0.1	0.2	•
Employee Benefits	17	0.4	0.3	•	0.3	0.3	0.4	0.4	0.3	0.4	0.7	0.8	0.6	•
Advertising	18	1.1	0.7	•	0.9	1.5	0.7	0.7	0.8	1.4	1.4	3.6	1.2	•
Other Expenses	19	6.8	5.1	•	11.5	9.5	6.8	6.5	5.9	6.2	6.4	7.3	3.7	•
Officers' Compensation	20	1.9	1.0	•	3.4	3.4	3.1	1.7	0.9	1.0	0.7	0.6	0.3	•
Operating Margin	21	3.2	0.7	•	2.9	3.7	4.4	3.1	3.8	3.6	2.6	0.3	2.7	•
Operating Margin Before Officers' Comp.	22	5.1	1.8	•	6.3	7.0	7.5	4.8	4.7	4.7	3.4	1.0	2.9	•

Selected Average Balance Sheet ($ in Thousands)

Item													
Net Receivables 23	609	0	•	162	585	2080	5124	12648	22100	43096	111218	187515	•
Inventories 24	644	0	•	251	804	2779	5697	13627	21805	38653	60240	18166	•
Net Property, Plant and Equipment 25	173	0	•	64	200	484	1273	2634	5019	14607	25175	95464	•
Total Assets 26	2137	0	•	664	2251	6874	15106	34850	66368	152680	310345	936191	•
Notes and Loans Payable 27	536	0	•	211	446	1660	4225	9783	15802	41690	51938	256816	•
All Other Liabilities 28	808	0	•	266	804	2464	5223	14887	24375	48622	115800	358539	•
Net Worth 29	794	0	•	187	1000	2749	5658	10180	26191	62367	142606	320836	•

Selected Financial Ratios (Times to 1)

Item												
Current Ratio 30	1.7	•	1.6	1.9	1.8	1.6	1.6	1.7	1.9	1.7	1.4	•
Quick Ratio 31	0.8	•	0.8	0.9	0.9	0.8	0.8	0.9	0.9	1.1	0.7	•
Net Sales to Working Capital 32	8.4	•	9.6	7.8	6.4	8.4	7.2	6.3	7.0	5.7	17.1	•
Coverage Ratio 33	7.2	5.9	10.1	9.4	8.9	6.9	5.5	8.0	5.0	5.2	5.4	•
Total Asset Turnover 34	2.5	•	3.1	3.0	2.4	2.6	2.2	2.2	2.2	1.6	2.3	•
Inventory Turnover 35	6.6	•	5.9	6.2	4.5	5.4	4.6	5.3	7.0	6.5	9.9	•
Receivables Turnover 36	8.8	•	10.8	11.7	7.4	7.0	6.2	•	7.7	4.3	•	•
Total Liabilities to Net Worth 37	1.7	•	2.5	1.2	1.5	2.4	1.7	1.5	1.4	1.2	1.9	•
Current Assets to Working Capital 38	2.5	•	2.5	2.1	2.3	2.7	2.6	2.4	2.1	2.5	3.8	•
Current Liabilities to Working Capital 39	1.5	•	1.5	1.1	1.3	1.7	1.6	1.4	1.1	1.5	2.8	•
Working Capital to Net Sales 40	0.1	•	0.1	0.1	0.2	0.1	0.1	0.2	0.1	0.2	0.1	•
Inventory to Working Capital 41	1.0	•	1.1	0.9	1.1	1.1	1.2	0.9	0.9	0.5	1.5	•
Total Receipts to Cash Flow 42	10.6	13.4	8.6	9.0	10.1	10.9	11.0	9.6	11.7	12.6	15.9	•
Cost of Goods to Cash Flow 43	8.4	11.2	6.2	6.6	7.7	8.8	8.7	7.7	9.3	9.9	13.5	•
Cash Flow to Total Debt 44	0.4	•	0.5	0.6	0.4	0.3	0.4	0.4	0.3	0.3	0.2	•

Selected Financial Factors (in Percentages)

Item												
Debt Ratio 45	62.8	•	71.8	55.6	60.0	70.8	62.5	60.5	59.2	54.0	65.7	•
Return on Total Assets 46	13.2	•	12.9	15.0	13.6	12.3	13.1	13.0	11.1	7.0	10.6	•
Return on Equity Before Income Taxes 47	30.7	•	41.3	30.1	30.1	34.3	30.0	28.8	21.6	12.2	25.3	•
Return on Equity After Income Taxes 48	26.2	•	38.1	28.1	27.5	30.8	27.4	24.8	16.3	8.8	16.5	•
Profit Margin (Before Income Tax) 49	4.5	3.8	3.8	4.4	5.0	4.5	4.3	5.2	4.0	3.5	3.8	•
Profit Margin (After Income Tax) 50	3.9	3.3	3.5	4.2	4.5	4.0	4.0	4.5	3.0	2.5	2.5	•

Table I

Corporations with and without Net Income

PAPER AND PAPER PRODUCT

MONEY AMOUNTS AND SIZE OF ASSETS IN THOUSANDS OF DOLLARS

Item Description for Accounting Period 7/07 Through 6/08	Total	Zero Assets	Under 500	500 to 1,000	1,000 to 5,000	5,000 to 10,000	10,000 to 25,000	25,000 to 50,000	50,000 to 100,000	100,000 to 250,000	250,000 to 500,000	500,000 to 2,500,000	2,500,000 and over
Number of Enterprises 1	10722	1079	7921	677	748	66	124	61	23	14	3	6	0
Revenues ($ in Thousands)													
Net Sales 2	53065566	1060184	3160272	2140756	5777957	1307663	5722442	6435604	4840896	9091023	1063716	12465052	0
Interest 3	31350	348	43	751	4079	1571	5200	1587	827	6446	932	9567	0
Rents 4	8110	31	0	0	1066	1956	50	304	1023	420	510	2750	0
Royalties 5	21086	0	0	0	3621	0	1062	0	306	0	2156	13941	0
Other Portfolio Income 6	74884	13943	0	298	14203	17	873	3034	11496	9748	14234	7038	0
Other Receipts 7	317360	2098	17280	9776	64273	6956	50255	43222	22638	64019	187	36654	0
Total Receipts 8	53518356	1076604	3177595	2151581	5865199	1318163	5779882	6483751	4877186	9171656	1081735	12535002	0
Average Total Receipts 9	4991	998	401	3178	7841	19972	46612	106291	212052	655118	360578	2089167	•
Operating Costs/Operating Income (%)													
Cost of Operations 10	82.2	84.7	57.1	76.7	74.2	79.7	78.8	85.4	83.2	89.8	80.1	87.3	•
Salaries and Wages 11	6.0	4.8	10.4	5.8	9.5	5.9	7.5	5.9	6.6	3.2	6.6	4.5	•
Taxes Paid 12	0.8	0.5	2.4	0.9	1.3	0.8	0.9	0.7	0.7	0.3	0.8	0.5	•
Interest Paid 13	0.9	0.1	0.6	0.1	1.0	0.5	0.7	0.5	0.8	0.7	4.4	1.5	•
Depreciation 14	0.5	0.1	0.4	0.5	0.7	0.4	0.5	0.4	0.4	0.2	3.7	0.5	•
Amortization and Depletion 15	0.2	0.0	0.1	0.2	0.1	0.0	0.1	0.1	0.1	0.1	2.0	0.5	•
Pensions and Other Deferred Comp. 16	0.3	0.7	0.1	1.1	0.4	0.4	0.3	0.2	0.2	0.1	0.3	0.2	•
Employee Benefits 17	0.4	0.0	0.5	0.1	0.5	0.4	0.5	0.6	0.5	0.2	0.7	0.3	•
Advertising 18	0.2	0.1	0.8	0.2	0.2	0.1	0.8	0.1	0.2	0.0	0.2	0.1	•
Other Expenses 19	6.4	5.1	17.5	7.7	9.9	7.0	5.7	4.7	6.1	5.0	9.8	3.9	•
Officers' Compensation 20	1.3	0.4	4.8	2.7	2.7	2.6	1.9	0.7	0.9	0.4	0.4	0.3	•
Operating Margin 21	0.8	3.5	5.4	4.1	•	2.2	2.3	0.7	0.2	•	•	0.3	•
Operating Margin Before Officers' Comp. 22	2.1	3.9	10.2	6.8	2.3	4.8	4.2	1.4	1.1	0.3	•	0.6	•

Selected Average Balance Sheet ($ in Thousands)

Net Receivables 23	561	0	28	245	917	2895	5540	13995	21233	79689	79178	229213
Inventories 24	333	0	17	151	642	2743	3296	8053	18078	33360	36368	130008
Net Property, Plant and Equipment 25	145	0	11	86	183	298	1544	2275	8615	10269	55833	68422
Total Assets 26	1594	0	94	704	2332	6390	14057	33434	66929	165631	321415	850363
Notes and Loans Payable 27	550	0	65	24	914	1497	4277	9677	19036	51543	148155	309468
All Other Liabilities 28	670	0	44	255	842	2290	4850	14492	23862	86416	123507	377518
Net Worth 29	374	0	-15	425	576	2603	4930	9265	24031	27672	49753	163378

Selected Financial Ratios (Times to 1)

Current Ratio 30	1.4	•	1.3	2.1	1.5	1.7	1.7	1.4	1.7	1.5	1.1	0.9
Quick Ratio 31	0.8	•	0.8	1.6	0.9	1.1	1.1	0.9	0.9	1.0	0.8	0.6
Net Sales to Working Capital 32	17.8	•	27.1	10.2	12.0	8.5	10.0	13.5	10.6	13.9	31.3	•
Coverage Ratio 33	2.8	36.5	11.0	39.0	2.2	7.3	6.5	3.8	2.1	2.1	•	1.6
Total Asset Turnover 34	3.1	•	4.3	4.5	3.3	3.1	3.3	3.2	3.1	3.9	1.1	2.4
Inventory Turnover 35	12.2	•	13.4	16.1	8.9	5.8	11.0	11.2	9.7	17.5	7.8	14.0
Receivables Turnover 36	8.8	•	16.4	11.9	7.9	5.3	8.6	8.2	9.8	8.7	4.5	8.7
Total Liabilities to Net Worth 37	3.3	•	•	0.7	3.0	1.5	1.9	2.6	1.8	5.0	5.5	4.2
Current Assets to Working Capital 38	3.9	•	4.3	1.9	2.9	2.5	2.4	3.4	2.4	2.9	12.2	•
Current Liabilities to Working Capital 39	2.9	•	3.3	0.9	1.9	1.5	1.4	2.4	1.4	1.9	11.2	•
Working Capital to Net Sales 40	0.1	•	0.0	0.1	0.1	0.1	0.1	0.1	0.1	0.1	0.0	•
Inventory to Working Capital 41	1.2	•	1.5	0.4	0.8	0.8	1.2	0.9	0.7	•	2.7	•
Total Receipts to Cash Flow 42	15.7	12.8	5.2	9.6	12.2	13.0	13.4	20.4	19.1	20.9	264.3	27.2
Cost of Goods to Cash Flow 43	12.9	10.8	3.0	7.4	9.1	10.4	10.5	17.4	15.9	18.8	211.7	23.7
Cash Flow to Total Debt 44	0.3	0.7	1.2	0.4	0.4	0.2	0.1	0.3	0.2	0.2	0.0	0.1

Selected Financial Factors (in Percentages)

Debt Ratio 45	76.5	•	116.4	39.6	75.3	59.3	64.9	72.3	64.1	83.3	84.5	80.8
Return on Total Assets 46	8.2	•	27.9	21.2	7.1	10.9	14.0	6.3	5.5	6.0	•	5.8
Return on Equity Before Income Taxes 47	22.3	•	•	34.3	16.0	23.2	33.8	16.7	8.1	18.4	•	10.8
Return on Equity After Income Taxes 48	19.0	•	•	34.1	13.8	18.7	31.0	14.1	7.1	15.8	•	4.5
Profit Margin (Before Income Tax) 49	1.7	5.0	5.9	4.6	1.2	3.0	3.6	1.5	0.9	0.8	•	0.8
Profit Margin (After Income Tax) 50	1.4	4.8	5.9	4.6	1.0	2.5	3.3	1.2	0.8	0.7	•	0.4

Table II

Corporations with Net Income

PAPER AND PAPER PRODUCT

MONEY AMOUNTS AND SIZE OF ASSETS IN THOUSANDS OF DOLLARS

Item Description for Accounting Period 7/07 Through 6/08	Total	Zero Assets	Under 500	500 to 1,000	1,000 to 5,000	5,000 to 10,000	10,000 to 25,000	25,000 to 50,000	50,000 to 100,000	100,000 to 250,000	250,000 to 500,000	500,000 to 2,500,000	2,500,000 and over
Number of Enterprises 1	7272	672	5190	625	540	48	118	48	•	•	0	3	0
Revenues ($ in Thousands)													
Net Sales 2	40879080	1036914	2369906	1987018	5164234	946898	5664564	4962127	•	•	0	6507475	0
Interest 3	17821	254	0	510	1127	820	5141	1414	•	•	0	2434	0
Rents 4	4866	31	0	0	1066	1956	50	304	•	•	0	16	0
Royalties 5	1154	0	0	0	0	0	1062	0	•	•	0	90	0
Other Portfolio Income 6	33080	13943	0	298	11032	17	868	3016	•	•	0	203	0
Other Receipts 7	282345	2105	14874	9146	61684	6947	50251	40344	•	•	0	16008	0
Total Receipts 8	41218346	1053247	2384780	1996972	5239143	956638	5721936	5007205	•	•	0	6526226	0
Average Total Receipts 9	5668	1567	459	3195	9702	19930	48491	104317	•	•	•	2175409	•
Operating Costs/Operating Income (%)													
Cost of Operations 10	81.5	86.0	54.9	76.7	74.5	77.7	78.8	83.7	•	•	•	85.1	•
Salaries and Wages 11	6.1	4.8	9.9	5.6	9.4	7.0	7.4	6.2	•	•	•	5.0	•
Taxes Paid 12	0.8	0.5	1.8	0.8	1.3	1.0	0.9	0.7	•	•	•	0.7	•
Interest Paid 13	0.6	0.1	0.6	0.1	1.0	0.3	0.6	0.6	•	•	•	1.0	•
Depreciation 14	0.4	0.1	0.4	0.5	0.7	0.3	0.4	0.4	•	•	•	0.2	•
Amortization and Depletion 15	0.2	0.0	0.1	0.2	0.1	0.0	0.1	0.1	•	•	•	0.5	•
Pensions and Other Deferred Comp. 16	0.3	0.4	0.1	1.1	0.3	0.5	0.3	0.3	•	•	•	0.4	•
Employee Benefits 17	0.4	0.0	0.6	0.0	0.5	0.4	0.5	0.6	•	•	•	0.5	•
Advertising 18	0.3	0.1	0.8	0.2	0.2	0.2	0.8	0.1	•	•	•	0.1	•
Other Expenses 19	6.1	3.8	16.3	7.5	9.3	6.0	5.7	5.1	•	•	•	3.6	•
Officers' Compensation 20	1.3	0.4	4.5	2.7	2.2	2.2	1.9	0.8	•	•	•	0.2	•
Operating Margin 21	2.2	3.9	9.8	4.5	0.6	4.4	2.7	1.3	•	•	•	2.8	•
Operating Margin Before Officers' Comp. 22	3.4	4.3	14.3	7.1	2.8	6.6	4.6	2.1	•	•	•	3.0	•

Selected Average Balance Sheet ($ in Thousands)

Net Receivables 23	600	0	25	245	1062	3091	5716	13305	•	215653
Inventories 24	363	0	11	154	511	3418	3245	9158	•	107376
Net Property, Plant and Equipment 25	119	0	14	91	236	255	1147	2563	•	20451
Total Assets 26	1546	0	93	712	2430	6342	14024	34181	•	754454
Notes and Loans Payable 27	395	0	37	26	820	995	3647	10021	•	170210
All Other Liabilities 28	657	0	31	268	1002	2181	4915	13312	•	375920
Net Worth 29	494	0	26	418	608	3166	5462	10847	•	208325

Selected Financial Ratios (Times to 1)

Current Ratio 30	1.4	•	1.5	2.0	1.3	2.0	1.8	1.5	•	0.8
Quick Ratio 31	0.9	•	1.1	1.5	0.8	1.3	1.2	0.8	•	0.5
Net Sales to Working Capital 32	18.0	•	27.0	10.8	21.4	7.0	9.4	11.7	•	•
Coverage Ratio 33	5.9	56.7	18.3	39.1	3.2	19.1	8.0	4.8	•	4.2
Total Asset Turnover 34	3.6	•	4.9	4.5	3.9	3.1	3.4	3.0	•	2.9
Inventory Turnover 35	12.6	•	22.0	15.9	13.9	4.5	11.7	9.5	•	17.2
Receivables Turnover 36	8.7	•	18.0	11.8	8.3	4.2	9.2	7.6	•	•
Total Liabilities to Net Worth 37	2.1	•	2.6	0.7	3.0	1.0	1.6	2.2	•	2.6
Current Assets to Working Capital 38	3.6	•	3.0	2.0	4.2	2.0	2.3	3.0	•	•
Current Liabilities to Working Capital 39	2.6	•	2.0	1.0	3.2	1.0	1.3	2.0	•	•
Working Capital to Net Sales 40	0.1	•	0.0	0.1	0.0	0.1	0.1	0.1	•	•
Inventory to Working Capital 41	1.1	•	0.6	0.4	1.4	0.6	0.7	1.1	•	•
Total Receipts to Cash Flow 42	13.3	14.5	4.3	9.3	11.5	9.9	12.7	16.6	•	18.2
Cost of Goods to Cash Flow 43	10.9	12.5	2.4	7.1	8.5	7.7	10.0	13.9	•	15.5
Cash Flow to Total Debt 44	0.4	•	1.6	1.2	0.5	0.6	0.4	0.3	•	0.2

Selected Financial Factors (in Percentages)

Debt Ratio 45	68.0	•	72.5	41.4	75.0	50.1	61.1	68.3	•	72.4
Return on Total Assets 46	13.3	•	53.7	22.8	12.0	17.9	15.7	8.4	•	11.6
Return on Equity Before Income Taxes 47	34.4	•	184.5	37.8	32.8	34.0	35.2	20.9	•	32.0
Return on Equity After Income Taxes 48	30.8	•	184.0	37.6	30.0	29.0	32.6	18.1	•	22.1
Profit Margin (Before Income Tax) 49	3.0	5.4	10.4	5.0	2.1	5.5	4.0	2.2	•	3.1
Profit Margin (After Income Tax) 50	2.7	5.1	10.4	4.9	1.9	4.6	3.7	1.9	•	2.1

184

Table I

Corporations with and without Net Income

DRUGS AND DRUGGISTS' SUNDRIES

MONEY AMOUNTS AND SIZE OF ASSETS IN THOUSANDS OF DOLLARS

Item Description for Accounting Period 7/07 Through 6/08	Total	Zero Assets	Under 500	500 to 1,000	1,000 to 5,000	5,000 to 10,000	10,000 to 25,000	25,000 to 50,000	50,000 to 100,000	100,000 to 250,000	250,000 to 500,000	500,000 to 2,500,000	2,500,000 and over
Number of Enterprises **1**	5479	687	2829	626	788	214	164	52	40	32	15	18	14
Revenues ($ in Thousands)													
Net Sales **2**	391773955	1295849	1214247	1453681	5550285	3707002	5697490	4478541	4965862	8388928	15831785	18858561	320331726
Interest **3**	1454713	8238	97	2653	2819	3327	12802	8638	15852	38290	22288	207086	1132623
Rents **4**	548898	0	0	37	693	0	143	922	460	447	648	3332	542215
Royalties **5**	2324182	11365	0	4140	19813	1297	537	682	20841	53357	289	118428	2093433
Other Portfolio Income **6**	1026996	11758	0	0	59	12233	23887	2966	16224	107344	15950	121888	714686
Other Receipts **7**	5554300	24244	4381	2772	57608	7280	53832	74270	101942	133226	61539	523325	4509881
Total Receipts **8**	402683044	1351454	1218725	1463283	5631277	3731139	5788691	4566019	5121181	8721592	15932499	19832620	329324564
Average Total Receipts **9**	73496	1967	431	2338	7146	17435	35297	87808	128030	272550	1062167	1101812	23523183
Operating Costs/Operating Income (%)													
Cost of Operations **10**	85.6	45.9	59.0	72.7	61.9	70.4	69.6	79.5	71.9	73.7	88.2	39.4	89.9
Salaries and Wages **11**	3.7	14.3	5.6	6.0	9.0	10.0	9.4	5.6	7.2	9.1	2.5	11.2	2.8
Taxes Paid **12**	0.4	2.9	1.3	2.0	1.3	1.2	1.2	0.6	1.0	0.8	0.5	1.4	0.3
Interest Paid **13**	0.6	0.9	0.6	1.3	1.3	0.7	0.9	0.8	1.1	1.1	1.0	1.5	0.5
Depreciation **14**	0.4	0.2	0.4	0.3	0.5	0.3	0.6	0.6	0.6	0.5	0.3	0.9	0.4
Amortization and Depletion **15**	0.2	0.4	0.2	0.0	0.1	0.4	0.2	0.3	1.3	0.7	0.2	1.0	0.2
Pensions and Other Deferred Comp. **16**	0.1	0.8	•	0.5	0.1	0.3	0.2	0.1	0.3	0.1	0.1	0.3	0.1
Employee Benefits **17**	0.4	0.7	0.1	0.5	0.4	0.8	0.6	0.5	0.7	0.5	0.2	1.6	0.3
Advertising **18**	0.8	4.7	1.2	2.0	1.4	0.5	1.4	1.2	3.9	1.7	0.2	4.1	0.6
Other Expenses **19**	6.3	8.7	20.6	12.1	19.5	10.3	11.0	9.9	12.0	11.2	5.0	26.3	4.5
Officers' Compensation **20**	0.5	0.5	6.0	4.6	4.9	4.5	1.6	1.3	1.2	1.5	0.2	0.6	0.3
Operating Margin **21**	0.9	20.0	5.1	•	•	0.7	3.2	•	•	•	1.6	11.6	0.2
Operating Margin Before Officers' Comp. **22**	1.4	20.5	11.1	2.5	4.4	5.1	4.8	1.0	0.2	0.5	1.8	12.2	0.5

Selected Average Balance Sheet ($ in Thousands)

Net Receivables **23**	5639	0	97	7	610	1476	5107	8626	16792	27800	95344	155423	1638773
Inventories **24**	5503	0	164	49	726	2067	3923	8381	13171	29685	88246	114638	1639317
Net Property, Plant and Equipment **25**	1828	0	51	6	191	477	1165	2497	6431	12577	18685	60505	525791
Total Assets **26**	32194	0	691	91	2465	7723	15816	32291	69129	147720	374393	1042787	9711147
Notes and Loans Payable **27**	7106	0	454	40	1136	1847	3852	7147	15595	44921	100090	208858	2065910
All Other Liabilities **28**	13891	0	238	51	1365	2647	7438	12565	26928	49473	170996	325358	4372552
Net Worth **29**	11198	0	-1	0	-36	3229	4526	12578	26606	53327	103307	508771	3272684

Selected Financial Ratios (Times to 1)

Current Ratio **30**	1.3	•	3.1	1.5	1.3	1.5	1.4	1.7	1.4	1.3	2.1	1.8	1.2
Quick Ratio **31**	0.7	•	1.3	0.7	0.7	0.7	0.8	0.9	0.9	0.7	1.2	0.9	0.7
Net Sales to Working Capital **32**	18.0	•	9.0	20.1	17.1	10.4	9.3	8.2	9.1	13.5	7.6	4.2	26.6
Coverage Ratio **33**	6.8	29.4	9.9	•	1.7	2.8	6.1	3.1	3.0	3.6	3.3	12.0	6.9
Total Asset Turnover **34**	2.2	•	4.7	3.4	2.9	2.2	2.2	2.7	1.8	1.8	2.8	1.0	2.4
Inventory Turnover **35**	11.1	•	5.1	10.3	6.0	5.9	6.2	8.2	6.8	6.5	10.5	3.6	12.6
Receivables Turnover **36**	11.6	•	33.2	23.8	11.2	13.5	7.7	9.4	8.5	8.8	11.0	7.0	12.3
Total Liabilities to Net Worth **37**	1.9	541.7	•	•	•	1.4	2.5	1.6	1.6	1.8	2.6	1.0	2.0
Current Assets to Working Capital **38**	4.3	1.5	3.2	3.2	4.8	3.2	3.4	2.4	3.2	5.0	1.9	2.3	5.7
Current Liabilities to Working Capital **39**	3.3	0.5	2.2	2.2	3.8	2.2	2.4	1.4	2.2	4.0	0.9	1.3	4.7
Working Capital to Net Sales **40**	0.1	0.1	0.0	0.0	0.1	0.1	0.1	0.1	0.1	0.1	0.1	0.2	0.0
Inventory to Working Capital **41**	1.4	0.8	1.7	•	1.5	1.5	1.2	0.9	1.0	1.5	0.6	0.4	1.9
Total Receipts to Cash Flow **42**	10.9	5.8	13.5	3.1	5.4	10.2	7.4	9.4	7.9	7.6	14.6	2.4	14.5
Cost of Goods to Cash Flow **43**	9.3	3.4	9.8	1.4	3.4	7.1	5.1	7.5	5.7	5.6	12.9	1.0	13.0
Cash Flow to Total Debt **44**	0.3	0.8	0.2	•	0.5	0.4	0.4	0.5	0.4	0.4	0.3	0.8	0.2

Selected Financial Factors (in Percentages)

Debt Ratio **45**	65.2	•	99.8	100.1	101.4	58.2	71.4	61.0	61.5	63.9	72.4	51.2	66.3
Return on Total Assets **46**	9.7	28.7	•	6.7	•	4.5	12.6	6.6	6.1	7.3	8.9	18.4	8.6
Return on Equity Before Income Taxes **47**	23.9	•	14018.9	5079.2	•	7.0	36.8	11.6	10.6	14.7	22.5	34.6	21.8
Return on Equity After Income Taxes **48**	16.0	•	13983.8	6221.8	•	5.6	33.5	8.4	4.0	11.0	15.0	22.5	14.5
Profit Margin (Before Income Tax) **49**	3.7	24.3	5.5	•	1.0	1.3	4.8	1.7	2.3	3.0	2.2	16.8	3.1
Profit Margin (After Income Tax) **50**	2.5	14.8	5.5	•	0.5	1.0	4.4	1.2	0.9	2.2	1.5	10.9	2.1

Table II

Corporations with Net Income

DRUGS AND DRUGGISTS' SUNDRIES

MONEY AMOUNTS AND SIZE OF ASSETS IN THOUSANDS OF DOLLARS

Item Description for Accounting Period 7/07 Through 6/08	Total	Zero Assets	Under 500	500 to 1,000	1,000 to 5,000	5,000 to 10,000	10,000 to 25,000	25,000 to 50,000	50,000 to 100,000	100,000 to 250,000	250,000 to 500,000	500,000 to 2,500,000	2,500,000 and over
Number of Enterprises 1	2359	9	1075	363	550	105	125	43	28	•	12	15	•

Revenues ($ in Thousands)

Item Description for Accounting Period 7/07 Through 6/08	Total	Zero Assets	Under 500	500 to 1,000	1,000 to 5,000	5,000 to 10,000	10,000 to 25,000	25,000 to 50,000	50,000 to 100,000	100,000 to 250,000	250,000 to 500,000	500,000 to 2,500,000	2,500,000 and over
Net Sales 2	370545545	1028656	718864	755144	4079296	1878743	4406177	4165124	4243752	•	11602501	17126045	•
Interest 3	1406469	8003	1	1953	2707	1677	8413	6614	13105	•	22288	200811	•
Rents 4	546458	0	0	0	693	0	143	560	460	•	648	3332	•
Royalties 5	2057135	11365	0	0	0	0	0	682	7580	•	289	109186	•
Other Portfolio Income 6	977066	4337	0	0	59	5855	6052	2928	13220	•	15948	121831	•
Other Receipts 7	5149321	22030	4291	2289	44406	8844	46015	73600	70203	•	32415	394053	•
Total Receipts 8	380681994	1074391	722956	759386	4127161	1895119	4466800	4249508	4348320	•	11674089	17955258	•
Average Total Receipts 9	161374	119377	673	2092	7504	18049	35734	98826	155297	•	972841	1197017	•

Operating Costs/Operating Income (%)

Item Description for Accounting Period 7/07 Through 6/08	Total	Zero Assets	Under 500	500 to 1,000	1,000 to 5,000	5,000 to 10,000	10,000 to 25,000	25,000 to 50,000	50,000 to 100,000	100,000 to 250,000	250,000 to 500,000	500,000 to 2,500,000	2,500,000 and over
Cost of Operations 10	87.0	33.3	58.9	73.4	56.7	73.2	68.0	80.3	76.3	•	85.0	37.2	•
Salaries and Wages 11	3.3	15.1	1.9	3.6	9.2	7.5	9.1	5.3	5.1	•	2.9	11.5	•
Taxes Paid 12	0.4	2.1	0.5	0.8	1.4	1.2	1.2	0.6	0.9	•	0.6	1.5	•
Interest Paid 13	0.6	0.6	1.0	1.7	1.3	0.6	0.7	0.7	0.6	•	1.0	1.5	•
Depreciation 14	0.4	0.3	0.2	0.2	0.4	0.3	0.5	0.4	0.5	•	0.3	0.9	•
Amortization and Depletion 15	0.2	0.5	0.0	0.0	0.0	0.0	0.2	0.1	0.2	•	0.3	0.9	•
Pensions and Other Deferred Comp. 16	0.1	1.0	•	0.9	0.1	0.2	0.2	0.1	0.3	•	0.1	0.3	•
Employee Benefits 17	0.3	0.9	•	0.1	0.5	0.3	0.5	0.5	0.5	•	0.2	1.6	•
Advertising 18	0.7	5.9	1.6	0.5	1.7	0.2	1.3	0.8	2.2	•	0.3	4.0	•
Other Expenses 19	5.2	8.3	21.5	10.9	19.9	7.1	10.2	8.9	8.1	•	6.3	25.8	•
Officers' Compensation 20	0.3	0.4	3.0	4.8	5.3	2.3	1.6	1.2	1.0	•	0.2	0.6	•
Operating Margin 21	1.4	31.6	11.4	3.1	3.3	7.3	6.5	1.1	4.3	•	2.7	14.3	•
Operating Margin Before Officers' Comp. 22	1.8	32.1	14.4	7.9	8.6	9.6	8.1	2.3	5.3	•	2.9	14.9	•

Selected Average Balance Sheet ($ in Thousands)

Net Receivables 23	12222	0	15	28	784	2026	5180	9520	19775	•	92608	166563
Inventories 24	12130	0	91	122	833	3170	4225	8980	15036		79851	124534
Net Property, Plant and Equipment 25	3612	0	10	25	213	305	946	2231	4873		17551	65757
Total Assets 26	67781	0	124	615	2636	7563	15100	31844	67056	•	352697	1121955
Notes and Loans Payable 27	14395	0	52	38	1204	1512	3082	6507	11529		90512	207987
All Other Liabilities 28	29337	0	114	243	1353	2508	5650	12570	27197		156088	354185
Net Worth 29	24049	0	-42	333	79	3543	6369	12767	28329	•	106097	559783

Selected Financial Ratios (Times to 1)

Current Ratio 30	1.3	3.5	1.2	1.5	1.5	1.7	1.8	1.8	1.6	•	2.0	1.8
Quick Ratio 31	0.7	•	1.6	0.5	0.8	0.6	1.0	0.9	1.0	•	1.3	0.9
Net Sales to Working Capital 32	17.1	•	7.6	42.7	10.9	8.6	6.8	8.6	8.7	•	7.6	4.2
Coverage Ratio 33	8.2	57.0	13.6	3.1	4.3	14.7	13.0	5.3	12.4	•	4.2	14.1
Total Asset Turnover 34	2.3	•	5.4	3.4	2.8	2.4	2.3	3.0	2.3	•	2.7	1.0
Inventory Turnover 35	11.3	•	4.3	12.5	5.0	4.1	5.7	8.7	7.7	•	10.3	3.4
Receivables Turnover 36	11.4	32.3	82.5	10.4	8.8	7.2	9.3		•	•		6.8
Total Liabilities to Net Worth 37	1.8	•	0.8	32.5	1.1	1.4	1.5	1.8	•		2.3	1.0
Current Assets to Working Capital 38	4.0	1.4	6.0	3.1	2.9	2.3	2.3			•	2.1	2.3
Current Liabilities to Working Capital 39	3.0	0.4	5.0	2.1	1.9	1.3	1.3			•	1.1	1.3
Working Capital to Net Sales 40	0.1	0.1	0.0	0.1	0.1	0.1	0.1			•	0.1	0.2
Inventory to Working Capital 41	1.3	0.8	3.5	1.2	1.6	0.8	0.9			•	0.6	0.4
Total Receipts to Cash Flow 42	11.5	2.3	4.1	9.9	4.5	7.4	6.3	0.9	9.1	•	10.8	2.3
Cost of Goods to Cash Flow 43	10.0	0.8	2.4	7.3	2.6	5.4	4.3	7.3	5.6	•	9.2	0.9
Cash Flow to Total Debt 44	0.3	1.0	0.7	0.6	0.6	0.6	0.6	0.5		•	0.4	0.9

Selected Financial Factors (in Percentages)

Debt Ratio 45	64.5	133.7	45.8	97.0	53.2	57.8	59.9	57.8		•	69.9	50.1
Return on Total Assets 46	11.2	69.8	18.0	16.3	20.7	19.8	11.7	16.9		•	11.8	21.0
Return on Equity Before Income Taxes 47	27.8	•	22.6	418.2	41.2	43.4	23.7	36.9		•	29.8	39.1
Return on Equity After Income Taxes 48	19.2	•	18.8	357.8	38.6	40.3	19.8	28.0		•	20.6	25.8
Profit Margin (Before Income Tax) 49	4.3	36.1	12.0	3.6	4.4	8.2	7.8	3.1	6.9	•	3.3	19.2
Profit Margin (After Income Tax) 50	2.9	24.1	12.0	3.0	3.8	7.6	7.3	2.6	5.2	•	2.3	12.7

186

Table I

Corporations with and without Net Income

APPAREL, PIECE GOODS, AND NOTIONS

Money Amounts and Size of Assets in Thousands of Dollars

Item Description for Accounting Period 7/07 Through 6/08	Total	Zero Assets	Under 500	500 to 1,000	1,000 to 5,000	5,000 to 10,000	10,000 to 25,000	25,000 to 50,000	50,000 to 100,000	100,000 to 250,000	250,000 to 500,000	500,000 to 2,500,000	2,500,000 and over
Number of Enterprises 1	24739	3370	16568	1744	2091	533	237	93	46	29	15	10	3
Revenues ($ in Thousands)													
Net Sales 2	101648500	1788800	12067744	5042173	12327454	8138049	8006379	7838910	5268992	7510951	7170751	10362273	16126023
Interest 3	219522	647	23506	1842	8858	9741	5286	4370	12722	30677	25287	28791	67794
Rents 4	59493	33	2995	0	2104	637	2493	1246	4873	26231	951	2009	15921
Royalties 5	1283616	2815	0	0	63	2729	151	3233	27175	29530	86529	279002	852390
Other Portfolio Income 6	553576	55589	3727	36	1291	1	32920	6226	10730	75529	20811	26389	320327
Other Receipts 7	1147959	8837	42944	78019	84362	14301	137973	85559	59696	47328	61094	51472	476375
Total Receipts 8	104912666	1856721	12140916	5122070	12424132	8165458	8185202	7939544	5384188	7720246	7365423	10749936	17858830
Average Total Receipts 9	4241	551	733	2937	5942	15320	34537	85371	117048	266215	491028	1074994	5952943
Operating Costs/Operating Income (%)													
Cost of Operations 10	66.6	76.2	71.5	57.8	72.8	71.7	75.4	73.5	65.5	64.7	59.8	61.2	57.3
Salaries and Wages 11	9.4	5.7	4.3	15.1	7.1	6.4	7.7	6.9	9.2	8.7	12.1	12.1	14.3
Taxes Paid 12	2.4	2.6	2.6	2.7	2.1	3.1	2.3	3.2	2.5	2.9	1.7	1.9	2.2
Interest Paid 13	1.2	2.1	0.4	0.5	0.8	1.0	1.1	1.0	1.4	1.6	1.6	2.3	1.1
Depreciation 14	0.8	0.3	0.3	0.3	0.4	0.3	0.3	0.5	0.8	0.9	1.2	1.5	2.0
Amortization and Depletion 15	0.2	0.1	0.0	0.1	0.1	0.1	0.1	0.1	0.4	0.2	0.2	0.7	0.4
Pensions and Other Deferred Comp. 16	0.3	0.1	0.2	0.6	0.3	0.1	0.2	0.2	0.4	0.2	0.3	0.2	0.4
Employee Benefits 17	0.6	1.5	0.3	0.5	0.5	0.5	0.5	0.3	0.7	0.9	0.8	0.8	0.7
Advertising 18	2.1	0.4	1.2	0.3	0.5	0.8	0.9	1.0	2.3	2.6	3.5	2.7	5.5
Other Expenses 19	13.0	19.6	12.1	17.4	11.9	9.5	9.1	9.2	13.4	11.3	16.2	13.8	16.4
Officers' Compensation 20	2.4	3.7	4.3	10.2	2.8	2.5	1.7	1.3	2.0	1.6	0.6	0.9	1.0
Operating Margin 21	1.0	•	2.7	•	0.7	3.8	1.7	2.7	1.4	4.3	1.9	1.7	•
Operating Margin Before Officers' Comp. 22	3.4	6.9	4.7	•	6.3	6.3	2.5	4.0	3.5	5.9	2.5	2.6	•

Selected Average Balance Sheet ($ in Thousands)

Net Receivables 23	476	0	20	128	576	1906	4047	9251	17272	36821	47801	264278	653109
Inventories 24	526	0	36	320	548	2289	5790	11971	18559	44635	89311	245124	716139
Net Property, Plant and Equipment 25	258	0	6	47	133	758	792	2401	6270	20470	40110	122921	797978
Total Assets 26	2431	0	108	704	2097	6824	14779	35121	69566	166386	356274	111406	5948610
Notes and Loans Payable 27	606	0	42	364	698	2232	4284	9791	21835	47668	80099	287673	875558
All Other Liabilities 28	743	0	36	382	761	2420	6350	13295	20122	40857	103088	367661	1387165
Net Worth 29	1082	0	30	-42	638	2171	4146	12035	27609	77860	173087	456072	3685888

Selected Financial Ratios (Times to 1)

Current Ratio 30	1.6	•	2.3	1.1	1.7	1.8	1.7	1.7	1.8	2.2	2.2	1.7	1.2
Quick Ratio 31	0.8	•	1.3	0.5	0.9	0.8	0.7	0.6	0.8	1.0	0.8	1.0	0.5
Net Sales to Working Capital 32	7.5	•	14.8	50.8	8.1	6.1	6.5	6.9	4.7	4.3	4.6	4.7	20.2
Coverage Ratio 33	4.9	•	9.8	•	2.8	5.1	3.6	4.9	3.7	5.3	3.9	3.5	11.7
Total Asset Turnover 34	1.7	•	6.8	4.1	2.8	2.2	2.3	2.4	1.6	1.6	1.3	0.9	0.9
Inventory Turnover 35	5.2	•	14.5	5.2	7.8	4.8	4.4	5.2	4.0	3.8	3.2	2.6	4.3
Receivables Turnover 36	9.1	•	37.7	17.3	11.7	8.2	8.6	9.3	7.2	7.4	9.6	3.2	16.5
Total Liabilities to Net Worth 37	1.2	•	2.6	•	2.3	2.1	2.6	1.9	1.5	1.1	1.1	1.4	0.6
Current Assets to Working Capital 38	2.6	•	1.8	11.2	2.3	2.3	2.5	2.5	2.2	1.8	1.9	2.5	7.1
Current Liabilities to Working Capital 39	1.6	•	0.8	10.2	1.3	1.3	1.5	1.5	1.2	0.8	0.9	1.5	6.1
Working Capital to Net Sales 40	0.1	•	0.1	0.0	0.1	0.2	0.2	0.1	0.2	0.2	0.2	0.2	0.0
Inventory to Working Capital 41	1.0	•	0.7	5.6	0.9	1.0	1.2	1.1	0.8	0.8	0.9	0.7	2.7
Total Receipts to Cash Flow 42	7.1	33.4	8.3	11.9	9.1	8.2	10.3	9.0	6.9	7.3	6.1	6.6	4.3
Cost of Goods to Cash Flow 43	4.8	25.5	5.9	6.9	6.6	5.9	7.8	6.6	4.5	4.7	3.6	4.1	2.4
Cash Flow to Total Debt 44	0.4	•	1.1	0.3	0.4	0.4	0.3	0.4	0.4	0.4	0.4	0.2	0.6

Selected Financial Factors (in Percentages)

Debt Ratio 45	55.5	•	72.1	105.9	69.6	68.2	72.0	65.7	60.3	53.2	51.4	59.0	38.0
Return on Total Assets 46	9.7	•	24.7	•	6.7	11.6	9.4	11.9	8.4	13.5	8.5	7.6	11.3
Return on Equity Before Income Taxes 47	17.3	•	79.5	264.0	14.1	29.4	24.3	27.6	15.6	23.5	13.0	13.3	16.7
Return on Equity After Income Taxes 48	12.7	•	78.4	266.4	13.4	27.4	22.7	24.6	12.8	18.0	8.7	9.0	10.6
Profit Margin (Before Income Tax) 49	4.6	•	3.3	•	1.5	4.2	3.0	3.9	3.8	7.1	4.7	5.8	11.4
Profit Margin (After Income Tax) 50	3.4	•	3.2	•	1.4	3.9	2.8	3.5	3.1	5.4	3.1	4.0	7.3

Table II

Corporations with Net Income

APPAREL, PIECE GOODS, AND NOTIONS

MONEY AMOUNTS AND SIZE OF ASSETS IN THOUSANDS OF DOLLARS

Item Description for Accounting Period 7/07 Through 6/08	Total	Zero Assets	Under 500	500 to 1,000	1,000 to 5,000	5,000 to 10,000	10,000 to 25,000	25,000 to 50,000	50,000 to 100,000	100,000 to 250,000	250,000 to 500,000	500,000 to 2,500,000	2,500,000 and over
Number of Enterprises **1**	14054	1333	9612	629	1668	477	181	79	32	25	8	10	0
Revenues ($ in Thousands)													
Net Sales **2**	78482767	198462	10493570	1756837	10413912	7368667	6387541	6722196	3759321	6377682	3797606	21206972	0
Interest **3**	181777	280	22617	1533	6057	4063	2948	3212	10176	27933	14471	88488	0
Rents **4**	40631	0	2995	0	1374	94	2002	1231	4838	25759	226	2111	0
Royalties **5**	1072008	0	0	0	57	2729	151	3233	17744	28789	75541	943765	0
Other Portfolio Income **6**	505464	20336	2722	0	813	1	31499	3634	7814	75084	20026	343536	0
Other Receipts **7**	939500	7906	41005	297	37852	1171	145830	81376	51422	44375	30177	498087	0
Total Receipts **8**	81222147	226984	10562909	1758667	10460065	7376725	6569971	6814882	3851315	6579622	3938047	23082959	0
Average Total Receipts **9**	5779	170	1099	2796	6271	15465	36298	86264	120354	263185	492256	2308296	•
Operating Costs/Operating Income (%)													
Cost of Operations **10**	67.0	40.4	72.7	78.0	71.7	71.8	76.1	74.3	63.2	63.8	57.7	57.8	•
Salaries and Wages **11**	8.8	3.6	3.6	6.0	7.0	6.2	6.9	6.3	8.7	8.2	12.5	14.1	•
Taxes Paid **12**	2.5	2.0	2.7	1.3	2.1	3.2	2.1	3.1	2.4	3.2	2.0	2.4	•
Interest Paid **13**	1.0	0.2	0.3	0.8	0.7	1.0	0.8	0.8	0.9	1.6	0.9	1.3	•
Depreciation **14**	0.8	1.2	0.3	0.2	0.3	0.2	0.2	0.4	0.9	1.0	1.3	1.9	•
Amortization and Depletion **15**	0.2	0.2	0.0	0.1	0.0	0.0	0.0	0.0	0.3	0.2	0.1	0.5	•
Pensions and Other Deferred Comp. **16**	0.2	0.4	0.3	0.0	0.4	0.1	0.1	0.1	0.4	0.2	0.4	0.2	•
Employee Benefits **17**	0.5	0.8	0.3	0.1	0.5	0.5	0.4	0.3	0.6	1.0	0.7	0.7	•
Advertising **18**	2.1	1.3	1.3	0.1	0.5	0.6	0.8	0.9	2.2	2.5	4.1	4.5	•
Other Expenses **19**	11.0	31.0	10.3	8.8	10.9	8.4	7.7	7.9	12.5	10.7	12.3	14.0	•
Officers' Compensation **20**	2.1	10.5	4.0	3.7	3.0	2.6	1.8	1.3	2.0	1.7	0.6	1.1	•
Operating Margin **21**	3.7	8.5	4.2	1.0	3.0	5.4	3.2	4.5	6.0	5.9	7.4	1.7	•
Operating Margin Before Officers' Comp. **22**	5.8	19.0	8.3	4.7	5.9	7.9	4.9	5.8	8.0	7.6	8.0	2.7.	•

Selected Average Balance Sheet ($ in Thousands)

Net Receivables 23	678	0	22	148	601	2049	3998	9583	17922	35868	54302	385910	•
Inventories 24	730	0	36	501	564	2268	5603	12760	19367	45895	97091	281538	•
Net Property, Plant and Equipment 25	366	0	8	31	124	751	592	2176	6921	21528	39584	312616	•
Total Assets 26	3375	0	126	744	2119	6775	14444	35753	69381	167902	347408	2434553	•
Notes and Loans Payable 27	705	0	30	204	753	2303	3412	9194	15015	43979	47101	383739	•
All Other Liabilities 28	1008	0	50	264	790	2335	5183	11395	20893	41102	92941	680812	•
Net Worth 29	1662	0	46	276	576	2138	5849	15163	33472	82821	207367	1370002	•

Selected Financial Ratios (Times to 1)

Current Ratio 30	1.7	•	2.0	1.9	1.7	1.9	1.8	1.9	1.9	2.3	2.4	1.4	•
Quick Ratio 31	0.8	•	1.1	0.8	0.9	0.8	0.7	0.9	1.1	1.0	0.8		•
Net Sales to Working Capital 32	6.9	134.1	22.2	8.7	8.8	5.6	5.9	5.9	4.7	4.2	4.0	7.9	•
Coverage Ratio 33	9.0	16.6	2.4	5.6	8.8	6.3	8.4	8.1	10.1	6.7	13.8	10.3	•
Total Asset Turnover 34	1.7	•	8.6	3.8	2.9	2.4	2.3	2.4	1.7	1.5	1.4	0.9	•
Inventory Turnover 35	5.1	•	22.0	4.4	7.9	4.8	4.9	5.0	3.8	3.5	2.8	4.4	•
Receivables Turnover 36	8.8	•	56.0	9.7	11.5	9.2	8.1	8.8	•	7.3	•	6.5	•
Total Liabilities to Net Worth 37	1.0	•	1.7	1.7	2.7	1.5	2.2	1.4	1.1	1.0	0.7	0.8	•
Current Assets to Working Capital 38	2.4	•	2.0	2.1	2.4	2.2	2.2	2.1	2.1	1.8	1.7	3.3	•
Current Liabilities to Working Capital 39	1.4	•	1.0	1.1	1.4	1.2	1.2	1.1	1.1	0.8	0.7	2.3	•
Working Capital to Net Sales 40	0.1	•	0.0	0.1	0.1	0.2	0.2	0.2	0.2	0.2	0.3	0.1	•
Inventory to Working Capital 41	0.9	•	0.8	0.9	1.0	1.0	0.9	0.9	0.8	0.7	0.8	1.1	•
Total Receipts to Cash Flow 42	6.4	2.5	8.1	14.6	8.3	8.4	8.0	8.3	5.3	6.7	5.1	4.7	•
Cost of Goods to Cash Flow 43	4.3	1.0	5.9	11.4	5.9	6.4	5.7	6.2	3.4	4.3	2.9	2.7	•
Cash Flow to Total Debt 44	0.5	•	1.7	0.4	0.5	0.5	0.4	0.5	0.6	0.4	0.7	0.4	•

Selected Financial Factors (in Percentages)

Debt Ratio 45	50.8	•	63.4	62.9	72.8	57.6	68.4	59.5	51.8	50.7	40.3	43.7	•
Return on Total Assets 46	14.3	•	45.0	7.2	12.2	16.0	14.8	16.7	15.9	16.2	16.5	11.7	•
Return on Equity Before Income Taxes 47	25.7	•	115.5	11.2	36.9	33.0	39.5	36.4	29.8	27.9	25.7	18.7	•
Return on Equity After Income Taxes 48	20.5	•	114.3	10.2	35.9	30.2	37.2	35.0	26.5	21.9	19.0	12.4	•
Profit Margin (Before Income Tax) 49	7.7	22.9	4.9	1.1	3.4	5.9	5.5	6.0	8.5	9.0	11.2	12.1	•
Profit Margin (After Income Tax) 50	6.1	21.9	4.8	1.0	3.3	5.4	5.2	5.8	7.5	7.1	8.3	8.0	•

Table I

Corporations with and without Net Income

GROCERY AND RELATED PRODUCT

MONEY AMOUNTS AND SIZE OF ASSETS IN THOUSANDS OF DOLLARS

Item Description for Accounting Period 7/07 Through 6/08		Total	Zero Assets	Under 500	500 to 1,000	1,000 to 5,000	5,000 to 10,000	10,000 to 25,000	25,000 to 50,000	50,000 to 100,000	100,000 to 250,000	250,000 to 500,000	500,000 to 2,500,000	2,500,000 and over
Number of Enterprises	1	34931	5335	20190	2056	5602	705	610	229	109	56	13	22	4
Revenues ($ in Thousands)														
Net Sales	2	525349539	6951767	20408144	8099366	61820669	22784443	44757001	28592157	27794940	26947373	22911464	77883126	176399090
Interest	3	7078847	9122	5473	2366	31902	14286	20510	15357	23819	18551	9936	79964	6847562
Rents	4	1213368	1451	1514	4312	23497	7586	12646	4784	9241	46980	7264	121665	972427
Royalties	5	671454	108	0	0	0	0	1733	0	220	714	70	5655	662954
Other Portfolio Income	6	7871175	28348	7499	22148	39100	2355	31973	21253	36031	96262	29498	86116	7470589
Other Receipts	7	4472914	57421	150229	60485	346483	-292494	329487	143425	149533	274070	78926	953217	2222133
Total Receipts	8	546657297	7048217	20572859	8188677	62261651	22516176	45153350	28776976	28013784	27383950	23037158	79129743	194574755
Average Total Receipts	9	15650	1321	1019	3983	11114	31938	74022	125664	257007	488999	1772089	3596806	48643689
Operating Costs/Operating Income (%)														
Cost of Operations	10	81.3	83.7	80.3	84.3	85.2	86.4	87.4	85.9	86.1	84.7	88.4	85.7	72.8
Salaries and Wages	11	5.7	5.7	4.2	3.4	3.8	3.5	4.4	4.5	4.5	4.3	3.5	5.2	8.4
Taxes Paid	12	1.4	0.7	1.0	0.9	0.9	0.8	0.6	0.7	0.9	1.5	0.5	0.7	2.4
Interest Paid	13	1.2	0.6	0.3	0.4	0.3	0.5	0.4	0.6	0.6	0.8	0.3	0.6	2.7
Depreciation	14	1.1	0.4	0.7	0.7	0.5	0.3	0.4	0.5	0.5	0.6	0.8	0.7	2.0
Amortization and Depletion	15	0.2	0.3	0.0	0.1	0.0	0.1	0.0	0.0	0.1	0.2	0.1	0.2	0.4
Pensions and Other Deferred Comp.	16	0.3	0.1	0.1	0.1	0.2	0.1	0.2	0.1	0.2	0.2	0.1	0.2	0.6
Employee Benefits	17	0.7	0.4	0.3	0.4	0.3	0.4	0.4	0.5	0.4	0.7	0.4	0.7	1.1
Advertising	18	0.5	0.1	0.4	0.3	0.2	0.3	0.2	0.3	0.6	1.2	0.4	0.6	0.7
Other Expenses	19	6.6	6.8	8.8	7.7	6.3	4.0	4.4	4.7	4.7	5.4	4.7	5.8	8.7
Officers' Compensation	20	0.8	1.3	3.0	1.8	1.5	1.1	1.0	0.8	1.1	0.5	0.3	0.1	0.4
Operating Margin	21	0.2	•	0.8	•	0.8	2.5	0.6	1.3	0.3	•	0.4	•	0.2
Operating Margin Before Officers' Comp.	22	1.0	1.2	3.8	1.7	2.3	3.6	1.6	2.1	1.5	0.5	0.7	•	0.2

Selected Average Balance Sheet ($ in Thousands)

Net Receivables 23	1171	0	27	187	745	2784	5783	11281	19017	35406	110365	139095	4792190
Inventories 24	840	0	20	133	428	2113	3517	8649	19632	40730	123984	195742	2575448
Net Property, Plant and Equipment 25	1594	0	22	204	305	781	1915	4955	9150	23475	103096	219524	10441903
Total Assets 26	14145	0	130	715	2050	7113	15460	33030	68676	143351	404792	1004509	103406506
Notes and Loans Payable 27	2486	0	53	342	641	2601	3976	10089	22905	49295	79493	315417	15415866
All Other Liabilities 28	3906	0	33	279	725	2312	6011	11954	23439	50904	203739	365589	26748054
Net Worth 29	7753	0	44	94	684	2200	5473	10987	22332	43152	121560	323502	61242586

Selected Financial Ratios (Times to 1)

Current Ratio 30	1.3	•	2.1	1.4	1.7	1.5	1.5	1.4	1.7	1.5	1.6	1.3	1.2
Quick Ratio 31	0.8	•	1.3	0.9	1.1	0.9	0.9	0.8	0.8	0.7	0.8	0.5	0.8
Net Sales to Working Capital 32	17.6	•	22.9	32.7	17.3	17.0	18.0	17.0	12.5	14.9	18.0	36.8	14.5
Coverage Ratio 33	4.5	3.2	6.8	3.5	5.8	3.6	5.1	4.4	2.7	3.0	3.7	2.8	4.8
Total Asset Turnover 34	1.1	•	7.8	5.5	5.4	4.5	4.7	3.8	3.7	3.4	4.4	3.5	0.4
Inventory Turnover 35	14.6	•	40.2	25.1	22.0	13.2	18.2	12.4	11.2	10.0	12.6	15.5	12.5
Receivables Turnover 36	13.0	•	34.1	18.6	14.8	9.7	13.8	12.2	14.1	14.8	14.5	28.1	9.2
Total Liabilities to Net Worth 37	0.8	•	2.0	6.6	2.0	2.2	1.8	2.0	2.1	2.3	2.3	2.1	0.7
Current Assets to Working Capital 38	4.7	•	2.0	3.6	2.4	2.9	2.9	3.3	2.5	2.9	2.6	4.7	7.2
Current Liabilities to Working Capital 39	3.7	•	1.0	2.6	1.4	1.9	1.9	2.3	1.5	1.9	1.6	3.7	6.2
Working Capital to Net Sales 40	0.1	•	0.0	0.0	0.1	0.1	0.1	0.1	0.1	0.1	0.1	0.0	0.1
Inventory to Working Capital 41	1.0	•	0.5	1.1	0.7	0.9	0.9	1.2	1.1	1.2	1.2	2.1	0.9
Total Receipts to Cash Flow 42	11.8	15.7	11.5	14.2	16.2	22.4	21.4	18.1	20.2	18.3	22.0	18.4	7.1
Cost of Goods to Cash Flow 43	9.6	13.1	9.2	11.9	13.8	19.4	18.7	15.6	17.4	15.5	19.5	15.8	5.1
Cash Flow to Total Debt 44	0.2	•	1.0	0.4	0.5	0.3	0.3	0.3	0.3	0.3	0.3	0.3	0.1

Selected Financial Factors (in Percentages)

Debt Ratio 45	45.2	•	66.5	86.8	66.6	69.1	64.6	66.7	67.5	69.9	70.0	67.8	40.8
Return on Total Assets 46	5.9	•	14.4	7.7	9.8	8.4	8.9	9.5	6.5	8.0	5.6	6.0	5.5
Return on Equity Before Income Taxes 47	8.4	•	36.7	41.4	24.3	19.6	20.2	22.0	12.6	17.8	13.7	11.9	7.3
Return on Equity After Income Taxes 48	5.9	•	36.2	40.6	22.7	17.8	18.6	20.0	10.3	12.4	9.6	7.3	4.9
Profit Margin (Before Income Tax) 49	4.3	1.2	1.6	1.0	1.5	1.3	1.5	1.9	1.1	1.6	0.9	1.1	10.2
Profit Margin (After Income Tax) 50	3.0	1.1	1.6	1.0	1.4	1.2	1.4	1.8	0.9	1.1	0.7	0.7	6.8

Table II

Corporations with Net Income

GROCERY AND RELATED PRODUCT

MONEY AMOUNTS AND SIZE OF ASSETS IN THOUSANDS OF DOLLARS

Item Description for Accounting Period 7/07 Through 6/08	Total	Zero Assets	Under 500	500 to 1,000	1,000 to 5,000	5,000 to 10,000	10,000 to 25,000	25,000 to 50,000	50,000 to 100,000	100,000 to 250,000	250,000 to 500,000	500,000 to 2,500,000	2,500,000 and over
Number of Enterprises **1**	21098	2481	11530	1450	4146	618	529	188	83	40	•	•	18
Revenues ($ in Thousands)													
Net Sales **2**	442147773	1964380	14899706	6792862	47233481	20529606	40146059	23738433	23004835	20995248	•	•	54627276
Interest **3**	7025680	3302	4720	280	27598	11939	17058	10032	18133	13262	•	•	65612
Rents **4**	1147600	1149	628	0	21905	7576	12120	4227	8776	5374	•	•	107001
Royalties **5**	666857	0	0	0	0	0	1685	0	0	251	•	•	1968
Other Portfolio Income **6**	7748763	27062	4221	7075	31678	1962	22877	21136	33914	43999	•	•	55688
Other Receipts **7**	4197749	52019	130869	39217	276005	50040	263089	118562	100494	219894	•	•	738948
Total Receipts **8**	462934422	2047912	15040144	6839434	47590667	20601123	40462888	23892390	23166152	21278028	•	•	55596493
Average Total Receipts **9**	21942	825	1304	4717	11479	33335	76489	127087	279110	531951	•	•	3088694
Operating Costs/Operating Income (%)													
Cost of Operations **10**	80.4	74.2	81.6	86.9	84.7	88.1	87.2	85.1	86.8	85.9	•	•	83.3
Salaries and Wages **11**	5.8	5.2	2.6	2.0	3.6	3.5	4.3	4.7	4.3	4.2	•	•	6.0
Taxes Paid **12**	1.4	0.8	1.0	0.7	1.0	0.8	0.6	0.7	0.9	0.6	•	•	0.9
Interest Paid **13**	1.3	0.6	0.2	0.3	0.3	0.5	0.3	0.6	0.6	0.6	•	•	0.6
Depreciation **14**	1.1	0.4	0.6	0.6	0.5	0.3	0.4	0.5	0.4	0.6	•	•	0.7
Amortization and Depletion **15**	0.2	0.1	0.1	0.1	0.0	0.1	0.0	0.0	0.1	0.1	•	•	0.2
Pensions and Other Deferred Comp. **16**	0.3	0.0	0.1	0.1	0.2	0.1	0.2	0.2	0.2	0.2	•	•	0.2
Employee Benefits **17**	0.7	0.3	0.3	0.2	0.3	0.3	0.4	0.5	0.4	0.6	•	•	0.8
Advertising **18**	0.6	0.2	0.1	0.3	0.1	0.2	0.2	0.3	0.7	1.4	•	•	0.7
Other Expenses **19**	6.6	8.7	7.8	6.2	5.7	3.5	4.3	4.7	3.7	4.4	•	•	6.3
Officers' Compensation **20**	0.7	3.9	2.9	1.7	1.7	1.2	0.9	0.9	0.6	0.5	•	•	0.2
Operating Margin **21**	0.7	5.6	2.7	1.1	1.9	1.4	1.1	1.9	1.2	1.1	•	•	0.1
Operating Margin Before Officers' Comp. **22**	1.5	9.5	5.6	2.8	3.6	2.6	2.1	2.8	1.8	1.6	•	•	0.3

Selected Average Balance Sheet ($ in Thousands)

Item												
Net Receivables 23	1687	0	32	209	758	2914	5945	11266	19904	36418	•	134979
Inventories 24	1199	0	16	136	428	2085	3511	8842	23390	43228	•	193991
Net Property, Plant and Equipment 25	2416	0	25	181	321	719	1708	4794	9084	23740	•	193941
Total Assets 26	22101	0	144	704	2012	7057	15436	32607	69402	146863	•	888962
Notes and Loans Payable 27	3542	0	45	276	548	2512	3471	9482	22967	46079	•	275592
All Other Liabilities 28	6006	0	34	311	658	2254	5988	11554	21829	50632	•	305262
Net Worth 29	12552	0	65	117	806	2292	5978	11571	24606	50152	•	309108

Selected Financial Ratios (Times to 1)

Item												
Current Ratio 30	1.3	•	2.3	1.3	2.0	1.5	1.6	1.5	1.7	1.6	•	1.3
Quick Ratio 31	0.8	•	1.6	0.8	1.3	1.0	1.0	0.8	0.8	0.7	•	0.6
Net Sales to Working Capital 32	15.9	•	24.3	40.8	14.9	16.9	16.7	16.5	12.7	14.0	•	28.0
Coverage Ratio 33	5.2	17.1	18.7	6.9	10.7	4.4	7.0	5.6	4.1	5.2	•	4.1
Total Asset Turnover 34	0.9	•	9.0	6.7	5.7	4.7	4.9	3.9	4.0	3.6	•	3.4
Inventory Turnover 35	14.0	•	65.2	29.9	22.6	14.0	18.9	12.1	10.3	10.4	•	13.0
Receivables Turnover 36	12.4	•	33.6	20.5	15.0	9.7	14.7	12.0	•	16.4	•	25.4
Total Liabilities to Net Worth 37	0.8	•	1.2	5.0	1.5	2.1	1.6	1.8	1.8	1.9	•	1.9
Current Assets to Working Capital 38	4.6	•	1.8	4.1	2.0	2.9	2.7	3.2	2.5	2.7	•	3.9
Current Liabilities to Working Capital 39	3.6	•	0.8	3.1	1.0	1.9	1.7	2.2	1.5	1.7	•	2.9
Working Capital to Net Sales 40	0.1	•	0.0	0.0	0.1	0.1	0.1	0.1	0.1	0.1	•	0.0
Inventory to Working Capital 41	0.9	•	0.3	1.5	0.6	0.9	0.8	1.2	1.1	1.2	•	1.7
Total Receipts to Cash Flow 42	10.6	6.1	10.1	15.2	14.6	22.1	20.0	16.4	20.4	17.4	•	15.3
Cost of Goods to Cash Flow 43	8.5	4.5	8.2	13.2	12.4	19.5	17.4	14.0	17.7	14.9	•	12.7
Cash Flow to Total Debt 44	0.2	•	1.6	0.5	0.6	0.3	0.4	0.4	0.3	0.3	•	0.3

Selected Financial Factors (in Percentages)

Item												
Debt Ratio 45	43.2	•	54.8	83.3	59.9	67.5	61.3	64.5	64.5	65.9	•	65.3
Return on Total Assets 46	6.4	•	34.8	13.7	16.9	10.5	11.0	12.2	10.0	10.7	•	8.4
Return on Equity Before Income Taxes 47	9.1	•	73.0	70.3	38.2	25.0	24.3	28.2	21.3	25.3	•	18.3
Return on Equity After Income Taxes 48	6.6	•	72.4	69.4	36.3	23.1	22.6	25.9	18.6	18.8	•	12.5
Profit Margin (Before Income Tax) 49	5.5	9.8	3.7	1.8	2.7	1.7	1.9	2.6	1.9	2.4	•	1.9
Profit Margin (After Income Tax) 50	4.0	9.5	3.7	1.7	2.6	1.6	1.8	2.4	1.7	1.8	•	1.3

Table I

Corporations with and without Net Income

FARM PRODUCT RAW MATERIAL

MONEY AMOUNTS AND SIZE OF ASSETS IN THOUSANDS OF DOLLARS

Item Description for Accounting Period 7/07 Through 6/08	Total	Zero Assets	Under 500	500 to 1,000	1,000 to 5,000	5,000 to 10,000	10,000 to 25,000	25,000 to 50,000	50,000 to 100,000	100,000 to 250,000	250,000 to 500,000	500,000 to 2,500,000	2,500,000 and over
Number of Enterprises **1**	4972	292	2476	863	828	235	166	63	18	16	6	5	3
Revenues ($ in Thousands)													
Net Sales **2**	142059243	1359813	6782274	2623279	8527819	5107715	6550019	7126694	2569622	6283732	14776249	13864581	66487446
Interest **3**	725779	851	424	6963	12893	4943	3421	3849	3141	11754	36767	30572	610202
Rents **4**	57234	474	0	989	9072	4020	4307	475	3662	1639	1483	2689	28424
Royalties **5**	78756	3147	0	0	0	1570	0	0	175	0	0	9882	63982
Other Portfolio Income **6**	750164	32063	122	26258	14795	2350	18153	6205	10556	7717	18668	19740	593540
Other Receipts **7**	922894	6395	2543	99578	99966	45866	86931	35018	25241	56335	27836	155740	281440
Total Receipts **8**	144594070	1402743	6785363	2757067	8664545	5166464	6662831	7172241	2612397	6361177	14861003	14083204	68065034
Average Total Receipts **9**	29082	4804	2740	3195	10464	21985	40138	113845	145133	397574	2476834	2816641	22688345
Operating Costs/Operating Income (%)													
Cost of Operations **10**	92.6	83.6	95.5	87.1	88.7	89.5	89.6	93.4	88.9	94.0	98.7	92.3	92.3
Salaries and Wages **11**	1.9	8.1	0.6	3.3	3.0	2.7	3.2	2.1	3.1	1.3	0.4	2.6	1.6
Taxes Paid **12**	0.4	1.0	0.2	0.7	0.6	0.5	0.5	0.4	0.5	0.3	0.1	0.3	0.5
Interest Paid **13**	1.2	1.5	0.1	0.3	0.9	0.7	0.9	0.8	1.4	1.0	0.4	0.5	1.9
Depreciation **14**	0.6	0.2	0.1	1.1	0.6	0.6	0.9	0.5	1.1	0.5	0.1	0.5	0.8
Amortization and Depletion **15**	0.0	0.1	0.0	0.0	0.1	0.0	0.0	0.0	0.0	0.0	0.0	0.0	0.0
Pensions and Other Deferred Comp. **16**	0.1	0.0	0.2	0.0	0.1	0.2	0.2	0.1	0.1	0.1	0.1	0.1	0.1
Employee Benefits **17**	0.3	0.7	0.1	0.2	0.2	0.2	0.2	0.2	0.2	0.1	0.0	0.4	0.4
Advertising **18**	0.1	0.1	0.1	0.1	0.1	0.2	0.1	0.0	0.1	0.3	0.0	0.1	0.1
Other Expenses **19**	2.5	1.8	2.3	5.6	6.0	3.9	3.7	2.1	4.3	2.1	0.5	2.7	2.1
Officers' Compensation **20**	0.8	3.5	0.9	2.3	1.6	1.0	0.8	0.4	0.5	0.4	0.1	0.2	1.0
Operating Margin **21**	•	•	•	•	•	0.4	•	•	•	•	•	0.3	•
Operating Margin Before Officers' Comp. **22**	0.3	2.9	0.9	1.5	1.4	1.4	0.8	0.3	0.2	0.3	•	0.5	0.2

Selected Average Balance Sheet ($ in Thousands)

Net Receivables 23	2707	0	57	95	580	1373	3603	9994	20668	43017	139710	266030	2658672
Inventories 24	2639	0	13	65	561	1748	4087	10919	22124	43325	123136	859029	3112119
Net Property, Plant and Equipment 25	1464	0	15	170	516	1083	2642	3691	14261	14458	23776	117603	1508211
Total Assets 26	16436	0	158	712	2418	6687	14140	34161	70688	152009	377537	1117207	20361456
Notes and Loans Payable 27	6784	0	135	178	1258	2360	5179	13370	33246	47601	212083	406234	8426909
All Other Liabilities 28	4322	0	96	117	650	2901	5365	14409	15350	65476	90036	497397	4593899
Net Worth 29	5330	0	-73	418	510	1427	3596	6382	22092	38933	75417	213577	7340647

Selected Financial Ratios (Times to 1)

Current Ratio 30	1.4	•	1.1	2.3	1.4	1.5	1.3	1.2	1.4	1.1	1.2	1.2	1.4
Quick Ratio 31	0.5	•	1.0	1.5	0.6	0.7	0.6	0.5	0.7	0.5	0.6	0.4	0.5
Net Sales to Working Capital 32	12.5	•	267.4	14.7	23.3	12.8	15.3	21.2	8.9	32.1	41.2	16.2	8.4
Coverage Ratio 33	2.3	2.7	1.3	15.7	0.9	3.1	2.8	1.7	2.0	2.2	1.4	4.6	2.2
Total Asset Turnover 34	1.7	•	17.3	4.3	4.3	3.3	2.8	3.3	2.0	2.6	6.5	2.5	1.1
Inventory Turnover 35	10.0	•	202.2	40.6	16.3	11.1	8.6	9.7	5.7	8.5	19.7	3.0	6.6
Receivables Turnover 36	12.2	•	54.9	44.2	13.7	12.2	9.8	14.4	7.1	12.3	21.4	3.8	16.7
Total Liabilities to Net Worth 37	2.1	•	•	0.7	3.7	3.7	2.9	4.4	2.2	2.9	4.0	4.2	1.8
Current Assets to Working Capital 38	3.8	•	12.3	1.8	3.7	3.1	4.2	5.5	3.3	9.0	5.6	5.2	3.4
Current Liabilities to Working Capital 39	2.8	•	11.3	0.8	2.7	2.1	3.2	4.5	2.3	8.0	4.6	4.2	2.4
Working Capital to Net Sales 40	0.1	•	0.0	0.1	0.0	0.1	0.1	0.0	0.1	0.0	0.0	0.1	0.1
Inventory to Working Capital 41	1.4	•	1.4	0.5	1.1	0.7	1.6	2.9	1.4	4.2	2.2	2.4	1.2
Total Receipts to Cash Flow 42	38.2	42.5	50.6	12.0	21.5	22.3	22.9	48.0	21.9	37.7	210.2	31.4	45.0
Cost of Goods to Cash Flow 43	35.4	35.5	48.3	10.5	19.0	19.9	20.5	44.9	19.5	35.5	207.4	29.0	41.6
Cash Flow to Total Debt 44	0.1	•	0.2	0.9	0.3	0.2	0.2	0.1	0.1	0.1	0.0	0.1	0.0

Selected Financial Factors (in Percentages)

Debt Ratio 45	67.6	•	145.8	41.4	78.9	78.7	74.6	81.3	68.7	74.4	80.0	80.9	63.9
Return on Total Assets 46	4.8	•	2.8	19.3	3.3	7.3	7.3	4.6	5.8	5.4	3.6	6.2	4.4
Return on Equity Before Income Taxes 47	8.3	•	•	30.9	•	23.1	18.5	10.0	9.3	11.6	5.1	25.2	6.5
Return on Equity After Income Taxes 48	5.7	•	•	30.2	•	20.7	17.4	7.5	7.8	7.5	•	15.9	4.5
Profit Margin (Before Income Tax) 49	1.6	2.5	0.0	4.2	•	1.5	1.7	0.6	1.4	1.2	0.2	1.9	2.2
Profit Margin (After Income Tax) 50	1.1	2.2	0.0	4.2	•	1.4	1.6	0.4	1.2	0.7	•	1.2	1.5

Table II

Corporations with Net Income

FARM PRODUCT RAW MATERIAL

MONEY AMOUNTS AND SIZE OF ASSETS IN THOUSANDS OF DOLLARS

Item Description for Accounting Period 7/07 Through 6/08	Total	Zero Assets	Under 500	500 to 1,000	1,000 to 5,000	5,000 to 10,000	10,000 to 25,000	25,000 to 50,000	50,000 to 100,000	100,000 to 250,000	250,000 to 500,000	500,000 to 2,500,000	2,500,000 and over
Number of Enterprises **1**	2802	27	1148	677	540	180	140	48	•	13	•	•	3

Revenues ($ in Thousands)

	Total	Zero Assets	Under 500	500 to 1,000	1,000 to 5,000	5,000 to 10,000	10,000 to 25,000	25,000 to 50,000	50,000 to 100,000	100,000 to 250,000	250,000 to 500,000	500,000 to 2,500,000	2,500,000 and over
Net Sales **2**	131237155	1331089	5832932	2359938	4135700	4184856	5865705	5314370	•	5823694	•	•	66487446
Interest **3**	711497	851	424	6576	5806	4478	2567	3293	•	8513	•	•	610202
Rents **4**	53428	474	0	989	8993	850	3784	441	•	1639	•	•	28424
Royalties **5**	77186	3147	0	0	0	0	0	0	•	0	•	•	63982
Other Portfolio Income **6**	744615	32063	122	26258	14741	1492	14891	6201	•	7410	•	•	593540
Other Receipts **7**	810849	6376	2543	99577	43345	43035	75370	31744	•	32358	•	•	281440
Total Receipts **8**	133634730	1374000	5836021	2493338	4208585	4234711	5962317	5356049	•	5873614	•	•	68065034
Average Total Receipts **9**	47693	50889	5084	3683	7794	23526	42588	111584	•	451816	•	•	22668345

Operating Costs/Operating Income (%)

	Total	Zero Assets	Under 500	500 to 1,000	1,000 to 5,000	5,000 to 10,000	10,000 to 25,000	25,000 to 50,000	50,000 to 100,000	100,000 to 250,000	250,000 to 500,000	500,000 to 2,500,000	2,500,000 and over
Cost of Operations **10**	92.3	85.4	96.1	87.6	81.7	88.0	88.8	93.6	•	93.9	•	•	92.3
Salaries and Wages **11**	1.9	8.3	0.5	3.4	4.5	3.1	3.5	1.6	•	1.1	•	•	1.6
Taxes Paid **12**	0.4	0.9	0.2	0.7	0.8	0.5	0.5	0.3	•	0.2	•	•	0.5
Interest Paid **13**	1.2	1.3	0.1	0.2	0.7	0.6	0.9	0.8	•	0.8	•	•	1.9
Depreciation **14**	0.6	0.2	0.1	0.7	0.9	0.7	0.8	0.6	•	0.5	•	•	0.8
Amortization and Depletion **15**	0.0	0.1	0.0	•	0.1	0.0	0.0	0.0	•	0.0	•	•	0.0
Pensions and Other Deferred Comp. **16**	0.1	0.0	0.2	0.0	0.1	0.3	0.2	0.1	•	0.1	•	•	0.1
Employee Benefits **17**	0.3	0.8	0.0	0.1	0.2	0.3	0.2	0.2	•	0.1	•	•	0.4
Advertising **18**	0.1	0.1	0.1	0.1	0.1	0.3	0.1	0.0	•	0.4	•	•	0.1
Other Expenses **19**	2.3	•	1.2	5.2	7.5	4.3	3.8	1.8	•	1.7	•	•	2.1
Officers' Compensation **20**	0.9	3.6	1.0	2.5	2.6	1.2	0.8	0.3	•	0.4	•	•	1.0
Operating Margin **21**	•	•	0.5	•	0.7	0.8	0.4	0.5	•	0.9	•	•	0.2
Operating Margin Before Officers' Comp. **22**	0.7	3.1	1.5	2.0	3.3	2.0	1.2	0.8	•	1.3	•	•	0.2

Selected Average Balance Sheet ($ in Thousands)

Net Receivables 23	4501	0	40	86	668	1659	3349	9101	46368	2658672
Inventories 24	4253	0	23	78	751	2102	4202	15545	35779	312119
Net Property, Plant and Equipment 25	2373	0	18	116	372	1067	2226	4276	13305	1508211
Total Assets 26	27739	0	156	677	2323	6743	13674	35119	150838	20361456
Notes and Loans Payable 27	11201	0	93	126	685	2077	5158	12459	49640	8426909
All Other Liabilities 28	7151	0	29	56	712	3014	4709	15083	58429	4593899
Net Worth 29	9388	0	34	495	926	1651	3806	7578	42769	7340647

Selected Financial Ratios (Times to 1)

Current Ratio 30	1.4	•	2.1	3.1	1.7	1.2	1.4	1.3	1.2	1.4
Quick Ratio 31	0.5	•	1.7	2.0	0.8	0.8	0.7	0.5	0.6	0.5
Net Sales to Working Capital 32	11.9	•	91.3	13.0	10.1	22.2	13.3	18.0	30.8	8.4
Coverage Ratio 33	2.6	3.1	4.7	34.1	4.5	4.1	3.3	2.6	3.3	2.2
Total Asset Turnover 34	1.7	•	32.5	5.1	3.3	3.4	3.1	3.2	3.0	1.1
Inventory Turnover 35	10.2	•	214.8	39.0	8.3	9.7	8.9	6.7	11.8	6.6
Receivables Turnover 36	12.4	•	83.4	56.7	9.6	10.6	12.1	•	14.6	16.7
Total Liabilities to Net Worth 37	2.0	•	3.6	0.4	1.5	3.1	2.6	3.6	2.5	1.8
Current Assets to Working Capital 38	3.6	•	1.9	1.5	2.4	5.1	3.4	4.7	7.4	3.4
Current Liabilities to Working Capital 39	2.6	•	0.9	0.5	1.4	4.1	2.4	3.7	6.4	2.4
Working Capital to Net Sales 40	0.1	•	0.0	0.1	0.1	0.0	0.1	0.1	0.0	0.1
Inventory to Working Capital 41	1.3	•	0.4	0.4	0.8	1.4	1.4	2.5	3.1	1.2
Total Receipts to Cash Flow 42	35.0	96.6	58.5	11.1	12.0	19.3	20.8	36.8	33.3	45.0
Cost of Goods to Cash Flow 43	32.3	82.4	56.3	9.7	9.8	17.0	18.4	34.5	31.3	41.6
Cash Flow to Total Debt 44	0.1	•	0.7	1.7	0.5	0.2	0.2	0.1	0.1	0.0

Selected Financial Factors (in Percentages)

Debt Ratio 45	66.2	•	78.4	26.8	60.2	75.5	72.2	78.4	71.6	63.9
Return on Total Assets 46	5.4	•	22.3	27.3	10.5	9.0	8.9	6.8	7.6	4.4
Return on Equity Before Income Taxes 47	9.9	•	81.1	36.2	20.5	27.8	22.1	19.4	18.7	6.5
Return on Equity After Income Taxes 48	7.3	•	77.5	35.5	17.4	25.1	20.9	16.6	14.1	4.5
Profit Margin (Before Income Tax) 49	2.0	2.8	0.5	5.1	2.5	2.0	2.0	1.3	1.8	2.2
Profit Margin (After Income Tax) 50	1.5	2.5	0.5	5.0	2.1	1.8	1.9	1.1	1.3	1.5

192

Table I

Corporations with and without Net Income

CHEMICAL AND ALLIED PRODUCTS

MONEY AMOUNTS AND SIZE OF ASSETS IN THOUSANDS OF DOLLARS

Item Description for Accounting Period 7/07 Through 6/08	Total	Zero Assets	Under 500	500 to 1,000	1,000 to 5,000	5,000 to 10,000	10,000 to 25,000	25,000 to 50,000	50,000 to 100,000	100,000 to 250,000	250,000 to 500,000	500,000 to 2,500,000	2,500,000 and over
Number of Enterprises **1**	7765	1736	3519	472	1443	235	218	64	38	24	5	8	3

Revenues ($ in Thousands)

	Total	Zero Assets	Under 500	500 to 1,000	1,000 to 5,000	5,000 to 10,000	10,000 to 25,000	25,000 to 50,000	50,000 to 100,000	100,000 to 250,000	250,000 to 500,000	500,000 to 2,500,000	2,500,000 and over
Net Sales **2**	73117415	1813434	2433490	1271808	9183294	5763401	7858082	5469887	5831089	8438901	1752779	11846233	11455018
Interest **3**	212163	32980	666	959	7569	7210	11369	5447	6468	15084	28167	62307	33939
Rents **4**	21294	438	0	0	1131	3670	1310	185	3114	6330	63	1050	4003
Royalties **5**	97190	159	0	0	0	0	101	49	268	121	0	96492	0
Other Portfolio Income **6**	286495	65485	3921	479	8820	40285	2202	6427	29421	3931	71275	26403	27847
Other Receipts **7**	716564	18462	5792	6	25438	28190	59019	61380	64922	-28152	51139	122208	308155
Total Receipts **8**	74451121	1918288	2456539	1273252	9226252	5842756	7932083	5543375	5935282	8436215	1903423	12154693	11828962
Average Total Receipts **9**	9588	1105	698	2698	6394	24863	36386	86615	156192	351509	380685	1519337	3942987

Operating Costs/Operating Income (%)

	Total	Zero Assets	Under 500	500 to 1,000	1,000 to 5,000	5,000 to 10,000	10,000 to 25,000	25,000 to 50,000	50,000 to 100,000	100,000 to 250,000	250,000 to 500,000	500,000 to 2,500,000	2,500,000 and over
Cost of Operations **10**	78.8	82.4	71.4	57.7	61.4	85.2	79.9	81.6	86.4	88.4	79.9	83.5	74.7
Salaries and Wages **11**	6.1	7.8	6.5	9.9	12.4	4.4	5.1	6.7	3.6	2.8	3.6	3.8	7.7
Taxes Paid **12**	1.0	1.5	0.5	1.8	1.5	0.6	1.1	1.1	0.7	0.6	0.7	1.1	1.3
Interest Paid **13**	1.2	3.3	0.8	1.0	0.5	0.5	0.7	0.7	0.7	0.7	2.1	2.3	1.4
Depreciation **14**	1.2	0.6	0.6	1.1	0.8	0.4	0.7	1.1	0.4	0.7	2.8	1.1	3.5
Amortization and Depletion **15**	0.3	0.2	0.0	0.0	0.1	0.0	0.2	0.1	0.1	0.2	0.6	0.4	1.1
Pensions and Other Deferred Comp. **16**	0.4	0.2	0.0	1.7	0.6	0.2	0.3	0.7	0.2	0.2	0.2	0.2	0.4
Employee Benefits **17**	0.8	0.5	0.5	1.2	0.8	0.2	0.5	0.6	0.5	0.5	0.6	0.6	2.3
Advertising **18**	0.2	0.1	0.2	0.3	0.4	0.1	0.3	0.2	0.1	0.1	0.8	0.1	0.1
Other Expenses **19**	6.5	4.4	13.3	15.0	10.8	5.4	6.4	5.6	4.0	3.4	8.8	6.3	5.3
Officers' Compensation **20**	1.5	3.2	3.2	9.8	3.8	1.8	1.5	1.2	1.0	0.5	0.3	0.5	0.5
Operating Margin **21**	2.0	•	3.0	0.4	6.9	1.1	3.3	0.3	2.3	2.1	•	•	1.9
Operating Margin Before Officers' Comp. **22**	3.6	•	6.2	10.2	10.7	2.9	4.8	1.5	3.3	2.5	•	•	2.4

Selected Average Balance Sheet ($ in Thousands)

Net Receivables 23	1153	0	29	330	721	2568	4961	10092	20658	51882	66647	230010	374427
Inventories 24	804	0	23	146	291	1463	4187	11237	16305	30682	62988	195649	307379
Net Property, Plant and Equipment 25	914	0	17	38	322	466	1966	6550	6309	18023	49096	132726	1206258
Total Assets 26	5329	0	119	755	2059	6785	15619	36235	65463	155542	388168	1189965	4210580
Notes and Loans Payable 27	1397	0	74	289	469	1716	4104	12314	15887	35206	117319	505282	536203
All Other Liabilities 28	2099	0	48	505	634	2783	4870	10659	22619	69484	131906	406554	2047926
Net Worth 29	1833	0	-2	-39	956	2287	6646	13262	26957	50852	138943	278128	1626451

Selected Financial Ratios (Times to 1)

Current Ratio 30	1.4	•	2.3	1.8	1.9	1.5	1.6	1.4	1.6	1.3	1.1	1.3	1.2
Quick Ratio 31	0.8	•	1.4	1.5	1.5	1.0	0.9	0.7	0.9	0.8	0.6	0.8	0.4
Net Sales to Working Capital 32	11.7	•	12.5	8.8	8.8	12.7	8.0	11.8	8.4	15.0	36.2	14.4	13.4
Coverage Ratio 33	4.3	1.4	6.2	1.5	14.4	6.3	6.7	3.3	6.7	3.8	4.8	2.1	4.6
Total Asset Turnover 34	1.8	•	5.8	3.6	3.1	3.6	2.3	2.4	2.3	2.3	0.9	1.2	0.9
Inventory Turnover 35	9.2	•	21.2	10.6	13.4	14.3	6.9	6.2	8.1	10.1	4.4	6.3	9.3
Receivables Turnover 36	8.5	•	23.6	5.4	9.2	8.7	7.7	6.7	7.6	8.4	3.7	6.0	20.4
Total Liabilities to Net Worth 37	1.9	•	•	•	1.2	2.0	1.4	1.7	1.4	2.1	1.8	3.3	1.6
Current Assets to Working Capital 38	3.4	•	1.8	2.2	2.1	3.0	2.6	3.4	2.6	4.4	15.0	4.3	5.4
Current Liabilities to Working Capital 39	2.4	•	0.8	1.2	1.1	2.0	1.6	2.4	1.6	3.4	14.0	3.3	4.4
Working Capital to Net Sales 40	0.1	•	0.1	0.1	0.1	0.1	0.1	0.1	0.1	0.1	0.0	0.1	0.1
Inventory to Working Capital 41	1.0	•	0.5	0.3	0.4	0.9	1.0	1.4	1.0	1.5	5.9	1.4	1.1
Total Receipts to Cash Flow 42	11.5	20.3	6.6	8.0	6.1	15.3	10.5	16.3	14.1	21.4	8.4	12.9	13.8
Cost of Goods to Cash Flow 43	9.1	16.7	4.7	4.6	3.7	13.0	8.4	13.3	12.2	18.9	6.8	10.7	10.3
Cash Flow to Total Debt 44	0.2	•	0.9	0.4	1.0	0.4	0.4	0.2	0.3	0.2	0.2	0.1	0.1

Selected Financial Factors (in Percentages)

Debt Ratio 45	65.6	•	101.9	105.2	53.6	66.3	57.5	63.4	58.8	67.3	64.2	76.6	61.4
Return on Total Assets 46	8.9	•	27.2	5.3	24.5	10.8	11.5	5.7	11.4	6.3	9.4	6.1	6.0
Return on Equity Before Income Taxes 47	19.9	•	•	•	49.2	26.9	22.9	10.8	23.6	14.2	20.8	14.0	12.1
Return on Equity After Income Taxes 48	17.0	•	•	25.8	47.9	24.1	19.6	9.1	19.0	9.6	18.9	8.7	10.6
Profit Margin (Before Income Tax) 49	3.9	1.5	3.9	0.5	7.4	2.5	4.2	1.7	4.1	2.1	8.2	2.6	5.2
Profit Margin (After Income Tax) 50	3.3	1.1	3.9	•	7.2	2.2	3.6	1.4	3.3	1.4	7.5	1.6	4.5

Table II

Corporations with Net Income

CHEMICAL AND ALLIED PRODUCTS

MONEY AMOUNTS AND SIZE OF ASSETS IN THOUSANDS OF DOLLARS

Item Description for Accounting Period 7/07 Through 6/08	Total	Zero Assets	Under 500	500 to 1,000	1,000 to 5,000	5,000 to 10,000	10,000 to 25,000	25,000 to 50,000	50,000 to 100,000	100,000 to 250,000	250,000 to 500,000	500,000 to 2,500,000	2,500,000 and over
Number of Enterprises **1**	4042	525	1485	•	1325	204	200	50	32	19	5	•	3

Revenues ($ in Thousands)

	Total	Zero Assets	Under 500	500 to 1,000	1,000 to 5,000	5,000 to 10,000	10,000 to 25,000	25,000 to 50,000	50,000 to 100,000	100,000 to 250,000	250,000 to 500,000	500,000 to 2,500,000	2,500,000 and over
Net Sales **2**	65633435	140755	1866204	•	8631128	5133869	7667080	5151189	5367807	6539833	1752779	•	11455018
Interest **3**	150352	0	666	•	6254	6526	11274	1414	5113	10943	28167	•	33939
Rents **4**	14913	438	0	•	1118	3670	1310	185	2998	78	63	•	4003
Royalties **5**	97140	159	0	•	0	0	101	0	268	121	0	•	0
Other Portfolio Income **6**	264009	63710	3921	•	5219	40037	2202	4916	28895	1133	71275	•	27847
Other Receipts **7**	732212	1901	18463	•	22601	21922	51016	61600	63121	17935	51139	•	308155
Total Receipts **8**	66892061	206963	1889254	•	8666320	5206024	7732983	5219304	5468202	6570043	1903423	•	11828962
Average Total Receipts **9**	16549	394	1272	•	6541	25520	38665	104386	170881	345792	380685	•	3942987

Operating Costs/Operating Income (%)

	Total	Zero Assets	Under 500	500 to 1,000	1,000 to 5,000	5,000 to 10,000	10,000 to 25,000	25,000 to 50,000	50,000 to 100,000	100,000 to 250,000	250,000 to 500,000	500,000 to 2,500,000	2,500,000 and over
Cost of Operations **10**	78.5	56.6	73.1	•	60.4	85.2	79.8	82.1	86.1	88.7	79.9	•	74.7
Salaries and Wages **11**	6.1	8.9	6.1	•	12.8	4.5	5.2	6.4	3.5	3.0	3.6	•	7.7
Taxes Paid **12**	1.0	0.8	0.4	•	1.5	0.5	1.1	1.1	0.7	0.6	0.7	•	1.3
Interest Paid **13**	1.0	0.1	0.3	•	0.5	0.5	0.7	0.6	0.7	0.6	2.1	•	1.4
Depreciation **14**	1.2	0.3	0.5	•	0.8	0.3	0.7	1.0	0.4	0.4	2.8	•	3.5
Amortization and Depletion **15**	0.3	•	0.0	•	0.0	0.0	0.1	0.0	0.1	0.1	0.6	•	1.1
Pensions and Other Deferred Comp. **16**	0.4	•	0.0	•	0.6	0.3	0.3	0.7	0.2	0.2	0.2	•	0.4
Employee Benefits **17**	0.8	0.0	0.0	•	0.8	0.2	0.5	0.6	0.5	0.4	0.6	•	2.3
Advertising **18**	0.2	0.0	0.2	•	0.4	0.1	0.3	0.2	0.1	0.1	0.8	•	0.1
Other Expenses **19**	6.1	8.6	10.2	•	11.0	5.0	6.2	4.6	3.8	2.7	8.8	•	5.3
Officers' Compensation **20**	1.4	3.5	3.1	•	3.7	1.9	1.5	1.0	1.1	0.6	0.3	•	0.5
Operating Margin **21**	2.9	21.1	6.2	•	7.6	1.6	3.8	1.7	3.0	2.6	•	•	1.9
Operating Margin Before Officers' Comp. **22**	4.3	24.6	9.3	•	11.2	3.4	5.3	2.8	4.0	3.2	•	•	2.4

Selected Average Balance Sheet ($ in Thousands)

Item													
Net Receivables **23**	2059	0	50	•	723	2549	5287	11984	21057	58438	66647	•	374427
Inventories **24**	1351	0	35	•	289	1523	4178	13014	16989	32759	57154	•	307379
Net Property, Plant and Equipment **25**	1559	0	25	•	321	409	1881	5724	5977	12596	49096	•	1206258
Total Assets **26**	9281	0	197	•	2052	6789	15521	35899	65394	147361	388168	•	4210580
Notes and Loans Payable **27**	2251	0	80	•	443	1456	3523	11131	15053	33706	117319	•	536203
All Other Liabilities **28**	3676	0	74	•	597	3001	5209	11264	22853	65622	131906	•	2047926
Net Worth **29**	3354	0	44	•	1011	2332	6789	13504	27488	48033	138943	•	1626451

Selected Financial Ratios (Times to 1)

Item												
Current Ratio **30**	1.4	•	3.0	•	2.0	1.6	1.7	1.7	1.4	1.1	1.2	
Quick Ratio **31**	0.8	•	1.9	•	1.6	1.1	0.9	0.9	0.9	0.6	0.4	
Net Sales to Working Capital **32**	10.9	•	11.4	•	8.6	12.3	8.0	9.0	8.7	10.2	36.2	13.4
Coverage Ratio **33**	5.9	585.7	25.1	•	17.8	7.4	8.0	6.0	8.4	6.3	4.8	4.6
Total Asset Turnover **34**	1.7	•	6.4	•	3.2	3.7	2.5	2.9	2.6	2.3	0.9	0.9
Inventory Turnover **35**	9.4	•	26.1	•	13.6	14.1	7.3	6.5	8.5	9.3	4.9	9.3
Receivables Turnover **36**	8.6	•	25.7	•	9.3	8.5	7.9	6.7	8.0	8.1	•	20.4
Total Liabilities to Net Worth **37**	1.8	•	3.5	•	1.0	1.9	1.3	1.7	1.4	2.1	1.8	1.6
Current Assets to Working Capital **38**	3.3	•	1.5	•	2.0	2.8	2.6	2.4	2.5	3.3	15.0	5.4
Current Liabilities to Working Capital **39**	2.3	•	0.5	•	1.0	1.8	1.6	1.4	1.5	2.3	14.0	4.4
Working Capital to Net Sales **40**	0.1	•	0.1	•	0.1	0.1	0.1	0.1	0.1	0.1	0.0	0.1
Inventory to Working Capital **41**	1.0	•	0.4	•	0.4	0.8	0.9	1.0	1.0	1.1	5.9	1.1
Total Receipts to Cash Flow **42**	10.8	1.3	6.2	•	5.8	15.5	10.3	14.8	13.1	19.4	8.4	13.8
Cost of Goods to Cash Flow **43**	8.5	0.7	4.5	•	3.5	13.2	8.2	12.1	11.3	17.2	6.8	10.3
Cash Flow to Total Debt **44**	0.3	•	1.3	•	1.1	0.4	0.4	0.3	0.3	0.2	0.2	0.1

Selected Financial Factors (in Percentages)

Item												
Debt Ratio **45**	63.9	•	77.9	•	50.7	65.7	56.3	62.4	58.0	67.4	64.2	61.4
Return on Total Assets **46**	10.2	•	49.5	•	26.9	12.7	13.1	10.5	14.3	8.5	9.4	6.0
Return on Equity Before Income Taxes **47**	23.4	•	215.0	•	51.5	32.0	26.2	23.3	29.9	22.0	20.8	12.1
Return on Equity After Income Taxes **48**	20.3	•	213.4	•	50.1	28.9	22.6	21.1	24.5	15.8	18.9	10.6
Profit Margin (Before Income Tax) **49**	4.8	68.1	7.5	•	8.0	3.0	4.6	3.0	4.9	3.1	8.2	5.2
Profit Margin (After Income Tax) **50**	4.2	63.3	7.4	•	7.8	2.7	4.0	2.8	4.0	2.2	7.5	4.5

Table I

Corporations with and without Net Income

PETROLEUM AND PETROLEUM PRODUCTS

MONEY AMOUNTS AND SIZE OF ASSETS IN THOUSANDS OF DOLLARS

Item Description for Accounting Period 7/07 Through 6/08		Total	Zero Assets	Under 500	500 to 1,000	1,000 to 5,000	5,000 to 10,000	10,000 to 25,000	25,000 to 50,000	50,000 to 100,000	100,000 to 250,000	250,000 to 500,000	500,000 to 2,500,000	2,500,000 and over
Number of Enterprises	1	8266	397	3602	724	2155	702	419	141	53	31	15	20	6
Revenues ($ in Thousands)														
Net Sales	2	536854544	37984915	3756280	4727924	40611852	49059492	50808094	36090750	25435891	38598460	33405328	83623913	132751646
Interest	3	669534	5651	2607	7319	14338	15727	25044	9743	7560	16613	20373	72281	472279
Rents	4	245235	0	0	563	27011	25377	41834	16033	8061	13067	15732	80872	16685
Royalties	5	23264	0	0	0	140	111	7	0	0	1630	808	65	20502
Other Portfolio Income	6	6513835	18095	10146	27757	20444	73206	58863	39022	43983	27784	50367	46055	6098114
Other Receipts	7	1637365	190414	4144	54877	175844	95139	156469	156173	44565	64588	-6480	579439	122189
Total Receipts	8	545943777	38199075	3773177	4818440	40849629	49269052	51090311	36311721	25540060	38722142	33486128	84402625	139481415
Average Total Receipts	9	66047	96219	1048	6655	18956	70184	121934	257530	481888	1249101	2232409	4220131	23246902
Operating Costs/Operating Income (%)														
Cost of Operations	10	93.3	99.9	79.8	92.1	91.7	93.5	94.7	94.7	95.3	97.3	95.9	97.7	86.2
Salaries and Wages	11	1.4	0.3	6.1	2.1	2.4	1.3	1.6	1.5	1.2	0.6	0.9	0.6	2.1
Taxes Paid	12	0.5	0.0	1.4	1.7	0.5	2.0	0.3	0.3	0.2	0.1	0.2	0.2	0.7
Interest Paid	13	0.6	0.3	0.2	0.3	0.2	0.2	0.3	0.3	0.3	0.2	0.3	0.5	1.7
Depreciation	14	0.6	0.0	1.4	0.5	0.4	0.3	0.5	0.5	0.4	0.2	0.4	0.3	1.5
Amortization and Depletion	15	0.2	0.0	0.1	0.1	0.0	0.0	0.0	0.0	0.0	0.0	0.0	0.0	0.6
Pensions and Other Deferred Comp.	16	0.1	0.0	0.1	0.0	0.1	0.0	0.0	0.0	0.0	0.0	0.1	0.1	0.1
Employee Benefits	17	0.1	0.0	0.1	0.2	0.1	0.1	0.1	0.1	0.1	0.0	0.2	0.1	0.3
Advertising	18	0.1	0.0	0.2	0.1	0.1	0.0	0.1	0.0	0.0	0.0	0.0	0.0	0.3
Other Expenses	19	2.4	0.2	6.5	3.7	3.4	2.0	2.1	2.4	1.7	0.8	1.6	0.8	4.8
Officers' Compensation	20	0.3	0.0	2.6	1.5	0.9	0.3	0.3	0.2	0.2	0.2	0.1	0.3	0.0
Operating Margin	21	0.3	•	1.5	•	0.0	0.1	0.0	•	0.4	0.4	0.3	•	1.7
Operating Margin Before Officers' Comp.	22	0.6	•	4.1	•	1.0	0.4	0.3	•	0.6	0.6	0.4	•	1.8

Selected Average Balance Sheet ($ in Thousands)

Net Receivables 23	4140	0	53	277	838	3241	5409	11041	25457	66478	125800	304493	2423280
Inventories 24	1548	0	29	85	400	808	1768	3899	8523	32377	60280	154135	744300
Net Property, Plant and Equipment 25	8783	0	51	111	501	1305	4345	11903	15648	23040	79006	112394	1031139
Total Assets 26	20076	0	220	729	2425	7137	15776	35869	69805	150202	352082	1050535	18012682
Notes and Loans Payable 27	5851	0	95	207	713	2360	4941	12067	21055	45782	98954	247024	5324553
All Other Liabilities 28	7948	0	41	259	893	2680	5921	12797	32610	66426	183423	520405	6720731
Net Worth 29	6277	0	84	262	819	2098	4914	11006	16140	37994	69705	283106	5967398

Selected Financial Ratios (Times to 1)

Current Ratio 30	1.1	•	3.6	1.6	1.8	1.4	1.3	1.1	1.2	1.2	1.4	1.2	0.9
Quick Ratio 31	0.7	•	3.0	1.2	1.2	1.1	0.9	0.8	0.8	0.7	0.9	0.8	0.6
Net Sales to Working Capital 32	89.6	•	9.2	34.9	25.7	49.2	54.4	215.7	52.9	41.4	72.7	49.0	•
Coverage Ratio 33	4.2	0.1	9.2	0.0	3.8	3.4	3.0	2.4	3.8	4.6	2.8	1.7	5.1
Total Asset Turnover 34	3.2	•	4.7	9.0	7.8	9.8	7.7	7.1	6.9	8.3	6.3	4.0	1.2
Inventory Turnover 35	39.1	•	28.8	71.1	43.2	80.9	64.9	62.2	53.7	37.4	35.4	26.5	25.6
Receivables Turnover 36	19.7	•	20.6	25.2	23.3	23.4	24.4	24.1	20.7	19.1	17.5	20.6	13.0
Total Liabilities to Net Worth 37	2.2	•	1.6	1.8	2.0	2.4	2.2	2.3	3.3	3.0	4.1	2.7	2.0
Current Assets to Working Capital 38	10.5	•	1.4	2.8	2.3	3.6	4.3	15.6	5.0	3.8	7.6	7.5	•
Current Liabilities to Working Capital 39	9.5	•	0.4	1.8	1.3	2.6	3.3	14.6	4.0	2.8	6.6	6.5	•
Working Capital to Net Sales 40	0.0	•	0.1	0.0	0.0	0.0	0.0	0.0	0.0	0.0	0.0	0.0	•
Inventory to Working Capital 41	2.5	•	0.3	0.4	0.6	0.6	0.8	3.1	1.1	1.1	2.1	2.2	•
Total Receipts to Cash Flow 42	30.1	•	14.1	35.2	32.6	51.5	49.0	48.1	56.8	86.1	62.0	110.5	11.8
Cost of Goods to Cash Flow 43	28.1	•	11.2	32.4	29.9	48.2	46.3	45.6	54.1	83.8	59.5	108.0	10.1
Cash Flow to Total Debt 44	0.2	•	0.5	0.4	0.4	0.3	0.2	0.2	0.2	0.1	0.1	0.0	0.2

Selected Financial Factors (in Percentages)

Debt Ratio 45	68.7	•	61.7	64.0	66.2	70.6	68.9	69.3	76.9	74.7	80.2	73.1	66.9
Return on Total Assets 46	8.7	•	10.4	0.0	6.3	7.3	6.2	5.0	7.1	7.3	5.0	3.5	10.5
Return on Equity Before Income Taxes 47	21.1	•	24.2	•	13.8	17.6	13.2	9.7	22.7	22.8	16.2	5.5	25.5
Return on Equity After Income Taxes 48	14.2	•	23.0	•	13.1	15.6	11.0	8.8	16.8	19.0	13.1	3.5	16.4
Profit Margin (Before Income Tax) 49	2.0	•	1.9	•	0.6	0.5	0.5	0.4	0.8	0.7	0.5	0.4	6.9
Profit Margin (After Income Tax) 50	1.4	•	1.9	•	0.6	0.5	0.4	0.4	0.6	0.6	0.4	0.2	4.4

Table II

Corporations with Net Income

PETROLEUM AND PETROLEUM PRODUCTS

MONEY AMOUNTS AND SIZE OF ASSETS IN THOUSANDS OF DOLLARS

Item Description for Accounting Period 7/07 Through 6/08	Total	Zero Assets	Under 500	500 to 1,000	1,000 to 5,000	5,000 to 10,000	10,000 to 25,000	25,000 to 50,000	50,000 to 100,000	100,000 to 250,000	250,000 to 500,000	500,000 to 2,500,000	2,500,000 and over
Number of Enterprises **1**	6480	384	3053	•	1545	572	337	97	45	22	10	15	•
Revenues ($ in Thousands)													
Net Sales **2**	401279711	442055	3459039	•	35629993	40058114	42182377	23563778	22934540	30543713	15160282	59649803	•
Interest **3**	634804	91	2527	•	10441	12577	22532	5802	6575	12016	18407	66734	•
Rents **4**	159811	0	0	•	23974	19433	39416	12544	7783	12175	15732	11945	•
Royalties **5**	23097	0	0	•	140	1	7	0	0	1630	808	9	•
Other Portfolio Income **6**	6437996	12092	10146	•	15900	63628	52645	25976	43721	25491	40044	44371	•
Other Receipts **7**	1276437	16715	4143	•	152107	78001	123557	120956	35103	40245	57520	543976	•
Total Receipts **8**	409811856	470953	3475855	•	35832555	40231754	42420534	23729056	23027722	30635270	15292793	60316838	•
Average Total Receipts **9**	63243	1226	1139	•	23193	70335	125877	244629	511727	1392512	1529279	4021123	•
Operating Costs/Operating Income (%)													
Cost of Operations **10**	91.9	95.3	78.4	•	91.9	92.8	94.7	94.7	95.3	97.3	93.4	98.0	•
Salaries and Wages **11**	1.6	1.3	6.4	•	2.1	1.4	1.6	1.5	1.2	0.6	1.6	0.5	•
Taxes Paid **12**	0.6	0.3	1.4	•	0.5	2.4	0.3	0.3	0.2	0.1	0.4	0.1	•
Interest Paid **13**	0.7	0.6	0.2	•	0.1	0.2	0.2	0.3	0.2	0.2	0.3	0.6	•
Depreciation **14**	0.7	0.8	1.4	•	0.4	0.4	0.4	0.5	0.4	0.2	0.5	0.1	•
Amortization and Depletion **15**	0.2	0.0	0.1	•	0.0	0.0	0.0	0.0	0.0	0.0	0.1	0.0	•
Pensions and Other Deferred Comp. **16**	0.1	0.0	0.1	•	0.1	0.1	0.0	0.0	0.0	0.0	0.1	0.0	•
Employee Benefits **17**	0.2	0.0	0.0	•	0.1	0.1	0.1	0.1	0.1	0.0	0.3	0.0	•
Advertising **18**	0.1	0.0	0.2	•	0.1	0.1	0.1	0.0	0.0	0.0	0.0	0.0	•
Other Expenses **19**	2.8	1.5	6.6	•	3.6	2.0	2.1	2.3	1.6	0.7	2.2	0.5	•
Officers' Compensation **20**	0.3	0.7	2.7	•	0.8	0.4	0.3	0.2	0.2	0.2	0.2	0.3	•
Operating Margin **21**	0.8	•	2.4	•	0.4	0.3	0.2	0.1	0.6	0.7	0.8	•	•
Operating Margin Before Officers' Comp. **22**	1.1	0.2	5.1	•	1.2	0.7	0.5	0.3	0.8	0.9	1.0	0.1	•

Selected Average Balance Sheet ($ in Thousands)

Net Receivables 23	4561	0	60	•	924	3226	5893	11779	28650	75878	120076	291673
Inventories 24	1560	0	31	•	440	811	1829	3926	8246	37016	58349	143074
Net Property, Plant and Equipment 25	9947	0	48	•	506	1294	4276	9621	14527	20120	82351	67562
Total Assets 26	22461	0	232	•	2516	7150	15817	34795	70209	156219	359323	1025897
Notes and Loans Payable 27	6018	0	100	•	597	2300	4673	10331	18768	39307	73678	217109
All Other Liabilities 28	9019	0	48	•	915	2536	5949	11795	31998	76057	189744	527859
Net Worth 29	7424	0	84	•	1003	2315	5194	12668	19443	40855	95901	280929

Selected Financial Ratios (Times to 1)

Current Ratio 30	1.1	•	3.5	1.9	1.4	1.3	1.2	1.2	1.3	1.4	1.2	1.2
Quick Ratio 31	0.7	•	2.8	1.2	1.1	1.0	0.9	0.9	0.9	0.9	0.8	0.8
Net Sales to Working Capital 32	74.2	•	9.2	26.7	46.1	51.4	71.3	48.2	40.6	36.7	30.7	
Coverage Ratio 33	5.0	11.4	16.5	8.3	4.7	4.0	4.1	5.4	6.6	5.8	2.6	
Total Asset Turnover 34	2.8	•	4.9	9.2	9.8	7.9	7.0	7.3	8.9	4.2	3.9	
Inventory Turnover 35	36.5	•	28.4	48.1	80.1	64.8	58.6	58.9	36.5	24.3	27.2	
Receivables Turnover 36	17.5	•	20.6	26.7	23.8	23.3	22.2	20.7	18.1	•	23.1	
Total Liabilities to Net Worth 37	2.0	•	1.8	1.5	2.1	2.0	1.7	2.6	2.8	2.7	2.7	
Current Assets to Working Capital 38	9.9	•	1.4	2.2	3.4	4.1	5.7	4.7	3.7	5.5	5.2	
Current Liabilities to Working Capital 39	8.9	•	0.4	1.2	2.4	3.1	4.7	3.7	2.7	4.5	4.2	
Working Capital to Net Sales 40	0.0	•	0.1	0.0	0.0	0.0	0.0	0.0	0.0	0.0	0.0	
Inventory to Working Capital 41	2.3	•	0.3	0.6	0.6	0.8	1.1	1.0	1.1	1.4	1.5	
Total Receipts to Cash Flow 42	23.0	13.6	12.2	27.7	46.4	45.0	38.8	52.4	74.6	32.5	81.1	
Cost of Goods to Cash Flow 43	21.1	12.9	9.6	25.4	43.0	42.6	36.8	49.9	72.6	30.4	79.5	
Cash Flow to Total Debt 44	0.2	•	0.6	0.6	0.3	0.3	0.3	0.2	0.2	0.2	0.1	

Selected Financial Factors (in Percentages)

Debt Ratio 45	66.9	63.8	•	60.1	67.6	67.2	63.6	72.3	73.8	73.3	72.6	
Return on Total Assets 46	10.2	15.2	•	10.4	9.4	7.8	7.3	8.9	10.0	8.5	5.7	
Return on Equity Before Income Taxes 47	24.7	39.5	•	22.9	22.8	17.9	15.1	26.2	32.6	26.3	12.9	
Return on Equity After Income Taxes 48	17.3	38.2	•	22.1	20.7	15.4	14.0	20.5	27.7	23.0	10.3	
Profit Margin (Before Income Tax) 49	3.0	6.0	2.9	1.0	0.8	0.7	0.8	1.0	1.0	1.7	0.9	
Profit Margin (After Income Tax) 50	2.1	5.9	2.8	1.0	0.7	0.6	0.7	0.8	0.8	1.5	0.7	

Table I

Corporations with and without Net Income

BEER, WINE, AND DISTILLED ALCOHOLIC BEVERAGE

MONEY AMOUNTS AND SIZE OF ASSETS IN THOUSANDS OF DOLLARS

Item Description for Accounting Period 7/07 Through 6/08	Total	Zero Assets	Under 500	500 to 1,000	1,000 to 5,000	5,000 to 10,000	10,000 to 25,000	25,000 to 50,000	50,000 to 100,000	100,000 to 250,000	250,000 to 500,000	500,000 to 2,500,000	2,500,000 and over
Number of Enterprises 1	3925	1105	686	334	902	424	293	81	51	28	8	12	0
Revenues ($ in Thousands)													
Net Sales 2	79071569	715797	311783	1378294	9348287	8945996	12037970	7461119	7318838	8790468	3763289	18999728	0
Interest 3	114155	2970	597	416	3931	5543	1397	2583	2936	5239	10450	78093	0
Rents 4	52216	0	0	831	0	777	0	61	384	9969	13792	26402	0
Royalties 5	6785	0	62	0	105	16	1229	0	0	0	2772	2600	0
Other Portfolio Income 6	391861	9572	0	205	45446	42187	81191	22932	46998	45279	49915	48136	0
Other Receipts 7	1131615	-1853	495	27400	84826	102173	87914	85274	152637	255756	59432	277562	0
Total Receipts 8	80768201	726486	312937	1407146	9482595	9096692	12209701	7571969	7521793	9106711	3899650	19432521	0
Average Total Receipts 9	20578	657	456	4213	10513	21454	41671	93481	147486	325240	487456	1619377	•
Operating Costs/Operating Income (%)													
Cost of Operations 10	75.8	70.1	19.4	76.7	75.3	76.1	74.6	76.7	75.0	75.4	80.9	77.1	•
Salaries and Wages 11	7.9	6.6	0.1	7.5	8.9	8.6	8.4	7.9	8.3	8.0	4.6	7.6	•
Taxes Paid 12	2.9	4.4	1.6	3.0	2.8	2.0	3.3	2.0	3.0	2.8	1.3	3.8	•
Interest Paid 13	1.0	5.0	0.0	0.6	0.3	0.4	0.9	0.6	0.9	0.7	1.7	1.6	•
Depreciation 14	0.6	0.7	0.1	2.4	0.4	0.6	0.6	0.5	1.0	0.6	0.5	0.4	•
Amortization and Depletion 15	0.6	0.9	0.1	0.1	0.1	0.3	0.6	0.5	0.6	0.5	1.4	0.9	•
Pensions and Other Deferred Comp. 16	0.5	0.4	5.1	0.1	0.3	1.8	0.3	0.4	0.3	0.3	0.8	0.3	•
Employee Benefits 17	0.7	0.6	0.0	0.5	1.0	0.7	0.8	0.6	0.8	0.7	0.6	0.6	•
Advertising 18	1.4	0.7	0.2	0.4	0.6	0.9	0.7	0.9	1.3	2.5	3.2	1.8	•
Other Expenses 19	6.0	14.3	12.6	8.0	6.3	5.3	5.7	6.8	5.8	6.8	3.8	5.4	•
Officers' Compensation 20	1.2	0.4	23.3	4.0	2.2	1.7	1.2	1.2	0.9	1.2	0.3	0.3	•
Operating Margin 21	1.4	•	37.5	•	1.8	1.5	2.9	1.9	2.3	0.5	1.1	0.3	•
Operating Margin Before Officers' Comp. 22	2.6	•	60.8	0.8	3.9	3.2	4.1	3.1	3.2	1.7	1.4	0.6	•

Selected Average Balance Sheet ($ in Thousands)

Net Receivables **23**	1463	0	11	118	488	1029	2032	6161	9082	29638	38932	176640
Inventories **24**	1889	0	20	317	740	1686	2885	7352	13314	33865	46027	206526
Net Property, Plant and Equipment **25**	1062	0	4	163	334	890	2131	3900	10534	19284	17953	105912
Total Assets **26**	10195		229	849	2240	6765	15533	34228	70316	144079	339516	1418895
Notes and Loans Payable **27**	3460	0	55	405	473	1297	5841	8392	22087	34702	152762	559894
All Other Liabilities **28**	2364	0	87	288	776	1655	2664	9814	12655	43941	80579	302180
Net Worth **29**	4371	0	87	156	991	3814	7028	16021	35575	65436	106174	556821

Selected Financial Ratios (Times to 1)

Current Ratio **30**	1.7	•	2.3	2.1	1.7	2.3	2.1	1.7	1.9	1.7	1.4	1.4
Quick Ratio **31**	0.8	•	1.5	0.6	0.9	1.2	1.2	0.8	0.9	0.9	0.7	0.6
Net Sales to Working Capital **32**	11.0	•	4.4	12.6	16.9	9.1	11.0	10.7	9.5	8.9	12.8	11.5
Coverage Ratio **33**	4.7	0.5	1019.4	•	10.6	8.4	5.7	6.3	6.8	6.4	3.8	2.6
Total Asset Turnover **34**	2.0	•	2.0	4.9	4.6	3.1	2.6	2.7	2.0	2.2	1.4	1.1
Inventory Turnover **35**	8.1	•	4.5	10.0	10.5	9.5	10.6	9.6	8.1	7.0	8.3	5.9
Receivables Turnover **36**	13.8	•	14.9	39.9	20.2	22.0	21.6	15.7	14.2	10.1	15.2	8.8
Total Liabilities to Net Worth **37**	1.3	•	1.6	4.4	1.3	0.8	1.2	1.1	1.0	1.2	2.2	1.5
Current Assets to Working Capital **38**	2.5	•	1.8	1.9	2.5	1.7	1.9	2.4	2.1	2.3	3.4	3.6
Current Liabilities to Working Capital **39**	1.5	•	0.8	0.9	1.5	0.7	0.9	1.4	1.1	1.3	2.4	2.6
Working Capital to Net Sales **40**	0.1	•	0.2	0.1	0.1	0.1	0.1	0.1	0.1	0.1	0.1	0.1
Inventory to Working Capital **41**	1.0	•	0.1	1.1	1.1	0.8	0.8	1.0	0.9	0.9	1.4	1.5
Total Receipts to Cash Flow **42**	12.7	10.4	2.1	18.0	13.3	14.6	12.7	11.7	11.1	10.2	15.5	14.8
Cost of Goods to Cash Flow **43**	9.6	7.3	0.4	13.8	10.0	11.1	9.4	8.9	8.3	7.7	12.5	11.4
Cash Flow to Total Debt **44**	0.3	•	1.5	0.3	0.6	0.5	0.4	0.4	0.4	0.4	0.1	0.1

Selected Financial Factors (in Percentages)

Debt Ratio **45**	57.1	•	62.1	81.6	55.7	43.6	54.8	53.2	49.4	54.6	68.7	60.8
Return on Total Assets **46**	9.0	•	75.4	•	16.3	11.3	13.7	10.8	12.0	10.4	8.9	4.7
Return on Equity Before Income Taxes **47**	16.5	•	198.6	•	33.4	17.7	25.0	19.5	20.3	19.3	20.9	7.4
Return on Equity After Income Taxes **48**	14.7	•	198.1	•	30.7	16.2	23.7	18.4	18.7	17.3	14.8	6.0
Profit Margin (Before Income Tax) **49**	3.6	•	37.9	•	3.2	3.2	4.3	3.4	5.0	4.0	4.7	2.6
Profit Margin (After Income Tax) **50**	3.2	•	37.8	•	2.9	2.9	4.0	3.2	4.6	3.6	3.3	2.1

Table II

Corporations with Net Income

BEER, WINE, AND DISTILLED ALCOHOLIC BEVERAGE

MONEY AMOUNTS AND SIZE OF ASSETS IN THOUSANDS OF DOLLARS

Item Description for Accounting Period 7/07 Through 6/08	Total	Zero Assets	Under 500	500 to 1,000	1,000 to 5,000	5,000 to 10,000	10,000 to 25,000	25,000 to 50,000	50,000 to 100,000	100,000 to 250,000	250,000 to 500,000	500,000 to 2,500,000	2,500,000 and over
Number of Enterprises **1**	2296	5	506	205	816	366	244	68	44	24	•	•	0
Revenues ($ in Thousands)													
Net Sales **2**	71328692	387774	255274	548311	8184815	7591469	10438155	6629743	6816448	7852295	•	•	0
Interest **3**	108211	0	594	416	3667	5439	1321	1541	2744	4108	•	•	0
Rents **4**	51918	0	0	831	0	520	0	61	342	9969	•	•	0
Royalties **5**	6601	0	0	0	0	0	1229	0	0	0	•	•	0
Other Portfolio Income **6**	360431	148	0	205	45446	42173	79394	9460	46476	39098	•	•	0
Other Receipts **7**	1077159	145	116	27307	84776	99851	79253	72285	141649	237949	•	•	0
Total Receipts **8**	72933012	388067	255984	577070	8318704	7739452	10599352	6713090	7007659	8143419	•	•	•
Average Total Receipts **9**	31765	77613	506	2815	10194	21146	43440	98722	159265	339309	•	•	•
Operating Costs/Operating Income (%)													
Cost of Operations **10**	75.6	71.4	4.7	73.1	72.7	76.1	74.4	76.0	74.8	76.7	•	•	•
Salaries and Wages **11**	7.9	0.9	0.1	12.5	9.8	8.3	8.2	7.7	8.2	7.7	•	•	•
Taxes Paid **12**	2.9	0.6	1.8	1.4	2.9	2.2	3.4	2.1	3.1	2.6	•	•	•
Interest Paid **13**	0.9	1.0	0.0	0.6	0.3	0.4	0.8	0.5	0.8	0.6	•	•	•
Depreciation **14**	0.6	0.8	0.1	3.4	0.5	0.6	0.6	0.5	1.0	0.4	•	•	•
Amortization and Depletion **15**	0.6	0.6	0.1	0.1	0.2	0.2	0.6	0.4	0.6	0.4	•	•	•
Pensions and Other Deferred Comp. **16**	0.4	0.6	6.2	•	0.3	0.9	0.3	0.4	0.3	0.2	•	•	•
Employee Benefits **17**	0.7	0.4	0.0	0.5	1.1	0.9	0.7	0.5	0.8	0.6	•	•	•
Advertising **18**	1.4	0.6	0.2	0.8	0.6	0.8	0.7	0.9	1.1	2.7	•	•	•
Other Expenses **19**	5.7	15.7	11.9	10.6	6.7	5.0	5.4	6.7	5.5	5.5	•	•	•
Officers' Compensation **20**	1.2	0.4	27.8	1.3	2.4	1.7	1.3	1.0	0.8	1.3	•	•	•
Operating Margin **21**	2.2	6.9	47.1	•	2.4	2.9	3.7	3.3	3.0	1.1	•	•	•
Operating Margin Before Officers' Comp. **22**	3.3	7.3	74.9	•	4.8	4.7	5.0	4.2	3.8	2.5	•	•	•

Selected Average Balance Sheet ($ in Thousands)

Net Receivables 23	2253	0	0	101	452	890	1935	6379	8906	31483
Inventories 24	2980	0	4	247	767	1796	2964	7704	12805	33643
Net Property, Plant and Equipment 25	1287	0	5	103	350	915	2211	4071	11302	18189
Total Assets 26	15530		227	776	2211	6926	15243	34085	71901	145122
Notes and Loans Payable 27	5088	0	1	224	408	1264	5402	7593	21076	29972
All Other Liabilities 28	3633	0	48	196	713	1596	2630	10155	12574	48192
Net Worth 29	6810	0	178	356	1090	4065	7211	16337	38251	66958

Selected Financial Ratios (Times to 1)

Current Ratio 30	1.7	•	4.5	2.8	1.8	2.3	2.2	1.7	1.9	1.7
Quick Ratio 31	0.8	•	3.1	0.8	1.0	1.2	1.2	0.8	0.9	0.9
Net Sales to Working Capital 32	11.0	•	3.0	7.3	15.6	9.0	11.6	11.3	10.1	9.3
Coverage Ratio 33	5.8	7.9	1164.3	2.3	12.8	12.5	7.4	9.4	8.7	8.4
Total Asset Turnover 34	2.0	•	2.2	3.4	4.5	3.0	2.8	2.9	2.2	2.3
Inventory Turnover 35	7.9	•	5.7	7.9	9.5	8.8	10.7	9.6	9.1	7.5
Receivables Turnover 36	13.9	•	10211.0	29.8	21.6	22.7	23.0	15.4	17.3	•
Total Liabilities to Net Worth 37	1.3	•	0.3	1.2	1.0	0.7	1.1	1.1	0.9	1.2
Current Assets to Working Capital 38	2.5	•	1.3	1.6	2.3	1.8	1.8	2.4	2.1	2.4
Current Liabilities to Working Capital 39	1.5	•	0.3	0.6	1.3	0.8	0.8	1.4	1.1	1.4
Working Capital to Net Sales 40	0.1	•	0.3	0.1	0.1	0.1	0.1	0.1	0.1	0.1
Inventory to Working Capital 41	1.1	•	0.0	0.9	1.0	0.8	0.8	1.0	0.9	1.0
Total Receipts to Cash Flow 42	11.8	4.6	1.8	10.6	11.5	12.2	11.9	10.4	10.5	10.7
Cost of Goods to Cash Flow 43	8.9	3.3	0.1	7.8	8.4	9.3	8.8	7.9	7.8	8.2
Cash Flow to Total Debt 44	0.3	•	5.9	0.6	0.8	0.6	0.4	0.5	0.4	0.4

Selected Financial Factors (in Percentages)

Debt Ratio 45	56.2	•	21.6	54.2	50.7	41.3	52.7	52.1	46.8	53.9
Return on Total Assets 46	10.7	•	105.3	5.1	20.0	15.9	16.8	14.4	14.2	12.3
Return on Equity Before Income Taxes 47	20.1	•	134.1	6.4	37.5	24.9	30.7	26.8	23.6	23.5
Return on Equity After Income Taxes 48	18.2	•	133.8	5.4	34.7	23.1	29.3	25.4	21.9	21.1
Profit Margin (Before Income Tax) 49	4.4	7.0	47.4	0.8	4.1	4.9	5.2	4.5	5.8	4.8
Profit Margin (After Income Tax) 50	4.0	6.9	47.3	0.7	3.8	4.5	4.9	4.3	5.4	4.3

Table I

Corporations with and without Net Income

MISCELLANEOUS NONDURABLE GOODS

MONEY AMOUNTS AND SIZE OF ASSETS IN THOUSANDS OF DOLLARS

Item Description for Accounting Period 7/07 Through 6/08	Total	Zero Assets	Under 500	500 to 1,000	1,000 to 5,000	5,000 to 10,000	10,000 to 25,000	25,000 to 50,000	50,000 to 100,000	100,000 to 250,000	250,000 to 500,000	500,000 to 2,500,000	2,500,000 and over
Number of Enterprises **1**	32358	4667	20159	3302	3140	520	313	132	61	36	16	12	0
Revenues ($ in Thousands)													
Net Sales **2**	146808521	1157529	14781906	9444430	26921857	14718239	15587390	13270039	9236161	10893854	7394238	23402877	0
Interest **3**	299509	91	5275	4656	17266	19023	9707	18652	12652	24187	12270	175729	0
Rents **4**	30082	5	5123	555	4086	2398	2008	1436	1174	3018	504	9775	0
Royalties **5**	79469	0	0	0	879	0	421	11038	6313	4621	1135	55061	0
Other Portfolio Income **6**	294436	21978	12311	27807	18907	17260	7456	7753	4879	8382	9232	158471	0
Other Receipts **7**	1463175	82511	52209	75999	236362	45345	204517	158037	96685	178441	124728	208344	0
Total Receipts **8**	148975192	1262114	14856824	9553447	27199357	14802265	15811499	13466955	9357864	11112503	7542107	24010257	0
Average Total Receipts **9**	4604	270	737	2893	8662	28466	50516	102022	153408	308681	471382	2000855	•
Operating Costs/Operating Income (%)													
Cost of Operations **10**	81.5	83.0	77.0	81.2	83.4	85.1	83.5	84.2	82.5	80.6	74.0	79.6	•
Salaries and Wages **11**	5.5	5.5	5.3	5.5	4.8	4.9	5.4	5.0	5.8	6.3	7.6	6.1	•
Taxes Paid **12**	1.2	0.7	1.2	1.6	1.5	0.8	2.0	1.1	0.9	0.9	1.0	0.9	•
Interest Paid **13**	0.9	0.4	0.3	0.5	0.6	0.7	0.6	0.6	1.1	1.2	1.1	2.0	•
Depreciation **14**	0.7	0.8	0.6	0.7	0.4	0.3	0.6	0.5	0.7	0.8	0.8	1.2	•
Amortization and Depletion **15**	0.2	0.0	0.1	0.0	0.0	0.0	0.1	0.1	0.3	0.1	0.5	0.4	•
Pensions and Other Deferred Comp. **16**	0.2	0.1	0.2	0.0	0.2	0.2	0.2	0.2	0.3	0.2	0.3	0.3	•
Employee Benefits **17**	0.5	0.1	0.4	0.4	0.3	0.3	0.5	0.4	0.4	0.6	0.8	0.8	•
Advertising **18**	0.6	0.2	0.4	0.6	0.4	0.5	0.3	0.6	0.6	0.9	1.9	0.9	•
Other Expenses **19**	6.9	14.4	11.4	7.0	7.0	5.0	4.6	5.4	5.6	6.6	7.1	7.7	•
Officers' Compensation **20**	1.4	2.8	3.6	2.2	1.6	1.1	1.4	1.1	0.9	0.6	0.7	0.4	•
Operating Margin **21**	0.5	•	•	0.2	•	1.3	0.8	0.9	0.7	1.2	4.4	•	•
Operating Margin Before Officers' Comp. **22**	1.9	•	3.4	2.4	1.3	2.4	2.3	2.0	1.6	1.8	5.1	0.0	•

Selected Average Balance Sheet ($ in Thousands)

Net Receivables 23	450	0	21	305	653	2568	4958	10864	15885	37733	68314	279220
Inventories 24	405	0	33	226	621	2402	4204	9143	18445	33339	51517	236243
Net Property, Plant and Equipment 25	212	0	20	83	176	529	1742	4645	8060	25271	27408	195380
Total Assets 26	1652	0	112	788	2167	7078	15257	34280	70141	144671	311290	1195282
Notes and Loans Payable 27	525	0	60	279	610	1946	4888	8815	21691	57383	72810	389345
All Other Liabilities 28	655	0	27	258	1124	2587	5952	12865	23384	66036	105358	489275
Net Worth 29	472	0	25	251	433	2545	4417	12600	25066	21252	133123	316662

Selected Financial Ratios (Times to 1)

Current Ratio 30	1.5	•	2.2	2.0	1.3	1.8	1.4	1.5	1.5	1.3	1.4	1.5
Quick Ratio 31	0.8	•	1.2	1.2	0.8	1.0	0.7	0.8	0.7	0.7	0.8	0.8
Net Sales to Working Capital 32	12.2	•	17.3	9.4	20.8	10.4	15.5	10.1	9.6	12.6	8.9	9.4
Coverage Ratio 33	3.2	3.8	2.0	3.5	2.3	3.8	4.5	5.2	2.8	3.6	6.8	2.3
Total Asset Turnover 34	2.7	•	6.6	3.6	4.0	4.0	3.3	2.9	2.2	2.1	1.5	1.6
Inventory Turnover 35	9.1	•	17.2	10.3	11.5	10.0	9.9	9.3	6.8	7.3	6.6	6.6
Receivables Turnover 36	10.6	•	34.0	11.3	14.7	9.8	10.1	9.8	9.5	8.6	8.8	7.1
Total Liabilities to Net Worth 37	2.5	•	3.6	2.1	4.0	1.8	2.5	1.7	1.8	5.8	1.3	2.8
Current Assets to Working Capital 38	3.0	•	1.9	2.0	4.0	2.2	3.7	2.9	2.9	4.0	3.2	2.9
Current Liabilities to Working Capital 39	2.0	•	0.9	1.0	3.0	1.2	2.7	1.9	1.9	3.0	2.2	1.9
Working Capital to Net Sales 40	0.1	•	0.1	0.1	0.0	0.1	0.1	0.1	0.1	0.1	0.1	0.1
Inventory to Working Capital 41	1.1	•	0.8	0.7	1.6	0.8	1.4	1.1	1.2	1.4	1.3	1.1
Total Receipts to Cash Flow 42	13.7	8.4	10.9	15.7	15.2	19.5	17.1	14.8	15.8	11.5	8.4	12.4
Cost of Goods to Cash Flow 43	11.2	7.0	8.4	12.7	12.7	16.6	14.2	12.5	13.0	9.3	6.2	9.9
Cash Flow to Total Debt 44	0.3	•	0.8	0.3	0.3	0.3	0.3	0.3	0.2	0.2	0.3	0.2

Selected Financial Factors (in Percentages)

Debt Ratio 45	71.4	•	78.1	68.2	80.0	64.0	71.0	63.2	64.3	85.3	57.2	73.5
Return on Total Assets 46	8.0	•	3.6	6.9	5.7	10.1	9.6	8.8	6.8	9.2	11.0	7.6
Return on Equity Before Income Taxes 47	19.4	•	8.1	15.5	15.9	20.7	25.8	19.3	12.3	45.5	21.9	16.3
Return on Equity After Income Taxes 48	16.3	•	6.6	14.6	14.8	19.3	23.3	16.5	10.1	37.1	19.6	10.8
Profit Margin (Before Income Tax) 49	2.0	1.1	0.3	1.4	0.8	1.9	2.3	2.4	2.0	3.2	6.3	2.7
Profit Margin (After Income Tax) 50	1.7	1.0	0.2	1.3	0.7	1.7	2.1	2.1	1.7	2.6	5.7	1.8

Table II
Corporations with Net Income

MISCELLANEOUS NONDURABLE GOODS

MONEY AMOUNTS AND SIZE OF ASSETS IN THOUSANDS OF DOLLARS

Item Description for Accounting Period 7/07 Through 6/08	Total	Zero Assets	Under 500	500 to 1,000	1,000 to 5,000	5,000 to 10,000	10,000 to 25,000	25,000 to 50,000	50,000 to 100,000	100,000 to 250,000	250,000 to 500,000	500,000 to 2,500,000	2,500,000 and over
Number of Enterprises 1	16113	1077	9559	2295	2249	466	252	111	47	32	•	•	0
Revenues ($ in Thousands)													
Net Sales 2	122107563	1030639	11279070	6583653	17597029	14274866	13072783	11890758	8385422	10388578	•	•	0
Interest 3	268007	5	4502	2446	14578	14087	8470	14054	8544	21642	•	•	0
Rents 4	25501	5	3119	55	3981	1361	1144	1436	1164	3018	•	•	0
Royalties 5	77679	0	0	0	0	0	421	10862	5578	4621	•	•	0
Other Portfolio Income 6	257763	21978	12311	23155	6560	9753	6262	7681	4047	7799	•	•	0
Other Receipts 7	1225413	82770	44114	57347	195863	40330	147434	81194	89769	176550	•	•	0
Total Receipts 8	123961926	1135397	11343116	6666656	17818011	14340397	13236514	12005985	8494524	10602208	•	•	0
Average Total Receipts 9	7693	1054	1187	2905	7923	30773	52526	108162	180735	331319	•	•	•
Operating Costs/Operating Income (%)													
Cost of Operations 10	81.7	83.2	79.9	80.1	80.9	85.3	83.0	84.2	83.7	82.0	•	•	•
Salaries and Wages 11	5.2	5.5	3.8	5.2	5.4	4.7	5.2	4.7	5.4	5.8	•	•	•
Taxes Paid 12	1.1	0.7	1.0	1.9	1.2	0.8	2.1	1.0	0.9	0.9	•	•	•
Interest Paid 13	0.9	0.4	0.2	0.5	0.6	0.6	0.7	0.5	0.8	1.2	•	•	•
Depreciation 14	0.6	0.7	0.3	0.8	0.5	0.3	0.5	0.5	0.7	0.8	•	•	•
Amortization and Depletion 15	0.1	0.0	0.1	0.0	0.0	0.0	0.1	0.1	0.2	0.1	•	•	•
Pensions and Other Deferred Comp. 16	0.2	0.1	0.2	0.0	0.3	0.1	0.2	0.2	0.3	0.2	•	•	•
Employee Benefits 17	0.5	0.1	0.5	0.5	0.3	0.3	0.5	0.4	0.4	0.6	•	•	•
Advertising 18	0.6	0.1	0.3	0.4	0.1	0.5	0.3	0.6	0.6	0.8	•	•	•
Other Expenses 19	6.0	7.5	7.9	6.5	6.5	4.7	4.2	5.1	4.1	5.4	•	•	•
Officers' Compensation 20	1.3	2.7	3.6	2.1	2.0	1.0	1.3	1.0	0.9	0.6	•	•	•
Operating Margin 21	1.8	•	2.4	2.0	2.1	1.8	1.9	1.9	2.1	1.7	•	•	•
Operating Margin Before Officers' Comp. 22	3.1	1.6	5.9	4.1	4.1	2.8	3.2	2.9	3.0	2.2	•	•	•

Selected Average Balance Sheet ($ in Thousands)

Net Receivables 23	775	0	34	348	635	2613	4699	11352	17892	40747
Inventories 24	671	0	38	236	633	2333	4326	9018	19970	33223
Net Property, Plant and Equipment 25	348	0	18	80	157	523	1473	4551	8641	27547
Total Assets 26	2721	0	148	782	2109	7151	15001	34892	70925	148455
Notes and Loans Payable 27	788	0	53	247	389	1885	4447	8372	19021	61801
All Other Liabilities 28	1051	0	37	260	1022	2573	4984	12775	23305	68786
Net Worth 29	882	0	58	275	699	2693	5570	13745	28599	17868

Selected Financial Ratios (Times to 1)

Current Ratio 30	1.6	•	2.4	2.2	1.5	1.9	1.6	1.6	1.7	1.4
Quick Ratio 31	0.9	•	1.4	1.4	0.8	1.1	0.8	0.8	0.8	0.7
Net Sales to Working Capital 32	10.8	•	17.9	7.7	14.0	10.3	11.8	10.3	8.7	12.1
Coverage Ratio 33	4.8	22.3	15.4	7.5	6.7	4.6	5.9	6.4	5.5	3.9
Total Asset Turnover 34	2.8	•	8.0	3.7	3.7	4.3	3.5	3.1	2.5	2.2
Inventory Turnover 35	9.2	•	24.9	9.7	10.0	11.2	10.0	10.0	7.5	8.0
Receivables Turnover 36	10.4	•	36.3	10.1	13.6	11.2	10.8	10.0	10.1	9.1
Total Liabilities to Net Worth 37	2.1	•	1.5	1.8	2.0	1.7	1.7	1.5	1.5	7.3
Current Assets to Working Capital 38	2.7	•	1.7	1.8	3.0	2.1	2.7	2.8	2.4	3.8
Current Liabilities to Working Capital 39	1.7	•	0.7	0.8	2.0	1.1	1.7	1.8	1.4	2.8
Working Capital to Net Sales 40	0.1	•	0.1	0.1	0.1	0.1	0.1	0.1	0.1	0.1
Inventory to Working Capital 41	1.0	•	0.7	0.7	1.2	0.8	1.0	1.0	1.0	1.2
Total Receipts to Cash Flow 42	12.8	7.5	11.0	12.7	11.6	18.6	15.6	14.2	15.9	12.5
Cost of Goods to Cash Flow 43	10.5	6.2	8.8	10.2	9.4	15.9	12.9	12.0	13.3	10.2
Cash Flow to Total Debt 44	0.3	•	1.2	0.4	0.5	0.4	0.4	0.4	0.3	0.2

Selected Financial Factors (in Percentages)

Debt Ratio 45	67.6	•	60.7	64.9	66.9	62.3	62.9	60.6	59.7	88.0
Return on Total Assets 46	11.7	•	24.9	13.7	14.6	12.4	13.3	10.5	10.6	10.8
Return on Equity Before Income Taxes 47	28.6	•	59.3	33.9	37.5	25.8	29.6	22.4	21.4	66.9
Return on Equity After Income Taxes 48	25.2	•	58.0	32.7	36.6	24.3	27.2	19.3	18.9	55.7
Profit Margin (Before Income Tax) 49	3.3	9.1	2.9	3.2	3.4	2.3	3.2	2.9	3.4	3.7
Profit Margin (After Income Tax) 50	2.9	9.0	2.9	3.1	3.3	2.1	2.9	2.5	3.0	3.1

WHOLESALE ELECTRONIC MARKETS AND AGENTS AND BROKERS

Table I

Corporations with and without Net Income

MONEY AMOUNTS AND SIZE OF ASSETS IN THOUSANDS OF DOLLARS

Item Description for Accounting Period 7/07 Through 6/08	Total	Zero Assets	Under 500	500 to 1,000	1,000 to 5,000	5,000 to 10,000	10,000 to 25,000	25,000 to 50,000	50,000 to 100,000	100,000 to 250,000	250,000 to 500,000	500,000 to 2,500,000	2,500,000 and over
Number of Enterprises **1**	16196	3530	12229	69	343	13	5	3	0	0	3	0	0

Revenues ($ in Thousands)

	Total	Zero Assets	Under 500	500 to 1,000	1,000 to 5,000	5,000 to 10,000	10,000 to 25,000	25,000 to 50,000	50,000 to 100,000	100,000 to 250,000	250,000 to 500,000	500,000 to 2,500,000	2,500,000 and over
Net Sales **2**	5607395	220143	3286888	141239	730285	0	15340	232	0	0	1213268	0	0
Interest **3**	45392	1515	4643	1195	1163	507	0	0	0	0	36369	0	0
Rents **4**	2887	0	0	0	0	0	0	0	0	0	2887	0	0
Royalties **5**	315	0	0	0	0	0	0	0	0	0	315	0	0
Other Portfolio Income **6**	2499	91	0	0	0	0	0	0	0	0	2408	0	0
Other Receipts **7**	153016	10231	50028	0	49822	507	11357	12940	0	0	18130	0	0
Total Receipts **8**	5811504	231980	3341559	142434	781270	1014	26697	13172	0	0	1273377	0	0
Average Total Receipts **9**	359	66	273	2064	2278	78	5339	4391	•	•	424459	•	•

Operating Costs/Operating Income (%)

	Total	Zero Assets	Under 500	500 to 1,000	1,000 to 5,000	5,000 to 10,000	10,000 to 25,000	25,000 to 50,000	50,000 to 100,000	100,000 to 250,000	250,000 to 500,000	500,000 to 2,500,000	2,500,000 and over
Cost of Operations **10**	4.7	0.2	•	•	35.9	•	•	•	•	•	49.0	•	•
Salaries and Wages **11**	22.5	9.3	11.8	25.2	29.3	•	38.3	•	•	•	4.4	•	•
Taxes Paid **12**	3.1	1.8	2.6	3.1	3.1	•	3.7	18.5	•	•	11.9	•	•
Interest Paid **13**	3.3	3.5	0.3	0.6	2.2	•	14.4	657.8	•	•	1.0	•	•
Depreciation **14**	0.5	1.0	0.3	0.7	0.6	•	0.7	•	•	•	2.0	•	•
Amortization and Depletion **15**	0.7	0.1	0.3	•	0.5	•	•	•	•	•	1.4	•	•
Pensions and Other Deferred Comp. **16**	1.3	1.1	1.6	•	0.2	•	•	•	•	•	4.7	•	•
Employee Benefits **17**	2.2	3.4	1.3	4.5	1.2	•	•	•	•	•	0.0	•	•
Advertising **18**	0.3	0.6	0.4	0.0	0.6	•	0.0	4.3	•	•	•	•	•
Other Expenses **19**	38.1	30.6	44.8	58.7	21.8	•	13.4	255.6	•	•	28.7	•	•
Officers' Compensation **20**	18.3	32.4	25.6	18.4	8.2	•	100.9	•	•	•	1.1	•	•
Operating Margin **21**	5.1	15.9	11.0	•	•	•	•	•	•	•	•	•	•
Operating Margin Before Officers' Comp. **22**	23.5	48.4	36.6	7.2	4.6	•	29.5	•	•	•	•	•	•

Selected Average Balance Sheet ($ in Thousands)

Net Receivables 23	25	0	9	1	290	2914	0	0	51676
Inventories 24	2	0	0	0	59	0	874	1	1194
Net Property, Plant and Equipment 25	11	0	6	59	82	0	0	0	27195
Total Assets 26	204	62	660	1593	6648	10826	26483		579679
Notes and Loans Payable 27	166	22	160	429	0	5091	7149		736771
All Other Liabilities 28	40	14	13	485	2808	6262	13		78692
Net Worth 29	-1	26	487	678	3840	-528	19321		-235785

Selected Financial Ratios (Times to 1)

Current Ratio 30	1.6	•	1.6	3.5	1.8	2.2	0.3	54.6	1.6
Quick Ratio 31	0.8	•	1.6	3.4	1.3	2.2	0.1	54.6	0.3
Net Sales to Working Capital 32	7.2	•	20.0	4.8	5.7	•	•	0.1	2.8
Coverage Ratio 33	3.7	7.0	44.3	•	2.5	1.2	8.2		1.1
Total Asset Turnover 34	1.7	•	4.3	3.1	1.3	0.3	0.0		0.7
Inventory Turnover 35	9.0	•	•	13.1	•	•			0.0
Receivables Turnover 36	9.8	•	51.4	1681.4	10.9	0.5	•		4.1
Total Liabilities to Net Worth 37	•	•	1.4	0.4	1.3	0.7	0.5	0.4	0.0
Current Assets to Working Capital 38	2.6	•	2.6	1.4	2.3	1.8	1.0		2.6
Current Liabilities to Working Capital 39	1.6	•	1.6	0.4	1.3	0.8	0.0		1.6
Working Capital to Net Sales 40	0.1	0.0	0.0	0.2	0.2	•	9.2		0.4
Inventory to Working Capital 41	0.1	•	0.0	•	0.3	•	0.0		0.0
Total Receipts to Cash Flow 42	2.3	2.1	1.9	2.2	4.8	7.2	0.0		3.9
Cost of Goods to Cash Flow 43	0.1	0.0	•	1.7	•	0.0			0.0
Cash Flow to Total Debt 44	0.7	•	4.0	5.3	0.5	0.0	0.0	0.5	0.1

Selected Financial Factors (in Percentages)

Debt Ratio 45	100.6	•	58.2	26.2	57.4	42.2	104.9	140.7
Return on Total Assets 46	20.4	•	56.3	7.4	•	4.8		15.8
Return on Equity Before Income Taxes 47	•	•	131.7	10.5	•			19.0
Return on Equity After Income Taxes 48	•	•	130.6	7.0	•			19.0
Profit Margin (Before Income Tax) 49	8.8	21.3	12.7	3.4	•	2.6	0.1	4740.9
Profit Margin (After Income Tax) 50	8.4	20.7	12.6	2.2	•	2.6	0.6	4740.9

Table II

Corporations with Net Income

WHOLESALE ELECTRONIC MARKETS AND AGENTS AND BROKERS

MONEY AMOUNTS AND SIZE OF ASSETS IN THOUSANDS OF DOLLARS

Item Description for Accounting Period 7/07 Through 6/08	Total	Zero Assets	Under 500	500 to 1000	251 to 500	501 to 1,000	1,001 to 5,000	5,001 to 10,000	10,001 to 25,000	25,001 to 50,000	50,001 to 100,000	100,001 to 250,000	250,001 and over
Number of Enterprises **1**	11470	2737	8425	54	242	4	5	3	0	0	0	0	0
Revenues ($ in Thousands)													
Net Sales **2**	4042547	220143	2800976	141239	454908	0	15340	409941	0	0	0	0	0
Interest **3**	39711	0	1558	1195	1163	0	0	35795	0	0	0	0	0
Rents **4**	2887	0	0	0	0	0	0	2887	0	0	0	0	0
Royalties **5**	315	0	0	0	0	0	0	315	0	0	0	0	0
Other Portfolio Income **6**	1475	0	0	0	0	0	0	1475	0	0	0	0	0
Other Receipts **7**	137178	7091	50028	0	51226	507	11357	16970	0	0	0	0	0
Total Receipts **8**	4224113	227234	2852562	142434	507297	507	26697	467383	0	0	0	0	0
Average Total Receipts **9**	368	83	339	2638	2096	127	5339	155794	•	•	•	•	•
Operating Costs/Operating Income (%)													
Cost of Operations **10**	0.0	0.2	0.2	•	•	•	•	•	•	•	•	•	•
Salaries and Wages **11**	20.7	6.0	12.5	22.5	45.6	•	38.3	56.2	•	•	•	•	•
Taxes Paid **12**	3.0	1.5	2.4	2.6	4.7	•	3.7	6.0	•	•	•	•	•
Interest Paid **13**	1.8	3.4	0.3	0.6	2.4	•	14.4	10.5	•	•	•	•	•
Depreciation **14**	0.4	0.8	0.2	0.6	0.6	•	•	1.3	•	•	•	•	•
Amortization and Depletion **15**	0.4	0.1	0.2	•	0.8	•	0.7	1.8	•	•	•	•	•
Pensions and Other Deferred Comp. **16**	1.1	1.1	1.1	•	0.3	•	•	2.9	•	•	•	•	•
Employee Benefits **17**	1.9	3.4	1.4	3.7	1.9	•	•	4.2	•	•	•	•	•
Advertising **18**	0.3	0.6	0.2	•	1.0	•	0.0	0.1	•	•	•	•	•
Other Expenses **19**	41.2	28.1	46.1	52.0	33.6	•	13.4	21.2	•	•	•	•	•
Officers' Compensation **20**	19.2	32.0	21.5	16.7	13.2	•	100.9	1.0	•	•	•	•	•
Operating Margin **21**	9.9	22.8	14.1	1.8	9.1	•	29.5	•	•	•	•	•	•
Operating Margin Before Officers' Comp. **22**	29.1	54.8	35.7	18.5	•	•	•	•	•	•	•	•	•

Selected Average Balance Sheet ($ in Thousands)

Net Receivables 23	24	0	11	2	342	9470	0	23653
Inventories 24	1	0	0	0	27	0	874	2
Net Property, Plant and Equipment 25	11	0	7	0	63	0	0	17974
Total Assets 26	208	0	75	704	1554	9488	10826	414026
Notes and Loans Payable 27	119	0	22	205	235	0	5091	360706
All Other Liabilities 28	36	0	18	15	503	9070	6262	25310
Net Worth 29	53	0	35	484	816	418	-528	28011

Selected Financial Ratios (Times to 1)

Current Ratio 30	1.6	•	1.4	3.2	1.6	1.0	0.3	1.8
Quick Ratio 31	0.6	•	1.4	3.2	1.1	1.0	0.1	0.2
Net Sales to Working Capital 32	6.6	•	27.6	5.4	6.5	•	•	0.9
Coverage Ratio 33	8.8	8.6	47.5	5.1	4.2	•	1.2	1.8
Total Asset Turnover 34	1.7	•	4.4	3.7	1.2	•	0.3	0.3
Inventory Turnover 35	0.0	•	•	•	•	•	•	•
Receivables Turnover 36	9.7	•	59.7	•	7.7	•	0.5	•
Total Liabilities to Net Worth 37	2.9	•	1.1	0.5	0.9	21.7	•	13.8
Current Assets to Working Capital 38	2.6	•	3.4	1.5	2.7	22.7	•	2.3
Current Liabilities to Working Capital 39	1.6	•	2.4	0.5	1.7	21.7	•	1.3
Working Capital to Net Sales 40	0.2	•	0.0	0.2	0.2	•	•	1.1
Inventory to Working Capital 41	0.0	•	0.0	•	0.2	•	•	0.0
Total Receipts to Cash Flow 42	1.9	2.0	1.7	1.9	2.8	•	7.2	3.9
Cost of Goods to Cash Flow 43	0.0	0.0	•	•	•	•	•	•
Cash Flow to Total Debt 44	1.2	•	4.9	6.1	0.9	0.0	0.0	0.1

Selected Financial Factors (in Percentages)

Debt Ratio 45	74.6	•	53.0	31.3	47.5	95.6	104.9	93.2
Return on Total Assets 46	27.5	•	72.2	12.0	11.9	1.3	4.8	6.4
Return on Equity Before Income Taxes 47	95.9	•	150.3	14.1	17.2	30.2	•	43.2
Return on Equity After Income Taxes 48	92.3	•	149.2	11.6	13.0	22.2	•	33.4
Profit Margin (Before Income Tax) 49	14.3	26.0	16.0	2.6	7.5	•	2.6	8.9
Profit Margin (After Income Tax) 50	13.8	25.4	15.9	2.1	5.6	•	2.6	6.8

Table I

Corporations with and without Net Income

NEW AND USED CAR DEALERS

MONEY AMOUNTS AND SIZE OF ASSETS IN THOUSANDS OF DOLLARS

Item Description for Accounting Period 7/07 Through 6/08		Total	Zero Assets	Under 500	500 to 1,000	1,000 to 5,000	5,000 to 10,000	10,000 to 25,000	25,000 to 50,000	50,000 to 100,000	100,000 to 250,000	250,000 to 500,000	500,000 to 2,500,000	2,500,000 and over
Number of Enterprises	1	47111	4182	20216	4068	8734	5297	3526	831	178	56	10	8	4
Revenues ($ in Thousands)														
Net Sales	2	677835534	5352905	15914929	11262952	78829473	142819496	200608930	96999450	38296721	22431116	7628743	25074461	32616357
Interest	3	1136185	1927	19422	30694	109319	123719	151339	102932	51448	83453	12809	241813	207312
Rents	4	335940	191	4895	1450	9389	14738	22130	35768	25606	46405	17993	22120	135254
Royalties	5	157721	0	0	0	0	1910	109	44	0	3594	0	725	151339
Other Portfolio Income	6	697675	171779	33243	14533	35822	82128	136195	45875	26373	66635	16581	30712	37799
Other Receipts	7	12298614	164968	196641	238298	1190917	2550388	3824833	1811547	807148	394301	166020	661805	291747
Total Receipts	8	692461669	5691770	16169130	11547927	80174920	145592379	204743536	98995616	39207296	23025504	7842146	26031636	33439808
Average Total Receipts	9	14699	1361	800	2839	9180	27486	58067	119128	220266	411170	784215	3253954	8359952
Operating Costs/Operating Income (%)														
Cost of Operations	10	87.6	91.6	82.5	84.7	86.8	88.3	88.5	88.3	88.0	85.4	87.1	87.5	83.6
Salaries and Wages	11	5.1	3.7	3.8	3.5	4.7	4.9	4.9	5.0	5.3	5.8	6.0	6.4	6.4
Taxes Paid	12	0.9	1.1	1.8	1.4	1.0	0.8	0.8	0.7	0.8	0.8	0.8	0.8	1.6
Interest Paid	13	1.0	0.9	1.0	0.8	1.1	0.9	0.8	0.9	0.9	1.1	1.3	1.3	2.2
Depreciation	14	0.4	0.9	0.3	0.3	0.2	0.3	0.3	0.4	0.5	0.8	0.7	1.2	0.5
Amortization and Depletion	15	0.1	0.0	0.1	0.0	0.0	0.1	0.1	0.1	0.1	0.1	0.1	0.4	0.7
Pensions and Other Deferred Comp.	16	0.1	0.0	0.0	0.1	0.1	0.1	0.1	0.1	0.1	0.1	0.1	0.1	0.1
Employee Benefits	17	0.4	0.3	0.2	0.3	0.4	0.5	0.4	0.4	0.4	0.4	0.6	0.5	0.4
Advertising	18	1.1	0.5	1.3	0.8	1.1	1.2	1.1	1.1	1.0	1.1	0.9	0.7	1.0
Other Expenses	19	4.2	4.6	9.4	8.5	4.8	3.9	3.7	3.6	3.7	5.4	3.9	3.2	4.7
Officers' Compensation	20	0.7	1.0	1.9	1.6	1.0	0.7	0.6	0.5	0.4	0.6	0.4	0.0	0.1
Operating Margin	21	•	•	•	•	•	•	•	•	•	•	•	•	•
Operating Margin Before Officers' Comp.	22	•	•	•	•	•	•	•	•	•	•	•	•	•

Selected Average Balance Sheet ($ in Thousands)

Net Receivables 23	472	0	24	106	369	654	1603	3851	8756	21881	47922	95050	442386
Inventories 24	2227	0	80	411	1629	4730	8852	16963	32226	53593	112518	393892	998432
Net Property, Plant and Equipment 25	490	0	15	59	152	487	1358	4385	10272	27303	77274	350073	815491
Total Assets 26	4203		151	675	2494	7009	14815	32884	66794	143016	303406	1454810	4791423
Notes and Loans Payable 27	2738	0	100	382	1524	5063	10774	22153	43458	90408	180956	593522	2384961
All Other Liabilities 28	534	0	32	147	414	748	1423	3476	7485	16428	36837	346254	758244
Net Worth 29	931	0	19	146	555	1198	2618	7255	15850	36180	85612	515033	1648218

Selected Financial Ratios (Times to 1)

Current Ratio 30	1.3	•	2.2	2.5	1.5	1.3	1.2	1.3	1.3	1.2	1.3	1.1	1.1
Quick Ratio 31	0.3	•	0.8	0.9	0.4	0.3	0.3	0.4	0.4	0.5	0.4	0.2	0.3
Net Sales to Working Capital 32	21.2	•	11.2	8.1	12.8	21.6	25.9	21.8	20.4	23.6	20.0	84.1	45.0
Coverage Ratio 33	1.7	2.8	0.3	1.5	1.5	1.3	1.9	2.2	2.2	1.9	1.7	2.2	1.6
Total Asset Turnover 34	3.4	•	5.2	4.1	3.6	3.8	3.8	3.5	3.2	2.8	2.5	2.2	1.7
Inventory Turnover 35	5.7	•	8.1	5.7	4.8	5.0	5.7	6.1	5.9	6.4	5.9	7.0	6.8
Receivables Turnover 36	29.8	•	28.1	19.7	25.1	36.1	34.6	30.6	23.1	19.9	16.1	35.9	20.6
Total Liabilities to Net Worth 37	3.5	•	7.1	3.6	3.5	4.8	4.7	3.5	3.2	3.0	2.5	1.8	1.9
Current Assets to Working Capital 38	4.6	•	1.8	1.7	3.1	4.9	5.6	4.7	4.7	5.7	4.5	14.7	8.9
Current Liabilities to Working Capital 39	3.6	•	0.8	0.7	2.1	3.9	4.6	3.7	3.7	4.7	3.5	13.7	7.9
Working Capital to Net Sales 40	0.0	•	0.1	0.1	0.0	0.0	0.0	0.0	0.0	0.0	0.1	0.0	0.0
Inventory to Working Capital 41	3.2	•	1.1	1.1	2.2	3.7	4.0	3.1	3.0	3.3	2.8	10.6	5.6
Total Receipts to Cash Flow 42	27.9	19.4	18.0	13.5	24.6	34.5	31.1	27.4	27.0	23.7	26.1	28.4	22.5
Cost of Goods to Cash Flow 43	24.4	17.8	14.8	11.4	21.4	30.4	27.5	24.2	23.8	20.2	22.7	24.9	18.8
Cash Flow to Total Debt 44	0.2	•	0.3	0.4	0.2	0.1	0.2	0.2	0.2	0.2	0.1	0.1	0.1

Selected Financial Factors (in Percentages)

Debt Ratio 45	77.9	•	87.7	78.4	77.7	82.9	82.3	77.9	76.3	74.7	71.8	64.6	65.6
Return on Total Assets 46	5.7	•	1.8	5.1	5.7	4.4	5.7	6.8	6.6	5.8	5.5	6.2	6.2
Return on Equity Before Income Taxes 47	10.7	•	•	8.1	8.0	5.3	14.9	16.7	15.0	10.8	8.0	9.6	6.9
Return on Equity After Income Taxes 48	9.4	•	•	7.5	7.6	4.8	14.1	16.0	13.8	9.3	5.6	5.8	4.4
Profit Margin (Before Income Tax) 49	0.7	1.6	•	0.4	0.5	0.2	0.7	1.0	1.1	1.0	0.9	1.6	1.4
Profit Margin (After Income Tax) 50	0.6	1.6	•	0.4	0.5	0.2	0.6	1.0	0.8	1.0	0.6	0.9	0.9

Table II

Corporations with Net Income

NEW AND USED CAR DEALERS

Money Amounts and Size of Assets in Thousands of Dollars

Item Description for Accounting Period 7/07 Through 6/08	Total	Zero Assets	Under 500	500 to 1,000	1,000 to 5,000	5,000 to 10,000	10,000 to 25,000	25,000 to 50,000	50,000 to 100,000	100,000 to 250,000	250,000 to 500,000	500,000 to 2,500,000	2,500,000 and over
Number of Enterprises 1	22434	1091	7255	2617	5153	3192	2352	580	136	42	•	•	•

Revenues ($ in Thousands)

Item	Total	Zero Assets	Under 500	500 to 1,000	1,000 to 5,000	5,000 to 10,000	10,000 to 25,000	25,000 to 50,000	50,000 to 100,000	100,000 to 250,000	250,000 to 500,000	500,000 to 2,500,000	2,500,000 and over
Net Sales 2	479208776	2239881	9337838	8096071	50037330	90462618	140611093	70293575	30722874	18268081	•	•	•
Interest 3	852888	676	7537	16516	72523	77487	116492	76626	45835	55465	•	•	•
Rents 4	246950	167	4844	0	5694	12690	13124	13461	7941	33599	•	•	•
Royalties 5	145586	0	0	0	0	0	109	44	0	3594	•	•	•
Other Portfolio Income 6	467884	140091	6870	11986	21461	54352	105070	34741	19334	37093	•	•	•
Other Receipts 7	8919035	135758	104545	79642	760933	1693302	2759864	1383068	649866	331971	•	•	•
Total Receipts 8	489841119	2516573	9461634	8204215	50897941	92300449	143612752	71801515	31445850	18729803	•	•	•
Average Total Receipts 9	21835	2307	1304	3135	9877	28916	61060	123796	231219	445948	•	•	•

Operating Costs/Operating Income (%)

Item	Total	Zero Assets	Under 500	500 to 1,000	1,000 to 5,000	5,000 to 10,000	10,000 to 25,000	25,000 to 50,000	50,000 to 100,000	100,000 to 250,000	250,000 to 500,000	500,000 to 2,500,000	2,500,000 and over
Cost of Operations 10	87.4	87.9	81.0	84.1	86.2	88.3	88.2	87.9	88.3	85.5	•	•	•
Salaries and Wages 11	5.0	4.4	3.4	3.9	4.7	4.7	4.9	5.0	5.2	5.7	•	•	•
Taxes Paid 12	0.9	1.8	2.2	1.3	1.0	0.7	0.8	0.7	0.7	0.8	•	•	•
Interest Paid 13	0.8	0.9	0.5	0.7	0.9	0.7	0.7	0.8	0.9	1.0	•	•	•
Depreciation 14	0.3	0.2	0.0	0.2	0.2	0.2	0.3	0.4	0.4	0.7	•	•	•
Amortization and Depletion 15	0.1	0.0	0.0	0.0	0.0	0.0	0.1	0.1	0.0	0.1	•	•	•
Pensions and Other Deferred Comp. 16	0.1	0.1	0.0	0.1	0.1	0.1	0.1	0.1	0.1	0.1	•	•	•
Employee Benefits 17	0.4	0.5	0.1	0.3	0.3	0.5	0.4	0.4	0.4	0.4	•	•	•
Advertising 18	1.0	0.7	1.0	0.8	1.1	1.1	1.1	1.1	1.0	1.1	•	•	•
Other Expenses 19	3.9	5.5	7.9	5.8	4.5	3.6	3.6	3.4	3.3	4.9	•	•	•
Officers' Compensation 20	0.6	1.0	1.3	1.7	1.1	0.8	0.6	0.6	0.4	0.6	•	•	•
Operating Margin 21	•	•	2.6	1.1	•	•	•	•	•	•	•	•	•
Operating Margin Before Officers' Comp. 22	0.1	•	3.9	2.9	1.0	0.1	•	0.1	•	0.1	•	•	•

Selected Average Balance Sheet ($ in Thousands)

Net Receivables **23**	676	0	37	74	421	686	1634	3859	8133	18184
Inventories **24**	3175	0	128	385	1515	4717	8980	17605	35682	58975
Net Property, Plant and Equipment **25**	701	0	9	21	157	503	1279	4277	9943	28700
Total Assets **26**	5957	0	213	650	2594	7043	14775	32665	66478	147336
Notes and Loans Payable **27**	3587	0	107	248	1468	4483	10276	21329	41708	91296
All Other Liabilities **28**	728	0	46	88	381	756	1360	3228	7399	16628
Net Worth **29**	1641	0	60	313	745	1804	3140	8109	17372	39412

Selected Financial Ratios (Times to 1)

Current Ratio **30**	1.3	•	2.7	3.3	1.7	1.4	1.3	1.3	1.3	1.3
Quick Ratio **31**	0.4	•	1.1	1.2	0.5	0.3	0.3	0.4	0.4	0.4
Net Sales to Working Capital **32**	18.7	•	10.7	7.8	10.7	17.4	23.3	20.4	20.1	21.4
Coverage Ratio **33**	2.9	11.3	8.8	4.8	2.8	2.9	3.1	3.1	2.8	2.5
Total Asset Turnover **34**	3.6	•	6.0	4.8	3.7	4.0	4.0	3.7	3.4	3.0
Inventory Turnover **35**	5.9	•	8.1	6.8	5.5	5.3	5.9	6.1	5.6	6.3
Receivables Turnover **36**	29.6	•	32.3	26.1	24.7	34.9	34.3	30.0	23.6	21.6
Total Liabilities to Net Worth **37**	2.6	•	2.6	1.1	2.5	2.9	3.7	3.0	2.8	2.7
Current Assets to Working Capital **38**	3.9	•	1.6	1.4	2.5	3.8	4.9	4.3	4.4	4.9
Current Liabilities to Working Capital **39**	2.9	•	0.6	0.4	1.5	2.8	3.9	3.3	3.4	3.9
Working Capital to Net Sales **40**	0.1	•	0.1	0.1	0.1	0.1	0.0	0.0	0.0	0.0
Inventory to Working Capital **41**	2.7	•	0.9	0.9	1.8	2.8	3.5	2.8	2.9	3.0
Total Receipts to Cash Flow **42**	23.5	7.9	10.6	15.0	19.8	26.8	25.7	24.3	25.2	24.6
Cost of Goods to Cash Flow **43**	20.6	6.9	8.6	12.6	17.0	23.7	22.7	21.4	22.3	21.1
Cash Flow to Total Debt **44**	0.2	•	0.8	0.6	0.3	0.2	0.2	0.2	0.2	0.2

Selected Financial Factors (in Percentages)

Debt Ratio **45**	72.5	•	71.9	51.8	71.3	74.4	78.8	75.2	73.9	73.3
Return on Total Assets **46**	8.8	•	26.9	14.9	9.8	8.2	8.6	9.2	8.2	7.5
Return on Equity Before Income Taxes **47**	21.1	•	84.7	24.4	21.9	21.0	27.2	25.3	20.4	16.8
Return on Equity After Income Taxes **48**	19.6	•	83.9	24.0	21.3	20.4	26.3	24.5	19.3	14.9
Profit Margin (Before Income Tax) **49**	1.6	9.3	3.9	2.5	1.7	1.3	1.4	1.7	1.6	1.5
Profit Margin (After Income Tax) **50**	1.5	9.2	3.9	2.4	1.6	1.3	1.4	1.6	1.5	1.4

Table I

Corporations with and without Net Income

OTHER MOTOR VEHICLE AND PARTS DEALERS

MONEY AMOUNTS AND SIZE OF ASSETS IN THOUSANDS OF DOLLARS

Item Description for Accounting Period 7/07 Through 6/08		Total	Zero Assets	Under 500	500 to 1,000	1,000 to 5,000	5,000 to 10,000	10,000 to 25,000	25,000 to 50,000	50,000 to 100,000	100,000 to 250,000	250,000 to 500,000	500,000 to 2,500,000	2,500,000 and over
Number of Enterprises	1	40568	5473	20005	5498	7556	1404	426	116	49	22	6	12	0
Revenues ($ in Thousands)														
Net Sales	2	149738576	1127393	13060671	8479667	41575467	20919313	14195304	9754161	7497523	5838684	2697229	24593165	0
Interest	3	170354	6	5731	7464	31203	15761	16137	7237	10533	8329	7758	60196	0
Rents	4	102898	89	1284	2359	12602	8840	9073	22285	24351	124	1678	20215	0
Royalties	5	29889	0	0	0	198	0	1635	0	4	0	207	27845	0
Other Portfolio Income	6	408632	10380	14622	13242	38586	47733	57811	15478	32830	50051	10489	117410	0
Other Receipts	7	1940140	8849	21702	106276	403966	327639	163925	132452	135358	50757	56854	532359	0
Total Receipts	8	152390489	1146717	13104010	8609008	42062022	21319286	14443885	9931613	7700599	5947945	2774215	25351190	0
Average Total Receipts	9	3756	210	655	1566	5567	15185	33906	85617	157155	270361	462369	2112599	•
Operating Costs/Operating Income (%)														
Cost of Operations	10	71.8	75.8	70.6	67.3	74.9	78.2	79.5	78.3	76.7	74.2	70.5	54.3	•
Salaries and Wages	11	9.6	7.5	8.1	9.9	8.0	7.7	7.1	8.3	8.7	8.9	10.6	17.0	•
Taxes Paid	12	1.8	2.3	2.7	2.2	1.6	1.4	1.1	1.1	1.3	1.3	1.3	3.0	•
Interest Paid	13	1.5	1.0	0.9	1.2	1.5	1.7	1.8	1.4	1.5	1.4	2.0	1.6	•
Depreciation	14	1.2	2.0	0.7	1.1	0.6	1.1	1.1	1.3	1.6	3.6	3.3	1.9	•
Amortization and Depletion	15	0.1	0.0	0.1	0.2	0.0	0.1	0.1	0.1	0.1	0.1	0.3	0.3	•
Pensions and Other Deferred Comp.	16	0.2	0.1	0.1	0.1	0.1	0.1	0.1	0.2	0.2	0.4	0.4	0.2	•
Employee Benefits	17	0.7	0.3	0.3	0.7	0.6	0.5	0.6	0.8	0.7	0.9	1.7	1.4	•
Advertising	18	1.4	1.2	1.3	1.1	1.3	1.8	1.1	0.9	1.4	0.6	1.2	1.9	•
Other Expenses	19	9.6	11.9	11.9	12.7	8.8	7.0	7.0	6.8	8.2	7.6	8.8	14.2	•
Officers' Compensation	20	1.5	4.0	3.6	3.3	2.1	1.1	1.0	0.6	0.4	0.5	0.4	0.3	•
Operating Margin	21	0.5	•	•	0.1	0.5	•	•	0.2	•	0.3	•	3.8	•
Operating Margin Before Officers' Comp.	22	2.0	•	3.3	3.4	2.6	0.4	0.5	0.8	0.8	0.8	•	4.1	•

Selected Average Balance Sheet ($ in Thousands)

Net Receivables 23	161	0	12	82	180	334	1389	4284	9304	21077	51059	142946
Inventories 24	930	0	81	356	1541	4320	9563	20821	34114	58016	87205	541488
Net Property, Plant and Equipment 25	316	0	24	120	240	1101	2618	5460	13752	40785	76550	378968
Total Assets 26	1809	0	155	707	2196	6951	15146	33411	68762	139577	333125	1771636
Notes and Loans Payable 27	769	0	100	357	822	2851	9778	19162	34255	66672	118503	564620
All Other Liabilities 28	556	0	37	209	773	2560	2855	8123	18450	28297	63856	596200
Net Worth 29	484	0	18	141	601	1540	2513	6126	16057	44608	150766	610816

Selected Financial Ratios (Times to 1)

Current Ratio 30	1.4	•	2.0	2.0	1.6	1.4	1.3	1.3	1.4	1.4	2.0	1.1
Quick Ratio 31	0.3	•	0.5	0.6	0.3	0.2	0.3	0.3	0.4	0.5	0.8	0.2
Net Sales to Working Capital 32	10.5	10.7	6.0	7.9	9.6	14.0	14.1	11.5	13.0	4.9	28.1	
Coverage Ratio 33	2.5	1.0	2.3	2.1	1.7	1.7	2.4	2.2	2.5	2.3	5.2	
Total Asset Turnover 34	2.0	4.2	2.2	2.5	2.1	2.2	2.5	2.2	1.9	1.3	1.2	
Inventory Turnover 35	2.8	5.7	2.9	2.7	2.7	2.8	3.2	3.4	3.4	3.6	2.1	
Receivables Turnover 36	22.4	45.4	19.9	29.8	30.8	22.3	18.9	15.9	10.5	11.2	16.8	
Total Liabilities to Net Worth 37	2.7	7.4	4.0	2.7	3.5	5.0	4.5	3.3	2.1	1.2	1.9	
Current Assets to Working Capital 38	3.5	2.0	2.0	2.7	3.4	4.9	4.3	3.6	3.9	2.0	11.0	
Current Liabilities to Working Capital 39	2.5	1.0	1.0	1.7	2.4	3.9	3.3	2.6	2.9	1.0	10.0	
Working Capital to Net Sales 40	0.1	0.1	0.2	0.1	0.1	0.1	0.1	0.1	0.1	0.2	0.0	
Inventory to Working Capital 41	2.6	1.4	1.4	2.1	2.9	3.7	3.2	2.5	2.3	1.1	7.9	
Total Receipts to Cash Flow 42	11.5	21.9	12.2	10.1	12.6	16.9	16.3	14.8	13.2	13.8	12.0	6.5
Cost of Goods to Cash Flow 43	8.3	16.6	8.6	6.8	9.5	13.2	13.0	11.6	10.1	10.2	8.4	3.5
Cash Flow to Total Debt 44	0.2	•	0.4	0.3	0.3	0.2	0.2	0.2	0.2	0.2	0.2	0.3

Selected Financial Factors (in Percentages)

Debt Ratio 45	73.2	•	88.1	80.0	72.7	77.8	83.4	81.7	76.6	68.0	54.7	65.5
Return on Total Assets 46	7.7	•	4.0	6.2	7.8	6.2	6.8	8.7	7.2	6.8	6.2	9.8
Return on Equity Before Income Taxes 47	17.4	0.5	17.6	14.9	11.5	17.2	27.9	16.9	12.7	7.6	23.0	
Return on Equity After Income Taxes 48	13.6	•	16.0	10.0	13.8	14.7	26.4	15.3	10.8	4.2	15.6	
Profit Margin (Before Income Tax) 49	2.3	0.0	1.6	1.2	1.6	1.3	2.0	1.8	2.1	2.6	6.9	
Profit Margin (After Income Tax) 50	1.8	•	1.5	1.0	1.5	1.1	1.9	1.6	1.8	1.4	4.6	

Table II

Corporations with Net Income

OTHER MOTOR VEHICLE AND PARTS DEALERS

MONEY AMOUNTS AND SIZE OF ASSETS IN THOUSANDS OF DOLLARS

Item Description for Accounting Period 7/07 Through 6/08	Total	Zero Assets	Under 500	500 to 1,000	1,000 to 5,000	5,000 to 10,000	10,000 to 25,000	25,000 to 50,000	50,000 to 100,000	100,000 to 250,000	250,000 to 500,000	500,000 to 2,500,000	2,500,000 and over
Number of Enterprises 1	20728	1458	9474	3471	4953	893	317	95	37	17	•	•	0
Revenues ($ in Thousands)													
Net Sales 2	112868083	251769	8147074	5690907	29593831	13601592	11478761	8072410	5860401	4497654	•	•	0
Interest 3	146397	0	5233	5371	25080	9299	12562	6095	9944	5275	•	•	0
Rents 4	90358	0	507	1564	11880	2115	9047	21757	23168	122	•	•	0
Royalties 5	29878	0	0	0	198	0	1635	0	4	0	•	•	0
Other Portfolio Income 6	327119	4	13180	5339	33860	44687	37125	13480	23707	38262	•	•	0
Other Receipts 7	1523543	50	5596	98182	309535	176984	123206	110086	82252	39988	•	•	0
Total Receipts 8	114985378	251823	8171590	5801363	29974384	13834677	11662336	8223828	5999476	4581301	•	•	0
Average Total Receipts 9	5547	173	863	1671	6052	15492	36790	86567	162148	269488	•	•	•
Operating Costs/Operating Income (%)													
Cost of Operations 10	70.5	63.4	71.5	65.9	74.2	76.9	80.3	79.7	76.7	73.2	•	•	•
Salaries and Wages 11	9.9	4.5	6.9	9.5	8.0	7.4	7.0	7.4	8.3	9.3	•	•	•
Taxes Paid 12	1.9	3.7	2.8	2.2	1.7	1.4	1.1	1.0	1.3	1.5	•	•	•
Interest Paid 13	1.3	1.4	0.6	0.8	1.2	1.5	1.4	1.3	1.2	1.4	•	•	•
Depreciation 14	1.2	0.5	0.6	0.8	0.7	1.3	1.0	1.2	1.3	2.9	•	•	•
Amortization and Depletion 15	0.1	•	0.1	0.1	0.0	0.1	0.1	0.0	0.1	0.1	•	•	•
Pensions and Other Deferred Comp. 16	0.2	0.0	0.1	0.1	0.2	0.1	0.1	0.2	0.3	0.5	•	•	•
Employee Benefits 17	0.8	•	0.2	0.8	0.5	0.5	0.6	0.8	0.7	0.9	•	•	•
Advertising 18	1.3	0.6	1.4	1.0	1.0	1.6	1.1	0.8	1.0	0.6	•	•	•
Other Expenses 19	9.4	10.0	10.1	12.6	8.6	6.8	5.6	6.1	8.1	7.2	•	•	•
Officers' Compensation 20	1.4	6.5	3.1	3.6	2.2	1.1	1.1	0.6	0.4	0.6	•	•	•
Operating Margin 21	2.1	9.3	2.7	2.5	1.8	1.2	0.7	0.9	0.5	1.8	•	•	•
Operating Margin Before Officers' Comp. 22	3.5	15.8	5.8	6.1	4.0	2.4	1.8	1.5	1.0	2.5	•	•	•

Selected Average Balance Sheet ($ in Thousands)

Net Receivables 23	245	0	16	105	203	363	1639	4151	10293	21459
Inventories 24	1378	0	87	391	1677	4684	9490	20599	35501	68881
Net Property, Plant and Equipment 25	489	0	24	112	262	1370	2315	5234	13113	34436
Total Assets 26	2697	0	184	705	2283	7239	14824	33104	67377	137093
Notes and Loans Payable 27	1003	0	73	283	725	2376	8604	18748	30412	62958
All Other Liabilities 28	844	0	37	227	820	2839	2928	7201	19066	33373
Net Worth 29	850	0	74	195	738	2024	3291	7155	17899	40762

Selected Financial Ratios (Times to 1)

Current Ratio 30	1.4	•	2.4	2.4	1.6	1.5	1.3	1.4	1.5	1.5
Quick Ratio 31	0.3	•	0.8	0.8	0.4	0.2	0.3	0.3	0.4	0.5
Net Sales to Working Capital 32	10.2	•	10.2	5.1	8.1	8.8	12.2	12.8	10.1	9.9
Coverage Ratio 33	4.1	7.8	6.0	6.6	3.7	3.0	2.6	3.2	3.3	3.7
Total Asset Turnover 34	2.0	•	4.7	2.3	2.6	2.1	2.4	2.6	2.4	1.9
Inventory Turnover 35	2.8	•	7.1	2.8	2.6	2.5	3.1	3.3	3.4	2.8
Receivables Turnover 36	20.4	•	45.6	16.5	26.1	23.7	21.3	19.2	14.5	9.1
Total Liabilities to Net Worth 37	2.2	•	1.5	2.6	2.1	2.6	3.5	3.6	2.8	2.4
Current Assets to Working Capital 38	3.3	•	1.7	1.7	2.6	3.1	3.9	3.8	3.1	3.1
Current Liabilities to Working Capital 39	2.3	•	0.7	0.7	1.6	2.1	2.9	2.8	2.1	2.1
Working Capital to Net Sales 40	0.1	•	0.1	0.2	0.1	0.1	0.1	0.1	0.1	0.1
Inventory to Working Capital 41	2.4	•	1.1	1.1	2.0	2.5	2.9	2.9	2.1	1.9
Total Receipts to Cash Flow 42	9.8	6.1	9.9	7.9	10.8	13.2	17.2	14.1	11.4	11.7
Cost of Goods to Cash Flow 43	6.9	3.9	7.0	5.2	8.0	10.1	13.8	11.3	8.7	8.6
Cash Flow to Total Debt 44	0.3	•	0.8	0.4	0.4	0.2	0.2	0.2	0.3	0.2

Selected Financial Factors (in Percentages)

Debt Ratio 45	68.5	•	59.9	72.3	67.7	72.0	77.8	78.4	73.4	70.3
Return on Total Assets 46	10.5	•	17.1	12.2	11.2	9.3	9.2	10.5	9.7	9.8
Return on Equity Before Income Taxes 47	25.3	•	35.5	37.2	25.3	22.0	25.3	33.2	25.6	24.0
Return on Equity After Income Taxes 48	21.1	•	34.7	35.4	23.8	20.3	22.8	31.7	23.7	21.3
Profit Margin (Before Income Tax) 49	4.0	9.4	3.0	4.4	3.1	2.9	2.3	2.8	2.9	3.7
Profit Margin (After Income Tax) 50	3.3	9.4	3.0	4.2	2.9	2.7	2.1	2.7	2.7	3.3

Table I

Corporations with and without Net Income

FURNITURE AND HOME FURNISHINGS STORES

MONEY AMOUNTS AND SIZE OF ASSETS IN THOUSANDS OF DOLLARS

Item Description for Accounting Period 7/07 Through 6/08	Total	Zero Assets	Under 500	500 to 1,000	1,000 to 5,000	5,000 to 10,000	10,000 to 25,000	25,000 to 50,000	50,000 to 100,000	100,000 to 250,000	250,000 to 500,000	500,000 to 2,500,000	2,500,000 and over
Number of Enterprises 1	40843	5543	28281	3381	2984	388	182	28	22	18	6	10	0
Revenues ($ in Thousands)													
Net Sales 2	92541918	806053	18022984	6910476	13535918	7644114	7730855	3262255	3841306	5196896	2790774	22800287	0
Interest 3	285574	251	4434	17796	47799	13622	17636	2194	1263	65525	84443	30611	0
Rents 4	40627	0	1174	1575	12273	2376	6134	383	9	6270	2430	8002	0
Royalties 5	22513	0	0	0	0	210	0	2896	0	152	1383	17872	0
Other Portfolio Income 6	242226	17852	11198	13518	22888	2535	11247	752	2891	4126	2309	152906	0
Other Receipts 7	1004764	56116	33953	29018	133155	78753	140132	65923	67452	146959	53001	200306	0
Total Receipts 8	94137622	880272	18073743	6972383	13752033	7741610	7906004	3334403	3912921	5419928	2934340	23209984	0
Average Total Receipts 9	2305	159	639	2062	4609	19953	43440	119086	177860	301107	489057	2320998	•
Operating Costs/Operating Income (%)													
Cost of Operations 10	57.9	55.7	59.8	61.7	59.5	62.0	62.4	63.1	55.8	53.7	52.9	52.6	•
Salaries and Wages 11	13.0	8.4	9.9	10.0	13.1	14.3	14.3	15.0	14.8	15.9	15.6	14.2	•
Taxes Paid 12	2.4	3.5	2.0	3.2	2.1	1.8	2.0	2.1	2.2	2.7	2.5	2.8	•
Interest Paid 13	0.9	0.5	0.6	0.8	0.9	1.0	0.8	0.7	0.8	1.3	1.5	1.2	•
Depreciation 14	1.2	0.8	0.7	0.7	0.9	0.9	0.8	0.8	1.4	1.6	1.6	2.0	•
Amortization and Depletion 15	0.2	0.2	0.2	0.1	0.1	0.1	0.3	0.0	0.1	0.3	0.1	0.2	•
Pensions and Other Deferred Comp. 16	0.2	0.1	0.1	0.2	0.1	0.3	0.1	0.2	0.2	0.2	0.2	0.3	•
Employee Benefits 17	0.9	0.5	0.6	0.8	0.5	1.0	0.8	1.1	1.0	1.0	1.3	1.2	•
Advertising 18	4.5	8.1	3.7	2.8	4.3	3.3	3.7	2.4	4.1	6.6	8.3	5.6	•
Other Expenses 19	16.2	41.4	16.7	16.2	15.0	12.5	14.7	15.8	18.8	18.9	19.5	16.0	•
Officers' Compensation 20	2.4	3.5	5.3	4.1	3.6	2.0	1.1	1.6	0.7	0.8	0.6	0.4	•
Operating Margin 21	0.3	•	0.4	•	•	0.8	1.1	•	0.1	•	•	3.6	•
Operating Margin Before Officers' Comp. 22	2.7	•	5.7	3.5	3.6	2.7	0.1	•	0.8	•	•	3.9	•

Selected Average Balance Sheet ($ in Thousands)

Line	C1	C2	C3	C4	C5	C6	C7	C8	C9	C10	C11	C12	
Net Receivables 23	145	0	22	149	337	979	2902	10313	5081	27460	105091	137471	•
Inventories 24	373	0	55	318	867	2927	6146	10617	30266	45703	93157	543202	•
Net Property, Plant and Equipment 25	286	0	30	151	356	1790	2959	3752	22357	56584	74050	599235	•
Total Assets 26	1059	0	155	705	2020	6881	15570	35137	76270	159989	337322	1737858	•
Notes and Loans Payable 27	333	0	89	282	774	2162	4097	8368	19405	52830	85429	411137	•
All Other Liabilities 28	400	0	53	172	723	2654	6580	15864	29884	48338	114262	721801	•
Net Worth 29	326	0	13	251	523	2064	4893	10905	26982	58821	137631	604919	•

Selected Financial Ratios (Times to 1)

Line	C1	C2	C3	C4	C5	C6	C7	C8	C9	C10	C11	C12	
Current Ratio 30	1.5	•	1.9	2.5	1.9	1.4	1.5	1.4	1.5	1.8	1.9	1.2	•
Quick Ratio 31	0.5	•	0.9	1.0	0.7	0.4	0.5	0.7	0.3	0.8	1.0	0.3	•
Net Sales to Working Capital 32	10.1	•	11.8	6.8	6.3	16.0	11.8	16.7	11.7	7.5	4.6	14.9	•
Coverage Ratio 33	3.0	•	2.1	1.4	2.6	3.1	2.6	0.3	3.5	1.9	1.6	5.1	•
Total Asset Turnover 34	2.1	•	4.1	2.9	2.2	2.9	2.7	3.3	2.3	1.8	1.4	1.3	•
Inventory Turnover 35	3.5	•	6.9	4.0	3.1	4.2	4.3	6.9	3.2	3.4	2.6	2.2	•
Receivables Turnover 36	16.7	•	30.7	13.7	14.4	20.8	14.7	10.8	35.7	9.5	5.4	19.8	•
Total Liabilities to Net Worth 37	2.3	•	10.8	1.8	2.9	2.3	2.2	2.2	1.8	1.7	1.5	1.9	•
Current Assets to Working Capital 38	2.9	•	2.1	1.7	2.1	3.8	3.2	3.8	2.9	2.3	2.1	5.7	•
Current Liabilities to Working Capital 39	1.9	•	1.1	0.7	1.1	2.8	2.2	2.8	1.9	1.3	1.1	4.7	•
Working Capital to Net Sales 40	0.1	•	0.1	0.1	0.2	0.1	0.1	0.1	0.1	0.1	0.2	0.1	•
Inventory to Working Capital 41	1.7	•	1.0	1.0	1.2	2.5	1.8	1.4	2.0	1.0	0.9	3.7	•
Total Receipts to Cash Flow 42	8.6	9.5	8.3	9.5	9.5	11.2	10.1	12.8	7.2	7.2	7.5	7.3	•
Cost of Goods to Cash Flow 43	5.0	5.3	5.1	5.7	5.7	7.0	6.3	8.0	4.0	3.8	4.0	3.8	•
Cash Flow to Total Debt 44	0.4	•	0.5	0.5	0.3	0.4	0.4	0.4	0.5	0.4	0.3	0.3	•

Selected Financial Factors (in Percentages)

Line	C1	C2	C3	C4	C5	C6	C7	C8	C9	C10	C11	C12	
Debt Ratio 45	69.2	91.5	64.4	74.1	70.0	68.6	69.0	64.6	63.2	59.2	65.2		•
Return on Total Assets 46	6.1	•	3.2	5.5	8.6	5.5	0.7	6.5	4.4	3.5	8.1		•
Return on Equity Before Income Taxes 47	13.3	33.6	2.5	13.2	19.6	10.9	13.2	•	5.7	3.3	18.7		•
Return on Equity After Income Taxes 48	8.5	31.5	1.4	11.6	17.5	9.3	11.6	•	3.4	1.8	10.1		•
Profit Margin (Before Income Tax) 49	1.9	0.7	0.3	1.5	2.0	1.3	1.5	•	2.0	1.2	1.0	5.0	•
Profit Margin (After Income Tax) 50	1.2	0.6	0.2	1.3	1.8	1.3	1.1	•	1.2	0.7	0.5	2.7	•

Table II

Corporations with Net Income

FURNITURE AND HOME FURNISHINGS STORES

MONEY AMOUNTS AND SIZE OF ASSETS IN THOUSANDS OF DOLLARS

Item Description for Accounting Period 7/07 Through 6/08	Total	Zero Assets	Under 500	500 to 1,000	1,000 to 5,000	5,000 to 10,000	10,000 to 25,000	25,000 to 50,000	50,000 to 100,000	100,000 to 250,000	250,000 to 500,000	500,000 to 2,500,000	2,500,000 and over
Number of Enterprises **1**	21468	1825	14702	2505	1901	361	115	21	16	12	3	7	0
Revenues ($ in Thousands)													
Net Sales **2**	67225731	297931	10376784	5836450	9649093	6973498	5443650	2431003	2992076	3908197	1604404	17712646	0
Interest **3**	211499	251	2336	5050	37731	13561	12134	1518	493	44874	71267	22285	0
Rents **4**	29492	0	55	596	8890	2258	4860	0	0	3430	2080	7324	0
Royalties **5**	4174	0	0	0	0	210	0	0	0	51	0	3913	0
Other Portfolio Income **6**	123567	3619	10410	12456	21970	2461	11149	688	2367	3986	2309	52152	0
Other Receipts **7**	771939	54583	12436	23993	47075	61979	116883	45397	55240	139934	40246	174171	0
Total Receipts **8**	68366402	356384	10402021	5878545	9764759	7053967	5588676	2478806	3050176	4100472	1720306	17972491	0
Average Total Receipts **9**	3185	195	708	2347	5137	19540	48597	118029	190636	341706	573435	2567499	•
Operating Costs/Operating Income (%)													
Cost of Operations **10**	56.9	43.1	60.4	60.1	58.5	61.4	62.5	63.7	54.3	53.2	53.8	50.2	•
Salaries and Wages **11**	12.6	7.3	7.8	9.7	12.6	14.6	14.0	14.8	14.7	15.6	15.1	13.9	•
Taxes Paid **12**	2.3	3.0	1.8	3.4	2.1	1.7	1.9	1.8	2.1	2.6	2.6	2.8	•
Interest Paid **13**	0.8	0.2	0.4	0.8	0.9	0.9	0.6	0.6	0.7	0.8	0.6	0.9	•
Depreciation **14**	1.2	0.7	0.7	0.7	0.6	0.9	0.7	0.5	1.4	1.5	1.7	2.0	•
Amortization and Depletion **15**	0.2	0.1	0.2	0.1	0.1	0.0	0.1	0.0	0.0	0.4	0.0	0.2	•
Pensions and Other Deferred Comp. **16**	0.2	0.3	0.1	0.2	0.1	0.3	0.2	0.3	0.2	0.2	0.3	0.1	•
Employee Benefits **17**	0.8	0.1	0.4	0.7	0.4	1.0	0.9	1.3	1.0	1.0	1.2	1.2	•
Advertising **18**	4.0	4.3	2.1	2.7	4.2	3.3	3.8	1.8	3.9	6.2	7.3	5.5	•
Other Expenses **19**	15.3	34.7	15.2	15.7	14.1	12.2	13.5	11.1	19.6	19.5	20.6	15.7	•
Officers' Compensation **20**	2.3	3.5	5.2	3.9	4.0	2.0	1.2	1.9	0.6	0.6	0.9	0.4	•
Operating Margin **21**	3.5	2.5	5.7	2.0	2.6	1.7	0.7	2.3	1.4	•	•	7.2	•
Operating Margin Before Officers' Comp. **22**	5.8	6.0	10.9	6.0	6.5	3.7	1.9	4.1	2.0	•	•	7.6	•

Selected Average Balance Sheet ($ in Thousands)

Net Receivables **23**	204	0	25	151	451	965	3585	13088	5719	29154	139610	125899	●
Inventories **24**	485	0	49	290	910	2912	5817	8210	32693	40370	143482	576593	●
Net Property, Plant and Equipment **25**	421	0	22	171	363	1767	3184	3351	18493	59984	100368	742764	●
Total Assets **26**	1459	0	143	707	2136	6744	16664	36194	77201	162845	386385	1990932	●
Notes and Loans Payable **27**	371	0	49	299	628	1776	3445	9213	15363	45568	82052	434358	●
All Other Liabilities **28**	524	0	31	165	743	2546	6720	13460	32097	46194	103924	800726	●
Net Worth **29**	565	0	63	243	766	2422	6499	13520	29740	71084	200409	755848	●

Selected Financial Ratios (Times to 1)

Current Ratio **30**	1.6	●	2.8	2.5	2.3	1.4	1.6	1.5	1.7	2.2	1.9	1.1	●
Quick Ratio **31**	0.6	●	1.5	1.0	0.9	0.4	0.7	0.9	0.4	1.1	1.1	0.3	●
Net Sales to Working Capital **32**	9.8	●	10.5	7.7	5.4	15.0	10.7	13.4	9.5	6.4	4.2	20.9	●
Coverage Ratio **33**	7.9	110.9	17.2	4.5	5.2	4.1	6.3	7.5	5.8	4.7	6.0	10.5	●
Total Asset Turnover **34**	2.1	●	4.9	3.3	2.4	2.9	2.8	3.2	2.4	2.0	1.4	1.3	●
Inventory Turnover **35**	3.7	●	8.7	4.8	3.3	4.1	5.1	9.0	3.1	4.3	2.0	2.2	●
Receivables Turnover **36**	16.0	●	30.8	●	12.8	22.9	12.4	●	33.2	8.8	3.9	21.8	●
Total Liabilities to Net Worth **37**	1.6	●	1.3	1.9	1.8	1.6	1.6	1.7	1.6	1.3	0.9	1.6	●
Current Assets to Working Capital **38**	2.8	●	1.6	1.7	1.8	2.8	2.8	3.1	2.3	1.8	2.1	7.9	●
Current Liabilities to Working Capital **39**	1.8	●	0.6	0.7	0.8	1.8	1.8	2.1	1.3	0.8	1.1	6.9	●
Working Capital to Net Sales **40**	0.1	●	0.1	0.1	0.2	0.1	0.1	0.1	0.1	0.2	0.2	0.0	●
Inventory to Working Capital **41**	1.5	●	0.7	1.0	1.0	2.3	1.3	0.9	1.6	0.8	0.8	5.0	●
Total Receipts to Cash Flow **42**	6.7	2.3	6.4	7.0	8.0	10.4	8.5	9.4	6.2	5.9	5.2	5.5	●
Cost of Goods to Cash Flow **43**	3.8	1.0	3.9	4.2	4.7	6.4	5.3	6.0	3.4	3.1	2.8	2.8	●
Cash Flow to Total Debt **44**	0.5	●	1.4	0.7	0.5	0.4	0.6	0.5	0.6	0.6	0.5	0.4	●

Selected Financial Factors (in Percentages)

Debt Ratio **45**	61.3	●	55.7	65.6	64.1	61.0	62.6	61.5	56.3	48.1	62.0	●
Return on Total Assets **46**	12.7	●	31.0	11.6	11.0	11.3	15.6	10.0	7.9	5.1	12.1	●
Return on Equity Before Income Taxes **47**	28.7	●	65.8	26.4	24.9	24.4	36.3	21.6	14.2	8.2	28.8	●
Return on Equity After Income Taxes **48**	23.4	●	65.0	24.9	23.2	22.5	34.2	20.5	11.3	6.1	19.0	●
Profit Margin (Before Income Tax) **49**	5.2	21.7	5.9	2.8	3.8	3.3	4.2	3.4	3.1	3.1	8.6	●
Profit Margin (After Income Tax) **50**	4.2	21.1	5.8	2.6	3.5	3.1	4.0	3.3	2.5	2.3	5.7	●

Table I

Corporations with and without Net Income

ELECTRONICS AND APPLIANCE STORES

MONEY AMOUNTS AND SIZE OF ASSETS IN THOUSANDS OF DOLLARS

Item Description for Accounting Period 7/07 Through 6/08	Total	Zero Assets	Under 500	500 to 1,000	1,000 to 5,000	5,000 to 10,000	10,000 to 25,000	25,000 to 50,000	50,000 to 100,000	100,000 to 250,000	250,000 to 500,000	500,000 to 2,500,000	2,500,000 and over
Number of Enterprises **1**	28942	4811	20233	1415	2085	223	93	23	27	12	10	10	0
Revenues ($ in Thousands)													
Net Sales **2**	116087796	1965568	11428397	3151267	12310206	3045081	3702890	2825479	4545240	3142766	7360160	62610743	0
Interest **3**	520380	15587	3895	7623	12595	7532	9203	2185	8788	18628	147158	287187	0
Rents **4**	70393	0	6686	395	564	1451	407	1318	342	0	3021	56209	0
Royalties **5**	52550	0	0	0	0	0	7895	0	0	97	0	44558	0
Other Portfolio Income **6**	244299	9286	4880	27255	16530	6238	10374	15	4441	8118	72389	84771	0
Other Receipts **7**	1457786	6774	140174	23516	53665	17822	20328	9188	46080	70909	75478	993853	0
Total Receipts **8**	118433204	1997215	11584032	3210056	12393560	3078124	3751097	2838185	4604891	3240518	7658206	64077321	0
Average Total Receipts **9**	4092	415	573	2269	5944	13803	40334	123399	170552	270043	765821	6407732	•
Operating Costs/Operating Income (%)													
Cost of Operations **10**	70.2	70.0	55.3	53.7	69.8	53.7	72.4	73.2	75.0	68.2	71.7	73.9	•
Salaries and Wages **11**	10.6	4.8	13.8	17.2	10.8	18.3	11.2	9.9	10.0	15.1	12.7	9.0	•
Taxes Paid **12**	1.6	1.4	2.8	2.5	2.0	2.1	1.3	1.1	1.3	1.5	1.5	1.3	•
Interest Paid **13**	0.7	0.1	0.6	0.6	0.6	0.7	0.9	0.6	0.6	0.3	1.7	0.7	•
Depreciation **14**	1.0	1.3	0.9	1.2	0.7	0.6	1.4	1.0	1.5	1.5	0.7	1.0	•
Amortization and Depletion **15**	0.1	0.1	0.1	0.0	0.1	0.4	0.1	0.1	0.2	0.1	0.6	0.1	•
Pensions and Other Deferred Comp. **16**	0.2	0.0	0.1	0.5	0.4	0.6	0.2	0.1	0.2	0.1	0.1	0.1	•
Employee Benefits **17**	0.5	0.5	0.7	1.9	0.7	1.3	0.5	0.3	0.6	0.8	0.3	0.4	•
Advertising **18**	1.9	3.9	1.6	1.5	2.1	2.0	1.5	1.3	0.8	1.4	1.6	2.1	•
Other Expenses **19**	10.4	13.2	18.0	13.3	8.7	10.0	8.3	11.3	6.3	9.6	10.1	9.5	•
Officers' Compensation **20**	1.8	1.2	6.5	7.4	3.8	4.9	1.3	0.7	0.9	1.4	1.5	0.3	•
Operating Margin **21**	1.0	3.5	•	0.2	0.4	5.5	0.8	0.6	2.6	•	•	1.5	•
Operating Margin Before Officers' Comp. **22**	2.8	4.8	6.0	7.7	4.1	10.3	2.1	1.2	3.5	1.4	•	1.8	•

Selected Average Balance Sheet ($ in Thousands)

Net Receivables 23	201	0	22	158	367	1208	3878	12384	18617	37399	62633	189071
Inventories 24	386	0	43	184	570	974	2834	11496	11500	21301	52912	701443
Net Property, Plant and Equipment 25	257	0	18	53	380	511	1931	3677	8726	16403	41872	496818
Total Assets 26	1514	0	130	707	1911	6462	15805	35862	73045	176660	360884	2476343
Notes and Loans Payable 27	294	0	69	174	513	1025	5152	7211	15983	8896	83106	353520
All Other Liabilities 28	674	0	60	367	753	3632	6384	21496	26182	62726	141950	1143947
Net Worth 29	546	0	1	167	644	1804	4268	7156	30880	105038	135829	978876

Selected Financial Ratios (Times to 1)

Current Ratio 30	1.3	•	1.4	1.5	1.6	1.3	1.5	1.1	1.5	1.7	1.4	1.1
Quick Ratio 31	0.5	•	0.7	0.8	0.9	1.0	0.8	0.6	0.9	1.2	0.7	0.3
Net Sales to Working Capital 32	21.4	•	22.6	13.2	11.1	10.8	11.6	36.0	11.1	5.9	13.0	45.9
Coverage Ratio 33	5.2	36.4	2.4	4.5	2.8	9.5	3.3	2.8	7.9	12.3	2.0	6.5
Total Asset Turnover 34	2.6	•	4.4	3.1	3.1	2.1	2.5	3.4	2.3	1.5	2.0	2.5
Inventory Turnover 35	7.3	•	7.2	6.5	7.2	7.5	10.2	7.8	11.0	8.4	10.0	6.6
Receivables Turnover 36	18.7	•	27.2	12.7	15.5	10.1	10.9	6.2	9.7	6.0	14.0	29.3
Total Liabilities to Net Worth 37	1.8	•	168.7	3.2	2.0	2.6	2.7	4.0	1.4	0.7	1.7	1.5
Current Assets to Working Capital 38	4.5	•	3.5	3.2	2.6	3.9	3.2	8.2	3.0	2.4	3.5	8.6
Current Liabilities to Working Capital 39	3.5	•	2.5	2.2	1.6	2.9	2.2	7.2	2.0	1.4	2.5	7.6
Working Capital to Net Sales 40	0.0	•	0.0	0.1	0.1	0.1	0.1	0.0	0.1	0.2	0.1	0.0
Inventory to Working Capital 41	2.1	•	1.7	1.1	1.1	0.8	0.9	3.1	0.9	0.5	1.1	5.1
Total Receipts to Cash Flow 42	10.1	6.9	7.5	8.9	13.2	7.1	12.3	11.0	11.9	9.2	12.4	10.2
Cost of Goods to Cash Flow 43	7.1	4.8	4.1	4.8	9.2	3.8	8.9	8.1	8.9	6.3	8.9	7.5
Cash Flow to Total Debt 44	0.4	•	0.6	0.5	0.4	0.4	0.3	0.4	0.3	0.4	0.3	0.4

Selected Financial Factors (in Percentages)

Debt Ratio 45	63.9	•	99.4	76.5	66.3	72.1	73.0	80.0	57.7	40.5	62.4	60.5
Return on Total Assets 46	9.9	•	6.5	8.5	5.0	15.0	7.4	5.3	10.1	5.0	6.7	11.5
Return on Equity Before Income Taxes 47	22.2	•	649.9	28.0	9.4	48.2	19.2	17.2	20.9	7.8	8.9	24.7
Return on Equity After Income Taxes 48	15.4	•	627.4	21.0	8.6	45.3	17.5	10.3	18.9	7.7	4.7	15.2
Profit Margin (Before Income Tax) 49	3.0	5.1	0.9	2.1	1.0	6.4	2.1	1.0	3.8	3.1	1.6	3.9
Profit Margin (After Income Tax) 50	2.1	5.1	0.8	1.6	0.9	6.0	1.9	0.6	3.5	3.1	0.9	2.4

Table II

Corporations with Net Income

ELECTRONICS AND APPLIANCE STORES

Money Amounts and Size of Assets in Thousands of Dollars

Item Description for Accounting Period 7/07 Through 6/08	Total	Zero Assets	Under 500	500 to 1,000	1,000 to 5,000	5,000 to 10,000	10,000 to 25,000	25,000 to 50,000	50,000 to 100,000	100,000 to 250,000	250,000 to 500,000	500,000 to 2,500,000	2,500,000 and over
Number of Enterprises **1**	14684	1118	10888	798	1568	175	69	•	22	•	6	•	0
Revenues ($ in Thousands)													
Net Sales **2**	93978075	1582192	7757354	2339916	10875704	2431211	2546358	•	3989334	•	5613634	•	0
Interest **3**	444767	14724	3551	5417	4962	5272	8117	•	7879	•	142761	•	0
Rents **4**	45644	0	6511	0	564	1451	197	•	333	•	2367	•	0
Royalties **5**	52453	0	0	0	0	0	7895	•	0	•	0	•	0
Other Portfolio Income **6**	217211	0	2281	27151	13866	3318	10357	•	4204	•	71919	•	0
Other Receipts **7**	1026192	66	67217	13453	42359	16887	12133	•	45962	•	57342	•	0
Total Receipts **8**	95764342	1596982	7836914	2385137	10937455	2458139	2585057	•	4047712	•	5888023	•	0
Average Total Receipts **9**	6522	1428	720	2989	6975	14047	37465	•	183987	•	981337	•	•
Operating Costs/Operating Income (%)													
Cost of Operations **10**	70.6	69.3	53.8	52.0	71.4	62.4	69.6	•	74.2	•	78.1	•	•
Salaries and Wages **11**	9.9	3.5	12.9	16.0	10.7	11.6	11.2	•	10.6	•	8.0	•	•
Taxes Paid **12**	1.5	0.8	2.7	2.6	1.5	1.6	1.4	•	1.2	•	1.2	•	•
Interest Paid **13**	0.7	0.0	0.4	0.4	0.5	0.8	0.6	•	0.4	•	1.7	•	•
Depreciation **14**	1.0	1.4	0.7	1.0	0.6	0.6	1.7	•	1.4	•	0.5	•	•
Amortization and Depletion **15**	0.1	0.0	0.1	0.0	0.1	0.4	0.2	•	0.1	•	0.4	•	•
Pensions and Other Deferred Comp. **16**	0.2	•	0.2	0.5	0.2	0.4	0.2	•	0.2	•	0.1	•	•
Employee Benefits **17**	0.5	0.6	0.6	1.9	0.6	0.7	0.5	•	0.6	•	0.2	•	•
Advertising **18**	1.7	4.6	1.6	1.2	1.6	2.1	1.7	•	0.7	•	1.4	•	•
Other Expenses **19**	9.3	9.6	16.3	13.4	7.4	9.5	8.4	•	6.2	•	7.8	•	•
Officers' Compensation **20**	1.5	0.5	6.8	8.1	2.9	2.8	1.4	•	0.9	•	1.0	•	•
Operating Margin **21**	3.0	9.7	3.9	3.0	2.5	7.2	3.1	•	3.4	•	•	•	•
Operating Margin Before Officers' Comp. **22**	4.5	10.2	10.7	11.1	5.4	10.0	4.5	•	4.4	•	0.5	•	•

Selected Average Balance Sheet ($ in Thousands)

Net Receivables 23	291	0	21	211	407	1177	3104	19415	69170
Inventories 24	639	0	50	149	630	1238	3273	13273	57938
Net Property, Plant and Equipment 25	388	0	16	64	301	629	1930	8915	50514
Total Assets 26	2366	0	136	755	2011	5890	15251	71308	370892
Notes and Loans Payable 27	398	0	48	135	474	980	2867	12486	86033
All Other Liabilities 28	1035	0	63	359	792	2414	6419	26497	151704
Net Worth 29	933	0	25	261	745	2495	5966	32325	133155

Selected Financial Ratios (Times to 1)

Current Ratio 30	1.3	•	1.6	1.7	1.8	1.7	1.6	1.6	1.4
Quick Ratio 31	0.5	•	0.8	1.1	0.9	1.0	0.9	1.0	0.8
Net Sales to Working Capital 32	21.3	•	19.0	13.5	10.3	8.7	9.3	10.3	14.8
Coverage Ratio 33	7.7	2411.4	13.0	12.6	6.9	11.4	8.7	12.7	3.5
Total Asset Turnover 34	2.7	•	5.2	3.9	3.4	2.4	2.4	2.5	2.5
Inventory Turnover 35	7.1	•	7.7	10.2	7.9	7.0	7.9	10.1	12.6
Receivables Turnover 36	19.3	•	28.1	12.2	17.8	9.6	13.4	10.3	17.1
Total Liabilities to Net Worth 37	1.5	•	4.5	1.9	1.7	1.4	1.6	1.2	1.8
Current Assets to Working Capital 38	4.3	•	2.6	2.5	2.3	2.5	2.8	2.7	3.4
Current Liabilities to Working Capital 39	3.3	•	1.6	1.5	1.3	1.5	1.8	1.7	2.4
Working Capital to Net Sales 40	0.0	•	0.1	0.1	0.1	0.1	0.1	0.1	0.1
Inventory to Working Capital 41	2.0	•	1.3	0.8	1.0	0.8	0.8	0.8	0.9
Total Receipts to Cash Flow 42	8.9	5.3	6.3	7.0	11.8	6.3	9.0	10.7	10.4
Cost of Goods to Cash Flow 43	6.3	3.7	3.4	3.7	8.4	3.9	6.3	8.0	8.1
Cash Flow to Total Debt 44	0.5	•	1.0	0.8	0.5	0.6	0.4	0.4	0.4

Selected Financial Factors (in Percentages)

Debt Ratio 45	60.6	•	81.7	65.4	62.9	57.6	60.9	54.7	64.1
Return on Total Assets 46	15.3	•	28.0	20.8	12.1	21.2	12.7	13.3	15.3
Return on Equity Before Income Taxes 47	33.7	•	140.8	55.5	27.9	45.6	28.8	27.0	30.3
Return on Equity After Income Taxes 48	25.9	•	139.5	47.6	26.9	43.0	27.2	24.7	23.2
Profit Margin (Before Income Tax) 49	4.9	10.7	4.9	4.9	3.0	8.2	4.7	4.8	4.3
Profit Margin (After Income Tax) 50	3.8	10.6	4.9	4.2	2.9	7.7	4.4	4.4	3.3

Table I

Corporations with and without Net Income

HOMES CENTERS; PAINT AND WALLPAPER STORES

MONEY AMOUNTS AND SIZE OF ASSETS IN THOUSANDS OF DOLLARS

Item Description for Accounting Period 7/07 Through 6/08	Total	Zero Assets	Under 500	500 to 1,000	1,000 to 5,000	5,000 to 10,000	10,000 to 25,000	25,000 to 50,000	50,000 to 100,000	100,000 to 250,000	250,000 to 500,000	500,000 to 2,500,000	2,500,000 and over
Number of Enterprises 1	3332	62	2171	526	415	85	57	9	6	0	0	0	3

Revenues ($ in Thousands)

Item	Total	Zero Assets	Under 500	500 to 1,000	1,000 to 5,000	5,000 to 10,000	10,000 to 25,000	25,000 to 50,000	50,000 to 100,000	100,000 to 250,000	250,000 to 500,000	500,000 to 2,500,000	2,500,000 and over
Net Sales 2	137368738	22609	1927523	673827	3050586	1306567	1701723	808654	1123226	0	0	0	126754025
Interest 3	151930	11	245	1581	3973	3165	1036	592	0	0	0	0	141326
Rents 4	439306	0	0	12	891	3886	942	0	0	0	0	0	433575
Royalties 5	220544	0	0	0	0	0	0	0	0	0	0	0	220544
Other Portfolio Income 6	100451	13403	1158	1575	1776	2801	671	374	314	0	0	0	78380
Other Receipts 7	3061013	12503	586	1727	10392	5823	16837	9808	9501	0	0	0	2993833
Total Receipts 8	141341982	48526	1929512	678722	3067618	1322242	1721209	819428	1133041	0	0	0	130621683
Average Total Receipts 9	42420	783	889	1290	7392	15556	30197	91048	188840	•	•	•	43540561

Operating Costs/Operating Income (%)

Item	Total	Zero Assets	Under 500	500 to 1,000	1,000 to 5,000	5,000 to 10,000	10,000 to 25,000	25,000 to 50,000	50,000 to 100,000	100,000 to 250,000	250,000 to 500,000	500,000 to 2,500,000	2,500,000 and over
Cost of Operations 10	66.8	76.5	62.8	68.2	71.1	73.0	69.2	72.2	71.2	•	•	•	66.6
Salaries and Wages 11	12.0	20.8	11.9	7.0	12.1	10.1	12.7	12.8	11.0	•	•	•	12.1
Taxes Paid 12	2.1	2.9	6.9	1.8	2.3	1.8	1.8	1.6	1.6	•	•	•	2.1
Interest Paid 13	0.9	6.0	0.4	3.3	0.7	0.4	1.2	1.0	1.0	•	•	•	0.9
Depreciation 14	2.4	3.5	0.5	1.5	0.7	0.7	1.0	1.7	1.6	•	•	•	2.5
Amortization and Depletion 15	0.1	6.6	0.0	0.0	0.0	0.0	0.2	0.1	0.0	•	•	•	0.1
Pensions and Other Deferred Comp. 16	0.2	0.0	0.0	0.2	0.5	0.3	0.2	0.2	0.8	•	•	•	0.2
Employee Benefits 17	1.2	0.1	0.4	0.6	0.7	0.9	0.9	1.0	1.3	•	•	•	1.2
Advertising 18	1.6	0.2	1.1	1.2	0.6	0.7	1.6	0.6	2.0	•	•	•	1.7
Other Expenses 19	6.8	37.5	12.3	11.0	8.0	4.9	9.2	7.0	8.4	•	•	•	6.7
Officers' Compensation 20	0.2	0.2	3.6	7.0	2.4	2.2	1.4	1.2	0.5	•	•	•	0.0
Operating Margin 21	5.5	•	0.1	•	0.8	5.0	0.6	0.6	0.6	•	•	•	5.9
Operating Margin Before Officers' Comp. 22	5.8	•	3.7	5.1	3.2	7.2	1.9	1.8	1.1	•	•	•	6.0

Selected Average Balance Sheet ($ in Thousands)

Net Receivables 23	7831	0	36	71	558	1064	3304	7946	13572	•	8437999
Inventories 24	6118	0	97	239	899	2012	4239	10061	25473	•	6318948
Net Property, Plant and Equipment 25	12223	0	17	371	212	926	2088	10313	28257	•	13316510
Total Assets 26	40953	0	162	806	2333	6480	13230	34996	89939	•	4418136
Notes and Loans Payable 27	16174	0	88	520	651	821	5266	11116	23933	•	17514650
All Other Liabilities 28	13708	0	70	118	469	948	2900	7584	18214	•	14947598
Net Worth 29	11071	0	4	168	1213	4711	5064	16296	47793	•	11721889

Selected Financial Ratios (Times to 1)

Current Ratio 30	1.1	•	1.9	2.4	3.4	4.1	1.9	2.5	4.1	•	1.0
Quick Ratio 31	0.6	•	0.6	0.8	1.9	2.1	0.9	0.9	1.3	•	0.6
Net Sales to Working Capital 32	34.5	•	12.7	5.9	5.3	4.1	6.7	7.0	4.6	•	57.4
Coverage Ratio 33	10.4	11.0	1.4	0.6	2.9	16.1	2.4	2.9	2.4	•	11.1
Total Asset Turnover 34	1.0	•	5.5	1.6	3.2	2.4	2.3	2.6	2.1	•	1.0
Inventory Turnover 35	4.5	•	5.8	3.7	5.8	5.6	4.9	6.4	5.2	•	4.5
Receivables Turnover 36	6.2	•	24.4	19.6	11.0	20.1	8.2	13.2	16.4	•	5.9
Total Liabilities to Net Worth 37	2.7	•	40.5	3.8	0.9	0.4	1.6	1.1	0.9	•	2.8
Current Assets to Working Capital 38	12.4	•	2.1	1.7	1.4	1.3	2.1	1.7	1.3	•	21.0
Current Liabilities to Working Capital 39	11.4	•	1.1	0.7	0.4	0.3	1.1	0.7	0.3	•	20.0
Working Capital to Net Sales 40	0.0	•	0.1	0.2	0.2	0.2	0.1	0.1	0.2	•	0.0
Inventory to Working Capital 41	5.2	•	1.4	1.1	0.5	0.6	1.0	0.9	0.8	•	8.7
Total Receipts to Cash Flow 42	7.7	1.4	13.3	14.5	13.7	10.4	12.5	13.8	13.5	•	7.5
Cost of Goods to Cash Flow 43	5.2	1.1	8.3	9.9	9.7	7.6	8.7	9.9	9.6	•	5.0
Cash Flow to Total Debt 44	0.2	•	0.4	0.1	0.5	0.8	0.3	0.3	0.3	•	0.2

Selected Financial Factors (in Percentages)

Debt Ratio 45	73.0	•	97.6	79.2	48.0	27.3	61.7	53.4	46.9	•	73.5
Return on Total Assets 46	9.5	•	3.4	3.3	6.7	15.2	6.6	7.5	5.3	•	9.6
Return on Equity Before Income Taxes 47	31.8	•	36.4	•	8.5	19.7	10.2	10.5	5.8	•	32.8
Return on Equity After Income Taxes 48	21.5	•	21.7	•	7.9	17.7	9.4	10.4	5.8	•	22.1
Profit Margin (Before Income Tax) 49	8.5	60.2	0.2	•	1.4	6.0	1.7	1.9	1.5	•	9.1
Profit Margin (After Income Tax) 50	5.8	60.2	0.1	•	1.3	5.4	1.6	1.9	1.5	•	6.1

Table II

Corporations with Net Income

HOMES CENTERS; PAINT AND WALLPAPER STORES

MONEY AMOUNTS AND SIZE OF ASSETS IN THOUSANDS OF DOLLARS

Item Description for Accounting Period 7/07 Through 6/08	Total	Zero Assets	Under 500	500 to 1,000	1,000 to 5,000	5,000 to 10,000	10,000 to 25,000	25,000 to 50,000	50,000 to 100,000	100,000 to 250,000	250,000 to 500,000	500,000 to 2,500,000	2,500,000 and over
Number of Enterprises **1**	1773	•	•	183	346	81	51	•	3	0	0	0	3
Revenues ($ in Thousands)													
Net Sales **2**	135269551	•	•	292854	2610459	1191857	1487683	•	675084	0	0	0	126754025
Interest **3**	150636	•	•	1199	3540	2975	903	•	0	0	0	0	141326
Rents **4**	439293	•	•	0	891	3886	940	•	0	0	0	0	433575
Royalties **5**	220544	•	•	0	0	0	0	•	0	0	0	0	220544
Other Portfolio Income **6**	98571	•	•	1524	1702	2527	596	•	113	0	0	0	78380
Other Receipts **7**	3047167	•	•	621	5982	3729	16638	•	3809	0	0	0	2993833
Total Receipts **8**	139225762	•	•	296198	2622574	1204974	1506760	•	679006	0	0	0	130621683
Average Total Receipts **9**	78526	•	•	1619	7580	14876	29544	•	226335	•	•	•	43540561
Operating Costs/Operating Income (%)													
Cost of Operations **10**	66.8	•	•	69.3	71.2	73.1	70.3	•	70.5	•	•	•	66.6
Salaries and Wages **11**	12.0	•	•	5.0	11.8	9.8	12.2	•	9.4	•	•	•	12.1
Taxes Paid **12**	2.1	•	•	2.1	1.8	1.8	1.7	•	1.6	•	•	•	2.1
Interest Paid **13**	0.9	•	•	0.6	0.7	0.4	1.1	•	1.1	•	•	•	0.9
Depreciation **14**	2.4	•	•	1.1	0.7	0.7	1.0	•	1.4	•	•	•	2.5
Amortization and Depletion **15**	0.1	•	•	0.0	0.0	0.0	0.0	•	0.0	•	•	•	0.1
Pensions and Other Deferred Comp. **16**	0.2	•	•	0.2	0.6	0.3	0.2	•	1.2	•	•	•	0.2
Employee Benefits **17**	1.2	•	•	0.5	0.6	0.8	0.9	•	1.4	•	•	•	1.2
Advertising **18**	1.6	•	•	0.7	0.6	0.6	1.5	•	2.9	•	•	•	1.7
Other Expenses **19**	6.8	•	•	10.7	7.8	4.7	8.6	•	7.2	•	•	•	6.7
Officers' Compensation **20**	0.2	•	•	9.9	2.4	2.2	1.4	•	0.3	•	•	•	0.0
Operating Margin **21**	5.7	•	•	•	1.8	5.7	1.2	•	3.1	•	•	•	5.9
Operating Margin Before Officers' Comp. **22**	5.9	•	•	9.8	4.2	7.9	2.5	•	3.4	•	•	•	6.0

Selected Average Balance Sheet ($ in Thousands)

Net Receivables 23	14636	•	91	538	1030	3546	13922	•	•	•	8437999
Inventories 24	11294	•	276	846	1719	4254	39388	•	•	•	6318948
Net Property, Plant and Equipment 25	22806	•	215	196	853	2013	35600	•	•	•	13316510
Total Assets 26	76387	•	844	2342	6319	12423	98921	•	•	•	44184136
Notes and Loans Payable 27	30073	•	255	666	695	4963	31531	•	•	•	17514650
All Other Liabilities 28	25645	•	105	499	890	2848	13701	•	•	•	14947598
Net Worth 29	20670	•	484	1177	4734	4612	53689	•	•	•	11721889

Selected Financial Ratios (Times to 1)

Current Ratio 30	1.1	•	4.8	3.8	4.5	1.9	3.4	•	•	•	1.0
Quick Ratio 31	0.6	•	2.1	2.1	2.4	1.0	0.9	•	•	•	0.6
Net Sales to Working Capital 32	37.4	•	4.0	5.2	3.9	6.4	5.4	•	•	•	57.4
Coverage Ratio 33	10.9	•	2.7	4.1	19.1	3.3	4.5	•	•	•	11.1
Total Asset Turnover 34	1.0	•	1.9	3.2	2.3	2.3	2.3	•	•	•	1.0
Inventory Turnover 35	4.5	•	4.0	6.3	6.3	4.8	4.0	•	•	•	4.5
Receivables Turnover 36	6.1	•	•	10.9	19.8	7.5	5.9	•	•	•	•
Total Liabilities to Net Worth 37	2.7	•	0.7	1.0	0.3	1.7	0.8	•	•	•	2.8
Current Assets to Working Capital 38	13.5	•	1.3	1.4	1.3	2.1	1.4	•	•	•	21.0
Current Liabilities to Working Capital 39	12.5	•	0.3	0.4	0.3	1.1	0.4	•	•	•	20.0
Working Capital to Net Sales 40	0.0	•	0.2	0.2	0.3	0.2	0.2	•	•	•	0.0
Inventory to Working Capital 41	5.6	•	0.7	0.5	0.5	0.9	0.9	•	•	•	8.7
Total Receipts to Cash Flow 42	7.7	•	15.6	12.5	10.0	12.0	12.4	•	•	•	7.5
Cost of Goods to Cash Flow 43	5.1	•	10.8	8.9	7.3	8.4	8.7	•	•	•	5.0
Cash Flow to Total Debt 44	0.2	•	0.3	0.5	0.9	0.3	0.4	•	•	•	0.2

Selected Financial Factors (in Percentages)

Debt Ratio 45	72.9	•	42.6	49.7	25.1	62.9	45.7	•	•	•	73.5
Return on Total Assets 46	9.6	•	2.9	9.5	16.3	8.2	10.7	•	•	•	9.6
Return on Equity Before Income Taxes 47	32.2	•	3.2	14.2	20.6	15.4	15.2	•	•	•	32.8
Return on Equity After Income Taxes 48	21.9	•	2.8	13.5	18.6	14.4	15.2	•	•	•	22.1
Profit Margin (Before Income Tax) 49	8.7	•	1.0	2.2	6.6	2.4	3.6	•	•	•	9.1
Profit Margin (After Income Tax) 50	5.9	•	0.9	2.1	6.0	2.3	3.6	•	•	•	6.1

Table I

Corporations with and without Net Income

HARDWARE STORES

MONEY AMOUNTS AND SIZE OF ASSETS IN THOUSANDS OF DOLLARS

Item Description for Accounting Period 7/07 Through 6/08	Total	Zero Assets	Under 500	500 to 1,000	1,000 to 5,000	5,000 to 10,000	10,000 to 25,000	25,000 to 50,000	50,000 to 100,000	100,000 to 250,000	250,000 to 500,000	500,000 to 2,500,000	2,500,000 and over
Number of Enterprises **1**	8470	322	3494	2418	2062	114	40	16	5	0	0	0	0
Revenues ($ in Thousands)													
Net Sales **2**	21356299	31334	2597539	4170746	8827327	1407922	1628863	1342971	1349596	0	0	0	0
Interest **3**	28801	35	6490	5975	10558	2324	244	2193	982	0	0	0	0
Rents **4**	22829	794	6060	4310	9892	0	32	770	970	0	0	0	0
Royalties **5**	26	0	0	25	1	0	0	0	0	0	0	0	0
Other Portfolio Income **6**	13307	97	492	2512	8505	1215	326	153	8	0	0	0	0
Other Receipts **7**	206792	135	19845	48411	92697	18395	10289	7525	9494	0	0	0	0
Total Receipts **8**	21628054	32395	2630426	4231979	8948980	1429856	1639754	1353612	1361050	0	0	0	0
Average Total Receipts **9**	2553	101	753	1750	4340	12543	40994	84601	272210	•	•	•	•
Operating Costs/Operating Income (%)													
Cost of Operations **10**	63.7	110.2	62.0	60.8	66.5	61.3	65.5	64.6	56.2	•	•	•	•
Salaries and Wages **11**	12.9	22.5	12.4	12.4	12.4	13.7	15.3	13.8	14.0	•	•	•	•
Taxes Paid **12**	2.4	6.3	2.6	2.5	2.3	2.1	1.9	2.7	2.4	•	•	•	•
Interest Paid **13**	1.1	4.4	0.8	1.1	1.0	0.4	1.0	0.8	2.8	•	•	•	•
Depreciation **14**	1.1	1.6	0.4	1.3	1.2	1.1	1.2	1.1	1.3	•	•	•	•
Amortization and Depletion **15**	0.0	•	0.0	0.0	0.0	•	0.1	0.1	0.3	•	•	•	•
Pensions and Other Deferred Comp. **16**	0.2	0.1	0.0	0.2	0.4	0.3	0.2	0.2	0.1	•	•	•	•
Employee Benefits **17**	1.1	1.4	1.2	0.8	1.1	0.5	1.4	1.6	1.1	•	•	•	•
Advertising **18**	1.5	2.3	1.0	1.9	1.3	1.3	1.6	1.7	3.1	•	•	•	•
Other Expenses **19**	11.4	25.1	13.8	13.1	10.1	9.4	10.5	9.7	13.8	•	•	•	•
Officers' Compensation **20**	3.7	9.0	8.9	4.7	3.2	3.5	1.2	0.6	0.4	•	•	•	•
Operating Margin **21**	0.8	•	•	1.3	0.4	6.5	0.2	2.9	4.4	•	•	•	•
Operating Margin Before Officers' Comp. **22**	4.6	•	5.8	6.0	3.6	10.0	1.4	3.5	4.8	•	•	•	•

Selected Average Balance Sheet ($ in Thousands)

Net Receivables	23	121	0	22	76	252	543	2398	2614	8536
Inventories	24	481	0	145	347	834	2015	5783	15831	58372
Net Property, Plant and Equipment	25	252	0	19	86	346	3872	5613	10436	63558
Total Assets	26	1145	0	252	721	1841	7649	17036	33250	238833
Notes and Loans Payable	27	389	0	114	275	599	409	5941	12043	104442
All Other Liabilities	28	220	0	77	107	354	829	3545	6647	53392
Net Worth	29	536	0	61	340	888	6411	7551	14560	80998

Selected Financial Ratios (Times to 1)

Current Ratio	30	2.5	•	1.8	4.2	2.7	3.4	2.1	1.8	1.1
Quick Ratio	31	0.7	•	0.4	1.3	0.9	1.2	0.6	0.3	0.2
Net Sales to Working Capital	32	5.8	•	8.6	4.0	5.2	5.6	7.7	9.3	48.1
Coverage Ratio	33	3.0	•	•	3.6	2.8	23.9	1.8	5.4	2.9
Total Asset Turnover	34	2.2	•	3.0	2.4	2.3	1.6	2.4	2.5	1.1
Inventory Turnover	35	3.3	•	3.2	3.0	3.4	3.8	4.6	3.4	2.6
Receivables Turnover	36	20.2	•	25.9	21.5	16.9	19.8	21.3	25.3	36.3
Total Liabilities to Net Worth	37	1.1	•	3.1	1.1	1.1	0.2	1.3	1.3	1.9
Current Assets to Working Capital	38	1.7	•	2.2	1.3	1.6	1.4	1.9	2.3	13.2
Current Liabilities to Working Capital	39	0.7	•	1.2	0.3	0.6	0.4	0.9	1.3	12.2
Working Capital to Net Sales	40	0.2	•	0.1	0.2	0.2	0.2	0.1	0.1	0.0
Inventory to Working Capital	41	1.1	•	1.6	0.9	1.0	0.7	1.3	1.8	10.2
Total Receipts to Cash Flow	42	11.0	•	13.7	10.1	12.0	6.5	15.4	10.8	8.1
Cost of Goods to Cash Flow	43	7.0	•	8.5	6.1	8.0	4.0	10.1	7.0	4.5
Cash Flow to Total Debt	44	0.4	•	0.3	0.4	0.4	1.5	0.3	0.4	0.2

Selected Financial Factors (in Percentages)

Debt Ratio	45	53.2	•	75.7	52.9	51.8	16.2	55.7	56.2	66.1
Return on Total Assets	46	7.0	•	•	9.3	6.6	13.5	4.4	11.4	9.1
Return on Equity Before Income Taxes	47	9.9	•	•	14.2	8.7	15.4	4.6	21.2	17.5
Return on Equity After Income Taxes	48	8.5	•	•	13.5	7.7	14.4	4.4	17.7	12.1
Profit Margin (Before Income Tax)	49	2.1	•	•	2.8	1.8	8.0	0.8	3.7	5.2
Profit Margin (After Income Tax)	50	1.8	•	•	2.7	1.6	7.5	0.8	3.1	3.6

213

Table II

Corporations with Net Income

HARDWARE STORES

MONEY AMOUNTS AND SIZE OF ASSETS IN THOUSANDS OF DOLLARS

Item Description for Accounting Period 7/07 Through 6/08	Total	Zero Assets	Under 500	500 to 1,000	1,000 to 5,000	5,000 to 10,000	10,000 to 25,000	25,000 to 50,000	50,000 to 100,000	100,000 to 250,000	250,000 to 500,000	500,000 to 2,500,000	2,500,000 and over
Number of Enterprises **1**	5722	0	1949	2077	1534	114	27	16	5	0	0	0	0
Revenues ($ in Thousands)													
Net Sales **2**	17526920	0	1351925	3787485	6881344	1407922	1405677	1342971	1349596	0	0	0	0
Interest **3**	22097	0	5857	4204	6537	2324	0	2193	982	0	0	0	0
Rents **4**	11605	0	92	2707	7066	0	0	770	970	0	0	0	0
Royalties **5**	1	0	0	0	1	0	0	0	0	0	0	0	0
Other Portfolio Income **6**	12042	0	492	2512	7547	1215	115	153	8	0	0	0	0
Other Receipts **7**	181221	0	19318	48160	72729	18395	5599	7525	9494	0	0	0	0
Total Receipts **8**	17753886	0	1377684	3845068	6975224	1429856	1411391	1353612	1361050	0	0	0	0
Average Total Receipts **9**	3103	•	707	1851	4547	12543	52274	84601	272210	•	•	•	•
Operating Costs/Operating Income (%)													
Cost of Operations **10**	63.2	•	58.0	61.0	66.7	61.3	63.9	64.6	56.2	•	•	•	•
Salaries and Wages **11**	12.6	•	12.4	12.5	11.4	13.7	15.4	13.8	14.0	•	•	•	•
Taxes Paid **12**	2.3	•	2.1	2.5	2.3	2.1	1.9	2.7	2.4	•	•	•	•
Interest Paid **13**	0.9	•	0.8	0.7	0.8	0.4	0.9	0.8	2.8	•	•	•	•
Depreciation **14**	1.1	•	0.5	1.0	1.1	1.1	1.1	1.1	1.3	•	•	•	•
Amortization and Depletion **15**	0.1	•	0.0	0.0	0.0	•	0.0	0.1	0.3	•	•	•	•
Pensions and Other Deferred Comp. **16**	0.3	•	0.1	0.2	0.4	0.3	0.2	0.2	0.1	•	•	•	•
Employee Benefits **17**	0.9	•	0.5	0.7	1.0	0.5	1.4	1.6	1.1	•	•	•	•
Advertising **18**	1.5	•	0.9	1.8	1.2	1.3	1.7	1.7	3.1	•	•	•	•
Other Expenses **19**	11.1	•	13.7	12.5	10.0	9.4	10.9	9.7	13.8	•	•	•	•
Officers' Compensation **20**	3.3	•	5.8	4.7	3.5	3.5	1.2	0.6	0.4	•	•	•	•
Operating Margin **21**	2.7	•	5.2	2.4	1.5	6.5	1.3	2.9	4.4	•	•	•	•
Operating Margin Before Officers' Comp. **22**	6.0	•	11.1	7.1	5.0	10.0	2.5	3.5	4.8	•	•	•	•

Selected Average Balance Sheet ($ in Thousands)

Item									
Net Receivables 23	147	•	21	80	272	543	2693	2614	8536
Inventories 24	558	•	153	314	852	1973	7150	16343	57267
Net Property, Plant and Equipment 25	309	•	16	84	310	3872	6007	10436	63558
Total Assets 26	1374	•	258	715	1815	7649	18260	33250	238833
Notes and Loans Payable 27	419	•	94	221	539	409	6059	12043	104442
All Other Liabilities 28	238	•	31	111	315	829	4504	6647	53392
Net Worth 29	717	•	132	383	961	6411	7697	14560	80998

Selected Financial Ratios (Times to 1)

Item									
Current Ratio 30	2.7	•	4.1	3.9	3.1	3.4	1.8	1.8	1.1
Quick Ratio 31	0.8	•	0.9	1.2	1.2	1.2	0.5	0.3	0.2
Net Sales to Working Capital 32	5.7	•	4.8	4.4	4.9	5.6	10.9	9.3	48.1
Coverage Ratio 33	5.4	•	10.3	6.6	4.6	23.9	3.0	5.4	2.9
Total Asset Turnover 34	2.2	•	2.7	2.6	2.5	1.6	2.9	2.5	1.1
Inventory Turnover 35	3.5	•	2.6	3.5	3.5	3.8	4.7	3.3	2.6
Receivables Turnover 36	19.8	•	21.6	23.9	15.5	20.9	21.6	•	•
Total Liabilities to Net Worth 37	0.9	•	0.9	0.9	0.9	0.2	1.4	1.3	1.9
Current Assets to Working Capital 38	1.6	•	1.3	1.3	1.5	1.4	2.3	2.3	13.2
Current Liabilities to Working Capital 39	0.6	•	0.3	0.3	0.5	0.4	1.3	1.3	12.2
Working Capital to Net Sales 40	0.2	•	0.2	0.2	0.2	0.2	0.1	0.1	0.0
Inventory to Working Capital 41	1.0	•	1.0	0.9	0.9	0.7	1.5	1.8	10.2
Total Receipts to Cash Flow 42	9.4	•	6.4	9.1	10.9	6.5	14.0	10.8	8.1
Cost of Goods to Cash Flow 43	5.9	•	3.7	5.5	7.3	4.0	8.9	7.0	4.5
Cash Flow to Total Debt 44	0.5	•	0.9	0.6	0.5	1.5	0.4	0.4	0.2

Selected Financial Factors (in Percentages)

Item									
Debt Ratio 45	47.8	•	48.6	46.4	47.0	16.2	57.8	56.2	66.1
Return on Total Assets 46	10.9	•	21.3	11.9	9.1	13.5	7.2	11.4	9.1
Return on Equity Before Income Taxes 47	17.1	•	37.4	18.8	13.5	15.4	11.4	21.2	17.5
Return on Equity After Income Taxes 48	15.5	•	36.4	18.1	12.2	14.4	11.2	17.7	12.1
Profit Margin (Before Income Tax) 49	4.0	•	7.2	4.0	2.9	8.0	1.7	3.7	5.2
Profit Margin (After Income Tax) 50	3.6	•	7.0	3.8	2.6	7.5	1.7	3.1	3.6

Table I

Corporations with and without Net Income

OTHER BUILDING MATERIAL DEALERS

MONEY AMOUNTS AND SIZE OF ASSETS IN THOUSANDS OF DOLLARS

Item Description for Accounting Period 7/07 Through 6/08	Total	Zero Assets	Under 500	500 to 1,000	1,000 to 5,000	5,000 to 10,000	10,000 to 25,000	25,000 to 50,000	50,000 to 100,000	100,000 to 250,000	250,000 to 500,000	500,000 to 2,500,000	2,500,000 and over
Number of Enterprises **1**	21852	1291	13360	2779	3675	453	202	59	17	10	0	7	0
Revenues ($ in Thousands)													
Net Sales **2**	76689758	1042177	7852163	6337385	22379323	8289221	7080151	4195072	2328458	3401822	0	13783985	0
Interest **3**	175927	5223	371	7025	25196	6923	13446	6473	3857	38695	0	68719	0
Rents **4**	36708	5809	3851	2166	6909	200	5208	7638	1576	880	0	2472	0
Royalties **5**	4686	0	3027	0	0	0	197	175	0	1286	0	0	0
Other Portfolio Income **6**	170739	21516	8777	6848	9294	1329	7045	9806	3945	12792	0	89386	0
Other Receipts **7**	744379	26606	12898	64729	154570	27976	52348	25575	15103	25118	0	339458	0
Total Receipts **8**	77822197	1101331	7881087	6418153	22575292	8325649	7158395	4244739	2352939	3480593	0	14284020	0
Average Total Receipts **9**	3561	853	590	2310	6143	18379	35438	71945	138408	348059	•	2040574	•
Operating Costs/Operating Income (%)													
Cost of Operations **10**	72.6	79.1	65.7	68.1	71.0	77.4	74.5	73.6	70.8	74.3	•	76.3	•
Salaries and Wages **11**	9.8	4.5	6.3	11.3	9.5	9.8	10.1	10.7	11.9	9.9	•	11.2	•
Taxes Paid **12**	1.6	1.4	1.9	2.0	1.8	1.7	1.5	1.7	1.7	1.6	•	1.1	•
Interest Paid **13**	1.2	1.6	0.5	0.5	0.6	0.6	0.7	0.9	1.1	1.8	•	3.5	•
Depreciation **14**	1.1	2.3	1.6	0.5	0.7	0.8	1.1	1.1	1.6	1.3	•	1.6	•
Amortization and Depletion **15**	0.2	0.9	0.0	0.0	0.0	0.0	0.1	0.1	0.1	0.1	•	1.0	•
Pensions and Other Deferred Comp. **16**	0.4	0.0	0.1	0.3	0.4	0.2	0.5	0.4	0.4	0.4	•	0.4	•
Employee Benefits **17**	1.1	0.0	0.6	0.7	0.9	1.3	0.9	1.0	0.8	1.1	•	2.0	•
Advertising **18**	0.8	0.2	1.8	0.7	0.9	0.4	0.6	0.5	0.7	2.4	•	0.2	•
Other Expenses **19**	9.1	9.4	15.8	9.0	8.6	6.1	7.4	7.5	8.9	7.3	•	9.9	•
Officers' Compensation **20**	2.4	1.3	5.4	4.6	3.4	1.6	1.3	0.9	0.9	0.7	•	0.2	•
Operating Margin **21**	•	•	0.3	2.4	2.1	•	1.4	1.6	1.2	•	•	•	•
Operating Margin Before Officers' Comp. **22**	2.1	0.6	5.7	7.0	5.5	1.6	2.7	2.6	2.1	•	•	•	•

Selected Average Balance Sheet ($ in Thousands)

Net Receivables 23	492	0	24	199	509	2116	4207	7528	15870	23983	748622	•
Inventories 24	398	0	40	245	725	2481	5340	8939	20639	36429	196675	•
Net Property, Plant and Equipment 25	272	0	39	75	308	1039	2668	5823	20197	49684	269550	•
Total Assets 26	1989	0	137	782	2086	7006	15123	34769	69174	167930	2952407	•
Notes and Loans Payable 27	727	0	73	166	545	1818	3786	8327	21255	22588	1398583	•
All Other Liabilities 28	546	0	35	219	480	1272	3365	7207	14827	33623	975319	•
Net Worth 29	716	0	29	398	1061	3916	7971	19236	33092	111718	578504	•

Selected Financial Ratios (Times to 1)

Current Ratio 30	1.8	•	1.8	2.6	2.6	2.2	2.1	1.9	2.2	1.7	1.3	•
Quick Ratio 31	1.0	•	0.8	1.4	1.3	1.2	1.0	0.9	1.1	0.7	0.9	•
Net Sales to Working Capital 32	6.9	•	14.7	5.9	6.1	6.1	6.3	6.7	6.3	9.9	7.0	•
Coverage Ratio 33	2.0	4.2	2.3	8.3	5.8	1.7	4.6	4.2	3.1	1.9	•	•
Total Asset Turnover 34	1.8	•	4.3	2.9	2.9	2.6	2.3	2.0	2.0	2.0	0.7	•
Inventory Turnover 35	6.4	•	9.5	6.3	6.0	5.7	4.9	5.9	4.7	6.9	7.6	•
Receivables Turnover 36	8.5	•	25.8	12.5	11.5	8.0	7.9	9.8	7.1	12.4	4.1	•
Total Liabilities to Net Worth 37	1.8	•	3.7	1.0	1.0	0.8	0.9	0.8	1.1	0.5	4.1	•
Current Assets to Working Capital 38	2.2	•	2.3	1.6	1.6	1.8	1.9	2.1	1.8	2.4	4.1	•
Current Liabilities to Working Capital 39	1.2	•	1.3	0.6	0.6	0.8	0.9	1.1	0.8	1.4	3.1	•
Working Capital to Net Sales 40	0.1	•	0.1	0.2	0.2	0.2	0.2	0.1	0.2	0.1	0.1	•
Inventory to Working Capital 41	0.8	•	1.1	0.7	0.8	0.7	0.9	0.9	0.8	1.1	0.8	•
Total Receipts to Cash Flow 42	13.5	9.2	8.3	10.1	11.4	22.9	13.4	12.1	12.2	14.1	37.9	•
Cost of Goods to Cash Flow 43	9.8	7.3	5.5	6.9	8.1	17.7	10.0	8.9	8.7	10.4	28.9	•
Cash Flow to Total Debt 44	0.2	•	0.7	0.6	0.5	0.3	0.4	0.4	0.3	0.4	0.0	•

Selected Financial Factors (in Percentages)

Debt Ratio 45	64.0	•	78.7	49.1	49.1	44.1	47.3	44.7	52.2	33.5	80.4	•
Return on Total Assets 46	4.3	•	5.1	12.1	10.5	2.7	7.6	7.4	6.5	6.8	•	•
Return on Equity Before Income Taxes 47	5.9	•	13.4	20.9	17.1	1.9	11.3	10.2	9.3	4.7	•	•
Return on Equity After Income Taxes 48	4.7	•	10.0	20.2	16.0	0.9	9.2	9.0	7.9	3.1	•	•
Profit Margin (Before Income Tax) 49	1.2	5.0	0.7	3.6	3.0	0.4	2.6	2.8	2.2	1.6	•	•
Profit Margin (After Income Tax) 50	1.0	4.8	0.5	3.5	2.8	0.2	2.1	2.4	1.9	1.0	•	•

Table II

Corporations with Net Income

OTHER BUILDING MATERIAL DEALERS

MONEY AMOUNTS AND SIZE OF ASSETS IN THOUSANDS OF DOLLARS

Item Description for Accounting Period 7/07 Through 6/08	Total	Zero Assets	Under 500	500 to 1,000	1,000 to 5,000	5,000 to 10,000	10,000 to 25,000	25,000 to 50,000	50,000 to 100,000	100,000 to 250,000	250,000 to 500,000	500,000 to 2,500,000	2,500,000 and over
Number of Enterprises 1	13546	•	•	2118	2932	202	166	•	13	6	0	4	0
Revenues ($ in Thousands)													
Net Sales 2	55494558	•	•	5460680	19131639	4429301	6036072	•	1719171	2328763	0	6563787	0
Interest 3	108834	•	•	6053	21590	4790	12616	•	3250	35504	0	14300	0
Rents 4	26814	•	•	2166	3300	102	5091	•	1177	556	0	2325	0
Royalties 5	4686	•	•	0	0	0	197	•	0	1286	0	0	0
Other Portfolio Income 6	151505	•	•	3936	7752	517	6143	•	3748	8209	0	86812	0
Other Receipts 7	628872	•	•	63545	139810	17180	49611	•	13557	25831	0	265106	0
Total Receipts 8	56415269	•	•	5536380	19304091	4451890	6109730	•	1740903	2400149	0	6932330	0
Average Total Receipts 9	4165	•	•	2614	6584	22039	36806	•	133916	400025	•	1733082	•
Operating Costs/Operating Income (%)													
Cost of Operations 10	72.4	•	•	69.1	71.4	77.0	74.5	•	70.6	72.2	•	78.4	•
Salaries and Wages 11	9.0	•	•	11.2	8.6	9.6	9.6	•	12.0	9.3	•	9.0	•
Taxes Paid 12	1.6	•	•	1.8	1.7	1.5	1.5	•	1.7	1.6	•	0.8	•
Interest Paid 13	0.7	•	•	0.3	0.5	0.6	0.6	•	1.0	2.1	•	1.3	•
Depreciation 14	1.0	•	•	0.4	0.6	0.8	1.1	•	1.8	1.5	•	1.8	•
Amortization and Depletion 15	0.1	•	•	0.0	0.0	0.0	0.1	•	0.0	0.0	•	0.6	•
Pensions and Other Deferred Comp. 16	0.4	•	•	0.2	0.4	0.2	0.4	•	0.6	0.4	•	0.5	•
Employee Benefits 17	0.8	•	•	0.5	0.8	0.5	0.8	•	0.9	0.6	•	1.5	•
Advertising 18	0.9	•	•	0.5	1.0	0.3	0.6	•	0.7	3.3	•	0.3	•
Other Expenses 19	8.2	•	•	7.3	8.2	5.0	7.2	•	7.5	7.8	•	8.2	•
Officers' Compensation 20	2.6	•	•	4.6	3.4	1.8	1.2	•	1.1	0.6	•	0.3	•
Operating Margin 21	2.3	•	•	4.1	3.2	2.5	2.4	•	2.1	0.6	•	•	•
Operating Margin Before Officers' Comp. 22	4.9	•	•	8.7	6.6	4.3	3.6	•	3.2	1.2	•	•	•

Selected Average Balance Sheet ($ in Thousands)

Net Receivables 23	352	220	508	2087	4157	14947	23296	182775
Inventories 24	507	248	767	4263	5654	22030	53728	253822
Net Property, Plant and Equipment 25	280	72	316	974	2702	21064	63230	213610
Total Assets 26	1474	777	2135	6916	15396	66721	188340	837734
Notes and Loans Payable 27	349	123	474	1915	3462	18415	17739	261915
All Other Liabilities 28	335	170	448	1356	3425	13540	36460	261336
Net Worth 29	790	484	1213	3645	8509	34767	134141	314482

Selected Financial Ratios (Times to 1)

Current Ratio 30	2.4	3.3	3.1	2.1	2.2	2.2	1.5	1.8
Quick Ratio 31	1.2	1.9	1.6	1.0	1.1	1.1	0.6	0.8
Net Sales to Working Capital 32	6.8	5.7	5.7	7.6	6.0	6.4	13.2	8.2
Coverage Ratio 33	6.8	21.5	8.7	5.8	6.8	4.3	2.8	3.3
Total Asset Turnover 34	2.8	3.3	3.1	3.2	2.4	2.0	2.1	2.0
Inventory Turnover 35	5.9	7.2	6.1	4.0	4.8	4.2	5.2	5.1
Receivables Turnover 36	9.7	12.5	11.8	6.0	8.0	7.4	10.4	6.1
Total Liabilities to Net Worth 37	0.9	0.6	0.8	0.9	0.8	0.9	0.4	1.7
Current Assets to Working Capital 38	1.7	1.4	1.5	1.9	1.8	1.8	3.2	2.3
Current Liabilities to Working Capital 39	0.7	0.4	0.5	0.9	0.8	0.8	2.2	1.3
Working Capital to Net Sales 40	0.1	0.2	0.2	0.1	0.2	0.2	0.1	0.1
Inventory to Working Capital 41	0.8	0.6	0.7	0.9	0.9	0.8	1.7	1.0
Total Receipts to Cash Flow 42	10.4	9.4	10.3	16.8	12.0	12.4	9.9	12.4
Cost of Goods to Cash Flow 43	7.5	6.5	7.4	13.0	8.9	8.8	7.1	9.7
Cash Flow to Total Debt 44	0.6	0.9	0.7	0.4	0.4	0.3	0.7	0.3

Selected Financial Factors (in Percentages)

Debt Ratio 45	46.4	37.7	43.2	47.3	44.7	47.9	28.8	62.5
Return on Total Assets 46	12.9	19.0	14.1	11.3	10.1	8.7	11.9	8.3
Return on Equity Before Income Taxes 47	20.6	29.0	22.0	17.8	15.6	12.8	10.7	15.4
Return on Equity After Income Taxes 48	18.8	28.3	20.7	15.4	13.3	11.1	8.5	13.1
Profit Margin (Before Income Tax) 49	4.0	5.4	4.1	3.0	3.7	3.4	3.7	3.0
Profit Margin (After Income Tax) 50	3.6	5.3	3.8	2.6	3.1	2.9	3.0	2.5

Table I

Corporations with and without Net Income

LAWN AND GARDEN EQUIPMENT AND SUPPLIES STORES

MONEY AMOUNTS AND SIZE OF ASSETS IN THOUSANDS OF DOLLARS

Item Description for Accounting Period 7/07 Through 6/08	Total	Zero Assets	Under 500	500 to 1,000	1,000 to 5,000	5,000 to 10,000	10,000 to 25,000	25,000 to 50,000	50,000 to 100,000	100,000 to 250,000	250,000 to 500,000	500,000 to 2,500,000	2,500,000 and over
Number of Enterprises **1**	9038	1137	4696	1932	1091	116	50	14	3	0	0	0	0
Revenues ($ in Thousands)													
Net Sales **2**	16894059	85076	2261562	3602178	5451201	1547950	1759705	1006655	1179732	0	0	0	0
Interest **3**	18812	0	681	1719	9858	3426	498	1275	1355	0	0	0	0
Rents **4**	4340	0	0	137	4036	0	0	168	0	0	0	0	0
Royalties **5**	1	0	0	1	0	0	0	0	0	0	0	0	0
Other Portfolio Income **6**	41335	0	26489	940	2304	1063	243	9981	314	0	0	0	0
Other Receipts **7**	80928	0	9368	3708	31009	14298	16926	2116	3504	0	0	0	0
Total Receipts **8**	17039475	85076	2298100	3608683	5498408	1566737	1777372	1020195	1184905	0	0	0	0
Average Total Receipts **9**	1885	75	489	1868	5040	13506	35547	72871	394968	•	•	•	•
Operating Costs/Operating Income (%)													
Cost of Operations **10**	72.3	73.7	70.5	65.2	72.5	83.1	71.0	67.7	87.9	•	•	•	•
Salaries and Wages **11**	8.7	22.8	7.0	11.1	9.2	6.0	7.7	11.7	4.5	•	•	•	•
Taxes Paid **12**	1.8	3.1	2.5	2.8	1.5	1.0	1.2	2.1	0.6	•	•	•	•
Interest Paid **13**	1.2	4.6	1.0	1.1	1.1	1.8	1.2	1.1	1.0	•	•	•	•
Depreciation **14**	1.4	9.7	1.3	1.1	1.4	0.6	1.2	4.3	0.6	•	•	•	•
Amortization and Depletion **15**	0.0	•	0.0	0.0	0.0	0.0	0.1	0.0	0.1	•	•	•	•
Pensions and Other Deferred Comp. **16**	0.1	•	0.0	0.1	0.1	0.1	0.4	0.2	0.0	•	•	•	•
Employee Benefits **17**	0.6	2.4	0.3	0.8	0.7	0.5	0.6	0.2	0.5	•	•	•	•
Advertising **18**	1.0	0.4	1.1	0.8	1.3	0.9	1.0	0.7	0.0	•	•	•	•
Other Expenses **19**	9.7	40.1	11.3	10.2	9.9	6.6	12.0	9.4	3.6	•	•	•	•
Officers' Compensation **20**	2.9	7.1	6.0	3.9	2.4	1.7	1.1	2.5	0.2	•	•	•	•
Operating Margin **21**	0.2	•	•	2.8	•	•	2.5	0.2	1.0	•	•	•	•
Operating Margin Before Officers' Comp. **22**	3.1	•	5.0	6.7	2.3	•	3.6	2.6	1.2	•	•	•	•

Selected Average Balance Sheet ($ in Thousands)

Net Receivables 23	104	0	13	87	219	530	2999	4842	64414
Inventories 24	378	0	79	334	1062	4882	7875	10667	34090
Net Property, Plant and Equipment 25	146	0	22	150	517	277	2596	12121	9135
Total Assets 26	806	0	193	701	2139	5777	16231	34740	242316
Notes and Loans Payable 27	328	0	77	214	804	2483	6404	14982	164124
All Other Liabilities 28	234	0	53	190	497	2730	5511	6891	89827
Net Worth 29	245	0	63	297	839	564	4316	12866	-11635

Selected Financial Ratios (Times to 1)

Current Ratio 30	1.7	•	3.2	2.6	1.9	1.4	1.4	1.3	0.8
Quick Ratio 31	0.5	•	0.7	1.0	0.5	0.2	0.4	0.4	0.5
Net Sales to Working Capital 32	7.6	•	5.0	5.7	6.7	9.4	9.0	16.6	•
Coverage Ratio 33	1.9	•	1.5	3.7	1.6	0.4	3.9	2.3	2.4
Total Asset Turnover 34	2.3	•	2.5	2.7	2.3	2.3	2.2	2.1	1.6
Inventory Turnover 35	3.6	•	4.3	3.6	3.4	2.3	3.2	4.6	10.1
Receivables Turnover 36	17.9	•	34.2	22.1	21.4	14.1	12.8	14.2	12.2
Total Liabilities to Net Worth 37	2.3	•	2.1	1.4	1.6	9.2	2.8	1.7	•
Current Assets to Working Capital 38	2.3	•	1.5	1.6	2.1	3.7	3.3	4.5	•
Current Liabilities to Working Capital 39	1.3	•	0.5	0.6	1.1	2.7	2.3	3.5	•
Working Capital to Net Sales 40	0.1	•	0.2	0.2	0.1	0.1	0.1	0.1	•
Inventory to Working Capital 41	1.5	•	1.1	1.0	1.3	3.2	2.2	2.8	•
Total Receipts to Cash Flow 42	12.4	•	12.2	10.2	12.7	27.7	7.6	12.0	23.4
Cost of Goods to Cash Flow 43	9.0	•	8.6	6.7	9.2	23.0	5.4	8.1	20.6
Cash Flow to Total Debt 44	0.3	•	0.3	0.5	0.3	0.1	0.4	0.3	0.1

Selected Financial Factors (in Percentages)

Debt Ratio 45	69.7	•	67.3	57.6	60.8	90.2	73.4	63.0	104.8
Return on Total Assets 46	5.2	•	3.9	11.0	4.1	1.6	10.2	5.4	4.1
Return on Equity Before Income Taxes 47	8.1	•	4.1	18.8	4.0	•	28.4	8.4	•
Return on Equity After Income Taxes 48	7.1	•	3.5	18.2	3.0	•	28.4	7.9	•
Profit Margin (Before Income Tax) 49	1.1	•	0.5	3.0	0.7	•	3.5	1.5	1.5
Profit Margin (After Income Tax) 50	0.9	•	0.5	2.9	0.5	•	3.5	1.4	1.0

Table II

Corporations with Net Income

LAWN AND GARDEN EQUIPMENT AND SUPPLIES STORES

MONEY AMOUNTS AND SIZE OF ASSETS IN THOUSANDS OF DOLLARS

Item Description for Accounting Period 7/07 Through 6/08	Total	Zero Assets	Under 500	500 to 1,000	1,000 to 5,000	5,000 to 10,000	10,000 to 25,000	25,000 to 50,000	50,000 to 100,000	100,000 to 250,000	250,000 to 500,000	500,000 to 2,500,000	2,500,000 and over
Number of Enterprises 1	3987	0	1967	1081	829	57	41	14	0	0	0	0	0
Revenues ($ in Thousands)													
Net Sales 2	11989435	0	1098387	2521158	3850623	812615	1558852	2147800	0	0	0	0	0
Interest 3	15865	0	681	1145	9381	2166	442	2049	0	0	0	0	0
Rents 4	2808	0	0	13	2627	0	0	168	0	0	0	0	0
Royalties 5	1	0	0	1	0	0	0	0	0	0	0	0	0
Other Portfolio Income 6	33358	0	26489	835	2010	481	234	3309	0	0	0	0	0
Other Receipts 7	49848	0	5377	3648	15895	3981	15601	5348	0	0	0	0	0
Total Receipts 8	12091315	0	1130934	2526800	3880536	819243	1575129	2158674	0	0	0	0	0
Average Total Receipts 9	3033	•	575	2337	4681	14373	38418	154191	•	•	•	•	•
Operating Costs/Operating Income (%)													
Cost of Operations 10	72.7	•	68.7	63.5	73.7	83.5	73.5	79.1	•	•	•	•	•
Salaries and Wages 11	8.5	•	9.4	10.8	8.1	5.0	7.6	7.8	•	•	•	•	•
Taxes Paid 12	1.6	•	2.2	2.0	1.5	0.9	1.3	1.3	•	•	•	•	•
Interest Paid 13	0.9	•	0.8	0.5	1.0	1.2	1.2	0.9	•	•	•	•	•
Depreciation 14	1.1	•	1.4	1.0	1.2	0.4	0.9	1.5	•	•	•	•	•
Amortization and Depletion 15	0.0	•	0.0	0.0	0.0	0.0	0.1	0.1	•	•	•	•	•
Pensions and Other Deferred Comp. 16	0.1	•	0.0	0.2	0.1	0.0	0.4	0.1	•	•	•	•	•
Employee Benefits 17	0.6	•	0.0	0.8	0.7	0.3	0.7	0.4	•	•	•	•	•
Advertising 18	0.9	•	1.0	0.9	1.4	0.4	0.9	0.3	•	•	•	•	•
Other Expenses 19	8.3	•	8.5	10.3	8.2	6.2	9.3	6.3	•	•	•	•	•
Officers' Compensation 20	2.8	•	2.8	4.6	3.2	2.2	1.0	1.2	•	•	•	•	•
Operating Margin 21	2.4	•	5.0	5.5	0.9	•	3.1	1.0	•	•	•	•	•
Operating Margin Before Officers' Comp. 22	5.2	•	7.9	10.0	4.1	1.9	4.1	2.3	•	•	•	•	•

Selected Average Balance Sheet ($ in Thousands)

Net Receivables **23**	159	•	8	96	208	453	1943	16955
Inventories **24**	592	•	132	370	959	4863	8420	18716
Net Property, Plant and Equipment **25**	188	•	10	85	509	191	1983	9064
Total Assets **26**	1266	•	263	774	2191	6516	15825	61343
Notes and Loans Payable **27**	382	•	51	135	674	2604	5221	25448
All Other Liabilities **28**	344	•	57	179	518	2550	5843	18022
Net Worth **29**	540	•	155	460	1000	1362	4761	17873

Selected Financial Ratios (Times to 1)

Current Ratio **30**	2.1	•	8.2	3.5	2.0	1.3	1.6	1.5
Quick Ratio **31**	0.6	•	1.0	1.6	0.5	0.1	0.4	0.7
Net Sales to Working Capital **32**	6.0	•	3.3	4.8	5.7	9.6	7.9	12.0
Coverage Ratio **33**	4.7	•	10.8	12.2	2.7	1.4	4.4	2.6
Total Asset Turnover **34**	2.4	•	2.1	3.0	2.1	2.2	2.4	2.5
Inventory Turnover **35**	3.7	•	2.9	4.0	3.6	2.4	3.3	6.5
Receivables Turnover **36**	18.5	•	40.5	•	20.3	21.0	19.0	•
Total Liabilities to Net Worth **37**	1.3	•	0.7	0.7	1.2	3.8	2.3	2.4
Current Assets to Working Capital **38**	1.9	•	1.1	1.4	2.0	3.9	2.7	3.0
Current Liabilities to Working Capital **39**	0.9	•	0.1	0.4	1.0	2.9	1.7	2.0
Working Capital to Net Sales **40**	0.2	•	0.3	0.2	0.2	0.1	0.1	0.1
Inventory to Working Capital **41**	1.3	•	1.0	0.8	1.2	3.5	2.0	1.5
Total Receipts to Cash Flow **42**	10.9	•	7.3	8.1	13.2	20.9	9.0	16.1
Cost of Goods to Cash Flow **43**	7.9	•	5.0	5.2	9.8	17.5	6.6	12.7
Cash Flow to Total Debt **44**	0.4	•	0.7	0.9	0.3	0.1	0.4	0.2

Selected Financial Factors (in Percentages)

Debt Ratio **45**	57.3	•	40.9	40.6	54.4	79.1	69.9	70.9
Return on Total Assets **46**	10.0	•	18.8	18.6	5.5	3.8	12.8	6.2
Return on Equity Before Income Taxes **47**	18.4	•	28.8	28.8	7.6	5.5	32.9	13.2
Return on Equity After Income Taxes **48**	17.3	•	28.2	28.1	6.4	4.3	32.9	10.6
Profit Margin (Before Income Tax) **49**	3.3	•	8.0	5.7	1.6	0.5	4.1	1.5
Profit Margin (After Income Tax) **50**	3.1	•	7.8	5.5	1.4	0.4	4.1	1.2

Table I

Corporations with and without Net Income

FOOD AND BEVERAGE STORES

MONEY AMOUNTS AND SIZE OF ASSETS IN THOUSANDS OF DOLLARS

Item Description for Accounting Period 7/07 Through 6/08		Total	Zero Assets	Under 500	500 to 1,000	1,000 to 5,000	5,000 to 10,000	10,000 to 25,000	25,000 to 50,000	50,000 to 100,000	100,000 to 250,000	250,000 to 500,000	500,000 to 2,500,000	2,500,000 and over
Number of Enterprises	1	74006	11610	52054	5155	4292	471	220	75	45	39	11	23	10
Revenues ($ in Thousands)														
Net Sales	2	472124460	6061996	40200288	12991275	35773570	13339070	16535976	10875433	11968959	23311107	10729241	84494581	205842965
Interest	3	884030	3196	3313	7947	13396	5870	3768	8573	6735	18692	6368	175163	631008
Rents	4	602187	17503	2649	11236	18849	10918	43506	9654	6351	26140	11332	113066	330984
Royalties	5	1872014	0	0	0	0	0	215	1025	50	33452	0	52998	1784274
Other Portfolio Income	6	1231390	97096	93846	46088	166201	7184	62033	82856	4057	133079	3977	69834	465136
Other Receipts	7	5473155	66715	492074	185258	539173	120429	191719	104386	140293	148259	135467	1369088	1980295
Total Receipts	8	482187236	6246506	40792170	13241804	36511189	13483471	16837217	11081927	12126445	23670729	10886385	86274730	211034662
Average Total Receipts	9	6516	538	784	2569	8507	28627	76533	147759	269477	606942	989671	3751075	21103466
Operating Costs/Operating Income (%)														
Cost of Operations	10	74.1	71.8	74.7	75.4	75.4	75.5	77.8	78.0	72.7	73.1	73.5	74.7	73.1
Salaries and Wages	11	9.8	10.2	6.9	7.5	9.3	10.1	8.9	8.3	11.3	11.6	11.5	10.4	10.0
Taxes Paid	12	1.6	1.7	2.1	1.5	1.5	1.4	1.3	1.4	2.2	1.7	1.3	1.5	1.5
Interest Paid	13	0.8	0.9	0.4	0.7	0.5	0.5	0.4	0.5	0.6	0.6	0.7	0.6	1.1
Depreciation	14	1.4	1.1	0.7	0.8	0.9	1.1	1.0	1.1	1.3	1.4	1.5	1.5	1.8
Amortization and Depletion	15	0.1	0.3	0.2	0.3	0.1	0.1	0.1	0.1	0.1	0.1	0.1	0.2	0.1
Pensions and Other Deferred Comp.	16	0.4	0.2	0.1	0.0	0.1	0.1	0.1	0.2	0.4	0.3	0.5	0.4	0.5
Employee Benefits	17	1.2	1.5	0.2	0.2	0.5	0.9	1.0	0.8	1.4	1.3	1.3	1.5	1.5
Advertising	18	0.7	0.6	0.5	0.6	1.1	0.8	0.8	0.9	0.9	0.9	0.8	0.7	0.6
Other Expenses	19	9.2	15.2	11.9	11.2	10.0	7.9	9.0	8.0	8.6	8.7	8.4	8.0	8.9
Officers' Compensation	20	0.5	1.9	2.3	1.7	0.9	1.0	0.5	0.6	0.4	0.3	0.3	0.2	0.0
Operating Margin	21	0.3	•	•	0.1	•	0.5	•	0.1	0.2	•	0.2	0.3	0.8
Operating Margin Before Officers' Comp.	22	0.8	•	2.2	1.8	0.6	1.4	•	0.7	0.6	0.3	0.4	0.5	0.8

Selected Average Balance Sheet ($ in Thousands)

Net Receivables 23	170	0	5	33	187	522	1675	2199	4351	7413	29752	50871	854777
Inventories 24	330	0	34	137	392	1512	3483	6822	13303	21715	54921	221106	1112340
Net Property, Plant and Equipment 25	951	0	34	188	665	2701	5756	14900	26458	70142	145615	581127	4220725
Total Assets 26	2275	0	124	659	1928	6755	15834	35652	71250	150708	378478	1214200	9974892
Notes and Loans Payable 27	632	0	83	402	736	2178	4792	10146	24185	44009	83448	264998	2454248
All Other Liabilities 28	907	0	19	111	471	1691	5829	12156	20362	55605	116039	418063	4656136
Net Worth 29	737	0	22	146	721	2886	5212	13350	26703	51094	178990	531138	2864508

Selected Financial Ratios (Times to 1)

Current Ratio 30	1.0	•	2.8	2.3	1.9	1.6	1.3	1.3	1.2	1.1	1.2	1.3	0.7
Quick Ratio 31	0.4	•	1.3	1.1	0.9	0.7	0.6	0.6	0.5	0.4	0.5	0.5	0.3
Net Sales to Working Capital 32	1278.7	•	18.2	16.6	17.6	23.9	44.2	38.7	59.3	117.3	42.4	36.3	•
Coverage Ratio 33	4.1	•	4.5	3.7	4.8	4.3	3.6	4.8	3.7	3.3	3.4	5.3	4.0
Total Asset Turnover 34	2.8	•	6.2	3.8	4.3	4.2	4.7	4.1	3.7	4.0	2.6	3.0	2.1
Inventory Turnover 35	14.3	•	16.8	13.9	16.0	14.1	16.8	16.6	14.5	20.1	13.1	12.4	13.5
Receivables Turnover 36	38.4	•	141.3	68.8	51.2	55.2	49.2	67.1	53.8	88.5	36.2	66.2	24.7
Total Liabilities to Net Worth 37	2.1	•	4.5	3.5	1.7	1.3	2.0	1.7	1.7	1.9	1.1	1.3	2.5
Current Assets to Working Capital 38	145.8	•	1.5	1.8	2.1	2.6	4.9	4.2	5.8	10.1	5.5	4.1	•
Current Liabilities to Working Capital 39	144.8	•	0.5	0.8	1.1	1.6	3.9	3.2	4.8	9.1	4.5	3.1	•
Working Capital to Net Sales 40	0.0	•	0.1	0.1	0.1	0.0	0.0	0.0	0.0	0.0	0.0	0.0	•
Inventory to Working Capital 41	66.5	•	0.8	0.9	0.9	1.3	2.2	1.9	2.7	5.2	2.5	1.9	•
Total Receipts to Cash Flow 42	11.8	16.9	11.8	10.8	11.9	14.2	14.9	15.3	14.3	14.6	14.1	12.8	10.5
Cost of Goods to Cash Flow 43	8.7	12.1	8.8	8.1	8.9	10.7	11.6	12.0	10.4	10.7	10.4	9.5	7.7
Cash Flow to Total Debt 44	0.4	•	0.6	0.5	0.6	0.5	0.5	0.4	0.4	0.4	0.3	0.4	0.3

Selected Financial Factors (in Percentages)

Debt Ratio 45	67.6	•	81.9	77.9	62.6	57.3	67.1	62.6	62.5	66.1	52.7	56.3	71.3
Return on Total Assets 46	8.9	•	11.3	10.2	9.5	8.4	6.3	10.4	7.8	8.5	5.9	8.9	9.0
Return on Equity Before Income Taxes 47	20.8	•	48.4	33.5	20.1	15.1	13.9	22.0	15.1	17.6	8.9	16.5	23.6
Return on Equity After Income Taxes 48	15.5	•	47.0	32.4	19.4	13.6	12.1	17.3	13.4	14.8	6.9	11.5	16.4
Profit Margin (Before Income Tax) 49	2.4	•	1.4	1.9	1.7	1.5	1.0	2.0	1.5	1.5	1.6	2.4	3.3
Profit Margin (After Income Tax) 50	1.8	•	1.4	1.9	1.7	1.4	0.8	1.6	1.3	1.3	1.3	1.7	2.3

Table II
Corporations with Net Income

FOOD AND BEVERAGE STORES

MONEY AMOUNTS AND SIZE OF ASSETS IN THOUSANDS OF DOLLARS

Item Description for Accounting Period 7/07 Through 6/08	Total	Zero Assets	Under 500	500 to 1,000	1,000 to 5,000	5,000 to 10,000	10,000 to 25,000	25,000 to 50,000	50,000 to 100,000	100,000 to 250,000	250,000 to 500,000	500,000 to 2,500,000	2,500,000 and over
Number of Enterprises 1	43831	4471	32367	3649	2664	363	155	61	35	29	8	19	10
Revenues ($ in Thousands)													
Net Sales 2	414039100	1742023	31564039	10821516	25879893	10517507	12515450	8785874	9540777	18254671	8526293	70048093	205842965
Interest 3	856021	1785	2211	4161	10571	5032	3069	8275	6664	15569	5489	162188	631008
Rents 4	520317	2009	75	8460	9166	4692	8803	9139	5618	17913	11332	112126	330984
Royalties 5	1865193	0	0	0	0	0	215	0	50	27656	0	52998	1784274
Other Portfolio Income 6	1138836	70027	93836	41402	122389	6707	52150	82335	3291	128868	3946	68746	465136
Other Receipts 7	4846337	42915	382965	157888	367334	104971	142710	86192	126608	99279	101455	1253726	1980295
Total Receipts 8	423265804	1858759	32043126	11033427	26389353	10638909	12722397	8971815	9683008	18543956	8648515	71697877	211034662
Average Total Receipts 9	9657	416	990	3024	9906	29308	82080	147079	276657	639447	1081064	3773572	21103466
Operating Costs/Operating Income (%)													
Cost of Operations 10	74.1	64.9	76.4	75.4	78.1	75.8	77.4	76.7	72.2	73.5	72.9	73.8	73.1
Salaries and Wages 11	9.7	10.5	6.1	7.4	7.5	9.7	9.0	8.9	11.9	11.0	12.0	10.6	10.0
Taxes Paid 12	1.5	2.3	2.0	1.4	1.2	1.3	1.3	1.5	1.6	1.7	1.3	1.6	1.5
Interest Paid 13	0.8	0.6	0.3	0.7	0.4	0.3	0.3	0.4	0.5	0.6	0.5	0.6	1.1
Depreciation 14	1.4	1.0	0.4	0.7	0.7	1.0	0.7	1.1	1.3	1.4	1.6	1.5	1.8
Amortization and Depletion 15	0.1	0.5	0.1	0.2	0.0	0.1	0.1	0.1	0.1	0.1	0.1	0.1	0.1
Pensions and Other Deferred Comp. 16	0.4	0.1	0.1	0.0	0.1	0.1	0.1	0.2	0.5	0.3	0.4	0.4	0.5
Employee Benefits 17	1.3	0.1	0.2	0.1	0.5	1.0	0.9	0.8	1.6	1.2	1.4	1.7	1.5
Advertising 18	0.7	0.9	0.5	0.4	0.9	0.9	0.7	0.8	0.9	0.8	0.8	0.7	0.6
Other Expenses 19	8.7	15.2	10.2	10.7	8.0	7.5	8.3	8.2	8.5	8.3	7.6	7.7	8.9
Officers' Compensation 20	0.4	3.5	2.0	1.8	0.9	1.1	0.5	0.6	0.4	0.3	0.3	0.2	0.0
Operating Margin 21	0.9	0.3	1.8	1.2	1.7	1.3	0.6	0.6	0.6	0.7	1.2	0.8	0.8
Operating Margin Before Officers' Comp. 22	1.3	3.9	3.8	2.9	2.6	2.3	1.1	1.3	1.0	1.0	1.5	1.0	0.8

Selected Average Balance Sheet ($ in Thousands)

Net Receivables 23	259	0	8	29	127	612	1735	1939	4352	8049	21171	49044	854777
Inventories 24	467	0	39	157	446	1589	3359	7148	12745	22533	54894	210830	1158073
Net Property, Plant and Equipment 25	1458	0	31	196	626	1983	4749	14636	26919	73161	178170	603693	4220725
Total Assets 26	3472	0	130	670	1928	6480	16312	35207	73454	149623	373776	1249135	9974892
Notes and Loans Payable 27	876	0	64	302	596	1260	3458	9297	20966	41032	86140	258906	2454248
All Other Liabilities 28	1408	0	17	106	484	1519	5611	10622	21120	54218	120685	397453	4656136
Net Worth 29	1189	0	49	262	848	3702	7242	15289	31369	54373	166951	592776	2864508

Selected Financial Ratios (Times to 1)

Current Ratio 30	1.0	•	3.6	2.9	2.0	2.0	1.5	1.5	1.2	1.1	1.2	1.3	0.7
Quick Ratio 31	0.4	•	1.7	1.4	1.0	1.0	0.7	0.7	0.5	0.5	0.4	0.6	0.3
Net Sales to Working Capital 32	•	•	16.9	16.4	18.3	16.7	27.7	26.3	53.8	98.2	56.3	36.2	•
Coverage Ratio 33	5.0	12.7	11.7	5.5	10.9	8.5	9.1	7.8	5.4	5.0	6.2	6.2	4.0
Total Asset Turnover 34	2.7	•	7.5	4.4	5.0	4.5	5.0	4.1	3.7	4.2	2.9	3.0	2.1
Inventory Turnover 35	15.0	•	19.2	14.2	17.0	13.8	18.6	15.5	15.4	20.5	14.2	12.9	13.0
Receivables Turnover 36	40.1	•	146.1	92.8	71.3	49.2	50.7	72.5	•	84.0	61.8	71.6	•
Total Liabilities to Net Worth 37	1.9	•	1.7	1.6	1.3	0.8	1.3	1.3	1.3	1.8	1.2	1.1	2.5
Current Assets to Working Capital 38	•	•	1.4	1.5	2.0	2.0	3.0	2.9	5.3	8.4	6.8	4.1	•
Current Liabilities to Working Capital 39	•	•	0.4	0.5	1.0	1.0	2.0	1.9	4.3	7.4	5.8	3.1	•
Working Capital to Net Sales 40	•	•	0.1	0.1	0.1	0.1	0.0	0.0	0.0	0.0	0.0	0.0	•
Inventory to Working Capital 41	•	•	0.7	0.8	1.0	0.9	1.3	1.4	2.5	4.0	3.2	1.8	•
Total Receipts to Cash Flow 42	11.1	6.6	10.5	10.0	11.0	13.4	13.0	13.6	13.3	13.5	13.7	11.8	10.5
Cost of Goods to Cash Flow 43	8.2	4.3	8.0	7.5	8.6	10.2	10.1	10.5	9.6	9.9	10.0	8.7	7.7
Cash Flow to Total Debt 44	0.4	•	1.1	0.7	0.8	0.8	0.7	0.5	0.5	0.5	0.4	0.5	0.3

Selected Financial Factors (in Percentages)

Debt Ratio 45	65.8	•	62.6	60.9	56.0	42.9	55.6	56.6	57.3	63.7	55.3	52.5	71.3
Return on Total Assets 46	10.7	•	27.4	16.4	20.2	12.2	12.4	12.9	9.5	11.7	9.0	11.2	9.0
Return on Equity Before Income Taxes 47	25.0	•	67.0	34.3	41.7	18.9	24.9	25.9	18.0	25.8	16.9	19.9	23.6
Return on Equity After Income Taxes 48	19.4	•	66.0	33.4	40.7	17.7	23.0	20.9	16.1	22.4	14.0	14.4	16.4
Profit Margin (Before Income Tax) 49	3.1	7.0	3.3	3.0	3.6	2.4	2.2	2.8	2.1	2.2	2.7	3.2	3.3
Profit Margin (After Income Tax) 50	2.4	7.0	3.3	3.0	3.5	2.3	2.1	2.2	1.9	1.9	2.2	2.3	2.3

Table I

Corporations with and without Net Income

BEER, WINE, AND LIQUOR STORES

MONEY AMOUNTS AND SIZE OF ASSETS IN THOUSANDS OF DOLLARS

Item Description for Accounting Period 7/07 Through 6/08	Total	Zero Assets	Under 500	500 to 1,000	1,000 to 5,000	5,000 to 10,000	10,000 to 25,000	25,000 to 50,000	50,000 to 100,000	100,000 to 250,000	250,000 to 500,000	500,000 to 2,500,000	2,500,000 and over
Number of Enterprises 1	20889	802	16848	2418	753	44	8	10	6	0	0	0	0
Revenues ($ in Thousands)													
Net Sales 2	25319753	112038	13047980	5017764	3784466	625457	155685	795470	1780894	0	0	0	0
Interest 3	6214	0	1375	757	3417	217	113	0	335	0	0	0	0
Rents 4	721	0	0	4	0	0	0	0	717	0	0	0	0
Royalties 5	0	0	0	0	0	0	0	0	0	0	0	0	0
Other Portfolio Income 6	39963	33421	4664	725	348	0	0	40	764	0	0	0	0
Other Receipts 7	373493	74	266813	28362	22187	1961	31868	4810	17418	0	0	0	•
Total Receipts 8	25740144	145533	13320832	5047612	3810418	627635	187666	800320	1800128	0	0	0	•
Average Total Receipts 9	1232	181	791	2088	5060	14264	23458	80032	300021	•	•	•	•
Operating Costs/Operating Income (%)													
Cost of Operations 10	78.4	91.1	77.1	78.6	81.3	88.4	85.2	76.9	77.2	•	•	•	•
Salaries and Wages 11	5.5	3.8	5.7	4.5	5.1	3.9	8.1	7.1	7.7	•	•	•	•
Taxes Paid 12	2.2	11.9	2.9	1.9	0.9	0.4	1.6	1.6	1.4	•	•	•	•
Interest Paid 13	0.8	4.4	0.7	0.9	0.6	0.3	3.3	0.7	1.2	•	•	•	•
Depreciation 14	0.5	0.0	0.6	0.3	0.3	0.2	0.6	0.4	1.1	•	•	•	•
Amortization and Depletion 15	0.3	•	0.3	0.5	0.2	0.1	0.0	0.1	0.1	•	•	•	•
Pensions and Other Deferred Comp. 16	0.1	•	0.1	0.1	0.1	0.2	0.0	0.0	0.1	•	•	•	•
Employee Benefits 17	0.2	•	0.2	0.1	0.3	0.2	0.1	0.1	0.9	•	•	•	•
Advertising 18	0.5	•	0.3	0.8	0.5	0.2	1.9	0.7	1.3	•	•	•	•
Other Expenses 19	9.3	6.9	10.2	9.0	6.5	3.1	18.2	9.3	12.1	•	•	•	•
Officers' Compensation 20	2.8	2.0	3.4	3.0	2.1	0.7	2.8	1.8	0.6	•	•	•	•
Operating Margin 21	•	•	•	0.5	2.3	2.4	•	1.1	•	•	•	•	•
Operating Margin Before Officers' Comp. 22	2.1	1.9	•	3.5	4.4	3.1	•	2.9	•	•	•	•	•

Selected Average Balance Sheet ($ in Thousands)

Net Receivables 23	14	0	1	6	100	2563	1487	1060	7192
Inventories 24	149	0	81	244	889	2114	1814	15313	39179
Net Property, Plant and Equipment 25	55	0	31	65	136	960	7851	2869	39949
Total Assets 26	370	0	185	671	1831	7709	17771	31019	136370
Notes and Loans Payable 27	187	0	110	349	843	3235	6811	8079	49438
All Other Liabilities 28	70	0	30	110	301	1779	4114	14130	36151
Net Worth 29	114	0	46	212	687	2694	6847	8810	50781

Selected Financial Ratios (Times to 1)

Current Ratio 30	2.4	•	3.1	3.4	2.4	1.7	0.8	1.4	1.5
Quick Ratio 31	0.7	•	0.8	1.0	0.6	1.1	0.2	0.1	0.3
Net Sales to Working Capital 32	8.6	•	9.5	7.5	6.0	5.3	•	11.5	15.1
Coverage Ratio 33	2.3	3.2	1.9	2.3	6.4	11.5	0.6	3.4	•
Total Asset Turnover 34	3.3	•	4.2	3.1	2.7	1.8	1.1	2.6	2.2
Inventory Turnover 35	6.4	•	7.4	6.7	4.6	5.9	9.1	4.0	5.8
Receivables Turnover 36	91.6	•	499.3	212.6	61.1	6.0	18.8	85.1	41.6
Total Liabilities to Net Worth 37	2.3	•	3.0	2.2	1.7	1.9	1.6	2.5	1.7
Current Assets to Working Capital 38	1.7	•	1.5	1.4	1.7	2.5	•	3.8	2.8
Current Liabilities to Working Capital 39	0.7	•	0.5	0.4	0.7	1.5	•	2.8	1.8
Working Capital to Net Sales 40	0.1	•	0.1	0.1	0.2	0.2	•	0.1	0.1
Inventory to Working Capital 41	1.2	•	1.0	1.0	1.2	0.9	•	2.7	2.1
Total Receipts to Cash Flow 42	15.3	•	15.1	15.0	14.7	19.3	6.7	14.0	19.2
Cost of Goods to Cash Flow 43	12.0	•	11.6	11.8	12.0	17.1	5.8	10.8	14.8
Cash Flow to Total Debt 44	0.3	•	0.4	0.3	0.3	0.1	0.3	0.3	0.2

Selected Financial Factors (in Percentages)

Debt Ratio 45	69.3	•	75.1	68.3	62.5	65.1	61.5	71.6	62.8
Return on Total Assets 46	5.7	•	5.5	6.1	9.7	5.6	2.2		6.4
Return on Equity Before Income Taxes 47	10.3	•	10.6	10.7	21.9	14.7	•		15.9
Return on Equity After Income Taxes 48	9.0	•	9.7	10.1	20.2	13.9	•		15.9
Profit Margin (Before Income Tax) 49	1.0	9.7	0.6	1.1	3.0	2.8	•	•	1.8
Profit Margin (After Income Tax) 50	0.8	3.4	0.6	1.0	2.8	2.6	•	•	1.8

Table II

Corporations with Net Income

BEER, WINE, AND LIQUOR STORES

MONEY AMOUNTS AND SIZE OF ASSETS IN THOUSANDS OF DOLLARS

Item Description for Accounting Period 7/07 Through 6/08	Total	Zero Assets	Under 500	500 to 1,000	1,000 to 5,000	5,000 to 10,000	10,000 to 25,000	25,000 to 50,000	50,000 to 100,000	100,000 to 250,000	250,000 to 500,000	500,000 to 2,500,000	2,500,000 and over
Number of Enterprises 1	13065	54	11031	1430	490	44	3	10	3	0	0	0	0

Revenues ($ in Thousands)

	Total	Zero Assets	Under 500	500 to 1,000	1,000 to 5,000	5,000 to 10,000	10,000 to 25,000	25,000 to 50,000	50,000 to 100,000	100,000 to 250,000	250,000 to 500,000	500,000 to 2,500,000	2,500,000 and over
Net Sales 2	17443606	30401	8387818	3619382	2947566	625457	62483	795470	975028	0	0	0	0
Interest 3	4042	0	560	678	2159	217	113	0	315	0	0	0	0
Rents 4	721	0	0	4	0	0	0	0	717	0	0	0	0
Royalties 5	0	0	0	0	0	0	0	0	0	0	0	0	0
Other Portfolio Income 6	25723	22762	1092	725	348	0	0	40	755	0	0	0	0
Other Receipts 7	300888	74	234353	8310	12265	1961	31757	4810	7359	0	0	0	0
Total Receipts 8	17774980	53237	8623823	3629099	2962338	627635	94353	800320	984174	0	0	0	0
Average Total Receipts 9	1361	986	782	2538	6046	14264	31451	80032	328058	•	•	•	•

Operating Costs/Operating Income (%)

	Total	Zero Assets	Under 500	500 to 1,000	1,000 to 5,000	5,000 to 10,000	10,000 to 25,000	25,000 to 50,000	50,000 to 100,000	100,000 to 250,000	250,000 to 500,000	500,000 to 2,500,000	2,500,000 and over
Cost of Operations 10	78.5	82.3	77.5	76.5	81.8	88.4	85.5	76.9	78.3	•	•	•	•
Salaries and Wages 11	5.0	9.7	4.8	4.6	4.5	3.9	10.5	7.1	8.1	•	•	•	•
Taxes Paid 12	1.5	2.2	2.2	0.8	0.7	0.4	2.2	1.6	1.3	•	•	•	•
Interest Paid 13	0.5	•	0.4	0.7	0.4	0.3	1.6	0.7	0.5	•	•	•	•
Depreciation 14	0.4	0.0	0.5	0.2	0.1	0.2	0.2	0.4	1.2	•	•	•	•
Amortization and Depletion 15	0.3	•	0.3	0.5	0.1	0.1	0.0	0.1	0.1	•	•	•	•
Pensions and Other Deferred Comp. 16	0.1	•	0.0	0.1	0.2	0.2	•	0.0	0.1	•	•	•	•
Employee Benefits 17	0.3	•	0.3	0.1	0.3	0.2	0.0	0.1	0.7	•	•	•	•
Advertising 18	0.5	•	0.3	1.0	0.6	0.2	3.0	0.7	0.7	•	•	•	•
Other Expenses 19	8.6	11.6	9.5	9.1	6.1	3.1	31.2	9.3	7.7	•	•	•	•
Officers' Compensation 20	2.9	•	3.7	3.1	1.6	0.7	7.0	1.8	0.4	•	•	•	•
Operating Margin 21	1.6	•	0.5	3.3	3.6	2.4	•	1.1	0.9	•	•	•	•
Operating Margin Before Officers' Comp. 22	4.4	•	4.2	6.4	5.2	3.1	•	2.9	1.3	•	•	•	•

Selected Average Balance Sheet ($ in Thousands)

Net Receivables 23	14	0	1	2	63	2563	3133	1060	3778
Inventories 24	184	0	97	302	1047	2114	2538	15313	48832
Net Property, Plant and Equipment 25	49	0	29	19	63	960	129	2869	62822
Total Assets 26	396	0	201	700	1728	7709	19122	31019	135831
Notes and Loans Payable 27	161	0	88	283	740	3235	7058	8079	40077
All Other Liabilities 28	80	0	30	122	355	1779	9175	14130	36522
Net Worth 29	156	0	83	295	634	2694	2888	8810	59232

Selected Financial Ratios (Times to 1)

Current Ratio 30	2.6	●	4.4	3.4	2.0	1.7	1.2	1.4	1.6
Quick Ratio 31	0.8	●	1.3	1.2	0.5	1.1	0.3	0.1	0.2
Net Sales to Working Capital 32	7.6	●	7.0	7.7	7.8	5.3	8.5	11.5	14.7
Coverage Ratio 33	8.1	●	9.0	6.4	10.5	11.5	7.2	3.4	5.0
Total Asset Turnover 34	3.4	●	3.8	3.6	3.5	1.8	1.1	2.6	2.4
Inventory Turnover 35	5.7	●	6.1	6.4	4.7	5.9	7.0	4.0	5.2
Receivables Turnover 36	85.5	●	774.6	●	74.9	6.0	8.9	85.1	●
Total Liabilities to Net Worth 37	1.5	●	1.4	1.4	1.7	1.9	5.6	2.5	1.3
Current Assets to Working Capital 38	1.6	●	1.3	1.4	2.0	2.5	7.4	3.8	2.7
Current Liabilities to Working Capital 39	0.6	●	0.3	0.4	1.0	1.5	6.4	2.8	1.7
Working Capital to Net Sales 40	0.1	●	0.1	0.1	0.1	0.2	0.1	0.1	0.1
Inventory to Working Capital 41	1.1	●	0.9	0.9	1.4	0.9	1.1	2.7	2.2
Total Receipts to Cash Flow 42	12.1	74.5	11.6	11.1	12.8	19.3	2.6	14.0	18.6
Cost of Goods to Cash Flow 43	9.5	61.3	9.0	8.5	10.4	17.1	2.2	10.8	14.6
Cash Flow to Total Debt 44	0.5	●	0.6	0.6	0.4	0.1	0.5	0.3	0.2

Selected Financial Factors (in Percentages)

Debt Ratio 45	60.6	●	58.8	57.9	63.3	65.1	84.9	71.6	56.4
Return on Total Assets 46	13.2	●	14.1	15.0	15.7	5.6	12.4	6.4	5.6
Return on Equity Before Income Taxes 47	29.5	●	30.4	30.1	38.6	14.7	70.8	15.9	10.3
Return on Equity After Income Taxes 48	28.0	●	29.6	29.3	35.8	13.9	46.7	15.9	9.2
Profit Margin (Before Income Tax) 49	3.4	69.3	3.3	3.5	4.1	2.8	9.8	1.8	1.9
Profit Margin (After Income Tax) 50	3.3	45.8	3.2	3.4	3.8	2.6	6.5	1.8	1.7

Table I
Corporations with and without Net Income

HEALTH AND PERSONAL CARE STORES

MONEY AMOUNTS AND SIZE OF ASSETS IN THOUSANDS OF DOLLARS

Item Description for Accounting Period 7/07 Through 6/08	Total	Zero Assets	Under 500	500 to 1,000	1,000 to 5,000	5,000 to 10,000	10,000 to 25,000	25,000 to 50,000	50,000 to 100,000	100,000 to 250,000	250,000 to 500,000	500,000 to 2,500,000	2,500,000 and over
Number of Enterprises 1	39767	5010	27457	3938	3103	144	49	24	10	16	8	4	6
Revenues ($ in Thousands)													
Net Sales 2	268148005	1791698	24606019	13618140	19010377	2859803	1377263	1493391	1691659	6769708	3950634	7537861	183441451
Interest 3	292738	336	3358	1988	9706	3969	4690	1949	509	5261	4282	7706	248984
Rents 4	122850	21	16	3681	3714	3876	273	1889	925	1413	2938	3875	100229
Royalties 5	67500	0	0	0	0	0	0	0	0	11129	1864	27915	26592
Other Portfolio Income 6	251568	7373	1920	1976	64558	45070	489	167	219	33266	5034	0	91494
Other Receipts 7	3887074	81246	22430	57204	123476	9428	44359	45293	3791	65769	45552	58806	3329722
Total Receipts 8	272769735	1880674	24633743	13682989	19211831	2922146	1427074	1542689	1697103	6886546	4010304	7636163	187238472
Average Total Receipts 9	6859	375	897	3475	6191	20293	29124	64279	169710	430409	501288	1909041	31206412
Operating Costs/Operating Income (%)													
Cost of Operations 10	73.4	72.3	68.8	71.6	73.3	73.0	57.4	60.2	67.8	68.7	57.5	66.4	75.3
Salaries and Wages 11	10.1	6.4	6.8	9.0	9.5	11.2	22.7	16.3	14.3	12.9	9.2	13.5	10.3
Taxes Paid 12	1.2	1.2	1.6	1.5	1.3	1.2	1.3	2.6	1.8	1.4	2.2	1.7	1.0
Interest Paid 13	0.9	0.4	0.4	0.2	0.6	0.6	0.6	2.2	3.3	1.2	2.9	1.8	0.9
Depreciation 14	0.9	0.7	0.4	0.4	0.6	1.1	0.8	1.1	0.9	1.0	2.3	1.3	1.0
Amortization and Depletion 15	0.3	0.0	0.1	0.0	0.2	0.2	0.0	0.2	0.3	0.3	1.1	0.8	0.4
Pensions and Other Deferred Comp. 16	0.3	0.4	0.2	0.6	0.5	0.2	0.6	0.2	0.3	0.1	0.2	0.3	0.2
Employee Benefits 17	0.6	0.4	0.4	0.5	0.5	1.0	1.7	0.6	1.4	1.4	1.0	1.2	0.5
Advertising 18	0.9	0.8	1.0	0.9	0.6	2.2	1.2	1.6	1.1	1.1	1.5	1.0	0.8
Other Expenses 19	8.3	15.4	10.9	8.5	7.2	9.3	13.2	14.3	9.8	9.9	20.0	10.8	7.5
Officers' Compensation 20	1.2	4.3	5.8	4.8	3.3	1.8	1.5	0.8	0.9	0.8	0.7	0.6	0.1
Operating Margin 21	2.0	•	3.7	1.8	2.5	•	•	•	•	1.2	1.2	0.6	2.0
Operating Margin Before Officers' Comp. 22	3.2	2.0	9.5	6.7	5.8	•	0.5	0.8	•	2.0	1.9	1.3	2.1

Selected Average Balance Sheet ($ in Thousands)

Net Receivables 23	482	0	18	116	358	1864	3183	6896	13394	23624	22722	135856	2546504
Inventories 24	642	0	65	226	393	1662	3196	7540	18916	46202	62888	200353	3139763
Net Property, Plant and Equipment 25	497	0	19	93	239	830	1102	6080	14254	28488	89321	251674	2584041
Total Assets 26	3426	0	145	706	1759	6440	13374	33346	78383	158777	397535	1346961	18290256
Notes and Loans Payable 27	909	0	71	169	575	2307	1669	12102	54201	60359	128165	511705	4408744
All Other Liabilities 28	1069	0	46	177	424	2212	22942	14985	31140	56181	99235	365010	5663308
Net Worth 29	1448	0	28	360	760	1921	-11238	6259	-6958	42237	170136	470246	8218203

Selected Financial Ratios (Times to 1)

Current Ratio 30	1.3	•	2.1	2.6	1.7	2.2	0.4	1.1	1.2	1.7	1.7	2.3	1.2
Quick Ratio 31	0.6	•	0.9	1.4	1.0	1.3	0.2	0.6	0.5	0.6	0.5	0.6	0.5
Net Sales to Working Capital 32	20.2	•	15.8	10.7	10.8	9.1	•	29.3	27.8	11.3	11.1	5.8	28.9
Coverage Ratio 33	5.4	7.4	10.8	10.7	1.4	6.9	5.1	2.5	0.5	3.5	1.9	2.1	5.7
Total Asset Turnover 34	2.0	•	6.2	4.9	3.1	3.5	2.1	1.9	2.2	2.7	1.2	1.4	1.7
Inventory Turnover 35	7.7	•	9.5	11.0	8.7	11.4	5.1	5.0	6.1	6.3	4.5	6.2	7.3
Receivables Turnover 36	16.1	•	48.4	35.2	10.7	16.9	8.7	8.5	10.1	16.8	22.8	17.0	14.3
Total Liabilities to Net Worth 37	1.4	•	4.1	1.0	2.4	1.3	•	4.3	•	2.8	1.3	1.9	1.2
Current Assets to Working Capital 38	4.1	•	1.9	1.6	2.4	1.8	•	8.5	6.4	2.4	2.4	1.8	6.2
Current Liabilities to Working Capital 39	3.1	•	0.9	0.6	1.4	0.8	•	7.5	5.4	1.4	1.4	0.8	5.2
Working Capital to Net Sales 40	0.0	•	0.1	0.1	0.1	0.1	•	0.0	0.0	0.1	0.1	0.2	0.0
Inventory to Working Capital 41	2.0	•	1.1	0.7	0.9	0.6	•	3.2	2.7	1.2	1.5	0.7	3.1
Total Receipts to Cash Flow 42	11.3	7.2	9.5	12.1	14.2	11.7	7.3	7.7	17.5	11.8	6.7	12.4	11.7
Cost of Goods to Cash Flow 43	8.3	5.2	6.5	8.6	10.4	8.6	4.2	4.6	11.9	8.1	3.8	8.2	8.8
Cash Flow to Total Debt 44	0.3	•	0.8	0.8	0.3	0.5	0.2	0.3	0.1	0.3	0.3	0.2	0.3

Selected Financial Factors (in Percentages)

Debt Ratio 45	57.7	•	80.6	49.0	70.2	56.8	184.0	81.2	108.9	73.4	57.2	65.1	55.1
Return on Total Assets 46	9.0	•	25.9	12.6	2.7	14.5	6.9	10.1	3.6	10.6	6.9	5.2	8.3
Return on Equity Before Income Taxes 47	17.4	•	121.0	22.3	2.6	28.6	•	32.2	38.8	28.4	7.7	7.7	15.3
Return on Equity After Income Taxes 48	12.2	•	119.1	21.2	•	26.1	•	29.2	40.7	20.6	5.5	5.8	9.7
Profit Margin (Before Income Tax) 49	3.7	2.6	3.8	2.3	2.6	3.6	2.6	3.2	•	2.8	2.6	1.9	4.1
Profit Margin (After Income Tax) 50	2.6	2.3	3.7	2.2	2.4	3.2	•	2.9	•	2.1	1.9	1.4	2.6

Table II

Corporations with Net Income

HEALTH AND PERSONAL CARE STORES

MONEY AMOUNTS AND SIZE OF ASSETS IN THOUSANDS OF DOLLARS

Item Description for Accounting Period 7/07 Through 6/08	Total	Zero Assets	Under 500	500 to 1,000	1,000 to 5,000	5,000 to 10,000	10,000 to 25,000	25,000 to 50,000	50,000 to 100,000	100,000 to 250,000	250,000 to 500,000	500,000 to 2,500,000	2,500,000 and over
Number of Enterprises 1	26961	2894	18031	3199	2638	120	35	14	5	12	5	•	•
Revenues ($ in Thousands)													
Net Sales 2	230128706	1427989	19587830	11830739	17108809	2643520	1145865	902321	690477	5597539	3270137	•	•
Interest 3	276624	336	1740	1905	7891	2547	1102	1238	242	3807	3403	•	•
Rents 4	80983	21	16	3586	3706	3876	273	1889	0	1413	2938	•	•
Royalties 5	57068	0	0	0	0	0	0	0	0	697	1864	•	•
Other Portfolio Income 6	241316	7373	484	1525	64558	45032	441	167	53	26741	3447	•	•
Other Receipts 7	3156858	75460	19439	43924	101977	7281	43028	44505	2576	61479	45549	•	•
Total Receipts 8	233941555	1511179	19609509	11881679	17286941	2702256	1190709	950120	693348	5691676	3327338	•	•
Average Total Receipts 9	8677	522	1088	3714	6553	22519	34020	67866	138670	474306	665468	•	•
Operating Costs/Operating Income (%)													
Cost of Operations 10	73.4	71.2	70.2	71.3	73.1	72.0	56.8	63.6	66.0	69.0	55.1	•	•
Salaries and Wages 11	9.7	5.5	6.1	9.2	9.7	10.4	23.8	16.1	12.6	12.4	10.0	•	•
Taxes Paid 12	1.1	1.3	1.4	1.5	1.3	1.2	1.2	2.3	1.5	1.4	2.3	•	•
Interest Paid 13	0.7	0.5	0.3	0.2	0.6	0.5	0.6	0.7	1.1	1.1	1.7	•	•
Depreciation 14	0.9	0.5	0.3	0.4	0.6	1.0	0.8	0.6	1.3	0.8	2.5	•	•
Amortization and Depletion 15	0.3	0.0	0.1	0.1	0.2	0.2	0.0	0.1	0.4	0.2	0.3	•	•
Pensions and Other Deferred Comp. 16	0.3	0.5	0.2	0.6	0.5	0.3	0.6	0.4	0.3	0.2	0.3	•	•
Employee Benefits 17	0.5	0.3	0.3	0.5	0.5	1.0	1.7	0.4	1.6	1.4	1.1	•	•
Advertising 18	0.8	0.8	0.8	1.0	0.4	2.1	0.5	0.5	1.3	1.2	1.7	•	•
Other Expenses 19	8.0	14.4	9.2	8.1	6.7	7.3	11.1	10.6	8.6	9.2	21.9	•	•
Officers' Compensation 20	1.1	4.4	5.3	4.7	2.9	1.7	1.6	1.0	0.8	0.8	0.6	•	•
Operating Margin 21	3.2	0.7	5.8	2.6	3.5	2.2	1.1	3.6	4.4	2.2	2.5	•	•
Operating Margin Before Officers' Comp. 22	4.2	5.0	11.1	7.3	6.4	4.0	2.7	4.6	5.3	3.0	3.1	•	•

Selected Average Balance Sheet ($ in Thousands)

Net Receivables 23	616	0	21	107	336	1992	3308	6313	14415	22629	14257	•
Inventories 24	826	0	72	240	371	1735	1998	5834	19998	52422	99612	•
Net Property, Plant and Equipment 25	595	0	12	65	269	659	1259	4159	15772	30447	130980	•
Total Assets 26	4386	0	160	714	1766	6368	13273	34283	82960	165093	403061	•
Notes and Loans Payable 27	987	0	45	121	536	1899	2031	9097	24730	58473	77234	•
All Other Liabilities 28	1303	0	43	158	444	2229	6459	7635	20840	63007	130515	•
Net Worth 29	2096	0	72	435	786	2241	4783	17552	37390	43613	195312	•

Selected Financial Ratios (Times to 1)

Current Ratio 30	1.3	•	2.7	3.3	2.1	2.0	1.8	1.6	1.6	1.7	1.7	•
Quick Ratio 31	0.6	•	1.2	1.7	1.2	1.2	1.1	0.8	0.9	0.6	0.3	•
Net Sales to Working Capital 32	20.0	•	13.3	9.4	10.1	10.1	7.5	9.8	10.4	11.8	11.7	•
Coverage Ratio 33	7.9	15.3	21.3	18.1	8.7	9.9	8.8	14.4	5.3	4.5	3.4	•
Total Asset Turnover 34	1.9	•	6.8	5.2	3.7	3.5	2.5	1.9	1.7	2.8	1.6	•
Inventory Turnover 35	7.6	•	10.6	11.0	12.8	9.1	9.3	7.0	4.6	6.1	3.6	•
Receivables Turnover 36	15.5	•	50.3	42.6	19.2	11.1	12.9	•	5.7	17.7	•	•
Total Liabilities to Net Worth 37	1.1	•	1.2	0.6	1.2	1.8	1.8	1.0	1.2	2.8	1.1	•
Current Assets to Working Capital 38	4.0	•	1.6	1.4	1.9	2.0	2.2	2.6	2.6	2.5	2.3	•
Current Liabilities to Working Capital 39	3.0	•	0.6	0.4	0.9	1.0	1.2	1.6	1.6	1.5	1.3	•
Working Capital to Net Sales 40	0.1	•	0.1	0.1	0.1	0.1	0.1	0.1	0.1	0.1	0.1	•
Inventory to Working Capital 41	1.9	•	0.9	0.7	0.6	0.7	0.7	0.9	1.0	1.3	1.8	•
Total Receipts to Cash Flow 42	10.2	5.9	8.6	11.9	11.0	10.6	7.1	6.1	8.5	10.8	5.8	•
Cost of Goods to Cash Flow 43	7.5	4.2	6.0	8.5	8.0	7.7	4.0	3.9	5.6	7.5	3.2	•
Cash Flow to Total Debt 44	0.4	1.4	1.1	0.6	0.5	0.5	0.6	0.4	0.4	0.5	•	•

Selected Financial Factors (in Percentages)

Debt Ratio 45	52.2	•	55.1	39.1	55.5	64.8	64.0	48.8	54.9	73.6	51.5	•
Return on Total Assets 46	10.7	•	42.0	16.7	19.0	17.1	14.0	17.9	9.9	14.1	9.5	•
Return on Equity Before Income Taxes 47	19.6	•	89.0	25.9	37.7	43.8	34.4	32.6	17.9	41.5	13.9	•
Return on Equity After Income Taxes 48	14.3	•	87.9	24.7	34.8	37.7	32.9	30.7	17.2	31.4	10.8	•
Profit Margin (Before Income Tax) 49	4.8	6.5	5.9	3.0	4.6	4.5	5.0	8.9	4.8	3.9	4.1	•
Profit Margin (After Income Tax) 50	3.5	6.0	5.8	2.9	4.2	3.8	4.8	8.4	4.7	2.9	3.2	•

224

Table I

Corporations with and without Net Income

GASOLINE STATIONS

MONEY AMOUNTS AND SIZE OF ASSETS IN THOUSANDS OF DOLLARS

Item Description for Accounting Period 7/07 Through 6/08		Total	Zero Assets	Under 500	500 to 1,000	1,000 to 5,000	5,000 to 10,000	10,000 to 25,000	25,000 to 50,000	50,000 to 100,000	100,000 to 250,000	250,000 to 500,000	500,000 to 2,500,000	2,500,000 and over
Number of Enterprises	1	41505	2291	26942	6206	5278	468	174	75	37	19	4	9	3
Revenues ($ in Thousands)														
Net Sales	2	320202097	1642811	59830872	28666191	57563330	17722937	18451622	20007749	14468195	13027144	10596911	46079423	32144913
Interest	3	104916	124	3885	3024	6765	4613	3287	8062	757	5070	2453	31372	35502
Rents	4	154331	1357	13945	11040	11157	13692	3824	8463	17415	3725	2816	4645	62252
Royalties	5	22665	0	0	13	0	0	0	2	0	2280	0	7716	12654
Other Portfolio Income	6	523821	25527	97648	65587	49520	25108	10097	25732	13637	6784	8125	7149	188912
Other Receipts	7	2007273	28465	789922	138395	208413	29677	166081	63710	82208	78478	126685	220538	74695
Total Receipts	8	323015103	1698284	60736272	28884250	57839185	17796027	18634911	20113718	14582212	13123481	10736990	46350843	32518928
Average Total Receipts	9	7783	741	2254	4654	10959	38026	107097	268183	394114	690710	2684248	5150094	10839643
Operating Costs/Operating Income (%)														
Cost of Operations	10	91.0	90.6	90.3	89.8	92.3	88.9	88.9	92.7	93.7	88.6	93.2	90.5	91.6
Salaries and Wages	11	2.7	2.5	2.5	2.4	2.1	3.3	4.2	2.5	2.0	4.0	2.6	3.3	2.5
Taxes Paid	12	0.8	1.1	0.9	1.3	0.9	1.8	0.7	0.5	0.4	0.7	0.3	0.6	0.3
Interest Paid	13	0.4	0.9	0.3	0.5	0.6	0.6	0.5	0.3	0.4	0.6	0.2	0.4	0.3
Depreciation	14	0.7	0.7	0.4	0.7	0.5	0.7	0.8	0.7	0.7	1.2	0.6	1.0	1.4
Amortization and Depletion	15	0.1	0.2	0.1	0.1	0.1	0.1	0.1	0.0	0.0	0.1	0.0	0.1	0.1
Pensions and Other Deferred Comp.	16	0.0	•	0.0	0.0	0.0	0.0	0.0	0.0	0.0	0.1	0.3	0.1	0.0
Employee Benefits	17	0.1	0.1	0.0	0.1	0.1	0.2	0.1	0.1	0.1	0.3	0.1	0.3	0.1
Advertising	18	0.1	0.1	0.1	0.0	0.1	0.1	0.2	0.1	0.1	0.2	0.1	0.2	0.1
Other Expenses	19	4.0	7.0	5.8	4.8	3.3	4.3	5.0	3.0	3.1	4.1	2.1	3.5	3.0
Officers' Compensation	20	0.4	0.9	0.9	0.7	0.4	0.5	0.3	0.3	0.2	0.2	0.0	0.1	0.0
Operating Margin	21	•	•	•	•	•	•	•	•	•	•	0.6	0.1	0.4
Operating Margin Before Officers' Comp.	22	•	•	0.2	0.2	0.1	0.1	•	0.1	•	0.2	0.7	0.1	0.4

Selected Average Balance Sheet ($ in Thousands)

Net Receivables 23	115	0	14	36	85	680	1583	3124	9778	17610	72934	99098	342376
Inventories 24	137	0	49	77	166	596	1833	3716	5741	14774	33497	115886	301953
Net Property, Plant and Equipment 25	623	0	55	347	1074	3384	7118	16205	33206	81415	126238	535682	1474439
Total Assets 26	1257	0	192	711	1761	7057	15789	34373	71444	155260	353407	968626	2969431
Notes and Loans Payable 27	594	0	108	417	1306	6037	6954	11791	28932	51914	53201	354208	629913
All Other Liabilities 28	371	0	46	120	234	3538	5504	12104	19541	56956	139882	313646	1155879
Net Worth 29	292	0	39	174	221	-2518	3331	10478	22971	46390	160325	300771	1183639

Selected Financial Ratios (Times to 1)

Current Ratio 30	1.2	•	2.0	1.9	1.7	0.7	0.9	1.2	1.1	0.9	0.9	1.1	1.1
Quick Ratio 31	0.7	•	0.8	0.9	0.8	0.5	0.5	0.6	0.7	0.5	0.6	0.7	0.7
Net Sales to Working Capital 32	100.5	•	44.6	41.4	61.4	•	•	134.2	129.4	•	•	165.9	105.9
Coverage Ratio 33	2.0	0.4	1.9	1.5	1.1	1.0	1.4	2.4	0.9	2.1	13.6	2.7	5.4
Total Asset Turnover 34	6.1	•	11.5	6.5	6.2	5.4	6.7	7.8	5.5	4.4	7.5	5.3	3.6
Inventory Turnover 35	51.3	•	40.7	53.8	60.8	56.5	51.4	66.6	63.8	41.1	73.7	40.0	32.5
Receivables Turnover 36	71.2	•	188.1	139.7	99.7	71.6	74.7	80.4	45.7	48.4	31.1	38.1	62.6
Total Liabilities to Net Worth 37	3.3	•	4.0	3.1	7.0	•	3.7	2.3	2.1	2.3	1.2	2.2	1.5
Current Assets to Working Capital 38	5.5	•	2.0	2.1	2.5	•	•	7.0	8.4	•	•	10.1	9.6
Current Liabilities to Working Capital 39	4.5	•	1.0	1.1	1.5	•	•	6.0	7.4	•	•	9.1	8.6
Working Capital to Net Sales 40	0.0	•	0.0	0.0	0.0	•	•	0.0	0.0	•	•	0.0	0.0
Inventory to Working Capital 41	2.0	•	1.1	0.8	1.0	•	•	2.0	1.9	•	•	2.8	3.0
Total Receipts to Cash Flow 42	33.0	43.3	27.2	28.7	45.9	37.2	27.1	38.2	47.8	28.8	29.9	35.9	28.1
Cost of Goods to Cash Flow 43	30.0	39.3	24.6	25.8	42.4	33.0	24.1	35.4	44.8	25.5	27.9	32.5	25.8
Cash Flow to Total Debt 44	0.2	•	0.5	0.3	0.2	0.1	0.3	0.3	0.2	0.2	0.5	0.2	0.2

Selected Financial Factors (in Percentages)

Debt Ratio 45	76.8	•	79.9	75.5	87.5	135.7	78.9	69.5	67.8	70.1	54.6	68.9	60.1
Return on Total Assets 46	5.4	•	6.5	5.4	4.1	3.1	4.6	5.4	1.9	5.7	15.5	5.4	6.5
Return on Equity Before Income Taxes 47	11.8	•	15.2	7.7	2.7	0.1	6.5	10.4	•	9.7	31.7	10.9	13.2
Return on Equity After Income Taxes 48	10.1	•	14.7	6.6	1.9	0.8	5.6	9.2	•	7.2	28.9	8.5	12.2
Profit Margin (Before Income Tax) 49	0.4	•	0.3	0.3	0.1	•	0.2	0.4	•	0.7	1.9	0.6	1.5
Profit Margin (After Income Tax) 50	0.4	•	0.3	0.2	0.0	•	0.2	0.4	0.2	0.5	1.8	0.5	1.3

Table II

Corporations with Net Income

GASOLINE STATIONS

MONEY AMOUNTS AND SIZE OF ASSETS IN THOUSANDS OF DOLLARS

Item Description for Accounting Period 7/07 Through 6/08	Total	Zero Assets	Under 500	500 to 1,000	1,000 to 5,000	5,000 to 10,000	10,000 to 25,000	25,000 to 50,000	50,000 to 100,000	100,000 to 250,000	250,000 to 500,000	500,000 to 2,500,000	2,500,000 and over
Number of Enterprises **1**	25296	642	•	3458	3009	272	112	55	21	14	4	•	3

Revenues ($ in Thousands)

Item Description for Accounting Period 7/07 Through 6/08	Total	Zero Assets	Under 500	500 to 1,000	1,000 to 5,000	5,000 to 10,000	10,000 to 25,000	25,000 to 50,000	50,000 to 100,000	100,000 to 250,000	250,000 to 500,000	500,000 to 2,500,000	2,500,000 and over
Net Sales **2**	241023936	415578	•	16997214	45402812	12051187	14225829	15487288	8806080	10716034	10596911	•	32144913
Interest **3**	80272	95	•	2139	4536	2295	3279	5333	-409	5070	2453	•	35502
Rents **4**	105769	1165	•	7467	6206	3831	2886	5312	5780	3725	2816	•	62252
Royalties **5**	14948	0	•	13	0	0	0	2	0	2280	0	•	12654
Other Portfolio Income **6**	442754	21564	•	55611	38710	18130	8200	25574	1860	5877	8125	•	188912
Other Receipts **7**	1345531	13505	•	66401	167068	23895	101964	46096	32345	64496	126685	•	74695
Total Receipts **8**	243013210	451907	•	17128845	45619332	12099338	14342158	15569605	8845656	10797482	10736990	•	32518928
Average Total Receipts **9**	9607	704	•	4953	15161	44483	128055	283084	421222	771249	2684248	•	10839643

Operating Costs/Operating Income (%)

Item Description for Accounting Period 7/07 Through 6/08	Total	Zero Assets	Under 500	500 to 1,000	1,000 to 5,000	5,000 to 10,000	10,000 to 25,000	25,000 to 50,000	50,000 to 100,000	100,000 to 250,000	250,000 to 500,000	500,000 to 2,500,000	2,500,000 and over
Cost of Operations **10**	91.0	87.0	•	89.2	93.0	89.0	90.6	92.3	93.7	88.7	93.2	•	91.6
Salaries and Wages **11**	2.5	2.9	•	2.4	1.9	3.1	2.8	2.5	1.9	4.1	2.6	•	2.5
Taxes Paid **12**	0.7	1.5	•	1.7	0.7	2.3	0.6	0.5	0.4	0.7	0.3	•	0.3
Interest Paid **13**	0.3	2.6	•	0.4	0.4	0.4	0.3	0.3	0.2	0.5	0.2	•	0.3
Depreciation **14**	0.7	1.2	•	0.6	0.4	0.5	0.6	0.6	0.6	1.2	0.6	•	1.4
Amortization and Depletion **15**	0.1	0.4	•	0.0	0.0	0.1	0.0	0.0	0.0	0.1	0.0	•	0.1
Pensions and Other Deferred Comp. **16**	0.0	•	•	0.0	0.0	0.0	0.0	0.0	0.0	0.1	0.3	•	0.0
Employee Benefits **17**	0.1	0.3	•	0.0	0.0	0.2	0.1	0.0	0.1	0.3	0.1	•	0.1
Advertising **18**	0.1	0.0	•	0.0	0.0	0.1	0.1	0.0	0.1	0.2	0.1	•	0.1
Other Expenses **19**	3.7	6.3	•	4.5	2.9	3.5	4.7	3.2	2.6	3.6	2.1	•	3.0
Officers' Compensation **20**	0.4	1.9	•	0.7	0.4	0.5	0.4	0.3	0.1	0.3	0.0	•	0.0
Operating Margin **21**	0.3	•	•	0.4	0.2	0.3	•	0.1	0.3	0.4	0.6	•	0.4
Operating Margin Before Officers' Comp. **22**	0.6	•	•	1.1	0.6	0.8	0.1	0.4	0.4	0.6	0.7	•	0.4

Selected Average Balance Sheet ($ in Thousands)

	1	2	3	4	5	6	7	8	9	10	11
Net Receivables 23	154	•	40	121	793	1923	3563	10583	21612	72934	342376
Inventories 24	167	•	95	167	740	2039	3997	6734	14528	33497	301953
Net Property, Plant and Equipment 25	695	•	305	924	3050	6884	16652	30593	76293	126238	1474439
Total Assets 26	1465	•	652	1760	7500	15918	35543	68758	160135	353407	2969431
Notes and Loans Payable 27	525	•	306	1000	3460	5663	10735	24271	46612	53201	629913
All Other Liabilities 28	438	•	120	286	1620	6102	12403	18598	65496	139882	1155879
Net Worth 29	502	•	226	474	2421	4153	12405	25889	48027	160325	1183639

Selected Financial Ratios (Times to 1)

	1	2	3	4	5	6	7	8	9	10	11
Current Ratio 30	1.3	•	2.1	1.9	1.7	1.1	1.2	1.2	0.9	0.9	1.1
Quick Ratio 31	0.7	•	1.0	1.1	1.0	0.6	0.6	0.8	0.6	0.6	0.7
Net Sales to Working Capital 32	75.0	•	34.3	58.9	39.0	180.2	124.1	87.7	•	•	105.9
Coverage Ratio 33	4.2	2.9	3.9	2.6	2.6	3.3	4.0	3.1	•	13.6	5.4
Total Asset Turnover 34	6.5	•	7.5	8.6	5.9	8.0	7.9	6.1	4.8	7.5	3.6
Inventory Turnover 35	52.0	•	46.4	83.8	53.3	56.4	65.0	58.3	46.7	73.7	32.5
Receivables Turnover 36	66.3	•	•	112.8	70.9	82.6	69.8	50.4	46.0	31.1	62.6
Total Liabilities to Net Worth 37	1.9	•	1.9	2.7	2.1	2.8	1.9	1.7	2.3	1.2	1.5
Current Assets to Working Capital 38	4.1	•	1.9	2.1	2.4	9.4	6.4	5.8	•	•	9.6
Current Liabilities to Working Capital 39	3.1	•	0.9	1.1	1.4	8.4	5.4	4.8	•	•	8.6
Working Capital to Net Sales 40	0.0	•	0.0	0.0	0.0	0.0	0.0	0.0	•	•	0.0
Inventory to Working Capital 41	1.4	•	0.7	0.7	0.7	3.3	1.9	1.3	•	•	3.0
Total Receipts to Cash Flow 42	29.1	24.8	23.5	41.3	34.8	26.2	33.1	41.0	27.8	29.9	28.1
Cost of Goods to Cash Flow 43	26.5	21.6	21.0	38.4	30.9	23.8	30.5	38.4	24.7	27.9	25.8
Cash Flow to Total Debt 44	0.3	•	0.5	0.3	0.3	0.4	0.4	0.2	0.2	0.5	0.2

Selected Financial Factors (in Percentages)

	1	2	3	4	5	6	7	8	9	10	11
Debt Ratio 45	65.7	•	65.4	73.1	67.7	73.9	65.1	62.3	70.0	54.6	60.1
Return on Total Assets 46	9.1	•	12.0	8.9	6.8	7.0	7.1	5.7	8.0	15.5	6.5
Return on Equity Before Income Taxes 47	20.3	•	25.9	20.4	13.0	17.7	14.2	11.4	17.9	31.7	13.2
Return on Equity After Income Taxes 48	18.8	•	24.4	19.8	11.9	16.6	12.8	10.5	14.6	28.9	12.2
Profit Margin (Before Income Tax) 49	1.1	4.8	1.2	0.6	0.6	0.6	0.6	0.7	1.1	1.9	1.5
Profit Margin (After Income Tax) 50	1.0	3.9	1.1	0.6	0.7	0.5	0.6	0.6	0.9	1.8	1.3

Table I

Corporations with and without Net Income

CLOTHING AND CLOTHING ACCESSORIES STORES

MONEY AMOUNTS AND SIZE OF ASSETS IN THOUSANDS OF DOLLARS

Item Description for Accounting Period 7/07 Through 6/08	Total	Zero Assets	Under 500	500 to 1,000	1,000 to 5,000	5,000 to 10,000	10,000 to 25,000	25,000 to 50,000	50,000 to 100,000	100,000 to 250,000	250,000 to 500,000	500,000 to 2,500,000	2,500,000 and over
Number of Enterprises **1**	52074	8455	36044	4312	2567	377	139	51	34	32	21	33	9
Revenues ($ in Thousands)													
Net Sales **2**	188067412	1815282	13183886	5488446	9024807	4548904	4193781	2791823	3991375	9882712	13851991	57247873	62046532
Interest **3**	910368	5772	4169	4515	12717	3580	20712	5947	4560	24844	78093	205957	539503
Rents **4**	120870	314	2997	239	4071	1176	16509	1719	1024	8479	1577	16630	66134
Royalties **5**	1147118	0	0	0	1297	0	6930	0	0	16509	9945	542002	570435
Other Portfolio Income **6**	1005236	81947	32231	2005	11711	869	849	3525	13714	17614	19096	182096	639573
Other Receipts **7**	2926598	9810	233250	29859	64308	16520	50782	15098	60455	143672	185037	958679	1159133
Total Receipts **8**	194177602	1913125	13456533	5525064	9118911	4571049	4289563	2818112	4071128	10093830	14145739	59153237	65021310
Average Total Receipts **9**	3729	226	373	1281	3552	12125	30860	55257	119739	315432	673607	1792522	7224590
Operating Costs/Operating Income (%)													
Cost of Operations **10**	54.2	59.7	53.1	58.2	59.0	61.8	54.4	60.8	49.6	50.4	53.0	53.5	54.1
Salaries and Wages **11**	13.9	8.3	8.5	12.7	11.8	12.4	15.2	13.3	17.3	16.6	15.1	14.1	14.6
Taxes Paid **12**	2.2	2.6	2.3	2.2	2.0	1.9	2.7	2.2	3.1	2.3	2.1	2.1	2.2
Interest Paid **13**	1.0	0.7	0.9	0.9	1.0	1.0	1.0	1.2	1.5	1.1	0.9	1.1	0.9
Depreciation **14**	2.0	1.2	0.7	0.7	0.9	0.8	1.3	1.3	1.8	1.8	2.2	2.6	2.3
Amortization and Depletion **15**	0.3	0.3	0.2	0.1	0.1	0.0	0.2	0.1	0.3	0.3	0.1	0.1	0.5
Pensions and Other Deferred Comp. **16**	0.2	0.0	0.2	0.2	0.4	0.3	0.1	0.2	0.1	0.1	0.2	0.2	0.2
Employee Benefits **17**	1.1	0.4	0.3	0.7	0.6	0.5	0.8	0.7	1.5	1.1	0.8	1.3	1.4
Advertising **18**	2.5	1.1	2.2	3.7	3.1	3.2	2.8	3.6	4.3	1.8	3.2	2.6	2.2
Other Expenses **19**	18.7	24.9	23.0	14.7	15.7	15.9	20.0	14.5	21.4	23.1	19.9	19.2	17.2
Officers' Compensation **20**	1.7	5.4	9.7	5.5	4.8	1.9	2.4	1.8	1.0	1.2	0.7	0.8	0.4
Operating Margin **21**	2.1	•	•	0.4	0.6	0.3	•	0.4	•	0.2	1.8	2.5	3.9
Operating Margin Before Officers' Comp. **22**	3.8	1.0	8.5	5.9	5.4	2.2	1.3	2.1	•	1.4	2.4	3.3	4.3

Selected Average Balance Sheet ($ in Thousands)

Net Receivables 23	181	0	3	34	100	454	1522	2727	5289	8196	12748	99359	489849
Inventories 24	676	0	76	426	1111	3588	6858	13466	28905	63458	119299	269478	1150553
Net Property, Plant and Equipment 25	542	0	13	77	285	1000	3542	5424	14631	43275	112719	318329	1201332
Total Assets 26	2226	0	137	673	1972	6492	15694	33891	69856	162067	373478	1160253	4773241
Notes and Loans Payable 27	512	0	70	246	606	2425	6235	7463	17441	33957	52438	220625	1035623
All Other Liabilities 28	898	0	40	167	559	2544	5877	14231	29609	68099	149653	472204	2086805
Net Worth 29	815	0	27	260	807	1523	3583	12197	22806	60012	171388	467424	1650813

Selected Financial Ratios (Times to 1)

Current Ratio 30	1.8	•	2.2	2.9	2.2	1.4	1.6	1.4	1.3	1.4	1.8	1.9	1.6
Quick Ratio 31	0.6	•	0.6	0.6	0.4	0.3	0.4	0.4	0.3	0.4	0.4	0.7	0.7
Net Sales to Working Capital 32	7.1	•	5.9	3.5	4.2	8.7	7.1	8.2	11.9	11.6	7.3	6.6	8.3
Coverage Ratio 33	6.6	3.3	1.9	2.3	2.7	1.8	2.3	2.1	1.0	3.0	5.0	6.6	11.1
Total Asset Turnover 34	1.6	•	2.7	1.9	1.8	1.9	1.9	1.6	1.7	1.9	1.8	1.5	1.4
Inventory Turnover 35	2.9	•	2.5	1.7	1.9	2.1	2.4	2.5	2.0	2.5	2.9	3.4	3.2
Receivables Turnover 36	25.0	•	127.8	38.5	37.6	23.5	19.7	21.3	21.3	38.8	57.6	25.2	17.5
Total Liabilities to Net Worth 37	1.7	•	4.1	1.6	1.4	3.3	3.4	1.8	2.1	1.7	1.2	1.5	1.9
Current Assets to Working Capital 38	2.3	•	1.8	1.5	1.8	3.7	2.8	3.3	4.4	3.5	2.2	2.1	2.7
Current Liabilities to Working Capital 39	1.3	•	0.8	0.5	0.8	2.7	1.8	2.3	3.4	2.5	1.2	1.1	1.7
Working Capital to Net Sales 40	0.1	•	0.2	0.3	0.2	0.1	0.1	0.1	0.1	0.1	0.1	0.2	0.1
Inventory to Working Capital 41	1.3	•	1.3	1.2	1.4	2.5	1.7	2.1	2.9	2.3	1.3	1.1	1.3
Total Receipts to Cash Flow 42	6.7	7.5	8.0	10.1	8.8	11.1	8.2	11.7	10.1	6.8	7.9	6.4	5.7
Cost of Goods to Cash Flow 43	3.6	4.5	4.3	5.9	5.2	6.9	4.5	7.1	5.0	3.4	4.2	3.4	3.1
Cash Flow to Total Debt 44	0.4	•	0.4	0.3	0.3	0.2	0.3	0.2	0.2	0.4	0.4	0.4	0.4

Selected Financial Factors (in Percentages)

Debt Ratio 45	63.4	•	80.3	61.3	59.1	76.5	77.2	64.0	67.4	63.0	54.1	59.7	65.4
Return on Total Assets 46	10.6	•	4.7	3.7	4.7	3.3	4.6	3.9	2.6	6.5	8.3	10.4	14.8
Return on Equity Before Income Taxes 47	24.6	•	11.5	5.4	7.2	6.2	11.6	5.7	0.1	11.7	14.4	22.0	39.1
Return on Equity After Income Taxes 48	16.4	•	10.7	4.6	6.2	4.2	9.0	3.1	•	8.5	9.2	14.4	26.1
Profit Margin (Before Income Tax) 49	5.5	1.5	0.8	1.1	1.7	0.8	1.4	1.3	0.0	2.3	3.8	5.9	9.4
Profit Margin (After Income Tax) 50	3.7	0.1	0.8	0.9	1.4	0.5	1.1	0.7	•	1.7	2.4	3.9	6.2

Table II

Corporations with Net Income

CLOTHING AND CLOTHING ACCESSORIES STORES

MONEY AMOUNTS AND SIZE OF ASSETS IN THOUSANDS OF DOLLARS

Item Description for Accounting Period 7/07 Through 6/08	Total	Zero Assets	Under 500	500 to 1,000	1,000 to 5,000	5,000 to 10,000	10,000 to 25,000	25,000 to 50,000	50,000 to 100,000	100,000 to 250,000	250,000 to 500,000	500,000 to 2,500,000	2,500,000 and over
Number of Enterprises 1	28483	3844	•	3207	2102	257	101	35	18	18	15	27	•
Revenues ($ in Thousands)													
Net Sales 2	156524880	1036371	•	4295108	8034759	2972255	3019976	2065971	1863118	6634006	10239557	50071008	•
Interest 3	835478	5539	•	3454	10975	2780	15545	3373	1853	22071	34130	200621	•
Rents 4	96886	0	•	239	3836	838	1897	1590	933	2933	342	16630	•
Royalties 5	1091080	0	•	0	0	0	0	0	0	15145	3829	535285	•
Other Portfolio Income 6	912399	81247	•	1685	10278	869	845	1459	4288	13909	18333	140948	•
Other Receipts 7	2497857	6688	•	23270	56922	9167	24595	14195	50146	38641	70687	873777	•
Total Receipts 8	161958580	1129845	•	4323756	8116770	2985909	3062858	2086588	1920338	6726705	10366878	51838269	•
Average Total Receipts 9	5686	294	•	1348	3861	11618	30325	59617	106685	373706	691125	1919936	•
Operating Costs/Operating Income (%)													
Cost of Operations 10	53.6	50.6	•	58.6	58.4	59.0	54.6	56.9	49.1	48.5	54.0	53.1	•
Salaries and Wages 11	13.8	10.9	•	11.1	11.4	11.9	13.7	12.3	16.8	15.7	14.4	14.1	•
Taxes Paid 12	2.2	3.6	•	2.2	2.0	1.8	2.6	2.5	2.7	2.3	2.1	2.1	•
Interest Paid 13	0.8	0.6	•	0.8	0.9	0.5	0.8	0.9	0.7	0.6	0.2	0.8	•
Depreciation 14	2.1	1.3	•	0.7	0.8	0.8	0.9	1.3	1.2	1.7	2.3	2.6	•
Amortization and Depletion 15	0.2	0.4	•	0.0	0.1	0.0	0.2	0.1	0.1	0.2	0.0	0.1	•
Pensions and Other Deferred Comp. 16	0.2	0.0	•	0.3	0.5	0.4	0.1	0.2	0.1	0.1	0.1	0.2	•
Employee Benefits 17	1.1	0.3	•	0.8	0.6	0.5	0.6	0.5	1.0	0.8	0.7	1.4	•
Advertising 18	2.4	0.7	•	2.9	3.2	3.5	2.5	2.8	4.2	1.1	2.3	2.7	•
Other Expenses 19	17.7	23.0	•	13.6	14.6	15.9	16.2	16.6	17.8	22.9	17.9	18.6	•
Officers' Compensation 20	1.7	8.5	•	5.9	5.0	1.8	2.4	1.5	1.6	1.2	0.6	0.8	•
Operating Margin 21	4.1	0.2	•	2.9	2.6	3.9	5.3	4.4	4.7	5.0	5.4	3.6	•
Operating Margin Before Officers' Comp. 22	5.8	8.7	•	8.8	7.5	5.7	7.7	5.9	6.3	6.2	6.0	4.4	•

Selected Average Balance Sheet ($ in Thousands)

	•	•	•	•	•	•	•	•	•	•	•
Net Receivables 23	291	0	33	116	177	1582	2709	5398	5593	9965	117797
Inventories 24	1028	0	424	1132	4180	6841	15090	37382	63315	127678	287322
Net Property, Plant and Equipment 25	853	0	80	282	900	3020	5271	11427	49219	120894	338905
Total Assets 26	3416	0	685	2010	6261	15682	35045	63998	165688	380847	1234432
Notes and Loans Payable 27	642	0	213	583	1845	5053	6071	9117	20008	26156	160695
All Other Liabilities 28	1388	0	167	534	1930	4802	11158	28672	58118	150329	518290
Net Worth 29	1386	0	305	893	2486	5827	17817	26209	87563	204362	555448

Selected Financial Ratios (Times to 1)

	•	•	•	•	•	•	•	•	•	•	•
Current Ratio 30	1.8	•	3.0	2.2	1.9	1.6	1.9	1.3	1.6	2.1	1.9
Quick Ratio 31	0.6	•	0.7	0.5	0.3	0.5	0.5	0.4	0.5	0.5	0.7
Net Sales to Working Capital 32	6.8	•	3.5	4.3	4.7	6.7	5.4	9.7	11.1	6.1	6.7
Coverage Ratio 33	10.7	18.0	5.4	5.2	9.7	9.7	7.0	12.1	11.5	41.0	9.7
Total Asset Turnover 34	1.6	•	2.0	1.9	1.8	1.9	1.7	1.6	2.2	1.8	1.5
Inventory Turnover 35	2.9	•	1.9	2.0	1.6	2.4	2.2	1.4	2.8	2.9	3.4
Receivables Turnover 36	23.3	•	37.7	25.8	18.4	20.0	14.1	53.9	72.3	•	•
Total Liabilities to Net Worth 37	1.5	•	1.2	1.3	1.5	1.7	1.0	1.4	0.9	0.9	1.2
Current Assets to Working Capital 38	2.2	•	1.5	1.8	2.1	2.6	2.1	3.9	2.6	1.9	2.1
Current Liabilities to Working Capital 39	1.2	•	0.5	0.8	1.1	1.6	1.1	2.9	1.6	0.9	1.1
Working Capital to Net Sales 40	0.1	•	0.3	0.2	0.2	0.1	0.2	0.1	0.1	0.2	0.1
Inventory to Working Capital 41	1.2	•	1.1	1.4	1.5	1.6	1.4	2.4	1.5	1.1	1.0
Total Receipts to Cash Flow 42	5.9	4.5	8.2	7.8	6.3	7.5	7.0	5.6	5.3	7.1	6.0
Cost of Goods to Cash Flow 43	3.2	2.3	4.8	4.5	3.4	3.4	4.0	2.8	2.6	3.8	3.2
Cash Flow to Total Debt 44	0.5	•	0.4	0.4	0.5	0.5	0.5	0.5	0.1	0.9	0.5

Selected Financial Factors (in Percentages)

	•	•	•	•	•	•	•	•	•	•	•
Debt Ratio 45	59.4	•	55.4	55.6	60.3	62.8	49.2	59.0	47.2	46.3	55.0
Return on Total Assets 46	13.8	•	8.6	8.5	9.0	14.2	10.6	13.6	15.4	11.9	12.0
Return on Equity Before Income Taxes 47	30.8	•	15.7	15.3	20.4	34.3	17.8	30.5	26.6	21.7	24.0
Return on Equity After Income Taxes 48	22.1	•	14.8	14.3	18.5	32.1	15.3	28.9	22.7	15.5	16.1
Profit Margin (Before Income Tax) 49	7.8	10.1	3.6	3.6	6.7	4.4	7.7	6.3	6.5	7.2	
Profit Margin (After Income Tax) 50	5.6	7.6	3.4	3.3	4.0	4.6	7.3	5.4	4.6	4.8	

Table I

Corporations with and without Net Income

SPORTING GOODS, HOBBY, BOOK, AND MUSIC STORES

MONEY AMOUNTS AND SIZE OF ASSETS IN THOUSANDS OF DOLLARS

Item Description for Accounting Period 7/07 Through 6/08	Total	Zero Assets	Under 500	500 to 1,000	1,000 to 5,000	5,000 to 10,000	10,000 to 25,000	25,000 to 50,000	50,000 to 100,000	100,000 to 250,000	250,000 to 500,000	500,000 to 2,500,000	2,500,000 and over
Number of Enterprises 1	30778	3061	22345	3174	1871	177	82	16	8	17	9	15	3
Revenues ($ in Thousands)													
Net Sales 2	88375172	2618531	11278410	4362443	6637024	2303634	2533539	805561	1174496	4297964	5615586	31551097	15196888
Interest 3	92466	2335	4397	1899	12778	3062	2228	3584	1042	7268	1567	19181	33125
Rents 4	379298	371	0	0	3935	1539	129	3085	1362	1098	128	7150	360499
Royalties 5	195450	1814	0	27	0	0	0	0	0	3199	8532	9201	172678
Other Portfolio Income 6	123791	0	1938	160	4150	216	1242	566	55	3925	80344	7352	23843
Other Receipts 7	1247755	10096	84490	6329	24974	85131	22368	-3465	14900	40520	42346	474315	445750
Total Receipts 8	90413932	2633147	11369235	4370858	6682861	2393582	2559506	809331	1191855	4353974	5748503	32068296	16232783
Average Total Receipts 9	2938	860	509	1377	3572	13523	31213	50583	148982	256116	638723	2137886	5410928
Operating Costs/Operating Income (%)													
Cost of Operations 10	62.0	65.2	65.1	59.8	60.9	77.3	68.5	64.7	56.1	62.7	61.1	58.5	64.7
Salaries and Wages 11	12.0	10.8	8.5	13.4	12.5	9.3	10.5	11.3	15.7	12.6	12.5	12.9	12.2
Taxes Paid 12	2.1	2.4	2.1	2.3	2.3	1.5	1.5	1.8	2.6	2.1	1.9	2.1	2.2
Interest Paid 13	1.9	0.7	0.9	1.0	0.8	1.0	0.9	1.9	1.6	1.5	1.2	2.3	3.5
Depreciation 14	1.7	1.4	0.7	0.8	1.3	0.6	0.6	2.1	1.2	1.3	1.9	2.2	2.0
Amortization and Depletion 15	0.1	0.4	0.1	0.2	0.2	0.0	0.3	0.8	0.6	0.6	0.5	•	0.2
Pensions and Other Deferred Comp. 16	0.1	0.0	0.1	0.0	0.4	0.1	0.3	0.2	0.3	0.1	0.1	0.1	0.2
Employee Benefits 17	0.6	0.2	0.5	0.5	0.5	0.3	0.4	0.6	1.0	0.8	0.4	0.8	0.5
Advertising 18	2.4	3.3	1.5	2.1	2.3	0.9	2.7	6.1	3.4	3.8	3.1	2.7	1.7
Other Expenses 19	16.2	14.7	16.5	16.3	13.5	7.8	13.5	21.9	16.6	14.4	15.9	17.3	16.9
Officers' Compensation 20	1.7	1.5	5.2	3.9	4.1	1.1	1.7	2.1	1.0	0.9	0.4	0.6	0.5
Operating Margin 21	•	•	•	1.2	0.1	•	•	•	•	•	1.1	0.5	•
Operating Margin Before Officers' Comp. 22	0.9	0.8	4.0	3.5	5.3	1.2	0.8	•	0.8	0.1	1.5	1.1	•

Selected Average Balance Sheet ($ in Thousands)

Net Receivables 23	84	0	3	39	120	402	1897	3669	3423	22230	34373	52297	128035
Inventories 24	662	0	76	387	984	2694	6310	10749	37483	69100	166784	646688	1180841
Net Property, Plant and Equipment 25	405	0	21	109	411	495	1882	3916	12140	23337	78382	330045	1479223
Total Assets 26	1638	0	127	702	1877	7253	14271	32557	72307	164783	333116	1248116	4593721
Notes and Loans Payable 27	691	0	85	305	616	1959	4142	11264	24603	57147	107424	570020	1895399
All Other Liabilities 28	652	0	41	183	521	2083	5546	14238	26770	56292	114498	510969	2220980
Net Worth 29	296	0	-0	214	740	3211	4583	7056	20934	51343	111194	167127	477341

Selected Financial Ratios (Times to 1)

Current Ratio 30	1.5	•	1.9	2.4	2.4	1.7	1.4	1.5	1.2	1.7	1.5	1.4	1.3
Quick Ratio 31	0.3	•	0.4	0.5	0.7	0.8	0.4	0.6	0.2	0.6	0.3	0.2	0.3
Net Sales to Working Capital 32	9.4	•	10.7	4.6	4.9	5.6	10.9	6.7	18.7	5.8	8.5	11.7	13.6
Coverage Ratio 33	1.8	0.8	0.6	0.8	3.3	5.0	1.1	•	1.8	1.4	3.9	1.9	1.8
Total Asset Turnover 34	1.8	•	4.0	2.0	1.9	1.8	2.2	1.5	2.0	1.5	1.9	1.7	1.1
Inventory Turnover 35	2.7	•	4.3	2.1	2.2	3.7	3.4	3.0	2.2	2.3	2.3	1.9	2.8
Receivables Turnover 36	31.7	•	159.6	40.3	25.4	24.7	16.6	15.0	28.9	11.5	17.8	28.0	79.1
Total Liabilities to Net Worth 37	4.5	•	•	2.3	1.5	1.3	2.1	3.6	2.5	2.2	2.0	6.5	8.6
Current Assets to Working Capital 38	3.0	•	2.1	1.7	1.7	2.5	3.5	3.2	5.3	2.3	3.0	3.8	4.7
Current Liabilities to Working Capital 39	2.0	•	1.1	0.7	0.7	1.5	2.5	2.2	4.3	1.3	2.0	2.8	3.7
Working Capital to Net Sales 40	0.1	•	0.1	0.2	0.2	0.2	0.1	0.1	0.1	0.2	0.1	0.1	0.1
Inventory to Working Capital 41	2.1	•	1.6	1.4	1.2	1.2	2.3	1.4	4.0	1.4	2.1	3.0	3.2
Total Receipts to Cash Flow 42	9.9	11.7	11.6	10.8	10.3	12.7	13.2	553.3	9.6	12.2	9.0	9.2	8.5
Cost of Goods to Cash Flow 43	6.1	7.7	7.5	6.5	6.3	9.8	9.0	357.9	5.4	7.6	5.5	5.4	5.5
Cash Flow to Total Debt 44	0.2	0.3	0.3	0.3	0.3	0.3	0.2	0.0	0.3	0.2	0.3	0.2	0.1

Selected Financial Factors (in Percentages)

Debt Ratio 45	82.0	•	100.1	69.5	60.6	55.7	67.9	78.3	71.0	68.8	66.6	86.6	89.6
Return on Total Assets 46	6.0	•	2.0	1.7	5.0	8.9	2.3	•	6.0	3.2	8.7	7.4	6.9
Return on Equity Before Income Taxes 47	15.0	•	1472.2	•	8.8	16.2	0.8	•	9.3	2.6	19.3	26.4	29.1
Return on Equity After Income Taxes 48	10.1	•	1723.7	•	7.7	15.8	•	•	6.4	0.5	14.5	18.5	20.5
Profit Margin (Before Income Tax) 49	1.5	•	•	1.8	1.8	4.0	•	•	1.3	0.5	3.4	2.1	2.7
Profit Margin (After Income Tax) 50	1.0	•	•	1.6	1.6	3.9	•	•	0.9	0.1	2.6	1.5	1.9

Table II

Corporations with Net Income

SPORTING GOODS, HOBBY, BOOK, AND MUSIC STORES

MONEY AMOUNTS AND SIZE OF ASSETS IN THOUSANDS OF DOLLARS

Item Description for Accounting Period 7/07 Through 6/08	Total	Zero Assets	Under 500	500 to 1,000	1,000 to 5,000	5,000 to 10,000	10,000 to 25,000	25,000 to 50,000	50,000 to 100,000	100,000 to 250,000	250,000 to 500,000	500,000 to 2,500,000	2,500,000 and over
Number of Enterprises **1**	15178	783	11085	1530	1575	122	42	8	4	9	•	•	0
Revenues ($ in Thousands)													
Net Sales **2**	68019431	1700743	7450047	2488281	5741679	1615638	1396533	263930	722901	2656058	•	•	0
Interest **3**	77229	1954	3713	1573	9034	2642	1208	2585	884	5470	•	•	0
Rents **4**	373166	0	0	0	3262	1539	0	3085	384	0	•	•	0
Royalties **5**	190326	0	0	27	0	0	0	0	0	3199	•	•	0
Other Portfolio Income **6**	116342	0	0	126	3905	216	420	99	51	3531	•	•	0
Other Receipts **7**	1082526	2365	37764	1781	15100	60809	2021	1469	1723	27180	•	•	0
Total Receipts **8**	69859020	1705062	7491524	2491788	5772980	1680844	1400182	271168	725943	2695438	•	•	0
Average Total Receipts **9**	4603	2178	676	1629	3665	13777	33338	33896	181486	299493	•	•	•
Operating Costs/Operating Income (%)													
Cost of Operations **10**	61.6	67.0	66.1	59.6	61.1	76.4	68.2	60.0	51.7	64.5	•	•	•
Salaries and Wages **11**	11.7	10.4	7.2	11.5	11.6	9.2	9.7	6.1	18.6	10.9	•	•	•
Taxes Paid **12**	2.1	2.0	1.9	1.6	2.3	1.7	1.3	2.0	2.7	1.9	•	•	•
Interest Paid **13**	1.9	0.5	0.6	0.5	0.7	0.4	0.7	3.0	1.0	1.0	•	•	•
Depreciation **14**	1.6	1.2	0.5	0.5	1.3	0.4	0.6	0.9	1.2	0.9	•	•	•
Amortization and Depletion **15**	0.1	0.2	0.1	0.1	0.2	0.0	0.2	1.7	0.0	0.3	•	•	•
Pensions and Other Deferred Comp. **16**	0.2	•	0.0	0.0	0.5	0.1	0.3	0.2	0.4	0.1	•	•	•
Employee Benefits **17**	0.6	0.0	0.5	0.3	0.5	0.4	0.5	0.6	1.2	0.7	•	•	•
Advertising **18**	2.5	3.6	1.0	2.2	2.1	0.9	2.7	0.9	2.6	4.2	•	•	•
Other Expenses **19**	15.2	10.5	13.2	15.4	11.8	7.1	10.2	20.1	16.7	12.3	•	•	•
Officers' Compensation **20**	1.7	1.7	5.0	4.5	4.5	1.4	1.4	1.3	0.8	1.0	•	•	•
Operating Margin **21**	0.9	2.9	3.9	3.9	3.4	2.0	4.2	3.3	3.0	2.4	•	•	•
Operating Margin Before Officers' Comp. **22**	2.5	4.6	8.9	8.4	7.8	3.4	5.6	4.5	3.9	3.4	•	•	•

Selected Average Balance Sheet ($ in Thousands)

Net Receivables 23	•	141	0	4	53	120	494	1979	5975	5015	36950
Inventories 24	•	976	0	87	467	845	2317	7838	12111	59182	86908
Net Property, Plant and Equipment 25	•	664	0	19	53	422	507	1509	3396	15287	18744
Total Assets 26	•	2431	0	144	722	1893	7581	13724	31693	72468	167849
Notes and Loans Payable 27	•	1076	0	50	212	599	648	3418	11609	23631	54605
All Other Liabilities 28	•	913	0	42	220	504	2339	4582	7640	21815	50845
Net Worth 29	•	442	0	53	290	790	4594	5724	12444	27021	62399

Selected Financial Ratios (Times to 1)

Current Ratio 30	•	1.6	•	2.3	2.3	2.5	2.3	1.7	2.0	1.5	2.3
Quick Ratio 31	•	0.4	•	0.6	0.5	0.8	1.5	0.6	0.8	0.3	1.0
Net Sales to Working Capital 32	•	9.3	•	10.2	4.4	4.8	4.1	8.2	3.2	10.6	4.0
Coverage Ratio 33	•	2.9	7.4	8.3	8.7	6.9	15.8	7.3	3.0	4.3	5.0
Total Asset Turnover 34	•	1.8	•	4.7	2.3	1.9	1.7	2.4	1.0	2.5	1.8
Inventory Turnover 35	•	2.8	•	5.1	2.1	2.6	4.4	2.9	1.6	1.6	2.2
Receivables Turnover 36	•	29.4	•	189.4	42.4	26.5	20.3	14.3	8.2	21.3	8.7
Total Liabilities to Net Worth 37	•	4.5	•	1.7	1.5	1.4	0.7	1.4	1.5	1.7	1.7
Current Assets to Working Capital 38	•	2.8	•	1.8	1.8	1.7	1.8	2.3	2.0	3.1	1.8
Current Liabilities to Working Capital 39	•	1.8	•	0.8	0.8	0.7	0.8	1.3	1.0	2.1	0.8
Working Capital to Net Sales 40	•	0.1	•	0.1	0.2	0.2	0.2	0.1	0.3	0.1	0.3
Inventory to Working Capital 41	•	1.9	•	1.3	1.3	1.1	0.5	1.5	0.8	2.5	0.9
Total Receipts to Cash Flow 42	•	8.3	9.7	8.3	7.7	9.0	10.4	9.6	4.3	8.2	9.2
Cost of Goods to Cash Flow 43	•	5.1	6.5	5.5	4.6	5.5	8.0	6.5	2.6	4.2	6.0
Cash Flow to Total Debt 44	•	0.3	•	0.9	0.5	0.4	0.4	0.4	0.4	0.5	0.3

Selected Financial Factors (in Percentages)

Debt Ratio 45	•	81.8	•	63.3	59.9	58.3	39.4	58.3	60.7	62.7	62.8
Return on Total Assets 46	•	10.3	•	23.5	10.2	8.8	11.2	12.5	9.4	11.2	8.6
Return on Equity Before Income Taxes 47	•	37.2	•	56.3	22.6	18.0	17.4	25.8	15.9	23.2	18.6
Return on Equity After Income Taxes 48	•	30.6	•	55.0	22.1	16.7	17.0	24.1	10.5	18.8	15.3
Profit Margin (Before Income Tax) 49	•	3.7	3.2	4.4	4.0	3.9	6.0	4.4	6.0	3.5	3.9
Profit Margin (After Income Tax) 50	•	3.0	2.3	4.3	3.9	3.6	5.9	4.2	4.0	2.8	3.2

Table I

Corporations with and without Net Income

GENERAL MERCHANDISE STORES

MONEY AMOUNTS AND SIZE OF ASSETS IN THOUSANDS OF DOLLARS

Item Description for Accounting Period 7/07 Through 6/08	Total	Zero Assets	Under 500	500 to 1,000	1,000 to 5,000	5,000 to 10,000	10,000 to 25,000	25,000 to 50,000	50,000 to 100,000	100,000 to 250,000	250,000 to 500,000	500,000 to 2,500,000	2,500,000 and over
Number of Enterprises **1**	9593	1730	6942	307	460	73	24	11	8	9	7	9	13
Revenues ($ in Thousands)													
Net Sales **2**	601250800	100823	2582620	395604	1930768	1543889	765569	834037	1076550	3001775	5488092	27530397	556000677
Interest **3**	3022286	0	3981	1244	1597	1137	508	2018	16040	13971	19531	55153	2907106
Rents **4**	1156801	3	199	0	940	289	576	10	7625	4172	1863	20214	1120909
Royalties **5**	2501285	0	0	0	434	0	0	0	515	8498	0	165214	2326624
Other Portfolio Income **6**	416977	0	125	346	980	8302	2372	500	42	46	3315	11800	389148
Other Receipts **7**	12675659	1	5919	12134	16324	19063	6618	27375	16456	61052	40775	576701	11893242
Total Receipts **8**	621023808	100827	2592844	409328	1951043	1572680	775643	863940	1117228	3089514	5553576	28359479	574637706
Average Total Receipts **9**	64737	58	374	1333	4241	21544	32318	78540	139654	343279	793368	3151053	44202900
Operating Costs/Operating Income (%)													
Cost of Operations **10**	73.9	74.6	56.1	83.3	62.7	66.2	68.4	78.1	66.4	63.6	66.7	72.1	74.3
Salaries and Wages **11**	10.8	3.6	11.3	5.4	14.4	14.4	11.4	9.4	13.6	12.0	13.8	10.6	10.8
Taxes Paid **12**	1.7	0.8	2.1	0.9	1.8	2.7	1.8	1.2	1.9	2.0	2.1	1.8	1.7
Interest Paid **13**	1.1	0.0	0.6	0.9	1.0	0.5	1.3	0.5	0.4	1.7	0.8	1.0	1.1
Depreciation **14**	1.6	0.3	1.0	0.1	0.6	0.5	0.7	0.6	1.1	1.4	1.5	1.8	1.6
Amortization and Depletion **15**	0.0	•	0.0	0.4	0.0	0.0	0.0	0.1	0.0	0.0	•	0.1	0.0
Pensions and Other Deferred Comp. **16**	0.4	•	0.0	•	0.9	0.2	0.1	0.1	0.2	0.1	0.1	0.1	0.4
Employee Benefits **17**	0.8	•	0.1	0.5	0.8	1.2	0.6	0.5	1.7	0.6	1.6	1.0	0.7
Advertising **18**	1.5	1.2	2.4	0.2	1.4	1.4	1.7	1.0	1.9	2.2	2.7	1.5	1.5
Other Expenses **19**	7.0	23.9	21.0	8.5	14.5	11.9	10.0	7.8	13.3	16.3	14.8	10.5	6.6
Officers' Compensation **20**	0.1	5.2	4.5	1.9	3.3	0.8	0.5	0.9	0.4	1.5	0.5	0.5	0.1
Operating Margin **21**	1.1	•	0.9	•	•	•	3.6	•	•	•	•	•	1.3
Operating Margin Before Officers' Comp. **22**	1.2	•	5.3	•	1.9	0.7	4.0	0.7	•	0.1	•	•	1.3

Selected Average Balance Sheet ($ in Thousands)

Net Receivables 23	1301	0	5	64	91	344	849	2851	8990	12863	40906	34418	886831
Inventories 24	7428	0	70	350	998	1924	10637	13500	25772	49950	116168	486855	4908715
Net Property, Plant and Equipment 25	11032	0	31	15	282	1134	2712	2981	12393	36258	90174	388687	7749155
Total Assets 26	35231	0	144	699	1722	6221	17513	31188	70627	157938	371123	1251421	24531041
Notes and Loans Payable 27	9498	0	66	399	612	1745	3318	6924	9412	22754	100692	320750	6623220
All Other Liabilities 28	13353	0	40	120	476	2282	5141	8099	124805	71859	101365	445425	9293488
Net Worth 29	12380	0	38	181	633	2194	9055	16165	-63590	63325	169066	485247	8614333

Selected Financial Ratios (Times to 1)

Current Ratio 30	0.9	•	2.2	1.8	2.5	2.2	2.0	2.4	0.4	1.3	1.7	1.7	0.8
Quick Ratio 31	0.2	•	0.6	0.7	0.5	0.7	0.3	0.5	0.2	0.3	0.4	0.2	0.2
Net Sales to Working Capital 32	•	•	7.2	8.0	5.6	8.5	5.5	6.8	•	14.1	7.8	11.7	•
Coverage Ratio 33	5.2	•	3.2	2.5	0.7	4.6	4.6	7.5	7.2	1.9	•	3.1	5.5
Total Asset Turnover 34	1.8	•	2.6	1.8	2.4	3.4	1.8	2.4	1.9	2.1	2.1	2.4	1.7
Inventory Turnover 35	6.2	•	3.0	3.1	2.6	7.3	2.1	4.4	3.5	4.2	4.5	4.5	6.5
Receivables Turnover 36	51.4	•	76.2	17.5	46.3	112.1	20.0	37.3	13.4	35.5	29.1	73.2	51.5
Total Liabilities to Net Worth 37	1.8	•	2.8	2.9	1.7	1.8	0.9	0.9	•	1.5	1.2	1.6	1.8
Current Assets to Working Capital 38	•	•	1.9	2.3	1.7	1.8	2.0	1.7	•	4.2	2.4	2.5	•
Current Liabilities to Working Capital 39	•	•	0.9	1.3	0.7	0.8	1.0	0.7	•	3.2	1.4	1.5	•
Working Capital to Net Sales 40	•	•	0.1	0.1	0.2	0.1	0.2	0.1	•	0.1	0.1	0.1	•
Inventory to Working Capital 41	•	•	1.2	0.9	1.3	1.1	1.4	1.3	•	2.6	1.4	2.0	•
Total Receipts to Cash Flow 42	11.0	24.7	7.7	15.4	12.9	12.8	9.7	13.6	9.3	9.3	26.9	12.6	10.9
Cost of Goods to Cash Flow 43	8.1	18.4	4.3	12.9	8.1	8.5	6.6	10.7	6.2	5.9	17.9	9.1	8.1
Cash Flow to Total Debt 44	0.2	•	0.5	0.2	0.3	0.4	0.4	0.4	0.1	0.4	0.1	0.3	0.2

Selected Financial Factors (in Percentages)

Debt Ratio 45	64.9	•	73.4	74.2	63.2	64.7	48.3	48.2	190.0	59.9	54.4	61.2	64.9
Return on Total Assets 46	9.8	•	4.8	4.2	1.7	7.9	10.6	9.5	5.7	6.6	7.3	7.3	10.1
Return on Equity Before Income Taxes 47	22.7	•	12.3	9.8	•	17.5	16.1	15.9	•	7.6	12.6	12.6	23.6
Return on Equity After Income Taxes 48	14.7	•	12.2	9.7	•	17.1	16.0	15.3	•	6.5	7.9	7.9	15.3
Profit Margin (Before Income Tax) 49	4.5	•	1.3	1.4	•	1.8	4.6	3.4	2.6	1.4	2.0	2.0	4.7
Profit Margin (After Income Tax) 50	2.9	•	1.3	1.4	•	1.8	4.5	3.3	1.8	1.2	1.3	1.3	3.1

Table II

Corporations with Net Income

GENERAL MERCHANDISE STORES

MONEY AMOUNTS AND SIZE OF ASSETS IN THOUSANDS OF DOLLARS

Item Description for Accounting Period 7/07 Through 6/08	Total	Zero Assets	Under 500	500 to 1,000	1,000 to 5,000	5,000 to 10,000	10,000 to 25,000	25,000 to 50,000	50,000 to 100,000	100,000 to 250,000	250,000 to 500,000	500,000 to 2,500,000	2,500,000 and over
Number of Enterprises **1**	5261	480	4178	255	228	56	16	•	•	•	3	•	•
Revenues ($ in Thousands)													
Net Sales **2**	575551924	67326	2130003	151044	1515651	908811	739793	•	•	•	1157443	•	•
Interest **3**	2862021	0	1551	475	1308	812	0	•	•	•	7501	•	•
Rents **4**	1154126	0	0	0	0	289	0	•	•	•	1058	•	•
Royalties **5**	2501285	0	0	0	434	0	0	•	•	•	0	•	•
Other Portfolio Income **6**	411335	0	0	342	208	8302	0	•	•	•	3290	•	•
Other Receipts **7**	12124933	0	2530	12098	14584	18592	5958	•	•	•	16516	•	•
Total Receipts **8**	594568624	67326	2134084	163959	1532185	936806	745751	•	•	•	1185808	•	•
Average Total Receipts **9**	113014	140	511	643	6720	16729	46609	•	•	•	395269	•	•
Operating Costs/Operating Income (%)													
Cost of Operations **10**	73.8	80.2	54.8	70.7	60.9	60.4	68.2	•	•	•	59.5	•	•
Salaries and Wages **11**	10.8	2.5	11.7	8.7	13.3	19.3	10.9	•	•	•	13.4	•	•
Taxes Paid **12**	1.7	0.6	1.7	1.1	1.7	3.3	1.6	•	•	•	2.3	•	•
Interest Paid **13**	1.0	•	0.3	2.3	0.8	0.9	0.7	•	•	•	0.5	•	•
Depreciation **14**	1.6	•	0.8	0.3	0.5	0.6	0.4	•	•	•	1.1	•	•
Amortization and Depletion **15**	0.0	•	0.0	0.9	0.0	0.0	0.0	•	•	•	0.0	•	•
Pensions and Other Deferred Comp. **16**	0.4	•	•	•	1.1	0.0	0.1	•	•	•	0.1	•	•
Employee Benefits **17**	0.8	•	0.1	1.0	0.8	0.9	0.5	•	•	•	0.9	•	•
Advertising **18**	1.5	•	2.5	0.3	1.5	1.2	1.7	•	•	•	0.2	•	•
Other Expenses **19**	6.8	10.7	18.1	14.3	13.4	11.8	8.4	•	•	•	12.8	•	•
Officers' Compensation **20**	0.1	5.2	4.5	4.0	3.2	1.1	0.5	•	•	•	1.3	•	•
Operating Margin **21**	1.4	0.8	5.4	•	2.7	0.4	6.8	•	•	•	7.8	•	•
Operating Margin Before Officers' Comp. **22**	1.5	6.0	9.9	0.4	5.9	1.5	7.3	•	•	•	9.1	•	•

Selected Average Balance Sheet ($ in Thousands)

Net Receivables **23**	2314	0	2	70	167	392	1120	•	25088
Inventories **24**	13165	0	75	131	1581	1664	13963	•	145187
Net Property, Plant and Equipment **25**	19537	0	32	18	130	816	1360	•	42881
Total Assets **26**	61505	0	142	677	1876	5498	17245	•	339836
Notes and Loans Payable **27**	16192	0	52	415	383	2263	3516	•	60877
All Other Liabilities **28**	23487	0	59	93	587	1205	2450	•	50110
Net Worth **29**	21826	0	30	168	906	2029	11280	•	228849

Selected Financial Ratios (Times to 1)

Current Ratio **30**	0.8	•	1.6	1.4	3.4	3.1	3.7	•	1.8
Quick Ratio **31**	0.2	•	0.5	0.7	0.8	1.3	0.7	•	0.3
Net Sales to Working Capital **32**	•	•	13.7	6.9	5.8	6.1	4.5	•	5.0
Coverage Ratio **33**	5.7	•	18.3	3.1	5.7	5.1	11.2	•	21.0
Total Asset Turnover **34**	1.8	•	3.6	0.9	3.5	3.0	2.7	•	1.1
Inventory Turnover **35**	6.1	•	3.7	3.2	2.6	5.9	2.3	•	1.6
Receivables Turnover **36**	50.2	•	190.8	•	41.7	74.5	20.9	•	13.9
Total Liabilities to Net Worth **37**	1.8	•	3.7	3.0	1.1	1.7	0.5	•	0.5
Current Assets to Working Capital **38**	•	•	2.7	3.2	1.4	1.5	1.4	•	2.3
Current Liabilities to Working Capital **39**	•	•	1.7	2.2	0.4	0.5	0.4	•	1.3
Working Capital to Net Sales **40**	•	•	0.1	0.1	0.2	0.2	0.2	•	0.2
Inventory to Working Capital **41**	•	•	1.7	1.5	1.1	0.8	1.1	•	1.0
Total Receipts to Cash Flow **42**	10.8	13.2	6.3	7.9	8.6	10.0	8.2	•	5.2
Cost of Goods to Cash Flow **43**	8.0	10.6	3.5	5.6	5.2	6.0	5.6	•	3.1
Cash Flow to Total Debt **44**	0.3	•	0.7	0.1	0.8	0.5	0.9	•	0.7

Selected Financial Factors (in Percentages)

Debt Ratio **45**	64.5	•	78.6	75.1	51.7	63.1	34.6	•	32.7
Return on Total Assets **46**	10.3	•	21.3	6.3	16.3	12.8	22.5	•	12.1
Return on Equity Before Income Taxes **47**	24.0	•	94.2	17.2	27.9	27.9	31.3	•	17.1
Return on Equity After Income Taxes **48**	15.8	•	94.0	17.1	23.5	27.3	31.2	•	15.0
Profit Margin (Before Income Tax) **49**	4.8	0.8	5.6	4.9	3.8	3.5	7.6	•	10.1
Profit Margin (After Income Tax) **50**	3.1	0.7	5.6	4.9	3.2	3.4	7.6	•	8.9

MISCELLANEOUS STORE RETAILERS

Table I

Corporations with and without Net Income

MONEY AMOUNTS AND SIZE OF ASSETS IN THOUSANDS OF DOLLARS

Item Description for Accounting Period 7/07 Through 6/08		Total	Zero Assets	Under 500	500 to 1,000	1,000 to 5,000	5,000 to 10,000	10,000 to 25,000	25,000 to 50,000	50,000 to 100,000	100,000 to 250,000	250,000 to 500,000	500,000 to 2,500,000	2,500,000 and over
Number of Enterprises	1	88956	18602	60770	4742	4037	454	230	49	31	16	8	12	3
Revenues ($ in Thousands)														
Net Sales	2	136569089	2086543	30116044	8387123	17022821	4601007	7297726	3222168	3034885	3009437	4491607	20217853	33081875
Interest	3	454533	816	10424	4370	38526	7862	7635	1947	5158	19861	11410	68195	278328
Rents	4	91807	0	1972	13449	7705	68	1285	829	3344	2343	3785	42765	14262
Royalties	5	168858	0	0	0	110	660	38685	2964	22541	0	4657	22404	76837
Other Portfolio Income	6	835946	8075	18699	27127	62887	23980	13902	1219	21203	6880	0	314482	337494
Other Receipts	7	1381075	39093	208449	43051	197775	83416	69194	58820	57352	55332	51088	442873	74632
Total Receipts	8	139501308	2134527	30355588	8475120	17329824	4716993	7428427	3287947	3144483	3093853	4562547	21108572	33863428
Average Total Receipts	9	1568	115	500	1787	4293	10390	32298	67101	101435	193366	570318	1759048	11287809
Operating Costs/Operating Income (%)														
Cost of Operations	10	63.5	58.7	59.1	64.2	66.5	67.4	67.7	56.3	65.6	58.6	64.7	58.7	68.5
Salaries and Wages	11	10.8	9.3	10.3	9.7	10.5	9.4	11.4	10.1	10.8	13.9	10.7	14.8	9.1
Taxes Paid	12	1.9	3.1	2.2	2.2	2.0	1.4	1.7	1.5	1.6	1.7	1.3	2.1	1.5
Interest Paid	13	1.2	1.0	0.8	1.0	1.2	1.1	1.1	1.4	2.3	3.5	2.1	2.0	0.9
Depreciation	14	1.3	1.1	0.9	1.3	1.0	0.7	1.6	1.3	2.5	1.3	1.6	2.0	1.5
Amortization and Depletion	15	0.3	0.3	0.1	0.1	0.1	0.1	0.1	0.1	0.4	0.2	1.0	0.8	0.2
Pensions and Other Deferred Comp.	16	0.2	0.0	0.1	0.1	0.2	0.6	0.3	0.3	0.3	0.1	0.0	0.2	0.1
Employee Benefits	17	0.9	0.6	0.4	0.5	0.7	0.8	0.7	0.8	0.8	1.5	1.2	1.3	1.1
Advertising	18	1.9	2.1	1.5	1.6	1.0	0.9	1.1	5.4	2.3	2.6	4.1	1.5	2.7
Other Expenses	19	14.7	30.2	19.6	13.7	12.8	12.8	10.7	19.4	14.5	15.9	9.6	15.4	11.4
Officers' Compensation	20	2.2	2.5	4.5	4.1	4.0	2.6	2.4	1.1	2.0	0.7	0.8	0.6	0.1
Operating Margin	21	1.1	•	0.4	1.4	•	2.0	1.3	2.3	•	0.1	2.9	0.6	3.0
Operating Margin Before Officers' Comp.	22	3.3	•	4.9	5.5	3.9	4.6	3.7	3.4	•	0.8	3.7	1.3	3.1

Selected Average Balance Sheet ($ in Thousands)

Net Receivables 23	86	0	12	76	286	884	2503	6801	10421	16581	22682	168158	449528
Inventories 24	214	0	43	332	816	2524	5035	15350	18738	60751	98021	189902	1277592
Net Property, Plant and Equipment 25	138	0	23	125	415	528	3036	4207	12559	22968	43203	273128	1017590
Total Assets 26	776	0	114	674	2047	6299	14882	35478	64692	163450	333638	1380237	6271534
Notes and Loans Payable 27	278	0	66	301	817	1780	4948	12208	25121	102545	124046	456285	1532044
All Other Liabilities 28	271	0	32	185	512	2059	5152	10623	22050	53794	102943	692646	1971066
Net Worth 29	226	0	15	188	718	2459	4781	12647	17520	7111	106648	231306	2768424

Selected Financial Ratios (Times to 1)

Current Ratio 30	1.4	•	1.9	2.5	1.8	2.0	1.5	1.6	1.4	1.3	1.9	0.8	1.4
Quick Ratio 31	0.5	•	0.8	0.8	0.7	0.5	0.6	0.7	0.5	0.6	0.5	0.3	0.4
Net Sales to Working Capital 32	12.2	•	13.9	5.9	6.7	3.8	9.3	6.5	8.1	9.2	6.1	•	12.5
Coverage Ratio 33	3.7	•	2.5	3.5	2.4	5.0	3.9	4.0	1.2	1.8	3.1	3.6	7.5
Total Asset Turnover 34	2.0	•	4.4	2.6	2.1	1.6	2.1	1.9	1.5	1.2	1.7	1.2	1.8
Inventory Turnover 35	4.6	•	6.8	3.4	3.4	2.7	4.3	2.4	3.4	1.8	3.7	5.2	5.9
Receivables Turnover 36	15.4	•	39.5	20.0	13.1	10.8	15.3	7.9	12.8	10.9	26.7	9.6	14.6
Total Liabilities to Net Worth 37	2.4	•	6.4	2.6	1.8	1.6	2.1	1.8	2.7	2.1	2.1	5.0	1.3
Current Assets to Working Capital 38	3.4	•	2.2	1.7	2.2	2.0	3.0	2.7	3.4	4.2	2.2	•	3.3
Current Liabilities to Working Capital 39	2.4	•	1.2	0.7	1.2	1.0	2.0	1.7	2.4	3.2	1.2	•	2.3
Working Capital to Net Sales 40	0.1	•	0.1	0.2	0.2	0.3	0.1	0.2	0.1	0.1	0.2	•	0.1
Inventory to Working Capital 41	1.7	•	1.2	1.1	1.2	1.3	1.6	1.2	1.8	2.0	1.4	•	1.4
Total Receipts to Cash Flow 42	8.1	10.3	7.7	9.3	9.3	7.6	10.3	5.0	9.9	7.7	13.5	7.3	7.9
Cost of Goods to Cash Flow 43	5.2	6.1	4.6	6.0	6.2	5.1	7.0	2.8	6.5	4.5	8.8	4.3	5.4
Cash Flow to Total Debt 44	0.3	•	0.7	0.4	0.3	0.3	0.3	0.6	0.2	0.2	0.2	0.2	0.4

Selected Financial Factors (in Percentages)

Debt Ratio 45	70.8	•	86.5	72.1	64.9	61.0	67.9	64.4	72.9	95.6	68.0	83.2	55.9
Return on Total Assets 46	9.0	•	8.7	8.9	6.0	9.1	9.0	10.6	4.2	7.3	11.1	8.9	11.5
Return on Equity Before Income Taxes 47	22.5	•	38.8	23.0	10.0	18.6	20.8	22.4	2.5	74.8	23.6	38.3	22.6
Return on Equity After Income Taxes 48	17.0	•	36.9	22.0	8.4	16.8	19.2	20.1	•	51.2	21.2	25.9	15.8
Profit Margin (Before Income Tax) 49	3.3	•	1.2	2.4	1.7	4.5	3.1	4.3	0.4	2.8	4.5	5.3	5.7
Profit Margin (After Income Tax) 50	2.5	•	1.1	2.3	1.4	4.1	2.9	3.9	•	1.9	4.0	3.6	4.0

Table II
Corporations with Net Income

MISCELLANEOUS STORE RETAILERS

MONEY AMOUNTS AND SIZE OF ASSETS IN THOUSANDS OF DOLLARS

Item Description for Accounting Period 7/07 Through 6/08		Total	Zero Assets	Under 500	500 to 1,000	1,000 to 5,000	5,000 to 10,000	10,000 to 25,000	25,000 to 50,000	50,000 to 100,000	100,000 to 250,000	250,000 to 500,000	500,000 to 2,500,000	2,500,000 and over
Number of Enterprises	1	44716	6125	31797	3488	2666	398	167	29	19	•	•	8	3
Revenues ($ in Thousands)														
Net Sales	2	109785581	1177035	18803695	6168869	12867446	4256793	6285933	2371193	1896296	•	•	16770744	33081875
Interest	3	430325	629	7938	3895	31337	7427	4687	1173	3588	•	•	63751	278328
Rents	4	45673	0	1972	13449	6060	68	1136	829	201	•	•	2997	14262
Royalties	5	159585	0	0	0	83	660	38685	2	20574	•	•	20745	76837
Other Portfolio Income	6	805556	6772	13093	26874	54808	23915	8967	307	13755	•	•	314328	337494
Other Receipts	7	1137222	26107	139128	34907	166897	75261	50594	40619	23162	•	•	440369	74632
Total Receipts	8	112363942	1210543	18965826	6247994	13126631	4364124	6390002	2414123	1957576	•	•	17612934	33863428
Average Total Receipts	9	2513	198	596	1791	4924	10965	38263	83246	103030	•	•	2201617	11287809
Operating Costs/Operating Income (%)														
Cost of Operations	10	63.4	61.9	56.0	62.9	66.9	66.8	67.8	51.2	65.4	•	•	57.5	68.5
Salaries and Wages	11	10.5	6.4	10.0	9.3	9.5	9.3	11.0	10.3	9.0	•	•	15.3	9.1
Taxes Paid	12	1.8	2.6	2.2	2.2	1.9	1.4	1.7	1.5	1.4	•	•	2.1	1.5
Interest Paid	13	1.1	0.5	0.7	0.9	1.0	1.0	0.9	1.2	1.1	•	•	1.9	0.9
Depreciation	14	1.3	0.7	0.8	1.3	0.7	0.7	1.5	1.2	2.0	•	•	2.0	1.5
Amortization and Depletion	15	0.2	0.3	0.1	0.1	0.0	0.0	0.1	0.1	0.1	•	•	0.5	0.2
Pensions and Other Deferred Comp.	16	0.2	•	0.1	0.2	0.3	0.7	0.2	0.4	0.4	•	•	0.2	0.1
Employee Benefits	17	0.9	0.7	0.5	0.5	0.6	0.8	0.6	1.0	1.0	•	•	1.3	1.1
Advertising	18	1.9	1.1	1.3	1.3	0.9	0.9	0.9	6.6	1.3	•	•	1.3	2.7
Other Expenses	19	13.6	21.4	18.7	13.7	12.2	12.8	9.7	20.0	11.3	•	•	15.5	11.4
Officers' Compensation	20	2.0	1.9	4.5	3.9	4.3	2.7	2.4	1.1	2.5	•	•	0.5	0.1
Operating Margin	21	3.2	2.4	5.0	3.8	1.8	2.9	3.2	5.6	4.4	•	•	1.9	3.0
Operating Margin Before Officers' Comp.	22	5.2	4.3	9.5	7.7	6.0	5.6	5.6	6.6	6.9	•	•	2.4	3.1

Selected Average Balance Sheet ($ in Thousands)

Net Receivables 23	143	•	18	84	351	909	2929	8721	11502	•	206124	449528
Inventories 24	324	0	46	259	899	2525	4902	17269	21667	•	245068	1277592
Net Property, Plant and Equipment 25	211	0	27	121	298	448	2806	4677	9756	•	363248	1017590
Total Assets 26	1225	0	135	659	2074	6290	15099	36849	63750	•	1608447	6271534
Notes and Loans Payable 27	384	0	61	236	656	1759	4461	9389	14684	•	533262	1532044
All Other Liabilities 28	441	0	33	176	566	1918	5513	13031	24680	•	872808	1971066
Net Worth 29	400	0	42	248	853	2614	5125	14429	24385	•	202377	2768424

Selected Financial Ratios (Times to 1)

Current Ratio 30	1.4	•	2.1	2.9	1.9	2.0	1.5	1.7	1.5	•	0.7	1.4
Quick Ratio 31	0.5	•	1.1	1.0	0.8	0.5	0.6	0.9	0.6	•	0.3	0.4
Net Sales to Working Capital 32	12.7	•	12.6	5.7	6.5	3.9	11.4	7.1	7.2	•	•	12.5
Coverage Ratio 33	6.2	12.0	9.9	6.6	5.0	6.7	6.6	7.4	7.8	•	4.9	7.5
Total Asset Turnover 34	2.0	•	4.4	2.7	2.3	1.7	2.5	2.2	1.6	•	1.3	1.8
Inventory Turnover 35	4.8	•	7.1	4.3	3.6	2.8	5.2	2.4	3.0	•	4.9	5.9
Receivables Turnover 36	14.5	•	33.5	18.7	11.8	11.1	16.0	6.7	11.3	•	•	14.6
Total Liabilities to Net Worth 37	2.1	•	2.2	1.7	1.4	1.4	1.9	1.6	1.6	•	6.9	1.3
Current Assets to Working Capital 38	3.5	•	1.9	1.5	2.1	2.0	3.2	2.4	3.1	•	•	3.3
Current Liabilities to Working Capital 39	2.5	•	0.9	0.5	1.1	1.0	2.2	1.4	2.1	•	•	2.3
Working Capital to Net Sales 40	0.1	•	0.1	0.2	0.2	0.3	0.1	0.1	0.1	•	•	0.1
Inventory to Working Capital 41	1.7	•	0.9	0.9	1.0	1.2	1.6	1.0	1.5	•	•	1.4
Total Receipts to Cash Flow 42	7.2	5.8	5.9	7.5	8.0	7.1	9.4	4.0	6.5	•	6.6	7.9
Cost of Goods to Cash Flow 43	4.6	3.6	3.3	4.7	5.3	4.8	6.4	2.0	4.3	•	3.8	5.4
Cash Flow to Total Debt 44	0.4	•	1.1	0.6	0.5	0.4	0.4	0.9	0.4	•	0.2	0.4

Selected Financial Factors (in Percentages)

Debt Ratio 45	67.4	•	69.1	62.4	58.5	58.9	66.1	60.8	61.7	•	87.4	55.9
Return on Total Assets 46	13.6	•	28.5	16.0	10.8	11.0	14.3	19.0	13.7	•	11.8	11.5
Return on Equity Before Income Taxes 47	34.9	•	82.9	36.2	22.2	21.4	35.7	41.9	31.2	•	74.7	22.6
Return on Equity After Income Taxes 48	28.7	•	81.6	35.3	20.2	19.4	33.7	38.5	28.2	•	53.5	15.8
Profit Margin (Before Income Tax) 49	5.7	5.3	5.9	5.1	5.4	3.8	4.9	7.4	7.6	•	7.2	5.7
Profit Margin (After Income Tax) 50	4.7	4.9	5.8	4.9	3.4	4.9	4.6	6.8	6.9	•	5.2	4.0

Table I

Corporations with and without Net Income

NONSTORE RETAILERS

MONEY AMOUNTS AND SIZE OF ASSETS IN THOUSANDS OF DOLLARS

Item Description for Accounting Period 7/07 Through 6/08	Total	Zero Assets	Under 500	500 to 1,000	1,000 to 5,000	5,000 to 10,000	10,000 to 25,000	25,000 to 50,000	50,000 to 100,000	100,000 to 250,000	250,000 to 500,000	500,000 to 2,500,000	2,500,000 and over
Number of Enterprises 1	55002	16723	31926	2942	2592	418	199	79	46	39	14	14	9
Revenues ($ in Thousands)													
Net Sales 2	161943321	1468028	18883252	9347484	20465140	8073346	8618578	6304748	6586572	14378743	11355757	15760163	40701508
Interest 3	1642752	13018	3028	8763	11536	6111	16186	13059	25539	43555	185102	186296	1130560
Rents 4	74847	48	3404	582	2253	3634	4268	7078	7014	4861	1347	39924	434
Royalties 5	644538	1391	0	0	19906	0	527	658	3244	272	2051	204918	411572
Other Portfolio Income 6	637224	116587	72674	24948	11321	27121	28720	15349	21339	26880	46108	49563	196614
Other Receipts 7	3430123	12096	33074	36836	99975	165700	111039	26498	107229	106548	105757	282395	2342978
Total Receipts 8	168372805	1611168	18995432	9418613	20610131	8275912	8779318	6367390	6750937	14560859	11696122	16523259	44783666
Average Total Receipts 9	3061	96	595	3201	7951	19799	44117	80600	146760	373355	835437	1180233	4975963
Operating Costs/Operating Income (%)													
Cost of Operations 10	67.1	59.2	64.1	66.5	70.4	61.4	72.9	64.2	67.0	71.5	73.1	61.1	66.7
Salaries and Wages 11	8.8	10.3	7.3	6.9	7.7	11.4	8.4	9.2	6.7	7.7	5.1	9.6	11.2
Taxes Paid 12	1.2	2.0	1.4	1.8	1.2	1.9	1.1	1.4	0.9	1.0	0.7	1.5	1.0
Interest Paid 13	1.9	2.4	0.5	0.4	0.6	0.8	0.6	0.9	1.2	1.0	1.0	2.1	4.9
Depreciation 14	1.3	1.7	0.9	1.3	1.1	2.1	1.3	1.8	1.2	1.0	0.6	1.5	1.5
Amortization and Depletion 15	0.4	0.4	0.2	0.0	0.2	0.1	0.2	0.4	0.4	0.7	0.6	0.6	0.7
Pensions and Other Deferred Comp. 16	0.2	0.1	0.2	0.6	0.2	0.2	0.3	0.2	0.3	0.2	0.1	0.3	0.2
Employee Benefits 17	0.8	1.3	0.3	0.7	0.6	0.8	0.7	1.3	0.8	0.7	0.5	1.0	1.0
Advertising 18	3.0	4.4	1.8	2.7	1.8	2.3	3.3	2.8	4.3	4.4	4.3	3.4	3.1
Other Expenses 19	14.3	24.2	16.8	13.1	13.1	16.9	11.9	16.4	14.4	11.4	12.6	14.5	14.7
Officers' Compensation 20	1.8	5.7	4.5	3.7	2.2	2.2	0.9	1.1	1.0	0.9	0.7	0.6	1.1
Operating Margin 21	•	•	2.1	2.5	0.9	•	•	0.4	1.7	•	0.7	3.7	•
Operating Margin Before Officers' Comp. 22	1.0	•	6.6	6.1	3.1	2.0	•	1.5	2.6	0.5	1.4	4.3	•

Selected Average Balance Sheet ($ in Thousands)

Net Receivables 23	299	0	11	137	538	1322	2882	7643	16212	23988	96295	83550	929850
Inventories 24	173	0	21	107	339	1271	2832	6547	11436	35358	61178	97485	211716
Net Property, Plant and Equipment 25	186	0	19	131	451	1652	2858	5500	9022	16009	24566	103983	394181
Total Assets 26	2840	0	91	723	2052	6783	15565	33247	70982	155352	386487	1042898	11999718
Notes and Loans Payable 27	770	0	46	262	763	2426	3856	10259	21713	49605	79850	275324	3071554
All Other Liabilities 28	888	0	29	223	727	1908	6329	11644	22621	47909	126699	276836	3760744
Net Worth 29	1182	0	16	238	562	2449	5381	11344	26648	57838	179938	490737	5167420

Selected Financial Ratios (Times to 1)

Current Ratio 30	1.0	•	1.9	1.4	1.8	1.5	1.5	1.3	1.7	1.2	0.8		
Quick Ratio 31	0.6	•	1.1	1.3	0.9	0.8	0.8	0.7	1.0	0.7	0.5		
Net Sales to Working Capital 32	113.1	•	19.4	13.9	21.4	11.0	12.2	10.5	10.7	15.9	9.8	20.2	•
Coverage Ratio 33	2.7	0.2	6.5	9.1	3.6	3.8	1.4	2.7	4.5	1.9	4.7	5.2	1.9
Total Asset Turnover 34	1.0	•	6.5	4.4	3.8	2.8	2.8	2.4	2.0	2.4	2.1	1.1	0.4
Inventory Turnover 35	11.4	•	17.8	19.7	16.4	9.3	11.1	7.8	8.4	7.5	9.7	7.1	14.3
Receivables Turnover 36	11.0	•	53.3	25.1	18.1	14.8	14.2	11.8	9.3	14.1	9.3	8.6	6.4
Total Liabilities to Net Worth 37	1.4	•	4.8	2.0	2.7	1.8	1.9	1.9	1.7	1.7	1.1	1.1	1.3
Current Assets to Working Capital 38	33.8	•	2.1	2.1	3.6	2.3	2.9	2.8	3.1	3.9	2.5	6.0	•
Current Liabilities to Working Capital 39	32.8	•	1.1	1.1	2.6	1.3	1.9	1.8	2.1	2.9	1.5	5.0	•
Working Capital to Net Sales 40	0.0	•	0.1	0.0	0.1	0.1	0.1	0.1	0.1	0.1	0.1	0.0	•
Inventory to Working Capital 41	7.1	•	0.7	0.5	0.6	0.8	0.8	0.8	1.0	1.5	0.8	1.6	•
Total Receipts to Cash Flow 42	6.4	5.2	6.2	6.7	7.8	5.8	9.6	6.3	5.8	9.3	6.8	4.8	5.8
Cost of Goods to Cash Flow 43	4.3	3.1	4.0	4.4	5.5	3.5	7.0	4.0	3.9	6.6	4.9	2.9	3.9
Cash Flow to Total Debt 44	0.3	•	1.3	1.0	0.7	0.8	0.4	0.6	0.6	0.4	0.6	0.4	0.1

Selected Financial Factors (in Percentages)

Debt Ratio 45	58.4	•	82.8	67.1	72.6	63.9	65.4	65.9	62.5	62.8	53.4	52.9	56.9
Return on Total Assets 46	5.5	•	20.4	15.9	8.6	8.8	2.4	5.5	11.0	4.5	9.7	11.8	3.5
Return on Equity Before Income Taxes 47	8.3	•	100.3	42.8	22.6	17.9	2.1	10.1	22.7	5.8	16.4	20.4	3.9
Return on Equity After Income Taxes 48	6.2	•	97.8	41.3	22.0	16.8	•	8.3	17.1	2.6	13.7	13.7	2.6
Profit Margin (Before Income Tax) 49	3.3	•	2.6	3.2	1.6	2.3	0.3	1.4	4.2	0.9	3.6	8.9	4.4
Profit Margin (After Income Tax) 50	2.5	•	2.6	3.1	1.6	2.1	•	1.2	3.2	0.4	3.0	6.0	3.0

Table II

Corporations with Net Income

NONSTORE RETAILERS

MONEY AMOUNTS AND SIZE OF ASSETS IN THOUSANDS OF DOLLARS

Item Description for Accounting Period 7/07 Through 6/08	Total	Zero Assets	Under 500	500 to 1,000	1,000 to 5,000	5,000 to 10,000	10,000 to 25,000	25,000 to 50,000	50,000 to 100,000	100,000 to 250,000	250,000 to 500,000	500,000 to 2,500,000	2,500,000 and over
Number of Enterprises **1**	25867	3816	17693	2209	1662	233	116	•	•	24	•	10	6
Revenues ($ in Thousands)													
Net Sales **2**	131487946	852617	14296311	7839448	15223812	4940983	5829573	•	•	10228595	•	13836625	38255198
Interest **3**	1542946	12861	460	6331	7950	3310	7597	•	•	27379	•	142884	1130362
Rents **4**	48626	48	0	582	107	6	191	•	•	823	•	39599	434
Royalties **5**	624516	1391	0	0	19906	0	0	•	•	168	•	187779	411572
Other Portfolio Income **6**	543189	83646	72674	24374	8434	24635	21840	•	•	3282	•	49497	190421
Other Receipts **7**	3112287	1836	8975	34025	38858	117048	94886	•	•	52417	•	268979	2275965
Total Receipts **8**	137359510	952399	14378420	7904760	15299067	5085982	5954087	•	•	10312664	•	14525363	42263952
Average Total Receipts **9**	5310	250	813	3578	9205	21828	51328	•	•	429694	•	1452536	7043992
Operating Costs/Operating Income (%)													
Cost of Operations **10**	66.9	59.4	62.8	67.4	72.5	60.3	72.0	•	•	72.5	•	59.1	66.6
Salaries and Wages **11**	8.4	7.6	7.7	6.8	6.4	8.7	6.8	•	•	7.1	•	9.8	10.9
Taxes Paid **12**	1.2	2.0	1.4	1.8	1.1	1.4	1.1	•	•	0.9	•	1.6	1.0
Interest Paid **13**	1.8	0.6	0.3	0.3	0.5	0.5	0.4	•	•	0.9	•	1.7	4.4
Depreciation **14**	1.1	0.7	0.8	1.2	0.8	1.6	1.0	•	•	0.7	•	1.6	1.4
Amortization and Depletion **15**	0.4	0.1	0.2	0.0	0.2	0.1	0.2	•	•	0.2	•	0.5	0.7
Pensions and Other Deferred Comp. **16**	0.2	0.1	0.2	0.6	0.2	0.3	0.2	•	•	0.2	•	0.4	0.1
Employee Benefits **17**	0.6	1.1	0.2	0.7	0.6	0.6	0.6	•	•	0.7	•	1.0	0.6
Advertising **18**	2.8	1.3	1.0	2.4	1.8	2.8	3.6	•	•	3.9	•	3.3	2.9
Other Expenses **19**	13.5	18.2	14.9	10.9	10.3	17.5	10.6	•	•	9.2	•	14.3	15.3
Officers' Compensation **20**	1.8	6.9	5.0	3.3	2.2	3.1	0.9	•	•	0.9	•	0.6	1.2
Operating Margin **21**	1.3	1.9	5.4	4.6	3.5	3.2	2.8	•	•	2.9	•	6.1	•
Operating Margin Before Officers' Comp. **22**	3.1	8.7	10.4	7.9	5.7	6.3	3.6	•	•	3.8	•	•	•

Selected Average Balance Sheet ($ in Thousands)

Net Receivables 23	527	0	16	142	671	1082	3619	•	27493	•	98440	1218508
Inventories 24	292	0	28	101	343	1432	2618	•	44609	•	130069	339098
Net Property, Plant and Equipment 25	281	0	23	133	380	1293	2366	•	14813	•	125073	498809
Total Assets 26	4888	0	125	720	2171	7071	15596	•	158047	•	1020812	15467114
Notes and Loans Payable 27	1113	0	38	192	700	1369	3023	•	48110	•	218624	3424440
All Other Liabilities 28	1644	0	34	214	592	1878	6628	•	49007	•	345296	5270742
Net Worth 29	2131	0	53	313	879	3824	5945	•	60930	•	456892	6771933

Selected Financial Ratios (Times to 1)

Current Ratio 30	1.0	•	2.6	2.1	1.7	2.0	1.5	•	1.6	•	1.3	0.7
Quick Ratio 31	0.6	•	1.6	1.4	1.2	1.0	0.8	•	0.9	•	0.7	0.5
Net Sales to Working Capital 32	•	•	14.1	14.1	15.3	9.6	14.0	•	11.2	•	16.5	•
Coverage Ratio 33	4.3	23.1	19.4	18.8	9.0	13.9	12.3	•	5.4	•	7.7	2.3
Total Asset Turnover 34	1.0	•	6.5	4.9	4.2	3.0	3.2	•	2.7	•	1.4	0.4
Inventory Turnover 35	11.6	•	18.0	23.7	19.4	8.9	13.8	•	6.9	•	6.3	12.5
Receivables Turnover 36	10.4	•	56.6	26.6	17.5	15.0	12.6	•	12.5	•	8.1	•
Total Liabilities to Net Worth 37	1.3	•	1.4	1.3	1.5	0.8	1.6	•	1.6	•	1.2	1.3
Current Assets to Working Capital 38	•	•	1.6	1.9	2.5	2.0	3.0	•	2.7	•	4.5	•
Current Liabilities to Working Capital 39	•	•	0.6	0.9	1.5	1.0	2.0	•	1.7	•	3.5	•
Working Capital to Net Sales 40	•	•	0.1	0.1	0.1	0.1	0.1	•	0.1	•	0.1	•
Inventory to Working Capital 41	•	•	0.5	0.5	0.6	0.6	0.7	•	1.0	•	1.4	•
Total Receipts to Cash Flow 42	5.6	3.3	5.7	6.6	7.7	4.6	7.1	•	8.4	•	4.3	5.1
Cost of Goods to Cash Flow 43	3.8	2.0	3.6	4.5	5.6	2.8	5.1	•	6.1	•	2.6	3.4
Cash Flow to Total Debt 44	0.3	•	2.0	1.3	0.9	1.4	0.7	•	0.5	•	0.6	0.1

Selected Financial Factors (in Percentages)

Debt Ratio 45	56.4	•	57.8	56.4	59.5	45.9	61.9	•	61.4	•	55.2	56.2
Return on Total Assets 46	8.1	•	41.0	28.3	18.8	19.7	17.2	•	12.3	•	17.6	4.3
Return on Equity Before Income Taxes 47	14.4	•	92.0	61.5	41.3	33.8	41.5	•	26.1	•	34.2	5.6
Return on Equity After Income Taxes 48	11.9	•	90.7	59.9	40.6	32.4	36.2	•	21.2	•	24.2	4.1
Profit Margin (Before Income Tax) 49	6.0	13.6	6.0	5.4	4.0	6.1	4.9	•	3.7	•	11.3	5.9
Profit Margin (After Income Tax) 50	5.0	13.5	5.9	5.3	3.9	5.8	4.3	•	3.0	•	8.0	4.4

Table I

Corporations with and without Net Income

AIR TRANSPORTATION

MONEY AMOUNTS AND SIZE OF ASSETS IN THOUSANDS OF DOLLARS

Item Description for Accounting Period 7/07 Through 6/08	Total	Zero Assets	Under 500	500 to 1,000	1,000 to 5,000	5,000 to 10,000	10,000 to 25,000	25,000 to 50,000	50,000 to 100,000	100,000 to 250,000	250,000 to 500,000	500,000 to 2,500,000	2,500,000 and over
Number of Enterprises **1**	7143	552	4223	996	844	249	155	56	19	11	6	18	12
Revenues ($ in Thousands)													
Net Sales **2**	152842697	1187012	432681	542615	1114454	1675664	3779533	1747122	1770247	2103527	2860155	16438751	119190936
Interest **3**	1662448	2034	39	533	1503	1310	2730	10126	16268	10210	29484	167291	1420922
Rents **4**	271193	1818	5	0	5363	0	0	1360	143	0	2747	5086	254671
Royalties **5**	311	0	0	0	0	0	0	254	0	0	0	57	0
Other Portfolio Income **6**	1625958	110416	70080	135122	73899	45045	76245	27012	9110	7718	114	155898	915298
Other Receipts **7**	521180	4732	813	1081	5307	19320	42452	15959	109822	34575	66649	570572	4349897
Total Receipts **8**	161623787	1306012	503618	679351	1200526	1741339	3900960	1801833	1905590	2156030	2959149	17337655	126131724
Average Total Receipts **9**	22627	2366	119	682	1422	6993	25167	32176	100294	196003	493192	963203	10510977
Operating Costs/Operating Income (%)													
Cost of Operations **10**	31.7	52.2	59.5	76.5	26.8	57.7	61.4	61.2	27.8	22.1	44.3	30.9	29.5
Salaries and Wages **11**	16.2	5.2	0.5	5.5	12.6	9.2	9.1	9.3	18.7	12.6	13.4	16.7	16.9
Taxes Paid **12**	2.3	1.4	3.3	0.8	3.0	1.8	1.5	2.8	2.3	1.4	1.1	2.8	2.3
Interest Paid **13**	2.9	1.3	0.5	1.0	2.8	2.2	2.2	2.1	1.4	1.8	2.5	2.9	3.0
Depreciation **14**	6.0	7.1	25.6	22.8	14.6	8.2	7.1	5.9	4.2	5.3	3.0	5.8	5.9
Amortization and Depletion **15**	0.4	•	0.2	0.0	0.4	0.1	0.4	0.2	0.2	0.1	•	1.0	0.3
Pensions and Other Deferred Comp. **16**	1.9	0.2	•	•	0.3	0.0	0.2	0.1	0.2	0.3	0.1	0.8	2.3
Employee Benefits **17**	2.4	0.6	0.0	0.2	0.8	0.5	0.8	1.1	2.1	1.3	1.2	1.7	2.7
Advertising **18**	0.7	0.1	0.0	0.0	0.2	0.3	0.2	0.6	1.2	0.3	0.9	0.6	0.8
Other Expenses **19**	43.6	39.9	31.8	29.8	50.6	33.0	25.9	21.4	53.9	54.8	40.9	40.3	44.8
Officers' Compensation **20**	0.3	2.7	1.3	3.9	2.2	1.1	1.5	0.9	0.8	2.1	0.3	0.6	0.2
Operating Margin **21**	•	•	•	•	•	•	•	•	•	•	•	•	•
Operating Margin Before Officers' Comp. **22**	•	•	•	•	•	•	•	•	•	0.1	•	•	•

Selected Average Balance Sheet ($ in Thousands)

Net Receivables 23	1181	0	7	150	253	490	3009	4233	10398	19429	21190	70895	450264
Inventories 24	489	0	18	0	7	109	390	1128	4359	7368	15436	24404	213727
Net Property, Plant and Equipment 25	13255	0	57	284	1152	3152	8568	15244	25871	66806	89752	431988	6723011
Total Assets 26	27840	0	95	650	2288	6998	15672	33313	69631	177899	308108	921342	14011217
Notes and Loans Payable 27	9745	0	195	147	1119	4179	8281	13086	30261	58437	98838	421844	4602790
All Other Liabilities 28	11739	0	5	116	358	1246	4364	10271	23309	57705	149704	310582	6190253
Net Worth 29	6356	0	-105	386	812	1573	3026	9956	16062	61757	59565	188916	3218174

Selected Financial Ratios (Times to 1)

Current Ratio 30	1.0	•	7.2	3.1	3.4	1.6	1.1	1.3	1.3	1.4	1.3	1.3	0.9
Quick Ratio 31	0.6	•	3.4	3.1	2.5	1.3	0.9	0.9	0.7	1.0	1.1	0.8	0.5
Net Sales to Working Capital 32	•	•	3.2	2.2	3.2	7.0	48.6	15.5	14.1	8.8	12.2	14.9	•
Coverage Ratio 33	0.1	0.4	•	•	•	•	•	•	•	1.2	•	1.4	0.0
Total Asset Turnover 34	0.8	•	1.1	0.8	0.6	1.0	1.6	0.9	1.3	1.1	1.5	1.0	0.7
Inventory Turnover 35	13.9	•	3.3	•	50.3	35.6	38.4	16.9	5.9	5.7	13.7	11.6	13.7
Receivables Turnover 36	18.5	•	9.5	5.1	5.3	6.8	8.4	7.9	9.0	9.0	13.3	14.2	23.1
Total Liabilities to Net Worth 37	3.4	•	•	0.7	1.8	3.4	4.2	2.3	3.3	1.9	4.2	3.9	3.4
Current Assets to Working Capital 38	•	•	1.2	1.5	1.4	2.6	10.9	4.7	4.9	3.4	3.9	4.8	•
Current Liabilities to Working Capital 39	•	•	0.2	0.5	0.4	1.6	9.9	3.7	3.9	2.4	2.9	3.8	•
Working Capital to Net Sales 40	•	•	0.3	0.5	0.3	0.1	0.0	0.1	0.1	0.1	0.1	0.1	•
Inventory to Working Capital 41	•	•	0.6	•	0.0	0.1	0.9	0.6	0.8	0.3	0.1	0.5	•
Total Receipts to Cash Flow 42	3.6	3.0	7.8	7.8	4.9	24.3	9.9	10.5	2.7	2.8	4.6	4.3	3.4
Cost of Goods to Cash Flow 43	1.2	1.6	4.7	6.0	1.3	14.0	6.1	6.4	0.8	0.6	2.0	1.3	1.0
Cash Flow to Total Debt 44	0.3	•	0.1	0.3	0.2	0.1	0.2	0.1	0.6	0.6	0.4	0.3	0.3

Selected Financial Factors (in Percentages)

Debt Ratio 45	77.2	•	211.2	40.6	64.5	77.5	80.7	70.1	76.9	65.3	80.7	79.5	77.0
Return on Total Assets 46	0.1	•	•	•	•	•	•	•	•	2.4	•	4.2	0.0
Return on Equity Before Income Taxes 47	•	6.1	•	•	•	•	•	•	•	1.3	•	•	6.3
Return on Equity After Income Taxes 48	•	6.1	•	•	•	•	•	•	•	0.0	•	•	1.8
Profit Margin (Before Income Tax) 49	•	•	•	•	•	•	•	•	•	0.4	•	•	1.3
Profit Margin (After Income Tax) 50	•	•	•	•	•	•	•	•	0.0	•	•	0.4	•

Table II

Corporations with Net Income

AIR TRANSPORTATION

MONEY AMOUNTS AND SIZE OF ASSETS IN THOUSANDS OF DOLLARS

Item Description for Accounting Period 7/07 Through 6/08	Total	Zero Assets	Under 500	500 to 1,000	1,000 to 5,000	5,000 to 10,000	10,000 to 25,000	25,000 to 50,000	50,000 to 100,000	100,000 to 250,000	250,000 to 500,000	500,000 to 2,500,000	2,500,000 and over
Number of Enterprises 1	1870	•	1156	175	289	58	57	16	7	6	•	•	•

Revenues ($ in Thousands)

Net Sales 2	103116435	•	111092	449845	878524	688543	2379763	612058	1155816	1915457			
Interest 3	1155517	•	39	533	1350	0	1673	5294	4061	977			
Rents 4	7785	•	5	0	0	0	0	1188	143	0			
Royalties 5	254	•	0	0	0	0	0	254	0	0			
Other Portfolio Income 6	1055056	•	42183	135122	73899	23669	64924	13080	1054	6716			
Other Receipts 7	2646516	•	379	1081	1529	2607	-12489	9016	106431	6796			
Total Receipts 8	107981563	•	153698	586581	955302	714819	2433871	640890	1267505	1929946			
Average Total Receipts 9	57744	•	133	3352	3306	12324	42699	40056	181072	321658			

Operating Costs/Operating Income (%)

Cost of Operations 10	34.4	•	20.4	92.3	32.8	40.1	60.9	66.1	24.4	21.5			
Salaries and Wages 11	16.9	•	1.1	6.0	12.6	7.2	7.6	13.7	22.3	12.0			
Taxes Paid 12	2.2	•	1.2	0.6	2.0	1.4	1.3	2.0	2.7	1.3			
Interest Paid 13	2.5	•	•	0.1	3.0	0.7	0.7	0.6	0.7	1.4			
Depreciation 14	5.2	•	3.6	12.0	7.2	0.5	1.9	2.6	2.5	3.3			
Amortization and Depletion 15	0.3	•	•	•	0.2	0.0	0.1	0.2	0.3	0.1			
Pensions and Other Deferred Comp. 16	1.8	•	•	•	0.3	0.0	0.1	0.2	0.3	0.3			
Employee Benefits 17	2.5	•	0.1	0.1	0.8	0.2	0.7	1.2	2.7	1.3			
Advertising 18	0.7	•	0.0	0.0	0.1	0.0	0.1	0.3	0.1	0.1			
Other Expenses 19	34.6	•	10.1	11.5	37.3	40.8	21.4	12.7	47.5	54.7			
Officers' Compensation 20	0.3	•	2.8	0.2	2.8	0.6	1.8	1.7	0.8	0.9			
Operating Margin 21	•	•	60.7	•	0.9	8.5	3.3	•	•	3.2			
Operating Margin Before Officers' Comp. 22	•	•	63.5	•	3.7	9.0	5.1	0.3	•	4.2			

Selected Average Balance Sheet ($ in Thousands)

Net Receivables	23	2867	•	0	145	691	532	4751	8048	20513	33531
Inventories	24	960	•	0	0	18	379	650	665	5106	11643
Net Property, Plant and Equipment	25	32637	•	2	311	530	948	4405	10644	22115	65110
Total Assets	26	61677	•	27	689	2101	6872	14183	30236	71653	196098
Notes and Loans Payable	27	21359	•	39	0	1216	1031	4452	10320	15465	67018
All Other Liabilities	28	28563	•	0	220	468	358	5890	6631	23936	82005
Net Worth	29	11755	•	-13	469	417	5483	3841	13285	32253	47074

Selected Financial Ratios (Times to 1)

Current Ratio	30	1.0	•	56.0	1.7	4.4	6.8	1.3	2.0	1.6	1.2
Quick Ratio	31	0.5	•	54.0	1.7	3.3	5.1	1.1	1.7	1.3	0.9
Net Sales to Working Capital	32	•	•	3.9	16.3	2.8	2.6	18.3	6.1	10.4	17.8
Coverage Ratio	33	2.4	•	•	118.4	4.2	18.4	8.8	6.3	8.3	3.9
Total Asset Turnover	34	0.9	•	3.5	3.7	1.4	1.7	2.9	1.3	2.3	1.6
Inventory Turnover	35	19.7	•	41.8	•	54.1	12.6	39.1	38.1	7.9	5.9
Receivables Turnover	36	21.4	•	420.8	22.5	7.8	6.2	10.1	5.9	9.4	•
Total Liabilities to Net Worth	37	4.2	•	•	0.5	4.0	0.3	2.7	1.3	1.2	3.2
Current Assets to Working Capital	38	•	•	1.0	2.4	1.3	1.2	4.0	2.0	2.7	5.2
Current Liabilities to Working Capital	39	•	•	0.0	1.4	0.3	0.2	3.0	1.0	1.7	4.2
Working Capital to Net Sales	40	•	•	0.3	0.1	0.4	0.4	0.1	0.2	0.1	0.1
Inventory to Working Capital	41	•	•	0.0	•	0.0	0.0	0.3	0.1	0.1	0.7
Total Receipts to Cash Flow	42	4.0	•	1.0	5.5	3.3	4.3	4.8	9.3	2.4	2.6
Cost of Goods to Cash Flow	43	1.4	•	0.2	5.1	1.1	1.7	2.9	6.1	0.6	0.6
Cash Flow to Total Debt	44	0.3	•	2.5	2.1	0.5	2.0	0.8	0.2	1.7	0.8

Selected Financial Factors (in Percentages)

Debt Ratio	45	80.9	•	145.7	31.9	80.1	20.2	72.9	56.1	55.0	76.0
Return on Total Assets	46	5.2	•	347.2	28.7	18.2	22.4	18.6	4.9	13.8	8.6
Return on Equity Before Income Taxes	47	15.8	•	•	41.8	70.0	26.6	60.8	9.4	27.1	26.7
Return on Equity After Income Taxes	48	14.3	•	•	41.8	60.5	25.1	56.3	8.6	24.0	23.6
Profit Margin (Before Income Tax)	49	3.4	•	99.1	7.6	9.6	12.3	5.6	3.3	5.3	3.9
Profit Margin (After Income Tax)	50	3.0	•	99.0	7.6	8.3	11.6	5.2	3.0	4.7	3.5

Table I

Corporations with and without Net Income

RAIL TRANSPORTATION

MONEY AMOUNTS AND SIZE OF ASSETS IN THOUSANDS OF DOLLARS

Item Description for Accounting Period 7/07 Through 6/08	Total	Zero Assets	Under 500	500 to 1,000	1,000 to 5,000	5,000 to 10,000	10,000 to 25,000	25,000 to 50,000	50,000 to 100,000	100,000 to 250,000	250,000 to 500,000	500,000 to 2,500,000	2,500,000 and over
Number of Enterprises **1**	373	10	200	0	68	35	17	11	8	8	3	4	9
Revenues ($ in Thousands)													
Net Sales **2**	62071146	241862	85742	0	122562	373004	166900	323760	230760	587896	579145	955793	58403724
Interest **3**	1613072	1389	1771	0	25	3083	114	2203	2509	2284	1976	89868	1507850
Rents **4**	496873	19442	1183	0	2908	4	606	2915	652	3750	4639	15953	444821
Royalties **5**	43657	0	0	0	0	278	0	0	0	359	0	•	43019
Other Portfolio Income **6**	767227	4831	308	0	4401	1299	1668	12820	1314	7148	4838	26482	702119
Other Receipts **7**	1544903	-4882	77	0	11232	2968	3995	26695	10413	6408	9022	87201	1391772
Total Receipts **8**	66536878	262642	89081	0	141128	380636	173283	368393	245648	607845	599620	1175297	62493305
Average Total Receipts **9**	178383	26264	445	•	2075	10875	10193	33490	30706	75981	199873	293824	6943701
Operating Costs/Operating Income (%)													
Cost of Operations **10**	18.4	0.7	5.5	•	•	0.6	20.6	50.3	12.1	37.8	39.8	3.9	18.3
Salaries and Wages **11**	20.9	10.6	15.1	•	18.6	13.8	8.0	10.4	21.4	12.3	8.5	25.2	21.3
Taxes Paid **12**	5.3	1.5	7.2	•	5.3	2.6	4.1	2.7	4.6	4.6	2.3	4.7	5.4
Interest Paid **13**	6.3	5.3	5.2	•	2.7	1.1	1.1	1.5	2.7	3.5	1.2	12.8	6.3
Depreciation **14**	8.1	12.0	5.4	•	10.7	2.0	7.3	7.9	9.9	8.3	8.5	8.9	8.1
Amortization and Depletion **15**	0.2	0.3	•	•	0.0	0.0	0.0	0.0	0.1	0.2	0.1	1.7	0.2
Pensions and Other Deferred Comp. **16**	0.8	3.6	0.3	•	•	0.4	•	0.2	1.8	0.8	0.0	0.7	0.8
Employee Benefits **17**	4.7	3.3	1.5	•	•	2.1	2.0	1.4	4.8	2.7	0.6	8.0	4.7
Advertising **18**	0.2	0.0	0.0	•	0.2	0.1	0.1	0.1	0.1	0.0	0.0	0.0	0.2
Other Expenses **19**	30.1	76.6	0.0	•	67.1	66.9	25.9	18.6	38.0	32.8	22.0	51.2	29.4
Officers' Compensation **20**	0.8	39.1	47.9	•	0.3	1.3	0.9	1.2	1.0	1.7	0.9	2.1	0.6
Operating Margin **21**	4.3	•	11.8	•	•	9.1	30.2	5.7	3.7	•	16.2	•	4.8
Operating Margin Before Officers' Comp. **22**	5.1	•	11.8	•	•	10.4	31.1	6.9	4.7	•	17.1	•	5.4

Selected Average Balance Sheet ($ in Thousands)

Net Receivables 23	15438	0	13	•	68	658	1628	6252	4738	20565	31403	139958	530577
Inventories 24	3195	0	1	•	0	2	178	557	360	3502	9920	4976	124066
Net Property, Plant and Equipment 25	359238	0	161	•	1139	1066	7489	20407	42616	102588	245289	640630	14337442
Total Assets 26	466507	0	296	•	1821	6352	16906	35171	69341	147018	339886	1343101	18311639
Notes and Loans Payable 27	105854	0	0	•	653	679	2864	7794	12698	57829	79349	398539	4098291
All Other Liabilities 28	194959	0	-243	•	144	1366	1520	9086	21660	47743	114972	280124	7840484
Net Worth 29	165694	0	539	•	1024	4307	12522	18291	34983	41446	145565	664438	6372865

Selected Financial Ratios (Times to 1)

Current Ratio 30	0.7	•	281.2	•	0.7	2.3	2.3	1.4	3.1	1.9	0.7	0.7	0.6
Quick Ratio 31	0.5	•	239.1	•	0.7	2.2	2.1	1.3	2.4	1.4	0.5	0.6	0.4
Net Sales to Working Capital 32	•	•	3.2	•	•	5.9	4.7	7.4	2.4	4.3	•	•	•
Coverage Ratio 33	2.8	•	4.0	4.7	11.1	31.8	14.1	4.8	0.6	17.9	1.3	•	2.9
Total Asset Turnover 34	0.4	•	1.4	1.0	1.7	0.6	0.8	0.4	0.5	0.6	0.2	0.2	0.4
Inventory Turnover 35	9.6	•	18.4	•	25.7	11.3	26.6	9.7	7.9	7.7	1.9	1.9	9.6
Receivables Turnover 36	10.3	•	23.5	4.6	26.9	5.4	5.5	9.7	5.1	12.3	1.4	2.7	11.8
Total Liabilities to Net Worth 37	1.8	•	•	0.8	0.5	0.9	0.4	5.5	1.0	3.5	1.3	1.0	1.9
Current Assets to Working Capital 38	•	•	1.0	•	1.8	1.7	3.5	1.0	1.5	2.2	1.3	1.0	1.9
Current Liabilities to Working Capital 39	•	•	0.0	•	0.8	0.7	2.5	0.5	0.5	1.2	0.5	•	•
Working Capital to Net Sales 40	•	•	0.3	•	0.2	0.2	0.4	0.4	0.2	0.4	0.2	•	•
Inventory to Working Capital 41	•	•	0.0	•	0.0	0.0	0.0	0.0	0.1	0.2	0.1	•	•
Total Receipts to Cash Flow 42	3.0	•	1.9	1.7	2.2	2.0	2.9	2.5	5.0	2.8	•	2.7	3.1
Cost of Goods to Cash Flow 43	0.6	•	0.1	•	0.0	0.4	0.0	0.3	1.9	1.1	•	0.1	0.6
Cash Flow to Total Debt 44	0.2	•	•	1.4	2.4	1.1	0.6	0.3	0.1	0.1	0.4	0.1	0.2

Selected Financial Factors (in Percentages)

Debt Ratio 45	64.5	•	•	•	43.8	25.9	32.2	48.0	49.6	71.8	57.2	50.5	65.2
Return on Total Assets 46	6.3	•	30.4	•	12.8	20.4	20.5	17.5	5.3	1.0	11.8	3.0	6.4
Return on Equity Before Income Taxes 47	11.5	•	12.5	•	17.9	26.7	27.5	31.3	8.3	•	26.1	1.5	12.0
Return on Equity After Income Taxes 48	7.3	•	8.4	•	12.3	24.4	27.5	22.6	6.6	•	22.1	0.4	7.6
Profit Margin (Before Income Tax) 49	11.5	•	15.7	•	10.2	34.0	11.1	19.5	10.1	•	19.7	4.0	11.8
Profit Margin (After Income Tax) 50	7.3	•	10.6	•	7.0	31.1	11.1	14.1	8.0	•	16.7	1.2	7.5

Table II

Corporations with Net Income

RAIL TRANSPORTATION

MONEY AMOUNTS AND SIZE OF ASSETS IN THOUSANDS OF DOLLARS

Item Description for Accounting Period 7/07 Through 6/08	Total	Zero Assets	Under 500	500 to 1,000	1,000 to 5,000	5,000 to 10,000	10,000 to 25,000	25,000 to 50,000	50,000 to 100,000	100,000 to 250,000	250,000 to 500,000	500,000 to 2,500,000	2,500,000 and over
Number of Enterprises **1**	346	•	200	0	68	32	13	•	5	5	•	0	•
Revenues ($ in Thousands)													
Net Sales **2**	59139481	•	85742	0	122562	373004	166900	•	127795	355908	•	0	•
Interest **3**	1487393	•	1771	0	25	3083	0	•	2484	2029	•	0	•
Rents **4**	423775	•	1183	0	2908	4	606	•	71	3750	•	0	•
Royalties **5**	43657	•	0	0	0	278	0	•	0	359	•	0	•
Other Portfolio Income **6**	750832	•	308	0	4401	1299	1668	•	361	3984	•	0	•
Other Receipts **7**	644370	•	77	0	11232	2968	3995	•	3981	4756	•	0	•
Total Receipts **8**	62489508	•	89081	0	141128	380636	173169	•	134692	370786	•	0	•
Average Total Receipts **9**	180606	•	445	•	2075	11895	13321	•	26938	74157	•	•	•
Operating Costs/Operating Income (%)													
Cost of Operations **10**	19.1	•	5.5	•	0.6	•	20.6	•	3.9	37.7	•	•	•
Salaries and Wages **11**	19.9	•	15.1	•	18.6	13.8	8.0	•	19.0	14.9	•	•	•
Taxes Paid **12**	5.1	•	7.2	•	5.3	2.6	4.1	•	4.0	4.2	•	•	•
Interest Paid **13**	6.1	•	5.2	•	2.7	1.1	1.1	•	4.2	1.6	•	•	•
Depreciation **14**	7.8	•	5.4	•	10.7	2.0	7.3	•	12.2	8.0	•	•	•
Amortization and Depletion **15**	0.1	•	•	•	0.0	0.0	0.0	•	0.1	0.0	•	•	•
Pensions and Other Deferred Comp. **16**	0.8	•	0.3	•	•	•	•	•	2.6	0.6	•	•	•
Employee Benefits **17**	4.4	•	1.5	•	•	2.1	2.0	•	3.8	3.2	•	•	•
Advertising **18**	0.0	•	0.0	•	0.2	0.1	0.1	•	0.1	0.0	•	•	•
Other Expenses **19**	28.8	•	47.9	•	67.1	66.9	25.0	•	33.4	27.2	•	•	•
Officers' Compensation **20**	0.6	•	•	•	0.3	1.3	0.9	•	0.8	1.5	•	•	•
Operating Margin **21**	7.4	•	11.8	•	9.1	31.2	31.2	•	15.9	1.1	•	•	•
Operating Margin Before Officers' Comp. **22**	8.0	•	11.8	•	10.4	32.0	32.0	•	16.7	2.6	•	•	•

Selected Average Balance Sheet ($ in Thousands)

Net Receivables 23	15456	13	68	719	2128	4332	7909
Inventories 24	3101	1	0	3	233	346	2217
Net Property, Plant and Equipment 25	356164	161	1139	1166	9793	39492	108716
Total Assets 26	463570	296	1821	6065	18238	63067	139799
Notes and Loans Payable 27	99474	0	653	743	2972	20080	27304
All Other Liabilities 28	199982	-243	144	1494	1963	13620	59134
Net Worth 29	164114	539	1024	3829	13303	29367	53360

Selected Financial Ratios (Times to 1)

Current Ratio 30	0.7	281.2	2.3	0.7	2.3	3.6	1.3
Quick Ratio 31	0.5	239.1	2.1	0.7	2.2	3.1	0.8
Net Sales to Working Capital 32		3.2	4.9		5.9	1.7	14.2
Coverage Ratio 33	3.2	4.0	11.1	32.5	4.7	6.1	4.2
Total Asset Turnover 34	0.4	1.4	0.7	1.0	1.9	0.4	0.5
Inventory Turnover 35	10.5	18.4	11.3	25.7		2.9	12.1
Receivables Turnover 36	10.6	23.5	5.4	26.9	11.4		5.5
Total Liabilities to Net Worth 37	1.8		0.4	0.6	0.8	1.1	1.6
Current Assets to Working Capital 38		1.0	1.8	1.8		1.4	4.7
Current Liabilities to Working Capital 39		0.0	0.8	0.8		0.4	3.7
Working Capital to Net Sales 40		0.3	0.2	0.2		0.6	0.1
Inventory to Working Capital 41		0.0	0.1	0.0		0.0	0.1
Total Receipts to Cash Flow 42	3.0	1.9	2.0	2.2	1.7	2.2	4.5
Cost of Goods to Cash Flow 43	0.6	0.1	0.4	0.0		0.1	1.7
Cash Flow to Total Debt 44	0.2		1.3	2.4	1.4	0.3	0.2

Selected Financial Factors (in Percentages)

Debt Ratio 45	64.6		43.8	36.9	27.1	53.4	61.8
Return on Total Assets 46	7.1	30.4	12.8	23.5	25.4	10.3	3.5
Return on Equity Before Income Taxes 47	13.6	12.5	17.9	33.9	33.7	18.5	7.0
Return on Equity After Income Taxes 48	9.0	8.4	12.3	33.9	30.9	15.3	4.9
Profit Margin (Before Income Tax) 49	13.1	15.7	10.2	11.1	34.9	21.3	5.2
Profit Margin (After Income Tax) 50	8.7	10.6	7.0	11.1	32.0	17.6	3.7

Table I

Corporations with and without Net Income

WATER TRANSPORTATION

MONEY AMOUNTS AND SIZE OF ASSETS IN THOUSANDS OF DOLLARS

Item Description for Accounting Period 7/07 Through 6/08	Total	Zero Assets	Under 500	500 to 1,000	1,000 to 5,000	5,000 to 10,000	10,000 to 25,000	25,000 to 50,000	50,000 to 100,000	100,000 to 250,000	250,000 to 500,000	500,000 to 2,500,000	2,500,000 and over
Number of Enterprises **1**	4360	395	2546	565	584	112	58	28	19	27	12	13	0
Revenues ($ in Thousands)													
Net Sales **2**	26703438	1586223	811202	919952	885822	1492050	1197665	854232	867010	2599250	1361113	14128919	0
Interest **3**	285509	7419	0	1380	2601	1232	3807	1683	1392	8986	60592	196418	0
Rents **4**	114378	60	0	0	0	0	695	1156	196	1608	167	110496	0
Royalties **5**	606	507	0	0	0	0	0	86	0	12	0	0	0
Other Portfolio Income **6**	660987	0	22403	1548	23891	31850	12865	12471	4705	49690	326231	175335	0
Other Receipts **7**	572913	-216015	147736	959	30481	6959	13465	62413	52884	34117	304444	135469	0
Total Receipts **8**	28337831	1378194	981341	923839	942795	1532091	1228497	932041	926187	2693663	2052547	14746637	0
Average Total Receipts **9**	6500	3489	385	1635	1614	13679	21181	33287	48747	99765	171046	1134357	•
Operating Costs/Operating Income (%)													
Cost of Operations **10**	37.1	23.1	37.0	0.1	34.0	55.0	47.7	35.9	42.3	37.3	53.3	36.7	•
Salaries and Wages **11**	10.2	5.4	12.7	10.0	15.4	12.3	8.9	12.5	6.7	8.2	9.7	10.6	•
Taxes Paid **12**	1.8	0.4	2.2	2.1	4.5	1.9	2.1	2.9	1.9	1.8	2.0	1.6	•
Interest Paid **13**	2.8	1.3	1.3	4.6	1.9	1.0	2.4	3.6	2.6	3.9	11.9	2.1	•
Depreciation **14**	7.0	3.4	2.1	6.9	11.6	3.1	6.4	8.0	7.9	10.0	14.5	6.6	•
Amortization and Depletion **15**	0.3	0.1	0.0	0.0	0.0	0.0	0.1	0.3	0.0	0.3	3.2	0.2	•
Pensions and Other Deferred Comp. **16**	0.6	0.1	1.3	0.0	1.4	0.1	0.7	1.2	0.5	0.6	0.6	0.6	•
Employee Benefits **17**	1.8	0.6	1.5	0.3	1.3	0.4	1.5	2.3	0.8	1.7	1.7	2.4	•
Advertising **18**	0.6	2.9	0.0	2.3	2.3	0.1	0.5	1.5	0.1	0.4	0.2	0.5	•
Other Expenses **19**	36.6	45.3	43.8	77.9	19.0	21.2	27.1	32.5	36.2	36.3	37.7	36.3	•
Officers' Compensation **20**	1.6	0.7	8.8	1.7	5.8	4.1	2.1	2.1	1.8	0.9	3.0	0.7	•
Operating Margin **21**	•	16.7	•	•	2.8	0.7	0.7	•	•	0.2	•	1.7	•
Operating Margin Before Officers' Comp. **22**	1.0	17.4	•	•	8.6	4.8	2.7	•	0.9	•	•	2.4	•

Selected Average Balance Sheet ($ in Thousands)

Net Receivables 23	792	0	0	67	167	1543	2101	4422	7876	12356	56811	133364
Inventories 24	93	0	8	0	2	14	109	312	832	459	2090	24777
Net Property, Plant and Equipment 25	4112	0	0	445	1078	3682	6601	20547	45005	91337	153322	803335
Total Assets 26	7938	0	115	801	2489	6666	15749	34405	73573	150289	356815	1542311
Notes and Loans Payable 27	3144	0	97	758	1218	2122	6388	18838	22835	63405	231874	481398
All Other Liabilities 28	1965	0	6	136	658	1438	3165	6861	17552	26357	87420	419782
Net Worth 29	2829	0	12	-94	613	3106	6195	8706	33185	60526	37520	641130

Selected Financial Ratios (Times to 1)

Current Ratio 30	1.2	•	4.0	1.2	0.9	0.8	2.0	1.3	1.2	1.1	2.3	1.1
Quick Ratio 31	0.9	•	3.3	0.9	0.4	0.7	1.5	0.9	0.9	0.8	1.7	0.8
Net Sales to Working Capital 32	18.6	•	9.0	31.9	•	•	7.1	12.6	12.1	39.9	1.8	44.9
Coverage Ratio 33	3.1	3.8	8.7	0.3	5.7	4.2	2.4	2.7	3.3	1.5	2.6	4.0
Total Asset Turnover 34	0.8	•	2.8	2.0	0.6	2.0	1.3	0.9	0.6	0.6	0.3	0.7
Inventory Turnover 35	24.5	•	14.3	•	213.3	512.3	90.6	35.2	23.2	78.3	28.9	16.1
Receivables Turnover 36	8.0	•	66.9	48.5	6.8	7.8	6.5	7.4	5.6	6.5	2.6	8.8
Total Liabilities to Net Worth 37	1.8	•	8.6	•	3.1	1.1	1.5	3.0	1.2	1.5	8.5	1.4
Current Assets to Working Capital 38	5.5	•	1.3	5.7	•	•	2.0	4.0	5.5	12.7	1.8	11.8
Current Liabilities to Working Capital 39	4.5	•	0.3	4.7	•	•	1.0	3.0	4.5	11.7	0.8	10.8
Working Capital to Net Sales 40	0.1	•	0.1	0.0	•	•	0.1	0.1	0.1	0.0	0.6	0.0
Inventory to Working Capital 41	0.3	•	0.2	0.0	•	•	0.1	0.1	0.2	0.0	0.0	1.1
Total Receipts to Cash Flow 42	2.9	2.1	2.3	•	5.3	4.8	4.3	3.1	3.3	3.1	0.0	1.1
Cost of Goods to Cash Flow 43	1.1	0.5	0.8	0.0	2.9	1.6	2.1	1.1	3.1	1.2	1.7	1.0
Cash Flow to Total Debt 44	0.4	•	1.3	0.8	0.7	0.2	0.5	0.4	0.3	0.3	0.1	0.4

Selected Financial Factors (in Percentages)

Debt Ratio 45	64.4	•	89.6	111.8	75.4	53.4	60.7	74.7	54.9	59.7	89.5	58.4
Return on Total Assets 46	6.7	•	31.6	2.5	6.8	8.9	7.3	8.8	5.3	3.8	10.0	5.8
Return on Equity Before Income Taxes 47	12.8	•	269.8	58.4	22.8	14.6	10.8	21.9	8.1	3.3	59.0	10.5
Return on Equity After Income Taxes 48	9.3	•	269.8	74.6	22.2	13.8	4.6	18.9	7.1	3.3	38.2	7.4
Profit Margin (Before Income Tax) 49	5.9	3.6	10.1	•	9.2	3.4	3.2	6.3	5.9	2.1	19.5	6.2
Profit Margin (After Income Tax) 50	4.3	3.1	10.1	•	9.0	3.2	1.4	5.4	5.2	1.1	12.6	4.4

Table II

Corporations with Net Income

WATER TRANSPORTATION

MONEY AMOUNTS AND SIZE OF ASSETS IN THOUSANDS OF DOLLARS

Item Description for Accounting Period 7/07 Through 6/08	Total	Zero Assets	Under 500	500 to 1,000	1,000 to 5,000	5,000 to 10,000	10,000 to 25,000	25,000 to 50,000	50,000 to 100,000	100,000 to 250,000	250,000 to 500,000	500,000 to 2,500,000	2,500,000 and over
Number of Enterprises **1**	2066	•	1354	201	320	82	34	•	11	15	7	•	0
Revenues ($ in Thousands)													
Net Sales **2**	21602244	•	569402	551676	865938	893661	876475	•	503202	1702890	936692	•	0
Interest **3**	264630	•	0	1	2601	1166	3807	•	1013	1961	48800	•	0
Rents **4**	113438	•	0	0	0	0	695	•	28	1080	167	•	0
Royalties **5**	593	•	0	0	0	0	0	•	0	0	0	•	0
Other Portfolio Income **6**	642954	•	22403	1548	23891	31787	12848	•	4528	38915	322592	•	0
Other Receipts **7**	485674	•	147704	870	18755	5770	18473	•	48887	34862	301788	•	0
Total Receipts **8**	23109533	•	739509	554095	911185	932384	912298	•	557658	1779708	1610039	•	•
Average Total Receipts **9**	11186	•	546	2757	2847	11371	26832	•	50696	118647	230006	•	•
Operating Costs/Operating Income (%)													
Cost of Operations **10**	38.1	•	43.8	0.1	34.8	49.4	46.6	•	49.5	39.5	51.5	•	•
Salaries and Wages **11**	9.6	•	10.8	4.5	15.0	15.7	9.3	•	6.8	7.7	11.4	•	•
Taxes Paid **12**	1.9	•	2.7	1.2	4.4	2.1	2.5	•	2.1	1.9	1.6	•	•
Interest Paid **13**	2.5	•	1.3	0.4	0.5	1.2	0.8	•	2.7	3.0	12.4	•	•
Depreciation **14**	5.9	•	2.9	6.0	4.3	3.9	2.6	•	8.1	9.3	9.4	•	•
Amortization and Depletion **15**	0.4	•	0.0	•	0.0	0.0	0.1	•	0.0	0.2	4.5	•	•
Pensions and Other Deferred Comp. **16**	0.6	•	1.9	0.1	1.4	0.1	0.4	•	0.5	0.7	0.4	•	•
Employee Benefits **17**	2.0	•	1.7	0.4	1.3	0.0	1.7	•	0.9	1.8	0.9	•	•
Advertising **18**	0.4	•	0.1	0.3	2.3	0.1	0.6	•	0.0	0.2	0.1	•	•
Other Expenses **19**	34.0	•	33.0	68.1	17.2	19.4	28.6	•	26.1	31.5	50.1	•	•
Officers' Compensation **20**	1.5	•	12.5	1.7	5.1	2.0	1.8	•	1.9	0.9	2.5	•	•
Operating Margin **21**	3.2	•	•	17.0	13.7	5.9	4.9	•	1.3	3.3	•	•	•
Operating Margin Before Officers' Comp. **22**	4.7	•	1.8	18.7	18.8	7.9	6.7	•	3.2	4.2	•	•	•

Selected Average Balance Sheet ($ in Thousands)

Net Receivables 23	1401	0	104	166	910	2401	8014	12549	84709
Inventories 24	161	15	0	4	20	185	793	417	1077
Net Property, Plant and Equipment 25	6435	50	271	913	3999	5892	46191	84830	108535
Total Assets 26	13170	137	911	1440	6595	17025	72867	155154	348354
Notes and Loans Payable 27	4473	93	105	284	1825	4081	23287	48820	249646
All Other Liabilities 28	3120	2	53	297	943	4444	12664	30769	99508
Net Worth 29	5577	43	752	859	3827	8499	36917	75565	-799

Selected Financial Ratios (Times to 1)

Current Ratio 30	1.5	5.1	4.8	0.9	0.8	2.0	2.0	1.1	2.3
Quick Ratio 31	1.1	3.8	3.1	0.9	0.7	1.5	1.5	0.7	1.7
Net Sales to Working Capital 32	9.8	8.3	5.5	•	•	6.8	4.0	68.3	1.5
Coverage Ratio 33	5.2	15.5	41.3	39.8	9.3	11.8	5.6	3.6	3.9
Total Asset Turnover 34	0.8	3.1	3.0	1.9	1.7	1.5	0.6	0.7	0.4
Inventory Turnover 35	24.8	11.9	•	213.3	275.3	64.8	28.6	107.5	64.0
Receivables Turnover 36	7.6	5694.0	52.7	8.1	7.2	5.8	•	5.9	•
Total Liabilities to Net Worth 37	1.4	2.2	0.2	0.7	0.7	1.0	1.0	1.1	•
Current Assets to Working Capital 38	3.0	1.2	1.3	•	•	2.0	2.0	21.0	1.8
Current Liabilities to Working Capital 39	2.0	0.2	0.3	•	•	1.0	1.0	20.0	0.8
Working Capital to Net Sales 40	0.1	0.1	0.2	•	•	0.1	0.2	0.0	0.7
Inventory to Working Capital 41	0.2	0.3	•	•	•	0.1	0.1	0.2	0.0
Total Receipts to Cash Flow 42	2.8	2.2	1.6	3.5	4.0	3.0	3.9	3.0	2.0
Cost of Goods to Cash Flow 43	1.1	1.0	0.0	1.2	2.0	1.4	1.9	1.2	1.0
Cash Flow to Total Debt 44	0.5	2.0	11.1	1.3	1.0	1.0	0.3	0.5	0.2

Selected Financial Factors (in Percentages)

Debt Ratio 45	57.7	69.1	17.4	40.4	42.0	50.1	49.3	51.3	100.2
Return on Total Assets 46	10.4	62.6	54.0	36.4	18.9	14.8	9.3	7.8	18.7
Return on Equity Before Income Taxes 47	19.9	189.2	63.8	59.6	29.1	27.1	15.1	11.5	•
Return on Equity After Income Taxes 48	16.1	189.2	58.1	58.7	28.2	19.4	13.5	9.1	•
Profit Margin (Before Income Tax) 49	10.6	19.1	17.5	18.9	10.2	8.9	12.2	7.6	36.2
Profit Margin (After Income Tax) 50	8.6	19.1	15.9	18.6	9.9	6.4	10.9	6.1	26.2

Table I

Corporations with and without Net Income

TRUCK TRANSPORTATION

MONEY AMOUNTS AND SIZE OF ASSETS IN THOUSANDS OF DOLLARS

Item Description for Accounting Period 7/07 Through 6/08		Total	Zero Assets	Under 500	500 to 1,000	1,000 to 5,000	5,000 to 10,000	10,000 to 25,000	25,000 to 50,000	50,000 to 100,000	100,000 to 250,000	250,000 to 500,000	500,000 to 2,500,000	2,500,000 and over
Number of Enterprises	1	110812	29676	67491	4779	7195	949	440	119	69	42	26	22	4
Revenues ($ in Thousands)														
Net Sales	2	237892055	5502720	38167357	15146027	49305206	18674066	16811847	9673813	8986950	10230678	13337079	31558395	20497917
Interest	3	605598	2794	11419	7869	33147	14876	13728	8830	5969	22766	12698	185671	285832
Rents	4	251981	0	1656	196	33836	8922	21558	28926	15000	42824	7187	51520	40357
Royalties	5	100403	0	0	0	70	0	67	5	16	2542	0	928	96775
Other Portfolio Income	6	1998087	73281	360805	193685	344481	120290	128440	59537	86428	68242	174817	255990	132091
Other Receipts	7	3600687	114057	364024	20701	482296	155838	172757	93469	60198	282796	404156	1144140	306252
Total Receipts	8	244448811	5692852	38905261	15368478	50199036	18973992	17148397	9864580	9154561	10649848	13935937	33196644	21359224
Average Total Receipts	9	2206	192	576	3216	6977	19994	38974	82896	132675	253568	535998	1508938	5339806
Operating Costs/Operating Income (%)														
Cost of Operations	10	33.9	27.3	28.2	34.0	43.1	36.8	43.6	41.0	26.9	23.2	24.2	41.0	13.9
Salaries and Wages	11	16.4	5.2	12.8	14.5	12.1	16.1	13.5	12.2	21.7	20.9	20.1	18.9	31.8
Taxes Paid	12	3.4	2.0	3.1	3.1	2.9	3.0	3.5	2.7	4.4	3.5	3.5	3.9	4.7
Interest Paid	13	1.4	1.0	1.0	1.0	1.1	1.2	1.3	1.3	1.7	1.9	1.7	1.6	3.1
Depreciation	14	4.7	3.9	3.9	4.1	4.1	4.6	5.1	5.0	6.0	6.6	7.5	5.1	4.4
Amortization and Depletion	15	0.1	0.2	0.0	0.0	0.1	0.0	0.1	0.1	0.1	0.1	0.3	0.3	0.0
Pensions and Other Deferred Comp.	16	0.3	0.0	0.2	0.4	0.3	0.4	0.1	0.3	0.2	0.5	0.3	0.4	1.0
Employee Benefits	17	2.5	0.7	1.0	1.6	1.5	2.0	1.8	1.6	2.8	3.1	2.0	3.4	8.5
Advertising	18	0.3	0.3	0.4	0.2	0.3	0.2	0.2	0.2	0.2	0.3	0.2	0.2	0.1
Other Expenses	19	35.9	37.5	45.9	38.6	32.5	35.2	30.4	34.9	35.8	42.3	42.6	26.6	35.7
Officers' Compensation	20	2.2	20.6	4.1	3.1	2.0	1.2	1.5	1.1	0.7	0.7	0.6	0.4	0.3
Operating Margin	21	•	1.1	•	•	•	•	•	•	•	•	•	•	•
Operating Margin Before Officers' Comp.	22	1.0	21.7	3.5	2.5	1.9	0.5	0.4	0.6	0.1	•	•	•	•

Selected Average Balance Sheet ($ in Thousands)

Net Receivables 23	200	0	12	111	522	2062	4078	9570	15360	32080	62630	167737	1095934
Inventories 24	12	0	1	14	25	83	281	570	1250	1995	2591	21500	13964
Net Property, Plant and Equipment 25	401	0	48	385	876	3050	7021	16267	35646	75137	190076	370374	1599594
Total Assets 26	917	0	90	715	2000	7261	15089	34470	70762	151137	346094	922172	4888519
Notes and Loans Payable 27	422	0	76	532	1106	3383	6949	14792	32305	68255	124030	331283	1860655
All Other Liabilities 28	255	0	20	103	383	1794	3618	9319	20440	35610	79472	263897	2101646
Net Worth 29	241	0	-6	79	512	2084	4522	10360	18017	47272	142592	326992	926218

Selected Financial Ratios (Times to 1)

Current Ratio 30	1.2	•	1.2	1.0	1.4	1.4	1.1	1.1	1.1	1.1	1.3	1.3	0.9
Quick Ratio 31	0.9	•	1.0	0.9	1.1	1.2	0.9	0.9	0.9	0.8	1.0	0.9	0.7
Net Sales to Working Capital 32	45.2	•	137.0	523.5	26.2	19.8	53.0	50.2	65.0	51.1	21.3	22.1	•
Coverage Ratio 33	2.1	5.8	2.4	1.8	2.5	1.7	1.7	2.2	1.8	1.5	1.8	3.1	1.2
Total Asset Turnover 34	2.3	•	6.3	4.4	3.4	2.7	2.5	2.4	1.8	1.6	1.5	1.6	1.0
Inventory Turnover 35	61.8	•	209.3	78.2	118.7	87.6	59.4	58.4	28.0	28.4	48.0	27.3	51.0
Receivables Turnover 36	10.9	•	51.3	26.2	14.9	8.9	9.3	8.1	9.2	6.7	9.0	5.3	9.4
Total Liabilities to Net Worth 37	2.8	•	8.0	•	2.9	2.5	2.3	2.3	2.9	2.2	1.4	1.8	4.3
Current Assets to Working Capital 38	7.2	•	7.6	34.4	3.5	3.7	8.4	9.4	12.4	11.0	4.0	4.8	•
Current Liabilities to Working Capital 39	6.2	•	6.6	33.4	2.5	2.7	7.4	8.4	11.4	10.0	3.0	3.8	•
Working Capital to Net Sales 40	0.0	•	0.0	0.0	0.0	0.0	0.0	0.0	0.0	0.0	0.0	0.0	•
Inventory to Working Capital 41	0.3	•	0.2	2.1	0.1	0.1	0.3	0.4	0.5	0.5	0.2	0.3	•
Total Receipts to Cash Flow 42	3.4	2.8	2.8	3.0	3.8	3.9	4.4	4.6	3.6	3.2	3.0	3.8	3.2
Cost of Goods to Cash Flow 43	1.2	0.8	0.8	1.0	1.6	1.4	1.9	1.9	1.0	0.7	0.7	1.5	0.4
Cash Flow to Total Debt 44	0.9	•	2.1	1.6	1.2	1.0	0.8	0.7	0.7	0.7	0.8	0.6	0.4

Selected Financial Factors (in Percentages)

Debt Ratio 45	73.7	•	106.5	88.9	74.4	71.3	70.0	69.9	74.5	68.7	58.8	64.5	81.1
Return on Total Assets 46	7.1	•	14.5	8.4	9.7	5.5	5.6	6.7	5.5	4.6	4.5	7.8	3.9
Return on Equity Before Income Taxes 47	14.1	•	•	34.6	22.6	8.0	7.7	12.1	9.3	4.8	4.7	14.8	3.5
Return on Equity After Income Taxes 48	11.0	•	•	31.4	20.3	6.1	5.3	10.5	7.7	2.9	3.6	8.9	1.6
Profit Margin (Before Income Tax) 49	1.6	4.6	1.3	0.9	1.7	0.9	0.9	1.5	1.3	0.9	1.3	3.4	0.6
Profit Margin (After Income Tax) 50	1.2	4.4	1.3	0.8	1.5	0.6	0.6	1.3	1.1	0.6	1.0	2.0	0.3

Table II

Corporations with Net Income

TRUCK TRANSPORTATION

MONEY AMOUNTS AND SIZE OF ASSETS IN THOUSANDS OF DOLLARS

Item Description for Accounting Period 7/07 Through 6/08	Total	Zero Assets	Under 500	500 to 1,000	1,000 to 5,000	5,000 to 10,000	10,000 to 25,000	25,000 to 50,000	50,000 to 100,000	100,000 to 250,000	250,000 to 500,000	500,000 to 2,500,000	2,500,000 and over
Number of Enterprises **1**	62416	15674	37737	3072	5085	457	234	68	•	•	14	•	•
Revenues ($ in Thousands)													
Net Sales **2**	155291557	3566565	22836299	8870327	33258537	8603069	11196867	6295525	•	•	7413533	•	•
Interest **3**	476196	4	10048	7709	23683	13852	10473	5132	•	•	11298	•	•
Rents **4**	166259	0	189	196	24978	7606	11644	14534	•	•	7160	•	•
Royalties **5**	97774	0	0	0	0	0	67	5	•	•	0	•	•
Other Portfolio Income **6**	1491382	59061	332563	130288	251630	92216	66446	35780	•	•	89479	•	•
Other Receipts **7**	2962693	111234	234010	-4931	408546	70359	93363	70212	•	•	370425	•	•
Total Receipts **8**	160485861	3736864	23413109	9003589	33967374	8787102	11378860	6421188	•	•	7891895	•	•
Average Total Receipts **9**	2571	238	620	2931	6680	19228	48628	94429	•	•	563707	•	•
Operating Costs/Operating Income (%)													
Cost of Operations **10**	32.9	24.4	26.6	30.4	42.3	40.4	46.9	50.0	•	•	24.2	•	•
Salaries and Wages **11**	16.7	3.4	13.4	14.8	12.1	13.6	11.2	9.4	•	•	16.8	•	•
Taxes Paid **12**	3.5	1.8	2.9	3.1	3.0	3.0	3.2	2.5	•	•	3.8	•	•
Interest Paid **13**	1.2	0.8	0.7	1.0	1.1	1.0	0.9	0.8	•	•	1.1	•	•
Depreciation **14**	4.3	2.6	3.2	4.0	3.9	4.3	3.6	3.4	•	•	6.9	•	•
Amortization and Depletion **15**	0.1	0.1	0.0	0.0	0.1	0.0	0.1	0.1	•	•	0.2	•	•
Pensions and Other Deferred Comp. **16**	0.4	0.1	0.1	0.1	0.4	0.6	0.1	0.3	•	•	0.3	•	•
Employee Benefits **17**	2.8	0.3	1.1	1.8	1.6	1.6	1.7	1.1	•	•	2.1	•	•
Advertising **18**	0.2	0.3	0.2	0.3	0.4	0.2	0.2	0.3	•	•	0.3	•	•
Other Expenses **19**	34.2	29.0	43.7	38.5	30.6	30.5	28.8	28.8	•	•	45.1	•	•
Officers' Compensation **20**	2.6	30.2	4.3	4.3	2.4	1.9	1.8	1.3	•	•	0.8	•	•
Operating Margin **21**	1.2	7.0	3.8	1.8	2.2	2.9	1.6	2.1	•	•	•	•	•
Operating Margin Before Officers' Comp. **22**	3.7	37.2	8.1	6.0	4.6	4.8	3.3	3.3	•	•	•	•	•

Selected Average Balance Sheet ($ in Thousands)

Item									
Net Receivables 23	244	0	9	96	492	2096	4936	9487	62940
Inventories 24	15	0	1	15	25	138	387	468	2936
Net Property, Plant and Equipment 25	440	0	39	385	837	2555	5790	13860	209482
Total Assets 26	1063	0	83	704	2035	7389	15385	33564	363592
Notes and Loans Payable 27	379	0	52	499	1033	2843	5440	11337	92626
All Other Liabilities 28	311	0	19	80	365	1324	4572	8702	79868
Net Worth 29	372	0	12	124	638	3221	5373	13525	191099

Selected Financial Ratios (Times to 1)

Item								
Current Ratio 30	1.3	•	1.3	1.1	1.6	1.8	1.3	1.5
Quick Ratio 31	1.0	•	1.1	0.9	1.3	1.5	1.1	1.3
Net Sales to Working Capital 32	25.3	•	85.8	128.6	18.2	10.2	29.7	18.9
Coverage Ratio 33	4.9	15.0	9.4	4.3	5.0	6.0	4.7	6.3
Total Asset Turnover 34	2.3	•	7.3	4.1	3.2	2.5	3.1	2.8
Inventory Turnover 35	55.0	•	144.2	57.9	108.6	55.2	58.0	99.0
Receivables Turnover 36	9.6	•	62.6	24.6	14.3	6.4	9.9	9.0
Total Liabilities to Net Worth 37	1.9	•	6.2	4.7	2.2	1.3	1.9	1.5
Current Assets to Working Capital 38	4.3	•	4.1	9.1	2.7	2.2	4.6	3.1
Current Liabilities to Working Capital 39	3.3	•	3.1	8.1	1.7	1.2	3.6	2.1
Working Capital to Net Sales 40	0.0	•	0.0	0.0	0.1	0.1	0.0	0.1
Inventory to Working Capital 41	0.1	•	0.2	0.8	0.1	0.1	0.1	0.1
Total Receipts to Cash Flow 42	3.2	2.8	2.5	2.9	3.7	3.8	4.3	5.2
Cost of Goods to Cash Flow 43	1.1	0.7	0.7	0.9	1.6	1.5	2.0	2.6
Cash Flow to Total Debt 44	1.1	•	3.4	1.7	1.3	1.2	1.1	0.9

Selected Financial Factors (in Percentages)

Item								
Debt Ratio 45	65.0	•	86.0	82.4	68.7	56.4	65.1	59.7
Return on Total Assets 46	13.2	•	51.5	17.4	17.2	15.4	12.6	13.2
Return on Equity Before Income Taxes 47	30.0	•	329.5	76.1	43.9	29.5	28.4	27.6
Return on Equity After Income Taxes 48	26.4	•	324.2	72.9	41.2	26.8	24.7	25.5
Profit Margin (Before Income Tax) 49	4.5	11.8	6.3	3.3	4.3	5.0	3.2	4.0
Profit Margin (After Income Tax) 50	4.0	11.5	6.2	3.1	4.0	4.6	2.8	3.7

Table I

Corporations with and without Net Income

TRANSIT AND GROUND PASSENGER TRANSPORTATION

MONEY AMOUNTS AND SIZE OF ASSETS IN THOUSANDS OF DOLLARS

Item Description for Accounting Period 7/07 Through 6/08	Total	Zero Assets	Under 500	500 to 1,000	1,000 to 5,000	5,000 to 10,000	10,000 to 25,000	25,000 to 50,000	50,000 to 100,000	100,000 to 250,000	250,000 to 500,000	500,000 to 2,500,000	2,500,000 and over
Number of Enterprises **1**	27417	•	16711	1737	1367	166	•	•	6	6	3	3	0
Revenues ($ in Thousands)													
Net Sales **2**	25080467	•	3232540	638342	5761738	2244327	•	•	461772	1480232	1485385	6604284	0
Interest **3**	212863	•	1528	-2102	1818	299	•	•	521	3957	4836	189969	0
Rents **4**	43528	•	20	0	5902	1122	•	•	145	5351	24643	5890	0
Royalties **5**	0	•	0	0	0	0	•	•	0	0	0	0	0
Other Portfolio Income **6**	330891	•	123330	6718	37666	95043	•	•	265	6782	14269	28295	0
Other Receipts **7**	199448	•	7979	13908	32500	8561	•	•	3565	965	9270	42992	0
Total Receipts **8**	25867197	•	3365397	656866	5839624	2349352	•	•	466268	1497287	1538403	6871430	0
Average Total Receipts **9**	943	•	201	378	4272	14153	•	•	77711	249548	512801	2290477	•
Operating Costs/Operating Income (%)													
Cost of Operations **10**	28.1	•	12.9	23.0	40.2	48.9	•	•	61.0	46.1	0.8	9.4	•
Salaries and Wages **11**	23.3	•	23.3	21.7	14.2	11.1	•	•	6.4	21.9	36.0	37.8	•
Taxes Paid **12**	4.6	•	3.9	3.9	3.6	7.0	•	•	4.0	4.9	6.5	5.3	•
Interest Paid **13**	3.4	•	2.7	6.5	1.4	2.6	•	•	2.1	5.0	4.7	5.9	•
Depreciation **14**	6.4	•	4.4	6.1	6.4	11.4	•	•	6.3	2.9	8.1	6.6	•
Amortization and Depletion **15**	0.6	•	1.0	1.0	0.2	0.0	•	•	0.2	0.6	0.8	1.2	•
Pensions and Other Deferred Comp. **16**	0.4	•	0.1	0.1	0.3	0.1	•	•	1.1	0.6	0.7	0.4	•
Employee Benefits **17**	1.6	•	1.0	0.8	0.8	1.2	•	•	1.8	5.6	4.9	1.2	•
Advertising **18**	0.6	•	1.0	0.6	0.8	0.2	•	•	0.5	0.2	0.5	0.5	•
Other Expenses **19**	30.7	•	44.5	32.6	25.8	20.2	•	•	14.0	16.8	42.4	36.4	•
Officers' Compensation **20**	1.9	•	3.3	3.6	4.2	1.1	•	•	1.3	0.4	0.1	0.1	•
Operating Margin **21**	•	•	2.0	0.1	2.1	•	•	•	1.2	•	•	•	•
Operating Margin Before Officers' Comp. **22**	0.4	•	5.3	3.7	6.3	•	•	•	2.5	•	•	•	•

Selected Average Balance Sheet ($ in Thousands)

Net Receivables 23	74	6	15	317	1260	6364	27195	72886	227167
Inventories 24	5	0	2	3	68	3566	1232	14163	30388
Net Property, Plant and Equipment 25	271	19	138	951	4873	27262	44640	181379	1079428
Total Assets 26	817	109	636	1886	7468	63777	171256	421794	3900521
Notes and Loans Payable 27	477	84	484	1109	5680	29107	98238	215131	2161421
All Other Liabilities 28	135	12	31	305	817	10089	51410	120154	643086
Net Worth 29	205	13	121	471	971	24581	21608	86509	1096014

Selected Financial Ratios (Times to 1)

Current Ratio 30	1.0	1.6	0.9	1.0	0.7	1.2	1.6	0.8	0.9
Quick Ratio 31	0.7	0.9	0.4	0.9	0.5	0.7	1.1	0.6	0.6
Net Sales to Working Capital 32	662.3	22.3	•	197.3	•	24.5	13.5	•	•
Coverage Ratio 33	1.5	3.2	1.5	3.5	1.3	2.0	0.3	0.5	0.8
Total Asset Turnover 34	1.1	1.8	0.6	2.2	1.8	1.2	1.4	1.2	0.6
Inventory Turnover 35	48.5	34766.2	41.6	547.9	97.1	13.2	92.3	0.3	6.8
Receivables Turnover 36	12.9	30.6	13.1	14.1	9.3	10.2	10.0	3.8	19.4
Total Liabilities to Net Worth 37	3.0	7.5	4.2	3.0	6.7	1.6	6.9	3.9	2.6
Current Assets to Working Capital 38	126.6	2.8	•	28.1	•	6.0	2.8	•	•
Current Liabilities to Working Capital 39	125.6	1.8	1.8	27.1	•	5.0	1.8	•	•
Working Capital to Net Sales 40	0.0	0.0	0.0	0.0	•	0.0	0.1	•	•
Inventory to Working Capital 41	4.4	0.0	0.0	0.1	•	1.2	0.1	•	•
Total Receipts to Cash Flow 42	3.9	2.3	3.7	4.8	8.1	8.9	11.8	3.3	3.3
Cost of Goods to Cash Flow 43	1.1	0.3	0.9	1.9	3.9	5.5	5.4	0.0	0.3
Cash Flow to Total Debt 44	0.4	0.2	0.2	0.6	0.3	0.2	0.1	0.5	0.2

Selected Financial Factors (in Percentages)

Debt Ratio 45	74.9	88.2	80.9	75.0	87.0	61.5	87.4	79.5	71.9
Return on Total Assets 46	5.6	15.5	5.5	10.9	5.9	5.2	2.2	3.0	2.8
Return on Equity Before Income Taxes 47	7.2	91.0	9.0	31.3	9.4	6.9	•	•	•
Return on Equity After Income Taxes 48	6.4	90.1	7.2	29.7	9.4	6.8	•	•	•
Profit Margin (Before Income Tax) 49	1.6	6.1	3.0	3.5	0.7	2.2	•	•	•
Profit Margin (After Income Tax) 50	1.4	6.0	2.4	3.3	0.7	2.2	•	•	•

Table II

Corporations with Net Income

TRANSIT AND GROUND PASSENGER TRANSPORTATION

MONEY AMOUNTS AND SIZE OF ASSETS IN THOUSANDS OF DOLLARS

Item Description for Accounting Period 7/07 Through 6/08		Total	Zero Assets	Under 500	500 to 1,000	1,000 to 5,000	5,000 to 10,000	10,000 to 25,000	25,000 to 50,000	50,000 to 100,000	100,000 to 250,000	250,000 to 500,000	500,000 to 2,500,000	2,500,000 and over
Number of Enterprises	1	13323	3174	7735	1246	995	96	63	•	•	0	•	0	0.
Revenues ($ in Thousands)														
Net Sales	2	16676775	381364	2420651	479536	4846850	1581591	1753921	•	•	0	•	0	0
Interest	3	37953	337	1242	-2132	3848	2	3965	•	•	0	•	0	0
Rents	4	27840	0	20	0	5902	0	222	•	•	0	•	0	0
Royalties	5	0	0	0	0	0	0	0	•	•	0	•	0	0
Other Portfolio Income	6	282269	149	102060	3884	33926	93289	16029	•	•	0	•	0	0
Other Receipts	7	150567	7862	1869	13082	27007	7744	57244	•	•	0	•	0	0
Total Receipts	8	17175404	389712	2525842	494370	4917533	1682626	1831381	•	•	0	•	0	0
Average Total Receipts	9	1289	123	327	397	4942	17527	29070	•	•	•	•	•	•
Operating Costs/Operating Income (%)														
Cost of Operations	10	31.5	20.3	12.8	30.6	47.4	45.4	58.3	•	•	•	•	•	•
Salaries and Wages	11	20.5	14.9	24.8	16.2	11.5	14.3	9.6	•	•	•	•	•	•
Taxes Paid	12	4.3	1.7	3.8	3.8	3.3	6.0	3.4	•	•	•	•	•	•
Interest Paid	13	2.2	0.5	1.6	5.3	1.5	1.0	1.3	•	•	•	•	•	•
Depreciation	14	6.4	1.4	3.2	8.0	6.4	11.0	6.0	•	•	•	•	•	•
Amortization and Depletion	15	0.2	0.1	0.1	0.0	0.2	0.0	0.1	•	•	•	•	•	•
Pensions and Other Deferred Comp.	16	0.3	1.1	0.0	0.1	0.1	0.1	0.6	•	•	•	•	•	•
Employee Benefits	17	1.3	0.0	0.5	0.8	0.8	1.0	1.8	•	•	•	•	•	•
Advertising	18	0.6	0.8	0.9	0.8	0.9	0.1	0.4	•	•	•	•	•	•
Other Expenses	19	29.3	52.2	43.0	24.3	22.8	23.1	15.4	•	•	•	•	•	•
Officers' Compensation	20	1.5	1.7	3.5	4.8	1.8	0.1	1.3	•	•	•	•	•	•
Operating Margin	21	2.0	5.3	5.7	5.2	3.3	•	1.7	•	•	•	•	•	•
Operating Margin Before Officers' Comp.	22	3.5	7.0	9.2	10.0	5.2	•	3.1	•	•	•	•	•	•

Selected Average Balance Sheet ($ in Thousands)

Net Receivables	23	94	0	7	19	374	1690	2276
Inventories	24	5	0	0	3	2	0	120
Net Property, Plant and Equipment	25	322	0	24	185	1095	4350	7226
Total Assets	26	720	0	116	604	2065	7305	15030
Notes and Loans Payable	27	341	0	69	406	1344	5131	4923
All Other Liabilities	28	135	0	15	30	271	903	2948
Net Worth	29	244	0	32	168	450	1272	7159

Selected Financial Ratios (Times to 1)

Current Ratio	30	1.2	•	2.4	1.7	1.1	0.7	1.4
Quick Ratio	31	0.8	•	1.1	0.8	0.9	0.6	1.2
Net Sales to Working Capital	32	35.3	•	13.6	10.4	57.0	•	15.6
Coverage Ratio	33	3.2	16.5	7.2	2.6	4.1	5.2	5.8
Total Asset Turnover	34	1.7	•	2.7	0.6	2.4	2.3	1.9
Inventory Turnover	35	72.7	•	25872.8	41.6	933.5	•	135.3
Receivables Turnover	36	13.4	•	41.2	18.9	13.3	8.3	11.1
Total Liabilities to Net Worth	37	2.0	•	2.6	2.6	3.6	4.7	1.1
Current Assets to Working Capital	38	6.6	•	1.7	2.4	8.1	•	3.2
Current Liabilities to Working Capital	39	5.6	•	0.7	1.4	7.1	•	2.2
Working Capital to Net Sales	40	0.0	•	0.1	0.1	0.0	•	0.1
Inventory to Working Capital	41	0.2	•	0.0	0.1	0.0	•	0.1
Total Receipts to Cash Flow	42	3.6	2.1	2.1	4.4	4.7	5.7	5.6
Cost of Goods to Cash Flow	43	1.1	0.4	0.3	1.3	2.2	2.6	3.3
Cash Flow to Total Debt	44	0.7	•	1.7	0.2	0.6	0.5	0.6

Selected Financial Factors (in Percentages)

Debt Ratio	45	66.2	•	72.5	72.2	78.2	82.6	52.4
Return on Total Assets	46	12.6	•	31.5	8.7	14.9	11.5	13.6
Return on Equity Before Income Taxes	47	25.7	•	98.5	18.9	51.8	53.2	23.6
Return on Equity After Income Taxes	48	24.2	•	97.7	17.2	49.6	53.2	19.6
Profit Margin (Before Income Tax)	49	5.0	7.5	10.1	8.3	4.8	4.1	6.1
Profit Margin (After Income Tax)	50	4.7	7.1	10.0	7.5	4.6	4.1	5.1

Table I

Corporations with and without Net Income

PIPELINE TRANSPORTATION

MONEY AMOUNTS AND SIZE OF ASSETS IN THOUSANDS OF DOLLARS

Item Description for Accounting Period 7/07 Through 6/08	Total	Zero Assets	Under 500	500 to 1,000	1,000 to 5,000	5,000 to 10,000	10,000 to 25,000	25,000 to 50,000	50,000 to 100,000	100,000 to 250,000	250,000 to 500,000	500,000 to 2,500,000	2,500,000 and over
Number of Enterprises 1	321	•	0	0	249	25	•	•	5	4	6	7	0
Revenues ($ in Thousands)													
Net Sales 2	10210083	•	0	0	815052	164937	•	•	545852	154098	1850083	5758495	0
Interest 3	220540	•	0	0	1748	1562	•	•	2427	5979	142680	64079	0
Rents 4	13001	•	0	0	0	0	•	•	0	5246	0	6233	0
Royalties 5	861	•	0	0	735	0	•	•	0	0	0	126	0
Other Portfolio Income 6	544502	•	0	0	2247	353	•	•	499	63	533457	7824	0
Other Receipts 7	73621	•	0	0	12233	15565	•	•	6676	6401	-106613	124677	0
Total Receipts 8	11062608	•	0	0	832015	182417	•	•	555454	171787	2419607	5961434	0
Average Total Receipts 9	34463	•	•	•	3341	7297	•	•	111091	42947	403268	851633	•
Operating Costs/Operating Income (%)													
Cost of Operations 10	62.8	•	•	•	52.3	10.5	•	•	48.6	4.8	81.2	61.3	•
Salaries and Wages 11	4.2	•	•	•	19.0	1.8	•	•	16.7	8.5	2.1	1.9	•
Taxes Paid 12	2.3	•	•	•	2.8	3.6	•	•	4.4	4.8	1.3	2.4	•
Interest Paid 13	7.1	•	•	•	0.1	1.5	•	•	0.8	16.8	10.4	8.5	•
Depreciation 14	5.7	•	•	•	2.7	3.7	•	•	3.2	15.6	4.9	6.6	•
Amortization and Depletion 15	0.4	•	•	•	2.0	•	•	•	0.0	•	0.1	0.4	•
Pensions and Other Deferred Comp. 16	0.2	•	•	•	0.1	0.0	•	•	0.6	0.6	0.1	0.3	•
Employee Benefits 17	0.5	•	•	•	0.2	1.1	•	•	3.0	1.7	0.2	0.4	•
Advertising 18	0.0	•	•	•	0.4	•	•	•	0.0	•	0.0	0.0	•
Other Expenses 19	11.5	•	•	•	15.9	57.7	•	•	15.6	34.7	11.0	9.2	•
Officers' Compensation 20	0.2	•	•	•	1.3	0.4	•	•	0.3	•	0.1	0.1	•
Operating Margin 21	4.8	•	•	•	3.2	19.6	•	•	6.7	12.5	•	8.9	•
Operating Margin Before Officers' Comp. 22	5.1	•	•	•	4.5	20.1	•	•	7.0	12.5	•	9.1	•

Selected Average Balance Sheet ($ in Thousands)

Net Receivables 23	5650	551	593	12139	3674	73796	151017
Inventories 24	644	87	86	150	2063	816	22193
Net Property, Plant and Equipment 25	29029	367	3324	31369	85462	115289	1097094
Total Assets 26	65384	2670	8355	65199	130461	331558	2393974
Notes and Loans Payable 27	37761	988	1610	12782	74718	276263	1383225
All Other Liabilities 28	7822	180	1079	26591	24472	-254035	511448
Net Worth 29	19801	1502	5666	25826	31272	309330	499302

Selected Financial Ratios (Times to 1)

Current Ratio 30	1.1	5.3	3.3	1.7	2.2	0.6	1.2
Quick Ratio 31	0.8	3.5	3.1	1.5	1.8	0.6	0.8
Net Sales to Working Capital 32	38.3	3.4	3.1	10.0	3.3	•	25.2
Coverage Ratio 33	2.9	40.8	20.4	12.2	2.4	2.9	2.5
Total Asset Turnover 34	0.5	1.2	0.8	1.7	0.3	0.9	0.3
Inventory Turnover 35	31.1	19.6	8.0	354.8	0.9	306.9	22.7
Receivables Turnover 36	6.1	5.7	13.8	12.9	2.3	4.5	6.2
Total Liabilities to Net Worth 37	2.3	0.8	0.5	1.5	3.2	0.1	3.8
Current Assets to Working Capital 38	11.5	1.2	1.4	2.5	1.8	•	7.5
Current Liabilities to Working Capital 39	10.5	0.2	0.4	1.5	0.8	•	6.5
Working Capital to Net Sales 40	0.0	0.3	0.3	0.1	0.3	•	0.0
Inventory to Working Capital 41	1.1	0.1	0.0	0.0	0.0	•	1.0
Total Receipts to Cash Flow 42	5.7	5.5	1.2	5.5	1.7	•	4.9
Cost of Goods to Cash Flow 43	3.6	2.9	0.1	2.7	0.1	•	3.0
Cash Flow to Total Debt 44	0.1	0.5	2.1	0.5	0.2	•	0.1

Selected Financial Factors (in Percentages)

Debt Ratio 45	69.7	43.7	32.2	60.4	76.0	6.7	79.1
Return on Total Assets 46	9.9	6.6	24.9	15.4	12.0	27.9	7.2
Return on Equity Before Income Taxes 47	21.2	11.5	35.0	35.8	29.6	19.5	20.5
Return on Equity After Income Taxes 48	15.5	10.2	31.3	25.8	17.2	18.1	13.2
Profit Margin (Before Income Tax) 49	13.2	5.3	30.0	8.5	24.0	19.6	12.4
Profit Margin (After Income Tax) 50	9.6	4.7	26.9	6.1	14.0	18.2	8.0

Table II

Corporations with Net Income

PIPELINE TRANSPORTATION

MONEY AMOUNTS AND SIZE OF ASSETS IN THOUSANDS OF DOLLARS

Item Description for Accounting Period 7/07 Through 6/08	Total	Zero Assets	Under 500	500 to 1,000	1,000 to 5,000	5,000 to 10,000	10,000 to 25,000	25,000 to 50,000	50,000 to 100,000	100,000 to 250,000	250,000 to 500,000	500,000 to 2,500,000	2,500,000 and over
Number of Enterprises **1**	232	0	0	0	177	25	•	•	5	•	0	•	0
Revenues ($ in Thousands)													
Net Sales **2**	5822748	0	0	0	797688	164937	•	•	545852	•	0	•	0
Interest **3**	166817	0	0	0	1748	1562	•	•	2427	•	0	•	0
Rents **4**	6671	0	0	0	0	0	•	•	0	•	0	•	0
Royalties **5**	861	0	0	0	735	0	•	•	0	•	0	•	0
Other Portfolio Income **6**	543509	0	0	0	2247	353	•	•	499	•	0	•	0
Other Receipts **7**	78197	0	0	0	26120	15565	•	•	6676	•	0	•	0
Total Receipts **8**	6618803	0	0	0	828538	182417	•	•	555454	•	0	•	0
Average Total Receipts **9**	28529	•	•	•	4681	7297	•	•	111091	•	•	•	•
Operating Costs/Operating Income (%)													
Cost of Operations **10**	41.2	•	•	•	53.4	10.5	•	•	48.6	•	•	•	•
Salaries and Wages **11**	7.1	•	•	•	19.4	1.8	•	•	16.7	•	•	•	•
Taxes Paid **12**	3.7	•	•	•	2.8	3.6	•	•	4.4	•	•	•	•
Interest Paid **13**	10.0	•	•	•	0.1	1.5	•	•	0.8	•	•	•	•
Depreciation **14**	7.8	•	•	•	1.7	3.7	•	•	3.2	•	•	•	•
Amortization and Depletion **15**	0.5	•	•	•	2.0	•	•	•	0.0	•	•	•	•
Pensions and Other Deferred Comp. **16**	0.4	•	•	•	0.1	0.0	•	•	0.6	•	•	•	•
Employee Benefits **17**	0.9	•	•	•	0.2	1.1	•	•	3.0	•	•	•	•
Advertising **18**	0.1	•	•	•	0.4	•	•	•	0.0	•	•	•	•
Other Expenses **19**	16.6	•	•	•	15.2	57.7	•	•	15.6	•	•	•	•
Officers' Compensation **20**	0.3	•	•	•	1.3	0.4	•	•	0.3	•	•	•	•
Operating Margin **21**	11.4	•	•	•	3.3	19.6	•	•	6.7	•	•	•	•
Operating Margin Before Officers' Comp. **22**	11.8	•	•	•	4.6	20.1	•	•	7.0	•	•	•	•

Selected Average Balance Sheet ($ in Thousands)

Net Receivables **23**	2690	268	593	12139
Inventories **24**	621	123	86	164
Net Property, Plant and Equipment **25**	34277	221	3324	31369
Total Assets **26**	69797	1971	8355	65199
Notes and Loans Payable **27**	44108	75	1610	12782
All Other Liabilities **28**	4564	253	1079	26591
Net Worth **29**	21124	1643	5666	25826

Selected Financial Ratios (Times to 1)

Current Ratio **30**	1.2	3.7	3.3	1.7
Quick Ratio **31**	0.8	1.9	3.1	1.5
Net Sales to Working Capital **32**	17.2	5.3	3.1	10.0
Coverage Ratio **33**	3.5	53.9	20.4	12.2
Total Asset Turnover **34**	0.4	2.3	0.8	1.7
Inventory Turnover **35**	16.7	19.6	8.0	323.7
Receivables Turnover **36**	10.0	8.2	13.8	
Total Liabilities to Net Worth **37**	2.3	0.2	0.5	1.5
Current Assets to Working Capital **38**	5.0	1.4	1.4	2.5
Current Liabilities to Working Capital **39**	4.0	0.4	0.4	1.5
Working Capital to Net Sales **40**	0.1	0.2	0.3	0.1
Inventory to Working Capital **41**	0.7	0.2	0.0	0.0
Total Receipts to Cash Flow **42**	3.4	5.2	1.2	5.5
Cost of Goods to Cash Flow **43**	1.4	2.8	0.1	2.7
Cash Flow to Total Debt **44**	0.2	2.6	2.1	0.5

Selected Financial Factors (in Percentages)

Debt Ratio **45**	69.7	16.7	32.2	60.4
Return on Total Assets **46**	12.6	16.7	24.9	15.4
Return on Equity Before Income Taxes **47**	29.8	19.7	35.0	35.8
Return on Equity After Income Taxes **48**	22.4	18.0	31.3	25.8
Profit Margin (Before Income Tax) **49**	25.1	7.2	30.0	8.5
Profit Margin (After Income Tax) **50**	18.8	6.6	26.9	6.1

Table I

Corporations with and without Net Income

OTHER TRANSPORTATION AND SUPPORT ACTIVITIES

MONEY AMOUNTS AND SIZE OF ASSETS IN THOUSANDS OF DOLLARS

Item Description for Accounting Period 7/07 Through 6/08	Total	Zero Assets	Under 500	500 to 1,000	1,000 to 5,000	5,000 to 10,000	10,000 to 25,000	25,000 to 50,000	50,000 to 100,000	100,000 to 250,000	250,000 to 500,000	500,000 to 2,500,000	2,500,000 and over
Number of Enterprises 1	44685	10228	28248	2884	2525	367	226	84	50	40	8	19	6
Revenues ($ in Thousands)													
Net Sales 2	212161652	2856163	15263563	8987060	21217537	8431566	9464490	6216847	6257155	8242363	3174411	9561432	112489065
Interest 3	815040	1146	4686	3751	15187	14345	7116	12563	14290	36627	32853	126323	546153
Rents 4	308037	2035	1808	15741	2848	5053	2361	1978	10980	29260	12481	34361	189131
Royalties 5	1327326	2042	0	0	0	0	0	889	1244	440	0	0	1322711
Other Portfolio Income 6	1153679	315888	16246	19295	49123	7021	7776	15232	57565	30876	176303	190894	267464
Other Receipts 7	1440127	8812	297237	29486	97666	42122	40087	68650	109575	139205	113350	163513	330420
Total Receipts 8	217205861	3186086	15583540	9055333	21382361	8500107	9521830	6316159	6450809	8478771	3509398	10076523	115144944
Average Total Receipts 9	4861	312	552	3140	8468	23161	42132	75192	129016	211969	438675	530343	19190824
Operating Costs/Operating Income (%)													
Cost of Operations 10	39.7	53.0	47.7	54.8	70.4	66.4	61.0	61.6	64.2	50.4	49.7	50.1	23.0
Salaries and Wages 11	17.2	12.0	13.1	9.1	10.4	10.7	10.0	13.8	13.2	14.9	18.7	17.6	21.5
Taxes Paid 12	2.7	3.4	2.2	4.1	1.8	3.2	2.2	1.8	2.4	4.3	2.7	2.3	2.9
Interest Paid 13	0.9	1.3	0.9	0.4	0.6	0.5	0.7	1.3	1.4	1.5	1.2	2.8	0.8
Depreciation 14	3.0	2.1	2.0	1.1	1.7	0.9	1.1	2.2	1.6	3.2	2.4	1.9	4.1
Amortization and Depletion 15	0.3	0.2	0.1	0.0	0.1	0.1	0.2	0.3	0.6	0.6	0.3	1.1	0.3
Pensions and Other Deferred Comp. 16	4.2	•	0.2	0.5	0.2	0.3	0.6	0.2	0.2	0.3	0.9	0.7	7.5
Employee Benefits 17	3.4	0.6	0.5	0.7	0.9	1.0	1.0	1.8	1.6	2.4	3.2	2.7	5.2
Advertising 18	0.4	0.1	0.3	0.4	0.3	0.2	0.2	0.1	0.3	0.2	0.1	0.3	0.6
Other Expenses 19	27.4	30.6	26.7	24.2	11.3	13.9	19.5	14.5	13.1	22.0	19.8	19.9	35.1
Officers' Compensation 20	1.3	6.7	5.6	3.4	1.9	1.7	1.5	1.0	0.9	0.8	1.2	1.5	0.3
Operating Margin 21	•	•	0.6	1.2	0.4	1.2	2.1	1.2	0.5	•	•	•	•
Operating Margin Before Officers' Comp. 22	0.8	•	6.1	4.7	2.3	2.8	3.6	2.2	1.4	0.2	1.0	0.5	•

Selected Average Balance Sheet ($ in Thousands)

Item													
Net Receivables 23	643	0	23	220	846	2657	5242	10197	20027	39858	93832	183367	2577438
Inventories 24	43	0	0	37	63	304	428	1256	2619	3802	1002	12354	121988
Net Property, Plant and Equipment 25	968	0	40	142	621	1680	5556	11389	16137	45968	76760	100587	5357230
Total Assets 26	2904	0	104	685	2395	7079	16532	35152	72344	155093	341282	965244	13105060
Notes and Loans Payable 27	934	0	64	231	1117	1823	4508	13918	20158	69318	61400	336524	3825090
All Other Liabilities 28	968	0	33	304	752	3259	5818	12737	23738	54071	106350	322038	4274554
Net Worth 29	1002	0	8	149	527	1998	6206	8497	28448	31703	173532	306682	5005416

Selected Financial Ratios (Times to 1)

Item													
Current Ratio 30	1.0	•	1.7	1.2	1.5	1.2	1.2	1.1	1.2	1.0	1.5	1.3	0.8
Quick Ratio 31	0.8	•	1.4	0.9	1.2	1.1	1.1	0.9	0.9	0.8	1.3	1.0	0.7
Net Sales to Working Capital 32	491.4	•	25.1	53.3	18.4	26.0	24.2	36.6	24.1	231.4	7.2	7.8	•
Coverage Ratio 33	3.1	4.3	3.9	6.0	2.8	5.1	4.9	3.1	3.7	2.5	10.2	2.7	2.5
Total Asset Turnover 34	1.6	•	5.2	4.5	3.5	3.2	2.5	2.1	1.7	1.3	1.2	0.5	1.4
Inventory Turnover 35	44.1	•	99.1	46.1	94.1	50.2	59.6	36.3	30.7	27.3	196.8	20.4	35.3
Receivables Turnover 36	7.8	•	22.2	17.2	9.8	10.3	7.2	8.5	5.9	6.7	3.9	2.5	8.1
Total Liabilities to Net Worth 37	1.9	•	12.1	3.6	3.5	2.5	1.7	3.1	1.5	3.9	1.0	2.1	1.6
Current Assets to Working Capital 38	104.7	•	2.4	7.6	3.0	5.1	5.0	8.8	7.1	71.3	3.0	4.8	•
Current Liabilities to Working Capital 39	103.7	•	1.4	6.6	2.0	4.1	4.0	7.8	6.1	70.3	2.0	3.8	•
Working Capital to Net Sales 40	0.0	•	0.0	0.0	0.1	0.0	0.0	0.0	0.0	0.0	0.1	0.1	•
Inventory to Working Capital 41	4.6	•	0.1	0.5	0.2	0.3	0.3	0.8	0.6	4.3	0.0	0.2	•
Total Receipts to Cash Flow 42	4.2	4.1	4.5	4.4	10.5	7.1	5.7	6.9	8.5	5.4	5.2	4.9	3.3
Cost of Goods to Cash Flow 43	1.7	2.2	2.2	2.4	7.4	4.7	3.5	4.3	5.5	2.7	2.6	2.5	0.8
Cash Flow to Total Debt 44	0.6	•	1.2	1.3	0.4	0.6	0.7	0.4	0.3	0.3	0.5	0.2	0.7

Selected Financial Factors (in Percentages)

Item													
Debt Ratio 45	65.5	•	92.4	78.2	78.0	71.8	62.5	75.8	60.7	79.6	49.2	68.2	61.8
Return on Total Assets 46	4.7	•	18.5	10.9	6.3	7.8	8.6	8.4	8.6	5.1	13.8	4.0	2.8
Return on Equity Before Income Taxes 47	9.2	•	179.8	41.4	18.6	22.2	18.3	23.6	15.8	15.2	24.5	7.9	4.5
Return on Equity After Income Taxes 48	5.4	•	176.6	39.1	14.4	19.8	15.6	17.3	12.2	8.4	15.9	2.1	1.7
Profit Margin (Before Income Tax) 49	1.9	4.3	2.7	2.0	1.2	1.9	2.7	2.7	3.6	2.3	10.7	4.8	1.2
Profit Margin (After Income Tax) 50	1.1	1.1	2.6	1.9	0.9	1.7	2.3	2.0	2.8	1.3	7.0	1.3	0.5

Table II

Corporations with Net Income

OTHER TRANSPORTATION AND SUPPORT ACTIVITIES

MONEY AMOUNTS AND SIZE OF ASSETS IN THOUSANDS OF DOLLARS

Item Description for Accounting Period 7/07 Through 6/08		Total	Zero Assets	Under 500	500 to 1,000	1,000 to 5,000	5,000 to 10,000	10,000 to 25,000	25,000 to 50,000	50,000 to 100,000	100,000 to 250,000	250,000 to 500,000	500,000 to 2,500,000	2,500,000 and over
Number of Enterprises	1	21180	4054	12762	2274	1523	247	•	67	38	29	•	•	8
Revenues ($ in Thousands)														
Net Sales	2	171457221	1372088	8948241	7511001	13519823	6733973	•	5024036	5029292	6952755	•	•	7588372
Interest	3	637537	945	3864	3720	13500	8847	•	10761	13485	30293	•	•	84723
Rents	4	217325	9	1808	15741	0	5053	•	1524	10265	28406	•	•	6383
Royalties	5	1325855	2042	0	0	0	0	•	889	1231	440	•	•	0
Other Portfolio Income	6	931779	177223	7422	19295	38323	6893	•	12922	56163	29425	•	•	164205
Other Receipts	7	924167	-861	32612	24082	44658	38409	•	43125	107025	145665	•	•	35596
Total Receipts	8	175493884	1551446	8993947	7573839	13616304	6793175	•	5093257	5217461	7186984	•	•	7879279
Average Total Receipts	9	8286	383	705	3331	8940	27503	•	76019	137302	247827	•	•	984910
Operating Costs/Operating Income (%)														
Cost of Operations	10	37.2	41.1	44.3	57.1	68.7	73.9	•	62.4	65.7	51.3	•	•	46.7
Salaries and Wages	11	18.1	13.3	15.3	8.3	11.2	8.2	•	15.0	12.1	13.3	•	•	18.6
Taxes Paid	12	2.8	2.1	2.1	4.5	1.4	3.5	•	2.0	1.7	4.5	•	•	2.2
Interest Paid	13	0.7	1.4	0.6	0.3	0.4	0.3	•	0.9	0.7	1.1	•	•	0.8
Depreciation	14	3.0	3.0	1.3	1.1	1.0	0.6	•	2.2	1.3	2.8	•	•	1.7
Amortization and Depletion	15	0.2	0.3	0.0	0.0	0.1	0.1	•	0.2	0.6	0.5	•	•	0.9
Pensions and Other Deferred Comp.	16	5.1	•	0.2	0.6	0.2	0.1	•	0.2	0.2	0.3	•	•	0.8
Employee Benefits	17	3.6	1.2	0.5	0.8	0.9	0.9	•	1.9	1.7	2.4	•	•	2.0
Advertising	18	0.5	0.1	0.3	0.3	0.3	0.2	•	0.1	0.4	0.1	•	•	0.3
Other Expenses	19	26.2	32.2	22.1	20.2	10.5	7.9	•	10.8	12.7	21.2	•	•	16.4
Officers' Compensation	20	1.1	1.4	5.1	3.7	1.9	1.8	•	1.0	0.9	0.8	•	•	0.9
Operating Margin	21	1.6	3.8	8.1	3.1	3.3	2.5	•	3.2	2.0	1.6	•	•	8.7
Operating Margin Before Officers' Comp.	22	2.7	5.3	13.2	6.8	5.2	4.4	•	4.2	3.0	2.4	•	•	9.5

Selected Average Balance Sheet ($ in Thousands)

Net Receivables **23**	983	0	21	251	848	3126	9787	21098	44050	•	344292
Inventories **24**	71	0	3	44	48	443	1059	3080	2707	•	19828
Net Property, Plant and Equipment **25**	1677	0	37	126	471	1372	11651	14597	39238	•	146530
Total Assets **26**	4519	0	113	688	2316	7280	34979	71772	153259	•	1053160
Notes and Loans Payable **27**	1086	0	51	227	582	1166	11583	15756	46806	•	145905
All Other Liabilities **28**	1519	0	26	271	831	3203	12218	23526	54927	•	416040
Net Worth **29**	1914	0	36	190	903	2911	11179	32490	51525	•	491215

Selected Financial Ratios (Times to 1)

Current Ratio **30**	1.0	•	2.0	1.3	1.6	1.4	1.1	1.5	1.1	•	1.3
Quick Ratio **31**	0.8	•	1.6	1.0	1.3	1.2	0.9	1.1	0.9	•	1.0
Net Sales to Working Capital **32**	•	17.3	23.6	29.7	16.0	18.3	37.2	9.1	38.5	•	8.4
Coverage Ratio **33**	7.1	•	16.0	12.2	10.8	13.7	5.8	9.5	5.4	•	16.4
Total Asset Turnover **34**	1.8	•	6.2	4.8	3.8	3.7	2.1	1.8	1.6	•	0.9
Inventory Turnover **35**	42.5	•	112.6	42.4	126.4	45.4	44.2	28.2	45.5	•	22.3
Receivables Turnover **36**	8.2	•	27.2	17.2	8.6	9.9	9.2	5.8	7.9	•	•
Total Liabilities to Net Worth **37**	1.4	•	2.1	2.6	1.6	1.5	2.1	1.2	2.0	•	1.1
Current Assets to Working Capital **38**	•	•	2.0	4.2	2.7	3.5	8.9	2.8	10.8	•	4.8
Current Liabilities to Working Capital **39**	•	•	1.0	3.2	1.7	2.5	7.9	1.8	9.8	•	3.8
Working Capital to Net Sales **40**	•	•	0.0	0.0	0.1	0.1	0.0	0.1	0.0	•	0.1
Inventory to Working Capital **41**	•	•	0.1	0.3	0.1	0.2	0.7	0.3	0.6	•	0.2
Total Receipts to Cash Flow **42**	4.0	2.5	4.0	4.7	8.3	10.3	8.1	7.4	4.6	•	4.0
Cost of Goods to Cash Flow **43**	1.5	1.0	1.8	2.7	5.7	7.6	5.1	4.9	2.3	•	1.8
Cash Flow to Total Debt **44**	0.8	•	2.3	1.4	0.8	0.6	0.4	0.5	0.5	•	0.4

Selected Financial Factors (in Percentages)

Debt Ratio **45**	57.6	•	68.1	72.4	61.0	60.0	68.0	54.7	66.4	•	53.4
Return on Total Assets **46**	8.6	•	56.9	20.6	16.8	13.6	11.7	11.9	9.7	•	12.4
Return on Equity Before Income Taxes **47**	17.5	•	167.5	68.3	39.0	31.6	30.3	23.4	23.5	•	24.9
Return on Equity After Income Taxes **48**	13.3	•	165.9	66.0	35.0	29.1	24.4	19.2	17.8	•	16.3
Profit Margin (Before Income Tax) **49**	4.1	23.0	8.6	3.9	4.0	3.4	4.5	5.8	5.1	•	12.9
Profit Margin (After Income Tax) **50**	3.1	16.2	8.5	3.8	3.6	3.1	3.6	4.7	3.8	•	8.5

WAREHOUSING AND STORAGE

Table I

Corporations with and without Net Income

MONEY AMOUNTS AND SIZE OF ASSETS IN THOUSANDS OF DOLLARS

Item Description for Accounting Period 7/07 Through 6/08		Total	Zero Assets	Under 500	500 to 1,000	1,000 to 5,000	5,000 to 10,000	10,000 to 25,000	25,000 to 50,000	50,000 to 100,000	100,000 to 250,000	250,000 to 500,000	500,000 to 2,500,000	2,500,000 and over
Number of Enterprises	1	5539	•	1667	812	1300	196	•	•	17	16	7	7	0
Revenues ($ in Thousands)														
Net Sales	2	21022125	•	461269	1547789	3494568	2007438	•	•	985625	2368351	1292633	3711913	0
Interest	3	139544	•	54	3070	7240	3770	•	•	3182	13863	19362	71253	0
Rents	4	50969	•	0	0	14094	781	•	•	3585	1561	6524	9913	0
Royalties	5	12477	•	0	0	0	0	•	•	0	1368	1106	0	0
Other Portfolio Income	6	239903	•	40524	133	4868	986	•	•	969	121001	3040	17586	0
Other Receipts	7	738537	•	547	10565	217435	6534	•	•	3473	80424	59125	184675	0
Total Receipts	8	22203555	•	502394	1561557	3738205	2019509	•	•	996834	2586568	1391790	3995340	0
Average Total Receipts	9	4009	•	301	1923	2876	10304	•	•	58637	161660	198827	570763	•
Operating Costs/Operating Income (%)														
Cost of Operations	10	34.2	•	2.5	46.8	42.8	34.5	•	•	51.5	22.4	38.1	17.9	•
Salaries and Wages	11	19.8	•	3.9	14.4	20.9	21.0	•	•	13.6	28.0	16.4	25.7	•
Taxes Paid	12	3.5	•	1.1	2.7	3.0	4.6	•	•	3.1	4.2	4.0	4.1	•
Interest Paid	13	3.9	•	5.7	1.6	2.1	1.5	•	•	2.0	2.1	5.8	10.8	•
Depreciation	14	4.3	•	1.0	1.9	3.3	2.4	•	•	3.2	3.8	7.5	7.2	•
Amortization and Depletion	15	0.9	•	1.8	0.0	0.3	0.0	•	•	0.6	1.0	0.6	3.3	•
Pensions and Other Deferred Comp.	16	0.8	•	•	0.2	0.6	1.8	•	•	0.7	1.2	0.9	0.3	•
Employee Benefits	17	2.4	•	0.0	1.9	0.9	3.1	•	•	3.1	4.3	2.0	3.4	•
Advertising	18	0.3	•	0.0	1.2	0.2	0.1	•	•	0.1	0.1	0.7	0.4	•
Other Expenses	19	30.4	•	78.6	29.8	28.7	23.0	•	•	17.2	32.7	31.5	31.7	•
Officers' Compensation	20	1.7	•	1.1	2.0	2.4	3.4	•	•	1.7	0.6	0.8	0.1	•
Operating Margin	21	•	•	4.0	•	•	4.5	•	•	3.2	•	•	•	•
Operating Margin Before Officers' Comp.	22	•	•	5.2	•	•	7.9	•	•	4.9	0.4	•	•	•

Selected Average Balance Sheet ($ in Thousands)

Net Receivables 23	532	10	143	329	1039	9662	31929	21501	121292
Inventories 24	90	4	19	109	166	6052	3004	3254	1539
Net Property, Plant and Equipment 25	1752	105	275	978	2641	28990	63887	167311	361643
Total Assets 26	5605	167	655	1917	7029	67445	155067	396825	2123020
Notes and Loans Payable 27	2315	121	528	772	1984	24224	45604	181683	896374
All Other Liabilities 28	1295	7	219	348	1144	11135	41595	99673	561492
Net Worth 29	1995	39	-92	798	3900	32086	67868	115468	665154

Selected Financial Ratios (Times to 1)

Current Ratio 30	1.3	7.2	1.1	1.8	1.8	1.6	1.5	0.9	0.8
Quick Ratio 31	1.0	4.8	0.9	1.3	1.5	0.9	1.3	0.7	0.6
Net Sales to Working Capital 32	15.0	8.7	61.0	6.9	8.9	6.0	7.6	•	1.3
Coverage Ratio 33	1.9	3.3	•	1.8	4.5	3.2	5.4	0.9	1.3
Total Asset Turnover 34	0.7	1.7	2.9	1.4	1.5	0.9	1.0	0.5	0.2
Inventory Turnover 35	14.4	1.8	48.1	10.5	21.3	4.9	11.0	21.6	61.8
Receivables Turnover 36	7.3	10.8	15.7	7.9	13.1	5.9	4.5	8.2	4.7
Total Liabilities to Net Worth 37	1.8	3.2	•	1.4	0.8	1.1	1.3	2.4	2.2
Current Assets to Working Capital 38	4.4	1.2	7.7	2.2	2.3	2.6	2.9	•	2.2
Current Liabilities to Working Capital 39	3.4	0.2	6.7	1.2	1.3	1.6	1.9	•	•
Working Capital to Net Sales 40	0.1	0.1	0.0	0.1	0.1	0.2	0.1	•	•
Inventory to Working Capital 41	0.4	0.0	0.9	0.3	0.1	0.7	0.2	•	•
Total Receipts to Cash Flow 42	4.6	6.3	5.2	4.7	6.3	6.4	3.4	3.7	4.6
Cost of Goods to Cash Flow 43	1.6	0.2	2.5	2.0	2.2	3.3	0.8	1.4	0.8
Cash Flow to Total Debt 44	0.2	0.3	0.5	0.5	0.5	0.3	0.5	0.2	0.1

Selected Financial Factors (in Percentages)

Debt Ratio 45	64.4	76.5	114.1	58.4	44.5	52.4	56.2	70.9	68.7
Return on Total Assets 46	5.0	30.9	•	5.2	9.6	5.5	10.7	2.4	3.4
Return on Equity Before Income Taxes 47	6.8	91.2	33.6	5.5	13.5	8.0	19.9	•	2.4
Return on Equity After Income Taxes 48	5.2	85.0	36.0	3.3	11.4	6.4	14.1	•	2.1
Profit Margin (Before Income Tax) 49	3.6	13.0	•	1.6	5.1	4.4	9.1	•	3.0
Profit Margin (After Income Tax) 50	2.7	12.1	•	1.0	4.3	3.6	6.5	•	2.6

Table II

Corporations with Net Income

WAREHOUSING AND STORAGE

MONEY AMOUNTS AND SIZE OF ASSETS IN THOUSANDS OF DOLLARS

Item Description for Accounting Period 7/07 Through 6/08	Total	Zero Assets	Under 500	500 to 1000	251 to 500	501 to 1,000	1,001 to 5,000	5,001 to 10,000	10,001 to 25,000	25,001 to 50,000	50,001 to 100,000	100,001 to 250,000	250,001 and over
Number of Enterprises 1	2687	106	1171	368	698	146	135	36	11	12	0	3	0
Revenues ($ in Thousands)													
Net Sales 2	14160096	315417	423926	729521	2125135	1962400	2023274	1147318	812361	2010245	0	2610499	0
Interest 3	120777	2161	54	3070	5879	2426	7617	3407	2636	26141	0	67385	0
Rents 4	29077	5941	0	0	14094	781	522	2296	3585	1850	0	8	0
Royalties 5	1632	0	0	0	0	0	3	0	0	1629	0	0	0
Other Portfolio Income 6	217813	7303	40524	133	2453	986	26177	14596	853	122433	0	2352	0
Other Receipts 7	611119	55614	3	1925	185521	7156	56705	46733	2354	83655	0	171458	0
Total Receipts 8	15140514	386436	464507	734649	2333082	1973749	2114298	1214350	821789	2245953	0	2851702	0
Average Total Receipts 9	5635	3646	397	1996	3343	13519	15661	33732	74708	187163	•	950567	•
Operating Costs/Operating Income (%)													
Cost of Operations 10	29.5	60.3	2.0	66.1	32.1	34.4	34.7	35.2	57.6	18.5	•	7.2	•
Salaries and Wages 11	21.7	20.2	1.1	5.0	25.6	21.0	14.0	19.1	9.7	29.4	•	32.1	•
Taxes Paid 12	3.7	2.4	1.1	1.5	3.4	4.4	3.4	3.4	3.0	4.3	•	4.5	•
Interest Paid 13	3.8	0.4	6.2	0.9	1.1	1.5	2.3	2.2	1.7	2.2	•	12.4	•
Depreciation 14	4.5	2.4	0.7	2.0	3.8	2.2	4.3	5.3	3.0	4.3	•	9.0	•
Amortization and Depletion 15	0.9	0.2	2.0	0.3	0.0	0.0	0.0	0.1	0.2	1.1	•	3.5	•
Pensions and Other Deferred Comp. 16	0.9	0.2	0.2	•	0.9	1.8	1.0	0.5	0.7	1.3	•	0.4	•
Employee Benefits 17	2.4	0.8	0.0	0.6	1.1	3.2	2.1	1.6	2.7	4.8	•	2.7	•
Advertising 18	0.3	0.0	0.0	1.2	0.2	0.1	0.6	0.2	0.1	0.1	•	0.6	•
Other Expenses 19	29.0	15.6	75.1	19.5	30.3	22.5	31.2	28.1	14.3	30.5	•	31.5	•
Officers' Compensation 20	1.8	0.2	1.2	2.0	3.1	2.8	2.3	3.1	1.9	0.6	•	0.1	•
Operating Margin 21	1.6	•	10.5	1.1	•	6.2	4.1	1.4	5.1	2.9	•	•	•
Operating Margin Before Officers' Comp. 22	3.4	•	11.7	3.2	1.2	9.0	6.4	4.5	7.0	3.5	•	•	•

Selected Average Balance Sheet ($ in Thousands)

Net Receivables 23	704	0	8	93	371	1309	1799	3482	10897	29921	183340	•
Inventories 24	120	0	6	22	39	221	412	902	9256	3983	2038	•
Net Property, Plant and Equipment 25	2442	0	135	354	901	3304	7286	14227	29337	93650	739334	•
Total Assets 26	8024	0	209	655	1954	7120	15328	33620	65464	207375	4061444	•
Notes and Loans Payable 27	3035	0	172	483	561	2574	5841	9901	18070	59655	165014	•
All Other Liabilities 28	1872	0	5	52	319	1432	1990	9418	11587	43590	1105103	•
Net Worth 29	3117	0	32	120	1074	3115	7497	14301	35807	104130	1306328	•

Selected Financial Ratios (Times to 1)

Current Ratio 30	1.3	•	8.2	3.4	2.1	1.6	1.9	1.1	1.6	1.4	0.7	•
Quick Ratio 31	1.0	•	4.5	2.5	1.9	1.3	1.4	0.8	0.8	1.1	0.6	•
Net Sales to Working Capital 32	14.9	•	10.7	14.0	6.0	12.8	7.0	42.5	6.0	10.1	•	•
Coverage Ratio 33	3.3	45.2	4.2	2.9	8.1	5.7	4.7	4.3	4.7	7.7	1.5	•
Total Asset Turnover 34	0.7	•	1.7	3.0	1.6	1.9	1.0	0.9	1.1	0.8	0.2	•
Inventory Turnover 35	13.0	•	1.3	59.0	24.7	20.9	12.6	12.5	4.6	7.8	30.6	•
Receivables Turnover 36	7.0	•	16.1	18.0	8.3	14.5	7.8	11.8	6.2	•	•	•
Total Liabilities to Net Worth 37	1.6	•	5.6	4.5	0.8	1.3	1.0	1.4	0.8	1.0	2.1	•
Current Assets to Working Capital 38	4.2	•	1.1	1.4	1.9	2.7	2.1	13.9	2.6	3.5	•	•
Current Liabilities to Working Capital 39	3.2	•	0.1	0.4	0.9	1.7	1.1	12.9	1.6	2.5	•	•
Working Capital to Net Sales 40	0.1	•	0.1	0.1	0.2	0.1	0.1	0.0	0.2	0.1	•	•
Inventory to Working Capital 41	0.4	•	•	0.3	0.1	0.2	0.2	2.2	0.9	0.2	•	•
Total Receipts to Cash Flow 42	4.0	3.8	4.6	5.5	3.5	5.9	3.7	4.0	6.1	3.0	4.2	•
Cost of Goods to Cash Flow 43	1.2	2.3	0.1	3.6	1.1	2.0	1.3	1.4	3.5	0.5	0.3	•
Cash Flow to Total Debt 44	0.3	•	0.4	0.7	1.0	0.6	0.5	0.4	0.4	0.5	0.1	•

Selected Financial Factors (in Percentages)

Debt Ratio 45	61.2	•	84.8	81.7	45.0	56.3	51.1	57.5	45.3	49.8	67.8	•
Return on Total Assets 46	8.2	•	45.5	8.4	13.9	15.6	10.6	8.9	9.2	13.7	4.0	•
Return on Equity Before Income Taxes 47	14.7	•	228.6	30.3	22.1	29.4	16.9	16.1	13.2	23.8	4.2	•
Return on Equity After Income Taxes 48	12.5	•	217.7	26.2	19.1	26.5	14.6	14.5	11.1	17.8	3.8	•
Profit Margin (Before Income Tax) 49	8.7	19.9	20.0	1.8	7.8	6.8	8.5	7.2	6.4	14.8	6.3	•
Profit Margin (After Income Tax) 50	7.4	17.5	19.1	1.6	6.8	7.3	6.5	5.4		11.1	5.8	•

Table I

Corporations with and without Net Income

NEWSPAPER PUBLISHERS

MONEY AMOUNTS AND SIZE OF ASSETS IN THOUSANDS OF DOLLARS

Item Description for Accounting Period 7/07 Through 6/08	Total	Zero Assets	Under 500	500 to 1,000	1,000 to 5,000	5,000 to 10,000	10,000 to 25,000	25,000 to 50,000	50,000 to 100,000	100,000 to 250,000	250,000 to 500,000	500,000 to 2,500,000	2,500,000 and over
Number of Enterprises **1**	5046	282	3211	869	410	81	83	37	23	12	13	13	12
Revenues ($ in Thousands)													
Net Sales **2**	50237553	75932	1190267	1057615	1744324	464777	1488899	1323819	1332268	1652290	2805520	6467925	30633916
Interest **3**	506995	217	85	726	274	624	6012	2917	8641	5575	19737	12574	449613
Rents **4**	176499	4	6	228	0	1133	969	4730	4360	10853	15364	15824	123029
Royalties **5**	277245	0	3	0	0	0	0	0	194	247	837	439	275525
Other Portfolio Income **6**	2117417	0	5	6107	23	12253	6241	7837	30924	16067	198648	341522	1497792
Other Receipts **7**	2255071	16549	15270	-7092	63149	44064	-4474	10328	86135	30479	12390	166748	1821523
Total Receipts **8**	55570780	92702	1205636	1057584	1807770	522851	1497647	1349631	1462522	1715511	3052496	7005032	34801398
Average Total Receipts **9**	11013	329	375	1217	4409	6455	18044	36477	63588	142959	277500	538849	2900116
Operating Costs/Operating Income (%)													
Cost of Operations **10**	24.9	7.1	52.4	31.6	26.8	19.6	35.8	21.1	30.3	29.6	13.7	21.6	24.5
Salaries and Wages **11**	25.1	16.2	20.9	22.2	31.9	32.3	22.3	29.9	26.5	23.1	28.1	24.5	24.8
Taxes Paid **12**	3.6	2.4	2.0	3.8	5.0	3.7	3.7	3.8	3.6	3.0	3.9	3.8	3.6
Interest Paid **13**	4.6	15.1	0.6	0.3	2.4	0.9	1.2	2.1	2.8	2.8	3.7	8.7	4.7
Depreciation **14**	3.6	1.9	0.7	0.9	2.9	2.9	3.0	3.0	5.2	5.1	5.7	4.2	3.4
Amortization and Depletion **15**	3.7	0.5	0.0	1.2	0.8	0.4	0.6	1.6	1.4	3.2	4.0	7.3	3.8
Pensions and Other Deferred Comp. **16**	1.1	•	0.0	0.5	0.3	0.8	0.9	2.1	1.6	0.8	2.2	1.3	1.0
Employee Benefits **17**	2.7	0.4	0.3	1.6	3.0	3.1	2.9	4.7	3.2	3.4	3.4	3.4	2.5
Advertising **18**	1.7	0.1	1.6	0.5	1.1	3.2	0.6	1.1	1.6	1.1	1.9	1.3	2.0
Other Expenses **19**	28.0	69.3	30.5	27.4	29.1	28.1	19.6	26.8	24.8	26.0	31.8	29.2	27.9
Officers' Compensation **20**	1.8	•	1.2	5.8	3.5	2.8	3.0	2.4	2.3	1.8	3.1	1.1	1.5
Operating Margin **21**	•	•	•	4.1	•	2.2	6.4	1.3	•	•	•	•	0.3
Operating Margin Before Officers' Comp. **22**	0.8	•	•	10.0	•	4.9	9.4	3.7	•	1.8	1.5	•	1.8

Selected Average Balance Sheet ($ in Thousands)

Net Receivables 23	2058	0	19	132	537	505	2014	3973	10349	18213	45972	73680	642714
Inventories 24	139	0	2	5	24	80	307	541	983	2812	3692	7899	35880
Net Property, Plant and Equipment 25	3223	0	18	45	1130	1163	4613	10520	21732	47173	96074	203806	838596
Total Assets 26	23000	0	62	594	2751	6267	16561	37455	65410	171167	358552	1077832	7452990
Notes and Loans Payable 27	7532	0	108	71	1515	621	2778	11687	23926	52383	123502	592646	2168355
All Other Liabilities 28	6390	0	44	335	539	905	3434	9159	19106	37231	86360	265881	2133440
Net Worth 29	9079	0	-90	187	697	4742	10349	16610	22378	81553	148690	219305	3151195

Selected Financial Ratios (Times to 1)

Current Ratio 30	1.1	•	1.7	1.1	1.1	4.4	3.5	1.9	1.7	1.8	1.5	1.4	0.9
Quick Ratio 31	0.8	•	1.4	1.0	1.0	2.3	2.5	1.3	1.3	1.1	1.2	1.2	0.7
Net Sales to Working Capital 32	41.5	•	26.4	59.1	64.5	2.2	3.7	7.1	6.8	6.0	9.7	12.9	•
Coverage Ratio 33	3.1	1.6	6.0	15.1	•	17.5	6.7	2.5	3.3	2.3	2.9	1.2	4.0
Total Asset Turnover 34	0.4	•	6.0	2.0	1.5	0.9	1.1	1.0	0.9	0.8	0.7	0.5	0.3
Inventory Turnover 35	17.8	•	86.7	72.4	47.5	14.0	20.9	14.0	17.9	14.5	9.5	13.6	17.4
Receivables Turnover 36	5.0	•	8.1	11.5	8.1	13.2	8.4	6.0	5.9	6.8	7.1	8.3	4.1
Total Liabilities to Net Worth 37	1.5	•	•	2.2	2.9	0.3	0.6	1.3	1.9	1.1	1.4	3.9	1.4
Current Assets to Working Capital 38	15.0	•	2.5	17.8	11.1	1.3	1.4	2.2	2.4	2.3	2.8	3.3	•
Current Liabilities to Working Capital 39	14.0	•	1.5	16.8	10.1	0.3	0.4	1.2	1.4	1.3	1.8	2.3	•
Working Capital to Net Sales 40	0.0	•	0.0	0.0	0.0	0.5	0.3	0.1	0.1	0.2	0.1	0.1	•
Inventory to Working Capital 41	0.6	•	0.3	0.2	0.3	0.0	0.1	0.1	0.1	0.1	0.1	0.2	•
Total Receipts to Cash Flow 42	3.2	•	5.4	3.7	4.4	2.5	4.1	3.6	3.9	3.9	3.4	3.9	2.8
Cost of Goods to Cash Flow 43	0.8	0.1	2.8	1.2	1.2	0.5	1.5	0.8	1.2	1.1	0.5	0.8	0.7
Cash Flow to Total Debt 44	0.2	•	0.5	0.8	0.5	1.5	0.7	0.5	0.3	0.4	0.4	0.1	0.2

Selected Financial Factors (in Percentages)

Debt Ratio 45	60.5	•	246.2	68.5	74.7	24.3	37.5	55.7	65.8	52.4	58.5	79.7	57.7
Return on Total Assets 46	6.3	•	•	9.1	•	14.2	8.7	5.0	8.2	5.2	7.7	4.9	6.5
Return on Equity Before Income Taxes 47	10.8	•	36.7	26.8	17.7	17.7	11.8	6.8	16.7	6.2	12.2	4.0	11.6
Return on Equity After Income Taxes 48	7.3	•	38.7	25.5	•	15.2	10.9	5.3	12.4	4.9	8.0	•	8.0
Profit Margin (Before Income Tax) 49	9.9	9.1	4.1	•	•	14.7	6.8	3.2	6.5	3.7	7.1	1.8	14.3
Profit Margin (After Income Tax) 50	6.6	8.1	•	3.9	•	12.6	6.3	2.5	4.8	2.9	4.6	•	9.9

Table II

Corporations with Net Income

NEWSPAPER PUBLISHERS

MONEY AMOUNTS AND SIZE OF ASSETS IN THOUSANDS OF DOLLARS

Item Description for Accounting Period 7/07 Through 6/08		Total	Zero Assets	Under 500	500 to 1,000	1,000 to 5,000	5,000 to 10,000	10,000 to 25,000	25,000 to 50,000	50,000 to 100,000	100,000 to 250,000	250,000 to 500,000	500,000 to 2,500,000	2,500,000 and over
Number of Enterprises	1	2434	32	1584	•	150	71	54	31	16	7	8	8	•
Revenues ($ in Thousands)														
Net Sales	2	42553073	35965	581056	•	514871	385647	1164705	1186631	1021841	842749	2181837	3639352	•
Interest	3	428480	217	83	•	248	624	5613	2570	6802	4864	18173	11007	•
Rents	4	165465	4	6	•	0	1133	942	4716	4360	6113	13259	11674	•
Royalties	5	276982	0	3	•	0	0	0	0	194	247	837	176	•
Other Portfolio Income	6	2076770	0	4	•	1	454	5970	7817	30886	14085	198381	321958	•
Other Receipts	7	2073768	16549	15167	•	62552	44157	9893	9132	63637	19333	11734	65544	•
Total Receipts	8	47574538	52735	596319	•	577672	432015	1187123	1210866	1127720	887391	2424221	4049711	•
Average Total Receipts	9	19546	1648	376	•	3851	6085	21984	39060	70482	126770	303028	506214	•
Operating Costs/Operating Income (%)														
Cost of Operations	10	24.9	15.0	50.9	•	39.4	21.7	37.7	21.7	32.3	44.0	9.3	24.3	•
Salaries and Wages	11	24.4	19.5	16.3	•	17.3	29.6	19.5	29.6	22.3	12.0	29.2	23.5	•
Taxes Paid	12	3.7	3.1	2.4	•	5.2	3.5	3.6	3.8	3.5	3.1	4.1	4.5	•
Interest Paid	13	4.1	31.8	0.5	•	2.5	0.8	0.6	1.2	2.3	2.5	3.5	4.7	•
Depreciation	14	3.5	4.0	0.8	•	3.8	3.0	2.7	3.0	3.4	3.1	6.2	4.3	•
Amortization and Depletion	15	3.4	1.0	0.0	•	0.2	0.3	0.2	1.4	0.8	2.8	4.0	4.4	•
Pensions and Other Deferred Comp.	16	1.1	•	0.0	•	0.4	0.5	1.0	2.3	1.9	0.5	2.4	1.0	•
Employee Benefits	17	2.6	0.9	0.6	•	1.9	3.4	2.5	4.9	3.0	3.2	3.3	2.5	•
Advertising	18	1.8	0.2	0.6	•	0.6	2.4	0.6	1.2	1.2	0.3	1.9	1.7	•
Other Expenses	19	27.2	50.9	23.9	•	30.3	20.1	18.2	26.7	23.2	21.0	33.0	27.1	•
Officers' Compensation	20	1.8	•	2.4	•	6.1	2.8	3.2	2.0	2.5	1.9	3.2	1.4	•
Operating Margin	21	1.4	•	1.7	•	•	11.8	10.3	2.2	3.8	5.5	0.0	0.5	•
Operating Margin Before Officers' Comp.	22	3.2	•	4.1	•	•	14.6	13.5	4.2	6.3	7.5	3.2	1.9	•

Selected Average Balance Sheet ($ in Thousands)

	•	•	•	•	•	•	•	•	•	•	•
Net Receivables 23	2920	0	17	506	567	2357	4140	10723	15638	55116	56775
Inventories 24	252	0	0	23	87	383	487	1104	1629	3466	9328
Net Property, Plant and Equipment 25	5647	0	7	1241	1076	5544	11101	21060	33692	103784	186600
Total Assets 26	41385	0	53	2951	5897	17587	37263	65396	161019	381461	756223
Notes and Loans Payable 27	12244	0	16	1407	621	1834	10411	15074	37065	99698	226282
All Other Liabilities 28	10721	0	27	387	920	4167	8817	14784	36739	103202	234996
Net Worth 29	18421	0	11	1157	4357	11587	18035	35539	87214	178560	294945

Selected Financial Ratios (Times to 1)

	•	•	•	•	•	•	•	•	•	•	•
Current Ratio 30	1.1	•	1.2	1.4	4.7	3.8	1.9	2.0	1.9	1.6	1.3
Quick Ratio 31	0.8	•	1.1	1.4	2.5	3.0	1.4	1.5	0.9	1.3	1.1
Net Sales to Working Capital 32	28.1	•	73.7	17.1	1.9	3.9	6.6	5.4	4.3	8.0	15.8
Coverage Ratio 33	4.3	1.6	10.6	2.8	30.1	4.6	7.1	7.1	5.3	4.2	3.5
Total Asset Turnover 34	0.4	•	6.9	1.2	0.9	1.2	1.0	1.0	0.7	0.7	0.6
Inventory Turnover 35	17.3	•	980.6	58.7	13.6	21.3	17.1	18.7	32.5	7.3	11.8
Receivables Turnover 36	6.0	•	6.5	7.3	13.4	8.9	7.4	6.0	•	6.9	7.7
Total Liabilities to Net Worth 37	1.2	•	4.0	1.5	0.4	0.5	1.1	0.8	0.8	1.1	1.6
Current Assets to Working Capital 38	9.2	•	6.2	3.6	1.3	1.4	2.1	2.0	2.1	2.6	4.0
Current Liabilities to Working Capital 39	8.2	•	5.2	2.6	0.3	0.4	1.1	1.0	1.1	1.6	3.0
Working Capital to Net Sales 40	0.0	•	0.0	0.1	0.5	0.3	0.2	0.2	0.2	0.1	0.1
Inventory to Working Capital 41	0.4	•	0.0	0.1	0.0	0.1	0.1	0.1	0.1	0.1	0.3
Total Receipts to Cash Flow 42	2.9	1.4	3.9	3.3	2.4	3.6	3.5	3.2	3.7	3.1	3.2
Cost of Goods to Cash Flow 43	0.7	0.2	2.0	1.3	0.5	1.3	0.8	1.0	1.6	0.3	0.8
Cash Flow to Total Debt 44	0.3	•	2.2	0.6	1.5	1.0	0.6	0.7	0.4	0.4	0.3

Selected Financial Factors (in Percentages)

	•	•	•	•	•	•	•	•	•	•	•
Debt Ratio 45	55.5	•	80.2	60.8	26.1	34.1	51.6	45.7	45.8	53.2	61.0
Return on Total Assets 46	7.4	•	32.9	8.2	22.7	15.5	5.4	16.0	9.9	10.4	9.8
Return on Equity Before Income Taxes 47	12.8	•	150.2	13.4	29.7	22.4	8.8	25.3	14.9	17.0	17.9
Return on Equity After Income Taxes 48	9.2	•	116.6	12.7	27.6	21.1	7.1	21.4	12.7	12.1	12.5
Profit Margin (Before Income Tax) 49	13.5	20.3	4.3	4.5	23.9	12.0	4.1	14.1	10.8	11.1	11.6
Profit Margin (After Income Tax) 50	9.7	18.2	3.3	4.3	22.1	11.3	3.4	11.9	9.2	7.9	8.1

Table I

Corporations with and without Net Income

PERIODICAL PUBLISHERS

MONEY AMOUNTS AND SIZE OF ASSETS IN THOUSANDS OF DOLLARS

Item Description for Accounting Period 7/07 Through 6/08		Total	Zero Assets	Under 500	500 to 1,000	1,000 to 5,000	5,000 to 10,000	10,000 to 25,000	25,000 to 50,000	50,000 to 100,000	100,000 to 250,000	250,000 to 500,000	500,000 to 2,500,000	2,500,000 and over
Number of Enterprises	1	7576	809	5254	723	531	100	65	31	21	11	15	15	0
Revenues ($ in Thousands)														
Net Sales	2	27383569	88344	1907654	582800	3178390	1029244	1785029	1546256	1416356	1308537	3040755	11500203	0
Interest	3	139498	799	1474	424	1610	6878	1127	60111	2922	7432	24018	32702	0
Rents	4	32757	0	0	157	0	0	1219	113	7368	665	3035	20200	0
Royalties	5	486368	0	0	0	0	1577	1963	246710	6	348	158795	76970	0
Other Portfolio Income	6	3097791	51202	0	0	3536	2266	9341	1277	19075	23758	864075	2123260	0
Other Receipts	7	673020	11607	2772	2135	2678	31402	7272	27466	65291	76017	164693	281689	0
Total Receipts	8	31813003	151952	1911900	585516	3186214	1071367	1805951	1881933	1511018	1416757	4255371	14035024	0
Average Total Receipts	9	4199	188	364	810	6000	10714	27784	60708	71953	128796	283691	935668	•
Operating Costs/Operating Income (%)														
Cost of Operations	10	37.7	28.0	22.4	29.9	50.9	42.7	51.8	40.8	35.9	35.9	30.1	36.3	•
Salaries and Wages	11	18.2	23.1	15.9	18.0	12.8	24.2	12.6	22.0	18.7	17.6	22.0	18.9	•
Taxes Paid	12	2.9	3.9	1.8	3.3	2.7	2.6	3.1	2.0	2.2	2.7	3.2	3.1	•
Interest Paid	13	9.2	5.1	0.1	3.0	0.8	0.2	1.2	1.0	2.5	2.3	8.8	18.3	•
Depreciation	14	1.7	0.4	0.4	1.0	0.8	1.4	2.4	2.5	1.7	2.0	2.9	1.8	•
Amortization and Depletion	15	3.7	0.9	0.0	2.1	0.8	0.4	0.9	0.5	2.2	1.9	5.5	6.3	•
Pensions and Other Deferred Comp.	16	1.0	13.8	0.5	1.3	0.4	1.8	0.4	0.6	0.6	1.1	1.0	1.2	•
Employee Benefits	17	1.9	1.3	1.0	2.7	1.2	1.7	2.5	2.4	1.8	1.3	2.5	1.9	•
Advertising	18	2.2	2.7	2.3	0.1	2.2	0.9	1.4	2.6	1.9	3.5	3.2	2.1	•
Other Expenses	19	24.8	50.6	41.4	39.8	22.0	19.6	20.7	36.3	28.8	27.7	33.2	18.4	•
Officers' Compensation	20	2.9	7.9	10.2	11.4	3.2	3.1	2.2	1.9	1.7	3.3	2.5	1.6	•
Operating Margin	21	•	•	4.1	•	2.0	1.4	0.8	•	2.1	0.8	•	•	•
Operating Margin Before Officers' Comp.	22	•	•	14.3	•	5.2	4.5	3.1	•	3.8	4.1	•	•	•

Selected Average Balance Sheet ($ in Thousands)

	1	2	3	4	5	6	7	8	9	10	11	12	13
Net Receivables 23	520	0	16	199	814	1087	3303	10875	10904	15779	29938	118036	•
Inventories 24	110	0	2	17	6	217	1298	1530	1975	5420	1798	20831	•
Net Property, Plant and Equipment 25	290	0	10	64	139	757	4628	9420	7222	16536	21265	47095	•
Total Assets 26	5382	74	672	2303	6248	16562	36255	66662	163898	336957		1839706	•
Notes and Loans Payable 27	3556	41	263	759	341	4850	8297	21943	41666	187440		1452984	•
All Other Liabilities 28	1411	32	456	1171	3083	7188	-26586	29390	52183	79705		482452	•
Net Worth 29	415	1	-47	373	2824	4525	54544	15329	70048	69812		-95731	•

Selected Financial Ratios (Times to 1)

	1	2	3	4	5	6	7	8	9	10	11	12	13
Current Ratio 30	1.3	•	1.6	0.9	1.4	1.6	1.5	2.2	1.1	1.4	1.5	1.2	•
Quick Ratio 31	0.9	•	1.2	0.8	1.1	1.5	0.9	1.9	0.7	1.1	1.2	0.5	•
Net Sales to Working Capital 32	9.8	•	16.9	•	16.9	5.9	11.3	2.1	17.6	6.5	6.5	16.1	•
Coverage Ratio 33	2.1	7.8	32.9	•	3.9	26.8	2.7	10.5	4.3	5.0	3.8	1.7	•
Total Asset Turnover 34	0.7	•	4.9	1.2	2.6	1.6	1.7	1.4	1.0	0.7	0.6	0.4	•
Inventory Turnover 35	12.4	•	34.0	14.3	485.6	20.3	11.0	13.3	12.3	7.9	33.9	13.4	•
Receivables Turnover 36	6.8	•	24.5	4.1	5.1	8.6	8.7	4.9	6.1	6.0	7.4	8.9	•
Total Liabilities to Net Worth 37	12.0	•	61.1	•	5.2	1.2	2.7	•	3.3	1.3	3.8	•	•
Current Assets to Working Capital 38	4.1	•	2.7	•	3.8	2.7	3.2	1.9	8.0	3.2	3.0	7.2	•
Current Liabilities to Working Capital 39	3.1	•	1.7	•	2.8	1.7	2.2	0.9	7.0	2.2	2.0	6.2	•
Working Capital to Net Sales 40	0.1	•	0.1	•	0.1	0.2	0.1	0.5	0.1	0.2	0.2	0.1	•
Inventory to Working Capital 41	0.2	•	0.1	•	0.0	0.1	0.6	0.1	0.5	0.3	0.1	0.5	•
Total Receipts to Cash Flow 42	4.7	1.2	2.3	4.6	5.0	4.4	4.9	2.4	2.9	3.0	3.7	9.6	•
Cost of Goods to Cash Flow 43	1.8	0.3	0.5	1.4	2.5	1.9	2.6	1.0	1.0	1.1	1.1	3.5	•
Cash Flow to Total Debt 44	0.2	•	2.2	0.2	0.6	0.7	0.5	•	0.5	0.4	0.2	0.0	•

Selected Financial Factors (in Percentages)

	1	2	3	4	5	6	7	8	9	10	11	12	13
Debt Ratio 45	92.3	•	98.4	106.9	83.8	54.8	72.7	•	77.0	57.3	79.3	105.2	•
Return on Total Assets 46	13.1	•	21.9	•	7.9	9.3	5.5	13.9	11.1	8.1	20.2	13.0	•
Return on Equity Before Income Taxes 47	89.6	•	1321.9	209.7	36.4	19.9	12.8	8.4	37.2	15.2	71.7	•	•
Return on Equity After Income Taxes 48	67.4	•	1318.7	210.4	36.1	18.5	12.5	5.9	33.8	12.7	61.4	•	•
Profit Margin (Before Income Tax) 49	10.3	34.2	4.3	•	2.3	5.5	2.1	9.2	8.5	9.0	24.7	12.9	•
Profit Margin (After Income Tax) 50	7.7	29.5	4.3	•	2.2	5.1	2.1	6.5	7.7	7.5	21.2	8.4	•

255

Table II

Corporations with Net Income

PERIODICAL PUBLISHERS

MONEY AMOUNTS AND SIZE OF ASSETS IN THOUSANDS OF DOLLARS

Item Description for Accounting Period 7/07 Through 6/08		Total	Zero Assets	Under 500	500 to 1,000	1,000 to 5,000	5,000 to 10,000	10,000 to 25,000	25,000 to 50,000	50,000 to 100,000	100,000 to 250,000	250,000 to 500,000	500,000 to 2,500,000	2,500,000 and over
Number of Enterprises	1	4757	19	4032	231	334	50	28	22	17	8	7	9	0
Revenues ($ in Thousands)														
Net Sales	2	21320369	69244	1704703	305808	2585705	932726	1239233	1271857	1258792	1132566	2018237	8801498	0
Interest	3	122924	799	1474	0	917	6322	622	58097	2824	7239	14932	29698	0
Rents	4	18250	0	0	0	0	0	40	72	7368	261	3035	7474	0
Royalties	5	365368	0	0	0	0	1577	0	246710	6	248	101081	15747	0
Other Portfolio Income	6	3031000	51202	0	0	7	2218	547	809	16053	3136	863905	2093121	0
Other Receipts	7	462007	11861	886	1951	118	31104	831	25159	53315	67345	127055	142383	0
Total Receipts	8	25319918	133106	1707063	307759	2586747	973947	1241273	1602704	1338358	1210795	3128245	11089921	0
Average Total Receipts	9	5323	7006	423	1332	7745	19479	44331	72850	78727	151349	446892	1232213	•
Operating Costs/Operating Income (%)														
Cost of Operations	10	36.2	21.2	21.4	24.5	53.8	37.2	55.5	41.8	35.7	34.7	29.4	32.7	•
Salaries and Wages	11	18.2	20.7	17.6	16.4	9.5	25.6	12.1	21.9	18.3	17.8	21.0	19.9	•
Taxes Paid	12	3.1	4.3	1.9	2.2	2.7	2.8	3.0	1.7	2.3	2.3	3.8	3.9	•
Interest Paid	13	8.8	1.1	0.0	0.7	0.5	0.1	1.0	0.6	1.7	0.4	5.4	19.2	•
Depreciation	14	1.6	0.3	0.4	0.9	0.8	0.6	1.9	2.5	1.7	1.9	1.7	2.0	•
Amortization and Depletion	15	3.2	0.0	0.0	3.5	0.6	0.4	0.7	0.5	1.6	0.7	3.6	6.1	•
Pensions and Other Deferred Comp.	16	1.1	17.1	0.3	1.5	0.5	2.0	0.5	0.7	0.7	1.2	1.4	1.4	•
Employee Benefits	17	1.8	1.7	0.6	0.8	1.3	1.8	2.7	2.7	1.8	1.1	2.8	1.8	•
Advertising	18	1.9	3.3	0.8	•	2.6	1.0	0.9	2.8	2.1	3.6	2.7	1.6	•
Other Expenses	19	22.5	60.6	32.3	36.9	19.4	20.5	12.6	35.3	28.3	27.1	34.0	16.3	•
Officers' Compensation	20	3.1	7.3	11.4	12.3	2.8	3.4	2.4	1.9	1.8	3.2	2.8	1.6	•
Operating Margin	21	•	•	13.4	0.3	5.5	4.4	6.7	•	4.1	5.9	•	•	•
Operating Margin Before Officers' Comp.	22	1.5	•	24.8	12.6	8.2	7.8	9.1	•	5.9	9.1	•	•	•

Selected Average Balance Sheet ($ in Thousands)

Net Receivables 23	629	0	20	155	1067	1612	4947	13790	11930	18832	40358	151330
Inventories 24	123	0	1	20	12	405	1958	1587	2259	7143	1752	15912
Net Property, Plant and Equipment 25	327	0	12	28	187	815	4812	9864	8598	17832	28918	61772
Total Assets 26	5426	0	82	740	2669	7103	18283	33825	65891	165548	360867	1981936
Notes and Loans Payable 27	3552	0	23	13	778	188	5606	6082	15451	20648	126354	1658728
All Other Liabilities 28	1380	0	1	193	1421	4485	7768	-44936	31529	59202	90095	549664
Net Worth 29	494	0	57	535	469	2430	4909	72679	18910	85699	144418	-226456

Selected Financial Ratios (Times to 1)

Current Ratio 30	1.5	•	4.9	1.0	1.5	1.1	1.4	2.3	1.2	1.4	1.7	1.4
Quick Ratio 31	0.9	•	4.1	1.0	1.2	0.9	1.0	2.1	0.8	1.0	1.4	0.6
Net Sales to Working Capital 32	7.1	•	8.0	324.6	13.2	56.9	16.0	2.0	12.6	7.8	4.9	7.3
Coverage Ratio 33	3.0	48.8	1079.4	2.4	11.7	90.9	8.0	23.8	7.0	31.7	9.5	2.0
Total Asset Turnover 34	0.8	•	5.2	1.8	2.9	2.6	2.4	1.7	1.1	0.9	0.8	0.5
Inventory Turnover 35	13.2	•	71.6	16.6	349.9	17.1	12.5	15.2	11.7	6.9	48.3	20.1
Receivables Turnover 36	7.4	•	24.6	3.5	11.5	9.6	9.6	5.0	5.8	6.6	8.2	8.9
Total Liabilities to Net Worth 37	10.0	•	0.4	0.4	4.7	1.9	2.7	•	2.5	0.9	1.5	•
Current Assets to Working Capital 38	2.9	•	1.3	48.7	2.9	14.2	3.7	1.8	5.6	3.6	2.4	3.5
Current Liabilities to Working Capital 39	1.9	•	0.3	47.7	1.9	13.2	2.7	0.8	4.6	2.6	1.4	2.5
Working Capital to Net Sales 40	0.1	•	0.1	0.0	0.1	0.0	0.1	0.5	0.1	0.1	0.2	0.1
Inventory to Working Capital 41	0.1	•	0.0	•	0.0	1.4	0.7	0.1	0.4	0.4	0.0	0.2
Total Receipts to Cash Flow 42	4.3	0.9	2.3	3.0	4.8	3.7	5.4	2.2	2.8	2.7	2.7	10.1
Cost of Goods to Cash Flow 43	1.5	0.2	0.5	0.7	2.6	1.4	3.0	0.9	1.0	0.9	0.8	3.3
Cash Flow to Total Debt 44	0.2	•	7.6	2.1	0.7	1.1	0.6	•	0.6	0.7	0.5	0.0

Selected Financial Factors (in Percentages)

Debt Ratio 45	90.9	•	29.5	27.8	82.4	65.8	73.1	•	71.3	48.2	60.0	111.4
Return on Total Assets 46	21.4	•	70.3	2.9	17.5	23.4	19.1	24.4	13.2	11.2	41.1	19.1
Return on Equity Before Income Taxes 47	155.9	•	99.6	2.4	91.0	67.7	62.1	10.9	39.4	21.0	91.8	•
Return on Equity After Income Taxes 48	126.1	•	99.5	2.2	90.5	64.5	61.5	8.3	36.0	18.2	81.2	•
Profit Margin (Before Income Tax) 49	17.2	54.6	13.5	1.0	5.5	8.8	6.9	13.7	10.1	12.7	46.0	19.4
Profit Margin (After Income Tax) 50	13.9	48.6	13.5	0.9	5.5	8.4	6.8	10.5	9.2	11.0	40.7	13.6

Table I

Corporations with and without Net Income

BOOK PUBLISHERS

MONEY AMOUNTS AND SIZE OF ASSETS IN THOUSANDS OF DOLLARS

Item Description for Accounting Period 7/07 Through 6/08	Total	Zero Assets	Under 500	500 to 1,000	1,000 to 5,000	5,000 to 10,000	10,000 to 25,000	25,000 to 50,000	50,000 to 100,000	100,000 to 250,000	250,000 to 500,000	500,000 to 2,500,000	2,500,000 and over
Number of Enterprises 1	6035	1421	3908	415	156	41	35	25	10	7	3	7	7

Revenues ($ in Thousands)

Item Description for Accounting Period 7/07 Through 6/08	Total	Zero Assets	Under 500	500 to 1,000	1,000 to 5,000	5,000 to 10,000	10,000 to 25,000	25,000 to 50,000	50,000 to 100,000	100,000 to 250,000	250,000 to 500,000	500,000 to 2,500,000	2,500,000 and over
Net Sales 2	35039334	1557232	239568	621683	622976	385015	514727	852488	522045	697456	1005846	2407594	25612706
Interest 3	1087203	4813	751	3809	647	96	2	6746	677	14195	2696	76044	976726
Rents 4	75702	0	0	0	255	0	0	1805	1013	0	0	0	72628
Royalties 5	855840	19355	0	0	0	0	0	4102	7953	901	0	49011	774518
Other Portfolio Income 6	3917692	5816	22	0	77	0	940	2359	2300	1722	0	66061	3838396
Other Receipts 7	918512	14355	10	11020	1892	1863	-10724	14592	2545	68711	46817	166750	600681
Total Receipts 8	41894283	1601571	240351	636512	625847	386974	504945	882092	536533	782985	1055359	2765460	31875655
Average Total Receipts 9	6942	1127	62	1534	4012	9438	14427	35284	53653	111855	351786	395066	4553665

Operating Costs/Operating Income (%)

Item Description for Accounting Period 7/07 Through 6/08	Total	Zero Assets	Under 500	500 to 1,000	1,000 to 5,000	5,000 to 10,000	10,000 to 25,000	25,000 to 50,000	50,000 to 100,000	100,000 to 250,000	250,000 to 500,000	500,000 to 2,500,000	2,500,000 and over
Cost of Operations 10	34.4	36.3	18.3	49.1	36.9	31.0	40.1	44.0	43.8	42.5	22.9	43.5	32.8
Salaries and Wages 11	20.3	18.5	29.8	11.4	8.6	26.1	12.9	18.8	17.2	20.4	20.3	19.5	21.1
Taxes Paid 12	2.7	2.0	3.5	1.4	1.3	2.8	2.2	2.9	1.7	1.9	2.0	2.6	2.9
Interest Paid 13	9.5	8.9	0.1	4.7	0.4	1.4	1.2	3.0	2.9	3.8	4.7	12.0	10.7
Depreciation 14	3.8	3.7	0.6	0.5	0.5	0.9	2.2	1.8	1.0	1.6	0.7	1.9	4.6
Amortization and Depletion 15	2.6	2.5	•	0.9	0.0	0.0	0.5	1.3	1.3	3.8	4.4	3.6	2.8
Pensions and Other Deferred Comp. 16	0.9	2.7	•	4.0	1.2	0.5	0.4	0.7	0.7	0.8	0.8	0.7	0.8
Employee Benefits 17	2.3	2.4	0.5	0.6	1.3	2.9	2.4	2.1	2.1	1.5	1.8	2.3	2.4
Advertising 18	1.8	1.9	4.3	0.4	1.0	2.2	4.0	2.9	4.8	3.8	0.9	4.8	1.3
Other Expenses 19	25.0	26.9	27.6	15.3	22.8	27.0	26.5	23.9	20.9	21.8	41.3	19.9	25.1
Officers' Compensation 20	1.6	0.2	13.5	11.5	6.4	3.2	1.6	3.3	2.3	3.8	1.8	2.0	1.0
Operating Margin 21	•	•	2.0	0.2	19.7	1.9	6.1	•	1.2	•	0.4	•	•
Operating Margin Before Officers' Comp. 22	•	•	15.5	11.7	26.1	5.1	7.7	•	3.5	•	•	•	•

Selected Average Balance Sheet ($ in Thousands)

Net Receivables 23	979	0	2	111	758	1919	2382	4856	11134	22926	103299	127356	568093
Inventories 24	577	0	19	277	632	1506	4227	10488	8517	20920	20745	59219	287167
Net Property, Plant and Equipment 25	565	0	8	146	57	630	2040	2635	4644	6298	18836	16600	412032
Total Assets 26	11254	0	54	705	2342	6928	12933	35404	64490	164812	302120	1004188	7955651
Notes and Loans Payable 27	4865	0	29	1064	338	1387	2944	8160	48672	54113	247520	500842	3324837
All Other Liabilities 28	3516	0	11	427	466	2114	4370	19874	20825	47306	123326	350576	2403728
Net Worth 29	2873	0	14	-785	1538	3426	5620	7370	-5006	63393	-68726	152770	2227085

Selected Financial Ratios (Times to 1)

Current Ratio 30	1.2	•	1.7	0.9	4.1	1.8	2.0	2.3	1.5	1.6	1.0	0.8	1.2
Quick Ratio 31	0.6	•	0.6	0.3	2.8	0.9	0.9	0.9	0.6	0.9	0.8	0.5	0.6
Net Sales to Working Capital 32	11.2	•	4.5	•	2.6	4.5	3.5	2.4	4.4	3.9	59.2	•	10.3
Coverage Ratio 33	2.6	0.7	29.2	1.6	55.3	2.7	4.5	0.5	2.5	2.7	1.8	1.2	2.8
Total Asset Turnover 34	0.5	•	1.1	2.1	1.7	1.4	1.1	1.0	0.8	0.6	1.1	0.3	0.5
Inventory Turnover 35	3.5	•	0.6	2.7	2.3	1.9	1.4	1.4	2.7	2.0	3.7	2.5	4.2
Receivables Turnover 36	5.8	•	10.7	9.7	5.8	2.2	7.3	5.6	5.8	3.3	4.2	2.5	6.5
Total Liabilities to Net Worth 37	2.9	•	2.9	•	0.5	1.0	1.3	3.8	•	1.6	•	5.6	2.6
Current Assets to Working Capital 38	6.4	•	2.5	•	1.3	2.2	2.0	1.7	2.9	2.6	30.4	•	6.2
Current Liabilities to Working Capital 39	5.4	•	1.5	•	0.3	1.2	1.0	0.7	1.9	1.6	29.4	•	5.2
Working Capital to Net Sales 40	0.1	•	0.2	•	0.4	0.2	0.3	0.4	0.2	0.3	0.0	•	0.1
Inventory to Working Capital 41	1.1	•	1.4	•	0.4	0.7	1.0	0.6	1.0	0.7	4.3	•	0.9
Total Receipts to Cash Flow 42	3.8	4.5	3.4	7.4	2.4	3.9	3.7	5.2	4.5	4.1	2.3	5.4	3.7
Cost of Goods to Cash Flow 43	1.3	1.6	0.6	3.6	0.9	1.2	1.5	2.3	2.0	1.7	0.5	2.3	1.2
Cash Flow to Total Debt 44	0.2	•	0.4	0.1	2.0	0.7	0.5	0.2	0.2	0.2	0.4	0.1	0.2

Selected Financial Factors (in Percentages)

Debt Ratio 45	74.5	•	74.1	211.3	34.3	50.5	56.5	79.2	107.8	61.5	122.7	84.8	72.0
Return on Total Assets 46	12.6	•	2.7	15.6	35.1	5.2	5.9	1.5	5.7	6.2	9.1	4.8	13.8
Return on Equity Before Income Taxes 47	30.0	•	10.0	•	52.4	6.6	10.6	•	•	10.0	•	4.8	31.6
Return on Equity After Income Taxes 48	19.0	•	9.8	•	52.0	3.9	9.8	•	•	7.8	•	3.1	19.9
Profit Margin (Before Income Tax) 49	14.9	•	2.3	2.6	20.2	2.4	4.0	4.2	4.2	6.4	3.5	2.1	19.3
Profit Margin (After Income Tax) 50	9.4	•	2.2	2.6	20.0	1.4	3.7	•	3.0	5.0	2.2	1.4	12.1

Table II

Corporations with Net Income

BOOK PUBLISHERS

MONEY AMOUNTS AND SIZE OF ASSETS IN THOUSANDS OF DOLLARS

Item Description for Accounting Period 7/07 Through 6/08	Total	Zero Assets	Under 500	500 to 1,000	1,000 to 5,000	5,000 to 10,000	10,000 to 25,000	25,000 to 50,000	50,000 to 100,000	100,000 to 250,000	250,000 to 500,000	500,000 to 2,500,000	2,500,000 and over
Number of Enterprises **1**	2677	503	1775	155	156	23	26	15	7	7	0	•	•
Revenues ($ in Thousands)													
Net Sales **2**	27512594	278074	120182	416444	622976	296124	451049	478537	371614	1326065	0	•	•
Interest **3**	568533	268	0	2393	647	7	2	2920	393	13572	0	•	•
Rents **4**	67954	0	0	0	255	0	0	1805	1013	0	0	•	•
Royalties **5**	411151	2241	0	0	0	0	0	3262	4033	0	0	•	•
Other Portfolio Income **6**	3885187	2201	0	0	77	0	940	1777	2300	1403	0	•	•
Other Receipts **7**	638111	1202	0	-1	1892	378	2854	12246	1769	110354	0	•	•
Total Receipts **8**	33083530	283986	120182	418836	625847	296509	454845	500547	381122	1451394	0	•	•
Average Total Receipts **9**	12358	565	68	2702	4012	12892	17494	33370	54446	207342	•	•	•
Operating Costs/Operating Income (%)													
Cost of Operations **10**	31.8	68.7	26.4	37.8	36.9	20.7	41.4	35.9	44.9	31.0	•	•	•
Salaries and Wages **11**	21.6	13.3	35.5	7.4	8.6	29.6	12.3	19.2	14.2	22.4	•	•	•
Taxes Paid **12**	2.9	0.8	0.4	1.4	1.3	3.2	2.4	2.7	1.9	2.2	•	•	•
Interest Paid **13**	7.5	11.1	0.1	0.5	0.4	1.0	0.8	1.0	2.3	2.2	•	•	•
Depreciation **14**	3.7	1.6	0.4	0.7	0.5	1.1	2.4	1.2	1.0	1.1	•	•	•
Amortization and Depletion **15**	2.6	5.6	•	0.0	0.0	0.0	0.4	1.5	1.2	1.1	•	•	•
Pensions and Other Deferred Comp. **16**	0.9	2.2	•	6.0	1.2	0.6	0.4	1.1	0.5	1.0	•	•	•
Employee Benefits **17**	2.5	2.3	•	0.3	1.3	3.1	2.0	2.0	1.6	1.8	•	•	•
Advertising **18**	1.5	0.0	5.7	•	1.0	1.8	3.9	3.3	6.0	2.6	•	•	•
Other Expenses **19**	21.8	•	17.2	11.7	22.8	26.0	24.9	21.5	19.9	33.3	•	•	•
Officers' Compensation **20**	1.6	1.1	•	16.1	6.4	3.6	1.8	3.6	2.2	2.6	•	•	•
Operating Margin **21**	1.7	4.9	14.2	18.2	19.7	9.3	7.2	7.0	4.2	•	•	•	•
Operating Margin Before Officers' Comp. **22**	3.3	6.0	14.2	34.2	26.1	12.8	9.0	10.6	6.4	1.2	•	•	•

Selected Average Balance Sheet ($ in Thousands)

Net Receivables 23	1753	0	5	1	758	3168	2239	4349	9759	59843
Inventories 24	987	0	37	4	627	1133	4664	10441	12880	17914
Net Property, Plant and Equipment 25	1011	0	0	389	57	1085	2699	2935	5422	12340
Total Assets 26	17168	0	53	652	2342	7143	13098	35043	64454	177646
Notes and Loans Payable 27	5804	0	6	146	338	972	3606	3168	20892	53307
All Other Liabilities 28	6455	0	4	168	466	2296	2361	15008	17324	83611
Net Worth 29	4910	0	43	339	1538	3875	7131	16867	26238	40728

Selected Financial Ratios (Times to 1)

Current Ratio 30	1.2	•	13.4	0.1	4.1	2.3	2.7	2.8	1.7	1.4
Quick Ratio 31	0.8	•	3.5	0.1	2.8	1.5	1.2	1.1	0.6	1.0
Net Sales to Working Capital 32	12.2	1.6	1.5	•	2.6	4.3	2.9	2.1	3.5	5.8
Coverage Ratio 33	4.0	1.6	116.2	37.5	55.3	10.1	10.2	12.9	4.0	4.6
Total Asset Turnover 34	0.6	•	1.3	4.1	1.7	1.8	1.3	0.9	0.8	1.1
Inventory Turnover 35	3.3	•	0.5	263.2	2.4	2.4	1.5	1.1	1.8	3.3
Receivables Turnover 36	5.6	•	5.4	16.7	5.8	1.9	9.2	5.3	•	3.4
Total Liabilities to Net Worth 37	2.5	•	0.2	0.9	0.5	0.8	0.8	1.1	1.5	3.4
Current Assets to Working Capital 38	5.9	•	1.1	•	1.3	1.8	1.6	1.5	2.5	3.2
Current Liabilities to Working Capital 39	4.9	•	0.1	•	0.3	0.8	0.6	0.5	1.5	2.2
Working Capital to Net Sales 40	0.1	•	0.7	0.4	0.4	0.2	0.3	0.5	0.3	0.2
Inventory to Working Capital 41	1.2	•	0.8	•	0.4	0.4	0.8	0.5	0.9	0.5
Total Receipts to Cash Flow 42	3.6	•	3.2	4.0	2.4	3.2	3.4	3.4	4.2	2.6
Cost of Goods to Cash Flow 43	1.2	•	0.8	1.5	0.9	0.7	1.4	1.2	1.9	0.8
Cash Flow to Total Debt 44	0.2	•	2.2	2.2	2.0	1.2	0.9	0.5	0.3	0.5

Selected Financial Factors (in Percentages)

Debt Ratio 45	71.4	•	18.6	48.1	34.3	45.8	45.6	51.9	59.3	77.1
Return on Total Assets 46	17.8	•	18.5	79.2	35.1	18.8	11.5	11.2	7.7	10.9
Return on Equity Before Income Taxes 47	46.7	•	22.5	148.5	52.4	31.3	19.0	21.5	14.3	37.0
Return on Equity After Income Taxes 48	32.2	•	22.3	147.7	52.0	27.0	18.2	18.3	11.0	29.0
Profit Margin (Before Income Tax) 49	22.3	7.0	14.2	18.7	20.2	9.4	7.8	11.4	7.0	8.0
Profit Margin (After Income Tax) 50	15.4	4.7	14.1	18.6	20.0	8.1	7.5	9.7	5.5	6.2

Table I

Corporations with and without Net Income

DATABASE, DIRECTORY, AND OTHER PUBLISHERS

MONEY AMOUNTS AND SIZE OF ASSETS IN THOUSANDS OF DOLLARS

Item Description for Accounting Period 7/07 Through 6/08	Total	Zero Assets	Under 500	500 to 1,000	1,000 to 5,000	5,000 to 10,000	10,000 to 25,000	25,000 to 50,000	50,000 to 100,000	100,000 to 250,000	250,000 to 500,000	500,000 to 2,500,000	2,500,000 and over
Number of Enterprises 1	4208	731	2712	446	174	73	28	11	6	11	3	8	4
Revenues ($ in Thousands)													
Net Sales 2	23494301	38920	880918	947200	1413670	742342	492489	514494	425368	1150181	244685	7285413	9358622
Interest 3	531321	209	115	1373	1664	1050	2974	2636	3122	5910	1525	101431	409312
Rents 4	64533	0	0	0	0	14	51	2121	0	0	0	1318	61028
Royalties 5	92490	3661	0	0	422	0	0	1	0	2495	419	42586	42905
Other Portfolio Income 6	99680	0	2121	0	376	0	48	2457	5266	6715	0	68352	14344
Other Receipts 7	729728	2555	53	15261	6147	660	-28612	4478	15777	46260	29154	280436	357561
Total Receipts 8	25012053	45345	883207	963834	1422279	744066	466950	526187	449533	1211561	275783	7779536	10243772
Average Total Receipts 9	5944	62	326	2161	8174	10193	16677	47835	74922	110142	91928	972442	2560943
Operating Costs/Operating Income (%)													
Cost of Operations 10	23.7	21.0	56.7	21.0	31.1	24.8	51.8	13.7	50.9	29.0	16.1	17.8	21.6
Salaries and Wages 11	19.7	41.9	18.1	28.9	18.7	35.9	20.9	22.0	16.1	18.1	20.0	20.0	17.5
Taxes Paid 12	3.4	5.0	1.7	3.9	2.2	3.5	4.0	3.4	1.8	2.5	2.2	2.3	4.6
Interest Paid 13	11.8	5.5	•	0.7	0.1	0.8	2.4	0.6	1.6	7.7	8.3	13.3	17.8
Depreciation 14	1.7	1.8	0.1	0.9	1.8	1.6	1.8	1.5	1.7	2.3	1.9	2.0	1.5
Amortization and Depletion 15	5.6	11.2	0.0	0.0	0.1	0.4	0.7	0.1	0.6	3.6	7.7	2.5	11.2
Pensions and Other Deferred Comp. 16	0.5	•	0.9	0.4	0.3	0.5	0.2	0.2	1.0	0.1	•	0.6	0.5
Employee Benefits 17	2.1	4.2	•	1.1	0.9	2.3	1.6	2.7	1.6	2.4	2.1	3.1	1.9
Advertising 18	2.7	1.1	0.8	0.3	1.3	7.6	0.5	4.8	3.1	1.8	1.2	3.0	2.9
Other Expenses 19	29.4	153.4	18.0	50.0	9.9	17.2	10.8	28.8	14.4	34.9	49.3	33.0	29.6
Officers' Compensation 20	3.3	15.5	3.9	8.6	29.0	6.5	2.4	5.6	1.5	1.7	2.6	0.6	0.8
Operating Margin 21	•	•	•	•	4.6	•	3.0	16.5	5.6	•	•	1.8	•
Operating Margin Before Officers' Comp. 22	•	•	3.7	•	5.5	33.6	5.4	22.1	7.2	•	•	2.4	•

Selected Average Balance Sheet ($ in Thousands)

Net Receivables 23	1299	0	11	211	1051	4183	4654	8915	10488	24387	30315	226676	596974
Inventories 24	283	0	15	39	16	367	852	174	737	4512	8929	13965	225061
Net Property, Plant and Equipment 25	478	0	3	35	406	551	1244	6527	8740	10123	4668	75724	247070
Total Assets 26	11333	0	82	675	2863	8519	16757	41695	71996	146209	321047	1258402	8011809
Notes and Loans Payable 27	7714	0	65	437	56	1400	4109	3909	13941	79722	122691	1610841	4401068
All Other Liabilities 28	3164	0	26	629	974	5124	7344	19087	24465	65502	93226	387007	1939872
Net Worth 29	455	0	-9	-391	1833	1995	5304	18698	33590	985	105131	-739446	1670868

Selected Financial Ratios (Times to 1)

Current Ratio 30	1.0	•	2.8	0.9	2.6	1.2	1.7	1.8	1.6	1.4	0.7	0.8	1.0
Quick Ratio 31	0.6	•	1.4	0.6	1.8	1.1	1.4	1.7	1.4	0.9	0.5	0.6	0.5
Net Sales to Working Capital 32	50.7	•	7.0	•	5.7	8.5	4.6	5.7	5.8	5.6	•	•	52.9
Coverage Ratio 33	1.3	•	•	•	44.5	0.0	0.1	34.0	7.9	1.2	1.2	1.7	1.0
Total Asset Turnover 34	0.5	•	4.0	3.1	2.8	1.2	1.0	1.1	1.0	0.7	0.3	0.7	0.3
Inventory Turnover 35	4.7	•	12.6	11.6	162.0	6.9	10.7	36.9	49.0	6.7	1.5	11.6	2.2
Receivables Turnover 36	4.3	•	44.8	8.3	6.6	2.1	3.9	4.7	8.5	3.6	5.4	5.5	3.4
Total Liabilities to Net Worth 37	23.9	•	•	•	0.6	3.3	2.2	1.2	1.1	147.4	2.1	•	3.8
Current Assets to Working Capital 38	23.1	•	1.6	•	1.6	5.3	2.4	2.2	2.6	3.2	•	•	30.0
Current Liabilities to Working Capital 39	22.1	•	0.6	•	0.6	4.3	1.4	1.2	1.6	2.2	•	•	29.0
Working Capital to Net Sales 40	0.0	•	0.1	•	0.2	0.2	0.2	0.2	0.2	0.2	•	•	0.0
Inventory to Working Capital 41	3.0	•	0.6	•	0.0	0.2	0.2	0.0	0.0	0.2	•	•	5.6
Total Receipts to Cash Flow 42	3.9	16.1	6.2	11.1	8.6	8.2	14.7	2.3	4.2	3.1	2.1	2.6	5.0
Cost of Goods to Cash Flow 43	0.9	3.4	3.5	2.3	2.7	2.0	7.6	0.3	2.1	0.9	0.3	0.5	1.1
Cash Flow to Total Debt 44	0.1	•	0.6	0.2	0.9	0.2	0.1	0.9	0.4	0.2	0.2	0.2	0.1

Selected Financial Factors (in Percentages)

Debt Ratio 45	96.0	•	111.6	157.9	36.0	76.6	68.3	55.2	53.3	99.3	67.3	158.8	79.1
Return on Total Assets 46	7.4	•	0.1	0.0	15.1	0.0	0.2	21.3	12.7	6.4	2.5	16.4	5.3
Return on Equity Before Income Taxes 47	39.0	•	•	77.8	23.1	•	•	46.2	23.8	128.7	1.1	•	0.6
Return on Equity After Income Taxes 48	14.6	•	•	77.9	20.8	•	•	41.2	20.7	65.1	1.0	•	•
Profit Margin (Before Income Tax) 49	3.2	•	0.0	•	5.2	•	•	18.5	11.3	1.2	1.4	9.4	0.4
Profit Margin (After Income Tax) 50	1.2	•	0.0	•	4.7	•	•	16.5	9.8	0.6	1.3	5.0	•

259

Table II

Corporations with Net Income

DATABASE, DIRECTORY, AND OTHER PUBLISHERS

MONEY AMOUNTS AND SIZE OF ASSETS IN THOUSANDS OF DOLLARS

Item Description for Accounting Period 7/07 Through 6/08	Total	Zero Assets	Under 500	500 to 1,000	1,000 to 5,000	5,000 to 10,000	10,000 to 25,000	25,000 to 50,000	50,000 to 100,000	100,000 to 250,000	250,000 to 500,000	500,000 to 2,500,000	2,500,000 and over
Number of Enterprises **1**	1887	0	1532	111	158	43	14	11	3	7	0	•	•
Revenues ($ in Thousands)													
Net Sales **2**	18653224	0	810711	221869	1413670	482142	258843	514494	172617	781885	0	•	•
Interest **3**	367557	0	115	1313	1664	484	2885	2636	1551	3987	0	•	•
Rents **4**	63682	0	0	0	0	0	51	2121	0	0	0	•	•
Royalties **5**	88401	0	0	0	422	0	0	1	0	2487	0	•	•
Other Portfolio Income **6**	90839	0	2121	0	376	0	48	2457	2976	1982	0	•	•
Other Receipts **7**	427087	0	0	0	5647	515	1682	4478	1520	69600	0	•	•
Total Receipts **8**	19690790	0	812947	223182	1421779	483141	263509	526187	178664	859941	0	•	•
Average Total Receipts **9**	10435	•	531	2011	8999	11236	18822	47835	59555	122849	•	•	•
Operating Costs/Operating Income (%)													
Cost of Operations **10**	24.5	•	59.9	26.9	31.1	12.3	28.5	13.7	7.7	22.2	•	•	•
Salaries and Wages **11**	20.1	•	14.4	9.2	18.7	46.5	27.2	22.0	29.4	17.0	•	•	•
Taxes Paid **12**	3.7	•	1.4	3.3	2.2	4.6	3.3	3.4	3.7	2.6	•	•	•
Interest Paid **13**	8.1	•	•	0.0	0.1	0.6	1.7	0.6	1.0	7.6	•	•	•
Depreciation **14**	1.5	•	0.0	0.1	1.8	0.3	2.9	1.5	1.5	2.2	•	•	•
Amortization and Depletion **15**	2.3	•	•	0.0	0.1	0.0	0.0	0.1	0.7	2.3	•	•	•
Pensions and Other Deferred Comp. **16**	0.5	•	1.0	•	0.3	0.8	0.3	0.2	1.8	0.1	•	•	•
Employee Benefits **17**	2.3	•	•	1.8	0.9	3.1	1.9	2.7	2.9	2.4	•	•	•
Advertising **18**	2.8	•	0.4	0.1	1.3	3.7	0.6	4.8	7.5	1.6	•	•	•
Other Expenses **19**	27.7	•	12.7	47.7	9.5	16.1	12.5	28.8	15.5	38.7	•	•	•
Officers' Compensation **20**	3.3	•	4.1	8.9	28.5	6.2	1.0	5.6	1.0	2.0	•	•	•
Operating Margin **21**	3.1	•	6.0	2.0	5.6	5.9	20.1	16.5	27.4	1.4	•	•	•
Operating Margin Before Officers' Comp. **22**	6.4	•	10.1	10.9	34.1	12.1	21.1	22.1	28.3	3.4	•	•	•

Selected Average Balance Sheet ($ in Thousands)

Net Receivables 23	2086	•	15	189	1157	6337	5534	8915	5808	29382
Inventories 24	435	•	43	155	9	474	959	174	0	5058
Net Property, Plant and Equipment 25	836	•	4	3	447	42	1949	6527	6440	11530
Total Assets 26	13379	•	123	710	2732	8225	16556	41695	59473	164945
Notes and Loans Payable 27	9784	•	0	0	62	1290	4213	3909	4546	91534
All Other Liabilities 28	3996	•	31	260	751	6247	4351	19087	17683	85654
Net Worth 29	-402	•	92	450	1919	688	7992	18698	37245	-12242

Selected Financial Ratios (Times to 1)

Current Ratio 30	1.2	•	3.9	1.5	2.9	1.3	2.9	1.8	3.9	1.5
Quick Ratio 31	0.7	•	1.9	1.4	2.3	1.2	2.7	1.7	3.3	1.0
Net Sales to Working Capital 32	11.4	•	6.0	16.1	6.0	6.6	3.1	5.7	2.3	5.0
Coverage Ratio 33	2.2	•	•	80.8	84.0	11.1	14.0	34.0	32.3	2.5
Total Asset Turnover 34	0.7	•	4.3	2.8	3.3	1.4	1.1	1.1	1.0	0.7
Inventory Turnover 35	5.6	•	7.3	3.5	318.4	2.9	5.5	36.9	•	4.9
Receivables Turnover 36	5.0	•	72.0	9.5	7.3	1.5	3.0	7.5	•	4.9
Total Liabilities to Net Worth 37	•	•	0.3	0.6	0.4	11.0	1.1	1.2	0.6	•
Current Assets to Working Capital 38	5.2	•	1.3	3.1	1.5	4.7	1.5	2.2	1.3	3.1
Current Liabilities to Working Capital 39	4.2	•	0.3	2.1	0.5	3.7	0.5	1.2	0.3	2.1
Working Capital to Net Sales 40	0.1	•	0.2	0.1	0.2	0.2	0.3	0.2	0.4	0.2
Inventory to Working Capital 41	0.8	•	0.5	•	0.0	•	0.0	0.0	•	0.4
Total Receipts to Cash Flow 42	3.3	•	5.7	2.0	8.2	5.5	3.1	2.3	2.2	2.1
Cost of Goods to Cash Flow 43	0.8	•	3.4	0.6	2.6	0.7	0.9	0.3	0.2	0.5
Cash Flow to Total Debt 44	0.2	•	3.0	3.7	1.3	0.3	0.7	0.9	1.2	0.3

Selected Financial Factors (in Percentages)

Debt Ratio 45	103.0	•	25.3	36.7	29.8	91.6	51.7	55.2	37.4	107.4
Return on Total Assets 46	12.9	•	26.8	7.3	20.3	9.2	26.3	21.3	30.8	12.9
Return on Equity Before Income Taxes 47	•	•	35.9	11.4	28.6	99.5	50.7	46.2	47.6	•
Return on Equity After Income Taxes 48	•	•	35.9	10.8	26.2	85.3	41.3	41.2	41.9	•
Profit Margin (Before Income Tax) 49	9.4	•	6.2	2.6	6.1	6.1	21.9	18.5	30.8	11.4
Profit Margin (After Income Tax) 50	6.9	•	6.2	2.4	5.6	5.2	17.9	16.5	27.1	10.5

Table I

Corporations with and without Net Income

SOFTWARE PUBLISHERS

MONEY AMOUNTS AND SIZE OF ASSETS IN THOUSANDS OF DOLLARS

Item Description for Accounting Period 7/07 Through 6/08	Total	Zero Assets	Under 500	500 to 1,000	1,000 to 5,000	5,000 to 10,000	10,000 to 25,000	25,000 to 50,000	50,000 to 100,000	100,000 to 250,000	250,000 to 500,000	500,000 to 2,500,000	2,500,000 and over
Number of Enterprises 1	10679	3532	5293	460	772	185	187	65	46	58	22	45	13
Revenues ($ in Thousands)													
Net Sales 2	112901368	1890479	2647079	711469	2378365	1565749	3128549	2266920	2452685	5059452	3520188	21919448	65360986
Interest 3	3282948	7231	1791	4794	20945	15216	45111	18972	52044	114232	93477	500433	2408703
Rents 4	227694	0	0	0	0	476	0	0	323	2637	6670	6713	210875
Royalties 5	8012000	16286	11264	0	39770	0	20100	646	61292	151834	5025	2145442	5560341
Other Portfolio Income 6	2803449	38230	25147	0	5070	1957	30730	22259	893	22297	72534	143412	2440920
Other Receipts 7	27447217	86341	27926	642	19080	35949	60752	-36777	55590	111047	41694	488610	26556360
Total Receipts 8	154674676	2038567	2713207	716905	2463230	1619347	3285242	2272020	2622827	5461499	3739588	25204058	102538185
Average Total Receipts 9	14484	577	513	1558	3191	8753	17568	34954	57018	94164	169981	560090	7887553
Operating Costs/Operating Income (%)													
Cost of Operations 10	29.1	42.7	2.1	4.6	27.1	27.6	16.8	35.8	20.4	17.6	12.7	34.7	30.8
Salaries and Wages 11	35.2	20.4	42.7	39.7	45.5	39.9	42.4	33.0	30.6	37.3	34.4	32.9	35.4
Taxes Paid 12	3.5	3.7	4.5	3.8	6.3	3.8	4.3	3.3	3.0	3.3	3.9	2.8	3.5
Interest Paid 13	5.2	2.1	1.0	1.1	3.4	1.7	1.0	1.1	2.5	2.1	2.6	3.4	7.2
Depreciation 14	2.8	1.0	1.2	1.3	2.9	2.8	2.4	2.2	2.0	2.1	2.1	2.2	3.2
Amortization and Depletion 15	1.6	1.4	0.4	0.7	1.4	1.0	0.8	0.8	1.9	2.2	2.6	1.7	1.5
Pensions and Other Deferred Comp. 16	0.4	0.5	0.3	5.3	0.4	0.2	0.5	0.5	2.0	0.4	1.2	0.7	0.2
Employee Benefits 17	3.3	1.3	2.9	2.7	3.9	3.0	3.3	2.6	2.6	3.2	3.9	3.2	3.4
Advertising 18	5.2	1.2	1.2	2.3	2.8	2.1	3.0	1.8	3.8	2.9	1.2	3.2	7.0
Other Expenses 19	31.9	36.4	43.0	45.1	37.6	30.2	39.6	23.3	38.3	31.4	26.0	26.1	32.9
Officers' Compensation 20	2.5	3.3	12.0	10.1	7.4	7.4	4.6	3.5	2.0	2.5	2.8	1.2	2.0
Operating Margin 21	•	•	•	•	•	•	•	•	•	•	6.6	•	•
Operating Margin Before Officers' Comp. 22	•	0.7	•	•	•	•	•	•	•	•	9.4	•	•

Selected Average Balance Sheet ($ in Thousands)

Net Receivables 23	2740	0	14	119	638	1685	4064	9564	16733	30912	44021	158347	1253156
Inventories 24	214	0	5	8	49	106	271	319	604	807	488	20432	86774
Net Property, Plant and Equipment 25	1259	0	11	38	220	672	914	2315	3853	6180	24609	45777	739252
Total Assets 26	26297	80	627	2127	7033	15750	33729	75232	156572	376360	1226165	15079255	
Notes and Loans Payable 27	4128	0	184	709	2144	2705	2395	4905	17151	24543	69430	246953	1923489
All Other Liabilities 28	14817	0	122	347	1591	3328	10221	24210	36309	48229	92703	402987	9804512
Net Worth 29	7351	0	-227	-429	-1608	1000	3135	4615	21772	83800	214227	576225	3351254

Selected Financial Ratios (Times to 1)

Current Ratio 30	0.5	•	0.3	0.9	0.7	1.8	1.4	1.2	1.2	1.8	2.1	1.5	0.3
Quick Ratio 31	0.4	•	0.2	0.9	0.6	1.5	1.2	1.0	0.9	1.5	1.9	1.2	0.2
Net Sales to Working Capital 32	•	•	•	•	•	4.4	5.4	13.8	8.5	2.3	1.9	3.3	•
Coverage Ratio 33	4.5	•	•	•	•	•	•	•	0.1	2.5	5.8	2.1	5.5
Total Asset Turnover 34	0.4	•	6.3	2.5	1.4	1.2	1.1	1.0	0.7	0.6	0.4	0.4	0.3
Inventory Turnover 35	14.4	•	2.2	9.1	17.1	22.1	10.4	39.2	18.0	19.0	41.6	8.3	17.9
Receivables Turnover 36	4.0	•	48.9	16.0	5.0	4.0	4.1	3.2	3.4	3.0	2.5	3.4	4.2
Total Liabilities to Net Worth 37	2.6	•	•	•	•	6.0	4.0	6.3	2.5	0.9	0.8	1.1	3.5
Current Assets to Working Capital 38	•	•	•	•	•	2.3	3.6	7.6	6.6	2.2	1.9	2.9	•
Current Liabilities to Working Capital 39	•	•	•	•	•	1.3	2.6	6.6	5.6	1.2	0.9	1.9	•
Working Capital to Net Sales 40	•	•	•	•	•	0.2	0.2	0.1	0.1	0.4	0.5	0.3	•
Inventory to Working Capital 41	•	•	•	•	•	0.0	0.1	0.1	0.1	0.0	0.0	0.1	•
Total Receipts to Cash Flow 42	2.3	3.8	3.3	3.7	9.5	4.7	8.9	3.0	3.3	3.0	3.9	1.8	
Cost of Goods to Cash Flow 43	0.7	1.6	0.1	0.2	2.6	0.8	3.2	0.6	0.6	0.4	1.4	0.6	
Cash Flow to Total Debt 44	0.2	0.5	0.4	•	0.1	0.3	0.1	0.3	0.4	0.3	0.2	0.2	

Selected Financial Factors (in Percentages)

Debt Ratio 45	72.0	•	384.4	168.4	175.6	85.8	80.1	86.3	71.1	46.5	43.1	53.0	77.8
Return on Total Assets 46	9.4	•	•	•	•	•	•	•	0.2	2.9	6.4	2.7	13.2
Return on Equity Before Income Taxes 47	26.0	•	19.4	57.3	67.4	•	•	•	3.2	9.4	3.0	48.8	
Return on Equity After Income Taxes 48	16.4	•	19.6	59.7	69.2	•	•	•	1.1	7.1	1.3	33.3	
Profit Margin (Before Income Tax) 49	18.1	•	•	•	•	•	•	•	3.1	12.6	3.5	32.5	
Profit Margin (After Income Tax) 50	11.4	•	•	•	•	•	•	•	1.1	9.5	1.5	22.2	

Table II

Corporations with Net Income

SOFTWARE PUBLISHERS

MONEY AMOUNTS AND SIZE OF ASSETS IN THOUSANDS OF DOLLARS

Item Description for Accounting Period 7/07 Through 6/08	Total	Zero Assets	Under 500	500 to 1,000	1,000 to 5,000	5,000 to 10,000	10,000 to 25,000	25,000 to 50,000	50,000 to 100,000	100,000 to 250,000	250,000 to 500,000	500,000 to 2,500,000	2,500,000 and over
Number of Enterprises **1**	4032	1444	1829	•	257	88	71	23	23	39	17	28	•
Revenues ($ in Thousands)													
Net Sales **2**	93034868	1382285	1099155	•	1086561	1001277	1594376	1027587	1384127	3718838	3160231	13654153	•
Interest **3**	2969510	3183	113	•	2533	4296	13776	5225	34916	80727	68939	431504	•
Rents **4**	224443	0	0	•	0	476	0	0	252	2508	6670	3663	•
Royalties **5**	7049659	2558	0	•	35487	0	0	614	19731	130106	1094	1326891	•
Other Portfolio Income **6**	2738620	36040	22599	•	3942	338	15233	21410	95	22244	64411	112638	•
Other Receipts **7**	27254643	-648	23854	•	6990	28071	33499	8706	36858	72842	8139	485449	•
Total Receipts **8**	133271743	1423418	1145721	•	1135513	1034458	1656884	1063542	1475979	4027265	3309484	16014298	•
Average Total Receipts **9**	33054	986	626	•	4418	11755	23336	46241	64173	103263	194676	571939	•
Operating Costs/Operating Income (%)													
Cost of Operations **10**	26.0	46.4	3.2	•	32.1	32.7	15.1	41.7	19.1	13.3	12.4	13.9	•
Salaries and Wages **11**	35.1	10.1	21.8	•	21.1	24.8	29.7	21.7	29.0	36.4	32.7	40.6	•
Taxes Paid **12**	3.5	3.9	2.7	•	4.5	2.4	2.2	2.5	3.0	3.3	3.8	3.5	•
Interest Paid **13**	5.7	0.8	1.5	•	0.8	0.4	0.6	0.4	1.4	1.9	2.7	3.2	•
Depreciation **14**	2.9	0.4	2.0	•	2.2	2.5	1.8	1.5	1.6	1.8	1.9	2.6	•
Amortization and Depletion **15**	1.5	0.1	0.0	•	1.1	0.1	0.4	0.2	1.7	1.6	2.4	1.8	•
Pensions and Other Deferred Comp. **16**	0.4	0.1	0.2	•	0.7	0.2	0.5	1.0	0.6	0.4	1.3	0.9	•
Employee Benefits **17**	3.4	0.7	2.0	•	3.0	2.1	2.2	2.2	2.6	3.3	3.8	4.2	•
Advertising **18**	5.4	0.4	0.9	•	0.8	2.3	2.0	1.3	3.9	2.1	1.2	2.3	•
Other Expenses **19**	31.6	27.7	49.7	•	19.6	17.8	34.5	18.3	29.1	30.0	23.0	27.5	•
Officers' Compensation **20**	2.2	0.5	10.1	•	6.1	4.2	3.1	4.0	2.1	2.2	2.8	1.3	•
Operating Margin **21**	•	8.9	5.8	•	8.0	10.5	7.9	5.2	6.0	3.7	12.0	•	•
Operating Margin Before Officers' Comp. **22**	•	9.4	15.9	•	14.1	14.7	11.0	9.2	8.1	5.9	14.8	•	•

Selected Average Balance Sheet ($ in Thousands)

Net Receivables 23	5981	0	24	773	2177	4638	9915	12306	27697	37921	182453
Inventories 24	331	0	3	113	92	359	129	535	397	502	4335
Net Property, Plant and Equipment 25	3027	0	11	283	904	990	3389	2708	6025	28978	57428
Total Assets 26	61589	0	68	2207	7086	16380	32790	73230	153420	387619	1383568
Notes and Loans Payable 27	8689	0	413	499	1076	1326	2193	7500	25567	80783	222811
All Other Liabilities 28	36074	0	303	700	3217	8293	24659	37940	46204	89539	452913
Net Worth 29	16825	0	-648	1008	2793	6761	5937	27790	81649	217297	707845

Selected Financial Ratios (Times to 1)

Current Ratio 30	0.4	•	0.1	2.3	1.9	1.4	1.4	1.5	1.8	1.9	1.7
Quick Ratio 31	0.3	•	0.1	1.8	1.6	1.2	1.2	1.2	1.4	1.7	1.4
Net Sales to Working Capital 32	•	•	•	5.0	5.1	7.1	9.0	4.8	3.0	3.0	2.2
Coverage Ratio 33	5.8	17.0	7.5	17.6	33.6	20.0	21.5	10.0	7.4	7.1	6.1
Total Asset Turnover 34	0.4	•	8.9	1.9	1.6	1.4	1.4	0.8	0.6	0.5	0.4
Inventory Turnover 35	18.1	•	5.7	12.1	40.4	9.4	144.3	21.4	31.9	45.9	15.7
Receivables Turnover 36	3.9	•	32.0	5.3	4.7	5.3	3.8	4.1	3.7	3.5	•
Total Liabilities to Net Worth 37	2.7	•	•	1.2	1.5	1.4	4.5	1.6	0.9	0.8	1.0
Current Assets to Working Capital 38	•	•	•	1.8	2.1	3.4	3.6	3.2	2.3	2.2	2.4
Current Liabilities to Working Capital 39	•	•	•	0.8	1.1	2.4	2.6	2.2	1.3	1.2	1.4
Working Capital to Net Sales 40	•	•	•	0.2	0.2	0.1	0.1	0.2	0.3	0.3	0.4
Inventory to Working Capital 41	•	•	•	0.1	0.0	0.2	0.0	0.0	0.0	0.0	0.0
Total Receipts to Cash Flow 42	2.0	2.7	1.8	3.5	3.4	2.3	4.5	2.6	2.6	2.9	2.6
Cost of Goods to Cash Flow 43	0.5	1.3	0.1	1.1	1.1	0.3	1.9	0.5	0.3	0.4	0.4
Cash Flow to Total Debt 44	0.3	•	0.5	1.0	0.8	1.0	0.4	0.5	0.5	0.4	0.3

Selected Financial Factors (in Percentages)

Debt Ratio 45	72.7	•	1054.7	54.3	60.6	58.7	81.9	62.1	46.8	43.9	48.8
Return on Total Assets 46	12.5	•	102.3	25.3	22.9	17.1	12.6	11.6	8.8	9.3	6.9
Return on Equity Before Income Taxes 47	37.8	•	•	52.3	56.3	39.4	66.1	27.5	14.2	14.2	11.3
Return on Equity After Income Taxes 48	26.8	•	•	43.9	44.2	35.3	61.8	24.5	11.0	11.2	9.1
Profit Margin (Before Income Tax) 49	27.6	12.0	10.0	12.5	13.8	11.8	8.8	12.7	12.2	16.6	16.3
Profit Margin (After Income Tax) 50	19.5	10.1	9.8	10.5	10.8	10.6	8.2	11.3	9.4	13.1	13.2

Table I

Corporations with and without Net Income

MOTION PICTURE AND VIDEO INDUSTRIES (EXCEPT VIDEO RENTAL)

MONEY AMOUNTS AND SIZE OF ASSETS IN THOUSANDS OF DOLLARS

Item Description for Accounting Period 7/07 Through 6/08	Total	Zero Assets	Under 500	500 to 1,000	1,000 to 5,000	5,000 to 10,000	10,000 to 25,000	25,000 to 50,000	50,000 to 100,000	100,000 to 250,000	250,000 to 500,000	500,000 to 2,500,000	2,500,000 and over
Number of Enterprises **1**	25710	4886	18907	660	859	167	138	34	23	11	7	10	9
Revenues ($ in Thousands)													
Net Sales **2**	65715212	525579	5104417	1615220	4426973	929014	2196043	848037	1096637	971832	932720	2728721	44340018
Interest **3**	11077348	2004	12155	1022	9341	4151	7393	1977	3106	16732	8256	198818	10812392
Rents **4**	188417	22291	0	454	0	0	0	0	264	2291	1406	158605	
Royalties **5**	855369	139148	14183	0	4	0	324	0	0	17982	0	37959	645769
Other Portfolio Income **6**	1766605	0	3165	259	20164	12435	6216	6417	27	11040	171503	68620	1466762
Other Receipts **7**	2911764	104968	-73088	-10384	29592	70291	24467	13659	19132	-758	55096	265115	2413674
Total Receipts **8**	82514715	793990	5060832	1606571	4486074	1015891	2234443	870090	1119166	1019919	1170681	3300639	59837220
Average Total Receipts **9**	3209	163	268	2434	5222	6083	16192	25591	48659	92647	167240	330064	6648580
Operating Costs/Operating Income (%)													
Cost of Operations **10**	29.1	47.8	21.4	45.2	28.6	44.6	44.9	28.5	26.1	50.1	24.1	24.3	28.2
Salaries and Wages **11**	10.3	0.9	5.6	16.0	13.7	14.9	14.6	12.1	10.7	5.3	7.7	13.3	10.0
Taxes Paid **12**	2.4	1.6	2.0	2.2	2.6	2.3	3.4	4.3	2.3	1.8	1.4	2.0	2.4
Interest Paid **13**	20.3	0.1	0.6	0.9	1.8	2.6	2.3	4.2	3.2	5.7	10.1	5.5	28.7
Depreciation **14**	6.6	2.1	3.6	2.3	1.9	5.1	4.0	5.0	3.0	1.6	6.3	5.3	8.0
Amortization and Depletion **15**	10.0	•	0.1	4.3	0.6	0.3	3.0	14.7	6.0	5.5	14.5	14.6	12.7
Pensions and Other Deferred Comp. **16**	0.5	1.7	1.7	0.9	0.4	0.4	0.2	0.3	0.4	0.1	0.0	1.3	0.3
Employee Benefits **17**	1.0	0.1	1.3	1.5	0.4	0.5	1.3	2.3	1.0	0.4	0.4	1.7	1.0
Advertising **18**	4.8	3.9	0.4	1.1	1.0	0.6	1.4	0.3	3.5	0.9	0.3	1.2	6.6
Other Expenses **19**	27.2	96.8	30.2	21.8	40.1	21.1	24.0	26.3	46.9	23.6	23.0	42.0	24.0
Officers' Compensation **20**	4.0	9.8	26.8	5.2	7.9	15.3	4.2	1.9	5.1	1.5	16.0	1.7	0.6
Operating Margin **21**	•	•	6.2	•	1.0	•	•	0.0	•	3.5	•	•	•
Operating Margin Before Officers' Comp. **22**	•	•	33.1	3.9	8.9	7.6	1.1	1.9	•	5.0	12.2	•	•

Selected Average Balance Sheet ($ in Thousands)

Net Receivables 23	442	0	6	79	208	672	3718	4086	8430	26360	36827	64326	985598
Inventories 24	194	0	2	40	95	186	958	173	1386	16136	11774	6755	479724
Net Property, Plant and Equipment 25	525	0	9	320	528	878	4424	7321	13649	23831	47532	127424	1051460
Total Assets 26	20888	0	55	733	1955	7098	16059	36533	70055	166378	299731	857353	57229139
Notes and Loans Payable 27	6325	0	91	726	1515	1847	7760	24569	20491	64188	167198	255690	16888045
All Other Liabilities 28	1813	0	20	155	570	2083	5235	5861	29052	52531	44566	202720	4532025
Net Worth 29	12750	0	-55	-148	-129	3168	3064	6103	20512	49659	87966	398942	35809069

Selected Financial Ratios (Times to 1)

Current Ratio 30	0.9	•	1.3	0.9	1.4	2.2	1.2	1.0	1.4	1.2	1.1	2.6	0.9
Quick Ratio 31	0.6	•	1.0	0.7	1.0	1.8	0.9	0.8	0.7	0.6	0.5	1.4	0.5
Net Sales to Working Capital 32	•	•	34.4	•	20.4	2.8	13.2	•	5.2	7.8	21.4	2.0	•
Coverage Ratio 33	1.5	•	9.4	•	2.3	1.1	0.4	1.6	•	2.5	3.1	2.4	1.4
Total Asset Turnover 34	0.1	•	4.9	3.3	2.6	0.8	1.0	0.7	0.7	0.5	0.4	0.3	0.1
Inventory Turnover 35	3.8	•	30.2	28.0	15.5	13.3	7.5	41.1	9.0	2.7	2.7	9.8	2.9
Receivables Turnover 36	5.4	•	51.7	22.2	18.5	9.6	4.5	4.6	7.1	3.6	3.5	4.4	4.6
Total Liabilities to Net Worth 37	0.6	•	•	•	•	1.2	4.2	5.0	2.4	2.4	2.4	1.1	0.6
Current Assets to Working Capital 38	•	•	4.2	•	3.6	1.8	6.3	•	3.4	6.4	17.8	1.6	•
Current Liabilities to Working Capital 39	•	•	3.2	•	2.6	0.8	5.3	•	2.4	5.4	16.8	0.6	•
Working Capital to Net Sales 40	•	•	0.0	•	0.0	0.4	0.1	•	0.2	0.1	0.0	0.5	•
Inventory to Working Capital 41	•	•	0.3	•	0.3	0.2	1.0	•	0.1	0.7	3.0	0.0	•
Total Receipts to Cash Flow 42	4.0	1.2	3.3	7.1	5.9	5.1	9.8	4.4	3.2	4.3	3.8	2.8	4.0
Cost of Goods to Cash Flow 43	1.2	0.6	0.7	3.2	1.7	2.3	4.4	1.3	0.8	2.1	0.9	0.7	1.1
Cash Flow to Total Debt 44	0.1	•	0.7	0.4	0.4	0.3	0.1	0.2	0.3	0.2	0.2	0.2	0.1

Selected Financial Factors (in Percentages)

Debt Ratio 45	39.0	•	199.9	120.2	106.6	55.4	80.9	83.3	70.7	70.2	70.7	53.5	37.4
Return on Total Assets 46	3.6	•	29.4	•	10.8	2.3	0.9	4.7	•	7.4	13.8	4.2	3.6
Return on Equity Before Income Taxes 47	1.9	•	•	30.6	•	0.6	•	10.8	•	14.8	31.7	5.1	1.7
Return on Equity After Income Taxes 48	1.3	•	•	37.5	•	0.6	•	8.0	•	10.0	31.2	3.6	1.1
Profit Margin (Before Income Tax) 49	9.5	•	5.4	•	2.3	0.4	•	2.7	•	8.3	20.9	7.5	12.6
Profit Margin (After Income Tax) 50	6.4	•	5.1	•	2.1	0.4	•	2.0	•	5.6	20.6	5.3	8.2

263

MOTION PICTURE AND VIDEO INDUSTRIES (EXCEPT VIDEO RENTAL)

Table II

Corporations with Net Income

MONEY AMOUNTS AND SIZE OF ASSETS IN THOUSANDS OF DOLLARS

Item Description for Accounting Period 7/07 Through 6/08	Total	Zero Assets	Under 500	500 to 1,000	1,000 to 5,000	5,000 to 10,000	10,000 to 25,000	25,000 to 50,000	50,000 to 100,000	100,000 to 250,000	250,000 to 500,000	500,000 to 2,500,000	2,500,000 and over
Number of Enterprises **1**	13396	2084	10466	245	429	66	65	•	6	7	4	7	•
Revenues ($ in Thousands)													
Net Sales **2**	56740954	380284	3373451	836258	2072917	610010	1440705	•	452530	812323	771035	1806936	•
Interest **3**	11015253	457	1994	955	6090	15	1136	•	713	16672	6849	183651	•
Rents **4**	163092	0	0	454	0	0	0	•	198	2104	3106	240	•
Royalties **5**	298267	0	836	0	4	0	253	•	0	17982	0	37959	•
Other Portfolio Income **6**	1745406	0	2958	0	19446	11752	307	•	27	10902	171503	55983	•
Other Receipts **7**	2886540	44428	14419	2930	28377	83237	28101	•	15272	-4497	49183	235422	•
Total Receipts **8**	72849512	425169	3393658	840597	2126834	705014	1470502	•	468740	855486	1001676	2320191	•
Average Total Receipts **9**	5438	204	324	3431	4958	10682	22623	•	78123	122212	250419	331456	•
Operating Costs/Operating Income (%)													
Cost of Operations **10**	28.7	59.8	23.2	22.7	27.2	44.5	48.3	•	6.0	57.6	28.2	24.2	•
Salaries and Wages **11**	10.0	0.6	4.8	24.8	15.1	9.0	14.0	•	2.3	4.4	7.0	9.9	•
Taxes Paid **12**	2.3	1.5	2.0	2.3	2.0	1.7	2.2	•	1.3	1.5	1.4	1.1	•
Interest Paid **13**	22.4	0.0	0.3	0.8	1.1	1.0	1.4	•	0.6	4.5	8.5	5.2	•
Depreciation **14**	5.8	0.8	1.9	2.5	1.1	1.1	2.6	•	0.9	0.7	1.6	4.2	•
Amortization and Depletion **15**	11.0	•	0.1	0.4	0.5	0.1	2.4	•	0.0	5.9	17.2	21.2	•
Pensions and Other Deferred Comp. **16**	0.5	2.3	0.8	1.7	0.8	0.4	0.2	•	0.1	0.1	0.0	1.9	•
Employee Benefits **17**	1.0	0.0	1.0	2.2	0.6	0.2	1.2	•	0.1	0.4	0.2	1.4	•
Advertising **18**	5.2	0.0	0.6	1.3	0.2	0.2	1.0	•	0.2	0.8	0.2	1.7	•
Other Expenses **19**	24.5	21.5	27.0	24.6	21.8	16.8	13.0	•	71.2	17.0	11.3	41.7	•
Officers' Compensation **20**	3.2	10.3	22.4	6.5	15.9	20.9	5.0	•	8.5	1.1	18.7	0.9	•
Operating Margin **21**	•	2.9	16.1	10.4	13.6	4.1	8.7	•	8.7	6.0	5.6	•	•
Operating Margin Before Officers' Comp. **22**	•	13.3	38.5	16.9	29.5	25.1	13.7	•	17.2	7.1	24.3	•	•

Selected Average Balance Sheet ($ in Thousands)

Net Receivables 23	745	0	52	4	271	564	4703	•	10076	26305	36207	76833
Inventories 24	335	0	44	0	52	6	209	•	212	5995	20376	6765
Net Property, Plant and Equipment 25	808	0	231	10	238	344	4463	•	19778	18923	14993	47154
Total Assets 26	39003	0	820	52	1716	7163	15988	•	61502	186133	289965	941146
Notes and Loans Payable 27	11363	0	299	43	538	1004	5412	•	11069	74476	147736	218749
All Other Liabilities 28	3204	0	124	22	490	1378	4487	•	22188	59053	33368	244636
Net Worth 29	24436	0	397	-13	687	4780	6089	•	28245	52603	108861	477761

Selected Financial Ratios (Times to 1)

Current Ratio 30	1.0	•	1.3	1.5	2.0	6.6	1.1	•	1.6	1.2	1.5	3.1
Quick Ratio 31	0.6	•	1.1	1.3	1.5	6.5	1.0	•	0.9	0.5	0.6	1.7
Net Sales to Working Capital 32	269.5	•	40.9	23.9	8.6	2.1	22.6	•	7.3	7.5	4.1	1.6
Coverage Ratio 33	1.6	367.4	52.7	15.4	15.2	19.2	8.6	•	21.6	3.5	5.1	3.7
Total Asset Turnover 34	0.1	•	6.1	4.2	2.8	1.3	1.4	•	1.2	0.6	0.7	0.3
Inventory Turnover 35	3.6	•	307.9	17.7	25.2	660.2	51.3	•	21.3	11.1	2.7	9.2
Receivables Turnover 36	5.3	•	56.3	•	16.4	13.2	4.3	•	9.2	5.1	7.7	4.9
Total Liabilities to Net Worth 37	0.6	•	•	1.1	1.5	0.5	1.6	•	1.2	2.5	1.7	1.0
Current Assets to Working Capital 38	188.3	•	4.4	2.8	2.0	1.2	7.9	•	2.6	6.3	2.8	1.5
Current Liabilities to Working Capital 39	187.3	•	3.4	1.8	1.0	0.2	6.9	•	1.6	5.3	1.8	0.5
Working Capital to Net Sales 40	0.0	•	0.0	0.0	0.1	0.5	0.0	•	0.1	0.1	0.2	0.6
Inventory to Working Capital 41	22.0	•	0.0	0.3	0.1	0.0	0.2	•	0.0	0.8	0.7	0.0
Total Receipts to Cash Flow 42	3.6	2.9	2.7	3.3	3.2	2.9	5.3	•	1.3	3.8	4.0	2.1
Cost of Goods to Cash Flow 43	1.0	1.7	0.6	0.8	0.9	1.3	2.6	•	0.1	2.2	1.1	0.5
Cash Flow to Total Debt 44	0.1	•	1.9	2.4	1.5	1.4	0.4	•	1.8	0.2	0.3	0.3

Selected Financial Factors (in Percentages)

Debt Ratio 45	37.3	•	124.4	51.6	59.9	33.3	61.9	•	54.1	71.7	62.5	49.2
Return on Total Assets 46	3.9	•	104.8	48.5	48.4	24.2	16.9	•	15.8	9.9	28.6	5.3
Return on Equity Before Income Taxes 47	2.4	•	•	93.6	112.8	34.4	39.3	•	32.9	25.0	61.1	7.7
Return on Equity After Income Taxes 48	1.8	•	•	86.7	109.6	34.4	39.2	•	30.4	17.8	60.5	5.8
Profit Margin (Before Income Tax) 49	14.0	14.7	16.7	10.9	16.0	17.8	10.8	•	12.3	11.3	34.5	14.2
Profit Margin (After Income Tax) 50	10.4	14.4	16.4	10.1	15.6	17.8	10.8	•	11.4	8.1	34.2	10.8

Table I

Corporations with and without Net Income

SOUND RECORDING INDUSTRIES

MONEY AMOUNTS AND SIZE OF ASSETS IN THOUSANDS OF DOLLARS

Item Description for Accounting Period 7/07 Through 6/08	Total	Zero Assets	Under 500	500 to 1,000	1,000 to 5,000	5,000 to 10,000	10,000 to 25,000	25,000 to 50,000	50,000 to 100,000	100,000 to 250,000	250,000 to 500,000	500,000 to 2,500,000	2,500,000 and over
Number of Enterprises 1	7409	2331	4651	112	200	88	12	9	0	4	0	3	0
Revenues ($ in Thousands)													
Net Sales 2	7304153	212880	907556	23648	197741	174362	31112	252848	0	47641	0	5456365	0
Interest 3	396691	2750	21	5420	1030	2903	368	3380	0	2570	0	378248	0
Rents 4	1175	0	0	631	0	0	0	543	0	0	0	0	0
Royalties 5	2671200	29	0	0	18039	0	0	84391	0	1404	0	2567337	0
Other Portfolio Income 6	23989	0	2649	0	0	0	0	37	0	7868	0	13436	0
Other Receipts 7	578179	-1	711	10	11910	5	29757	9309	0	4067	0	522412	0
Total Receipts 8	10975387	215658	910937	29709	228720	177270	61237	350508	0	63550	0	8937798	0
Average Total Receipts 9	1481	93	196	265	1144	2014	5103	38945	•	15888	•	2979266	•
Operating Costs/Operating Income (%)													
Cost of Operations 10	37.3	7.9	20.5	54.4	0.5	44.2	33.6	58.9	•	40.8	•	41.3	•
Salaries and Wages 11	16.4	2.8	9.2	18.6	14.5	7.6	69.1	14.4	•	16.2	•	18.3	•
Taxes Paid 12	2.0	0.9	2.6	4.3	1.9	1.6	13.7	2.0	•	2.6	•	1.9	•
Interest Paid 13	9.5	•	0.7	0.1	2.1	2.3	12.0	2.7	•	13.9	•	12.1	•
Depreciation 14	6.2	0.5	4.0	1.6	2.8	2.8	3.1	1.1	•	1.3	•	7.3	•
Amortization and Depletion 15	4.4	7.9	0.0	•	•	1.2	21.8	4.8	•	23.5	•	4.9	•
Pensions and Other Deferred Comp. 16	1.3	•	1.9	•	1.6	•	3.1	0.8	•	0.0	•	1.3	•
Employee Benefits 17	2.0	0.1	2.5	•	•	•	5.8	1.9	•	2.6	•	2.1	•
Advertising 18	3.0	0.2	0.8	2.4	0.1	0.2	9.7	4.5	•	13.4	•	3.5	•
Other Expenses 19	59.2	99.4	30.5	35.5	35.6	19.1	82.5	32.6	•	25.1	•	66.1	•
Officers' Compensation 20	4.8	0.7	30.2	22.0	4.4	2.3	49.4	5.6	•	6.3	•	0.4	•
Operating Margin 21	•	•	•	•	36.4	18.7	•	•	•	•	•	•	•
Operating Margin Before Officers' Comp. 22	•	•	27.2	•	40.8	21.0	•	•	•	•	•	•	•

Selected Average Balance Sheet ($ in Thousands)

Net Receivables 23	1403	0	2	91	264	106	2066	3759	•	1952	•	3414456
Inventories 24	71	0	0	108	20	223	524	3124	•	971	•	144717
Net Property, Plant and Equipment 25	103	0	29	64	142	1433	635	3778	•	2014	•	139369
Total Assets 26	7741	0	66	597	2243	6661	19508	40922	•	180684	•	18206513
Notes and Loans Payable 27	1499	0	147	90	560	4156	6035	13723	•	74624	•	3146783
All Other Liabilities 28	3908	0	10	284	111	603	20632	14384	•	40809	•	9419371
Net Worth 29	2334	0	-92	223	1572	1903	-7158	12815	•	65251	•	5640359

Selected Financial Ratios (Times to 1)

Current Ratio 30	0.5	•	1.1	10.0	17.4	8.3	0.6	1.3	•	2.8	•	0.4
Quick Ratio 31	0.4	•	0.9	5.4	14.7	2.0	0.3	0.6	•	2.4	•	0.4
Net Sales to Working Capital 32	•	•	73.5	1.0	0.8	0.5	•	5.2	•	0.5	•	•
Coverage Ratio 33	1.6	•	•	•	25.8	9.7	•	5.5	•	0.1	•	1.5
Total Asset Turnover 34	0.1	•	3.0	0.4	0.4	0.3	0.1	0.7	•	0.1	•	0.1
Inventory Turnover 35	5.2	•	581.7	1.1	0.2	3.9	1.7	5.3	•	5.0	•	5.2
Receivables Turnover 36	0.6	•	96.5	4.6	4.0	21.2	0.6	8.3	•	12.2	•	0.5
Total Liabilities to Net Worth 37	2.3	•	1.7	1.1	0.4	2.5	•	2.2	•	1.8	•	2.2
Current Assets to Working Capital 38	•	•	10.7	1.1	1.1	1.1	•	4.2	•	1.6	•	•
Current Liabilities to Working Capital 39	•	•	9.7	0.1	0.1	0.1	•	3.2	•	0.6	•	•
Working Capital to Net Sales 40	•	•	0.0	1.0	1.3	2.2	•	0.2	•	1.9	•	•
Inventory to Working Capital 41	•	•	•	0.5	0.0	0.1	•	0.8	•	0.0	•	•
Total Receipts to Cash Flow 42	1.7	1.3	5.0	17.6	1.2	2.6	2.6	2.6	•	130.5	•	1.5
Cost of Goods to Cash Flow 43	0.6	0.1	1.0	9.6	0.0	1.2	0.0	1.5	•	53.2	•	0.6
Cash Flow to Total Debt 44	0.1	•	0.2	0.0	1.3	0.2	0.2	0.4	•	0.0	•	0.1

Selected Financial Factors (in Percentages)

Debt Ratio 45	69.9	•	240.3	62.6	29.9	71.4	136.7	68.7	•	63.9	•	69.0
Return on Total Assets 46	1.9	•	•	•	23.9	6.7	•	10.3	•	0.1	•	1.8
Return on Equity Before Income Taxes 47	2.4	•	5.6	32.8	21.2	38.8	•	26.8	•	•	•	2.0
Return on Equity After Income Taxes 48	2.3	•	5.6	32.1	19.0	39.1	•	21.6	•	•	•	2.0
Profit Margin (Before Income Tax) 49	5.6	•	•	52.1	20.3	•	•	12.2	•	•	•	6.3
Profit Margin (After Income Tax) 50	5.4	•	•	51.0	18.3	•	•	9.8	•	•	•	6.3

Table II

Corporations with Net Income

SOUND RECORDING INDUSTRIES

MONEY AMOUNTS AND SIZE OF ASSETS IN THOUSANDS OF DOLLARS

Item Description for Accounting Period 7/07 Through 6/08	Total	Zero Assets	Under 500	500 to 1,000	1,000 to 5,000	5,000 to 10,000	10,000 to 25,000	25,000 to 50,000	50,000 to 100,000	100,000 to 250,000	250,000 to 500,000	500,000 to 2,500,000	2,500,000 and over
Number of Enterprises **1**	3720	820	2579	58	200	51	0	•	•	•	0	0	0
Revenues ($ in Thousands)													
Net Sales **2**	6304377	29793	719560	0	197741	185995	0	•	•	•	0	0	0
Interest **3**	365537	2750	10	5250	1030	3205	0	•	•	•	0	0	0
Rents **4**	543	0	0	0	0	0	0	•	•	•	0	0	0
Royalties **5**	2140004	0	0	0	18039	0	0	•	•	•	0	0	0
Other Portfolio Income **6**	15052	0	1984	0	0	0	0	•	•	•	0	0	0
Other Receipts **7**	478780	0	573	0	11910	4599	0	•	•	•	0	0	0
Total Receipts **8**	9304293	32543	722127	5250	228720	193799	0	•	•	•	0	0	0
Average Total Receipts **9**	2501	40	280	91	1144	3800	•	•	•	•	•	•	•
Operating Costs/Operating Income (%)													
Cost of Operations **10**	39.1	36.0	25.2	•	0.5	46.1	•	•	•	•	•	•	•
Salaries and Wages **11**	15.1	•	3.8	•	14.5	8.1	•	•	•	•	•	•	•
Taxes Paid **12**	1.9	2.4	1.8	•	1.9	1.6	•	•	•	•	•	•	•
Interest Paid **13**	10.0	•	0.1	•	2.1	2.3	•	•	•	•	•	•	•
Depreciation **14**	5.7	•	1.2	•	2.8	1.9	•	•	•	•	•	•	•
Amortization and Depletion **15**	4.0	•	•	•	•	1.1	•	•	•	•	•	•	•
Pensions and Other Deferred Comp. **16**	1.4	•	2.4	•	1.6	•	•	•	•	•	•	•	•
Employee Benefits **17**	1.8	•	2.7	•	•	0.1	•	•	•	•	•	•	•
Advertising **18**	3.1	0.1	0.7	•	0.1	1.1	•	•	•	•	•	•	•
Other Expenses **19**	51.5	51.6	24.9	•	35.6	19.6	•	•	•	•	•	•	•
Officers' Compensation **20**	3.7	•	27.5	•	4.4	2.6	•	•	•	•	•	•	•
Operating Margin **21**	•	9.8	9.8	•	36.4	15.4	•	•	•	•	•	•	•
Operating Margin Before Officers' Comp. **22**	•	9.8	37.3	•	40.8	18.0	•	•	•	•	•	•	•

Selected Average Balance Sheet ($ in Thousands)

Net Receivables 23	2729	0	4	0	264	199
Inventories 24	128	0	0	0	20	396
Net Property, Plant and Equipment 25	129	0	5	0	142	1567
Total Assets 26	14579	0	45	514	2243	6414
Notes and Loans Payable 27	2459	0	33	0	560	1626
All Other Liabilities 28	7547	0	17	517	111	1248
Net Worth 29	4573	0	-5	-3	1572	3540

Selected Financial Ratios (Times to 1)

Current Ratio 30	0.5	•	1.2	0.8	17.4	3.7
Quick Ratio 31	0.4	•	1.2	0.8	14.7	1.7
Net Sales to Working Capital 32	•	•	39.8	•	0.8	1.1
Coverage Ratio 33	2.2	•	123.9	•	25.8	9.6
Total Asset Turnover 34	0.1	•	6.2	•	0.4	0.6
Inventory Turnover 35	5.2	•	567.1	•	0.2	4.2
Receivables Turnover 36	0.6	•	117.8	•	4.1	21.6
Total Liabilities to Net Worth 37	2.2	•	•	•	0.4	0.8
Current Assets to Working Capital 38	•	•	5.6	•	1.1	1.4
Current Liabilities to Working Capital 39	•	•	4.6	•	0.1	0.4
Working Capital to Net Sales 40	•	•	0.0	•	1.3	0.9
Inventory to Working Capital 41	•	•	•	•	0.0	0.2
Total Receipts to Cash Flow 42	1.7	2.0	3.6	•	1.2	2.6
Cost of Goods to Cash Flow 43	0.7	0.7	0.9	•	0.0	1.2
Cash Flow to Total Debt 44	0.1	•	1.6	0.1	1.3	0.5

Selected Financial Factors (in Percentages)

Debt Ratio 45	68.6	•	112.0	100.6	29.9	44.8
Return on Total Assets 46	2.5	•	64.0	2.9	23.9	12.5
Return on Equity Before Income Taxes 47	4.3	•	•	•	32.8	20.2
Return on Equity After Income Taxes 48	4.2	•	•	•	32.1	18.1
Profit Margin (Before Income Tax) 49	11.7	19.1	10.2	•	52.1	19.6
Profit Margin (After Income Tax) 50	11.4	17.0	10.2	•	51.0	17.5

Table I

Corporations with and without Net Income

BROADCASTING (EXCEPT INTERNET)

MONEY AMOUNTS AND SIZE OF ASSETS IN THOUSANDS OF DOLLARS

Item Description for Accounting Period 7/07 Through 6/08	Total	Zero Assets	Under 500	500 to 1,000	1,000 to 5,000	5,000 to 10,000	10,000 to 25,000	25,000 to 50,000	50,000 to 100,000	100,000 to 250,000	250,000 to 500,000	500,000 to 2,500,000	2,500,000 and over
Number of Enterprises 1	8297	2045	4353	458	991	146	133	43	35	32	19	28	13
Revenues ($ in Thousands)													
Net Sales 2	109563864	411967	942839	380264	1767289	734921	1491877	593276	1238048	1617080	3866024	8797743	87722535
Interest 3	2803628	1830	10	1541	6014	3978	10939	5205	9621	25807	232844	150771	2355068
Rents 4	391283	0	0	4	4075	406	0	1941	713	11031	7379	13081	352654
Royalties 5	4142837	0	0	0	56946	0	6	1	730	3335	37155	58387	3986276
Other Portfolio Income 6	3238324	97326	166	306	22902	1615	1396	43306	77612	50610	79904	303754	2559428
Other Receipts 7	3924707	-243248	7830	2574	103158	10426	19568	27818	73202	89732	216008	73400	3544238
Total Receipts 8	124064643	267875	950845	384689	1960384	751346	1523786	671547	1399926	1797595	4439314	9397136	100520199
Average Total Receipts 9	14953	131	218	840	1978	5146	11457	15617	39998	56175	233648	335612	7732323
Operating Costs/Operating Income (%)													
Cost of Operations 10	14.9	1.3	13.5	19.6	18.6	24.5	31.6	5.3	14.4	17.5	54.4	13.2	12.9
Salaries and Wages 11	14.1	30.5	13.7	26.1	26.9	28.2	21.9	23.3	21.0	21.1	10.0	23.1	12.4
Taxes Paid 12	2.6	5.0	14.5	5.5	5.3	1.9	3.7	4.2	3.1	2.7	2.0	3.5	2.3
Interest Paid 13	7.5	39.5	0.3	2.8	5.1	2.4	6.0	4.8	8.0	9.7	8.1	15.7	6.6
Depreciation 14	4.8	2.5	1.6	2.0	6.1	5.8	3.5	5.6	3.5	7.4	4.4	5.3	4.8
Amortization and Depletion 15	9.1	6.6	0.4	1.6	3.2	1.6	7.4	7.3	6.4	7.9	5.8	13.3	9.3
Pensions and Other Deferred Comp. 16	0.4	0.0	1.1	0.0	0.1	0.1	0.5	0.8	0.4	0.7	0.3	0.6	0.4
Employee Benefits 17	2.8	2.2	1.1	5.0	3.3	2.2	1.0	1.7	1.5	1.4	1.2	1.4	3.0
Advertising 18	3.2	3.2	0.6	1.3	1.4	0.6	3.3	2.8	3.3	3.3	0.8	2.2	3.5
Other Expenses 19	44.4	53.6	33.5	31.8	41.8	32.7	30.7	53.0	32.3	35.7	54.4	39.9	45.3
Officers' Compensation 20	1.6	7.7	13.7	1.7	6.2	5.3	1.8	9.3	10.3	2.5	1.1	1.1	1.2
Operating Margin 21	•	•	6.1	2.6	•	•	•	•	•	•	•	•	•
Operating Margin Before Officers' Comp. 22	•	•	19.8	4.4	•	•	•	•	6.1	•	•	•	•

Selected Average Balance Sheet ($ in Thousands)

Net Receivables **23**	4078	0	10	82	296	581	2252	1879	8554	15593	59944	82331	2212013
Inventories **24**	153	0	0	6	29	13	54	99	449	1810	1052	1293	84299
Net Property, Plant and Equipment **25**	4332	0	20	114	596	1024	2305	4535	10342	20716	62362	117907	2234695
Total Assets **26**	33687	0	69	635	2142	6735	14845	38558	70448	148186	359312	1208952	17252860
Notes and Loans Payable **27**	11084	0	69	591	2249	4960	12702	11080	32935	61799	226181	627584	4713722
All Other Liabilities **28**	11317	0	28	611	687	1225	5035	2283	13688	43612	489167	302728	5555878
Net Worth **29**	11285	0	-27	-567	-795	550	-2892	25194	23825	42776	-356037	278640	6983259

Selected Financial Ratios (Times to 1)

Current Ratio **30**	1.1	•	1.9	0.3	0.5	3.0	1.4	2.0	1.5	1.0	1.0	1.7	1.0
Quick Ratio **31**	0.8	•	1.8	0.1	0.5	2.6	1.2	1.1	1.2	0.8	0.8	1.2	0.8
Net Sales to Working Capital **32**	24.0	•	12.3	•	•	2.0	6.7	3.1	5.3	30.5	84.0	3.8	45.4
Coverage Ratio **33**	2.1	•	24.6	2.3	•	•	•	•	2.1	1.1	•	0.2	3.0
Total Asset Turnover **34**	0.4	•	3.1	1.3	0.8	0.7	0.8	0.4	0.5	0.3	0.6	0.3	0.4
Inventory Turnover **35**	12.8	•	•	27.8	11.2	94.8	65.5	7.3	11.4	4.9	105.3	32.2	10.3
Receivables Turnover **36**	4.0	•	30.2	5.1	6.0	8.5	6.5	5.9	4.9	3.2	3.8	4.2	3.8
Total Liabilities to Net Worth **37**	2.0	•	•	•	•	11.2	•	0.5	2.0	2.5	•	3.3	1.5
Current Assets to Working Capital **38**	12.5	•	2.1	•	•	1.5	3.7	2.0	2.8	22.8	38.2	2.5	23.1
Current Liabilities to Working Capital **39**	11.5	•	1.1	•	•	0.5	2.7	1.0	1.8	21.8	37.2	1.5	22.1
Working Capital to Net Sales **40**	0.0	•	0.1	•	•	0.5	0.2	0.3	0.2	0.0	0.0	0.3	0.0
Inventory to Working Capital **41**	0.2	•	•	•	•	0.0	0.0	0.0	0.1	2.2	0.4	0.0	0.4
Total Receipts to Cash Flow **42**	2.1	•	2.7	4.6	3.3	4.3	7.1	2.9	3.1	3.2	4.9	4.3	1.9
Cost of Goods to Cash Flow **43**	0.3	•	0.4	0.9	0.6	1.1	2.3	0.2	0.4	0.6	2.7	0.6	0.2
Cash Flow to Total Debt **44**	0.3	•	0.8	0.1	0.2	0.2	0.1	0.4	0.2	0.2	0.1	0.1	0.3

Selected Financial Factors (in Percentages)

Debt Ratio **45**	66.5	•	139.5	189.3	137.1	91.8	119.5	34.7	66.2	71.1	199.1	77.0	59.5
Return on Total Assets **46**	6.1	•	22.5	8.6	•	•	•	•	8.4	3.5	•	0.8	7.7
Return on Equity Before Income Taxes **47**	9.4	•	•	•	15.4	•	35.7	•	13.0	0.8	15.8	•	12.6
Return on Equity After Income Taxes **48**	5.0	•	•	•	16.9	•	40.2	•	8.7	•	16.4	•	8.3
Profit Margin (Before Income Tax) **49**	8.0	•	6.9	3.8	•	•	•	•	8.7	0.6	•	•	13.0
Profit Margin (After Income Tax) **50**	4.3	•	6.9	3.7	•	•	•	•	5.9	•	•	•	8.6

Table II

Corporations with Net Income

BROADCASTING (EXCEPT INTERNET)

MONEY AMOUNTS AND SIZE OF ASSETS IN THOUSANDS OF DOLLARS

Item Description for Accounting Period 7/07 Through 6/08	Total	Zero Assets	Under 500	500 to 1,000	1,000 to 5,000	5,000 to 10,000	10,000 to 25,000	25,000 to 50,000	50,000 to 100,000	100,000 to 250,000	250,000 to 500,000	500,000 to 2,500,000	2,500,000 and over
Number of Enterprises **1**	4255	1507	1841	246	473	53	64	18	16	14	6	7	10
Revenues ($ in Thousands)													
Net Sales **2**	93698026	321729	616373	238283	1197795	446363	950519	309133	842424	1042848	1018155	1849047	84865357
Interest **3**	2389567	1830	5	1540	1357	3388	5860	1988	3425	13547	13891	5219	2337517
Rents **4**	372243	0	0	4	1017	243	0	1860	256	9939	5935	2036	350953
Royalties **5**	4043412	0	0	0	56946	0	0	1	0	24	162	2	3986276
Other Portfolio Income **6**	2982522	84172	166	0	21479	994	356	40772	71156	41060	48104	163092	2511171
Other Receipts **7**	3949906	38915	3828	2495	74298	9774	15446	2345	65510	70559	216611	99468	3350659
Total Receipts **8**	107435676	620372	446646	242322	1352892	460762	972181	356099	982771	1177977	1302858	2118864	97401933
Average Total Receipts **9**	25249	296	337	985	2860	8694	15190	19783	61423	84141	217143	302695	9740193
Operating Costs/Operating Income (%)													
Cost of Operations **10**	13.3	1.6	•	0.1	19.9	24.6	22.5	9.4	19.0	24.6	15.1	16.8	13.0
Salaries and Wages **11**	13.1	25.9	12.3	32.7	25.1	28.8	21.2	21.7	14.2	17.4	18.9	25.1	12.2
Taxes Paid **12**	2.4	2.3	20.9	4.4	4.9	1.6	4.0	4.1	2.4	2.5	3.6	4.4	2.2
Interest Paid **13**	5.8	12.6	0.2	2.3	1.7	0.8	6.3	4.8	1.2	4.1	5.8	8.4	5.9
Depreciation **14**	4.5	2.3	0.6	1.6	3.9	2.3	2.7	6.1	1.6	7.0	9.4	3.5	4.5
Amortization and Depletion **15**	8.9	8.1	•	2.4	0.7	0.2	1.1	4.2	2.6	5.4	9.7	9.9	9.4
Pensions and Other Deferred Comp. **16**	0.4	0.1	1.6	0.1	0.2	0.2	0.2	0.5	0.4	1.0	0.6	1.4	0.4
Employee Benefits **17**	3.0	1.3	1.6	5.8	4.4	1.2	1.0	1.6	1.1	1.0	2.6	1.7	3.1
Advertising **18**	3.4	4.1	0.7	2.1	0.9	0.4	2.8	2.6	3.6	3.2	1.7	2.2	3.6
Other Expenses **19**	44.0	46.5	29.0	37.8	36.2	26.5	24.2	36.5	26.7	29.0	44.3	22.3	45.4
Officers' Compensation **20**	1.6	9.8	13.6	0.8	6.3	4.9	1.7	2.8	13.8	2.8	1.7	1.4	1.3
Operating Margin **21**	•	•	19.6	10.0	•	8.5	12.3	5.6	13.5	2.1	2.8	2.8	•
Operating Margin Before Officers' Comp. **22**	1.1	•	•	2.1	10.8	13.4	14.0	8.5	27.3	4.9	4.2	•	0.4

Selected Average Balance Sheet ($ in Thousands)

Net Receivables 23	7107	0	12	64	483	1078	2441	2615	11975	17910	83994	53158	2839652
Inventories 24	267	0	0	4	30	23	49	29	676	72	3166	38	80859
Net Property, Plant and Equipment 25	6882	0	7	89	428	1164	2477	6430	6233	27348	98886	64225	2718391
Total Assets 26	51999	0	68	707	1799	7026	13918	35526	73512	162358	406430	1100336	20461248
Notes and Loans Payable 27	14497	0	4	476	1586	3781	9111	11612	9333	35142	239250	289461	5571552
All Other Liabilities 28	14997	0	8	184	1075	1765	3976	4080	19351	46467	85592	166316	6018491
Net Worth 29	22504	0	56	46	-863	1480	831	19834	44828	80748	81587	644559	8871205

Selected Financial Ratios (Times to 1)

Current Ratio 30	1.1	•	6.4	0.4	0.5	3.4	2.9	1.3	1.5	1.4	0.8	1.5	1.1
Quick Ratio 31	0.9	•	6.1	0.3	0.4	2.4	2.8	1.0	1.2	1.0	0.6	1.4	0.8
Net Sales to Working Capital 32	21.9	•	7.6	•	•	2.5	3.0	7.2	5.7	5.8	•	4.0	23.2
Coverage Ratio 33	3.5	2.9	133.8	6.0	5.9	15.5	3.3	5.3	26.9	4.6	3.5	3.0	3.4
Total Asset Turnover 34	0.4	•	4.9	1.4	1.4	1.2	1.1	0.5	0.7	0.5	0.4	0.2	0.4
Inventory Turnover 35	11.0	•	•	0.3	16.6	90.1	68.3	55.8	14.8	254.4	8.1	1164.4	13.6
Receivables Turnover 36	3.8	•	43.7	•	5.4	13.3	6.9	5.4	5.1	3.7	2.2	3.7	•
Total Liabilities to Net Worth 37	1.3	•	0.2	14.2	3.7	3.7	15.7	0.8	0.6	1.0	4.0	0.7	1.3
Current Assets to Working Capital 38	11.0	•	1.2	•	1.4	1.4	1.5	3.9	2.9	3.6	•	3.2	11.5
Current Liabilities to Working Capital 39	10.0	•	0.2	•	0.4	0.4	0.5	2.9	1.9	2.6	•	2.2	10.5
Working Capital to Net Sales 40	0.0	•	0.1	•	0.4	0.4	0.3	0.1	0.2	0.2	•	0.2	0.0
Inventory to Working Capital 41	0.2	•	•	•	0.0	0.0	0.0	0.0	0.0	0.0	•	0.0	0.2
Total Receipts to Cash Flow 42	1.9	2.5	2.2	3.4	2.4	2.9	2.7	2.6	2.1	2.6	2.0	2.9	1.9
Cost of Goods to Cash Flow 43	0.3	0.0	•	0.0	0.5	0.7	0.6	0.2	0.4	0.6	0.3	0.5	0.2
Cash Flow to Total Debt 44	0.4	•	12.6	0.4	0.4	0.5	0.4	0.4	0.9	0.3	0.3	0.2	0.4

Selected Financial Factors (in Percentages)

Debt Ratio 45	56.7	•	18.1	93.4	148.0	78.9	94.0	44.2	39.0	50.3	79.9	41.4	56.6
Return on Total Assets 46	8.5	•	100.2	19.2	14.6	15.1	22.3	12.4	22.4	8.7	8.4	6.1	8.3
Return on Equity Before Income Taxes 47	14.0	•	121.5	243.8	•	66.9	260.5	18.0	35.3	13.6	29.9	6.9	13.4
Return on Equity After Income Taxes 48	9.7	•	121.5	241.8	•	63.0	228.0	14.0	30.4	10.9	21.3	5.6	9.0
Profit Margin (Before Income Tax) 49	14.3	24.3	20.2	11.7	8.6	11.8	14.6	20.8	30.1	14.7	14.4	16.9	14.0
Profit Margin (After Income Tax) 50	9.9	21.7	20.2	11.6	7.7	11.1	12.8	16.2	25.9	11.8	10.2	13.7	9.5

Table I

Corporations with and without Net Income

TELECOMMUNICATIONS (WIRED, WIRELESS, SATELLITE, INTERNET PROVIDERS)

MONEY AMOUNTS AND SIZE OF ASSETS IN THOUSANDS OF DOLLARS

Item Description for Accounting Period 7/07 Through 6/08	Total	Zero Assets	Under 500	500 to 1,000	1,000 to 5,000	5,000 to 10,000	10,000 to 25,000	25,000 to 50,000	50,000 to 100,000	100,000 to 250,000	250,000 to 500,000	500,000 to 2,500,000	2,500,000 and over
Number of Enterprises **1**	19181	5011	10154	1167	1485	450	349	209	144	86	41	53	32
Revenues ($ in Thousands)													
Net Sales **2**	452745035	2194125	10165168	2110297	9473079	6207773	5543594	6524994	5441173	9427592	9220308	30248897	356188036
Interest **3**	29435165	16293	4024	3231	22993	116842	58422	43375	92435	170276	123941	651332	28132003
Rents **4**	10333945	1920	0	1851	4400	3540	7294	7120	13054	27727	41298		10212524
Royalties **5**	14134165	0	0	0	0	0	682	814	9784	20091	16991		13881665
Other Portfolio Income **6**	6380877	207563	34828	23152	49104	18894	22924	35090	229191	78661	156730	930810	4593927
Other Receipts **7**	23093718	-516973	155004	18016	58030	723694	178092	269789	244193	186554	191959	912701	20672658
Total Receipts **8**	536112905	1902928	10359024	2156547	9607606	7070743	5811008	6881182	6029830	10094949	9726247	32802029	433680813
Average Total Receipts **9**	27951	380	1020	1848	6470	15713	16650	32924	41874	117383	237226	618906	13552525
Operating Costs/Operating Income (%)													
Cost of Operations **10**	21.7	16.2	72.1	59.6	72.5	69.7	47.3	47.2	39.8	54.5	42.4	42.7	13.6
Salaries and Wages **11**	13.5	23.3	6.6	14.5	9.4	11.8	14.4	14.3	11.5	10.2	15.4	15.7	13.6
Taxes Paid **12**	2.6	1.7	1.0	2.0	1.4	2.5	2.3	2.2	2.8	1.9	2.9	2.5	2.7
Interest Paid **13**	10.8	13.7	0.3	5.2	0.5	8.4	1.5	3.7	3.4	3.1	4.7	7.8	12.5
Depreciation **14**	9.5	7.8	0.9	2.3	1.5	3.1	6.0	6.5	9.8	7.1	10.8	10.1	10.2
Amortization and Depletion **15**	2.5	5.0	0.2	0.4	0.3	1.0	1.0	1.3	1.3	1.0	2.6	3.2	2.7
Pensions and Other Deferred Comp. **16**	0.8	0.5	0.6	•	0.1	0.3	0.3	0.4	0.3	0.3	0.4	0.4	0.9
Employee Benefits **17**	2.1	6.0	0.4	0.9	0.9	0.4	1.3	1.1	1.5	1.3	2.0	2.0	2.3
Advertising **18**	2.6	2.9	0.3	0.7	0.7	0.8	1.0	1.3	0.8	0.9	3.2	3.5	2.8
Other Expenses **19**	43.4	47.1	14.3	15.0	11.3	27.3	30.4	23.6	33.4	21.9	25.3	22.6	49.1
Officers' Compensation **20**	0.7	2.9	3.0	4.0	2.8	1.7	1.9	2.1	1.9	1.5	1.0	1.0	0.4
Operating Margin **21**	•	•	0.1	•	•	•	•	•	•	•	•	•	•
Operating Margin Before Officers' Comp. **22**	1.4	•	3.2	•	•	•	•	•	•	•	•	•	•

Selected Average Balance Sheet ($ in Thousands)

Net Receivables 23	6645	0	11	150	519	1714	2327	5104	6517	18863	32587	109643	3563735
Inventories 24	612	0	9	31	97	135	500	836	1584	4624	3938	15592	295173
Net Property, Plant and Equipment 25	16848	0	10	103	450	1874	5332	11513	24506	47234	118166	306073	9015516
Total Assets 26	77147	0	83	669	2228	7203	16290	35163	69771	159335	365167	1066907	42602563
Notes and Loans Payable 27	22689	0	34	1200	423	3185	3760	10220	19327	45383	122605	551961	12093397
All Other Liabilities 28	21737	0	53	1039	1021	3080	2411	10669	15610	42439	123942	318903	11916644
Net Worth 29	32721	0	-3	-1570	784	938	10119	14274	34834	71513	118620	196043	18592521

Selected Financial Ratios (Times to 1)

Current Ratio 30	0.9	•	1.2	0.4	1.3	1.3	1.8	1.4	1.6	1.6	2.3	1.2	0.8
Quick Ratio 31	0.7	•	0.9	0.3	1.0	1.0	1.4	1.0	1.2	1.1	1.5	0.9	0.6
Net Sales to Working Capital 32	•	•	92.2	•	20.4	15.1	5.0	8.6	4.6	4.9	3.1	11.1	•
Coverage Ratio 33	1.8	•	7.0	0.5	1.1	•	1.5	1.5	2.2	2.0	•	0.6	1.9
Total Asset Turnover 34	0.3	•	12.0	2.7	2.9	1.9	1.0	0.9	0.5	0.7	0.6	0.5	0.3
Inventory Turnover 35	8.4	•	78.3	34.5	47.8	71.4	15.0	17.6	9.5	12.9	24.2	15.6	5.1
Receivables Turnover 36	3.5	•	94.4	11.3	12.0	9.8	7.3	6.6	5.8	6.0	6.1	5.9	3.1
Total Liabilities to Net Worth 37	1.4	•	•	1.8	6.7	0.6	1.5	1.0	1.2	2.1	4.4	•	1.3
Current Assets to Working Capital 38	•	•	5.2	•	4.4	4.5	2.3	3.6	2.6	2.6	1.8	5.5	•
Current Liabilities to Working Capital 39	•	•	4.2	•	3.4	3.5	1.3	2.6	1.6	1.6	0.8	4.5	•
Working Capital to Net Sales 40	•	•	0.0	•	0.0	0.1	0.2	0.1	0.2	0.2	0.3	0.1	•
Inventory to Working Capital 41	•	•	0.9	•	0.3	0.2	0.1	0.3	0.2	0.3	0.1	0.3	•
Total Receipts to Cash Flow 42	2.2	•	7.3	14.3	11.6	8.3	4.4	5.1	3.5	4.6	7.1	8.2	1.9
Cost of Goods to Cash Flow 43	0.5	•	5.2	8.5	8.4	5.8	2.1	2.4	1.4	2.5	3.0	3.5	0.3
Cash Flow to Total Debt 44	0.2	•	1.6	0.1	0.4	0.3	0.6	0.3	0.3	0.3	0.1	0.1	0.2

Selected Financial Factors (in Percentages)

Debt Ratio 45	57.6	•	103.9	334.5	64.8	87.0	37.9	59.4	50.1	55.1	67.5	81.6	56.4
Return on Total Assets 46	5.8	•	28.7	7.2	1.6	•	•	4.8	4.1	4.3	•	2.5	6.2
Return on Equity Before Income Taxes 47	5.9	•	•	2.9	0.5	•	•	3.8	4.5	4.9	•	•	6.6
Return on Equity After Income Taxes 48	4.0	•	•	2.9	•	•	•	0.4	1.1	2.4	•	•	4.8
Profit Margin (Before Income Tax) 49	8.2	•	2.1	•	0.1	•	•	1.7	4.1	3.2	•	•	11.1
Profit Margin (After Income Tax) 50	5.5	•	2.0	•	•	•	•	0.2	1.0	1.5	•	•	8.0

Table II

Corporations with Net Income

TELECOMMUNICATIONS (WIRED, WIRELESS, SATELLITE, INTERNET PROVIDERS)

MONEY AMOUNTS AND SIZE OF ASSETS IN THOUSANDS OF DOLLARS

Item Description for Accounting Period 7/07 Through 6/08	Total	Zero Assets	Under 500	500 to 1,000	1,000 to 5,000	5,000 to 10,000	10,000 to 25,000	25,000 to 50,000	50,000 to 100,000	100,000 to 250,000	250,000 to 500,000	500,000 to 2,500,000	2,500,000 and over
Number of Enterprises **1**	9557	1521	5763	427	960	322	203	145	93	56	21	24	22
Revenues ($ in Thousands)													
Net Sales **2**	408440597	265082	8888354	530328	7717638	5503178	3325155	5131233	3654462	6170137	3553217	14294507	349407306
Interest **3**	28358869	5848	2772	693	12529	23848	36031	31595	50379	98156	66191	364657	27666171
Rents **4**	10319484	783	0	1851	3956	3152	7098	6879	11879	26550	13041	32909	10211386
Royalties **5**	13913625	0	0	0	0	0	0	814	9784	6422	389	14551	13881665
Other Portfolio Income **6**	6006030	207293	34143	19619	46819	18438	18196	26199	203176	75722	144325	769288	4442812
Other Receipts **7**	22546662	16601	151554	18770	32746	133602	154522	220895	214374	129575	91266	725513	20657243
Total Receipts **8**	489585267	495607	9076823	571261	7813688	5568218	3541002	5417615	4144054	6506562	3868429	16201425	426266583
Average Total Receipts **9**	51228	326	1575	1338	8139	17647	17443	37363	44560	116189	184211	675059	19375754
Operating Costs/Operating Income (%)													
Cost of Operations **10**	19.1	12.5	74.6	29.7	76.4	71.9	43.5	48.3	39.1	49.1	33.6	38.0	13.3
Salaries and Wages **11**	13.2	27.0	5.0	12.1	6.6	9.2	10.7	12.5	7.3	8.1	14.2	15.6	13.6
Taxes Paid **12**	2.6	1.8	0.8	3.2	1.0	1.2	2.1	2.0	3.0	2.3	2.7	2.9	2.7
Interest Paid **13**	11.0	2.4	0.3	0.7	0.3	0.5	0.9	1.7	2.9	3.0	3.0	8.1	12.3
Depreciation **14**	9.4	11.3	0.8	3.6	1.0	2.5	5.5	4.9	9.8	7.9	10.0	9.4	10.0
Amortization and Depletion **15**	2.4	0.2	0.1	1.2	0.1	0.2	0.2	0.6	1.0	0.9	1.3	2.9	2.7
Pensions and Other Deferred Comp. **16**	0.9	2.5	0.6	•	0.0	0.3	0.3	0.4	0.4	0.3	0.3	0.5	1.0
Employee Benefits **17**	2.1	4.6	0.3	1.6	0.5	0.2	0.8	1.0	1.2	1.2	2.1	2.5	2.3
Advertising **18**	2.5	0.3	0.2	0.8	0.5	0.7	0.7	1.0	0.8	0.9	0.5	1.7	2.8
Other Expenses **19**	44.8	40.8	12.1	19.7	7.4	9.7	31.1	20.4	29.8	21.6	25.1	20.2	49.3
Officers' Compensation **20**	0.6	1.9	2.5	7.4	1.7	1.4	1.1	1.7	1.4	1.3	1.1	1.2	0.4
Operating Margin **21**	•	•	2.7	20.0	4.5	2.3	3.2	5.5	3.4	3.5	6.1	•	•
Operating Margin Before Officers' Comp. **22**	•	•	5.2	27.4	6.2	3.6	4.2	7.2	4.8	4.8	7.2	•	•

Selected Average Balance Sheet ($ in Thousands)

Net Receivables 23	12465	0	7	116	542	1869	2382	5555	6994	18535	26776	113033	5075432
Inventories 24	1074	0	11	43	97	114	337	921	1606	5578	3622	8915	413736
Net Property, Plant and Equipment 25	31216	0	11	60	371	2060	5444	11472	28696	55975	125879	324935	12645813
Total Assets 26	139812	0	100	591	2297	7293	15740	34499	70526	158909	353685	1107988	57869335
Notes and Loans Payable 27	40245	0	34	385	239	1386	2672	7506	19536	46123	85209	533448	1649852
All Other Liabilities 28	40623	0	41	307	1092	2521	-537	8895	12759	33366	75860	360389	16887652
Net Worth 29	58944	0	25	-101	967	3386	13605	18097	38230	79421	192616	214151	24483151

Selected Financial Ratios (Times to 1)

Current Ratio 30	0.8	•	2.0	0.5	1.4	1.6	2.0	1.7	1.8	1.7	3.9	1.1	0.8
Quick Ratio 31	0.7	•	1.5	0.4	1.1	1.2	1.6	1.2	1.3	1.2	2.0	0.8	0.6
Net Sales to Working Capital 32	•	43.1	•	17.4	10.6	4.9	6.2	4.2	4.7	1.5	•	23.5	•
Coverage Ratio 33	2.0	35.4	18.3	38.2	20.2	12.5	11.6	7.6	6.7	3.9	6.0	2.3	2.0
Total Asset Turnover 34	0.3	•	15.5	2.1	3.5	2.3	1.0	1.0	0.6	0.7	0.5	0.5	0.3
Inventory Turnover 35	7.6	•	105.9	8.5	63.5	108.2	21.1	18.5	9.6	9.7	15.7	25.4	5.1
Receivables Turnover 36	3.4	•	191.4	6.9	14.5	11.5	7.6	7.8	5.6	6.1	5.4	6.5	3.1
Total Liabilities to Net Worth 37	1.4	•	3.0	•	1.4	1.2	0.2	0.9	0.8	1.0	0.8	4.2	1.4
Current Assets to Working Capital 38	•	•	2.0	•	3.2	2.6	2.0	2.5	2.3	2.4	1.3	9.9	•
Current Liabilities to Working Capital 39	•	•	1.0	•	2.2	1.6	1.0	1.5	1.3	1.4	0.3	8.9	•
Working Capital to Net Sales 40	•	•	0.0	•	0.1	0.1	0.2	0.2	0.2	0.2	0.7	0.0	•
Inventory to Working Capital 41	•	•	0.4	•	0.2	0.1	0.1	0.2	0.1	0.3	0.0	0.3	•
Total Receipts to Cash Flow 42	2.0	1.9	6.6	2.7	9.2	7.6	2.9	3.9	2.7	3.7	3.1	4.6	1.8
Cost of Goods to Cash Flow 43	0.4	0.2	4.9	0.8	7.0	5.4	1.2	1.9	1.1	1.8	1.0	1.7	0.2
Cash Flow to Total Debt 44	0.3	•	3.1	0.7	0.7	0.6	2.7	0.6	0.4	0.4	0.3	0.1	0.3

Selected Financial Factors (in Percentages)

Debt Ratio 45	57.8	•	74.7	117.1	57.9	53.6	13.6	47.5	45.8	50.0	45.5	80.7	57.7
Return on Total Assets 46	6.8	•	79.0	59.8	21.0	14.1	10.9	13.0	10.9	8.2	8.5	10.0	6.6
Return on Equity Before Income Taxes 47	8.3	•	295.7	•	47.4	27.9	11.6	21.6	17.1	12.2	13.0	29.2	7.6
Return on Equity After Income Taxes 48	6.1	•	290.7	•	43.3	23.6	8.7	17.8	12.2	8.8	9.7	25.2	5.5
Profit Margin (Before Income Tax) 49	11.4	82.2	4.8	27.7	5.7	5.5	9.6	11.0	16.6	8.8	14.8	10.5	11.7
Profit Margin (After Income Tax) 50	8.4	62.8	4.7	27.5	5.2	4.7	7.2	9.1	11.9	6.4	11.1	9.1	8.5

Table I

Corporations with and without Net Income

DATA PROCESSING, HOSTING AND RELATED SERVICES

MONEY AMOUNTS AND SIZE OF ASSETS IN THOUSANDS OF DOLLARS

Item Description for Accounting Period 7/07 Through 6/08	Total	Zero Assets	Under 500	500 to 1,000	1,000 to 5,000	5,000 to 10,000	10,000 to 25,000	25,000 to 50,000	50,000 to 100,000	100,000 to 250,000	250,000 to 500,000	500,000 to 2,500,000	2,500,000 and over
Number of Enterprises 1	8722	1250	6354	254	637	90	51	30	22	13	5	9	6
Revenues ($ in Thousands)													
Net Sales 2	43144923	157681	3045746	518001	2525276	882979	992141	808756	1278472	1358593	1107192	2852379	27617708
Interest 3	1132435	9392	1870	1351	7482	6366	8124	8727	7192	24470	9822	43323	1004317
Rents 4	229711	0	3383	0	0	0	5876	257	1142	0	0	0	219052
Royalties 5	933271	0	0	0	0	121	142	0	2250	1069	2025	10683	916981
Other Portfolio Income 6	812193	2082	16325	199	12872	5335	622	8315	3376	11391	4893	223470	523315
Other Receipts 7	1523640	37744	108697	12616	39335	3217	11405	4897	45637	-21280	5545	18135	1257690
Total Receipts 8	47776173	206899	3176021	532167	2584965	898018	1018310	830952	1338069	1374243	1129477	3147990	31539063
Average Total Receipts 9	5478	166	500	2095	4058	9978	19967	27698	60821	105711	225895	349777	5256510
Operating Costs/Operating Income (%)													
Cost of Operations 10	15.4	10.5	31.2	17.0	27.9	45.4	38.3	28.1	20.7	34.7	27.6	20.0	8.2
Salaries and Wages 11	29.3	27.7	16.3	37.8	25.1	14.1	26.6	29.9	28.7	21.8	23.4	33.8	31.7
Taxes Paid 12	3.3	3.2	4.0	3.8	1.9	4.0	2.8	3.3	3.7	2.1	4.9	2.7	3.3
Interest Paid 13	5.2	6.2	1.1	4.1	0.6	1.7	2.2	2.2	4.2	4.7	1.2	6.5	6.5
Depreciation 14	5.8	3.4	1.4	1.2	4.0	3.5	4.1	3.0	3.7	2.5	7.0	6.3	7.0
Amortization and Depletion 15	2.7	17.1	0.0	0.2	0.7	1.9	1.2	3.1	1.8	1.5	1.5	7.8	2.8
Pensions and Other Deferred Comp. 16	0.6	0.0	0.1	•	1.2	0.2	0.7	0.7	0.9	0.3	0.1	0.5	0.7
Employee Benefits 17	2.5	1.6	1.2	0.8	1.1	1.3	3.1	3.9	2.0	2.3	2.3	2.6	2.8
Advertising 18	0.9	1.2	2.2	0.4	3.4	2.1	1.3	1.3	0.9	1.0	5.3	0.8	0.3
Other Expenses 19	39.1	38.2	38.8	29.9	29.3	31.2	28.8	27.8	31.5	26.1	19.4	23.3	44.6
Officers' Compensation 20	2.1	22.2	9.1	7.5	8.1	5.8	3.4	4.5	2.9	1.8	4.2	1.8	0.2
Operating Margin 21	•	•	•	•	•	•	•	•	•	1.2	3.2	•	•
Operating Margin Before Officers' Comp. 22	•	•	3.8	4.9	4.8	•	•	1.9	3.0	7.4	•	•	•

Selected Average Balance Sheet ($ in Thousands)

Net Receivables 23	793	21	179	163	742	4216	4572	11343	27597	76727	68006	768738
Inventories 24	19	0	13	7	76	129	524	262	246	4	3762	12302
Net Property, Plant and Equipment 25	1368	11	101	659	853	2801	4421	10062	11324	66487	87171	1596939
Total Assets 26	12794	97	688	1603	6786	15363	34503	66577	153259	377082	790360	15815695
Notes and Loans Payable 27	2857	164	1046	683	1587	4207	9614	24864	59898	56620	309111	3022433
All Other Liabilities 28	7143	42	794	737	1118	7301	13434	19039	44889	144253	171373	9536682
Net Worth 29	2795	-109	-1152	182	4080	3855	11455	22674	48471	176208	309876	3256580

Selected Financial Ratios (Times to 1)

Current Ratio 30	0.7	1.1	1.1	0.9	1.9	1.3	1.6	1.0	1.4	2.1	1.3	0.6
Quick Ratio 31	0.5	0.7	0.9	0.8	1.7	1.1	1.3	0.8	1.2	1.4	1.2	0.3
Net Sales to Working Capital 32	•	76.4	35.8	•	5.2	10.7	5.3	51.9	6.5	1.8	6.5	•
Coverage Ratio 33	2.1	0.0	1.0	•	•	•	•	1.9	1.4	5.1	1.7	2.3
Total Asset Turnover 34	0.4	4.9	3.0	2.5	1.4	1.3	0.8	0.9	0.7	0.6	0.4	0.3
Inventory Turnover 35	41.1	118.1	27.7	156.8	58.5	57.8	14.5	45.9	147.6	15263.0	16.8	30.7
Receivables Turnover 36	•	•	•	•	•	•	•	•	•	•	•	•
Total Liabilities to Net Worth 37	3.6	•	•	7.8	0.7	3.0	2.0	1.9	2.2	1.1	1.6	3.9
Current Assets to Working Capital 38	•	11.4	8.8	•	2.1	4.8	2.6	21.2	3.3	1.9	3.9	•
Current Liabilities to Working Capital 39	•	10.4	7.8	•	1.1	3.8	1.6	20.2	2.3	0.9	2.9	•
Working Capital to Net Sales 40	•	0.0	0.0	•	0.2	0.1	0.2	0.0	0.2	0.5	0.2	•
Inventory to Working Capital 41	•	0.2	0.2	•	0.0	0.1	0.1	0.2	0.0	0.0	0.1	•
Total Receipts to Cash Flow 42	2.8	2.9	5.1	4.2	7.1	6.7	6.6	3.2	4.0	4.7	6.3	2.3
Cost of Goods to Cash Flow 43	0.4	0.9	0.9	1.2	3.2	2.6	1.9	0.7	1.4	1.3	1.3	0.2
Cash Flow to Total Debt 44	0.2	0.8	0.2	0.7	0.5	0.3	0.2	0.4	0.3	0.2	0.1	0.2

Selected Financial Factors (in Percentages)

Debt Ratio 45	78.2	212.6	267.4	88.6	39.9	74.9	66.8	65.9	68.4	53.3	60.8	79.4
Return on Total Assets 46	4.1	0.3	12.3	•	•	•	•	6.8	4.6	3.7	4.4	4.4
Return on Equity Before Income Taxes 47	9.8	4.6	•	•	•	•	•	9.2	4.3	6.3	4.6	12.3
Return on Equity After Income Taxes 48	3.8	5.8	•	•	•	•	•	5.3	3.0	4.3	4.3	5.3
Profit Margin (Before Income Tax) 49	5.5	•	0.1	•	•	•	•	3.6	2.0	5.0	4.5	8.7
Profit Margin (After Income Tax) 50	2.1	•	0.1	•	•	•	•	2.1	1.4	3.4	4.2	3.7

Table II

Corporations with Net Income

DATA PROCESSING, HOSTING AND RELATED SERVICES

MONEY AMOUNTS AND SIZE OF ASSETS IN THOUSANDS OF DOLLARS

Item Description for Accounting Period 7/07 Through 6/08	Total	Zero Assets	Under 500	500 to 1,000	1,000 to 5,000	5,000 to 10,000	10,000 to 25,000	25,000 to 50,000	50,000 to 100,000	100,000 to 250,000	250,000 to 500,000	500,000 to 2,500,000	2,500,000 and over
Number of Enterprises 1	4247	803	2996	60	294	26	22	13	15	•	•	•	3
Revenues ($ in Thousands)													
Net Sales 2	32947116	100217	1932048	301192	2081545	481478	573846	441731	1088884	•	•	•	1554712
Interest 3	986606	3846	1165	1	1339	926	5605	2656	4686	•	•	•	16878
Rents 4	215304	0	3383	0	0	0	5521	0	1142	•	•	•	0
Royalties 5	921290	0	0	0	0	0	0	0	2250	•	•	•	68
Other Portfolio Income 6	751421	2082	15574	0	12317	105	374	1050	913	•	•	•	222773
Other Receipts 7	1297517	37748	90849	11963	18907	3852	11588	637	34964	•	•	•	6154
Total Receipts 8	37119254	143893	2043019	313156	2114108	486361	596934	446074	1132839	•	•	•	1800585
Average Total Receipts 9	8740	179	682	5219	7191	18706	27133	34313	75523	•	•	•	600195
Operating Costs/Operating Income (%)													
Cost of Operations 10	8.9	8.2	26.4	21.7	23.3	34.6	34.2	16.5	18.2	•	•	•	24.4
Salaries and Wages 11	31.4	15.3	16.8	28.7	24.9	14.1	23.2	27.0	29.1	•	•	•	30.7
Taxes Paid 12	3.3	3.1	4.1	2.7	1.3	2.0	3.0	2.4	3.8	•	•	•	2.8
Interest Paid 13	2.8	4.8	0.6	4.5	0.6	2.2	0.9	2.6	3.1	•	•	•	3.4
Depreciation 14	4.0	1.4	0.9	0.3	3.3	3.0	3.9	2.4	3.5	•	•	•	6.3
Amortization and Depletion 15	2.6	26.7	0.0	•	0.7	0.1	0.4	2.0	1.4	•	•	•	10.6
Pensions and Other Deferred Comp. 16	0.6	•	0.1	•	0.2	0.3	1.1	0.8	0.9	•	•	•	0.6
Employee Benefits 17	2.8	1.1	0.8	0.1	0.9	1.0	3.7	5.1	1.9	•	•	•	3.0
Advertising 18	0.8	0.6	3.1	0.0	3.9	1.8	1.1	0.2	0.5	•	•	•	1.0
Other Expenses 19	41.0	36.8	40.3	30.7	26.4	29.2	25.2	24.8	28.7	•	•	•	16.5
Officers' Compensation 20	1.6	8.5	6.7	2.6	7.0	3.2	3.1	4.8	2.6	•	•	•	2.3
Operating Margin 21	0.3	•	0.2	8.6	7.6	8.5	0.2	11.4	6.3	•	•	•	0.8
Operating Margin Before Officers' Comp. 22	1.8	2.1	6.9	11.2	14.6	11.7	3.4	16.3	8.9	•	•	•	0.8

Selected Average Balance Sheet ($ in Thousands)

	C1	C2	C3	C4	C5	C6	C7	C8	C9	C10	C11	C12
Net Receivables **23**	1281	17	0	40	170	2145	6032	5436	10269	•	69445	•
Inventories **24**	23	2	0	23	3	264	117	286	137	•	44	•
Net Property, Plant and Equipment **25**	972	9	0	55	743	1661	4368	3469	12576	•	88707	•
Total Assets **26**	21278	115	0	633	1502	6757	15450	32801	67636	•	831948	•
Notes and Loans Payable **27**	3284	146	0	469	625	1287	3174	10046	25810	•	215776	•
All Other Liabilities **28**	12861	38	0	632	519	2933	10010	9209	15278	•	222242	•
Net Worth **29**	5133	-69	0	-468	358	2537	2265	13545	26548	•	393929	•

Selected Financial Ratios (Times to 1)

	C1	C2	C3	C4	C5	C6	C7	C8	C9	C10	C11	C12
Current Ratio **30**	0.6	•	•	1.6	1.1	1.4	1.0	2.7	1.2	•	1.6	•
Quick Ratio **31**	0.4	•	•	1.1	0.9	1.2	0.9	2.0	0.9	•	1.4	•
Net Sales to Working Capital **32**	•	•	•	20.7	210.9	16.2	•	4.0	15.4	•	4.5	•
Coverage Ratio **33**	6.4	8.8	•	11.6	17.4	5.3	6.0	5.8	4.3	•	5.2	•
Total Asset Turnover **34**	0.4	•	•	5.6	4.7	2.7	1.7	1.0	1.1	•	0.6	•
Inventory Turnover **35**	30.1	•	•	100.8	525.5	24.3	76.3	19.6	96.2	•	2891.3	•
Receivables Turnover **36**	•	•	•	•	•	•	•	•	•	•	•	•
Total Liabilities to Net Worth **37**	3.1	•	•	•	3.2	1.7	5.8	1.4	1.5	•	1.1	•
Current Assets to Working Capital **38**	•	•	•	2.7	19.8	3.7	•	1.6	5.0	•	2.6	•
Current Liabilities to Working Capital **39**	•	•	•	1.7	18.8	2.7	•	0.6	4.0	•	1.6	•
Working Capital to Net Sales **40**	•	•	•	0.0	0.0	0.1	•	0.3	0.1	•	0.2	•
Inventory to Working Capital **41**	•	•	•	0.1	0.1	0.2	•	0.0	0.0	•	0.0	•
Total Receipts to Cash Flow **42**	2.1	1.4	•	2.3	3.3	2.7	3.8	3.0	2.8	•	6.3	•
Cost of Goods to Cash Flow **43**	0.2	0.1	•	0.6	0.7	0.9	1.3	0.5	0.5	•	1.5	•
Cash Flow to Total Debt **44**	0.2	•	•	1.5	1.4	1.6	0.5	0.6	0.6	•	0.2	•

Selected Financial Factors (in Percentages)

	C1	C2	C3	C4	C5	C6	C7	C8	C9	C10	C11	C12
Debt Ratio **45**	75.9	•	160.4	173.9	76.2	62.5	85.3	58.7	60.7	•	52.6	•
Return on Total Assets **46**	6.5	•	36.9	136.1	45.7	32.2	8.6	15.5	14.4	•	11.0	•
Return on Equity Before Income Taxes **47**	22.7	•	•	180.8	69.8	48.6	31.0	28.2	•	•	18.8	•
Return on Equity After Income Taxes **48**	16.0	•	•	171.6	58.8	42.4	29.2	23.4	•	•	18.3	•
Profit Margin (Before Income Tax) **49**	15.0	37.1	6.0	12.6	9.1	9.6	4.2	12.4	10.3	•	14.3	•
Profit Margin (After Income Tax) **50**	10.6	33.5	5.5	12.6	8.7	8.1	3.7	11.6	8.5	•	13.9	•

Table I

Corporations with and without Net Income

OTHER INFORMATION SERVICES, INTERNET PUBLISHING, WEB PORTALS

MONEY AMOUNTS AND SIZE OF ASSETS IN THOUSANDS OF DOLLARS

Item Description for Accounting Period 7/07 Through 6/08	Total	Zero Assets	Under 500	500 to 1,000	1,000 to 5,000	5,000 to 10,000	10,000 to 25,000	25,000 to 50,000	50,000 to 100,000	100,000 to 250,000	250,000 to 500,000	500,000 to 2,500,000	2,500,000 and over
Number of Enterprises 1	19507	4486	13630	532	461	212	89	23	25	18	7	18	5
Revenues ($ in Thousands)													
Net Sales 2	46551537	1101672	4720463	1299912	942743	2268436	1159367	545222	1329681	1811718	1293892	11129928	18948501
Interest 3	1033274	44439	2298	2960	13642	18278	13774	8482	14691	23753	14217	304511	572229
Rents 4	18212	1767	0	0	0	914	0	0	0	0	0	3048	12483
Royalties 5	1112713	2178	23	0	59	33333	0	307	1038	7872	0	656057	411845
Other Portfolio Income 6	544230	29739	2177	447	53485	7276	6512	19343	78951	23834	4528	160516	157424
Other Receipts 7	3221324	86440	12437	1370	22368	27619	57111	17071	15727	108528	937386	456437	1478831
Total Receipts 8	52481290	1266235	4737398	1304689	1032297	2355856	1236764	590425	1440088	1975705	2250023	12710497	21581313
Average Total Receipts 9	2690	282	348	2452	2239	11113	13896	25671	57604	109761	321432	706139	4316263
Operating Costs/Operating Income (%)													
Cost of Operations 10	20.7	30.9	34.5	71.0	16.9	40.3	32.0	12.1	21.5	16.3	11.2	22.4	10.7
Salaries and Wages 11	26.8	16.1	14.0	11.9	46.9	26.4	30.2	30.9	22.1	30.6	21.1	28.7	29.5
Taxes Paid 12	2.3	1.5	1.9	1.5	4.8	4.2	2.8	3.8	2.7	3.2	2.5	1.9	2.2
Interest Paid 13	2.6	5.8	1.2	0.7	1.6	0.8	3.0	3.1	2.0	2.5	0.8	4.7	2.0
Depreciation 14	3.2	3.1	0.9	0.3	2.5	1.5	2.7	6.7	3.3	2.6	2.6	2.5	4.6
Amortization and Depletion 15	2.2	1.1	0.1	0.4	1.9	1.5	2.6	2.6	2.3	3.2	2.9	2.7	2.5
Pensions and Other Deferred Comp. 16	0.5	0.1	0.7	0.1	0.2	0.9	0.0	0.5	0.4	0.4	1.8	0.5	0.4
Employee Benefits 17	2.2	2.8	0.8	0.4	3.1	2.1	2.6	2.4	2.3	3.0	2.0	3.5	1.6
Advertising 18	2.0	3.7	1.2	1.9	5.2	1.0	2.8	3.0	2.9	10.8	4.7	1.0	1.4
Other Expenses 19	39.1	42.0	34.6	14.8	53.3	34.3	27.7	46.8	40.1	27.8	106.9	39.9	38.0
Officers' Compensation 20	3.0	5.5	10.3	1.8	16.9	3.4	4.6	5.3	2.5	2.0	1.7	2.0	1.0
Operating Margin 21	•	•	•	•	•	•	•	•	•	•	•	•	6.0
Operating Margin Before Officers' Comp. 22	•	10.1	•	•	•	•	•	•	0.3	•	•	•	7.0

Selected Average Balance Sheet ($ in Thousands)

Net Receivables 23	494	0	5	108	254	1620	2600	12942	9226	15552	49951	213975	761752
Inventories 24	18	0	0	2	8	34	98	38	1840	1366	9	14236	921
Net Property, Plant and Equipment 25	396	0	14	30	169	543	1261	4388	4963	11331	27030	61896	1097973
Total Assets 26	4278	0	48	660	2340	6985	14644	39617	74494	167727	372283	1233835	9594379
Notes and Loans Payable 27	997	0	90	477	1225	1177	5445	3576	10036	37460	22880	338670	1883200
All Other Liabilities 28	1110	0	31	189	607	1889	7120	15979	26085	58725	108037	424669	1867024
Net Worth 29	2171	-73	-73	-6	508	3919	2080	20062	38373	71542	241366	470496	5844156

Selected Financial Ratios (Times to 1)

Current Ratio 30	1.5	•	1.0	1.8	1.8	2.7	1.3	3.2	1.5	1.4	1.3	1.4	1.5
Quick Ratio 31	0.8	•	0.7	1.7	1.5	2.4	1.1	2.9	1.0	1.2	0.9	1.1	0.6
Net Sales to Working Capital 32	4.2	•	484.3	10.1	3.2	3.2	7.6	1.4	4.0	5.7	5.3	5.1	3.0
Coverage Ratio 33	4.2	1.4	1.1	•	•	•	•	•	4.0	3.7	20.5	1.9	10.8
Total Asset Turnover 34	0.6	•	7.3	3.7	0.9	1.5	0.9	0.6	0.7	0.6	0.5	0.5	0.4
Inventory Turnover 35	26.9	•	300.5	890.3	43.8	125.4	42.6	74.5	6.2	12.0	2270.7	9.7	439.1
Receivables Turnover 36	6.2	•	77.3	38.0	6.3	6.6	6.7	2.8	7.0	7.1	3.3	3.4	7.8
Total Liabilities to Net Worth 37	1.0	•	•	•	3.6	0.8	6.0	1.0	0.9	1.3	0.5	1.6	0.6
Current Assets to Working Capital 38	3.1	•	42.5	2.2	2.3	1.6	5.0	1.5	2.9	3.8	4.3	3.3	3.1
Current Liabilities to Working Capital 39	2.1	•	41.5	1.2	1.3	0.6	4.0	0.5	1.9	2.8	3.3	2.3	2.1
Working Capital to Net Sales 40	0.2	•	0.0	0.1	0.3	0.3	0.1	0.7	0.3	0.2	0.2	0.2	0.3
Inventory to Working Capital 41	0.0	•	0.9	0.0	0.0	0.0	0.1	0.0	0.2	0.1	0.0	0.1	0.0
Total Receipts to Cash Flow 42	2.3	2.8	3.1	13.0	•	5.4	4.9	3.5	2.6	3.6	0.8	2.5	1.8
Cost of Goods to Cash Flow 43	0.5	0.9	1.1	9.2	•	2.2	1.6	0.4	0.6	0.6	0.1	0.6	0.2
Cash Flow to Total Debt 44	0.5	•	0.9	0.3	•	0.7	0.2	0.4	0.6	0.3	1.7	0.3	0.6

Selected Financial Factors (in Percentages)

Debt Ratio 45	49.3	•	253.6	100.9	78.3	43.9	85.8	49.4	48.5	57.3	35.2	61.9	39.1
Return on Total Assets 46	6.1	•	9.8	•	•	•	•	•	5.8	5.5	8.3	4.6	8.7
Return on Equity Before Income Taxes 47	9.1	•	•	1997.7	•	•	•	•	8.5	9.4	12.2	5.7	12.9
Return on Equity After Income Taxes 48	5.7	•	•	2059.0	•	•	•	•	4.8	4.9	7.5	3.1	9.6
Profit Margin (Before Income Tax) 49	8.3	2.4	0.1	•	•	•	•	•	6.1	6.7	15.9	4.4	19.9
Profit Margin (After Income Tax) 50	5.2	2.3	0.0	•	•	•	•	•	3.5	3.5	9.8	2.4	14.7

Table II

Corporations with Net Income

OTHER INFORMATION SERVICES, INTERNET PUBLISHING, WEB PORTALS

MONEY AMOUNTS AND SIZE OF ASSETS IN THOUSANDS OF DOLLARS

Item Description for Accounting Period 7/07 Through 6/08		Total	Zero Assets	Under 500	500 to 1,000	1,000 to 5,000	5,000 to 10,000	10,000 to 25,000	25,000 to 50,000	50,000 to 100,000	100,000 to 250,000	250,000 to 500,000	500,000 to 2,500,000	2,500,000 and over
Number of Enterprises	1	9568	2523	6441	291	112	105	44	12	8	11	3	14	5
Revenues ($ in Thousands)														
Net Sales	2	41506114	814490	3947483	797828	603441	1941902	869134	273733	704914	1409724	959097	10235867	18948501
Interest	3	918908	43151	718	1327	3190	2321	4834	3953	5908	17941	11678	251659	572229
Rents	4	16278	213	0	0	0	873	0	0	0	0	0	2708	12483
Royalties	5	1075500	2178	23	0	0	0	0	307	1038	7872	0	652237	411845
Other Portfolio Income	6	518301	29675	743	447	53309	3513	6481	637	78455	23760	3740	160117	157424
Other Receipts	7	2080802	79500	11770	302	12320	1179	8535	16050	3455	6547	31011	431303	1478831
Total Receipts	8	46115903	969207	3960737	799904	672260	1949788	888984	294680	793770	1465844	1005526	11733891	21581313
Average Total Receipts	9	4820	384	615	2749	6002	18569	20204	24557	99221	133259	335175	838135	4316263
Operating Costs/Operating Income (%)														
Cost of Operations	10	20.0	34.2	37.3	81.5	21.0	39.5	31.2	2.5	15.9	11.1	•	23.7	10.7
Salaries and Wages	11	25.3	14.6	9.0	2.4	35.5	19.6	21.5	18.5	18.7	28.5	23.8	27.6	29.5
Taxes Paid	12	2.1	1.5	1.1	1.2	2.9	3.9	2.2	1.8	2.6	3.2	2.5	1.8	2.2
Interest Paid	13	2.2	7.1	0.2	0.2	1.0	0.1	2.9	2.7	0.4	2.5	0.5	3.6	2.0
Depreciation	14	3.1	3.0	0.7	0.1	1.1	0.9	2.2	3.7	3.2	2.2	2.6	2.3	4.6
Amortization and Depletion	15	1.8	0.6	0.1	0.0	0.4	0.3	0.7	2.1	1.7	2.1	1.3	1.8	2.5
Pensions and Other Deferred Comp.	16	0.5	0.1	0.7	0.1	0.2	1.0	0.0	0.9	0.5	0.4	2.3	0.6	0.4
Employee Benefits	17	2.0	3.5	0.4	0.5	1.9	1.6	2.1	1.5	2.2	2.2	2.0	3.4	1.6
Advertising	18	1.5	4.6	0.9	•	2.5	0.2	2.2	1.1	1.6	9.0	2.3	0.6	1.4
Other Expenses	19	35.4	27.1	29.4	6.6	20.2	24.7	18.6	50.2	38.8	26.5	43.0	40.1	38.0
Officers' Compensation	20	2.5	7.3	9.5	2.4	8.8	2.3	3.4	5.0	1.6	1.9	1.1	2.0	1.0
Operating Margin	21	3.6	•	10.7	4.9	4.4	5.9	13.0	10.1	12.8	10.5	18.6	•	6.0
Operating Margin Before Officers' Comp.	22	6.1	3.8	20.2	7.3	13.2	8.2	16.4	15.2	14.4	12.3	19.7	•	7.0

Selected Average Balance Sheet ($ in Thousands)

Line Item													
Net Receivables 23	895	0	7	55	566	2876	3371	14943	10954	19767	37808	256169	761752
Inventories 24	28	0	0	0	6	19	134	14	1122	24	0	18023	921
Net Property, Plant and Equipment 25	732	0	17	2	197	501	1606	3559	6762	13900	28696	65834	1097973
Total Assets 26	7481	0	50	653	3120	6770	14599	40581	71150	165162	337648	1250471	9594379
Notes and Loans Payable 27	1503	0	32	202	1070	412	5532	3839	6868	42444	24007	261035	1883200
All Other Liabilities 28	1863	0	14	63	895	2044	8426	18724	31182	51151	43578	466261	1867024
Net Worth 29	4115	0	4	389	1155	4314	642	18017	33100	71566	270063	523175	5844156

Selected Financial Ratios (Times to 1)

Line Item													
Current Ratio 30	1.5	•	2.0	9.8	0.9	2.1	1.5	9.6	1.5	1.8	1.9	1.6	1.5
Quick Ratio 31	0.8	•	1.3	9.7	0.8	2.0	1.3	8.6	1.3	1.5	1.9	1.2	0.6
Net Sales to Working Capital 32	4.0	•	30.7	5.0	•	7.3	6.7	1.1	5.5	3.9	5.3	4.3	3.0
Coverage Ratio 33	7.8	3.2	52.1	32.5	16.7	47.8	6.3	7.7	59.9	6.7	51.2	3.0	10.8
Total Asset Turnover 34	0.6	•	12.2	4.2	1.7	2.7	1.4	0.6	1.2	0.8	0.9	0.6	0.4
Inventory Turnover 35	30.4	•	2249.7	•	186.8	380.7	46.0	41.7	12.5	587.0	•	9.6	439.1
Receivables Turnover 36	6.9	•	77.3	•	7.7	6.8	7.7	2.3	6.5	7.9	•	4.2	7.8
Total Liabilities to Net Worth 37	0.8	•	12.0	0.7	1.7	0.6	21.8	1.3	1.1	1.3	0.3	1.4	0.6
Current Assets to Working Capital 38	2.9	•	2.0	1.1	•	1.9	3.1	1.1	3.0	2.2	2.1	2.7	3.1
Current Liabilities to Working Capital 39	1.9	•	1.0	0.1	•	0.9	2.1	0.1	2.0	1.2	1.1	1.7	2.1
Working Capital to Net Sales 40	0.2	•	0.0	0.2	•	0.1	0.1	1.0	0.2	0.3	0.2	0.2	0.3
Inventory to Working Capital 41	0.0	•	0.0	•	•	•	0.0	•	0.0	0.0	•	0.1	0.0
Total Receipts to Cash Flow 42	2.1	3.0	2.6	11.9	4.5	3.5	3.2	1.5	1.9	3.0	1.6	2.3	1.8
Cost of Goods to Cash Flow 43	0.4	1.0	1.0	9.7	0.9	1.4	1.0	0.0	0.3	0.3	•	0.6	0.2
Cash Flow to Total Debt 44	0.6	•	5.1	0.9	0.6	2.2	0.4	0.7	1.2	0.5	3.0	0.4	0.6

Selected Financial Factors (in Percentages)

Line Item													
Debt Ratio 45	45.0	•	92.3	40.5	63.0	36.3	95.6	55.6	53.5	56.7	20.0	58.2	39.1
Return on Total Assets 46	9.8	•	138.2	22.0	29.1	17.6	24.6	11.5	32.0	13.0	22.9	6.2	8.7
Return on Equity Before Income Taxes 47	15.5	•	1768.3	35.9	73.9	27.1	471.0	22.5	67.5	25.6	28.0	9.8	12.9
Return on Equity After Income Taxes 48	11.9	•	1748.5	34.2	62.4	26.1	442.3	19.7	54.4	18.3	18.2	6.8	9.6
Profit Margin (Before Income Tax) 49	14.7	15.5	11.1	5.1	15.8	6.3	15.3	17.8	25.4	14.3	23.7	7.0	19.9
Profit Margin (After Income Tax) 50	11.3	15.3	10.9	4.8	13.4	6.1	14.4	15.6	20.5	10.2	15.4	4.9	14.7

Table I

Corporations with and without Net Income

CREDIT INTERMEDIATION

MONEY AMOUNTS AND SIZE OF ASSETS IN THOUSANDS OF DOLLARS

Item Description for Accounting Period 7/07 Through 6/08	Total	Zero Assets	Under 500	500 to 1,000	1,000 to 5,000	5,000 to 10,000	10,000 to 25,000	25,000 to 50,000	50,000 to 100,000	100,000 to 250,000	250,000 to 500,000	500,000 to 2,500,000	2,500,000 and over
Number of Enterprises **1**	59093	12295	32980	3517	4987	1123	1025	704	740	830	382	368	141
Revenues ($ in Thousands)													
Net Sales **2**	656082766	109632612	13964270	6762985	8326324	3646000	6513358	4004952	6048159	14420454	13578012	39329286	429856353
Interest **3**	435646695	97359576	1586813	57223	759849	189721	352068	947373	2247259	6169094	6644680	21736522	297596516
Rents **4**	898719	199824	0	1	12468	2052	2381	6883	10824	18055	18318	113849	514064
Royalties **5**	479852	59300	858	0	137	0	0	143	12665	34423	3	19215	353108
Other Portfolio Income **6**	11697392	1807985	14734	25719	59057	12680	180339	41791	104856	260183	319162	1052626	7818262
Other Receipts **7**	207360108	10205927	12361865	6680042	7494813	3441547	5978570	3008762	3672555	7938699	6595849	16407074	123574403
Total Receipts **8**	656082766	109632612	13964270	6762985	8326324	3646000	6513358	4004952	6048159	14420454	13578012	39329286	429856353
Average Total Receipts **9**	11103	8917	423	1923	1670	3247	6354	5689	8173	17374	35545	106873	3048627
Operating Costs/Operating Income (%)													
Cost of Operations **10**	1.6	0.6	6.4	55.7	18.7	6.8	7.9	2.4	4.0	6.4	0.3	0.7	0.3
Salaries and Wages **11**	8.4	7.9	33.9	18.2	21.0	30.8	33.7	23.6	19.3	17.6	16.5	14.2	5.3
Taxes Paid **12**	1.1	1.5	2.9	1.6	2.6	3.5	3.8	2.8	2.6	2.6	2.5	1.9	0.7
Interest Paid **13**	56.1	82.6	12.2	1.4	13.3	9.8	10.6	22.3	27.6	31.4	33.5	32.6	57.9
Depreciation **14**	1.9	0.6	0.7	0.6	1.8	2.5	1.6	1.7	1.9	2.9	2.7	1.7	2.3
Amortization and Depletion **15**	2.1	0.2	0.1	0.1	0.5	0.4	•	0.6	0.6	0.9	0.8	1.2	3.0
Pensions and Other Deferred Comp. **16**	0.3	0.2	0.3	0.3	0.4	0.2	0.4	0.5	0.7	0.7	0.9	0.9	0.3
Employee Benefits **17**	0.8	0.6	0.8	0.3	1.0	1.5	1.5	1.7	2.0	1.9	2.0	1.5	0.7
Advertising **18**	1.2	0.1	1.3	0.9	1.8	3.8	3.4	1.6	1.3	1.6	1.8	3.0	1.2
Other Expenses **19**	24.5	20.0	33.3	17.3	31.1	43.1	36.3	35.8	31.7	35.7	25.5	31.6	23.8
Officers' Compensation **20**	0.9	0.7	6.8	2.5	4.7	4.3	4.2	5.7	5.8	4.2	2.6	1.5	0.3
Operating Margin **21**	1.0	•	1.4	0.9	3.0	•	•	1.2	2.5	•	10.9	9.2	4.3
Operating Margin Before Officers' Comp. **22**	2.0	•	8.2	3.4	7.7	•	1.0	7.0	8.3	•	13.5	10.8	4.6

Selected Average Balance Sheet ($ in Thousands)

Net Receivables 23	13499	0	18	201	913	3557	6247	16721	32870	68580	104116	268574	3899344
Inventories 24	•	•	•	•	•	•	•	•	•	•	•	•	•
Net Property, Plant and Equipment 25	984	0	17	115	226	601	604	868	1745	3602	6868	14681	296810
Total Assets 26	81029	0	106	783	2172	7084	15564	36474	71485	158302	351736	1003438	28607568
Notes and Loans Payable 27	45315	0	52	417	1120	4111	7239	9224	9879	21750	51635	236798	17860061
All Other Liabilities 28	28448	0	55	52	984	1812	5248	21544	50110	116431	257127	622722	8443059
Net Worth 29	7266	0	-2	315	68	1160	3078	5705	11496	20121	42973	143918	2304447

Selected Financial Ratios (Times to 1)

Current Ratio 30	0.6	•	1.5	2.8	1.1	1.4	1.2	1.0	0.9	0.8	0.6	0.6	0.5
Quick Ratio 31	0.4	•	1.0	2.4	1.0	1.3	1.0	1.0	0.8	0.7	0.6	0.5	0.4
Net Sales to Working Capital 32	•	•	19.8	5.8	12.3	2.3	3.7	4.9	•	•	•	•	•
Coverage Ratio 33	1.0	0.8	1.1	1.7	1.2	0.3	0.7	1.0	1.1	0.8	1.3	1.3	1.1
Total Asset Turnover 34	0.1	•	4.0	2.5	0.8	0.5	0.4	0.2	0.1	0.1	0.1	0.1	0.1
Inventory Turnover 35	•	•	•	•	•	•	•	•	•	•	•	•	•
Receivables Turnover 36	•	•	•	•	•	•	•	•	•	•	•	•	•
Total Liabilities to Net Worth 37	10.2	•	•	1.5	31.0	5.1	4.1	5.4	5.2	6.9	7.2	6.0	11.4
Current Assets to Working Capital 38	•	•	3.1	1.5	10.9	3.5	5.7	21.6	•	•	•	•	•
Current Liabilities to Working Capital 39	•	•	2.1	0.5	9.9	2.5	4.7	20.6	•	•	•	•	•
Inventory to Working Capital 41	•	•	•	0.0	0.0	0.0	0.0	0.0	•	•	•	•	•
Working Capital to Net Sales 40	•	•	0.1	0.2	0.1	0.4	0.3	0.2	0.1	0.1	0.1	0.1	0.1
Total Receipts to Cash Flow 42	4.5	58.8	3.5	7.6	3.4	3.4	3.9	3.2	3.3	4.1	3.2	2.7	3.9
Cost of Goods to Cash Flow 43	0.1	0.3	0.2	4.2	0.6	0.2	0.3	0.1	0.1	0.3	0.0	0.0	0.0
Cash Flow to Total Debt 44	0.0	•	1.1	0.5	0.2	0.2	0.1	0.1	0.0	0.0	0.0	0.0	0.0

Selected Financial Factors (in Percentages)

Debt Ratio 45	91.0	101.7	59.8	96.9	83.6	80.2	84.4	83.9	87.3	87.8	85.7	91.9
Return on Total Assets 46	7.8	54.6	5.8	12.5	1.4	3.0	3.6	3.4	2.7	4.4	4.4	6.6
Return on Equity Before Income Taxes 47	1.0	•	5.7	73.9	•	•	0.9	1.2	•	8.4	6.7	5.3
Return on Equity After Income Taxes 48	•	•	4.8	63.7	•	•	•	0.1	•	5.2	3.6	2.1
Profit Margin (Before Income Tax) 49	0.7	1.4	0.9	3.0	•	•	0.9	1.8	•	10.2	9.0	4.0
Profit Margin (After Income Tax) 50	•	1.4	0.8	2.6	•	•	•	0.2	•	6.3	4.9	1.6

Table II

Corporations with Net Income

CREDIT INTERMEDIATION

Money Amounts and Size of Assets in Thousands of Dollars

Item Description for Accounting Period 7/07 Through 6/08	Total	Zero Assets	Under 500	500 to 1,000	1,000 to 5,000	5,000 to 10,000	10,000 to 25,000	25,000 to 50,000	50,000 to 100,000	100,000 to 250,000	250,000 to 500,000	500,000 to 2,500,000	2,500,000 and over
Number of Enterprises 1	32141	4623	18392	2237	3138	706	649	473	507	658	337	312	108
Revenues ($ in Thousands)													
Net Sales 2	518176192	61822110	8047313	5214900	5052202	1799218	3716949	2820225	4307361	10139363	12127127	32212813	370918611
Interest 3	340559425	48199440	100051	53889	639811	78325	250151	467560	1479712	4740153	5845693	17647336	261057305
Rents 4	775250	154807	213	0	7033	572	1760	5134	5530	12829	17382	98698	471293
Royalties 5	395700	12	0	0	0	0	0	143	102	34284	3	8393	352763
Other Portfolio Income 6	8563641	470771	7605	24532	50885	6782	126919	32241	76988	225473	280094	927372	6333983
Other Receipts 7	167882176	12997080	7939444	5136479	4354473	1711539	3338119	2315147	2745029	5126624	5983955	13531014	102703267
Total Receipts 8	518176192	61822110	8047313	5214900	5052202	1799218	3716949	2820225	4307361	10139363	12127127	32212813	370918611
Average Total Receipts 9	16122	13373	438	2331	1610	2546	5727	5962	8496	15409	35986	103246	3434432
Operating Costs/Operating Income (%)													
Cost of Operations 10	1.2	0.2	5.8	67.3	8.3	3.0	6.4	2.5	3.9	4.4	0.3	0.8	0.1
Salaries and Wages 11	6.7	5.8	41.7	8.7	19.2	24.2	24.8	21.9	16.0	15.1	16.3	13.6	4.3
Taxes Paid 12	1.0	2.0	2.4	1.4	2.3	2.3	2.8	2.9	2.4	2.4	2.7	2.0	0.6
Interest Paid 13	53.5	68.3	1.1	1.0	15.4	9.3	11.1	18.4	23.7	29.7	31.0	31.2	58.0
Depreciation 14	0.7	0.5	0.6	0.4	0.9	1.6	1.6	1.5	1.7	2.1	2.0	1.7	0.5
Amortization and Depletion 15	2.4	0.1	0.1	0.0	0.2	0.2	0.3	0.3	0.4	0.9	0.7	0.9	3.2
Pensions and Other Deferred Comp. 16	0.3	0.2	0.3	0.4	0.6	0.3	0.4	0.6	0.8	0.8	0.9	1.0	0.2
Employee Benefits 17	0.7	0.3	0.6	0.3	0.7	1.2	1.4	1.4	1.9	1.8	2.0	1.5	0.6
Advertising 18	1.3	0.1	1.4	1.0	1.6	1.7	2.4	1.4	0.8	1.4	1.9	3.1	1.2
Other Expenses 19	21.1	9.8	25.3	10.4	28.9	34.0	29.1	25.6	28.6	22.3	23.1	25.8	22.2
Officers' Compensation 20	0.9	0.5	8.6	2.9	5.5	6.1	4.3	5.8	5.5	4.1	2.7	1.5	0.3
Operating Margin 21	10.3	12.3	12.2	6.0	16.5	16.1	15.5	17.7	14.4	15.0	16.5	17.0	8.8
Operating Margin Before Officers' Comp. 22	11.2	12.8	20.7	9.0	22.0	22.2	19.7	23.6	19.8	19.1	19.2	18.5	9.1

Selected Average Balance Sheet ($ in Thousands)

Net Receivables 23	18688	0	12	270	962	3674	7010	17529	33152	70914	106675	266854	3691538
Inventories 24	•	•	•	•	•	•	•	•	•	•	•	•	•
Net Property, Plant and Equipment 25	763	0	15	55	141	365	576	680	1651	3396	7118	14942	116735
Total Assets 26	122088	0	113	774	2164	7077	15719	37141	72135	158466	354091	988319	30667950
Notes and Loans Payable 27	69505	0	24	341	806	4557	6713	8584	9116	17168	42881	192861	19704280
All Other Liabilities 28	40701	0	22	33	432	815	5590	20556	51915	119179	263464	642438	8318879
Net Worth 29	11882	0	67	401	927	1705	3417	8001	11104	22119	47747	153020	2644791

Selected Financial Ratios (Times to 1)

Current Ratio 30	0.5	•	3.6	4.9	2.2	1.5	1.3	1.1	0.9	0.8	0.6	0.6	0.5
Quick Ratio 31	0.4	•	2.2	4.0	1.9	1.4	1.1	1.0	0.8	0.8	0.5	0.5	0.4
Net Sales to Working Capital 32	•	•	8.5	4.5	1.9	1.5	2.6	3.1	•	•	•	•	•
Coverage Ratio 33	1.2	1.2	11.8	7.3	2.1	2.7	2.4	1.9	1.6	1.5	1.5	1.5	1.1
Total Asset Turnover 34	0.1	•	3.9	3.0	0.7	0.4	0.4	0.2	0.1	0.1	0.1	0.1	0.1
Inventory Turnover 35	•	•	•	•	•	•	•	•	•	•	•	•	•
Receivables Turnover 36	•	•	•	•	•	•	•	•	•	•	•	•	•
Total Liabilities to Net Worth 37	9.3	•	0.7	0.9	1.3	3.2	3.6	3.6	5.5	6.2	6.4	5.5	10.6
Current Assets to Working Capital 38	•	•	1.4	1.3	1.8	2.8	4.6	14.0	•	•	•	•	•
Current Liabilities to Working Capital 39	•	•	0.4	0.3	0.8	1.8	3.6	13.0	•	•	•	•	•
Working Capital to Net Sales 40	•	•	0.1	0.2	0.5	0.6	0.4	0.3	•	•	•	•	•
Inventory to Working Capital 41	•	•	•	0.0	•	•	•	0.0	•	•	•	•	•
Total Receipts to Cash Flow 42	3.4	4.9	3.1	7.3	2.4	2.2	2.6	2.5	2.5	2.9	2.9	2.5	3.4
Cost of Goods to Cash Flow 43	0.0	0.0	0.2	4.9	0.2	0.1	0.2	0.1	0.1	0.1	0.0	0.0	0.0
Cash Flow to Total Debt 44	0.0	•	3.0	0.9	0.5	0.2	0.2	0.1	0.1	0.0	0.0	0.0	0.0

Selected Financial Factors (in Percentages)

Debt Ratio 45	90.3	•	40.7	48.3	57.2	75.9	78.3	78.5	84.6	86.0	86.5	84.5	91.4
Return on Total Assets 46	8.4	•	51.2	21.1	23.8	9.1	9.6	5.7	4.4	4.2	4.8	5.0	7.4
Return on Equity Before Income Taxes 47	13.6	•	79.0	35.1	28.7	24.0	25.8	12.9	10.3	9.7	11.9	11.2	11.0
Return on Equity After Income Taxes 48	9.5	•	77.8	34.0	27.8	22.0	23.5	11.3	8.6	7.5	8.6	7.9	7.4
Profit Margin (Before Income Tax) 49	10.0	12.2	12.1	6.0	16.5	16.1	15.4	17.3	13.5	13.9	15.8	16.7	8.5
Profit Margin (After Income Tax) 50	7.0	8.5	12.0	5.8	16.0	14.7	14.0	15.2	11.3	10.7	11.5	11.7	5.7

Table I

Corporations with and without Net Income

COMMERCIAL BANKING

MONEY AMOUNTS AND SIZE OF ASSETS IN THOUSANDS OF DOLLARS

Item Description for Accounting Period 7/07 Through 6/08	Total	Zero Assets	Under 500	500 to 1,000	1,000 to 5,000	5,000 to 10,000	10,000 to 25,000	25,000 to 50,000	50,000 to 100,000	100,000 to 250,000	250,000 to 500,000	500,000 to 2,500,000	2,500,000 and over
Number of Enterprises **1**	1733	227	0	0	34	11	159	281	418	419	114	60	9
Revenues ($ in Thousands)													
Net Sales **2**	108809364	91857729	0	0	24357	15414	226317	687942	1943679	4598576	2832089	4305852	2317407
Interest **3**	99103820	88465505	0	0	3273	3965	118113	348482	1215971	2716847	1739362	2765432	1726870
Rents **4**	324005	175174	0	0	5157	27	166	629	1976	4804	5060	10598	120413
Royalties **5**	165	35	0	0	0	0	0	0	0	82	3	0	45
Other Portfolio Income **6**	1728254	1318299	0	0	106	5	4287	14405	57985	116710	64770	83817	67868
Other Receipts **7**	7653120	1898716	0	0	15821	11417	103751	324426	667747	1760133	1022894	1446005	402211
Total Receipts **8**	108809364	91857729	0	0	24357	15414	226317	687942	1943679	4598576	2832089	4305852	2317407
Average Total Receipts **9**	62787	404660	•	•	716	1401	1423	2448	4650	10975	24843	71764	257490
Operating Costs/Operating Income (%)													
Cost of Operations **10**	0.0	•	•	•	•	0.4	•	•	•	•	•	•	•
Salaries and Wages **11**	6.3	5.1	•	•	14.5	22.7	18.8	14.9	14.8	13.6	13.0	12.8	8.2
Taxes Paid **12**	1.6	1.5	•	•	4.7	2.7	2.8	2.9	2.8	2.6	2.4	2.5	2.3
Interest Paid **13**	83.5	91.6	•	•	36.4	1.1	21.9	32.4	37.6	38.5	41.1	41.4	43.8
Depreciation **14**	0.9	0.5	•	•	7.3	1.3	2.5	2.9	2.8	2.3	2.3	1.8	7.7
Amortization and Depletion **15**	0.2	0.1	•	•	1.9	•	0.3	0.6	0.7	0.7	0.3	0.3	0.4
Pensions and Other Deferred Comp. **16**	0.3	0.2	•	•	0.6	0.3	0.6	0.9	0.7	0.7	0.6	0.8	0.6
Employee Benefits **17**	0.6	0.3	•	•	2.4	1.9	3.4	3.1	2.7	2.2	1.8	1.6	1.7
Advertising **18**	0.2	0.1	•	•	0.6	0.4	1.2	1.2	1.2	0.9	0.8	0.6	0.5
Other Expenses **19**	18.1	18.2	•	•	13.2	108.2	30.0	24.8	20.8	19.1	16.1	15.0	13.4
Officers' Compensation **20**	1.3	0.5	•	•	7.2	12.5	9.3	11.5	9.0	6.0	5.2	2.6	6.0
Operating Margin **21**	•	•	•	•	11.1	•	9.3	4.7	7.0	13.5	16.3	20.6	15.4
Operating Margin Before Officers' Comp. **22**	•	•	•	•	18.3	•	18.5	16.2	16.0	19.5	21.5	23.2	21.5

Selected Average Balance Sheet ($ in Thousands)

Net Receivables 23	78976	•	1377	878	8970	22134	44307	99397	222041	500487	1517012
Inventories 24	•	•	•	•	•	•	•	•	•	•	•
Net Property, Plant and Equipment 25	2353	0	2101	267	342	784	1498	3155	5842	13588	33295
Total Assets 26	140623	•	4404	7215	18196	37167	71245	153605	350559	1003935	3976866
Notes and Loans Payable 27	7449	0	0	51	130	566	1608	5187	16356	80007	357707
All Other Liabilities 28	116474	0	2808	68926	13781	29805	59278	129640	298355	816594	3147041
Net Worth 29	16700	0	1596	-61762	4284	6796	10360	18779	35847	107335	472118

Selected Financial Ratios (Times to 1)

Current Ratio 30	1.0	•	0.7	0.1	1.3	1.1	1.0	1.0	0.9	0.9	1.0
Quick Ratio 31	0.9	•	0.7	0.1	1.2	1.1	1.0	1.0	0.9	0.9	0.9
Net Sales to Working Capital 32	•	0.8	•	•	0.4	0.7	3.2	•	•	•	•
Coverage Ratio 33	0.8	•	1.3	•	1.3	1.1	1.3	1.3	1.4	1.5	1.3
Total Asset Turnover 34	0.4	•	0.2	0.2	0.1	0.1	0.1	0.1	0.1	0.1	0.1
Inventory Turnover 35	•	•	•	•	•	•	•	•	•	•	•
Receivables Turnover 36	•	•	•	•	•	•	•	•	•	•	•
Total Liabilities to Net Worth 37	7.4	•	1.8	•	3.2	4.5	5.9	7.2	8.8	8.4	7.4
Current Assets to Working Capital 38	•	•	•	•	4.6	9.8	42.6	•	•	•	•
Current Liabilities to Working Capital 39	•	•	•	•	3.6	8.8	41.6	•	•	•	•
Working Capital to Net Sales 40	•	•	•	•	2.5	1.4	0.3	•	•	•	•
Inventory to Working Capital 41	•	•	•	•	•	•	0.0	•	•	•	•
Total Receipts to Cash Flow 42	51.8	•	4.5	1.9	2.8	3.8	4.1	3.4	3.4	3.0	3.9
Cost of Goods to Cash Flow 43	0.0	•	•	0.0	•	•	•	•	•	•	•
Cash Flow to Total Debt 44	0.0	•	0.1	0.0	0.0	0.0	0.0	0.0	0.0	0.0	0.0

Selected Financial Factors (in Percentages)

Debt Ratio 45	88.1	•	63.8	956.0	76.5	81.7	85.5	87.8	89.8	89.3	88.1
Return on Total Assets 46	31.3	•	7.7	•	2.3	2.3	2.8	3.6	4.0	4.3	3.8
Return on Equity Before Income Taxes 47	•	•	4.8	1.2	2.5	1.1	2.3	6.7	10.3	12.7	8.1
Return on Equity After Income Taxes 48	•	•	4.8	1.2	2.2	0.4	1.5	5.1	7.7	9.4	5.6
Profit Margin (Before Income Tax) 49	•	•	10.7	•	7.6	3.0	5.2	11.5	14.8	19.0	14.9
Profit Margin (After Income Tax) 50	•	•	10.7	•	6.6	1.1	3.3	8.8	11.2	14.1	10.3

Table II

Corporations with Net Income

COMMERCIAL BANKING

Money Amounts and Size of Assets in Thousands of Dollars

Item Description for Accounting Period 7/07 Through 6/08	Total	Zero Assets	Under 500	500 to 1,000	1,000 to 5,000	5,000 to 10,000	10,000 to 25,000	25,000 to 50,000	50,000 to 100,000	100,000 to 250,000	250,000 to 500,000	500,000 to 2,500,000	2,500,000 and over
Number of Enterprises **1**	1265	154	0	0	3	0	•	190	285	356	105	•	9

Revenues ($ in Thousands)

	Total	Zero Assets	Under 500	500 to 1,000	1,000 to 5,000	5,000 to 10,000	10,000 to 25,000	25,000 to 50,000	50,000 to 100,000	100,000 to 250,000	250,000 to 500,000	500,000 to 2,500,000	2,500,000 and over
Net Sales **2**	66665930	51305087	0	0	27692	0	•	535848	1419210	4085463	2629582	•	2317407
Interest **3**	49742264	40304094	0	0	585	0	•	228444	799484	2327957	1609993	•	1726870
Rents **4**	293729	151195	0	0	27	0	•	502	1639	4461	4800	•	120413
Royalties **5**	142	12	0	0	0	0	•	0	0	82	3	•	45
Other Portfolio Income **6**	797113	416949	0	0	19	0	•	12357	45502	109437	58237	•	67868
Other Receipts **7**	15832682	10432837	0	0	27061	0	•	294545	572585	1643526	956549	•	402211
Total Receipts **8**	66665930	51305087	0	0	27692	0	•	535848	1419210	4085463	2629582	•	2317407
Average Total Receipts **9**	52700	333150	•	•	9231	•	•	2820	4980	11476	25044	•	257490

Operating Costs/Operating Income (%)

	Total	Zero Assets	Under 500	500 to 1,000	1,000 to 5,000	5,000 to 10,000	10,000 to 25,000	25,000 to 50,000	50,000 to 100,000	100,000 to 250,000	250,000 to 500,000	500,000 to 2,500,000	2,500,000 and over
Cost of Operations **10**	0.0	•	•	•	0.2	•	•	•	•	•	•	•	•
Salaries and Wages **11**	5.7	3.8	•	•	20.5	•	•	13.0	12.4	12.7	12.6	•	8.2
Taxes Paid **12**	2.1	2.0	•	•	3.0	•	•	2.6	2.7	2.6	2.4	•	2.3
Interest Paid **13**	64.4	71.9	•	•	18.8	•	•	31.0	36.4	37.5	40.7	•	43.8
Depreciation **14**	1.0	0.5	•	•	1.5	•	•	1.8	2.3	2.1	2.3	•	7.7
Amortization and Depletion **15**	0.1	0.1	•	•	0.6	•	•	0.2	0.3	0.7	0.3	•	0.4
Pensions and Other Deferred Comp. **16**	0.3	0.2	•	•	0.7	•	•	1.0	0.7	0.7	0.6	•	0.6
Employee Benefits **17**	0.7	0.3	•	•	2.2	•	•	2.9	2.5	2.1	1.8	•	1.7
Advertising **18**	0.2	0.0	•	•	0.6	•	•	0.9	0.9	0.8	0.8	•	0.5
Other Expenses **19**	11.3	9.9	•	•	24.5	•	•	18.4	17.1	18.2	14.7	•	13.4
Officers' Compensation **20**	1.5	0.4	•	•	11.5	•	•	9.4	8.2	5.9	5.0	•	6.0
Operating Margin **21**	12.6	10.9	•	•	15.9	•	•	18.9	16.5	16.7	18.7	•	15.4
Operating Margin Before Officers' Comp. **22**	14.1	11.3	•	•	27.5	•	•	28.3	24.7	22.6	23.8	•	21.5

Selected Average Balance Sheet ($ in Thousands)

Net Receivables 23	94852	0	2807	22707	43286	101094	225657	1517012
Inventories 24	•	•	•	•	•	•	•	•
Net Property, Plant and Equipment 25	2597	0	1225	582	1382	3092	5693	33295
Total Assets 26	170095	0	6656	38328	72095	155443	355096	3976866
Notes and Loans Payable 27	9507	0	85	584	1714	5338	16381	357707
All Other Liabilities 28	141057	0	3232	31676	61530	131653	301850	3147041
Net Worth 29	19531	0	3339	6068	8852	18452	36865	472118

Selected Financial Ratios (Times to 1)

Current Ratio 30	1.0	1.5	1.1	1.0	1.0	1.0	1.0	1.0
Quick Ratio 31	0.9	1.5	1.1	1.0	1.0	1.0	0.9	0.9
Net Sales to Working Capital 32	•	5.7	1.0	55.6	•	•	•	•
Coverage Ratio 33	1.2	1.8	1.5	1.4	1.4	1.4	1.4	1.3
Total Asset Turnover 34	0.3	1.4	0.1	0.1	0.1	0.1	0.1	0.1
Inventory Turnover 35	•	•	•	•	•	•	•	•
Receivables Turnover 36	•	•	•	•	•	•	•	•
Total Liabilities to Net Worth 37	7.7	1.0	5.3	7.1	7.4	7.4	8.6	7.4
Current Assets to Working Capital 38	•	3.0	11.8	696.1	•	•	•	•
Current Liabilities to Working Capital 39	•	2.0	10.8	695.1	•	•	•	•
Working Capital to Net Sales 40	•	0.2	1.0	0.0	•	•	•	•
Inventory to Working Capital 41	•	•	•	1.0	•	•	•	•
Total Receipts to Cash Flow 42	4.5	2.7	2.9	3.2	3.1	3.1	3.3	3.9
Cost of Goods to Cash Flow 43	0.0	0.0	0.0	0.0	0.0	0.0	0.0	0.0
Cash Flow to Total Debt 44	0.1	1.0	0.0	0.0	0.0	0.0	0.0	0.0

Selected Financial Factors (in Percentages)

Debt Ratio 45	88.5	49.8	84.2	87.7	88.1	89.6	88.1	88.1
Return on Total Assets 46	23.7	48.0	3.5	3.5	3.8	4.1	3.8	3.8
Return on Equity Before Income Taxes 47	32.8	43.8	7.9	8.1	9.1	11.7	8.1	8.1
Return on Equity After Income Taxes 48	23.4	43.7	6.8	6.6	7.1	9.0	6.6	5.6
Profit Margin (Before Income Tax) 49	12.1	10.8	15.8	17.0	14.4	14.6	17.2	14.9
Profit Margin (After Income Tax) 50	8.7	7.5	14.5	11.8	11.5	13.2	11.8	10.3

Table I

Corporations with and without Net Income

SAVINGS INSTITUTIONS AND OTHER DEPOSITORY CREDIT

MONEY AMOUNTS AND SIZE OF ASSETS IN THOUSANDS OF DOLLARS

Item Description for Accounting Period 7/07 Through 6/08		Total	Zero Assets	Under 500	500 to 1,000	1,000 to 5,000	5,000 to 10,000	10,000 to 25,000	25,000 to 50,000	50,000 to 100,000	100,000 to 250,000	250,000 to 500,000	500,000 to 2,500,000	2,500,000 and over
Number of Enterprises	1	1195	27	7	0	45	14	53	124	156	282	214	212	61
Revenues ($ in Thousands)														
Net Sales	2	103809061	8639035	16321	0	158227	18142	77220	634971	720690	3189240	5264785	14122728	70967703
Interest	3	78525930	7097959	166	0	80193	5765	39958	438220	593677	2407847	3973154	10519398	53369593
Rents	4	254937	3685	0	0	213	22	1054	733	1884	7693	9795	64732	165128
Royalties	5	2327	0	0	0	0	0	0	23	0	0	0	1414	889
Other Portfolio Income	6	3216135	14225	0	0	165	24	12582	7336	22663	76876	213139	483869	2385255
Other Receipts	7	21809732	1523166	16155	0	77656	12331	23626	188659	102466	696824	1068697	3053315	15046838
Total Receipts	8	103809061	8639035	16321	0	158227	18142	77220	634971	720690	3189240	5264785	14122728	70967703
Average Total Receipts	9	86870	319964	2332	•	3516	1296	1457	5121	4620	11309	24602	66617	1163405
Operating Costs/Operating Income (%)														
Cost of Operations	10	0.1	•	•	•	•	•	•	0.0	0.2	0.2	•	0.2	0.1
Salaries and Wages	11	13.1	14.9	0.9	•	21.1	9.5	9.3	20.0	12.9	17.2	14.1	13.8	12.4
Taxes Paid	12	1.7	2.0	0.2	•	3.5	2.0	1.8	1.4	2.8	2.7	2.3	2.2	1.5
Interest Paid	13	52.5	54.3	235.0	•	75.5	49.0	39.5	34.8	44.5	40.7	44.3	46.4	54.8
Depreciation	14	1.6	0.5	0.3	•	1.4	0.6	1.4	1.4	2.1	2.0	4.0	1.9	1.4
Amortization and Depletion	15	2.7	0.1	0.8	•	0.2	•	0.2	1.5	0.1	0.1	0.3	1.1	3.7
Pensions and Other Deferred Comp.	16	0.6	0.2	•	•	1.0	0.0	0.7	0.8	1.7	1.7	1.4	1.3	0.4
Employee Benefits	17	1.8	0.7	•	•	2.1	•	1.9	2.4	2.4	2.4	2.4	2.1	1.8
Advertising	18	1.3	0.3	•	•	0.3	0.3	0.7	0.8	1.0	1.3	1.0	1.2	1.4
Other Expenses	19	20.2	8.1	80.9	•	34.0	13.8	13.7	60.5	19.0	18.3	19.7	16.7	22.1
Officers' Compensation	20	1.1	1.0	0.7	•	0.9	5.4	5.7	4.0	6.7	5.3	3.1	2.0	0.5
Operating Margin	21	3.4	17.9	•	•	•	19.3	25.0	•	6.5	8.1	7.4	11.2	•
Operating Margin Before Officers' Comp.	22	4.5	18.9	•	•	•	24.8	30.7	•	13.2	13.5	10.5	13.2	0.5

Selected Average Balance Sheet ($ in Thousands)

Net Receivables 23	70277	0	9	975	826	1668	4505	6605	19285	38395	85904	825932
Inventories 24	•	•	•	•	•	•	•	•	•	•	•	•
Net Property, Plant and Equipment 25	12508	0	0	27	259	94	725	1587	3236	6586	15402	147633
Total Assets 26	1126028	•	234	2200	7177	16949	37359	74157	164666	358449	967404	16394573
Notes and Loans Payable 27	215852	0	2	406	501	2242	1784	4942	14576	33016	114441	3629001
All Other Liabilities 28	825609	145842	65848	5758	11447	27512	58361	129190	280527	739915	•	11739168
Net Worth 29	84567	-145610	-64054	918	3259	8064	10854	20900	44905	113048	•	1026404

Selected Financial Ratios (Times to 1)

Current Ratio 30	0.3	•	0.0	0.0	0.2	0.3	0.4	0.3	0.3	0.3	0.3	0.2
Quick Ratio 31	0.2	•	0.0	0.0	0.2	0.3	0.4	0.3	0.3	0.3	0.2	0.1
Net Sales to Working Capital 32	•	•	•	•	•	•	•	•	•	•	•	•
Coverage Ratio 33	1.1	1.3	0.1	0.5	1.4	1.6	0.2	1.1	1.2	1.1	1.2	1.0
Total Asset Turnover 34	0.1	0.1	10.0	1.6	0.2	0.1	0.1	0.1	0.1	0.1	0.1	0.1
Inventory Turnover 35	•	•	•	•	•	•	•	•	•	•	•	•
Receivables Turnover 36	•	•	•	•	•	•	•	•	•	•	•	•
Total Liabilities to Net Worth 37	12.3	•	•	6.8	4.2	3.6	5.8	6.9	7.0	7.6	•	15.0
Current Assets to Working Capital 38	•	•	•	•	•	•	•	•	•	•	•	•
Current Liabilities to Working Capital 39	•	•	•	•	•	•	•	•	•	•	•	•
Working Capital to Net Sales 40	•	•	•	•	•	•	•	•	•	•	•	•
Inventory to Working Capital 41	•	•	•	•	•	•	•	•	•	•	•	•
Total Receipts to Cash Flow 42	6.8	4.3	•	3.1	4.5	5.6	4.6	4.3	4.6	5.6	4.1	9.3
Cost of Goods to Cash Flow 43	0.0	0.0	•	•	0.0	0.0	0.0	0.0	0.0	0.0	0.0	0.0
Cash Flow to Total Debt 44	0.0	0.0	•	0.1	0.0	0.0	0.0	0.0	0.0	0.0	0.0	0.0

Selected Financial Factors (in Percentages)

Debt Ratio 45	92.5	62288.5	3011.2	80.8	87.2	78.4	85.4	87.3	87.5	88.3	•	93.7
Return on Total Assets 46	4.3	161.8	56.6	5.5	12.3	0.9	3.1	3.3	3.5	3.9	•	•
Return on Equity Before Income Taxes 47	3.0	3.5	2.2	2.4	27.3	11.2	2.4	3.9	3.5	6.2	•	•
Return on Equity After Income Taxes 48	0.1	3.5	2.4	27.3	10.6	1.2	2.2	1.7	4.1	•	•	•
Profit Margin (Before Income Tax) 49	2.9	17.9	19.3	24.9	5.6	7.1	6.4	10.5	•	•	•	•
Profit Margin (After Income Tax) 50	0.1	11.7	19.3	23.8	2.7	4.1	3.2	7.0	•	•	•	•

Table II

Corporations with Net Income

SAVINGS INSTITUTIONS AND OTHER DEPOSITORY CREDIT

MONEY AMOUNTS AND SIZE OF ASSETS IN THOUSANDS OF DOLLARS

Item Description for Accounting Period 7/07 Through 6/08	Total	Zero Assets	Under 500	500 to 1,000	1,000 to 5,000	5,000 to 10,000	10,000 to 25,000	25,000 to 50,000	50,000 to 100,000	100,000 to 250,000	250,000 to 500,000	500,000 to 2,500,000	2,500,000 and over
Number of Enterprises **1**	902	12	•	0	0	0	42	77	118	222	188	•	51
Revenues ($ in Thousands)													
Net Sales **2**	88664768	8514061	•	0	0	0	72093	215306	563070	2532103	4379955	•	59982104
Interest **3**	66057575	7011107	•	0	0	0	35190	145186	468776	1863950	3422148	•	43533125
Rents **4**	238974	3597	•	0	0	0	1054	394	1262	6495	9119	•	161371
Royalties **5**	2091	0	•	0	0	0	0	23	0	0	0	•	654
Other Portfolio Income **6**	2919381	13266	•	0	0	0	12548	6379	19609	62147	189138	•	2224820
Other Receipts **7**	19446747	1486091	•	0	0	0	23301	63324	73423	599511	759550	•	14062134
Total Receipts **8**	88664768	8514061	•	0	0	0	72093	215306	563070	2532103	4379955	•	59982104
Average Total Receipts **9**	98298	709505	•	•	•	•	1716	2796	4772	11406	23298	•	1176120
Operating Costs/Operating Income (%)													
Cost of Operations **10**	0.1	•	•	•	•	•	•	0.1	0.0	•	•	•	0.1
Salaries and Wages **11**	12.5	14.8	•	•	•	•	8.3	15.5	11.1	17.1	13.4	•	11.8
Taxes Paid **12**	1.7	2.0	•	•	•	•	1.6	2.7	2.7	2.8	2.5	•	1.5
Interest Paid **13**	51.2	54.5	•	•	•	•	40.0	36.1	44.1	38.5	45.2	•	52.9
Depreciation **14**	1.4	0.5	•	•	•	•	1.1	1.7	1.9	2.0	2.0	•	1.4
Amortization and Depletion **15**	2.9	0.1	•	•	•	•	0.0	0.1	0.0	0.1	0.2	•	4.0
Pensions and Other Deferred Comp. **16**	0.7	0.2	•	•	•	•	0.7	1.3	1.8	1.6	1.5	•	0.5
Employee Benefits **17**	1.8	0.6	•	•	•	•	1.5	2.4	2.3	2.3	2.4	•	1.8
Advertising **18**	1.2	0.3	•	•	•	•	0.5	0.8	0.8	1.2	1.1	•	1.4
Other Expenses **19**	14.2	7.7	•	•	•	•	10.6	18.7	15.4	16.9	14.2	•	14.8
Officers' Compensation **20**	1.1	0.7	•	•	•	•	4.1	7.6	6.8	4.8	3.4	•	0.5
Operating Margin **21**	11.3	18.6	•	•	•	•	31.4	13.0	13.1	12.6	14.1	•	9.4
Operating Margin Before Officers' Comp. **22**	12.3	19.4	•	•	•	•	35.5	20.5	19.9	17.4	17.5	•	9.9

Selected Average Balance Sheet ($ in Thousands)

Net Receivables 23	75487	•	•	1787	5368	7140	18648	36318	789697
Inventories 24	•	•	•	•	•	•	•	•	•
Net Property, Plant and Equipment 25	14191	•	•	174	608	1445	3201	6702	150739
Total Assets 26	1250480	•	•	16770	38197	75063	164498	359272	16314267
Notes and Loans Payable 27	232515	•	•	2707	1810	4133	14537	31423	3510463
All Other Liabilities 28	918843	•	•	11240	28840	59999	128189	283741	11770962
Net Worth 29	99122	•	•	2823	7547	10931	21772	44108	1032842

Selected Financial Ratios (Times to 1)

Current Ratio 30	0.3	•	•	0.3	0.4	0.3	0.3	0.3	0.2
Quick Ratio 31	0.2	•	•	0.3	0.4	0.3	0.3	0.3	0.1
Net Sales to Working Capital 32	•	•	•	•	•	•	•	•	•
Coverage Ratio 33	1.2	1.3	•	1.8	1.3	1.3	1.3	1.3	1.2
Total Asset Turnover 34	0.1	•	•	0.1	0.1	0.1	0.1	0.1	0.1
Inventory Turnover 35	•	•	•	•	•	•	•	•	•
Receivables Turnover 36	•	•	•	•	•	•	•	•	•
Total Liabilities to Net Worth 37	11.6	•	•	4.9	4.1	5.9	6.6	7.1	14.8
Current Assets to Working Capital 38	•	•	•	•	•	•	•	•	•
Current Liabilities to Working Capital 39	•	•	•	•	•	•	•	•	•
Working Capital to Net Sales 40	•	•	•	•	•	•	•	•	•
Inventory to Working Capital 41	•	•	•	•	•	•	•	•	•
Total Receipts to Cash Flow 42	5.1	4.3	•	4.0	3.4	4.0	3.7	4.1	5.9
Cost of Goods to Cash Flow 43	0.0	•	•	0.0	0.0	0.0	0.0	•	0.0
Cash Flow to Total Debt 44	0.0	•	•	0.0	0.0	0.0	0.0	0.0	0.0

Selected Financial Factors (in Percentages)

Debt Ratio 45	92.1	•	•	83.2	80.2	85.4	86.8	87.7	93.7
Return on Total Assets 46	4.9	•	•	7.3	3.5	3.6	3.5	3.8	4.5
Return on Equity Before Income Taxes 47	10.7	•	•	19.1	4.5	5.3	6.1	6.9	10.1
Return on Equity After Income Taxes 48	7.4	•	•	18.3	3.4	3.7	4.2	4.9	7.1
Profit Margin (Before Income Tax) 49	10.8	18.6	•	31.4	12.1	12.2	11.7	13.1	8.9
Profit Margin (After Income Tax) 50	7.5	12.4	•	30.1	9.2	8.6	8.0	9.2	6.2

Table I

Corporations with and without Net Income

CREDIT CARD ISSUING AND OTHER CONSUMER CREDIT

MONEY AMOUNTS AND SIZE OF ASSETS IN THOUSANDS OF DOLLARS

Item Description for Accounting Period 7/07 Through 6/08	Total	Zero Assets	Under 500	500 to 1,000	1,000 to 5,000	5,000 to 10,000	10,000 to 25,000	25,000 to 50,000	50,000 to 100,000	100,000 to 250,000	250,000 to 500,000	500,000 to 2,500,000	2,500,000 and over
Number of Enterprises 1	8179	1101	3806	433	1875	440	266	83	57	43	25	29	21
Revenues ($ in Thousands)													
Net Sales 2	103116981	228939	923176	127451	1913169	1940996	1563307	724108	1160782	2116648	3258987	9159512	79999905
Interest 3	36380277	22122	177488	635	66358	105729	73154	43727	289605	324324	602823	3693428	30980885
Rents 4	51579	0	0	1	3299	479	739	477	1191	1762	2	1504	42125
Royalties 5	57584	0	0	0	0	0	0	0	12563	34199	0	10822	0
Other Portfolio Income 6	1876377	14623	536	49	13358	3910	60803	11171	12610	13730	28333	29214	1688043
Other Receipts 7	64751164	192194	745152	126766	1830154	1830878	1428611	668733	844813	1742633	2627829	5424544	47288852
Total Receipts 8	103116981	228939	923176	127451	1913169	1940996	1563307	724108	1160782	2116648	3258987	9159512	79999905
Average Total Receipts 9	12608	208	243	294	1020	4411	5877	8724	20365	49224	130359	315845	3809519
Operating Costs/Operating Income (%)													
Cost of Operations 10	0.2	•	•	•	•	0.1	0.0	0.5	0.5	0.7	0.1	0.1	0.3
Salaries and Wages 11	9.2	13.0	15.8	3.9	18.9	22.5	26.4	20.7	18.2	15.5	22.4	14.3	6.7
Taxes Paid 12	1.1	1.0	1.0	6.9	2.2	2.7	2.5	2.7	2.2	2.3	3.5	1.6	0.8
Interest Paid 13	27.5	18.4	21.6	6.1	8.6	10.8	14.2	12.7	23.2	19.7	18.3	17.7	30.6
Depreciation 14	7.9	0.7	0.7	0.2	3.9	3.3	2.2	1.1	1.5	1.5	1.3	1.5	9.7
Amortization and Depletion 15	0.9	0.7	•	0.0	1.0	0.7	•	0.6	1.0	2.2	0.5	0.9	1.0
Pensions and Other Deferred Comp. 16	0.4	0.1	0.1	•	0.7	0.1	0.5	0.5	0.8	0.1	0.3	0.1	0.5
Employee Benefits 17	0.7	0.2	0.2	0.0	0.4	1.1	1.5	1.2	1.4	1.2	2.0	0.6	0.7
Advertising 18	2.8	0.0	1.2	1.0	1.4	4.8	2.0	3.3	2.0	2.5	1.8	2.9	2.9
Other Expenses 19	42.7	91.2	44.7	53.6	48.6	50.3	45.0	36.8	38.4	44.4	36.2	50.6	41.6
Officers' Compensation 20	0.7	0.8	9.6	0.1	6.1	2.3	6.0	3.8	4.8	3.6	0.8	0.6	0.2
Operating Margin 21	5.7	•	5.3	28.2	8.1	1.2	1.1	15.9	6.0	6.2	12.7	9.0	5.1
Operating Margin Before Officers' Comp. 22	6.4	•	14.9	28.3	14.2	3.5	7.1	19.8	10.7	9.9	13.6	9.6	5.3

Selected Average Balance Sheet ($ in Thousands)

	1	2	3	4	5	6	7	8	9	10	11	12
Net Receivables 23	44882	104	384	1462	6071	10481	25104	45062	103225	189579	757214	15358905
Inventories 24	•	0	0	0	0	•	•	•	•	•	•	•
Net Property, Plant and Equipment 25	3534	9	1	61	715	860	695	3515	2370	7165	8887	1305552
Total Assets 26	75305	225	799	2058	6922	15313	34522	70244	160857	330151	1198748	26044512
Notes and Loans Payable 27	42014	137	277	911	3802	9359	19111	40351	90969	207109	775399	14364694
All Other Liabilities 28	23226	62	63	319	536	2591	6268	12753	30505	74497	186723	8492374
Net Worth 29	10065	26	459	827	2584	3362	9143	17140	39384	48545	236627	3187444

Selected Financial Ratios (Times to 1)

	1	2	3	4	5	6	7	8	9	10	11	12
Current Ratio 30	1.7	4.0	5.7	3.0	4.9	2.0	2.3	2.1	2.3	2.0	1.7	1.7
Quick Ratio 31	1.7	2.9	3.3	2.9	4.6	1.8	2.0	1.8	2.0	1.9	1.7	1.7
Net Sales to Working Capital 32	0.6	1.8	0.4	0.9	0.8	1.0	0.5	0.7	0.7	1.2	0.9	0.5
Coverage Ratio 33	1.2	1.2	5.6	1.9	1.1	1.1	2.2	1.3	1.3	1.7	1.5	1.2
Total Asset Turnover 34	0.2	1.1	0.4	0.5	0.6	0.4	0.3	0.3	0.3	0.4	0.3	0.1
Inventory Turnover 35	•	•	•	•	•	•	•	•	•	•	•	•
Receivables Turnover 36	•	•	•	•	•	•	•	•	•	•	•	•
Total Liabilities to Net Worth 37	6.5	7.8	0.7	1.5	1.7	3.6	2.8	3.1	3.1	5.8	4.1	7.2
Current Assets to Working Capital 38	2.4	1.3	1.2	1.5	1.3	2.0	1.8	1.9	1.8	2.0	2.4	2.4
Current Liabilities to Working Capital 39	1.4	0.3	0.2	0.5	0.3	1.0	0.8	0.9	0.8	1.0	1.4	1.4
Working Capital to Net Sales 40	1.8	0.6	2.2	1.2	1.3	1.0	1.9	1.5	1.5	0.9	1.2	1.9
Inventory to Working Capital 41	0.0	•	•	•	•	•	•	•	•	•	0.0	0.0
Total Receipts to Cash Flow 42	2.2	2.4	1.3	1.9	2.3	2.4	2.1	2.4	2.2	2.4	1.7	2.2
Cost of Goods to Cash Flow 43	0.0	•	•	•	0.0	0.0	0.0	0.0	0.0	0.0	0.0	0.0
Cash Flow to Total Debt 44	0.1	0.5	0.7	0.4	0.4	0.2	0.2	0.2	0.2	0.2	0.2	0.1

Selected Financial Factors (in Percentages)

	1	2	3	4	5	6	7	8	9	10	11	12
Debt Ratio 45	86.6	88.6	42.5	59.8	62.7	78.0	73.5	75.6	75.5	85.3	80.3	87.8
Return on Total Assets 46	5.6	28.9	12.6	8.3	7.6	5.9	7.2	8.4	7.9	12.3	7.0	5.3
Return on Equity Before Income Taxes 47	7.4	49.6	18.1	10.0	2.1	1.9	15.2	7.0	7.8	34.3	12.0	6.4
Return on Equity After Income Taxes 48	3.6	49.4	16.8	9.3	1.0	0.4	12.5	5.6	5.8	17.3	7.7	2.7
Profit Margin (Before Income Tax) 49	5.9	5.2	28.2	8.1	1.2	1.1	15.9	5.9	6.2	12.8	9.0	5.4
Profit Margin (After Income Tax) 50	2.9	5.2	26.2	7.6	0.6	0.2	13.1	4.7	4.6	6.4	5.8	2.2

Table II

Corporations with Net Income

CREDIT CARD ISSUING AND OTHER CONSUMER CREDIT

MONEY AMOUNTS AND SIZE OF ASSETS IN THOUSANDS OF DOLLARS

Item Description for Accounting Period 7/07 Through 6/08	Total	Zero Assets	Under 500	500 to 1,000	1,000 to 5,000	5,000 to 10,000	10,000 to 25,000	25,000 to 50,000	50,000 to 100,000	100,000 to 250,000	250,000 to 500,000	500,000 to 2,500,000	2,500,000 and over
Number of Enterprises 1	4706	647	1548	376	1428	319	206	56	40	29	20	23	13
Revenues ($ in Thousands)													
Net Sales 2	73576546	208369	667903	84846	1375808	973378	1246395	654609	828520	1179978	3104450	6783049	56465241
Interest 3	25270710	21355	3270	635	57993	58654	38997	37315	123221	243426	537591	1942954	22205298
Rents 4	46763	0	0	0	3242	11	308	374	249	0	2	452	42125
Royalties 5	34199	0	0	0	0	0	0	0	0	34199	0	0	0
Other Portfolio Income 6	1135777	14623	458	12	12309	3883	16085	7516	9658	11763	28333	29140	1001996
Other Receipts 7	47089097	172391	664175	84199	1302264	910830	1191005	609404	695392	890590	2538524	4810503	33219822
Total Receipts 8	73576546	208369	667903	84846	1375808	973378	1246395	654609	828520	1179978	3104450	6783049	56465241
Average Total Receipts 9	15635	322	431	226	963	3051	6050	11689	20713	40689	155222	294915	4343788
Operating Costs/Operating Income (%)													
Cost of Operations 10	0.1	•	•	•	•	•	•	0.6	•	1.2	0.1	0.2	0.1
Salaries and Wages 11	10.0	12.8	13.1	5.7	18.1	19.3	19.9	20.4	20.3	14.1	23.0	17.0	7.5
Taxes Paid 12	1.4	0.9	0.6	9.7	2.7	1.7	2.1	2.8	2.7	2.4	3.6	2.0	1.0
Interest Paid 13	20.1	16.7	0.4	8.7	8.1	11.3	12.8	10.4	13.2	17.5	11.9	13.9	22.5
Depreciation 14	0.8	0.1	0.1	0.3	1.4	1.6	2.1	0.9	1.6	1.6	1.4	1.7	0.6
Amortization and Depletion 15	1.1	0.1	•	0.0	0.4	0.3	0.4	0.7	0.3	3.7	0.5	1.0	1.1
Pensions and Other Deferred Comp. 16	0.4	0.1	•	•	0.9	0.1	0.6	0.6	1.1	0.1	0.3	0.1	0.4
Employee Benefits 17	0.7	0.1	0.2	0.0	0.3	1.2	1.3	1.1	1.7	1.2	2.1	0.7	0.6
Advertising 18	3.5	0.0	0.9	1.0	1.5	1.8	1.9	3.2	0.7	1.1	1.8	1.9	4.0
Other Expenses 19	47.4	55.5	42.9	30.9	37.6	40.3	37.1	33.5	35.6	37.9	33.7	44.2	49.7
Officers' Compensation 20	0.8	0.8	12.4	0.1	7.8	3.8	5.2	3.7	5.7	1.4	0.8	0.7	0.2
Operating Margin 21	13.7	13.1	29.4	43.5	21.2	18.4	16.7	22.1	17.1	17.6	20.7	16.5	12.2
Operating Margin Before Officers' Comp. 22	14.5	13.9	41.8	43.6	28.9	22.2	21.9	25.8	22.7	19.0	21.5	17.3	12.4

Selected Average Balance Sheet ($ in Thousands)

Net Receivables 23	50492	0	55	368	1445	5089	11120	24337	47252	97360	196209	738130	15725963
Inventories 24	•	•	•	•	•	•	•	•	•	•	•	•	•
Net Property, Plant and Equipment 25	598	•	0	0	1	171	817	906	4080	2074	8915	7776	147734
Total Assets 26	84624	250	840	2066	6844	15055	36047	68235	155111	332737	1063369		26841934
Notes and Loans Payable 27	37020	60	296	812	3983	8935	20087	42983	85881	126030	615376		11363944
All Other Liabilities 28	32419	61	23	224	438	2793	4681	11572	27834	88445	182187		11071704
Net Worth 29	15186	129	521	1029	2423	3327	11278	13680	41397	118261	265807		4406285

Selected Financial Ratios (Times to 1)

Current Ratio 30	1.7	•	10.7	7.5	3.9	3.8	2.2	2.2	2.3	2.1	1.9	2.0	1.7
Quick Ratio 31	1.7	•	4.8	4.1	3.7	3.5	2.0	1.9	2.2	1.9	1.8	2.0	1.6
Net Sales to Working Capital 32	0.6	•	2.2	0.3	0.7	0.7	0.9	0.7	0.7	0.6	1.5	0.7	0.6
Coverage Ratio 33	1.7	1.8	67.4	6.0	3.6	2.6	2.3	3.1	2.3	2.0	2.7	2.2	1.6
Total Asset Turnover 34	0.2	•	1.7	0.3	0.5	0.4	0.4	0.3	0.3	0.3	0.5	0.3	0.2
Inventory Turnover 35	•	•	•	•	•	•	•	•	•	•	•	•	•
Receivables Turnover 36	•	•	•	•	•	•	•	•	•	•	•	•	•
Total Liabilities to Net Worth 37	4.6	•	0.9	0.6	1.0	1.8	3.5	2.2	4.0	2.7	1.8	3.0	5.1
Current Assets to Working Capital 38	2.4	•	1.1	1.2	1.3	1.4	1.9	1.9	1.7	1.9	2.2	2.0	2.5
Current Liabilities to Working Capital 39	1.4	•	0.1	0.2	0.3	0.4	0.9	0.9	0.7	0.9	1.2	1.0	1.5
Working Capital to Net Sales 40	1.6	•	0.5	3.2	1.4	1.5	1.1	1.3	1.5	1.6	0.7	1.4	1.7
Inventory to Working Capital 41	0.0	•	•	•	•	•	•	•	•	0.0	0.0	0.0	0.0
Total Receipts to Cash Flow 42	1.7	1.6	1.4	1.4	1.9	1.8	2.0	1.9	2.0	2.0	2.1	1.7	1.6
Cost of Goods to Cash Flow 43	0.0	•	0.0	0.0	0.0	0.0	0.0	0.0	0.0	0.0	0.0	0.0	0.0
Cash Flow to Total Debt 44	0.1	•	2.5	0.5	0.5	0.4	0.3	0.2	0.2	0.2	0.3	0.2	0.1

Selected Financial Factors (in Percentages)

Debt Ratio 45	82.1	•	48.3	37.9	50.2	64.6	77.9	68.7	80.0	73.3	64.5	75.0	83.6
Return on Total Assets 46	6.3	•	51.3	14.0	13.6	13.3	11.8	10.5	9.2	9.2	15.2	8.4	5.7
Return on Equity Before Income Taxes 47	14.4	•	97.8	18.8	19.8	23.2	30.4	22.9	25.7	17.3	27.2	18.3	12.4
Return on Equity After Income Taxes 48	10.1	•	97.6	17.5	19.1	21.6	28.4	19.8	23.1	14.5	18.4	13.5	8.1
Profit Margin (Before Income Tax) 49	14.0	13.0	29.3	43.5	21.2	18.4	16.7	22.1	17.0	17.6	20.7	16.5	12.6
Profit Margin (After Income Tax) 50	9.8	11.3	29.3	40.5	20.4	17.1	15.6	19.1	15.2	14.7	14.0	12.2	8.2

REAL ESTATE CREDIT INCL. MORTGAGE BANKERS AND ORIGINATORS

Table I

Corporations with and without Net Income

MONEY AMOUNTS AND SIZE OF ASSETS IN THOUSANDS OF DOLLARS

Item Description for Accounting Period 7/07 Through 6/08	Total	Zero Assets	Under 500	500 to 1,000	1,000 to 5,000	5,000 to 10,000	10,000 to 25,000	25,000 to 50,000	50,000 to 100,000	100,000 to 250,000	250,000 to 500,000	500,000 to 2,500,000	2,500,000 and over
Number of Enterprises **1**	13649	3085	7837	684	1170	344	317	99	41	34	11	19	7
Revenues ($ in Thousands)													
Net Sales **2**	42182314	429299	4176329	1020526	1928175	698892	2729828	850632	696943	2115698	521973	4141687	22872332
Interest **3**	20177708	214395	17358	4632	41442	49729	71638	44567	54737	400626	170505	2273047	16835033
Rents **4**	21787	0	0	0	1	787	318	4503	4066	780	1970	8919	444
Royalties **5**	140	0	0	0	0	0	0	0	0	140	0	0	0
Other Portfolio Income **6**	1039799	27639	11049	10575	9203	4814	19600	2066	7555	5786	1124	304653	635730
Other Receipts **7**	20942880	187265	4147922	1005319	1877529	643562	2638272	799496	630585	1708366	348374	1555068	5401125
Total Receipts **8**	42182314	429299	4176329	1020526	1928175	698892	2729828	850632	696943	2115698	521973	4141687	22872332
Average Total Receipts **9**	3091	139	533	1492	1648	2032	8611	8592	16999	62226	47452	217984	3267476
Operating Costs/Operating Income (%)													
Cost of Operations **10**	5.7	17.2	4.7	25.0	11.1	12.5	6.9	4.2	6.9	22.3	6.1	0.0	3.6
Salaries and Wages **11**	26.0	111.3	54.1	26.8	36.1	39.1	43.2	35.5	39.0	28.5	6.9	17.8	16.9
Taxes Paid **12**	2.8	11.9	3.5	2.4	3.2	6.3	5.2	3.5	3.7	3.6	1.0	1.5	2.2
Interest Paid **13**	38.1	71.5	0.6	2.4	9.7	13.2	9.0	21.0	23.5	32.1	39.7	25.3	56.5
Depreciation **14**	1.5	3.2	0.3	1.2	0.8	1.8	0.9	1.0	1.4	6.2	1.2	1.5	1.4
Amortization and Depletion **15**	2.3	•	0.0	0.6	0.0	0.1	0.2	0.2	0.1	1.3	0.6	0.8	4.0
Pensions and Other Deferred Comp. **16**	0.5	1.2	0.2	0.9	0.8	0.3	0.3	0.2	0.3	0.4	0.2	0.3	0.6
Employee Benefits **17**	1.6	4.6	0.9	1.3	1.2	3.0	1.6	1.7	1.5	2.4	0.4	2.0	1.5
Advertising **18**	2.4	4.6	1.6	2.3	2.7	5.5	5.9	1.9	1.5	1.5	2.2	5.8	1.5
Other Expenses **19**	38.1	194.4	23.1	42.9	25.4	44.1	33.1	32.7	40.5	93.1	37.1	63.5	29.7
Officers' Compensation **20**	2.5	17.1	8.3	2.1	6.8	7.3	2.7	4.3	3.9	1.6	1.4	1.4	0.9
Operating Margin **21**	•	•	2.9	•	2.2	•	•	•	•	•	3.1	•	•
Operating Margin Before Officers' Comp. **22**	•	•	11.2	9.0	•	•	•	•	•	4.5	•	•	•

Selected Average Balance Sheet ($ in Thousands)

Item													
Net Receivables 23	1537	0	4	163	749	1021	3587	9524	8624	36164	9874	259389	1559155
Inventories 24	•	•	•	•	•	•	•	•	•	•	•	•	•
Net Property, Plant and Equipment 25	249	0	8	46	335	483	337	1346	2453	5554	2836	14665	272325
Total Assets 26	22168	0	111	798	2580	7381	14714	34380	68880	150268	331672	1006509	36689289
Notes and Loans Payable 27	10662	0	27	311	1703	5022	9221	25554	28177	94617	222327	507277	17066274
All Other Liabilities 28	9732	0	16	55	244	959	3205	17981	33607	66661	74778	364797	16836521
Net Worth 29	1774	0	67	432	633	1400	2288	-9155	7097	-11010	34567	134435	2786494

Selected Financial Ratios (Times to 1)

Item													
Current Ratio 30	0.8	•	3.5	1.9	0.9	0.5	0.9	0.8	0.5	0.7	0.4	0.8	0.9
Quick Ratio 31	0.5	•	2.1	1.7	0.6	0.4	0.6	0.6	0.4	0.5	0.1	0.7	0.5
Net Sales to Working Capital 32	•	•	11.2	8.6	•	•	•	•	•	•	•	•	•
Coverage Ratio 33	0.4	•	6.0	•	1.2	•	•	0.7	0.0	1.1	•	0.2	0.7
Total Asset Turnover 34	0.1	•	4.8	1.9	0.6	0.3	0.6	0.2	0.2	0.4	0.1	0.2	0.1
Inventory Turnover 35	•	•	•	•	•	•	•	•	•	•	•	•	•
Receivables Turnover 36	•	•	•	•	•	•	•	•	•	•	•	•	•
Total Liabilities to Net Worth 37	11.5	•	0.7	0.8	3.1	4.3	5.4	8.7	8.7	•	8.6	6.5	12.2
Current Assets to Working Capital 38	•	•	1.4	2.1	•	•	•	•	•	•	•	•	•
Current Liabilities to Working Capital 39	•	•	0.4	1.1	•	•	•	•	•	•	•	•	•
Working Capital to Net Sales 40	•	•	0.1	0.1	•	•	•	•	•	•	•	•	•
Inventory to Working Capital 41	•	•	•	•	•	•	•	•	•	•	•	•	•
Total Receipts to Cash Flow 42	10.7	•	5.0	3.5	4.4	38.3	6.4	4.8	8.7	•	2.6	3.2	16.5
Cost of Goods to Cash Flow 43	0.6	•	0.2	0.9	0.5	4.8	0.4	0.2	0.6	•	0.2	0.0	0.6
Cash Flow to Total Debt 44	0.0	•	2.4	1.2	0.2	0.0	0.1	0.0	0.0	•	0.1	0.1	0.0

Selected Financial Factors (in Percentages)

Item													
Debt Ratio 45	92.0	•	39.6	45.9	75.5	81.0	84.5	126.6	89.7	107.3	89.6	86.6	92.4
Return on Total Assets 46	2.3	•	16.5	7.6	5.7	3.7	5.8	5.9	0.3	•	6.1	1.1	3.4
Return on Equity Before Income Taxes 47	•	•	22.8	5.7	•	•	•	524.3	•	•	5.8	4.0	•
Return on Equity After Income Taxes 48	•	•	22.4	5.4	•	•	•	526.2	•	•	5.9	3.8	•
Profit Margin (Before Income Tax) 49	•	•	2.9	2.2	•	•	•	•	•	•	2.9	•	•
Profit Margin (After Income Tax) 50	•	•	2.8	2.1	•	•	•	•	•	•	2.7	•	•

Table II

Corporations with Net Income

REAL ESTATE CREDIT INCL. MORTGAGE BANKERS AND ORIGINATORS

MONEY AMOUNTS AND SIZE OF ASSETS IN THOUSANDS OF DOLLARS

Item Description for Accounting Period 7/07 Through 6/08	Total	Zero Assets	Under 500	500 to 1,000	1,000 to 5,000	5,000 to 10,000	10,000 to 25,000	25,000 to 50,000	50,000 to 100,000	100,000 to 250,000	250,000 to 500,000	500,000 to 2,500,000	2,500,000 and over
Number of Enterprises **1**	7519	950	4797	376	885	228	180	48	18	17	•	11	•
Revenues ($ in Thousands)													
Net Sales **2**	16076472	216972	3282583	446798	1309840	351241	1068771	439031	234582	402160	•	2987273	•
Interest **3**	4157648	5037	16217	4230	25106	17020	60192	3227	18266	63928	•	1629226	•
Rents **4**	16120	0	0	0	0	123	303	3328	1557	457	•	8372	•
Royalties **5**	0	0	0	0	0	0	0	0	0	0	•	0	•
Other Portfolio Income **6**	531270	203	5879	10575	3547	1331	16841	309	421	3271	•	304653	•
Other Receipts **7**	11371434	211732	3260487	431993	1281187	332767	991435	432167	214338	334504	•	1045022	•
Total Receipts **8**	16076472	216972	3282583	446798	1309840	351241	1068771	439031	234582	402160	•	2987273	•
Average Total Receipts **9**	2138	228	684	1188	1480	1541	5938	9146	13032	23656	•	271570	•
Operating Costs/Operating Income (%)													
Cost of Operations **10**	3.1	14.6	1.7	0.1	5.1	9.3	8.8	3.3	5.9	0.1	•	•	•
Salaries and Wages **11**	27.7	13.2	60.8	39.7	32.9	21.0	30.0	36.6	23.4	23.4	•	12.7	•
Taxes Paid **12**	1.9	1.4	1.7	3.6	3.0	3.5	3.7	3.4	3.1	2.8	•	1.2	•
Interest Paid **13**	16.7	3.6	0.3	2.7	8.5	10.3	10.4	17.5	17.8	25.1	•	15.6	•
Depreciation **14**	1.1	0.5	0.2	2.4	0.7	0.8	0.7	0.8	0.6	1.8	•	1.3	•
Amortization and Depletion **15**	1.1	•	0.0	•	0.1	0.2	0.3	0.4	0.1	2.0	•	0.2	•
Pensions and Other Deferred Comp. **16**	0.4	0.6	0.2	2.0	1.1	0.4	0.3	0.2	0.5	0.5	•	0.3	•
Employee Benefits **17**	1.0	0.7	0.1	2.3	0.9	1.0	1.5	0.9	0.9	1.9	•	1.3	•
Advertising **18**	2.6	1.6	1.6	4.1	3.1	2.2	4.4	1.8	0.7	1.8	•	7.5	•
Other Expenses **19**	32.6	13.9	18.7	33.8	23.7	26.9	23.3	23.5	27.2	26.7	•	45.1	•
Officers' Compensation **20**	2.9	3.7	5.9	3.8	7.7	8.7	3.0	4.3	3.1	3.2	•	1.1	•
Operating Margin **21**	9.1	46.2	8.8	5.5	13.3	15.8	13.6	7.4	16.6	10.8	•	13.7	•
Operating Margin Before Officers' Comp. **22**	12.0	49.9	14.6	9.3	21.0	24.5	16.6	11.7	19.7	14.1	•	14.8	•

Selected Average Balance Sheet ($ in Thousands)

	•	•	•	•	•	•	•	•	•	•	•	•	•
Net Receivables **23**	1741	•	0	6	297	375	1324	3602	10224	17701	43624	477444	•
Inventories **24**	•	•	•	•	•	•	•	•	•	•	•	•	•
Net Property, Plant and Equipment **25**	171	•	0	7	63	352	498	372	587	976	8357	22944	•
Total Assets **26**	7739	•	0	118	814	2521	7147	15237	33144	65288	141457	1050659	•
Notes and Loans Payable **27**	3299	•	0	15	409	1208	5821	9232	23827	22599	57931	280602	•
All Other Liabilities **28**	3064	•	0	23	43	642	532	2255	5222	28409	56554	547719	•
Net Worth **29**	1376	•	0	80	362	671	794	3750	4095	14280	26972	222339	•

Selected Financial Ratios (Times to 1)

	•	•	•	•	•	•	•	•	•	•	•	•	•
Current Ratio **30**	1.2	•	2.8	2.2	1.0	0.9	0.4	0.9	1.1	0.7	1.0	1.0	•
Quick Ratio **31**	1.0	•	1.8	2.0	0.6	0.7	0.4	0.7	0.7	0.6	0.8	0.9	•
Net Sales to Working Capital **32**	5.3	•	14.0	3.8	•	•	•	•	8.9	•	7.9	•	•
Coverage Ratio **33**	1.6	13.7	30.9	3.1	2.6	2.3	2.5	1.4	1.4	1.9	1.4	1.9	•
Total Asset Turnover **34**	0.3	•	5.8	1.5	0.6	0.4	0.2	0.4	0.3	0.2	0.2	0.3	•
Inventory Turnover **35**	•	•	•	•	•	•	•	•	•	•	•	•	•
Receivables Turnover **36**	•	•	•	•	•	•	•	•	•	•	•	•	•
Total Liabilities to Net Worth **37**	4.6	•	0.5	1.2	2.8	3.1	8.0	3.1	7.1	3.6	4.2	3.7	•
Current Assets to Working Capital **38**	6.5	•	1.5	1.8	•	•	•	•	16.2	•	21.4	•	•
Current Liabilities to Working Capital **39**	5.5	•	0.5	0.8	•	•	•	•	15.2	20.4	•	•	•
Working Capital to Net Sales **40**	0.2	•	0.1	0.3	0.3	•	•	•	0.1	0.1	•	0.1	•
Inventory to Working Capital **41**	0.0	•	•	•	•	•	•	•	•	•	•	•	•
Total Receipts to Cash Flow **42**	2.8	1.7	4.4	3.0	3.0	3.1	2.5	3.8	3.8	2.4	3.0	1.8	•
Cost of Goods to Cash Flow **43**	0.1	0.3	0.1	0.0	0.2	0.3	0.2	0.1	0.1	0.1	0.0	•	•
Cash Flow to Total Debt **44**	0.1	•	4.1	0.9	0.3	0.2	0.1	0.1	0.1	0.1	0.1	0.2	•

Selected Financial Factors (in Percentages)

	•	•	•	•	•	•	•	•	•	•	•	•	•
Debt Ratio **45**	82.2	•	32.4	55.5	73.4	75.4	88.9	87.6	78.1	80.9	78.8	•	•
Return on Total Assets **46**	7.3	•	52.6	11.9	12.8	9.4	5.6	6.9	6.8	5.9	7.5	•	•
Return on Equity Before Income Taxes **47**	14.9	•	75.3	18.1	29.4	21.6	30.7	16.4	15.1	9.0	16.4	•	•
Return on Equity After Income Taxes **48**	12.4	•	74.8	17.5	29.0	19.2	27.9	15.8	13.2	7.8	11.4	•	•
Profit Margin (Before Income Tax) **49**	9.6	46.1	8.8	5.5	13.3	13.6	15.8	7.3	16.5	10.3	13.4	•	•
Profit Margin (After Income Tax) **50**	8.0	45.9	8.7	5.3	13.1	12.2	14.4	7.1	14.5	8.9	9.3	•	•

Table I
Corporations with and without Net Income

INTL. TRADE, SECONDARY FINANCING, OTHER NONDEPOSITORY CREDIT

MONEY AMOUNTS AND SIZE OF ASSETS IN THOUSANDS OF DOLLARS

Item Description for Accounting Period 7/07 Through 6/08		Total	Zero Assets	Under 500	500 to 1,000	1,000 to 5,000	5,000 to 10,000	10,000 to 25,000	25,000 to 50,000	50,000 to 100,000	100,000 to 250,000	250,000 to 500,000	500,000 to 2,500,000	2,500,000 and over
Number of Enterprises	1	6962	1071	3850	875	768	94	112	55	37	29	7	30	34
Revenues ($ in Thousands)														
Net Sales	2	248217542	1566777	3125514	371491	1413343	305111	696824	410182	367507	827693	167945	3556987	235408166
Interest	3	196479930	1370176	1374548	44754	547678	6694	24225	51003	75507	267819	49189	1970215	190698122
Rents	4	49501	16	0	0	3704	0	0	532	92	2924	0	1416	40816
Royalties	5	8112	0	858	0	137	0	0	120	0	2	0	6979	16
Other Portfolio Income	6	2593660	25811	1616	15090	31529	1446	66574	3852	2195	1452	3814	60759	2379519
Other Receipts	7	49086339	170774	1748492	311647	830295	296971	606025	354675	289713	555496	114942	1517618	42289693
Total Receipts	8	248217542	1566777	3125514	371491	1413343	305111	696824	410182	367507	827693	167945	3556987	235408166
Average Total Receipts	9	35653	1463	812	425	1840	3246	6222	7458	9933	28541	23992	118566	6923770
Operating Costs/Operating Income (%)														
Cost of Operations	10	0.4	4.7	•	17.0	32.3	3.8	20.5	0.9	11.0	0.6	1.1	6.0	•
Salaries and Wages	11	1.4	1.8	4.5	17.1	7.4	35.9	21.5	17.4	23.2	14.7	6.3	9.4	1.0
Taxes Paid	12	0.1	0.5	0.8	4.8	1.3	2.0	2.8	3.2	2.0	1.3	0.9	1.3	0.1
Interest Paid	13	70.3	74.7	44.2	12.0	40.8	8.0	9.8	22.5	26.7	29.6	48.1	37.9	72.0
Depreciation	14	0.1	0.1	0.3	1.3	1.6	2.9	1.2	2.3	0.8	1.8	1.7	1.1	0.1
Amortization and Depletion	15	3.4	0.0	0.0	0.0	0.8	0.3	0.3	1.0	1.2	0.8	0.6	0.8	3.6
Pensions and Other Deferred Comp.	16	0.1	•	0.2	•	•	0.4	0.5	0.4	0.2	0.3	0.2	0.3	0.1
Employee Benefits	17	0.2	0.1	0.0	0.3	0.5	1.1	0.9	0.8	1.3	0.9	0.4	0.5	0.2
Advertising	18	0.1	0.0	0.4	2.5	1.3	1.2	1.2	0.6	1.1	1.0	1.2	1.1	0.0
Other Expenses	19	17.5	4.5	47.0	32.0	15.7	33.8	36.9	24.3	26.9	40.3	25.2	21.7	16.9
Officers' Compensation	20	0.3	•	1.8	6.6	2.9	3.5	5.1	5.6	5.2	1.8	1.4	1.3	0.2
Operating Margin	21	6.1	13.7	0.7	6.3	•	7.1	•	21.0	0.3	6.8	12.7	18.5	6.0
Operating Margin Before Officers' Comp.	22	6.4	13.7	2.6	12.9	•	10.6	4.4	26.5	5.5	8.6	14.1	19.8	6.2

Selected Average Balance Sheet ($ in Thousands)

Line Item													
Net Receivables 23	21387	0	22	380	677	4041	6369	19692	37040	114414	119727	646975	3554336
Inventories 24	•	•	•	•	•	•	•	•	•	•	•	•	•
Net Property, Plant and Equipment 25	419	0	4	16	548	486	397	713	487	8399	1861	11333	50619
Total Assets 26	300866	0	80	725	1977	7232	15202	36500	71006	166209	331327	1096650	60150267
Notes and Loans Payable 27	265283	0	36	525	1361	4422	8494	17194	38182	109960	195745	654988	53450613
All Other Liabilities 28	17679	0	8	46	261	1270	2252	6541	14033	32145	72329	159955	3391899
Net Worth 29	17903	0	35	154	355	1540	4456	12766	18792	24104	63253	281707	3307755

Selected Financial Ratios (Times to 1)

Line Item													
Current Ratio 30	0.4	•	3.3	4.1	2.0	1.3	1.7	1.7	1.7	1.3	1.1	1.3	0.4
Quick Ratio 31	0.3	•	1.7	3.4	1.7	1.2	1.4	1.5	1.3	1.1	0.8	1.2	0.2
Net Sales to Working Capital 32	•	•	16.9	0.9	3.1	2.8	1.6	0.7	0.5	0.9	1.3	0.7	•
Coverage Ratio 33	1.1	1.2	1.0	1.5	0.9	1.9	0.9	1.9	1.0	1.2	1.3	1.5	1.1
Total Asset Turnover 34	0.1	•	10.2	0.6	0.9	0.4	0.4	0.2	0.1	0.2	0.1	0.1	0.1
Inventory Turnover 35	•	•	•	•	•	•	•	•	•	•	•	•	•
Receivables Turnover 36	•	•	•	•	•	•	•	•	•	•	•	•	•
Total Liabilities to Net Worth 37	15.8	•	1.3	3.7	4.6	3.7	2.4	1.9	2.8	5.9	4.2	2.9	17.2
Current Assets to Working Capital 38	•	•	1.4	1.3	2.0	4.4	2.5	2.5	2.5	4.4	11.4	4.1	•
Current Liabilities to Working Capital 39	•	•	0.4	0.3	1.0	3.4	1.5	1.5	1.5	3.4	10.4	3.1	•
Working Capital to Net Sales 40	•	•	0.1	1.1	0.3	0.4	0.6	1.5	2.1	1.1	0.8	1.5	•
Inventory to Working Capital 41	•	•	•	0.0	•	•	•	•	0.0	0.0	•	0.0	•
Total Receipts to Cash Flow 42	4.3	5.6	2.2	3.9	11.1	2.8	4.5	2.4	4.1	2.3	2.7	2.7	4.4
Cost of Goods to Cash Flow 43	0.0	0.3	•	0.7	3.6	0.1	0.9	0.0	0.5	0.0	0.0	0.2	•
Cash Flow to Total Debt 44	0.0	•	8.4	0.2	0.1	0.2	0.1	0.1	0.0	0.1	0.0	0.1	0.0

Selected Financial Factors (in Percentages)

Line Item													
Debt Ratio 45	94.0	•	55.8	78.7	82.0	78.7	70.7	65.0	73.5	85.5	80.9	74.3	94.5
Return on Total Assets 46	9.0	•	456.0	10.7	33.7	6.8	3.7	8.9	3.8	6.2	4.4	6.2	8.9
Return on Equity Before Income Taxes 47	10.9	•	17.0	17.4	•	15.0	•	12.3	0.1	8.0	4.8	8.0	11.2
Return on Equity After Income Taxes 48	7.1	•	16.4	13.1	•	12.1	•	9.8	•	2.8	4.1	5.4	7.2
Profit Margin (Before Income Tax) 49	5.5	13.7	0.7	6.3	7.1	7.1	•	21.0	0.3	6.8	12.7	19.1	5.3
Profit Margin (After Income Tax) 50	3.6	9.6	0.7	4.8	5.7	5.7	•	16.7	•	2.4	10.9	12.8	3.5

Table II

Corporations with Net Income

INTL. TRADE, SECONDARY FINANCING, OTHER NONDEPOSITORY CREDIT

MONEY AMOUNTS AND SIZE OF ASSETS IN THOUSANDS OF DOLLARS

Item Description for Accounting Period 7/07 Through 6/08	Total	Zero Assets	Under 500	500 to 1,000	1,000 to 5,000	5,000 to 10,000	10,000 to 25,000	25,000 to 50,000	50,000 to 100,000	100,000 to 250,000	250,000 to 500,000	500,000 to 2,500,000	2,500,000 and over
Number of Enterprises **1**	4082	664	2102	697	352	72	45	50	23	21	7	24	24
Revenues ($ in Thousands)													
Net Sales **2**	238923115	1051572	398516	358039	1071866	293210	194860	377191	226162	732679	167945	3086583	230964490
Interest **3**	190852315	856778	2053	44754	538932	348	8196	39906	55834	205262	49189	1580707	187470356
Rents **4**	47711	16	0	0	3704	0	0	532	6	1323	0	1313	40816
Royalties **5**	7118	0	0	0	0	0	0	120	0	2	0	6979	16
Other Portfolio Income **6**	2511851	24177	0	13939	31331	60	62375	3852	46	302	3814	60353	2311601
Other Receipts **7**	45504120	170601	396463	299346	497899	292802	124289	332781	170276	525790	114942	1437231	41141701
Total Receipts **8**	238923115	1051572	398516	358039	1071866	293210	194860	377191	226162	732679	167945	3086583	230964490
Average Total Receipts **9**	58531	1584	190	514	3045	4072	4330	7544	9833	34889	23992	128608	9623520
Operating Costs/Operating Income (%)													
Cost of Operations **10**	0.3	6.9	•	17.7	30.1	4.0	•	1.0	3.6	0.7	1.1	6.5	•
Salaries and Wages **11**	1.3	2.7	31.4	17.2	1.3	37.3	10.9	17.1	21.7	15.9	6.3	8.6	0.9
Taxes Paid **12**	0.1	0.6	5.1	4.9	0.2	2.1	4.3	3.4	2.3	1.3	0.9	1.3	0.1
Interest Paid **13**	70.8	63.9	0.1	7.2	50.3	3.8	11.6	16.0	21.2	19.7	48.1	35.7	72.0
Depreciation **14**	0.1	0.1	0.2	0.9	0.3	3.0	0.9	2.5	0.8	1.9	1.7	1.1	0.1
Amortization and Depletion **15**	3.5	0.0	0.3	0.0	0.3	0.1	0.4	0.3	0.5	0.7	0.6	0.9	3.6
Pensions and Other Deferred Comp. **16**	0.1	•	1.5	•	•	0.4	0.4	0.4	0.2	0.1	0.2	0.3	0.1
Employee Benefits **17**	0.2	0.1	0.4	0.2	0.4	1.2	0.4	0.9	1.3	1.0	0.4	0.4	0.2
Advertising **18**	0.1	0.0	2.7	2.6	0.0	1.3	1.7	0.6	0.8	1.1	1.2	1.2	0.0
Other Expenses **19**	16.5	2.9	42.9	24.9	10.7	28.6	28.2	24.2	22.9	37.5	25.2	20.1	16.4
Officers' Compensation **20**	0.3	•	8.8	6.8	1.4	3.6	4.9	5.8	4.9	1.8	1.4	1.3	0.2
Operating Margin **21**	6.8	22.8	6.7	17.5	5.0	14.6	36.2	27.9	19.7	18.3	12.7	22.5	6.4
Operating Margin Before Officers' Comp. **22**	7.1	22.8	15.5	24.3	6.5	18.2	41.2	33.7	24.6	20.1	14.1	23.8	6.6

Selected Average Balance Sheet ($ in Thousands)

Net Receivables 23	33365	0	30	389	926	5103	8382	17998	42865	118341	119727	633060	4766178
Inventories 24	•	•	•	•	•	•	•	•	•	•	•	•	•
Net Property, Plant and Equipment 25	514	0	1	18	95	400	298	738	461	3581	1861	12803	65168
Total Assets 26	491636	0	89	706	1534	7334	17005	34939	71287	162492	331327	1098029	82036366
Notes and Loans Payable 27	435390	0	23	284	423	3478	7312	14651	35792	94237	195745	642967	73164562
All Other Liabilities 28	25499	0	0	54	363	1531	3000	6193	13541	27894	72329	120790	4127627
Net Worth 29	30747	0	66	368	748	2325	6693	14095	21954	40361	63253	334272	4744177

Selected Financial Ratios (Times to 1)

Current Ratio 30	0.4	•	5.8	8.7	3.7	1.7	2.1	1.7	1.9	1.7	1.1	1.5	0.4
Quick Ratio 31	0.3	•	2.3	7.0	3.2	1.6	1.8	1.5	1.5	1.5	0.8	1.4	0.2
Net Sales to Working Capital 32	•	•	2.8	0.9	3.3	1.5	0.7	0.7	0.4	0.6	1.3	0.5	•
Coverage Ratio 33	1.1	1.4	88.5	3.4	1.1	4.8	4.1	2.7	1.9	1.9	1.3	1.6	1.1
Total Asset Turnover 34	0.1	•	2.1	0.7	2.0	0.6	0.3	0.2	0.1	0.2	0.1	0.1	0.1
Inventory Turnover 35	•	•	•	•	•	•	•	•	•	•	•	•	•
Receivables Turnover 36	•	•	•	•	•	•	•	•	•	•	•	•	•
Total Liabilities to Net Worth 37	15.0	•	0.4	0.9	1.1	2.2	1.5	1.5	2.2	3.0	4.2	2.3	16.3
Current Assets to Working Capital 38	•	•	1.2	1.1	1.4	2.4	1.9	2.4	2.2	2.5	11.4	2.9	•
Current Liabilities to Working Capital 39	•	•	0.2	0.1	0.4	1.4	0.9	1.4	1.2	1.5	10.4	1.9	•
Working Capital to Net Sales 40	•	•	0.4	1.1	0.3	0.7	1.4	1.4	2.8	1.6	0.8	1.9	•
Inventory to Working Capital 41	•	•	•	0.0	•	•	•	•	•	0.0	•	0.0	•
Total Receipts to Cash Flow 42	4.4	3.9	2.6	3.4	7.4	2.6	3.5	2.1	2.6	1.9	2.7	2.5	4.4
Cost of Goods to Cash Flow 43	0.0	0.3	0.6	0.6	2.2	0.1	•	0.0	0.1	0.0	0.0	0.2	•
Cash Flow to Total Debt 44	0.0	•	3.1	0.4	0.5	0.3	0.1	0.2	0.1	0.2	0.0	0.1	0.0

Selected Financial Factors (in Percentages)

Debt Ratio 45	93.7	•	26.1	47.9	51.3	68.3	60.6	59.7	69.2	75.2	80.9	69.6	94.2
Return on Total Assets 46	9.2	•	14.4	18.0	109.8	10.2	12.2	9.5	5.6	8.2	4.4	6.9	9.1
Return on Equity Before Income Taxes 47	11.9	•	19.2	24.4	20.5	25.5	23.4	14.9	8.8	15.8	4.8	8.9	11.8
Return on Equity After Income Taxes 48	8.1	•	18.7	22.2	17.9	23.0	19.6	12.5	7.6	11.5	4.1	6.1	7.9
Profit Margin (Before Income Tax) 49	6.3	22.8	6.7	17.5	5.0	14.6	36.2	27.9	19.7	18.3	12.7	23.2	5.8
Profit Margin (After Income Tax) 50	4.3	16.7	6.5	15.9	4.4	13.1	30.3	23.3	16.9	13.3	10.9	15.9	3.9

Table I

Corporations with and without Net Income

ACTIVITIES RELATED TO CREDIT INTERMEDIATION

MONEY AMOUNTS AND SIZE OF ASSETS IN THOUSANDS OF DOLLARS

Item Description for Accounting Period 7/07 Through 6/08	Total	Zero Assets	Under 500	500 to 1,000	1,000 to 5,000	5,000 to 10,000	10,000 to 25,000	25,000 to 50,000	50,000 to 100,000	100,000 to 250,000	250,000 to 500,000	500,000 to 2,500,000	2,500,000 and over
Number of Enterprises **1**	27376	6785	17481	1525	1095	219	118	62	30	23	11	18	9
Revenues ($ in Thousands)													
Net Sales **2**	49947505	6910833	5722930	5243517	2889052	667445	1219862	697117	1158557	1572600	1532233	4042520	18290840
Interest **3**	4979032	189419	17254	7202	20905	17840	24981	21373	17762	51631	109648	515003	396014
Rents **4**	196910	20949	0	0	94	737	104	9	1615	93	1490	26680	145139
Royalties **5**	411524	59265	0	0	0	0	0	0	102	0	0	0	352157
Other Portfolio Income **6**	1243169	407388	1534	5	4694	2481	16492	2961	1847	45631	7981	90310	661847
Other Receipts **7**	43116870	6233812	5704142	5236310	2863359	646387	1178285	672774	1137231	1475245	1413114	3410527	13145683
Total Receipts **8**	49947505	6910833	5722930	5243517	2889052	667445	1219862	697117	1158557	1572600	1532233	4042520	18290840
Average Total Receipts **9**	1824	1019	327	3438	2638	3048	10338	11244	38619	68374	139294	224584	2032316
Operating Costs/Operating Income (%)													
Cost of Operations **10**	13.2	6.7	12.1	65.8	30.8	22.0	14.9	7.4	12.8	27.3	0.0	0.8	0.5
Salaries and Wages **11**	21.0	31.4	38.2	17.0	19.1	44.5	33.1	27.7	18.9	20.2	22.8	17.4	12.0
Taxes Paid **12**	2.3	0.7	3.8	1.0	3.0	3.6	2.9	3.2	2.0	2.3	2.4	1.5	2.7
Interest Paid **13**	7.3	3.0	1.1	0.4	1.7	3.3	6.1	12.3	7.5	7.2	11.1	11.4	12.6
Depreciation **14**	1.4	1.8	1.2	0.5	1.0	0.8	2.6	1.9	1.5	4.1	2.8	1.8	1.2
Amortization and Depletion **15**	1.3	1.9	0.1	0.1	0.5	0.1	0.6	0.0	0.6	0.9	3.6	3.9	1.5
Pensions and Other Deferred Comp. **16**	0.8	0.6	0.6	0.2	0.2	0.3	0.3	0.4	0.5	0.3	1.4	2.5	0.8
Employee Benefits **17**	1.7	4.1	1.2	0.2	1.4	1.3	1.4	0.9	1.4	1.1	1.6	2.1	1.5
Advertising **18**	4.6	0.4	1.7	0.6	1.8	0.4	1.4	0.9	0.7	3.4	6.3	11.1	8.0
Other Expenses **19**	33.4	48.8	31.3	10.4	30.9	24.7	34.3	33.6	47.4	28.5	36.2	34.2	34.7
Officers' Compensation **20**	2.2	1.3	8.1	2.3	3.5	7.2	3.7	5.3	2.3	2.2	0.6	1.0	0.4
Operating Margin **21**	10.8	•	0.8	1.6	6.2	•	•	6.4	4.6	2.5	11.2	12.5	24.2
Operating Margin Before Officers' Comp. **22**	13.0	0.5	8.8	3.9	9.6	•	2.4	11.7	6.8	4.7	11.8	13.5	24.6

Selected Average Balance Sheet ($ in Thousands)

Net Receivables 23	1457	0	5	64	299	2609	2117	14252	16002	36945	50633	238762	3497121
Inventories 24	•	•	•	•	•	•	•	•	•	•	•	•	•
Net Property, Plant and Equipment 25	143	0	26	234	115	657	1449	1147	3288	9592	29540	24770	166780
Total Assets 26	6788	0	83	805	2000	6896	14593	37494	69823	162969	315439	952924	16548615
Notes and Loans Payable 27	2590	0	49	441	750	3622	7763	16964	33319	63115	163731	350289	6137438
All Other Liabilities 28	1707	0	23	50	700	2333	5287	11621	19161	59863	89633	342187	3837629
Net Worth 29	2491	0	12	313	550	941	1544	8908	17343	39991	62075	260449	6573547

Selected Financial Ratios (Times to 1)

Current Ratio 30	1.0	•	1.5	2.2	1.2	2.0	0.9	1.2	1.1	1.1	0.5	1.7	1.0
Quick Ratio 31	0.8	•	1.2	2.0	1.0	1.9	0.6	0.9	0.9	0.8	0.5	1.4	0.7
Net Sales to Working Capital 32	18.1	•	24.4	14.0	17.2	1.3	•	2.6	18.6	7.1	•	1.2	•
Coverage Ratio 33	2.4	•	1.7	5.1	4.6	•	0.8	1.5	1.6	1.3	2.0	2.2	3.0
Total Asset Turnover 34	0.3	•	3.9	4.3	1.3	0.4	0.7	0.3	0.6	0.4	0.4	0.2	0.1
Inventory Turnover 35	•	•	•	•	•	•	•	•	•	•	•	•	•
Receivables Turnover 36	•	•	•	•	•	•	•	•	•	•	•	•	•
Total Liabilities to Net Worth 37	1.7	6.2	1.6	2.6	•	6.3	8.5	3.2	3.0	3.1	4.1	2.7	1.5
Current Assets to Working Capital 38	25.3	•	2.9	1.9	6.9	•	2.0	5.5	16.0	8.0	•	2.4	•
Current Liabilities to Working Capital 39	24.3	•	1.9	0.9	5.9	•	1.0	4.5	15.0	7.0	•	1.4	•
Working Capital to Net Sales 40	0.1	•	0.0	0.1	0.1	•	0.8	0.4	0.1	0.1	•	0.8	•
Inventory to Working Capital 41	0.0	•	0.0	•	•	•	0.0	0.0	0.0	0.0	•	0.0	•
Total Receipts to Cash Flow 42	2.5	2.2	4.1	13.0	3.1	7.5	3.6	2.7	2.1	3.9	2.5	2.3	1.8
Cost of Goods to Cash Flow 43	0.3	0.1	0.5	8.6	1.0	1.7	0.5	0.2	0.3	1.1	0.0	0.0	0.0
Cash Flow to Total Debt 44	0.2	•	1.1	0.5	0.6	0.1	0.2	0.1	0.4	0.1	0.0	0.2	0.1

Selected Financial Factors (in Percentages)

Debt Ratio 45	63.3	•	86.1	61.1	72.5	86.4	89.4	76.2	75.2	75.5	80.3	72.7	60.3
Return on Total Assets 46	4.8	•	7.3	8.5	10.3	•	3.3	5.6	6.6	4.1	9.8	5.9	4.6
Return on Equity Before Income Taxes 47	7.7	•	21.5	17.7	29.5	•	8.0	10.1	4.3	25.1	11.7	•	7.7
Return on Equity After Income Taxes 48	4.8	•	19.0	17.5	28.1	•	7.9	7.5	1.6	18.9	6.5	•	5.0
Profit Margin (Before Income Tax) 49	10.5	0.8	1.6	6.1	•	6.3	7.9	4.5	2.5	1.6	11.2	13.5	24.8
Profit Margin (After Income Tax) 50	6.6	0.7	1.6	5.8	•	6.3	7.5	3.4	2.5	1.6	8.4	7.6	16.1

287

Table II

Corporations with Net Income

ACTIVITIES RELATED TO CREDIT INTERMEDIATION

MONEY AMOUNTS AND SIZE OF ASSETS IN THOUSANDS OF DOLLARS

Item Description for Accounting Period 7/07 Through 6/08	Total	Zero Assets	Under 500	500 to 1,000	1,000 to 5,000	5,000 to 10,000	10,000 to 25,000	25,000 to 50,000	50,000 to 100,000	100,000 to 250,000	250,000 to 500,000	500,000 to 2,500,000	2,500,000 and over
Number of Enterprises **1**	13667	2196	•	789	470	86	•	52	23	13	•	•	9
Revenues ($ in Thousands)													
Net Sales **2**	34269362	526049	•	4325218	1266996	179390	•	598239	1035816	1206980	•	•	2904706
Interest **3**	4478913	1070	•	4270	17194	2302	•	13483	14131	35629	•	•	341305
Rents **4**	131953	0	•	0	59	437	•	4	817	93	•	•	22494
Royalties **5**	352149	0	•	0	0	0	•	0	102	0	•	•	0
Other Portfolio Income **6**	668248	1552	•	5	3678	1507	•	1826	1752	38554	•	•	58083
Other Receipts **7**	28638099	523427	•	4320943	1246065	175144	•	582926	1019014	1132704	•	•	2482824
Total Receipts **8**	34269362	526049	•	4325218	1266996	179390	•	598239	1035816	1206980	•	•	2904706
Average Total Receipts **9**	2507	240	•	5482	2696	2086	•	11505	45035	92845	•	•	322745
Operating Costs/Operating Income (%)													
Cost of Operations **10**	13.8	•	•	79.7	2.2	5.3	•	8.2	14.0	35.3	•	•	0.9
Salaries and Wages **11**	14.9	49.3	•	4.8	21.3	35.2	•	26.0	17.1	16.5	•	•	14.9
Taxes Paid **12**	2.4	1.9	•	0.8	2.8	3.4	•	2.8	1.7	2.0	•	•	1.7
Interest Paid **13**	7.0	0.5	•	0.1	1.0	5.3	•	11.6	5.3	4.5	•	•	5.1
Depreciation **14**	1.2	0.6	•	0.1	1.1	1.3	•	1.6	1.3	2.7	•	•	1.2
Amortization and Depletion **15**	0.9	0.1	•	0.0	0.0	0.0	•	0.0	0.6	0.2	•	•	1.5
Pensions and Other Deferred Comp. **16**	0.9	0.0	•	0.3	0.3	0.9	•	0.3	0.5	0.4	•	•	3.4
Employee Benefits **17**	1.0	0.2	•	0.2	1.1	1.4	•	0.7	1.3	0.9	•	•	1.9
Advertising **18**	6.3	0.4	•	0.6	1.5	1.0	•	0.5	0.7	4.2	•	•	14.8
Other Expenses **19**	28.7	31.3	•	6.4	40.1	22.6	•	28.1	47.7	21.4	•	•	30.9
Officers' Compensation **20**	2.2	3.7	•	2.6	4.0	17.2	•	5.4	1.6	1.0	•	•	1.1
Operating Margin **21**	20.6	12.1	•	4.4	24.6	6.4	•	14.8	8.2	10.9	•	•	22.6
Operating Margin Before Officers' Comp. **22**	22.9	15.7	•	7.0	28.6	23.6	•	20.2	9.8	11.9	•	•	23.6

Selected Average Balance Sheet ($ in Thousands)

Net Receivables 23	1878	•	105	618	3499	•	15576	18897	37089	•	142814
Inventories 24	•	0	•	•	•	•	•	•	•	•	•
Net Property, Plant and Equipment 25	165	0	110	123	709	•	929	3547	11225	•	27450
Total Assets 26	8608	•	783	2238	7624	•	38227	70587	161495	•	1069109
Notes and Loans Payable 27	2630	0	379	319	4295	•	15550	30271	54945	•	234582
All Other Liabilities 28	1555	0	15	701	2372	•	12725	18236	56874	•	454991
Net Worth 29	4424	0	390	1218	957	•	9952	22080	49676	•	379536

Selected Financial Ratios (Times to 1)

Current Ratio 30	1.0	•	4.5	2.2	1.7	•	1.2	1.2	1.2	•	1.3
Quick Ratio 31	0.8	•	4.4	1.9	1.7	•	0.9	1.0	0.9	•	1.1
Net Sales to Working Capital 32	•	•	11.7	2.8	1.0	•	3.7	9.1	6.5	•	3.2
Coverage Ratio 33	4.0	27.4	38.1	25.4	2.2	•	2.3	2.5	3.4	•	5.7
Total Asset Turnover 34	0.3	•	7.0	1.2	0.3	•	0.3	0.6	0.6	•	0.3
Inventory Turnover 35	•	•	•	•	•	•	•	•	•	•	•
Receivables Turnover 36	•	•	•	•	•	•	•	•	•	•	•
Total Liabilities to Net Worth 37	0.9	•	1.0	0.8	7.0	•	2.8	2.2	2.3	•	1.8
Current Assets to Working Capital 38	•	•	1.3	1.8	2.4	•	7.6	7.2	5.5	•	3.9
Current Liabilities to Working Capital 39	•	•	0.3	0.8	1.4	•	6.6	6.2	4.5	•	2.9
Working Capital to Net Sales 40	•	•	0.1	0.4	1.0	•	0.3	0.1	0.2	•	0.3
Inventory to Working Capital 41	•	•	•	•	•	•	0.0	0.0	0.0	•	0.0
Total Receipts to Cash Flow 42	2.2	2.7	11.0	1.7	4.2	•	2.5	1.9	3.7	•	2.0
Cost of Goods to Cash Flow 43	0.3	•	8.7	0.0	0.2	•	0.2	0.3	1.3	•	0.0
Cash Flow to Total Debt 44	0.3	•	1.3	1.6	0.1	•	0.2	0.5	0.2	•	0.2

Selected Financial Factors (in Percentages)

Debt Ratio 45	48.6	•	50.2	45.6	87.4	•	74.0	68.7	69.2	•	64.5
Return on Total Assets 46	8.2	•	31.6	30.8	3.2	•	7.9	8.6	8.8	•	8.8
Return on Equity Before Income Taxes 47	12.0	•	61.9	54.4	14.0	•	17.1	16.6	20.3	•	20.4
Return on Equity After Income Taxes 48	8.8	•	61.7	53.1	10.9	•	17.0	14.0	16.5	•	13.3
Profit Margin (Before Income Tax) 49	21.2	11.9	4.4	24.6	6.4	•	14.8	8.2	10.9	•	24.0
Profit Margin (After Income Tax) 50	15.6	11.5	4.4	24.0	5.0	•	14.7	6.9	8.8	•	15.7

Table I

Corporations with and without Net Income

INVESTMENT BANKING AND SECURITIES DEALING

MONEY AMOUNTS AND SIZE OF ASSETS IN THOUSANDS OF DOLLARS

Item Description for Accounting Period 7/07 Through 6/08	Total	Zero Assets	Under 500	500 to 1,000	1,000 to 5,000	5,000 to 10,000	10,000 to 25,000	25,000 to 50,000	50,000 to 100,000	100,000 to 250,000	250,000 to 500,000	500,000 to 2,500,000	2,500,000 and over
Number of Enterprises 1	3251	1577	1162	201	142	44	30	21	23	17	9	12	13
Revenues ($ in Thousands)													
Net Sales 2	303637618	1236766	647393	42838	89760	113941	131727	114235	510461	609622	516892	2627704	296996279
Interest 3	216076386	27109	1797	3319	4615	1072	10116	2040	36524	42080	170144	631662	215145906
Rents 4	455318	7760	0	0	0	0	33	0	0	175	44833	0	398654
Royalties 5	94070	0	0	0	0	0	0	0	0	0	50986	0	43084
Other Portfolio Income 6	9454947	6023	2989	855	1199	0	20393	12699	49507	34144	14852	275366	9036920
Other Receipts 7	77556897	1195874	642607	38664	80083	112869	101185	99496	424430	533223	236077	1720676	72371715
Total Receipts 8	303637618	1236766	647393	42838	89760	113941	131727	114235	510461	609622	516892	2627704	296996279
Average Total Receipts 9	93398	784	557	213	632	2590	4391	5440	22194	35860	57432	218975	22845868
Operating Costs/Operating Income (%)													
Cost of Operations 10	3.9	•	•	•	•	•	•	•	•	•	•	•	4.0
Salaries and Wages 11	7.9	9.4	11.8	63.9	3.6	32.6	7.3	43.0	31.2	36.5	13.7	28.1	7.6
Taxes Paid 12	0.7	0.7	2.6	4.8	3.3	3.0	2.8	4.8	2.9	2.6	1.9	2.5	0.7
Interest Paid 13	69.8	65.7	0.3	3.6	3.7	0.1	5.4	1.2	5.1	5.6	32.5	29.8	70.7
Depreciation 14	0.6	0.2	0.5	0.1	0.9	0.4	1.0	0.9	1.1	0.8	2.4	0.9	0.5
Amortization and Depletion 15	0.3	0.6	•	•	0.0	•	0.0	0.0	0.5	1.5	0.1	0.3	0.2
Pensions and Other Deferred Comp. 16	1.1	0.1	0.4	1.7	0.2	0.2	0.7	1.7	0.8	1.4	0.1	0.3	1.1
Employee Benefits 17	0.4	0.2	1.2	1.2	0.5	1.5	1.6	2.1	1.5	0.8	0.4	1.3	0.3
Advertising 18	0.1	0.0	1.7	0.1	0.1	0.3	0.1	0.1	4.6	0.3	0.2	0.4	0.1
Other Expenses 19	13.7	21.1	52.1	56.7	15.7	22.1	37.5	41.0	28.9	34.8	45.6	41.2	13.2
Officers' Compensation 20	0.7	2.6	12.2	59.4	16.9	3.4	28.5	7.8	6.6	2.4	1.7	1.3	0.7
Operating Margin 21	0.9	•	17.0	•	55.1	36.3	15.1	•	16.9	13.3	1.4	•	0.9
Operating Margin Before Officers' Comp. 22	1.6	2.2	29.3	•	72.0	39.7	43.6	5.2	23.4	15.7	3.1	•	1.5

Selected Average Balance Sheet ($ in Thousands)

Item													
Net Receivables 23	472639	0	2	60	16	128	3517	1994	15518	24641	72472	272766	117821420
Inventories 24	•	•	•	•	•	•	•	•	•	•	•	•	•
Net Property, Plant and Equipment 25	3160	0	27	5	46	67	216	194	2819	2199	5924	8448	766369
Total Assets 26	1758854	0	183	740	1907	5195	17645	31893	71707	157385	366525	1192417	438003382
Notes and Loans Payable 27	298612	0	26	268	341	51	1972	815	12495	7660	130782	67187	74475118
All Other Liabilities 28	1372808	0	23	18	134	141	4227	6530	14354	77184	159174	664737	342432962
Net Worth 29	87434	0	133	454	1431	5003	11446	24548	44858	72542	76569	460493	21095302

Selected Financial Ratios (Times to 1)

Item													
Current Ratio 30	0.9	•	3.2	31.1	6.1	21.1	2.5	3.0	1.6	1.0	1.3	1.6	0.9
Quick Ratio 31	0.4	•	2.3	28.5	3.7	19.2	1.7	1.6	1.0	0.8	0.8	0.9	0.4
Net Sales to Working Capital 32	•	•	6.2	0.4	0.8	0.7	0.5	1.6	1.6	1.7	59.0	0.8	•
Coverage Ratio 33	1.0	1.0	56.2	15.8	431.6	3.8	0.2	4.2	3.2	1.0	0.8	•	1.0
Total Asset Turnover 34	0.1	•	3.1	0.3	0.3	0.2	0.2	0.3	0.2	0.2	0.2	0.2	0.1
Inventory Turnover 35	•	•	•	•	•	•	•	•	•	•	•	•	•
Receivables Turnover 36	•	•	•	•	•	•	•	•	•	•	•	•	19.8
Total Liabilities to Net Worth 37	19.1	•	•	0.4	0.6	0.3	0.0	0.5	0.3	0.6	1.2	3.8	1.6
Current Assets to Working Capital 38	•	•	1.5	1.0	1.2	1.0	1.7	1.5	2.7	4.6	198.4	2.7	•
Current Liabilities to Working Capital 39	•	•	0.5	0.0	0.2	0.0	0.7	0.5	1.7	3.6	197.4	1.7	•
Working Capital to Net Sales 40	•	•	0.2	2.5	1.3	1.5	1.5	2.2	0.6	0.6	0.0	1.2	•
Inventory to Working Capital 41	•	•	•	•	•	•	0.0	•	•	•	•	•	•
Total Receipts to Cash Flow 42	8.6	6.0	1.6	1.5	1.8	2.1	4.0	3.4	2.5	4.6	2.4	•	8.9
Cost of Goods to Cash Flow 43	0.3	•	•	•	•	•	•	•	•	•	•	•	0.4
Cash Flow to Total Debt 44	0.0	7.2	•	0.9	7.4	0.3	0.2	0.2	0.2	0.1	•	0.1	0.0

Selected Financial Factors (in Percentages)

Item													
Debt Ratio 45	95.0	•	26.9	38.6	25.0	3.7	35.1	23.0	37.4	53.9	79.1	61.4	95.2
Return on Total Assets 46	3.9	•	52.7	19.5	18.1	5.1	6.6	4.2	5.3	4.2	•	•	3.8
Return on Equity Before Income Taxes 47	3.1	•	70.9	24.3	18.8	5.8	8.1	6.2	1.1	•	•	•	3.1
Return on Equity After Income Taxes 48	1.4	•	67.8	24.3	16.1	3.8	4.8	4.5	0.0	•	•	•	1.4
Profit Margin (Before Income Tax) 49	2.9	•	17.0	55.0	36.3	15.0	16.3	12.6	1.4	•	•	•	2.9
Profit Margin (After Income Tax) 50	1.3	•	16.2	55.0	31.2	9.9	9.7	9.1	0.0	•	•	•	1.3

Table II

Corporations with Net Income

INVESTMENT BANKING AND SECURITIES DEALING

MONEY AMOUNTS AND SIZE OF ASSETS IN THOUSANDS OF DOLLARS

Item Description for Accounting Period 7/07 Through 6/08	Total	Zero Assets	Under 500	500 to 1,000	1,000 to 5,000	5,000 to 10,000	10,000 to 25,000	25,000 to 50,000	50,000 to 100,000	100,000 to 250,000	250,000 to 500,000	500,000 to 2,500,000	2,500,000 and over
Number of Enterprises **1**	1288	113	844	112	110	•	12	8	13	•	•	•	7

Revenues ($ in Thousands)

Net Sales **2**	133800726	1064220	648306	11240	89959	•	87391	70246	274731	•	•	•	128622290
Interest **3**	94236900	1730	1797	2005	4581	•	3284	1785	13064	•	•	•	93476421
Rents **4**	225004	0	0	0	0		33	0	0			•	179963
Royalties **5**	25135	0	0	0	0		0	0	0				25104
Other Portfolio Income **6**	6881906	3301	2989	855	1106		19991	11419	48591	•	•	•	6630779
Other Receipts **7**	32431781	1059189	643520	8380	84272		64083	57042	213076	•	•	•	28310023
Total Receipts **8**	133800726	1064220	648306	11240	89959	•	87391	70246	274731	•	•	•	128622290
Average Total Receipts **9**	103883	9418	768	100	818	•	7283	8781	21133	•	•	•	18374613

Operating Costs/Operating Income (%)

Cost of Operations **10**	0.0	•	•	•	•	•	•	•	•	•	•	•	0.0
Salaries and Wages **11**	11.1	3.3	11.8	•	3.6	•	4.9	21.5	16.9	•	•	•	10.8
Taxes Paid **12**	1.0	0.3	2.6	6.0	1.6	•	2.6	4.6	3.3	•	•	•	0.9
Interest Paid **13**	69.3	73.9	0.3	•	2.1	•	2.8	1.3	3.3	•	•	•	71.0
Depreciation **14**	0.8	0.0	0.5	•	0.5	•	1.5	0.3	0.5	•	•	•	0.8
Amortization and Depletion **15**	0.4	0.0	•		0.0	•	0.1	•	0.2	•	•	•	0.4
Pensions and Other Deferred Comp. **16**	0.3	0.1	0.4	6.3	0.2	•	0.9	1.2	0.5	•	•	•	0.3
Employee Benefits **17**	0.5	0.2	1.2		0.5	•	1.4	0.6	0.7	•	•	•	0.4
Advertising **18**	0.1	0.0	1.7		0.1	•	0.0	0.2	8.0	•	•	•	0.0
Other Expenses **19**	7.6	13.6	51.9	29.9	12.9	•	14.5	18.5	21.9	•	•	•	6.7
Officers' Compensation **20**	1.2	1.2	12.2	42.3	1.4	•	41.0	11.3	5.9	•	•	•	1.1
Operating Margin **21**	7.8	7.4	17.3	15.4	77.1	•	30.4	40.6	38.8	•	•	•	7.5
Operating Margin Before Officers' Comp. **22**	9.0	8.6	29.5	57.7	78.6	•	71.4	51.9	44.7	•	•	•	8.5

Selected Average Balance Sheet ($ in Thousands)

Net Receivables 23	274151	•	0	3	8	20	3413	2821	24142	•	49866271
Inventories 24	•	•	•	•	•	•	•	•	•	•	•
Net Property, Plant and Equipment 25	4979	0	37	0	0	483	170	719	•	•	893014
Total Assets 26	1723068	0	151	758	1777	18700	30090	74982	•	•	314537057
Notes and Loans Payable 27	430187	0	36	254	289	201	723	17345	•	•	78888268
All Other Liabilities 28	1237999	0	31	31	50	8519	14187	14692	•	•	226442625
Net Worth 29	54883	0	84	473	1437	9981	15181	42944	•	•	9206164

Selected Financial Ratios (Times to 1)

Current Ratio 30	0.8	•	1.4	20.2	12.7	2.2	2.1	1.8	•	•	0.8
Quick Ratio 31	0.3	•	0.6	17.6	9.7	2.0	1.3	1.1	•	•	0.3
Net Sales to Working Capital 32	•	•	30.9	0.2	1.0	1.1	0.6	1.0	•	•	•
Coverage Ratio 33	1.2	1.1	57.2	•	38.3	12.0	29.8	12.5	•	•	1.1
Total Asset Turnover 34	0.1	•	5.1	0.1	0.5	0.4	0.3	0.3	•	•	0.1
Inventory Turnover 35	•	•	•	•	•	•	•	•	•	•	•
Receivables Turnover 36	•	•	•	•	•	•	•	•	•	•	•
Total Liabilities to Net Worth 37	30.4	•	0.8	0.6	0.2	0.9	1.0	0.7	•	•	33.2
Current Assets to Working Capital 38	•	•	3.3	1.1	1.1	1.8	1.9	2.3	•	•	•
Current Liabilities to Working Capital 39	•	•	2.3	0.1	0.1	0.8	0.9	1.3	•	•	•
Working Capital to Net Sales 40	•	•	0.0	6.0	1.0	0.9	1.8	1.0	•	•	•
Inventory to Working Capital 41	•	•	•	•	•	0.0	•	•	•	•	•
Total Receipts to Cash Flow 42	9.5	5.0	1.6	2.5	1.2	2.4	2.3	2.3	•	•	10.8
Cost of Goods to Cash Flow 43	0.0	•	•	•	•	•	•	•	•	•	0.0
Cash Flow to Total Debt 44	0.0	•	7.2	0.1	2.1	0.3	0.3	0.3	•	•	0.0

Selected Financial Factors (in Percentages)

Debt Ratio 45	96.8	•	44.7	37.6	19.1	46.6	49.5	42.7	•	•	97.1
Return on Total Assets 46	4.8	•	88.9	2.0	36.4	12.9	10.9	11.7	•	•	4.8
Return on Equity Before Income Taxes 47	20.2	•	158.1	3.3	43.8	22.2	20.8	18.8	•	•	20.8
Return on Equity After Income Taxes 48	13.6	•	151.5	3.0	43.8	16.6	15.4	12.7	•	•	13.9
Profit Margin (Before Income Tax) 49	10.7	7.4	17.2	15.4	77.0	30.4	36.0	38.1	•	•	10.4
Profit Margin (After Income Tax) 50	7.2	4.8	16.5	13.9	77.0	22.7	26.6	25.8	•	•	6.9

Table I

Corporations with and without Net Income

SECURITIES BROKERAGE

MONEY AMOUNTS AND SIZE OF ASSETS IN THOUSANDS OF DOLLARS

Item Description for Accounting Period 7/07 Through 6/08	Total	Zero Assets	Under 500	500 to 1,000	1,000 to 5,000	5,000 to 10,000	10,000 to 25,000	25,000 to 50,000	50,000 to 100,000	100,000 to 250,000	250,000 to 500,000	500,000 to 2,500,000	2,500,000 and over
Number of Enterprises 1	7603	1823	3736	868	840	106	106	26	28	15	9	16	30
Revenues ($ in Thousands)													
Net Sales 2	318382008	3828388	1390282	1869989	3003880	1120832	2053055	915300	1634298	1425410	1721868	5345921	294072786
Interest 3	204535587	500346	1379	4551	9827	12540	33898	14877	81411	63993	61123	442274	203309368
Rents 4	734718	35397	0	0	472	0	924	0	1720	1919	803	4551	688932
Royalties 5	43830	0	0	0	0	0	12200	0	37	0	6	7368	24219
Other Portfolio Income 6	6476792	104578	244	4400	5090	10811	57667	5756	15178	33598	32473	127698	6079301
Other Receipts 7	106591081	3188067	1388659	1861038	2988491	1097481	1948366	894667	1535952	1325900	1627463	4764030	83970966
Total Receipts 8	318382008	3828388	1390282	1869989	3003880	1120832	2053055	915300	1634298	1425410	1721868	5345921	294072786
Average Total Receipts 9	41876	2100	372	2154	3576	10574	19368	35204	58368	95027	191319	334120	9802426
Operating Costs/Operating Income (%)													
Cost of Operations 10	0.7	•	•	•	•	•	•	•	•	2.3	•	0.1	0.7
Salaries and Wages 11	11.7	40.4	26.0	20.2	35.4	7.6	19.8	48.2	36.4	29.2	46.1	40.3	9.9
Taxes Paid 12	0.9	2.3	2.5	1.7	2.4	1.1	2.3	2.9	4.3	1.8	6.7	3.9	0.7
Interest Paid 13	61.2	8.7	1.4	0.2	1.1	0.4	1.3	0.7	1.6	4.5	2.3	6.7	65.9
Depreciation 14	0.5	0.7	1.6	0.2	0.2	0.4	0.7	0.5	0.6	1.3	1.0	1.2	0.5
Amortization and Depletion 15	0.3	0.7	0.0	0.0	0.1	0.1	0.1	0.1	0.5	0.8	0.2	1.2	0.3
Pensions and Other Deferred Comp. 16	0.3	1.3	0.4	0.3	0.8	0.3	0.4	0.5	1.1	0.4	1.2	0.8	0.3
Employee Benefits 17	0.5	1.5	0.4	1.1	1.8	0.6	1.2	1.5	1.0	0.9	1.8	1.2	0.5
Advertising 18	0.3	0.9	1.5	0.0	0.3	0.2	0.4	0.3	0.8	0.8	0.6	0.6	0.3
Other Expenses 19	26.7	30.6	31.2	59.3	39.8	78.3	62.7	35.5	26.7	58.4	24.6	25.7	25.7
Officers' Compensation 20	1.2	3.3	10.8	9.3	10.3	6.6	7.9	5.4	7.9	2.3	0.7	1.9	0.9
Operating Margin 21	•	9.7	24.2	7.6	7.9	4.4	3.2	4.5	19.2	14.8	•	16.4	•
Operating Margin Before Officers' Comp. 22	•	12.9	35.0	16.9	18.2	11.0	11.1	9.9	27.1	15.5	•	18.3	•

Selected Average Balance Sheet ($ in Thousands)

Item													
Net Receivables 23	127282	0	1	82	206	258	1235	7503	13565	28050	57779	257251	32056298
Inventories 24	•	•	•	•	•	•	•	•	•	•	•	•	•
Net Property, Plant and Equipment 25	1031	0	13	48	55	143	673	1204	1515	5019	11300	15173	237488
Total Assets 26	469149	0	59	634	1860	7071	14888	37242	68714	155777	309705	1288319	117788337
Notes and Loans Payable 27	79175	0	64	46	109	762	1121	1085	9785	19464	11146	144175	19946400
All Other Liabilities 28	360854	0	11	181	497	2359	6462	13915	28206	59897	153700	807184	90855642
Net Worth 29	29121	0	-16	406	1253	3950	7305	22241	30723	76417	144859	336960	6986296

Selected Financial Ratios (Times to 1)

Item													
Current Ratio 30	1.2	•	2.6	2.4	4.5	5.0	2.0	1.6	1.5	1.5	1.3	0.9	1.2
Quick Ratio 31	0.5	•	2.2	2.1	3.0	3.5	1.4	1.1	1.2	1.2	1.1	0.5	0.5
Net Sales to Working Capital 32	0.8	•	19.2	9.4	3.1	3.1	2.8	5.5	3.7	3.8	5.0	•	0.7
Coverage Ratio 33	0.9	2.1	17.9	34.0	8.1	11.2	7.2	3.2	12.8	0.4	7.4	3.4	0.9
Total Asset Turnover 34	0.1	•	6.3	3.4	1.9	1.5	0.9	1.3	0.8	0.6	0.6	0.3	0.1
Inventory Turnover 35	•	•	•	•	•	•	•	•	•	•	•	•	•
Receivables Turnover 36	•	•	•	•	•	•	•	•	•	•	•	•	•
Total Liabilities to Net Worth 37	15.1	•	•	0.6	0.5	0.8	0.7	1.0	1.2	1.0	1.1	2.8	15.9
Current Assets to Working Capital 38	6.1	•	•	1.6	1.7	1.3	1.3	2.0	2.8	2.9	3.1	4.8	6.1
Current Liabilities to Working Capital 39	5.1	•	•	0.6	0.7	0.3	0.3	1.0	1.8	1.9	2.1	3.8	5.1
Working Capital to Net Sales 40	1.3	•	0.1	0.1	0.3	0.3	0.2	0.2	0.3	0.3	0.2	0.2	1.4
Inventory to Working Capital 41	0.0	•	0.1	0.1	0.0	0.0	0.0	0.0	0.0	0.0	0.0	0.0	0.0
Total Receipts to Cash Flow 42	5.4	3.0	2.1	1.6	2.3	1.3	1.6	2.8	2.3	2.0	3.0	2.7	6.1
Cost of Goods to Cash Flow 43	0.0	•	•	•	•	•	•	•	•	•	•	0.0	0.0
Cash Flow to Total Debt 44	0.0	•	2.3	6.1	2.6	2.7	1.6	0.8	0.7	0.6	0.4	0.1	0.0

Selected Financial Factors (in Percentages)

Item													
Debt Ratio 45	93.8	•	126.4	35.9	32.6	44.1	50.9	40.3	55.3	50.9	53.2	73.8	94.1
Return on Total Assets 46	5.1	•	160.5	26.6	17.2	7.0	5.4	4.9	17.4	1.0	10.4	5.9	5.1
Return on Equity Before Income Taxes 47	•	•	•	40.3	22.4	11.4	7.5	7.1	35.8	•	19.2	16.0	•
Return on Equity After Income Taxes 48	•	•	•	37.9	21.4	9.7	4.7	4.7	24.4	•	12.7	10.6	•
Profit Margin (Before Income Tax) 49	9.4	24.2	24.2	7.6	7.8	4.3	2.8	4.5	18.9	0.0	14.5	16.2	•
Profit Margin (After Income Tax) 50	4.6	24.2	24.2	7.1	7.5	3.6	1.8	2.9	12.8	0.0	9.6	10.6	•

Table II

Corporations with Net Income

SECURITIES BROKERAGE

MONEY AMOUNTS AND SIZE OF ASSETS IN THOUSANDS OF DOLLARS

Item Description for Accounting Period 7/07 Through 6/08	Total	Zero Assets	Under 500	500 to 1,000	1,000 to 5,000	5,000 to 10,000	10,000 to 25,000	25,000 to 50,000	50,000 to 100,000	100,000 to 250,000	250,000 to 500,000	500,000 to 2,500,000	2,500,000 and over
Number of Enterprises 1	5969	1289	3087	726	624	•	79	19	22	11	•	13	22
Revenues ($ in Thousands)													
Net Sales 2	78000858	3164648	1027848	1168028	1910627	•	1765737	842064	1297180	822292	•	5062540	58497007
Interest 3	31789653	133539	0	3285	7456	•	31407	10890	32017	57355	•	407410	31047552
Rents 4	128591	31223	0	0	0	•	924	0	0	233	•	4551	90858
Royalties 5	27060	0	0	0	0	•	12200	0	37	0	•	7368	7449
Other Portfolio Income 6	2510582	92705	0	4400	727	•	22575	5330	14910	33506	•	117595	2185341
Other Receipts 7	43544972	2907181	1027848	1160343	1902444	•	1698631	825844	1250216	731198	•	4525616	25165807
Total Receipts 8	78000858	3164648	1027848	1168028	1910627	•	1765737	842064	1297180	822292	•	5062540	58497007
Average Total Receipts 9	13068	2455	333	1609	3062	•	22351	44319	58963	74754	•	389426	2658955
Operating Costs/Operating Income (%)													
Cost of Operations 10	0.0	•	•	•	•	•	•	•	•	•	•	•	0.0
Salaries and Wages 11	18.3	39.0	15.4	30.3	27.5	•	14.2	45.0	33.1	27.0	•	39.9	13.7
Taxes Paid 12	1.8	2.7	2.8	2.2	1.9	•	2.0	2.8	4.8	1.9	•	4.0	1.3
Interest Paid 13	37.3	0.7	1.5	0.4	1.2	•	0.8	0.5	1.3	6.5	•	6.4	48.8
Depreciation 14	0.5	0.7	2.1	0.3	0.2	•	0.5	0.5	0.5	1.7	•	1.2	0.4
Amortization and Depletion 15	1.0	0.9	0.0	0.0	0.1	•	0.1	0.1	0.3	1.3	•	1.3	1.1
Pensions and Other Deferred Comp. 16	0.6	1.5	0.5	0.5	1.2	•	0.3	0.4	1.2	0.4	•	0.7	0.5
Employee Benefits 17	0.9	1.5	0.3	1.6	1.4	•	1.0	1.3	0.9	1.4	•	1.1	0.8
Advertising 18	0.9	1.1	1.1	0.0	0.2	•	0.3	0.3	0.6	0.8	•	0.6	1.0
Other Expenses 19	23.4	29.0	27.9	36.8	35.5	•	64.6	35.3	21.4	46.4	•	25.3	19.6
Officers' Compensation 20	2.0	2.5	14.6	14.9	13.0	•	5.7	4.5	6.4	3.5	•	2.0	0.8
Operating Margin 21	13.4	20.5	33.8	12.8	17.9	•	10.5	9.2	29.6	9.0	•	17.5	11.9
Operating Margin Before Officers' Comp. 22	15.4	23.0	48.4	27.7	30.9	•	16.3	13.7	35.9	12.6	•	19.5	12.8

Selected Average Balance Sheet ($ in Thousands)

Net Receivables 23	12800	0	0	58	236	•	1273	9265	12844	31144	•	308588	3216513
Inventories 24	•	•	•	•	•	•	•	•	•	•	•	•	•
Net Property, Plant and Equipment 25	425	0	16	46	48	•	699	1446	1011	2257	•	16854	89892
Total Assets 26	100240	0	55	607	1744	•	15111	36966	65790	151953	•	1336572	25978484
Notes and Loans Payable 27	8682	0	66	14	145	•	1448	1485	6211	21045	•	76458	2268911
All Other Liabilities 28	83504	0	10	151	421	•	5703	13929	27305	62651	•	954656	21924124
Net Worth 29	8054	0	-21	442	1179	•	7961	21552	32274	68257	•	305457	1785448

Selected Financial Ratios (Times to 1)

Current Ratio 30	0.9	•	2.8	2.5	5.2	•	1.9	2.0	1.6	1.2	•	0.8	0.9
Quick Ratio 31	0.3	•	2.3	2.2	3.8	•	1.3	1.7	1.2	0.9	•	0.5	0.2
Net Sales to Working Capital 32	•	20.3	7.2	2.5	•	4.4	3.6	3.6	5.7	•	•	•	•
Coverage Ratio 33	1.4	•	23.1	36.1	16.2	•	13.7	17.7	24.3	2.4	•	3.7	1.2
Total Asset Turnover 34	0.1	30.8	6.0	2.6	1.8	•	1.5	1.2	0.9	0.5	•	0.3	0.1
Inventory Turnover 35	•	•	•	•	•	•	•	•	•	•	•	•	•
Receivables Turnover 36	•	•	•	•	•	•	•	•	•	•	•	•	•
Total Liabilities to Net Worth 37	11.4	•	•	0.4	0.5	•	0.9	0.7	1.0	1.2	•	3.4	13.6
Current Assets to Working Capital 38	•	1.6	1.7	1.2	•	2.1	2.0	2.6	5.8	•	•	•	•
Current Liabilities to Working Capital 39	•	0.6	0.7	0.2	•	1.1	1.0	1.6	4.8	•	•	•	•
Working Capital to Net Sales 40	•	0.0	0.1	0.4	•	0.2	0.3	0.3	0.2	•	•	•	•
Inventory to Working Capital 41	•	•	0.0	•	•	0.0	•	0.0	•	•	•	•	•
Total Receipts to Cash Flow 42	3.1	2.4	1.9	2.2	2.0	•	1.4	2.5	2.1	2.0	•	2.7	3.7
Cost of Goods to Cash Flow 43	0.0	•	•	•	•	•	•	•	•	•	•	0.0	0.0
Cash Flow to Total Debt 44	0.0	2.3	4.5	2.8	•	2.3	1.2	0.9	0.4	•	•	0.1	0.0

Selected Financial Factors (in Percentages)

Debt Ratio 45	92.0	137.2	27.2	32.4	•	47.3	41.7	50.9	55.1	•	•	77.1	93.1
Return on Total Assets 46	6.6	212.7	34.8	33.6	•	16.2	11.6	27.2	7.6	•	•	6.9	6.2
Return on Equity Before Income Taxes 47	21.7	•	46.4	46.6	•	28.5	18.8	53.2	9.7	•	•	22.1	17.8
Return on Equity After Income Taxes 48	15.6	•	43.7	45.2	•	25.1	15.4	39.4	7.8	•	•	14.7	12.3
Profit Margin (Before Income Tax) 49	13.4	20.1	33.8	12.8	17.9	•	10.2	9.2	29.1	8.9	•	17.3	12.0
Profit Margin (After Income Tax) 50	9.6	14.3	33.8	12.0	17.4	•	9.0	7.5	21.6	7.2	•	11.5	8.3

Table I

Corporations with and without Net Income

COMMODITY CONTRACTS DEALING AND BROKERAGE

MONEY AMOUNTS AND SIZE OF ASSETS IN THOUSANDS OF DOLLARS

Item Description for Accounting Period 7/07 Through 6/08	Total	Zero Assets	Under 500	500 to 1,000	1,000 to 5,000	5,000 to 10,000	10,000 to 25,000	25,000 to 50,000	50,000 to 100,000	100,000 to 250,000	250,000 to 500,000	500,000 to 2,500,000	2,500,000 and over
Number of Enterprises 1	1970	266	1432	70	93	15	31	17	14	7	11	6	7
Revenues ($ in Thousands)													
Net Sales 2	8065786	92254	198468	23561	280509	103231	43216	64018	182193	150312	592324	640676	5695025
Interest 3	3485332	11798	4452	316	4708	0	3176	2634	6435	13634	36506	77648	3324023
Rents 4	15070	0	0	0	0	0	0	0	193	0	261	0	11338
Royalties 5	0	0	0	0	0	0	0	0	0	0	0	0	0
Other Portfolio Income 6	488640	0	0	1	1027	0	43	1143	15945	31384	68159	13065	357871
Other Receipts 7	4076744	80456	194016	23244	274774	103231	39997	56963	159620	105294	487398	549963	2001793
Total Receipts 8	8065786	92254	198468	23561	280509	103231	43216	64018	182193	150312	592324	640676	5695025
Average Total Receipts 9	4094	347	139	337	3016	6882	1394	3766	13014	21473	53848	106779	813575
Operating Costs/Operating Income (%)													
Cost of Operations 10	0.4	•	•	•	•	•	•	•	•	0.7	1.1	3.1	0.1
Salaries and Wages 11	15.9	14.3	3.3	7.3	23.6	13.1	60.8	43.2	29.5	21.6	20.5	43.6	11.2
Taxes Paid 12	1.7	2.1	2.7	14.7	3.3	3.8	6.7	4.9	3.7	3.8	1.8	4.8	1.0
Interest Paid 13	41.3	33.0	1.6	•	4.4	3.1	9.3	5.1	7.6	12.5	10.2	14.8	54.3
Depreciation 14	0.7	0.6	0.2	1.6	0.6	0.1	1.0	1.6	0.8	0.9	0.5	0.3	0.7
Amortization and Depletion 15	1.4	0.1	0.0	•	2.4	•	0.1	1.9	0.2	0.1	1.2	0.2	1.7
Pensions and Other Deferred Comp. 16	0.5	0.2	1.6	•	1.6	1.2	0.5	0.4	6.6	1.8	0.3	0.7	0.2
Employee Benefits 17	1.1	0.0	1.0	22.3	2.2	0.4	6.0	3.7	1.5	0.6	1.9	1.0	0.8
Advertising 18	0.1	•	0.5	•	0.6	0.1	0.9	0.0	0.1	0.9	0.3	0.2	0.0
Other Expenses 19	30.9	46.9	76.8	80.1	38.6	6.8	95.3	52.2	44.8	37.7	18.9	43.1	27.4
Officers' Compensation 20	4.6	4.9	28.0	26.4	38.2	8.0	8.9	1.9	9.9	6.4	4.3	7.3	1.5
Operating Margin 21	1.3	•	•	•	•	63.2	•	•	•	13.0	38.9	•	1.0
Operating Margin Before Officers' Comp. 22	5.9	2.8	12.2	•	22.8	71.2	•	•	5.3	19.4	43.2	•	2.5

Selected Average Balance Sheet ($ in Thousands)

Net Receivables 23	10134	0	•	0	967	3356	2952	2376	17753	13029	31475	397068	2374802
Inventories 24	•	•	•	•	•	•	•	•	•	•	•	•	•
Net Property, Plant and Equipment 25	151	5	•	1	60	30	100	1072	952	666	10548	1053	17464
Total Assets 26	48877	49	•	809	2765	9317	17422	36837	67161	162508	343724	953467	11859873
Notes and Loans Payable 27	2809	5	•	3	1223	2510	7214	10614	18246	15292	45073	24974	566117
All Other Liabilities 28	42542	6	•	761	595	3538	8151	4557	35779	111642	223198	742886	10730298
Net Worth 29	3527	38	•	44	948	3269	2056	21666	13136	35575	75453	185607	563457

Selected Financial Ratios (Times to 1)

Current Ratio 30	1.2	3.8	•	1.1	4.0	1.8	1.7	1.5	1.2	0.7	1.0	1.2	1.2
Quick Ratio 31	0.6	2.4	•	0.4	3.6	1.1	0.8	0.8	0.8	0.5	0.4	0.8	0.6
Net Sales to Working Capital 32	0.6	8.2	•	7.8	1.5	2.3	0.3	0.6	2.1	•	•	0.7	0.4
Coverage Ratio 33	1.0	•	0.9	•	•	21.3	•	0.6	0.4	2.0	4.8	•	1.0
Total Asset Turnover 34	0.1	2.8	•	0.4	1.1	0.7	0.1	0.1	0.2	0.1	0.2	0.1	0.1
Inventory Turnover 35	•	•	•	•	•	•	•	•	•	•	•	•	•
Receivables Turnover 36	•	•	•	•	•	•	•	•	•	•	•	•	•
Total Liabilities to Net Worth 37	12.9	0.3	•	17.2	1.9	1.8	7.5	0.7	4.1	3.6	3.6	4.1	20.0
Current Assets to Working Capital 38	5.6	1.4	•	18.6	1.3	2.3	2.5	3.1	7.0	•	5.5	5.5	5.3
Current Liabilities to Working Capital 39	4.6	0.4	•	17.6	0.3	1.3	1.5	2.1	6.0	•	4.5	4.5	4.3
Working Capital to Net Sales 40	1.8	0.1	•	0.1	0.7	0.4	3.4	1.8	0.5	•	1.5	1.5	2.3
Inventory to Working Capital 41	0.0	•	•	•	•	•	•	•	•	•	•	•	0.0
Total Receipts to Cash Flow 42	3.9	1.8	2.3	6.8	1.5	1.5	•	3.4	3.7	2.1	2.2	4.9	4.5
Cost of Goods to Cash Flow 43	0.0	•	•	•	•	•	•	•	•	0.0	0.0	0.2	0.0
Cash Flow to Total Debt 44	0.0	7.2	•	0.2	0.8	0.8	0.1	0.1	0.1	0.1	0.0	0.0	0.0

Selected Financial Factors (in Percentages)

Debt Ratio 45	92.8	22.1	•	94.5	65.7	64.9	88.2	41.2	80.4	78.1	78.0	80.5	95.2
Return on Total Assets 46	3.6	•	•	•	•	49.0	•	0.6	3.4	7.7	•	•	3.8
Return on Equity Before Income Taxes 47	1.6	•	•	•	133.0	133.0	•	•	•	27.7	7.9	•	1.7
Return on Equity After Income Taxes 48	•	•	•	•	133.0	133.0	•	•	•	16.6	•	•	•
Profit Margin (Before Income Tax) 49	1.4	•	•	•	63.2	63.2	•	•	13.0	38.9	13.0	•	1.2
Profit Margin (After Income Tax) 50	•	•	•	63.2	63.2	•	•	23.2	•	•	•	•	•

Table II

Corporations with Net Income

COMMODITY CONTRACTS DEALING AND BROKERAGE

MONEY AMOUNTS AND SIZE OF ASSETS IN THOUSANDS OF DOLLARS

Item Description for Accounting Period 7/07 Through 6/08	Total	Zero Assets	Under 500	500 to 1,000	1,000 to 5,000	5,000 to 10,000	10,000 to 25,000	25,000 to 50,000	50,000 to 100,000	100,000 to 250,000	250,000 to 500,000	500,000 to 2,500,000	2,500,000 and over
Number of Enterprises **1**	939	256	489	54	77	15	8	13	9	•	6	•	3
Revenues ($ in Thousands)													
Net Sales **2**	5278496	92253	117936	23219	148745	103231	35502	25879	157984	•	523388	•	3456127
Interest **3**	2050353	11798	4452	316	1936	0	2812	1471	6417	•	34019	•	1905587
Rents **4**	14849	0	0	0	0	0	0	3278	193	•	40	•	11338
Royalties **5**	0	0	0	0	0	0	0	0	0	•	0	•	0
Other Portfolio Income **6**	308830	0	0	0	766	0	43	762	15928	•	67969	•	180776
Other Receipts **7**	2904464	80455	113484	22903	146043	103231	32647	20368	135446	•	421360	•	1358426
Total Receipts **8**	5278496	92253	117936	23219	148745	103231	35502	25879	157984	•	523388	•	3456127
Average Total Receipts **9**	5621	360	241	430	1932	6882	4438	1991	17554	•	87231	•	1152042
Operating Costs/Operating Income (%)													
Cost of Operations **10**	0.5	•	•	•	•	•	•	•	•	•	1.3	•	
Salaries and Wages **11**	9.8	14.3	0.3	7.3	14.3	13.1	44.0	4.4	26.0	•	13.9	•	8.5
Taxes Paid **12**	1.3	2.1	0.9	2.5	2.6	3.8	4.4	4.0	3.5	•	1.8	•	0.7
Interest Paid **13**	38.0	33.0	1.3	•	7.7	3.1	1.7	5.9	6.1	•	8.7	•	53.2
Depreciation **14**	0.7	0.6	0.2	0.2	0.3	0.1	0.4	1.8	0.7	•	0.5	•	0.9
Amortization and Depletion **15**	0.4	0.1	•	•	4.4	•	0.1	0.4	0.1	•	1.4	•	0.1
Pensions and Other Deferred Comp. **16**	0.5	0.2	0.7	•	0.9	1.2	0.6	0.6	7.4	•	0.3	•	0.2
Employee Benefits **17**	0.9	0.0	0.9	22.7	2.8	0.4	6.0	•	1.2	•	2.0	•	0.5
Advertising **18**	0.1	•	0.1	•	•	0.1	0.1	•	0.0	•	0.4	•	0.0
Other Expenses **19**	26.2	23.2	44.7	34.8	13.1	6.8	24.7	4.6	24.0	•	14.6	•	26.1
Officers' Compensation **20**	3.0	4.9	10.3	26.8	43.3	8.0	2.5	4.0	4.0	•	4.3	•	0.4
Operating Margin **21**	18.6	21.6	40.6	5.7	10.5	63.2	15.6	78.1	26.9	•	51.0	•	9.4
Operating Margin Before Officers' Comp. **22**	21.6	26.5	50.8	32.5	53.8	71.2	18.1	78.1	30.9	•	55.3	•	9.7

Selected Average Balance Sheet ($ in Thousands)

Net Receivables **23**	12051	0	0	953	3356	1180	2798	15737	56560	2785135
Inventories **24**	•	•	•	•	•	•	•	•	•	•
Net Property, Plant and Equipment **25**	219	0	13	18	30	205	1214	1385	18976	15454
Total Assets **26**	53800	764	86	2655	9317	16367	36743	66580	350632	13927979
Notes and Loans Payable **27**	2382	0	14	1298	2510	2626	13465	22386	66364	346911
All Other Liabilities **28**	46916	0	1	529	3538	7010	1359	40342	174280	12711583
Net Worth **29**	4502	0	71	828	3269	6731	21919	3853	109987	869485

Selected Financial Ratios (Times to 1)

Current Ratio **30**	1.7	61.5	•	2.4	1.8	0.8	1.7	1.2	0.9	1.9
Quick Ratio **31**	0.9	58.4	•	2.3	1.1	0.3	0.9	0.6	0.5	0.9
Net Sales to Working Capital **32**	0.3	5.7	•	2.0	2.3	•	0.2	2.6	•	0.2
Coverage Ratio **33**	1.5	33.3	1.7	2.4	21.3	10.2	14.1	5.4	6.9	1.2
Total Asset Turnover **34**	0.1	2.8	•	0.7	0.7	0.3	0.1	0.3	0.2	0.1
Inventory Turnover **35**	•	•	•	•	•	•	•	•	•	•
Receivables Turnover **36**	•	•	•	•	•	•	•	•	•	•
Total Liabilities to Net Worth **37**	11.0	0.2	•	2.2	1.8	1.4	0.7	16.3	2.2	15.0
Current Assets to Working Capital **38**	2.5	1.0	•	1.7	2.3	2.5	2.5	6.9	•	2.2
Current Liabilities to Working Capital **39**	1.5	0.0	•	0.7	1.3	1.5	1.5	5.9	•	1.2
Working Capital to Net Sales **40**	3.5	0.2	•	0.5	0.4	4.6	4.6	0.4	•	5.3
Inventory to Working Capital **41**	0.0	•	•	•	•	•	•	•	•	•
Total Receipts to Cash Flow **42**	2.6	1.2	2.3	4.7	1.5	3.1	1.2	2.6	1.9	3.3
Cost of Goods to Cash Flow **43**	0.0	•	•	•	•	•	•	•	0.0	•
Cash Flow to Total Debt **44**	0.0	13.4	1.5	0.2	0.8	0.1	0.1	0.1	0.2	0.0

Selected Financial Factors (in Percentages)

Debt Ratio **45**	91.6	•	17.0	14.7	68.8	58.9	40.3	94.2	68.6	93.8
Return on Total Assets **46**	5.9	•	117.7	3.2	13.3	4.7	4.5	8.8	14.8	5.2
Return on Equity Before Income Taxes **47**	23.5	•	137.5	3.8	24.5	10.3	7.1	123.6	40.5	12.8
Return on Equity After Income Taxes **48**	16.8	•	137.5	3.2	20.8	10.2	6.7	90.6	26.4	8.5
Profit Margin (Before Income Tax) **49**	18.8	21.6	40.6	5.7	10.5	15.6	77.7	27.1	51.0	9.6
Profit Margin (After Income Tax) **50**	13.5	14.0	40.6	4.9	8.9	15.4	74.1	19.9	33.3	6.4

Table I

Corporations with and without Net Income

SECURITIES & COMMODITY EXCHANGES, OTHER FINANCIAL INVESTMENT

MONEY AMOUNTS AND SIZE OF ASSETS IN THOUSANDS OF DOLLARS

Item Description for Accounting Period 7/07 Through 6/08	Total	Zero Assets	Under 500	500 to 1,000	1,000 to 5,000	5,000 to 10,000	10,000 to 25,000	25,000 to 50,000	50,000 to 100,000	100,000 to 250,000	250,000 to 500,000	500,000 to 2,500,000	2,500,000 and over
Number of Enterprises 1	42937	6667	29752	1646	2861	686	627	280	162	120	42	60	33
Revenues ($ in Thousands)													
Net Sales 2	145012272	20658483	10258574	1687238	6948272	3924811	3865222	5828196	4500606	5652743	3438882	16559904	61689343
Interest 3	21247083	1495468	29706	6532	298201	61568	64659	123510	150612	213830	246292	1357657	17199046
Rents 4	560852	354140	2971	0	1115	805	5006	1335	7586	5732	596	32082	149484
Royalties 5	66520	96	35305	7198	13879	1027	24	2179	890	2236	40	3586	60
Other Portfolio Income 6	3199450	102369	21659	33451	102124	211110	362267	375261	119398	341150	228529	342846	959288
Other Receipts 7	119938367	18706410	10168933	1640057	6532953	3650301	3433266	5325911	4222120	5089795	2963425	14823733	43381465
Total Receipts 8	145012272	20658483	10258574	1687238	6948272	3924811	3865222	5828196	4500606	5652743	3438882	16559904	61689343
Average Total Receipts 9	3377	3099	345	1025	2429	5721	6165	20815	27782	47106	81878	275998	1869374
Operating Costs/Operating Income (%)													
Cost of Operations 10	0.6	0.7	•	1.7	0.0	0.2	1.0	2.4	1.3	0.2	0.0	0.3	0.7
Salaries and Wages 11	19.5	19.0	20.1	18.7	20.6	27.4	25.3	25.1	25.9	20.6	26.2	24.1	15.8
Taxes Paid 12	2.2	1.6	2.7	2.5	2.3	2.6	2.8	2.5	2.7	2.8	3.4	2.4	1.9
Interest Paid 13	12.8	5.8	0.6	1.0	0.9	3.2	2.6	2.9	3.6	3.7	5.9	7.2	24.4
Depreciation 14	1.1	0.6	0.6	4.1	0.9	1.3	1.0	1.6	1.1	1.5	1.3	1.0	1.1
Amortization and Depletion 15	0.9	0.4	0.1	0.2	0.2	1.4	0.2	0.6	0.5	0.5	1.3	2.0	1.0
Pensions and Other Deferred Comp. 16	1.2	1.7	2.6	2.5	1.3	0.6	0.9	1.0	0.6	0.9	0.7	0.5	1.1
Employee Benefits 17	1.5	1.9	2.0	1.6	1.4	2.0	1.2	1.1	0.9	1.0	1.2	1.9	1.3
Advertising 18	1.1	1.3	1.3	0.3	0.2	0.4	0.4	1.2	1.0	0.5	0.2	0.8	1.3
Other Expenses 19	36.8	56.9	33.0	14.0	34.5	32.4	33.2	27.6	27.4	24.1	38.5	36.6	34.8
Officers' Compensation 20	8.5	1.7	23.1	35.5	25.3	15.1	12.5	14.8	20.2	22.5	6.6	7.9	2.7
Operating Margin 21	13.9	8.2	13.8	18.1	12.3	13.3	19.0	19.3	14.9	21.8	14.7	15.2	13.9
Operating Margin Before Officers' Comp. 22	22.4	9.9	36.9	53.6	37.6	28.5	31.5	34.1	35.1	44.3	21.3	23.1	16.5

Selected Average Balance Sheet ($ in Thousands)

Net Receivables 23	1828	0	4	60	206	545	1185	4284	6558	14402	38616	138604	1897297
Inventories 24	•	•	•	•	•	•	•	•	•	•	•	•	•
Net Property, Plant and Equipment 25	281	0	10	107	355	691	763	2198	4498	5287	13850	19225	179010
Total Assets 26	14755	0	68	696	2283	7046	16024	35513	67774	151678	351225	1040037	14929825
Notes and Loans Payable 27	4928	0	35	129	597	2275	4356	11136	15486	31247	94248	264802	5306275
All Other Liabilities 28	5208	0	19	185	586	2200	1555	6200	11386	26183	54179	353164	5708181
Net Worth 29	4620	0	13	382	1100	2572	10112	18177	40901	94248	202798	422070	3915368

Selected Financial Ratios (Times to 1)

Current Ratio 30	1.1	•	1.7	2.4	2.3	1.1	2.1	2.3	2.3	2.2	1.4	1.1	
Quick Ratio 31	0.8	•	1.6	2.1	1.8	0.7	1.4	1.7	1.8	1.6	0.8	0.7	
Net Sales to Working Capital 32	3.8	•	24.1	4.9	5.3	34.5	2.4	2.6	1.9	1.5	2.5	3.8	
Coverage Ratio 33	2.1	2.4	23.5	19.7	14.8	5.2	8.3	7.7	5.1	6.8	3.7	3.1	1.6
Total Asset Turnover 34	0.2	•	5.1	1.5	1.1	0.8	0.4	0.6	0.4	0.3	0.2	0.3	0.1
Inventory Turnover 35	•	•	•	•	•	•	•	•	•	•	•	•	•
Receivables Turnover 36	•	•	•	•	•	•	•	•	•	•	•	•	•
Total Liabilities to Net Worth 37	2.2	•	4.0	0.8	1.1	1.7	0.6	1.0	0.7	0.6	0.7	1.5	2.8
Current Assets to Working Capital 38	7.7	•	2.5	1.7	1.8	14.5	1.9	1.8	1.8	1.8	1.8	3.4	15.0
Current Liabilities to Working Capital 39	6.7	•	1.5	0.7	0.8	13.5	0.9	0.8	0.8	0.8	0.8	2.4	14.0
Working Capital to Net Sales 40	0.3	•	0.0	0.2	0.2	0.0	0.4	0.4	0.5	0.7	0.9	0.4	0.3
Inventory to Working Capital 41	0.0	•	0.0	0.0	0.0	•	0.0	0.0	0.0	0.0	0.0	0.0	0.0
Total Receipts to Cash Flow 42	2.2	1.6	2.4	3.5	2.4	2.8	2.4	2.6	2.6	2.5	2.1	2.1	2.2
Cost of Goods to Cash Flow 43	0.0	0.0	1.6	0.1	0.0	0.0	0.0	0.1	0.0	0.0	0.0	0.0	0.0
Cash Flow to Total Debt 44	0.2	•	2.7	0.9	0.8	0.5	0.4	0.5	0.4	0.3	0.2	0.2	0.1

Selected Financial Factors (in Percentages)

Debt Ratio 45	68.7	•	80.1	45.1	51.8	63.5	36.9	48.8	39.7	42.3	59.4	73.8	
Return on Total Assets 46	6.2	•	73.1	27.8	13.9	13.4	8.2	12.9	7.5	7.8	5.0	4.9	
Return on Equity Before Income Taxes 47	10.4	•	351.7	48.0	26.9	29.6	11.4	22.0	9.9	10.7	6.4	7.0	
Return on Equity After Income Taxes 48	7.5	•	348.6	45.7	25.4	26.4	8.6	16.7	8.7	8.9	3.3	4.9	
Profit Margin (Before Income Tax) 49	14.2	8.1	13.8	17.9	12.2	13.3	18.7	19.2	14.6	21.4	15.8	15.1	14.7
Profit Margin (After Income Tax) 50	10.2	5.3	13.6	17.0	11.5	11.9	14.1	14.6	12.7	17.7	8.2	7.3	10.3

Table II

Corporations with Net Income

SECURITIES & COMMODITY EXCHANGES, OTHER FINANCIAL INVESTMENT

MONEY AMOUNTS AND SIZE OF ASSETS IN THOUSANDS OF DOLLARS

Item Description for Accounting Period 7/07 Through 6/08	Total	Zero Assets	Under 500	500 to 1,000	1,000 to 5,000	5,000 to 10,000	10,000 to 25,000	25,000 to 50,000	50,000 to 100,000	100,000 to 250,000	250,000 to 500,000	500,000 to 2,500,000	2,500,000 and over
Number of Enterprises **1**	26282	2119	20153	1369	1572	333	324	158	99	65	23	40	27
Revenues ($ in Thousands)													
Net Sales **2**	121360648	20059948	8726060	1652238	6060512	2862480	3144932	4540809	4006597	4741163	2444855	14065493	49055559
Interest **3**	8573096	1442424	24227	6181	47070	54289	45190	88610	105855	173369	167541	1081866	5336473
Rents **4**	556134	354096	2971	0	707	805	1844	1281	6966	5320	595	32065	149484
Royalties **5**	54317	47	35305	0	13872	1	0	0	890	526	40	3576	60
Other Portfolio Income **6**	2845477	89608	21403	32547	77107	180410	331141	367798	94044	266396	203843	260753	920426
Other Receipts **7**	109331624	18173773	8642154	1613510	5921756	2626975	2766757	4083120	3798842	4295552	2072836	12687233	42649116
Total Receipts **8**	121360648	20059948	8726060	1652238	6060512	2862480	3144932	4540809	4006597	4741163	2444855	14065493	49055559
Average Total Receipts **9**	4618	9467	433	1207	3855	8596	9707	28739	40471	72941	106298	351637	1816873
Operating Costs/Operating Income (%)													
Cost of Operations **10**	0.6	0.6	•	•	•	0.3	1.1	3.1	1.1	0.0	•	0.0	0.8
Salaries and Wages **11**	19.1	18.2	16.5	18.8	20.4	17.7	18.8	24.5	25.4	19.1	20.2	18.2	19.0
Taxes Paid **12**	2.3	1.6	2.5	2.4	2.4	2.6	2.9	2.5	2.6	2.6	4.1	2.5	2.3
Interest Paid **13**	4.9	5.6	0.5	0.8	0.5	3.0	1.7	2.3	1.9	2.2	6.4	5.4	7.0
Depreciation **14**	1.1	0.6	0.5	4.1	0.7	0.9	0.7	1.5	0.9	1.6	1.5	0.8	1.4
Amortization and Depletion **15**	0.7	0.2	0.1	0.1	0.2	0.7	0.1	0.6	0.3	0.2	1.7	1.5	1.1
Pensions and Other Deferred Comp. **16**	1.2	1.5	2.4	2.6	1.4	0.8	0.9	0.7	0.6	0.5	0.8	0.5	1.2
Employee Benefits **17**	1.6	1.8	2.0	1.6	1.4	1.8	1.0	1.0	0.7	0.8	1.4	1.9	1.6
Advertising **18**	1.1	1.2	1.1	0.2	0.2	0.4	0.4	1.5	0.9	0.4	0.3	0.7	1.6
Other Expenses **19**	38.3	57.0	31.2	13.6	24.7	29.2	24.1	19.8	22.3	14.7	26.6	35.4	42.5
Officers' Compensation **20**	8.2	1.7	24.3	34.5	26.3	16.1	10.5	8.4	20.0	23.3	7.3	3.9	3.1
Operating Margin **21**	20.9	10.2	19.0	21.3	22.0	26.6	37.9	34.0	23.3	34.5	29.7	29.3	18.4
Operating Margin Before Officers' Comp. **22**	29.1	11.9	43.2	55.8	48.3	42.7	48.3	42.5	43.3	57.9	37.0	33.1	21.5

Selected Average Balance Sheet ($ in Thousands)

Net Receivables 23	2750	0	4	69	182	586	1382	5102	7743	15560	60468	168950	2238372
Inventories 24	•	•	•	•	•	•	•	•	•	•	•	•	•
Net Property, Plant and Equipment 25	372	0	12	119	403	590	823	2327	3938	6102	20760	21585	214127
Total Assets 26	15372	0	81	704	2167	6969	15886	36247	67682	155936	356478	1053744	11763566
Notes and Loans Payable 27	3642	0	30	110	331	1387	3528	11161	10290	25800	80091	220519	2878639
All Other Liabilities 28	5738	0	18	214	498	2903	1706	5099	12229	29026	61147	327514	4794124
Net Worth 29	5991	0	33	379	1338	2679	10651	19987	45163	101109	215240	505712	4090804

Selected Financial Ratios (Times to 1)

Current Ratio 30	1.6	•	2.1	2.1	2.3	1.0	2.4	3.5	2.4	2.7	2.5	1.4	1.5
Quick Ratio 31	1.2	•	1.9	1.9	2.0	0.6	1.5	2.7	2.0	1.9	1.8	0.9	1.2
Net Sales to Working Capital 32	1.8	•	19.8	7.0	7.5	•	2.8	2.4	2.4	1.8	1.0	2.9	1.0
Coverage Ratio 33	5.3	2.8	36.4	27.0	49.7	9.9	22.9	15.9	13.5	16.6	5.9	6.4	3.8
Total Asset Turnover 34	0.3	•	5.3	1.7	1.8	1.2	0.6	0.8	0.6	0.5	0.3	0.3	0.2
Inventory Turnover 35	•	•	•	•	•	•	•	•	•	•	•	•	•
Receivables Turnover 36	•	•	•	•	•	•	•	•	•	•	•	•	•
Total Liabilities to Net Worth 37	1.6	•	1.5	0.9	0.6	1.6	0.5	0.8	0.5	0.5	0.7	1.1	1.9
Current Assets to Working Capital 38	2.8	•	2.0	1.9	1.8	•	1.7	1.4	1.7	1.6	1.7	3.2	2.9
Current Liabilities to Working Capital 39	1.8	•	1.0	0.9	0.8	0.7	0.7	0.4	0.7	0.6	0.7	2.2	1.9
Working Capital to Net Sales 40	0.6	•	0.1	0.1	0.1	0.4	0.4	0.4	0.4	0.5	1.0	0.3	1.0
Inventory to Working Capital 41	0.0	•	•	•	•	•	0.0	0.0	0.0	•	•	0.0	0.0
Total Receipts to Cash Flow 42	1.8	1.6	2.2	3.2	2.5	2.1	1.9	2.2	2.4	2.3	2.0	1.6	1.8
Cost of Goods to Cash Flow 43	0.0	0.0	•	•	•	0.0	0.0	0.1	0.0	0.0	•	0.0	0.0
Cash Flow to Total Debt 44	0.3	•	4.1	1.2	1.9	1.0	0.8	0.8	0.7	0.4	0.4	0.4	0.1

Selected Financial Factors (in Percentages)

Debt Ratio 45	61.0	•	59.5	46.1	38.2	61.6	33.0	44.9	33.3	35.2	39.6	52.0	65.2
Return on Total Assets 46	7.9	•	103.9	37.5	39.8	36.4	24.0	28.7	15.0	17.1	11.3	11.5	4.1
Return on Equity Before Income Taxes 47	16.4	•	249.1	67.0	63.1	85.2	34.3	48.8	20.8	24.8	15.5	20.3	8.7
Return on Equity After Income Taxes 48	12.8	•	247.2	64.2	60.9	79.0	29.2	40.3	18.9	22.1	10.3	13.9	6.2
Profit Margin (Before Income Tax) 49	21.3	10.2	19.0	21.1	21.9	26.6	37.6	33.9	23.2	34.4	31.5	29.2	19.5
Profit Margin (After Income Tax) 50	16.6	7.2	18.8	20.2	21.1	24.6	32.1	28.0	21.1	30.7	20.9	20.0	13.9

Table I

Corporations with and without Net Income

LIFE INSURANCE

MONEY AMOUNTS AND SIZE OF ASSETS IN THOUSANDS OF DOLLARS

Item Description for Accounting Period 7/07 Through 6/08	Total	Zero Assets	Under 500	500 to 1,000	1,000 to 5,000	5,000 to 10,000	10,000 to 25,000	25,000 to 50,000	50,000 to 100,000	100,000 to 250,000	250,000 to 500,000	500,000 to 2,500,000	2,500,000 and over
Number of Enterprises **1**	1027	44	•	99	155	54	96	54	41	35	40	58	90
Revenues ($ in Thousands)													
Net Sales **2**	999629247	1274637	•	36715	161499	115643	1731791	1195358	1329127	1720764	5307317	13874601	972837662
Interest **3**	179628710	100696	•	3727	31730	11244	1053344	92098	157555	212400	654492	2890813	174418330
Rents **4**	3627227	0	•	0	551	394	3179	673	6950	7299	13943	24760	3569478
Royalties **5**	13100	0	•	0	0	0	0	0	0	732	42	133	12192
Other Portfolio Income **6**	27583916	20910	•	171	4263	5969	16477	10340	13396	36223	82674	230789	27161764
Other Receipts **7**	788776294	1153031	•	32817	124955	98036	658791	1092247	1151226	1464110	4556166	10728106	767675898
Total Receipts **8**	999629247	1274637	•	36715	161499	115643	1731791	1195358	1329127	1720764	5307317	13874601	972837662
Average Total Receipts **9**	973349	28969	•	371	1042	2142	18039	22136	32418	49165	132683	239217	10809307
Operating Costs/Operating Income (%)													
Cost of Operations **10**	56.7	9.0	•	32.1	27.0	26.7	13.2	44.9	47.2	43.2	43.3	48.9	57.1
Salaries and Wages **11**	2.1	•	•	•	•	•	0.0	0.3	1.2	0.3	0.4	0.9	2.1
Taxes Paid **12**	0.8	1.0	•	0.8	1.3	1.2	0.5	1.0	1.6	1.6	1.2	1.2	0.8
Interest Paid **13**	3.9	•	•	0.6	0.2	0.0	0.1	0.6	0.2	3.7	0.7	0.9	4.0
Depreciation **14**	0.6	0.1	•	0.1	0.1	0.5	0.2	0.2	0.4	0.4	0.3	0.4	0.6
Amortization and Depletion **15**	1.0	0.8	•	0.6	1.4	1.4	0.7	1.4	2.7	2.6	2.0	2.1	1.0
Pensions and Other Deferred Comp. **16**	0.3	0.2	•	•	0.2	0.2	0.1	0.3	1.4	0.6	0.5	0.7	0.3
Employee Benefits **17**	0.3	0.0	•	•	0.0	0.4	0.1	0.2	0.6	0.2	0.1	0.3	0.3
Advertising **18**	0.3	0.0	•	•	0.0	0.7	0.0	0.1	1.0	0.1	0.4	0.7	0.3
Other Expenses **19**	30.8	92.4	•	38.8	49.2	49.7	33.8	44.5	40.3	52.0	45.6	46.1	30.3
Officers' Compensation **20**	0.1	•	•	•	•	•	0.0	0.1	0.0	•	0.2	0.2	0.1
Operating Margin **21**	3.0	•	•	27.1	20.5	19.1	51.1	6.4	3.5	•	5.1	•	3.0
Operating Margin Before Officers' Comp. **22**	3.1	•	•	27.1	20.5	19.1	51.2	6.4	3.5	•	5.3	•	3.1

Selected Average Balance Sheet ($ in Thousands)

Net Receivables 23	103514	•	29	67	231	1224	1976	5071	1186	3897	31173	1153809
Inventories 24	•	•	•	•	•	•	•	•	•	•	•	•
Net Property, Plant and Equipment 25	56046	0	0	9	121	106	109	783	699	1747	3477	635630
Total Assets 26	5735681	•	749	2649	7341	16462	35773	72430	159273	351729	1193202	64380912
Notes and Loans Payable 27	243400	0	0	0	0	141	108	421	9430	•	4247	2770239
All Other Liabilities 28	4694915	0	487	1287	4520	10103	22629	50858	139056	284455	997323	52697374
Net Worth 29	797366	0	262	1362	2821	6359	13003	21464	19796	57844	191632	8913299

Selected Financial Ratios (Times to 1)

Current Ratio 30	0.4	•	4.3	8.4	4.0	2.0	2.6	2.8	0.8	1.5	1.1	0.4
Quick Ratio 31	0.3	•	3.6	6.3	3.2	1.5	1.9	2.3	0.6	1.2	0.8	0.3
Net Sales to Working Capital 32	•	•	0.9	0.6	0.9	4.1	2.2	1.4	•	3.1	5.5	•
Coverage Ratio 33	1.8	•	44.2	126.1	907.1	620.2	11.8	19.4	•	7.8	•	1.8
Total Asset Turnover 34	0.2	•	0.5	0.4	0.3	1.1	0.6	0.4	0.3	0.4	0.2	0.2
Inventory Turnover 35	•	•	•	•	•	•	•	•	•	•	•	•
Receivables Turnover 36	•	•	•	•	•	•	•	•	•	•	•	•
Total Liabilities to Net Worth 37	6.2	•	1.9	0.9	1.6	1.6	1.8	2.4	7.0	5.1	5.2	6.2
Current Assets to Working Capital 38	•	•	1.3	1.1	2.0	2.0	1.6	1.5	•	3.1	9.6	•
Current Liabilities to Working Capital 39	•	•	0.3	0.1	0.3	1.0	0.6	0.5	•	2.1	8.6	•
Working Capital to Net Sales 40	•	•	1.1	1.6	1.2	0.2	0.5	0.7	•	0.3	0.2	•
Inventory to Working Capital 41	•	•	•	•	•	•	•	•	•	•	•	•
Total Receipts to Cash Flow 42	3.1	1.1	1.5	1.5	1.6	1.2	2.0	2.4	2.2	2.0	2.4	3.2
Cost of Goods to Cash Flow 43	1.8	0.1	0.5	0.4	0.4	0.2	0.9	1.1	1.0	0.9	1.2	1.8
Cash Flow to Total Debt 44	0.1	•	0.5	0.6	0.3	1.5	0.5	0.3	0.2	0.2	0.1	0.1

Selected Financial Factors (in Percentages)

Debt Ratio 45	86.1	•	65.0	48.6	61.6	61.4	63.7	70.4	87.6	83.6	83.9	86.2
Return on Total Assets 46	1.2	•	13.7	8.0	5.5	56.1	4.2	1.6	•	2.2	0.8	1.2
Return on Equity Before Income Taxes 47	3.8	•	38.3	15.5	14.3	145.1	10.6	5.2	•	11.6	•	3.8
Return on Equity After Income Taxes 48	2.5	•	36.6	13.3	11.4	93.3	7.9	3.0	•	8.6	•	2.5
Profit Margin (Before Income Tax) 49	3.1	•	27.1	20.3	18.8	51.1	6.2	3.5	•	5.0	•	3.1
Profit Margin (After Income Tax) 50	2.0	•	25.9	17.4	15.1	32.9	4.6	2.0	•	3.7	•	2.1

Table II
Corporations with Net Income

LIFE INSURANCE

MONEY AMOUNTS AND SIZE OF ASSETS IN THOUSANDS OF DOLLARS

Item Description for Accounting Period 7/07 Through 6/08		Total	Zero Assets	Under 500	500 to 1,000	1,000 to 5,000	5,000 to 10,000	10,000 to 25,000	25,000 to 50,000	50,000 to 100,000	100,000 to 250,000	250,000 to 500,000	500,000 to 2,500,000	2,500,000 and over
Number of Enterprises	1	795	19	181	94	131	44	79	40	28	27	32	47	72
Revenues ($ in Thousands)														
Net Sales	2	895977902	269313	25339	36391	141899	96891	1583805	1086528	733160	1377984	4132246	11822779	874671567
Interest	3	163307970	94895	1531	3632	29094	9454	1044078	75258	80178	171199	477184	2451724	158869744
Rents	4	3266347	0	0	0	551	328	2144	646	4549	7208	11179	23627	3216116
Royalties	5	8580	0	0	0	0	0	0	0	0	732	42	131	7675
Other Portfolio Income	6	24608439	3893	52	150	3861	5182	16291	8658	9912	14216	75389	156966	24313869
Other Receipts	7	704786566	170525	23756	32609	108393	81927	521292	1001966	638521	1184629	3568452	9190331	688264163
Total Receipts	8	895977902	269313	25339	36391	141899	96891	1583805	1086528	733160	1377984	4132246	11822779	874671567
Average Total Receipts	9	1127016	14174	140	387	1083	2202	20048	27163	26184	51036	129133	251548	12148216
Operating Costs/Operating Income (%)														
Cost of Operations	10	56.0	42.2	22.9	32.3	28.4	24.7	9.7	44.0	41.0	46.6	45.2	46.9	56.3
Salaries and Wages	11	2.2	•	•	•	•	•	0.0	0.3	2.1	0.3	0.5	0.9	2.2
Taxes Paid	12	0.8	1.1	0.7	0.8	1.2	1.4	0.4	0.8	1.5	1.8	1.3	1.2	0.8
Interest Paid	13	4.2	•	0.0	0.5	0.2	0.0	0.1	0.2	0.2	0.4	0.9	0.6	4.3
Depreciation	14	0.7	0.2	0.1	0.1	0.1	0.5	0.1	0.2	0.5	0.3	0.3	0.4	0.7
Amortization and Depletion	15	1.0	2.9	0.5	0.5	1.5	1.0	0.4	1.3	2.0	2.7	2.2	2.0	0.9
Pensions and Other Deferred Comp.	16	0.3	0.3	•	•	0.1	0.2	0.1	0.2	1.9	0.6	0.5	0.7	0.3
Employee Benefits	17	0.3	•	•	•	0.0	0.5	0.1	0.1	1.0	0.3	0.1	0.3	0.3
Advertising	18	0.3	•	•	•	0.0	0.2	0.0	0.1	0.3	0.1	0.4	0.7	0.3
Other Expenses	19	30.2	40.8	38.6	38.3	43.7	44.9	29.5	44.7	38.1	40.2	41.4	38.4	30.0
Officers' Compensation	20	0.1	•	•	•	•	•	0.0	•	0.1	•	0.3	0.2	0.1
Operating Margin	21	3.9	12.5	37.1	27.5	24.8	26.7	59.5	8.0	11.3	6.7	6.8	7.7	3.7
Operating Margin Before Officers' Comp.	22	4.0	12.5	37.1	27.5	24.8	26.7	59.5	8.0	11.4	6.7	7.1	7.9	3.8

Selected Average Balance Sheet ($ in Thousands)

Net Receivables 23	133061	0	13	25	78	282	1480	1332	4778	1489	4827	38083	1437055
Inventories 24	•	•	•	•	•	•	•	•	•	•	•	•	•
Net Property, Plant and Equipment 25	71712	0	0	0	0	84	47	79	706	870	1848	3871	787721
Total Assets 26	6504212	0	203	759	2640	6875	16328	36819	71583	159652	349145	1173629	70759458
Notes and Loans Payable 27	302689	0	0	0	0	0	0	112	157	433	11787	4798	3333536
All Other Liabilities 28	5243080	0	194	489	1177	3856	9342	22018	49529	135363	274428	945636	57054949
Net Worth 29	958443	0	9	270	1463	3018	6986	14688	21897	23856	62930	223195	10370973

Selected Financial Ratios (Times to 1)

Current Ratio 30	0.4	•	6.3	5.0	11.8	3.2	2.5	2.4	3.6	1.0	1.3	1.2	0.4
Quick Ratio 31	0.3	•	5.4	4.2	9.1	2.5	1.8	1.7	2.9	0.8	1.1	0.9	0.3
Net Sales to Working Capital 32	•	•	1.0	0.9	0.6	1.1	3.7	2.6	1.1	•	3.8	4.2	•
Coverage Ratio 33	1.9	•	1044.4	54.1	136.4	1074.7	659.9	35.0	57.9	17.3	8.3	14.4	1.9
Total Asset Turnover 34	0.2	•	0.7	0.5	0.4	0.3	1.2	0.7	0.4	0.3	0.4	0.2	0.2
Inventory Turnover 35	•	•	•	•	•	•	•	•	•	•	•	•	•
Receivables Turnover 36	•	•	•	•	•	•	•	•	•	•	•	•	•
Total Liabilities to Net Worth 37	5.8	•	22.2	1.8	0.8	1.3	1.5	1.5	2.3	5.7	4.5	4.3	5.8
Current Assets to Working Capital 38	•	•	1.2	1.2	1.1	1.5	1.7	1.7	1.4	•	4.0	6.8	•
Current Liabilities to Working Capital 39	•	•	0.2	0.2	0.1	0.5	0.7	0.7	0.4	•	3.0	5.8	•
Working Capital to Net Sales 40	•	•	1.0	1.2	1.6	0.9	0.3	0.4	0.9	•	0.3	0.2	•
Inventory to Working Capital 41	•	•	•	•	•	•	•	•	•	•	•	•	•
Total Receipts to Cash Flow 42	3.1	1.9	1.3	1.5	1.5	1.5	1.9	1.9	2.2	2.2	2.2	2.2	3.2
Cost of Goods to Cash Flow 43	1.7	0.8	0.3	0.5	0.4	0.4	0.1	0.8	0.9	1.0	1.0	1.0	1.8
Cash Flow to Total Debt 44	0.1	•	0.5	0.5	0.6	0.4	1.9	0.6	0.2	0.2	0.2	0.1	0.1

Selected Financial Factors (in Percentages)

Debt Ratio 45	85.3	•	95.7	64.4	44.6	56.1	57.2	60.1	69.4	85.1	82.0	81.0	85.3
Return on Total Assets 46	1.4	•	25.6	14.3	10.2	8.5	73.2	5.9	4.2	2.3	2.8	1.8	1.4
Return on Equity Before Income Taxes 47	4.6	•	592.9	39.3	18.2	19.4	170.7	14.5	13.5	14.3	13.8	8.7	4.4
Return on Equity After Income Taxes 48	3.2	12.4	571.7	37.5	15.8	16.1	113.5	11.3	10.3	10.4	10.4	5.9	3.1
Profit Margin (Before Income Tax) 49	4.0	12.4	37.1	27.4	24.6	26.6	59.5	7.8	11.3	6.7	6.7	7.7	3.8
Profit Margin (After Income Tax) 50	2.7	8.4	35.7	26.2	21.3	22.1	39.6	6.1	8.6	4.8	5.1	5.3	2.6

Table I

Corporations with and without Net Income

LIFE INSURANCE, STOCK COMPANIES (FORM 1120L)

MONEY AMOUNTS AND SIZE OF ASSETS IN THOUSANDS OF DOLLARS

Item Description for Accounting Period 7/07 Through 6/08	Total	Zero Assets	Under 500	500 to 1,000	1,000 to 5,000	5,000 to 10,000	10,000 to 25,000	25,000 to 50,000	50,000 to 100,000	100,000 to 250,000	250,000 to 500,000	500,000 to 2,500,000	2,500,000 and over
Number of Enterprises 1	969	39	•	97	147	49	96	49	41	29	34	49	80
Revenues ($ in Thousands)													
Net Sales 2	888138179	1274539	•	36642	158259	92425	1731791	1138949	1329127	1391145	4722177	11211237	865007827
Interest 3	156568484	100685	•	3662	30677	9340	1053344	78832	157555	162750	511107	2198860	152259446
Rents 4	2639292	0	•	0	479	386	3179	651	6950	6897	9285	21774	2589692
Royalties 5	7411	0	•	0	0	0	0	0	0	5	42	132	7231
Other Portfolio Income 6	23703755	20910	•	171	3899	5128	16477	9340	13396	31439	76824	198634	23326597
Other Receipts 7	705219237	1152944	•	32809	123204	77571	658791	1050126	1151226	1190054	4124919	8791837	686824861
Total Receipts 8	888138179	1274539	•	36642	158259	92425	1731791	1138949	1329127	1391145	4722177	11211237	865007827
Average Total Receipts 9	916551	32680	•	378	1077	1886	18039	23244	32418	47971	138888	228801	10812598
Operating Costs/Operating Income (%)													
Cost of Operations 10	57.5	8.9	•	32.1	27.2	29.3	13.2	44.2	47.2	39.8	42.8	49.5	57.9
Salaries and Wages 11	2.3	•	•	•	•	•	0.0	0.3	1.2	0.3	0.5	1.1	2.3
Taxes Paid 12	0.8	1.0	•	0.8	1.2	1.0	0.5	1.0	1.6	1.4	1.1	1.2	0.8
Interest Paid 13	4.3	•	•	0.6	0.2	0.0	0.1	0.6	0.2	4.5	0.8	0.8	4.4
Depreciation 14	0.7	0.1	•	0.1	0.1	0.2	0.2	0.2	0.4	0.4	0.3	0.4	0.7
Amortization and Depletion 15	0.9	0.8	•	0.6	1.4	1.3	0.7	1.3	2.7	2.3	1.9	2.0	0.9
Pensions and Other Deferred Comp. 16	0.3	0.2	•	0.2	0.2	0.3	0.1	0.3	1.4	0.6	0.5	0.6	0.3
Employee Benefits 17	0.3	0.0	•	•	0.0	0.1	0.1	0.2	0.6	0.2	0.1	0.3	0.4
Advertising 18	0.3	0.0	•	•	0.0	0.9	0.0	0.1	1.0	0.1	0.4	0.8	0.3
Other Expenses 19	29.7	92.4	•	38.8	48.5	45.0	33.8	45.5	40.3	57.1	45.8	47.3	29.2
Officers' Compensation 20	0.1	•	•	•	•	•	0.0	0.1	0.0	•	0.3	0.2	0.1
Operating Margin 21	2.8	•	•	27.1	21.2	21.9	51.1	6.2	3.5	•	5.6	•	2.8
Operating Margin Before Officers' Comp. 22	2.9	•	•	27.1	21.2	21.9	51.2	6.3	3.5	•	5.9	•	2.9

Selected Average Balance Sheet ($ in Thousands)

Net Receivables **23**	106415	•	29	71	251	1224	2177	5071	729	4541	36761	1258490
Inventories **24**	•	•	•	•	•	•	•	•	•	•	•	•
Net Property, Plant and Equipment **25**	57036	0	0	9	80	106	86	783	643	1761	3628	686991
Total Assets **26**	5443295	•	740	2640	6908	16462	33958	72430	154106	353589	1155923	64929502
Notes and Loans Payable **27**	256268	0	0	0	0		156	108	508	11094	5022	3095924
All Other Liabilities **28**	4408231	0	492	1267	3887	10103	20441	50858	132849	281525	949204	52588811
Net Worth **29**	778796	0	248	1374	3021	6359	13361	21464	60969		201698	9244767

Selected Financial Ratios (Times to 1)

Current Ratio **30**	0.4	•	4.3	9.3	3.6	2.0	2.6	2.8	0.7	1.5	1.3	0.4
Quick Ratio **31**	0.3	•	3.6	7.0	2.8	1.5	1.9	2.3	0.6	1.1	0.9	0.3
Net Sales to Working Capital **32**	•	•	0.9	0.6	0.9	4.1	2.3	1.4	•	3.2	2.7	•
Coverage Ratio **33**	1.7	•	44.1	127.7	839.2	620.2	11.1	19.4	•	7.8		1.7
Total Asset Turnover **34**	0.2	•	0.5	0.4	0.3	1.1	0.7	0.4	0.3	0.4	0.2	0.2
Inventory Turnover **35**	•	•	•	•	•	•	•	•	•	•	•	•
Receivables Turnover **36**	•	•	•	•	•	•	•	•	•	•	•	•
Total Liabilities to Net Worth **37**	6.0	•	2.0	0.9	1.3	1.6	1.5	2.4	6.4	4.8	4.7	6.0
Current Assets to Working Capital **38**	•	•	1.3	1.1	1.4	2.0	1.6	1.5	•	3.1	4.9	•
Current Liabilities to Working Capital **39**	•	•	0.3	0.1	0.4	1.0	0.6	0.5	•	2.1	3.9	•
Working Capital to Net Sales **40**	•	•	1.1	1.7	1.2	0.2	0.4	0.7	0.3	0.3	0.4	•
Inventory to Working Capital **41**	•	•	•	•	•	•	•	•	•	•	0.0	•
Total Receipts to Cash Flow **42**	3.2	1.1	1.5	1.5	1.6	1.2	2.0	2.4	2.1	2.0	2.4	3.3
Cost of Goods to Cash Flow **43**	1.9	0.1	0.5	0.4	0.5	0.2	0.9	1.1	0.8	0.9	1.2	1.9
Cash Flow to Total Debt **44**	0.1	•	0.5	0.6	0.3	1.5	0.6	0.3	0.2	0.2	0.1	0.1

Selected Financial Factors (in Percentages)

Debt Ratio **45**	85.7	•	66.5	48.0	56.3	61.4	60.7	70.4	86.5	82.8	82.6	85.8
Return on Total Assets **46**	1.2	•	14.1	8.6	6.0	56.1	4.6	1.6	•	2.5		1.2
Return on Equity Before Income Taxes **47**	3.4	•	41.2	16.4	13.6	145.1	10.6	5.2	•	12.7		3.4
Return on Equity After Income Taxes **48**	2.2	•	39.3	14.1	10.8	93.3	7.9	3.0	•	9.4		2.2
Profit Margin (Before Income Tax) **49**	2.9	•	27.1	21.0	21.8	51.1	6.1	3.5	•	5.6		2.9
Profit Margin (After Income Tax) **50**	1.9	•	25.8	18.0	17.3	32.9	4.5	2.0	•	4.1		1.9

Table II
Corporations with Net Income

LIFE INSURANCE, STOCK COMPANIES (FORM 1120L)

MONEY AMOUNTS AND SIZE OF ASSETS IN THOUSANDS OF DOLLARS

Item Description for Accounting Period 7/07 Through 6/08	Total	Zero Assets	Under 500	500 to 1,000	1,000 to 5,000	5,000 to 10,000	10,000 to 25,000	25,000 to 50,000	50,000 to 100,000	100,000 to 250,000	250,000 to 500,000	500,000 to 2,500,000	2,500,000 and over
Number of Enterprises **1**	753	•	179	92	129	•	79	35	28	•	29	38	65
Revenues ($ in Thousands)													
Net Sales **2**	789616859	•	25266	36317	141016	•	1583805	1030119	733160	•	3936379	9159414	771483953
Interest **3**	141101500	•	1478	3567	28482	•	1044078	61991	80178	•	429410	1759770	137454745
Rents **4**	2325524	•	0	0	479	•	2144	624	4549	•	8451	20641	2281411
Royalties **5**	7409	•	0	0	0	•	0	0	0	•	42	131	7231
Other Portfolio Income **6**	20752063	•	52	150	3819	•	16291	7659	9912	•	71434	124811	20498243
Other Receipts **7**	625430363	•	23736	32600	108236	•	521292	959845	638521	•	3427042	7254061	611242323
Total Receipts **8**	789616859	•	25266	36317	141016	•	1583805	1030119	733160	•	3936379	9159414	771483953
Average Total Receipts **9**	1048628	•	141	395	1093	•	20048	29432	26184	•	135737	241037	11868984
Operating Costs/Operating Income (%)													
Cost of Operations **10**	57.0	•	23.0	32.4	28.5	•	9.7	43.3	41.0	•	45.3	47.0	57.4
Salaries and Wages **11**	2.4	•	•	•	•	•	0.0	0.3	2.1	•	0.6	1.2	2.4
Taxes Paid **12**	0.8	•	0.7	0.8	1.2	•	0.4	0.7	1.5	•	1.2	1.2	0.8
Interest Paid **13**	4.6	•	0.0	0.5	0.2	•	0.1	0.2	0.2	•	1.0	0.5	4.7
Depreciation **14**	0.7	•	0.1	0.1	0.1	•	0.1	0.1	0.5	•	0.3	0.4	0.7
Amortization and Depletion **15**	0.9	•	0.6	0.5	1.5	•	0.4	1.2	2.0	•	2.2	1.9	0.9
Pensions and Other Deferred Comp. **16**	0.3	•	•	•	0.1	•	0.1	0.2	1.9	•	0.5	0.7	0.3
Employee Benefits **17**	0.4	•	•	•	0.0	•	0.1	0.1	1.0	•	0.1	0.4	0.4
Advertising **18**	0.3	•	•	•	0.0	•	0.0	0.1	0.3	•	0.4	0.9	0.3
Other Expenses **19**	28.8	•	38.6	38.3	43.5	•	29.5	45.7	38.1	•	41.2	37.6	28.6
Officers' Compensation **20**	0.1	•	•	•	•	•	0.0	•	0.1	•	0.3	0.2	0.1
Operating Margin **21**	3.7	•	37.0	27.4	24.9	•	59.5	7.9	11.3	•	6.9	8.1	3.5
Operating Margin Before Officers' Comp. **22**	3.8	•	37.0	27.4	24.9	•	59.5	7.9	11.4	•	7.3	8.4	3.6

Selected Average Balance Sheet ($ in Thousands)

Net Receivables 23	136270	13	26	80	1480	1523	4778	•	5320	46925	1543415
Inventories 24	•	•	•	•	•	•	•	•	•	•	•
Net Property, Plant and Equipment 25	73109	0	0	0	47	43	706	•	1988	4159	842945
Total Assets 26	6089227	199	750	2615	16328	34426	71583	•	348885	1120924	69596847
Notes and Loans Payable 27	317384	0	0	0	0	128	157	•	13007	5927	3667184
All Other Liabilities 28	4843385	190	494	1130	9342	18867	49529	•	271278	871346	55385529
Net Worth 29	928459	9	256	1485	6986	15431	21897	•	64600	243651	10544135

Selected Financial Ratios (Times to 1)

Current Ratio 30	0.4	6.0	5.0	12.5	2.5	2.4	3.6	•	1.4	1.4	0.4
Quick Ratio 31	0.3	5.2	4.2	9.7	1.8	1.6	2.9	•	1.1	1.1	0.3
Net Sales to Working Capital 32	•	1.0	0.9	0.6	3.7	2.9	1.1	•	3.2	2.1	•
Coverage Ratio 33	1.8	1039.1	54.0	135.7	659.9	33.2	57.9	•	8.1	18.6	1.8
Total Asset Turnover 34	0.2	0.7	0.5	0.4	1.2	0.9	0.4	•	0.4	0.2	0.2
Inventory Turnover 35	•	•	•	•	•	•	•	•	•	•	•
Receivables Turnover 36	•	•	•	•	•	•	•	•	•	•	•
Total Liabilities to Net Worth 37	5.6	21.5	1.9	0.8	1.3	1.2	2.3	•	4.4	3.6	5.6
Current Assets to Working Capital 38	•	1.2	1.2	1.1	1.7	1.7	1.4	•	3.3	3.5	•
Current Liabilities to Working Capital 39	•	0.2	0.2	0.1	0.7	0.7	0.4	•	2.3	2.5	•
Working Capital to Net Sales 40	•	1.0	1.1	1.7	0.3	0.3	0.9	•	0.3	0.5	•
Inventory to Working Capital 41	•	•	•	•	•	•	•	•	•	•	•
Total Receipts to Cash Flow 42	3.2	1.3	1.5	1.5	1.1	1.9	2.2	•	2.2	2.3	3.3
Cost of Goods to Cash Flow 43	1.9	0.3	0.5	0.4	0.1	0.8	0.9	•	1.0	1.1	1.9
Cash Flow to Total Debt 44	0.1	0.6	0.5	0.6	1.9	0.8	0.2	•	0.2	0.1	0.1

Selected Financial Factors (in Percentages)

Debt Ratio 45	84.8	95.5	65.9	43.2	57.2	55.2	69.4	•	81.5	78.3	84.8
Return on Total Assets 46	1.4	26.3	14.7	10.4	73.2	6.9	4.2	•	3.1	1.8	1.4
Return on Equity Before Income Taxes 47	4.3	589.8	42.3	18.1	170.7	14.9	13.5	•	14.5	8.0	4.0
Return on Equity After Income Taxes 48	3.0	568.8	40.4	15.7	113.5	11.6	10.3	•	10.9	5.4	2.8
Profit Margin (Before Income Tax) 49	3.8	37.0	27.4	24.7	59.5	7.8	11.3	•	6.9	8.0	3.6
Profit Margin (After Income Tax) 50	2.6	35.7	26.2	21.3	39.6	6.1	8.6	•	5.2	5.5	2.5

Table I

Corporations with and without Net Income

LIFE INSURANCE, MUTUAL COMPANIES (FORM 1120L)

MONEY AMOUNTS AND SIZE OF ASSETS IN THOUSANDS OF DOLLARS

Item Description for Accounting Period 7/07 Through 6/08	Total	Zero Assets	Under 500	500 to 1,000	1,000 to 5,000	5,000 to 10,000	10,000 to 25,000	25,000 to 50,000	50,000 to 100,000	100,000 to 250,000	250,000 to 500,000	500,000 to 2,500,000	2,500,000 and over
Number of Enterprises **1**	59	5	3	3	8	5	0	5	0	6	6	9	10
Revenues ($ in Thousands)													
Net Sales **2**	111491068	98	73	74	3240	23218	0	56409	0	329619	585140	2663365	107829834
Interest **3**	23060227	12	53	65	1053	1904	0	13267	0	49651	143385	691954	22158884
Rents **4**	987935	0	0	0	72	8	0	22	0	402	4659	2986	979786
Royalties **5**	5689	0	0	0	0	0	0	0	0	727	0	1	4961
Other Portfolio Income **6**	3880162	0	0	0	364	841	0	1000	0	4784	5850	32155	3835169
Other Receipts **7**	83557055	86	20	9	1751	20465	0	42120	0	274055	431246	1936269	80851034
Total Receipts **8**	111491068	98	73	74	3240	23218	0	56409	0	329619	585140	2663365	107829834
Average Total Receipts **9**	1889679	20	24	25	405	4644	•	11282	•	54936	97523	295929	10782983
Operating Costs/Operating Income (%)													
Cost of Operations **10**	49.9	76.5	6.8	1.4	19.3	16.4	•	58.1	•	57.4	47.7	46.3	50.0
Salaries and Wages **11**	0.8	•	•	•	•	•	•	•	•	•	0.1	0.0	0.8
Taxes Paid **12**	0.9	1.0	2.7	•	2.8	2.2	•	2.1	•	2.7	2.1	1.2	0.9
Interest Paid **13**	1.3	•	•	•	•	•	•	0.0	•	0.3	0.1	1.0	1.3
Depreciation **14**	0.3	•	•	•	0.2	1.6	•	1.5	•	0.3	0.4	0.3	0.3
Amortization and Depletion **15**	1.4	•	•	•	1.8	1.8	•	3.1	•	3.8	3.1	2.5	1.4
Pensions and Other Deferred Comp. **16**	0.7	•	•	•	1.2	•	•	0.2	•	0.9	1.0	0.9	0.7
Employee Benefits **17**	0.1	•	•	•	•	1.6	•	0.0	•	0.5	0.2	0.2	0.1
Advertising **18**	0.3	•	•	•	•	0.1	•	0.0	•	0.2	0.1	0.2	0.3
Other Expenses **19**	39.2	79.6	24.7	62.2	85.2	68.2	•	26.0	•	30.3	44.3	41.1	39.1
Officers' Compensation **20**	0.1	•	•	•	•	•	•	•	•	•	0.0	0.0	0.1
Operating Margin **21**	5.0	65.8	•	36.5	•	8.0	•	8.9	•	3.3	0.7	6.5	5.0
Operating Margin Before Officers' Comp. **22**	5.0	65.8	•	36.5	•	8.0	•	8.9	•	3.3	0.7	6.5	5.0

Selected Average Balance Sheet ($ in Thousands)

Net Receivables 23	54108	0	0	0	38	2	•	3398	247	748	316356
Inventories 24	•	•	•	•	•	•	•	•	•	•	•
Net Property, Plant and Equipment 25	38838	•	0	382	530	330	•	970	1664	2658	224744
Total Assets 26	10440539	382	791	2810	11589	53567	•	184248	341190	1396162	59992193
Notes and Loans Payable 27	27930	0	0	0	0	0.	•	0	0	30	164762
All Other Liabilities 28	9323765	382	164	1666	10729	44074	•	169058	301054	1259307	53565875
Net Worth 29	1088843	0	627	1143	861	9493	•	15191	40137	136825	6261555

Selected Financial Ratios (Times to 1)

Current Ratio 30	3.0	•	•	1.5	1.8	2.4	•	1.5	1.5	0.7	3.5
Quick Ratio 31	2.3	•	•	1.0	1.0	2.1	•	1.2	1.3	0.6	2.7
Net Sales to Working Capital 32	1.5	0.1	0.3	0.9	0.8	0.9	•	2.2	2.7	•	1.5
Coverage Ratio 33	4.9	•	0.0	0.1	0.4	1152.5	•	11.1	7.5	7.7	4.8
Total Asset Turnover 34	0.2	0.1	0.0	0.1	0.4	0.2	•	0.3	0.3	0.2	0.2
Inventory Turnover 35	•	•	•	•	•	•	•	•	•	•	•
Receivables Turnover 36	•	•	•	•	•	•	•	•	•	•	•
Total Liabilities to Net Worth 37	8.6	•	0.3	1.5	12.5	4.6	•	11.1	7.5	9.2	8.6
Current Assets to Working Capital 38	1.5	1.0	1.0	2.2	1.1	1.7	•	3.0	3.1	•	1.4
Current Liabilities to Working Capital 39	0.5	0.0	0.0	1.2	0.1	0.7	•	2.0	2.1	•	0.4
Working Capital to Net Sales 40	0.7	15.7	3.4	1.1	1.2	1.1	•	0.5	0.4	0.7	0.7
Inventory to Working Capital 41	0.0	•	•	•	•	•	•	•	•	•	0.0
Total Receipts to Cash Flow 42	2.4	4.7	1.1	1.0	1.4	3.0	•	3.2	2.3	2.2	2.5
Cost of Goods to Cash Flow 43	1.2	3.6	0.0	0.3	0.2	1.8	•	1.9	1.1	1.0	1.2
Cash Flow to Total Debt 44	0.1	•	0.1	0.2	0.3	0.1	•	0.1	0.1	0.1	0.1

Selected Financial Factors (in Percentages)

Debt Ratio 45	89.6	100.0	20.7	59.3	92.6	82.3	•	91.8	88.2	90.2	89.6
Return on Total Assets 46	1.1	4.2	1.1	•	2.8	1.7	•	1.1	0.2	1.6	1.1
Return on Equity Before Income Taxes 47	8.6	•	1.4	•	37.9	9.7	•	12.0	1.7	14.0	8.5
Return on Equity After Income Taxes 48	5.7	•	1.4	•	32.2	8.1	•	6.4	1.2	9.5	5.6
Profit Margin (Before Income Tax) 49	5.0	65.8	36.5	•	7.0	8.2	•	3.3	0.7	6.5	5.0
Profit Margin (After Income Tax) 50	3.3	61.6	36.5	•	6.0	6.8	•	1.8	0.5	4.4	3.2

Table II

Corporations with Net Income

LIFE INSURANCE, MUTUAL COMPANIES (FORM 1120L)

MONEY AMOUNTS AND SIZE OF ASSETS IN THOUSANDS OF DOLLARS

Item Description for Accounting Period 7/07 Through 6/08	Total	Zero Assets	Under 500	500 to 1000	251 to 500	501 to 1,000	1,001 to 5,000	5,001 to 10,000	10,001 to 25,000	25,001 to 50,000	50,001 to 100,000	100,001 to 250,000	250,001 and over
Number of Enterprises 1	42	•	3	3	3	•	0	5	0	•	3	9	7
Revenues ($ in Thousands)													
Net Sales 2	106361043	•	73	74	883	•	0	56409	0	•	195867	2663365	103187614
Interest 3	22206470	•	53	65	612	•	0	13267	0	•	47774	691954	21414999
Rents 4	940823	•	0	0	72	•	0	22	0	•	2728	2986	934705
Royalties 5	1172	•	0	0	0	•	0	0	0	•	0	1	444
Other Portfolio Income 6	3856377	•	0	0	41	•	0	1000	0	•	3955	32155	3815625
Other Receipts 7	79356201	•	20	9	158	•	0	42120	0	•	141410	1936269	77021841
Total Receipts 8	106361043	•	73	74	883	•	0	56409	0	•	195867	2663365	103187614
Average Total Receipts 9	2252406	•	24	25	294	•	•	11282	•	•	65289	295929	14741088
Operating Costs/Operating Income (%)													
Cost of Operations 10	48.5	•	6.8	1.4	6.5	•	•	58.1	•	•	43.6	46.3	48.6
Salaries and Wages 11	0.9	•	•	•	•	•	•	•	•	•	0.1	0.0	0.9
Taxes Paid 12	0.9	•	2.7	•	4.2	•	•	2.1	•	•	1.8	1.2	0.9
Interest Paid 13	1.3	•	•	•	•	•	•	0.0	•	•	•	1.0	1.4
Depreciation 14	0.3	•	•	•	0.6	•	•	1.5	•	•	0.5	0.3	0.3
Amortization and Depletion 15	1.5	•	•	•	1.5	•	•	3.1	•	•	2.9	2.5	1.4
Pensions and Other Deferred Comp. 16	0.7	•	•	•	4.4	•	•	0.2	•	•	0.6	0.9	0.7
Employee Benefits 17	0.1	•	•	•	•	•	•	0.0	•	•	0.5	0.2	0.1
Advertising 18	0.3	•	•	•	•	•	•	0.0	•	•	0.0	0.2	0.3
Other Expenses 19	40.2	•	24.7	62.2	63.8	•	•	26.0	•	•	46.1	41.1	40.2
Officers' Compensation 20	0.1	•	•	•	•	•	•	•	•	•	•	0.0	0.1
Operating Margin 21	5.3	•	65.8	36.5	19.1	•	•	8.9	•	•	3.9	6.5	5.2
Operating Margin Before Officers' Comp. 22	5.3	•	65.8	36.5	19.1	•	•	8.9	•	•	3.9	6.5	5.3

Selected Average Balance Sheet ($ in Thousands)

Net Receivables **23**	75534	•	0	0	•	2	•	61	748	449426
Inventories **24**	•	•	•	•	•	•	•	•	•	•
Net Property, Plant and Equipment **25**	46653	•	0	0	•	330	•	488	2658	274926
Total Assets **26**	13944286	•	382	791	2816	53567	•	351658	1396162	81555132
Notes and Loans Payable **27**	39236	•	0	0	0	0	•	0	30	235375
All Other Liabilities **28**	12409038	•	382	164	2816	44074	•	304880	1259307	72556709
Net Worth **29**	1496012	•	0	627	0	9493	•	46778	136825	8763048

Selected Financial Ratios (Times to 1)

Current Ratio **30**	3.1	•	29.1	0.1	•	2.4	•	•	0.7	3.7
Quick Ratio **31**	2.4	•	•	0.1	•	2.1	•	•	0.6	2.8
Net Sales to Working Capital **32**	1.5	0.1	0.3	•	•	0.9	•	•	•	1.4
Coverage Ratio **33**	4.9	•	•	•	•	1152.5	•	•	7.7	4.9
Total Asset Turnover **34**	0.2	0.1	0.0	0.1	•	0.2	•	•	0.2	0.2
Inventory Turnover **35**	•	•	•	•	•	•	•	•	•	•
Receivables Turnover **36**	•	•	•	•	•	•	•	•	•	•
Total Liabilities to Net Worth **37**	8.3	•	0.3	•	•	4.6	•	•	6.5	8.3
Current Assets to Working Capital **38**	1.5	1.0	1.0	•	•	1.7	•	•	9.2	1.4
Current Liabilities to Working Capital **39**	0.5	•	0.0	•	•	0.7	•	•	•	0.4
Working Capital to Net Sales **40**	0.7	15.7	3.4	•	•	1.1	•	•	7.7	0.7
Inventory to Working Capital **41**	0.0	•	•	•	•	•	•	•	•	0.0
Total Receipts to Cash Flow **42**	2.4	1.1	1.0	1.3	•	3.0	•	•	2.1	2.4
Cost of Goods to Cash Flow **43**	1.2	0.1	0.0	0.1	•	1.8	•	•	0.9	1.2
Cash Flow to Total Debt **44**	0.1	0.1	0.1	0.1	•	0.1	•	•	0.1	0.1

Selected Financial Factors (in Percentages)

Debt Ratio **45**	89.3	100.0	20.7	100.0	•	82.3	•	86.7	90.2	89.3
Return on Total Assets **46**	1.2	4.2	1.1	2.0	•	1.7	•	0.7	1.6	1.2
Return on Equity Before Income Taxes **47**	8.9	•	1.4	•	•	9.7	•	5.2	14.0	8.8
Return on Equity After Income Taxes **48**	5.9	•	1.4	•	•	8.1	•	4.3	9.5	5.8
Profit Margin (Before Income Tax) **49**	5.3	65.8	36.5	18.8	•	8.2	•	3.7	6.5	5.2
Profit Margin (After Income Tax) **50**	3.5	61.6	36.5	17.8	•	6.8	•	3.1	4.4	3.5

Table I

Corporations with and without Net Income

MUTUAL PROPERTY AND CASUALTY COMPANIES (FORM 1120-PC)

MONEY AMOUNTS AND SIZE OF ASSETS IN THOUSANDS OF DOLLARS

Item Description for Accounting Period 7/07 Through 6/08	Total	Zero Assets	Under 500	500 to 1,000	1,000 to 5,000	5,000 to 10,000	10,000 to 25,000	25,000 to 50,000	50,000 to 100,000	100,000 to 250,000	250,000 to 500,000	500,000 to 2,500,000	2,500,000 and over
Number of Enterprises 1	1565	22	101	71	540	168	232	119	88	74	56	70	24
Revenues ($ in Thousands)													
Net Sales 2	229550025	18562	3622	37049	477491	556118	1537860	1992394	2676667	4925031	10533100	45641411	161150719
Interest 3	13275608	2245	676	1099	49447	38057	111645	126000	196629	302098	503619	2012991	9931103
Rents 4	527133	0	0	48	1741	506	1940	1302	3145	11258	12226	73648	421319
Royalties 5	939	0	0	0	0	0	0	0	23	0	1	816	98
Other Portfolio Income 6	9210423	116	126	415	11423	10935	43302	49115	81982	192130	343230	1371220	7106431
Other Receipts 7	206535922	16201	2820	35487	414880	506620	1380973	1815977	2394888	4419545	9674024	42182736	143691768
Total Receipts 8	229550025	18562	3622	37049	477491	556118	1537860	1992394	2676667	4925031	10533100	45641411	161150719
Average Total Receipts 9	146677	844	36	522	884	3310	6629	16743	30417	66554	188091	652020	6714613
Operating Costs/Operating Income (%)													
Cost of Operations 10	57.9	62.9	34.7	38.8	41.7	50.7	51.9	54.1	48.7	48.2	57.0	62.5	57.2
Salaries and Wages 11	12.5	15.4	0.1	12.6	16.6	10.3	9.2	11.1	15.3	15.7	13.7	13.0	12.2
Taxes Paid 12	2.3	3.4	0.1	1.2	2.5	2.4	2.7	2.8	3.0	3.0	2.3	2.1	2.4
Interest Paid 13	0.4	0.2	•	0.5	0.1	0.1	0.3	0.2	0.5	0.3	0.2	0.2	0.4
Depreciation 14	1.0	0.1	•	0.4	0.5	0.2	0.4	0.4	0.6	1.3	1.0	1.0	1.0
Amortization and Depletion 15	0.2	•	•	•	0.0	0.0	1.2	0.1	0.0	0.1	0.2	0.0	0.2
Pensions and Other Deferred Comp. 16	1.3	0.5	•	•	0.2	0.1	0.2	0.3	0.3	0.2	0.6	0.5	1.6
Employee Benefits 17	1.4	0.7	0.1	0.2	1.0	0.5	0.6	1.3	1.0	2.6	1.7	1.7	1.3
Advertising 18	0.5	0.8	•	0.4	0.3	0.2	0.1	0.4	0.4	0.8	0.2	0.3	0.6
Other Expenses 19	13.4	24.4	61.3	11.1	21.1	26.0	26.6	20.0	20.6	16.3	12.0	9.8	14.1
Officers' Compensation 20	0.3	•	•	•	2.4	1.2	0.7	1.0	1.1	0.8	0.7	0.3	0.2
Operating Margin 21	8.8	3.8	3.8	34.7	13.5	8.1	6.1	8.4	8.4	10.7	10.3	8.6	8.7
Operating Margin Before Officers' Comp. 22	9.1	•	3.8	34.7	15.9	9.3	6.8	9.4	9.5	11.5	11.0	8.9	8.9

Selected Average Balance Sheet ($ in Thousands)

Item													
Net Receivables **23**	25159	0	0	23	105	334	1178	2523	4594	14219	34387	115500	1134093
Inventories **24**	•	•	•	•	•	•	•	•	•	•	•	•	•
Net Property, Plant and Equipment **25**	4497	0	37	9	68	71	120	225	968	2992	6635	24815	188154
Total Assets **26**	357778		156	811	2769	7065	16382	35575	70340	164744	338482	1211870	17790242
Notes and Loans Payable **27**	3107	0	28	6	57	103	58	349	428	1003	7174		174841
All Other Liabilities **28**	218697	47	560	1006	3893	11031	24510	45739	94440	209790	697466		1098267
Net Worth **29**	135974	108	222	1757	3115	5248	11006	24251	69876	127690	507229		6617135

Selected Financial Ratios (Times to 1)

Item													
Current Ratio **30**	0.8	•	3.4	1.2	1.9	1.0	0.9	0.9	1.0	1.0	0.9		0.8
Quick Ratio **31**	0.8	•	3.4	1.0	1.8	0.8	0.7	0.8	0.9	0.9	0.8		0.7
Net Sales to Working Capital **32**	•	•	0.4	5.2	1.0	2.3	61.9	•	•	32.1	•		•
Coverage Ratio **33**	22.0	•	•	65.3	98.7	20.4	52.2	48.0	15.3	33.7	40.0	32.2	19.2
Total Asset Turnover **34**	0.4	0.2	0.6	0.3	0.5	0.4	0.5	0.4	0.4	0.6	0.5		0.4
Inventory Turnover **35**	•	•	•	•	•	•	•	•	•	•	•	•	•
Receivables Turnover **36**	•	•	•	•	•	•	•	•	•	•	•	•	•
Total Liabilities to Net Worth **37**	1.6	•	2.6	0.6	2.1	1.3	2.2	1.9	2.2	1.7	1.4		1.7
Current Assets to Working Capital **38**	•	•	1.4	6.5	2.1	3.2	98.5	•	33.1	33.1	•		•
Current Liabilities to Working Capital **39**	•	•	0.4	5.5	1.1	2.2	97.5	•	32.1	32.1	•		•
Working Capital to Net Sales **40**	•	•	2.4	0.2	1.0	0.4	0.0	•	0.0	0.0	•		•
Inventory to Working Capital **41**	0.2	•	•	0.0	•	0.2	•	•	•	•	•		•
Total Receipts to Cash Flow **42**	5.1	7.3	1.6	2.2	3.0	3.2	3.8	3.8	4.0	5.0	6.2		5.0
Cost of Goods to Cash Flow **43**	2.9	4.6	0.5	0.9	1.3	1.7	2.0	2.0	2.9	3.9	2.8		
Cash Flow to Total Debt **44**	0.1	•	0.5	0.4	0.3	0.2	0.2	0.2	0.2	0.1	0.1		

Selected Financial Factors (in Percentages)

Item													
Debt Ratio **45**	62.0	•	30.5	72.6	36.5	55.9	68.0	69.1	65.5	57.6	62.3	58.1	62.8
Return on Total Assets **46**	3.2	•	0.9	22.7	4.1	3.5	2.3	3.7	3.6	3.8	5.2	4.2	2.9
Return on Equity Before Income Taxes **47**	8.1	•	1.3	81.5	6.5	7.7	6.8	11.8	9.8	8.7	13.6	9.8	7.4
Return on Equity After Income Taxes **48**	5.3	•	1.1	78.2	4.4	5.4	3.7	7.9	6.6	5.8	9.0	6.5	4.8
Profit Margin (Before Income Tax) **49**	7.5	•	3.8	34.7	12.9	7.3	5.4	7.8	7.8	9.1	9.2	7.6	7.2
Profit Margin (After Income Tax) **50**	4.9	•	3.4	33.3	8.8	5.1	2.9	5.2	5.3	6.1	6.1	5.0	4.7

Table II

Corporations with Net Income

MUTUAL PROPERTY AND CASUALTY COMPANIES (FORM 1120-PC)

MONEY AMOUNTS AND SIZE OF ASSETS IN THOUSANDS OF DOLLARS

Item Description for Accounting Period 7/07 Through 6/08	Total	Zero Assets	Under 500	500 to 1,000	1,000 to 5,000	5,000 to 10,000	10,000 to 25,000	25,000 to 50,000	50,000 to 100,000	100,000 to 250,000	250,000 to 500,000	500,000 to 2,500,000	2,500,000 and over
Number of Enterprises **1**	1272	•	70	71	461	•	177	90	73	65	52	65	•
Revenues ($ in Thousands)													
Net Sales **2**	216387369	•	2272	37049	375936	•	1215114	1391029	2078717	4092780	10125441	42778164	•
Interest **3**	12632217	•	220	1099	42183	•	87331	97713	158255	253732	462381	1890788	•
Rents **4**	491787	•	0	48	976	•	889	898	2894	10208	10538	73648	•
Royalties **5**	939	•	0	0	0	•	0	0	23	0	1	816	•
Other Portfolio Income **6**	9063762	•	126	415	9835	•	36462	41747	77211	180360	332056	1305819	•
Other Receipts **7**	194198664	•	1926	35487	322942	•	1090432	1250671	1840334	3648480	9320465	39507093	•
Total Receipts **8**	216387369	•	2272	37049	375936	•	1215114	1391029	2078717	4092780	10125441	42778164	•
Average Total Receipts **9**	170116	•	32	522	815	•	6865	15456	28476	62966	194720	658126	•
Operating Costs/Operating Income (%)													
Cost of Operations **10**	57.2	•	50.4	38.8	36.2	•	48.7	46.1	42.1	44.5	56.7	61.0	•
Salaries and Wages **11**	12.9	•	0.1	12.6	14.8	•	10.6	12.7	17.6	16.5	13.8	13.4	•
Taxes Paid **12**	2.4	•	0.1	1.2	2.3	•	2.4	2.5	3.4	3.1	2.3	2.1	•
Interest Paid **13**	0.4	•	•	0.5	0.1	•	0.3	0.2	0.4	0.2	0.2	0.3	•
Depreciation **14**	1.0	•	0.4	0.4	0.5	•	0.4	0.5	0.6	1.3	1.0	1.0	•
Amortization and Depletion **15**	0.2	•	•	•	•	•	0.0	0.1	0.0	0.1	0.2	0.0	•
Pensions and Other Deferred Comp. **16**	1.4	•	•	•	0.2	•	0.2	0.3	0.3	0.2	0.7	0.5	•
Employee Benefits **17**	1.5	•	0.1	0.2	1.0	•	0.7	1.5	1.2	2.9	1.8	1.7	•
Advertising **18**	0.6	•	•	0.4	0.4	•	0.2	0.4	0.3	1.0	0.2	0.3	•
Other Expenses **19**	12.7	•	6.9	11.1	19.3	•	22.5	19.1	20.5	15.9	11.6	10.1	•
Officers' Compensation **20**	0.3	•	•	•	2.5	•	0.8	1.2	1.3	0.9	0.7	0.3	•
Operating Margin **21**	9.6	•	42.4	34.7	22.7	•	13.2	15.4	12.4	13.3	10.8	9.4	•
Operating Margin Before Officers' Comp. **22**	9.9	•	42.4	34.7	25.2	•	14.0	16.6	13.7	14.2	11.5	9.7	•

Selected Average Balance Sheet ($ in Thousands)

Line Item														
Net Receivables 23	29341	•	•	0	23	86	•	1216	2431	4541	14864	31508	121120	•
Inventories 24	•	•	•	•	•	•	•	•	•	•	•	•	•	•
Net Property, Plant and Equipment 25	5143	•	•	53	9	57	•	124	240	1037	2796	6923	26225	•
Total Assets 26	419748	•	•	140	811	2767	•	16658	35860	70297	165431	342032	1244660	•
Notes and Loans Payable 27	3733	•	•	0	28	4	•	130	58	421	481	1079	7649	•
All Other Liabilities 28	254772	•	•	35	560	947	•	9882	22968	43166	94109	208428	710549	•
Net Worth 29	161242	•	•	105	222	1816	•	6646	12834	26710	70841	132525	526462	•

Selected Financial Ratios (Times to 1)

Line Item														
Current Ratio 30	0.8	•	•	4.2	1.2	2.1	•	1.1	1.0	0.9	1.0	1.0	0.9	•
Quick Ratio 31	0.7	•	•	4.2	1.0	2.0	•	0.9	0.9	0.7	0.9	0.9	0.8	•
Net Sales to Working Capital 32	•	•	•	0.5	5.2	0.8	•	5.6	•	•	•	24.8	•	•
Coverage Ratio 33	23.3	•	•	65.3	164.1	74.9	•	43.1	29.2	48.4	42.2	33.6	•	•
Total Asset Turnover 34	0.4	•	•	0.2	0.6	0.3	•	0.4	0.4	0.4	0.6	0.5	•	•
Inventory Turnover 35	•	•	•	•	•	•	•	•	•	•	•	•	•	•
Receivables Turnover 36	•	•	•	•	•	•	•	•	•	•	•	•	•	•
Total Liabilities to Net Worth 37	1.6	•	•	0.3	2.6	0.5	•	1.5	1.8	1.6	1.3	1.6	1.4	•
Current Assets to Working Capital 38	•	•	•	1.3	6.5	1.9	•	8.8	•	•	•	24.6	•	•
Current Liabilities to Working Capital 39	•	•	•	0.3	5.5	0.9	•	7.8	•	•	•	23.6	•	•
Working Capital to Net Sales 40	•	•	•	2.0	0.2	1.2	•	0.2	•	•	•	0.0	•	•
Inventory to Working Capital 41	•	•	•	•	0.0	•	•	0.0	•	•	•	•	•	•
Total Receipts to Cash Flow 42	5.1	•	•	2.2	2.2	2.5	•	3.0	3.1	3.3	3.8	5.0	5.8	•
Cost of Goods to Cash Flow 43	2.9	•	•	1.1	0.9	0.9	•	1.4	1.4	1.4	1.7	2.8	3.5	•
Cash Flow to Total Debt 44	0.1	•	•	0.4	0.4	0.3	•	0.2	0.2	0.2	0.2	0.2	0.2	•

Selected Financial Factors (in Percentages)

Line Item														
Debt Ratio 45	61.6	•	•	24.9	72.6	34.4	•	60.1	64.2	62.0	57.2	61.3	57.7	•
Return on Total Assets 46	3.5	•	•	9.9	22.7	6.5	•	5.2	6.4	4.9	4.5	5.7	4.6	•
Return on Equity Before Income Taxes 47	8.7	•	•	13.1	81.5	9.9	•	12.8	17.6	12.4	10.3	14.3	10.5	•
Return on Equity After Income Taxes 48	5.8	•	•	12.9	78.2	7.6	•	9.5	13.2	9.0	7.0	9.5	7.1	•
Profit Margin (Before Income Tax) 49	8.2	•	•	42.4	34.7	22.1	•	12.4	14.6	11.6	11.6	9.7	8.4	•
Profit Margin (After Income Tax) 50	5.5	•	•	41.7	33.3	17.0	•	9.2	11.0	8.4	7.9	6.5	5.6	•

Table I

Corporations with and without Net Income

STOCK PROPERTY AND CASUALTY COMPANIES (FORM 1120-PC)

MONEY AMOUNTS AND SIZE OF ASSETS IN THOUSANDS OF DOLLARS

Item Description for Accounting Period 7/07 Through 6/08	Total	Zero Assets	Under 500	500 to 1,000	1,000 to 5,000	5,000 to 10,000	10,000 to 25,000	25,000 to 50,000	50,000 to 100,000	100,000 to 250,000	250,000 to 500,000	500,000 to 2,500,000	2,500,000 and over
Number of Enterprises **1**	5610	164	1810	846	1360	414	342	170	128	118	76	101	81
Revenues ($ in Thousands)													
Net Sales **2**	688264367	1624978	48834	65276	14920529	1601543	3373664	4019214	7748570	12621985	15603683	72463103	554172989
Interest **3**	45033208	128319	11691	17917	369969	96663	157145	169349	257292	556218	651578	2875502	39741566
Rents **4**	1116929	3431	0	164	1125	3495	2655	1731	3735	9692	10369	39765	1040768
Royalties **5**	600686	0	0	0	0	217	0	0	0	0	8077	39968	552423
Other Portfolio Income **6**	20293787	83397	3940	6476	93633	19975	64053	67415	99699	170412	267727	1231766	18185298
Other Receipts **7**	621219757	1409831	33203	40719	14455802	1481193	3149811	3780719	7387844	11885663	14665932	68276102	494652934
Total Receipts **8**	688264367	1624978	48834	65276	14920529	1601543	3373664	4019214	7748570	12621985	15603683	72463103	554172989
Average Total Receipts **9**	122685	9908	27	77	10971	3868	9865	23642	60536	106966	205312	717456	6841642
Operating Costs/Operating Income (%)													
Cost of Operations **10**	59.2	35.0	53.0	53.1	85.9	56.1	56.9	59.1	69.5	51.8	49.8	60.9	58.7
Salaries and Wages **11**	12.6	27.0	11.7	0.6	6.6	15.4	10.9	10.8	8.6	16.3	17.3	13.8	12.4
Taxes Paid **12**	2.0	2.1	0.9	0.2	0.7	1.5	1.8	2.5	2.1	2.4	2.4	2.0	2.0
Interest Paid **13**	1.7	1.6	0.8	0.0	0.1	0.3	0.4	0.2	0.3	0.6	0.9	0.7	2.0
Depreciation **14**	0.7	0.5	•	•	0.5	0.3	0.3	0.3	0.7	0.6	0.7	0.8	0.7
Amortization and Depletion **15**	0.3	0.8	0.7	•	0.8	0.1	0.0	0.0	0.1	2.8	0.2	0.2	0.3
Pensions and Other Deferred Comp. **16**	0.3	0.0	•	•	0.4	0.0	0.1	0.1	0.1	0.1	0.2	0.4	0.3
Employee Benefits **17**	1.0	0.4	0.1	•	0.4	0.4	0.4	0.5	1.5	0.9	1.3	1.0	1.1
Advertising **18**	0.6	0.7	•	•	0.0	0.6	0.3	0.3	0.4	0.3	0.8	0.5	0.6
Other Expenses **19**	12.3	19.9	11.0	9.7	8.0	11.6	21.3	19.9	10.9	16.3	18.9	13.6	11.9
Officers' Compensation **20**	0.4	0.1	•	•	0.2	0.5	0.9	0.8	0.5	0.8	0.7	0.6	0.4
Operating Margin **21**	8.8	11.8	21.8	36.3	•	13.2	6.7	5.5	5.3	7.1	6.6	5.6	9.7
Operating Margin Before Officers' Comp. **22**	9.2	11.9	21.8	36.3	•	13.7	7.6	6.3	5.7	7.9	7.3	6.1	10.1

Selected Average Balance Sheet ($ in Thousands)

Net Receivables 23	20956	0	16	124	364	1204	1970	6301	14183	28487	98461	1257915
Inventories 24	•	•	•	•	•	•	•	•	•	•	•	•
Net Property, Plant and Equipment 25	4360	0	0	21	91	119	329	583	2881	5846	18697	266021
Total Assets 26	337088	189	723	2402	7242	16498	34436	70984	156765	345168	1125093	21048142
Notes and Loans Payable 27	25429	0	1	9	41	171	317	292	1909	6912	24427	1649737
All Other Liabilities 28	189523	175	454	1564	3898	11367	23030	50909	99021	208740	630095	11768817
Net Worth 29	122136	12	260	796	3173	4814	11114	18166	50832	112001	437385	7629588

Selected Financial Ratios (Times to 1)

Current Ratio 30	0.7	•	0.7	1.0	1.2	1.0	1.0	1.0	0.9	1.0	1.0	0.7
Quick Ratio 31	0.6	•	0.6	0.8	1.0	0.8	0.8	0.8	0.8	0.9	0.8	0.5
Net Sales to Working Capital 32	•	•	•	•	4.7	•	•	•	•	•	•	•
Coverage Ratio 33	5.6	6.6	29.0	876.2	37.8	18.9	22.0	15.7	12.1	7.5	8.4	5.4
Total Asset Turnover 34	0.4	•	0.1	0.1	0.5	0.6	0.7	0.9	0.7	0.6	0.6	0.3
Inventory Turnover 35	•	•	•	•	•	•	•	•	•	•	•	•
Receivables Turnover 36	•	•	•	•	•	•	•	•	•	•	•	•
Total Liabilities to Net Worth 37	1.8	•	14.4	1.8	2.0	2.4	2.1	2.9	2.1	2.1	1.6	1.8
Current Assets to Working Capital 38	•	•	•	•	5.3	•	•	•	•	•	•	•
Current Liabilities to Working Capital 39	•	•	•	•	4.3	•	•	•	•	•	•	•
Working Capital to Net Sales 40	•	•	•	•	0.2	•	•	•	•	•	•	•
Inventory to Working Capital 41	•	•	•	•	•	•	•	•	•	•	•	•
Total Receipts to Cash Flow 42	5.3	3.5	3.8	2.4	4.3	3.8	4.2	6.8	4.6	4.2	5.8	5.2
Cost of Goods to Cash Flow 43	3.1	1.2	2.0	1.3	2.4	2.2	2.5	4.7	2.4	2.1	3.6	3.0
Cash Flow to Total Debt 44	0.1	0.0	0.1	0.2	0.2	0.2	0.2	0.2	0.2	0.2	0.2	0.1

Selected Financial Factors (in Percentages)

Debt Ratio 45	63.8	93.5	64.1	66.9	56.2	70.8	67.7	74.4	67.6	67.6	61.1	63.8
Return on Total Assets 46	3.5	3.2	3.9	•	7.1	4.0	3.7	4.4	4.9	4.1	3.7	3.5
Return on Equity Before Income Taxes 47	7.9	47.8	10.8	•	15.7	12.9	10.8	16.3	13.9	11.0	8.4	7.8
Return on Equity After Income Taxes 48	5.1	38.3	9.2	•	10.9	7.0	5.2	9.2	9.0	6.2	5.1	5.1
Profit Margin (Before Income Tax) 49	7.9	21.8	36.2	•	12.9	6.3	5.1	4.9	6.6	6.0	5.1	8.7
Profit Margin (After Income Tax) 50	5.1	17.4	31.1	•	8.9	3.4	2.5	2.8	4.3	3.4	3.1	5.7

Table II

Corporations with Net Income

STOCK PROPERTY AND CASUALTY COMPANIES (FORM 1120-PC)

MONEY AMOUNTS AND SIZE OF ASSETS IN THOUSANDS OF DOLLARS

Item Description for Accounting Period 7/07 Through 6/08	Total	Zero Assets	Under 500	500 to 1,000	1,000 to 5,000	5,000 to 10,000	10,000 to 25,000	25,000 to 50,000	50,000 to 100,000	100,000 to 250,000	250,000 to 500,000	500,000 to 2,500,000	2,500,000 and over
Number of Enterprises **1**	4834	141	1558	785	1223	316	262	135	96	101	60	82	75
Revenues ($ in Thousands)													
Net Sales **2**	650452692	1618481	16593	56473	13338128	774545	2302858	2926086	5876372	10856213	13161993	52172636	547352314
Interest **3**	41769658	125853	11243	17787	224476	76866	125686	129921	195016	461868	516491	2272811	37611641
Rents **4**	1082215	3431	0	164	847	1557	2582	472	2084	9661	5913	25812	1029692
Royalties **5**	600265	0	0	0	0	217	0	0	0	0	8074	39551	552422
Other Portfolio Income **6**	19589406	83090	3835	6476	93143	17967	49179	52043	81135	148343	234255	1016697	17803247
Other Receipts **7**	587411148	1406107	1515	32046	13019662	677938	2125411	2743650	5598137	10236341	12397260	48817765	490355312
Total Receipts **8**	650452692	1618481	16593	56473	13338128	774545	2302858	2926086	5876372	10856213	13161993	52172636	547352314
Average Total Receipts **9**	134558	11479	11	72	10906	2451	8790	21675	61212	107487	219367	636252	7298031
Operating Costs/Operating Income (%)													
Cost of Operations **10**	58.6	35.1	2.0	47.7	82.5	42.9	47.4	53.1	65.2	51.1	49.7	59.4	58.4
Salaries and Wages **11**	12.3	27.0	0.7	0.7	4.4	8.9	10.3	11.1	8.4	14.9	14.1	12.5	12.4
Taxes Paid **12**	2.0	2.1	0.2	0.1	0.8	1.8	1.9	2.4	2.3	2.3	2.6	2.0	2.0
Interest Paid **13**	1.6	1.6	0.4	0.0	0.1	0.4	0.3	0.2	0.2	0.6	0.7	0.7	1.8
Depreciation **14**	0.7	0.5	•	•	0.6	0.2	0.3	0.3	0.8	0.5	0.7	0.7	0.7
Amortization and Depletion **15**	0.3	0.8	0.1	•	0.1	0.1	0.0	0.0	0.1	3.2	0.2	0.2	0.3
Pensions and Other Deferred Comp. **16**	0.3	0.0	•	•	0.5	0.0	0.1	0.1	0.1	0.2	0.2	0.4	0.3
Employee Benefits **17**	1.0	0.4	•	•	0.5	0.3	0.5	0.5	1.7	0.9	1.2	0.9	1.1
Advertising **18**	0.6	0.7	•	•	0.0	0.4	0.2	0.3	0.5	0.3	0.7	0.4	0.6
Other Expenses **19**	12.1	19.8	6.7	8.6	8.7	10.0	22.0	19.1	10.9	15.7	18.7	13.3	11.8
Officers' Compensation **20**	0.4	0.1	•	•	0.2	0.5	1.0	0.9	0.5	0.8	0.7	0.6	0.4
Operating Margin **21**	10.1	11.9	89.8	42.9	1.7	34.5	16.0	12.0	9.4	9.4	10.5	8.9	10.4
Operating Margin Before Officers' Comp. **22**	10.5	12.0	89.8	42.9	1.9	34.9	17.0	12.9	9.8	10.3	11.2	9.5	10.7

Selected Average Balance Sheet ($ in Thousands)

Line	1	2	3	4	5	6	7	8	9	10	11	12	13	14
Net Receivables **23**	17467	0	•	3	13	89	344	1030	2076	6209	14112	29165	90771	965847
Inventories **24**	•	•	•	•	•	•	•	•	•	•	•	•	•	•
Net Property, Plant and Equipment **25**	4767	•	0	0	11	33	96	289	539	2439	6291	12706		283158
Total Assets **26**	361911	0	203	727	2377	7192	16445	34157	71320	154365	345255	1107476		21340332
Notes and Loans Payable **27**	24195	0	1	10	15	97	234	218	1187	5839	16425	55712		1474011
All Other Liabilities **28**	197851	0	146	469	1320	3412	9942	22482	47786	92679	202046	598043		11631670
Net Worth **29**	139865	0	55	249	1042	3683	6269	11457	22347	55847	126784	453720		8234651

Selected Financial Ratios (Times to 1)

Line	1	2	3	4	5	6	7	8	9	10	11	12	13	14
Current Ratio **30**	0.7	•	0.9	0.9	1.1	1.4	1.1	1.0	1.1	1.1	1.0	1.0	1.0	0.6
Quick Ratio **31**	0.6	•	0.7	0.7	0.9	1.1	0.9	0.8	0.9	0.9	0.9	0.9	0.9	0.5
Net Sales to Working Capital **32**	•	•	•	70.3	2.2	11.6	•	19.6	27.5	34.3	•	•	•	•
Coverage Ratio **33**	6.8	6.7	223.2	894.8	15.0	90.6	53.3	60.1	37.0	17.2	14.5	12.4		6.3
Total Asset Turnover **34**	0.4	•	0.1	0.1	4.6	0.3	0.5	0.6	0.9	0.7	0.6	0.6	0.6	0.3
Inventory Turnover **35**	•	•	•	•	•	•	•	•	•	•	•	•	•	•
Receivables Turnover **36**	•	•	•	•	•	•	•	•	•	•	•	•	•	•
Total Liabilities to Net Worth **37**	1.6	2.7	1.9	•	1.3	1.0	3.8	2.0	2.2	1.8	1.7	1.4		1.6
Current Assets to Working Capital **38**	•	•	•	9.1	3.8	13.2	14.8	•	24.8	30.3	•	•	•	•
Current Liabilities to Working Capital **39**	•	•	•	8.1	2.8	12.2	13.8	•	23.8	29.3	•	•	•	•
Working Capital to Net Sales **40**	•	•	•	0.0	0.5	0.1	0.1	•	0.0	0.0	•	0.0	0.0	•
Inventory to Working Capital **41**	•	•	•	0.0	•	0.0	0.0	•	0.0	0.0	•	0.0	0.0	•
Total Receipts to Cash Flow **42**	5.0	1.2	2.2	10.6	2.3	2.7	3.4	5.3	4.2	3.6	4.9	5.0		
Cost of Goods to Cash Flow **43**	2.9	0.0	1.0	8.7	1.0	1.8	1.3	3.5	2.2	1.8	2.9	2.9		
Cash Flow to Total Debt **44**	0.1	0.1	0.1	0.8	0.3	0.3	0.3	0.2	0.3	0.3	0.2	0.1		

Selected Financial Factors (in Percentages)

Line	1	2	3	4	5	6	7	8	9	10	11	12
Debt Ratio **45**	61.4	72.7	65.8	56.2	48.8	61.9	66.5	68.7	63.8	63.3	59.0	61.4
Return on Total Assets **46**	4.0	4.7	4.2	8.0	11.7	8.5	7.5	7.9	6.6	6.7	5.2	3.8
Return on Equity Before Income Taxes **47**	8.8	17.3	12.4	17.0	22.5	21.8	22.0	24.4	17.1	17.0	11.7	8.3
Return on Equity After Income Taxes **48**	6.0	14.8	10.6	12.7	17.1	15.8	15.1	16.8	11.9	11.7	7.8	5.6
Profit Margin (Before Income Tax) **49**	9.2	89.7	42.7	1.6	33.9	15.5	11.6	8.9	8.9	9.8	8.4	9.3
Profit Margin (After Income Tax) **50**	6.2	76.9	36.8	1.2	25.7	11.3	8.0	6.1	6.2	6.7	5.6	6.3

Table I

Corporations with and without Net Income

INSURANCE AGENCIES AND BROKERAGES

MONEY AMOUNTS AND SIZE OF ASSETS IN THOUSANDS OF DOLLARS

Item Description for Accounting Period 7/07 Through 6/08	Total	Zero Assets	Under 500	500 to 1,000	1,000 to 5,000	5,000 to 10,000	10,000 to 25,000	25,000 to 50,000	50,000 to 100,000	100,000 to 250,000	250,000 to 500,000	500,000 to 2,500,000	2,500,000 and over
Number of Enterprises **1**	89533	17104	62530	4815	4113	546	257	76	38	27	9	13	5
Revenues ($ in Thousands)													
Net Sales **2**	88330030	2753061	26305797	5115125	12483920	3635104	4825385	2866558	2680375	2123213	929947	5470811	19141232
Interest **3**	1357145	13901	21972	16194	46181	26807	36406	27894	21388	69398	42130	77408	957466
Rents **4**	105232	2912	4906	3290	5820	10460	1724	1254	1894	329	0	61382	11259
Royalties **5**	30185	0	0	15815	0	0	6	274	0	0	0	0	14089
Other Portfolio Income **6**	4552789	104761	32896	12818	32949	36308	77823	10959	10729	64684	42552	52687	4073622
Other Receipts **7**	82284679	2631487	26246023	5067008	12398970	3561529	4709426	2826177	2646364	1988802	844765	5279334	14084796
Total Receipts **8**	88330030	2753061	26305797	5115125	12483920	3635104	4825385	2866558	2680375	2123213	929947	5470811	19141232
Average Total Receipts **9**	987	161	421	1062	3035	6658	18776	37718	70536	78638	103272	420832	3828246
Operating Costs/Operating Income (%)													
Cost of Operations **10**	12.2	3.1	17.9	1.4	13.8	8.9	25.0	21.1	24.0	7.6	3.6	•	6.5
Salaries and Wages **11**	27.1	28.1	21.6	25.6	29.4	35.2	27.7	26.6	23.6	35.7	20.4	34.3	29.8
Taxes Paid **12**	2.9	3.9	2.6	3.4	2.8	3.5	2.8	2.5	1.8	3.0	3.1	2.9	3.3
Interest Paid **13**	2.4	1.7	0.7	1.8	0.7	0.9	0.7	1.2	0.9	6.2	5.2	5.7	5.9
Depreciation **14**	0.8	1.6	0.6	0.9	0.6	0.9	0.8	1.1	1.0	1.3	1.0	1.4	0.9
Amortization and Depletion **15**	1.2	0.5	0.4	1.5	0.9	0.5	0.6	0.8	0.8	2.2	1.4	5.0	1.6
Pensions and Other Deferred Comp. **16**	1.3	0.8	1.1	1.3	1.3	1.0	1.2	1.2	0.9	1.1	0.4	0.5	2.0
Employee Benefits **17**	1.9	1.9	1.5	2.2	2.0	2.0	1.8	1.9	2.0	3.2	2.0	3.2	1.9
Advertising **18**	1.3	3.9	1.7	1.7	0.8	0.9	1.5	0.6	2.6	1.7	0.2	0.6	0.6
Other Expenses **19**	26.3	40.5	25.3	31.3	23.9	20.8	21.9	29.4	30.7	28.9	46.7	34.0	23.6
Officers' Compensation **20**	9.5	8.1	13.9	16.2	12.9	15.2	7.5	7.9	6.0	4.1	1.7	4.8	2.2
Operating Margin **21**	13.0	6.0	12.7	12.9	11.0	10.1	8.5	5.7	5.8	4.9	14.4	7.8	21.8
Operating Margin Before Officers' Comp. **22**	22.5	14.0	26.6	29.1	23.9	25.3	16.0	13.6	11.8	9.0	16.1	12.6	24.0

Selected Average Balance Sheet ($ in Thousands)

Net Receivables 23	311	0	8	36	320	1297	2635	8418	13780	31246	45959	209908	3870541
Inventories 24	•	•	•	•	•	•	•	•	•	•	•	•	•
Net Property, Plant and Equipment 25	45	0	12	83	113	490	862	2890	3388	5726	8771	26233	204118
Total Assets 26	1377	0	82	679	1971	7182	14195	35422	68777	147458	331847	1418856	13695059
Notes and Loans Payable 27	233	0	37	266	350	980	2562	7741	9632	45143	98396	426138	1201074
All Other Liabilities 28	616	0	23	151	987	4217	8557	19029	42005	66888	136684	574271	6164482
Net Worth 29	528	0	21	262	634	1985	3077	8652	17140	35427	96766	418446	6329502

Selected Financial Ratios (Times to 1)

Current Ratio 30	1.1	•	1.5	1.7	1.3	1.2	1.2	1.2	1.1	1.0	1.0	1.0	1.0
Quick Ratio 31	0.9	•	1.4	1.5	1.1	0.9	1.0	1.0	0.8	0.9	0.6	0.9	0.9
Net Sales to Working Capital 32	19.5	•	31.9	9.4	10.9	11.4	10.4	8.4	34.0	28.6	•	28.1	34.3
Coverage Ratio 33	6.5	4.5	20.1	8.2	16.0	11.8	13.2	5.8	7.2	1.8	3.7	2.4	5.1
Total Asset Turnover 34	0.7	•	5.1	1.6	1.5	0.9	1.3	1.1	1.0	0.5	0.3	0.3	0.3
Inventory Turnover 35	•	•	•	•	•	•	•	•	•	•	•	•	•
Receivables Turnover 36	•	•	•	•	•	•	•	•	•	•	•	•	•
Total Liabilities to Net Worth 37	1.6	•	2.9	1.6	2.1	2.6	3.6	3.1	3.0	3.2	2.4	2.4	1.2
Current Assets to Working Capital 38	11.3	•	3.1	2.4	4.5	7.0	5.3	5.1	20.0	24.1	•	24.7	46.4
Current Liabilities to Working Capital 39	10.3	•	2.1	1.4	3.5	6.0	4.3	4.1	19.0	23.1	•	23.7	45.4
Working Capital to Net Sales 40	0.1	•	0.0	0.1	0.1	0.1	0.1	0.1	0.0	0.0	•	0.0	0.0
Inventory to Working Capital 41	0.0	•	•	•	0.0	•	0.0	•	0.1	•	•	•	•
Total Receipts to Cash Flow 42	3.3	2.7	3.0	2.6	3.3	3.8	3.7	3.1	3.0	3.6	1.7	2.7	4.4
Cost of Goods to Cash Flow 43	0.4	0.1	0.5	0.0	0.5	0.3	0.9	0.7	0.7	0.3	0.1	•	0.3
Cash Flow to Total Debt 44	0.4	•	2.3	1.0	0.7	0.3	0.5	0.5	0.5	0.2	0.3	0.2	0.1

Selected Financial Factors (in Percentages)

Debt Ratio 45	61.6	•	74.4	61.4	67.8	72.4	78.3	75.6	75.1	76.0	70.8	70.5	53.8
Return on Total Assets 46	11.4	•	68.9	23.0	18.0	10.2	12.1	7.2	6.7	5.9	5.9	3.9	8.4
Return on Equity Before Income Taxes 47	25.1	•	255.8	52.3	52.4	33.8	51.5	24.4	23.3	10.7	14.7	7.7	14.5
Return on Equity After Income Taxes 48	20.6	•	253.2	51.3	51.1	30.3	45.9	19.4	19.9	5.4	9.4	4.3	9.5
Profit Margin (Before Income Tax) 49	13.4	6.0	12.7	12.9	10.9	10.1	8.4	5.6	5.7	4.8	13.8	7.7	24.0
Profit Margin (After Income Tax) 50	11.0	4.6	12.6	12.7	10.7	9.0	7.5	4.5	4.8	2.4	8.8	4.2	15.7

Table II

Corporations with Net Income

INSURANCE AGENCIES AND BROKERAGES

MONEY AMOUNTS AND SIZE OF ASSETS IN THOUSANDS OF DOLLARS

Item Description for Accounting Period 7/07 Through 6/08		Total	Zero Assets	Under 500	500 to 1,000	1,000 to 5,000	5,000 to 10,000	10,000 to 25,000	25,000 to 50,000	50,000 to 100,000	100,000 to 250,000	250,000 to 500,000	500,000 to 2,500,000	2,500,000 and over
Number of Enterprises	1	65861	11446	46460	3733	3452	459	201	52	28	13	6	6	5
Revenues ($ in Thousands)														
Net Sales	2	72397553	1849878	19249970	4014471	10628565	3436890	4357561	2081159	2205875	1311048	690146	3430757	19141232
Interest	3	1258792	13752	12034	12203	42104	24323	25749	22325	17536	48800	27193	55309	957466
Rents	4	41492	2912	4885	3134	1573	10351	1724	1254	1894	329	0	2176	11259
Royalties	5	30185	0	0	15815	0	0	6	274	0	0	0	0	14089
Other Portfolio Income	6	4436797	35769	10401	12560	22132	35823	76590	7290	10007	64309	39987	48309	4073622
Other Receipts	7	66630287	1797445	19222650	3970759	10562756	3366393	4253492	2050016	2176438	1197610	622966	3324963	14084796
Total Receipts	8	72397553	1849878	19249970	4014471	10628565	3436890	4357561	2081159	2205875	1311048	690146	3430757	19141232
Average Total Receipts	9	1099	162	414	1075	3079	7488	21679	40022	78781	100850	115024	571793	3828246
Operating Costs/Operating Income (%)														
Cost of Operations	10	11.1	4.5	14.6	1.7	14.4	8.8	26.9	15.3	20.7	3.0	4.8	•	6.5
Salaries and Wages	11	26.1	21.5	21.2	26.1	24.8	34.2	28.1	26.3	23.1	35.0	21.7	27.9	29.8
Taxes Paid	12	2.9	2.9	2.4	3.2	2.8	3.5	2.6	2.5	1.7	3.4	3.5	3.1	3.3
Interest Paid	13	2.3	2.1	0.6	2.1	0.5	0.6	0.7	1.1	0.8	3.7	6.1	2.3	5.9
Depreciation	14	0.8	0.9	0.5	0.8	0.6	0.9	0.7	1.1	1.1	1.4	1.1	1.4	0.9
Amortization and Depletion	15	1.1	0.2	0.4	1.6	0.6	0.4	0.4	0.9	0.8	1.0	1.7	4.9	1.6
Pensions and Other Deferred Comp.	16	1.3	0.9	0.8	1.2	1.4	1.0	1.3	1.2	0.9	1.3	0.5	0.6	2.0
Employee Benefits	17	1.8	1.3	1.2	2.3	1.9	2.0	1.9	2.2	2.1	2.6	2.4	2.8	1.9
Advertising	18	1.2	2.8	1.8	1.8	0.7	0.9	1.1	0.5	3.0	0.9	0.1	0.5	0.6
Other Expenses	19	24.9	35.9	24.2	26.4	23.5	19.7	17.8	30.2	30.5	29.1	34.1	36.2	23.6
Officers' Compensation	20	9.0	6.2	13.2	14.2	13.8	15.6	7.5	8.4	6.3	4.7	1.8	4.3	2.2
Operating Margin	21	17.6	20.6	19.1	18.5	15.1	12.3	11.1	10.2	9.0	13.8	22.2	15.9	21.8
Operating Margin Before Officers' Comp.	22	26.7	26.8	32.4	32.7	28.9	27.9	18.5	18.6	15.3	18.6	24.0	20.2	24.0

Selected Average Balance Sheet ($ in Thousands)

Net Receivables 23	379	•	5	36	338	1454	2933	9434	14899	25869	51336	205840	3870541
Inventories 24	•	•	•	•	•	•	•	•	•	•	•	•	•
Net Property, Plant and Equipment 25	48	0	11	87	93	547	961	3206	4098	7918	4616	22862	204118
Total Assets 26	1571	0	79	681	1962	7392	13927	35578	68478	142011	318009	1383026	13695059
Notes and Loans Payable 27	190	0	28	267	284	849	2526	6203	9856	26589	62029	174197	1201074
All Other Liabilities 28	708	0	16	159	982	4187	8129	19466	37570	67060	140963	626033	6164482
Net Worth 29	673	0	35	255	696	2355	3273	9909	21051	48361	115017	582796	6329502

Selected Financial Ratios (Times to 1)

Current Ratio 30	1.1	•	1.9	1.8	1.3	1.2	1.1	1.4	1.1	1.0	1.2	1.1	1.0
Quick Ratio 31	1.0	•	1.8	1.6	1.2	0.9	0.9	1.1	0.9	0.7	1.0	1.0	0.9
Net Sales to Working Capital 32	16.5	•	21.9	7.8	10.7	9.1	17.9	6.4	23.0	83.9	4.9	13.2	34.3
Coverage Ratio 33	8.8	10.9	35.0	9.9	30.4	20.6	17.8	10.3	11.6	4.7	4.6	7.7	5.1
Total Asset Turnover 34	0.7	•	5.3	1.6	1.6	1.0	1.6	1.1	1.2	0.7	0.4	0.4	0.3
Inventory Turnover 35	•	•	•	•	•	•	•	•	•	•	•	•	•
Receivables Turnover 36	•	•	•	•	•	•	•	•	•	•	•	•	•
Total Liabilities to Net Worth 37	1.3	•	1.2	1.7	1.8	2.1	3.3	2.6	2.3	1.9	1.8	1.4	1.2
Current Assets to Working Capital 38	9.9	•	2.1	2.2	4.4	5.5	7.8	3.8	11.6	57.1	5.7	8.7	46.4
Current Liabilities to Working Capital 39	8.9	•	1.1	1.2	3.4	4.5	6.8	2.8	10.6	56.1	4.7	7.7	45.4
Working Capital to Net Sales 40	0.1	•	0.0	0.1	0.1	0.1	0.1	0.2	0.0	0.0	0.2	0.1	0.0
Inventory to Working Capital 41	0.0	•	•	•	•	•	0.1	•	•	0.7	•	•	•
Total Receipts to Cash Flow 42	3.0	2.0	2.6	2.5	2.9	3.6	3.9	2.7	2.7	2.9	1.9	2.1	4.4
Cost of Goods to Cash Flow 43	0.3	0.1	0.4	0.0	0.4	0.3	1.1	0.4	0.6	0.1	0.1	•	0.3
Cash Flow to Total Debt 44	0.4	•	3.7	1.0	0.8	0.4	0.5	0.6	0.6	0.4	0.3	0.3	0.1

Selected Financial Factors (in Percentages)

Debt Ratio 45	57.2	•	54.9	62.5	64.5	68.1	76.5	72.1	69.3	65.9	63.8	57.9	53.8
Return on Total Assets 46	14.4	•	103.9	32.4	24.4	13.1	18.2	12.7	11.2	12.4	10.1	7.5	8.4
Return on Equity Before Income Taxes 47	29.8	•	223.8	77.8	66.5	39.0	72.9	41.2	33.3	28.6	21.7	15.4	14.5
Return on Equity After Income Taxes 48	25.0	•	221.7	76.5	65.0	35.5	66.3	34.9	29.6	20.6	15.0	10.1	9.5
Profit Margin (Before Income Tax) 49	18.2	20.6	19.1	18.5	15.0	12.3	11.0	10.2	8.9	13.7	21.7	15.7	24.0
Profit Margin (After Income Tax) 50	15.3	19.9	18.9	18.2	14.7	11.2	10.0	8.6	7.9	9.9	15.0	10.2	15.7

Table I

Corporations with and without Net Income

OTHER INSURANCE RELATED ACTIVITIES

MONEY AMOUNTS AND SIZE OF ASSETS IN THOUSANDS OF DOLLARS

Item Description for Accounting Period 7/07 Through 6/08	Total	Zero Assets	Under 500	500 to 1,000	1,000 to 5,000	5,000 to 10,000	10,000 to 25,000	25,000 to 50,000	50,000 to 100,000	100,000 to 250,000	250,000 to 500,000	500,000 to 2,500,000	2,500,000 and over
Number of Enterprises 1	13428	3217	8585	660	540	152	134	39	35	28	13	18	7
Revenues ($ in Thousands)													
Net Sales 2	59763610	4417902	3439848	1290518	1947663	1964393	1991476	1871009	1773765	3525520	5009471	8020917	24511128
Interest 3	7108941	39043	6941	4377	16005	6224	21912	23690	37791	75065	87463	288624	6501805
Rents 4	98964	284	0	0	9665	120	2204	968	1228	10851	0	9979	63666
Royalties 5	46972	30946	0	0	0	0	0	0	0	0	0	15975	50
Other Portfolio Income 6	1617531	22344	12776	1	3263	8298	25147	4856	20874	58125	12224	225726	1223898
Other Receipts 7	50891202	4325285	3420131	1286140	1918730	1949751	1942213	1841495	1713872	3381479	4909784	7480613	16721709
Total Receipts 8	59763610	4417902	3439848	1290518	1947663	1964393	1991476	1871009	1773765	3525520	5009471	8020917	24511128
Average Total Receipts 9	4451	1373	401	1955	3607	12924	14862	47975	50679	125911	385344	445606	3501590
Operating Costs/Operating Income (%)													
Cost of Operations 10	19.3	58.0	60.4	6.2	0.3	0.9	15.6	17.8	19.0	11.5	10.1	39.8	6.9
Salaries and Wages 11	13.5	16.4	8.9	11.3	23.8	16.9	32.9	21.9	22.8	25.5	10.3	18.9	7.0
Taxes Paid 12	1.6	0.7	1.6	0.7	2.6	1.6	3.0	2.9	2.5	2.6	1.3	1.7	1.2
Interest Paid 13	10.4	4.4	0.5	1.6	0.9	0.7	0.6	0.8	2.7	2.7	3.7	2.6	21.9
Depreciation 14	0.7	0.7	0.4	0.2	0.9	0.4	1.1	1.3	1.1	1.3	0.9	1.0	0.5
Amortization and Depletion 15	0.7	1.3	0.0	0.0	0.2	0.0	0.4	0.4	2.2	1.0	0.9	1.3	0.5
Pensions and Other Deferred Comp. 16	0.5	0.4	0.4	3.0	1.8	0.2	1.2	0.3	0.5	0.4	0.1	0.6	0.3
Employee Benefits 17	2.3	0.3	1.4	0.7	2.6	1.4	2.1	9.7	9.2	7.1	1.5	2.8	1.1
Advertising 18	0.5	0.8	0.4	0.2	2.2	0.2	0.6	1.7	0.2	0.5	0.3	0.4	0.4
Other Expenses 19	40.6	16.3	14.4	71.2	54.8	68.8	30.4	35.5	49.6	40.1	67.7	20.1	45.6
Officers' Compensation 20	2.1	4.6	7.0	4.2	7.9	2.5	6.0	2.5	1.8	3.2	1.1	1.1	0.5
Operating Margin 21	7.8	•	4.6	0.7	1.9	6.5	6.1	5.2	•	4.1	2.0	9.8	14.2
Operating Margin Before Officers' Comp. 22	10.0	0.8	11.6	5.0	9.7	9.0	12.1	7.6	•	7.2	3.2	10.8	14.7

Selected Average Balance Sheet ($ in Thousands)

Net Receivables **23**	329496	166980	19708	21228	6650	5721	2638	852	620	53	5	559
Inventories **24**	•	•	•	•	•	•	•	•	•	•	•	•
Net Property, Plant and Equipment **25**	85243	30507	22010	9194	4026	1723	685	357	224	11	15	171
Total Assets **26**	20224807	909213	361175	163249	69291	36476	13645	7615	2148	625	54	13112
Notes and Loans Payable **27**	3631031	190109	206147	41822	14410	3918	1748	674	648	333	46	2580
All Other Liabilities **28**	10625169	799393	81936	89924	53991	15616	7454	5546	1644	361	10	7291
Net Worth **29**	5968608	-80288	73092	31504	890	16942	4443	1395	-145	-70	-2	3241

Selected Financial Ratios (Times to 1)

Current Ratio **30**	1.7	1.2	1.0	1.5	1.4	1.3	1.5	1.3	1.3	0.8	1.8	1.5
Quick Ratio **31**	1.4	1.0	0.6	1.1	1.1	0.7	1.2	1.2	1.2	0.5	1.7	1.3
Net Sales to Working Capital **32**	1.7	9.6	215.4	4.9	5.2	11.6	5.5	13.2	10.2	•	31.6	3.6
Coverage Ratio **33**	1.5	4.6	1.5	2.4	•	7.2	10.9	10.0	2.9	1.5	10.0	1.7
Total Asset Turnover **34**	0.2	0.5	1.1	0.8	0.7	1.3	1.1	1.7	1.7	3.1	7.5	0.3
Inventory Turnover **35**	•	•	•	•	•	•	•	•	•	•	•	•
Receivables Turnover **36**	•	•	•	•	•	•	•	•	•	•	•	•
Total Liabilities to Net Worth **37**	2.4	6.3	3.9	4.2	76.8	1.2	2.1	4.5	•	•	•	3.0
Current Assets to Working Capital **38**	2.5	6.3	66.1	3.0	3.4	5.0	3.2	4.2	4.4	2.3	•	2.9
Current Liabilities to Working Capital **39**	1.5	5.3	65.1	2.0	2.4	4.0	2.2	3.2	3.4	1.3	•	1.9
Working Capital to Net Sales **40**	0.6	0.1	0.0	0.2	0.2	0.1	0.2	0.1	0.1	0.0	•	0.3
Inventory to Working Capital **41**	0.0	0.0	0.6	0.0	0.0	•	0.0	0.0	0.0	•	•	0.0
Total Receipts to Cash Flow **42**	1.7	3.7	1.5	2.4	2.9	2.6	3.0	1.4	2.0	1.5	6.4	2.2
Cost of Goods to Cash Flow **43**	0.1	1.5	0.1	0.3	0.6	0.5	0.5	0.0	0.0	0.1	3.8	0.4
Cash Flow to Total Debt **44**	0.1	0.1	0.9	0.4	0.3	0.9	0.5	1.5	0.8	1.9	1.1	0.2

Selected Financial Factors (in Percentages)

Debt Ratio **45**	70.5	108.8	79.8	80.7	98.7	53.6	67.4	81.7	106.8	111.2	103.9	75.3
Return on Total Assets **46**	5.8	5.9	6.0	5.1	•	7.9	7.2	12.2	4.6	7.4	38.1	5.9
Return on Equity Before Income Taxes **47**	6.9	•	10.0	15.4	•	14.6	20.0	60.0	•	•	•	9.5
Return on Equity After Income Taxes **48**	4.6	•	6.4	9.1	•	9.6	16.1	54.3	•	•	•	6.1
Profit Margin (Before Income Tax) **49**	11.8	9.4	1.9	3.9	•	5.1	6.0	6.5	1.8	0.7	4.6	6.9
Profit Margin (After Income Tax) **50**	7.8	6.0	1.2	2.3	•	3.4	4.8	5.9	1.5	0.6	4.4	4.5

Table II

Corporations with Net Income

OTHER INSURANCE RELATED ACTIVITIES

MONEY AMOUNTS AND SIZE OF ASSETS IN THOUSANDS OF DOLLARS

Item Description for Accounting Period 7/07 Through 6/08	Total	Zero Assets	Under 500	500 to 1,000	1,000 to 5,000	5,000 to 10,000	10,000 to 25,000	25,000 to 50,000	50,000 to 100,000	100,000 to 250,000	250,000 to 500,000	500,000 to 2,500,000	2,500,000 and over
Number of Enterprises 1	9338	•	6157	368	400	•	87	28	25	•	5	12	•
Revenues ($ in Thousands)													
Net Sales 2	47345899	•	893091	1211125	1679771	•	1506198	1587506	1224678	•	3666507	6960355	•
Interest 3	6338630	•	3786	3159	11700	•	14739	15950	32235	•	58961	226996	•
Rents 4	92654	•	0	0	7126	•	1206	968	977	•	0	7740	•
Royalties 5	14431	•	0	0	0	•	0	0	0	•	0	14380	•
Other Portfolio Income 6	1177036	•	12776	1	3262	•	23874	4437	20729	•	11808	210432	•
Other Receipts 7	39723148	•	876529	1207965	1657683	•	1466379	1566151	1170737	•	3595738	6500807	•
Total Receipts 8	47345899	•	893091	1211125	1679771	•	1506198	1587506	1224678	•	3666507	6960355	•
Average Total Receipts 9	5070	•	145	3291	4199	•	17313	56697	48987	•	733301	580030	•
Operating Costs/Operating Income (%)													
Cost of Operations 10	13.8	•	7.6	6.5	0.3	•	13.9	20.2	13.9	•	•	45.2	•
Salaries and Wages 11	11.8	•	7.1	7.6	21.1	•	33.9	16.9	19.4	•	6.1	15.3	•
Taxes Paid 12	1.4	•	2.8	0.2	2.2	•	2.9	3.0	2.4	•	1.0	1.5	•
Interest Paid 13	11.3	•	0.4	1.5	0.5	•	0.3	0.5	2.1	•	2.5	1.7	•
Depreciation 14	0.7	•	0.9	0.0	0.6	•	1.0	1.1	1.1	•	0.7	0.8	•
Amortization and Depletion 15	0.5	•	0.2	0.0	0.0	•	0.3	0.3	0.9	•	0.4	0.8	•
Pensions and Other Deferred Comp. 16	0.5	•	0.4	3.1	1.9	•	1.3	0.4	0.2	•	0.1	0.3	•
Employee Benefits 17	2.3	•	0.9	0.2	2.5	•	2.1	10.6	12.3	•	0.9	2.5	•
Advertising 18	0.5	•	1.0	0.2	1.8	•	0.5	1.9	0.2	•	0.2	0.4	•
Other Expenses 19	43.3	•	30.1	68.0	53.7	•	25.7	32.1	37.2	•	82.6	18.2	•
Officers' Compensation 20	1.9	•	18.2	3.8	8.4	•	6.3	2.6	1.7	•	0.8	0.2	•
Operating Margin 21	12.1	•	30.5	8.8	7.0	•	12.0	10.4	8.4	•	4.8	13.2	•
Operating Margin Before Officers' Comp. 22	14.0	•	48.7	12.7	15.4	•	18.3	13.0	10.1	•	5.6	13.4	•

Selected Average Balance Sheet ($ in Thousands)

	1	2	3	4	5	6	7	8	9	10	11	12	13
Net Receivables 23	690	•	•	1	90	758	•	2208	6276	6149	•	28706	216752
Inventories 24	•	•	•	•	•	•	•	•	•	•	•	•	•
Net Property, Plant and Equipment 25	169	•	•	9	4	107	•	458	1704	4064	•	35213	24098
Total Assets 26	14851	•	•	36	680	2030	•	13134	35706	67953	•	359984	913000
Notes and Loans Payable 27	2188	•	•	6	444	411	•	713	3519	10073	•	309825	188531
All Other Liabilities 28	8033	•	•	3	156	2062	•	9342	14792	34625	•	-85597	369772
Net Worth 29	4629	•	•	27	81	-444	•	3080	17395	23255	•	135756	354697

Selected Financial Ratios (Times to 1)

	1	2	3	4	5	6	7	8	9	10	11	12	13
Current Ratio 30	1.3	•	•	4.4	1.0	1.2	•	1.4	1.5	1.3	•	1.6	1.2
Quick Ratio 31	1.1	•	•	4.2	0.8	1.1	•	1.1	0.9	1.1	•	1.3	1.0
Net Sales to Working Capital 32	5.6	•	•	9.0	•	15.8	•	6.6	7.3	•	•	10.8	12.8
Coverage Ratio 33	2.0	•	•	79.3	7.1	14.3	•	46.2	21.4	6.9	•	2.9	8.5
Total Asset Turnover 34	0.3	•	•	4.0	4.8	2.1	•	1.3	1.6	0.7	•	2.0	0.6
Inventory Turnover 35	•	•	•	•	•	•	•	•	•	•	•	•	•
Receivables Turnover 36	•	•	•	•	•	•	•	•	•	•	•	•	•
Total Liabilities to Net Worth 37	2.2	•	•	0.3	7.4	•	•	3.3	1.1	1.9	•	1.7	1.6
Current Assets to Working Capital 38	3.9	•	•	1.3	6.5	3.0	•	3.5	3.0	4.3	•	2.8	7.6
Current Liabilities to Working Capital 39	2.9	•	•	0.3	5.5	2.0	•	2.5	2.0	3.3	•	1.8	6.6
Working Capital to Net Sales 40	0.2	•	•	0.1	0.1	0.2	•	0.2	0.1	0.1	•	0.1	0.1
Inventory to Working Capital 41	0.0	•	•	0.0	0.0	0.0	•	0.0	0.0	0.0	•	0.0	0.0
Total Receipts to Cash Flow 42	1.9	•	•	1.9	1.4	1.8	•	2.8	2.5	2.4	•	1.2	3.5
Cost of Goods to Cash Flow 43	0.3	•	•	0.1	0.1	0.0	•	0.4	0.5	0.3	•	•	1.6
Cash Flow to Total Debt 44	0.3	•	•	9.0	4.0	0.9	•	0.6	1.3	•	•	2.8	0.5

Selected Financial Factors (in Percentages)

	1	2	3	4	5	6	7	8	9	10	11	12	13
Debt Ratio 45	68.8	•	•	24.2	88.1	121.9	•	76.5	51.3	65.8	•	62.3	61.2
Return on Total Assets 46	7.8	•	•	124.1	49.7	15.5	•	16.0	17.2	10.2	•	14.5	9.2
Return on Equity Before Income Taxes 47	12.7	•	•	161.6	359.4	•	•	66.6	33.7	25.4	•	25.1	20.9
Return on Equity After Income Taxes 48	9.4	•	•	158.5	353.7	•	•	57.9	26.9	18.9	•	20.0	14.4
Profit Margin (Before Income Tax) 49	11.6	•	•	30.5	8.8	7.0	•	11.8	10.3	12.1	•	4.6	12.8
Profit Margin (After Income Tax) 50	8.6	•	•	29.9	8.7	6.6	•	10.3	8.3	9.0	•	3.7	8.8

Table I

Corporations with and without Net Income

OPEN-END INVESTMENT FUNDS (FORM 1120-RIC)

MONEY AMOUNTS AND SIZE OF ASSETS IN THOUSANDS OF DOLLARS

Item Description for Accounting Period 7/07 Through 6/08	Total	Zero Assets	Under 500	500 to 1,000	1,000 to 5,000	5,000 to 10,000	10,000 to 25,000	25,000 to 50,000	50,000 to 100,000	100,000 to 250,000	250,000 to 500,000	500,000 to 2,500,000	2,500,000 and over
Number of Enterprises 1	12083	564	55	80	516	558	888	937	1283	1981	1541	2604	1076
Revenues ($ in Thousands)													
Net Sales 2	536567685	2126263	233251	1689	60330	194096	585614	1533372	4016874	13336543	22676993	111451457	380351204
Interest 3	238734491	890499	232152	696	8698	48802	138203	394819	1305296	4330061	7550808	37356292	186478165
Rents 4	0	0	0	0	0	0	0	0	0	0	0	0	0
Royalties 5	0	0	0	0	0	0	0	0	0	0	0	0	0
Other Portfolio Income 6	120781091	803072	353	400	27156	69137	197441	615679	1483347	5135607	8253976	36493680	67700742
Other Receipts 7	177052103	432692	746	593	24476	76157	249970	522874	1227731	3870875	6872209	37601485	126172297
Total Receipts 8	536567685	2126263	233251	1689	60330	194096	585614	1533372	4016874	13336543	22676993	111451457	380351204
Average Total Receipts 9	44407	3770	4241	21	117	348	659	1636	3131	6732	14716	42800	353486
Operating Costs/Operating Income (%)													
Cost of Operations 10	•	•	•	•	•	•	•	•	•	•	•	•	•
Salaries and Wages 11	0.0	0.1	0.0	1.3	0.4	0.1	0.0	0.1	0.1	0.1	0.0	0.0	0.0
Taxes Paid 12	0.2	0.1	0.0	0.2	0.3	0.3	0.3	0.3	0.2	0.3	0.3	0.3	0.2
Interest Paid 13	0.4	0.2	•	•	0.0	0.4	1.6	0.4	0.8	0.7	1.0	0.7	0.3
Depreciation 14	0.0	0.0	•	•	•	•	•	0.0	0.0	0.0	0.0	0.0	0.0
Amortization and Depletion 15	0.0	0.0	0.0	1.2	0.6	0.6	0.3	0.0	0.1	0.0	0.0	0.0	0.0
Pensions and Other Deferred Comp. 16	•	•	•	•	•	•	•	•	•	•	•	•	•
Employee Benefits 17	•	•	•	•	•	•	•	•	•	•	•	•	•
Advertising 18	0.0	0.0	•	•	•	•	•	•	0.0	0.0	0.0	0.0	0.0
Other Expenses 19	15.6	17.0	0.8	81.4	21.4	14.0	20.7	22.1	19.9	19.8	19.2	19.2	14.2
Officers' Compensation 20	0.0	0.0	0.3	•	•	0.0	0.0	0.0	0.0	0.0	0.0	0.0	0.0
Operating Margin 21	83.7	82.6	98.9	15.9	77.3	84.6	77.1	77.1	78.9	79.0	79.4	79.7	85.3
Operating Margin Before Officers' Comp. 22	83.7	82.6	99.2	15.9	77.3	84.6	77.1	77.1	79.0	79.1	79.4	79.7	85.3

Selected Average Balance Sheet ($ in Thousands)

Line Item	Total												
Net Receivables 23	19265	0	0	12	23	101	302	708	1166	2792	4976	20159	152964
Inventories 24	•	•	•	•	•	•	•	•	•	•	•	•	•
Net Property, Plant and Equipment 25	1	•	0	0	0	1	4	0	0	0	•	2	1
Total Assets 26	1212123	0	154	748	3035	7094	16470	36844	73023	165038	359087	1104920	9981552
Notes and Loans Payable 27	1833	0	0	0	16	8	45	217	556	1790	2272	•	11187
All Other Liabilities 28	65905	0	35	31	120	387	620	1685	4006	10450	24671	84865	473108
Net Worth 29	1144386	0	118	718	2915	6691	15843	35114	68801	154032	332627	1017782	9497257

Selected Financial Ratios (Times to 1)

Line Item	Total												
Current Ratio 30	2.6	•	1.3	1.5	2.1	2.0	3.3	3.4	3.4	3.0	2.7	2.0	2.8
Quick Ratio 31	2.3	•	1.1	0.9	1.7	1.6	2.9	3.0	3.0	2.7	2.4	1.8	2.5
Net Sales to Working Capital 32	0.4	•	487.0	1.3	0.9	0.9	0.5	0.4	0.3	0.3	0.3	0.5	0.4
Coverage Ratio 33	184.8	•	250.9	•	8176.6	215.6	45.0	161.8	83.0	87.4	64.2	96.6	292.5
Total Asset Turnover 34	0.0	•	250.9	27.5	0.0	0.0	0.0	0.0	0.0	0.0	0.0	0.0	0.0
Inventory Turnover 35	•	•	•	•	•	•	•	•	•	•	•	•	•
Receivables Turnover 36	•	•	•	•	•	•	•	•	•	•	•	•	•
Total Liabilities to Net Worth 37	0.1	•	0.3	0.0	0.1	0.0	0.0	0.0	0.1	0.1	0.1	0.1	0.1
Current Assets to Working Capital 38	1.6	•	4.7	1.9	2.0	1.4	1.4	1.4	1.5	1.6	2.0	1.6	•
Current Liabilities to Working Capital 39	0.6	•	3.7	0.9	1.0	0.4	0.4	0.4	0.5	0.6	1.0	0.6	•
Working Capital to Net Sales 40	2.3	•	0.0	0.0	1.1	1.2	2.2	2.6	3.0	3.1	2.9	2.0	2.4
Inventory to Working Capital 41	•	•	•	•	•	•	•	•	•	•	•	•	•
Total Receipts to Cash Flow 42	1.2	•	1.2	1.0	1.6	1.5	1.4	1.4	1.3	1.3	1.3	1.3	1.2
Cost of Goods to Cash Flow 43	•	•	•	•	•	•	•	•	•	•	•	•	•
Cash Flow to Total Debt 44	0.5	•	119.0	0.5	0.6	0.6	0.8	0.7	0.6	0.5	0.4	0.4	0.6

Selected Financial Factors (in Percentages)

Line Item	Total												
Debt Ratio 45	5.6	•	23.0	4.1	3.9	5.7	3.8	4.7	5.8	6.7	7.4	7.9	4.9
Return on Total Assets 46	2.8	•	2725.0	0.4	2.6	4.0	2.9	2.8	2.7	2.6	2.7	2.7	2.9
Return on Equity Before Income Taxes 47	3.0	•	3540.9	0.5	2.7	4.2	2.9	3.0	2.9	2.8	2.8	2.9	3.0
Return on Equity After Income Taxes 48	3.0	•	3540.9	0.5	2.7	4.2	2.9	3.0	2.9	2.8	2.8	2.9	3.0
Profit Margin (Before Income Tax) 49	76.9	57.8	98.9	15.9	67.8	81.5	69.7	63.6	63.3	63.8	64.3	69.8	80.4
Profit Margin (After Income Tax) 50	76.8	57.8	98.9	15.9	67.8	81.5	69.7	63.6	63.3	63.8	64.2	69.8	80.4

Table II

Corporations with Net Income

OPEN-END INVESTMENT FUNDS (FORM 1120-RIC)

MONEY AMOUNTS AND SIZE OF ASSETS IN THOUSANDS OF DOLLARS

Item Description for Accounting Period 7/07 Through 6/08	Total	Zero Assets	Under 500	500 to 1,000	1,000 to 5,000	5,000 to 10,000	10,000 to 25,000	25,000 to 50,000	50,000 to 100,000	100,000 to 250,000	250,000 to 500,000	500,000 to 2,500,000	2,500,000 and over
Number of Enterprises 1	10514	427	49	61	424	466	751	763	1077	1722	1370	2375	1028
Revenues ($ in Thousands)													
Net Sales 2	522935857	1982553	232637	1562	53806	187003	545137	1355947	3652346	12412556	21421733	106397518	374693058
Interest 3	238060953	860202	232152	679	8374	47060	135252	391092	1293491	4297282	7518166	37019716	186257486
Rents 4	0	0	0	0	0	0	0	0	0	0	0	0	0
Royalties 5	0	0	0	0	0	0	0	0	0	0	0	0	0
Other Portfolio Income 6	111042903	727403	353	374	21857	63059	169325	471033	1185366	4431809	7276652	32919045	63776629
Other Receipts 7	173832001	394948	132	509	23575	76884	240560	493822	1173489	3683465	6626915	36458757	124658943
Total Receipts 8	522935857	1982553	232637	1562	53806	187003	545137	1355947	3652346	12412556	21421733	106397518	374693058
Average Total Receipts 9	49737	4643	4748	26	127	401	726	1777	3391	7208	15636	44799	364487
Operating Costs/Operating Income (%)													
Cost of Operations 10	•	•	•	•	•	•	•	•	•	•	•	•	•
Salaries and Wages 11	0.0	0.1	0.0	•	0.4	0.1	0.0	0.1	0.1	0.1	0.0	0.0	0.0
Taxes Paid 12	0.2	0.1	0.0	0.3	0.3	0.3	0.3	0.3	0.2	0.3	0.3	0.3	0.2
Interest Paid 13	0.4	0.2	•	•	0.0	0.4	1.1	0.4	0.7	0.8	1.1	0.5	0.3
Depreciation 14	0.0	0.0	•	•	0.0	•	•	0.0	0.0	0.0	0.0	0.0	0.0
Amortization and Depletion 15	0.0	0.0	0.0	0.4	0.7	0.2	0.2	0.0	0.1	0.0	0.0	0.0	0.0
Pensions and Other Deferred Comp. 16	•	•	•	•	•	•	•	•	•	•	•	•	•
Employee Benefits 17	•	•	•	•	•	•	•	•	•	•	•	•	•
Advertising 18	0.0	0.0	0.0	•	•	•	•	•	0.0	0.0	0.0	0.0	0.0
Other Expenses 19	14.9	13.1	0.8	26.1	19.3	11.4	18.0	21.1	18.5	18.4	18.1	13.7	13.7
Officers' Compensation 20	0.0	0.0	•	•	0.0	0.0	0.0	0.0	0.1	0.0	0.0	0.0	0.0
Operating Margin 21	84.4	86.5	99.2	73.3	79.4	87.5	80.4	78.0	80.3	80.4	80.3	81.0	85.8
Operating Margin Before Officers' Comp. 22	84.4	86.5	99.2	73.3	79.4	87.5	80.4	78.1	80.4	80.4	80.3	81.0	85.8

Selected Average Balance Sheet ($ in Thousands)

Net Receivables 23	21403	•	0	0	15	19	77	313	608	1222	2887	5066	20823	157199
Inventories 24	•	•	•	•	•	•	•	•	•	•	•	•	•	•
Net Property, Plant and Equipment 25	1	0	0	0	0	0	0	5	0	0	0	0	3	2
Total Assets 26	1326848		160	791	2931	7067	16523	36417	73026	165559	359032		1112598	10124177
Notes and Loans Payable 27	2055		0	0	0	0	19	0	38	231	552	1970	2373	11709
All Other Liabilities 28	71671		27	36	116	341	574	1705	3754	10528	24501		86014	478197
Net Worth 29	1253121		133	755	2815	6707	15948	34674	69041	154479	332561		1024211	9634271

Selected Financial Ratios (Times to 1)

Current Ratio 30	2.4	•	1.4	1.6	2.4	1.5	2.9	2.2	2.9	2.6	2.5	1.9	2.7
Quick Ratio 31	2.2	•	1.2	1.0	1.9	1.2	2.7	2.0	2.4	2.4	2.2	1.6	2.4
Net Sales to Working Capital 32	0.5	•	484.7	1.1	0.8	2.2	0.7	0.8	0.5	0.4	0.4	0.6	0.5
Coverage Ratio 33	211.6	258.4	•	8438.6	226.8	70.9	171.7	100.0	93.7	65.3	136.4	301.5	
Total Asset Turnover 34	0.0	•	29.6	0.0	0.0	0.1	0.0	0.0	0.0	0.0	0.0	0.0	0.0
Inventory Turnover 35	•	•	•	•	•	•	•	•	•	•	•	•	•
Receivables Turnover 36	•	•	•	•	•	•	•	•	•	•	•	•	•
Total Liabilities to Net Worth 37	0.1	•	0.2	0.0	0.0	0.1	0.0	0.0	0.1	0.1	0.1	0.1	0.1
Current Assets to Working Capital 38	1.7	•	3.4	2.6	1.7	3.0	1.5	1.8	1.5	1.6	1.7	2.2	1.6
Current Liabilities to Working Capital 39	0.7	•	2.4	1.6	0.7	2.0	0.5	0.8	0.5	0.6	0.7	1.2	0.6
Working Capital to Net Sales 40	2.1	•	0.0	0.9	1.3	0.5	1.5	1.2	2.1	2.4	2.4	1.7	2.2
Inventory to Working Capital 41	•	•	•	•	•	•	•	•	•	•	•	•	•
Total Receipts to Cash Flow 42	1.2	1.2	1.0	1.3	1.7	1.5	1.4	1.3	1.3	1.4	1.3	1.3	1.2
Cost of Goods to Cash Flow 43	•	•	•	•	•	•	•	•	•	•	•	•	•
Cash Flow to Total Debt 44	0.6	•	173.5	0.5	0.6	0.7	0.9	0.7	0.6	0.5	0.4	0.4	0.4	0.6

Selected Financial Factors (in Percentages)

Debt Ratio 45	5.6	•	17.0	4.6	3.5	5.1	3.5	4.8	5.5	6.7	7.4	7.9	4.8
Return on Total Assets 46	3.0	•	29377.7	2.4	3.4	5.0	3.4	3.6	3.3	3.1	3.0	3.0	3.0
Return on Equity Before Income Taxes 47	3.1	•	3540.9	2.5	3.5	5.2	3.5	3.8	3.5	3.2	3.2	3.2	3.1
Return on Equity After Income Taxes 48	3.1	•	3540.9	2.5	3.5	5.2	3.5	3.8	3.5	3.2	3.2	3.2	3.1
Profit Margin (Before Income Tax) 49	79.2	63.8	99.2	73.3	78.4	87.5	77.2	73.4	71.3	69.6	68.8	73.9	81.8
Profit Margin (After Income Tax) 50	79.2	63.8	99.2	73.3	78.4	87.5	77.2	73.4	71.3	69.6	68.7	73.9	81.8

Table I

Corporations with and without Net Income

OTHER FINANCIAL VEHICLES

MONEY AMOUNTS AND SIZE OF ASSETS IN THOUSANDS OF DOLLARS

Item Description for Accounting Period 7/07 Through 6/08	Total	Zero Assets	Under 500	500 to 1,000	1,000 to 5,000	5,000 to 10,000	10,000 to 25,000	25,000 to 50,000	50,000 to 100,000	100,000 to 250,000	250,000 to 500,000	500,000 to 2,500,000	2,500,000 and over
Number of Enterprises 1	13231	2462	7853	449	1207	242	227	124	117	114	100	206	131

Revenues ($ in Thousands)

	Total	Zero Assets	Under 500	500 to 1,000	1,000 to 5,000	5,000 to 10,000	10,000 to 25,000	25,000 to 50,000	50,000 to 100,000	100,000 to 250,000	250,000 to 500,000	500,000 to 2,500,000	2,500,000 and over
Net Sales 2	101268785	7464184	2534434	68427	1324329	915531	591839	606318	677590	1583140	2952912	16441864	66108219
Interest 3	83065634	6064748	2145781	9142	552767	218818	159673	485755	412749	769443	2259311	14374288	55613158
Rents 4	2966971	86117	9428	0	1612	0	21987	29449	78977	212137	642272		1663285
Royalties 5	14000	6	32	0	0	0	13443	360	16	0	43	61	38
Other Portfolio Income 6	5640732	855161	27265	35751	435386	194072	207815	41408	81956	220581	226685	418987	2895667
Other Receipts 7	9581448	458152	351928	23534	334564	502641	188921	49346	103892	380979	245167	1006256	5936071
Total Receipts 8	101268785	7464184	2534434	68427	1324329	915531	591839	606318	677590	1583140	2952912	16441864	66108219
Average Total Receipts 9	7654	3032	323	152	1097	3783	2607	4890	5791	13887	29529	79815	504643

Operating Costs/Operating Income (%)

	Total	Zero Assets	Under 500	500 to 1,000	1,000 to 5,000	5,000 to 10,000	10,000 to 25,000	25,000 to 50,000	50,000 to 100,000	100,000 to 250,000	250,000 to 500,000	500,000 to 2,500,000	2,500,000 and over
Cost of Operations 10	0.0	•	•	•	1.4	•	•	•	0.0	•	•	0.0	•
Salaries and Wages 11	0.4	0.1	0.0	1.0	1.3	0.1	1.7	0.1	1.0	0.5	1.2	0.2	0.4
Taxes Paid 12	0.3	0.1	0.4	0.5	1.4	0.9	2.9	1.4	2.1	1.6	1.5	0.3	0.2
Interest Paid 13	39.8	55.8	85.0	1.4	46.6	17.4	24.6	43.7	25.8	22.9	42.4	38.3	37.3
Depreciation 14	0.5	0.4	0.1	0.2	0.2	0.3	0.8	1.0	1.7	2.3	1.4	0.6	0.5
Amortization and Depletion 15	0.2	0.0	0.0	1.1	0.3	0.0	0.2	4.1	0.4	0.5	0.3	0.3	0.2
Pensions and Other Deferred Comp. 16	0.0	0.0	0.0	•	0.3	•	0.0	0.0	0.0	0.0	•	•	•
Employee Benefits 17	0.2	•	0.4	0.7	0.1	•	0.3	•	0.0	0.0	0.1	•	0.2
Advertising 18	0.0	0.0	0.0	•	0.0	0.0	0.0	0.0	0.1	0.0	0.1	0.0	0.0
Other Expenses 19	11.1	14.6	12.8	38.2	29.0	75.5	45.7	49.7	38.4	28.8	14.3	13.1	7.4
Officers' Compensation 20	0.1	0.1	1.4	0.8	2.4	0.5	2.1	0.0	0.2	0.3	0.1	0.0	0.1
Operating Margin 21	47.3	28.9	•	56.0	16.8	5.4	21.6	0.1	30.2	43.1	38.8	47.1	53.8
Operating Margin Before Officers' Comp. 22	47.4	29.0	1.2	56.8	19.2	5.9	23.7	0.1	30.4	43.4	38.9	47.1	53.8

Selected Average Balance Sheet ($ in Thousands)

Net Receivables **23**	6880	0	1	•	6	125	629	399	1338	4139	5658	26404	78269	538726
Inventories **24**	•	•	•	•	•	•	•	•	•	•	•	•	•	•
Net Property, Plant and Equipment **25**	1782	0	2	0	10	46	200	1450	1793	3236	9740	17148	31281	101155
Total Assets **26**	104305	86	2	10	669	2155	7045	16027	36480	70714	167163	357039	1167627	8114882
Notes and Loans Payable **27**	31309	0	23	67	1046	1843	4581	10349	12893	35072	95636	324052	•	2505224
All Other Liabilities **28**	13684	0	38	7	145	1577	1937	5984	9794	15033	43629	151505	•	1073177
Net Worth **29**	59311	0	25	595	964	3625	9508	20147	48028	117058	217775	692070	•	4536481

Selected Financial Ratios (Times to 1)

Current Ratio **30**	0.8	•	2.3	6.1	2.5	1.5	1.8	1.8	1.6	1.6	1.3	0.9	0.8
Quick Ratio **31**	0.6	•	1.6	5.4	2.1	1.5	1.3	1.0	1.4	1.0	1.1	0.6	0.6
Net Sales to Working Capital **32**	•	•	28.2	0.6	3.1	7.9	2.2	1.0	1.1	1.0	1.7	0.6	0.8
Coverage Ratio **33**	2.2	1.5	1.0	39.6	1.4	1.3	1.9	1.0	2.1	2.8	1.9	2.2	2.4
Total Asset Turnover **34**	0.1	•	3.7	0.2	0.5	0.5	0.2	0.1	0.1	0.1	0.1	0.1	0.1
Inventory Turnover **35**	•	•	•	•	•	•	•	•	•	•	•	•	•
Receivables Turnover **36**	•	•	•	•	•	•	•	•	•	•	•	•	•
Total Liabilities to Net Worth **37**	0.8	2.4	•	0.1	1.2	0.9	0.7	0.8	0.5	0.4	0.6	0.7	0.8
Current Assets to Working Capital **38**	•	•	1.8	1.2	1.7	2.8	2.3	2.2	2.8	2.5	4.4	0.6	0.8
Current Liabilities to Working Capital **39**	•	0.8	0.2	0.7	1.8	1.3	1.8	1.2	1.8	1.5	3.4	•	•
Working Capital to Net Sales **40**	•	0.0	1.7	0.0	0.3	0.1	0.4	1.0	0.9	1.0	0.6	•	0.1
Inventory to Working Capital **41**	•	•	0.0	0.0	0.0	0.1	0.4	1.0	0.9	1.0	0.6	•	0.1
Total Receipts to Cash Flow **42**	1.9	3.1	9.2	2.5	8.2	2.0	3.4	2.3	1.7	1.8	2.2	1.7	1.7
Cost of Goods to Cash Flow **43**	0.0	•	•	•	0.1	0.1	0.0	0.0	0.0	•	•	0.0	•
Cash Flow to Total Debt **44**	0.1	0.6	0.8	0.1	0.6	0.1	0.1	0.1	0.1	0.2	0.1	0.1	0.1

Selected Financial Factors (in Percentages)

Debt Ratio **45**	43.1	•	70.9	11.1	55.3	48.5	40.7	44.8	32.1	30.0	39.0	40.7	44.1
Return on Total Assets **46**	6.4	•	317.4	13.1	32.1	12.1	7.5	5.8	4.5	5.4	6.7	5.8	5.6
Return on Equity Before Income Taxes **47**	6.1	•	•	14.3	18.6	5.4	5.8	3.6	5.0	5.3	5.4	•	5.9
Return on Equity After Income Taxes **48**	5.7	•	•	13.6	15.3	•	3.9	2.8	4.7	5.0	5.4	•	5.7
Profit Margin (Before Income Tax) **49**	47.0	28.9	56.0	•	16.4	5.2	21.3	29.5	42.1	38.7	47.1	•	53.4
Profit Margin (After Income Tax) **50**	44.4	26.3	53.2	•	13.4	14.1	23.2	39.7	42.1	36.8	43.1	•	51.1

Table II

Corporations with Net Income

OTHER FINANCIAL VEHICLES

MONEY AMOUNTS AND SIZE OF ASSETS IN THOUSANDS OF DOLLARS

Item Description for Accounting Period 7/07 Through 6/08	Total	Zero Assets	Under 500	500 to 1,000	1,000 to 5,000	5,000 to 10,000	10,000 to 25,000	25,000 to 50,000	50,000 to 100,000	100,000 to 250,000	250,000 to 500,000	500,000 to 2,500,000	2,500,000 and over
Number of Enterprises 1	5518	1179	2761	234	606	80	89	58	72	81	72	168	118

Revenues ($ in Thousands)

Net Sales 2	85951274	6109960	1033983	65023	980503	456839	496509	542657	574773	1197980	2013962	12518487	59960598
Interest 3	69106275	4770464	692526	6721	255424	210089	129527	436855	299157	567753	1446914	10705010	49585836
Rents 4	2745257	68768	0	0	1612	0	8667	0	67322	172120	210602	552881	1663285
Royalties 5	13548	5	0	0	0	0	13443	0	16	0	43	3	38
Other Portfolio Income 6	5348705	828141	5563	35564	430379	191803	199132	35420	64652	207002	167034	288347	2895667
Other Receipts 7	8737489	442582	335894	22738	293088	54947	145740	70382	143626	251105	189369	972246	5815772
Total Receipts 8	85951274	6109960	1033983	65023	980503	456839	496509	542657	574773	1197980	2013962	12518487	59960598
Average Total Receipts 9	15577	5182	374	278	1618	5710	5579	9356	7983	14790	27972	74515	508141

Operating Costs/Operating Income (%)

Cost of Operations 10	0.0	•	•	•	•	•	•	•	0.0	•	•	•	0.0
Salaries and Wages 11	0.4	0.0	0.0	•	0.0	0.1	1.6	0.0	0.6	0.6	1.7	0.1	0.5
Taxes Paid 12	0.3	0.1	0.4	0.2	1.8	1.1	2.4	0.5	2.1	1.8	1.8	0.4	0.2
Interest Paid 13	31.4	51.0	72.1	72.1	27.1	30.6	19.5	37.0	14.2	14.7	20.5	22.6	31.6
Depreciation 14	0.6	0.2	0.0	0.0	0.2	0.5	0.6	0.0	1.6	2.5	1.6	0.7	0.5
Amortization and Depletion 15	0.2	0.0	0.0	0.1	0.2	0.0	0.1	0.3	0.3	0.4	0.3	0.2	0.2
Pensions and Other Deferred Comp. 16	0.0	0.0	0.0	•	0.5	0.0	0.0	0.0	0.0	0.0	•	•	0.3
Employee Benefits 17	0.2	•	0.8	•	•	•	0.2	•	0.0	0.0	0.1	0.0	0.0
Advertising 18	0.0	0.0	0.0	•	•	•	0.0	0.0	0.1	0.0	0.0	0.0	0.0
Other Expenses 19	7.1	3.9	5.5	7.0	6.4	19.1	14.0	22.5	9.3	12.2	9.0	6.3	7.2
Officers' Compensation 20	0.1	0.0	3.4	•	2.9	•	2.0	0.0	0.2	0.3	0.1	0.0	0.1
Operating Margin 21	59.6	44.7	17.6	92.7	60.9	48.5	59.6	39.7	71.4	67.4	64.9	69.7	59.5
Operating Margin Before Officers' Comp. 22	59.8	44.8	21.0	92.7	63.8	48.5	61.6	39.7	71.7	67.6	65.1	69.7	59.6

Selected Average Balance Sheet ($ in Thousands)

Net Receivables 23	13772	0	0	4	243	388	499	989	4337	4362	14281	58554	543904
Inventories 24	•	•	•	•	•	•	•	3	•	•	•	•	•
Net Property, Plant and Equipment 25	3812	0	3	7	90	591	957	3481	4481	10851	20181	29783	112290
Total Assets 26	218892	0	146	633	1865	7102	17392	37233	71374	166764	345491	1141661	8191249
Notes and Loans Payable 27	51952	0	12	0	435	1182	2938	8473	8039	18840	60699	223558	2046562
All Other Liabilities 28	27924	0	6	3	114	1129	1990	9103	8929	15557	24795	107126	1114542
Net Worth 29	139016	0	128	630	1316	4790	12464	19656	54406	132368	259997	810977	5030146

Selected Financial Ratios (Times to 1)

Current Ratio 30	1.2	•	5.6	129.0	14.5	3.3	1.5	1.2	1.5	2.4	2.2	1.1	1.1
Quick Ratio 31	0.9	•	4.0	123.6	13.4	2.9	1.2	0.6	1.4	1.6	1.6	0.8	0.9
Net Sales to Working Capital 32	3.0	•	18.8	0.7	2.2	6.5	5.9	5.6	1.8	0.8	0.8	4.2	3.0
Coverage Ratio 33	2.9	1.9	1.2	60276.0	3.2	2.6	4.1	2.1	6.0	5.6	4.2	4.1	2.9
Total Asset Turnover 34	0.1	•	2.6	0.4	0.9	0.8	0.3	0.3	0.1	0.1	0.1	0.1	0.1
Inventory Turnover 35	•	•	•	•	•	•	•	•	•	•	•	•	•
Receivables Turnover 36	•	•	•	•	•	•	•	•	•	•	•	•	•
Total Liabilities to Net Worth 37	0.6	•	0.1	0.0	0.4	0.5	0.4	0.9	0.3	0.3	0.3	0.4	0.6
Current Assets to Working Capital 38	7.4	•	1.2	1.0	1.1	1.4	3.1	5.8	2.9	1.7	1.8	9.0	8.5
Current Liabilities to Working Capital 39	6.4	•	0.2	0.0	0.1	0.4	2.1	4.8	1.9	0.7	0.8	8.0	7.5
Working Capital to Net Sales 40	0.3	•	0.1	1.5	0.5	0.2	0.2	0.2	0.6	1.3	1.2	0.2	0.3
Inventory to Working Capital 41	•	•	•	•	•	•	•	•	•	•	•	•	•
Total Receipts to Cash Flow 42	1.6	2.7	4.6	2.2	4.1	3.9	3.1	1.8	1.4	1.6	1.5	1.3	1.6
Cost of Goods to Cash Flow 43	0.0	•	•	•	•	•	•	•	0.0	0.0	•	0.0	•
Cash Flow to Total Debt 44	0.1	•	4.7	39.0	0.7	0.6	0.4	0.3	0.3	0.3	0.2	0.2	0.1

Selected Financial Factors (in Percentages)

Debt Ratio 45	36.5	•	11.9	0.5	29.4	32.5	28.3	47.2	23.8	20.6	24.7	29.0	38.6
Return on Total Assets 46	6.5	•	230.4	40.7	76.1	63.6	25.3	19.3	9.6	7.3	6.9	6.0	5.6
Return on Equity Before Income Taxes 47	6.7	•	51.2	40.9	74.4	57.8	26.7	18.9	10.5	7.5	7.0	6.4	6.0
Return on Equity After Income Taxes 48	6.3	•	49.9	39.6	69.5	42.7	22.8	17.6	9.4	7.2	6.7	5.9	5.7
Profit Margin (Before Income Tax) 49	59.4	44.7	17.5	92.7	60.6	48.5	59.6	39.6	71.3	67.2	64.9	69.7	59.2
Profit Margin (After Income Tax) 50	56.3	41.6	17.1	89.8	56.6	35.9	37.0	63.8	64.0	62.1	64.9	64.5	56.6

Table I

Corporations with and without Net Income

LESSORS OF BUILDINGS

MONEY AMOUNTS AND SIZE OF ASSETS IN THOUSANDS OF DOLLARS

Item Description for Accounting Period 7/07 Through 6/08	Total	Zero Assets	Under 500	500 to 1,000	1,000 to 5,000	5,000 to 10,000	10,000 to 25,000	25,000 to 50,000	50,000 to 100,000	100,000 to 250,000	250,000 to 500,000	500,000 to 2,500,000	2,500,000 and over
Number of Enterprises 1	218959	24743	110534	36479	39226	4573	2277	544	267	146	70	73	27
Revenues ($ in Thousands)													
Net Sales 2	69319668	8761860	3905684	2233701	6864248	2420566	3490723	2473152	2669914	2656144	2856948	8448601	22538127
Interest 3	2785659	100731	55306	42792	160580	68558	84775	74926	93312	113309	125059	636653	1229659
Rents 4	20236193	399160	26546	11734	44340	24237	123013	188060	336732	687824	1052659	3408782	13933103
Royalties 5	29392	78	20	10040	14834	2768	104	641	647	259	0	0	0
Other Portfolio Income 6	10720232	3565691	215352	161007	486892	161852	222033	336100	193141	375174	408605	1826786	2767599
Other Receipts 7	35548192	4696200	3608460	2008128	6157602	2163151	3060798	1873425	2046082	1479578	1270625	2576380	4607766
Total Receipts 8	69319668	8761860	3905684	2233701	6864248	2420566	3490723	2473152	2669914	2656144	2856948	8448601	22538127
Average Total Receipts 9	317	354	35	61	175	529	1533	4546	10000	18193	40814	115734	834745
Operating Costs/Operating Income (%)													
Cost of Operations 10	7.8	1.0	13.6	0.8	9.4	6.6	16.0	14.0	21.6	12.2	20.0	4.5	5.4
Salaries and Wages 11	5.0	0.7	12.4	4.8	11.3	8.2	8.8	5.9	11.3	5.8	4.9	4.7	1.9
Taxes Paid 12	7.2	9.5	9.5	13.2	12.7	11.4	8.1	8.1	7.2	5.9	5.6	6.2	3.6
Interest Paid 13	12.7	14.4	5.6	12.1	13.0	14.5	14.8	13.8	13.6	19.5	17.7	18.1	9.0
Depreciation 14	9.5	3.9	5.8	9.4	9.0	9.8	9.5	7.5	7.8	9.8	8.7	9.4	13.0
Amortization and Depletion 15	0.9	0.4	0.1	1.2	0.5	0.6	0.7	0.7	0.9	1.5	0.9	1.0	1.2
Pensions and Other Deferred Comp. 16	0.2	0.0	0.1	0.4	0.6	0.7	0.6	0.3	0.3	0.2	0.0	0.1	0.0
Employee Benefits 17	0.4	0.0	0.4	0.8	1.6	0.8	0.9	0.8	0.9	0.4	0.3	0.4	0.0
Advertising 18	0.3	0.0	0.2	0.9	0.3	0.5	0.4	0.3	0.3	0.5	0.6	0.4	0.3
Other Expenses 19	27.0	12.8	40.3	43.7	32.1	35.0	30.3	30.8	30.7	30.2	19.7	23.6	26.6
Officers' Compensation 20	2.3	0.2	5.5	5.5	6.8	6.0	3.5	3.8	1.4	1.7	0.7	2.1	0.5
Operating Margin 21	26.7	57.1	6.3	7.2	2.6	6.0	6.5	13.9	4.0	12.3	20.8	29.6	38.5
Operating Margin Before Officers' Comp. 22	29.0	57.3	11.8	12.6	9.4	12.0	10.1	17.7	5.4	14.0	21.5	31.6	39.0

Selected Average Balance Sheet ($ in Thousands)

Net Receivables 23	67	0	3	20	41	178	352	778	2847	6471	8582	24790	220385
Inventories 24	•	•	•	•	•	•	•	•	•	•	•	•	•
Net Property, Plant and Equipment 25	1641	0	143	504	1444	4412	9474	20622	37936	88746	176418	591361	5067175
Total Assets 26	2542	0	192	706	2038	6783	14757	34954	68980	153077	354310	1061850	7516276
Notes and Loans Payable 27	1261	0	121	486	1439	4417	9641	19467	35765	80765	149795	520761	2446243
All Other Liabilities 28	188	0	4	49	140	330	1241	3057	5677	9915	33492	92077	572899
Net Worth 29	1092	0	67	171	459	2036	3876	12430	27538	62396	171024	449012	4497134

Selected Financial Ratios (Times to 1)

Current Ratio 30	1.4	•	2.9	2.5	2.0	2.8	1.7	2.3	1.9	2.0	2.0	1.3	0.7
Quick Ratio 31	0.9	•	2.2	1.9	1.3	1.9	1.1	1.5	1.3	1.4	1.1	0.9	0.5
Net Sales to Working Capital 32	4.5	•	1.9	0.9	1.2	0.8	1.6	1.4	1.9	1.9	2.3	6.2	•
Coverage Ratio 33	3.1	5.0	2.1	1.6	1.2	1.3	1.4	2.0	1.3	1.6	2.2	2.6	5.2
Total Asset Turnover 34	0.1	•	0.2	0.1	0.1	0.1	0.1	0.1	0.1	0.1	0.1	0.1	0.1
Inventory Turnover 35	•	•	•	•	•	•	•	•	•	•	•	•	•
Receivables Turnover 36	•	•	•	•	•	•	•	•	•	•	•	•	•
Total Liabilities to Net Worth 37	1.3	•	1.9	3.1	3.4	2.3	2.8	1.8	1.5	1.5	1.1	1.4	0.7
Current Assets to Working Capital 38	3.8	•	1.5	1.7	2.0	1.5	2.4	1.8	2.1	2.0	2.0	4.8	•
Current Liabilities to Working Capital 39	2.8	•	0.5	0.7	1.0	0.5	1.4	0.8	1.1	1.0	1.0	3.8	•
Working Capital to Net Sales 40	0.2	•	0.5	1.1	0.8	1.2	0.6	0.7	0.5	0.5	0.4	0.2	•
Inventory to Working Capital 41	0.0	•	•	•	0.0	0.0	0.0	0.0	0.0	0.1	0.0	0.0	•
Total Receipts to Cash Flow 42	3.2	3.6	3.4	3.7	4.5	3.6	4.1	3.7	4.1	4.3	4.4	3.6	2.4
Cost of Goods to Cash Flow 43	0.2	0.0	0.5	0.0	0.4	0.2	0.7	0.5	0.9	0.5	0.9	0.2	0.1
Cash Flow to Total Debt 44	0.1	•	0.1	0.0	0.0	0.0	0.0	0.1	0.1	0.0	0.1	0.1	0.1

Selected Financial Factors (in Percentages)

Debt Ratio 45	57.0	•	65.2	75.8	77.5	70.0	73.7	64.4	60.1	59.2	51.7	57.7	40.2
Return on Total Assets 46	4.9	•	2.2	1.7	1.3	1.5	2.1	3.5	2.5	3.8	4.4	5.2	5.3
Return on Equity Before Income Taxes 47	7.7	•	3.3	2.5	0.9	1.3	2.3	4.8	1.3	3.5	4.9	7.6	7.1
Return on Equity After Income Taxes 48	6.9	•	2.2	1.9	0.4	0.4	1.2	3.2	0.4	3.0	4.7	7.1	7.1
Profit Margin (Before Income Tax) 49	26.5	57.1	6.3	7.1	2.3	4.9	5.9	13.2	3.7	12.1	20.6	29.4	38.4
Profit Margin (After Income Tax) 50	23.7	45.5	4.2	5.2	•	1.5	3.0	8.6	1.0	10.2	19.5	27.7	38.3

315

Table II

Corporations with Net Income

LESSORS OF BUILDINGS

MONEY AMOUNTS AND SIZE OF ASSETS IN THOUSANDS OF DOLLARS

Item Description for Accounting Period 7/07 Through 6/08		Total	Zero Assets	Under 500	500 to 1,000	1,000 to 5,000	5,000 to 10,000	10,000 to 25,000	25,000 to 50,000	50,000 to 100,000	100,000 to 250,000	250,000 to 500,000	500,000 to 2,500,000	2,500,000 and over
Number of Enterprises	1	49664	4825	25886	8046	8484	1173	705	246	115	77	38	•	•
Revenues ($ in Thousands)														
Net Sales	2	56613855	8198609	2993533	1668615	4415264	1518986	2437888	1736995	1721319	1759400	1726209	•	•
Interest	3	2422804	82640	33902	30361	120668	38948	53767	49187	67194	96090	80654	•	•
Rents	4	18488615	384542	26023	2639	25559	10716	65668	101410	233237	483989	764876	•	•
Royalties	5	14040	3	0	26	12314	422	0	375	641	259	0	•	•
Other Portfolio Income	6	10318459	3526610	178451	156336	444939	136876	209489	312716	159116	262626	388386	•	•
Other Receipts	7	25369937	4204814	2755157	1479253	3811784	1332024	2108964	1273307	1261131	916436	492293	•	•
Total Receipts	8	56613855	8198609	2993533	1668615	4415264	1518986	2437888	1736995	1721319	1759400	1726209	•	•
Average Total Receipts	9	1140	1699	116	207	520	1295	3458	7061	14968	22849	45427	•	•
Operating Costs/Operating Income (%)														
Cost of Operations	10	6.0	1.0	12.4	1.0	10.4	3.7	17.0	6.4	19.9	7.0	1.0	•	•
Salaries and Wages	11	3.9	0.6	13.2	3.3	11.4	8.3	8.2	5.1	7.3	4.7	3.2	•	•
Taxes Paid	12	6.1	9.0	7.2	10.3	9.1	9.7	5.8	8.2	7.1	6.2	6.0	•	•
Interest Paid	13	10.1	12.8	3.2	8.0	7.9	9.1	9.6	9.8	10.3	13.9	15.6	•	•
Depreciation	14	8.6	3.0	3.9	6.9	5.5	7.3	6.1	6.1	6.1	9.4	8.0	•	•
Amortization and Depletion	15	0.7	0.2	0.0	0.5	0.3	0.3	0.5	0.5	0.8	0.9	0.9	•	•
Pensions and Other Deferred Comp.	16	0.1	0.0	0.1	0.5	0.5	0.5	0.5	0.4	0.2	0.2	0.0	•	•
Employee Benefits	17	0.3	0.0	0.5	0.5	1.5	0.5	0.8	0.6	0.6	0.5	0.1	•	•
Advertising	18	0.3	0.0	0.2	1.1	0.2	0.6	0.3	0.3	0.2	0.4	0.3	•	•
Other Expenses	19	22.6	7.3	29.3	39.0	23.5	24.5	26.4	27.8	24.6	25.7	19.9	•	•
Officers' Compensation	20	1.7	0.2	3.7	5.5	8.0	5.0	3.3	2.1	1.0	1.6	0.8	•	•
Operating Margin	21	39.6	65.8	26.2	23.4	21.6	30.6	21.4	32.6	21.8	29.5	44.1	•	•
Operating Margin Before Officers' Comp.	22	41.3	66.0	29.9	28.9	29.6	35.6	24.7	34.7	22.8	31.2	45.0	•	•

Selected Average Balance Sheet ($ in Thousands)

Line Item												
Net Receivables 23	190	0		77	21	7	236	285	1012	3758	8346	5503
Inventories 24												
Net Property, Plant and Equipment 25	4042	0		119	446	1240	4176	8889	20657	38652	84310	164294
Total Assets 26	6534	0		195	699	2022	6661	15721	35247	69406	159254	374526
Notes and Loans Payable 27	2366	0		90	350	1113	2871	8659	16240	34414	68721	129899
All Other Liabilities 28	519	0		15	50	193	360	1474	3925	5042	10283	33535
Net Worth 29	3650	0		89	299	716	3430	5588	15082	29949	80250	211092

Selected Financial Ratios (Times to 1)

Line Item											
Current Ratio 30	1.1		4.0	4.1	2.6	3.0	1.7	2.0	2.6	2.2	1.7
Quick Ratio 31	0.8		3.4	3.7	2.0	2.2	1.2	1.5	2.1	1.9	0.9
Net Sales to Working Capital 32	36.9		3.2	1.8	2.1	1.7	3.0	2.5	2.0	2.0	3.5
Coverage Ratio 33	4.9	6.1	9.1	3.9	3.7	4.3	3.2	4.3	3.1	3.1	3.8
Total Asset Turnover 34	0.2		0.6	0.3	0.3	0.2	0.2	0.2	0.2	0.1	0.1
Inventory Turnover 35											
Receivables Turnover 36											
Total Liabilities to Net Worth 37	0.8		1.2	1.3	1.8	0.9	1.3	2.0	1.3	1.0	0.8
Current Assets to Working Capital 38	19.6		1.3	1.3	1.6	1.5	2.4	2.0	1.6	1.8	2.5
Current Liabilities to Working Capital 39	18.6		0.3	0.3	0.6	0.5	1.4	1.0	0.6	0.8	1.5
Working Capital to Net Sales 40	0.0		0.3	0.6	0.5	0.6	0.3	0.4	0.5	0.5	0.3
Inventory to Working Capital 41	0.1		0.0	0.0	0.0	0.0	0.0	0.0	0.0	0.0	0.0
Total Receipts to Cash Flow 42	2.7	3.3	2.4	2.8	3.2	3.0	2.4	2.5	2.9	2.6	2.7
Cost of Goods to Cash Flow 43	0.2	0.0	0.3	0.0	0.3	0.5	0.1	0.2	0.6	0.2	0.0
Cash Flow to Total Debt 44	0.1		0.5	0.2	0.1	0.1	0.2	0.1	0.1	0.1	0.1

Selected Financial Factors (in Percentages)

Line Item											
Debt Ratio 45	44.1		54.4	57.2	64.6	48.5	64.5	57.2	56.8	49.6	43.6
Return on Total Assets 46	8.7		17.5	9.3	7.5	7.6	6.7	8.4	6.9	6.2	7.2
Return on Equity Before Income Taxes 47	12.3		34.1	16.2	15.6	11.2	12.9	15.0	10.8	8.3	9.5
Return on Equity After Income Taxes 48	11.3		30.6	14.4	12.6	9.2	10.4	12.0	8.8	7.5	9.1
Profit Margin (Before Income Tax) 49	39.5	65.8	26.2	23.3	21.4	29.8	20.8	32.0	21.7	29.3	44.1
Profit Margin (After Income Tax) 50	36.1	53.4	23.5	20.8	17.4	24.3	16.8	25.6	17.5	26.4	42.4

Table I

Corporations with and without Net Income

LESSORS OF MINIWAREHOUSES, SELF-STORAGE, OTHER REAL ESTATE

MONEY AMOUNTS AND SIZE OF ASSETS IN THOUSANDS OF DOLLARS

Item Description for Accounting Period 7/07 Through 6/08	Total	Zero Assets	Under 500	500 to 1,000	1,000 to 5,000	5,000 to 10,000	10,000 to 25,000	25,000 to 50,000	50,000 to 100,000	100,000 to 250,000	250,000 to 500,000	500,000 to 2,500,000	2,500,000 and over
Number of Enterprises **1**	79715	13468	44660	8028	10267	1643	829	270	184	144	82	103	39
Revenues ($ in Thousands)													
Net Sales **2**	59014935	11480049	3759580	669514	2037247	1726610	1522914	1357969	2019882	2617351	3210732	10500607	18112479
Interest **3**	3027481	179692	21101	15940	107031	43319	97957	64558	119997	113238	200305	740154	1324190
Rents **4**	20514336	26773	42326	5701	12123	84556	306323	205612	514041	930594	1626569	5597548	11162169
Royalties **5**	103064	0	0	4041	34114	8436	32904	9989	13566	14	0	0	0
Other Portfolio Income **6**	18038087	10301941	119448	93281	275971	598933	397486	413324	571207	507816	625418	2087396	2045868
Other Receipts **7**	17331967	971643	3576705	550551	1608008	991366	688244	664486	801071	1065689	758440	2075509	3580252
Total Receipts **8**	59014935	11480049	3759580	669514	2037247	1726610	1522914	1357969	2019882	2617351	3210732	10500607	18112479
Average Total Receipts **9**	740	852	84	83	198	1051	1837	5030	10978	18176	39155	101948	464423
Operating Costs/Operating Income (%)													
Cost of Operations **10**	2.3	0.3	11.8	3.2	6.1	11.0	0.7	0.8	10.0	5.1	3.6	0.9	•
Salaries and Wages **11**	3.6	0.4	11.1	4.5	9.8	5.6	4.3	11.3	3.7	7.6	4.5	1.7	2.8
Taxes Paid **12**	4.4	2.5	4.9	10.4	8.2	5.2	6.1	4.3	3.7	4.2	4.0	4.5	4.6
Interest Paid **13**	12.1	1.6	2.2	14.1	16.5	10.7	17.0	10.8	10.1	17.9	13.7	13.9	18.1
Depreciation **14**	7.7	0.5	2.0	5.9	10.4	6.2	5.3	5.5	5.7	8.0	6.9	10.4	12.5
Amortization and Depletion **15**	0.7	0.0	0.1	0.4	0.4	0.4	0.8	0.6	0.6	1.0	1.6	1.0	1.0
Pensions and Other Deferred Comp. **16**	0.2	0.0	1.9	•	0.2	0.3	0.3	0.5	0.1	0.1	0.1	0.0	•
Employee Benefits **17**	0.3	0.2	1.5	0.4	0.4	0.5	0.5	0.7	1.0	0.5	0.2	0.0	•
Advertising **18**	0.4	0.1	1.5	0.8	0.9	0.3	0.3	0.8	0.2	0.7	0.2	0.3	0.3
Other Expenses **19**	26.0	6.0	47.4	37.2	47.7	30.9	38.8	38.1	33.1	37.7	98.1	27.6	12.9
Officers' Compensation **20**	1.6	0.6	7.1	4.0	4.5	3.7	2.9	7.0	2.7	1.0	0.9	0.5	0.7
Operating Margin **21**	40.8	87.9	8.4	19.1	•	25.2	22.9	19.6	29.1	16.1	•	39.3	47.0
Operating Margin Before Officers' Comp. **22**	42.4	88.5	15.5	23.1	•	28.9	25.8	26.6	31.8	17.1	•	39.8	47.8

Selected Average Balance Sheet ($ in Thousands)

Net Receivables 23	136043	18885	6639	3015	2056	663	1078	153	62	20	4	0	137
Inventories 24	•	•	•	•	•	•	•	•	•	•	•	•	•
Net Property, Plant and Equipment 25	3393162	468719	108328	47142	22220	11516	5381	2734	1133	401	81	0	2897
Total Assets 26	5387490	1067362	361317	151102	71317	35313	15523	6873	2173	703	152	0	5683
Notes and Loans Payable 27	2307111	272430	88479	49630	23884	11359	7399	3315	1234	350	75	0	2136
All Other Liabilities 28	340766	56382	33306	8661	10880	3746	2368	790	224	59	22	0	415
Net Worth 29	2739613	738550	239533	92811	36553	20208	5757	2768	715	294	55	0	3131

Selected Financial Ratios (Times to 1)

Current Ratio 30	1.9	1.9	1.3	1.8	1.4	2.2	2.3	2.7	1.7	2.9	1.2	•	1.8
Quick Ratio 31	1.6	1.4	0.7	1.1	0.8	1.3	1.3	1.4	1.2	2.0	0.8	•	1.3
Net Sales to Working Capital 32	2.9	2.5	5.6	2.6	4.3	1.5	0.8	1.2	1.1	1.0	18.0	•	3.0
Coverage Ratio 33	3.6	3.8	•	1.9	3.9	2.7	2.3	3.3	0.7	2.3	4.8	56.0	4.4
Total Asset Turnover 34	0.1	0.1	0.1	0.1	0.2	0.1	0.1	0.2	0.1	0.1	0.6	•	0.1
Inventory Turnover 35	•	•	•	•	•	•	•	•	•	•	•	•	•
Receivables Turnover 36	•	•	•	•	•	•	•	•	•	•	•	•	•
Total Liabilities to Net Worth 37	1.0	0.4	0.5	0.6	1.0	0.7	1.7	1.5	2.0	1.4	1.8	•	0.8
Current Assets to Working Capital 38	2.2	2.1	4.0	2.2	3.6	1.9	1.8	1.6	2.4	1.5	6.6	•	2.2
Current Liabilities to Working Capital 39	1.2	1.1	3.0	1.2	2.6	0.9	0.8	0.6	1.4	0.5	5.6	•	1.2
Working Capital to Net Sales 40	0.3	0.4	0.2	0.4	0.2	0.7	1.3	0.8	0.9	1.0	0.1	•	0.3
Inventory to Working Capital 41	0.0	0.0	0.0	0.0	0.0	0.0	0.0	•	0.0	•	•	•	0.0
Total Receipts to Cash Flow 42	2.2	2.2	3.0	3.0	3.1	3.9	3.1	5.4	4.7	3.4	2.2	21.4	3.3
Cost of Goods to Cash Flow 43	•	0.0	0.2	0.2	0.3	0.0	0.0	0.6	0.3	0.1	0.3	0.1	0.1
Cash Flow to Total Debt 44	0.1	0.1	•	0.1	0.1	0.1	0.1	0.0	0.0	0.1	0.4	•	0.1

Selected Financial Factors (in Percentages)

Debt Ratio 45	49.1	30.8	33.7	38.6	48.7	42.8	62.9	59.7	67.1	58.1	63.9	•	44.9
Return on Total Assets 46	5.6	5.1	•	4.1	6.0	4.2	4.7	5.4	1.0	3.9	5.8	•	6.9
Return on Equity Before Income Taxes 47	8.0	5.4	•	3.1	8.7	4.6	7.2	9.3	•	5.4	12.8	•	9.6
Return on Equity After Income Taxes 48	8.0	5.2	•	2.7	7.9	3.6	5.6	8.0	•	4.2	11.4	•	9.0
Profit Margin (Before Income Tax) 49	47.0	39.4	•	16.0	28.9	18.4	22.7	24.5	•	19.0	8.3	87.9	40.7
Profit Margin (After Income Tax) 50	47.0	37.5	•	13.7	26.2	14.3	17.5	21.0	•	14.9	7.4	81.3	38.2

Table II

Corporations with Net Income

LESSORS OF MINIWAREHOUSES, SELF-STORAGE, OTHER REAL ESTATE

MONEY AMOUNTS AND SIZE OF ASSETS IN THOUSANDS OF DOLLARS

Item Description for Accounting Period 7/07 Through 6/08	Total	Zero Assets	Under 500	500 to 1,000	1,000 to 5,000	5,000 to 10,000	10,000 to 25,000	25,000 to 50,000	50,000 to 100,000	100,000 to 250,000	250,000 to 500,000	500,000 to 2,500,000	2,500,000 and over
Number of Enterprises **1**	24772	4081	13060	3407	2823	598	361	•	101	74	49	75	•
Revenues ($ in Thousands)													
Net Sales **2**	52674475	11161606	3001522	609897	1379006	1260715	1237552		1794687	2062659	2513577	9231532	•
Interest **3**	2696907	152156	14290	14925	64473	32946	74729		100179	71385	171724	642223	•
Rents **4**	17911862	26250	42024	4816	9099	81149	165755		419864	590928	1080831	5046353	•
Royalties **5**	103007	0	0	3998	34114	8436	32904		13566	0	0	0	•
Other Portfolio Income **6**	17628097	10292597	116150	92835	236412	556169	377876		562054	468818	549269	1940972	•
Other Receipts **7**	14334602	690603	2829058	493323	1034908	582015	586288		699024	931528	711753	1601984	•
Total Receipts **8**	52674475	11161606	3001522	609897	1379006	1260715	1237552		1794687	2062659	2513577	9231532	•
Average Total Receipts **9**	2126	2735	230	179	488	2108	3428		17769	27874	51297	123087	•
Operating Costs/Operating Income (%)													
Cost of Operations **10**	1.6	0.0	10.3	3.5	5.8	0.5	0.9	•	11.0	5.7	4.6	0.1	•
Salaries and Wages **11**	2.8	0.1	7.4	4.5	5.0	2.5	2.9		2.7	7.9	4.3	1.4	•
Taxes Paid **12**	3.8	2.3	4.0	7.3	6.6	3.9	4.7		2.8	3.7	3.4	4.3	•
Interest Paid **13**	9.1	0.9	1.0	10.5	7.7	7.8	9.7		5.8	10.1	7.7	10.0	•
Depreciation **14**	6.8	0.1	1.7	4.1	8.4	4.0	3.2		3.8	6.5	4.5	9.1	•
Amortization and Depletion **15**	0.5	0.0	0.1	0.4	0.4	0.4	0.8		0.5	0.6	1.2	0.5	•
Pensions and Other Deferred Comp. **16**	0.2	0.0	2.3	•	0.1	0.4	0.3		0.1	0.1	0.2	0.0	•
Employee Benefits **17**	0.2	0.0	1.5	0.5	0.4	0.3	0.4		1.1	0.5	0.2	0.0	•
Advertising **18**	0.3	0.1	1.1	0.8	0.7	0.2	0.2		0.1	0.6	0.1	0.3	•
Other Expenses **19**	17.0	3.3	41.4	32.6	24.6	21.5	22.1		25.7	24.3	34.2	23.2	•
Officers' Compensation **20**	1.2	0.1	4.5	2.7	4.0	2.9	2.6		2.7	0.8	1.0	0.3	•
Operating Margin **21**	56.4	93.1	24.6	33.1	36.3	55.7	52.2		43.6	39.3	38.8	51.0	•
Operating Margin Before Officers' Comp. **22**	57.5	93.2	29.1	35.8	40.3	58.6	54.8		46.3	40.1	39.8	51.2	•

Selected Average Balance Sheet ($ in Thousands)

	1	2	3	4	5	6	7	8	9	10	11
Net Receivables 23	361	0	8	40	114	185	1158	2413	3467	2907	25051
Inventories 24	•	•	•	•	•	•	•	•	•	•	•
Net Property, Plant and Equipment 25	7134	0	79	327	998	3122	4894	19388	46950	95406	518318
Total Assets 26	13546	0	154	717	2173	7122	15788	71833	154486	362932	1090328
Notes and Loans Payable 27	4497	0	31	304	959	2462	5559	17848	37667	66161	228642
All Other Liabilities 28	928	0	20	90	207	780	2523	10906	8941	23782	69297
Net Worth 29	8121	0	103	323	1007	3880	7705	43079	107877	272989	792389

Selected Financial Ratios (Times to 1)

	1	2	3	4	5	6	7	8	9	10	11
Current Ratio 30	2.0	•	2.1	3.5	3.6	2.2	3.3	1.9	1.6	1.2	2.0
Quick Ratio 31	1.5	•	1.5	2.4	3.0	1.4	2.1	1.3	1.2	0.5	1.6
Net Sales to Working Capital 32	3.6	•	9.7	1.2	1.4	3.4	1.0	3.4	4.2	15.9	2.6
Coverage Ratio 33	7.2	106.2	25.2	4.1	5.7	8.1	6.4	8.5	4.9	6.0	6.1
Total Asset Turnover 34	0.2	•	1.5	0.2	0.2	0.3	0.2	0.2	0.2	0.1	0.1
Inventory Turnover 35	•	•	•	•	•	•	•	•	•	•	•
Receivables Turnover 36	•	•	•	•	•	•	•	•	•	•	•
Total Liabilities to Net Worth 37	0.7	•	0.5	1.2	1.2	0.8	1.0	0.7	0.4	0.3	0.4
Current Assets to Working Capital 38	2.0	•	1.9	1.4	1.4	1.8	1.4	2.1	2.7	7.1	2.0
Current Liabilities to Working Capital 39	1.0	•	0.9	0.4	0.4	0.8	0.4	1.1	1.7	6.1	1.0
Working Capital to Net Sales 40	0.3	•	0.1	0.8	0.7	0.3	1.1	0.3	0.2	0.1	0.4
Inventory to Working Capital 41	0.0	•	•	•	0.0	•	0.0	0.0	0.0	0.0	0.0
Total Receipts to Cash Flow 42	2.6	20.3	1.7	2.6	2.4	3.2	2.2	2.7	2.4	2.0	2.0
Cost of Goods to Cash Flow 43	0.0	0.0	0.2	0.1	0.1	0.0	0.0	0.3	0.1	0.1	0.0
Cash Flow to Total Debt 44	0.1	•	2.6	0.2	0.2	0.2	0.2	0.2	0.2	0.3	0.2

Selected Financial Factors (in Percentages)

	1	2	3	4	5	6	7	8	9	10	11
Debt Ratio 45	40.0	•	33.2	55.0	53.7	45.5	51.2	40.0	30.2	24.8	27.3
Return on Total Assets 46	10.3	•	38.1	10.9	9.9	18.7	13.4	12.2	8.9	6.6	6.9
Return on Equity Before Income Taxes 47	14.7	•	54.8	18.3	17.5	30.1	23.2	17.9	10.1	7.3	7.9
Return on Equity After Income Taxes 48	14.0	•	52.2	15.8	14.3	27.5	20.4	16.7	9.4	7.0	7.6
Profit Margin (Before Income Tax) 49	56.3	93.1	24.5	33.0	36.1	55.5	52.1	43.5	39.2	38.8	51.0
Profit Margin (After Income Tax) 50	53.6	86.3	23.4	28.5	29.4	50.6	45.8	40.4	36.4	37.2	48.9

Table I

Corporations with and without Net Income

OFFICES OF REAL ESTATE AGENTS AND BROKERS

MONEY AMOUNTS AND SIZE OF ASSETS IN THOUSANDS OF DOLLARS

Item Description for Accounting Period 7/07 Through 6/08	Total	Zero Assets	Under 500	500 to 1,000	1,000 to 5,000	5,000 to 10,000	10,000 to 25,000	25,000 to 50,000	50,000 to 100,000	100,000 to 250,000	250,000 to 500,000	500,000 to 2,500,000	2,500,000 and over
Number of Enterprises **1**	130320	32558	90555	4013	2756	226	139	31	16	15	3	6	3
Revenues ($ in Thousands)													
Net Sales **2**	65689805	2073680	28936307	6731981	4722260	752209	2426452	960265	1120455	2052192	1074830	3683396	11155778
Interest **3**	481050	3135	28162	4213	29121	16385	6263	2729	19127	66279	2123	113018	190495
Rents **4**	314759	4097	21302	13372	32073	32342	5711	5130	221	27979	0	42712	129822
Royalties **5**	1047962	0	0	0	5	35	453	1102	1496	177945	854	11275	854798
Other Portfolio Income **6**	1213267	2523	42554	10896	90908	32655	19657	18158	3918	47224	5361	133926	805486
Other Receipts **7**	62632767	2063925	2844289	6703500	4570153	670792	2394368	933146	1095693	1732765	1066492	3382465	9175177
Total Receipts **8**	65689805	2073680	28936307	6731981	4722260	752209	2426452	960265	1120455	2052192	1074830	3683396	11155778
Average Total Receipts **9**	504	64	320	1678	1713	3328	17456	30976	70028	136813	358277	613899	3718593
Operating Costs/Operating Income (%)													
Cost of Operations **10**	16.8	5.6	12.6	13.9	17.1	6.6	17.4	56.4	28.7	40.6	58.5	4.9	22.9
Salaries and Wages **11**	33.1	6.9	34.1	36.0	28.8	29.0	45.0	12.1	19.8	16.7	13.0	48.1	36.3
Taxes Paid **12**	2.0	2.0	1.8	1.8	1.5	4.0	1.9	2.3	2.3	2.2	1.4	2.8	2.5
Interest Paid **13**	2.2	1.6	0.3	0.9	1.9	7.5	2.0	1.8	2.2	5.6	2.6	4.3	6.6
Depreciation **14**	1.0	1.3	0.7	1.1	0.9	1.9	1.7	1.0	1.5	2.1	1.6	1.4	1.0
Amortization and Depletion **15**	0.6	0.1	0.1	0.4	0.1	0.1	0.2	0.5	0.8	3.0	2.3	1.1	2.0
Pensions and Other Deferred Comp. **16**	0.7	0.6	1.0	1.0	0.3	0.5	0.3	0.1	0.4	0.5	0.3	0.1	0.3
Employee Benefits **17**	1.0	0.5	0.7	0.8	0.7	0.6	0.9	0.9	1.2	1.4	0.8	1.6	2.2
Advertising **18**	3.7	4.4	4.2	4.9	5.2	2.2	4.5	3.3	3.3	4.1	4.2	0.6	1.9
Other Expenses **19**	25.6	50.9	26.6	21.0	32.5	37.4	24.2	15.8	34.8	30.4	15.2	28.8	16.7
Officers' Compensation **20**	7.2	13.3	10.7	13.0	3.2	3.1	3.0	2.0	4.4	0.8	1.2	2.3	0.4
Operating Margin **21**	6.0	13.0	7.2	5.2	7.8	7.1	•	3.9	0.7	•	•	4.1	7.1
Operating Margin Before Officers' Comp. **22**	13.2	26.2	17.9	18.2	11.0	10.2	1.9	6.0	5.1	0.2	•	6.4	7.6

Selected Average Balance Sheet ($ in Thousands)

Item													
Net Receivables 23	32	0	3	64	156	555	1166	1849	9089	12121	69783	252485	302726
Inventories 24	•	0	•	•	•	•	•	•	•	•	•	•	•
Net Property, Plant and Equipment 25	72	0	17	217	600	3241	4190	6494	12677	44606	18917	77440	788202
Total Assets 26	386	0	63	725	1918	7562	14320	34223	69679	145923	290876	1359610	6431856
Notes and Loans Payable 27	197	0	42	322	1294	5103	7750	15300	14936	85393	33650	438775	3370601
All Other Liabilities 28	103	0	12	166	321	1071	3072	5459	16547	33301	104437	373359	2194149
Net Worth 29	85	0	8	237	303	1389	3498	13464	38196	27229	152789	547476	867105

Selected Financial Ratios (Times to 1)

Item													
Current Ratio 30	1.3	•	1.7	2.1	1.7	1.9	1.5	2.2	1.4	1.1	1.4	2.1	0.8
Quick Ratio 31	0.8	•	1.4	1.1	0.8	1.1	0.6	0.6	0.9	0.5	1.0	1.5	0.4
Net Sales to Working Capital 32	15.0	•	27.8	11.6	5.2	3.4	10.2	3.3	9.0	20.7	7.7	2.4	•
Coverage Ratio 33	3.7	9.3	22.2	7.0	5.1	1.9	0.4	3.1	1.2	0.9	0.5	2.0	2.1
Total Asset Turnover 34	1.3	•	5.1	2.3	0.9	0.4	1.2	0.9	1.0	0.9	1.2	0.5	0.6
Inventory Turnover 35	•	•	•	•	•	•	•	•	•	•	•	•	•
Receivables Turnover 36	•	•	•	•	•	•	•	•	•	•	•	•	•
Total Liabilities to Net Worth 37	3.5	•	6.5	2.1	5.3	4.4	3.1	1.5	0.8	4.4	0.9	1.5	6.4
Current Assets to Working Capital 38	3.9	•	2.5	1.9	2.5	2.1	3.2	1.8	3.7	12.3	3.3	1.9	•
Current Liabilities to Working Capital 39	2.9	•	1.5	0.9	1.5	1.1	2.2	0.8	2.7	11.3	2.3	0.9	•
Working Capital to Net Sales 40	0.1	•	0.0	0.1	0.2	0.3	0.1	0.3	0.1	0.0	0.1	0.4	•
Inventory to Working Capital 41	0.1	•	•	•	0.0	0.0	0.0	•	0.4	•	•	0.2	•
Total Receipts to Cash Flow 42	3.9	1.7	3.5	4.4	3.0	2.8	6.0	8.1	3.3	6.2	11.2	3.7	7.2
Cost of Goods to Cash Flow 43	0.7	0.1	0.4	0.6	0.5	0.2	1.0	4.6	1.0	2.5	6.6	0.2	1.7
Cash Flow to Total Debt 44	0.4	•	1.7	0.8	0.4	0.2	0.3	0.2	0.7	0.2	0.2	0.2	0.1

Selected Financial Factors (in Percentages)

Item													
Debt Ratio 45	77.9	•	86.6	67.3	84.2	81.6	75.6	60.7	45.2	81.3	47.5	59.7	86.5
Return on Total Assets 46	10.7	•	38.3	14.0	8.6	6.4	1.1	5.2	2.7	•	1.6	3.8	8.1
Return on Equity Before Income Taxes 47	35.3	•	273.0	36.6	43.6	16.6	•	8.9	1.0	•	•	4.6	31.4
Return on Equity After Income Taxes 48	30.4	•	270.7	35.8	41.0	12.7	•	8.6	•	•	•	2.3	16.4
Profit Margin (Before Income Tax) 49	6.0	13.0	7.2	5.2	7.7	6.9	•	3.9	0.5	•	•	4.1	7.3
Profit Margin (After Income Tax) 50	5.2	12.8	7.1	5.1	7.3	5.3	3.7	3.7	•	•	•	2.0	3.8

Table II

Corporations with Net Income

OFFICES OF REAL ESTATE AGENTS AND BROKERS

MONEY AMOUNTS AND SIZE OF ASSETS IN THOUSANDS OF DOLLARS

Item Description for Accounting Period 7/07 Through 6/08	Total	Zero Assets	Under 500	500 to 1,000	1,000 to 5,000	5,000 to 10,000	10,000 to 25,000	25,000 to 50,000	50,000 to 100,000	100,000 to 250,000	250,000 to 500,000	500,000 to 2,500,000	2,500,000 and over
Number of Enterprises 1	77425	19364	54165	2537	1160	115	41	•	8	10	0	•	0
Revenues ($ in Thousands)													
Net Sales 2	41509662	1732806	19483063	5858188	2948519	548175	412855	•	738670	1260856	0	•	0
Interest 3	256681	2392	21291	3604	20540	14825	680	•	8823	16674	0	•	0
Rents 4	239560	1978	19549	120	13941	30509	553	•	162	27219	0	•	0
Royalties 5	316257	0	0	0	5	0	0	•	0	0	0	•	0
Other Portfolio Income 6	1090667	2523	36179	1956	81273	30647	19400	•	1872	13201	0	•	0
Other Receipts 7	39606497	1725913	19406044	5852508	2832760	472194	392222	•	727813	1203762	0	•	0
Total Receipts 8	41509662	1732806	19483063	5858188	2948519	548175	412855	•	738670	1260856	0	•	0
Average Total Receipts 9	536	89	360	2309	2542	4767	10070	•	92334	126086	•	•	•
Operating Costs/Operating Income (%)													
Cost of Operations 10	9.7	4.2	7.9	9.8	8.0	8.0	18.8	•	41.3	51.9	•	•	•
Salaries and Wages 11	34.9	4.2	32.9	39.3	39.5	13.8	28.7	•	17.9	13.9	•	•	•
Taxes Paid 12	2.0	1.8	1.8	1.7	1.4	4.3	2.4	•	1.9	2.0	•	•	•
Interest Paid 13	1.2	0.8	0.3	0.5	1.3	5.9	3.7	•	1.7	2.6	•	•	•
Depreciation 14	0.8	1.0	0.6	0.9	0.8	1.7	0.6	•	1.3	2.2	•	•	•
Amortization and Depletion 15	0.3	0.1	0.1	0.3	0.1	0.1	0.1	•	0.1	1.0	•	•	•
Pensions and Other Deferred Comp. 16	0.8	0.7	1.1	1.1	0.4	0.6	0.3	•	0.5	0.3	•	•	•
Employee Benefits 17	0.9	0.3	0.5	0.8	0.7	0.6	0.5	•	0.9	1.0	•	•	•
Advertising 18	3.6	3.4	4.0	4.7	7.3	2.2	2.3	•	3.6	2.3	•	•	•
Other Expenses 19	21.9	40.3	23.4	18.3	18.8	41.2	22.7	•	18.8	16.7	•	•	•
Officers' Compensation 20	8.8	12.6	11.9	14.0	3.6	3.5	2.4	•	4.7	2.1	•	•	•
Operating Margin 21	15.2	30.7	15.5	8.7	18.1	18.2	17.4	•	7.3	4.1	•	•	•
Operating Margin Before Officers' Comp. 22	24.0	43.3	27.5	22.6	21.7	21.6	19.8	•	12.0	6.2	•	•	•

Selected Average Balance Sheet ($ in Thousands)

Net Receivables 23	35	0	2	40	132	1024	1814	•	7846	20386
Inventories 24	•	•	•	•	•	•	•	•	•	•
Net Property, Plant and Equipment 25	65	0	16	181	518	1914	4009	•	10191	38475
Total Assets 26	297	0	60	716	1961	7737	13286	•	62340	170792
Notes and Loans Payable 27	111	0	22	217	757	3216	7692	•	17623	33667
All Other Liabilities 28	81	0	8	157	322	1774	3191	•	15796	54475
Net Worth 29	105	0	30	342	881	2746	2402	•	28920	82650

Selected Financial Ratios (Times to 1)

Current Ratio 30	1.6	•	2.6	2.1	2.3	2.7	1.4	•	1.5	1.4
Quick Ratio 31	1.2	•	2.4	1.1	1.8	2.0	0.5	•	1.1	0.9
Net Sales to Working Capital 32	11.5	•	19.5	15.5	6.3	2.6	5.6	•	9.2	4.5
Coverage Ratio 33	14.1	37.4	52.8	18.8	14.5	4.0	5.7	•	5.1	2.5
Total Asset Turnover 34	1.8	•	6.0	3.2	1.3	0.6	0.8	•	1.5	0.7
Inventory Turnover 35	•	•	•	•	•	•	•	•	•	•
Receivables Turnover 36	•	•	•	•	•	•	•	•	•	•
Total Liabilities to Net Worth 37	1.8	•	1.0	1.1	1.2	1.8	4.5	•	1.2	1.1
Current Assets to Working Capital 38	2.6	•	1.6	1.9	1.8	1.6	3.8	•	3.1	3.2
Current Liabilities to Working Capital 39	1.6	•	0.6	0.9	0.8	0.6	2.8	•	2.1	2.2
Working Capital to Net Sales 40	0.1	•	0.1	0.1	0.2	0.4	0.2	•	0.1	0.2
Inventory to Working Capital 41	0.0	•	•	•	•	•	•	•	0.0	•
Total Receipts to Cash Flow 42	3.2	1.5	2.9	4.2	3.2	2.0	2.9	•	4.9	6.7
Cost of Goods to Cash Flow 43	0.3	0.1	0.2	0.4	0.3	0.2	0.5	•	2.0	3.5
Cash Flow to Total Debt 44	0.9	•	4.2	1.5	0.7	0.5	0.3	•	0.6	0.2

Selected Financial Factors (in Percentages)

Debt Ratio 45	64.7	•	50.0	52.3	55.0	64.5	81.9	•	53.6	51.6
Return on Total Assets 46	29.7	•	94.9	29.5	25.1	14.7	16.0	•	13.0	4.8
Return on Equity Before Income Taxes 47	78.2	•	186.1	58.5	51.9	31.1	72.9	•	22.6	6.0
Return on Equity After Income Taxes 48	71.6	•	185.0	57.7	49.9	27.2	71.1	•	19.8	5.1
Profit Margin (Before Income Tax) 49	15.3	30.7	15.5	8.7	18.0	17.9	17.4	•	7.1	3.9
Profit Margin (After Income Tax) 50	14.0	30.5	15.4	8.5	17.3	15.7	17.0	•	6.2	3.3

Table I

Corporations with and without Net Income

OTHER REAL ESTATE ACTIVITIES

MONEY AMOUNTS AND SIZE OF ASSETS IN THOUSANDS OF DOLLARS

Item Description for Accounting Period 7/07 Through 6/08		Total	Zero Assets	Under 500	500 to 1,000	1,000 to 5,000	5,000 to 10,000	10,000 to 25,000	25,000 to 50,000	50,000 to 100,000	100,000 to 250,000	250,000 to 500,000	500,000 to 2,500,000	2,500,000 and over
Number of Enterprises	1	177911	39854	112797	8920	12866	1529	1243	361	194	92	31	18	4
Revenues ($ in Thousands)														
Net Sales	2	65775061	4244281	21955418	2225689	12087600	3166540	4228055	2218630	2541747	2370456	4470582	2486318	3779746
Interest	3	1628022	44696	56966	44668	105278	62579	94278	68860	104899	155596	99056	87204	703944
Rents	4	2081796	125674	343988	171975	139953	69429	205096	176988	173284	155951	149327	138510	231622
Royalties	5	267668	0	884	0	250	6858	16005	10	0	3241	2411	0	238009
Other Portfolio Income	6	4334293	757490	262226	96861	401175	155275	316257	168392	296702	188300	143211	609107	939298
Other Receipts	7	57463282	3316421	21291354	1912185	11440944	2872399	3596419	1804380	1966862	1867368	4076577	1651497	1666873
Total Receipts	8	65775061	4244281	21955418	2225689	12087600	3166540	4228055	2218630	2541747	2370456	4470582	2486318	3779746
Average Total Receipts	9	370	106	195	250	939	2071	3401	6146	13102	25766	144212	138129	944936
Operating Costs/Operating Income (%)														
Cost of Operations	10	13.6	9.2	14.3	14.1	16.1	16.0	27.5	30.2	14.8	7.6	3.3	2.3	1.3
Salaries and Wages	11	23.2	14.2	19.4	22.2	37.8	23.6	20.1	14.0	12.8	21.8	29.6	12.9	25.2
Taxes Paid	12	3.5	4.6	2.8	4.2	4.3	4.3	4.4	4.2	4.1	4.8	2.5	2.9	2.7
Interest Paid	13	5.3	4.3	1.0	4.4	4.3	5.4	8.8	15.8	10.3	10.8	6.3	9.4	14.0
Depreciation	14	2.0	1.4	0.9	1.9	1.5	3.9	2.9	3.2	3.4	4.1	3.2	2.9	3.6
Amortization and Depletion	15	0.4	0.5	0.1	0.0	0.2	0.2	0.4	0.7	0.5	1.0	0.5	0.6	1.5
Pensions and Other Deferred Comp.	16	0.6	0.4	0.8	2.2	0.5	0.2	0.5	0.3	0.3	0.2	0.2	1.0	0.2
Employee Benefits	17	2.1	0.6	1.7	2.7	2.9	1.7	1.1	1.1	1.3	0.9	5.2	0.5	3.5
Advertising	18	1.4	1.3	1.3	0.4	0.6	1.0	0.4	1.4	1.8	1.0	5.1	0.4	2.7
Other Expenses	19	34.6	32.7	36.6	37.1	25.6	38.0	27.9	27.9	43.7	30.6	41.1	46.1	43.3
Officers' Compensation	20	7.8	9.9	14.0	9.7	5.2	5.1	5.8	3.0	2.1	1.5	2.3	2.7	1.4
Operating Margin	21	5.5	20.9	7.2	1.1	1.1	0.6	0.3	•	4.9	15.7	0.9	18.2	0.7
Operating Margin Before Officers' Comp.	22	13.3	30.8	21.2	10.8	6.3	5.6	6.1	1.1	7.0	17.2	3.2	20.9	2.1

Selected Average Balance Sheet ($ in Thousands)

Net Receivables 23	85	0	4	34	148	598	939	2394	3959	8046	25485	68536	1476108
Inventories 24	•	•	•	•	•	•	•	•	•	•	•	•	•
Net Property, Plant and Equipment 25	245	0	18	260	692	2008	4419	10990	23258	42686	111408	174980	666705
Total Assets 26	926	0	77	722	2072	7031	15094	34627	70037	150883	344534	810847	7060322
Notes and Loans Payable 27	488	0	58	495	1214	3982	8550	20945	32702	76496	172863	442101	2321038
All Other Liabilities 28	187	0	20	86	323	910	2409	6633	15491	21193	76537	222832	1993627
Net Worth 29	252	0	-0	141	535	2140	4135	7050	21843	53194	95135	145915	2745657

Selected Financial Ratios (Times to 1)

Current Ratio 30	1.9	•	2.0	2.3	2.4	2.6	1.7	1.5	1.3	1.8	1.4	1.2	2.6
Quick Ratio 31	1.0	•	1.4	1.3	1.3	1.6	0.8	0.7	0.7	1.0	0.9	0.5	1.6
Net Sales to Working Capital 32	2.4	•	10.0	1.6	1.9	1.5	1.7	1.5	2.6	1.3	6.0	2.5	0.6
Coverage Ratio 33	2.0	5.8	7.9	1.3	1.2	0.6	1.0	0.9	1.4	2.4	1.1	2.9	1.1
Total Asset Turnover 34	0.4	•	2.5	0.3	0.5	0.3	0.2	0.2	0.2	0.2	0.4	0.2	0.1
Inventory Turnover 35	•	•	•	•	•	•	•	•	•	•	•	•	•
Receivables Turnover 36	•	•	•	•	•	•	•	•	•	•	•	•	•
Total Liabilities to Net Worth 37	2.7	•	4.1	2.9	2.3	2.7	3.9	2.2	1.8	2.6	3.0	4.6	1.6
Current Assets to Working Capital 38	2.2	•	2.0	1.8	1.6	2.4	3.0	4.0	2.2	2.2	3.4	5.9	1.6
Current Liabilities to Working Capital 39	1.2	•	1.0	0.7	0.6	1.4	2.0	3.0	1.2	1.2	2.4	4.9	0.6
Working Capital to Net Sales 40	0.4	•	0.1	0.6	0.6	0.6	0.7	0.4	0.4	0.8	0.2	0.4	1.7
Inventory to Working Capital 41	0.0	•	•	0.0	•	0.0	0.0	0.0	0.0	0.1	0.1	0.2	•
Total Receipts to Cash Flow 42	3.3	3.1	2.8	3.9	5.1	3.4	5.4	6.6	3.3	2.8	2.7	2.1	2.5
Cost of Goods to Cash Flow 43	0.4	0.3	0.4	0.6	0.8	0.5	1.5	2.0	0.5	0.2	0.1	0.0	0.0
Cash Flow to Total Debt 44	0.2	•	0.9	0.1	0.1	0.1	0.1	0.0	0.1	0.1	0.2	0.0	0.1

Selected Financial Factors (in Percentages)

Debt Ratio 45	72.8	•	100.3	80.4	74.2	69.6	72.6	79.6	68.8	64.7	72.4	82.0	61.1
Return on Total Assets 46	4.2	•	20.6	1.9	2.4	0.9	2.0	2.4	2.8	4.5	3.0	4.7	2.0
Return on Equity Before Income Taxes 47	7.8	•	•	2.0	1.9	•	0.1	•	2.7	7.4	1.2	17.1	0.4
Return on Equity After Income Taxes 48	5.2	•	•	0.7	0.8	•	•	•	0.3	4.8	4.8	8.8	•
Profit Margin (Before Income Tax) 49	5.3	20.8	7.2	1.1	1.1	0.1	•	•	4.5	15.4	0.8	18.1	1.0
Profit Margin (After Income Tax) 50	3.5	15.4	6.8	0.5	0.4	•	•	•	0.5	9.8	•	9.3	•

Table II

Corporations with Net Income

OTHER REAL ESTATE ACTIVITIES

MONEY AMOUNTS AND SIZE OF ASSETS IN THOUSANDS OF DOLLARS

Item Description for Accounting Period 7/07 Through 6/08		Total	Zero Assets	Under 500	500 to 1,000	1,000 to 5,000	5,000 to 10,000	10,000 to 25,000	25,000 to 50,000	50,000 to 100,000	100,000 to 250,000	250,000 to 500,000	500,000 to 2,500,000	2,500,000 and over
Number of Enterprises	1	82859	19326	54886	3050	4350	545	404	144	83	45	14	13	0
Revenues ($ in Thousands)														
Net Sales	2	45773058	3399897	16257980	1526080	8928742	1689513	2720580	1227392	1496783	1846696	3648196	3031200	0
Interest	3	736192	35624	39316	38610	81176	24215	59399	48800	46728	103378	58940	200004	0
Rents	4	1240831	81257	284195	67773	51481	67524	123140	115659	103808	62624	40946	242423	0
Royalties	5	26003	0	469	0	250	6858	16005	10	0	0	2411	0	0
Other Portfolio Income	6	2981285	751884	233121	95647	383097	55492	240357	148458	273418	157884	100504	541422	0
Other Receipts	7	40788747	2531132	15700879	1324050	8412738	1535424	2281679	914465	1072829	1522810	3445395	2047351	0
Total Receipts	8	45773058	3399897	16257980	1526080	8928742	1689513	2720580	1227392	1496783	1846696	3648196	3031200	0
Average Total Receipts	9	552	176	296	500	2053	3100	6734	8524	18034	41038	260585	233169	•
Operating Costs/Operating Income (%)														
Cost of Operations	10	9.5	2.3	8.3	5.3	12.8	26.0	29.6	4.1	10.8	9.6	0.7	1.5	•
Salaries and Wages	11	21.6	13.7	19.1	15.0	38.3	16.7	14.2	14.4	9.5	18.3	25.7	13.1	•
Taxes Paid	12	3.1	4.1	2.6	2.6	3.5	3.2	3.0	4.6	4.3	4.0	2.3	3.2	•
Interest Paid	13	2.9	2.7	0.5	2.5	2.7	3.8	4.4	10.2	7.3	6.0	2.2	9.6	•
Depreciation	14	1.3	1.1	0.8	0.8	0.7	2.5	1.3	4.0	2.5	1.8	1.6	2.4	•
Amortization and Depletion	15	0.2	0.4	0.0	0.0	0.1	0.3	0.2	0.4	0.4	0.7	0.3	0.3	•
Pensions and Other Deferred Comp.	16	0.6	0.5	0.9	1.3	0.5	0.3	0.5	0.2	0.1	0.2	0.1	0.9	•
Employee Benefits	17	2.0	0.3	1.3	2.8	3.4	1.6	0.7	1.5	1.0	0.9	6.0	1.5	•
Advertising	18	1.2	0.8	1.5	0.1	0.3	0.6	0.2	0.8	0.7	0.3	5.6	0.5	•
Other Expenses	19	28.9	23.3	34.0	26.3	18.0	20.2	17.9	27.7	33.5	24.7	43.2	40.4	•
Officers' Compensation	20	8.1	9.9	14.6	11.3	4.2	5.6	4.2	4.2	1.9	1.5	2.7	2.0	•
Operating Margin	21	20.4	40.9	16.4	32.0	15.5	19.2	23.7	28.0	28.0	31.9	9.6	24.7	•
Operating Margin Before Officers' Comp.	22	28.6	50.8	31.0	43.3	19.7	24.7	27.9	32.2	29.9	33.3	12.3	26.7	•

Selected Average Balance Sheet ($ in Thousands)

Net Receivables 23	69	0	5	56	201	1154	1194	2314	3905	10979	36644	128237
Inventories 24	•	0	0	•	•	•	•	•	•	•	•	•
Net Property, Plant and Equipment 25	178	0	15	187	495	1231	3238	8774	23548	34881	69041	264936
Total Assets 26	828	0	90	743	2153	6942	14931	34137	71358	150650	344639	1522639
Notes and Loans Payable 27	359	0	28	277	1095	3954	6776	15510	30729	59608	154409	617843
All Other Liabilities 28	200	0	20	104	484	815	2661	4339	17002	24748	122989	510743
Net Worth 29	270	0	42	362	575	2173	5494	14287	23627	66294	67241	394053

Selected Financial Ratios (Times to 1)

Current Ratio 30	1.7	•	2.5	3.3	3.3	2.0	2.0	2.2	1.3	1.9	1.2	1.1
Quick Ratio 31	1.0	•	1.8	2.0	2.2	1.4	1.0	1.3	0.8	1.2	0.7	0.4
Net Sales to Working Capital 32	4.0	•	9.4	1.7	2.8	1.9	2.3	1.1	3.4	1.7	13.9	6.5
Coverage Ratio 33	7.9	15.9	34.4	13.8	6.9	6.0	6.4	3.7	4.8	6.3	5.3	3.6
Total Asset Turnover 34	0.7	3.3	3.3	0.7	1.0	0.4	0.5	0.2	0.3	0.3	0.8	0.2
Inventory Turnover 35	•	•	•	•	•	•	•	•	•	•	•	•
Receivables Turnover 36	•	•	•	•	•	•	•	•	•	•	•	•
Total Liabilities to Net Worth 37	2.1	•	1.2	1.1	2.7	2.2	1.7	1.4	2.0	1.3	4.1	2.9
Current Assets to Working Capital 38	2.4	•	1.7	1.4	1.4	2.0	2.0	1.8	4.1	2.1	6.1	13.9
Current Liabilities to Working Capital 39	1.4	•	0.7	0.4	0.4	1.0	1.0	0.8	3.1	1.1	5.1	12.9
Working Capital to Net Sales 40	0.2	•	0.1	0.6	0.4	0.5	0.4	0.9	0.3	0.6	0.1	0.2
Inventory to Working Capital 41	0.0	•	0.1	•	0.0	0.0	0.0	0.0	0.0	0.1	0.4	0.3
Total Receipts to Cash Flow 42	2.5	2.5	2.3	2.1	3.5	2.9	3.2	2.4	2.6	2.2	2.1	1.9
Cost of Goods to Cash Flow 43	0.2	0.1	0.2	0.1	0.5	0.7	1.0	0.1	0.3	0.2	0.0	0.0
Cash Flow to Total Debt 44	0.4	•	2.6	0.6	0.4	0.2	0.2	0.2	0.1	0.2	0.0	0.1

Selected Financial Factors (in Percentages)

Debt Ratio 45	67.4	•	53.6	51.3	73.3	68.7	63.2	58.1	66.9	56.0	80.5	74.1
Return on Total Assets 46	15.6	•	55.7	23.3	17.3	10.2	12.6	9.4	8.8	10.2	8.9	5.2
Return on Equity Before Income Taxes 47	41.7	•	116.4	44.3	55.4	27.2	28.9	16.5	21.1	19.6	37.1	14.6
Return on Equity After Income Taxes 48	36.9	•	113.4	42.9	52.6	25.1	24.9	14.1	16.0	15.2	29.3	10.3
Profit Margin (Before Income Tax) 49	20.4	40.9	16.4	32.0	15.5	19.1	23.6	27.7	27.7	31.6	9.6	24.6
Profit Margin (After Income Tax) 50	18.0	34.1	16.0	31.0	14.7	17.6	20.4	23.7	20.9	24.5	7.6	17.4

Table I

Corporations with and without Net Income

AUTOMOTIVE EQUIPMENT RENTAL AND LEASING

MONEY AMOUNTS AND SIZE OF ASSETS IN THOUSANDS OF DOLLARS

Item Description for Accounting Period 7/07 Through 6/08	Total	Zero Assets	Under 500	500 to 1,000	1,000 to 5,000	5,000 to 10,000	10,000 to 25,000	25,000 to 50,000	50,000 to 100,000	100,000 to 250,000	250,000 to 500,000	500,000 to 2,500,000	2,500,000 and over
Number of Enterprises **1**	7528	943	4402	917	802	148	193	66	26	18	0	5	8
Revenues ($ in Thousands)													
Net Sales **2**	53820241	36188	1897736	464529	1106320	615810	2059817	2064959	1230569	1788873	0	2317955	40237484
Interest **3**	1134964	0	845	2	3807	524	3753	3494	-300	8342	0	42594	1071902
Rents **4**	133779	0	0	0	49	11	2362	11880	11813	75	0	352	107238
Royalties **5**	163300	0	0	0	0	0	0	0	0	0	0	0	163300
Other Portfolio Income **6**	2061981	18475	38622	4812	131387	71604	115451	52428	56306	154469	0	46611	1371811
Other Receipts **7**	50326217	17713	1858269	459715	971077	543671	1938251	1997157	1162750	1625987	0	2228398	37523233
Total Receipts **8**	53820241	36188	1897736	464529	1106320	615810	2059817	2064959	1230569	1788873	0	2317955	40237484
Average Total Receipts **9**	7149	38	431	507	1379	4161	10673	31287	47330	99382	•	463591	5029686
Operating Costs/Operating Income (%)													
Cost of Operations **10**	17.7	3.6	8.1	9.8	16.7	16.9	34.2	49.5	48.2	24.0	•	1.5	15.6
Salaries and Wages **11**	12.6	8.9	3.1	22.6	7.0	7.6	7.3	7.2	7.1	6.1	•	4.2	14.6
Taxes Paid **12**	2.8	8.6	2.5	3.0	2.1	4.2	2.0	2.2	2.0	2.2	•	0.3	3.1
Interest Paid **13**	7.5	1.3	1.7	6.0	6.6	6.7	6.2	5.2	6.7	6.6	•	9.6	7.9
Depreciation **14**	27.1	4.6	8.7	12.7	34.1	23.7	29.5	19.5	23.6	34.0	•	68.9	25.7
Amortization and Depletion **15**	0.2	•	•	0.1	0.1	0.1	0.0	0.1	0.2	0.1	•	0.2	0.3
Pensions and Other Deferred Comp. **16**	0.3	0.0	0.1	•	0.3	0.0	0.2	0.2	0.3	0.1	•	0.1	0.3
Employee Benefits **17**	1.4	0.0	0.2	0.1	0.3	0.1	0.7	0.4	0.7	1.1	•	0.4	1.7
Advertising **18**	1.4	0.9	0.2	5.6	1.0	0.7	0.7	1.3	0.4	0.3	•	0.1	1.6
Other Expenses **19**	25.7	29.2	74.1	34.3	19.5	27.0	14.8	15.3	11.1	22.4	•	5.7	26.3
Officers' Compensation **20**	0.8	1.5	3.0	4.6	2.5	2.9	2.8	1.1	1.0	1.3	•	0.4	0.5
Operating Margin **21**	2.5	41.2	•	1.1	9.8	10.2	1.6	•	•	1.7	•	8.5	2.4
Operating Margin Before Officers' Comp. **22**	3.3	42.8	1.3	5.7	12.3	13.1	4.4	•	•	3.0	•	9.0	2.9

Selected Average Balance Sheet ($ in Thousands)

Net Receivables **23**	1280	0	16	43	137	1630	1408	4313	5256	9704	150092	944095
Inventories **24**	•	•	•	•	•	•	•	•	•	•	•	•
Net Property, Plant and Equipment **25**	6398	0	71	471	1393	4756	10088	18602	43836	114143	625130	4513063
Total Assets **26**	10837	0	140	738	2035	7445	15799	35873	64670	157461	1175688	7717288
Notes and Loans Payable **27**	5839	0	131	377	1535	4327	10607	27674	47845	104599	933966	3687094
All Other Liabilities **28**	2731	0	2	83	85	1053	1571	4111	5473	23661	118220	2314278
Net Worth **29**	2266	0	8	278	414	2064	3621	4088	11352	29201	123503	1715915

Selected Financial Ratios (Times to 1)

Current Ratio **30**	0.6	•	1.0	1.1	1.5	2.2	0.9	0.9	0.9	0.4	0.3	0.7
Quick Ratio **31**	0.5	•	0.8	0.8	0.9	1.9	0.6	0.5	0.6	0.6	0.2	0.5
Net Sales to Working Capital **32**	•	32.8	724.9	37.0	9.7	3.1	•	•	•	•	•	•
Coverage Ratio **33**	1.3	•	0.0	1.2	2.5	1.5	1.3	0.6	0.8	1.3	1.9	1.3
Total Asset Turnover **34**	0.7	•	3.1	0.7	0.7	0.6	0.7	0.9	0.7	0.6	0.4	0.7
Inventory Turnover **35**	•	•	•	•	•	•	•	•	•	•	•	•
Receivables Turnover **36**	•	•	•	•	•	•	•	•	•	•	•	•
Total Liabilities to Net Worth **37**	3.8	•	17.5	1.7	3.9	2.6	3.4	7.8	4.7	4.4	8.5	3.5
Current Assets to Working Capital **38**	•	•	53.3	15.9	3.0	1.8	•	•	•	•	•	•
Current Liabilities to Working Capital **39**	•	•	52.3	14.9	2.0	0.8	•	•	•	•	•	•
Working Capital to Net Sales **40**	•	•	0.0	0.0	0.1	0.3	•	•	•	•	•	•
Inventory to Working Capital **41**	•	•	•	•	0.2	0.1	•	•	•	•	•	•
Total Receipts to Cash Flow **42**	5.1	1.7	1.7	4.1	7.4	5.7	8.8	19.8	19.4	6.1	8.8	5.0
Cost of Goods to Cash Flow **43**	0.9	0.1	0.1	0.4	1.2	1.0	3.0	9.8	9.4	1.5	0.1	0.8
Cash Flow to Total Debt **44**	0.2	•	1.9	0.3	0.1	0.1	0.1	0.0	0.0	0.1	0.0	0.2

Selected Financial Factors (in Percentages)

Debt Ratio **45**	79.1	•	94.6	62.4	79.6	72.3	77.1	88.6	82.4	81.5	89.5	77.8
Return on Total Assets **46**	6.5	•	0.1	4.8	11.1	5.5	5.2	2.8	4.0	5.3	7.2	6.8
Return on Equity Before Income Taxes **47**	7.7	•	•	2.0	32.6	6.3	4.7	•	•	5.9	32.1	7.2
Return on Equity After Income Taxes **48**	4.8	•	•	1.5	29.4	5.5	4.4	•	•	3.1	28.9	4.0
Profit Margin (Before Income Tax) **49**	2.4	41.2	•	1.1	9.8	3.1	1.6	•	•	1.7	8.5	2.5
Profit Margin (After Income Tax) **50**	1.5	41.2	•	0.8	8.8	2.7	1.5	•	•	0.9	7.7	1.4

AUTOMOTIVE EQUIPMENT RENTAL AND LEASING

Table II

Corporations with Net Income

MONEY AMOUNTS AND SIZE OF ASSETS IN THOUSANDS OF DOLLARS

Item Description for Accounting Period 7/07 Through 6/08	Total	Zero Assets	Under 500	500 to 1,000	1,000 to 5,000	5,000 to 10,000	10,000 to 25,000	25,000 to 50,000	50,000 to 100,000	100,000 to 250,000	250,000 to 500,000	500,000 to 2,500,000	2,500,000 and over
Number of Enterprises 1	2908	•	1573	442	632	•	111	37	12	12	0	0	5
Revenues ($ in Thousands)													
Net Sales 2	36811277	•	115610	111954	997439	•	1249296	952774	575365	1209904	0	0	2317955
Interest 3	1074138	•	368	2	3547	•	3304	3286	-1226	7566	0	0	42594
Rents 4	120578	•	0	0	49	•	2072	11880	1556	15	0	0	352
Royalties 5	57883	•	0	0	0	•	0	0	0	0	0	0	0
Other Portfolio Income 6	1715765	•	25213	4812	120543	•	73938	29335	35075	99587	0	0	46611
Other Receipts 7	33842913	•	90029	107140	873300	•	1169982	908273	539960	1102736	0	0	2228398
Total Receipts 8	36811277	•	115610	111954	997439	•	1249296	952774	575365	1209904	0	0	2317955
Average Total Receipts 9	12659	•	73	253	1578	•	11255	25751	47947	100825	•	•	463591
Operating Costs/Operating Income (%)													
Cost of Operations 10	19.3	•	0.5	0.3	16.9	•	31.6	49.0	48.8	19.0	•	•	1.5
Salaries and Wages 11	12.0	•	•	19.4	7.3	•	6.6	4.6	6.6	5.8	•	•	4.2
Taxes Paid 12	2.6	•	2.0	2.8	2.1	•	2.4	1.5	1.3	2.4	•	•	0.3
Interest Paid 13	7.1	•	3.7	8.2	6.0	•	6.4	6.0	6.1	6.2	•	•	9.6
Depreciation 14	26.7	•	52.6	16.6	30.7	•	30.3	17.7	23.8	32.0	•	•	68.9
Amortization and Depletion 15	0.1	•	•	0.3	0.0	•	0.0	0.1	0.2	0.1	•	•	0.2
Pensions and Other Deferred Comp. 16	0.3	•	•	•	0.3	•	0.2	0.4	0.0	0.1	•	•	0.1
Employee Benefits 17	1.5	•	•	0.5	0.2	•	0.7	0.6	0.6	1.0	•	•	0.4
Advertising 18	0.7	•	•	2.2	1.1	•	0.9	0.5	0.3	0.2	•	•	0.1
Other Expenses 19	23.6	•	17.0	15.0	20.7	•	13.2	12.5	8.8	26.1	•	•	5.7
Officers' Compensation 20	0.8	•	10.9	12.0	2.2	•	2.6	1.4	0.9	1.5	•	•	0.4
Operating Margin 21	5.4	•	13.3	22.8	12.4	•	5.2	5.7	2.5	5.5	•	•	8.5
Operating Margin Before Officers' Comp. 22	6.2	•	24.2	34.8	14.6	•	7.7	7.1	3.4	7.0	•	•	9.0

Selected Average Balance Sheet ($ in Thousands)

Item										
Net Receivables 23	2264	•	3	42	81	1820	6097	7425	8955	150092
Inventories 24	•	•	•	•	•	•	•	•	•	•
Net Property, Plant and Equipment 25	12093	•	55	474	1347	10524	14665	43158	11195	625130
Total Assets 26	18743	•	97	840	2046	16187	36700	65293	159913	1175688
Notes and Loans Payable 27	9605	•	49	229	1465	10349	25384	44826	107970	933966
All Other Liabilities 28	4812	•	1	5	100	1185	5271	6176	20046	118220
Net Worth 29	4326	•	48	606	481	4653	6045	14291	31898	123503

Selected Financial Ratios (Times to 1)

Item										
Current Ratio 30	0.5	•	2.1	144.7	1.7	1.3	0.9	0.7	0.4	0.3
Quick Ratio 31	0.4	•	1.8	103.4	0.9	0.9	0.6	0.5	0.3	0.2
Net Sales to Working Capital 32	•	•	7.3	0.7	8.6	11.2	•	•	•	•
Coverage Ratio 33	1.8	•	4.6	3.8	3.1	1.8	2.0	1.4	1.9	1.9
Total Asset Turnover 34	0.7	•	0.8	0.3	0.8	0.7	0.7	0.7	0.6	0.4
Inventory Turnover 35	•	•	•	•	•	•	•	•	•	•
Receivables Turnover 36	•	•	•	•	•	•	•	•	•	•
Total Liabilities to Net Worth 37	3.3	•	1.0	0.4	3.3	2.5	5.1	3.6	4.0	8.5
Current Assets to Working Capital 38	•	•	1.9	1.0	2.4	4.9	•	•	•	•
Current Liabilities to Working Capital 39	•	•	0.9	0.0	1.4	3.9	•	•	•	•
Working Capital to Net Sales 40	•	•	0.1	1.4	0.1	0.1	•	•	•	•
Inventory to Working Capital 41	•	•	•	•	0.2	0.5	•	•	•	•
Total Receipts to Cash Flow 42	4.5	•	6.6	2.9	6.2	7.5	7.2	12.6	4.4	8.8
Cost of Goods to Cash Flow 43	0.9	•	0.0	0.0	1.1	2.4	3.5	6.2	0.8	0.1
Cash Flow to Total Debt 44	0.2	•	0.2	0.4	0.2	0.1	0.1	0.1	0.2	0.0

Selected Financial Factors (in Percentages)

Item										
Debt Ratio 45	76.9	•	51.1	27.9	76.5	71.3	83.5	78.1	80.1	89.5
Return on Total Assets 46	8.4	•	12.8	9.4	14.2	8.0	8.2	6.3	7.4	7.2
Return on Equity Before Income Taxes 47	15.8	•	20.6	9.5	40.8	12.5	24.5	8.4	17.3	32.1
Return on Equity After Income Taxes 48	11.9	•	20.5	9.1	37.2	12.1	22.7	5.6	13.4	28.9
Profit Margin (Before Income Tax) 49	5.4	•	13.3	22.8	12.4	5.2	5.7	2.5	5.5	8.5
Profit Margin (After Income Tax) 50	4.1	•	13.3	21.8	11.4	5.0	5.3	1.7	4.2	7.7

Table I

Corporations with and without Net Income

OTHER CONSUMER GOODS AND GENERAL RENTAL CENTERS

MONEY AMOUNTS AND SIZE OF ASSETS IN THOUSANDS OF DOLLARS

Item Description for Accounting Period 7/07 Through 6/08	Total	Zero Assets	Under 500	500 to 1,000	1,000 to 5,000	5,000 to 10,000	10,000 to 25,000	25,000 to 50,000	50,000 to 100,000	100,000 to 250,000	250,000 to 500,000	500,000 to 2,500,000	2,500,000 and over
Number of Enterprises **1**	12778	963	9974	1058	584	125	43	19	0	6	0	6	0
Revenues ($ in Thousands)													
Net Sales **2**	21229828	67102	3143770	1363768	1429297	993948	882601	561452	0	729227	0	12058663	0
Interest **3**	37935	1271	971	927	1155	0	602	858	0	2730	0	29422	0
Rents **4**	8160	0	1080	0	1592	0	0	1895	0	2640	0	953	0
Royalties **5**	118995	0	0	0	0	0	0	0	0	0	0	118995	0
Other Portfolio Income **6**	80782	0	6753	11082	11438	10385	12348	7874	0	6005	0	14899	0
Other Receipts **7**	20983956	65831	3134966	1351759	1415112	983563	869651	550825	0	717852	0	11894394	0
Total Receipts **8**	21229828	67102	3143770	1363768	1429297	993948	882601	561452	0	729227	0	12058663	0
Average Total Receipts **9**	1661	70	315	1289	2447	7952	20526	29550	•	121538	•	2009777	•
Operating Costs/Operating Income (%)													
Cost of Operations **10**	25.6	47.3	25.7	21.3	28.8	29.2	33.6	38.1	•	29.4	•	23.8	•
Salaries and Wages **11**	19.9	15.3	18.7	26.9	16.1	18.2	22.9	15.9	•	15.2	•	20.2	•
Taxes Paid **12**	3.7	2.7	4.1	3.9	5.7	4.3	2.3	3.4	•	4.2	•	3.4	•
Interest Paid **13**	2.7	0.7	1.0	2.7	4.0	2.3	2.5	5.9	•	7.2	•	2.7	•
Depreciation **14**	12.5	4.2	5.3	11.1	14.1	9.8	15.2	12.9	•	10.2	•	14.5	•
Amortization and Depletion **15**	1.3	•	0.1	0.6	0.2	0.3	0.2	2.3	•	14.2	•	1.2	•
Pensions and Other Deferred Comp. **16**	0.1	•	0.2	•	0.3	0.5	0.0	0.1	•	0.0	•	0.1	•
Employee Benefits **17**	1.0	•	0.7	0.1	0.6	1.9	0.8	1.0	•	0.8	•	1.1	•
Advertising **18**	3.1	0.0	2.0	2.3	2.0	2.6	2.0	1.5	•	0.5	•	3.9	•
Other Expenses **19**	27.7	27.9	32.7	26.7	24.7	24.0	16.6	23.7	•	18.0	•	28.7	•
Officers' Compensation **20**	2.4	•	7.0	4.7	4.0	3.5	1.1	1.8	•	1.3	•	0.8	•
Operating Margin **21**	0.1	1.8	2.6	•	•	3.4	2.7	•	•	•	•	•	•
Operating Margin Before Officers' Comp. **22**	2.5	1.8	9.6	4.5	3.4	6.9	3.8	•	•	0.3	•	0.3	•

Selected Average Balance Sheet ($ in Thousands)

Item										
Net Receivables 23	52	0	3	47	66	613	3002	1267	9426	42694
Inventories 24	•	0	•	•	•	•	•	•	•	•
Net Property, Plant and Equipment 25	536	0	50	424	1065	2989	8196	25009	84604	593345
Total Assets 26	1304	0	116	731	1476	5544	15363	41725	211360	1743085
Notes and Loans Payable 27	607	0	54	625	1533	2442	8948	20340	117284	647113
All Other Liabilities 28	445	0	21	109	231	828	2609	3835	36735	786592
Net Worth 29	252	0	41	-2	-288	2274	3806	17550	57342	309380

Selected Financial Ratios (Times to 1)

Item										
Current Ratio 30	0.5	•	2.1	2.6	1.0	2.7	1.4	1.2	0.5	0.3
Quick Ratio 31	0.3	•	1.4	1.1	0.6	1.0	1.1	0.8	0.3	0.1
Net Sales to Working Capital 32	•	•	11.5	9.0	•	5.3	15.0	35.6	•	•
Coverage Ratio 33	1.2	3.4	3.6	0.9	0.9	2.5	2.0	•	0.9	1.0
Total Asset Turnover 34	1.3	•	2.7	1.8	1.7	1.4	1.3	0.7	0.6	1.2
Inventory Turnover 35	•	•	•	•	•	•	•	•	•	•
Receivables Turnover 36	•	•	•	•	•	•	•	•	2.7	4.6
Total Liabilities to Net Worth 37	4.2	•	1.8	•	1.4	1.4	3.0	1.4	2.7	4.6
Current Assets to Working Capital 38	•	•	1.9	1.6	•	1.6	3.8	7.6	•	•
Current Liabilities to Working Capital 39	•	•	0.9	0.6	•	0.6	2.8	6.6	•	•
Working Capital to Net Sales 40	•	•	0.1	0.1	•	0.2	0.1	0.0	•	•
Inventory to Working Capital 41	•	•	0.5	0.9	•	0.5	0.6	1.4	•	•
Total Receipts to Cash Flow 42	6.2	5.2	4.7	6.7	7.9	5.9	6.8	9.6	15.4	6.1
Cost of Goods to Cash Flow 43	1.6	2.5	1.2	1.4	2.3	1.7	2.3	3.7	4.5	1.5
Cash Flow to Total Debt 44	0.3	•	0.9	0.3	0.2	0.4	0.3	0.1	0.1	0.2

Selected Financial Factors (in Percentages)

Item										
Debt Ratio 45	80.7	•	64.4	100.3	119.5	59.0	75.2	57.9	72.9	82.3
Return on Total Assets 46	4.1	•	9.8	4.5	5.7	8.1	6.9	•	3.6	3.2
Return on Equity Before Income Taxes 47	2.9	•	19.9	114.3	11.8	11.8	14.1	•	•	0.4
Return on Equity After Income Taxes 48	•	•	17.8	125.1	7.6	11.8	12.7	•	•	•
Profit Margin (Before Income Tax) 49	0.4	1.8	2.6	•	•	3.4	2.6	•	•	0.1
Profit Margin (After Income Tax) 50	•	1.0	2.3	•	•	3.4	2.4	•	•	•

Table II

Corporations with Net Income

OTHER CONSUMER GOODS AND GENERAL RENTAL CENTERS

MONEY AMOUNTS AND SIZE OF ASSETS IN THOUSANDS OF DOLLARS

Item Description for Accounting Period 7/07 Through 6/08	Total	Zero Assets	Under 500	500 to 1,000	1,000 to 5,000	5,000 to 10,000	10,000 to 25,000	25,000 to 50,000	50,000 to 100,000	100,000 to 250,000	250,000 to 500,000	500,000 to 2,500,000	2,500,000 and over
Number of Enterprises **1**	4244	•	3248	304	334	•	24	•	3	0	0	3	0

Revenues ($ in Thousands)

Net Sales **2**	10555005	•	2218513	504172	856606	•	626907	•	402581	0	0	5495392	0
Interest **3**	22241	•	971	38	777	•	18	•	2705	0	0	16462	0
Rents **4**	6265	•	1080	0	1592	•	0	•	2640	0	0	953	0
Royalties **5**	35375	•	0	0	0	•	0	•	0	0	0	35375	0
Other Portfolio Income **6**	34055	•	4635	5633	4244	•	8325	•	3475	0	0	2317	0
Other Receipts **7**	10457069	•	2211827	498501	849993	•	618564	•	393761	0	0	5440285	0
Total Receipts **8**	10555005	•	2218513	504172	856606	•	626907	•	402581	0	0	5495392	0
Average Total Receipts **9**	2487	•	683	1658	2565	•	26121	•	134194	•	•	1831797	•

Operating Costs/Operating Income (%)

Cost of Operations **10**	22.3	•	27.2	30.9	30.8	•	36.2	•	2.5	•	•	17.2	•
Salaries and Wages **11**	19.5	•	18.1	16.7	16.7	•	19.4	•	22.9	•	•	20.4	•
Taxes Paid **12**	3.4	•	4.0	3.2	5.0	•	1.8	•	5.7	•	•	2.9	•
Interest Paid **13**	1.9	•	0.7	2.6	2.7	•	2.3	•	5.3	•	•	1.9	•
Depreciation **14**	15.1	•	3.7	12.6	6.7	•	13.1	•	8.8	•	•	22.7	•
Amortization and Depletion **15**	1.5	•	0.0	•	0.0	•	0.2	•	22.3	•	•	1.1	•
Pensions and Other Deferred Comp. **16**	0.2	•	0.0	•	0.3	•	0.1	•	0.2	•	•	0.2	•
Employee Benefits **17**	1.4	•	0.8	0.1	0.4	•	0.7	•	1.1	•	•	2.0	•
Advertising **18**	3.4	•	1.9	2.2	2.2	•	1.0	•	0.4	•	•	5.1	•
Other Expenses **19**	22.2	•	29.7	16.4	26.0	•	15.3	•	21.6	•	•	20.8	•
Officers' Compensation **20**	2.3	•	5.4	5.6	3.5	•	1.1	•	1.9	•	•	0.6	•
Operating Margin **21**	6.9	•	8.4	9.7	5.6	•	8.8	•	7.3	•	•	5.2	•
Operating Margin Before Officers' Comp. **22**	9.2	•	13.8	15.4	9.1	•	9.8	•	9.2	•	•	5.8	•

Selected Average Balance Sheet ($ in Thousands)

Net Receivables 23	77	4	16	62	5097	2081	40722
Inventories 24							
Net Property, Plant and Equipment 25	901	86	625	1017	5876	127881	747944
Total Assets 26	2234	207	878	1481	15836	166360	2229592
Notes and Loans Payable 27	674	69	687	1411	7791	86575	481722
All Other Liabilities 28	822	35	36	149	2565	38832	1028343
Net Worth 29	738	103	156	-78	5479	40954	719526

Selected Financial Ratios (Times to 1)

Current Ratio 30	0.5	2.3	4.7	1.5	1.6	0.1	0.2
Quick Ratio 31	0.3	1.7	2.9	0.8	1.3	0.1	0.2
Net Sales to Working Capital 32	12.2	12.7	19.8	9.6			
Coverage Ratio 33	4.7	12.7	4.7	3.0	4.7	2.4	3.7
Total Asset Turnover 34	1.1	3.3	1.9	1.7	1.6	0.8	0.8
Inventory Turnover 35							
Receivables Turnover 36							
Total Liabilities to Net Worth 37	2.0	1.0	4.6	1.9	1.9	3.1	2.1
Current Assets to Working Capital 38	1.7	1.3	2.9	2.7			
Current Liabilities to Working Capital 39	0.7	0.3	1.9	1.7			
Working Capital to Net Sales 40	0.1	0.1	0.1	0.1			
Inventory to Working Capital 41	0.3	0.5	1.1	0.4			
Total Receipts to Cash Flow 42	4.9	4.2	5.4	5.0	5.4	5.7	5.3
Cost of Goods to Cash Flow 43	1.1	1.1	1.7	1.8	1.7	0.1	0.9
Cash Flow to Total Debt 44	0.3	1.6	0.4	0.5	0.3	0.2	0.2

Selected Financial Factors (in Percentages)

Debt Ratio 45	67.0	50.2	82.3	105.3	65.4	75.4	67.7
Return on Total Assets 46	9.7	30.0	23.3	14.4	18.1	10.1	5.8
Return on Equity Before Income Taxes 47	23.2	55.6	103.5		41.2	23.9	13.2
Return on Equity After Income Taxes 48	20.1	53.0	102.9		39.5	17.3	9.9
Profit Margin (Before Income Tax) 49	6.9	8.4	9.7	5.6	8.6	7.3	5.2
Profit Margin (After Income Tax) 50	6.0	8.0	9.7	5.1	8.3	5.3	3.9

COMMERCIAL AND INDUSTRIAL MACHINERY AND EQUIPMENT RENTAL

Table I

Corporations with and without Net Income

MONEY AMOUNTS AND SIZE OF ASSETS IN THOUSANDS OF DOLLARS

Item Description for Accounting Period 7/07 Through 6/08	Total	Zero Assets	Under 500	500 to 1,000	1,000 to 5,000	5,000 to 10,000	10,000 to 25,000	25,000 to 50,000	50,000 to 100,000	100,000 to 250,000	250,000 to 500,000	500,000 to 2,500,000	2,500,000 and over
Number of Enterprises 1	28373	2878	18020	2405	3816	600	343	145	72	40	13	32	7
Revenues ($ in Thousands)													
Net Sales 2	52722684	530273	4096713	1555910	5692169	4072502	3450678	4044419	2798047	3016551	2358688	10512045	10594689
Interest 3	1144481	5520	19698	4994	22240	8681	10856	20309	53248	87976	97667	470776	342515
Rents 4	168908	3693	0	617	2172	114	15	1849	11091	1638	2011	145707	0
Royalties 5	10104	0	0	1	392	0	0	1118	0	814	0	7779	0
Other Portfolio Income 6	2941920	69034	53170	18328	151615	117832	217830	155258	77930	462119	57684	930401	630719
Other Receipts 7	48457271	452026	4023845	1531970	5515875	3945875	3221977	3865885	2655778	2464004	2201326	8957382	9621455
Total Receipts 8	52722684	530273	4096713	1555910	5692169	4072502	3450678	4044419	2798047	3016551	2358688	10512045	10594689
Average Total Receipts 9	1858	184	227	647	1492	6788	10060	27893	38862	75414	181438	328501	1513527
Operating Costs/Operating Income (%)													
Cost of Operations 10	28.2	15.7	37.6	30.3	23.6	38.5	34.3	48.7	31.4	22.3	40.3	25.9	14.1
Salaries and Wages 11	10.4	16.3	9.3	14.7	12.1	9.9	8.3	7.5	9.4	9.1	9.7	9.2	13.0
Taxes Paid 12	2.1	2.3	2.8	2.9	2.8	3.3	2.2	1.7	2.0	1.3	1.3	2.0	1.6
Interest Paid 13	7.6	11.3	2.3	2.1	3.1	2.9	4.5	3.5	6.4	12.5	6.2	11.7	12.2
Depreciation 14	20.6	32.0	7.6	10.8	15.6	14.5	19.0	15.0	18.8	24.2	16.1	25.0	30.1
Amortization and Depletion 15	0.7	0.3	0.0	0.2	0.1	0.1	0.1	0.5	0.2	0.7	1.0	1.4	1.5
Pensions and Other Deferred Comp. 16	0.3	0.1	0.4	0.1	0.3	0.4	0.2	0.2	0.2	0.3	0.4	0.4	0.4
Employee Benefits 17	1.3	1.2	1.5	1.0	1.0	0.8	1.0	0.9	0.8	1.1	1.6	1.1	2.0
Advertising 18	0.4	0.6	0.5	0.7	0.5	0.4	0.3	0.5	0.3	0.4	0.4	0.3	0.3
Other Expenses 19	20.4	20.9	23.6	28.3	33.3	18.7	19.1	14.1	23.1	15.3	16.8	15.2	21.2
Officers' Compensation 20	2.3	6.9	8.5	4.4	3.6	3.2	1.9	1.4	1.6	2.0	1.4	1.1	0.3
Operating Margin 21	5.7	•	6.0	4.5	3.9	7.4	9.1	6.1	5.7	10.7	4.7	6.8	3.1
Operating Margin Before Officers' Comp. 22	8.0	•	14.5	8.8	7.6	10.6	11.0	7.4	7.3	12.8	6.1	7.9	3.4

Selected Average Balance Sheet ($ in Thousands)

Net Receivables 23	668	0	14	71	248	546	1851	4399	13934	33924	69493	126209	1240563
Inventories 24	•	•	•	•	•	•	•	•	•	•	•	•	•
Net Property, Plant and Equipment 25	1717	0	53	400	1133	3810	8049	14413	28040	44460	109568	402901	2463039
Total Assets 26	4020	0	132	733	2043	6899	14850	34760	68964	155903	358540	1022784	5609763
Notes and Loans Payable 27	2159	0	134	467	1001	3583	6893	15836	35030	96638	160395	541362	3040171
All Other Liabilities 28	868	0	14	87	336	510	2439	7268	11972	24992	89955	261303	1327189
Net Worth 29	994	0	-16	180	706	2807	5518	11656	21962	34272	108190	220118	1242403

Selected Financial Ratios (Times to 1)

Current Ratio 30	1.7	•	2.6	1.5	1.4	2.1	1.5	1.4	1.4	1.9	2.7	2.1	1.4
Quick Ratio 31	1.3	•	2.2	1.1	0.9	0.9	1.1	0.7	1.0	1.1	1.7	1.7	1.3
Net Sales to Working Capital 32	3.8	•	6.0	10.8	8.6	5.2	6.3	7.6	5.4	2.5	1.9	2.3	3.6
Coverage Ratio 33	1.7	0.3	3.6	3.1	2.2	3.6	3.0	2.7	1.9	1.9	1.7	1.6	1.2
Total Asset Turnover 34	0.5	•	1.7	0.9	0.7	1.0	0.7	0.8	0.6	0.5	0.5	0.3	0.3
Inventory Turnover 35	•	•	•	•	•	•	•	•	•	•	•	•	•
Receivables Turnover 36	•	•	•	•	•	•	•	•	•	•	•	•	•
Total Liabilities to Net Worth 37	3.0	•	•	3.1	1.9	1.5	1.7	2.0	2.1	3.5	2.3	3.6	3.5
Current Assets to Working Capital 38	2.5	1.6	•	3.1	3.6	1.9	2.9	3.6	3.5	2.2	1.6	1.9	3.5
Current Liabilities to Working Capital 39	1.5	0.6	•	2.1	2.6	0.9	1.9	2.6	2.5	1.2	0.6	0.9	2.5
Working Capital to Net Sales 40	0.3	0.2	•	0.1	0.1	0.2	0.2	0.1	0.2	0.4	0.5	0.4	0.3
Inventory to Working Capital 41	0.2	0.0	•	0.5	0.3	0.2	0.4	1.1	0.5	0.2	0.4	0.1	0.1
Total Receipts to Cash Flow 42	6.3	59.7	4.5	4.1	4.3	5.3	6.1	7.2	5.4	5.0	6.0	11.1	7.8
Cost of Goods to Cash Flow 43	1.8	9.4	1.7	1.3	1.0	2.0	2.1	3.5	1.7	1.1	2.4	2.9	1.1
Cash Flow to Total Debt 44	0.1	•	0.3	0.3	0.3	0.3	0.2	0.2	0.2	0.1	0.1	0.0	0.0

Selected Financial Factors (in Percentages)

Debt Ratio 45	75.3	•	112.5	75.4	65.5	59.3	62.8	66.5	68.2	78.0	69.8	78.5	77.9
Return on Total Assets 46	6.1	•	14.2	5.8	5.2	10.2	9.2	7.7	6.8	11.2	5.5	5.9	4.1
Return on Equity Before Income Taxes 47	10.6	•	•	15.8	8.3	17.9	16.5	14.5	10.0	23.5	7.8	10.2	3.7
Return on Equity After Income Taxes 48	8.2	•	•	13.4	6.4	17.0	14.1	12.8	8.4	21.3	5.2	6.4	2.1
Profit Margin (Before Income Tax) 49	5.7	•	5.9	4.4	3.9	7.4	9.1	6.0	5.6	10.7	4.6	6.8	3.0
Profit Margin (After Income Tax) 50	4.4	•	5.8	3.7	3.0	7.0	7.8	4.7	5.4	9.7	3.1	4.3	1.7

327

Table II

Corporations with Net Income

COMMERCIAL AND INDUSTRIAL MACHINERY AND EQUIPMENT RENTAL

MONEY AMOUNTS AND SIZE OF ASSETS IN THOUSANDS OF DOLLARS

Item Description for Accounting Period 7/07 Through 6/08	Total	Zero Assets	Under 500	500 to 1,000	1,000 to 5,000	5,000 to 10,000	10,000 to 25,000	25,000 to 50,000	50,000 to 100,000	100,000 to 250,000	250,000 to 500,000	500,000 to 2,500,000	2,500,000 and over
Number of Enterprises 1	14814	•	9861	920	2181	344	204	•	46	22	9	18	•
Revenues ($ in Thousands)													
Net Sales 2	40536364	•	3451318	960608	3961367	3571436	2725539	•	1718038	2201880	2170480	7277364	•
Interest 3	904761		2735	4388	12020	5849	9114		50329	51715	80371	343654	
Rents 4	165861		0	229	2064	114	8		10467	44	2011	145634	
Royalties 5	10103		0	0	392	0	0		0	814	0	7779	
Other Portfolio Income 6	2599692		48260	13604	117295	106600	188819		57900	394786	52871	874586	
Other Receipts 7	36855947		3400323	942387	3829596	3458873	2527598		1599342	1754521	2035227	5905711	
Total Receipts 8	40536364		3451318	960608	3961367	3571436	2725539		1718038	2201880	2170480	7277364	
Average Total Receipts 9	2736	•	350	1044	1816	10382	13360	•	37349	100085	241164	404298	•
Operating Costs/Operating Income (%)													
Cost of Operations 10	29.1	•	40.7	20.8	20.8	38.5	34.7	•	27.0	24.6	42.8	28.5	•
Salaries and Wages 11	10.5	•	7.2	15.8	12.6	9.7	8.3	•	10.3	8.2	9.9	10.1	•
Taxes Paid 12	2.1	•	2.5	2.4	2.6	3.5	2.1	•	2.3	1.3	1.4	2.4	•
Interest Paid 13	6.1	•	1.4	2.0	2.4	1.9	2.7	•	6.8	8.7	4.8	7.7	•
Depreciation 14	17.0	•	4.3	12.0	15.4	11.3	13.7	•	19.4	21.8	14.9	13.7	•
Amortization and Depletion 15	0.7	•	0.0	0.0	0.1	0.0	0.1	•	0.2	0.4	1.0	1.4	•
Pensions and Other Deferred Comp. 16	0.3	•	0.4	0.2	0.3	0.4	0.2	•	0.2	0.4	0.4	0.4	•
Employee Benefits 17	1.3	•	1.1	0.2	1.0	0.8	1.1	•	0.7	1.1	1.6	1.4	•
Advertising 18	0.4	•	0.4	0.2	0.5	0.2	0.3	•	0.3	0.5	0.4	0.3	•
Other Expenses 19	18.5	•	19.6	26.1	27.0	18.5	18.1	•	18.9	12.5	15.4	17.0	•
Officers' Compensation 20	2.0	•	6.6	4.3	3.1	3.2	1.9	•	1.6	2.0	1.5	0.9	•
Operating Margin 21	12.1	•	15.9	16.0	14.4	12.2	16.9	•	12.3	18.4	5.9	16.2	•
Operating Margin Before Officers' Comp. 22	14.1	•	22.5	20.3	17.4	15.3	18.7	•	14.0	20.4	7.4	17.1	•

Selected Average Balance Sheet ($ in Thousands)

Net Receivables 23	1040	24	62	320	658	2492	17066	26475	64647	156278
Inventories 24										
Net Property, Plant and Equipment 25	1704	58	372	1159	4154	7435	22576	47697	90530	304820
Total Assets 26	4868	158	777	2086	6917	14586	68685	147986	344089	1006053
Notes and Loans Payable 27	2366	93	454	855	3152	5664	34826	73573	150572	437352
All Other Liabilities 28	1116	13	109	255	623	2340	11985	28534	81457	273831
Net Worth 29	1387	52	214	977	3143	6582	21873	45879	112059	294871

Selected Financial Ratios (Times to 1)

Current Ratio 30	1.7	3.6	1.3	1.8	1.4	1.7	1.3	1.4	2.1	2.6
Quick Ratio 31	1.4	3.1	0.9	1.4	1.0	1.4	1.1	0.8	1.2	2.2
Net Sales to Working Capital 32	3.8	5.6	18.7	5.8	18.7	5.9	5.5	7.7	3.0	1.9
Coverage Ratio 33	3.0	12.4	8.8	7.0	7.5	7.3	2.8	3.1	2.2	3.1
Total Asset Turnover 34	0.6	2.2	1.3	0.9	1.5	0.9	0.5	0.7	0.7	0.4
Inventory Turnover 35										
Receivables Turnover 36										
Total Liabilities to Net Worth 37	2.5	2.0	2.6	1.1	1.2	1.2	2.1	2.2	2.1	2.4
Current Assets to Working Capital 38	2.4	1.4	4.3	2.2	3.6	2.4	3.9	3.7	1.9	1.6
Current Liabilities to Working Capital 39	1.4	0.4	3.3	1.2	2.6	1.4	2.9	2.7	0.9	0.6
Working Capital to Net Sales 40	0.3	0.2	0.1	0.2	0.1	0.2	0.2	0.1	0.3	0.5
Inventory to Working Capital 41	0.2	0.0	0.3	0.1	0.5	0.2	0.3	0.8	0.7	0.1
Total Receipts to Cash Flow 42	4.8	3.2	2.9	4.0	4.3	4.4	4.3	3.9	5.4	5.9
Cost of Goods to Cash Flow 43	1.4	1.3	0.6	0.8	1.6	1.5	1.2	1.0	2.3	1.7
Cash Flow to Total Debt 44	0.2	1.0	0.6	0.4	0.6	0.4	0.2	0.3	0.2	0.1

Selected Financial Factors (in Percentages)

Debt Ratio 45	71.5	66.9	72.5	53.2	54.6	54.9	68.2	69.0	67.4	70.7
Return on Total Assets 46	10.2	38.2	24.1	14.6	21.0	17.9	10.3	18.3	7.5	9.6
Return on Equity Before Income Taxes 47	23.9	106.1	77.6	26.7	40.1	34.2	20.8	40.1	12.6	22.1
Return on Equity After Income Taxes 48	20.6	105.0	72.5	24.3	38.7	30.9	18.3	37.2	9.0	17.2
Profit Margin (Before Income Tax) 49	12.1	15.9	15.9	14.3	12.1	16.9	12.2	18.4	5.9	16.1
Profit Margin (After Income Tax) 50	10.5	15.7	14.8	13.0	11.7	15.2	10.7	17.0	4.2	12.5

Table I

Corporations with and without Net Income

LESSORS OF NONFINAN. INTANGIBLE ASSETS (EX. COPYRIGHTED WORKS)

MONEY AMOUNTS AND SIZE OF ASSETS IN THOUSANDS OF DOLLARS

Item Description for Accounting Period 7/07 Through 6/08	Total	Zero Assets	Under 500	500 to 1,000	1,000 to 5,000	5,000 to 10,000	10,000 to 25,000	25,000 to 50,000	50,000 to 100,000	100,000 to 250,000	250,000 to 500,000	500,000 to 2,500,000	2,500,000 and over
Number of Enterprises 1	1363	61	969	234	33	18	20	8	3	6	3	7	0
Revenues ($ in Thousands)													
Net Sales 2	3986446	89782	148154	81739	90390	90107	267660	177212	73007	284565	242947	2440883	0
Interest 3	103667	6552	0	26	1121	1882	1965	6874	3283	8242	19036	54685	0
Rents 4	26712	0	0	0	0	0	0	0	0	2628	0	24084	0
Royalties 5	1541548	34079	6446	0	0	25486	67069	0	69723	59084	117855	1161805	0
Other Portfolio Income 6	86614	20270	16994	1692	14	321	358	18703	0	5373	4730	18160	0
Other Receipts 7	2227905	28881	124714	80021	89255	62418	198268	151635	1	209238	101326	1182149	0
Total Receipts 8	3986446	89782	148154	81739	90390	90107	267660	177212	73007	284565	242947	2440883	0
Average Total Receipts 9	2925	1472	153	349	2739	5006	13383	22152	24336	47428	80982	348698	•
Operating Costs/Operating Income (%)													
Cost of Operations 10	3.7	2.5	•	24.2	14.5	0.6	3.9	12.8	•	0.1	2.0	3.1	•
Salaries and Wages 11	16.2	6.6	0.2	15.5	27.5	22.9	16.2	4.5	0.2	0.9	12.9	20.3	•
Taxes Paid 12	2.5	2.8	1.2	2.0	4.6	3.2	1.9	3.9	1.4	2.7	3.1	2.4	•
Interest Paid 13	7.0	0.0	0.2	0.1	1.1	0.0	2.9	2.0	1.7	3.5	0.0	10.5	•
Depreciation 14	2.2	1.0	•	1.1	3.8	1.4	1.4	0.8	0.0	0.5	1.0	3.0	•
Amortization and Depletion 15	4.5	•	0.5	•	3.9	0.5	4.5	2.9	9.9	0.2	12.3	4.9	•
Pensions and Other Deferred Comp. 16	0.4	0.3	•	•	•	1.9	0.6	0.6	•	0.1	0.4	0.4	•
Employee Benefits 17	1.5	0.1	0.1	•	3.3	1.1	1.2	0.2	0.1	0.2	0.7	2.1	•
Advertising 18	1.6	0.4	0.5	0.6	2.5	0.4	3.2	1.1	0.0	0.1	1.2	1.8	•
Other Expenses 19	30.8	22.4	17.5	47.4	40.3	47.4	45.5	20.4	92.1	42.4	26.9	26.7	•
Officers' Compensation 20	3.4	6.8	•	3.3	20.2	10.9	3.5	6.3	•	0.2	5.5	2.6	•
Operating Margin 21	26.1	57.0	79.7	5.7	•	9.6	15.0	44.5	•	49.2	34.0	22.2	•
Operating Margin Before Officers' Comp. 22	29.6	63.9	79.7	9.0	•	20.6	18.6	50.8	•	49.3	39.5	24.8	•

Selected Average Balance Sheet ($ in Thousands)

	1	2	3	4	5	6	7	8	9	10	11	12
Net Receivables 23	1082	0	2	78	1108	672	1418	1750	33	2528	31285	179206
Inventories 24	•	•	•	•	•	•	•	•	•	•	•	•
Net Property, Plant and Equipment 25	671	•	•	1	336	191	2079	486	0	10710	5192	110656
Total Assets 26	14928	0	31	615	2705	7413	18791	40682	144222	130699	331699	2464780
Notes and Loans Payable 27	2932	0	127	55	429	14	4052	4389	72111	12700	40926	504383
All Other Liabilities 28	5417	0	134	86	642	3761	2759	8300	-13528	21098	89188	952746
Net Worth 29	6579	0	-231	475	1634	3639	11980	27993	85639	96901	201584	1007651

Selected Financial Ratios (Times to 1)

	1	2	3	4	5	6	7	8	9	10	11	12
Current Ratio 30	0.6	•	0.2	1.6	2.5	2.6	2.1	2.0	1.4	1.5	1.6	0.6
Quick Ratio 31	0.4	•	0.2	1.5	2.1	2.2	1.8	1.2	0.5	1.4	1.3	0.3
Net Sales to Working Capital 32	•	•	•	8.3	2.4	2.5	5.1	2.6	54.6	8.7	1.8	•
Coverage Ratio 33	4.7	3582.4	320.9	45.1	•	379.9	6.1	23.0	•	14.6	1949.2	3.1
Total Asset Turnover 34	0.2	•	5.0	0.6	1.0	0.7	0.7	0.5	0.3	0.4	0.2	0.1
Inventory Turnover 35	•	•	•	•	•	•	•	•	•	•	•	•
Receivables Turnover 36	•	•	•	•	•	•	•	•	•	•	•	•
Total Liabilities to Net Worth 37	1.3	•	0.3	0.3	0.7	1.0	0.6	0.5	•	0.3	0.6	1.4
Current Assets to Working Capital 38	•	•	2.7	1.7	1.7	1.6	1.9	2.0	3.8	2.9	2.6	•
Current Liabilities to Working Capital 39	•	•	1.7	0.7	0.7	0.6	0.9	1.0	2.8	1.9	1.6	•
Working Capital to Net Sales 40	•	•	0.1	0.4	0.4	0.4	0.2	0.4	0.0	0.1	0.6	•
Inventory to Working Capital 41	•	•	•	•	•	0.0	0.1	0.0	0.0	0.0	0.1	•
Total Receipts to Cash Flow 42	1.9	1.8	1.2	2.1	8.1	1.8	1.7	1.9	1.2	1.1	1.7	2.3
Cost of Goods to Cash Flow 43	0.1	0.0	•	0.5	1.2	0.0	0.1	0.2	0.0	0.0	0.0	0.1
Cash Flow to Total Debt 44	0.2	•	1.2	1.2	0.3	0.7	1.1	0.9	•	1.3	0.4	0.1

Selected Financial Factors (in Percentages)

	1	2	3	4	5	6	7	8	9	10	11	12
Debt Ratio 45	55.9	•	850.1	22.9	39.6	50.9	36.2	31.2	•	25.9	39.2	59.1
Return on Total Assets 46	6.4	•	397.3	3.3	•	6.3	12.7	25.3	•	18.4	7.8	4.6
Return on Equity Before Income Taxes 47	11.4	•	•	4.2	•	12.7	16.7	35.2	•	23.1	12.9	7.6
Return on Equity After Income Taxes 48	8.5	•	•	2.8	•	6.0	14.7	26.8	•	20.0	7.2	5.3
Profit Margin (Before Income Tax) 49	25.6	55.8	79.7	5.7	•	9.3	14.9	44.5	47.3	•	32.1	21.9
Profit Margin (After Income Tax) 50	19.1	36.6	75.6	3.8	•	4.4	13.1	33.9	40.9	•	18.0	15.5

329

LESSORS OF NONFINAN. INTANGIBLE ASSETS (EX. COPYRIGHTED WORKS)

Table II

Corporations with Net Income

MONEY AMOUNTS AND SIZE OF ASSETS IN THOUSANDS OF DOLLARS

Item Description for Accounting Period 7/07 Through 6/08	Total	Zero Assets	Under 500	500 to 1,000	1,000 to 5,000	5,000 to 10,000	10,000 to 25,000	25,000 to 50,000	50,000 to 100,000	100,000 to 250,000	250,000 to 500,000	500,000 to 2,500,000	2,500,000 and over
Number of Enterprises **1**	779	61	591	58	21	13	14	8	0	6	0	7	0
Revenues ($ in Thousands)													
Net Sales **2**	3750469	89782	148154	83454	66048	89808	196277	183115	0	452946	0	2440883	0
Interest **3**	95629	6552	0	26	686	1882	1334	6061	0	24403	0	54685	0
Rents **4**	26712	0	0	0	0	0	0	0	0	2628	0	24084	0
Royalties **5**	1478830	34079	6446	0	0	25486	67069	7005	0	176939	0	1161805	0
Other Portfolio Income **6**	81491	20270	16994	1692	14	35	340	18703	0	5285	0	18160	0
Other Receipts **7**	2067807	28881	124714	81736	65348	62405	127534	151346	0	243691	0	1182149	0
Total Receipts **8**	3750469	89782	148154	83454	66048	89808	196277	183115	0	452946	0	2440883	0
Average Total Receipts **9**	4814	1472	251	1439	3145	6908	14020	22889	•	75491	•	348698	•
Operating Costs/Operating Income (%)													
Cost of Operations **10**	3.6	2.5	•	23.7	•	0.6	5.3	12.2	•	0.9	•	3.1	•
Salaries and Wages **11**	15.8	6.6	0.2	15.2	28.5	20.2	12.1	1.5	•	3.5	•	20.3	•
Taxes Paid **12**	2.4	2.8	1.1	1.8	4.8	2.1	1.7	4.1	•	2.1	•	2.4	•
Interest Paid **13**	7.2	0.0	0.2	0.1	0.4	0.0	3.2	2.6	•	0.9	•	10.5	•
Depreciation **14**	2.2	1.0	•	1.1	1.5	1.4	1.4	0.4	•	0.7	•	3.0	•
Amortization and Depletion **15**	3.4	•	0.5	•	1.9	0.5	0.7	2.6	•	0.3	•	4.9	•
Pensions and Other Deferred Comp. **16**	0.4	0.3	•	•	•	1.9	0.7	0.6	•	0.2	•	0.4	•
Employee Benefits **17**	1.5	0.1	0.1	•	3.4	1.1	1.6	0.2	•	0.2	•	2.1	•
Advertising **18**	1.6	0.4	0.5	0.6	3.1	0.4	4.3	1.0	•	0.4	•	1.8	•
Other Expenses **19**	28.4	22.4	17.5	46.5	31.8	46.3	40.0	16.0	•	35.1	•	26.7	•
Officers' Compensation **20**	3.3	6.8	•	3.2	19.8	11.0	3.2	5.6	•	2.2	•	2.6	•
Operating Margin **21**	30.0	57.0	79.8	7.8	4.7	14.4	25.7	53.2	•	53.5	•	22.2	•
Operating Margin Before Officers' Comp. **22**	33.2	63.9	79.8	11.0	24.5	25.4	28.9	58.8	•	55.7	•	24.8	•

Selected Average Balance Sheet ($ in Thousands)

Net Receivables 23	1853	0	313	1634	931	1959	1762	13566	179206	•
Inventories 24	•	•	•	•	•	•	•	•	•	•
Net Property, Plant and Equipment 25	1133	0	6	152	265	1965	256	11857	110656	•
Total Assets 26	24806	50	587	2589	6539	17485	43755	212118	2464780	•
Notes and Loans Payable 27	4948	208	220	168	19	5482	4389	12133	504383	•
All Other Liabilities 28	9428	220	334	540	1729	3770	10715	58852	952746	•
Net Worth 29	10430	-379	32	1882	4791	8233	28651	141132	1007651	•

Selected Financial Ratios (Times to 1)

Current Ratio 30	0.6	0.2	1.7	3.5	2.6	1.8	1.9	1.2	0.6	•
Quick Ratio 31	0.4	0.2	1.6	2.9	2.1	1.5	1.1	1.0	0.3	•
Net Sales to Working Capital 32	•	•	8.0	2.0	2.6	5.3	3.2	9.2	•	•
Coverage Ratio 33	5.1	3582.4	321.4	62.9	11.6	587.1	9.0	21.2	58.2	3.1
Total Asset Turnover 34	0.2	5.0	2.5	1.2	1.1	0.8	0.5	0.4	0.1	•
Inventory Turnover 35	•	•	•	•	•	•	•	•	•	•
Receivables Turnover 36	•	•	•	•	•	•	•	•	•	•
Total Liabilities to Net Worth 37	1.4	•	17.3	0.4	0.4	1.1	0.5	0.5	1.4	•
Current Assets to Working Capital 38	•	•	2.5	1.4	1.6	2.2	2.1	6.2	•	•
Current Liabilities to Working Capital 39	•	•	1.5	0.4	0.6	1.2	1.1	5.2	•	•
Working Capital to Net Sales 40	•	•	0.1	0.5	0.4	0.2	0.3	0.1	•	•
Inventory to Working Capital 41	•	•	•	•	0.0	0.1	0.0	0.0	•	•
Total Receipts to Cash Flow 42	1.9	1.8	2.1	3.0	1.7	1.6	1.8	1.1	2.3	•
Cost of Goods to Cash Flow 43	0.1	0.0	0.5	0.0	0.0	0.1	0.2	0.0	0.1	•
Cash Flow to Total Debt 44	0.2	0.5	1.2	1.5	2.3	0.9	0.9	0.9	0.1	•

Selected Financial Factors (in Percentages)

Debt Ratio 45	58.0	860.4	94.5	27.3	26.7	52.9	34.5	33.5	59.1	•
Return on Total Assets 46	7.1	403.1	19.4	6.2	15.2	23.1	29.2	19.0	4.6	•
Return on Equity Before Income Taxes 47	13.7	•	350.6	7.8	20.7	43.6	42.5	28.0	7.6	•
Return on Equity After Income Taxes 48	10.4	•	266.1	7.4	13.7	39.4	33.8	21.8	5.3	•
Profit Margin (Before Income Tax) 49	29.6	55.8	79.8	7.8	4.7	14.4	25.6	53.2	52.4	21.9
Profit Margin (After Income Tax) 50	22.6	36.6	75.7	5.9	4.4	9.5	23.1	42.3	40.8	15.5

Table I

Corporations with and without Net Income

LEGAL SERVICES

MONEY AMOUNTS AND SIZE OF ASSETS IN THOUSANDS OF DOLLARS

Item Description for Accounting Period 7/07 Through 6/08	Total	Zero Assets	Under 500	500 to 1,000	1,000 to 5,000	5,000 to 10,000	10,000 to 25,000	25,000 to 50,000	50,000 to 100,000	100,000 to 250,000	250,000 to 500,000	500,000 to 2,500,000	2,500,000 and over
Number of Enterprises **1**	109074	20225	82665	2858	2973	185	126	25	12	5	0	0	0
Revenues ($ in Thousands)													
Net Sales **2**	91831520	2413327	46836345	7940258	16418884	4464888	6893508	3748373	1249690	1866247	0	0	0
Interest **3**	159730	2570	26724	16397	21682	11796	10337	8034	7614	54576	0	0	0
Rents **4**	41526	0	12707	9228	7267	7174	121	3631	673	724	0	0	0
Royalties **5**	2564	0	2118	0	0	0	45	39	361	0	0	0	0
Other Portfolio Income **6**	191166	573	124345	5866	37765	3469	1681	7883	4019	5564	0	0	0
Other Receipts **7**	2864764	65653	1831735	194548	245813	7634	318441	177862	16660	6421	0	0	0
Total Receipts **8**	95091270	2482123	48833974	8166297	16731411	4494961	7224133	3945822	1279017	1933532	0	0	0
Average Total Receipts **9**	872	123	591	2857	5628	24297	57334	157833	106585	386706	•	•	•
Operating Costs/Operating Income (%)													
Cost of Operations **10**	4.4	1.6	5.8	5.3	4.2	1.4	0.0	0.1	1.2	6.3	•	•	•
Salaries and Wages **11**	31.0	15.8	22.7	33.1	35.4	39.5	54.4	57.4	53.5	38.3	•	•	•
Taxes Paid **12**	3.5	4.4	3.5	3.7	3.5	3.3	3.4	3.5	4.0	3.3	•	•	•
Interest Paid **13**	0.5	0.6	0.5	0.6	0.5	0.5	0.7	0.6	1.1	1.1	•	•	•
Depreciation **14**	0.8	1.0	0.6	0.5	0.8	0.9	1.1	1.5	1.5	2.2	•	•	•
Amortization and Depletion **15**	0.0	0.0	0.0	0.0	0.0	0.1	0.0	0.0	0.1	1.1	•	•	•
Pensions and Other Deferred Comp. **16**	2.1	1.1	1.9	1.8	2.3	2.0	2.9	4.0	1.9	0.6	•	•	•
Employee Benefits **17**	2.2	1.7	1.9	2.8	2.5	2.0	2.3	2.5	3.1	2.4	•	•	•
Advertising **18**	2.3	4.0	2.4	2.0	3.5	1.4	0.9	0.5	0.9	0.7	•	•	•
Other Expenses **19**	26.1	39.6	28.0	20.9	22.8	23.5	22.9	22.3	21.5	40.5	•	•	•
Officers' Compensation **20**	21.6	15.8	24.7	27.2	20.3	22.5	12.0	11.5	6.0	1.3	•	•	•
Operating Margin **21**	5.5	14.5	8.1	2.1	4.3	3.1	•	•	5.2	2.2	•	•	•
Operating Margin Before Officers' Comp. **22**	27.1	30.3	32.8	29.2	24.5	25.5	11.3	7.5	11.2	3.5	•	•	•

Selected Average Balance Sheet ($ in Thousands)

	•	•	•	•	•	•	•	•	•	•
	•	•	•	•	•	•	•	•	•	•
Net Receivables 23	11	0	2	18	127	145	982	6840	6565	24394
Inventories 24	1	0	0	0	3	0	32	584	1	12314
Net Property, Plant and Equipment 25	32	0	14	95	300	1126	3612	11671	7922	28866
Total Assets 26	184	0	83	696	1814	6708	15367	35577	60813	214615
Notes and Loans Payable 27	71	0	41	339	550	3031	4176	9395	15643	40649
All Other Liabilities 28	81	0	37	308	838	2299	6494	13568	19926	117575
Net Worth 29	33	0	5	48	426	1379	4696	12614	25244	56392

Selected Financial Ratios (Times to 1)

	•	•	•	•	•	•	•	•	•	•
Current Ratio 30	1.2	•	1.1	1.0	1.3	1.4	1.2	1.3	1.5	1.1
Quick Ratio 31	0.7	•	0.8	0.7	0.8	0.7	0.6	0.9	0.7	0.7
Net Sales to Working Capital 32	52.1	•	134.6	•	21.6	24.6	36.6	36.8	8.3	31.9
Coverage Ratio 33	18.2	31.2	28.4	9.6	12.3	9.1	7.2	3.0	7.9	6.3
Total Asset Turnover 34	4.6	•	6.8	4.0	3.0	3.6	3.6	4.2	1.7	1.7
Inventory Turnover 35	42.7	•	222.9	428.9	79.5	747.5	0.1	0.1	1729.7	1.9
Receivables Turnover 36	84.9	•	229.0	125.0	48.7	295.2	72.0	24.9	14.4	14.5
Total Liabilities to Net Worth 37	4.6	•	15.5	13.5	3.3	3.9	2.3	1.8	1.4	2.8
Current Assets to Working Capital 38	6.9	•	11.4	•	4.8	3.6	6.0	4.5	3.0	9.0
Current Liabilities to Working Capital 39	5.9	•	10.4	•	3.8	2.6	5.0	3.5	2.0	8.0
Working Capital to Net Sales 40	0.0	•	0.0	•	0.0	0.0	0.0	0.0	0.1	0.0
Inventory to Working Capital 41	0.1	•	0.0	•	0.0	0.0	0.0	0.1	•	1.1
Total Receipts to Cash Flow 42	3.5	2.0	2.9	5.0	4.4	4.6	4.9	6.4	4.6	2.4
Cost of Goods to Cash Flow 43	0.2	0.0	0.2	0.3	0.2	0.1	0.0	0.0	0.1	0.2
Cash Flow to Total Debt 44	1.6	•	2.5	0.9	0.9	1.0	1.0	1.0	0.6	1.0

Selected Financial Factors (in Percentages)

	•	•	•	•	•	•	•	•	•	•
Debt Ratio 45	82.3	•	93.9	93.1	76.5	79.4	69.4	64.5	58.5	73.7
Return on Total Assets 46	43.7	•	87.4	21.9	20.4	15.1	17.1	8.0	14.7	11.7
Return on Equity Before Income Taxes 47	233.0	•	1388.8	285.1	79.7	65.5	48.1	15.0	31.0	37.5
Return on Equity After Income Taxes 48	227.7	•	1375.7	271.2	78.0	57.7	44.5	12.0	27.3	27.9
Profit Margin (Before Income Tax) 49	9.1	17.4	12.4	4.9	6.1	3.7	4.1	1.3	7.5	5.7
Profit Margin (After Income Tax) 50	8.8	17.2	12.3	4.7	6.0	3.3	3.8	1.0	6.6	4.2

Table II

Corporations with Net Income

LEGAL SERVICES

MONEY AMOUNTS AND SIZE OF ASSETS IN THOUSANDS OF DOLLARS

Item Description for Accounting Period 7/07 Through 6/08	Total	Zero Assets	Under 500	500 to 1,000	1,000 to 5,000	5,000 to 10,000	10,000 to 25,000	25,000 to 50,000	50,000 to 100,000	100,000 to 250,000	250,000 to 500,000	500,000 to 2,500,000	2,500,000 and over
Number of Enterprises **1**	77618	10640	62916	1689	2128	110	105	16	•	•	0	0	0

Revenues ($ in Thousands)

	Total	Zero Assets	Under 500	500 to 1,000	1,000 to 5,000	5,000 to 10,000	10,000 to 25,000	25,000 to 50,000	50,000 to 100,000	100,000 to 250,000	250,000 to 500,000	500,000 to 2,500,000	2,500,000 and over
Net Sales **2**	70768346	1615979	36445474	5768520	11646484	3125019	6477107	3460327	•	•	0	0	0
Interest **3**	80962	131	21620	13711	14754	9966	8982	7103	•	•	0	0	0
Rents **4**	39238	0	12287	8514	6824	7174	121	3631	•	•	0	0	0
Royalties **5**	400	0	0	0	0	0	0	39	•	•	0	0	0
Other Portfolio Income **6**	82760	573	26907	1913	34221	3464	1674	7468	•	•	0	0	0
Other Receipts **7**	2422265	61607	1759467	174314	242173	7003	117848	42757	•	•	0	0	0
Total Receipts **8**	73393971	1678290	38265755	5966972	11944456	3152626	6605732	3521325	•	•	0	0	0
Average Total Receipts **9**	946	158	608	3533	5613	28660	62912	220083	•	•	•	•	•

Operating Costs/Operating Income (%)

	Total	Zero Assets	Under 500	500 to 1,000	1,000 to 5,000	5,000 to 10,000	10,000 to 25,000	25,000 to 50,000	50,000 to 100,000	100,000 to 250,000	250,000 to 500,000	500,000 to 2,500,000	2,500,000 and over
Cost of Operations **10**	3.5	•	4.4	7.0	3.3	2.0	•	•	•	•	•	•	•
Salaries and Wages **11**	29.7	16.9	22.0	27.3	32.6	35.7	54.6	55.2	•	•	•	•	•
Taxes Paid **12**	3.4	4.8	3.4	3.3	3.3	3.1	3.3	3.3	•	•	•	•	•
Interest Paid **13**	0.4	0.5	0.3	0.3	0.6	0.3	0.6	0.5	•	•	•	•	•
Depreciation **14**	0.7	1.0	0.5	0.5	0.7	0.8	1.0	1.1	•	•	•	•	•
Amortization and Depletion **15**	0.0	0.0	0.0	0.0	0.0	0.0	0.0	0.0	•	•	•	•	•
Pensions and Other Deferred Comp. **16**	2.0	0.4	1.8	1.3	2.1	2.3	3.1	3.1	•	•	•	•	•
Employee Benefits **17**	1.9	1.2	1.7	2.1	2.2	1.4	2.3	2.5	•	•	•	•	•
Advertising **18**	2.2	4.2	2.2	2.5	3.5	1.5	0.9	0.5	•	•	•	•	•
Other Expenses **19**	24.9	31.6	26.6	18.2	23.1	22.5	21.8	22.2	•	•	•	•	•
Officers' Compensation **20**	21.3	10.7	24.3	32.0	20.4	24.8	9.2	11.3	•	•	•	•	•
Operating Margin **21**	9.9	28.7	12.7	5.5	8.2	5.6	3.0	0.2	•	•	•	•	•
Operating Margin Before Officers' Comp. **22**	31.2	39.4	37.0	37.4	28.6	30.5	12.3	11.5	•	•	•	•	•

Selected Average Balance Sheet ($ in Thousands)

Net Receivables 23	11	0	3	19	145	171	1055	6477
Inventories 24	0	0	0	0	4	1	38	0
Net Property, Plant and Equipment 25	31	0	12	91	258	1450	4004	11086
Total Assets 26	189	0	85	756	1744	6950	15125	35531
Notes and Loans Payable 27	49	0	24	252	392	1264	4606	7724
All Other Liabilities 28	85	0	40	390	787	2877	5395	15617
Net Worth 29	55	0	21	114	565	2809	5125	12189

Selected Financial Ratios (Times to 1)

Current Ratio 30	1.3	•	1.3	1.0	1.4	1.6	1.3	1.3
Quick Ratio 31	0.9	•	1.0	0.8	0.8	0.9	0.7	0.9
Net Sales to Working Capital 32	34.1	•	52.4	278.4	15.2	18.1	31.7	40.1
Coverage Ratio 33	33.2	71.5	57.6	29.3	19.3	21.6	9.2	5.0
Total Asset Turnover 34	4.8	•	6.8	4.5	3.1	4.1	4.1	6.1
Inventory Turnover 35	97.6	•	133.0	•	45.0	734.8	•	•
Receivables Turnover 36	85.4	•	223.3	153.8	42.6	281.9	72.6	31.1
Total Liabilities to Net Worth 37	2.5	•	3.0	5.6	2.1	1.5	2.0	1.9
Current Assets to Working Capital 38	4.4	•	4.6	42.1	3.4	2.7	4.5	4.0
Current Liabilities to Working Capital 39	3.4	•	3.6	41.1	2.4	1.7	3.5	3.0
Working Capital to Net Sales 40	0.0	•	0.0	0.0	0.1	0.1	0.0	0.0
Inventory to Working Capital 41	0.0	•	0.0	•	0.0	0.0	•	•
Total Receipts to Cash Flow 42	3.1	1.7	2.6	4.6	3.5	4.1	4.9	6.2
Cost of Goods to Cash Flow 43	0.1	•	0.1	0.3	0.1	0.1	•	•
Cash Flow to Total Debt 44	2.2	•	3.5	1.2	1.3	1.7	1.3	1.5

Selected Financial Factors (in Percentages)

Debt Ratio 45	71.1	•	75.2	84.9	67.6	59.6	66.1	65.7
Return on Total Assets 46	67.7	•	122.2	41.8	35.5	27.9	23.0	15.1
Return on Equity Before Income Taxes 47	226.8	•	484.1	266.7	103.8	65.8	60.5	35.3
Return on Equity After Income Taxes 48	222.4	•	480.0	256.8	102.0	59.3	56.5	30.5
Profit Margin (Before Income Tax) 49	13.6	32.5	17.7	8.9	10.7	6.5	5.0	2.0
Profit Margin (After Income Tax) 50	13.3	32.3	17.5	8.6	10.5	5.9	4.7	1.7

Table I

Corporations with and without Net Income

ACCOUNTING, TAX PREPARATION, BOOKKEEPING, AND PAYROLL SERVICES

MONEY AMOUNTS AND SIZE OF ASSETS IN THOUSANDS OF DOLLARS

Item Description for Accounting Period 7/07 Through 6/08		Total	Zero Assets	Under 500	500 to 1,000	1,000 to 5,000	5,000 to 10,000	10,000 to 25,000	25,000 to 50,000	50,000 to 100,000	100,000 to 250,000	250,000 to 500,000	500,000 to 2,500,000	2,500,000 and over
Number of Enterprises	1	77416	19368	55993	1168	668	133	55	13	3	13	0	3	0
Revenues ($ in Thousands)														
Net Sales	2	38000489	1694402	19402266	2761241	3296976	2918239	2507005	180130	170680	1215025	0	3854526	0
Interest	3	998743	1859	18567	3673	10584	8010	2514	9372	90	29595	0	914479	0
Rents	4	17116	0	4684	8127	1562	47	1865	0	0	0	0	831	0
Royalties	5	335362	13399	2114	0	0	0	712	0	0	431	0	318705	0
Other Portfolio Income	6	110466	200	98975	155	950	5821	777	230	0	184	0	3174	0
Other Receipts	7	583312	135165	113766	21073	9335	16988	16495	760	14	36097	0	233619	0
Total Receipts	8	40045488	1845025	19640372	2794269	3319407	2949105	2529368	190492	170784	1281332	0	5325334	0
Average Total Receipts	9	517	95	351	2392	4969	22174	45989	14653	56928	98564	•	1775111	•
Operating Costs/Operating Income (%)														
Cost of Operations	10	15.1	0.3	4.5	15.8	13.8	70.4	68.9	8.2	71.4	2.0	•	0.7	•
Salaries and Wages	11	31.7	23.6	33.6	28.6	41.6	6.4	8.5	27.8	9.0	45.4	•	50.3	•
Taxes Paid	12	4.8	3.2	5.0	3.7	4.4	3.7	6.4	3.8	1.3	2.8	•	5.9	•
Interest Paid	13	2.0	0.9	0.5	0.9	0.8	0.5	0.5	3.3	2.8	4.7	•	13.0	•
Depreciation	14	1.1	1.6	0.8	1.2	0.7	0.3	1.0	2.5	0.6	2.0	•	3.3	•
Amortization and Depletion	15	1.5	0.3	0.3	0.1	0.5	0.1	0.2	1.1	0.0	2.7	•	11.4	•
Pensions and Other Deferred Comp.	16	1.5	0.9	2.1	1.4	1.4	0.3	0.2	0.4	0.1	0.3	•	0.9	•
Employee Benefits	17	2.1	2.9	2.1	2.8	2.5	0.5	2.1	0.5	0.9	2.7	•	2.6	•
Advertising	18	1.1	0.9	0.8	0.2	0.6	1.9	0.2	0.5	0.1	1.5	•	3.9	•
Other Expenses	19	25.8	67.2	18.7	23.0	19.6	9.4	8.8	36.3	8.3	32.6	•	72.1	•
Officers' Compensation	20	16.1	15.8	25.3	15.3	10.5	3.0	2.6	4.0	1.5	1.5	•	0.2	•
Operating Margin	21	•	•	6.4	7.0	3.8	3.6	0.5	11.6	4.0	1.7	•	•	•
Operating Margin Before Officers' Comp.	22	13.4	•	31.7	22.3	14.3	6.6	3.2	15.6	5.5	3.2	•	•	•

Selected Average Balance Sheet ($ in Thousands)

	1	2	3	4	5	6	7	8	9	10	11	12
Net Receivables 23	137	0	6	142	125	908	4180	1504	10774	38659	3042898	•
Inventories 24	1	0	0	0	2	0	59	18	304	474	9774	•
Net Property, Plant and Equipment 25	26	0	13	318	206	349	1172	1087	1960	9319	161346	•
Total Assets 26	417	0	59	724	1746	6292	15441	34342	57158	161339	7519571	•
Notes and Loans Payable 27	177	0	30	312	747	985	4764	829	11635	39561	3397803	•
All Other Liabilities 28	175	0	11	150	486	3025	7387	28945	27989	69019	3421532	•
Net Worth 29	65	0	18	263	514	2283	3289	4568	17534	52759	700236	•

Selected Financial Ratios (Times to 1)

	1	2	3	4	5	6	7	8	9	10	11	12
Current Ratio 30	1.1	•	1.6	1.3	1.4	1.4	1.7	0.9	1.2	1.5	0.9	•
Quick Ratio 31	0.9	•	1.4	1.0	1.2	0.7	1.1	0.9	1.0	1.0	0.8	•
Net Sales to Working Capital 32	36.8	•	32.2	32.7	17.0	16.5	8.7	•	12.4	3.3	•	•
Coverage Ratio 33	2.3	•	15.4	10.4	6.9	11.1	4.0	6.2	2.5	2.5	•	•
Total Asset Turnover 34	1.2	•	5.8	3.3	2.8	3.5	3.0	0.4	1.0	0.6	0.2	•
Inventory Turnover 35	137.6	•	1460.5	2499.2	381.6	•	529.6	62.3	133.6	4.0	0.9	•
Receivables Turnover 36	5.7	•	64.9	19.4	17.6	29.6	11.8	3.4	2.7	3.6	0.7	•
Total Liabilities to Net Worth 37	5.4	•	2.2	1.8	2.4	1.8	3.7	6.5	2.3	2.1	9.7	•
Current Assets to Working Capital 38	16.6	•	2.7	4.5	3.5	3.8	2.4	•	6.2	2.9	•	•
Current Liabilities to Working Capital 39	15.6	•	1.7	3.5	2.5	2.8	1.4	•	5.2	1.9	•	•
Working Capital to Net Sales 40	0.0	•	0.0	0.0	0.1	0.1	0.1	•	0.1	0.3	•	•
Inventory to Working Capital 41	0.0	•	0.0	0.0	0.0	0.0	0.0	•	0.1	0.0	•	•
Total Receipts to Cash Flow 42	4.5	2.1	5.1	3.6	5.4	10.1	11.2	2.0	10.0	2.7	3.0	•
Cost of Goods to Cash Flow 43	0.7	0.0	0.2	0.6	0.7	7.1	7.7	0.2	7.1	0.1	0.0	•
Cash Flow to Total Debt 44	0.3	•	1.7	1.4	0.7	0.5	0.3	0.2	0.1	0.3	0.1	•

Selected Financial Factors (in Percentages)

	1	2	3	4	5	6	7	8	9	10	11	12
Debt Ratio 45	84.3	•	69.1	63.7	70.6	63.7	78.7	86.7	69.3	67.3	90.7	•
Return on Total Assets 46	5.4	•	47.7	29.7	14.7	17.7	5.6	8.3	6.8	6.9	•	•
Return on Equity Before Income Taxes 47	19.7	•	144.4	73.9	42.8	44.4	19.7	52.6	13.1	12.7	•	•
Return on Equity After Income Taxes 48	16.7	•	141.6	73.0	40.3	42.2	14.6	50.8	8.7	8.4	•	•
Profit Margin (Before Income Tax) 49	2.6	•	7.6	8.2	4.5	4.6	1.4	17.4	4.0	7.2	•	•
Profit Margin (After Income Tax) 50	2.2	•	7.5	8.1	4.2	4.4	1.1	16.7	2.7	4.8	•	•

ACCOUNTING, TAX PREPARATION, BOOKKEEPING, AND PAYROLL SERVICES

Table II

Corporations with Net Income

MONEY AMOUNTS AND SIZE OF ASSETS IN THOUSANDS OF DOLLARS

Item Description for Accounting Period 7/07 Through 6/08	Total	Zero Assets	Under 500	500 to 1,000	1,000 to 5,000	5,000 to 10,000	10,000 to 25,000	25,000 to 50,000	50,000 to 100,000	100,000 to 250,000	250,000 to 500,000	500,000 to 2,500,000	2,500,000 and over
Number of Enterprises **1**	55939	13306	41008	876	562	123	40	10	3	10	0	0	0
Revenues ($ in Thousands)													
Net Sales **2**	28178835	1197634	15322996	2707359	2402802	2860881	2254305	157736	170680	1104443	0	0	0
Interest **3**	62759	1412	15762	3673	6840	8010	597	2045	90	24331	0	0	0
Rents **4**	14420	0	4684	8127	1562	47	0	0	0	0	0	0	0
Royalties **5**	84307	0	2114	0	0	0	0	0	0	82193	0	0	0
Other Portfolio Income **6**	93950	177	86174	155	933	5821	488	17	0	184	0	0	0
Other Receipts **7**	215628	952	110121	16710	5601	12604	10083	794	14	58749	0	0	0
Total Receipts **8**	28649899	1200175	15541851	2736024	2417738	2887363	2265473	160592	170784	1269900	0	0	0
Average Total Receipts **9**	512	90	379	3123	4302	23474	56637	16059	56928	126990	•	•	•
Operating Costs/Operating Income (%)													
Cost of Operations **10**	18.0	0.2	1.7	16.2	18.9	71.7	76.6	4.3	71.4	0.3	•	•	•
Salaries and Wages **11**	25.1	12.2	29.4	28.3	39.0	5.2	3.6	28.5	9.0	40.0	•	•	•
Taxes Paid **12**	4.2	2.8	4.3	3.6	4.4	3.8	6.6	3.6	1.3	3.0	•	•	•
Interest Paid **13**	0.7	1.1	0.5	0.9	0.5	0.1	0.3	0.0	2.8	5.6	•	•	•
Depreciation **14**	0.9	1.5	0.8	1.1	0.7	0.3	0.4	2.6	0.6	2.5	•	•	•
Amortization and Depletion **15**	0.4	0.5	0.3	0.1	0.4	0.1	0.1	1.2	0.0	2.9	•	•	•
Pensions and Other Deferred Comp. **16**	1.5	0.8	2.2	1.4	1.4	0.3	0.1	0.3	0.1	0.5	•	•	•
Employee Benefits **17**	1.9	2.5	2.0	2.8	1.8	0.3	1.9	0.0	0.9	2.4	•	•	•
Advertising **18**	0.7	0.6	0.6	0.2	0.3	1.9	0.2	0.5	0.1	1.5	•	•	•
Other Expenses **19**	21.7	41.6	24.0	22.5	18.6	8.9	5.6	37.2	8.3	39.1	•	•	•
Officers' Compensation **20**	16.7	13.9	24.9	15.2	7.2	3.0	1.1	3.0	1.5	1.3	•	•	•
Operating Margin **21**	8.2	22.5	9.3	7.8	6.9	4.4	3.7	18.7	4.0	0.8	•	•	•
Operating Margin Before Officers' Comp. **22**	24.9	36.3	34.2	23.0	14.1	7.4	4.7	21.6	5.5	2.1	•	•	•

Selected Average Balance Sheet ($ in Thousands)

	1	2	3	4	5	6	7	8	9	10
Net Receivables 23	17	0	5	93	146	867	5007	1943	10774	25084
Inventories 24	1	0	0	0	2	0	76	24	302	616
Net Property, Plant and Equipment 25	21	0	15	275	192	365	453	1236	1960	12278
Total Assets 26		143	62	661	1668	6392	15226	33580	57158	201384
Notes and Loans Payable 27		48	28	359	579	418	1608	92	11635	75427
All Other Liabilities 28		49	11	200	524	3172	8154	26704	27989	74842
Net Worth 29		46	24	102	565	2802	5464	6784	17534	51114

Selected Financial Ratios (Times to 1)

	1	2	3	4	5	6	7	8	9	10
Current Ratio 30	1.5	•	1.8	1.0	1.7	1.6	1.5	1.1	1.2	1.3
Quick Ratio 31	1.1	•	1.6	0.7	1.5	0.8	1.0	1.1	1.0	0.8
Net Sales to Working Capital 32	21.1	•	30.0	•	10.6	11.8	12.6	6.0	12.4	7.9
Coverage Ratio 33	14.4	21.2	21.2	11.3	14.7	40.5	16.6	449.4	2.5	3.8
Total Asset Turnover 34	3.5	•	6.0	4.7	2.6	3.6	3.7	0.5	1.0	0.5
Inventory Turnover 35	140.7	•	1070.2	2499.2	381.6	•	567.0	28.6	134.6	0.5
Receivables Turnover 36	16.9	•	79.5	32.7	20.8	44.4	12.1	3.0	2.9	6.8
Total Liabilities to Net Worth 37	2.1	•	1.6	5.5	2.0	1.3	1.8	3.9	2.3	2.9
Current Assets to Working Capital 38	3.2	•	2.3	•	2.5	2.7	2.8	11.1	6.2	4.7
Current Liabilities to Working Capital 39	2.2	•	1.3	•	1.5	1.7	1.8	10.1	5.2	3.7
Working Capital to Net Sales 40	0.0	•	0.0	•	0.1	0.1	0.1	0.2	0.1	0.1
Inventory to Working Capital 41	0.0	•	•	•	0.0	•	0.0	0.0	0.0	0.0
Total Receipts to Cash Flow 42	3.8	1.9	3.5	3.6	4.7	9.8	10.9	1.8	10.0	2.0
Cost of Goods to Cash Flow 43	0.7	0.0	0.1	0.6	0.9	7.0	8.3	0.1	7.1	0.0
Cash Flow to Total Debt 44	1.4	•	2.7	1.5	0.8	0.7	0.5	0.3	0.1	0.4

Selected Financial Factors (in Percentages)

	1	2	3	4	5	6	7	8	9	10
Debt Ratio 45	67.8	•	61.9	84.6	66.2	56.2	64.1	79.8	69.3	74.6
Return on Total Assets 46	37.5	•	67.3	45.3	20.6	19.7	16.3	9.6	6.8	11.7
Return on Equity Before Income Taxes 47	108.3	•	168.6	268.8	56.8	43.9	42.8	47.6	13.1	34.0
Return on Equity After Income Taxes 48	103.6	•	165.7	265.8	54.2	42.0	38.5	46.0	8.7	23.3
Profit Margin (Before Income Tax) 49	9.9	22.7	10.7	8.8	7.5	5.3	4.1	20.5	4.0	15.7
Profit Margin (After Income Tax) 50	9.5	22.0	10.5	8.7	7.2	5.1	3.7	19.8	2.7	10.8

Table I

Corporations with and without Net Income

ARCHITECTURAL, ENGINEERING, AND RELATED SERVICES

MONEY AMOUNTS AND SIZE OF ASSETS IN THOUSANDS OF DOLLARS

Item Description for Accounting Period 7/07 Through 6/08	Total	Zero Assets	Under 500	500 to 1,000	1,000 to 5,000	5,000 to 10,000	10,000 to 25,000	25,000 to 50,000	50,000 to 100,000	100,000 to 250,000	250,000 to 500,000	500,000 to 2,500,000	2,500,000 and over
Number of Enterprises **1**	100699	16529	76002	3567	3293	638	372	123	65	55	23	25	7
Revenues ($ in Thousands)													
Net Sales **2**	214650452	2189635	63953896	8501023	21480888	12056390	12491933	7691776	8090498	12666388	9999273	26479461	29049292
Interest **3**	947406	1517	49728	4499	29465	17741	48520	16086	22124	80387	67915	258776	350648
Rents **4**	132177	58	13099	0	10174	2102	1006	5321	8541	16254	12493	25807	37321
Royalties **5**	85318	17	0	0	0	1920	70	2203	193	10502	2019	24220	44172
Other Portfolio Income **6**	525710	4699	16664	25940	55216	32068	10211	8517	9880	84333	40146	152242	85797
Other Receipts **7**	2336932	82744	90176	131509	144142	91119	157306	54929	129268	414513	179541	444856	416829
Total Receipts **8**	218677995	2278670	64123563	8662971	21719885	12201340	12709046	7778832	8260504	13272377	10301387	27385362	29984059
Average Total Receipts **9**	2172	138	844	2429	6596	19124	34164	63243	127085	241316	447886	1095414	4283437
Operating Costs/Operating Income (%)													
Cost of Operations **10**	41.0	12.4	27.8	30.9	32.1	36.3	32.4	45.7	42.7	53.4	49.6	57.1	63.0
Salaries and Wages **11**	19.4	28.6	21.3	19.0	23.2	23.2	25.9	17.7	20.7	16.8	18.5	12.6	14.7
Taxes Paid **12**	2.8	3.9	3.4	2.9	3.8	3.4	3.6	3.0	2.5	2.4	2.3	1.9	1.4
Interest Paid **13**	1.0	1.0	0.4	1.4	0.5	0.6	0.7	0.7	0.7	1.4	2.3	2.0	1.7
Depreciation **14**	1.2	1.5	0.9	1.6	1.6	1.7	1.6	1.6	1.5	1.7	1.8	0.8	1.1
Amortization and Depletion **15**	0.3	0.0	0.0	0.1	0.1	0.2	0.4	0.2	0.3	0.5	1.4	0.5	0.7
Pensions and Other Deferred Comp. **16**	1.2	1.7	1.3	0.8	1.6	1.4	1.4	1.2	1.2	1.2	0.9	0.6	1.0
Employee Benefits **17**	2.2	2.1	1.7	1.5	2.2	2.4	3.0	2.1	3.1	2.3	3.3	2.3	2.6
Advertising **18**	0.3	0.7	0.4	0.8	0.4	0.3	0.4	0.3	0.2	0.2	0.2	0.2	0.0
Other Expenses **19**	20.2	32.2	22.4	27.8	20.7	19.6	22.6	19.6	22.1	18.2	16.3	19.6	13.5
Officers' Compensation **20**	7.2	12.2	15.3	9.4	7.3	5.4	5.6	3.4	3.2	2.0	1.5	1.8	0.8
Operating Margin **21**	3.1	3.8	5.0	3.8	6.4	5.5	2.5	4.3	1.8	0.0	1.9	0.6	•
Operating Margin Before Officers' Comp. **22**	10.3	15.9	20.4	13.2	13.7	11.0	8.0	7.7	5.0	2.0	3.4	2.4	0.2

Selected Average Balance Sheet ($ in Thousands)

Net Receivables 23	279	0	10	187	695	2604	6381	15007	24013	47445	96010	256791	807378
Inventories 24	33	0	1	22	83	170	530	1332	2278	5792	13341	16626	181002
Net Property, Plant and Equipment 25	132	0	27	185	409	1310	2832	4934	10527	21188	40615	83277	261437
Total Assets 26	1123	0	86	711	2208	6940	15231	34402	69268	158403	364572	1025711	5020024
Notes and Loans Payable 27	312	0	54	309	552	1857	3666	8964	14401	32936	94648	261260	1325457
All Other Liabilities 28	396	0	28	237	560	2232	5191	14359	28641	61071	123981	371939	1800226
Net Worth 29	415	0	4	165	1096	2851	6374	11079	26226	64395	145943	392512	1894341

Selected Financial Ratios (Times to 1)

Current Ratio 30	1.4	•	1.3	1.2	2.2	1.8	1.6	1.5	1.5	1.5	1.6	1.4	1.1
Quick Ratio 31	1.0	•	1.1	0.9	1.8	1.5	1.3	1.2	1.1	1.2	1.3	1.0	0.6
Net Sales to Working Capital 32	13.3	•	96.6	28.9	8.2	10.0	8.5	7.7	8.8	7.1	6.7	7.7	23.6
Coverage Ratio 33	5.9	9.0	13.7	5.2	14.6	11.5	7.2	8.4	6.5	4.6	3.2	3.1	2.7
Total Asset Turnover 34	1.9	•	9.7	3.4	3.0	2.7	2.2	1.8	1.8	1.5	1.2	1.0	0.8
Inventory Turnover 35	26.4	•	323.4	33.5	25.2	40.2	20.6	21.4	23.3	21.2	16.2	36.3	14.4
Receivables Turnover 36	8.1	•	85.3	13.4	10.3	7.3	6.1	4.6	4.9	5.6	4.5	4.6	5.0
Total Liabilities to Net Worth 37	1.7	•	18.4	3.3	1.0	1.4	1.4	2.1	1.6	1.5	1.5	1.6	1.7
Current Assets to Working Capital 38	3.5	•	4.9	5.1	1.9	2.3	2.7	3.0	3.1	2.9	2.5	3.3	11.6
Current Liabilities to Working Capital 39	2.5	•	3.9	4.1	0.9	1.3	1.7	2.0	2.1	1.9	1.5	2.3	10.6
Working Capital to Net Sales 40	0.1	•	0.0	0.0	0.1	0.1	0.1	0.1	0.1	0.1	0.1	0.1	0.0
Inventory to Working Capital 41	0.2	•	0.1	0.4	0.1	0.1	0.2	0.2	0.1	0.2	0.2	0.1	1.1
Total Receipts to Cash Flow 42	4.7	2.8	4.3	3.5	4.1	4.5	4.4	4.6	4.5	5.4	5.8	4.8	7.8
Cost of Goods to Cash Flow 43	1.9	0.4	1.2	1.1	1.3	1.6	1.4	1.4	1.9	2.9	2.9	2.7	4.9
Cash Flow to Total Debt 44	0.6	•	2.4	1.2	1.4	1.0	0.9	0.6	0.6	0.5	0.3	0.4	0.2

Selected Financial Factors (in Percentages)

Debt Ratio 45	63.1	•	94.8	76.8	50.4	58.9	58.2	67.8	62.1	59.3	60.0	61.7	62.3
Return on Total Assets 46	11.5	•	55.4	23.7	23.7	20.0	10.8	11.2	8.7	9.0	8.6	6.3	3.7
Return on Equity Before Income Taxes 47	25.7	•	996.1	82.3	44.5	44.5	22.3	30.6	19.5	17.2	14.7	11.1	6.2
Return on Equity After Income Taxes 48	22.3	•	980.3	80.7	42.2	40.7	17.3	24.9	14.9	11.6	9.5	7.9	4.3
Profit Margin (Before Income Tax) 49	5.0	7.8	5.3	5.7	7.5	6.7	4.2	5.4	4.1	4.8	4.9	4.1	2.8
Profit Margin (After Income Tax) 50	4.3	7.1	5.2	5.6	7.1	6.1	3.3	4.4	3.1	3.2	3.2	2.9	2.0

Table II

Corporations with Net Income

ARCHITECTURAL, ENGINEERING, AND RELATED SERVICES

MONEY AMOUNTS AND SIZE OF ASSETS IN THOUSANDS OF DOLLARS

Item Description for Accounting Period 7/07 Through 6/08		Total	Zero Assets	Under 500	500 to 1,000	1,000 to 5,000	5,000 to 10,000	10,000 to 25,000	25,000 to 50,000	50,000 to 100,000	100,000 to 250,000	250,000 to 500,000	500,000 to 2,500,000	2,500,000 and over
Number of Enterprises	1	69792	8842	54719	2626	2556	526	288	100	51	45	•	18	•
Revenues ($ in Thousands)														
Net Sales	2	185156643	1613079	54540059	6764712	17324515	10020317	10364216	6818185	7183681	11633067	•	23719067	•
Interest	3	729329	815	45124	3956	26242	14805	42296	11528	13050	71004	•	169536	•
Rents	4	107083	17	12137	0	2771	2102	960	5281	8366	16228	•	10840	•
Royalties	5	53747	17	0	0	0	1920	56	2203	185	10431	•	4759	•
Other Portfolio Income	6	434776	1115	8520	25776	54560	31878	9865	7375	7718	82965	•	96486	•
Other Receipts	7	2209101	81471	110664	128050	135450	85762	149404	77057	89604	408069	•	360554	•
Total Receipts	8	188690679	1696514	54716504	6922494	17543538	10156784	10566797	6921629	7302604	12221764	•	24361242	•
Average Total Receipts	9	2704	192	1000	2636	6864	19309	36690	69216	143188	271595	•	1353402	•
Operating Costs/Operating Income (%)														
Cost of Operations	10	40.7	13.5	28.2	29.3	26.7	28.9	31.0	45.0	41.2	53.0	•	54.4	•
Salaries and Wages	11	19.3	24.0	20.5	18.7	25.7	25.8	25.9	17.9	20.2	17.1	•	13.6	•
Taxes Paid	12	2.7	3.3	3.1	2.7	3.9	3.8	3.7	3.0	2.4	2.4	•	2.0	•
Interest Paid	13	0.7	0.5	0.3	1.1	0.3	0.5	0.6	0.6	0.7	0.7	•	1.3	•
Depreciation	14	1.1	1.2	0.7	1.6	1.5	1.6	1.4	1.4	1.4	1.3	•	0.8	•
Amortization and Depletion	15	0.2	0.0	0.0	0.1	0.0	0.1	0.2	0.2	0.2	0.4	•	0.3	•
Pensions and Other Deferred Comp.	16	1.1	1.4	1.3	0.6	1.4	1.7	1.5	1.3	1.2	1.3	•	0.5	•
Employee Benefits	17	2.2	1.8	1.6	1.5	2.1	2.7	3.1	2.2	3.1	2.3	•	2.5	•
Advertising	18	0.3	0.6	0.3	0.9	0.3	0.3	0.3	0.3	0.2	0.2	•	0.2	•
Other Expenses	19	19.6	27.1	21.6	27.3	20.5	20.9	22.2	18.8	22.6	18.4	•	20.4	•
Officers' Compensation	20	7.1	10.5	15.2	8.8	8.0	6.2	5.7	3.6	2.9	2.1	•	1.6	•
Operating Margin	21	4.9	16.0	7.1	7.3	9.3	7.4	4.5	5.6	3.9	0.9	•	2.4	•
Operating Margin Before Officers' Comp.	22	11.9	26.5	22.3	16.1	17.4	13.7	10.2	9.2	6.8	2.9	•	4.0	•

Selected Average Balance Sheet ($ in Thousands)

	•	•	•	•	•	•	•	•	•	•	•
Net Receivables 23	342	0	9	167	726	2843	6284	16073	25750	50171	306319
Inventories 24	41	0	1	25	88	119	536	1481	2427	6132	20282
Net Property, Plant and Equipment 25	141	0	25	177	359	1359	2812	5209	10257	20386	86783
Total Assets 26	1250	0	79	714	2199	7144	15447	34881	69105	155470	1004764
Notes and Loans Payable 27	312	0	40	311	365	1582	3214	7835	13401	24187	233636
All Other Liabilities 28	444	0	26	171	439	2412	5003	13611	28745	61298	367259
Net Worth 29	494	0	13	232	1394	3151	7230	13435	26959	69985	403868

Selected Financial Ratios (Times to 1)

	•	•	•	•	•	•	•	•	•	•	•
Current Ratio 30	1.5	•	1.2	1.4	3.0	1.9	1.7	1.8	1.5	1.6	1.5
Quick Ratio 31	1.1	•	1.1	1.1	2.7	1.6	1.3	1.5	1.1	1.3	1.1
Net Sales to Working Capital 32	12.0	•	125.2	21.3	6.6	8.7	8.4	6.1	10.0	7.0	7.2
Coverage Ratio 33	10.2	45.9	26.0	9.5	32.7	18.9	12.3	12.6	9.4	9.2	5.1
Total Asset Turnover 34	2.1	•	12.6	3.6	3.1	2.7	2.3	2.0	2.0	1.7	1.3
Inventory Turnover 35	26.2	•	347.8	30.1	20.6	46.3	20.8	20.7	23.9	22.3	35.3
Receivables Turnover 36	8.2	•	109.6	15.3	10.3	7.4	6.2	4.7	5.2	6.0	4.7
Total Liabilities to Net Worth 37	1.5	•	4.9	2.1	0.6	1.3	1.1	1.6	1.6	1.2	1.5
Current Assets to Working Capital 38	3.1	•	5.4	3.4	1.5	2.2	2.5	2.2	3.1	2.6	2.9
Current Liabilities to Working Capital 39	2.1	•	4.4	2.4	0.5	1.2	1.5	1.2	2.1	1.6	1.9
Working Capital to Net Sales 40	0.1	•	0.0	0.0	0.2	0.1	0.1	0.2	0.1	0.1	0.1
Inventory to Working Capital 41	0.2	•	0.0	0.3	0.1	0.1	0.1	0.1	0.1	0.2	0.1
Total Receipts to Cash Flow 42	4.4	2.3	4.0	3.2	3.6	3.9	4.1	4.5	4.1	5.0	4.4
Cost of Goods to Cash Flow 43	1.8	0.3	1.1	0.9	1.0	1.1	1.3	2.0	1.7	2.7	2.4
Cash Flow to Total Debt 44	0.8	•	3.8	1.7	2.3	1.2	1.1	0.7	0.8	0.6	0.5

Selected Financial Factors (in Percentages)

	•	•	•	•	•	•	•	•	•	•	•
Debt Ratio 45	60.5	•	83.1	67.5	36.6	55.9	53.2	61.5	61.0	55.0	59.8
Return on Total Assets 46	16.1	•	96.9	38.8	33.7	24.7	16.4	15.2	13.4	11.1	8.5
Return on Equity Before Income Taxes 47	36.9	•	550.2	106.8	51.5	53.1	32.1	36.3	30.8	21.9	17.0
Return on Equity After Income Taxes 48	32.7	•	542.9	105.2	49.2	48.9	26.5	30.6	25.1	15.6	12.6
Profit Margin (Before Income Tax) 49	6.9	21.2	7.4	9.6	10.6	8.8	6.4	7.2	5.9	5.9	5.2
Profit Margin (After Income Tax) 50	6.1	20.2	7.3	9.5	10.1	8.1	5.3	6.0	4.8	4.2	3.9

Table I

Corporations with and without Net Income

SPECIALIZED DESIGN SERVICES

MONEY AMOUNTS AND SIZE OF ASSETS IN THOUSANDS OF DOLLARS

Item Description for Accounting Period 7/07 Through 6/08	Total	Zero Assets	Under 500	500 to 1,000	1,000 to 5,000	5,000 to 10,000	10,000 to 25,000	25,000 to 50,000	50,000 to 100,000	100,000 to 250,000	250,000 to 500,000	500,000 to 2,500,000	2,500,000 and over
Number of Enterprises **1**	42570	11741	28967	851	817	139	29	20	0	7	0	0	0
Revenues ($ in Thousands)													
Net Sales **2**	21966439	839538	12018764	1199368	2879479	1292657	783187	684154	0	2269292	0	0	0
Interest **3**	68588	2	8161	840	3944	6834	1115	7706	0	39984	0	0	0
Rents **4**	12833	0	11453	723	460	0	0	100	0	98	0	0	0
Royalties **5**	13509	0	0	0	0	3	606	0	0	12900	0	0	0
Other Portfolio Income **6**	50378	2802	20484	0	1372	3219	18076	0	0	4426	0	0	0
Other Receipts **7**	459495	291	39782	154121	16300	39174	-21860	6382	0	225304	0	0	0
Total Receipts **8**	22571242	842633	12098644	1355052	2901555	1341887	781124	698342	0	2552004	0	0	0
Average Total Receipts **9**	530	72	418	1592	3551	9654	26935	34917	•	364572	•	•	•
Operating Costs/Operating Income (%)													
Cost of Operations **10**	41.2	22.2	38.4	64.7	59.9	46.6	40.2	50.9	•	21.2	•	•	•
Salaries and Wages **11**	18.1	3.3	11.3	10.4	14.4	15.1	27.9	23.6	•	64.7	•	•	•
Taxes Paid **12**	2.6	2.9	2.5	2.3	1.8	2.5	2.7	2.1	•	4.1	•	•	•
Interest Paid **13**	0.7	1.7	0.6	0.8	0.4	0.5	0.6	1.1	•	0.9	•	•	•
Depreciation **14**	1.4	1.2	0.9	1.0	0.9	1.2	0.5	1.1	•	5.5	•	•	•
Amortization and Depletion **15**	0.1	0.0	0.0	0.4	0.1	0.1	0.3	0.0	•	0.5	•	•	•
Pensions and Other Deferred Comp. **16**	0.7	0.1	0.7	0.8	1.0	0.4	0.3	0.9	•	0.4	•	•	•
Employee Benefits **17**	1.3	0.5	0.7	1.6	0.9	1.4	1.2	2.4	•	4.4	•	•	•
Advertising **18**	1.0	0.9	1.4	0.1	1.0	0.3	0.5	0.3	•	0.7	•	•	•
Other Expenses **19**	24.6	52.0	28.6	17.3	15.2	16.7	16.4	10.1	•	20.4	•	•	•
Officers' Compensation **20**	7.9	11.4	9.6	10.3	5.8	2.8	2.4	7.3	•	3.9	•	•	•
Operating Margin **21**	0.4	3.8	5.1	•		12.5	6.9	0.3	•	•	•	•	•
Operating Margin Before Officers' Comp. **22**	8.3	15.2	14.7	0.5	4.4	15.3	9.3	7.6	•	•	•	•	•

Selected Average Balance Sheet ($ in Thousands)

Net Receivables 23	46	0	12	374	289	1186	3885	6673	•	96052
Inventories 24	24	0	6	196	541	548	498	2433	•	15053
Net Property, Plant and Equipment 25	35	0	17	105	314	396	766	2216	•	72472
Total Assets 26	227	0	68	745	1906	7490	15188	34255	•	477702
Notes and Loans Payable 27	68	0	58	265	689	979	1259	5607	•	22459
All Other Liabilities 28	97	0	24	358	1054	4247	7441	12580	•	171288
Net Worth 29	63	0	-13	122	164	2265	6488	16068	•	283955

Selected Financial Ratios (Times to 1)

Current Ratio 30	1.4	•	1.2	1.3	1.4	0.9	1.7	2.3	•	1.7
Quick Ratio 31	1.0	•	0.9	1.0	0.6	0.6	1.5	1.4	•	1.5
Net Sales to Working Capital 32	12.6	•	58.9	10.7	9.5	•	6.0	2.1	•	3.2
Coverage Ratio 33	5.8	3.5	10.1	4.9	•	35.1	11.6	3.1	•	3.1
Total Asset Turnover 34	2.3	•	6.1	1.9	1.8	1.2	1.8	1.0	•	0.7
Inventory Turnover 35	8.8	•	24.6	4.7	3.9	7.9	21.8	7.1	•	4.6
Receivables Turnover 36	10.9	•	27.7	4.8	10.9	7.7	8.2	8.1	•	6.8
Total Liabilities to Net Worth 37	2.6	•	•	5.1	10.7	2.3	1.3	1.1	•	0.7
Current Assets to Working Capital 38	3.5	•	6.0	4.3	3.8	•	2.3	1.8	•	2.4
Current Liabilities to Working Capital 39	2.5	•	5.0	3.3	2.8	•	1.3	0.8	•	1.4
Working Capital to Net Sales 40	0.1	•	0.0	0.1	0.1	•	0.2	0.5	•	0.3
Inventory to Working Capital 41	0.6	•	0.8	0.8	1.6	•	0.2	0.2	•	0.1
Total Receipts to Cash Flow 42	4.5	2.0	3.4	6.7	10.6	3.5	5.3	10.5	•	
Cost of Goods to Cash Flow 43	1.8	0.4	1.3	4.4	6.4	1.7	2.1	5.4	•	
Cash Flow to Total Debt 44	0.7	•	1.5	0.3	0.2	0.5	0.6	0.2	•	0.2

Selected Financial Factors (in Percentages)

Debt Ratio 45	72.4	•	119.4	83.6	91.4	69.8	57.3	53.1	•	40.6
Return on Total Assets 46	9.0	•	38.8	7.6	•	20.5	12.8	3.5	•	3.5
Return on Equity Before Income Taxes 47	27.2	•	•	37.0	•	65.9	27.4	•	•	5.0
Return on Equity After Income Taxes 48	25.3	•	•	35.9	•	58.5	27.3	•	•	1.6
Profit Margin (Before Income Tax) 49	3.3	4.2	5.7	3.2	16.1	6.6	•	•	•	2.3
Profit Margin (After Income Tax) 50	3.1	4.2	5.7	3.1	14.3	6.5	•	•	•	0.8

Table II

Corporations with Net Income

SPECIALIZED DESIGN SERVICES

MONEY AMOUNTS AND SIZE OF ASSETS IN THOUSANDS OF DOLLARS

Item Description for Accounting Period 7/07 Through 6/08	Total	Zero Assets	Under 500	500 to 1,000	1,000 to 5,000	5,000 to 10,000	10,000 to 25,000	25,000 to 50,000	50,000 to 100,000	100,000 to 250,000	250,000 to 500,000	500,000 to 2,500,000	2,500,000 and over
Number of Enterprises **1**	28477	6999	20261	595	454	128	23	12	0	4	0	0	0
Revenues ($ in Thousands)													
Net Sales **2**	15817779	550002	8393503	833333	1792711	1195006	738535	514660	0	1800030	0	0	0
Interest **3**	20709	2	6360	803	3409	6649	1099	1583	0	804	0	0	0
Rents **4**	12011	0	11453	0	460	0	0	0	0	98	0	0	0
Royalties **5**	12900	0	0	0	0	0	0	0	0	12900	0	0	0
Other Portfolio Income **6**	30497	2802	20423	0	902	3219	1011	0	0	2140	0	0	0
Other Receipts **7**	209671	131	35894	130728	14343	39173	-21914	5779	0	5535	0	0	0
Total Receipts **8**	16103567	552937	8467633	964864	1811825	1244047	718731	522022	0	1821507	0	0	0
Average Total Receipts **9**	565	79	418	1622	3991	9719	31249	43502	•	455377	•	•	•
Operating Costs/Operating Income (%)													
Cost of Operations **10**	38.7	24.0	35.3	65.8	59.9	43.4	41.7	41.6	•	20.0	•	•	•
Salaries and Wages **11**	13.6	3.0	8.9	10.8	12.6	16.1	26.0	26.2	•	30.5	•	•	•
Taxes Paid **12**	2.5	2.4	2.6	2.6	1.6	2.6	2.4	2.1	•	3.0	•	•	•
Interest Paid **13**	0.5	0.7	0.3	0.9	0.4	0.4	0.0	0.3	•	1.0	•	•	•
Depreciation **14**	1.1	0.7	0.9	0.9	1.1	1.3	0.4	0.9	•	2.0	•	•	•
Amortization and Depletion **15**	0.1	0.1	0.0	0.4	0.1	0.1	0.0	0.0	•	0.6	•	•	•
Pensions and Other Deferred Comp. **16**	0.7	0.2	0.9	0.0	1.1	0.4	0.3	1.1	•	0.5	•	•	•
Employee Benefits **17**	1.1	0.1	0.5	1.5	0.7	1.4	1.0	2.5	•	3.9	•	•	•
Advertising **18**	0.6	1.2	0.8	0.1	0.4	0.3	0.5	0.3	•	0.6	•	•	•
Other Expenses **19**	25.2	41.6	29.6	18.2	12.3	16.9	13.5	8.1	•	31.1	•	•	•
Officers' Compensation **20**	7.3	7.7	9.8	7.2	6.2	2.6	2.5	9.4	•	1.3	•	•	•
Operating Margin **21**	8.5	18.3	10.3	•	3.7	14.4	11.7	7.7	•	5.4	•	•	•
Operating Margin Before Officers' Comp. **22**	15.9	26.0	20.1	•	9.9	17.1	14.1	17.1	•	6.7	•	•	•

Selected Average Balance Sheet ($ in Thousands)

Net Receivables 23	39	•	0	8	433	326	1062	4540	9355	•	44569
Inventories 24	20	•	0	7	89	475	383	621	2048	•	14295
Net Property, Plant and Equipment 25	34	•	0	20	107	475	400	902	2092	•	48477
Total Assets 26	192	•	0	66	709	2115	7447	16009	33565	•	255661
Notes and Loans Payable 27	43	•	0	28	187	556	986	150	1805	•	36392
All Other Liabilities 28	72	•	0	19	269	831	4159	7624	8538	•	76406
Net Worth 29	77	•	0	19	253	729	2302	8234	23222	•	142864

Selected Financial Ratios (Times to 1)

Current Ratio 30	1.5	•	1.6	1.4	1.7	0.9	2.1	3.3	•	1.5
Quick Ratio 31	1.1	•	1.2	1.4	0.9	0.6	1.8	2.8	•	1.1
Net Sales to Working Capital 32	14.7	•	28.6	10.3	6.7	•	5.2	2.3	•	14.3
Coverage Ratio 33	23.7	26.7	33.0	9.5	14.1	43.7	196.4	32.8	•	7.5
Total Asset Turnover 34	2.9	•	6.3	2.0	1.9	1.3	2.0	1.3	•	1.8
Inventory Turnover 35	10.9	•	20.4	10.3	5.0	10.6	21.5	8.7	•	6.3
Receivables Turnover 36	14.5	•	29.1	5.5	11.3	10.3	8.7	5.1	•	9.4
Total Liabilities to Net Worth 37	1.5	•	2.4	1.8	1.9	2.2	0.9	0.4	•	0.8
Current Assets to Working Capital 38	3.0	•	2.7	3.7	2.4	•	1.9	1.4	•	3.1
Current Liabilities to Working Capital 39	2.0	•	1.7	2.7	1.4	•	0.9	0.4	•	2.1
Working Capital to Net Sales 40	0.1	•	0.0	0.1	0.2	•	0.2	0.4	•	0.1
Inventory to Working Capital 41	0.5	•	0.5	0.0	0.6	•	0.2	0.1	•	0.5
Total Receipts to Cash Flow 42	3.2	1.8	2.8	5.0	7.5	3.3	4.8	7.0	•	3.1
Cost of Goods to Cash Flow 43	1.2	0.4	1.0	3.3	4.5	1.4	2.0	2.9	•	0.6
Cash Flow to Total Debt 44	1.5	•	3.2	0.6	0.4	0.6	0.9	0.6	•	1.3

Selected Financial Factors (in Percentages)

Debt Ratio 45	59.7	•	70.9	64.4	65.6	69.1	48.6	30.8	•	44.1
Return on Total Assets 46	31.2	•	71.9	16.3	9.5	23.4	17.9	12.0	•	13.3
Return on Equity Before Income Taxes 47	74.0	•	239.1	40.9	25.7	74.1	34.7	16.8	•	20.6
Return on Equity After Income Taxes 48	71.8	•	237.8	40.1	23.0	66.5	34.5	12.9	•	20.5
Profit Margin (Before Income Tax) 49	10.3	18.8	11.1	7.4	4.7	18.3	8.9	9.1	•	6.5
Profit Margin (After Income Tax) 50	10.0	18.8	11.1	7.2	4.2	16.4	8.9	7.0	•	6.5

338

Table I

Corporations with and without Net Income

COMPUTER SYSTEMS DESIGN AND RELATED SERVICES

MONEY AMOUNTS AND SIZE OF ASSETS IN THOUSANDS OF DOLLARS

Item Description for Accounting Period 7/07 Through 6/08		Total	Zero Assets	Under 500	500 to 1,000	1,000 to 5,000	5,000 to 10,000	10,000 to 25,000	25,000 to 50,000	50,000 to 100,000	100,000 to 250,000	250,000 to 500,000	500,000 to 2,500,000	2,500,000 and over
Number of Enterprises	1	123245	27469	85216	3759	4636	990	634	230	122	104	31	48	6
Revenues ($ in Thousands)														
Net Sales	2	193773838	8019617	26952112	7259204	26596330	20473364	14236696	8909553	9078596	12637662	6471731	27138295	26000678
Interest	3	1696958	21331	18914	10169	70143	55608	74083	57702	68095	167317	129351	414462	609782
Rents	4	53726	740	8781	38	3114	1305	1252	3643	2102	5027	2812	20089	4823
Royalties	5	1697120	336	0	0	36410	10	15179	31253	6548	107873	79099	1070952	349460
Other Portfolio Income	6	986700	70991	77725	30	99390	55304	91935	85812	26518	37592	109423	160124	171857
Other Receipts	7	3206655	213182	145781	68214	229333	213664	106555	231476	238438	213864	149928	697548	698671
Total Receipts	8	201414997	8326197	27203313	7337655	27034720	20799255	14525700	9319439	9420297	13169335	6942344	29501470	27835271
Average Total Receipts	9	1634	303	319	1952	5831	21009	22911	40519	77216	126628	223947	614614	4639212
Operating Costs/Operating Income (%)														
Cost of Operations	10	34.8	19.9	24.5	39.1	43.2	62.1	45.5	43.3	40.9	41.6	45.1	26.3	10.7
Salaries and Wages	11	25.5	38.8	19.1	27.3	24.7	20.2	26.3	25.1	27.0	26.7	21.4	27.1	30.8
Taxes Paid	12	3.5	3.8	3.3	2.9	3.3	1.8	2.8	2.9	2.7	2.8	2.8	2.8	7.8
Interest Paid	13	2.1	1.0	0.7	0.8	1.0	0.6	1.1	1.4	1.8	2.1	3.0	3.1	5.9
Depreciation	14	1.4	0.6	0.9	1.1	0.8	0.8	1.6	1.7	1.8	1.8	2.1	2.0	2.4
Amortization and Depletion	15	1.2	0.1	0.2	0.5	0.3	0.6	0.7	1.1	1.4	2.0	3.3	1.9	2.6
Pensions and Other Deferred Comp.	16	0.8	0.4	1.4	0.5	0.8	0.7	0.6	0.6	0.3	0.3	0.4	1.0	0.7
Employee Benefits	17	2.4	1.7	1.1	2.2	2.1	1.5	2.4	3.3	1.9	2.6	2.7	3.2	4.0
Advertising	18	0.8	0.9	0.7	0.8	0.9	0.7	1.4	1.4	0.8	0.8	0.9	0.7	0.3
Other Expenses	19	25.5	31.1	28.6	20.6	20.1	13.5	20.8	20.8	22.9	20.4	21.3	33.8	36.5
Officers' Compensation	20	4.6	5.8	14.3	8.5	6.6	2.6	3.1	3.2	2.0	1.9	2.6	1.1	0.7
Operating Margin	21	•	•	5.3	•	•	•	•	•	•	•	•	•	•
Operating Margin Before Officers' Comp.	22	2.0	1.6	19.6	4.3	2.8	•	•	•	•	•	•	•	•

Selected Average Balance Sheet ($ in Thousands)

Item													
Net Receivables 23	395	0	12	233	857	2640	5486	8835	15598	30527	49426	203824	3044219
Inventories 24	15	0	2	34	40	176	349	459	1354	1951	4898	4913	24999
Net Property, Plant and Equipment 25	90	0	9	50	176	470	1095	2373	3420	7727	19491	64895	448556
Total Assets 26	1586	0	58	718	2340	7175	15589	34052	67760	162091	361993	1097090	10533861
Notes and Loans Payable 27	438	0	46	288	936	1405	3664	8241	13651	30672	84876	222347	3480349
All Other Liabilities 28	538	0	24	334	1047	4442	7284	13837	25147	50525	108627	340461	2998195
Net Worth 29	610	0	-12	96	358	1327	4641	11974	28963	80894	168489	534282	4055317

Selected Financial Ratios (Times to 1)

Item													
Current Ratio 30	1.4	•	1.2	1.4	1.6	1.2	1.5	1.3	1.4	1.5	1.5	1.8	1.1
Quick Ratio 31	1.2	•	1.0	1.3	1.4	1.0	1.3	1.0	1.1	1.1	1.2	1.4	1.0
Net Sales to Working Capital 32	7.8	•	51.6	12.6	8.6	24.7	6.0	9.4	6.8	5.6	4.9	3.2	8.7
Coverage Ratio 33	1.8	0.6	10.3	1.6	•	•	1.4	1.0	1.1	1.2	1.7	3.1	1.9
Total Asset Turnover 34	1.0	•	5.5	2.7	2.5	2.9	1.4	1.1	1.1	0.7	0.6	0.5	0.4
Inventory Turnover 35	35.8	•	40.3	22.4	61.7	73.1	29.3	36.5	22.5	25.9	19.2	30.3	18.6
Receivables Turnover 36	4.3	•	31.0	8.8	6.4	9.3	4.8	4.9	5.1	4.2	3.5	3.5	1.5
Total Liabilities to Net Worth 37	1.6	•	•	6.5	5.5	4.4	2.4	1.8	1.3	1.0	1.1	1.1	1.6
Current Assets to Working Capital 38	3.6	•	6.7	3.3	2.6	6.1	3.0	4.6	3.3	3.2	3.1	2.3	8.0
Current Liabilities to Working Capital 39	2.6	•	5.7	2.3	1.6	5.1	2.0	3.6	2.3	2.2	2.1	1.3	7.0
Working Capital to Net Sales 40	0.1	•	0.0	0.1	0.1	0.0	0.2	0.1	0.1	0.2	0.2	0.3	0.1
Inventory to Working Capital 41	0.1	•	0.3	0.3	0.1	0.2	0.1	0.1	0.1	0.1	0.1	0.0	0.1
Total Receipts to Cash Flow 42	4.2	3.6	3.2	7.2	6.6	11.8	7.4	5.8	4.9	5.3	5.4	2.8	2.7
Cost of Goods to Cash Flow 43	1.5	0.7	0.8	2.8	2.8	7.3	3.4	2.5	2.0	2.2	2.4	0.7	0.3
Cash Flow to Total Debt 44	0.4	•	1.4	0.4	0.4	0.3	0.3	0.3	0.4	0.3	0.2	0.4	0.3

Selected Financial Factors (in Percentages)

Item													
Debt Ratio 45	61.5	•	120.1	86.6	84.7	81.5	70.2	64.8	57.3	50.1	53.5	51.3	61.5
Return on Total Assets 46	3.6	377	•	•	•	•	•	1.5	2.3	2.6	3.0	4.9	4.7
Return on Equity Before Income Taxes 47	4.1	•	•	•	•	•	•	•	0.8	2.0	2.7	6.8	5.9
Return on Equity After Income Taxes 48	1.8	•	•	•	•	•	•	•	•	0.7	1.3	5.1	3.8
Profit Margin (Before Income Tax) 49	1.6	6.2	•	•	•	•	•	•	0.3	1.3	2.1	6.4	5.5
Profit Margin (After Income Tax) 50	0.7	6.1	•	•	•	•	•	•	•	0.5	1.0	4.8	3.6

Table II

Corporations with Net Income

COMPUTER SYSTEMS DESIGN AND RELATED SERVICES

MONEY AMOUNTS AND SIZE OF ASSETS IN THOUSANDS OF DOLLARS

Item Description for Accounting Period 7/07 Through 6/08	Total	Zero Assets	Under 500	500 to 1,000	1,000 to 5,000	5,000 to 10,000	10,000 to 25,000	25,000 to 50,000	50,000 to 100,000	100,000 to 250,000	250,000 to 500,000	500,000 to 2,500,000	2,500,000 and over
Number of Enterprises 1	73009	12771	53673	2570	2845	499	362	112	•	•	17	•	38
Revenues ($ in Thousands)													
Net Sales 2	152380863	6265651	21226894	5722821	21723091	16294866	10829510	5828882	•	•	3374046	•	24025587
Interest 3	928052	3390	9079	4544	28179	11881	25150	23003	•	•	99277	•	387526
Rents 4	31308	0	0	17	728	72	645	890	•	•	1951	•	19122
Royalties 5	1403631	0	0	0	29984	3	14813	31253	•	•	77689	•	1067491
Other Portfolio Income 6	785629	70988	75855	30	88624	55222	65956	71126	•	•	103475	•	156936
Other Receipts 7	2447746	67153	150960	26065	177548	185552	75899	80038	•	•	49908	•	688918
Total Receipts 8	157977229	6407182	21462788	5753477	22048154	16547596	11011973	6035192	•	•	3706346	•	26345580
Average Total Receipts 9	2164	502	400	2239	7750	33162	30420	53886	•	•	218020	•	693305
Operating Costs/Operating Income (%)													
Cost of Operations 10	33.7	15.2	25.3	42.1	45.1	67.4	49.7	44.4	•	•	38.1	•	26.1
Salaries and Wages 11	23.5	37.7	16.4	21.7	20.5	14.7	20.5	20.4	•	•	21.7	•	27.8
Taxes Paid 12	3.5	4.0	2.9	2.3	2.9	1.4	2.4	2.8	•	•	3.0	•	2.8
Interest Paid 13	1.5	0.2	0.3	0.3	0.6	0.2	0.5	0.8	•	•	2.6	•	2.6
Depreciation 14	1.2	0.2	0.5	0.9	0.6	0.4	1.0	1.2	•	•	2.2	•	1.8
Amortization and Depletion 15	1.0	0.1	0.0	0.1	0.2	0.1	0.3	0.5	•	•	2.4	•	1.6
Pensions and Other Deferred Comp. 16	0.8	0.3	1.4	0.6	0.8	0.9	0.7	0.7	•	•	0.6	•	0.9
Employee Benefits 17	2.3	1.0	0.9	1.4	1.8	1.2	2.0	3.5	•	•	2.7	•	3.4
Advertising 18	0.5	0.4	0.5	0.5	0.5	0.3	0.9	1.4	•	•	1.3	•	0.7
Other Expenses 19	23.0	25.2	26.3	14.4	14.7	8.2	14.0	15.6	•	•	21.3	•	33.5
Officers' Compensation 20	4.0	5.0	12.8	7.1	5.5	1.9	2.3	2.0	•	•	2.6	•	1.1
Operating Margin 21	4.9	10.7	12.6	8.6	6.7	3.3	5.8	6.7	•	•	1.6	•	•
Operating Margin Before Officers' Comp. 22	8.9	15.8	25.5	15.7	12.2	5.2	8.1	8.7	•	•	4.2	•	•

Selected Average Balance Sheet ($ in Thousands)

Net Receivables 23	451	0	14	248	1005	3429	6996	10821	•	50110	226674
Inventories 24	15	0	2	39	40	188	400	681	•	3610	3648
Net Property, Plant and Equipment 25	108	0	6	48	160	398	799	2819	•	15184	73831
Total Assets 26	1910	0	63	727	2368	7210	15511	33869	•	365815	1149497
Notes and Loans Payable 27	418	0	17	159	942	594	2926	6846	•	71450	210123
All Other Liabilities 28	619	0	16	187	978	3780	7370	12165	•	89294	340163
Net Worth 29	872	0	29	381	448	2836	5214	14858	•	205071	599212

Selected Financial Ratios (Times to 1)

Current Ratio 30	1.6	•	2.5	2.5	1.7	1.5	1.6	1.6	•	1.7	2.0
Quick Ratio 31	1.3	•	2.2	2.2	1.5	1.3	1.4	1.3	•	1.4	1.6
Net Sales to Working Capital 32	6.9	•	12.9	7.2	9.8	17.0	6.9	6.9	•	3.5	2.8
Coverage Ratio 33	6.7	74.5	46.9	28.1	14.6	25.2	15.7	13.9	•	5.8	4.1
Total Asset Turnover 34	1.1	•	6.3	3.1	3.2	4.5	1.9	1.5	•	0.5	0.6
Inventory Turnover 35	46.0	•	44.6	23.9	86.1	117.0	37.1	33.9	•	21.0	45.2
Receivables Turnover 36	4.6	•	32.2	9.1	6.8	10.6	5.2	5.4	•	3.0	3.8
Total Liabilities to Net Worth 37	1.2	•	1.1	0.9	4.3	1.5	2.0	1.3	•	0.8	0.9
Current Assets to Working Capital 38	2.7	•	1.7	1.7	2.4	2.9	2.7	2.8	•	2.4	2.0
Current Liabilities to Working Capital 39	1.7	•	0.7	0.7	1.4	1.9	1.7	1.8	•	1.4	1.0
Working Capital to Net Sales 40	0.1	•	0.1	0.1	0.1	0.1	0.1	0.1	•	0.3	0.4
Inventory to Working Capital 41	0.0	•	0.1	0.2	0.1	0.0	0.1	0.1	•	0.0	0.0
Total Receipts to Cash Flow 42	3.5	2.8	2.7	4.8	4.8	8.3	5.3	4.4	•	3.7	2.7
Cost of Goods to Cash Flow 43	1.2	0.4	0.7	2.0	2.2	5.6	2.6	2.0	•	1.4	0.7
Cash Flow to Total Debt 44	0.6	•	4.4	1.3	0.8	0.9	0.6	0.6	•	0.3	0.4

Selected Financial Factors (in Percentages)

Debt Ratio 45	54.3	•	53.1	47.6	81.1	60.7	66.4	56.1	•	43.9	47.9
Return on Total Assets 46	11.3	•	88.7	28.9	28.4	23.0	15.6	16.9	•	8.1	6.0
Return on Equity Before Income Taxes 47	20.9	•	185.2	53.3	140.0	56.1	43.3	35.8	•	12.0	8.7
Return on Equity After Income Taxes 48	18.2	•	183.9	50.8	131.5	52.2	36.1	31.1	•	9.9	6.8
Profit Margin (Before Income Tax) 49	8.8	13.0	13.8	9.1	8.2	4.9	7.5	10.2	•	12.4	8.3
Profit Margin (After Income Tax) 50	7.6	11.8	13.7	8.7	7.7	4.5	6.3	8.9	•	10.3	6.4

340

Table I

Corporations with and without Net Income

MANAGEMENT, SCIENTIFIC, AND TECHNICAL CONSULTING SERVICES

MONEY AMOUNTS AND SIZE OF ASSETS IN THOUSANDS OF DOLLARS

Item Description for Accounting Period 7/07 Through 6/08		Total	Zero Assets	Under 500	500 to 1,000	1,000 to 5,000	5,000 to 10,000	10,000 to 25,000	25,000 to 50,000	50,000 to 100,000	100,000 to 250,000	250,000 to 500,000	500,000 to 2,500,000	2,500,000 and over
Number of Enterprises	1	233615	50981	170011	6052	4954	674	530	169	103	72	32	30	7
Revenues ($ in Thousands)														
Net Sales	2	210906490	9773521	54205051	14380146	26830820	9546949	13488330	4861407	7581754	8965053	11028438	29023912	21221110
Interest	3	1296740	8732	43569	22400	47226	27891	33947	53186	58732	89261	113927	431090	366777
Rents	4	92923	210	8443	2282	1039	1549	4220	4059	9463	16021	8380	16311	20945
Royalties	5	651674	221	579	0	90331	0	5021	2991	11186	35915	191	75671	429568
Other Portfolio Income	6	1162918	201387	153718	25497	116393	73295	62062	121079	32510	167425	73039	55734	80779
Other Receipts	7	4761023	286569	779682	194275	881768	463261	199882	431445	200839	209541	180314	446457	486991
Total Receipts	8	218871768	10270640	55191042	14624600	27967577	10112945	13793462	5474167	7894484	9483216	11404289	30049175	22606170
Average Total Receipts	9	937	201	325	2416	5645	15004	26025	32392	76645	131711	356384	1001639	3229453
Operating Costs/Operating Income (%)														
Cost of Operations	10	33.7	53.2	19.5	43.1	56.6	24.1	45.0	26.2	35.3	34.6	53.0	22.9	28.7
Salaries and Wages	11	23.4	11.0	19.8	20.6	14.8	28.2	19.4	30.5	30.7	27.2	19.8	36.3	30.0
Taxes Paid	12	2.8	1.6	3.1	2.1	1.8	3.7	2.4	3.3	3.3	2.7	2.7	2.9	3.7
Interest Paid	13	1.1	0.3	0.4	1.4	0.4	0.7	0.8	1.7	1.6	2.8	2.4	2.0	1.7
Depreciation	14	1.0	0.8	0.7	0.7	0.5	0.6	1.4	1.7	1.8	1.6	1.0	1.5	1.2
Amortization and Depletion	15	0.5	0.2	0.0	0.1	0.2	0.2	0.2	0.8	0.8	1.5	1.1	1.0	0.8
Pensions and Other Deferred Comp.	16	1.4	0.6	2.0	0.6	0.6	1.1	1.1	1.5	1.3	1.0	0.3	1.9	2.3
Employee Benefits	17	1.9	2.1	1.6	0.9	1.1	2.2	1.8	2.5	2.9	2.5	2.5	2.9	1.6
Advertising	18	0.7	0.4	1.1	1.0	0.7	0.2	0.5	0.6	0.4	1.1	0.7	0.6	0.1
Other Expenses	19	23.1	21.3	25.3	22.2	16.5	25.0	18.2	30.6	22.8	24.4	13.7	24.7	30.1
Officers' Compensation	20	7.8	8.0	18.0	3.9	6.9	13.0	3.5	4.5	3.8	2.0	1.0	3.0	0.7
Operating Margin	21	2.6	0.5	8.5	3.5	•	1.0	5.6	•	•	•	1.8	0.3	•
Operating Margin Before Officers' Comp.	22	10.4	8.5	26.5	7.4	6.8	14.0	9.2	0.6	0.6	0.6	2.7	3.3	•

Selected Average Balance Sheet ($ in Thousands)

Line Item												
Net Receivables 23	129	7	188	442	1711	4887	6851	17473	34555	70030	236901	1025126
Inventories 24	10	0	12	52	84	422	461	862	3274	7490	22961	20695
Net Property, Plant and Equipment 25	50	0	121	294	563	1828	3224	8203	13176	27163	71751	159470
Total Assets 26	585	58	693	2107	7056	15149	35195	69310	150127	355114	1089022	4488762
Notes and Loans Payable 27	189	42	746	678	1688	4396	8151	18565	49227	97350	255543	1150118
All Other Liabilities 28	217	16	212	709	2651	4831	10484	23087	44539	124136	448514	2000735
Net Worth 29	179	-0	-264	720	2718	5922	16560	27658	56361	133628	384965	1337909

Selected Financial Ratios (Times to 1)

Line Item													
Current Ratio 30	1.5	•	1.9	1.8	1.7	1.5	1.5	1.4	1.3	1.5	1.2	1.4	1.4
Quick Ratio 31	1.2	•	1.6	1.5	1.3	1.2	1.0	1.1	1.1	1.1	0.9	1.0	1.2
Net Sales to Working Capital 32	9.9	•	18.3	12.5	11.6	9.5	8.7	5.8	8.8	5.8	17.7	7.7	4.5
Coverage Ratio 33	6.7	19.3	29.8	4.8	10.4	10.5	6.2	0.8	0.8	2.6	3.2	3.2	4.3
Total Asset Turnover 34	1.5	•	5.5	3.4	2.6	2.0	1.7	0.8	1.1	0.8	1.0	0.9	0.7
Inventory Turnover 35	31.1	•	51.8	88.3	58.8	40.8	27.1	16.4	30.1	13.2	24.4	9.6	42.1
Receivables Turnover 36	7.7	•	44.3	14.8	11.3	8.5	5.6	4.7	4.3	3.7	6.8	4.5	3.5
Total Liabilities to Net Worth 37	2.3	•	•	1.9	1.6	1.6	1.1	1.1	1.5	1.7	1.8	2.4	
Current Assets to Working Capital 38	3.2	•	2.1	2.2	2.5	2.8	3.0	3.3	4.0	3.0	6.4	3.8	3.7
Current Liabilities to Working Capital 39	2.2	•	1.1	1.2	1.5	1.8	2.0	2.3	3.0	2.0	5.4	2.8	2.7
Working Capital to Net Sales 40	0.1	•	0.1	0.1	0.1	0.1	0.1	0.2	0.1	0.2	0.1	0.1	0.2
Inventory to Working Capital 41	0.1	•	0.1	0.1	0.1	0.1	0.2	0.1	0.1	0.2	0.2	0.3	0.0
Total Receipts to Cash Flow 42	3.9	4.0	3.1	4.8	5.4	4.0	4.4	3.0	5.4	4.0	6.0	4.0	3.1
Cost of Goods to Cash Flow 43	1.3	2.1	0.6	2.1	3.0	1.0	2.0	0.8	1.9	1.4	3.2	0.9	0.9
Cash Flow to Total Debt 44	0.6	•	1.7	0.5	0.7	0.8	0.6	0.5	0.3	0.3	0.3	0.9	0.3

Selected Financial Factors (in Percentages)

Line Item													
Debt Ratio 45	69.4	•	100.1	138.2	65.8	61.5	60.9	52.9	60.1	62.5	62.4	64.7	70.2
Return on Total Assets 46	11.7	•	58.4	22.4	11.8	15.2	14.6	8.5	1.4	6.1	7.4	5.6	5.1
Return on Equity Before Income Taxes 47	32.5	•	•	•	31.1	35.7	33.8	15.1	•	10.0	13.4	11.0	13.1
Return on Equity After Income Taxes 48	28.1	•	•	•	28.5	33.0	31.8	12.1	•	7.2	9.9	6.5	7.9
Profit Margin (Before Income Tax) 49	6.4	5.6	10.3	5.2	4.1	6.8	7.9	8.7	•	4.5	5.2	4.4	5.8
Profit Margin (After Income Tax) 50	5.6	4.7	10.2	5.1	3.8	6.3	7.0	7.0	•	3.3	3.8	2.6	3.5

Table II

Corporations with Net Income

MANAGEMENT, SCIENTIFIC, AND TECHNICAL CONSULTING SERVICES

MONEY AMOUNTS AND SIZE OF ASSETS IN THOUSANDS OF DOLLARS

Item Description for Accounting Period 7/07 Through 6/08		Total	Zero Assets	Under 500	500 to 1,000	1,000 to 5,000	5,000 to 10,000	10,000 to 25,000	25,000 to 50,000	50,000 to 100,000	100,000 to 250,000	250,000 to 500,000	500,000 to 2,500,000	2,500,000 and over
Number of Enterprises	1	141026	24808	108652	3410	3043	466	381	110	60	44	•	•	•
Revenues ($ in Thousands)														
Net Sales	2	151948933	3256195	40549543	11058269	13406214	7365660	11163246	3892504	4844179	5680135	•	•	•
Interest	3	995786	5464	29572	17157	29150	15198	22414	41397	37970	39603	•	•	•
Rents	4	55979	210	3067	2282	421	1549	2898	3608	9055	5321	•	•	•
Royalties	5	557738	0	0	0	0	0	5021	2991	11076	33230	•	•	•
Other Portfolio Income	6	809849	34937	133059	24456	111440	29885	58401	120558	14921	136883	•	•	•
Other Receipts	7	3591451	248373	803501	81365	479607	473530	259379	249896	159752	148914	•	•	•
Total Receipts	8	157959736	3545179	41151742	11183529	14026832	7885822	11980359	4310954	5076953	6044086	•	•	•
Average Total Receipts	9	1120	143	382	3280	4610	16922	31445	39190	84616	137366	•	•	•
Operating Costs/Operating Income (%)														
Cost of Operations	10	28.5	13.8	16.5	50.9	35.3	23.4	47.4	26.4	26.8	35.7	•	•	•
Salaries and Wages	11	23.4	8.7	19.6	9.5	18.1	27.8	17.6	26.6	28.4	22.5	•	•	•
Taxes Paid	12	2.9	2.8	2.9	1.3	2.4	3.3	2.3	2.8	3.6	2.7	•	•	•
Interest Paid	13	0.9	0.6	0.3	0.5	0.5	0.3	0.6	1.3	1.4	2.3	•	•	•
Depreciation	14	1.0	0.8	0.6	0.5	0.7	0.6	1.0	1.6	1.8	1.5	•	•	•
Amortization and Depletion	15	0.4	0.1	0.0	0.0	0.2	0.0	0.2	0.7	0.4	1.7	•	•	•
Pensions and Other Deferred Comp.	16	1.6	0.6	2.2	0.7	0.6	1.1	1.1	1.0	1.6	0.6	•	•	•
Employee Benefits	17	1.7	0.8	0.9	0.6	1.3	2.1	1.8	2.0	3.2	2.3	•	•	•
Advertising	18	0.5	0.8	0.7	0.5	0.6	0.2	0.4	0.6	0.3	1.2	•	•	•
Other Expenses	19	22.7	34.3	23.1	22.2	22.6	27.0	14.6	26.9	24.3	22.8	•	•	•
Officers' Compensation	20	8.0	12.3	18.6	4.2	8.2	9.4	3.4	4.6	4.4	1.4	•	•	•
Operating Margin	21	8.3	24.4	14.6	9.0	9.5	4.7	9.5	5.5	3.8	5.3	•	•	•
Operating Margin Before Officers' Comp.	22	16.3	36.7	33.2	13.2	17.7	14.2	12.9	10.1	8.3	6.7	•	•	•

Selected Average Balance Sheet ($ in Thousands)

Net Receivables 23	173	0	8	176	453	1775	5396	7417	21283	35369
Inventories 24	11	0	1	17	68	120	394	635	1051	1638
Net Property, Plant and Equipment 25	53	0	9	78	268	593	1574	2783	8899	12154
Total Assets 26	706	0	64	706	2022	7256	14997	35170	70718	145277
Notes and Loans Payable 27	174	0	23	263	477	1273	3727	7410	18140	42389
All Other Liabilities 28	272	0	17	238	594	2025	5019	9907	25104	42873
Net Worth 29	260	0	24	204	951	3959	6251	17854	27474	60015

Selected Financial Ratios (Times to 1)

Current Ratio 30	1.5	•	2.4	1.9	2.1	1.9	1.6	1.7	1.3	1.4
Quick Ratio 31	1.3	•	2.1	1.7	1.6	1.6	1.3	1.2	1.1	1.2
Net Sales to Working Capital 32	8.2	•	15.2	15.0	7.0	7.2	9.2	4.6	9.1	6.9
Coverage Ratio 33	14.4	52.1	65.9	21.5	30.7	38.3	21.0	13.3	7.3	6.1
Total Asset Turnover 34	1.5	•	5.8	4.6	2.2	2.2	2.0	1.0	1.1	0.9
Inventory Turnover 35	27.6	•	48.7	95.4	22.9	30.9	36.7	14.7	20.6	28.1
Receivables Turnover 36	6.7	•	51.4	17.7	8.0	8.2	6.3	5.0	3.7	3.3
Total Liabilities to Net Worth 37	1.7	•	1.7	2.5	1.1	0.8	1.4	1.0	1.6	1.4
Current Assets to Working Capital 38	2.9	•	1.7	2.1	1.9	2.1	2.8	2.4	4.3	3.4
Current Liabilities to Working Capital 39	1.9	•	0.7	1.1	0.9	1.1	1.8	1.4	3.3	2.4
Working Capital to Net Sales 40	0.1	•	0.1	0.1	0.1	0.1	0.1	0.2	0.1	0.1
Inventory to Working Capital 41	0.1	•	0.1	0.0	0.1	0.0	0.1	0.1	0.1	0.1
Total Receipts to Cash Flow 42	3.2	1.6	2.7	4.0	2.9	3.2	4.2	2.6	3.4	3.2
Cost of Goods to Cash Flow 43	0.9	0.2	0.4	2.1	1.0	0.7	2.0	0.7	0.9	1.1
Cash Flow to Total Debt 44	0.8	•	3.5	1.6	1.4	1.5	0.8	0.8	0.5	0.5

Selected Financial Factors (in Percentages)

Debt Ratio 45	63.2	•	62.7	71.1	53.0	45.4	58.3	49.2	61.1	58.7
Return on Total Assets 46	20.4	•	101.0	49.0	31.7	26.3	26.5	17.7	11.9	12.6
Return on Equity Before Income Taxes 47	51.6	•	266.8	161.4	65.1	47.0	60.6	32.3	26.5	25.4
Return on Equity After Income Taxes 48	46.6	•	264.1	159.5	61.9	44.4	57.9	28.0	21.3	21.2
Profit Margin (Before Income Tax) 49	12.4	33.2	17.0	10.2	14.1	11.8	12.4	16.3	9.0	11.8
Profit Margin (After Income Tax) 50	11.2	31.4	16.9	10.0	13.4	11.1	11.9	14.1	7.2	9.8

Table I

Corporations with and without Net Income

SCIENTIFIC RESEARCH AND DEVELOPMENT SERVICES

MONEY AMOUNTS AND SIZE OF ASSETS IN THOUSANDS OF DOLLARS

Item Description for Accounting Period 7/07 Through 6/08	Total	Zero Assets	Under 500	500 to 1,000	1,000 to 5,000	5,000 to 10,000	10,000 to 25,000	25,000 to 50,000	50,000 to 100,000	100,000 to 250,000	250,000 to 500,000	500,000 to 2,500,000	2,500,000 and over
Number of Enterprises 1	12598	1892	6679	1211	1487	465	414	186	132	74	24	30	3
Revenues ($ in Thousands)													
Net Sales 2	35381961	1510002	1155221	2299134	4281519	2281201	2015698	2273806	2857391	2814955	3528478	7144928	3219629
Interest 3	1828200	27337	5808	10457	48372	59094	163152	157534	272319	315749	172642	441158	154578
Rents 4	24453	0	0	0	2545	303	2714	877	1020	7099	2888	7007	0
Royalties 5	2294960	69786	0	3674	315	13374	48521	17742	153151	195261	52894	1233098	507144
Other Portfolio Income 6	849625	259	1474	0	21394	30959	38522	59467	35011	121387	110647	312083	118425
Other Receipts 7	3640150	111144	6332	27230	602708	99821	255334	171232	291205	646651	164895	1246911	16684
Total Receipts 8	44019349	1718528	1168835	2340495	4956853	2484752	2523941	2680658	3610097	4101102	4032444	10385185	4016460
Average Total Receipts 9	3494	908	175	1933	3333	5344	6096	14412	27349	55420	168018	346173	1338820
Operating Costs/Operating Income (%)													
Cost of Operations 10	25.6	9.6	19.5	17.3	32.5	34.9	21.8	38.0	35.4	17.8	30.1	21.3	21.4
Salaries and Wages 11	36.1	20.5	27.1	23.3	31.5	38.0	55.7	41.0	42.0	40.1	36.3	35.1	38.1
Taxes Paid 12	4.2	4.7	3.2	3.5	4.0	5.5	6.6	5.5	5.5	5.6	2.9	3.9	2.0
Interest Paid 13	3.6	1.7	0.5	1.1	1.7	1.9	5.1	2.6	4.6	4.0	3.7	5.2	5.6
Depreciation 14	4.3	1.6	1.6	1.5	2.5	3.7	7.0	5.1	5.3	4.7	4.1	6.7	2.7
Amortization and Depletion 15	3.5	5.6	1.3	0.1	1.0	1.3	3.2	5.0	5.9	6.6	1.8	4.0	6.0
Pensions and Other Deferred Comp. 16	2.1	3.2	2.3	2.4	0.9	2.1	1.0	0.7	1.1	0.4	0.8	5.1	1.7
Employee Benefits 17	4.1	2.4	1.9	1.9	3.6	5.1	6.5	4.8	4.5	4.8	3.9	5.1	2.6
Advertising 18	1.6	0.8	3.5	2.2	1.0	2.0	1.7	1.8	1.9	1.7	0.9	1.5	1.6
Other Expenses 19	60.2	70.4	52.6	33.6	55.5	45.2	103.7	80.0	82.3	94.7	40.7	52.7	40.6
Officers' Compensation 20	7.2	9.9	13.5	13.5	11.7	9.5	12.5	9.6	7.5	6.2	3.5	3.0	1.1
Operating Margin 21	•	•	•	•	•	•	•	•	•	•	•	•	•
Operating Margin Before Officers' Comp. 22	•	12.9	•	•	•	•	•	•	•	•	•	•	•

Selected Average Balance Sheet ($ in Thousands)

Net Receivables 23	696	0	3	78	488	1420	1370	3042	4903	9598	27281	79973	575267
Inventories 24	182	0	1	19	62	275	377	746	1126	2663	6605	13216	283183
Net Property, Plant and Equipment 25	778	0	9	120	337	660	1857	3915	6504	12927	37619	140997	113714
Total Assets 26	7013	0	89	725	2250	7019	15726	35146	70284	149402	332849	938183	3584067
Notes and Loans Payable 27	1776	0	221	607	998	2220	2295	5709	10101	16154	112341	274949	721840
All Other Liabilities 28	1988	0	40	200	893	2290	3626	8542	20081	53378	69769	222074	1370789
Net Worth 29	3249	0	-172	-83	358	2509	9805	20895	40102	79870	150738	441161	1491438

Selected Financial Ratios (Times to 1)

Current Ratio 30	2.6	•	0.8	1.1	1.7	2.1	3.4	2.8	2.7	3.2	2.5	3.0	2.3
Quick Ratio 31	1.9	•	0.7	1.0	1.5	1.8	2.8	2.1	1.9	2.1	1.8	2.0	1.5
Net Sales to Working Capital 32	1.1	•	•	73.8	4.9	1.8	0.6	0.8	0.8	0.6	1.3	0.8	1.0
Coverage Ratio 33	•	•	•	2.1	•	•	•	•	•	•	•	1.4	1.4
Total Asset Turnover 34	0.4	•	1.9	2.6	1.3	0.7	0.3	0.3	0.3	0.3	0.4	0.3	0.3
Inventory Turnover 35	3.9	•	51.3	17.1	15.2	6.2	2.8	6.2	6.8	2.5	6.7	3.8	0.8
Receivables Turnover 36	3.6	•	57.3	19.5	5.9	3.8	3.8	4.0	4.2	4.7	4.5	3.3	1.1
Total Liabilities to Net Worth 37	1.2	•	•	•	5.3	1.8	0.6	0.7	0.8	0.9	1.2	1.1	1.4
Current Assets to Working Capital 38	1.6	•	•	20.7	2.5	1.9	1.4	1.5	1.6	1.5	1.7	1.5	1.8
Current Liabilities to Working Capital 39	0.6	•	•	19.7	1.5	0.9	0.4	0.5	0.6	0.5	0.7	0.5	0.8
Working Capital to Net Sales 40	0.9	•	•	0.0	0.2	0.5	1.6	1.2	1.3	1.7	0.7	1.2	1.0
Inventory to Working Capital 41	0.1	•	•	0.6	0.1	0.1	0.1	0.1	0.0	0.0	0.1	0.1	0.2
Total Receipts to Cash Flow 42	4.3	2.1	5.3	3.4	5.6	•	•	•	26.7	2.4	5.4	2.3	2.7
Cost of Goods to Cash Flow 43	1.1	0.2	1.0	0.6	1.8	•	•	•	9.4	0.4	1.6	0.5	0.6
Cash Flow to Total Debt 44	0.2	•	0.1	0.7	0.3	•	•	•	0.0	0.2	0.1	0.2	0.2

Selected Financial Factors (in Percentages)

Debt Ratio 45	53.7	•	293.3	111.4	84.1	64.3	37.7	40.5	42.9	46.5	54.7	53.0	58.4
Return on Total Assets 46	•	•	•	6.1	•	•	•	•	•	•	•	1.8	2.4
Return on Equity Before Income Taxes 47	•	•	26.1	•	•	•	•	•	•	•	•	1.1	1.8
Return on Equity After Income Taxes 48	•	•	26.2	•	•	•	•	•	•	•	•	•	1.6
Profit Margin (Before Income Tax) 49	•	•	•	1.2	•	•	•	•	•	•	•	2.1	2.5
Profit Margin (After Income Tax) 50	•	•	•	0.9	•	•	•	•	•	•	•	•	2.3

Table II

Corporations with Net Income

SCIENTIFIC RESEARCH AND DEVELOPMENT SERVICES

MONEY AMOUNTS AND SIZE OF ASSETS IN THOUSANDS OF DOLLARS

Item Description for Accounting Period 7/07 Through 6/08	Total	Zero Assets	Under 500	500 to 1,000	1,000 to 5,000	5,000 to 10,000	10,000 to 25,000	25,000 to 50,000	50,000 to 100,000	100,000 to 250,000	250,000 to 500,000	500,000 to 2,500,000	2,500,000 and over
Number of Enterprises 1	5227	733	2697	772	628	189	100	33	23	21	13	18	0
Revenues ($ in Thousands)													
Net Sales 2	23913172	1116483	1036979	2109590	2619398	1961629	1197479	1391627	1336767	1598586	2989111	6555523	0
Interest 3	533916	1959	681	1778	5132	9356	31904	11655	29316	104470	63826	273839	0
Rents 4	4437	0	0	0	2372	303	1261	35	0	81	385	0	0
Royalties 5	1275034	0	0	0	91	1558	28680	7986	112439	179893	28100	916287	0
Other Portfolio Income 6	472263	7	0	0	0	30146	35296	44798	1792	8098	63788	272479	0
Other Receipts 7	2608891	85804	2105	18808	543820	18934	173464	42407	98925	443170	42515	1138938	0
Total Receipts 8	28807713	1204253	1039765	2130176	3186674	2021926	1468084	1498508	1579239	2334298	3187725	9157066	0
Average Total Receipts 9	5511	1643	386	2759	5074	10698	14681	45409	68663	111157	245210	508726	•
Operating Costs/Operating Income (%)													
Cost of Operations 10	25.8	3.7	16.7	18.2	25.8	31.3	19.9	41.8	45.5	17.7	33.4	24.1	•
Salaries and Wages 11	25.5	12.1	18.3	19.4	26.8	24.5	26.8	19.4	18.0	22.4	24.3	34.3	•
Taxes Paid 12	3.0	5.1	2.4	3.1	3.3	3.6	3.6	3.0	2.6	2.8	2.1	2.8	•
Interest Paid 13	2.2	0.3	0.1	0.8	0.6	0.5	1.4	1.3	0.9	1.7	1.4	5.6	•
Depreciation 14	2.9	0.2	0.9	1.0	1.4	2.0	3.5	2.8	1.9	2.5	3.2	5.1	•
Amortization and Depletion 15	1.2	0.2	•	0.0	0.3	0.1	0.7	0.2	0.6	2.6	0.9	2.8	•
Pensions and Other Deferred Comp. 16	1.4	3.6	2.6	2.4	1.0	2.4	1.4	0.8	1.8	0.5	0.7	1.0	•
Employee Benefits 17	3.0	0.5	1.5	1.7	2.8	4.3	3.5	2.3	1.9	2.3	3.0	4.3	•
Advertising 18	1.0	0.8	3.8	2.2	0.9	0.6	0.3	0.3	0.5	0.4	0.4	1.0	•
Other Expenses 19	32.4	62.2	20.3	23.5	38.6	15.9	37.5	16.8	24.2	52.5	28.7	35.4	•
Officers' Compensation 20	5.0	9.7	11.8	12.1	10.1	4.8	6.3	3.4	3.3	3.4	1.4	1.5	•
Operating Margin 21	•	1.5	21.6	15.6	•	10.0	•	8.2	•	•	0.5	•	•
Operating Margin Before Officers' Comp. 22	1.7	11.1	33.4	27.6	•	14.8	1.5	11.6	2.1	•	1.8	•	•

Selected Average Balance Sheet ($ in Thousands)

Net Receivables 23	1167	0	0	98	782	2993	3041	9392	15484	18722	45145	167679	•
Inventories 24	281	0	2	8	64	402	423	1108	1762	3937	9918	28295	•
Net Property, Plant and Equipment 25	859	0	7	147	314	599	3035	8341	8539	13084	43225	135207	•
Total Assets 26	7508		100	712	1958	6697	15893	37444	74182	157790	344730	1311416	•
Notes and Loans Payable 27	1515		16	275	496	1076	2812	8078	7267	10273	77214	289560	•
All Other Liabilities 28	2294	0	16	187	612	3106	4730	9143	21858	54653	77547	411072	•
Net Worth 29	3699	0	67	250	851	2515	8350	20223	45057	92864	189969	610784	•

Selected Financial Ratios (Times to 1)

Current Ratio 30	2.3	•	1.9	2.8	2.1	1.7	2.4	1.8	2.8	3.6	1.6	2.4	•
Quick Ratio 31	1.6	•	1.7	2.7	1.9	1.5	2.1	1.5	1.9	2.2	1.2	1.5	•
Net Sales to Working Capital 32	2.1	•	14.3	7.5	5.9	4.5	2.4	5.0	1.8	1.1	3.8	1.0	•
Coverage Ratio 33	8.7	32.6	161.8	21.0	16.4	27.6	13.7	13.6	19.5	22.8	6.2	5.0	•
Total Asset Turnover 34	0.6	•	3.9	3.8	2.1	1.5	0.8	1.1	0.8	0.5	0.7	0.3	•
Inventory Turnover 35	4.2	•	35.2	64.8	16.8	8.1	5.6	15.9	15.0	3.4	7.7	3.1	•
Receivables Turnover 36	3.4	•	195.1	30.9	6.2	4.7	4.4	4.2	3.5	4.9	•	3.1	•
Total Liabilities to Net Worth 37	1.0	•	0.5	1.8	1.3	1.7	0.9	0.9	0.6	0.7	0.8	1.1	•
Current Assets to Working Capital 38	1.8	•	2.1	1.5	1.9	2.4	1.7	2.2	1.5	1.4	2.7	1.7	•
Current Liabilities to Working Capital 39	0.8	•	1.1	0.5	0.9	1.4	0.7	1.2	0.5	0.4	1.7	0.7	•
Working Capital to Net Sales 40	0.5	•	0.1	0.1	0.2	0.2	0.4	0.2	0.6	0.9	0.3	1.0	•
Inventory to Working Capital 41	0.1	•	0.1	0.0	0.1	0.2	0.1	0.2	0.1	0.1	0.2	0.1	•
Total Receipts to Cash Flow 42	2.3	1.5	2.6	2.9	2.3	4.2	2.2	3.9	2.7	1.2	3.3	2.0	•
Cost of Goods to Cash Flow 43	0.6	0.1	0.4	0.5	0.6	1.3	0.4	1.6	1.2	0.2	1.1	0.5	•
Cash Flow to Total Debt 44	0.5	•	4.6	2.1	1.6	0.6	0.7	0.6	0.8	1.0	0.5	0.3	•

Selected Financial Factors (in Percentages)

Debt Ratio 45	50.7	•	32.4	64.9	56.6	62.4	47.5	46.0	39.3	41.1	44.9	53.4	•
Return on Total Assets 46	11.9	•	84.8	66.7	22.6	20.9	14.5	19.3	14.0	18.8	6.0	7.7	•
Return on Equity Before Income Taxes 47	21.4	•	124.6	180.9	48.8	53.6	25.6	33.0	21.8	30.5	9.1	13.3	•
Return on Equity After Income Taxes 48	18.8	•	123.6	177.8	48.0	47.7	22.7	29.0	20.7	27.4	7.5	10.8	•
Profit Margin (Before Income Tax) 49	17.3	9.3	21.9	16.6	9.9	13.0	17.8	15.8	16.9	37.2	7.5	22.3	•
Profit Margin (After Income Tax) 50	15.2	8.1	21.7	16.3	9.8	11.6	15.8	13.9	16.0	33.4	6.2	18.1	•

ADVERTISING AND RELATED SERVICES

Table I

Corporations with and without Net Income

MONEY AMOUNTS AND SIZE OF ASSETS IN THOUSANDS OF DOLLARS

Item Description for Accounting Period 7/07 Through 6/08	Total	Zero Assets	Under 500	500 to 1,000	1,000 to 5,000	5,000 to 10,000	10,000 to 25,000	25,000 to 50,000	50,000 to 100,000	100,000 to 250,000	250,000 to 500,000	500,000 to 2,500,000	2,500,000 and over
Number of Enterprises 1	47682	7300	36423	1659	1597	341	217	63	30	27	10	10	5
Revenues ($ in Thousands)													
Net Sales 2	85692443	1443847	18840811	4605216	10056616	6115424	6661227	4222139	1934253	3836931	2388402	7518194	18069382
Interest 3	2294854	12284	10664	8239	29990	12257	32661	12040	13159	16856	16513	62247	2067945
Rents 4	92366	0	393	1889	3083	0	0	348	115	7	914	961	84657
Royalties 5	66167	0	0	0	46	0	0	39974	1109	0	3229	2455	19354
Other Portfolio Income 6	1112546	547	59967	1860	25072	703	1530	16647	23910	20092	46013	456156	460050
Other Receipts 7	1193682	-17446	154984	10492	91019	34803	101883	32894	98977	69923	49357	118973	447819
Total Receipts 8	90452058	1439232	19066819	4627696	10205826	6163187	6797301	4324042	2071523	3943809	2504428	8158986	21149207
Average Total Receipts 9	1897	197	523	2789	6391	18074	31324	68636	69051	146067	250443	815899	4229841
Operating Costs/Operating Income (%)													
Cost of Operations 10	40.4	27.6	45.0	60.4	53.9	61.6	60.0	53.8	46.0	49.9	52.9	35.1	4.4
Salaries and Wages 11	21.0	61.4	8.3	8.5	14.4	16.2	15.9	11.5	21.3	17.9	16.7	25.4	42.9
Taxes Paid 12	2.3	3.2	1.8	1.9	1.7	1.7	1.6	1.5	2.0	1.7	2.1	3.0	3.8
Interest Paid 13	4.6	2.2	0.5	0.2	0.9	0.6	0.3	1.0	2.2	2.6	2.5	5.7	16.6
Depreciation 14	1.4	2.1	0.6	1.0	0.9	0.7	0.8	0.7	1.9	1.2	3.0	2.5	2.3
Amortization and Depletion 15	1.0	0.9	0.1	0.2	0.3	0.1	0.1	0.8	1.3	1.4	1.2	2.3	2.6
Pensions and Other Deferred Comp. 16	0.6	0.3	0.6	1.1	0.5	0.4	0.3	0.3	0.4	0.6	0.6	0.3	1.0
Employee Benefits 17	1.2	1.2	1.0	1.3	0.9	0.6	0.8	1.1	1.1	1.3	1.1	1.9	1.9
Advertising 18	2.9	0.9	2.8	6.1	4.8	0.4	2.0	9.8	1.3	5.9	0.3	4.4	0.3
Other Expenses 19	21.7	31.4	26.5	14.0	15.3	10.8	15.3	19.6	20.7	16.6	17.0	17.1	31.9
Officers' Compensation 20	4.4	3.5	8.6	7.4	4.4	3.6	3.1	2.3	2.5	2.2	2.1	0.7	3.2
Operating Margin 21	•	•	4.3	•	1.9	3.4	•	•	•	•	0.5	1.7	•
Operating Margin Before Officers' Comp. 22	2.8	•	12.9	5.3	6.3	7.0	2.9	•	1.8	1.0	2.6	2.3	•

Selected Average Balance Sheet ($ in Thousands)

	1	2	3	4	5	6	7	8	9	10	11	12	13
Net Receivables 23	687	13	159	931	3264	6244	11766	21122	36667	58039	195872		4635937
Inventories 24	39	0	19	217	85	120	1369	1008	740	4586	9934		208779
Net Property, Plant and Equipment 25	140	2	17	183	293	474	1177	2075	6829	8110	33698	116069	564607
Total Assets 26	2757	71	729	2493	7328	15439	37046	71779	158061	336894	1289724		18565744
Notes and Loans Payable 27	472	42	76	689	1224	1612	7432	18960	43964	82238	504520		2181986
All Other Liabilities 28	1322	28	392	1342	3186	9615	20803	33976	60295	151997	453811		9210219
Net Worth 29	963	1	260	462	2919	4211	8811	18842	53801	102659	331392		7173539

Selected Financial Ratios (Times to 1)

	1	2	3	4	5	6	7	8	9	10	11	12	13
Current Ratio 30	0.9	•	1.2	1.1	1.2	1.9	1.1	1.2	1.1	1.1	0.6	1.1	0.8
Quick Ratio 31	0.8	•	1.0	1.0	1.0	1.7	1.0	1.0	0.9	0.8	0.4	0.8	0.7
Net Sales to Working Capital 32	•	86.5	72.2	18.5	6.9	27.3	17.1	14.1	37.9	•	16.5	•	
Coverage Ratio 33	2.0	12.8	•	4.7	8.5	6.5	1.1	3.8	1.6	3.7	2.7		1.5
Total Asset Turnover 34	0.7	•	7.3	3.8	2.5	2.4	2.0	1.8	0.9	0.9	0.7	0.6	0.2
Inventory Turnover 35	18.8	109.7	87.8	15.6	129.8	153.1	26.3	29.4	95.7	27.5	26.6		0.8
Receivables Turnover 36	2.8	39.1	24.0	7.4	6.0	5.6	5.8	3.1	4.6	3.4	3.9		0.8
Total Liabilities to Net Worth 37	1.9	62.4	1.8	4.4	1.5	2.7	3.2	2.8	1.9	2.3	2.9		1.6
Current Assets to Working Capital 38	•	7.1	12.0	5.6	2.1	9.9	6.2	9.9	18.4	•	8.6	•	
Current Liabilities to Working Capital 39	•	6.1	11.0	4.6	1.1	8.9	5.2	8.9	17.4	•	7.6	•	
Working Capital to Net Sales 40	•	0.0	0.0	0.1	0.1	0.0	0.1	0.1	0.0	•	0.1	•	
Inventory to Working Capital 41	•	0.4	0.1	0.7	0.0	0.7	0.3	0.2	0.2	•	0.2	•	
Total Receipts to Cash Flow 42	4.7	3.4	10.3	6.2	8.6	6.6	5.9	4.4	6.3	5.4	5.2		3.3
Cost of Goods to Cash Flow 43	1.9	1.5	6.2	3.4	5.3	4.0	3.1	2.0	3.1	2.8	1.8		0.1
Cash Flow to Total Debt 44	0.2	2.1	0.6	0.5	0.5	0.4	0.4	0.3	0.2	0.2	0.2		0.1

Selected Financial Factors (in Percentages)

	1	2	3	4	5	6	7	8	9	10	11	12	13
Debt Ratio 45	65.1	•	98.4	64.3	81.5	60.2	72.7	76.2	73.7	66.0	69.5	74.3	61.4
Return on Total Assets 46	5.9	•	43.3	•	10.9	11.5	4.3	2.0	7.6	3.8	6.6	9.1	4.8
Return on Equity Before Income Taxes 47	8.2	•	2531.3	•	46.3	25.5	13.3	0.6	21.2	4.4	15.7	22.4	4.2
Return on Equity After Income Taxes 48	6.6	•	2515.1	•	43.0	23.7	11.0	•	15.7	2.5	11.7	18.2	3.0
Profit Margin (Before Income Tax) 49	4.4	5.5	3.4	•	3.4	4.2	1.8	0.1	6.2	1.7	6.8	9.9	8.3
Profit Margin (After Income Tax) 50	3.5	5.5	3.2	•	3.2	3.9	1.5	•	0.9	1.7	5.0	8.0	6.1

Table II
Corporations with Net Income

ADVERTISING AND RELATED SERVICES

MONEY AMOUNTS AND SIZE OF ASSETS IN THOUSANDS OF DOLLARS

Item Description for Accounting Period 7/07 Through 6/08	Total	Zero Assets	Under 500	500 to 1,000	1,000 to 5,000	5,000 to 10,000	10,000 to 25,000	25,000 to 50,000	50,000 to 100,000	100,000 to 250,000	250,000 to 500,000	500,000 to 2,500,000	2,500,000 and over
Number of Enterprises **1**	29440	3218	23753	750	1199	265	164	34	17	18	•	•	5
Revenues ($ in Thousands)													
Net Sales **2**	69668241	497754	14379535	2540346	7978121	5123680	6011041	2932294	1246545	2458556	•	•	18069382
Interest **3**	2237952	1179	8699	7481	25160	6729	21097	5679	10331	13816	•	•	2067945
Rents **4**	90550	0	341	1889	1401	0	0	271	115	7	•	•	84657
Royalties **5**	62914	0	0	0	46	0	0	36721	1109	0	•	•	19354
Other Portfolio Income **6**	1066767	0	59962	67	22361	406	906	300	6187	20092	•	•	460050
Other Receipts **7**	989082	9	26735	7766	121336	33996	93698	10976	66297	55585	•	•	447819
Total Receipts **8**	74115506	498942	14475272	2557549	8148425	5164811	6126742	2986241	1330584	2548056	•	•	21149207
Average Total Receipts **9**	2518	155	609	3410	6796	19490	37358	87831	78270	141559	•	•	4229841
Operating Costs/Operating Income (%)													
Cost of Operations **10**	35.6	22.6	37.3	53.7	53.6	59.6	59.4	54.1	49.6	50.0	•	•	4.4
Salaries and Wages **11**	22.0	14.0	9.1	9.3	14.1	15.7	14.3	10.3	19.7	18.8	•	•	42.9
Taxes Paid **12**	2.4	1.3	1.9	1.6	1.6	1.7	1.4	1.7	1.8	2.0	•	•	3.8
Interest Paid **13**	5.1	0.2	0.4	0.0	0.6	0.6	0.2	0.6	0.4	2.4	•	•	16.6
Depreciation **14**	1.3	0.2	0.6	0.3	0.6	0.7	0.5	0.5	1.1	1.0	•	•	2.3
Amortization and Depletion **15**	1.0	0.0	0.1	0.0	0.2	0.1	0.1	0.2	0.4	1.7	•	•	2.6
Pensions and Other Deferred Comp. **16**	0.6	0.3	0.6	0.8	0.5	0.4	0.4	0.4	0.4	0.6	•	•	1.0
Employee Benefits **17**	1.2	0.3	0.8	1.3	0.8	0.5	0.7	1.0	0.6	1.0	•	•	1.9
Advertising **18**	2.0	1.6	1.3	7.0	0.7	0.4	1.9	13.5	0.2	2.4	•	•	0.3
Other Expenses **19**	22.7	20.2	30.1	14.1	16.4	10.8	13.8	13.0	17.3	17.2	•	•	31.9
Officers' Compensation **20**	4.2	5.5	8.9	5.5	4.4	3.5	2.7	2.3	1.6	1.6	•	•	3.2
Operating Margin **21**	1.8	33.8	8.9	6.3	6.6	5.9	4.6	2.4	6.8	1.4	•	•	•
Operating Margin Before Officers' Comp. **22**	6.0	39.3	17.8	11.8	11.0	9.4	7.2	4.7	8.4	3.0	•	•	•

Selected Average Balance Sheet ($ in Thousands)

Item														
Net Receivables **23**	1045	0	12	132	1002	3409	6979	13660	31683	30906	•	•	•	4635937
Inventories **24**	55	0	1	276	92	130	1560	1408	709	•	•	•	•	210327
Net Property, Plant and Equipment **25**	180	0	20	246	462	933	2391	3742	8190	•	•	•	•	564607
Total Assets **26**	4146	74	644	2455	7185	15783	35981	72151	153695	•	•	•	•	18565744
Notes and Loans Payable **27**	608	28	4	447	1249	1183	7627	10755	30969	•	•	•	•	2181986
All Other Liabilities **28**	2007	30	296	1357	3106	11006	20922	47056	58225	•	•	•	•	9210219
Net Worth **29**	1531	16	345	651	2831	3594	7432	14340	64502	•	•	•	•	7173539

Selected Financial Ratios (Times to 1)

Item														
Current Ratio **30**	0.9	•	1.1	1.7	1.4	1.9	1.1	1.1	1.2	1.1	•	•	•	0.8
Quick Ratio **31**	0.8	•	1.0	1.4	1.2	1.7	1.0	1.0	0.9	1.0	•	•	•	0.7
Net Sales to Working Capital **32**	•	167.1	133.4	16.2	11.6	7.3	53.4	43.5	9.2	19.7	•	•	•	•
Coverage Ratio **33**	2.7	24.9	245.1	19.3	11.5	28.7	8.7	32.9	3.1	•	•	•	•	1.5
Total Asset Turnover **34**	0.6	8.1	5.3	2.7	2.7	2.3	2.4	1.0	0.9	•	•	•	•	0.2
Inventory Turnover **35**	15.3	390.6	2640.0	12.9	125.6	167.8	29.9	25.8	96.4	•	•	•	•	0.8
Receivables Turnover **36**	2.5	48.9	30.0	7.7	6.4	5.7	5.3	2.4	5.1	•	•	•	•	0.8
Total Liabilities to Net Worth **37**	1.7	3.5	0.9	2.8	1.5	3.4	3.8	4.0	5.1	•	•	•	•	1.6
Current Assets to Working Capital **38**	•	9.4	2.4	3.5	2.1	17.3	12.6	7.2	8.8	•	•	•	•	•
Current Liabilities to Working Capital **39**	•	8.4	1.4	2.5	1.1	16.3	11.6	6.2	7.8	•	•	•	•	•
Working Capital to Net Sales **40**	•	0.0	0.1	0.1	0.1	0.0	0.0	0.1	0.1	•	•	•	•	0.1
Inventory to Working Capital **41**	•	0.1	0.0	0.5	0.0	0.2	0.7	0.2	0.2	•	•	•	•	0.2
Total Receipts to Cash Flow **42**	3.8	2.0	2.7	4.5	7.2	5.4	6.5	3.5	5.1	•	•	•	•	5.1
Cost of Goods to Cash Flow **43**	1.4	0.4	2.8	2.4	4.3	3.2	3.5	1.8	2.5	•	•	•	•	3.3
Cash Flow to Total Debt **44**	0.2	•	2.1	0.8	0.6	0.5	0.4	0.3	•	•	•	•	•	0.1

Selected Financial Factors (in Percentages)

Item														
Debt Ratio **45**	63.1	•	77.9	46.5	73.5	60.6	77.2	79.3	80.1	58.0	•	•	•	61.4
Return on Total Assets **46**	7.9	•	80.8	36.6	24.9	19.6	15.6	11.5	14.1	6.6	•	•	•	4.8
Return on Equity Before Income Taxes **47**	13.4	•	350.8	68.1	88.9	45.5	66.1	49.4	69.0	10.7	•	•	•	4.2
Return on Equity After Income Taxes **48**	11.9	•	349.1	67.4	85.8	43.1	62.6	46.1	56.2	8.3	•	•	•	3.0
Profit Margin (Before Income Tax) **49**	8.7	34.0	9.5	6.9	8.7	6.7	6.1	6.5	13.5	5.1	•	•	•	8.3
Profit Margin (After Income Tax) **50**	7.7	33.8	9.5	6.9	8.4	6.3	6.1	4.3	11.0	3.9	•	•	•	6.1

Table I

Corporations with and without Net Income

OTHER PROFESSIONAL, SCIENTIFIC, AND TECHNICAL SERVICES

MONEY AMOUNTS AND SIZE OF ASSETS IN THOUSANDS OF DOLLARS

Item Description for Accounting Period 7/07 Through 6/08	Total	Zero Assets	Under 500	500 to 1,000	1,000 to 5,000	5,000 to 10,000	10,000 to 25,000	25,000 to 50,000	50,000 to 100,000	100,000 to 250,000	250,000 to 500,000	500,000 to 2,500,000	2,500,000 and over
Number of Enterprises **1**	88939	18501	63854	3314	2517	258	291	87	58	30	15	15	0
Revenues ($ in Thousands)													
Net Sales **2**	81532134	4114172	28574556	6360234	7851321	3656276	5847605	3865141	4985141	6393550	2278742	7605397	0
Interest **3**	915554	13698	11165	3883	30676	14453	36176	15786	27940	40574	8766	712439	0
Rents **4**	43008	478	1925	0	3047	0	395	1614	1657	20699	3863	9331	0
Royalties **5**	253061	15788	347	0	12999	3602	368	1503	684	12326	21523	183922	0
Other Portfolio Income **6**	1469172	27247	31637	5811	34064	1506	63641	54216	27274	15563	1495	1206720	0
Other Receipts **7**	1685810	66083	186138	22095	247037	35918	514960	64039	110906	69391	15930	353308	0
Total Receipts **8**	85898739	4237466	28805768	6392023	8179144	3711755	6463145	4002299	5153602	6552103	2330319	10071117	0
Average Total Receipts **9**	966	229	451	1929	3250	14387	22210	46003	88855	218403	155355	671408	•
Operating Costs/Operating Income (%)													
Cost of Operations **10**	29.3	13.8	21.3	41.7	27.3	45.8	40.5	35.5	34.4	50.9	26.3	18.6	•
Salaries and Wages **11**	20.2	11.2	19.4	20.4	20.5	18.0	23.1	22.1	15.6	16.5	32.9	27.7	•
Taxes Paid **12**	3.0	2.0	3.1	3.3	2.7	1.9	3.8	2.5	2.1	2.0	3.5	4.3	•
Interest Paid **13**	3.3	0.4	0.7	0.9	1.1	0.8	1.7	1.6	1.8	1.4	3.4	24.6	•
Depreciation **14**	1.5	1.2	1.1	1.0	1.4	1.1	1.4	2.0	1.7	1.3	2.8	2.9	•
Amortization and Depletion **15**	0.7	0.3	0.3	0.3	0.2	0.3	0.4	0.8	0.8	0.7	2.0	3.8	•
Pensions and Other Deferred Comp. **16**	1.1	0.4	1.2	1.3	1.5	0.4	0.8	0.6	0.5	0.9	2.4	1.6	•
Employee Benefits **17**	1.6	1.0	1.1	1.4	1.2	4.3	2.3	1.8	1.4	1.6	2.9	2.6	•
Advertising **18**	1.1	0.5	1.2	0.7	1.6	2.0	0.4	1.2	1.7	0.3	2.3	1.4	•
Other Expenses **19**	29.5	61.6	28.8	17.3	28.9	18.7	29.7	29.8	41.9	21.5	19.6	32.0	•
Officers' Compensation **20**	7.7	6.6	12.4	9.3	12.4	5.2	4.3	2.1	1.8	1.7	1.0	1.8	•
Operating Margin **21**	1.0	1.1	9.3	2.4	1.2	1.5	•	0.1	•	1.1	0.9	•	•
Operating Margin Before Officers' Comp. **22**	8.7	7.7	21.8	11.7	13.6	6.7	•	2.2	•	2.8	1.9	•	•

Selected Average Balance Sheet ($ in Thousands)

Net Receivables **23**	97	0	7	137	335	3179	3751	8274	11298	33878	47560	125529
Inventories **24**	14	0	4	44	85	368	257	467	1166	8490	3905	4204
Net Property, Plant and Equipment **25**	81	0	21	135	278	676	1964	5144	7935	12394	36780	143125
Total Assets **26**	675	0	85	676	1885	7086	15007	34088	70121	156104	322204	1655468
Notes and Loans Payable **27**	264	0	54	231	639	1988	4610	11675	16191	47034	84145	745033
All Other Liabilities **28**	224	0	18	194	819	2665	5425	11140	22970	47138	115432	558430
Net Worth **29**	186	0	13	252	427	2433	4972	11273	30960	61932	122627	352005

Selected Financial Ratios (Times to 1)

Current Ratio **30**	1.3	•	1.9	1.6	1.4	1.7	1.4	1.4	1.4	1.5	1.0	0.8
Quick Ratio **31**	1.0	•	1.6	1.1	1.2	1.5	1.1	1.1	1.0	1.1	0.7	0.5
Net Sales to Working Capital **32**	17.3	•	23.0	14.1	9.5	5.8	9.2	8.7	10.1	8.0	•	•
Coverage Ratio **33**	3.0	11.6	16.0	4.3	5.9	4.6	2.2	3.3	0.8	3.6	1.9	1.6
Total Asset Turnover **34**	1.4	•	5.3	2.8	1.7	2.0	1.3	1.2	1.2	1.4	0.5	0.3
Inventory Turnover **35**	18.6	•	22.4	18.3	10.0	17.6	31.7	33.8	25.4	12.8	10.2	22.4
Receivables Turnover **36**	9.9	•	66.7	18.6	8.1	4.7	5.4	5.8	7.0	6.3	3.4	4.8
Total Liabilities to Net Worth **37**	2.6	•	5.8	1.7	3.4	1.9	2.0	2.0	1.3	1.5	1.6	3.7
Current Assets to Working Capital **38**	4.5	•	2.1	2.7	3.2	2.4	3.8	3.2	3.4	3.0	•	•
Current Liabilities to Working Capital **39**	3.5	•	1.1	1.7	2.2	1.4	2.8	2.2	2.4	2.0	•	•
Working Capital to Net Sales **40**	0.1	•	0.0	0.1	0.1	0.2	0.1	0.1	0.1	0.1	0.5	0.3
Inventory to Working Capital **41**	0.3	•	0.2	0.4	0.3	0.1	0.2	0.1	0.2	0.3	•	•
Total Receipts to Cash Flow **42**	3.3	1.6	3.2	6.6	3.5	5.3	3.7	3.4	2.6	4.3	5.4	2.7
Cost of Goods to Cash Flow **43**	1.0	0.2	0.7	2.8	1.0	2.4	1.5	1.2	0.9	2.2	1.4	0.5
Cash Flow to Total Debt **44**	0.6	•	1.9	0.7	0.6	0.6	0.5	0.6	0.8	0.5	0.1	0.1

Selected Financial Factors (in Percentages)

Debt Ratio **45**	72.4	•	85.2	62.8	77.3	65.7	66.9	66.9	55.8	60.3	61.9	78.7
Return on Total Assets **46**	13.5	•	56.8	10.7	10.6	7.6	4.8	6.9	1.8	6.6	3.1	12.2
Return on Equity Before Income Taxes **47**	33.0	•	360.1	22.1	38.9	17.3	7.8	14.4	12.0	•	3.9	21.9
Return on Equity After Income Taxes **48**	28.7	•	355.4	21.1	37.5	12.5	4.8	9.3	8.9	•	3.8	14.1
Profit Margin (Before Income Tax) **49**	6.7	4.1	10.1	2.9	5.3	3.0	1.9	3.7	•	3.5	3.1	15.2
Profit Margin (After Income Tax) **50**	5.8	3.6	10.0	2.8	5.1	2.1	1.2	2.4	•	2.6	3.1	9.8

Table II

Corporations with Net Income

OTHER PROFESSIONAL, SCIENTIFIC, AND TECHNICAL SERVICES

MONEY AMOUNTS AND SIZE OF ASSETS IN THOUSANDS OF DOLLARS

Item Description for Accounting Period 7/07 Through 6/08	Total	Zero Assets	Under 500	500 to 1,000	1,000 to 5,000	5,000 to 10,000	10,000 to 25,000	25,000 to 50,000	50,000 to 100,000	100,000 to 250,000	250,000 to 500,000	500,000 to 2,500,000	2,500,000 and over
Number of Enterprises **1**	57249	11382	41252	2764	1420	152	160	48	34	19	5	11	0
Revenues ($ in Thousands)													
Net Sales **2**	58790638	1840994	22477154	5948484	5810305	2924425	4464479	2969740	3832113	2792750	1039871	4690322	0
Interest **3**	458642	2530	7283	3079	20487	5824	5841	10964	17818	31225	4637	348954	0
Rents **4**	11313	478	458	0	683	0	233	1530	331	0	0	7599	0
Royalties **5**	169347	4153	347	0	0	0	0	1503	683	10989	0	151672	0
Other Portfolio Income **6**	1422340	26685	22004	5811	31939	1457	52948	50072	25063	5466	1121	1199776	0
Other Receipts **7**	1463694	68779	232124	21650	188408	31630	407448	58803	41608	50436	8850	353957	0
Total Receipts **8**	62315974	1943619	22739370	5979024	6051822	2963336	4930949	3092612	3917616	2890866	1054479	6752280	0
Average Total Receipts **9**	1089	171	551	2163	4262	19496	30818	64429	115224	152151	210896	613844	•
Operating Costs/Operating Income (%)													
Cost of Operations **10**	27.4	26.7	20.5	41.4	20.8	47.9	44.6	28.2	31.7	31.8	11.0	18.7	•
Salaries and Wages **11**	19.8	12.5	19.0	19.6	18.9	17.8	21.8	23.0	12.5	25.8	31.8	25.0	•
Taxes Paid **12**	3.0	2.4	3.0	3.3	2.7	2.0	3.5	2.6	1.8	2.9	2.9	5.1	•
Interest Paid **13**	2.2	0.3	0.6	0.8	0.9	0.5	1.0	1.4	0.9	1.4	3.0	17.9	•
Depreciation **14**	1.2	1.7	0.9	0.8	1.4	0.8	0.8	1.9	1.1	2.1	2.2	2.7	•
Amortization and Depletion **15**	0.6	0.3	0.2	0.3	0.2	0.1	0.2	0.8	0.3	0.9	2.5	3.0	•
Pensions and Other Deferred Comp. **16**	1.2	0.8	1.3	1.4	1.8	0.4	0.7	0.6	0.5	2.0	1.2	2.0	•
Employee Benefits **17**	1.4	1.7	1.0	1.4	1.0	0.8	2.3	2.1	1.0	2.2	1.7	2.5	•
Advertising **18**	1.2	0.7	1.2	0.6	1.5	0.7	0.3	1.4	2.0	0.5	3.9	2.1	•
Other Expenses **19**	26.0	23.5	25.4	16.2	26.6	14.5	22.9	30.2	44.3	19.8	27.6	36.9	•
Officers' Compensation **20**	8.7	12.8	13.1	9.0	14.1	3.5	3.7	2.1	1.5	3.5	0.8	1.5	•
Operating Margin **21**	7.3	16.6	13.8	5.2	10.0	11.0	•	5.7	2.2	7.0	11.4	•	•
Operating Margin Before Officers' Comp. **22**	16.0	29.4	26.9	14.2	24.1	14.5	1.8	7.7	3.7	10.5	12.3	•	•

Selected Average Balance Sheet ($ in Thousands)

Net Receivables 23	89	0	8	155	303	2920	5038	10590	12352	24463	50549	91401
Inventories 24	12	0	5	49	59	405	381	347	1130	554	3154	3798
Net Property, Plant and Equipment 25	84	0	23	141	340	689	1624	5526	8419	13709	18827	154371
Total Assets 26	607	0	101	658	1996	7169	14578	34403	68048	159706	313765	1265392
Notes and Loans Payable 27	192	0	43	223	552	1261	3852	12678	12375	23410	86325	465082
All Other Liabilities 28	209	0	21	178	931	3165	5102	12847	25437	41469	126593	459138
Net Worth 29	206	0	37	256	513	2743	5625	8878	30236	94827	100847	341172

Selected Financial Ratios (Times to 1)

Current Ratio 30	1.4	•	2.2	1.9	1.6	1.6	1.6	1.6	1.3	1.8	1.2	0.8
Quick Ratio 31	1.0	•	1.9	1.4	1.5	1.4	1.3	1.3	0.9	1.3	0.7	0.4
Net Sales to Working Capital 32	16.1	•	19.1	11.4	10.2	8.3	8.1	8.7	14.1	5.0	9.5	•
Coverage Ratio 33	7.3	66.4	27.8	8.3	16.7	24.5	9.4	7.9	5.9	8.7	5.3	2.8
Total Asset Turnover 34	1.7	•	5.4	3.3	2.0	2.7	1.9	1.8	1.7	0.9	0.7	0.3
Inventory Turnover 35	24.2	•	23.0	18.2	14.4	22.8	32.6	50.3	31.7	84.5	7.3	21.0
Receivables Turnover 36	11.3	•	61.8	18.7	8.8	7.0	5.5	6.7	10.1	5.1	3.4	5.0
Total Liabilities to Net Worth 37	1.9	•	1.8	1.6	2.9	2.5	1.6	2.9	1.3	0.7	2.1	2.7
Current Assets to Working Capital 38	3.7	•	1.8	2.1	2.5	2.7	2.7	2.8	4.0	2.3	5.3	•
Current Liabilities to Working Capital 39	2.7	•	0.8	1.1	1.7	1.5	1.7	1.8	3.0	1.3	4.3	•
Working Capital to Net Sales 40	0.1	•	0.1	0.1	0.1	0.1	0.1	0.1	0.1	0.2	0.1	•
Inventory to Working Capital 41	0.2	•	0.1	0.3	0.1	0.1	0.1	0.1	0.2	0.0	0.2	•
Total Receipts to Cash Flow 42	3.0	2.5	2.9	6.0	2.9	4.1	3.7	2.8	2.2	3.7	2.9	1.8
Cost of Goods to Cash Flow 43	0.8	0.7	0.6	2.5	0.6	2.0	1.7	0.8	0.7	1.2	0.3	0.3
Cash Flow to Total Debt 44	0.9	•	2.9	0.9	1.0	1.1	0.8	0.9	1.4	0.6	0.3	0.3

Selected Financial Factors (in Percentages)

Debt Ratio 45	66.1	•	63.7	61.1	74.3	61.7	61.4	74.2	55.6	40.6	67.9	73.0
Return on Total Assets 46	27.1	•	83.8	21.1	30.9	34.4	18.2	20.2	9.0	10.9	10.4	17.2
Return on Equity Before Income Taxes 47	68.9	•	222.5	47.8	113.2	86.3	42.2	68.2	16.8	16.2	26.4	41.3
Return on Equity After Income Taxes 48	62.9	•	220.0	46.6	111.3	79.2	37.4	56.4	13.4	13.0	26.2	30.3
Profit Margin (Before Income Tax) 49	13.8	22.2	15.0	5.7	14.2	12.3	8.5	9.8	4.5	10.5	12.8	33.1
Profit Margin (After Income Tax) 50	12.6	21.2	14.8	5.5	13.9	11.3	7.5	8.1	3.6	8.4	12.7	24.3

Table I

Corporations with and without Net Income

OFFICES OF BANK HOLDING COMPANIES

MONEY AMOUNTS AND SIZE OF ASSETS IN THOUSANDS OF DOLLARS

Item Description for Accounting Period 7/07 Through 6/08	Total	Zero Assets	Under 500	500 to 1,000	1,000 to 5,000	5,000 to 10,000	10,000 to 25,000	25,000 to 50,000	50,000 to 100,000	100,000 to 250,000	250,000 to 500,000	500,000 to 2,500,000	2,500,000 and over
Number of Enterprises **1**	5059	103	0	8	32	45	219	573	944	1494	800	666	175
Revenues ($ in Thousands)													
Net Sales **2**	198238723	3869943	0	0	446	11229	37850	352595	1472591	4223439	3919813	8680658	175670160
Interest **3**	773286492	13438935	0	1827	2390	7568	290516	520118	1957402	8560065	11667511	32278261	704561899
Rents **4**	22611839	427073	0	0	0	34	215	1621	7029	33599	44889	210441	21886937
Royalties **5**	289319	0	0	0	0	0	8	8	433	194	330	8462	279883
Other Portfolio Income **6**	42160370	2550121	0	0	542	9503	9918	57111	154411	566029	711156	1475102	3662477
Other Receipts **7**	85841571	672934	0	485	1997	2228	56740	481545	1359973	3838367	4015923	7586203	67825177
Total Receipts **8**	1122428314	20959006	0	2312	5375	30562	395247	1412998	4951839	17221693	20359622	50239127	1006850533
Average Total Receipts **9**	221868	203485	•	289	168	679	1805	2466	5246	11527	25450	75434	5753432
Operating Costs/Operating Income (%)													
Cost of Operations **10**	1.6	•	•	•	•	•	•	•	0.7	0.2	0.4	0.1	1.7
Salaries and Wages **11**	67.6	57.7	•	•	303.4	20.1	135.7	48.0	41.2	53.2	69.0	82.4	67.7
Taxes Paid **12**	7.8	7.8	•	•	225.3	7.0	23.4	11.1	8.7	10.3	12.8	14.3	7.3
Interest Paid **13**	269.2	246.0	•	•	164.6	44.9	469.2	134.8	117.4	155.7	211.8	233.9	277.0
Depreciation **14**	13.6	15.2	•	•	14.8	5.0	15.4	7.9	8.4	9.8	11.4	13.3	13.8
Amortization and Depletion **15**	4.7	1.1	•	•	0.4	0.2	20.7	1.2	1.1	1.2	1.7	2.4	5.0
Pensions and Other Deferred Comp. **16**	2.5	2.8	•	•	7.0	0.6	9.3	3.9	3.0	3.6	4.2	5.1	2.3
Employee Benefits **17**	8.8	5.6	•	•	14.3	9.7	30.5	12.0	9.0	9.4	10.7	10.6	8.7
Advertising **18**	5.0	2.7	•	•	4.7	0.5	11.4	3.7	3.2	5.4	4.6	5.6	5.0
Other Expenses **19**	123.4	126.7	•	•	3003.8	68.5	239.7	78.1	70.3	71.5	82.4	98.4	127.2
Officers' Compensation **20**	5.5	4.8	•	•	6782.3	7.0	100.3	42.5	27.7	26.0	25.2	18.4	3.6
Operating Margin **21**	•	•	•	•	•	•	•	•	•	•	•	•	•
Operating Margin Before Officers' Comp. **22**	•	•	•	•	•	•	•	•	•	•	•	•	•

Selected Average Balance Sheet ($ in Thousands)

Net Receivables 23	1375414	0	•	208	575	9946	23538	46208	104991	228269	615860	35138655
Inventories 24	32	0	•	0	0	0	0	0	0	1	10	873
Net Property, Plant and Equipment 25	24610	0	•	1	11	209	614	1611	3628	7385	20298	558495
Total Assets 26	3335056	732		2168	8047	18782	37658	74316	162772	352450	1003372	89042182
Notes and Loans Payable 27	575930	271		0	272	435	753	3206	8103	20523	77082	16172573
All Other Liabilities 28	2303400	461		20	1473	13278	31408	63054	138010	298454	835806	60404593
Net Worth 29	455727	0		2148	6302	5069	5497	8056	16659	33472	90484	12465016

Selected Financial Ratios (Times to 1)

Current Ratio 30	0.8	•	•	1.6	2438.1	3.4	1.1	1.0	1.0	1.0	0.9	0.8
Quick Ratio 31	0.8	•	•	1.6	2438.1	1.6	1.0	1.0	1.0	1.0	0.9	0.7
Net Sales to Working Capital 32	•	•	•	•	0.0	0.3	0.1	1.1	7.9	•	•	•
Coverage Ratio 33	1.2	1.3	•	•	3.4	1.3	0.9	1.3	1.3	1.3	1.4	1.2
Total Asset Turnover 34	0.0	•	•	0.0	0.0	0.0	0.0	0.0	0.0	0.0	0.0	0.0
Inventory Turnover 35	19.2	•	•	•	•	•	•	•	16.0	13.9	19.7	20.1
Receivables Turnover 36	0.0	•	•	0.1	0.0	0.4	0.0	0.0	0.0	0.0	0.0	0.0
Total Liabilities to Net Worth 37	6.3	•	•	0.0	0.3	2.7	5.9	8.2	8.8	9.5	10.1	6.1
Current Assets to Working Capital 38	•	•	•	2.7	1.0	1.4	9.6	17.8	44.5	392.4	•	•
Current Liabilities to Working Capital 39	•	•	•	1.7	0.0	0.4	8.6	16.8	43.5	391.4	•	•
Working Capital to Net Sales 40	•	•	•	•	142.1	13.4	9.1	3.0	0.9	0.1	1.3	•
Inventory to Working Capital 41	•	•	•	•	•	0.0	0.0	0.0	0.0	0.0	•	•
Total Receipts to Cash Flow 42	0.6	0.5	•	•	0.6	0.8	0.5	0.8	0.8	0.7	0.6	0.6
Cost of Goods to Cash Flow 43	0.0	•	•	•	•	0.0	0.0	0.0	0.0	0.0	0.0	0.0
Cash Flow to Total Debt 44	0.0	•	•	0.4	0.3	0.0	0.0	0.0	0.0	0.0	0.0	0.0

Selected Financial Factors (in Percentages)

Debt Ratio 45	86.3	100.0	•	0.9	21.7	73.0	85.4	89.2	89.8	90.5	91.0	86.0
Return on Total Assets 46	3.8	33.9	•	21.7	4.7	4.1	3.0	3.2	3.6	3.9	4.1	3.7
Return on Equity Before Income Taxes 47	4.9	•	•	•	4.3	•	5.2	7.1	8.6	10.6	12.0	4.5
Return on Equity After Income Taxes 48	3.3	•	•	•	2.7	•	4.4	5.9	6.8	8.0	8.7	2.9
Profit Margin (Before Income Tax) 49	57.0	67.0	•	108.1	•	•	46.4	36.7	50.9	72.1	83.6	55.5
Profit Margin (After Income Tax) 50	38.0	43.9	•	68.4	•	•	39.0	40.2	54.7	60.1	36.4	

Table II

Corporations with Net Income

OFFICES OF BANK HOLDING COMPANIES

MONEY AMOUNTS AND SIZE OF ASSETS IN THOUSANDS OF DOLLARS

Item Description for Accounting Period 7/07 Through 6/08	Total	Zero Assets	Under 500	500 to 1,000	1,000 to 5,000	5,000 to 10,000	10,000 to 25,000	25,000 to 50,000	50,000 to 100,000	100,000 to 250,000	250,000 to 500,000	500,000 to 2,500,000	2,500,000 and over
Number of Enterprises 1	4441	47	0	•	•	27	158	476	821	1334	745	625	170
Revenues ($ in Thousands)													
Net Sales 2	196598935	3468059	0	•	•	7360	25157	303321	1342115	3894579	3741134	8397457	175419753
Interest 3	76414348	12015148	0	•	•	7532	120929	411602	1636160	7598271	10944992	30282929	701121717
Rents 4	22077920	346117	0	•	•	34	140	928	6316	29427	43885	202511	21448561
Royalties 5	289078	0	0	•	•	0	0	8	433	194	330	8229	279883
Other Portfolio Income 6	41680988	2497786	0	•	•	9159	8369	51402	135658	494175	660691	1430657	36392847
Other Receipts 7	84293115	496290	0	•	•	2183	36554	420412	1257573	3463486	3738233	7067429	67810473
Total Receipts 8	1109083534	18823400	0	•	•	26268	191149	1187673	4378255	15480132	19129265	47389212	1002473234
Average Total Receipts 9	249737	400498	•	•	•	973	1210	2495	5333	11604	25677	75823	5896901
Operating Costs/Operating Income (%)													
Cost of Operations 10	1.6	•	•	•	•	•	•	•	0.0	0.2	0.5	0.1	1.7
Salaries and Wages 11	67.1	48.3	•	•	•	22.4	71.7	43.4	37.8	50.4	66.7	79.7	67.6
Taxes Paid 12	7.7	6.3	•	•	•	2.6	20.1	10.4	8.4	10.0	12.7	14.0	7.3
Interest Paid 13	268.3	253.7	•	•	•	47.5	230.9	126.1	111.0	149.0	206.6	225.7	276.0
Depreciation 14	13.1	13.6	•	•	•	6.8	12.6	7.0	7.3	9.2	11.0	12.8	13.3
Amortization and Depletion 15	4.7	1.1	•	•	•	0.3	1.9	0.9	0.9	1.1	1.6	2.4	5.0
Pensions and Other Deferred Comp. 16	2.4	2.0	•	•	•	0.2	13.5	3.7	3.0	3.5	4.2	5.0	2.2
Employee Benefits 17	8.7	4.0	•	•	•	14.1	24.5	11.3	8.7	9.1	10.5	10.3	8.6
Advertising 18	5.0	2.4	•	•	•	0.3	4.6	3.3	2.9	5.3	4.4	5.5	5.0
Other Expenses 19	122.3	123.0	•	•	•	87.2	121.1	64.1	63.5	64.1	76.5	89.3	126.7
Officers' Compensation 20	5.3	3.1	•	•	•	7.1	113.7	40.5	26.3	25.2	24.5	17.8	3.6
Operating Margin 21	•	•	•	•	•	•	•	•	•	•	•	•	•
Operating Margin Before Officers' Comp. 22	•	•	•	•	•	•	•	•	•	•	•	•	•

Selected Average Balance Sheet ($ in Thousands)

Net Receivables 23	1547835	•	958	11183	23425	46514	105263	230963	624542	35999823
Inventories 24	36	•	0	0	0	1	0	1	11	898
Net Property, Plant and Equipment 25	26878	•	19	223	505	1467	3534	7251	20361	559071
Total Assets 26	3763808	•	7926	19695	37643	74523	162849	352184	1007533	91313221
Notes and Loans Payable 27	652828	•	453	558	685	3043	7930	20221	77360	1660169
All Other Liabilities 28	2595330	•	2252	15253	31695	63757	138205	299026	838493	61910329
Net Worth 29	515651	•	5221	3884	5263	7723	16715	32937	91679	12801200

Selected Financial Ratios (Times to 1)

Current Ratio 30	0.8	•	3.6	1.1	1.1	1.0	1.0	1.0	0.9	0.8
Quick Ratio 31	0.8	•	1.6	1.1	1.0	1.0	1.0	1.0	0.9	0.7
Net Sales to Working Capital 32	•	•	0.1	0.1	0.3	1.0	6.9	•	•	•
Coverage Ratio 33	1.2	1.3	4.5	1.6	1.6	1.4	1.4	1.4	1.4	1.2
Total Asset Turnover 34	0.0	•	0.0	0.0	0.0	0.0	0.0	0.0	0.0	0.0
Inventory Turnover 35	19.2	•	•	•	•	0.0	15.1	19.7	1.3	20.1
Receivables Turnover 36	0.0	•	•	0.0	0.0	0.0	0.0	0.0	0.0	0.0
Total Liabilities to Net Worth 37	6.3	•	0.5	4.1	6.2	8.7	8.7	9.7	10.0	6.1
Current Assets to Working Capital 38	•	•	1.4	12.2	18.1	39.6	330.6	•	•	•
Current Liabilities to Working Capital 39	•	•	0.4	11.2	17.1	38.6	329.6	•	•	•
Working Capital to Net Sales 40	•	•	20.0	8.6	2.9	1.0	0.1	•	•	•
Inventory to Working Capital 41	•	•	•	0.0	0.0	0.0	0.0	•	•	•
Total Receipts to Cash Flow 42	0.6	0.5	0.4	0.4	0.7	0.9	0.8	0.6	0.6	0.6
Cost of Goods to Cash Flow 43	0.0	•	•	•	0.0	0.0	0.0	0.0	0.0	0.0
Cash Flow to Total Debt 44	0.0	•	0.3	0.0	0.0	0.0	0.0	0.0	0.0	0.0

Selected Financial Factors (in Percentages)

Debt Ratio 45	86.3	•	34.1	80.3	86.0	89.6	89.7	90.6	90.9	86.0
Return on Total Assets 46	3.8	•	7.4	2.9	3.3	3.5	3.8	4.1	4.2	3.8
Return on Equity Before Income Taxes 47	5.0	•	8.8	5.3	8.4	10.1	10.5	12.1	13.3	4.5
Return on Equity After Income Taxes 48	3.4	•	6.1	4.5	7.4	8.7	8.5	9.4	9.8	3.0
Profit Margin (Before Income Tax) 49	58.4	81.7	168.2	128.3	69.7	47.8	60.2	79.6	91.0	55.9
Profit Margin (After Income Tax) 50	39.2	56.3	117.7	109.2	61.2	41.0	48.6	61.4	66.7	36.8

Table I

Corporations with and without Net Income

OFFICES OF OTHER HOLDING COMPANIES

MONEY AMOUNTS AND SIZE OF ASSETS IN THOUSANDS OF DOLLARS

Item Description for Accounting Period 7/07 Through 6/08		Total	Zero Assets	Under 500	500 to 1,000	1,000 to 5,000	5,000 to 10,000	10,000 to 25,000	25,000 to 50,000	50,000 to 100,000	100,000 to 250,000	250,000 to 500,000	500,000 to 2,500,000	2,500,000 and over
Number of Enterprises	1	42807	8877	23055	3184	4502	1130	968	422	262	218	84	82	25
Revenues ($ in Thousands)														
Net Sales	2	1442168	27700	14401	29355	12708	193023	87367	22709	146927	72466	442690	246232	146593
Interest	3	6692630	181723	35515	36470	112025	56987	136541	168596	278992	424101	478136	2148545	2634999
Rents	4	219220	1936	3215	3827	9042	21558	7869	51922	32482	22974	14990	33224	16182
Royalties	5	118034	774	905	14	10430	1650	92	10972	4098	60335	20390	3686	4689
Other Portfolio Income	6	6863489	656052	319080	176218	740760	227115	443350	380017	463869	646680	444682	1327402	1038264
Other Receipts	7	8055991	333045	96721	66296	666322	628687	531504	715718	470139	15432	1129735	2693823	708564
Total Receipts	8	23391532	1201230	469837	312180	1551287	1129020	1206723	1349934	1396507	1241988	2530623	6452912	4549291
Average Total Receipts	9	546	135	20	98	345	999	1247	3199	5330	5697	30126	78694	181972
Operating Costs/Operating Income (%)														
Cost of Operations	10	16.0	101.7	•	•	12.8	2.0	5.6	•	66.5	50.5	8.8	7.8	•
Salaries and Wages	11	80.1	222.1	136.7	16.1	335.7	76.5	57.1	178.2	55.5	320.5	42.6	79.0	63.1
Taxes Paid	12	46.7	299.0	101.4	52.2	461.8	21.1	37.4	171.6	24.8	77.1	15.1	80.2	22.1
Interest Paid	13	396.0	536.3	318.9	19.8	621.2	32.7	140.7	691.8	167.6	475.3	87.1	806.9	1449.4
Depreciation	14	12.0	42.2	4.6	4.3	116.2	3.8	12.1	45.1	13.7	43.6	8.3	10.9	1.3
Amortization and Depletion	15	23.1	103.7	23.5	1.8	155.5	1.8	12.1	135.7	41.9	40.0	10.1	40.8	0.5
Pensions and Other Deferred Comp.	16	2.7	0.3	•	0.7	44.9	2.5	2.7	14.5	5.3	5.0	1.6	1.8	0.1
Employee Benefits	17	5.8	10.5	34.6	3.1	63.8	4.7	3.3	13.7	2.9	24.4	3.8	2.9	4.2
Advertising	18	1.2	0.1	0.5	•	0.5	0.3	2.3	1.3	4.9	1.3	0.8	1.0	0.4
Other Expenses	19	665.3	5163.7	1577.8	1075.0	3504.6	196.6	606.9	2718.9	537.8	951.1	147.3	1208.6	369.4
Officers' Compensation	20	25.2	39.3	71.0	23.9	645.9	26.9	49.6	77.8	7.6	46.6	3.0	19.0	24.3
Operating Margin	21	•	•	•	•	•	•	•	•	•	•	•	•	•
Operating Margin Before Officers' Comp.	22	•	•	•	•	•	•	•	•	•	•	•	•	•

Selected Average Balance Sheet ($ in Thousands)

Item													
Net Receivables 23	506	0	7	16	64	182	545	1386	2618	6197	9354	26222	594245
Inventories 24	2	0	0	0	2	0	2	64	57	152	98	240	0
Net Property, Plant and Equipment 25	135	0	0	8	77	314	318	1314	1671	4945	4701	27241	1115
Total Assets 26	8949	0	130	710	2196	7078	16019	35134	69530	149820	349494	1140699	6233548
Notes and Loans Payable 27	1733	0	50	76	785	731	3080	5655	11107	25270	65312	268300	1085904
All Other Liabilities 28	1229	0	13	82	296	510	2149	2637	7354	16895	40052	122129	1119564
Net Worth 29	5987	0	68	553	1115	5836	10790	26843	51069	107656	244131	750270	4028079

Selected Financial Ratios (Times to 1)

Item													
Current Ratio 30	1.2	•	1.5	6.6	1.9	4.7	1.9	2.4	3.9	2.3	2.7	1.5	0.7
Quick Ratio 31	0.9	•	1.2	3.9	1.1	2.8	1.3	1.4	2.8	1.8	1.9	1.0	0.6
Net Sales to Working Capital 32	0.1	•	0.0	0.0	0.0	0.1	0.1	0.0	0.1	0.0	0.1	0.0	•
Coverage Ratio 33	1.9	•	4.0	•	10.9	7.4	3.8	3.6	1.1	0.4	4.1	1.5	1.8
Total Asset Turnover 34	0.0	•	0.0	0.0	0.0	0.0	0.0	0.0	0.0	0.0	0.0	0.0	0.0
Inventory Turnover 35	2.3	•	•	•	0.2	•	3.4	•	6.6	1.1	4.7	1.0	•
Receivables Turnover 36	0.1	•	•	0.0	1.3	0.1	0.1	•	0.2	0.1	0.4	0.1	0.0
Total Liabilities to Net Worth 37	0.5	•	0.3	1.0	0.2	0.5	0.5	0.3	0.4	0.4	0.4	0.5	0.5
Current Assets to Working Capital 38	5.2	•	1.2	2.1	1.3	1.3	2.1	1.7	1.3	1.8	1.6	2.8	•
Current Liabilities to Working Capital 39	4.2	•	2.2	1.1	0.3	0.7	1.1	0.7	0.3	0.8	0.6	1.8	•
Working Capital to Net Sales 40	9.2	•	24.7	98.3	19.2	7.9	87.7	19.3	47.4	6.7	22.3	1.8	•
Inventory to Working Capital 41	0.0	•	•	0.0	0.0	0.0	0.0	0.0	0.0	0.0	0.0	0.0	•
Total Receipts to Cash Flow 42	0.1	0.3	0.2	0.0	0.3	0.3	0.0	0.3	0.0	0.4	0.3	0.1	•
Cost of Goods to Cash Flow 43	0.0	0.3	•	0.0	0.0	•	0.0	0.2	0.0	0.0	0.0	0.0	•
Cash Flow to Total Debt 44	0.1	•	0.3	0.1	0.4	0.1	0.1	0.2	0.1	0.4	0.2	0.1	0.0

Selected Financial Factors (in Percentages)

Item													
Debt Ratio 45	33.1	•	48.2	22.2	49.2	17.5	32.6	23.6	26.6	28.1	30.1	34.2	35.4
Return on Total Assets 46	2.9	•	6.1	•	8.7	5.9	3.0	3.8	1.5	0.5	5.4	3.2	2.5
Return on Equity Before Income Taxes 47	2.0	•	8.7	•	15.6	6.2	3.3	3.6	0.2	•	5.8	1.6	1.8
Return on Equity After Income Taxes 48	0.7	•	6.1	•	11.6	4.2	1.6	2.5	•	•	3.8	•	1.4
Profit Margin (Before Income Tax) 49	363.9	•	945.9	6165.8	210.4	392.3	1801.0	17.0	•	•	268.5	405.2	1231.0
Profit Margin (After Income Tax) 50	126.2	•	662.9	4571.0	143.5	193.2	1262.2	•	•	•	174.8	•	988.0

Table II

Corporations with Net Income

OFFICES OF OTHER HOLDING COMPANIES

MONEY AMOUNTS AND SIZE OF ASSETS IN THOUSANDS OF DOLLARS

Item Description for Accounting Period 7/07 Through 6/08	Total	Zero Assets	Under 500	500 to 1000	251 to 500	501 to 1,000	1,001 to 5,000	5,001 to 10,000	10,001 to 25,000	25,001 to 50,000	50,001 to 100,000	100,001 to 250,000	250,001 and over
Number of Enterprises **1**	14522	3044	5904	•	•	551	435	188	126	122	48	54	20
Revenues ($ in Thousands)													
Net Sales **2**	1165304	336	370	•	•	189934	68805	3626	87230	54941	419439	233585	65008
Interest **3**	5018783	40088	13617	•	•	25563	80100	118667	207333	291723	342779	1854828	1915546
Rents **4**	168015	1633	1382	•	•	21114	6952	51192	24502	6191	14990	11139	16182
Royalties **5**	49313	245	706	•	•	1646	76	10710	5	19608	0	2239	4689
Other Portfolio Income **6**	6294281	614364	294225	•	•	203140	399925	328517	352693	571959	360159	1267168	1037008
Other Receipts **7**	11032282	1482682	194380	•	•	684435	781683	775013	945007	946277	1021572	2460451	704674
Total Receipts **8**	23727978	2139348	504680	•	•	1125832	1337541	1287725	1616770	1890699	2158939	5829410	3743107
Average Total Receipts **9**	1634	703	85	•	•	2043	3075	6850	12832	15498	44978	107952	187155
Operating Costs/Operating Income (%)													
Cost of Operations **10**	12.6	•	•	•	•	2.0	1.6	•	58.1	64.5	9.2	6.4	•
Salaries and Wages **11**	54.5	1183.6	890.8	•	•	68.1	53.1	462.1	80.4	27.4	35.9	41.9	142.2
Taxes Paid **12**	45.1	19358.3	2365.9	•	•	17.3	36.0	834.7	33.2	72.7	14.3	65.7	47.5
Interest Paid **13**	272.6	13744.3	2727.0	•	•	9.2	72.8	1804.8	149.8	303.7	57.2	520.6	1821.8
Depreciation **14**	10.1	1153.3	19.2	•	•	3.4	5.0	138.7	15.8	35.5	8.5	7.7	2.9
Amortization and Depletion **15**	10.1	3000.3	126.8	•	•	1.2	12.0	116.9	6.9	37.9	4.2	19.0	1.2
Pensions and Other Deferred Comp. **16**	2.1	•	•	•	•	0.7	2.9	68.7	6.2	2.2	1.0	1.4	0.3
Employee Benefits **17**	3.7	56.0	226.2	•	•	2.6	1.4	45.2	2.8	2.1	3.5	2.8	9.5
Advertising **18**	0.9	0.3	15.4	•	•	0.3	1.1	3.7	3.9	1.5	0.5	1.0	1.0
Other Expenses **19**	196.5	32914.0	10290.8	•	•	57.3	205.1	3833.3	245.6	304.8	67.0	185.5	688.9
Officers' Compensation **20**	22.3	1977.1	2144.6	•	•	13.8	28.1	357.0	8.4	21.1	2.2	18.3	54.8
Operating Margin **21**	•	•	•	•	•	•	•	•	•	•	•	•	•
Operating Margin Before Officers' Comp. **22**	•	•	•	•	•	•	•	•	•	•	•	•	•

Selected Average Balance Sheet ($ in Thousands)

Net Receivables 23	1327	0	8	•	144	386	1347	2975	7160	10789	39088	738383
Inventories 24	4	0	0	•	0	1	0	74	83	277	339	0
Net Property, Plant and Equipment 25	183	0	0	•	529	250	1065	2205	2800	7852	18134	1394
Total Assets 26	17761	0	135	•	6887	16124	34833	70823	148847	339736	1220765	6229356
Notes and Loans Payable 27	1960	0	28	•	571	1651	4518	8463	22230	61795	242879	291785
All Other Liabilities 28	2934	0	3	•	328	865	3267	8559	18329	36329	147401	1399508
Net Worth 29	12867	0	104	•	5988	13609	27047	53802	108288	241612	830485	4538063

Selected Financial Ratios (Times to 1)

Current Ratio 30	1.7	•	3.3	•	10.9	3.2	2.8	3.6	3.0	2.8	1.9	1.3
Quick Ratio 31	1.4	•	2.4	•	5.9	2.6	1.6	2.8	2.4	2.3	1.3	1.1
Net Sales to Working Capital 32	0.1	•	0.0	•	0.2	0.1	0.0	0.1	0.0	0.2	0.0	0.0
Coverage Ratio 33	6.3	41.9	44.0	•	46.0	21.7	16.2	9.8	9.8	7.0	4.2	2.7
Total Asset Turnover 34	0.0	•	0.0	•	0.1	0.0	0.0	0.0	0.0	0.0	0.0	0.0
Inventory Turnover 35	2.8	•	•	•	•	4.9	•	5.4	3.5	2.9	0.8	•
Receivables Turnover 36	0.1	•	•	•	•	0.3	•	0.2	0.1	0.8	0.1	0.0
Total Liabilities to Net Worth 37	0.4	•	0.3	•	0.2	0.2	0.3	0.3	0.4	0.4	0.5	0.4
Current Assets to Working Capital 38	2.4	•	1.4	•	1.1	1.5	1.6	1.4	1.5	1.6	2.2	4.4
Current Liabilities to Working Capital 39	1.4	•	0.4	•	0.1	0.5	0.6	0.4	0.5	0.6	1.2	3.4
Working Capital to Net Sales 40	19.9	•	780.8	•	4.7	13.5	312.7	17.8	49.8	4.4	28.5	86.9
Inventory to Working Capital 41	0.0	•	•	•	•	0.0	0.0	0.0	0.0	0.0	0.0	•
Total Receipts to Cash Flow 42	0.1	0.0	0.0	•	0.3	0.1	0.1	0.1	0.0	0.3	0.1	0.0
Cost of Goods to Cash Flow 43	0.0	•	•	•	0.0	0.0	•	0.0	0.0	0.0	0.0	•
Cash Flow to Total Debt 44	0.2	•	1.4	•	1.5	0.8	0.6	0.5	0.2	0.3	0.2	0.1

Selected Financial Factors (in Percentages)

Debt Ratio 45	27.6	•	23.1	•	13.1	15.6	22.4	24.0	27.2	28.9	32.0	27.2
Return on Total Assets 46	7.7	•	55.8	•	21.3	15.5	16.2	14.3	9.0	10.2	7.8	2.6
Return on Equity Before Income Taxes 47	9.0	•	70.9	•	24.0	17.5	19.6	16.9	11.1	12.3	8.7	2.2
Return on Equity After Income Taxes 48	7.2	•	64.3	•	21.6	14.6	17.2	14.2	8.7	8.8	6.2	1.8
Profit Margin (Before Income Tax) 49	1440.3	562619.6	117212.2	•	416.1	1506.2	27504.3	1313.5	2673.8	340.6	1668.3	3130.6
Profit Margin (After Income Tax) 50	1151.6	464525.3	106196.5	•	374.5	1255.4	24146.0	1104.2	2098.1	243.5	1189.2	2582.5

Administrative and Support and Waste Management and Remediation Services
561300

Table I
Corporations with and without Net Income

EMPLOYMENT SERVICES

MONEY AMOUNTS AND SIZE OF ASSETS IN THOUSANDS OF DOLLARS

Item Description for Accounting Period 7/07 Through 6/08	Total	Zero Assets	Under 500	500 to 1,000	1,000 to 5,000	5,000 to 10,000	10,000 to 25,000	25,000 to 50,000	50,000 to 100,000	100,000 to 250,000	250,000 to 500,000	500,000 to 2,500,000	2,500,000 and over
Number of Enterprises 1	29208	3356	22283	1536	1580	234	114	32	25	16	15	17	0
Revenues ($ in Thousands)													
Net Sales 2	174020713	3279517	44929171	5607938	28956231	5204125	10235110	3262770	8888650	7984430	10184740	45480032	0
Interest 3	300944	1515	3952	447	9194	1657	9502	6369	6118	2673	25479	234037	0
Rents 4	6817	0	0	0	359	564	1710	2553	0	728	0	903	0
Royalties 5	367629	0	0	0	0	0	0	0	0	2558	56197	308873	0
Other Portfolio Income 6	212027	276	3694	571	21677	644	3073	8143	10634	2338	44378	116602	0
Other Receipts 7	1694983	15551	22593	2837	163575	20594	12550	11065	140866	13024	47974	1244353	0
Total Receipts 8	176603113	3296859	44959410	5611793	29151036	5227584	10261945	3290900	9046268	8005751	10358768	47392800	0
Average Total Receipts 9	6046	982	2018	3654	18450	22340	90017	102841	361851	500359	690585	2787812	•
Operating Costs/Operating Income (%)													
Cost of Operations 10	48.2	55.9	32.9	52.8	55.0	47.8	48.9	46.4	43.7	64.2	55.6	54.4	•
Salaries and Wages 11	29.0	27.0	40.0	28.5	23.2	30.2	29.9	31.7	40.9	20.7	24.8	21.5	•
Taxes Paid 12	6.5	7.4	7.6	4.8	6.0	4.6	6.1	7.5	5.8	7.1	4.6	6.4	•
Interest Paid 13	0.5	0.2	0.2	0.2	0.3	0.4	0.3	0.7	0.5	1.2	1.1	0.7	•
Depreciation 14	0.3	0.1	0.1	0.2	0.2	0.3	0.2	0.5	0.2	0.3	0.5	0.5	•
Amortization and Depletion 15	0.3	0.0	0.0	0.2	0.0	0.1	0.2	0.2	0.2	0.7	1.0	0.6	•
Pensions and Other Deferred Comp. 16	0.2	0.5	0.5	0.1	0.0	0.4	0.0	0.1	0.1	0.1	0.2	0.1	•
Employee Benefits 17	2.6	3.3	3.1	0.8	2.2	2.5	2.6	4.3	2.6	1.6	1.6	2.9	•
Advertising 18	0.3	0.1	0.4	0.6	0.2	0.6	0.5	0.4	0.2	0.2	0.3	0.3	•
Other Expenses 19	9.1	3.3	9.4	7.9	10.3	6.6	8.5	7.4	4.5	3.5	8.5	11.2	•
Officers' Compensation 20	1.7	1.8	4.2	1.3	1.2	2.3	1.6	1.3	0.3	0.4	0.6	0.5	•
Operating Margin 21	1.2	1.0	1.5	2.8	1.4	4.2	1.1	•	1.0	0.1	1.1	0.9	•
Operating Margin Before Officers' Comp. 22	3.0	2.8	5.7	4.1	2.5	6.5	2.7	0.9	1.3	0.4	1.7	1.3	•

Selected Average Balance Sheet ($ in Thousands)

Net Receivables 23	420	0	17	316	716	2726	6164	11608	25870	38734	120320	322929	•
Inventories 24	3	0	0	0	8	0	57	7	250	216	219	2583	•
Net Property, Plant and Equipment 25	93	0	12	48	112	470	859	2550	3256	4995	14403	90461	•
Total Assets 26	1458	0	97	620	2214	7053	15518	33416	69627	160150	378474	1264022	•
Notes and Loans Payable 27	323	0	50	99	835	1490	3078	9019	19461	67958	99954	164449	•
All Other Liabilities 28	512	0	44	243	869	2112	6496	14780	26453	64055	120075	414001	•
Net Worth 29	622	0	4	278	509	3451	5944	9617	23713	28137	158444	685572	•

Selected Financial Ratios (Times to 1)

Current Ratio 30	1.3	•	1.0	1.7	1.3	1.5	1.4	1.6	1.5	1.0	1.7	1.2	•
Quick Ratio 31	1.1	•	0.8	1.5	1.0	1.1	1.1	1.2	1.4	0.8	1.5	1.0	•
Net Sales to Working Capital 32	39.5	•	•	20.8	61.8	13.6	30.5	14.2	29.5	180.0	9.2	34.1	•
Coverage Ratio 33	7.0	8.4	8.9	16.0	8.7	13.6	5.5	1.4	6.5	1.2	3.5	9.0	•
Total Asset Turnover 34	4.1	•	20.7	5.9	8.3	3.2	5.8	3.1	5.1	3.1	1.8	2.1	•
Inventory Turnover 35	1094.6	•	•	25980.5	1236.2	•	766.4	7060.1	620.4	1480.0	1721.7	563.5	•
Receivables Turnover 36	14.8	•	89.8	17.4	31.7	8.7	15.6	7.9	17.0	11.4	6.8	8.1	•
Total Liabilities to Net Worth 37	1.3	•	25.7	1.2	3.3	1.0	1.6	2.5	1.9	4.7	1.4	0.8	•
Current Assets to Working Capital 38	4.5	•	•	2.5	4.7	2.9	3.6	2.8	2.9	22.1	2.5	5.9	•
Current Liabilities to Working Capital 39	3.5	•	•	1.5	3.7	1.9	2.6	1.8	1.9	21.1	1.5	4.9	•
Working Capital to Net Sales 40	0.0	•	•	0.0	0.0	0.0	0.0	0.1	0.0	0.0	0.1	0.0	•
Inventory to Working Capital 41	0.0	•	•	0.0	0.0	•	0.0	0.0	0.0	0.0	0.0	0.0	•
Total Receipts to Cash Flow 42	9.4	22.5	10.2	10.3	8.7	9.9	11.2	16.1	15.0	31.6	10.2	6.8	•
Cost of Goods to Cash Flow 43	4.5	12.6	3.4	5.5	4.8	4.7	5.5	7.5	6.6	20.3	5.7	3.7	•
Cash Flow to Total Debt 44	0.8	2.1	2.1	1.0	1.2	0.6	0.8	0.3	0.5	0.1	0.3	0.7	•

Selected Financial Factors (in Percentages)

Debt Ratio 45	57.3	•	96.3	55.1	77.0	51.1	61.7	71.2	65.9	82.4	58.1	45.8	•
Return on Total Assets 46	13.7	•	35.3	18.0	19.0	15.9	9.9	3.2	16.5	4.6	7.1	13.5	•
Return on Equity Before Income Taxes 47	27.6	•	838.3	37.5	73.0	30.1	21.1	3.3	41.1	5.2	12.1	22.2	•
Return on Equity After Income Taxes 48	22.5	•	827.1	35.8	70.2	28.3	16.6	0.5	40.0	0.9	9.0	16.0	•
Profit Margin (Before Income Tax) 49	2.9	1.5	1.5	2.9	2.0	4.7	1.4	0.3	2.7	0.3	2.8	5.7	•
Profit Margin (After Income Tax) 50	2.4	1.4	1.5	2.7	1.9	4.4	1.1	0.0	2.7	0.1	2.1	4.1	•

Table II
Corporations with Net Income

EMPLOYMENT SERVICES

MONEY AMOUNTS AND SIZE OF ASSETS IN THOUSANDS OF DOLLARS

Item Description for Accounting Period 7/07 Through 6/08	Total	Zero Assets	Under 500	500 to 1,000	1,000 to 5,000	5,000 to 10,000	10,000 to 25,000	25,000 to 50,000	50,000 to 100,000	100,000 to 250,000	250,000 to 500,000	500,000 to 2,500,000	2,500,000 and over
Number of Enterprises 1	17516	359	14631	1295	885	•	92	19	19	9	10	•	0
Revenues ($ in Thousands)													
Net Sales 2	129590754	2113163	29861668	4103173	12104396	•	7811862	2374802	7954333	6209608	8413610	•	0
Interest 3	288050	372	2982	369	7514	•	8279	5072	3962	1539	23310	•	0
Rents 4	4596	0	0	0	359	•	76	2553	0	728	0	•	0
Royalties 5	363597	0	0	0	0	•	0	0	0	0	54723	•	0
Other Portfolio Income 6	182989	276	417	571	17182	•	3073	2783	6413	2192	32838	•	0
Other Receipts 7	1631385	15551	19527	2684	142774	•	8831	2730	139844	10431	29543	•	0
Total Receipts 8	132061371	2129362	29884594	4106797	12272225	•	7832121	2387940	8104552	6224498	8554024	•	0
Average Total Receipts 9	7539	5931	2043	3171	13867	•	85132	125681	426555	691611	855402	•	•
Operating Costs/Operating Income (%)													
Cost of Operations 10	47.7	86.7	27.7	53.1	55.3	•	45.6	54.9	42.4	66.3	54.3	•	•
Salaries and Wages 11	28.0	1.4	42.5	27.6	13.6	•	31.4	22.9	42.4	20.0	24.7	•	•
Taxes Paid 12	6.6	4.3	9.1	4.5	3.9	•	6.1	8.0	5.8	7.5	5.0	•	•
Interest Paid 13	0.5	0.1	0.2	0.2	0.3	•	0.3	0.4	0.3	0.7	1.2	•	•
Depreciation 14	0.3	0.0	0.1	0.2	0.2	•	0.2	0.3	0.1	0.2	0.5	•	•
Amortization and Depletion 15	0.3	0.0	0.0	0.1	0.0	•	0.2	0.1	0.1	0.3	1.0	•	•
Pensions and Other Deferred Comp. 16	0.3	0.0	0.7	0.1	0.1	•	0.0	0.1	0.1	0.2	0.2	•	•
Employee Benefits 17	2.3	2.3	2.1	0.5	1.4	•	2.2	5.3	2.8	1.5	1.4	•	•
Advertising 18	0.4	0.0	0.5	0.7	0.4	•	0.5	0.3	0.1	0.1	0.3	•	•
Other Expenses 19	9.5	1.7	8.4	7.0	17.8	•	9.2	5.0	3.8	2.2	8.6	•	•
Officers' Compensation 20	1.9	0.8	5.4	1.4	1.7	•	2.0	1.4	0.2	0.3	0.7	•	•
Operating Margin 21	2.4	2.7	3.4	4.6	5.4	•	2.2	1.4	1.8	0.8	2.2	•	•
Operating Margin Before Officers' Comp. 22	4.4	3.4	8.7	6.1	7.0	•	4.2	2.8	2.0	1.0	2.8	•	•

Selected Average Balance Sheet ($ in Thousands)

	•	•	•	•	•	•	•	•	•	•	•
Net Receivables 23	601	0	22	324	983	•	6299	13056	27621	36494	133142
Inventories 24	3	0	0	0	0	•	71	11	416	203	0
Net Property, Plant and Equipment 25	134	0	12	53	115	•	788	3140	3340	5379	14542
Total Assets 26	2037	0	119	632	2191	•	14824	34789	70430	169662	409139
Notes and Loans Payable 27	389	0	49	73	657	•	3096	9925	17448	50553	109048
All Other Liabilities 28	665	0	28	241	613	•	6180	15378	30498	77032	133666
Net Worth 29	982	0	43	318	922	•	5548	9486	22485	42077	166424

Selected Financial Ratios (Times to 1)

	•	•	•	•	•	•	•	•	•	•	•
Current Ratio 30	1.4	•	1.4	1.7	1.9	•	1.4	1.8	1.4	0.9	1.7
Quick Ratio 31	1.2	•	1.2	1.5	1.6	•	1.1	1.5	1.3	0.8	1.6
Net Sales to Working Capital 32	29.3	•	83.8	18.9	16.1	•	28.5	12.9	38.3	•	9.3
Coverage Ratio 33	10.3	64.3	18.2	21.5	21.3	•	9.4	5.7	11.5	2.4	4.3
Total Asset Turnover 34	3.6	•	17.1	5.0	6.2	•	5.7	3.6	5.9	4.1	2.1
Inventory Turnover 35	1075.9	•	19125.2	743806.0	•	•	544.9	6080.9	426.2	2257.9	•
Receivables Turnover 36	13.5	•	86.6	14.3	19.4	•	15.4	8.0	20.3	16.4	•
Total Liabilities to Net Worth 37	1.1	•	1.8	1.0	1.4	•	1.7	2.7	2.1	3.0	1.5
Current Assets to Working Capital 38	3.8	•	3.2	2.5	2.1	•	3.5	2.2	3.4	•	2.3
Current Liabilities to Working Capital 39	2.8	•	2.2	1.5	1.1	•	2.5	1.2	2.4	•	1.3
Working Capital to Net Sales 40	0.0	•	0.0	0.1	0.1	•	0.0	0.1	0.0	•	0.1
Inventory to Working Capital 41	0.0	•	•	0.0	0.0	•	0.0	0.0	0.0	•	•
Total Receipts to Cash Flow 42	8.0	20.1	9.4	9.5	4.3	•	9.3	17.3	14.2	36.5	9.3
Cost of Goods to Cash Flow 43	3.8	17.4	2.6	5.0	2.4	•	4.2	9.5	6.0	24.2	5.1
Cash Flow to Total Debt 44	0.9	2.8	1.1		2.5	•	1.0	0.3	0.6	0.1	0.4

Selected Financial Factors (in Percentages)

	•	•	•	•	•	•	•	•	•	•	•
Debt Ratio 45	51.8	•	64.2	49.7	57.9	•	62.6	72.7	68.1	75.2	59.3
Return on Total Assets 46	18.4	•	62.1	24.8	44.3	•	15.9	8.3	23.9	6.9	10.2
Return on Equity Before Income Taxes 47	34.5	•	164.2	47.1	100.4	•	37.9	25.2	68.2	16.2	19.4
Return on Equity After Income Taxes 48	29.1	•	162.7	45.3	97.7	•	32.0	20.4	66.7	11.1	14.9
Profit Margin (Before Income Tax) 49	4.6	3.4	3.4	4.7	6.8	•	2.5	1.9	3.7	1.0	3.8
Profit Margin (After Income Tax) 50	3.9	3.3	3.4	4.5	6.6	•	2.1	1.6	3.6	0.7	3.0

TRAVEL ARRANGEMENT AND RESERVATION SERVICES

Table I

Corporations with and without Net Income

MONEY AMOUNTS AND SIZE OF ASSETS IN THOUSANDS OF DOLLARS

Item Description for Accounting Period 7/07 Through 6/08	Total	Zero Assets	Under 500	500 to 1,000	1,000 to 5,000	5,000 to 10,000	10,000 to 25,000	25,000 to 50,000	50,000 to 100,000	100,000 to 250,000	250,000 to 500,000	500,000 to 2,500,000	2,500,000 and over
Number of Enterprises 1	23639	5637	16901	327	567	50	61	32	26	17	9	8	3
Revenues ($ in Thousands)													
Net Sales 2	41109595	2408249	14369260	1959426	2654276	808428	2624757	1584376	2442059	3067042	2454696	2942108	3794916
Interest 3	210203	492	566	1947	6148	2298	7472	7245	17465	11888	40698	65568	48416
Rents 4	35891	131	39	0	137	0	336	231	2230	5011	2433	22141	3204
Royalties 5	58090	0	0	0	0	0	0	0	2435	0	0	54185	1470
Other Portfolio Income 6	306447	1635	56	0	14	1635	14622	30724	62198	47747	43496	89312	15010
Other Receipts 7	2044877	1895	95516	6715	65762	2512	69413	116756	68377	71756	411463	1019074	115636
Total Receipts 8	43765103	2412402	14465437	1968088	2726337	814873	2716600	1739332	2594764	3203444	2952786	4192388	3978652
Average Total Receipts 9	1851	428	856	6019	4808	16297	44534	54354	99799	188438	328087	524048	1326217
Operating Costs/Operating Income (%)													
Cost of Operations 10	56.9	79.8	73.3	82.4	61.6	71.9	26.8	61.0	55.2	53.3	57.9	20.8	10.7
Salaries and Wages 11	14.1	3.7	6.2	4.6	16.2	9.2	22.4	15.7	13.6	14.4	19.7	43.8	21.9
Taxes Paid 12	1.7	0.7	1.2	0.6	1.7	1.2	2.0	2.2	2.2	1.9	1.9	4.3	1.7
Interest Paid 13	1.1	0.3	0.4	0.0	0.2	0.2	0.1	1.1	1.2	0.3	2.5	4.5	3.0
Depreciation 14	0.8	0.4	0.4	0.1	0.6	0.8	0.8	1.1	1.4	1.5	1.0	1.9	1.0
Amortization and Depletion 15	0.5	0.0	0.0	•	0.1	0.1	0.1	0.5	1.8	0.6	1.0	1.8	1.2
Pensions and Other Deferred Comp. 16	0.6	0.1	0.2	0.5	0.4	0.2	0.5	0.5	0.5	0.5	2.2	2.0	0.4
Employee Benefits 17	1.3	0.3	0.4	0.6	0.7	1.4	1.6	1.7	2.2	1.5	2.5	5.2	1.2
Advertising 18	3.1	0.6	0.6	0.1	1.1	1.8	2.2	3.9	1.8	3.4	1.9	6.8	16.1
Other Expenses 19	22.4	11.9	14.4	5.8	17.2	7.6	42.8	16.6	21.8	19.2	27.3	50.9	41.1
Officers' Compensation 20	2.6	3.2	2.1	3.4	3.6	1.6	1.0	1.5	1.3	1.3	0.6	1.2	8.9
Operating Margin 21	•	•	0.7	1.8	•	3.8	•	•	•	2.2	•	•	•
Operating Margin Before Officers' Comp. 22	•	2.2	2.8	5.3	0.1	5.4	0.6	•	•	3.5	•	•	1.6

Selected Average Balance Sheet ($ in Thousands)

Net Receivables 23	135	0	6	106	293	929	3948	6006	10993	30143	9905	36272	410175
Inventories 24	6	0	1	10	39	225	267	213	1075	287	2324	1467	2795
Net Property, Plant and Equipment 25	105	0	14	13	241	1057	2455	2598	9198	23016	18490	67459	160815
Total Assets 26	1497	0	68	640	2268	7475	17070	34038	72779	156207	361378	865898	5170076
Notes and Loans Payable 27	271	0	56	34	252	365	1230	8159	18328	6076	109069	165411	687072
All Other Liabilities 28	669	0	31	232	1679	3824	11892	25073	36237	92872	116863	369049	2002846
Net Worth 29	557	0	-20	374	337	3287	3948	806	18215	57259	135446	331438	2480158

Selected Financial Ratios (Times to 1)

Current Ratio 30	0.8	•	1.3	2.7	1.2	1.2	0.9	0.9	1.0	1.0	1.0	0.6	0.6
Quick Ratio 31	0.6	•	1.1	2.5	0.9	0.9	0.7	0.5	0.8	0.8	0.3	0.3	0.5
Net Sales to Working Capital 32	•	•	69.0	15.2	14.7	25.2	•	•	65.0	648.7	•	•	•
Coverage Ratio 33	2.3	•	4.0	757.0	•	20.3	28.5	4.6	3.6	20.2	1.6	1.0	0.2
Total Asset Turnover 34	1.2	•	12.5	9.4	2.1	2.2	2.5	1.5	1.3	1.2	0.8	0.4	0.2
Inventory Turnover 35	154.6	•	483.6	516.1	73.6	51.7	43.2	141.6	48.3	335.1	68.0	52.0	48.6
Receivables Turnover 36	14.7	•	92.3	55.5	17.4	10.4	9.0	11.8	8.1	7.8	18.0	5.8	6.2
Total Liabilities to Net Worth 37	1.7	•	•	0.7	5.7	1.3	3.3	41.2	3.0	1.7	1.7	1.6	1.1
Current Assets to Working Capital 38	•	•	4.0	1.6	5.0	6.9	•	•	21.7	294.3	•	•	•
Current Liabilities to Working Capital 39	•	•	3.0	0.6	4.0	5.9	•	•	20.7	293.3	•	•	•
Working Capital to Net Sales 40	•	•	0.0	0.1	0.1	0.0	•	•	0.0	0.0	•	•	•
Inventory to Working Capital 41	•	•	0.1	0.2	0.2	0.3	•	•	0.5	1.1	•	•	•
Total Receipts to Cash Flow 42	4.7	10.3	7.4	13.5	7.4	9.7	2.3	5.6	4.6	4.4	4.1	2.4	2.7
Cost of Goods to Cash Flow 43	2.7	8.2	5.4	11.1	4.6	7.0	0.6	3.4	2.5	2.4	2.3	0.5	0.3
Cash Flow to Total Debt 44	0.4	1.3	1.7	1.7	0.3	0.4	1.4	0.3	0.4	0.4	0.3	0.3	0.2

Selected Financial Factors (in Percentages)

Debt Ratio 45	62.8	•	128.9	41.5	85.1	56.0	76.9	97.6	75.0	63.3	62.5	61.7	52.0
Return on Total Assets 46	3.0	•	22.1	21.3	•	10.1	8.3	7.3	5.8	7.7	3.1	1.9	0.2
Return on Equity Before Income Taxes 47	4.6	•	36.4	•	21.8	34.6	242.8	16.7	20.0	3.2	•	•	•
Return on Equity After Income Taxes 48	3.0	•	32.8	•	20.5	33.1	206.1	10.2	15.6	1.7	•	•	•
Profit Margin (Before Income Tax) 49	1.5	1.3	2.3	•	4.4	3.2	4.0	3.2	3.2	6.3	1.6	1.6	0.8
Profit Margin (After Income Tax) 50	1.0	1.3	2.1	•	4.2	3.0	3.4	2.0	3.0	4.9	1.3	1.3	0.8

355

Table II

=Corporations with Net Income

TRAVEL ARRANGEMENT AND RESERVATION SERVICES

MONEY AMOUNTS AND SIZE OF ASSETS IN THOUSANDS OF DOLLARS

Item Description for Accounting Period 7/07 Through 6/08	Total	Zero Assets	Under 500	500 to 1,000	1,000 to 5,000	5,000 to 10,000	10,000 to 25,000	25,000 to 50,000	50,000 to 100,000	100,000 to 250,000	250,000 to 500,000	500,000 to 2,500,000	2,500,000 and over
Number of Enterprises 1	12758	1887	10096	327	289	•	56	27	16	12	4	•	0
Revenues ($ in Thousands)													
Net Sales 2	26286565	598755	9606292	1959426	988063	•	2594759	1381088	1793364	2713750	767625	•	0
Interest 3	139579	400	232	1947	4566	•	6783	5219	15671	11837	15766	•	0
Rents 4	15909	131	39	0	0	•	336	231	2230	5011	2343	•	0
Royalties 5	56620	0	0	0	0	•	0	0	2435	0	0	•	0
Other Portfolio Income 6	233598	1635	56	0	14	•	14614	30724	42494	43738	33836	•	0
Other Receipts 7	1669080	1422	95348	6715	58689	•	68950	110976	53716	71201	83177	•	0
Total Receipts 8	28401351	602343	9701967	1968088	1051332	•	2685442	1528238	1909910	2845537	902747	•	0
Average Total Receipts 9	2226	319	961	6019	3638	•	47954	56601	119369	237128	225687	•	•
Operating Costs/Operating Income (%)													
Cost of Operations 10	56.8	67.7	71.5	82.4	53.8	•	26.1	67.3	55.4	58.6	33.0	•	•
Salaries and Wages 11	12.2	4.0	4.5	4.6	19.8	•	22.6	13.5	13.2	11.5	21.5	•	•
Taxes Paid 12	1.6	0.9	1.1	0.6	2.4	•	2.0	1.5	2.4	1.7	2.5	•	•
Interest Paid 13	0.6	0.1	0.1	0.0	0.1	•	0.1	0.2	1.0	0.3	4.4	•	•
Depreciation 14	0.7	0.9	0.4	0.1	0.5	•	0.8	0.8	1.5	0.8	1.2	•	•
Amortization and Depletion 15	0.4	•	0.0	•	0.0	•	0.2	0.3	0.6	0.6	1.7	•	•
Pensions and Other Deferred Comp. 16	0.6	0.2	0.3	0.5	1.2	•	0.5	0.5	0.5	0.6	3.6	•	•
Employee Benefits 17	1.1	0.8	0.2	0.6	0.9	•	1.6	1.5	2.6	1.1	2.7	•	•
Advertising 18	3.4	1.1	0.6	0.1	0.8	•	2.1	3.8	1.9	3.3	2.8	•	•
Other Expenses 19	22.3	16.5	15.8	5.8	14.2	•	43.2	14.5	19.4	16.8	32.9	•	•
Officers' Compensation 20	3.0	2.6	2.8	3.4	5.2	•	1.0	0.9	1.5	1.3	1.4	•	•
Operating Margin 21	•	5.2	2.7	1.8	1.1	•	1.0	•	0.1	3.6	•	•	•
Operating Margin Before Officers' Comp. 22	0.3	7.8	5.5	5.3	6.3	•	0.8	•	1.5	4.9	•	•	•

Selected Average Balance Sheet ($ in Thousands)

Net Receivables 23	139	0	6	106	335	•	4300	5739	8150	26176	11750
Inventories 24	8	0	1	10	41	•	289	44	996	292	4152
Net Property, Plant and Equipment 25	98	0	10	13	64	•	2673	2345	12470	15625	16898
Total Assets 26	1394	0	71	640	1912	•	17390	32409	69584	155704	365025
Notes and Loans Payable 27	175	0	30	34	34	•	781	3661	10776	458	105400
All Other Liabilities 28	573	0	23	232	1295	•	12591	22156	35233	85369	98653
Net Worth 29	646	0	19	374	583	•	4018	6593	23576	69877	160972

Selected Financial Ratios (Times to 1)

Current Ratio 30	0.9	•	2.4	2.7	2.8	•	0.9	0.8	1.0	1.2	2.6
Quick Ratio 31	0.7	•	2.2	2.5	1.9	•	0.7	0.5	0.8	1.0	0.4
Net Sales to Working Capital 32	•	•	30.2	15.2	3.0	•	•	34.7	•	16.6	2.1
Coverage Ratio 33	10.4	43.0	46.6	757.0	63.1	•	29.7	34.7	7.3	32.3	3.2
Total Asset Turnover 34	1.5	•	13.3	9.4	1.8	•	2.7	1.6	1.6	1.5	0.5
Inventory Turnover 35	152.2	•	822.0	516.1	45.0	•	42.0	782.4	62.3	454.8	15.2
Receivables Turnover 36	15.8	•	190.8	58.0	9.4	•	9.9	•	10.5	10.7	•
Total Liabilities to Net Worth 37	1.2	•	2.8	0.7	2.3	•	3.3	3.9	2.0	1.2	1.3
Current Assets to Working Capital 38	•	•	1.7	1.6	1.6	•	•	•	6.2	•	1.6
Current Liabilities to Working Capital 39	•	•	0.7	0.6	0.6	•	•	•	5.2	•	0.6
Working Capital to Net Sales 40	•	•	0.0	0.1	0.3	•	•	•	0.1	•	0.5
Inventory to Working Capital 41	•	•	0.0	0.0	0.0	•	•	•	0.0	•	0.0
Total Receipts to Cash Flow 42	4.0	5.2	5.6	13.5	5.3	•	2.2	5.5	4.5	4.5	2.7
Cost of Goods to Cash Flow 43	2.3	3.5	4.0	11.1	2.9	•	0.6	3.7	2.5	2.6	0.9
Cash Flow to Total Debt 44	0.7	•	3.2	1.7	0.5	•	1.5	0.4	0.5	0.6	0.3

Selected Financial Factors (in Percentages)

Debt Ratio 45	53.6	•	73.9	41.5	69.5	•	76.9	79.7	66.1	55.1	55.9
Return on Total Assets 46	8.6	•	50.0	21.3	13.6	•	9.2	9.5	12.1	12.3	7.5
Return on Equity Before Income Taxes 47	16.8	•	187.7	36.4	44.0	•	38.6	45.5	30.7	26.6	11.8
Return on Equity After Income Taxes 48	14.2	•	186.3	32.8	37.7	•	36.9	40.2	22.6	21.4	8.9
Profit Margin (Before Income Tax) 49	5.3	5.8	3.7	2.3	7.5	•	3.4	5.9	6.5	8.2	9.9
Profit Margin (After Income Tax) 50	4.5	5.4	3.6	2.1	6.4	•	3.2	5.2	4.8	6.6	7.5

Table I

Corporations with and without Net Income

OTHER ADMINISTRATIVE AND SUPPORT SERVICES

MONEY AMOUNTS AND SIZE OF ASSETS IN THOUSANDS OF DOLLARS

Item Description for Accounting Period 7/07 Through 6/08	Total	Zero Assets	Under 500	500 to 1,000	1,000 to 5,000	5,000 to 10,000	10,000 to 25,000	25,000 to 50,000	50,000 to 100,000	100,000 to 250,000	250,000 to 500,000	500,000 to 2,500,000	2,500,000 and over
Number of Enterprises 1	206159	44613	147915	6772	5568	589	364	119	93	56	31	35	4
Revenues ($ in Thousands)													
Net Sales 2	204899657	4125620	60324389	12235139	29058887	12552356	11332966	6042472	7101955	9254556	15191497	30975172	6721547
Interest 3	1362965	49353	39604	14443	36833	29768	23330	22651	34583	144251	65761	366067	536321
Rents 4	104385	0	4591	6738	9987	0	4277	3057	3248	16300	5977	36674	13535
Royalties 5	293581	0	0	7235	599	0	678	100765	6518	458	10	177318	0
Other Portfolio Income 6	1215393	50666	151243	43948	162574	20875	35133	10788	67330	43600	20282	505912	103040
Other Receipts 7	3794127	215216	343370	68764	92782	382462	180501	187506	291728	380504	631450	998501	21346
Total Receipts 8	211667008	4440855	60863197	12376267	29361662	12965461	11576885	6367239	7505362	9839669	15914977	33059644	7395789
Average Total Receipts 9	1027	100	411	1828	5273	22013	31805	53506	80703	175708	513386	944561	1848947
Operating Costs/Operating Income (%)													
Cost of Operations 10	39.1	19.3	32.4	47.8	52.8	58.2	48.4	43.0	47.2	35.5	47.3	25.3	22.4
Salaries and Wages 11	20.3	17.9	19.4	14.2	14.8	14.7	23.7	22.5	21.6	25.5	21.8	27.3	24.1
Taxes Paid 12	3.7	3.1	3.5	3.4	2.9	3.5	4.3	3.6	3.3	3.3	5.1	4.6	3.1
Interest Paid 13	2.2	1.1	0.8	0.9	1.3	0.9	1.1	1.7	2.5	3.4	2.3	4.4	14.3
Depreciation 14	2.0	3.3	2.0	2.3	1.8	1.3	1.8	1.7	1.8	2.5	1.5	2.6	1.7
Amortization and Depletion 15	1.0	0.6	0.1	0.1	0.2	0.2	0.2	0.7	0.8	1.1	1.5	2.4	9.4
Pensions and Other Deferred Comp. 16	0.4	0.2	0.3	0.5	0.3	0.4	0.3	0.4	0.3	0.3	0.5	0.5	0.5
Employee Benefits 17	2.1	1.5	0.8	1.2	1.7	2.7	2.2	3.0	2.9	2.6	4.9	3.4	2.6
Advertising 18	1.2	4.3	1.6	1.1	0.6	0.2	0.5	0.7	1.2	2.1	0.4	1.6	2.0
Other Expenses 19	22.3	25.9	25.9	18.9	17.1	16.0	14.0	23.3	20.7	24.7	17.6	26.3	23.6
Officers' Compensation 20	4.1	8.8	7.8	7.1	4.1	2.3	2.0	2.1	2.1	1.7	0.5	0.9	0.5
Operating Margin 21	1.5	2.2	5.4	2.5	2.5	•	1.4	•	•	•	•	0.5	•
Operating Margin Before Officers' Comp. 22	5.6	11.0	13.1	9.6	6.5	1.7	3.4	•	•	•	•	•	1.4

Selected Average Balance Sheet ($ in Thousands)

Net Receivables 23	108	0	9	113	618	2327	4764	7850	15283	36634	52738	192265	201023
Inventories 24	10	0	3	31	71	132	346	761	2462	3452	2467	6010	29657
Net Property, Plant and Equipment 25	105	0	24	242	429	1265	2610	3982	8882	16675	56634	174287	548975
Total Assets 26	600	0	80	687	1979	6803	15248	34452	68145	158351	349916	1089164	4602274
Notes and Loans Payable 27	261	0	50	303	906	3054	4703	10754	23968	45166	121053	443364	2619276
All Other Liabilities 28	180	0	21	161	668	1813	5860	13552	21564	53682	114398	319975	1140138
Net Worth 29	159	0	8	223	405	1937	4685	10146	22612	59504	114464	325826	842861

Selected Financial Ratios (Times to 1)

Current Ratio 30	1.2	•	1.3	1.7	1.4	1.5	1.3	1.4	1.5	1.5	1.1	1.3	0.3
Quick Ratio 31	0.9	•	1.1	1.2	1.1	1.2	1.0	1.2	1.0	1.1	0.8	1.0	0.2
Net Sales to Working Capital 32	29.5	•	49.2	13.4	14.4	13.4	16.9	11.0	7.5	7.0	80.1	11.5	•
Coverage Ratio 33	3.2	9.7	8.6	5.0	3.6	4.2	4.4	2.6	1.4	2.1	1.6	2.7	1.5
Total Asset Turnover 34	1.7	•	5.1	2.6	2.6	3.1	2.0	1.5	1.1	1.0	1.4	0.8	0.4
Inventory Turnover 35	37.6	•	48.7	28.2	38.6	93.7	43.6	28.7	14.6	17.0	94.0	37.2	12.7
Receivables Turnover 36	8.4	•	43.5	15.6	9.1	9.1	6.9	6.4	5.4	4.5	10.4	5.0	1.7
Total Liabilities to Net Worth 37	2.8	•	8.6	2.1	3.9	2.5	2.3	2.4	2.0	1.7	2.1	2.3	4.5
Current Assets to Working Capital 38	6.6	•	4.4	2.5	3.3	3.0	4.8	3.6	3.2	3.0	18.7	4.2	•
Current Liabilities to Working Capital 39	5.6	•	3.4	1.5	2.3	2.0	3.8	2.6	2.2	2.0	17.7	3.2	•
Working Capital to Net Sales 40	0.0	•	0.0	0.1	0.1	0.1	0.1	0.1	0.1	0.1	0.0	0.1	•
Inventory to Working Capital 41	0.3	•	0.3	0.2	0.2	0.1	0.3	0.3	0.3	0.2	0.2	0.1	•
Total Receipts to Cash Flow 42	4.4	2.5	3.7	5.9	6.0	6.3	7.0	4.4	5.4	4.1	6.7	3.4	3.7
Cost of Goods to Cash Flow 43	1.7	0.5	1.2	2.8	3.2	3.7	3.4	1.9	2.5	1.5	3.2	0.8	0.8
Cash Flow to Total Debt 44	0.5	•	1.6	0.7	0.5	0.7	0.4	0.5	0.3	0.4	0.3	0.3	0.1

Selected Financial Factors (in Percentages)

Debt Ratio 45	73.5	•	89.6	67.5	79.5	71.5	69.3	70.6	66.8	62.4	67.3	70.1	81.7
Return on Total Assets 46	11.7	•	36.0	12.0	12.7	11.7	9.4	6.4	4.0	7.4	5.1	9.7	7.6
Return on Equity Before Income Taxes 47	30.3	•	305.6	29.5	45.1	31.4	23.6	13.2	3.7	10.2	5.8	20.5	13.0
Return on Equity After Income Taxes 48	25.8	•	302.2	28.7	43.1	29.5	21.0	10.5	1.1	7.5	3.2	13.0	9.5
Profit Margin (Before Income Tax) 49	4.8	9.8	6.2	3.6	3.5	2.9	3.5	2.6	1.1	3.7	1.3	7.6	6.5
Profit Margin (After Income Tax) 50	4.1	8.6	6.1	3.5	3.3	2.7	3.2	2.1	0.3	2.7	0.7	4.8	4.8

OTHER ADMINISTRATIVE AND SUPPORT SERVICES

Table II

Corporations with Net Income

MONEY AMOUNTS AND SIZE OF ASSETS IN THOUSANDS OF DOLLARS

Item Description for Accounting Period 7/07 Through 6/08		Total	Zero Assets	Under 500	500 to 1,000	1,000 to 5,000	5,000 to 10,000	10,000 to 25,000	25,000 to 50,000	50,000 to 100,000	100,000 to 250,000	250,000 to 500,000	500,000 to 2,500,000	2,500,000 and over
Number of Enterprises	1	145256	27509	107786	4931	4170	413	241	74	56	•	19	23	•
Revenues ($ in Thousands)														
Net Sales	2	159485368	2963127	47455231	9699065	23928049	9385436	8493765	4347298	5112281	•	12359852	24554939	•
Interest	3	1139541	41607	35218	10908	25856	16801	10662	15004	22834	•	47306	263824	•
Rents	4	55739	0	1274	2276	4340	0	1344	3045	2859	•	5977	17790	•
Royalties	5	280800	0	0	0	0	0	678	100765	6470	•	0	172887	•
Other Portfolio Income	6	1055532	44251	140079	40915	126432	16644	31183	7151	25378	•	16405	504283	•
Other Receipts	7	3279279	241839	134167	60341	78364	265408	162376	132325	248160	•	612504	923068	•
Total Receipts	8	165296259	3290824	47765969	9813505	24163041	9684289	8700008	4605588	5417982	•	13042044	26436791	•
Average Total Receipts	9	1138	120	443	1990	5794	23449	36100	62238	96750	•	686423	1149426	•
Operating Costs/Operating Income (%)														
Cost of Operations	10	40.2	14.7	31.3	47.5	55.9	60.0	45.6	41.6	48.5	•	51.9	29.6	•
Salaries and Wages	11	19.1	16.8	18.6	12.6	13.1	14.1	22.6	21.2	17.9	•	19.3	27.2	•
Taxes Paid	12	3.7	3.4	3.4	3.3	2.7	3.1	4.6	3.8	2.5	•	5.4	5.1	•
Interest Paid	13	1.6	1.0	0.7	0.8	1.1	0.7	0.8	0.7	2.0	•	1.6	2.6	•
Depreciation	14	1.8	2.0	1.7	2.4	1.5	0.9	1.5	1.7	1.5	•	1.5	2.8	•
Amortization and Depletion	15	0.8	0.8	0.1	0.0	0.1	0.0	0.3	0.5	0.5	•	0.9	1.5	•
Pensions and Other Deferred Comp.	16	0.5	0.3	0.3	0.5	0.4	0.3	0.4	0.6	0.2	•	0.5	0.9	•
Employee Benefits	17	2.1	1.4	0.7	1.1	1.5	2.6	1.8	3.2	2.8	•	4.8	3.7	•
Advertising	18	1.0	1.1	1.6	1.0	0.6	0.2	0.6	0.7	1.6	•	0.5	0.4	•
Other Expenses	19	20.1	34.5	24.0	18.5	13.7	13.5	15.1	21.5	19.6	•	15.7	22.2	•
Officers' Compensation	20	4.1	8.5	7.7	6.9	4.0	2.3	2.2	2.3	1.8	•	0.5	0.8	•
Operating Margin	21	5.0	15.5	9.8	5.4	5.4	2.2	4.5	2.1	1.1	•	•	3.2	•
Operating Margin Before Officers' Comp.	22	9.1	24.0	17.5	12.3	9.4	4.6	6.7	4.4	2.8	•	•	4.0	•

Selected Average Balance Sheet ($ in Thousands)

Net Receivables 23	107	0	9	119	600	2546	5088	8508	19015	51830	202418	•
Inventories 24	10	0	3	17	62	153	374	684	3063	3342	6491	•
Net Property, Plant and Equipment 25	113	0	23	243	400	990	2759	4160	8995	66465	236387	•
Total Assets 26	598	0	82	684	1960	6892	15085	34120	68005	371016	1142883	•
Notes and Loans Payable 27	212	0	39	265	745	2682	4196	9129	22407	95418	358498	•
All Other Liabilities 28	168	0	13	146	677	1550	4281	13094	23427	132149	301985	•
Net Worth 29	219	0	30	273	538	2660	6608	11898	22170	143448	482400	•

Selected Financial Ratios (Times to 1)

Current Ratio 30	1.2	•	1.8	1.9	1.5	2.0	1.6	1.5	1.5	0.9	1.6	•
Quick Ratio 31	0.9	•	1.5	1.3	1.2	1.6	1.3	1.2	1.1	0.6	1.2	•
Net Sales to Working Capital 32	24.5	•	26.5	12.4	14.2	8.7	10.0	8.8	6.9	•	7.8	•
Coverage Ratio 33	6.3	28.4	15.5	9.0	7.0	9.1	9.3	11.9	4.5	2.9	5.3	•
Total Asset Turnover 34	1.8	•	5.4	2.9	2.9	3.3	2.3	1.7	1.3	1.8	0.9	•
Inventory Turnover 35	43.0	•	51.8	54.1	51.4	89.0	42.9	35.8	14.4	101.1	48.8	•
Receivables Turnover 36	8.5	•	51.3	17.3	9.8	8.9	7.0	•	5.3	13.3	•	•
Total Liabilities to Net Worth 37	1.7	•	1.7	1.5	2.6	1.3	1.3	1.9	2.1	1.6	1.4	•
Current Assets to Working Capital 38	5.1	•	2.3	2.1	3.0	2.6	2.6	2.9	2.9	•	2.6	•
Current Liabilities to Working Capital 39	4.1	•	1.3	1.1	2.0	1.6	1.6	1.9	1.9	•	1.6	•
Working Capital to Net Sales 40	0.0	•	0.0	0.1	0.1	0.1	0.1	0.1	0.1	•	0.1	•
Inventory to Working Capital 41	0.2	•	0.2	0.1	0.2	0.0	0.1	0.1	0.2	•	0.0	•
Total Receipts to Cash Flow 42	4.0	1.8	3.3	5.2	6.1	6.1	5.3	3.8	4.2	6.5	3.4	•
Cost of Goods to Cash Flow 43	1.6	0.3	1.0	2.5	3.4	3.7	2.4	1.6	2.0	3.4	1.0	•
Cash Flow to Total Debt 44	0.7	•	2.6	0.9	0.7	0.9	0.8	0.7	0.5	0.4	0.5	•

Selected Financial Factors (in Percentages)

Debt Ratio 45	63.5	•	63.3	60.1	72.6	61.4	56.2	65.1	67.4	61.3	57.8	•
Return on Total Assets 46	18.9	•	59.5	21.3	21.7	20.0	18.1	15.0	12.1	8.1	12.8	•
Return on Equity Before Income Taxes 47	43.6	•	151.5	47.4	67.8	46.1	36.8	39.5	29.0	13.8	24.7	•
Return on Equity After Income Taxes 48	39.0	•	150.2	46.5	65.8	44.2	34.1	35.9	24.6	10.4	16.9	•
Profit Margin (Before Income Tax) 49	8.7	26.6	10.4	6.6	6.4	5.4	6.9	8.0	7.0	3.0	11.1	•
Profit Margin (After Income Tax) 50	7.8	24.9	10.3	6.5	6.2	5.2	6.4	7.3	6.0	2.3	7.6	•

358

Table I

Corporations with and without Net Income

WASTE MANAGEMENT AND REMEDIATION SERVICES

MONEY AMOUNTS AND SIZE OF ASSETS IN THOUSANDS OF DOLLARS

Item Description for Accounting Period 7/07 Through 6/08		Total	Zero Assets	Under 500	500 to 1,000	1,000 to 5,000	5,000 to 10,000	10,000 to 25,000	25,000 to 50,000	50,000 to 100,000	100,000 to 250,000	250,000 to 500,000	500,000 to 2,500,000	2,500,000 and over
Number of Enterprises	1	15365	2099	8834	1930	2053	185	140	42	30	24	9	13	5
Revenues ($ in Thousands)														
Net Sales	2	63722256	420865	5918157	2772040	10420622	2550634	2898060	1633710	2126065	2573447	2039790	6296572	24077295
Interest	3	387626	265	1616	4257	8206	769	6523	6668	10471	20474	4908	152087	171384
Rents	4	51858	558	0	1066	2305	2	518	4576	2146	751	152	1658	38127
Royalties	5	13456	134	0	0	1070	0	0	0	0	0	10580	555	1116
Other Portfolio Income	6	467715	24786	5005	54394	86656	72677	4704	6339	11069	6258	2685	1476	191669
Other Receipts	7	1044832	18493	146575	5988	23971	25462	32704	36437	17167	14412	76176	68279	579163
Total Receipts	8	65692743	465101	6071353	2837745	10542830	2649544	2942509	1687730	2166918	2615342	2134291	6520627	25058754
Average Total Receipts	9	4275	222	687	1470	5135	14322	21018	40184	72231	108973	237143	501587	5011751
Operating Costs/Operating Income (%)														
Cost of Operations	10	38.7	36.2	37.8	35.6	44.5	55.8	48.4	55.7	43.0	41.8	31.3	30.7	34.7
Salaries and Wages	11	15.6	15.4	12.2	11.0	12.9	6.9	9.4	9.4	13.2	14.3	17.1	16.7	20.1
Taxes Paid	12	3.5	2.7	2.8	2.3	3.1	2.0	2.0	2.6	2.4	2.6	3.8	2.6	4.8
Interest Paid	13	3.8	2.7	0.5	2.2	1.1	1.2	1.8	1.3	2.3	3.8	5.3	7.5	5.7
Depreciation	14	5.3	3.2	2.2	5.4	3.7	3.2	4.9	4.0	3.9	5.7	6.6	5.2	7.3
Amortization and Depletion	15	1.4	1.3	0.1	0.1	0.1	0.1	0.5	1.5	0.7	1.3	2.3	3.5	2.2
Pensions and Other Deferred Comp.	16	0.4	0.1	0.3	0.4	0.5	0.4	0.4	0.6	0.8	0.4	2.5	0.2	0.3
Employee Benefits	17	1.9	1.9	0.8	1.8	1.4	1.0	1.8	2.2	2.3	2.1	4.1	1.9	2.2
Advertising	18	0.4	0.3	1.0	0.5	0.6	0.1	0.7	0.1	0.3	0.2	0.1	0.4	0.3
Other Expenses	19	23.0	27.9	32.5	24.7	28.1	23.2	24.3	17.1	27.3	25.2	29.1	30.7	15.4
Officers' Compensation	20	2.1	9.6	6.3	4.3	3.6	3.2	3.2	2.8	1.6	1.3	1.3	1.2	0.2
Operating Margin	21	3.8	•	3.4	11.7	0.4	2.9	2.6	2.7	2.3	1.2	•	•	7.0
Operating Margin Before Officers' Comp.	22	5.9	8.4	9.8	16.0	4.1	6.1	5.8	5.5	3.9	2.5	0.7	0.7	7.2

Selected Average Balance Sheet ($ in Thousands)

Net Receivables 23	552	0	11	115	394	2876	2817	4753	14819	17326	39509	120074	690640
Inventories 24	52	0	3	23	26	270	433	1259	1204	329	958	6609	75488
Net Property, Plant and Equipment 25	1891	0	63	268	818	2233	6047	10935	17598	45497	110051	249561	3745287
Total Assets 26	5013	0	114	700	2100	6681	16121	32593	70229	151244	372989	972411	8751603
Notes and Loans Payable 27	2202	0	61	370	772	2745	5972	10827	27644	77621	164331	421175	3910357
All Other Liabilities 28	1462	0	13	98	848	2693	4414	13629	19859	24833	122746	223633	2705440
Net Worth 29	1349	0	41	232	480	1243	5735	8137	22727	48790	85911	327603	2135806

Selected Financial Ratios (Times to 1)

Current Ratio 30	1.1	•	2.1	2.1	1.2	1.5	1.7	1.5	1.5	1.3	0.8	0.9	1.0
Quick Ratio 31	0.8	•	1.7	1.6	1.0	1.3	1.3	1.2	1.2	1.0	0.7	0.6	0.7
Net Sales to Working Capital 32	35.5	•	34.8	8.3	32.1	10.7	7.6	10.7	6.6	12.5	•	•	129.5
Coverage Ratio 33	2.8	4.4	12.7	7.4	2.5	6.5	3.2	5.4	2.9	1.7	1.2	1.5	2.9
Total Asset Turnover 34	0.8	•	5.9	2.1	2.4	2.1	1.3	1.2	1.0	0.7	0.6	0.5	0.6
Inventory Turnover 35	30.6	•	82.5	22.1	86.1	28.6	23.1	17.2	25.3	136.4	73.9	22.5	22.1
Receivables Turnover 36	8.0	•	46.4	16.3	13.9	5.4	7.4	6.3	5.3	4.9	5.7	5.6	7.0
Total Liabilities to Net Worth 37	2.7	•	1.8	2.0	3.4	4.4	1.8	3.0	2.1	2.1	3.3	2.0	3.1
Current Assets to Working Capital 38	9.6	•	1.9	1.9	6.4	3.2	2.5	2.9	2.8	4.1	•	•	39.5
Current Liabilities to Working Capital 39	8.6	•	0.9	0.9	5.4	2.2	1.5	1.9	1.8	3.1	•	•	38.5
Working Capital to Net Sales 40	0.0	•	0.1	0.1	0.0	0.1	0.1	0.1	0.2	0.1	•	•	0.0
Inventory to Working Capital 41	0.3	•	0.2	0.1	0.2	0.2	0.2	0.2	0.2	0.0	•	•	0.9
Total Receipts to Cash Flow 42	4.1	3.4	3.0	3.1	4.1	4.5	4.3	5.3	3.7	4.2	4.0	3.4	4.8
Cost of Goods to Cash Flow 43	1.6	1.2	1.1	1.1	1.8	2.5	2.1	2.9	1.6	1.8	1.2	1.0	1.7
Cash Flow to Total Debt 44	0.3	•	3.0	1.0	0.8	0.6	0.5	0.3	0.4	0.2	0.2	0.2	0.2

Selected Financial Factors (in Percentages)

Debt Ratio 45	73.1	•	64.4	66.9	77.1	81.4	64.4	75.0	67.6	67.7	77.0	66.3	75.6
Return on Total Assets 46	8.8	•	38.3	33.4	6.5	16.6	7.6	8.6	6.6	4.7	3.9	5.4	9.2
Return on Equity Before Income Taxes 47	21.2	•	99.2	87.2	17.1	75.4	14.7	28.0	13.2	6.1	3.0	5.0	24.9
Return on Equity After Income Taxes 48	16.8	•	99.0	86.1	13.2	70.7	13.3	23.2	9.2	3.4	1.1	3.2	18.5
Profit Margin (Before Income Tax) 49	6.9	9.3	6.0	14.1	1.6	6.8	4.1	5.9	4.2	2.8	1.1	3.4	11.0
Profit Margin (After Income Tax) 50	5.5	9.2	6.0	13.9	1.2	6.4	3.7	4.9	2.9	1.5	0.4	2.2	8.2

WASTE MANAGEMENT AND REMEDIATION SERVICES
562000

Table II
Corporations with Net Income

MONEY AMOUNTS AND SIZE OF ASSETS IN THOUSANDS OF DOLLARS

Item Description for Accounting Period 7/07 Through 6/08	Total	Zero Assets	Under 500	500 to 1,000	1,000 to 5,000	5,000 to 10,000	10,000 to 25,000	25,000 to 50,000	50,000 to 100,000	100,000 to 250,000	250,000 to 500,000	500,000 to 2,500,000	2,500,000 and over
Number of Enterprises 1	9604	1019	5240	1591	1477	96	92	35	21	•	4	•	8
Revenues ($ in Thousands)													
Net Sales 2	55518184	316262	4266275	2601427	9067020	1415311	2042445	1510240	1889465	•	1176302	•	5322756
Interest 3	274587	55	578	4002	7342	663	3281	5906	6686	•	1584	•	60852
Rents 4	50473	498	0	392	1769	2	431	4551	2146	•	149	•	1658
Royalties 5	13456	134	0	0	1070	0	0	0	0	•	10580	•	555
Other Portfolio Income 6	441818	24722	2776	48168	80868	72237	3933	2570	9991	•	2342	•	1476
Other Receipts 7	953089	18335	146411	5757	18572	18906	29202	36232	14909	•	20034	•	44600
Total Receipts 8	57251607	360006	4416040	2659746	9176641	1507119	2079292	1559499	1923197	•	1210991	•	5431897
Average Total Receipts 9	5961	353	843	1672	6213	15699	22601	44557	91581	•	302748	•	678987
Operating Costs/Operating Income (%)													
Cost of Operations 10	35.7	23.6	34.3	33.6	42.4	33.5	36.8	56.0	44.1	•	6.7	•	27.3
Salaries and Wages 11	16.0	16.2	13.3	11.0	11.0	10.2	10.7	8.9	13.0	•	22.1	•	17.7
Taxes Paid 12	3.6	3.2	3.0	2.2	2.8	2.2	2.1	2.5	2.5	•	5.7	•	2.7
Interest Paid 13	3.6	3.2	0.4	2.3	0.9	1.1	1.4	1.3	1.9	•	4.0	•	4.8
Depreciation 14	5.4	3.9	2.1	5.2	3.0	2.8	5.7	3.9	3.8	•	7.9	•	5.0
Amortization and Depletion 15	1.4	1.6	0.1	0.1	0.1	0.1	0.2	0.4	0.5	•	1.8	•	3.2
Pensions and Other Deferred Comp. 16	0.4	0.1	0.5	0.5	0.4	0.6	0.5	0.6	0.9	•	4.3	•	0.2
Employee Benefits 17	1.9	2.5	0.8	1.8	1.5	1.3	2.0	2.2	2.4	•	4.8	•	1.9
Advertising 18	0.4	0.4	0.9	0.6	0.3	0.2	0.7	0.1	0.2	•	0.2	•	0.4
Other Expenses 19	22.7	28.6	31.2	24.5	27.9	34.6	28.7	15.8	22.9	•	38.0	•	32.3
Officers' Compensation 20	2.0	11.4	7.1	4.5	3.5	5.1	3.4	2.6	1.7	•	1.1	•	1.3
Operating Margin 21	6.6	5.4	6.3	13.7	6.3	8.2	7.9	5.7	6.2	•	3.5	•	3.3
Operating Margin Before Officers' Comp. 22	8.7	16.8	13.4	18.2	9.7	13.2	11.3	8.3	7.8	•	4.6	•	4.6

Selected Average Balance Sheet ($ in Thousands)

Net Receivables 23	734	0	12	100	415	2519	2902	5455	18124	•	38352	153338
Inventories 24	45	0	4	25	28	56	369	893	1652	•	447	6482
Net Property, Plant and Equipment 25	2751	0	56	309	875	2102	7097	11588	20847	•	158728	317111
Total Assets 26	6827	0	128	718	2132	6555	16686	32754	73490	•	406499	993729
Notes and Loans Payable 27	2955	0	58	422	871	1953	4463	12415	25203	•	180590	395536
All Other Liabilities 28	2006	0	13	101	556	3012	4321	11750	20250	•	131611	272719
Net Worth 29	1866	0	57	195	706	1590	7902	8590	28036	•	94298	325474

Selected Financial Ratios (Times to 1)

Current Ratio 30	1.1	•	2.8	1.8	1.4	1.3	2.4	1.5	1.5	•	1.1	1.0
Quick Ratio 31	0.9	•	2.2	1.5	1.1	1.2	2.0	1.2	1.2	•	0.9	0.8
Net Sales to Working Capital 32	30.9	•	28.9	12.5	24.6	16.4	5.5	11.4	8.8	•	71.0	•
Coverage Ratio 33	3.7	7.0	26.8	8.0	9.1	14.8	7.9	7.6	5.2	•	2.6	2.1
Total Asset Turnover 34	0.8	•	6.4	2.3	2.9	2.2	1.3	1.3	1.2	•	0.7	0.7
Inventory Turnover 35	46.0	•	67.7	21.8	93.0	88.6	22.1	27.0	24.0	•	44.4	28.0
Receivables Turnover 36	8.9	•	49.7	20.7	15.8	•	7.6	6.8	5.6	•	6.6	6.5
Total Liabilities to Net Worth 37	2.7	•	1.3	2.7	2.0	3.1	1.1	2.8	1.6	•	3.3	2.1
Current Assets to Working Capital 38	7.8	•	1.6	2.3	3.7	4.7	1.7	3.0	3.2	•	13.6	•
Current Liabilities to Working Capital 39	6.8	•	0.6	1.3	2.7	3.7	0.7	2.0	2.2	•	12.6	•
Working Capital to Net Sales 40	0.0	•	0.0	0.1	0.0	0.1	0.2	0.1	0.1	•	0.0	•
Inventory to Working Capital 41	0.3	•	0.3	0.2	0.1	0.1	0.1	0.2	0.3	•	0.1	•
Total Receipts to Cash Flow 42	3.7	2.4	2.8	3.0	3.3	2.6	3.1	4.6	3.8	•	2.6	3.0
Cost of Goods to Cash Flow 43	1.3	0.6	1.0	1.0	1.4	0.9	1.1	2.6	1.7	•	0.2	0.8
Cash Flow to Total Debt 44	0.3	•	4.1	1.0	1.3	1.1	0.8	0.4	0.5	•	0.4	0.3

Selected Financial Factors (in Percentages)

Debt Ratio 45	72.7	•	55.6	72.8	66.9	75.7	52.6	73.8	61.9	•	76.8	67.2
Return on Total Assets 46	11.3	•	64.8	41.5	24.2	35.3	14.7	13.5	12.0	•	7.6	6.8
Return on Equity Before Income Taxes 47	30.2	•	140.5	133.5	64.9	135.8	27.1	44.9	25.5	•	20.2	11.0
Return on Equity After Income Taxes 48	25.1	•	140.4	131.8	61.2	128.8	25.5	39.5	20.9	•	16.3	8.1
Profit Margin (Before Income Tax) 49	9.7	19.2	9.8	15.9	7.5	14.6	9.7	8.9	8.0	•	6.5	5.4
Profit Margin (After Income Tax) 50	8.1	19.0	9.8	15.7	7.0	13.9	9.1	7.9	6.5	•	5.2	4.0

Table I

Corporations with and without Net Income

EDUCATIONAL SERVICES

MONEY AMOUNTS AND SIZE OF ASSETS IN THOUSANDS OF DOLLARS

Item Description for Accounting Period 7/07 Through 6/08	Total	Zero Assets	Under 500	500 to 1,000	1,000 to 5,000	5,000 to 10,000	10,000 to 25,000	25,000 to 50,000	50,000 to 100,000	100,000 to 250,000	250,000 to 500,000	500,000 to 2,500,000	2,500,000 and over
Number of Enterprises **1**	49240	12615	34304	931	1030	134	114	32	33	25	12	6	3
Revenues ($ in Thousands)													
Net Sales **2**	40438008	1043057	9132483	1194418	4883504	1472802	2230006	1653052	2529598	4107496	2218692	7242979	2729922
Interest **3**	302924	1782	5521	2177	9966	1016	10258	8814	11885	18613	20681	93855	118356
Rents **4**	30743	0	0	88	14	894	0	229	4195	10381	990	11788	2164
Royalties **5**	216531	0	0	0	0	67681	398	2807	1068	5920	71217	47565	19875
Other Portfolio Income **6**	141013	69	15532	9	1093	112	3098	1054	25341	6772	19141	57221	11571
Other Receipts **7**	556413	3256	74309	36689	24623	80448	72000	18766	51172	19647	5775	157795	11932
Total Receipts **8**	41685632	1048164	9227845	1233381	4919200	1622953	2315760	1684722	2623259	4168829	2336496	7611203	2893820
Average Total Receipts **9**	847	83	269	1325	4776	12112	20314	52648	79493	166753	194708	1268534	964607
Operating Costs/Operating Income (%)													
Cost of Operations **10**	13.6	23.3	11.4	18.6	18.0	14.0	30.9	17.0	8.7	17.4	9.0	6.3	12.3
Salaries and Wages **11**	28.9	7.8	26.6	29.7	24.2	38.9	24.7	27.0	33.2	31.5	28.6	32.9	33.9
Taxes Paid **12**	3.3	2.8	3.7	4.1	4.3	3.2	2.8	2.8	4.0	3.1	3.2	2.6	2.0
Interest Paid **13**	2.5	0.5	1.1	1.1	0.6	0.5	1.2	0.8	2.7	1.9	6.9	1.2	15.7
Depreciation **14**	2.2	1.9	1.5	1.4	1.3	1.7	1.9	2.4	3.7	2.8	2.2	2.3	3.8
Amortization and Depletion **15**	1.1	0.4	0.4	0.1	0.1	0.1	1.4	0.9	1.1	2.0	4.8	0.5	3.1
Pensions and Other Deferred Comp. **16**	0.4	0.1	0.7	0.3	0.4	0.5	0.3	0.7	0.3	0.5	0.4	0.2	0.3
Employee Benefits **17**	2.1	0.5	1.5	2.3	0.9	1.3	1.8	3.0	2.0	2.2	3.0	3.1	3.9
Advertising **18**	5.4	1.8	1.9	2.6	1.9	5.0	5.2	7.6	6.5	3.9	4.0	12.7	8.4
Other Expenses **19**	32.7	48.3	37.7	30.3	38.0	30.9	25.2	32.6	34.3	31.3	40.8	25.9	20.3
Officers' Compensation **20**	5.0	5.8	12.6	6.4	5.8	2.9	3.3	1.7	2.4	1.2	1.6	1.7	1.8
Operating Margin **21**	2.8	6.9	0.9	2.9	4.4	1.0	1.5	3.5	1.0	2.2	•	10.5	•
Operating Margin Before Officers' Comp. **22**	7.8	12.7	13.5	9.3	10.2	3.9	4.8	5.2	3.4	3.4	•	12.2	•

Selected Average Balance Sheet ($ in Thousands)

Net Receivables 23	118	0	6	144	418	1902	2797	5573	11536	22828	69303	82624	666980
Inventories 24	9	0	3	9	22	317	313	945	1326	2619	2233	6901	13816
Net Property, Plant and Equipment 25	125	0	20	248	667	1085	2611	8106	21896	32003	35795	214998	193157
Total Assets 26	760	0	73	662	2081	6325	15221	34500	70754	155912	372896	864350	4192297
Notes and Loans Payable 27	246	0	65	215	492	1139	4458	6805	30317	31478	140988	105042	1386005
All Other Liabilities 28	285	0	27	223	1190	3629	6203	14131	25028	50013	115862	312388	1564207
Net Worth 29	229	0	-19	224	399	1557	4560	13564	15409	74421	116046	446919	1242086

Selected Financial Ratios (Times to 1)

Current Ratio 30	1.2	0.8	•	1.6	1.0	2.0	1.3	1.1	1.2	1.2	1.2	1.2	1.5
Quick Ratio 31	1.0	0.7	•	1.4	0.9	1.7	1.1	0.9	0.9	0.9	1.1	0.8	1.4
Net Sales to Working Capital 32	17.0	•	•	10.2	85.6	4.8	9.8	27.9	17.1	21.3	9.5	20.8	3.1
Coverage Ratio 33	3.3	2.8	14.7	6.6	10.2	21.9	5.6	7.5	2.7	2.9	1.2	13.1	1.0
Total Asset Turnover 34	1.1	3.6	•	1.9	2.3	1.7	1.3	1.5	1.1	1.1	0.5	1.4	0.2
Inventory Turnover 35	12.8	11.4	•	27.3	39.7	4.9	19.3	9.3	5.0	10.9	7.4	11.1	8.1
Receivables Turnover 36	7.8	37.7	•	11.3	12.0	5.6	7.5	9.6	7.1	6.6	3.1	7.2	2.7
Total Liabilities to Net Worth 37	2.3	•	•	2.0	4.2	3.1	2.3	1.5	3.6	1.1	2.2	0.9	2.4
Current Assets to Working Capital 38	5.6	•	•	2.7	22.2	2.0	4.1	9.3	6.1	7.4	5.5	6.4	2.9
Current Liabilities to Working Capital 39	4.6	•	•	1.7	21.2	1.0	3.1	8.3	5.1	6.4	4.5	5.4	1.9
Working Capital to Net Sales 40	0.1	•	•	0.1	0.0	0.2	0.1	0.0	0.1	0.0	0.1	0.0	0.3
Inventory to Working Capital 41	0.2	•	•	0.1	0.6	0.1	0.2	0.6	0.3	0.4	0.1	0.1	0.0
Total Receipts to Cash Flow 42	3.4	3.5	2.4	3.5	3.2	2.7	3.9	3.1	3.4	3.6	2.9	3.0	7.4
Cost of Goods to Cash Flow 43	0.5	0.4	0.6	0.7	0.6	0.4	1.2	0.5	0.3	0.6	0.3	0.2	0.9
Cash Flow to Total Debt 44	0.5	•	0.8	0.8	0.9	0.9	0.5	0.8	0.4	0.6	0.2	1.0	0.0

Selected Financial Factors (in Percentages)

Debt Ratio 45	69.8	•	126.5	66.1	80.8	75.4	70.0	60.7	78.2	52.3	68.9	48.3	70.4
Return on Total Assets 46	8.9	•	11.1	14.1	13.0	20.5	8.4	9.3	8.0	5.7	4.0	22.6	3.4
Return on Equity Before Income Taxes 47	20.7	•	•	35.3	61.2	79.5	23.1	20.6	23.2	7.8	1.9	40.3	0.1
Return on Equity After Income Taxes 48	15.3	•	•	34.2	59.1	75.2	20.4	16.3	15.9	5.8	•	26.2	•
Profit Margin (Before Income Tax) 49	5.8	7.4	2.0	6.2	5.1	11.3	5.4	5.4	4.7	3.5	1.2	14.9	0.2
Profit Margin (After Income Tax) 50	4.3	6.8	1.9	6.0	5.0	10.6	4.8	4.3	3.2	2.6	•	9.7	•

Table II

Corporations with Net Income

EDUCATIONAL SERVICES

MONEY AMOUNTS AND SIZE OF ASSETS IN THOUSANDS OF DOLLARS

Item Description for Accounting Period 7/07 Through 6/08	Total	Zero Assets	Under 500	500 to 1,000	1,000 to 5,000	5,000 to 10,000	10,000 to 25,000	25,000 to 50,000	50,000 to 100,000	100,000 to 250,000	250,000 to 500,000	500,000 to 2,500,000	2,500,000 and over
Number of Enterprises 1	26986	6079	19011	825	789	120	82	26	26	•	•	•	0
Revenues ($ in Thousands)													
Net Sales 2	32461391	824420	6190501	1003161	4221352	1401636	1932352	1496482	2019714	•	•	•	0
Interest 3	233262	1652	3399	2138	2934	889	6184	7925	10274	•	•	•	0
Rents 4	26546	0	0	88	14	886	0	229	2111	•	•	•	0
Royalties 5	169624	0	0	0	0	67681	27	201	1068	•	•	•	0
Other Portfolio Income 6	123826	69	13530	9	1093	32	3080	1054	23647	•	•	•	0
Other Receipts 7	502588	3085	44645	36688	10369	80356	71788	17752	48554	•	•	•	0
Total Receipts 8	33517237	829226	6252075	1042084	4235762	1551480	2013431	1523643	2105368	•	•	•	•
Average Total Receipts 9	1242	136	329	1263	5369	12929	24554	58602	80976	•	•	•	•
Operating Costs/Operating Income (%)													
Cost of Operations 10	13.9	27.9	10.5	21.0	18.8	12.5	33.8	16.9	8.8	•	•	•	•
Salaries and Wages 11	28.3	7.7	26.0	29.5	22.1	39.8	21.3	25.9	32.5	•	•	•	•
Taxes Paid 12	3.2	2.5	3.8	4.2	4.3	3.3	2.5	2.7	3.9	•	•	•	•
Interest Paid 13	1.9	0.2	0.6	0.9	0.4	0.5	0.7	0.6	2.4	•	•	•	•
Depreciation 14	2.0	1.8	1.0	1.7	1.1	0.9	1.6	2.2	3.1	•	•	•	•
Amortization and Depletion 15	0.7	0.0	0.2	0.2	0.1	0.0	1.4	0.7	0.8	•	•	•	•
Pensions and Other Deferred Comp. 16	0.4	0.1	0.7	0.2	0.5	0.5	0.3	0.7	0.3	•	•	•	•
Employee Benefits 17	2.2	0.3	1.7	2.1	0.8	1.2	1.7	3.0	2.1	•	•	•	•
Advertising 18	5.6	1.6	1.1	2.7	1.6	5.1	4.7	6.9	5.8	•	•	•	•
Other Expenses 19	30.0	37.7	34.3	26.4	37.9	30.3	23.5	32.4	33.0	•	•	•	•
Officers' Compensation 20	4.4	6.5	11.6	6.8	5.1	2.8	3.3	1.7	2.5	•	•	•	•
Operating Margin 21	7.4	13.7	8.5	4.3	7.5	3.0	5.3	6.3	4.8	•	•	•	•
Operating Margin Before Officers' Comp. 22	11.8	20.2	20.1	11.1	12.7	5.8	8.6	7.9	7.3	•	•	•	•

Selected Average Balance Sheet ($ in Thousands)

Net Receivables 23	166	0	7	138	406	1717	3103	6349	13045
Inventories 24	12	0	4	5	30	282	380	969	1303
Net Property, Plant and Equipment 25	183	0	18	276	617	1003	3040	8323	21370
Total Assets 26	908	0	73	665	1922	6235	15274	35042	71670
Notes and Loans Payable 27	222	0	43	185	499	1249	4435	5518	28849
All Other Liabilities 28	381	0	32	201	698	3600	5312	15142	24688
Net Worth 29	305	0	-3	278	725	1387	5528	14382	18134

Selected Financial Ratios (Times to 1)

Current Ratio 30	1.3	•	0.9	1.8	1.6	2.2	1.5	1.3	1.3
Quick Ratio 31	1.1	•	0.8	1.7	1.5	1.8	1.2	1.0	1.0
Net Sales to Working Capital 32	13.5	•	•	8.2	12.1	4.7	7.6	14.6	10.7
Coverage Ratio 33	6.5	80.8	18.3	10.0	19.1	26.7	14.2	14.9	4.7
Total Asset Turnover 34	1.3	•	4.5	1.8	2.8	1.9	1.5	1.6	1.1
Inventory Turnover 35	14.3	•	9.4	54.2	33.9	5.2	20.9	10.1	5.2
Receivables Turnover 36	8.6	•	44.1	12.9	•	10.0	8.9	10.6	6.4
Total Liabilities to Net Worth 37	2.0	•	•	1.4	1.7	3.5	1.8	1.4	3.0
Current Assets to Working Capital 38	4.3	•	•	2.2	2.7	1.8	3.0	4.9	4.3
Current Liabilities to Working Capital 39	3.3	•	•	1.2	1.7	0.8	2.0	3.9	3.3
Working Capital to Net Sales 40	0.1	•	•	0.1	0.1	0.2	0.1	0.1	0.1
Inventory to Working Capital 41	0.2	•	•	0.0	0.1	0.1	0.2	0.3	0.2
Total Receipts to Cash Flow 42	3.1	2.4	2.9	3.9	2.9	2.6	3.6	2.8	3.0
Cost of Goods to Cash Flow 43	0.4	0.7	0.3	0.8	0.6	0.3	1.2	0.5	0.3
Cash Flow to Total Debt 44	0.6	•	1.5	0.8	1.5	0.9	0.7	1.0	0.5

Selected Financial Factors (in Percentages)

Debt Ratio 45	66.4	•	103.6	58.2	62.3	77.8	63.8	59.0	74.7
Return on Total Assets 46	16.4	•	45.2	16.6	23.2	26.7	15.8	14.2	12.4
Return on Equity Before Income Taxes 47	41.2	•	•	35.7	58.3	115.7	40.6	32.3	38.5
Return on Equity After Income Taxes 48	33.8	•	•	34.7	56.8	110.2	37.6	27.2	30.6
Profit Margin (Before Income Tax) 49	10.4	14.2	9.5	8.2	7.9	13.7	9.5	8.1	9.0
Profit Margin (After Income Tax) 50	8.6	13.5	9.4	7.9	7.7	13.1	8.8	6.8	7.2

Table I

Corporations with and without Net Income

OFFICES OF PHYSICIANS

MONEY AMOUNTS AND SIZE OF ASSETS IN THOUSANDS OF DOLLARS

Item Description for Accounting Period 7/07 Through 6/08	Total	Zero Assets	Under 500	500 to 1,000	1,000 to 5,000	5,000 to 10,000	10,000 to 25,000	25,000 to 50,000	50,000 to 100,000	100,000 to 250,000	250,000 to 500,000	500,000 to 2,500,000	2,500,000 and over
Number of Enterprises 1	149536	14872	125997	4601	3463	365	140	49	29	15	0	4	0
Revenues ($ in Thousands)													
Net Sales 2	229822487	2822505	128275595	22242498	40165797	8387764	7355181	4756365	3013419	4223465	0	8579898	0
Interest 3	213980	3085	64424	17535	33227	11413	14126	13268	14661	21933	0	20308	0
Rents 4	139720	1503	45159	7736	27006	10901	2556	22264	9221	12534	0	840	0
Royalties 5	19386	3637	651	0	0	0	175	0	0	14923	0	0	0
Other Portfolio Income 6	669239	45085	92951	25723	99654	569	7230	35083	11476	8408	0	343063	0
Other Receipts 7	6339776	158629	3854237	424811	743207	75673	296778	184588	156168	55485	0	390197	0
Total Receipts 8	237204588	3034444	132333017	22718303	41068891	8486320	7676046	5011568	3204945	4336748	0	9334306	0
Average Total Receipts 9	1586	204	1050	4938	11859	23250	54829	102277	110515	289117	•	2333576	•
Operating Costs/Operating Income (%)													
Cost of Operations 10	5.3	1.1	4.3	4.9	6.7	0.9	17.2	15.7	11.3	9.3	•	0.7	•
Salaries and Wages 11	29.0	25.3	25.5	25.1	30.9	46.4	37.5	41.8	39.0	31.0	•	48.6	•
Taxes Paid 12	3.1	4.4	3.1	2.9	2.9	2.9	2.7	2.9	2.6	2.2	•	4.2	•
Interest Paid 13	0.5	0.7	0.4	0.3	0.5	1.0	0.5	1.0	1.1	1.4	•	1.0	•
Depreciation 14	1.1	1.4	0.8	0.9	1.6	2.6	1.7	1.4	1.9	1.7	•	0.3	•
Amortization and Depletion 15	0.1	0.4	0.0	0.1	0.1	0.2	0.2	0.2	0.4	0.1	•	0.4	•
Pensions and Other Deferred Comp. 16	3.4	2.5	3.7	2.4	3.2	2.3	2.4	3.1	1.8	1.6	•	6.8	•
Employee Benefits 17	2.1	1.1	1.8	1.7	2.0	2.0	2.8	3.7	2.7	2.8	•	5.5	•
Advertising 18	0.6	0.5	0.7	0.4	0.7	1.5	0.4	0.2	0.4	1.8	•	0.1	•
Other Expenses 19	31.6	36.4	29.9	36.3	30.0	32.7	32.4	31.9	44.5	47.9	•	35.3	•
Officers' Compensation 20	21.6	29.5	27.5	19.8	20.0	6.5	5.3	2.1	1.0	0.6	•	0.5	•
Operating Margin 21	1.7	•	2.3	5.1	1.5	1.0	•	•	•	•	•	•	•
Operating Margin Before Officers' Comp. 22	23.3	26.3	29.8	24.9	21.5	7.5	2.2	•	•	0.2	•	•	•

Selected Average Balance Sheet ($ in Thousands)

Net Receivables 23	26	0	3	31	303	914	2542	9424	14773	35761	52219
Inventories 24	1	0	0	7	12	21	197	351	412	663	1383
Net Property, Plant and Equipment 25	70	0	29	188	756	2286	4645	11285	20089	38585	27681
Total Assets 26	243	0	92	688	1939	6477	14089	35496	68397	160143	1092040
Notes and Loans Payable 27	111	0	55	285	979	3613	9765	11409	21086	41158	134810
All Other Liabilities 28	112	0	33	269	845	2011	4544	12656	28867	62998	1179759
Net Worth 29	19	0	5	134	115	853	-219	11431	18444	55986	-222528

Selected Financial Ratios (Times to 1)

Current Ratio 30	1.1	•	1.0	1.6	0.9	0.9	0.9	1.1	1.0	1.6	1.5
Quick Ratio 31	0.9	•	0.9	1.4	0.8	0.7	0.7	0.8	0.8	1.4	1.2
Net Sales to Working Capital 32	268.2	•	•	35.2	•	•	•	81.9	1285.0	12.1	20.3
Coverage Ratio 33	11.1	7.4	16.2	22.3	8.5	3.2	3.5	2.3	0.9	2.5	6.0
Total Asset Turnover 34	6.3	•	11.0	7.0	6.0	3.5	3.7	2.7	1.5	1.8	2.0
Inventory Turnover 35	58.8	•	115.0	33.3	63.1	9.5	45.8	43.3	28.5	39.4	11.6
Receivables Turnover 36	61.2	•	391.6	167.2	41.3	26.1	21.7	10.2	7.3	8.9	36.9
Total Liabilities to Net Worth 37	11.5	•	19.5	4.1	15.9	6.6	•	2.1	2.7	1.9	•
Current Assets to Working Capital 38	17.8	•	•	2.6	•	•	•	13.2	330.7	2.7	3.1
Current Liabilities to Working Capital 39	16.8	•	•	1.6	•	•	•	12.2	329.7	1.7	2.1
Working Capital to Net Sales 40	0.0	•	•	0.0	•	•	•	0.0	0.0	0.1	0.0
Inventory to Working Capital 41	0.2	•	•	0.1	•	•	•	0.4	4.9	0.0	0.0
Total Receipts to Cash Flow 42	3.2	3.0	3.3	2.6	3.6	3.5	3.7	3.3	2.5	2.1	3.1
Cost of Goods to Cash Flow 43	0.2	0.0	0.1	0.1	0.2	0.0	0.6	0.5	0.3	0.2	0.0
Cash Flow to Total Debt 44	2.1	•	3.5	3.4	1.8	1.2	1.0	1.2	0.8	1.3	0.5

Selected Financial Factors (in Percentages)

Debt Ratio 45	92.0	•	95.1	80.6	94.1	86.8	101.6	67.8	73.0	65.0	120.4
Return on Total Assets 46	33.7	•	64.6	53.2	25.3	11.1	6.4	6.3	1.4	6.3	12.4
Return on Equity Before Income Taxes 47	383.7	•	1244.3	261.3	376.2	57.6	•	11.2	329.7	10.6	•
Return on Equity After Income Taxes 48	370.3	•	1229.3	259.2	372.0	54.8	•	6.0	6.0	6.0	•
Profit Margin (Before Income Tax) 49	4.9	4.3	5.5	7.2	3.7	2.1	1.2	1.3	2.1	2.1	5.2
Profit Margin (After Income Tax) 50	4.7	4.0	5.4	7.2	3.7	2.0	1.1	0.7	1.2	1.2	3.5

Table II

Corporations with Net Income

OFFICES OF PHYSICIANS

MONEY AMOUNTS AND SIZE OF ASSETS IN THOUSANDS OF DOLLARS

Item Description for Accounting Period 7/07 Through 6/08	Total	Zero Assets	Under 500	500 to 1,000	1,000 to 5,000	5,000 to 10,000	10,000 to 25,000	25,000 to 50,000	50,000 to 100,000	100,000 to 250,000	250,000 to 500,000	500,000 to 2,500,000	2,500,000 and over
Number of Enterprises 1	98567	8118	83897	3786	2367	265	77	25	17	•	0	•	0
Revenues ($ in Thousands)													
Net Sales 2	158406567	1923325	87208908	15623256	25180749	7723000	4500992	2788124	2007760	•	0	•	0
Interest 3	149863	898	32892	12854	20403	11082	13049	10362	11668	•	0	•	0
Rents 4	73119	1054	26340	80	6610	10901	2291	18336	1428	•	0	•	0
Royalties 5	15098	0	0	0	0	0	175	0	0	•	0	•	0
Other Portfolio Income 6	619450	43957	67011	24053	93802	568	6694	29801	2757	•	0	•	0
Other Receipts 7	4562546	122335	2684865	382936	374080	62876	206073	153239	134971	•	0	•	0
Total Receipts 8	163826643	2091569	90020016	16043179	25675644	7808427	4729274	2999862	2158584	•	0	•	0
Average Total Receipts 9	1662	258	1073	4238	10847	29466	61419	119994	126976	•	•	•	•
Operating Costs/Operating Income (%)													
Cost of Operations 10	5.4	1.0	4.6	5.9	8.8	0.8	12.1	8.6	7.6	•	•	•	•
Salaries and Wages 11	27.2	25.3	23.0	26.2	25.7	46.6	38.1	37.5	32.2	•	•	•	•
Taxes Paid 12	3.0	4.4	3.0	3.3	2.8	2.9	2.5	3.0	2.4	•	•	•	•
Interest Paid 13	0.5	0.3	0.4	0.4	0.5	0.6	0.5	1.0	0.4	•	•	•	•
Depreciation 14	1.0	0.5	0.7	1.1	1.5	2.0	1.7	1.2	1.3	•	•	•	•
Amortization and Depletion 15	0.1	0.0	0.0	0.2	0.1	0.2	0.1	0.1	0.3	•	•	•	•
Pensions and Other Deferred Comp. 16	3.1	2.5	3.1	2.5	3.0	2.4	2.5	4.0	1.6	•	•	•	•
Employee Benefits 17	1.9	1.0	1.5	1.9	1.7	2.0	2.8	3.5	2.0	•	•	•	•
Advertising 18	0.8	0.5	0.8	0.5	0.8	1.6	0.5	0.2	0.4	•	•	•	•
Other Expenses 19	30.8	32.0	30.1	28.1	28.2	31.5	36.1	40.6	54.2	•	•	•	•
Officers' Compensation 20	20.9	24.1	26.3	21.7	21.8	7.0	3.8	2.8	0.9	•	•	•	•
Operating Margin 21	5.2	8.1	6.5	8.4	5.3	2.3	•	•	•	•	•	•	•
Operating Margin Before Officers' Comp. 22	26.2	32.2	32.8	30.1	27.1	9.4	2.9	0.4	•	•	•	•	•

Selected Average Balance Sheet ($ in Thousands)

Net Receivables 23	26	0	2	25	318	837	2356	8431	17327
Inventories 24	1	0	0	8	9	22	240	308	270
Net Property, Plant and Equipment 25	69	0	29	192	661	2150	3918	10921	19005
Total Assets 26	264	0	99	694	1922	6437	13774	34762	67280
Notes and Loans Payable 27	97	0	44	261	822	3028	6099	11176	17689
All Other Liabilities 28	107	0	26	168	561	1846	4640	13728	23686
Net Worth 29	60	0	29	265	539	1563	3035	9858	25905

Selected Financial Ratios (Times to 1)

Current Ratio 30	1.4	•	1.3	2.1	1.3	1.0	1.2	1.3	1.2
Quick Ratio 31	1.2	•	1.1	1.9	1.1	0.8	1.0	0.9	1.0
Net Sales to Working Capital 32	53.0	•	102.8	22.4	56.3	237.0	51.7	30.0	22.7
Coverage Ratio 33	18.8	50.0	27.9	29.5	15.1	6.5	8.7	6.2	11.0
Total Asset Turnover 34	6.1	•	10.5	5.9	5.5	4.5	4.2	3.2	1.8
Inventory Turnover 35	60.0	•	115.7	30.6	109.8	10.2	29.5	31.2	33.3
Receivables Turnover 36	64.5	•	453.5	263.2	•	39.8	23.0	11.1	7.4
Total Liabilities to Net Worth 37	3.4	•	2.4	1.6	2.6	3.1	3.5	2.5	1.6
Current Assets to Working Capital 38	3.8	•	4.4	1.9	4.7	22.8	6.3	4.8	5.6
Current Liabilities to Working Capital 39	2.8	•	3.4	0.9	3.7	21.8	5.3	3.8	4.6
Working Capital to Net Sales 40	0.0	•	0.0	0.0	0.0	0.0	0.0	0.0	0.0
Inventory to Working Capital 41	0.0	•	0.0	0.0	0.0	0.2	0.1	0.1	0.0
Total Receipts to Cash Flow 42	3.0	2.4	2.9	2.9	3.4	3.4	2.9	2.4	1.8
Cost of Goods to Cash Flow 43	0.2	0.0	0.1	0.2	0.3	0.0	0.4	0.2	0.1
Cash Flow to Total Debt 44	2.7	•	5.1	3.3	2.3	1.8	1.9	1.9	1.6

Selected Financial Factors (in Percentages)

Debt Ratio 45	77.3	•	70.6	61.8	72.0	75.7	78.0	71.6	61.5
Return on Total Assets 46	55.5	•	106.6	68.3	43.0	18.5	19.4	19.6	8.3
Return on Equity Before Income Taxes 47	231.3	•	349.5	172.8	143.3	64.4	78.0	58.0	19.5
Return on Equity After Income Taxes 48	224.7	•	346.0	171.6	142.0	62.4	73.4	46.3	13.6
Profit Margin (Before Income Tax) 49	8.6	16.8	9.7	11.1	7.3	3.5	4.1	5.1	4.3
Profit Margin (After Income Tax) 50	8.4	16.4	9.6	11.0	7.2	3.3	3.8	4.1	3.0

Table I

Corporations with and without Net Income

OFFICES OF DENTISTS

MONEY AMOUNTS AND SIZE OF ASSETS IN THOUSANDS OF DOLLARS

Item Description for Accounting Period 7/07 Through 6/08	Total	Zero Assets	Under 500	500 to 1,000	1,000 to 5,000	5,000 to 10,000	10,000 to 25,000	25,000 to 50,000	50,000 to 100,000	100,000 to 250,000	250,000 to 500,000	500,000 to 2,500,000	2,500,000 and over
Number of Enterprises **1**	71779	3499	61937	5218	1092	10	12	6	0	5	0	0	0

Revenues ($ in Thousands)

	Total	Zero Assets	Under 500	500 to 1,000	1,000 to 5,000	5,000 to 10,000	10,000 to 25,000	25,000 to 50,000	50,000 to 100,000	100,000 to 250,000	250,000 to 500,000	500,000 to 2,500,000	2,500,000 and over
Net Sales **2**	58813025	1019019	43691617	9006259	2814131	441728	499165	253366	0	1087739	0	0	0
Interest **3**	22628	796	11199	6047	3055	12	147	164	0	1210	0	0	0
Rents **4**	4684	0	3990	0	51	0	642	0	0	0	0	0	0
Royalties **5**	0	0	0	0	0	0	0	0	0	0	0	0	0
Other Portfolio Income **6**	98582	26314	64434	5425	788	0	1517	104	0	0	0	0	0
Other Receipts **7**	955204	43460	633357	231284	28592	7316	7751	144	0	3301	0	0	0
Total Receipts **8**	59894123	1089589	44404597	9249015	2846617	449056	509222	253778	0	1092250	0	0	0
Average Total Receipts **9**	834	311	717	1773	2607	44906	42435	42296	•	218450	•	•	•

Operating Costs/Operating Income (%)

	Total	Zero Assets	Under 500	500 to 1,000	1,000 to 5,000	5,000 to 10,000	10,000 to 25,000	25,000 to 50,000	50,000 to 100,000	100,000 to 250,000	250,000 to 500,000	500,000 to 2,500,000	2,500,000 and over
Cost of Operations **10**	5.8	0.0	5.7	6.4	8.9	•	•	11.6	•	5.7	•	•	•
Salaries and Wages **11**	23.4	14.9	22.2	25.3	27.4	33.3	38.5	46.7	•	37.0	•	•	•
Taxes Paid **12**	3.5	4.0	3.6	3.3	3.9	1.9	2.6	1.9	•	3.9	•	•	•
Interest Paid **13**	1.2	0.9	0.9	1.8	2.1	0.1	0.4	5.3	•	4.7	•	•	•
Depreciation **14**	1.8	1.6	1.7	1.9	3.7	0.1	0.6	3.8	•	2.4	•	•	•
Amortization and Depletion **15**	0.5	0.3	0.4	0.7	0.4	0.1	0.0	0.9	•	3.7	•	•	•
Pensions and Other Deferred Comp. **16**	2.1	1.5	2.3	2.0	1.2	0.5	4.6	0.1	•	0.2	•	•	•
Employee Benefits **17**	1.1	1.0	1.0	1.5	1.1	•	2.3	2.0	•	1.7	•	•	•
Advertising **18**	1.8	1.1	1.8	1.8	1.8	1.5	0.3	2.4	•	2.9	•	•	•
Other Expenses **19**	31.6	40.8	32.1	26.8	25.0	68.9	51.9	17.4	•	36.6	•	•	•
Officers' Compensation **20**	19.8	19.1	21.4	19.6	10.8	•	0.3	1.1	•	1.6	•	•	•
Operating Margin **21**	7.4	14.7	6.9	9.0	13.6	•	•	6.7	•	•	•	•	•
Operating Margin Before Officers' Comp. **22**	27.2	33.9	28.3	28.6	24.4	•	•	7.9	•	1.3	•	•	•

Selected Average Balance Sheet ($ in Thousands)

	1	2	3	4	5	6	7	8	9
Net Receivables 23	11	0	2	55	43	5919	3481	11886	33197
Inventories 24	1	0	1	1	0	35	0	777	953
Net Property, Plant and Equipment 25	75	0	57	204	500	256	1790	8621	32994
Total Assets 26	205	•	130	646	1422	6743	12656	36634	252337
Notes and Loans Payable 27	135	•	95	444	685	10	1500	21763	120347
All Other Liabilities 28	40	•	21	159	115	7353	7827	22597	50613
Net Worth 29	30	•	14	42	622	-621	3330	-7726	81377

Selected Financial Ratios (Times to 1)

	1	2	3	4	5	6	7	8	9
Current Ratio 30	1.2	•	1.1	0.9	2.9	1.0	0.8	1.1	1.4
Quick Ratio 31	1.0	•	1.0	0.8	2.2	0.9	0.7	0.9	1.1
Net Sales to Working Capital 32	108.1	•	156.3	•	8.9	•	20.9	•	14.7
Coverage Ratio 33	8.9	25.5	10.5	7.4	8.1	•	2.5	2.3	1.0
Total Asset Turnover 34	4.0	•	5.4	2.7	1.8	6.6	3.3	1.2	0.9
Inventory Turnover 35	56.7	51.6	156.8	628.0	•	6.6	•	6.3	13.0
Receivables Turnover 36	72.5	•	352.7	32.7	70.2	10.1	14.7	5.1	4.4
Total Liabilities to Net Worth 37	5.7	•	8.1	14.3	1.3	•	2.8	•	2.1
Current Assets to Working Capital 38	7.5	•	7.9	•	1.5	•	8.2	•	3.4
Current Liabilities to Working Capital 39	6.5	•	6.9	•	0.5	•	7.2	•	2.4
Working Capital to Net Sales 40	0.0	•	0.0	•	0.1	•	0.0	•	0.1
Inventory to Working Capital 41	0.1	•	0.2	•	•	•	0.6	•	0.1
Total Receipts to Cash Flow 42	2.9	1.8	2.9	3.1	2.9	1.6	1.9	5.3	3.3
Cost of Goods to Cash Flow 43	0.2	0.0	0.2	0.2	0.3	•	0.2	0.6	0.2
Cash Flow to Total Debt 44	1.6	•	2.1	0.9	1.1	3.7	2.3	0.2	0.4

Selected Financial Factors (in Percentages)

	1	2	3	4	5	6	7	8	9
Debt Ratio 45	85.2	•	89.0	93.5	56.3	109.2	73.7	121.1	67.8
Return on Total Assets 46	41.7	•	51.3	36.0	30.5	•	3.0	14.0	4.1
Return on Equity Before Income Taxes 47	249.0	•	422.1	476.6	61.1	344.3	6.7	•	0.1
Return on Equity After Income Taxes 48	246.8	•	420.7	474.1	60.5	344.3	6.7	•	•
Profit Margin (Before Income Tax) 49	9.2	21.7	8.6	11.7	14.8	•	0.5	6.9	0.0
Profit Margin (After Income Tax) 50	9.1	20.4	8.5	11.6	14.6	•	0.5	3.6	•

Table II

Corporations with Net Income

OFFICES OF DENTISTS

MONEY AMOUNTS AND SIZE OF ASSETS IN THOUSANDS OF DOLLARS

Item Description for Accounting Period 7/07 Through 6/08	Total	Zero Assets	Under 500	500 to 1,000	1,000 to 5,000	5,000 to 10,000	10,000 to 25,000	25,000 to 50,000	50,000 to 100,000	100,000 to 250,000	250,000 to 500,000	500,000 to 2,500,000	2,500,000 and over
Number of Enterprises **1**	52428	2864	44327	4377	848	0	9	3	0	0	0	0	0
Revenues ($ in Thousands)													
Net Sales **2**	44080655	861351	32750467	7044778	2645186	0	362233	416640	0	0	0	0	0
Interest **3**	14356	796	8355	2111	2773	0	127	194	0	0	0	0	0
Rents **4**	4632	0	3990	0	0	0	642	0	0	0	0	0	0
Royalties **5**	0	0	0	0	0	0	0	0	0	0	0	0	0
Other Portfolio Income **6**	56190	26314	26550	2537	788	0	0	0	0	0	0	0	0
Other Receipts **7**	808255	43459	497391	230974	28589	0	5854	1989	0	0	0	0	0
Total Receipts **8**	44964088	931920	33286753	7280400	2677336	0	368856	418823	0	0	0	0	0
Average Total Receipts **9**	858	325	751	1663	3157	•	40984	139608	•	•	•	•	•
Operating Costs/Operating Income (%)													
Cost of Operations **10**	6.5	0.0	6.4	7.4	9.0	•	•	5.9	•	•	•	•	•
Salaries and Wages **11**	22.2	12.9	21.2	24.9	27.2	•	27.2	34.7	•	•	•	•	•
Taxes Paid **12**	3.4	3.0	3.5	3.3	3.9	•	1.7	4.2	•	•	•	•	•
Interest Paid **13**	1.0	0.6	0.8	1.9	1.5	•	0.3	2.3	•	•	•	•	•
Depreciation **14**	1.5	1.7	1.3	1.8	3.3	•	0.8	3.2	•	•	•	•	•
Amortization and Depletion **15**	0.4	0.4	0.4	0.8	0.4	•	0.0	2.2	•	•	•	•	•
Pensions and Other Deferred Comp. **16**	1.9	1.8	2.1	1.7	1.1	•	0.4	0.5	•	•	•	•	•
Employee Benefits **17**	1.0	1.2	0.9	1.5	1.0	•	1.3	2.8	•	•	•	•	•
Advertising **18**	1.6	0.8	1.6	1.8	1.9	•	0.4	3.7	•	•	•	•	•
Other Expenses **19**	30.5	39.1	31.2	26.4	25.2	•	68.9	29.3	•	•	•	•	•
Officers' Compensation **20**	18.1	18.6	19.5	16.7	10.4	•	•	1.1	•	•	•	•	•
Operating Margin **21**	11.6	19.8	11.2	12.0	15.1	•	•	10.2	•	•	•	•	•
Operating Margin Before Officers' Comp. **22**	29.8	38.4	30.7	28.6	25.5	•	•	11.3	•	•	•	•	•

Selected Average Balance Sheet ($ in Thousands)

Net Receivables 23	9	0	2	62	47		2079	13545
Inventories 24	1	0	1	0	0		0	723
Net Property, Plant and Equipment 25	69	0	52	198	394		2156	33771
Total Assets 26	198		130	638	1404		9879	187410
Notes and Loans Payable 27	113	0	81	395	447		2000	68641
All Other Liabilities 28	36	0	19	173	107		5777	48946
Net Worth 29	49	0	30	70	850		2103	69824

Selected Financial Ratios (Times to 1)

Current Ratio 30	1.3		1.4	0.9	5.4		0.5	0.8
Quick Ratio 31	1.2		1.3	0.8	4.0		0.5	0.5
Net Sales to Working Capital 32	55.5		61.3		7.1			
Coverage Ratio 33	14.3	45.5	17.0	9.0	11.7		3.8	5.6
Total Asset Turnover 34	4.2		5.7	2.5	2.2		4.1	0.7
Inventory Turnover 35	68.8		56.2	473.5				11.3
Receivables Turnover 36	95.5		288.7	27.5			38.7	12.3
Total Liabilities to Net Worth 37	3.0		3.4	8.2	0.7		3.7	1.7
Current Assets to Working Capital 38	4.0		3.3	1.2				
Current Liabilities to Working Capital 39	3.0		2.3	0.2				
Working Capital to Net Sales 40	0.0		0.0	0.1				
Inventory to Working Capital 41	0.1		0.1					
Total Receipts to Cash Flow 42	2.6	1.6	2.6	2.8	2.8		1.4	3.2
Cost of Goods to Cash Flow 43	0.2	0.0	0.2	0.2	0.2			0.2
Cash Flow to Total Debt 44	2.2		2.8	1.0	2.0		3.6	0.4

Selected Financial Factors (in Percentages)

Debt Ratio 45	75.3		77.1	89.1	39.5		78.7	62.7
Return on Total Assets 46	62.1		77.6	43.4	39.7		4.9	9.7
Return on Equity Before Income Taxes 47	233.6		319.4	353.4	59.9		16.8	21.3
Return on Equity After Income Taxes 48	231.7		318.5	351.6	59.3		16.8	14.8
Profit Margin (Before Income Tax) 49	13.6	28.0	12.8	15.3	16.3		0.9	10.7
Profit Margin (After Income Tax) 50	13.5	26.5	12.8	15.2	16.2		0.9	7.4

Table I

Corporations with and without Net Income

OFFICES OF OTHER HEALTH PRACTITIONERS

MONEY AMOUNTS AND SIZE OF ASSETS IN THOUSANDS OF DOLLARS

Item Description for Accounting Period 7/07 Through 6/08	Total	Zero Assets	Under 500	500 to 1,000	1,000 to 5,000	5,000 to 10,000	10,000 to 25,000	25,000 to 50,000	50,000 to 100,000	100,000 to 250,000	250,000 to 500,000	500,000 to 2,500,000	2,500,000 and over
Number of Enterprises **1**	99760	17423	79564	1701	889	72	50	27	18	10	5	0	0
Revenues ($ in Thousands)													
Net Sales **2**	53241301	1351907	29953094	3817644	6635716	1148342	1878785	968724	1223710	2944674	3318704	0	0
Interest **3**	127829	1185	2800	1356	1196	2983	4520	7155	13571	12703	80360	0	0
Rents **4**	18406	0	3210	0	2135	0	288	8309	3893	504	68	0	0
Royalties **5**	0	0	0	0	0	0	0	0	0	0	0	0	0
Other Portfolio Income **6**	315316	40	197851	507	5969	3812	13252	64122	6511	22753	499	0	0
Other Receipts **7**	846945	6535	183930	39450	16101	4467	22179	28245	504009	11096	30933	0	0
Total Receipts **8**	54549797	1359667	30340885	3858957	6661117	1159604	1919024	1076555	1751694	2291730	3430564	0	0
Average Total Receipts **9**	547	78	381	2269	7493	16106	38380	39872	97316	299173	686113	•	•
Operating Costs/Operating Income (%)													
Cost of Operations **10**	18.7	7.3	10.8	37.1	35.4	44.1	38.5	15.5	24.8	35.9	3.8	•	•
Salaries and Wages **11**	20.7	11.8	19.3	17.2	19.6	25.0	22.9	43.6	35.5	29.8	19.5	•	•
Taxes Paid **12**	3.3	3.4	3.7	2.4	4.3	3.2	1.7	3.7	2.8	1.9	1.5	•	•
Interest Paid **13**	1.1	1.3	0.7	0.7	0.7	1.9	0.7	2.3	3.1	1.2	5.1	•	•
Depreciation **14**	1.2	2.7	1.1	1.2	1.1	0.4	1.8	1.6	2.4	0.9	0.6	•	•
Amortization and Depletion **15**	0.3	0.1	0.2	0.3	0.3	0.2	0.2	0.6	0.8	0.6	1.3	•	•
Pensions and Other Deferred Comp. **16**	0.9	1.7	1.0	1.6	1.1	0.4	0.4	0.6	0.5	0.2	0.1	•	•
Employee Benefits **17**	1.7	1.4	1.1	1.7	2.1	2.0	4.2	5.2	3.7	3.9	1.4	•	•
Advertising **18**	1.5	1.0	2.0	0.7	1.1	0.6	2.0	0.2	0.9	0.5	0.6	•	•
Other Expenses **19**	36.5	43.5	37.5	17.9	30.7	16.4	23.7	31.9	74.3	25.4	68.6	•	•
Officers' Compensation **20**	9.9	17.1	14.2	12.7	1.9	3.7	1.9	1.4	1.9	0.4	0.5	•	•
Operating Margin **21**	4.3	8.7	8.4	6.6	1.9	2.0	2.1	•	•	•	•	•	•
Operating Margin Before Officers' Comp. **22**	14.1	25.8	22.6	19.3	3.8	5.7	4.0	•	•	•	•	•	•

Selected Average Balance Sheet ($ in Thousands)

Net Receivables 23	24	0	5	129	367	2021	1674	8403	15593	29053	85140
Inventories 24	3	0	3	15	30	6	389	570	430	982	541
Net Property, Plant and Equipment 25	35	0	26	130	364	531	3297	6853	13100	13652	31673
Total Assets 26	153	0	72	694	1599	6866	14332	38170	74781	139504	394137
Notes and Loans Payable 27	75	0	39	406	592	6896	3234	9308	36459	38010	247371
All Other Liabilities 28	41	0	14	187	287	2013	4220	9055	22193	60947	158234
Net Worth 29	37	0	19	101	719	-2043	6879	19807	16128	40548	-11468

Selected Financial Ratios (Times to 1)

Current Ratio 30	1.4	•	1.6	1.4	2.4	0.7	1.4	1.8	1.1	1.1	1.3
Quick Ratio 31	1.2	•	1.4	1.4	2.0	0.7	1.0	1.3	0.9	0.8	1.2
Net Sales to Working Capital 32	25.4	•	33.0	19.8	13.6	•	19.6	3.6	26.7	86.3	22.2
Coverage Ratio 33	6.9	8.0	14.8	12.3	4.4	2.5	7.0	2.9	•	1.7	1.1
Total Asset Turnover 34	3.5	•	5.2	3.2	4.7	2.3	2.6	0.9	0.9	2.1	1.7
Inventory Turnover 35	32.2	•	16.1	55.6	87.4	1233.4	37.2	9.8	39.1	107.7	47.0
Receivables Turnover 36	23.4	•	63.0	24.6	23.2	9.5	16.4	4.2	5.6	10.9	8.3
Total Liabilities to Net Worth 37	3.1	•	2.8	5.9	1.2	•	1.1	0.9	3.6	2.4	•
Current Assets to Working Capital 38	3.2	•	2.6	3.3	1.7	•	3.6	2.3	11.0	19.5	4.1
Current Liabilities to Working Capital 39	2.2	•	1.6	2.3	0.7	•	2.6	1.3	10.0	18.5	3.1
Working Capital to Net Sales 40	0.0	•	0.0	0.1	0.1	•	0.1	0.3	0.0	0.0	0.0
Inventory to Working Capital 41	0.2	•	0.2	0.1	0.0	•	0.2	0.1	0.2	0.2	0.0
Total Receipts to Cash Flow 42	2.8	2.4	2.6	4.7	3.6	6.3	4.5	3.8	1.7	4.0	1.5
Cost of Goods to Cash Flow 43	0.5	0.2	0.3	1.8	1.3	2.8	1.7	0.6	0.4	1.5	0.1
Cash Flow to Total Debt 44	1.7	•	2.7	0.8	2.4	0.3	1.1	0.5	0.7	0.7	1.1

Selected Financial Factors (in Percentages)

Debt Ratio 45	75.7	•	73.4	85.4	55.0	129.8	52.0	48.1	78.4	70.9	102.9
Return on Total Assets 46	27.3	•	54.2	27.2	13.6	11.4	13.1	6.2	•	4.4	9.1
Return on Equity Before Income Taxes 47	96.2	•	189.8	171.5	23.4	•	23.3	7.8	•	6.4	•
Return on Equity After Income Taxes 48	93.8	•	189.2	168.2	23.0	•	18.4	4.2	0.0	4.8	5.8
Profit Margin (Before Income Tax) 49	6.7	9.3	9.7	7.7	2.3	2.9	4.3	4.3	0.9	0.9	0.3
Profit Margin (After Income Tax) 50	6.5	9.3	9.7	7.6	2.2	2.2	3.4	2.3	0.9	0.7	0.3

367

Table II
Corporations with Net Income

OFFICES OF OTHER HEALTH PRACTITIONERS

MONEY AMOUNTS AND SIZE OF ASSETS IN THOUSANDS OF DOLLARS

Item Description for Accounting Period 7/07 Through 6/08		Total	Zero Assets	Under 500	500 to 1,000	1,000 to 5,000	5,000 to 10,000	10,000 to 25,000	25,000 to 50,000	50,000 to 100,000	100,000 to 250,000	250,000 to 500,000	500,000 to 2,500,000	2,500,000 and over
Number of Enterprises	1	71965	11067	58930	1040	794	64	31	•	10	•	•	0	0
Revenues ($ in Thousands)														
Net Sales	2	3889126	959565	22986639	1838960	5179505	997302	1369646	•	828382	•	•	0	0
Interest	3	111939	9	740	1186	1119	2357	2839	•	6255	•	•	0	0
Rents	4	11297	0	3204	0	2135	0	288	•	1323	•	•	0	0
Royalties	5	0	0	0	0	0	0	0	•	0	•	•	0	0
Other Portfolio Income	6	291377	0	186932	507	5919	10	13004	•	899	•	•	0	0
Other Receipts	7	448199	67	176767	30318	13707	3629	8309	•	163113	•	•	0	0
Total Receipts	8	40753938	959641	23354282	1870971	5202385	1003298	1394086	•	999972	•	•	0	0
Average Total Receipts	9	566	87	396	1799	6552	15677	44971	•	99997	•	•	•	•
Operating Costs/Operating Income (%)														
Cost of Operations	10	17.3	7.3	10.2	11.2	38.5	50.6	43.0	•	5.1	•	•	•	•
Salaries and Wages	11	20.9	8.6	20.3	23.1	21.4	20.6	17.1	•	39.3	•	•	•	•
Taxes Paid	12	3.5	2.5	3.8	3.1	4.9	3.1	1.6	•	2.9	•	•	•	•
Interest Paid	13	1.1	0.4	0.6	1.2	0.7	2.1	0.5	•	2.1	•	•	•	•
Depreciation	14	1.0	1.1	1.0	1.6	1.2	0.3	1.4	•	2.8	•	•	•	•
Amortization and Depletion	15	0.3	0.1	0.1	0.5	0.4	0.1	0.1	•	0.9	•	•	•	•
Pensions and Other Deferred Comp.	16	0.9	0.6	1.1	1.6	1.3	0.1	0.5	•	0.8	•	•	•	•
Employee Benefits	17	1.7	1.3	1.2	1.8	2.5	1.6	3.2	•	4.1	•	•	•	•
Advertising	18	1.6	0.8	2.1	1.3	1.2	0.7	1.5	•	1.1	•	•	•	•
Other Expenses	19	32.8	38.8	32.6	23.3	21.7	10.4	24.0	•	56.9	•	•	•	•
Officers' Compensation	20	9.9	15.0	14.5	15.9	2.0	3.5	1.8	•	0.4	•	•	•	•
Operating Margin	21	8.9	23.5	12.5	15.3	4.3	6.7	5.3	•	•	•	•	•	•
Operating Margin Before Officers' Comp.	22	18.8	38.5	27.1	31.2	6.3	10.3	7.1	•	•	•	•	•	•

Selected Average Balance Sheet ($ in Thousands)

Net Receivables 23	22	0	4	79	317	1900	895	17116
Inventories 24	3	0	3	24	34	6	104	430
Net Property, Plant and Equipment 25	34	0	25	119	321	559	3309	17684
Total Assets 26	157	0	74	689	1534	6681	14802	75198
Notes and Loans Payable 27	63	0	29	299	431	5276	2504	30804
All Other Liabilities 28	36	0	10	135	221	1791	3285	18562
Net Worth 29	58	0	35	255	882	-386	9014	25832

Selected Financial Ratios (Times to 1)

Current Ratio 30	1.8	•	2.1	2.0	3.5	1.4	1.7	1.3
Quick Ratio 31	1.5	•	1.8	1.8	2.7	1.3	1.4	1.2
Net Sales to Working Capital 32	17.6	•	23.0	12.3	10.5	19.8	14.5	12.4
Coverage Ratio 33	10.8	53.3	23.5	15.6	7.9	4.4	16.3	3.1
Total Asset Turnover 34	3.5	•	5.2	2.6	4.3	2.3	3.0	1.1
Inventory Turnover 35	29.2	•	14.9	8.4	75.0	1388.9	182.7	9.8
Receivables Turnover 36	26.7	•	68.6	41.7	28.4	10.2	64.1	5.7
Total Liabilities to Net Worth 37	1.7	•	1.1	1.7	0.7	•	0.6	1.9
Current Assets to Working Capital 38	2.2	•	1.9	2.0	1.4	3.8	2.4	4.3
Current Liabilities to Working Capital 39	1.2	•	0.9	1.0	0.4	2.8	1.4	3.3
Working Capital to Net Sales 40	0.1	•	0.0	0.1	0.1	0.1	0.1	0.1
Inventory to Working Capital 41	0.1	•	0.1	0.2	0.0	0.0	0.0	0.1
Total Receipts to Cash Flow 42	2.7	1.9	2.6	3.0	4.8	6.6	3.8	1.8
Cost of Goods to Cash Flow 43	0.5	0.1	0.3	0.3	1.9	3.4	1.6	0.1
Cash Flow to Total Debt 44	2.1	•	3.7	1.3	2.1	0.3	2.0	0.9

Selected Financial Factors (in Percentages)

Debt Ratio 45	62.8	•	53.1	63.0	42.5	105.8	39.1	65.6
Return on Total Assets 46	42.9	•	77.4	46.8	23.0	22.1	22.5	7.2
Return on Equity Before Income Taxes 47	104.7	•	158.1	118.4	35.0	•	34.7	14.3
Return on Equity After Income Taxes 48	102.6	•	157.6	116.3	34.7	•	28.7	11.5
Profit Margin (Before Income Tax) 49	11.0	23.5	14.1	17.0	4.7	7.3	7.1	4.5
Profit Margin (After Income Tax) 50	10.8	23.5	14.1	16.7	4.7	6.5	5.8	3.6

Table I

Corporations with and without Net Income

OUTPATIENT CARE CENTERS

MONEY AMOUNTS AND SIZE OF ASSETS IN THOUSANDS OF DOLLARS

Item Description for Accounting Period 7/07 Through 6/08	Total	Zero Assets	Under 500	500 to 1,000	1,000 to 5,000	5,000 to 10,000	10,000 to 25,000	25,000 to 50,000	50,000 to 100,000	100,000 to 250,000	250,000 to 500,000	500,000 to 2,500,000	2,500,000 and over
Number of Enterprises 1	7062	1390	4811	368	371	49	26	10	12	4	8	10	3
Revenues ($ in Thousands)													
Net Sales 2	34418021	907486	2379356	1600378	3470657	919955	497603	1070596	1655819	321296	3438122	6674090	11252663
Interest 3	397210	9194	1098	3272	7020	641	3772	10003	12153	3081	27918	137827	181230
Rents 4	25478	0	648	0	95	637	555	849	1809	1	2684	3897	14304
Royalties 5	460	197	0	0	0	0	99	22	0	0	0	142	0
Other Portfolio Income 6	297143	32664	26086	61	619	4901	1802	22470	1966	629	6849	3031	196065
Other Receipts 7	1691394	48871	25751	1828	6833	-9906	983	11806	17642	22129	828866	165912	570680
Total Receipts 8	36599706	998412	2432939	1605539	3485224	916228	504814	1115746	1689389	347136	4304439	6984899	12214942
Average Total Receipts 9	5183	718	506	4363	9394	18699	19416	111575	140782	86784	538055	698490	4071647
Operating Costs/Operating Income (%)													
Cost of Operations 10	31.1	61.5	10.3	10.5	17.8	4.4	15.5	55.6	9.3	18.3	54.7	32.0	36.4
Salaries and Wages 11	22.2	12.1	12.5	19.2	41.1	23.6	25.3	3.9	17.5	30.5	18.1	29.7	18.4
Taxes Paid 12	3.2	4.0	2.4	2.5	3.7	2.2	2.6	0.6	1.7	3.3	1.8	4.4	3.7
Interest Paid 13	4.1	3.6	0.4	0.3	0.8	0.9	2.9	0.1	1.8	4.4	1.6	5.0	7.8
Depreciation 14	2.1	1.0	0.8	0.9	1.9	1.5	1.0	0.3	1.2	6.7	1.0	1.7	3.5
Amortization and Depletion 15	1.5	0.5	0.0	0.0	0.1	0.2	0.6	0.1	0.6	4.8	1.0	2.2	2.7
Pensions and Other Deferred Comp. 16	0.8	0.1	0.2	0.1	4.9	0.9	0.0	0.1	0.3	0.4	0.1	0.2	0.7
Employee Benefits 17	5.2	1.1	2.5	0.8	4.8	1.5	2.2	15.8	1.8	1.5	21.1	2.3	3.7
Advertising 18	0.4	0.3	0.6	0.2	0.3	0.2	0.7	0.3	0.5	8.3	0.2	0.8	0.1
Other Expenses 19	29.1	25.6	51.5	59.8	16.8	61.4	54.4	24.1	64.6	36.2	18.4	21.6	23.1
Officers' Compensation 20	1.9	8.6	7.0	1.4	6.2	1.3	1.2	0.2	0.9	1.0	0.7	0.9	0.5
Operating Margin 21	•	•	11.8	4.2	1.9	1.9	•	•	•	•	•	•	•
Operating Margin Before Officers' Comp. 22	0.2	•	18.8	5.7	8.1	3.2	•	0.5	•	•	•	•	0.2

Selected Average Balance Sheet ($ in Thousands)

Net Receivables 23	536	0	5	104	935	1055	3041	2954	9080	8166	37227	91084	619929
Inventories 24	60	0	3	7	208	56	62	120	527	1824	590	15663	101842
Net Property, Plant and Equipment 25	633	0	46	169	553	1519	2146	2352	12622	20598	33975	102330	766370
Total Assets 26	7432	0	97	781	2563	6522	14116	34759	70175	161024	344386	985828	11882463
Notes and Loans Payable 27	4120	0	160	201	1365	2239	6976	1852	22509	86180	92674	440800	7224336
All Other Liabilities 28	1343	0	27	118	1126	2587	3804	19413	29290	24532	85679	168903	1882271
Net Worth 29	1969	0	-90	462	72	1696	3336	13493	18375	50311	166032	376124	2775856

Selected Financial Ratios (Times to 1)

Current Ratio 30	1.2	•	0.7	4.6	1.3	1.0	2.0	1.5	0.7	1.1	1.6	1.6	1.0
Quick Ratio 31	0.9	•	0.5	2.0	1.0	0.9	1.4	1.3	0.6	0.7	1.2	1.4	0.8
Net Sales to Working Capital 32	22.1	•	•	10.0	23.0	269.8	4.0	13.4	•	50.7	9.7	9.0	126.7
Coverage Ratio 33	2.3	•	38.6	18.1	4.1	2.6	•	23.7	1.9	•	5.2	1.8	2.0
Total Asset Turnover 34	0.7	•	5.1	5.6	3.6	2.9	1.4	3.1	2.0	0.5	1.2	0.7	0.3
Inventory Turnover 35	25.1	•	17.5	66.1	8.0	14.9	48.3	494.4	24.3	8.0	398.5	13.7	13.4
Receivables Turnover 36	9.6	•	98.3	79.9	13.2	20.1	8.4	9.5	20.0	19.7	9.0	4.1	12.1
Total Liabilities to Net Worth 37	2.8	•	•	0.7	34.8	2.8	3.2	1.6	2.8	2.2	1.1	1.6	3.3
Current Assets to Working Capital 38	6.6	•	•	1.3	4.8	40.9	2.0	3.0	15.3	•	2.7	2.7	58.9
Current Liabilities to Working Capital 39	5.6	•	•	0.3	3.8	39.9	1.0	2.0	14.3	•	1.7	1.7	57.9
Working Capital to Net Sales 40	0.0	•	•	0.1	0.0	0.0	0.2	0.1	0.0	0.0	0.1	0.1	0.0
Inventory to Working Capital 41	0.3	•	•	0.0	0.5	1.5	0.0	0.0	•	1.2	0.0	0.0	3.4
Total Receipts to Cash Flow 42	3.4	7.5	1.6	1.9	5.9	1.7	2.4	4.1	1.6	4.4	4.5	4.3	4.3
Cost of Goods to Cash Flow 43	1.1	4.6	0.2	0.2	1.0	0.1	0.4	2.3	0.1	0.8	2.5	1.4	1.6
Cash Flow to Total Debt 44	0.3	•	1.4	8.4	0.6	2.3	0.7	1.2	1.7	0.2	0.5	0.3	0.1

Selected Financial Factors (in Percentages)

Debt Ratio 45	73.5	•	193.3	40.9	97.2	74.0	76.4	61.2	73.8	68.8	51.8	61.8	76.6
Return on Total Assets 46	6.1	•	73.7	26.8	11.2	6.8	•	10.0	6.7	•	10.1	6.0	5.0
Return on Equity Before Income Taxes 47	13.1	•	•	42.8	302.4	16.2	•	24.6	12.0	•	17.0	7.0	10.8
Return on Equity After Income Taxes 48	9.4	•	•	42.4	291.5	16.2	•	19.3	6.8	•	13.2	4.4	6.7
Profit Margin (Before Income Tax) 49	5.3	•	14.0	4.5	2.3	1.5	•	3.1	1.6	•	6.6	3.9	8.0
Profit Margin (After Income Tax) 50	3.8	•	13.9	4.5	2.2	1.5	•	2.4	0.9	•	5.1	2.5	4.9

Table II

Corporations with Net Income

OUTPATIENT CARE CENTERS

MONEY AMOUNTS AND SIZE OF ASSETS IN THOUSANDS OF DOLLARS

Item Description for Accounting Period 7/07 Through 6/08	Total	Zero Assets	Under 500	500 to 1,000	1,000 to 5,000	5,000 to 10,000	10,000 to 25,000	25,000 to 50,000	50,000 to 100,000	100,000 to 250,000	250,000 to 500,000	500,000 to 2,500,000	2,500,000 and over
Number of Enterprises **1**	3878	386	2853	364	195	35	16	•	6	0	•	•	0

Revenues ($ in Thousands)

Net Sales **2**	27689882	134219	1881819	1600378	2460626	631759	200185	•	943494	0	•	•	0
Interest **3**	194895	0	333	3173	3632	609	3524	•	5902	0	•	•	0
Rents **4**	6445	0	648	0	95	637	192	•	76	0	•	•	0
Royalties **5**	263	0	0	0	0	0	99	•	0	0	•	•	0
Other Portfolio Income **6**	115019	32563	26086	61	619	4901	1802	•	1966	0	•	•	0
Other Receipts **7**	1442013	0	25616	1450	5944	6280	449	•	1493	0	•	•	0
Total Receipts **8**	29448517	166782	1934502	1605062	2470916	644186	206251	•	952931	0	•	•	0
Average Total Receipts **9**	7594	432	678	4410	12671	18405	12891	•	158822	•	•	•	•

Operating Costs/Operating Income (%)

Cost of Operations **10**	35.5	90.6	13.1	10.5	24.6	6.5	9.4	•	5.8	•	•	•	•
Salaries and Wages **11**	19.1	•	9.1	19.2	36.9	8.3	9.0	•	14.4	•	•	•	•
Taxes Paid **12**	3.2	0.5	2.1	2.5	4.0	1.2	1.0	•	1.4	•	•	•	•
Interest Paid **13**	3.1	2.5	0.4	0.2	0.4	0.9	3.1	•	0.4	•	•	•	•
Depreciation **14**	1.9	0.9	0.8	0.9	1.4	1.3	0.8	•	0.9	•	•	•	•
Amortization and Depletion **15**	1.3	•	•	0.0	0.0	0.0	1.2	•	0.0	•	•	•	•
Pensions and Other Deferred Comp. **16**	0.8	•	0.2	0.1	5.2	0.3	•	•	0.5	•	•	•	•
Employee Benefits **17**	5.2	•	2.8	0.8	5.6	0.2	0.7	•	1.6	•	•	•	•
Advertising **18**	0.4	0.4	0.6	0.2	0.3	0.1	0.8	•	0.7	•	•	•	•
Other Expenses **19**	25.4	26.4	42.5	59.2	9.3	75.6	73.2	•	68.7	•	•	•	•
Officers' Compensation **20**	1.8	•	8.5	1.4	6.6	0.9	0.5	•	1.2	•	•	•	•
Operating Margin **21**	2.2	•	19.9	4.9	5.7	4.6	0.4	•	4.4	•	•	•	•
Operating Margin Before Officers' Comp. **22**	4.0	•	28.4	6.4	12.3	5.5	0.9	•	5.6	•	•	•	•

Selected Average Balance Sheet ($ in Thousands)

	1	2	3	4	5	6	7	8	9	10
Net Receivables **23**	748	•	0	0	106	1132	959	448	•	9188
Inventories **24**	106	•	0	5	13	395	78	2	•	319
Net Property, Plant and Equipment **25**	895	•	0	64	171	721	1443	1114	•	14037
Total Assets **26**	11211	•	0	126	780	3225	6365	12820	•	61140
Notes and Loans Payable **27**	5935	•	0	84	198	652	2295	4128	•	10260
All Other Liabilities **28**	1311	•	0	10	106	1797	2954	2424	•	21828
Net Worth **29**	3964	•	0	33	475	777	1116	6268	•	29052

Selected Financial Ratios (Times to 1)

	1	2	3	4	5	6	7	8	9	10
Current Ratio **30**	1.4	•	0.8	5.1	1.1	1.0	1.0	2.5	•	1.1
Quick Ratio **31**	1.1	•	0.4	2.1	0.9	1.0	1.5	•	•	1.0
Net Sales to Working Capital **32**	12.6	•	•	9.9	73.2	126.2	2.2	•	•	93.1
Coverage Ratio **33**	3.7	2.2	57.7	25.2	15.8	8.7	2.1	•	•	15.4
Total Asset Turnover **34**	0.6	•	5.2	5.6	3.9	2.8	1.0	•	•	2.6
Inventory Turnover **35**	24.0	•	17.5	34.9	7.9	14.9	537.1	•	•	28.7
Receivables Turnover **36**	9.9	•	418182.0	82.8	12.3	22.1	19.3	•	•	24.2
Total Liabilities to Net Worth **37**	1.8	•	2.8	0.6	3.2	4.7	1.0	•	•	1.1
Current Assets to Working Capital **38**	3.2	•	•	1.2	14.3	21.8	1.7	•	•	15.6
Current Liabilities to Working Capital **39**	2.2	•	•	0.2	13.3	20.8	0.7	•	•	14.6
Working Capital to Net Sales **40**	0.1	•	•	0.1	0.0	0.0	0.4	•	•	0.0
Inventory to Working Capital **41**	0.2	•	•	0.0	2.0	1.0	0.0	•	•	0.2
Total Receipts to Cash Flow **42**	3.3	4.8	1.8	1.6	7.5	1.3	1.3	•	•	1.4
Cost of Goods to Cash Flow **43**	1.2	4.3	0.2	0.2	1.8	0.1	0.1	•	•	0.1
Cash Flow to Total Debt **44**	0.3	•	3.9	8.9	0.7	2.7	1.4	•	•	3.5

Selected Financial Factors (in Percentages)

	1	2	3	4	5	6	7	8	9	10
Debt Ratio **45**	64.6	•	73.7	39.1	75.9	82.5	51.1	•	•	52.5
Return on Total Assets **46**	7.4	•	120.6	30.7	25.5	21.1	6.4	•	•	14.5
Return on Equity Before Income Taxes **47**	15.4	•	450.6	48.4	99.1	106.6	6.9	•	•	28.6
Return on Equity After Income Taxes **48**	12.0	•	447.9	48.0	97.2	106.5	6.8	•	•	22.0
Profit Margin (Before Income Tax) **49**	8.5	3.0	22.7	5.2	6.1	6.6	3.4	•	•	5.3
Profit Margin (After Income Tax) **50**	6.7	3.0	22.6	5.2	6.0	6.6	3.4	•	•	4.1

Table I

Corporations with and without Net Income

MISC. HEALTH CARE AND SOCIAL ASSISTANCE

MONEY AMOUNTS AND SIZE OF ASSETS IN THOUSANDS OF DOLLARS

Item Description for Accounting Period 7/07 Through 6/08	Total	Zero Assets	Under 500	500 to 1,000	1,000 to 5,000	5,000 to 10,000	10,000 to 25,000	25,000 to 50,000	50,000 to 100,000	100,000 to 250,000	250,000 to 500,000	500,000 to 2,500,000	2,500,000 and over
Number of Enterprises **1**	61048	10539	44740	2988	2196	276	137	52	49	36	13	21	0
Revenues ($ in Thousands)													
Net Sales **2**	95007485	4275688	25506156	6227312	7747562	5861829	4432611	3003351	3739684	5049543	4126477	25037273	0
Interest **3**	330814	4167	9897	4537	7795	14755	11343	13784	22697	54420	13990	173429	0
Rents **4**	32117	0	10471	0	4224	798	98	205	1436	8048	2220	4617	0
Royalties **5**	105234	4340	0	0	0	0	49	0	50349	44280	3098	3119	0
Other Portfolio Income **6**	440763	49455	79352	4615	77393	10654	24740	17201	73668	18994	16599	68093	0
Other Receipts **7**	1462582	94415	421642	83368	109663	196856	43859	26271	41717	155933	78911	209944	0
Total Receipts **8**	97378995	4428065	26027518	6319832	7946637	6084892	4512700	3060812	3929551	5331218	4241295	25496475	0
Average Total Receipts **9**	1595	420	582	2115	3619	22047	32939	58862	80195	148089	326253	1214118	•
Operating Costs/Operating Income (%)													
Cost of Operations **10**	17.6	9.1	9.2	11.8	15.0	40.3	26.0	27.0	34.1	25.2	17.9	18.0	•
Salaries and Wages **11**	30.4	37.4	34.6	31.4	36.3	29.7	23.1	30.1	30.5	26.9	29.0	25.2	•
Taxes Paid **12**	3.8	4.2	4.7	3.3	4.7	2.6	3.6	3.7	3.9	4.0	3.0	3.1	•
Interest Paid **13**	2.1	1.8	0.6	0.8	2.3	0.8	1.0	2.3	2.8	4.7	3.9	3.6	•
Depreciation **14**	2.1	0.9	1.0	1.2	1.8	3.3	2.0	1.8	2.2	3.2	2.9	3.2	•
Amortization and Depletion **15**	0.8	0.6	0.2	0.3	0.1	0.1	0.5	1.4	1.6	2.3	1.1	1.3	•
Pensions and Other Deferred Comp. **16**	0.4	0.1	0.6	0.2	0.6	0.9	0.3	0.4	0.4	0.3	0.4	0.3	•
Employee Benefits **17**	2.5	2.3	1.4	1.5	2.1	2.4	1.5	6.9	2.7	2.1	3.1	3.7	•
Advertising **18**	0.6	0.3	0.8	1.4	0.5	0.6	0.5	0.5	0.7	0.4	0.3	0.4	•
Other Expenses **19**	32.4	45.6	32.3	30.2	26.8	20.3	36.3	30.3	24.4	35.6	37.9	34.6	•
Officers' Compensation **20**	4.7	2.8	10.9	9.1	5.4	1.6	2.3	2.1	2.0	1.3	0.7	0.8	•
Operating Margin **21**	2.5	•	3.7	8.8	4.5	•	2.8	•	•	•	•	5.7	•
Operating Margin Before Officers' Comp. **22**	7.2	•	14.6	17.9	9.8	5.1	5.1	•	•	•	0.5	6.5	•

Selected Average Balance Sheet ($ in Thousands)

Net Receivables 23	144	0	8	91	329	1463	3171	10135	12352	26229	62107	177039
Inventories 24	12	0	1	5	32	123	333	750	1832	3333	6638	8854
Net Property, Plant and Equipment 25	185	0	29	216	750	1895	3434	4439	7125	22768	56752	218765
Total Assets 26	998	0	74	700	1892	6897	16337	37726	69002	159710	313322	1525802
Notes and Loans Payable 27	422	0	56	283	1127	3698	6498	15147	24229	62061	156935	561338
All Other Liabilities 28	247	0	16	147	215	1641	4876	11958	20092	45943	62007	395615
Net Worth 29	328	0	2	271	551	1559	4964	10621	24681	51705	94379	568849

Selected Financial Ratios (Times to 1)

Current Ratio 30	1.5	•	1.7	2.0	2.4	1.3	1.2	1.2	1.4	1.3	1.7	1.4
Quick Ratio 31	1.1	•	1.5	1.8	2.0	1.1	0.9	0.9	1.0	1.0	1.2	1.0
Net Sales to Working Capital 32	15.0	•	49.2	13.9	6.8	26.3	27.1	14.6	10.7	9.9	7.2	11.3
Coverage Ratio 33	3.3	0.1	10.5	13.1	4.0	2.6	5.5	•	0.9	0.9	1.6	3.1
Total Asset Turnover 34	1.6	•	7.7	3.0	1.9	3.1	2.0	1.5	1.1	0.9	1.0	0.8
Inventory Turnover 35	23.3	•	73.6	46.4	16.6	69.7	25.3	20.8	14.2	10.6	8.6	24.2
Receivables Turnover 36	11.5	•	61.3	22.9	11.9	13.0	9.7	5.6	6.0	6.0	4.7	8.0
Total Liabilities to Net Worth 37	2.0	•	30.7	1.6	2.4	3.4	2.3	2.6	1.8	2.1	2.3	1.7
Current Assets to Working Capital 38	3.1	•	2.5	2.0	1.7	4.4	6.9	5.1	3.9	4.0	2.4	3.5
Current Liabilities to Working Capital 39	2.1	•	1.5	1.0	0.7	3.4	5.9	4.1	2.9	3.0	1.4	2.5
Working Capital to Net Sales 40	0.1	•	0.0	0.1	0.1	0.0	0.0	0.1	0.1	0.1	0.1	0.1
Inventory to Working Capital 41	0.1	•	0.0	0.0	0.1	0.2	0.3	0.3	0.2	0.3	0.1	0.1
Total Receipts to Cash Flow 42	3.1	2.5	3.2	2.9	3.6	5.4	2.9	4.7	5.8	3.3	2.8	2.7
Cost of Goods to Cash Flow 43	0.6	0.2	0.3	0.3	0.5	2.2	0.7	1.3	2.0	0.8	0.5	0.5
Cash Flow to Total Debt 44	0.7	•	2.5	1.7	0.7	0.7	1.0	0.5	0.3	0.4	0.5	0.5

Selected Financial Factors (in Percentages)

Debt Ratio 45	67.1	•	96.8	61.3	70.9	77.4	69.6	71.8	64.2	67.6	69.9	62.7
Return on Total Assets 46	11.0	•	49.1	33.1	17.5	6.2	11.2	•	2.7	3.9	6.6	8.7
Return on Equity Before Income Taxes 47	23.5	•	1411.4	79.2	45.0	16.9	30.1	•	•	•	8.6	15.8
Return on Equity After Income Taxes 48	18.8	•	1398.7	77.8	41.3	11.7	27.1	•	•	•	6.0	10.3
Profit Margin (Before Income Tax) 49	4.9	•	5.8	10.3	7.0	1.2	4.6	•	•	•	2.6	7.5
Profit Margin (After Income Tax) 50	4.0	•	5.7	10.1	6.4	0.9	4.2	•	•	•	1.8	4.9

Table II
Corporations with Net Income

MISC. HEALTH CARE AND SOCIAL ASSISTANCE

MONEY AMOUNTS AND SIZE OF ASSETS IN THOUSANDS OF DOLLARS

Item Description for Accounting Period 7/07 Through 6/08	Total	Zero Assets	Under 500	500 to 1,000	1,000 to 5,000	5,000 to 10,000	10,000 to 25,000	25,000 to 50,000	50,000 to 100,000	100,000 to 250,000	250,000 to 500,000	500,000 to 2,500,000	2,500,000 and over
Number of Enterprises 1	37310	4647	28279	2423	1564	205	98	24	27	21	9	14	0
Revenues ($ in Thousands)													
Net Sales 2	75276749	3378362	20817808	5562464	5941000	3362273	3924283	1971166	2579784	3247305	2897115	21595190	0
Interest 3	175587	1731	5042	4254	6414	6368	5536	5850	9437	17099	13180	100676	0
Rents 4	23322	0	7909	0	4209	545	98	0	135	5038	850	4537	0
Royalties 5	7623	4340	0	0	0	0	0	0	0	186	3098	0	0
Other Portfolio Income 6	362578	49416	36407	4615	72773	7351	24461	13140	63541	13347	9848	67679	0
Other Receipts 7	1132926	76189	328634	82070	104871	214755	27609	15913	21328	72268	62281	127007	0
Total Receipts 8	76978785	3510038	21195800	5653403	6129267	3591292	3981987	2006069	2674225	3355243	2986372	21895089	0
Average Total Receipts 9	2063	755	750	2333	3919	17518	40633	83586	99045	159773	331819	1563935	•
Operating Costs/Operating Income (%)													
Cost of Operations 10	16.5	9.5	10.6	12.4	16.1	11.1	26.6	23.5	29.6	27.5	18.7	19.2	•
Salaries and Wages 11	29.0	32.4	33.0	30.2	33.7	45.6	21.1	32.6	31.7	21.0	28.8	22.4	•
Taxes Paid 12	3.7	4.1	4.5	3.3	4.2	3.8	3.5	3.9	3.9	4.2	3.2	2.6	•
Interest Paid 13	1.6	0.9	0.5	0.8	1.6	1.0	0.7	1.4	1.5	2.7	3.0	2.9	•
Depreciation 14	1.9	0.5	0.8	0.9	1.4	5.5	1.9	1.0	2.1	2.4	2.1	2.9	•
Amortization and Depletion 15	0.6	0.3	0.1	0.4	0.1	0.1	0.2	0.8	0.9	1.5	0.7	1.4	•
Pensions and Other Deferred Comp. 16	0.5	0.0	0.7	0.2	0.6	1.5	0.3	0.3	0.5	0.2	0.4	0.3	•
Employee Benefits 17	2.5	2.6	1.5	1.4	2.0	3.7	1.3	2.8	2.4	1.7	3.0	4.0	•
Advertising 18	0.5	0.2	0.7	0.8	0.4	0.4	0.4	0.4	0.5	0.5	0.3	0.4	•
Other Expenses 19	31.2	45.9	29.4	29.9	24.3	25.5	35.2	28.4	20.7	33.5	37.5	33.5	•
Officers' Compensation 20	4.7	1.9	10.7	8.8	5.5	2.0	2.1	1.1	1.9	1.0	0.7	0.8	•
Operating Margin 21	7.3	1.6	7.3	10.9	10.1	•	6.6	3.8	4.3	3.7	1.7	9.6	•
Operating Margin Before Officers' Comp. 22	12.0	3.5	18.0	19.6	15.6	1.8	8.7	5.0	6.2	4.7	2.4	10.4	•

Selected Average Balance Sheet ($ in Thousands)

	•	•	•	•	•	•	•	•	•	•	•
Net Receivables 23	186	112	12	261	1602	3640	13108	15236	29120	65157	235374
Inventories 24	13	5	1	38	150	289	878	1181	4070	8136	10742
Net Property, Plant and Equipment 25	204	221	32	768	2344	3257	5032	8442	24033	49997	204351
Total Assets 26	1180	707	89	1956	7060	16145	35008	65906	154361	302318	1795317
Notes and Loans Payable 27	424	301	60	847	3510	5528	14406	17930	43525	130396	564256
All Other Liabilities 28	299	116	15	220	1426	4440	13153	20889	43211	66390	500447
Net Worth 29	457	290	15	889	2124	6177	7449	27087	67625	105531	730614

Selected Financial Ratios (Times to 1)

	•	•	•	•	•	•	•	•	•	•	•
Current Ratio 30	1.6	•	2.0	2.3	3.1	1.3	1.4	1.5	1.5	2.4	1.3
Quick Ratio 31	1.2	•	1.8	2.1	2.6	1.0	1.1	1.2	1.1	1.7	0.9
Net Sales to Working Capital 32	14.6	37.2	12.7	5.7	24.7	17.6	11.7	9.9	8.3	4.6	16.5
Coverage Ratio 33	6.9	7.4	18.6	17.0	9.1	7.7	13.1	4.9	6.2	2.6	4.8
Total Asset Turnover 34	1.7	•	8.3	3.2	1.9	2.5	2.3	1.4	1.0	1.1	0.9
Inventory Turnover 35	25.2	118.9	53.5	16.0	12.2	36.9	22.0	23.9	10.5	7.4	27.6
Receivables Turnover 36	12.0	62.7	31.2	•	8.8	11.3	6.5	6.7	•	4.6	•
Total Liabilities to Net Worth 37	1.6	5.1	1.4	1.2	2.3	1.6	3.7	1.4	1.3	1.9	1.5
Current Assets to Working Capital 38	2.8	2.0	1.8	1.5	4.8	3.8	3.1	3.2	3.0	1.7	4.4
Current Liabilities to Working Capital 39	1.8	1.0	0.8	0.5	3.8	2.8	2.1	2.2	2.0	0.7	3.4
Working Capital to Net Sales 40	0.1	0.0	0.1	0.2	0.0	0.1	0.1	0.1	0.1	0.2	0.1
Inventory to Working Capital 41	0.1	0.0	0.0	0.1	0.3	0.2	0.2	0.1	0.2	0.1	0.1
Total Receipts to Cash Flow 42	2.8	3.1	2.7	3.2	3.5	2.7	3.3	4.4	2.7	2.5	2.5
Cost of Goods to Cash Flow 43	0.5	0.3	0.3	0.5	0.4	0.7	0.8	1.3	0.7	0.5	0.5
Cash Flow to Total Debt 44	1.0	3.2	2.1	1.1	0.9	1.5	0.9	0.6	0.7	0.6	0.6

Selected Financial Factors (in Percentages)

	•	•	•	•	•	•	•	•	•	•	•
Debt Ratio 45	61.3	•	83.6	59.0	54.6	69.9	61.7	78.7	58.9	65.1	59.3
Return on Total Assets 46	19.0	79.7	43.1	28.9	17.5	21.7	16.4	13.8	9.9	8.2	11.9
Return on Equity Before Income Taxes 47	42.0	459.2	98.9	56.6	50.6	52.5	61.6	28.1	16.4	14.4	23.1
Return on Equity After Income Taxes 48	36.5	456.0	97.3	53.3	45.5	49.1	41.4	21.6	12.6	11.1	16.8
Profit Margin (Before Income Tax) 49	9.5	9.1	12.5	13.2	6.6	8.1	5.6	8.0	7.2	4.7	10.9
Profit Margin (After Income Tax) 50	8.3	5.4	12.3	12.5	5.9	7.6	3.8	6.1	5.5	3.6	7.9

Table I

Corporations with and without Net Income

HOSPITALS, NURSING, AND RESIDENTIAL CARE FACILITIES

MONEY AMOUNTS AND SIZE OF ASSETS IN THOUSANDS OF DOLLARS

Item Description for Accounting Period 7/07 Through 6/08	Total	Zero Assets	Under 500	500 to 1,000	1,000 to 5,000	5,000 to 10,000	10,000 to 25,000	25,000 to 50,000	50,000 to 100,000	100,000 to 250,000	250,000 to 500,000	500,000 to 2,500,000	2,500,000 and over
Number of Enterprises 1	16403	2413	10566	1167	1544	296	234	69	39	27	13	24	10
Revenues ($ in Thousands)													
Net Sales 2	118944648	4642719	6990372	3444966	6617884	3326682	6507023	3567879	4398003	5693103	4250141	24420399	45085477
Interest 3	1420985	8333	1574	455	5190	2405	10785	6188	5249	25553	24796	446104	884352
Rents 4	433154	15176	0	16	410	0	4911	65	8828	34626	68319	55834	244969
Royalties 5	11	0	0	0	0	0	0	0	0	0	0	11	0
Other Portfolio Income 6	668042	3103	98775	1205	210	25889	57461	25474	6648	32686	2247	115511	298834
Other Receipts 7	7030365	133102	23489	8551	554454	119599	89176	82575	83412	394529	53117	1132625	4355736
Total Receipts 8	128497205	4802433	7114210	3455193	7178148	3474575	6669356	3682181	4502140	6180497	4398620	26170484	50869368
Average Total Receipts 9	7834	1990	673	2961	4649	11738	28502	53365	115439	228907	338355	1090437	5086937
Operating Costs/Operating Income (%)													
Cost of Operations 10	5.0	0.3	6.9	•	12.5	4.1	16.7	4.0	8.2	6.3	8.8	4.2	2.4
Salaries and Wages 11	39.4	12.8	31.1	27.0	44.3	36.9	33.1	42.8	42.2	45.9	41.5	40.7	42.4
Taxes Paid 12	4.8	1.3	4.5	4.1	6.5	4.9	6.5	5.0	4.9	6.0	5.3	5.1	4.3
Interest Paid 13	5.4	2.4	1.2	1.2	1.9	1.9	2.3	2.4	2.1	2.3	3.1	4.9	9.2
Depreciation 14	2.8	2.1	1.2	0.6	1.4	1.6	1.5	1.8	1.5	2.1	3.1	2.3	4.2
Amortization and Depletion 15	0.7	0.2	0.1	0.0	0.2	0.1	0.2	0.2	0.5	0.2	0.5	1.3	0.9
Pensions and Other Deferred Comp. 16	0.6	0.1	0.1	0.3	0.2	0.2	0.3	0.2	0.3	0.3	0.2	0.2	1.1
Employee Benefits 17	4.1	0.2	1.1	1.7	3.1	3.4	4.4	2.9	3.6	4.8	3.1	3.9	5.6
Advertising 18	0.4	0.4	0.5	0.2	0.3	0.4	0.3	0.3	0.4	0.4	0.2	0.4	0.4
Other Expenses 19	41.5	78.9	43.8	65.2	31.5	42.4	34.7	40.3	36.3	40.0	34.4	41.8	39.1
Officers' Compensation 20	1.2	3.4	5.8	2.4	1.5	4.8	1.0	0.8	1.0	0.5	0.4	0.9	0.3
Operating Margin 21	•	•	3.7	•	•	•	•	•	•	•	•	•	•
Operating Margin Before Officers' Comp. 22	•	1.3	9.5	•	•	4.3	•	0.1	0.1	•	•	•	•

Selected Average Balance Sheet ($ in Thousands)

	1	2	3	4	5	6	7	8	9	10	11	12
Net Receivables 23	945	7	252	590	1905	2934	6558	17044	29924	49997	123206	743801
Inventories 24	12	0	2	3	8	84	118	648	1731	1430	2392	1658
Net Property, Plant and Equipment 25	2888	58	224	693	2670	5589	14098	27078	63490	162426	359500	2885855
Total Assets 26	8700	105	650	2008	6638	15516	35127	70787	157033	331640	1257592	8822734
Notes and Loans Payable 27	5256	171	572	1106	3309	9286	20738	43358	64329	185006	577139	5776420
All Other Liabilities 28	2032	37	292	554	2568	5319	11846	25230	54756	52521	295150	1868748
Net Worth 29	1412	-103	-215	347	762	911	2543	2199	37947	94113	385303	1177566

Selected Financial Ratios (Times to 1)

	1	2	3	4	5	6	7	8	9	10	11	12
Current Ratio 30	1.2	•	1.0	0.9	0.9	1.1	1.1	1.0	0.7	1.7	1.5	1.3
Quick Ratio 31	0.9	•	0.8	0.7	0.8	0.8	0.8	0.8	0.6	1.5	1.3	0.9
Net Sales to Working Capital 32	24.3	•	•	•	•	50.7	44.5	277.2	•	9.1	10.6	14.4
Coverage Ratio 33	1.4	1.5	•	3.5	3.1	1.6	2.1	1.7	0.9	1.9	1.3	1.3
Total Asset Turnover 34	0.8	•	4.5	2.1	1.7	1.8	1.5	1.6	1.3	1.0	0.8	0.5
Inventory Turnover 35	29.3	6.3	•	194.5	55.4	55.5	17.4	14.2	7.7	20.2	17.8	65.7
Receivables Turnover 36	8.1	3519.8	12.8	7.7	8.3	9.4	8.4	7.0	5.5	8.6	8.5	6.5
Total Liabilities to Net Worth 37	5.2	78.3	•	4.8	7.7	16.0	12.8	31.2	3.1	2.5	2.3	6.5
Current Assets to Working Capital 38	6.0	•	•	•	•	11.5	11.5	74.2	•	2.3	3.0	4.3
Current Liabilities to Working Capital 39	5.0	•	•	•	•	10.5	10.5	73.2	•	1.3	2.0	3.3
Working Capital to Net Sales 40	0.0	•	•	•	•	0.0	0.0	0.0	•	0.1	0.1	0.1
Inventory to Working Capital 41	0.0	•	•	•	•	0.2	0.1	1.8	•	0.1	0.0	0.0
Total Receipts to Cash Flow 42	2.7	•	1.9	3.4	2.4	3.3	2.7	3.1	2.9	3.5	2.7	2.7
Cost of Goods to Cash Flow 43	0.1	1.3	0.0	0.4	0.1	0.6	0.1	0.3	0.2	0.3	0.1	0.1
Cash Flow to Total Debt 44	0.4	0.0	•	0.8	0.8	0.6	0.6	0.5	0.6	0.4	0.4	0.2

Selected Financial Factors (in Percentages)

	1	2	3	4	5	6	7	8	9	10	11	12
Debt Ratio 45	83.8	198.5	133.0	82.7	88.5	94.1	92.8	96.9	75.8	71.6	69.4	86.7
Return on Total Assets 46	6.4	•	42.1	14.7	9.8	6.7	7.1	5.6	2.6	5.9	5.2	6.2
Return on Equity Before Income Taxes 47	12.1	•	•	32.1	61.0	57.8	44.4	50.9	74.8	9.8	5.9	11.0
Return on Equity After Income Taxes 48	7.8	•	•	32.2	58.9	53.8	38.3	42.4	68.4	7.4	2.9	4.5
Profit Margin (Before Income Tax) 49	2.4	1.3	5.4	•	4.9	3.9	1.5	2.5	1.5	2.8	1.4	2.9
Profit Margin (After Income Tax) 50	1.5	1.0	5.3	•	4.8	3.6	1.3	2.1	1.3	2.1	0.9	1.2

Table II

Corporations with Net Income

HOSPITALS, NURSING, AND RESIDENTIAL CARE FACILITIES

MONEY AMOUNTS AND SIZE OF ASSETS IN THOUSANDS OF DOLLARS

Item Description for Accounting Period 7/07 Through 6/08	Total	Zero Assets	Under 500	500 to 1,000	1,000 to 5,000	5,000 to 10,000	10,000 to 25,000	25,000 to 50,000	50,000 to 100,000	100,000 to 250,000	250,000 to 500,000	500,000 to 2,500,000	2,500,000 and over
Number of Enterprises **1**	9989	1257	6615	740	924	169	173	48	24	14	8	15	3
Revenues ($ in Thousands)													
Net Sales **2**	78751693	4097296	5253287	1534985	4698323	2332967	4679572	2072884	2954170	3533359	3208336	20553946	23832568
Interest **3**	569898	8160	1009	86	4413	2045	9080	4894	3887	10628	10916	374406	140373
Rents **4**	250340	15051	0	0	410	0	2844	55	505	1590	63827	52630	113428
Royalties **5**	11	0	0	0	0	0	0	0	0	0	0	11	0
Other Portfolio Income **6**	435295	3103	98758	16	210	22591	14491	426	3074	15886	2239	39664	234838
Other Receipts **7**	6336817	132761	23255	946	550387	128240	71859	75504	55613	100635	57742	951470	4188404
Total Receipts **8**	86344054	4256371	5376309	1536033	5253743	2485843	4777846	2153763	3017249	3362098	3343060	21972127	28509611
Average Total Receipts **9**	8644	3386	813	2076	5686	14709	27618	44870	125719	261578	417882	1464808	9503204
Operating Costs/Operating Income (%)													
Cost of Operations **10**	5.1	0.4	3.6	•	14.1	3.3	21.9	5.5	8.8	6.6	9.8	4.0	1.3
Salaries and Wages **11**	37.5	3.6	31.9	11.5	44.8	25.8	28.1	45.8	38.1	44.2	43.5	40.2	42.9
Taxes Paid **12**	4.7	1.4	4.5	2.5	6.6	4.5	6.7	6.3	4.6	5.9	5.6	4.8	4.2
Interest Paid **13**	4.8	2.7	1.1	1.4	1.4	1.8	2.0	2.0	1.4	1.4	2.0	4.6	9.6
Depreciation **14**	2.3	2.4	0.9	0.4	1.3	1.6	1.7	2.1	1.5	1.9	2.6	1.8	3.7
Amortization and Depletion **15**	0.6	0.2	0.0	0.0	0.2	0.0	0.2	0.2	0.2	0.2	0.3	1.2	0.8
Pensions and Other Deferred Comp. **16**	0.6	0.1	0.1	0.5	0.2	0.3	0.3	0.3	0.3	0.4	0.2	0.2	1.4
Employee Benefits **17**	4.0	0.2	1.3	0.5	3.2	3.4	4.2	3.3	3.9	5.0	3.0	3.8	5.9
Advertising **18**	0.3	0.4	0.6	0.1	0.3	0.4	0.3	0.3	0.5	0.3	0.2	0.4	0.3
Other Expenses **19**	42.2	86.7	41.9	78.3	30.2	51.2	31.3	29.9	37.4	34.7	31.6	42.0	40.2
Officers' Compensation **20**	1.3	3.9	6.1	4.3	1.1	5.2	0.9	1.1	0.9	0.4	0.4	0.9	0.1
Operating Margin **21**	•	•	8.2	0.6	•	2.4	2.4	3.1	2.3	•	0.8	•	•
Operating Margin Before Officers' Comp. **22**	•	1.8	14.3	4.9	•	7.7	3.3	4.2	3.1	•	1.2	•	•

Selected Average Balance Sheet ($ in Thousands)

Net Receivables 23	939	0	9	315	703	1775	2797	6646	17965	28298	56902	175053	1141190
Inventories 24	12	0	0	1	2	7	88	113	677	1739	1142	2193	10632
Net Property, Plant and Equipment 25	2083	0	48	205	712	3200	6070	15173	26840	65286	158829	273185	3478310
Total Assets 26	7447	0	99	632	2366	7359	15537	34419	73526	155769	313570	1175067	13803087
Notes and Loans Payable 27	4507	0	112	280	813	3685	8641	17592	35284	51413	161119	508796	9958975
All Other Liabilities 28	1419	0	25	284	636	2589	5167	10017	28768	49242	51604	288768	1755121
Net Worth 29	1521	0	-37	68	917	1085	1729	6711	9473	55114	100848	377503	2088991

Selected Financial Ratios (Times to 1)

Current Ratio 30	1.4	•	1.2	1.3	1.9	1.0	1.1	1.2	1.2	1.3	1.8	1.6	1.2
Quick Ratio 31	1.1	•	1.2	1.3	1.6	0.9	0.8	1.0	1.0	1.0	1.6	1.4	0.8
Net Sales to Working Capital 32	18.8	•	101.9	27.0	8.5	•	58.8	20.1	25.8	19.1	9.2	10.1	35.9
Coverage Ratio 33	2.2	1.7	10.8	1.5	7.0	6.1	3.2	4.4	4.1	2.8	3.5	1.6	2.0
Total Asset Turnover 34	1.1	•	8.0	3.3	2.1	1.9	1.7	1.3	1.7	1.6	1.3	1.2	0.6
Inventory Turnover 35	32.5	•	2270.9	•	339.3	63.7	67.6	20.9	16.1	9.6	34.5	25.1	9.8
Receivables Turnover 36	7.8	•	64.4	8.6	•	9.3	10.4	6.3	7.3	5.6	8.9	8.4	•
Total Liabilities to Net Worth 37	3.9	•	•	8.3	•	5.8	8.0	4.1	6.8	1.8	2.1	2.1	5.6
Current Assets to Working Capital 38	3.9	•	5.1	4.4	2.1	•	13.0	5.7	6.6	4.0	2.2	2.6	7.2
Current Liabilities to Working Capital 39	2.9	•	4.1	3.4	1.1	•	12.0	4.7	5.6	3.0	1.2	1.6	6.2
Working Capital to Net Sales 40	0.1	•	0.0	0.0	0.1	•	0.0	0.0	0.0	0.1	0.1	0.1	0.0
Inventory to Working Capital 41	0.0	•	0.0	0.0	0.0	•	0.3	0.1	0.2	0.0	0.0	0.0	0.0
Total Receipts to Cash Flow 42	2.4	1.2	2.6	1.3	3.2	1.8	3.2	3.2	2.8	3.1	3.6	2.5	2.2
Cost of Goods to Cash Flow 43	0.1	0.0	0.1	•	0.5	0.1	0.7	0.2	0.2	0.2	0.4	0.1	0.0
Cash Flow to Total Debt 44	0.6	•	2.3	2.9	1.1	1.2	0.6	0.5	0.7	0.8	0.5	0.7	0.3

Selected Financial Factors (in Percentages)

Debt Ratio 45	79.6	•	137.5	89.3	61.2	85.3	88.9	80.5	87.1	64.6	67.8	67.9	84.9
Return on Total Assets 46	11.5	•	92.6	6.8	21.1	20.2	11.4	11.3	9.7	6.5	9.0	8.7	10.8
Return on Equity Before Income Taxes 47	31.3	•	•	20.6	46.8	114.2	70.4	44.9	57.0	11.8	19.9	10.4	34.8
Return on Equity After Income Taxes 48	24.6	•	•	19.9	45.4	109.3	66.0	40.3	54.6	10.6	16.3	8.0	22.6
Profit Margin (Before Income Tax) 49	6.0	1.9	10.5	0.7	8.4	9.0	4.5	7.0	4.4	2.6	5.0	2.9	9.1
Profit Margin (After Income Tax) 50	4.7	1.5	10.3	0.6	8.2	8.6	4.2	6.3	4.2	2.3	4.1	2.2	6.0

Table I

Corporations with and without Net Income

OTHER ARTS, ENTERTAINMENT, AND RECREATION

MONEY AMOUNTS AND SIZE OF ASSETS IN THOUSANDS OF DOLLARS

Item Description for Accounting Period 7/07 Through 6/08	Total	Zero Assets	Under 500	500 to 1,000	1,000 to 5,000	5,000 to 10,000	10,000 to 25,000	25,000 to 50,000	50,000 to 100,000	100,000 to 250,000	250,000 to 500,000	500,000 to 2,500,000	2,500,000 and over
Number of Enterprises 1	68653	13487	52282	1377	1060	224	94	53	23	26	15	11	0
Revenues ($ in Thousands)													
Net Sales 2	40856485	714692	14217207	1969902	4230779	1712186	1484159	1130782	1600838	3465611	2873848	7456482	0
Interest 3	337659	453	13407	2278	8663	2708	5653	13189	6738	30907	39759	213905	0
Rents 4	110184	0	1275	876	3020	402	502	675	881	27316	24566	50672	0
Royalties 5	258851	0	0	89267	0	0	17271	0	84	71016	61641	19572	0
Other Portfolio Income 6	304103	49734	38747	8517	11204	30984	22950	22997	209	14046	39289	65429	0
Other Receipts 7	2899192	87650	283429	12772	94300	307760	159551	120786	120433	757914	781722	172869	0
Total Receipts 8	44766474	852529	14554065	2083612	4347966	2054040	1690086	1288429	1729183	4366810	3820825	7978929	0
Average Total Receipts 9	652	63	278	1513	4102	9170	17980	24310	75182	167954	254722	725357	•
Operating Costs/Operating Income (%)													
Cost of Operations 10	20.3	9.1	9.7	17.5	19.3	20.2	24.7	25.0	25.2	20.8	27.9	37.1	•
Salaries and Wages 11	18.1	5.8	13.5	15.0	11.7	14.3	27.9	16.8	33.0	44.0	30.1	11.8	•
Taxes Paid 12	3.6	2.5	2.3	2.5	2.6	2.1	3.6	3.2	2.8	3.7	11.8	4.4	•
Interest Paid 13	2.1	0.3	0.7	0.9	0.1	2.9	0.7	0.8	2.8	3.0	4.5	5.3	•
Depreciation 14	2.5	0.4	1.8	1.3	1.5	2.5	1.8	1.8	1.5	3.1	3.5	4.5	•
Amortization and Depletion 15	1.0	0.0	0.0	0.2	0.1	0.1	0.1	0.3	2.1	2.5	4.6	1.8	•
Pensions and Other Deferred Comp. 16	1.5	0.4	1.8	0.7	2.3	0.1	0.4	0.9	1.0	2.7	2.0	0.6	•
Employee Benefits 17	1.2	0.8	0.7	1.1	0.4	0.3	1.6	2.3	1.0	3.0	2.5	1.3	•
Advertising 18	2.0	1.1	0.8	6.6	2.0	0.9	1.7	1.7	2.5	1.6	1.5	3.8	•
Other Expenses 19	37.7	63.4	43.7	36.7	35.8	47.2	31.1	36.9	26.7	35.8	30.3	30.4	•
Officers' Compensation 20	11.9	13.0	22.1	14.3	15.5	10.6	6.1	6.7	5.8	1.6	2.5	1.6	•
Operating Margin 21	•	3.4	2.8	3.2	8.6	•	0.3	3.5	•	•	•	•	•
Operating Margin Before Officers' Comp. 22	10.0	16.3	24.9	17.5	24.1	9.3	6.3	10.2	1.5	•	•	•	•

Selected Average Balance Sheet ($ in Thousands)

Net Receivables 23	36	0	2	46	108	564	1716	4236	5490	22412	15432	68067
Inventories 24	8	0	3	7	175	140	147	129	1027	2442	973	3072
Net Property, Plant and Equipment 25	140	0	12	176	218	1413	3654	5956	15714	39988	93306	431079
Total Assets 26	540	0	54	651	2019	7049	13969	34710	68497	174983	349117	1373142
Notes and Loans Payable 27	237	0	55	261	597	3538	4657	11704	49430	74341	142536	486474
All Other Liabilities 28	174	0	17	115	630	2338	3394	11546	27770	83289	87943	425452
Net Worth 29	129	0	-18	276	793	1172	5918	11460	-8702	17353	118638	461215

Selected Financial Ratios (Times to 1)

Current Ratio 30	1.4	•	1.7	1.4	1.9	2.0	2.3	1.6	0.9	1.2	1.2	1.2
Quick Ratio 31	0.9	•	1.1	1.1	1.1	1.8	1.5	1.2	0.7	0.8	0.7	0.5
Net Sales to Working Capital 32	10.6	•	18.4	16.5	5.5	3.2	4.1	3.7	•	11.1	11.3	15.0
Coverage Ratio 33	4.6	74.4	8.2	10.5	97.5	7.2	20.2	22.2	2.4	2.4	3.5	1.9
Total Asset Turnover 34	1.1	•	5.0	2.2	2.0	1.1	1.1	0.6	1.0	0.8	0.5	0.5
Inventory Turnover 35	15.6	•	9.2	34.7	4.4	11.1	26.5	41.3	17.1	11.3	55.0	81.8
Receivables Turnover 36	17.2	•	140.7	45.9	30.0	12.3	8.0	6.3	9.5	6.1	13.8	11.7
Total Liabilities to Net Worth 37	3.2	•	•	1.4	1.5	5.0	1.4	2.0	2.0	9.1	1.9	2.0
Current Assets to Working Capital 38	3.5	•	2.4	3.3	2.1	2.0	1.8	2.8	•	5.9	5.7	6.6
Current Liabilities to Working Capital 39	2.5	•	1.4	2.3	1.1	1.0	0.8	1.8	•	4.9	4.7	5.6
Working Capital to Net Sales 40	0.1	•	0.1	0.1	0.2	0.3	0.2	0.3	•	0.1	0.1	0.1
Inventory to Working Capital 41	0.1	•	0.2	0.1	0.2	0.1	0.0	0.0	•	0.2	0.1	0.1
Total Receipts to Cash Flow 42	2.5	1.4	2.3	2.5	2.3	1.6	2.5	2.0	3.7	2.9	2.7	3.4
Cost of Goods to Cash Flow 43	0.5	0.1	0.2	0.4	0.5	0.3	0.6	0.5	0.9	0.6	0.7	1.2
Cash Flow to Total Debt 44	0.6	•	1.7	1.5	1.4	0.8	0.8	0.5	0.2	0.3	0.3	0.2

Selected Financial Factors (in Percentages)

Debt Ratio 45	76.2	•	132.6	57.7	60.7	83.4	57.6	67.0	112.7	90.1	66.0	66.4
Return on Total Assets 46	10.8	•	29.4	21.8	22.7	22.8	16.7	11.1	6.6	5.5	8.6	5.0
Return on Equity Before Income Taxes 47	35.6	•	•	46.6	57.2	118.0	37.4	32.1	•	32.1	18.1	7.0
Return on Equity After Income Taxes 48	31.4	•	•	45.4	55.9	116.5	33.9	29.5	•	23.9	13.9	3.9
Profit Margin (Before Income Tax) 49	7.7	22.5	5.1	9.0	11.4	18.1	14.0	17.3	3.8	4.2	11.2	4.8
Profit Margin (After Income Tax) 50	6.8	18.5	5.1	8.8	11.1	17.9	12.7	15.8	2.7	3.1	8.6	2.7

Table II

Corporations with Net Income

OTHER ARTS, ENTERTAINMENT, AND RECREATION

MONEY AMOUNTS AND SIZE OF ASSETS IN THOUSANDS OF DOLLARS

Item Description for Accounting Period 7/07 Through 6/08	Total	Zero Assets	Under 500	500 to 1,000	1,000 to 5,000	5,000 to 10,000	10,000 to 25,000	25,000 to 50,000	50,000 to 100,000	100,000 to 250,000	250,000 to 500,000	500,000 to 2,500,000	2,500,000 and over
Number of Enterprises 1	32438	4933	25621	995	601	162	50	29	12	16	•	•	0
Revenues ($ in Thousands)													
Net Sales 2	28794247	538528	9769143	1703436	3596725	1222584	1200511	782093	1075549	2502237	•	•	0
Interest 3	194243	187	10355	1248	4844	2291	4675	5463	3915	27009	•	•	0
Rents 4	88396	0	244	815	3005	402	502	0	881	26183	•	•	0
Royalties 5	257885	0	0	89267	0	0	17270	0	84	71016	•	•	0
Other Portfolio Income 6	243948	48907	36147	7678	6634	30984	19058	21520	22	13946	•	•	0
Other Receipts 7	2613620	129300	146062	12093	68905	305305	174959	111410	33887	721774	•	•	0
Total Receipts 8	32192339	716922	9961951	1814537	3680113	1561566	1416975	920486	1114338	3362165	•	•	0
Average Total Receipts 9	992	145	389	1824	6123	9639	28340	31741	92862	210135	•	•	•
Operating Costs/Operating Income (%)													
Cost of Operations 10	15.4	10.7	7.2	16.9	16.7	27.4	20.5	17.7	24.5	27.2	•	•	•
Salaries and Wages 11	17.3	4.2	11.4	13.1	10.4	13.8	28.6	17.6	28.5	40.0	•	•	•
Taxes Paid 12	3.5	2.1	2.2	2.3	2.8	1.8	3.8	3.4	2.5	3.3	•	•	•
Interest Paid 13	1.6	0.3	0.4	1.0	0.1	0.3	0.5	0.3	2.1	3.2	•	•	•
Depreciation 14	1.9	0.4	0.8	0.9	0.8	1.3	1.4	1.3	1.3	3.5	•	•	•
Amortization and Depletion 15	1.2	0.0	0.0	0.2	0.1	0.1	0.0	0.2	0.5	2.7	•	•	•
Pensions and Other Deferred Comp. 16	1.4	0.5	1.9	0.8	1.3	0.1	0.5	0.5	0.8	2.3	•	•	•
Employee Benefits 17	1.1	0.6	0.7	0.9	0.4	0.2	1.7	2.4	0.7	2.8	•	•	•
Advertising 18	1.5	1.0	0.7	7.5	0.8	0.5	1.4	1.1	3.1	1.5	•	•	•
Other Expenses 19	35.7	44.7	38.6	34.3	31.8	31.3	27.3	33.4	14.7	34.2	•	•	•
Officers' Compensation 20	13.3	14.3	23.5	15.7	16.7	14.2	6.8	6.7	7.5	1.4	•	•	•
Operating Margin 21	6.0	21.3	12.6	6.4	18.2	9.0	7.6	15.4	13.8	•	•	•	•
Operating Margin Before Officers' Comp. 22	19.3	35.6	36.1	22.2	34.9	23.2	14.4	22.1	21.4	•	•	•	•

Selected Average Balance Sheet ($ in Thousands)

Net Receivables 23	46	0	3	28	155	451	1814	2153	4078	16236
Inventories 24	12	0	1	7	294	189	184	113	811	3884
Net Property, Plant and Equipment 25	184	0	12	215	188	513	3045	3786	22565	49995
Total Assets 26	697	0	61	682	2220	7547	14004	34675	71245	186669
Notes and Loans Payable 27	230	0	24	304	781	642	1671	3890	64648	84243
All Other Liabilities 28	204	0	17	148	716	1302	4218	9392	5616	73708
Net Worth 29	263	0	20	231	724	5603	8115	21394	981	28717

Selected Financial Ratios (Times to 1)

Current Ratio 30	1.4	•	2.2	1.2	1.7	4.4	2.0	1.8	2.1	1.1
Quick Ratio 31	1.0	•	1.5	0.9	1.0	3.9	1.4	1.4	1.6	0.7
Net Sales to Working Capital 32	12.6	•	17.8	32.6	8.9	1.6	6.4	3.3	7.6	19.6
Coverage Ratio 33	12.4	216.0	36.2	14.5	278.3	136.3	54.4	131.0	9.2	4.7
Total Asset Turnover 34	1.3	•	6.3	2.5	2.7	1.0	1.7	0.8	1.3	0.8
Inventory Turnover 35	11.8	•	18.2	42.8	3.4	10.9	26.7	42.1	27.0	11.0
Receivables Turnover 36	19.8	•	142.5	82.6	37.5	20.4	11.1	15.1	10.2	8.5
Total Liabilities to Net Worth 37	1.6	•	2.1	2.0	2.1	0.3	0.7	0.6	71.6	5.5
Current Assets to Working Capital 38	3.7	•	1.9	5.8	2.5	1.3	2.0	2.2	1.9	9.1
Current Liabilities to Working Capital 39	2.7	•	0.9	4.8	1.5	0.3	1.0	1.2	0.9	8.1
Working Capital to Net Sales 40	0.1	•	0.1	0.0	0.1	0.6	0.2	0.3	0.1	0.1
Inventory to Working Capital 41	0.2	•	0.1	0.0	0.5	0.0	0.1	0.0	0.0	0.5
Total Receipts to Cash Flow 42	2.0	1.2	2.1	2.4	2.1	1.6	2.1	1.6	3.4	2.5
Cost of Goods to Cash Flow 43	0.3	0.1	0.1	0.4	0.3	0.4	0.4	0.3	0.8	0.7
Cash Flow to Total Debt 44	1.0	•	4.6	1.6	1.9	2.4	2.0	1.3	0.4	0.4

Selected Financial Factors (in Percentages)

Debt Ratio 45	62.2	•	67.3	66.1	67.4	25.8	42.1	38.3	98.6	84.6
Return on Total Assets 46	24.6	•	94.5	34.9	55.4	36.2	44.5	25.7	24.6	12.8
Return on Equity Before Income Taxes 47	59.9	•	280.9	96.0	169.2	48.4	75.5	41.4	1590.6	65.9
Return on Equity After Income Taxes 48	55.6	•	280.0	94.1	166.8	48.0	70.7	38.8	1452.5	57.8
Profit Margin (Before Income Tax) 49	17.8	54.4	14.6	13.0	20.5	35.9	25.5	32.8	17.4	12.1
Profit Margin (After Income Tax) 50	16.5	49.1	14.5	12.7	20.2	35.6	23.9	30.8	15.9	10.6

Table I

Corporations with and without Net Income

AMUSEMENT, GAMBLING, AND RECREATION INDUSTRIES

MONEY AMOUNTS AND SIZE OF ASSETS IN THOUSANDS OF DOLLARS

Item Description for Accounting Period 7/07 Through 6/08		Total	Zero Assets	Under 500	500 to 1,000	1,000 to 5,000	5,000 to 10,000	10,000 to 25,000	25,000 to 50,000	50,000 to 100,000	100,000 to 250,000	250,000 to 500,000	500,000 to 2,500,000	2,500,000 and over
Number of Enterprises	1	54732	8369	36670	4348	4077	600	401	164	44	30	12	14	3
Revenues ($ in Thousands)														
Net Sales	2	50476178	479338	10326928	3412747	7226939	3399967	3503412	2796420	1761162	2457779	3403930	7452730	4254827
Interest	3	563150	60	5310	6500	18323	7894	10922	10335	4562	28687	28608	58822	383125
Rents	4	181045	166	4835	11298	7493	19563	5976	8659	9856	6848	12969	68677	24703
Royalties	5	89443	0	0	0	4174	0	0	0	0	18545	4723	2591	59411
Other Portfolio Income	6	919383	85618	162530	9759	94772	30534	89202	21081	33258	239023	20703	17846	115057
Other Receipts	7	4158357	26372	210235	861014	615566	189576	288497	247356	170006	164670	236414	961773	186879
Total Receipts	8	56387556	591554	10709838	4301318	7967267	3647534	3898009	3083851	1978844	2915552	3707347	8562439	5024002
Average Total Receipts	9	1030	71	292	989	1954	6079	9721	18804	44974	97185	308946	611603	1674667
Operating Costs/Operating Income (%)														
Cost of Operations	10	24.2	22.6	25.7	15.8	30.3	13.2	28.8	25.5	24.7	21.2	34.7	17.3	26.8
Salaries and Wages	11	22.2	18.7	16.2	24.1	19.5	32.5	23.6	26.1	25.9	20.7	22.7	30.7	12.1
Taxes Paid	12	7.9	4.8	4.3	6.1	6.3	8.8	6.3	6.8	7.8	7.1	4.7	11.9	18.0
Interest Paid	13	5.9	3.2	1.1	3.1	4.0	4.1	4.5	3.1	3.9	5.6	7.2	10.2	20.6
Depreciation	14	6.7	9.4	3.5	6.1	6.3	7.1	7.9	7.6	5.9	8.3	6.7	9.5	7.6
Amortization and Depletion	15	0.8	0.1	0.4	0.5	0.4	0.5	0.6	0.9	1.1	1.0	1.1	1.4	2.0
Pensions and Other Deferred Comp.	16	0.2	0.5	0.1	0.2	0.2	0.5	0.3	0.3	0.2	0.2	0.5	0.2	0.2
Employee Benefits	17	1.7	2.0	0.8	0.9	1.5	1.5	2.1	1.8	1.6	2.2	1.2	2.3	3.9
Advertising	18	2.7	5.1	2.2	2.0	1.6	3.0	3.5	2.8	2.4	3.0	2.0	3.3	4.2
Other Expenses	19	35.0	64.1	40.6	52.9	35.6	34.6	29.6	29.5	34.9	34.2	30.0	32.8	19.1
Officers' Compensation	20	3.1	12.2	7.5	2.0	2.8	4.6	1.6	1.2	1.1	1.8	0.7	0.8	1.8
Operating Margin	21	•	•	•	•	•	•	•	•	•	•	•	•	•
Operating Margin Before Officers' Comp.	22	•	5.1	•	•	•	•	•	•	•	•	•	•	•

Selected Average Balance Sheet ($ in Thousands)

Net Receivables 23	100	0	5	32	116	620	887	2602	4156	5327	18120	53950	739768
Inventories 24	31	0	4	8	73	141	388	761	1597	2027	2924	45505	20585
Net Property, Plant and Equipment 25	678	0	50	473	1111	4353	9206	20781	35818	84162	170222	668614	1147843
Total Assets 26	1390	0	107	717	2044	7106	14622	36000	69717	162576	344574	1354963	4551172
Notes and Loans Payable 27	854	0	66	400	1538	4465	7174	9858	26511	58697	265762	903970	3448077
All Other Liabilities 28	235	0	25	68	291	1139	2488	6122	19933	34584	113886	230616	426280
Net Worth 29	301	0	15	250	215	1502	4959	20020	23273	69294	-35074	220377	676816

Selected Financial Ratios (Times to 1)

Current Ratio 30	1.2	•	1.5	1.6	1.4	1.0	1.4	1.5	1.3	1.1	0.6	1.2	1.2
Quick Ratio 31	0.9	•	1.1	1.4	0.8	0.7	1.0	1.1	0.9	0.7	0.4	0.7	1.2
Net Sales to Working Capital 32	16.5	•	22.6	14.1	11.8	87.0	8.3	6.7	10.3	20.6	•	14.3	8.9
Coverage Ratio 33	1.3	•	2.2	4.9	1.4	0.3	1.6	2.5	1.7	3.4	0.6	0.4	1.3
Total Asset Turnover 34	0.7	•	2.6	1.1	0.9	0.8	0.6	0.5	0.6	0.5	0.8	0.4	0.3
Inventory Turnover 35	7.2	•	18.2	15.4	7.4	5.3	6.5	5.7	6.2	8.6	33.6	2.0	18.4
Receivables Turnover 36	10.2	•	67.9	29.3	16.3	9.5	10.4	6.8	13.1	13.9	22.2	9.2	2.3
Total Liabilities to Net Worth 37	3.6	•	5.9	1.9	8.5	3.7	1.9	0.8	2.0	1.3	•	5.1	5.7
Current Assets to Working Capital 38	5.4	•	3.0	2.6	3.7	31.0	3.3	3.2	4.3	8.6	•	6.1	5.5
Current Liabilities to Working Capital 39	4.4	•	2.0	1.6	2.7	30.0	2.3	2.2	3.3	7.6	•	5.1	4.5
Working Capital to Net Sales 40	0.1	•	0.0	0.1	0.1	0.0	0.1	0.1	0.1	0.0	•	0.1	0.1
Inventory to Working Capital 41	0.6	•	0.3	0.1	0.4	1.0	0.4	0.3	0.4	0.4	•	1.4	0.1
Total Receipts to Cash Flow 42	4.3	9.1	4.2	2.1	4.2	4.5	4.1	4.0	3.9	3.2	6.5	6.0	6.1
Cost of Goods to Cash Flow 43	1.0	2.1	1.1	0.3	1.3	0.6	1.2	1.0	1.0	0.7	2.3	1.0	1.6
Cash Flow to Total Debt 44	0.2	•	0.7	0.8	0.2	0.2	0.2	0.3	0.2	0.3	0.1	0.1	0.1

Selected Financial Factors (in Percentages)

Debt Ratio 45	78.3	•	85.5	65.2	89.5	78.9	66.1	44.4	66.6	57.4	110.2	83.7	85.1
Return on Total Assets 46	5.0	•	6.6	16.9	4.9	0.9	4.2	3.6	3.8	9.5	3.8	1.8	8.3
Return on Equity Before Income Taxes 47	5.0	•	24.6	38.6	13.6	•	4.4	3.9	4.9	15.8	20.8	•	12.4
Return on Equity After Income Taxes 48	3.1	•	22.4	38.4	10.4	•	3.6	3.1	4.4	13.2	25.9	•	7.9
Profit Margin (Before Income Tax) 49	1.6	•	1.3	12.3	1.7	•	2.5	4.6	2.8	13.4	•	•	5.9
Profit Margin (After Income Tax) 50	1.0	•	1.2	12.2	1.3	•	2.1	3.6	2.6	11.2	•	•	3.7

377

Table II

Corporations with Net Income

AMUSEMENT, GAMBLING, AND RECREATION INDUSTRIES

MONEY AMOUNTS AND SIZE OF ASSETS IN THOUSANDS OF DOLLARS

Item Description for Accounting Period 7/07 Through 6/08		Total	Zero Assets	Under 500	500 to 1,000	1,000 to 5,000	5,000 to 10,000	10,000 to 25,000	25,000 to 50,000	50,000 to 100,000	100,000 to 250,000	250,000 to 500,000	500,000 to 2,500,000	2,500,000 and over
Number of Enterprises	1	27011	3131	18699	2678	1979	252	154	69	21	15	•	•	0
Revenues ($ in Thousands)														
Net Sales	2	30525355	355157	6928603	2764830	4881065	1889896	1839401	1469435	1090171	1250600	•	•	0
Interest	3	304011	45	2698	3898	14585	5783	4719	5579	2768	12391	•	•	0
Rents	4	86356	137	1277	2506	5833	14622	1476	8262	9661	5705	•	•	0
Royalties	5	77574	0	0	0	4174	0	0	0	0	13297	•	•	0
Other Portfolio Income	6	750216	82417	159673	2749	81755	27158	85309	16913	25373	233865	•	•	0
Other Receipts	7	1546423	27715	18686	178104	457443	78029	137005	114327	103306	140793	•	•	0
Total Receipts	8	33289935	465471	7110937	2952087	5444855	2015488	2067910	1614516	1231279	1656651	•	•	0
Average Total Receipts	9	1232	149	380	1102	2751	7998	13428	23399	58632	110443	•	•	•
Operating Costs/Operating Income (%)														
Cost of Operations	10	22.0	6.4	24.4	13.4	32.6	14.3	24.7	16.2	27.2	15.9	•	•	•
Salaries and Wages	11	19.7	18.0	14.8	22.7	17.1	35.1	20.4	24.9	25.1	23.1	•	•	•
Taxes Paid	12	7.9	3.4	3.7	5.6	6.1	6.3	5.8	6.7	7.1	6.0	•	•	•
Interest Paid	13	4.1	1.6	0.6	2.6	2.3	2.3	3.8	1.6	3.3	3.7	•	•	•
Depreciation	14	5.2	5.2	2.7	5.4	3.7	4.3	7.0	6.4	5.2	7.1	•	•	•
Amortization and Depletion	15	0.7	0.2	0.2	0.3	0.1	0.3	0.5	0.2	0.6	0.5	•	•	•
Pensions and Other Deferred Comp.	16	0.2	0.5	0.1	0.2	0.3	0.6	0.4	0.5	0.4	0.3	•	•	•
Employee Benefits	17	1.6	1.0	0.6	0.8	1.0	1.9	1.9	2.0	1.5	3.1	•	•	•
Advertising	18	2.3	4.0	2.1	2.0	1.4	2.5	3.3	3.2	2.2	2.9	•	•	•
Other Expenses	19	30.3	56.3	37.2	32.1	32.1	24.2	26.4	28.7	27.1	31.6	•	•	•
Officers' Compensation	20	3.6	9.0	7.4	2.0	2.7	6.7	1.7	1.7	1.4	2.6	•	•	•
Operating Margin	21	2.5	•	6.3	12.9	0.5	1.4	4.0	7.9	•	3.2	•	•	•
Operating Margin Before Officers' Comp.	22	6.1	3.3	13.6	14.9	3.2	8.1	5.6	9.6	0.4	5.8	•	•	•

Selected Average Balance Sheet ($ in Thousands)

Net Receivables 23	129	0	7	24	185	96	635	2392	3827	6853
Inventories 24	25	0	4	8	101	238	359	1270	587	2305
Net Property, Plant and Equipment 25	638	0	43	553	1095	3605	9429	17073	39806	77314
Total Assets 26	1452	0	104	745	2101	7148	14679	36441	70974	160321
Notes and Loans Payable 27	756	0	38	314	938	2932	8368	7507	22729	37963
All Other Liabilities 28	223	0	20	29	307	1358	2159	6090	15835	27329
Net Worth 29	473	0	46	402	856	2858	4152	22844	32411	95029

Selected Financial Ratios (Times to 1)

Current Ratio 30	1.5	•	2.7	2.3	1.9	1.4	1.4	1.5	1.8	1.6
Quick Ratio 31	1.1	•	2.1	2.0	1.5	0.6	1.0	1.0	1.5	0.9
Net Sales to Working Capital 32	10.6	•	12.7	11.4	8.1	10.3	14.2	6.1	6.2	4.7
Coverage Ratio 33	4.0	16.7	15.0	8.6	6.2	4.6	5.3	12.1	4.6	10.7
Total Asset Turnover 34	0.8	•	3.6	1.4	1.2	1.0	0.8	0.6	0.7	0.5
Inventory Turnover 35	9.8	•	23.7	16.6	7.9	4.5	8.2	2.7	24.0	5.8
Receivables Turnover 36	11.3	•	57.5	43.8	15.3	47.6	15.7	8.9	15.2	11.1
Total Liabilities to Net Worth 37	2.1	•	1.3	0.9	1.5		2.5	0.6	1.2	0.7
Current Assets to Working Capital 38	3.2	•	1.6	1.8	2.1	3.7	3.7	2.9	2.2	2.7
Current Liabilities to Working Capital 39	2.2	•	0.6	0.8	1.1	2.7	2.7	1.9	1.2	1.7
Working Capital to Net Sales 40	0.1	•	0.1	0.1	0.1	0.1	0.1	0.2	0.2	0.2
Inventory to Working Capital 41	0.2	•	0.1	0.1	0.4	0.1	0.5	0.3	0.1	0.1
Total Receipts to Cash Flow 42	3.3	2.1	3.2	2.3	3.3	4.0	2.9	2.7	3.4	1.9
Cost of Goods to Cash Flow 43	0.7	0.1	0.8	0.3	1.1	0.6	0.7	0.4	0.9	0.3
Cash Flow to Total Debt 44	0.4	•	2.0	1.3	0.6	0.4	0.4	0.6	0.4	0.7

Selected Financial Factors (in Percentages)

Debt Ratio 45	67.5	•	56.2	46.1	59.3	60.0	71.7	37.3	54.3	40.7
Return on Total Assets 46	12.6	•	34.0	30.8	16.8	10.9	16.4	11.4	11.1	20.5
Return on Equity Before Income Taxes 47	29.0	•	72.4	50.5	34.6	21.2	47.0	16.7	19.1	31.3
Return on Equity After Income Taxes 48	26.6	•	71.0	50.3	33.0	19.7	44.4	14.9	18.4	27.6
Profit Margin (Before Income Tax) 49	12.1	25.4	8.9	19.6	12.0	8.1	16.3	17.9	11.9	35.7
Profit Margin (After Income Tax) 50	11.1	22.0	8.7	19.6	11.4	7.5	15.4	15.9	11.5	31.5

Table I

Corporations with and without Net Income

ACCOMMODATION

MONEY AMOUNTS AND SIZE OF ASSETS IN THOUSANDS OF DOLLARS

Item Description for Accounting Period 7/07 Through 6/08	Total	Zero Assets	Under 500	500 to 1,000	1,000 to 5,000	5,000 to 10,000	10,000 to 25,000	25,000 to 50,000	50,000 to 100,000	100,000 to 250,000	250,000 to 500,000	500,000 to 2,500,000	2,500,000 and over
Number of Enterprises 1	33871	4776	15625	4359	7380	1025	393	132	72	43	26	26	15
Revenues ($ in Thousands)													
Net Sales 2	95912333	5482395	4249523	2810886	7820233	3589585	3802521	3431906	5961097	6974337	4637419	8351173	38801258
Interest 3	2646744	162558	1641	5573	20928	5699	10929	17371	39523	69419	71234	274864	1967004
Rents 4	615879	73196	27	0	4081	5182	14438	5168	14634	39275	18051	58461	383365
Royalties 5	1871032	3323	0	0	0	0	2053	0	276	1960	223394	16656	1623369
Other Portfolio Income 6	3610197	405332	64421	450	102802	196759	45413	123520	118439	245089	106474	508324	1693174
Other Receipts 7	11583559	1805397	49836	33021	140984	44227	184625	79814	140751	381928	204491	606541	7911946
Total Receipts 8	116239744	7932201	4365448	2849930	8089028	3841452	4059979	3657779	6274720	7712008	5261063	9816019	52380116
Average Total Receipts 9	3432	1661	279	654	1096	3748	10331	27710	87149	179349	202349	377539	3492008
Operating Costs/Operating Income (%)													
Cost of Operations 10	16.7	34.7	7.4	8.6	19.5	13.7	32.5	23.1	13.8	28.8	21.8	13.3	11.8
Salaries and Wages 11	27.0	37.6	17.2	21.2	16.3	17.3	21.2	13.0	15.4	15.1	12.6	22.6	38.4
Taxes Paid 12	7.4	6.4	8.9	7.9	6.7	6.8	4.8	4.3	3.0	3.5	4.2	9.4	9.5
Interest Paid 13	9.3	11.3	2.8	5.7	10.2	9.1	4.6	3.6	2.3	2.7	5.0	10.5	13.4
Depreciation 14	5.4	4.9	3.1	3.5	7.1	6.5	5.9	4.0	2.8	3.5	5.5	7.5	5.9
Amortization and Depletion 15	0.8	0.9	0.7	0.6	0.5	0.5	0.4	0.3	0.2	0.3	0.2	1.7	1.1
Pensions and Other Deferred Comp. 16	0.5	1.8	0.0	•	0.1	0.2	0.2	0.1	0.2	0.2	0.5	0.6	0.8
Employee Benefits 17	2.6	0.7	0.2	0.8	0.9	2.0	2.0	1.3	2.1	1.4	0.8	2.8	4.2
Advertising 18	3.3	0.9	1.7	2.0	1.5	1.4	1.5	1.7	4.7	2.9	3.8	3.4	4.6
Other Expenses 19	41.0	55.1	61.3	48.0	32.4	40.7	31.1	51.4	57.9	45.6	51.5	39.6	33.8
Officers' Compensation 20	2.3	8.4	2.4	1.9	3.2	1.9	1.3	1.3	0.7	0.6	1.0	0.9	2.5
Operating Margin 21	•	•	•	•	1.7	0.0	•	•	•	•	•	•	•
Operating Margin Before Officers' Comp. 22	1.7	•	1.7	•	4.9	1.9	•	•	•	•	•	•	•

Selected Average Balance Sheet ($ in Thousands)

Net Receivables 23	311	0	2	21	53	397	966	1817	4913	11248	18710	56092	415268
Inventories 24	82	0	2	4	14	21	81	426	719	1730	1528	15629	130605
Net Property, Plant and Equipment 25	3303	0	104	564	1623	4646	9240	19537	36558	87090	165658	562507	3969473
Total Assets 26	8429	0	154	750	2186	6426	14869	34680	70613	167454	325856	1079126	13191378
Notes and Loans Payable 27	4105	0	147	585	1905	5262	8755	18925	31480	61405	123621	559805	5742319
All Other Liabilities 28	2285	0	23	95	114	548	2055	9154	15298	35340	70062	181260	4269885
Net Worth 29	2039	0	-16	70	167	616	4058	6601	23835	70709	132173	338061	3179173

Selected Financial Ratios (Times to 1)

Current Ratio 30	1.1	•	0.7	1.3	1.8	1.8	1.5	0.9	1.5	1.6	1.5	1.2	1.0
Quick Ratio 31	0.8	•	0.6	1.0	1.2	1.3	1.0	0.6	1.1	1.2	1.1	0.7	0.7
Net Sales to Working Capital 32	27.0	•	•	23.8	8.6	6.0	10.0	•	13.7	10.1	7.0	12.0	•
Coverage Ratio 33	1.6	•	•	1.2	1.5	1.8	1.3	2.0	1.9	3.2	2.3	1.5	1.8
Total Asset Turnover 34	0.3	•	1.8	0.9	0.5	0.5	0.7	0.7	1.2	1.0	0.5	0.3	0.2
Inventory Turnover 35	5.8	•	10.7	13.5	15.2	22.9	39.1	14.1	15.9	27.0	25.5	2.7	2.3
Receivables Turnover 36	9.9	•	103.7	29.4	18.9	12.3	13.0	18.6	16.9	15.6	9.4	6.2	6.7
Total Liabilities to Net Worth 37	3.1	•	•	9.7	12.1	9.4	2.7	4.3	2.0	1.4	1.5	2.2	3.1
Current Assets to Working Capital 38	9.4	•	•	4.4	2.2	2.3	3.1	•	3.2	2.8	3.2	7.0	•
Current Liabilities to Working Capital 39	8.4	•	•	3.4	1.2	1.3	2.1	•	2.2	1.8	2.2	6.0	•
Working Capital to Net Sales 40	0.0	•	•	0.0	0.1	0.2	0.1	•	0.1	0.1	0.1	0.1	•
Inventory to Working Capital 41	0.9	•	•	0.2	0.1	0.0	0.1	•	0.1	0.1	0.1	0.6	•
Total Receipts to Cash Flow 42	3.2	4.0	3.9	3.1	3.4	3.5	4.1	3.7	3.5	3.8	2.6	3.8	2.9
Cost of Goods to Cash Flow 43	0.5	1.4	0.3	0.3	0.7	0.5	1.3	0.9	0.5	1.1	0.6	0.5	0.3
Cash Flow to Total Debt 44	0.1	•	0.4	0.3	0.2	0.2	0.2	0.3	0.5	0.4	0.3	0.1	0.1

Selected Financial Factors (in Percentages)

Debt Ratio 45	75.8	•	110.7	90.7	92.3	90.4	72.7	81.0	66.2	57.8	59.4	68.7	75.9
Return on Total Assets 46	5.0	•	•	5.9	7.4	8.8	3.9	5.5	5.1	8.3	6.4	4.7	4.9
Return on Equity Before Income Taxes 47	7.9	•	47.1	11.2	32.2	40.0	3.1	14.6	7.0	13.6	8.9	4.9	9.2
Return on Equity After Income Taxes 48	4.3	•	52.3	9.7	29.7	28.9	1.3	9.5	4.1	8.7	5.9	2.5	5.6
Profit Margin (Before Income Tax) 49	5.7	•	•	1.2	5.1	7.0	1.3	3.7	2.0	5.9	6.6	5.2	11.3
Profit Margin (After Income Tax) 50	3.1	•	•	1.1	4.7	5.1	0.6	2.4	1.2	3.8	4.4	2.7	6.8

Table II

Corporations with Net Income

ACCOMMODATION

MONEY AMOUNTS AND SIZE OF ASSETS IN THOUSANDS OF DOLLARS

Item Description for Accounting Period 7/07 Through 6/08	Total	Zero Assets	Under 500	500 to 1,000	1,000 to 5,000	5,000 to 10,000	10,000 to 25,000	25,000 to 50,000	50,000 to 100,000	100,000 to 250,000	250,000 to 500,000	500,000 to 2,500,000	2,500,000 and over
Number of Enterprises 1	17136	2123	7717	2371	3921	592	232	70	40	30	16	•	•
Revenues ($ in Thousands)													
Net Sales 2	69885888	1196917	3147591	1338385	5171471	2752242	2556639	2266174	2467571	5610593	1838248	•	•
Interest 3	2310285	20742	1571	4716	17156	5198	12229	11008	28923	47677	62301	•	•
Rents 4	450275	37441	27	0	1675	3969	8508	1363	10429	38041	17637	•	•
Royalties 5	1861081	0	0	0	0	0	2053	0	276	1960	223394	•	•
Other Portfolio Income 6	3164391	113901	51627	450	100478	196737	32236	110701	111104	241859	33096	•	•
Other Receipts 7	9250183	62370	28640	11143	106377	39973	81343	54682	92887	366228	195583	•	•
Total Receipts 8	86922103	1431371	3229456	1354694	5397157	2998119	2693008	2443928	2711190	6306358	2370259	•	•
Average Total Receipts 9	5072	674	418	571	1376	5064	11608	34913	67780	210212	148141	•	•
Operating Costs/Operating Income (%)													
Cost of Operations 10	15.5	11.2	6.3	2.8	19.2	11.9	38.4	26.8	16.6	33.4	23.7	•	•
Salaries and Wages 11	28.4	10.1	16.8	15.7	13.5	17.1	18.4	12.8	14.2	14.8	21.9	•	•
Taxes Paid 12	7.9	5.7	8.8	7.7	6.1	6.4	4.7	5.3	4.1	3.2	5.6	•	•
Interest Paid 13	9.2	16.3	2.1	7.3	8.6	7.2	4.8	2.9	3.6	1.6	5.2	•	•
Depreciation 14	5.1	6.5	2.0	4.7	5.6	5.1	5.3	3.4	3.5	3.0	6.2	•	•
Amortization and Depletion 15	0.7	0.7	0.1	1.2	0.4	0.4	0.2	0.2	0.3	0.2	0.3	•	•
Pensions and Other Deferred Comp. 16	0.5	0.1	0.1	•	0.0	0.2	0.2	0.1	0.2	0.2	1.1	•	•
Employee Benefits 17	2.7	1.2	0.3	0.8	0.8	2.4	1.0	1.5	1.8	1.5	1.1	•	•
Advertising 18	3.7	1.8	1.9	2.7	1.3	1.3	1.3	1.7	5.6	3.2	5.3	•	•
Other Expenses 19	36.3	47.2	52.8	41.9	28.8	38.1	20.4	42.5	49.1	41.9	33.8	•	•
Officers' Compensation 20	1.8	1.2	2.7	3.0	3.8	2.2	1.5	1.0	1.1	0.6	2.2	•	•
Operating Margin 21	•	•	6.1	12.0	11.8	7.7	3.7	1.6	•	•	•	•	•
Operating Margin Before Officers' Comp. 22	•	•	8.8	15.1	15.6	9.9	5.2	2.6	0.9	•	•	•	•

Selected Average Balance Sheet ($ in Thousands)

Item											
Net Receivables 23	488	0	2	9	73	365	973	2359	4751	12522	11743
Inventories 24	140	0	1	2	17	19	97	568	704	1629	1694
Net Property, Plant and Equipment 25	4850	0	102	607	1525	4842	9458	19608	36988	81876	162308
Total Assets 26	13539	0	169	754	2229	6779	14731	32959	70544	169467	340109
Notes and Loans Payable 27	5949	0	172	677	1711	5393	8365	13709	31642	46386	110996
All Other Liabilities 28	4005	0	26	35	117	526	1287	6452	12291	36730	61812
Net Worth 29	3585	0	-29	42	401	860	5079	12798	26611	86352	167301

Selected Financial Ratios (Times to 1)

Item											
Current Ratio 30	1.2	0.7	1.5	2.4	1.3	1.2	2.1	1.2	2.0	1.5	1.1
Quick Ratio 31	0.8	0.5	1.3	1.5	1.2	0.9	1.5	0.9	1.5	1.2	0.9
Net Sales to Working Capital 32	20.1	•	19.2	5.7	15.3	23.9	7.2	5.5	10.8	21.2	
Coverage Ratio 33	2.5	2.1	2.8	2.9	3.3	4.9	2.9	3.7	6.5	5.3	
Total Asset Turnover 34	0.3	2.4	0.7	0.6	0.7	1.0	0.7	0.9	1.1	0.3	
Inventory Turnover 35	4.5	42.3	8.3	14.7	28.6	43.8	15.3	14.6	38.3	16.1	
Receivables Turnover 36	8.8	•	35.0	15.0	16.4	12.6	22.6	13.3	19.4	5.6	
Total Liabilities to Net Worth 37	2.8	•	17.1	4.6	6.9	1.9	1.6	1.0	1.7	1.0	
Current Assets to Working Capital 38	7.5	•	3.1	1.7	4.2	1.9	6.6	2.0	3.0	13.2	
Current Liabilities to Working Capital 39	6.5	•	2.1	0.7	3.2	0.9	5.6	1.0	2.0	12.2	
Working Capital to Net Sales 40	0.0	•	0.1	0.2	0.1	0.1	0.0	0.2	0.1	0.0	
Inventory to Working Capital 41	0.8	•	0.1	0.1	0.0	0.1	0.5	0.0	0.1	0.3	
Total Receipts to Cash Flow 42	2.8	3.0	2.4	2.6	2.9	4.0	3.8	2.8	3.8	2.0	
Cost of Goods to Cash Flow 43	0.4	0.2	0.5	0.3	0.3	1.5	0.5	0.5	1.3	0.5	
Cash Flow to Total Debt 44	0.1	0.7	0.3	0.3	0.3	0.4	0.5	1.0	0.6	0.3	

Selected Financial Factors (in Percentages)

Item											
Debt Ratio 45	73.5	•	116.9	94.5	82.0	87.3	65.5	61.2	62.3	49.0	50.8
Return on Total Assets 46	6.9	26.1	15.4	14.6	16.3	10.3	14.0	11.6	11.5	9.4	
Return on Equity Before Income Taxes 47	15.7	•	179.2	52.9	89.9	19.6	28.7	22.4	19.1	15.5	
Return on Equity After Income Taxes 48	11.7	•	174.5	51.0	76.2	17.2	24.4	17.8	13.4	11.8	
Profit Margin (Before Income Tax) 49	13.8	17.7	8.7	13.3	16.1	16.6	9.0	11.3	9.7	8.8	22.6
Profit Margin (After Income Tax) 50	10.2	14.8	8.3	12.9	15.5	14.1	7.9	9.7	6.2	7.7	17.1

FOOD SERVICES AND DRINKING PLACES

Table I

Corporations with and without Net Income

MONEY AMOUNTS AND SIZE OF ASSETS IN THOUSANDS OF DOLLARS

Item Description for Accounting Period 7/07 Through 6/08	Total	Zero Assets	Under 500	500 to 1,000	1,000 to 5,000	5,000 to 10,000	10,000 to 25,000	25,000 to 50,000	50,000 to 100,000	100,000 to 250,000	250,000 to 500,000	500,000 to 2,500,000	2,500,000 and over
Number of Enterprises **1**	254078	42787	186079	14174	9601	710	390	143	65	51	28	36	12
Revenues ($ in Thousands)													
Net Sales **2**	328087029	9896953	100386556	22907617	41867071	10467015	9839882	7468776	7533733	11739028	11792435	34122521	60065442
Interest **3**	1483304	86268	18198	12324	28462	6703	14217	525	7479	21981	39922	517345	729879
Rents **4**	614829	3930	19476	8572	12191	2966	9083	17161	11216	44607	52266	254800	178560
Royalties **5**	4532139	171204	7057	18	1680	4519	81475	52587	78131	202419	517077	1571129	1844842
Other Portfolio Income **6**	2285949	253708	277641	72394	73517	51414	23056	17043	30379	17892	162717	609925	696264
Other Receipts **7**	8115275	398292	659136	156641	442308	148819	317186	72008	4758	188264	116165	1687930	3923770
Total Receipts **8**	345118525	10810355	101368064	23157566	42425229	10681436	10284899	7628100	7665696	12214191	12680582	38763650	67438757
Average Total Receipts **9**	1358	253	545	1634	4419	15044	26372	53343	117934	239494	452878	1076768	5619896
Operating Costs/Operating Income (%)													
Cost of Operations **10**	41.7	38.3	42.6	38.2	42.2	43.1	44.7	40.7	35.7	44.1	40.1	43.4	40.8
Salaries and Wages **11**	19.5	22.2	16.5	20.9	18.1	16.0	20.3	19.6	20.6	19.5	23.3	24.1	21.3
Taxes Paid **12**	4.2	4.8	4.4	4.5	3.6	3.8	3.9	4.2	3.4	3.7	4.0	4.1	4.7
Interest Paid **13**	1.9	2.2	0.7	1.3	1.2	1.4	1.9	1.9	1.9	3.1	3.4	3.6	3.4
Depreciation **14**	2.5	2.6	1.6	2.3	1.9	2.2	2.8	3.0	2.7	3.2	3.2	4.2	3.0
Amortization and Depletion **15**	0.5	1.2	0.3	0.4	0.5	0.6	0.6	0.5	0.3	0.8	0.9	0.6	0.7
Pensions and Other Deferred Comp. **16**	0.2	0.0	0.1	0.1	0.0	0.1	0.5	0.2	0.2	0.1	0.3	0.4	0.3
Employee Benefits **17**	1.2	1.2	0.5	0.7	0.8	0.7	1.2	1.1	1.3	1.4	1.5	1.9	2.4
Advertising **18**	2.4	1.4	1.7	1.9	3.3	3.4	3.2	3.3	2.1	2.7	3.1	3.0	2.2
Other Expenses **19**	24.4	36.4	25.6	23.6	23.4	24.8	22.3	25.2	30.6	22.5	22.8	22.2	22.6
Officers' Compensation **20**	2.5	2.2	4.6	4.0	2.6	1.3	1.5	1.1	1.2	0.9	0.9	0.8	0.7
Operating Margin **21**	•	•	1.5	2.0	2.3	2.7	•	•	•	•	•	•	•
Operating Margin Before Officers' Comp. **22**	1.6	•	6.0	6.1	5.0	3.9	•	0.4	1.2	•	•	•	•

Selected Average Balance Sheet ($ in Thousands)

Item													
Net Receivables 23	44	0	3	41	91	152	821	1807	5954	5837	12796	56160	453285
Inventories 24	22	0	7	26	54	163	605	695	2030	4173	8474	19230	130918
Net Property, Plant and Equipment 25	306	0	59	328	935	3524	7229	16226	32030	75005	144901	446002	1633513
Total Assets 26	839	0	121	653	1819	6718	14903	34261	68789	152234	335199	1034074	7474009
Notes and Loans Payable 27	365	0	91	393	932	3330	8837	15209	27122	72391	186556	337174	2540836
All Other Liabilities 28	263	0	25	140	416	1511	3243	8118	20202	43911	106132	397765	2642292
Net Worth 29	211	0	4	121	471	1877	2823	10935	21466	35933	42512	299135	2290880

Selected Financial Ratios (Times to 1)

Item													
Current Ratio 30	0.8	•	1.1	1.4	1.0	1.0	1.1	0.9	0.8	0.7	0.6	0.7	0.7
Quick Ratio 31	0.5	•	0.7	1.0	0.7	0.8	0.7	0.6	0.6	0.4	0.4	0.5	0.4
Net Sales to Working Capital 32	•	•	137.5	32.1	•	244.0	69.0	•	•	•	•	•	•
Coverage Ratio 33	3.3	•	4.6	3.4	4.1	4.3	1.8	1.8	1.9	1.6	2.2	2.6	4.3
Total Asset Turnover 34	1.5	•	4.5	2.5	2.4	2.2	1.7	1.5	1.7	1.5	1.3	0.9	0.7
Inventory Turnover 35	24.9	•	32.6	23.6	34.0	39.0	18.7	30.6	20.4	24.3	19.9	21.4	15.6
Receivables Turnover 36	26.5	•	169.5	46.1	49.1	96.2	27.0	30.0	19.2	28.5	31.1	15.8	9.4
Total Liabilities to Net Worth 37	3.0	•	28.5	4.4	2.9	2.6	4.3	2.1	2.2	3.2	6.9	2.5	2.3
Current Assets to Working Capital 38	•	•	9.1	3.7	•	25.4	12.1	•	•	•	•	•	•
Current Liabilities to Working Capital 39	•	•	8.1	2.7	•	24.4	11.1	•	•	•	•	•	•
Working Capital to Net Sales 40	•	•	0.0	0.0	•	0.0	0.0	•	•	•	•	•	•
Inventory to Working Capital 41	•	•	1.8	0.5	•	2.9	1.4	•	•	•	•	•	•
Total Receipts to Cash Flow 42	5.2	•	5.6	5.6	5.4	5.1	5.9	5.4	4.0	6.0	5.3	5.4	4.4
Cost of Goods to Cash Flow 43	2.2	•	2.4	2.1	2.3	2.2	2.6	2.2	1.4	2.7	2.1	2.3	1.8
Cash Flow to Total Debt 44	0.4	•	0.8	0.5	0.6	0.6	0.4	0.4	0.6	0.3	0.3	0.2	0.2

Selected Financial Factors (in Percentages)

Item													
Debt Ratio 45	74.8	•	96.6	81.5	74.1	72.1	81.1	68.1	68.8	76.4	87.3	71.1	69.3
Return on Total Assets 46	9.8	•	14.0	10.9	11.7	13.5	6.1	5.0	6.0	7.8	9.3	8.6	9.7
Return on Equity Before Income Taxes 47	27.3	•	322.7	41.8	34.0	37.2	14.6	6.8	8.9	13.0	39.4	18.4	24.2
Return on Equity After Income Taxes 48	20.7	•	315.6	39.9	33.0	35.1	12.6	5.5	6.9	9.1	29.0	11.9	15.7
Profit Margin (Before Income Tax) 49	4.5	•	2.5	3.1	3.7	4.7	1.6	1.4	1.7	2.0	4.0	5.8	11.1
Profit Margin (After Income Tax) 50	3.4	•	2.4	3.0	3.6	4.5	1.4	1.2	1.3	1.4	2.9	3.7	7.2

Table II

Corporations with Net Income

FOOD SERVICES AND DRINKING PLACES

MONEY AMOUNTS AND SIZE OF ASSETS IN THOUSANDS OF DOLLARS

Item Description for Accounting Period 7/07 Through 6/08	Total	Zero Assets	Under 500	500 to 1,000	1,000 to 5,000	5,000 to 10,000	10,000 to 25,000	25,000 to 50,000	50,000 to 100,000	100,000 to 250,000	250,000 to 500,000	500,000 to 2,500,000	2,500,000 and over
Number of Enterprises **1**	126564	13916	97082	7788	6683	618	253	91	38	31	24	•	•
Revenues ($ in Thousands)													
Net Sales **2**	254307134	6271448	66063262	16475055	33145495	9178674	7028019	4897492	5383632	7373414	10317053		
Interest **3**	1259016	82695	9150	9874	19386	6186	8519	-3361	5258	17380	35457		
Rents **4**	493476	73	14783	8554	7593	2966	6013	2724	5559	31060	41501		
Royalties **5**	4215104	171204	0	18	1639	0	70635	32374	58712	156738	477151		
Other Portfolio Income **6**	2098981	233236	200725	71413	53415	50379	15426	14890	26564	16535	162717		
Other Receipts **7**	7363414	330618	426504	108952	271987	141963	259229	56796	-23936	189314	100999		
Total Receipts **8**	269737125	7089274	66714424	16673866	33499515	9380168	7387841	5000915	5455789	7784441	11134878		
Average Total Receipts **9**	2131	509	687	2141	5013	15178	29201	54955	143573	251111	463953		
Operating Costs/Operating Income (%)													
Cost of Operations **10**	40.9	31.9	40.7	37.0	41.5	41.5	46.2	42.2	33.9	41.7	42.0	•	•
Salaries and Wages **11**	19.5	23.9	16.6	20.7	17.9	16.8	19.5	17.6	19.7	21.8	22.9	•	•
Taxes Paid **12**	4.2	4.2	4.2	4.4	3.5	3.7	3.9	4.1	3.2	3.9	4.1	•	•
Interest Paid **13**	1.8	2.3	0.5	0.8	1.0	1.3	1.2	1.5	1.6	2.0	3.3	•	•
Depreciation **14**	2.3	2.2	1.1	1.4	1.6	2.0	2.7	2.8	2.3	3.1	3.2	•	•
Amortization and Depletion **15**	0.5	1.0	0.2	0.2	0.5	0.6	0.4	0.5	0.3	0.6	0.7	•	•
Pensions and Other Deferred Comp. **16**	0.2	0.0	0.1	0.2	0.0	0.1	0.2	0.2	0.2	0.2	0.3	•	•
Employee Benefits **17**	1.3	1.5	0.6	0.8	0.8	0.7	1.3	1.0	1.1	1.5	1.5	•	•
Advertising **18**	2.4	1.4	1.8	1.6	3.3	3.6	3.0	3.6	2.0	2.5	3.2	•	•
Other Expenses **19**	23.4	35.3	23.8	22.1	22.4	24.4	20.6	22.5	32.1	21.9	21.1	•	•
Officers' Compensation **20**	2.3	1.5	4.4	4.4	2.6	1.3	1.6	0.9	1.3	0.9	0.9	•	•
Operating Margin **21**	1.3	•	5.9	6.5	4.9	4.1	•	3.1	2.5	0.0	•	•	•
Operating Margin Before Officers' Comp. **22**	3.6	•	10.4	10.9	7.5	5.4	1.0	4.0	3.7	0.9	•	•	•

Selected Average Balance Sheet ($ in Thousands)

Net Receivables 23	73	0	3	49	115	163	973	1818	6742	7019	13121
Inventories 24	34	0	8	35	57	145	668	680	2195	4075	8056
Net Property, Plant and Equipment 25	460	0	56	274	846	3314	6977	15459	35170	72545	148539
Total Assets 26	1311	0	129	651	1810	6588	14805	34046	70714	146449	336348
Notes and Loans Payable 27	487	0	62	279	791	3050	6407	13504	25354	53746	188449
All Other Liabilities 28	409	0	24	137	381	1117	3793	6305	22777	37569	109883
Net Worth 29	415	0	43	236	639	2421	4605	14236	22583	55135	38016

Selected Financial Ratios (Times to 1)

Current Ratio 30	0.9	•	1.5	2.1	1.3	1.2	1.2	1.1	0.9	0.9	0.6
Quick Ratio 31	0.6	•	1.0	1.5	0.9	0.9	0.9	0.7	0.7	0.6	0.4
Net Sales to Working Capital 32	•	•	43.3	16.3	41.2	65.0	31.6	78.7	•	•	•
Coverage Ratio 33	5.2	4.3	14.5	10.8	6.9	5.7	4.6	4.4	3.4	3.8	2.5
Total Asset Turnover 34	1.5	•	5.3	3.2	2.7	2.3	1.9	1.6	2.0	1.6	1.3
Inventory Turnover 35	24.5	•	36.1	22.5	35.8	42.5	19.2	33.4	21.9	24.3	22.4
Receivables Turnover 36	25.5	•	•	47.5	46.8	97.2	24.1	30.0	22.5	28.8	35.7
Total Liabilities to Net Worth 37	2.2	•	2.0	1.8	1.8	1.7	2.2	1.4	2.1	1.7	7.8
Current Assets to Working Capital 38	•	•	3.0	2.0	4.6	6.8	5.6	11.6	•	•	•
Current Liabilities to Working Capital 39	•	•	2.0	1.0	3.6	5.8	4.6	10.6	•	•	•
Working Capital to Net Sales 40	•	•	0.0	0.1	0.0	0.0	0.0	0.0	•	•	•
Inventory to Working Capital 41	•	•	0.5	0.2	0.5	0.7	0.6	0.9	•	•	•
Total Receipts to Cash Flow 42	4.6	2.7	4.7	4.7	5.0	4.8	5.5	4.8	3.4	4.9	5.7
Cost of Goods to Cash Flow 43	1.9	0.9	1.9	1.8	2.1	2.0	2.5	2.0	1.2	2.1	2.4
Cash Flow to Total Debt 44	0.5	•	1.7	1.1	0.9	0.7	0.5	0.6	0.9	0.5	0.3

Selected Financial Factors (in Percentages)

Debt Ratio 45	68.4	•	66.7	63.8	64.7	63.2	68.9	58.2	68.1	62.4	88.7
Return on Total Assets 46	14.5	•	39.1	27.5	19.0	17.2	10.8	10.6	10.8	12.1	10.4
Return on Equity Before Income Taxes 47	37.1	•	109.2	68.8	46.0	38.6	27.2	19.6	23.8	23.7	54.4
Return on Equity After Income Taxes 48	30.4	•	108.0	67.0	44.9	36.8	25.3	18.4	20.5	19.6	40.8
Profit Margin (Before Income Tax) 49	7.7	7.6	6.9	7.7	5.9	6.3	4.5	5.2	3.8	5.5	4.8
Profit Margin (After Income Tax) 50	6.3	7.0	6.8	7.5	5.8	6.0	4.2	4.9	3.3	4.5	3.6

Table I
Corporations with and without Net Income

AUTOMOTIVE REPAIR AND MAINTENANCE

MONEY AMOUNTS AND SIZE OF ASSETS IN THOUSANDS OF DOLLARS

Item Description for Accounting Period 7/07 Through 6/08	Total	Zero Assets	Under 500	500 to 1,000	1,000 to 5,000	5,000 to 10,000	10,000 to 25,000	25,000 to 50,000	50,000 to 100,000	100,000 to 250,000	250,000 to 500,000	500,000 to 2,500,000	2,500,000 and over
Number of Enterprises 1	110557	17018	82751	7349	3140	211	57	12	11	5	3	0	0
Revenues ($ in Thousands)													
Net Sales 2	69351178	2107344	39015810	12649791	9438237	1511139	1027652	780150	1127882	440976	1252198	0	0
Interest 3	52034	214	16127	4779	11221	1471	1041	3976	9187	2206	1811	0	0
Rents 4	17715	22	7074	318	2346	2504	2587	1560	673	68	563	0	0
Royalties 5	86596	0	1664	0	0	0	1227	0	1388	82318	0	0	0
Other Portfolio Income 6	396323	51473	193157	9035	57928	1482	4295	19072	10431	47359	2091	0	•
Other Receipts 7	346702	19080	128849	27079	29162	-32673	11328	1389	153242	8293	953	0	•
Total Receipts 8	70250548	2178133	39362681	12691002	9538894	1483923	1048130	806147	1302803	581220	1257616	0	•
Average Total Receipts 9	635	128	476	1727	3038	7033	18388	67179	118437	116244	419205	•	•
Operating Costs/Operating Income (%)													
Cost of Operations 10	51.2	42.5	47.0	61.0	54.4	68.8	45.6	45.5	61.5	39.7	56.3	•	•
Salaries and Wages 11	12.8	14.3	13.6	8.1	14.8	5.6	16.9	21.1	17.5	19.1	9.9	•	•
Taxes Paid 12	3.5	3.7	3.7	2.8	3.3	6.5	3.8	2.1	3.3	3.5	2.2	•	•
Interest Paid 13	1.4	1.0	1.0	1.5	2.3	1.0	1.2	2.5	2.0	15.7	3.1	•	•
Depreciation 14	1.8	1.8	1.6	1.6	2.4	1.1	3.4	4.5	2.1	3.3	2.0	•	•
Amortization and Depletion 15	0.4	0.5	0.2	0.5	0.5	0.3	0.2	1.1	0.8	5.8	2.3	•	•
Pensions and Other Deferred Comp. 16	0.2	0.1	0.1	0.1	0.3	0.0	0.4	0.1	0.2	0.3	0.5	•	•
Employee Benefits 17	1.1	0.6	1.0	1.3	0.9	0.6	1.3	1.7	1.7	2.4	1.9	•	•
Advertising 18	1.5	1.3	1.5	1.3	1.7	0.4	1.8	1.1	0.9	2.8	2.8	•	•
Other Expenses 19	19.0	30.0	20.8	15.5	14.4	13.7	16.6	22.7	21.2	29.2	17.3	•	•
Officers' Compensation 20	6.0	6.0	7.7	4.4	4.1	1.4	2.1	0.8	0.3	3.1	0.5	•	•
Operating Margin 21	1.2	•	1.7	1.9	1.0	0.6	6.7	•	•	•	1.4	•	•
Operating Margin Before Officers' Comp. 22	7.1	4.2	9.4	6.3	5.1	2.0	8.8	•	1.8	•	1.8	•	•

Selected Average Balance Sheet ($ in Thousands)

Net Receivables 23	19	0	8	74	144	887	944	4988	10805	11362	7135
Inventories 24	21	0	11	60	138	1480	777	3380	2721	2620	40956
Net Property, Plant and Equipment 25	90	0	41	299	778	2040	7596	13147	22924	55036	120335
Total Assets 26	221	0	101	680	1671	6748	16708	35926	72719	208717	399105
Notes and Loans Payable 27	134	0	75	445	902	3131	5438	16161	24927	100868	197367
All Other Liabilities 28	44	0	25	111	259	751	492	5818	26778	69135	86479
Net Worth 29	43	0	1	124	510	2867	10779	13948	21014	38714	115258

Selected Financial Ratios (Times to 1)

Current Ratio 30	1.5	•	1.3	1.5	2.2	1.4	1.4	1.3	1.7	0.8	0.8
Quick Ratio 31	1.0	•	0.9	1.0	1.6	0.7	0.7	0.9	1.1	0.5	0.1
Net Sales to Working Capital 32	27.1	•	50.7	24.2	9.9	8.7	13.5	25.6	10.1	•	•
Coverage Ratio 33	2.7	2.6	3.7	2.5	1.9	•	8.1	1.0	3.0	1.5	1.6
Total Asset Turnover 34	2.8	•	4.7	2.5	1.8	1.1	1.1	1.8	1.4	0.4	1.0
Inventory Turnover 35	15.4	•	21.1	17.5	11.8	3.3	10.6	8.8	23.2	13.4	5.7
Receivables Turnover 36	30.8	•	55.3	24.0	18.2	8.7	20.8	12.2	8.5	9.8	37.3
Total Liabilities to Net Worth 37	4.2	•	147.6	4.5	2.3	1.4	0.6	1.6	2.5	4.4	2.5
Current Assets to Working Capital 38	3.2	•	4.2	3.1	1.8	3.4	3.5	4.7	2.5	•	•
Current Liabilities to Working Capital 39	2.2	•	3.2	2.1	0.8	2.4	2.5	3.7	1.5	•	•
Working Capital to Net Sales 40	0.0	•	0.0	0.0	0.1	0.1	0.1	0.0	0.1	•	•
Inventory to Working Capital 41	0.9	•	1.1	0.8	0.4	1.5	0.6	1.2	0.3	•	•
Total Receipts to Cash Flow 42	6.9	4.3	6.5	7.9	9.3	11.0	4.9	6.4	5.4	6.2	8.7
Cost of Goods to Cash Flow 43	3.5	1.8	3.0	4.8	5.1	7.6	2.2	2.9	3.3	2.5	4.9
Cash Flow to Total Debt 44	0.5	•	0.7	0.4	0.3	0.2	0.6	0.5	0.4	0.1	0.2

Selected Financial Factors (in Percentages)

Debt Ratio 45	80.6	•	99.3	81.7	69.5	57.5	35.5	61.2	71.1	81.5	71.1
Return on Total Assets 46	11.0	•	16.9	9.3	7.8	•	10.6	4.3	8.3	9.8	5.2
Return on Equity Before Income Taxes 47	36.1	•	1833.7	30.8	12.0	•	14.4	•	19.1	17.3	6.5
Return on Equity After Income Taxes 48	34.7	•	1809.0	30.3	11.4	•	14.1	•	17.5	16.0	3.1
Profit Margin (Before Income Tax) 49	2.5	1.5	2.6	2.2	2.0	•	8.6	•	3.9	7.6	1.8
Profit Margin (After Income Tax) 50	2.4	1.4	2.6	2.2	1.9	•	8.4	•	3.6	7.0	0.9

Table II

Corporations with Net Income

AUTOMOTIVE REPAIR AND MAINTENANCE

MONEY AMOUNTS AND SIZE OF ASSETS IN THOUSANDS OF DOLLARS

Item Description for Accounting Period 7/07 Through 6/08	Total	Zero Assets	Under 500	500 to 1,000	1,000 to 5,000	5,000 to 10,000	10,000 to 25,000	25,000 to 50,000	50,000 to 100,000	100,000 to 250,000	250,000 to 500,000	500,000 to 2,500,000	2,500,000 and over
Number of Enterprises **1**	62168	7170	48565	4594	1647	137	36	•	7	•	0	0	0
Revenues ($ in Thousands)													
Net Sales **2**	47783801	1096045	26859810	9329622	6642504	1378296	900371	•	634027	•	•	0	0
Interest **3**	37545	210	12909	3708	6144	1471	877	•	9086	•	0	0	0
Rents **4**	11466	0	5612	0	1631	2504	0	•	182	•	0	0	0
Royalties **5**	61213	0	1664	0	0	0	1227	•	1388	•	0	0	0
Other Portfolio Income **6**	369269	44468	178861	8660	57917	1482	4250	•	9365	•	0	0	•
Other Receipts **7**	334123	18276	103329	21725	26738	4952	6922	•	150791	•	0	0	•
Total Receipts **8**	48597417	1158999	27162185	9363715	6734934	1388705	913647	•	804839	•	•	0	•
Average Total Receipts **9**	782	162	559	2038	4089	10137	25379	•	114977	•	•	•	•
Operating Costs/Operating Income (%)													
Cost of Operations **10**	50.8	47.0	45.8	62.2	53.3	75.5	43.1	•	52.1	•	•	•	•
Salaries and Wages **11**	12.3	10.8	12.9	8.0	15.2	4.9	18.0	•	23.0	•	•	•	•
Taxes Paid **12**	3.3	2.6	3.6	2.6	3.3	1.8	4.1	•	4.1	•	•	•	•
Interest Paid **13**	1.0	1.2	0.8	1.2	1.3	1.1	0.8	•	2.6	•	•	•	•
Depreciation **14**	1.5	0.8	1.2	1.4	1.8	1.2	2.9	•	2.2	•	•	•	•
Amortization and Depletion **15**	0.3	0.2	0.2	0.3	0.4	0.3	0.2	•	1.0	•	•	•	•
Pensions and Other Deferred Comp. **16**	0.2	•	0.1	0.2	0.2	0.0	0.5	•	0.3	•	•	•	•
Employee Benefits **17**	1.1	0.7	1.0	1.1	1.1	0.6	1.5	•	2.8	•	•	•	•
Advertising **18**	1.5	1.4	1.7	0.8	2.0	0.4	1.8	•	0.3	•	•	•	•
Other Expenses **19**	17.2	19.5	19.1	13.8	12.8	9.8	15.5	•	30.2	•	•	•	•
Officers' Compensation **20**	6.2	6.4	7.9	4.9	3.9	1.6	2.3	•	0.5	•	•	•	•
Operating Margin **21**	4.7	9.6	5.6	3.6	4.6	2.8	9.5	•	•	•	•	•	•
Operating Margin Before Officers' Comp. **22**	10.9	16.0	13.5	8.5	8.6	4.4	11.7	•	•	•	•	•	•

Selected Average Balance Sheet ($ in Thousands)

Line Item								
Net Receivables 23	24	0	9	96	195	537	1250	16079
Inventories 24	19	0	8	51	164	1005	796	1474
Net Property, Plant and Equipment 25	93	0	38	301	729	3138	8723	12569
Total Assets 26	229	0	103	684	1854	6248	16067	73592
Notes and Loans Payable 27	111	0	54	408	755	2673	4218	25727
All Other Liabilities 28	39	0	20	91	222	1133	3439	24157
Net Worth 29	78	0	29	185	876	2443	8410	23708

Selected Financial Ratios (Times to 1)

Line Item								
Current Ratio 30	1.9	•	1.7	2.0	3.2	2.0	1.3	1.7
Quick Ratio 31	1.4	•	1.3	1.4	2.5	1.1	0.9	1.3
Net Sales to Working Capital 32	18.1	•	29.5	16.8	7.7	8.4	23.3	7.3
Coverage Ratio 33	7.2	13.9	9.2	4.3	5.8	4.3	14.9	4.0
Total Asset Turnover 34	3.4	•	5.4	3.0	2.2	1.6	1.6	1.2
Inventory Turnover 35	20.9	•	31.8	24.7	13.1	7.6	13.6	32.0
Receivables Turnover 36	30.8	•	56.6	21.6	16.8	15.5	29.1	8.5
Total Liabilities to Net Worth 37	1.9	•	2.5	2.7	1.1	1.6	0.9	2.1
Current Assets to Working Capital 38	2.1	•	2.4	2.0	1.5	2.0	4.6	2.4
Current Liabilities to Working Capital 39	1.1	•	1.4	1.0	0.5	1.0	3.6	1.4
Working Capital to Net Sales 40	0.1	•	0.0	0.1	0.1	0.1	0.0	0.1
Inventory to Working Capital 41	0.4	•	0.4	0.4	0.2	0.9	0.8	0.2
Total Receipts to Cash Flow 42	5.8	3.4	5.4	7.3	7.2	10.2	4.7	3.4
Cost of Goods to Cash Flow 43	3.0	1.6	2.5	4.6	3.8	7.7	2.0	1.8
Cash Flow to Total Debt 44	0.9	•	1.4	0.6	0.6	0.3	0.7	0.5

Selected Financial Factors (in Percentages)

Line Item								
Debt Ratio 45	65.7	•	71.8	72.9	52.7	60.9	47.7	67.8
Return on Total Assets 46	24.8	•	40.5	15.5	15.8	7.5	18.2	13.0
Return on Equity Before Income Taxes 47	62.2	•	127.6	44.0	27.8	14.8	32.4	30.2
Return on Equity After Income Taxes 48	60.9	•	126.6	43.4	27.0	11.6	31.7	28.1
Profit Margin (Before Income Tax) 49	6.4	15.3	6.7	4.0	6.0	3.6	10.9	7.9
Profit Margin (After Income Tax) 50	6.2	15.0	6.7	4.0	5.9	2.8	10.7	7.3

Table I

Corporations with and without Net Income

OTHER REPAIR AND MAINTENANCE

MONEY AMOUNTS AND SIZE OF ASSETS IN THOUSANDS OF DOLLARS

Item Description for Accounting Period 7/07 Through 6/08		Total	Zero Assets	Under 500	500 to 1,000	1,000 to 5,000	5,000 to 10,000	10,000 to 25,000	25,000 to 50,000	50,000 to 100,000	100,000 to 250,000	250,000 to 500,000	500,000 to 2,500,000	2,500,000 and over
Number of Enterprises	1	57857	12091	42430	1171	1894	112	106	30	13	6	4	0	0
Revenues ($ in Thousands)														
Net Sales	2	45319546	952638	22572134	2242701	8611875	1746600	3703756	1717683	1201096	1093092	1477970	0	0
Interest	3	62040	593	3880	3308	10448	2211	5897	2800	4568	2734	25601	0	0
Rents	4	15363	0	9074	0	4389	213	1301	321	0	23	42	0	0
Royalties	5	68707	0	0	0	0	0	0	0	300	41	68366	0	0
Other Portfolio Income	6	48724	0	1508	3050	15456	9056	7101	2599	2185	359	7411	0	0
Other Receipts	7	280638	3402	16907	29020	124016	31652	13174	9143	5099	2833	45390	0	0
Total Receipts	8	45795018	956633	22603503	2278079	8766184	1789732	3731229	1732546	1213248	1099082	1624780	0	0
Average Total Receipts	9	792	79	533	1945	4628	15980	35200	57752	93327	183180	406195	•	•
Operating Costs/Operating Income (%)														
Cost of Operations	10	57.0	28.4	54.3	44.9	60.8	62.4	66.0	69.0	62.1	60.0	63.6	•	•
Salaries and Wages	11	11.5	2.4	12.8	12.2	10.4	9.4	11.2	7.6	10.6	14.3	7.9	•	•
Taxes Paid	12	2.5	2.0	2.4	3.4	2.8	2.3	2.1	2.2	2.4	3.2	2.6	•	•
Interest Paid	13	1.4	1.4	0.5	0.9	1.4	0.5	0.9	1.2	2.4	2.1	16.0	•	•
Depreciation	14	1.5	3.0	1.2	2.1	1.6	1.3	2.1	2.0	2.1	1.6	1.5	•	•
Amortization and Depletion	15	0.3	0.1	0.2	0.2	0.2	0.0	0.1	0.1	0.5	0.8	5.1	•	•
Pensions and Other Deferred Comp.	16	0.2	0.3	0.1	0.2	0.3	0.8	0.4	0.4	0.2	0.1	0.2	•	•
Employee Benefits	17	1.6	0.2	0.8	1.7	2.3	3.4	1.3	3.4	2.8	5.9	1.3	•	•
Advertising	18	0.6	1.0	0.8	0.6	0.5	0.2	0.5	0.3	0.1	0.2	0.7	•	•
Other Expenses	19	15.3	45.2	17.3	19.8	12.1	11.0	8.8	6.3	14.6	8.9	14.0	•	•
Officers' Compensation	20	4.5	5.4	5.5	6.9	4.7	3.4	2.3	1.4	1.0	0.7	0.6	•	•
Operating Margin	21	3.5	10.6	4.0	7.1	2.9	5.1	4.3	6.1	1.1	2.0	•	•	•
Operating Margin Before Officers' Comp.	22	8.1	16.0	9.5	14.1	7.6	8.6	6.6	7.6	2.1	2.8	•	•	•

Selected Average Balance Sheet ($ in Thousands)

Net Receivables 23	68	0	18	188	419	2082	4724	9262	18481	55966	133181
Inventories 24	41	0	13	103	368	1257	4505	6605	9693	10931	2405
Net Property, Plant and Equipment 25	49	0	23	180	363	1026	2912	5667	12161	13844	32825
Total Assets 26	378	0	85	695	1932	7200	15852	32966	69142	174501	2084082
Notes and Loans Payable 27	193	0	53	281	801	1565	4008	9481	28654	61452	1355927
All Other Liabilities 28	89	0	25	148	510	1947	5389	7627	22261	72782	291630
Net Worth 29	96	0	7	267	621	3688	6455	15858	18227	40267	436525

Selected Financial Ratios (Times to 1)

Current Ratio 30	1.4	•	1.4	2.9	1.7	1.9	1.7	3.1	1.5	1.9	0.5
Quick Ratio 31	0.9	•	1.0	2.3	1.0	1.3	0.9	2.0	0.9	1.5	0.4
Net Sales to Working Capital 32	17.9	•	32.7	7.7	9.6	6.4	7.1	3.5	8.3	3.8	•
Coverage Ratio 33	4.3	9.1	8.7	10.8	4.3	15.1	6.8	6.8	1.9	2.2	0.8
Total Asset Turnover 34	2.1	•	6.2	2.8	2.4	2.2	2.2	1.7	1.3	1.0	0.2
Inventory Turnover 35	10.9	•	22.5	8.4	7.5	7.7	5.1	6.0	5.9	10.0	97.8
Receivables Turnover 36	12.7	•	32.4	8.5	10.5	8.1	7.2	6.6	6.0	3.4	5.5
Total Liabilities to Net Worth 37	2.9	•	12.1	1.6	2.1	1.0	1.5	1.1	2.8	3.3	3.8
Current Assets to Working Capital 38	3.7	•	3.2	1.5	2.4	2.1	2.4	1.5	3.0	2.2	•
Current Liabilities to Working Capital 39	2.7	•	2.2	0.5	1.4	1.1	1.4	0.5	2.0	1.2	•
Working Capital to Net Sales 40	0.1	•	0.0	0.1	0.1	0.2	0.1	0.3	0.1	0.3	•
Inventory to Working Capital 41	1.0	•	0.9	0.2	0.8	0.5	1.0	0.5	0.9	0.1	•
Total Receipts to Cash Flow 42	6.1	2.0	5.7	4.0	7.2	6.6	9.1	9.2	8.3	9.9	12.4
Cost of Goods to Cash Flow 43	3.5	0.6	3.1	1.8	4.4	4.1	6.0	6.4	5.1	5.9	7.9
Cash Flow to Total Debt 44	0.5	•	1.2	1.1	0.5	0.7	0.4	0.4	0.2	0.1	0.0

Selected Financial Factors (in Percentages)

Debt Ratio 45	74.5	•	92.4	61.6	67.9	48.8	59.3	51.9	73.6	76.9	79.1
Return on Total Assets 46	12.4	•	29.0	26.4	14.5	17.6	13.0	14.2	6.1	5.0	2.2
Return on Equity Before Income Taxes 47	37.3	•	335.9	62.5	34.6	32.1	27.1	25.2	10.9	11.9	•
Return on Equity After Income Taxes 48	34.1	•	331.4	57.4	31.6	28.5	19.7	20.8	7.0	7.2	•
Profit Margin (Before Income Tax) 49	4.6	11.0	4.1	8.7	4.7	7.6	5.0	7.0	2.1	2.6	•
Profit Margin (After Income Tax) 50	4.2	10.3	4.1	8.0	4.3	6.7	3.6	5.8	1.4	1.6	•

Table II

Corporations with Net Income

OTHER REPAIR AND MAINTENANCE

MONEY AMOUNTS AND SIZE OF ASSETS IN THOUSANDS OF DOLLARS

Item Description for Accounting Period 7/07 Through 6/08	Total	Zero Assets	Under 500	500 to 1,000	1,000 to 5,000	5,000 to 10,000	10,000 to 25,000	25,000 to 50,000	50,000 to 100,000	100,000 to 250,000	250,000 to 500,000	500,000 to 2,500,000	2,500,000 and over
Number of Enterprises **1**	37167	7387	26993	1032	1522	99	94	•	9	•	0	0	0
Revenues ($ in Thousands)													
Net Sales **2**	38942009	772636	19090564	2108917	7678737	1607637	3410182	•	838505	•	0	0	0
Interest **3**	24787	593	2511	3304	7227	1956	5157	•	-1406	•	0	0	0
Rents **4**	14493	0	9068	0	3555	206	1301	•	0	•	0	0	0
Royalties **5**	219	0	0	0	0	0	0	•	179	•	0	0	0
Other Portfolio Income **6**	34390	0	504	3050	13205	9056	4215	•	2185	•	0	0	0
Other Receipts **7**	229623	3363	16001	29019	122574	31652	12302	•	3096	•	0	0	0
Total Receipts **8**	39245521	776592	19118648	2144290	7825298	1650507	3433157	•	842559	•	0	0	0
Average Total Receipts **9**	1056	105	708	2078	5141	16672	36523	•	93618	•	•	•	•
Operating Costs/Operating Income (%)													
Cost of Operations **10**	57.1	27.4	54.0	44.8	60.6	62.3	67.8	•	59.1	•	•	•	•
Salaries and Wages **11**	11.5	0.9	13.5	11.9	9.6	9.0	10.8	•	11.2	•	•	•	•
Taxes Paid **12**	2.4	1.9	2.4	3.2	2.6	2.5	1.8	•	2.1	•	•	•	•
Interest Paid **13**	0.8	1.5	0.4	0.7	1.3	0.5	0.6	•	2.0	•	•	•	•
Depreciation **14**	1.3	2.8	0.9	2.0	1.6	1.2	1.4	•	2.6	•	•	•	•
Amortization and Depletion **15**	0.1	0.1	0.0	0.1	0.2	0.0	0.0	•	0.5	•	•	•	•
Pensions and Other Deferred Comp. **16**	0.2	0.4	0.1	0.2	0.3	0.7	0.5	•	0.2	•	•	•	•
Employee Benefits **17**	1.5	0.1	0.7	1.5	2.4	3.3	1.1	•	2.7	•	•	•	•
Advertising **18**	0.5	0.9	0.7	0.6	0.5	0.2	0.5	•	0.2	•	•	•	•
Other Expenses **19**	14.0	40.2	16.0	20.2	11.5	9.0	8.1	•	13.7	•	•	•	•
Officers' Compensation **20**	4.3	5.3	4.9	6.9	4.8	3.6	2.1	•	1.3	•	•	•	•
Operating Margin **21**	6.2	18.4	6.5	7.9	4.6	7.8	5.2	•	4.5	•	•	•	•
Operating Margin Before Officers' Comp. **22**	10.4	23.8	11.4	14.8	9.4	11.4	7.3	•	5.7	•	•	•	•

Selected Average Balance Sheet ($ in Thousands)

Net Receivables 23	84	0	24	207	433	2177	4786	18138
Inventories 24	52	0	13	43	381	1401	4773	10796
Net Property, Plant and Equipment 25	59	0	26	161	403	864	2409	14153
Total Assets 26	320	0	103	701	2030	6992	15998	70132
Notes and Loans Payable 27	123	0	43	240	811	1127	3303	29478
All Other Liabilities 28	81	0	26	159	477	2024	5757	21980
Net Worth 29	116	0	33	301	741	3842	6938	18674

Selected Financial Ratios (Times to 1)

Current Ratio 30	1.7	•	1.9	3.0	1.8	2.1	1.8	1.5
Quick Ratio 31	1.1	•	1.4	2.5	1.0	1.4	1.0	0.8
Net Sales to Working Capital 32	13.6	•	22.5	7.3	10.3	5.9	6.7	7.8
Coverage Ratio 33	9.7	13.7	18.1	14.2	6.0	20.9	10.3	3.5
Total Asset Turnover 34	3.3	•	6.9	2.9	2.5	2.3	2.3	1.3
Inventory Turnover 35	11.6	•	29.3	21.5	8.0	7.2	5.2	5.1
Receivables Turnover 36	13.4	•	33.6	9.5	11.4	7.9	7.2	6.4
Total Liabilities to Net Worth 37	1.8	•	2.1	1.3	1.7	0.8	1.3	2.8
Current Assets to Working Capital 38	2.5	•	2.1	1.5	2.3	2.0	2.3	3.0
Current Liabilities to Working Capital 39	1.5	•	1.1	0.5	1.3	1.0	1.3	2.0
Working Capital to Net Sales 40	0.1	•	0.0	0.1	0.1	0.2	0.1	0.1
Inventory to Working Capital 41	0.7	•	0.4	0.2	0.9	0.5	0.9	1.0
Total Receipts to Cash Flow 42	5.5	1.8	5.1	3.8	6.5	5.7	8.8	6.9
Cost of Goods to Cash Flow 43	3.2	0.5	2.8	1.7	4.0	3.6	6.0	4.1
Cash Flow to Total Debt 44	0.9	•	2.0	1.3	0.6	0.9	0.5	0.3

Selected Financial Factors (in Percentages)

Debt Ratio 45	63.7	•	67.7	57.0	63.5	45.1	56.6	73.4
Return on Total Assets 46	25.3	•	48.6	30.0	19.6	25.5	14.7	9.2
Return on Equity Before Income Taxes 47	62.6	•	142.4	64.9	44.7	44.1	30.7	24.7
Return on Equity After Income Taxes 48	58.6	•	141.0	59.7	41.5	40.2	22.9	19.1
Profit Margin (Before Income Tax) 49	6.9	18.9	6.7	9.6	6.6	10.4	5.9	4.9
Profit Margin (After Income Tax) 50	6.5	18.1	6.6	8.8	6.1	9.5	4.4	3.8

Table I

Corporations with and without Net Income

PERSONAL AND LAUNDRY SERVICES

MONEY AMOUNTS AND SIZE OF ASSETS IN THOUSANDS OF DOLLARS

Item Description for Accounting Period 7/07 Through 6/08	Total	Zero Assets	Under 500	500 to 1,000	1,000 to 5,000	5,000 to 10,000	10,000 to 25,000	25,000 to 50,000	50,000 to 100,000	100,000 to 250,000	250,000 to 500,000	500,000 to 2,500,000	2,500,000 and over
Number of Enterprises **1**	154875	36219	106469	6654	4914	377	146	48	19	9	8	8	3
Revenues ($ in Thousands)													
Net Sales **2**	77838211	3081094	27299678	10076198	13249524	4115965	2442828	1737196	1256981	973449	1522889	4098943	7983466
Interest **3**	176533	200	14005	4799	12164	4319	8933	9968	3564	5346	1098	40933	71202
Rents **4**	46306	0	1184	3636	5503	371	6249	871	680	0	6636	10189	10987
Royalties **5**	133618	0	0	0	1	434	94	236	235	2470	0	82414	47735
Other Portfolio Income **6**	1045980	165688	152098	109589	47619	11752	4790	10510	1016	7721	2404	150058	382734
Other Receipts **7**	1587140	17134	316007	67547	507302	94443	62224	31451	39968	143641	15731	209319	82375
Total Receipts **8**	80827788	3264116	27782972	10261769	13822113	4227284	2525118	1790232	1302444	1132627	1548758	4591856	8578499
Average Total Receipts **9**	522	90	261	1542	2813	11213	17295	37296	68550	125847	193595	573982	2859500
Operating Costs/Operating Income (%)													
Cost of Operations **10**	28.0	19.8	22.9	20.1	34.4	39.7	31.6	28.0	35.9	20.7	41.3	29.2	37.1
Salaries and Wages **11**	21.4	17.7	22.1	17.5	23.6	17.0	23.5	22.4	17.3	28.1	22.2	23.2	21.5
Taxes Paid **12**	3.9	3.5	3.7	3.0	4.6	4.2	2.5	4.0	3.6	3.7	3.3	4.3	5.2
Interest Paid **13**	2.1	1.9	1.2	1.7	2.3	1.7	2.2	2.1	3.0	3.3	4.3	5.2	3.1
Depreciation **14**	3.1	4.0	2.3	2.8	2.8	5.4	4.1	3.2	3.6	2.5	6.4	4.1	4.0
Amortization and Depletion **15**	1.0	1.5	0.5	0.3	0.5	0.3	0.8	0.7	0.7	1.1	3.3	6.2	1.9
Pensions and Other Deferred Comp. **16**	0.5	0.1	0.3	0.3	0.4	0.4	0.3	0.6	0.4	0.8	0.7	1.2	1.2
Employee Benefits **17**	1.5	0.5	0.9	1.0	1.4	1.2	2.8	2.1	5.1	4.5	1.8	3.6	2.3
Advertising **18**	2.0	1.7	2.5	2.0	1.8	1.5	1.8	1.6	1.9	1.3	0.7	0.8	1.5
Other Expenses **19**	31.1	47.4	32.6	45.2	27.1	26.2	27.4	32.7	30.1	45.1	17.0	20.7	17.8
Officers' Compensation **20**	5.3	8.7	8.8	5.3	4.6	2.3	2.1	2.5	1.8	1.6	0.7	0.5	1.0
Operating Margin **21**	0.2	•	2.2	0.9	•	0.1	0.8	•	•	•	•	1.0	3.5
Operating Margin Before Officers' Comp. **22**	5.5	1.9	11.0	6.1	1.0	2.3	2.8	2.4	•	•	•	1.5	4.5

Selected Average Balance Sheet ($ in Thousands)

Net Receivables 23	26	0	3	53	211	761	2796	3868	5624	18388	22271	63965	165307
Inventories 24	16	0	3	25	40	404	476	1990	4769	4964	10875	98751	268367
Net Property, Plant and Equipment 25	110	0	29	312	804	2748	4692	7566	27482	18665	99178	205677	890874
Total Assets 26	351	0	75	674	1875	7164	14684	33245	70396	142881	332159	970784	4423644
Notes and Loans Payable 27	158	0	61	394	958	2532	5708	11010	23746	37541	101554	393830	1180269
All Other Liabilities 28	108	0	12	124	452	1302	4272	12660	20545	77143	85410	413255	1877388
Net Worth 29	85	0	1	157	465	3330	4705	9575	26106	28196	145196	163699	1365988

Selected Financial Ratios (Times to 1)

Current Ratio 30	1.4	•	1.7	1.2	1.5	1.9	1.6	1.5	1.2	0.8	1.8	1.0	1.3
Quick Ratio 31	0.9	•	1.2	0.9	1.1	1.5	1.2	0.6	0.7	0.6	0.9	0.5	0.4
Net Sales to Working Capital 32	20.8	•	27.8	50.4	14.8	7.7	7.9	7.2	22.9	•	6.8	•	18.9
Coverage Ratio 33	3.0	0.6	4.4	2.6	1.3	2.6	2.8	2.4	1.1	2.1	1.0	3.7	4.6
Total Asset Turnover 34	1.4	•	3.4	2.2	1.4	1.5	1.1	1.1	0.9	0.8	0.6	0.5	0.6
Inventory Turnover 35	8.9	•	18.1	12.4	23.5	10.7	11.1	5.1	5.0	4.5	7.2	1.5	3.7
Receivables Turnover 36	18.8	•	84.8	24.8	13.6	15.8	6.1	11.5	8.9	6.4	10.2	4.3	32.2
Total Liabilities to Net Worth 37	3.1	•	69.1	3.3	3.0	1.2	2.1	2.5	1.7	4.1	1.3	4.9	2.2
Current Assets to Working Capital 38	3.7	•	2.5	6.4	3.1	2.2	2.7	3.2	7.4	•	2.3	•	4.5
Current Liabilities to Working Capital 39	2.7	•	1.5	5.4	2.1	1.2	1.7	2.2	6.4	•	1.3	•	3.5
Working Capital to Net Sales 40	0.0	•	0.0	0.0	0.1	0.1	0.1	0.1	0.0	0.1	0.1	•	0.1
Inventory to Working Capital 41	0.6	•	0.3	0.8	0.2	0.3	0.3	0.5	1.2	0.8	0.4	•	1.9
Total Receipts to Cash Flow 42	4.3	3.8	4.4	2.5	6.7	4.8	4.1	4.9	5.1	3.8	7.0	3.8	5.5
Cost of Goods to Cash Flow 43	1.2	0.7	1.0	0.5	2.3	1.9	1.3	1.4	1.8	0.8	2.9	1.1	2.0
Cash Flow to Total Debt 44	0.4	•	0.8	1.2	0.3	0.6	0.4	0.3	0.3	0.3	0.1	0.2	0.2

Selected Financial Factors (in Percentages)

Debt Ratio 45	75.8	•	98.6	76.7	75.2	53.5	68.0	71.2	62.9	80.3	56.3	83.1	69.1
Return on Total Assets 46	8.8	•	17.6	9.9	4.3	6.7	7.2	5.5	3.0	5.4	2.5	10.0	8.5
Return on Equity Before Income Taxes 47	24.1	•	956.2	26.3	8.9	14.6	11.2	0.5	•	14.7	0.1	43.2	21.4
Return on Equity After Income Taxes 48	20.6	•	947.7	25.1	8.1	12.0	8.1	•	•	11.8	0.0	31.7	16.2
Profit Margin (Before Income Tax) 49	4.1	•	4.0	2.7	0.7	2.7	4.1	3.0	0.2	3.8	0.1	13.8	11.0
Profit Margin (After Income Tax) 50	3.5	•	3.9	2.6	0.5	2.5	3.4	2.1	•	3.1	0.0	10.1	8.3

Table II
Corporations with Net Income

PERSONAL AND LAUNDRY SERVICES

MONEY AMOUNTS AND SIZE OF ASSETS IN THOUSANDS OF DOLLARS

Item Description for Accounting Period 7/07 Through 6/08	Total	Zero Assets	Under 500	500 to 1,000	1,000 to 5,000	5,000 to 10,000	10,000 to 25,000	25,000 to 50,000	50,000 to 100,000	100,000 to 250,000	250,000 to 500,000	500,000 to 2,500,000	2,500,000 and over
Number of Enterprises 1	84117	17626	59137	4185	2739	276	92	33	10	•	0	•	3
Revenues ($ in Thousands)													
Net Sales 2	53462676	2076946	17203367	7656319	5803430	3323401	1886403	1188437	714140	•	0	•	7983466
Interest 3	153084	116	5532	4593	10015	1346	6155	8469	1605	•	0	•	71202
Rents 4	36584	0	192	2232	5501	16	6160	871	435	•	0	•	10987
Royalties 5	130818	0	0	0	0	434	0	236	0	•	0	•	47735
Other Portfolio Income 6	978784	151640	135887	97673	37767	4640	1110	9009	125	•	0	•	382734
Other Receipts 7	1320422	11208	202588	45336	444638	86619	48752	18726	30271	•	0	•	82375
Total Receipts 8	56082368	2239910	17547566	7806153	6301351	3416456	1948580	1225748	746576	•	0	•	8578499
Average Total Receipts 9	667	127	297	1865	2301	12378	21180	37144	74658	•	•	•	2859500
Operating Costs/Operating Income (%)													
Cost of Operations 10	26.7	22.7	20.4	18.9	33.9	38.8	30.1	26.4	41.0	•	•	•	37.1
Salaries and Wages 11	20.5	14.9	21.7	14.2	23.4	16.0	25.0	19.6	7.1	•	•	•	21.5
Taxes Paid 12	3.6	3.4	3.3	2.3	4.0	4.2	2.3	2.9	3.5	•	•	•	5.2
Interest Paid 13	1.9	0.9	0.9	1.1	2.7	1.2	1.6	1.8	2.2	•	•	•	3.1
Depreciation 14	2.9	1.9	1.8	1.9	2.6	5.5	4.0	4.0	3.5	•	•	•	4.0
Amortization and Depletion 15	1.2	0.7	0.5	0.2	1.0	0.4	0.4	0.5	0.7	•	•	•	1.9
Pensions and Other Deferred Comp. 16	0.5	•	0.2	0.2	0.9	0.3	0.3	0.9	0.3	•	•	•	1.2
Employee Benefits 17	1.5	0.5	0.7	0.6	1.3	0.7	3.1	2.5	6.0	•	•	•	2.3
Advertising 18	1.9	1.3	2.7	2.1	1.4	1.6	2.1	1.2	2.5	•	•	•	1.5
Other Expenses 19	29.4	35.3	30.0	48.9	23.4	24.8	24.2	32.0	31.2	•	•	•	17.8
Officers' Compensation 20	5.0	8.5	8.3	5.1	6.6	2.5	1.8	3.1	1.1	•	•	•	1.0
Operating Margin 21	5.0	10.0	9.6	4.4	•	3.8	5.0	5.1	0.9	•	•	•	3.5
Operating Margin Before Officers' Comp. 22	10.0	18.5	17.9	9.5	5.6	6.3	6.9	8.1	2.0	•	•	•	4.5

Selected Average Balance Sheet ($ in Thousands)

Net Receivables 23	36	0	3	66	274	488	3039	4156	4113	165307
Inventories 24	23	0	4	22	43	427	481	2203	4106	268367
Net Property, Plant and Equipment 25	132	0	25	276	657	2789	4496	9175	26474	890874
Total Assets 26	477	0	75	681	1826	7232	14910	33892	73437	4423644
Notes and Loans Payable 27	172	0	49	259	729	1861	3984	8562	24755	1180269
All Other Liabilities 28	155	0	8	106	475	996	4425	15266	15788	1877388
Net Worth 29	150	0	18	316	622	4375	6501	10063	32893	1365988

Selected Financial Ratios (Times to 1)

Current Ratio 30	1.6	•	2.4	1.7	1.9	2.6	2.1	1.4	1.6	1.3
Quick Ratio 31	1.0	•	1.8	1.3	1.3	2.2	1.6	0.6	1.1	0.4
Net Sales to Working Capital 32	14.7	•	18.8	18.2	6.6	6.4	6.1	7.2	11.4	18.9
Coverage Ratio 33	6.3	21.4	14.4	6.8	3.8	6.4	6.1	5.4	3.5	4.6
Total Asset Turnover 34	1.3	•	3.9	2.7	1.2	1.7	1.4	1.1	1.0	0.6
Inventory Turnover 35	7.4	•	16.5	15.5	16.6	11.0	12.8	4.3	7.1	3.7
Receivables Turnover 36	16.8	•	83.4	24.8	8.6	19.5	7.1	10.1	9.7	32.2
Total Liabilities to Net Worth 37	2.2	•	3.1	1.2	1.9	0.7	1.3	2.4	1.2	2.2
Current Assets to Working Capital 38	2.8	•	1.7	2.5	2.1	1.6	1.9	3.5	2.6	4.5
Current Liabilities to Working Capital 39	1.8	•	0.7	1.5	1.1	0.6	0.9	2.5	1.6	3.5
Working Capital to Net Sales 40	0.1	•	0.1	0.1	0.2	0.2	0.2	0.1	0.1	0.1
Inventory to Working Capital 41	0.5	•	0.2	0.2	0.1	0.2	0.1	0.6	0.2	1.9
Total Receipts to Cash Flow 42	3.5	2.6	3.4	2.0	4.4	4.4	3.8	4.2	4.4	5.5
Cost of Goods to Cash Flow 43	0.9	0.6	0.7	0.4	1.5	1.7	1.1	1.1	1.8	2.0
Cash Flow to Total Debt 44	0.6	•	1.5	2.4	0.4	1.0	0.6	0.4	0.4	0.2

Selected Financial Factors (in Percentages)

Debt Ratio 45	68.5	•	75.6	53.5	65.9	39.5	56.4	70.3	55.2	69.1
Return on Total Assets 46	15.8	•	48.6	20.1	11.7	13.0	13.7	10.7	7.4	8.5
Return on Equity Before Income Taxes 47	42.2	•	185.6	36.9	25.3	18.1	26.2	29.3	11.8	21.4
Return on Equity After Income Taxes 48	38.5	•	184.7	35.9	24.1	17.2	23.2	25.0	10.5	16.2
Profit Margin (Before Income Tax) 49	10.0	17.8	11.6	6.4	7.4	6.6	8.3	8.2	5.4	11.0
Profit Margin (After Income Tax) 50	9.1	17.7	11.6	6.2	7.1	6.3	7.3	7.0	4.8	8.3

RELIGIOUS, GRANTMAKING, CIVIC AND PROFESSIONAL ORGANIZATIONS

Table I

Corporations with and without Net Income

MONEY AMOUNTS AND SIZE OF ASSETS IN THOUSANDS OF DOLLARS

Item Description for Accounting Period 7/07 Through 6/08	Total	Zero Assets	Under 500	500 to 1,000	1,000 to 5,000	5,000 to 10,000	10,000 to 25,000	25,000 to 50,000	50,000 to 100,000	100,000 to 250,000	250,000 to 500,000	500,000 to 2,500,000	2,500,000 and over
Number of Enterprises **1**	48760	6545	35959	3549	2350	238	92	16	10	0	0	0	0
Revenues ($ in Thousands)													
Net Sales **2**	12837881	279158	4778202	1166239	2390401	554604	750812	341744	2576721	0	0	0	0
Interest **3**	318008	5725	91649	60624	114978	17863	15080	3282	8807	0	0	0	0
Rents **4**	37649	0	16208	3459	7483	3902	4489	253	1855	0	0	0	0
Royalties **5**	3038	0	0	3025	12	0	0	0	0	0	0	0	0
Other Portfolio Income **6**	49520	0	19133	5697	9982	1675	3263	4009	5761	0	0	0	0
Other Receipts **7**	2333386	8	583022	561992	619525	271193	179388	52005	66254	0	0	0	0
Total Receipts **8**	15579482	284891	5488214	1801036	3142381	849237	953032	401293	2659398	0	0	0	0
Average Total Receipts **9**	320	44	153	507	1337	3568	10359	25081	265940	•	•	•	•
Operating Costs/Operating Income (%)													
Cost of Operations **10**	29.3	14.2	10.5	10.9	17.8	7.3	51.4	19.2	84.2	•	•	•	•
Salaries and Wages **11**	12.0	2.1	8.4	14.0	18.7	18.2	15.5	35.4	7.3	•	•	•	•
Taxes Paid **12**	2.0	1.6	1.7	3.0	2.9	3.1	2.5	3.4	0.8	•	•	•	•
Interest Paid **13**	0.7	0.0	0.6	1.3	0.8	1.7	2.2	0.8	0.1	•	•	•	•
Depreciation **14**	1.7	0.1	0.8	2.0	2.3	6.1	4.1	4.9	0.8	•	•	•	•
Amortization and Depletion **15**	0.1	•	0.0	0.0	0.0	0.1	0.1	0.0	0.2	•	•	•	•
Pensions and Other Deferred Comp. **16**	0.2	•	0.1	0.0	0.1	0.2	0.5	1.3	0.3	•	•	•	•
Employee Benefits **17**	1.2	•	1.2	1.0	1.4	2.4	2.0	2.4	0.7	•	•	•	•
Advertising **18**	0.8	4.6	1.2	0.1	1.0	0.3	0.1	0.5	0.4	•	•	•	•
Other Expenses **19**	70.6	61.9	88.1	120.1	83.3	112.4	44.0	42.9	7.4	•	•	•	•
Officers' Compensation **20**	1.5	13.5	2.0	0.3	0.4	1.5	2.2	5.1	0.3	•	•	•	•
Operating Margin **21**	•	1.9	•	•	•	•	•	•	•	•	•	•	•
Operating Margin Before Officers' Comp. **22**	•	15.5	•	•	•	•	•	•	•	•	•	•	•

Selected Average Balance Sheet ($ in Thousands)

Net Receivables 23	23	0	5	44	133	592	734	3497	19932
Inventories 24	2	0	0	0	10	20	328	321	192
Net Property, Plant and Equipment 25	80	0	10	81	445	3940	8214	12881	30412
Total Assets 26	320		106	711	1981	7137	15354	32901	97607
Notes and Loans Payable 27	39	0	14	73	160	1707	2747	2961	4686
All Other Liabilities 28	70	0	19	108	414	1639	3255	12255	47977
Net Worth 29	211	0	73	530	1407	3791	9352	17684	44945

Selected Financial Ratios (Times to 1)

Current Ratio 30	3.3	•	4.8	7.5	3.5	1.4	1.6		1.2
Quick Ratio 31	2.9	•	4.5	7.2	3.1	1.0	0.9		1.0
Net Sales to Working Capital 32	1.8	•	1.9	0.7	1.0	3.3	5.9	4.7	37.2
Coverage Ratio 33	2.6	273.0	1.3	2.3	4.7	0.9	2.1	2.5	14.7
Total Asset Turnover 34	0.8	•	1.3	0.5	0.5	0.3	0.5	0.6	2.6
Inventory Turnover 35	47.3	•	97.3	192.0	18.0	8.6	12.8	12.8	1128.5
Receivables Turnover 36	11.9	•	32.8	8.7	8.8	2.5	16.9	5.5	17.1
Total Liabilities to Net Worth 37	0.5	•	0.5	0.3	0.4	0.9	0.6	0.9	1.2
Current Assets to Working Capital 38	1.4	•	1.3	1.2	1.4	3.8	3.3	2.6	5.7
Current Liabilities to Working Capital 39	0.4	•	0.3	0.2	0.4	2.8	2.3	1.6	4.7
Working Capital to Net Sales 40	0.5	•	0.5	1.5	1.0	0.3	0.2	0.2	0.0
Inventory to Working Capital 41	0.0	•	0.0	0.0	0.0	0.0	0.3	0.1	0.0
Total Receipts to Cash Flow 42	1.7	1.8	1.4	1.0	1.4	1.3	2.4	2.8	15.6
Cost of Goods to Cash Flow 43	0.5	0.3	0.1	0.1	0.2	0.1	1.3	0.5	13.1
Cash Flow to Total Debt 44	1.4	•	2.8	1.8	1.3	0.6	0.6	0.5	0.3

Selected Financial Factors (in Percentages)

Debt Ratio 45	34.0	•	31.4	25.4	29.0	46.9	39.1	46.3	54.0
Return on Total Assets 46	1.5	•	1.0	1.4	1.8	0.5	2.4	1.3	2.4
Return on Equity Before Income Taxes 47	1.5	•	0.4	1.0	2.0	•	2.0	1.5	4.9
Return on Equity After Income Taxes 48	0.7	•	•	0.6	1.4	•	1.1	•	3.1
Profit Margin (Before Income Tax) 49	1.2	4.0	0.2	1.7	2.8		2.3	1.2	0.9
Profit Margin (After Income Tax) 50	0.6	3.8	•	1.0	1.9		1.3	•	0.5

389

Table II

Corporations with Net Income

RELIGIOUS, GRANTMAKING, CIVIC AND PROFESSIONAL ORGANIZATIONS

MONEY AMOUNTS AND SIZE OF ASSETS IN THOUSANDS OF DOLLARS

Item Description for Accounting Period 7/07 Through 6/08	Total	Zero Assets	Under 500	500 to 1,000	1,000 to 5,000	5,000 to 10,000	10,000 to 25,000	25,000 to 50,000	50,000 to 100,000	100,000 to 250,000	250,000 to 500,000	500,000 to 2,500,000	2,500,000 and over
Number of Enterprises **1**	27514	3010	19657	2891	1791	99	48	13	5	0	0	0	0
Revenues ($ in Thousands)													
Net Sales **2**	6416686	162914	2348633	692016	1718797	330327	359972	241444	562584	0	0	0	0
Interest **3**	256614	4633	77265	53733	91379	8176	10409	3282	7737	0	0	0	0
Rents **4**	16289	0	4064	3423	5190	413	1147	253	1800	0	0	0	0
Royalties **5**	3025	0	0	3025	0	0	0	0	0	0	0	0	0
Other Portfolio Income **6**	47478	0	19133	5697	9559	1675	1645	4009	5761	0	0	0	0
Other Receipts **7**	1699623	8	442606	452308	433453	169979	129930	52005	19332	0	0	0	0
Total Receipts **8**	8439715	167555	2891701	1210202	2258378	510570	503103	300993	597214	0	0	0	0
Average Total Receipts **9**	307	56	147	419	1261	5157	10481	23153	119443	•	•	•	•
Operating Costs/Operating Income (%)													
Cost of Operations **10**	15.3	2.8	11.3	18.4	10.9	6.9	48.2	8.3	32.1	•	•	•	•
Salaries and Wages **11**	13.2	3.7	4.1	12.4	18.0	11.9	15.3	33.4	30.9	•	•	•	•
Taxes Paid **12**	2.5	2.6	1.5	3.6	3.0	1.7	2.3	4.7	2.9	•	•	•	•
Interest Paid **13**	0.6	0.0	0.4	2.1	0.3	0.4	1.6	1.1	0.1	•	•	•	•
Depreciation **14**	1.6	0.7	0.7	1.9	2.1	1.8	2.7	6.0	1.8	•	•	•	•
Amortization and Depletion **15**	0.1	•	0.0	0.0	0.1	0.0	0.0	0.0	1.1	•	•	•	•
Pensions and Other Deferred Comp. **16**	0.3	•	•	•	0.0	0.0	0.9	1.9	1.4	•	•	•	•
Employee Benefits **17**	1.5	•	1.7	0.5	1.2	1.1	1.9	3.3	3.2	•	•	•	•
Advertising **18**	0.9	7.1	0.3	0.2	1.3	0.2	0.2	0.6	1.8	•	•	•	•
Other Expenses **19**	87.3	53.3	95.6	127.2	88.5	122.5	54.8	51.7	24.7	•	•	•	•
Officers' Compensation **20**	1.8	23.2	1.3	•	0.2	1.9	3.8	7.2	1.4	•	•	•	•
Operating Margin **21**	•	7.2	•	•	•	•	•	•	•	•	•	•	•
Operating Margin Before Officers' Comp. **22**	•	30.4	•	•	•	•	•	•	0.1	•	•	•	•

Selected Average Balance Sheet ($ in Thousands)

Net Receivables 23	23	0	5	33	114	1129	1189	4265	4090
Inventories 24	2	0	0	0	42	403	327	242	
Net Property, Plant and Equipment 25	64	0	11	56	331	2570	4863	15249	20923
Total Assets 26	390	0	143	702	1973	6764	15046	33055	108300
Notes and Loans Payable 27	30	0	8	76	114	756	2323	3599	550
All Other Liabilities 28	81	0	13	82	451	2948	4605	10083	56900
Net Worth 29	279	0	122	544	1407	3060	8118	19374	50850

Selected Financial Ratios (Times to 1)

Current Ratio 30	4.2	•	11.4	7.8	3.7	1.5	1.2	1.9	1.5
Quick Ratio 31	3.8	•	10.8	7.5	3.3	1.2	0.6	1.1	0.9
Net Sales to Working Capital 32	1.1	•	1.0	0.5	0.9	2.9	8.3	2.8	10.1
Coverage Ratio 33	11.5	401.6	17.4	5.1	18.2	17.0	6.0	6.3	72.1
Total Asset Turnover 34	0.6	•	0.8	0.3	0.5	0.5	0.5	0.6	1.0
Inventory Turnover 35	17.8	•	390.7	1149.2	11.0	5.4	9.0	4.7	148.8
Receivables Turnover 36	11.3	•	•	8.5	10.9	•	10.1	•	47.8
Total Liabilities to Net Worth 37	0.4	•	0.2	0.3	0.4	1.2	0.9	0.7	1.1
Current Assets to Working Capital 38	1.3	•	1.1	1.1	1.4	3.2	6.1	2.1	3.0
Current Liabilities to Working Capital 39	0.3	•	0.1	0.1	0.4	2.2	5.1	1.1	2.0
Working Capital to Net Sales 40	0.9	•	1.0	2.0	1.1	0.3	0.1	0.4	0.1
Inventory to Working Capital 41	0.0	•	0.0	•	0.0	0.0	0.9	0.0	0.0
Total Receipts to Cash Flow 42	1.3	1.9	1.2	1.0	1.3	1.0	1.8	2.1	4.1
Cost of Goods to Cash Flow 43	0.2	0.1	0.1	0.2	0.1	0.1	0.9	0.2	1.3
Cash Flow to Total Debt 44	1.6	•	4.6	1.6	1.3	0.9	0.6	0.7	0.5

Selected Financial Factors (in Percentages)

Debt Ratio 45	28.4	•	14.7	22.6	28.7	54.8	46.0	41.4	53.0
Return on Total Assets 46	4.2	•	5.4	3.7	3.0	3.2	4.7	3.8	5.1
Return on Equity Before Income Taxes 47	5.3	•	6.0	3.8	4.0	6.6	7.3	5.5	10.7
Return on Equity After Income Taxes 48	4.4	•	5.3	3.3	3.2	5.1	5.2	3.7	7.5
Profit Margin (Before Income Tax) 49	6.4	10.1	6.1	8.6	5.9	6.0	7.9	5.7	4.9
Profit Margin (After Income Tax) 50	5.3	9.7	5.4	7.4	4.7		5.7	3.9	3.4

Index

Index